Fodor's 2000

D0288424

Australia

Fodor's Travel Publications, Inc. • New York, Toronto, London, Sydney, Auckland

www.fodors.com/australia

CONTENTS

MAPS

Circled letters in text correspond to letters on the photographs. For more information on the sights pictured, turn
to the indicated page number Ⓐ▷ on each photograph.

DESTINATION AUSTRALIA

Those who live in Australia call it "Oz." The name fits. This is a land so different from any other that it can sometimes seem as if it were conjured rather than created. It casts its spell through paradoxes: It is a developed nation, poised for the Century of the Pacific Rim, yet it is largely unpopulated, a land of vast frontiers—and with a frontier spirit in its people that was lost in other nations long ago, when life became crowded or comfortable or both. Its cities can be at once sophisticated and unpretentious, as can its people. If you love outdoor recreation, imaginative cuisine, natural beauty seemingly without limit, and the idea of an English-speaking nation actually being exotic, Australia was made (or conjured) for you.

343

A > 58

With nearly 4 million people, Sydney is Australia's largest metropolis, and like most big cities, it moves at a fast, hard-driving pace. Visitors from New York and Los Angeles feel

SYDNEY

B > 50

right at home, dining in first-class restaurants, admiring the Ⓑ **Sydney Harbour Bridge** and the city's skyline, and enjoying performances in the Ⓒ **Sydney Opera House** (or simply studying its architecture). Even outdoorsy Angelenos are surprised by the Sydney beach scene and the gusto with which Sydneysiders pursue it. Between wide, wonderful Ⓓ **Bondi Beach** and peaceful Palm Beach there are 30-plus strands, and on many of these, sun-lovers regularly trade business suits for birthday suits (although most beaches do have a dress code, if only thong bikinis, tops op-

C > 59

Ⓓ 74

tional). Surf carnivals in which teams of lifeguards match muscle power are big. So are such legacies of Empire as cricket and rugby, not to mention Australian Rules Football—very rough, a bit self-consciously manly, and a window on the Aussie soul; catch a match. More contemplative outings take you to the fine Taronga Zoo, the splendid Ⓐ**Royal Botanic Gardens,** oh-so-English Argyle Place, or nearby Ⓔ**Cadman's Cottage,** the oldest building in town, once the home of a convict-settler who got lucky. Ponder that for a minute—Britain used to send people to Australia as a punishment.

Ⓔ 48

If Sydney were nothing more than one of the loveliest, most cosmopolitan cities of the Pacific Rim, that would be quite enough. But as capital of New South Wales, it's also gateway to some of Australia's finest scenery. The town of Katoomba is charming, surrounded by the magnificent Blue Mountains, a trail-crossed area of towering eucalyptus groves and rugged sandstone cliffs. Nearby is Echo Point, with its commanding view of the stone pillars called the Ⓐ**Three Sisters.** Farther north are the vine-

NEW SOUTH
WALES

Ⓐ 121

Ⓑ 136

© 160

yards of ⑧**Hunter Valley,** which draws many weekend visitors for wine-tastings, good food, historic towns, and dazzling fall foliage (in April). At ©**Kosciuszko National Park** in the rugged, alpine

Ⓓ 148

Snowy Mountains, look for some of the country's most scenic cross-country skiing and bushwalking (as Aussies call hiking). Back at sea level, near the North Coast resort town of Coffs Harbour, is Ⓓ**Big Banana Leisure Park,** hinting strongly at the main product from these parts (and it's not Carmen Miranda figurines). Perhaps the best of New South Wales is a two-hour plane ride away in the South Pacific: those who have known the beauty and peace of coral-fringed Ⓔ**Lord Howe Island** would travel two weeks by kayak to know it again.

Ⓔ 154

CANBERRA
AND THE A.C.T.

Much like other great purpose-built capitals, the city of Canberra is too often underappreciated. Its detractors call it, together with the surrounding Australian Capital Territory (A.C.T.), soulless and sterile. True, it's not the place to come seeking the cutting-edge. But in this gem of urban planning you will find some of the most vigorous cultural life in the land, in a setting of great natural beauty. The city itself is calm, orderly, clean, and

green, free of billboards and other evidence of urban chaos. You are rewarded with a surprisingly extensive array of museums and galleries as well as festivals, performing arts events, and, lately, an increasingly vibrant food scene. Some of the country's finest modern architecture is also here, including the vast Parliament House, the gleaming

ⒶHigh Court of Australia, the Ⓒ National Carillon, and the National Gallery of Australia, with its fine Australian collection—all just a walk from the city's hotels. And the town is an easy drive from some of Australia's most scenic national parks, including Kosciuszko and the New South Wales snowfields, ⒷNamadgi National Park, and historic ⒹLanyon Homestead National Park. After your tour, if you find yourself in Perth or Adelaide or Melbourne and the pub chatter turns to Canberra, you'll be able to say, "Well, I've been there." You might even hear yourself adding, "And I'd go back."

MELBOURNE AND VICTORIA

Melbourne prides itself on many things—too many, if you ask Sydneysiders. Many think the city a bit formal, even stuffy, and see Melburnians as overly class-conscious, as sedate as their streetcars, as Victorian as circa-1860 ⒷComo House. At least to visitors, Melbourne more than justifies the city's good opinion of itself. As the self-styled cultural capital of Australia, it is home to the impressive ⒻVictorian Arts Centre, whose program includes first-class companies such as the Australian Opera and the Australian Ballet, and the ⒹSidney Myer Music Bowl, for al fresco entertainment. Melbourne is also ground zero for Australian sports fans, from January's Australian Open, one of the tennis world's four Grand Slam events, to the first Tuesday of November and the ⒶMelbourne Cup. Australia's Kentucky Derby or Grand National, it draws Melbourne society, dressed to the nines, along with working-class punters and wags in outlandish get-ups. It's almost as good a show as a Sunday afternoon spent along the waterfront Esplanade and elsewhere in

Ⓐ 221

Ⓑ 207

Ⓒ 259

Ⓓ 218

suburban Ⓔ**St. Kilda,** where Melburnians from every walk of life rub shoulders in cosmopolitan nosheries, on the Ferris wheel and roller coaster, and in the audiences gathered around mimes and street musicians. Beyond Melbourne the state of Victoria's countryside beckons. Bushwalkers head for Ⓒ**Alpine,** Wilson's Promontory, and Grampians national parks. The dramatic Great Ocean Road down Victoria's spectacular west coast takes in Port Campbell National Park and its famous rock formations, the Ⓖ**Twelve Apostles.** Much of the region, including the area around the mighty Murray River, the country's largest stream, showcases wineries and old goldfields towns such as Ballarat, Maldon, Bendigo, Beechworth, Chiltern, and others. They boomed in the late 19th century, when gold was discovered, and fell fast asleep when the metal ran out. Few early miners got rich. It was the merchants who sold them supplies who made the fortunes. All the same, be grateful to those early diggers. Without them and the veins they tapped, Melbourne would not be what it is today.

TASMANIA

281

Even by Australian standards, Tasmania's beauty is rare and different. This most favored destination of trout fishermen, bushwalkers, and other outdoors lovers reveals no sprawling Outback vistas, no endless red-sand desert. The weather is cool and moist, the landscape rugged, mountainous, and green, recalling what used to be the Mother Country. The brilliant fruits in the orchards, the mist shrouding harbors like the one in sleepy E**Strahan,** and even the architecture, from colonial Hobart to the Midland's Georgian villages, are classically British. So are strands like the one near the ©**Nut,** an an-

Ⓐ 278

© 291

cient volcanic plug up north, totally ringed by the sea. But just when you think you've ended up in the wrong hemisphere, Tasmania assures you otherwise. Cradle Mountain–Lake St. Clair National Park is magnificently alpine. In rain-forested Ⓓ**Southwest National Park,** the exotic cushion plants on the northeast ridge of Mt. Anne are as at home as gorse in Scotland. And at places such as Wineglass Bay in Ⓑ**Freycinet National Park,** soft white sand and panhandling marsupials act as reality checks. The beauty all around is in poignant contrast to Tasmania's doleful history. Aborigines were slaughtered here in an ethnic cleansing that raised few European eyebrows. Australia's cruelest penal colony was at Ⓐ**Port Arthur,** whose surrounding parkland is as uplifting as a tour of the prison is sobering. The prisoners' resting place is one of the most beautiful islands in the world.

Ⓔ 293

15

ⒶＲＦ 307

Australia goes tropical in Queensland, the self-proclaimed Sunshine State that inspired Crocodile Dundee. Easygoing even by the standards of an easygoing nation, Queenslanders see themselves as more archetypally Australian than their countrymen. And the frontier never feels far away, even if most citizens make their living in reptile-free zones such as contemporary Brisbane's **ⒶKing George Square** and the glitzy Gold Coast. As you

QUEENSLAND

ⒷＲＦ 354

ⒸＲＦ 335

continue north, wilderness Queensland comes into focus. On the Sunshine Coast it's quieter and more understated, except for kitschy spots like the ©**Big Pineapple.** It's wilder still in Far North Queensland, as close to Papua New Guinea as it is to the rest of Australia. You can get a feeling for the landscape of rain forests, canyons, lakes, and waterfalls aboard the Ⓔ**Kuranda Scenic Railway,** which runs out of mellow, tropical Cairns. Here you are close to the Ⓑ**Tjapukai Aboriginal Cultural Park** and not far from the densely forested Bellenden Ker National Park, pristine Cape Tribulation National Park, and ⒟**Daintree National Park.** In these parts, humans are guests, and koalas—and crocodiles—are right at home.

GREAT
BARRIER REEF

As befits a land apart, Australia's most dazzling feature lies apart from land, in the shallow turquoise seas off the Queensland coast. The Great Barrier Reef is one of the world's natural wonders—1,200 miles long, up to 50 miles wide, and very much alive, made up of billions of tiny, brilliantly colored organisms whose skeletons have fused. The reef supports a rich array of other life as well, including clown fish, whose symbiosis with the sea anemone is but one of the strange relation-

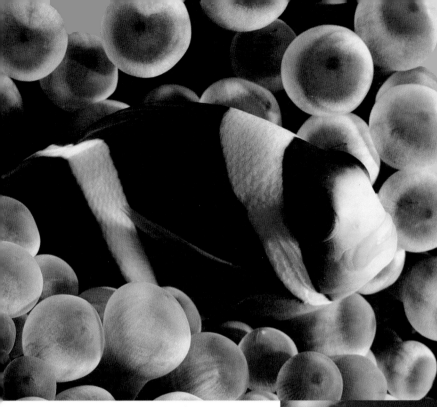

ships in this surprising environment. These waters constitute one of the best snorkeling and diving areas on earth, but you don't have to immerse yourself to have a great time—hiking and tennis are part of the picture, along with perfect beaches. It helps that all the reef's island-resorts have distinct personalities of their own. Some getaways are big on peace, solitude, and natural splendor; others are hives of sports and sociability. Landfalls such as Great Keppel Island offer endless recreational activities. The ⒷWhitsunday Islands—among them spectacular Hayman Island and ⒶHamilton Island—are extraordinary, and hikes here can yield unforgettable views. Heron Island is a wildlife sanctuary. On idyllic, upscale Lizard Island, a trek to ©Cook's Look lets you survey the surrounding area as Captain Cook did, and a stroll to the water's edge on low-key ⒹLady Elliot Island can feed your soul with a glorious, back-to-basics tropical sunset.

©⟩ 393

Ⓓ⟩ 375

Ⓐ▷ 442

ADELAIDE AND SOUTH AUSTRALIA

Ⓑ▷ 402

Travelers know that every nation has its well-kept secrets. Australia's finest may be Ⓑ**Adelaide** and the state of South Australia. The capital is known as the city of churches for its houses of worship: Ⓓ**St. Cyprian's Anglican Church** is just one of them. But Adelaide could as easily be known as the city of parks. Its huge, rambling green spaces give it a pastoral feeling, almost as if its brilliant planner, William Light, couldn't decide whether he wanted a city abundantly supplied with parks or a gigantic park punctuated by buildings. Either way, Adelaide is lovely—and the natu-

Ⓒ▷ 433

ral launch point for trips into the surrounding countryside. The nearby Adelaide Hills are as verdant as the city itself, and the Clare and Barossa valleys produce wines of international fame. At Grant Burge and other wineries you can have a sip or three on the house. Beyond, in the parched Outback, the town of Ⓐ**Coober Pedy** supplies opals to the world, and you can dig for your own. Offshore, on folksy, friendly ©Ⓔ**Kangaroo Island,** you can lunch with locals: Beaches can be thronged with pelicans, sea lions, fairy penguins, kangaroos, koalas, and other natives.

Ⓓ▷ 405

Ⓔ▷ 433

THE RED CENTRE

The hues of the desert give the Red Centre its name, and Ⓐ**Uluru,** referred to less often these days as Ayers Rock, gives the whole world a place to treasure. To Aborigines this is sacred ground, and others who come here soon see why. The great sandstone monolith commands awe, never more than when low, slanting sunlight paints it a deep, rich red. Improbably suburban Alice Springs, the Red Centre's unofficial capital-by-default, is worth seeing itself—as the only town around in a landscape of unforgettable beauty and power.

Ⓐ 488

In the pecking order of Australian hardiness, residents of the Far North bow to no one—and not only because everyone else is so far away. Many in these parts think nothing of "going bush" for the weekend, sleeping under the stars in

Ⓑ 485

DARWIN, THE TOP END, AND THE KIMBERLEY

country many Southerners know only in their dreams. Darwin is the hub, a fascinating, cosmopolitan city where Anglo, Aboriginal, and Asian cultures interweave. It is also the major departure point for side trips to dramatic Litchfield National Park, site of Ⓐ**Wangi Falls,** and to Ⓑ**Kakadu National Park.** Crocs have been cranky in this tropical wilderness for aeons and Aboriginal art has graced rocks here for millennia, as it has in the wild, remote Ⓒ**Kimberley** region. Locals say this is what Australia is all about, and, although it's not quite that simple, something basic to the spirit of Australia undeniably resides here.

Ⓒ 491

Ⓐ 500

PERTH AND
WESTERN AUSTRALIA

Ⓑ 524

Although Perth is the world's most isolated city (2,000 miles, across ocean or desert, from any other city of size) it seems invigorated, not isolated, by its solitude. And why not? Good cheer is a classic Aussie trait, all the stronger in Perth because the population is so young, with a median age of 25. Perth's zest is infectious, especially if you love water sports or golf, both of which are passions here. A walkable city sprinkled with landmarks such as ⒸHis Majesty's Theatre, Perth is a fine base for side trips to beautifully restored York, monastic New Norcia, and otherworldly ⒷNambung National Park. And the rest of Western Australia is magnificent. You might travel to leafy Fremantle, explore rough-

and-ready goldfields towns like Kalgoorlie and Coolgardie, or venture to the remote ⒶPilbara region, where, long ago, human hands decorated the rocks. Or see nature's creations: the cave systems of the Cape Leeuwin–Naturaliste National Park and the panoramic ⒹStirling Range National Park,

Ⓒ 507

Ⓓ▷ 538

famous for the wildflowers that carpet the area with brilliant colors in September and October. Renowned for its marine life, including huge manta rays, nesting turtles, and giant but harmless whale sharks, is Ⓔ**Ningaloo Reef Marine Park,** a long way north of Perth but worth the trip—like Perth and Western Australia themselves.

Ⓔ▷ 544

GREET ITINERARIES

Highlights of Australia
16 or 17 days

This tour surveys the misty heights of Tasmania's Cradle Mountain, the steamy wetlands of Kakadu, the central deserts, and the northern rain forests. It finishes in Port Douglas, where you can linger if time permits.

(A) 59

Darwin ○ 256 km Kakadu NP

3 hrs 45 min

2 hrs

2 hrs

NORTHERN TERRITORY

Western MacDonnell Ranges — Finke Gorge NP — **Alice Springs**

Kings Canyon — 450 km

Ayers Rock/ Uluru NP/ Olgas/Kata Tjuta Domes — 440 km

4 hrs

Flinders Ranges NP

2 hrs

St. Mary's Peak
Wilpena Pound

Port Augusta — 460 km

Barossa Valley

Adelaide — 70 km

SYDNEY
2 or 3 days. Spend a day cruising the harbor and exploring the Rocks. Take an evening stroll past the Ⓐ Opera House to the Royal Botanic Gardens. The next day take a Sydney Explorer bus tour and visit Darling Harbour, followed by dinner at Cockle Bay Wharf or Chinatown. Day three could be spent in Paddington, with a trip to Bondi Beach.
☞ *Exploring Sydney and Beaches in Chapter 1*

BLUE MOUNTAINS
1 day. Stop at Wentworth Falls for a view across the Jamison Valley and the National Pass trail. Pause for refreshments at Leura, then continue along Cliff Drive to Blackheath.
☞ *The Blue Mountains in Chapter 2*

TASMANIA
6 days. Spend the first afternoon strolling Hobart's waterfront. The following day, drive to Port Arthur and explore Australia's convict past. On day three, head for Freycinet National Park and hike to Ⓑ Wineglass Bay, then overnight in Launceston.

The next morning, drive to Cradle Mountain–Lake St. Clair National Park and spend two days hiking. Drive back to Hobart for your final night.
☞ *Exploring Hobart, Port Arthur, Freycinet National Park, Launceston, and Central Tasmania National Parks in Chapter 5*

ULURU
2 days. Fly into Alice Springs to experience Ⓓ Ayers Rock/Uluru, a monolith that resonates with mystical force. Explore its base the first day, spend the night in town, and visit the vast Olgas/Kata Tjuta Domes on day two.
☞ *Uluru and Kata Tjuta in Chapter 9*

KAKADU
2 days. Fly into Darwin and head for Kakadu National Park, with its escarpments, wetlands, and ancient Aboriginal rock art.
☞ *Kakadu National Park in Chapter 10*

Ⓑ 281

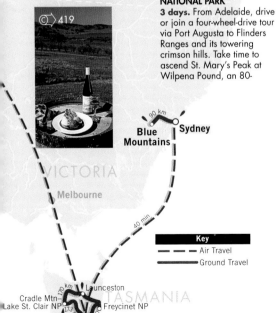

Into the Outback
13 to 16 days

In the raw, brooding Outback, with a little imagination you can go back to a time when the earth was created by the giant ancestral beings from whom the Aboriginal people trace their lineage.

PORT DOUGLAS
3 days. From Cairns drive north to small, glamorous Port Douglas, where catamarans and sloops cruise to the Great Barrier Reef. Take one day to explore the surrounding rain forest and another for a four-wheel-drive tour to Cape Tribulation.
☞ *North from Cairns in Chapter 6*

Transportation
Daily flights depart from Sydney to Hobart (40 min), from Hobart to Alice Springs via Melbourne (4 hrs), from Alice Springs to Darwin (2 hrs), and from Darwin to Cairns (3 hrs, 45 min). From each hub you can rent a car or join a tour to get around.

ADELAIDE
2 days. Begin the day with a visit to the Central Market area and a tour of the historic buildings along North Terrace. Stroll through the Botanic Gardens before catching a PopEye launch back to the city center. Later head for the cafés in Rundle Mall. Next day tour the wineries of the ©Barossa Valley.
☞ *Exploring Adelaide and The Barossa Valley in Chapter 8*

FLINDERS RANGES NATIONAL PARK
3 days. From Adelaide, drive or join a four-wheel-drive tour via Port Augusta to Flinders Ranges and its towering crimson hills. Take time to ascend St. Mary's Peak at Wilpena Pound, an 80-square-km (31-square-mi) bowl ringed by quartzite hills.
☞ *The Outback in Chapter 8*

ALICE SPRINGS
4 days. Spend the afternoon viewing Aboriginal art in the galleries or on an excursion into the Western MacDonnell Ranges. The next day head out from Alice Springs on the scenic Mereenie Track, which also links Kings Canyon and Finke Gorge National Park, to visit Ayers Rock/Uluru.
☞ *Exploring Alice Springs and Side Trips from Alice Springs in Chapter 9*

ULURU
2 to 4 days. In the afternoon take a half-day trip to the Olgas/Kata Tjuta and hike through the Valley of the Winds. Spend one or more days on an Aboriginal guided tour learning about indigenous culture and lifestyle.
☞ *Uluru and Kata Tjuta in Chapter 9*

KAKADU
2 or 3 days. Kick back and enjoy the warm climate, abundant wildlife, and sandstone caves. When Aborigines camped here aeons ago they daubed the walls with ocher, clay, and charcoal.
☞ *Kakadu National Park in Chapter 10*

Transportation
Flights depart daily from Adelaide to Alice Springs (2 hrs), Alice Springs to Darwin (2 hrs), and Darwin back to Adelaide (4½ hrs). Use these cities as bases—either rent a car or take day tours of the sights mentioned.

Cape Tribulation
Port Douglas
Cairns

©419

Blue Mountains
90 km
Sydney

VICTORIA
Melbourne

40 min

Key
--- Air Travel
— Ground Travel

Launceston
Cradle Mtn. Lake St. Clair NP
Freycinet NP
TASMANIA
Hobart
Port Arthur

Wines and Scenery of the Southeast
10 days

The continent's southeast corner offers serenity, grace, and some wonderful wines along with quiet country towns, Victorian architecture, and a rugged coastline.

RUTHERGLEN
1 day. Near the Murray River, Rutherglen's vineyards produce Australia's finest fortified wines. A half-day tour introduces you to tokays, muscats, and ports underpinned with subtle layers of fruit.
☞ *Murray River Region in Chapter 4*

BENDIGO
2 days. At the northern extremity of Victoria's goldfields region, Bendigo prospered most from the gold rush of the 1850s and has a rich legacy of Victorian architecture. Ballarat, another goldrush settlement, hosts reenactments of prosperous days. Between Bendigo and Ballarat is Maldon, also well-preserved. Down the road the Hepburn Springs Mineral Spa has flotation tanks, saunas, a relaxation pool, and hot tubs.
☞ *Gold Country in Chapter 4*

MELBOURNE
2 days. In Australia's serene and gracious second-largest city spend a day exploring the riverside Southgate complex and the parks and gardens to the east, then head for the bayside suburb of St. Kilda for a walk along the Esplanade. Next day tour the Dandenongs, driving through the cool, moist hills of Belgrave and Sherbrooke.
☞ *Exploring Melbourne in Chapter 4*

GREAT OCEAN ROAD
2 days. Pause at the pretty village of Lorne, then circle rain-forested Otway National Park and head for Port Campbell National Park's huge limestone stacks. Overnight in Port Fairy and cross the South Australian border, stopping at Mount Gambier's Blue Lake. Continue to Kingston and drive along the Coorong, a lagoon protected from the ocean by the Younghusband Peninsula dunes and a bird sanctuary.
☞ *West Coast Region in Chapter 4*

ADELAIDE
3 days. Devote a day to walking along the North Terrace to the Botanic Gardens and zoo, and another in the Adelaide Hills. Founded by German settlers during the 19th century, the village of Hahndorf is full of stone and timber structures. In the evening visit Ⓔ Warrawong Sanctuary for wildlife. Spend another day seeing the Barossa Valley's wineries, fine restaurants, and historic inns.
☞ *Exploring Adelaide, The Adelaide Hills, and The Barossa Valley in Chapter 8*

Transportation
A rental car is the best means of transportation.

Tropical Wonders
13 or 14 days

The East Coast's riotous greenery, tropical islands, and year-round warmth, not to mention the Ⓖ Great Barrier Reef, are difficult to resist.

BRISBANE
1 day. Explore the Queensland capital's city center and the Ⓕ South Bank Parklands. In the evening head for one of the riverside restaurants at Eagle Street Pier.
☞ *Exploring Brisbane in Chapter 6*

THE SUNSHINE COAST
2 days. Drive an hour north to stylish Noosa Heads, with its balmy climate and scenic beaches. On sophisticated Hastings Street are boutiques, cafés, and restaurants.
☞ *Sunshine Coast in Chapter 6*

FRASER ISLAND
2 days. Fly to Hervey Bay and then to Fraser Island to join a four-wheel-drive tour of rocky headlands, the rusting wreck of the *Maheno*, and towering sand dunes. In the interior you'll see paperbark swamps, freshwater lakes, and forests of brush box trees.
☞ *Fraser Island in Chapter 6*

HERON ISLAND
2 days. Back at Hervey Bay, fly to Gladstone and then head on to this Great Barrier Reef island, where you can

Ⓔ 417

spend your time diving or bird-watching.
☞ *Heron Island* in Chapter 7

PORT DOUGLAS

3 days. Fly from Gladstone to Cairns, drive to Port Douglas, and spend the first day exploring this relaxed town. Devote another day to hiking the Mossman Gorge trails or cruising the Great Barrier Reef. If the weather sours, head toward Cairns and take the train through the rain forest to Kuranda. Return via the Skyway Rain Forest Cableway.
☞ *Cairns and North from Cairns* in Chapter 6

CAPE TRIBULATION

2 days. Keep driving north from Port Douglas to this area of untamed beaches and rain forests. As the spirit moves you, stop for hiking, horse-back riding, and beachcomb-ing on half-deserted strands.
☞ *North from Cairns* in Chapter 6

COOKTOWN

1 or 2 days. North from Cape Tribulation, the rough Bloomfield Track and numer-ous river crossings make the four-wheel-drive journey to Cooktown an adventure. Stop along the way at Mission Creek Falls, Black Mountain National Park, and the Lion's Den Hotel, a rough pub.
☞ *North from Cairns* in Chapter 6

Transportation

Fly from Brisbane to Hervey Bay (1 hr), where car ferries chug to Fraser Island from Mary River Heads and Inskip Point. Daily flights connect Hervey Bay with Gladstone (1 hr), and it's a 2-hr boat trip or 25-min helicopter ride from there to Heron Island. Daily flights link Gladstone to Cairns (1 hr), where you can rent a car to tour Port Douglas and the north. In each region, the best way to get around is to rent a four-wheel-drive vehicle or join a tour.

Black Mountain NP
Lion's Den Hotel
Mission Creek Falls
Cape Tribulation
Mossman
Kuranda
Cairns
Cooktown
Port Douglas

Heron Island
Gladstone

Fraser Island
Hervey Bay
Noosa Heads

Brisbane

Sydney

Adelaide
Warrawong Sanctuary
Barossa Valley
Adelaide Hills
Coorong NP
Hahndorf
Kingston
Mt. Gambier
Port Fairy
Port Campbell NP
Otway NP
Bendigo
Maldon
Ballarat
Hepburn Springs
Melbourne
Lorne
The Dandenongs
Rutherglen

VICTORIA

TASMANIA

Key	
- - - -	Air Travel
————	Ground Travel

FODOR'S
CHOICE

Even with so many special places in Australia, Fodor's writers and editors have their favorites. Here are a few that stand out.

THE REAL OZ

Ⓓ **Harbour Ferry Ride, Sydney.** The journey to Manly captures stunning, breezy views of the city. ☞ p. 108

Lygon Street, Melbourne. Have coffee at an open-air café here in Carlton, on the bohemian fringe of the inner city. ☞ p. 206

Ⓕ **Salamanca Place, Hobart.** One of this city's liveliest gathering spots showcases the island's best crafts and antiques. ☞ p. 271

Ⓔ **Skyrail Rain Forest Cableway, Queensland.** The journey takes you 7 ½ km (5 mi) over rain-forest canopy to the village of Kuranda, near Cairns. ☞ p. 359

Vineyards of Margaret River, Western Australia. Wine-tasting amid the scenic backdrop here is an experience you'll never forget. ☞ p. 533

Zig Zag Railway, New South Wales. Riding this vintage steam engine along cliff-side precipices through the Blue Mountains is thrilling. ☞ p. 125

NATURAL WONDERS

Cape Leeuwin–Naturaliste National Park, Western Australia. Human and animal relics, as well as more than 360 caves, are part of the rugged coastal scenery here. ☞ p. 532

Ⓗ **Great Barrier Reef.** The world's richest marine area gathers wondrous undersea life. ☞ p. 371

Snowy Mountains, New South Wales. Part of Kosciuszko National Park, this area is Australia's largest alpine region. ☞ p. 159

Three Sisters, Blue Mountains, New South Wales. The name of these sandstone pillars comes from an Aboriginal legend of sisters who were saved from a monster by their transformation into stone. ☞ p. 121

Ⓒ **Uluru (Ayers Rock) and Kata Tjuta (the Olgas), the Red Centre.** This area's best-known natural formations are classic sights. ☞ p. 461

EXPERIENCING WILDLIFE

Cradle Mountain–Lake St. Clair National Park, Tasmania. Watch the infamous Tasmanian devil feed at the Cradle Mountain Lodge here. ☞ p. 296

Exmouth, Western Australia. Whales, sharks, and turtles abound in these waters, and travelers can help tag the huge turtles that nest on the shore. ☞ p. 544

Kakadu National Park, the Top End. The water holes (billabongs) at Yellow Water, South Alligator River, and Magella Creek offer the opportunity to see more than 280 species of birds. ☞ p. 485

Lizard Island, Great Barrier Reef. The boat crew feed the giant potato cod and the Maori wrasse at Cod Hole, just off the outer reef of this island. ☞ p. 393

Lone Pine Koala Sanctuary, Brisbane, Queensland. You can pet the animals at this fauna park and even have your picture taken while cuddling a koala. ☞ p. 310

Monkey Mia, Western Australia. Dolphins show up in Shark Bay at all times of day to be hand-fed by the rangers, who will share the job with you. ☞ p. 543

Phillip Island, Victoria. The twilight return of the fairy penguins here is a spectacular sight. ☞ p. 231

Seal Bay Conservation Park, Kangaroo Island, South Australia. Members of Seal Bay's sea lion colony relax on the beach between fishing trips. ☞ p. 435

Warrawong Sanctuary, Adelaide Hills, South Australia. Rangers lead night walks through this rain forest, which is home to bandicoots, wallabies, and platypuses. ☞ p. 417

FLAVORS

Ⓙ **Rockpool, Sydney.** The cuisine of this chrome-and-glass restaurant is famous for its fusion of Mediterranean, Middle Eastern, Chinese, and Thai flavors. $$$$ ☞ p. 79

Mead's Fish Gallery, Perth. Views of yachts and pelicans make this Perth restaurant irresistible. $$$ ☞ p. 514

Ⓖ **Melbourne Wine Room Restaurant.** Serene, romantic, and modestly glamorous, this is the perfect place to try wines by the glass, paired with stylish Italian cooking. $$ ☞ p. 211

Hanuman Thai and Nonya Restaurant, Darwin. Thai-Malaysian flavors have made this dazzling restaurant the city's Asian sensation. $$–$$$ ☞ p. 480

Ⓑ **Pier 9 Oyster Bar and Seafood Grill, Brisbane, Queensland.** Broad river views, fresh seafood, and a late-harvest Australian riesling make for a fine Brisbane evening. $$–$$$ ☞ p. 314

COMFORTS

Ⓘ **Lizard Island Lodge, Great Barrier Reef.** This is the reef's most idyllic island retreat—the perfect tropical getaway. $$$$ ☞ p. 394

Ⓐ **Silky Oaks Lodge, Mossman, Queensland.** Open-air living and delicious food in a tropical rain-forest setting are unforgettable. $$$$ ☞ p. 364

El Questro Cattle Station, the Kimberley, Western Australia. You can join a roundup, hike in gorges, and dunk in a river at this working ranch. $–$$$$ ☞ p. 493

Apple Tree Cottage and Gum Tree Cottage, Adelaide Hills, South Australia. Set in rolling countryside, this inn resembles a 19th-century pioneer's home. $$ ☞ p. 418

Lenna of Hobart. Canopy beds and wicker chairs create a comfortable, romantic setting. $$$ ☞ p. 274

The Russell, the Rocks, Sydney. For Old World character—and a view of the harbor from the roof garden—the Russell is a classy, charming Victorian. $$ ☞ p. 92

1   SYDNEY

Wrapped around its majestic harbor, Sydney is the vibrant, cosmopolitan gateway to Australia. A city of captivating natural beauty—whose charms include a superb array of beaches—Sydney is also well equipped for the good life, as a visit to some of the city's world-class restaurants will prove. The year 2000, when Sydney hosts the Olympic Games, will provide special memories for any visitor to the city. You're bound to spend at least a couple of days here—take hold of them with both hands.

TAKE A TAXI FROM SYDNEY AIRPORT and chances are that the driver will not say "G'day" with the broad accent you might expect. Probe a little further and you will probably discover that he was not born in Australia. Like the United States, Australia is a society of immigrants, and Sydney has been a preferred destination for many of these new arrivals. Over the past half century the Anglo-Irish immigrants who made up the city's original population base have been joined by successive waves of Italians, Greeks, Turks, Lebanese, and, more recently, Asians. Today, more than half of all Australians were either born overseas or have at least one parent who was. This intermingling has created a cultural vibrancy and energy that were missing only a generation ago.

Updated by
Michael
Gebicki

Sydney is a city in a hurry. Compared with the rest of Australia, Sydney's traffic is fast and impatient. This city of over 4 million people works hard and plays harder—moderation is something practiced by the citizens of Melbourne. Sydney has the tallest buildings, the most expensive real estate, the finest beaches, and the seediest nightlife of any Australian city. Most Australians regard its loud, brash ways with a mixture of fear and fascination, although Sydneysiders prefer to think of their city as virile rather than vulgar.

British writer Lawrence Durrell once lamented that Americans seem to live out of sync with their natural surroundings. The same could be said of Sydney, which seems a strident contrast to the barren, unforgiving continent at its door. For the average Sydneysider, life unfolds in one of the red-roofed suburbs that surround the city. The outback is as foreign to most Sydneysiders as the Mojave Desert is to the inhabitants of Boston.

Sydney may have forsaken the hinterland, but it embraces its harbor with passion. The harbor is a shining gem, studded with small bays and inlets and crowned by the billowing sails of the Opera House. When he first set eyes on this harbor on January 26, 1788, Captain Arthur Phillip, the commander of the First Fleet, wrote in his diary: "We had the satisfaction of finding the finest harbor in the world, in which a thousand ships of the line may ride in the most perfect security." It was not an easy beginning, however. Passengers on board the 11 ships of the First Fleet were not the "huddled masses yearning to breathe free" that populated the United States, but wretched inmates flushed from overcrowded jails in England and sent halfway around the globe. It says much of those early days that when the women prisoners came ashore two weeks after the men, an orgy ensued.

Sydney has long since outgrown the stigma of its convict origins, but the passage of time has not tamed its spirit. Other Australian cities may lay claim to the title of the nation's cultural capital, but Sydney's panache and appetite for life are unchallenged. A walk among the scantily clad bathers at Bondi Beach or through the raucous nightlife district of Kings Cross provides evidence enough.

Visiting Sydney is an essential part of an Australian experience, but the city is no more representative of Australia than New York is of the United States. Sydney has joined the ranks of the great cosmopolitan cities whose characters are essentially international. What Sydney has to offer is style, sophistication, and great looks—an exhilarating prelude to the unique continent that lies at its back door. In 2000, the year that the Olympic Games comes to Sydney, this promises to be one of the fashionable destinations of the new millennium.

Pleasures and Pastimes

Although Sydney is well endowed with galleries, museums, and some splendid examples of Georgian and Victorian architecture, its warm, sunny climate, spectacular setting, and addiction to the great outdoors are its prime attractions. Sydney is also a superb city in which to wine, dine, or shop till you drop.

Beaches and Waterways

The boom of the surf could well be Sydney's summer theme song: Forty beaches, including world-famous Bondi, lie within the Sydney metropolitan area. With their fine, golden sand, average water temperature of 68°F, and a choice of sheltered harbor waters or crashing breakers, it's little wonder that Sydneysiders are addicted to the pleasures of sun, sea, sand, and surfing. If you wish to try your hand at the latter, surfboards can be rented at some ocean beaches.

The city is also a paradise for other water-based activities. A journey along the many inlets of Sydney Harbour reveals a natural wonderland of beaches, sheltered coves, high cliffs, and bays, which are ideal for boating, sailing, windsurfing, and diving. You can rent watercraft of all types, or join a skippered sailing excursion to explore these delightful waters.

Dining

In the new world order, Sydney has suddenly become one of the glamorous global food centers, ranking up there with London and New York. Sydney-trained chefs are making their presence felt as far away as Great Britain, while the Australian food magazines are giddy about what's going on at home.

So what's to eat in Sydney? There's tuna tartare with flying fish roe and wasabi; emu prosciutto; five-spice duck; shiitake mushroom pie; and sweet turmeric barramundi curry. This is the stuff of mod-Oz (modern Australian) cooking, and Sydney is where it flourishes—fueled by local produce and guided by Mediterranean and Asian techniques. Sydney's dining scene is now as sunny and cosmopolitan as the city itself, and there are diverse and exotic culinary adventures to suit every appetite. A meal at Tetsuya's, Paramount, Darley Street Thai, or Rockpool constitute a crash course in this dazzling culinary language.

Food lovers on holiday in Sydney are especially in luck, for many of Sydney's top sightseeing spots are of equal food interest. The Opera House has the Bennelong, Cockle Bay has Ampersand, the Museum of Contemporary Art has MCA Café, and the Art Gallery of New South Wales has Pavilion on the Park. Then there are the food 'burbs of Bondi, Leichhardt, Surry Hills, and Darlinghurst, where the smells of good espresso, a sizzling grill, or an aromatic stir-fry hover in the air.

Seafood is a highlight. You'll find a variety of fish and shellfish that nearly boggles the mind: rudderfish, warehou, barramundi, blue-eye cod, kingfish, John Dory, ocean perch, and parrot fish; then Yamba prawns, Balmain bugs, sweet Sydney rock oysters, mud crab, spanner crab, yabbies (small lobsters), and marrons (freshwater lobsters). A visit to the city's fish markets at Pyrmont, just five minutes from the city center, will tell you much about Sydney's diet.

Of course, Sydney food tastes so much better when taken outdoors—at a sidewalk table, in a sun-drenched courtyard, or best of all, in full view of that glorious harbor. Keep in mind the general rule: the better the view, the bigger the bill.

National Parks and Wildlife

Anyone who wishes to sample the sights and sounds of wild Australia or experience the country's Aboriginal heritage can choose from several national parks (and numerous nature reserves) in the Greater Sydney region. Close to the heart of the city, Sydney Harbour National Park is relaxing and inspirational. Ku-ring-gai Chase National Park to the north and Royal National Park to the south encompass large tracts of natural coastline, foreshore, and bushland.

Although Sydney's wildlife is generally restricted to birds and such small creatures as lizards and possums, several wildlife parks around the city display a more extensive range of native fauna. These are ideal places to learn more about koalas, kangaroos, the strange egg-laying mammals (the echidna and the platypus), birds, and reptiles.

Sports

Whether it's watching or playing, Sydneysiders are devoted to sports, and the city's benign climate makes outdoor sports a year-round possibility. There are some 80 golf courses within easy reach of the city. Many of these are open to the public, and greens fees are modest compared with most other countries. Tennis is also popular, and dozens of centers rent out courts for day and night use.

By far the most popular summer sport is cricket; Australia plays international test matches against England, the West Indies, Sri Lanka, Pakistan, South Africa, and India at the Sydney Cricket Ground. The biggest winter game is rugby league, but rugby union, soccer, and Australian rules football also attract passionate followings. Many of these winter matches take place at the Sydney Football Stadium.

Shopping

Sydney is a great place to shop for knitwear and woolen goods, sheepskin items, Aboriginal art and artifacts, opals, crafts, and innovative beach, leisure, and resort wear (raised to a virtual art form in this city of beaches). There are also plenty of outlets for local clothing designers, ranging from high fashion to bush- and country-wear manufacturers. Look for such names as Carla Zampatti, Trent Nathan, George Gross, Simona, R. M. Williams, Dorian Scott, and Adele Weiss. Duty-free shopping is excellent in Sydney—prices are very competitive in the dozens of duty-free shops.

EXPLORING SYDNEY

Sydney is a giant, stretching almost 97 km (60 mi) from top to bottom and about 55 km (34 mi) across. It is divided into north and south by the harbor, with most of the headline attractions located on the south shore. The area bounded by Chinatown in the south, the Harbour Bridge in the north, Darling Harbour to the west, and the beaches and coastline to the east has plenty to occupy any visitor for several days. North of the Harbour Bridge lie the important commercial center of North Sydney and the pleasant, leafy, north-shore suburbs. Ocean beaches, Taronga Zoo, and Ku-ring-gai Chase National Park are the only reasons most visitors find to venture north of the harbor.

We have divided Sydney into seven exploring areas and an Around Sydney section. Tours cover sights old and new, from the city's earliest convict days to the Victorian era to the Sydney Opera House, the very symbol of cosmopolitan, contemporary Australia. Walks begin at Circular Quay, a central point in Sydney as well as the docking area for harbor ferries, and the Pitt Street Mall, the heart of the main shopping district. Sydney Harbour is a ferry tour, and the Kings Cross and Paddington itinerary requires some bus travel, but the rest can be done easily on foot. Around Sydney covers various places of interest that are farther afield.

There are areas of spectacular scenic beauty outside Sydney, and the city's ever-improving road system makes it practical to make day tours to areas such as the Blue Mountains or the vineyards of the Hunter Valley (both of which are covered in Chaper 2) (☞ Guided Tours *in* Sydney A to Z, *below*). However, if you want to get the most out of these places, you would do far better to plan an overnight stop.

Numbers in the text correspond to numbers in the margin and on the Sydney Harbour, Central Sydney, and Greater Sydney maps.

Great Itineraries

You really need three days in Sydney to see the essential city center, while six days would allow more time to explore the beaches and inner suburbs. A stay of 10 days would allow trips outside the city and give you time to explore a few of Sydney's lesser known delights.

IF YOU HAVE 3 DAYS

Start with an afternoon **Sydney Harbour Explorer cruise** for one of the best impressions of the city (☞ Guided Tours *in* Sydney A to Z, *below*). Follow the cruise with a walking tour of the historic **Rocks,** the nation's birthplace, and take a walk up onto the **Sydney Harbour Bridge** for great views. The following day, take a **Sydney Explorer** tour (☞ Guided Tours *in* Sydney A to Z, *below*). If you're feeling energetic, there will still be enough time to see the famous **Sydney Opera House** and relax at sunset in the nearby **Royal Botanic Gardens** and **Domain** parkland. On day three, explore the **city center** highlights, with another spectacular panorama from the top of **Sydney Tower.** Include a walk around the **Macquarie Street** area, a living reminder of Sydney's colonial history, and the contrasting experience of futuristic **Darling Harbour,** with its museums, aquarium, cafés, and lively shopping center.

IF YOU HAVE 6 DAYS

Follow the three-day itinerary above, then take the **Kings Cross, Darlinghurst, and Paddington** bus and walking trip on day four. You could also continue to **Bondi,** Australia's most famous beach. The next day, catch the ferry to **Manly** to visit that beach and the historic **Quarantine Station.** From here, take an afternoon bus tour to the **northern beaches,** or return to the city to shop or spend more time in one of the many museums. Day six options could include a visit to a **wildlife** or **national park, Taronga Zoo,** or take a trip west of the city to tour the Sydney 2000 **Olympic Games site.**

IF YOU HAVE 10 DAYS

In this amount of time it is possible to see most of the above, then travel farther afield by rental car or with an organized tour. Take day trips to the **Blue Mountains** (☞ Chapter 2), **Ku-ring-gai Chase National Park,** the **Hawkesbury River,** or the historic city of **Parramatta** to Sydney's west. You may also like to explore some lesser known corners of the city. Travel on the **Bondi & Bay Explorer** bus around the eastern suburbs to Vaucluse House, the charming harborside village of **Watsons Bay,** and its beaches. You could take a boat tour to the historic harbor island of **Fort Denison,** play a round of golf or some tennis, or just spend a day shopping or do more relaxing on the beach.

When to Tour Sydney

The best times to visit Sydney are late spring and early fall. October and November are pleasantly warm, although the ocean is a bit too cold in October for swimming. December through February is hot and humid, with the likelihood of fierce, tropical downpours especially likely in January and February. In March and April, weather is typically stable and comfortable, outdoor city life is still in full swing, and the ocean is at its warmest.

If you're interested in two of the city's major festivals, you'll just have to live with the heat. January is the month of the Sydney Festival, with outdoor music, theater, circuses, and general mayhem. All of this takes an interesting turn in late February and early March during the Sydney Gay and Lesbian Mardi Gras, which culminates with a glittering and raunchy parade.

Sydney Harbour

Captain Arthur Phillip, commander of the first European fleet to sail into these waters, called Sydney Harbour "in extent and security, very superior to any other that I have ever seen—containing a considerable number of coves, formed by narrow necks of land, mostly rocks, covered with timber." Two centuries later, few would dispute that the harbor is one of nature's extraordinary creations.

Officially titled Port Jackson, the harbor is in its depths a river valley carved by the Parramatta and Lane Cove rivers and the many creeks that flow in from the north. The rising sea level at the end of the last Ice Age submerged the floor of the valley, leaving only the walls. In the earliest days of the colony, the military laid claim to much of the harbor's 240 km (149 mi) of shoreline. Few of these military areas were ever fortified or cleared, and as a result, much of the foreshore has survived in its natural splendor. Several pockets of land are now protected within Sydney Harbour National Park. Such areas as North, South, and Middle heads, and the harbor islands that you'll pass on the harbor cruise, are still much as they were in Governor Phillip's day.

This tour is based on the route followed by the State Transit Authority ferries on their daily Afternoon Harbour Cruise (☞ Contacts and Resources *in* Sydney A to Z, *below*). The Coffee Cruise run by Captain Cook Cruises follows a similar course. The tour takes in the eastern half of the harbor, from the city to the Heads and Middle Harbour. This is the glamorous side of the waterway, but the western shore has its own areas of historic and natural distinction, as well as Homebush Bay, the main site for the Olympic Summer Games in 2000 (☞ Around Sydney, *below*).

A Good Cruise

As the vessel leaves the ferry wharves at Circular Quay, it crosses **Sydney Cove** ①, where the ships of the First Fleet dropped anchor in January 1788. After rounding Bennelong Point (named after an early Aboriginal inhabitant who was a favorite of Governor Phillip) site of the Sydney Opera House, the boat turns east and crosses **Farm Cove** ②, passing the Royal Botanic Gardens. The tall, Gothic Revival chimneys just visible above the trees belong to Government House, the former official residence of the state governor and now frequently open to the public.

Garden Island ③, the country's largest naval dockyard, is easily identifiable across Woolloomooloo (say "*wool*-uh-muh-loo") Bay by its squadrons of sleek, gray warships. Visiting ships of the U.S. Navy's Pacific fleet can often be seen tied up here. Darling Point is the next headland, dominated by several tall apartment blocks and marking the beginning of Sydney's desirable eastern suburbs. Across Double Bay, **Point Piper** ④ is famous as the ritziest address in the country. The large expanse of water to the east of Point Piper is **Rose Bay** ⑤, bordered by

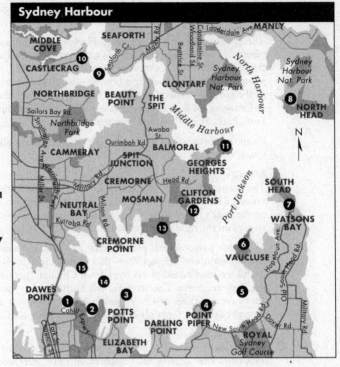

Sydney Harbour

---

another highly desirable, but somewhat more affordable, harborside suburb.

Vaucluse ⑥ is yet another suburb that conveys social stature, beyond Rose Bay. The area is named after **Vaucluse House,** the sandstone mansion built by 19th-century explorer, publisher, and politician William Wentworth. The house is hidden from view, but you can see the Grecian columns of Strickland House, which was used as a convalescent home until a few years ago. To the east is Shark Bay, part of **Nielsen Park,** and one of the most popular of the harbor bathing beaches (☞ Beaches, *below*). **Watsons Bay** ⑦, a former fishing village, is the easternmost suburb on the harbor's south side. Beyond, South Head presides over the meeting of harbor and ocean. It is one of the two giant sandstone headlands that protect Port Jackson.

North Head is the boat's next landmark, followed by the beachside suburb of **Manly** ㉛, and the **Quarantine Station** ⑧. The station was once used to protect Sydney from disease, and is a remnant of a fascinating chapter in the nation's history. The vessel then enters **Middle Harbour** ⑨—formed by creeks that spring from the forested peaks of Ku-ring-gai Chase National Park (☞ Around Sydney, *below*)—where you'll pass the beach at Clontarf and sail through the opening in the Spit Bridge. On the way back to the bridge after exploring Middle Harbour, you'll cruise by the suburb of **Castlecrag** ⑩, founded by Walter Burley Griffin, the American architect responsible for the layout of Canberra.

On returning to the main body of the harbor, look to your right for the popular beach at Balmoral and **Middle Head** ⑪, part of Sydney Harbour National Park and the site of mid-19th-century cannons and fortifications. During that period, Sydney Harbour became a regular port of call for American whaling ships, the crews of which were responsible for the name of nearby **Chowder Bay** ⑫. Sailing deeper into the harbor, the vessel passes **Taronga Zoo** ⑬, where you might catch a glimpse of some of the animals through the foliage.

The vessel now heads back toward Harbour Bridge, passing the tiny island of **Fort Denison** ⑭, Sydney's most prominent fortification. On the point at **Kirribilli** ⑮, almost opposite the Opera House, you will catch glimpses of two colonial-style houses—the official Sydney residences of the governor-general and prime minister, who are otherwise based in Canberra. Still on the north side, but west of Harbour Bridge, lies Luna Park, Sydney's defunct amusement park.

From the north side of the harbor, the vessel crosses back to Circular Quay, where the tour ends.

TIMING

This scenic cruise, aboard one of the State Transit Authority ferries, takes 2½ hours and operates year-round. Refreshments are available on the boat's lower deck and, for the best view, you should begin the voyage on the right side of the vessel.

The cruise passes several places—such as Vaucluse House, the Quarantine Station, and Taronga Zoo—that you may wish to visit later. These can all be reached either via ferry from Circular Quay, or on one of the Explorer buses. The State Transit Authority ferry tour described above departs Circular Quay weekdays at 1, weekends at 1:30. Sunset and city-lights tours ply the waters on different scenic routes.

Sights to See

⑩ **Castlecrag.** This Middle Harbour suburb was founded by Walter Burley Griffin after he designed Canberra. In 1924, after working on the national capital and in Melbourne, the American architect moved to Sydney and built a number of houses that are notable for their harmony with the surrounding bushland. About eight of his houses survive, although none are visible from the harbor.

⑫ **Chowder Bay.** The oysters and other shellfish collected from these rocky shores decades ago have their part in the naming of this bay. Nineteenth-century American whalers made their chowder here. They once anchored off what is now army land to the southwest of Middle Head. The bay's location is identifiable by a cluster of wooden buildings at water's edge and twin oil-storage tanks.

❷ **Farm Cove.** Now the location of the **Royal Botanic Gardens** (☞ *below*), the shore of this bay was where the first, unsuccessful attempts were made to establish gardens to feed the convict settlers. The long sea wall was constructed from the 1840s onward to enclose the previously swampy foreshore.

⑭ **Fort Denison.** For a brief time in the early days of the colony, convicts who committed petty offenses were kept on this harbor island. The island was progressively fortified from 1841, when it was also decided to strengthen the existing defenses at Dawes Point Battery, under the Harbour Bridge. Work was abandoned when cash ran out and not completed until 1857, when fears of Russian expansion in the Pacific spurred further fortification. Today, the firing of the fort's cannon signals not an imminent invasion, but merely the hour—one o'clock. The National Parks and Wildlife Service runs two-hour-long tours to Fort Denison; however, these are occasionally suspended due to ongoing conservation work on the island. Tours depart from Cadman's Cottage, 110 George Street, The Rocks. ⊠ *Sydney Harbour,* ☎ *02/9247–5033.* ⊡ *$12–14.* ☉ *Tour Sat. at noon and 6, Sun. at noon, Thurs. and Fri. at 5:30.*

③ Garden Island. During the 1941–45 War of the Pacific, Garden Island, Sydney's large naval base and dockyard, was a frontline port for Allied ships. On the night of May 31, 1942, this battle fleet was the target of three Japanese midget submarines that were launched from a mother submarine at sea. Two of the three penetrated the antisubmarine net that had been laid across the harbor and one sank the HMAS *Kuttabul*, a ferry being used as a naval depot ship, with a loss of 21 lives. Despite the ensuing chaos, two of the midget submarines were confirmed sunk.

Garden Island isn't open to the public, but the naval base may eventually be relocated outside Sydney, and there are plans to transform this prime harborside location into a recreational area.

⑮ Kirribilli. Residents of this attractive suburb opposite the city and Opera House have million-dollar views, an excellent little theater, and two of Sydney's most important mansions. The more modest of the two is **Kirribilli House,** which is the official Sydney home of the prime minister and not open to the public. Next door and far more prominent is **Admiralty House**—the Sydney residence of the governor-general, the Queen's representative in Australia. This impressive residence is occasionally open for inspection. ⊠ *Carabella St. and Kirribilli Ave.* ☎ *02/9955–4095.*

⑨ Middle Harbour. Except for the sight of yachts moored in the sandy coves, the upper reaches of Middle Harbour are exactly as they were when the first Europeans set eyes on Port Jackson, just over 200 years ago. This area of bush and parkland also has tranquil, desirable residential suburbs that are only a short drive from the city. Many of the houses here on the northern side of the harbor are set back from the waterline behind bushland; by the time these were built, planning authorities no longer allowed direct water frontage.

⑪ Middle Head. Despite its benign appearance now, Sydney Harbour once bristled with armaments. In the middle of the last century, faced with expansionist European powers hungry for new colonies, artillery positions were erected on the headlands to guard harbor approaches. At Middle Head you can still see the rectangular gun emplacements set into the cliff face.

④ Point Piper. Many of this exclusive harborside suburb's magnificent dwellings are home to Sydney's rich and famous. Tom Cruise and Nicole Kidman purchased a home here in 1998, and waterfront mansions change hands for close to $20 million.

⑧ Quarantine Station. From the 1830s onward, ships and passengers that arrived with contagious diseases were isolated on this outpost in the shadow of North Head until pronounced free of illness. Among the last to be quartered here were the victims of Cyclone Tracy, which devastated Darwin in 1974. Ten years later, after its brief use as a staging post for a group of Vietnamese orphans, the Quarantine Station was closed, its grim purpose finally brought to an end by modern medicine. You can take a 90-minute guided tour of the station with a ranger from the National Parks and Wildlife Service, caretakers of the site. Another interesting option is a three-hour nocturnal Ghost Tour—the station reputedly has its fair share of ghosts. The tour includes supper, and reservations are essential. The basic tour departs from Manly Wharf and the Ghost Tour departs from the visitor center at the Quarantine Station. Catch a ferry to Manly from Circular Quay, then take a taxi from Manly Wharf, or take Bus 135 from Stand No. 4 at the wharf. ⊠ *North Head, Manly,* ☎ *02/9977–6229.* ⌑ *$10 basic tour, $17–$20 Ghost Tour.* ☉ *Basic tour Mon., Wed., and Fri. at 10:40, Sat. at 1:25; Ghost Tour Wed., Fri., and weekends at 7:30.*

⑤ Rose Bay. This large bay was once a base for the Qantas flying boats that provided the only passenger air service between Australia and America and Europe. The last flying boat departed Rose Bay in the 1960s, but the "airstrip" is still used by floatplanes on scenic flights connecting Sydney with the Hawkesbury River and the Central Coast.

① Sydney Cove. Enclosed by Bennelong Point and the Sydney Opera House to the east and Circular Quay West and the Rocks to the west, the cove was named after Lord Sydney, the British Home Secretary at the time the colony was founded. The settlement itself was to be known as New Albion, but the name never caught on. Instead the city took its name from this tiny bay.

★ ☺ ⑬ **Taronga Zoo.** In a natural bush setting on the northern shore of the harbor, Sydney's zoo has an especially extensive collection of Australian fauna, including everybody's favorite marsupial—the koala. The zoo has gone to great effort to create spacious enclosures that closely simulate natural habitats. It is set on a hillside, and a complete tour can be tiring, so you may want to pick up the free map at the entrance gate that outlines a less strenuous route. Children's strollers are provided free of charge, but they are rather basic.

The easiest way to get to the zoo from the city is by ferry. From Taronga Wharf, a bus or the cable car will take you up the hill to the main entrance. The ZooPass, a combined ferry-zoo ticket, is available at Circular Quay. ⊠ *Bradleys Head Rd., Mosman,* ☎ *02/9969–2777.* ☜ *$16.* ☉ *Daily 9–5.*

⑥ Vaucluse. One of the most attractive harbor suburbs, the palatial homes of Vaucluse offer a glimpse of Sydney's high society. The small beaches at Nielsen Park and Parsley Bay offer safe swimming and are packed with families in summer.

A large part of this area once belonged to the estate of **Vaucluse House,** one of Sydney's most illustrious remaining historic mansions. Most of the Gothic Revival building was constructed in the 1830s for William Charles Wentworth, the "Father of the Australian Constitution," and his family. The 15-room house is furnished in period style, and its delightful gardens are managed by the Historic Houses Trust and open to the public. There are also famous old-style tearooms on the grounds. You can get to the house on the Bondi & Bay Explorer bus. ⊠ *Wentworth Rd., Vaucluse,* ☎ *02/9388–7922.* ☜ *$6.* ☉ *Tues.–Sun. 10–4:30.*

⑦ Watsons Bay. Established as a military base and fishing settlement in the colony's early years, Watsons Bay is a charming suburb that has held onto its rare, village atmosphere. Camp Cove, the main beach here, is of some historical importance: It was intended that the convicts who were to be Australia's first settlers would establish a community at Botany Bay, which had been explored by Captain Cook in 1770. However, as Captain Phillip found when he arrived 18 years later, the lack of fresh water at that site made settlement impossible. After a few days, he set off to explore Port Jackson, which had been named but not visited by Cook. Phillip rounded the Heads and landed on a beach that he named Camp Cove. The walkway that runs along the top of The Gap, the sheer cliffs at the southern approach to Port Jackson, commands a spectacular view of the surging sea far below.

The Rocks and Sydney Harbour Bridge

The Rocks is the birthplace not just of Sydney but of modern Australia. It was here that the 11 ships of the First Fleet dropped anchor in 1788, and this stubby peninsula enclosing the western side of Sydney Cove became known simply as the Rocks.

The first crude wooden huts erected by the convicts were followed by simple houses made from mud bricks cemented together by a mixture of sheep's wool and mud. The rain soon washed this rough mortar away, and no buildings in the Rocks survive from the earliest period of convict settlement. Most of the architecture dates from the Victorian era, by which time Sydney had become a thriving port. Warehouses lining the waterfront were backed by a row of tradesmen's shops, banks, and taverns, and above them ascending Observatory Hill rose a tangled mass of alleyways lined with the cottages of seamen and wharf laborers. By the late 1800s all who could afford to had moved out of the area, and it was widely regarded as a rough, tough, squalid part of town. As late as 1900 bubonic plague swept through the Rocks, prompting the government to offer a bounty for dead rats in an effort to exterminate their disease-carrying fleas.

The character of the Rocks area changed considerably when the Sydney Harbour Bridge was built during the 1920s and '30s, when many old houses, and even entire streets, were demolished to make room for the bridge's southern approach route. The bridge took almost nine years to build and replaced the ferries that once carried passengers and freight across the harbor.

It is only since the 1980s that the Rocks has become appreciated for its historic significance and extensive restoration has transformed the area. Here you can see the evolution of a society almost from its inception to the present, and yet the Rocks is anything but a stuffy tutorial. History stands side by side with shops, outdoor cafés, and some excellent museums.

A Good Walk

Begin at **Circular Quay,** the lively waterfront area where Sydney's ferry, bus, and train systems converge. Follow the quay toward Harbour Bridge and, as you round the curve, turn left and walk about 20 paces into First Fleet Park. The map on the platform in front of you describes the colony of 1808. The **Tank Stream** entered Sydney Cove at this very spot. This tiny watercourse brought the colony its fresh water—the necessity that decided the location of the first European settlement on Australian soil.

Return to the waterfront and take the paved walkway toward Harbour Bridge. The massive art deco–style building to your left is the **Museum of Contemporary Art** ⑯, which is devoted to painting, sculpture, film, video, and kinetic art made during the past 20 years.

Continue on this walkway around **Circular Quay West,** and when you reach the fig trees in the circular bed, look left. The bronze statue beneath the trees is the figure of **William Bligh** ⑰ of HMAV *Bounty* fame. To the right is a two-story, cream-color stone house. This is **Cadman's Cottage** ⑱. Built in 1816, it is the oldest surviving house in the city of Sydney. The large modern building ahead of you on the waterfront is the **Overseas Passenger Terminal** ⑲, the main mooring for passenger liners in Sydney.

Have a look inside Cadman's Cottage and then climb the stairs leading to George Street. Note the original gas streetlamp at the top of these steps. Turn right and immediately on the right is the **Sydney Visitors Information Centre** ⑳, which has a bookshop and an information counter that can provide you with useful leaflets about the city.

44

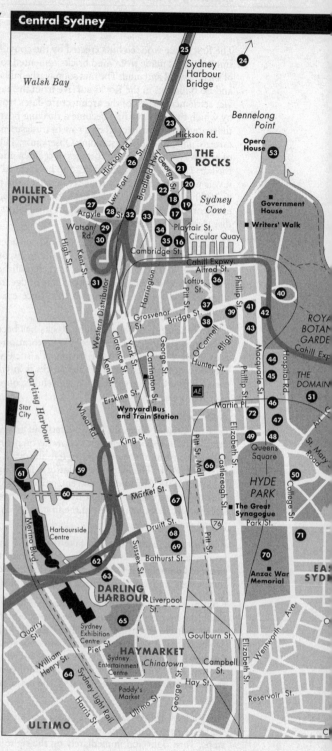

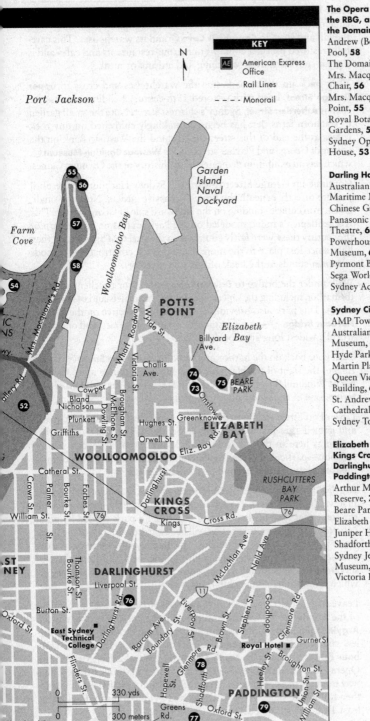

KEY

AE American Express Office

— Rail Lines

- - - Monorail

N

Port Jackson

Garden Island Naval Dockyard

Farm Cove

POTTS POINT

Elizabeth Bay

Billyard Ave.

Challis Ave.

Wharf Road

Wylde St.

Victoria St.

Kingsway

BEARE PARK

Onslow

Greenknowe

ELIZABETH BAY

Cowper
Bland
Nicholson
Plunkett
Griffiths

Broughton St.
McElhone St.
Dowling St.

Hughes St.

Orwell St.

Eliz. Bay Rd.

WOOLLOOMOOLOO

RUSHCUTTERS BAY PARK

Darlinghurst Rd.

KINGS CROSS

Kings Cross Rd.

Catheral St.

Crown St.

Palmer St.

Bourke St.

Forbes St.

William St.

ST
NEY

Thomson St.

Bourke St.

DARLINGHURST

Liverpool St.

Burton St.

Oxford St.

East Sydney Technical College

Darlinghurst Rd.

Barcom Ave.

Boundary St.

Liverpool St.

McLachlan Ave.

Neild Ave.

Stephen St.

Brown St.

Goodhope St.

Glenmore Rd.

Royal Hotel ■

Gurner St.

Flinders St.

Hopewell St.

Shadforth St.

Glenmore Rd.

Oxford St.

Heeley St.

Broughton St.

Union St.

PADDINGTON

William St.

Greens Rd.

0 ———— 330 yds

0 ———— 300 meters

Cleveland St.

The Opera House, the RBG, and the Domain North
Andrew (Boy) Charlton Pool, **58**
The Domain north, **57**
Mrs. Macquarie's Chair, **56**
Mrs. Macquarie's Point, **55**
Royal Botanic Gardens, **54**
Sydney Opera House, **53**

Darling Harbour
Australian National Maritime Museum, **61**
Chinese Garden, **65**
Panasonic IMAX Theatre, **62**
Powerhouse Museum, **64**
Pyrmont Bridge, **60**
Sega World, **63**
Sydney Aquarium, **59**

Sydney City Center
AMP Tower, **66**
Australian Museum, **71**
Hyde Park, **70**
Martin Place, **72**
Queen Victoria Building, **67**
St. Andrew's Cathedral, **69**
Sydney Town Hall, **68**

Elizabeth Bay and Kings Cross, Darlinghurst, and Paddington
Arthur McElhone Reserve, **74**
Beare Park, **75**
Elizabeth Bay House, **73**
Juniper Hall, **79**
Shadforth Street, **78**
Sydney Jewish Museum, **76**
Victoria Barracks, **77**

After leaving the Information Centre, turn right past the redbrick façade of the Australian Steam Navigation Company. Continue down the hill and steps to **Campbells Cove** ㉑ and its warehouses. This carefully restored precinct contains numerous restaurants and cafés and is a great spot for harbor watching and a drink or meal.

Walk back up the steps beside the warehouses and cross to **upper George Street,** lined with restored 19th-century buildings. Across the road is **Atherden Street,** Sydney's shortest street. Note the small garden of staghorn ferns that has been painstakingly cultivated on tiny rock ledges at the end of this street. Just behind the Westpac Bank on the corner of George and Playfair streets is the **Westpac Banking Museum** ㉒, which has an exhibition dedicated to the history of the Olympic Games.

Continue up George Street toward the Sydney Harbour Bridge until you are directly beneath the bridge's massive girders. Note the small, green, iron cubicle standing on the landward side of George Street. This is a gentlemen's toilet, modeled on the Parisian pissoir. At the turn of the century these were fairly common on the streets of Sydney, but they have since lost place to the more discreet brick constructions (a modern toilet stands at the back of this sole survivor).

Walk under the bridge to **Dawes Point Park** ㉓ for excellent views of the harbor, including the Opera House and the small island of **Fort Denison** ㉔. This park also provides an unusual perspective on the **Sydney Harbour Bridge** ㉕—an unmistakable symbol of the city, and one of the world's widest long-span bridges.

Turn your back on the harbor and walk up **Lower Fort Street** ㉖, which runs to the right of the Harbour View Hotel. Continue up to the corner of Windmill Street, where you'll find the wedge-shaped **Hero of Waterloo,** one of the oldest pubs in the city.

Lower Fort Street ends at **Argyle Place** ㉗, built by Governor Macquarie and named after his home county in Scotland. The houses and other buildings here in the minisuburb of Millers Point are worth an inspection—particularly **Holy Trinity Church** ㉘ on the left-hand side, and the **Lord Nelson Hotel** beyond the "village" green.

Argyle Place is dominated by **Observatory Hill** ㉙, the site of the colony's first windmill and, later, a signal station. If you have the energy to climb the steps that lead to the hill, you will reach a park shaded by giant Moreton Bay fig trees, where you will be rewarded with one of the finest views in Sydney. On top of the hill is the **Sydney Observatory** ㉚, now a museum of astronomy. You can also follow the path behind the Observatory to the National Trust Centre and the **S. H. Ervin Gallery** ㉛, which mounts changing exhibitions with Australian themes.

Leave Argyle Place and walk down **Argyle Street** into the dark tunnel of the **Argyle Cut** ㉜. On the lower side of the cut and to the left, the **Argyle Stairs** lead up through an archway. Don't take these steps unless you intend to tackle several flights of stairs that lead to the Harbour Bridge and into the **South East Pylon** for a dizzying view of the Opera House and the city. To get to the Sydney Harbour Bridge walkway from the top of the stairs, cross the road and walk left for 20 yards, then follow the signs to the walkway and pylon. You should allow at least 1½ hours for this detour.

The walk resumes at the foot of the steps on Argyle Street. Continue down the street and turn left under the archway inscribed with the words **Argyle Stores** ㉝. The old warehouses around this courtyard have been converted to upmarket fashion shops and galleries. Leave the Argyle Stores and cross onto Harrington Street.

The **Gumnut Café** on the left-hand side of this street is a good place for a refreshment stop. Ten yards beyond the café is the **Suez Canal** ㉞, a narrow laneway that runs down the incline toward George Street. Turn right at **Nurses Walk** ㉟, another of the area's historic and atmospheric back streets, then left into Surgeons Court and left again into George Street. On the left is the handsome sandstone facade of the former **Rocks Police Station,** now a crafts gallery. From this point, Circular Quay is only a short walk away.

TIMING

The attractions of the Rocks are many, so to walk this route—even without lingering in museums or galleries, or walking up to the Sydney Harbour Bridge—you should allow about a half day. If you spend a reasonable amount of time in the Museum of Contemporary Art, Sydney Observatory, and the S. H. Ervin Gallery, a full day is required.

The area is often very crowded on weekends, when the Rocks Market in George Street with its crafts, souvenir items, and handmade Australiana presents a serious distraction from sightseeing. The Rocks is also packed with interesting shops, so be forewarned that your time can disappear rapidly if you succumb to shopping fever.

Sights to See

㉜ Argyle Cut. Argyle Street links Argyle Place with George Street, and the thoroughfare is dominated by the Argyle Cut and its massive walls. In the days before the cut was made, the sandstone ridge here was a major barrier to traffic crossing between Circular Quay and Millers Point. In 1843, convict work gangs hacked at the sandstone with hand tools for 2½ years before the project was abandoned due to lack of progress. Work restarted in 1857, when drills, explosives, and paid labor completed the job. The **Argyle Stairs** lead off this street up to the Sydney Harbour Bridge walkway, and a spectacular view from the South East Pylon (☞ Sydney Harbour Bridge, *below,* for details).

㉗ Argyle Place. Unusual for Sydney, this charming enclave in the suburb of Millers Point has all the traditional requirements of an English green: a pub at one end, church at the other, and grass in between. Argyle Place is lined with 19th-century houses and cottages on its northern side and overlooked by Observatory Hill to the south.

NEED A BREAK?	While in the west end of Argyle Place, consider the liquid temptations of the **Lord Nelson,** Sydney's oldest hotel, which has been licensed to serve alcohol since 1842. The sandstone pub has its own brewery on the premises. One of its specialties is Quayle Ale, named after the U.S. vice president who "sank a schooner" here during his 1989 visit to Australia—a decade later and they're still serving it. ⊠ *19 Kent St., Millers Point,* ☎ *02/9251–4044.*

㉝ Argyle Stores. These solid sandstone warehouses date from the late 1820s. The building emerged from a total refit at the end of 1996 and now houses several chic gift and souvenir shops, clothes boutiques, and cafés. ⊠ *Argyle St. opposite Harrington St.*

⑰ William Bligh statue. Yes, this is the infamous captain—cursed both at sea and on land. After his incident on the *Bounty,* Bligh became governor of New South Wales in 1806. Two years later he faced his second mutiny. Bligh had made himself unpopular with the soldiers of the New South Wales Corps, commonly known as the Rum Corps, who were the real power in the colony. When he threatened to end their lucrative liquor trade monopoly, he was imprisoned in an incident known as the Rum Rebellion. He spent the next two years as a captive until his successor, Lachlan Macquarie, arrived. Ironically, the statue's gaze frequently rests on HMAV *Bounty,* a replica of Bligh's ship, as it sails around the harbor on daily sightseeing cruises.

⑱ Cadman's Cottage. Although of modest proportions, the city's oldest building has an interesting history. John Cadman was a convict who was sentenced for life to New South Wales for stealing a horse. He later became superintendent of government boats, a position that entitled him to live in the upper story of this house. The water once lapped almost at Cadman's doorstep, and the original seawall still stands at the front of the house. The small extension on the side of the cottage was built to lock up the oars of Cadman's boats, since oars would have been a necessity for any convict attempting to escape by sea. The upper floor of Cadman's Cottage now contains a National Parks and Wildlife Service bookshop and information center for Sydney Harbour National Park. ⊠ *110 George St.,* ☎ *02/9247–8861.* ☉ *Mon. 10–3, Tues.–Fri. 9–4:30, weekends 11–4.*

㉑ Campbells Cove. Robert Campbell was a Scottish merchant who is sometimes referred to as the "father of Australian commerce." Campbell broke the stranglehold that the British East India Company exercised over seal and whale products, which were New South Wales's only exports in those early days. The cove's atmospheric, sandstone **Campbells Storehouse,** built from 1838 onward, now serves as a home for waterside restaurants. The pulleys that were used to hoist cargoes still hang on the upper level of the warehouses.

The cove is also the mooring for Sydney's fully operational tall ships— the **HMAV** *Bounty,* an authentic replica of the original 18th-century vessel, and the rebuilt 1902 *Solway Lass*—which offer theme cruises around the harbor (☞ Guided Tours *in* Sydney A to Z, *below*).

㉓ Dawes Point Park. Named after William Dawes, a First Fleet marine and astronomer who established the colony's first basic observatory nearby in 1788, this was also once the site of a fortification known as Dawes Battery. The cannon on the hillside pointing toward the Opera House came from the ships of the First Fleet. The park provides wonderful views of the harbor, Fort Denison, and the Harbour Bridge.

㉛ S. H. Ervin Gallery. Housed in the impressive National Trust Centre just behind Observatory Hill, this gallery concentrates on Australian art and architecture from a historical perspective. The changing exhibitions are of a consistently high standard and have shown the work of such well-known Australian artists as Lloyd Rees, Sidney Nolan, Hans Heysen, and Russell Drysdale. The gallery has a bookshop, and there is a very good National Trust gift shop next door. ⊠ *National Trust Centre, Observatory Hill, Watson Rd., Millers Point,* ☎ *02/9258– 0123.* ▧ *$6.* ☉ *Tues.–Fri. 11–5, weekends noon–5.*

Harrington Street area. The small precinct around this street forms one of the Rocks's most interesting areas. Many old cottages, houses, and even warehouses here have been converted to hotel accommodations, and there are some fascinating lanes and alleyways to explore. ☞ **Suez Canal** and ☞ **Nurses Walk** are among them.

㉘ Holy Trinity Church. Every morning redcoats would march to this 1840 Argyle Place church from Dawes Point Battery, and it became commonly known as the Garrison Church. As the regimental plaques and colors around the walls testify, it still retains a close association with the military. The tattered ensign on the left wall was carried into battle by Australian troops during the Boer War, in which Australians were enlisted to help the British Empire fight Dutch South Africans. ⊠ *Argyle Pl., Millers Point.* ☼ *Daily, generally 9–5, but times vary.*

26 **Lower Fort Street.** At one time the handsome Georgian houses along this street, originally a rough track leading from the Dawes Point Battery to Observatory Hill, were among the best addresses in Sydney. Elaborate wrought-iron lacework still graces many of the facades—restoration is under way, but many of the houses are rather run-down.

Hero of Waterloo, which dates from 1844, is Sydney's second-oldest hotel. Gold fever struck the colony during the middle of the 19th century, and it was not uncommon for an entire ship's crew to desert and head for the goldfields as soon as the ship reached Sydney. Captains often resorted to skulduggery to recruit a new crew, and legend has it that many a lad who drank with a generous sea captain in the Hero would awake the next morning on a heaving deck, already out of sight of land. ⊠ *81 Lower Fort St.,* ☎ *02/9252–4553.* ☼ *Daily 10 AM–11 PM.*

16 **Museum of Contemporary Art.** Andy Warhol, Roy Lichtenstein, Cindy Sherman, and local artists Juan Devila, Maria Kozic, and Imants Tillers are just some of the well-known names whose works hang in this ponderous art deco building on Circular Quay West. The MCA houses one of Australia's most important collections of modern art, and its special exhibitions are as worthwhile as the permanent collection. The museum's café, with outdoor seating beside the harbor, is pleasant for breakfast and lunch. ⊠ *Circular Quay W,* ☎ *02/9252–4033.* 💲 *$9.* ☼ *Daily 10–6.*

35 **Nurses Walk.** Cutting across the area of the colony's first hospital, Nurses Walk bears its name out of the colony's earliest illnesses. Seven hundred and thirty-six convicts survived the voyage from Portsmouth, England, aboard the First Fleet's 11 ships. Many of them arrived suffering from dysentery, smallpox, scurvy, and typhoid. A few days after he landed at Sydney Cove, Governor Phillip established a tent hospital to care for the worst cases.

Only 40 convicts had died onboard Phillip's ships during the long voyage from England, a mortality rate (5%) that was considered a triumph at the time. In comparison, by the time the Second Fleet dropped anchor in Sydney Cove in 1790, a quarter of its convicts had died and a great many more were critically ill. One of the ships in the Second Fleet carried a prefabricated hospital, which was erected and filled almost immediately.

Beyond Nurses Walk, the old **Rocks Police Station** on George Street dates from 1882 and now contains a variety of good crafts shops. Note the police truncheon thrust into the lion's mouth above the doorway, an architectural motif that appears on at least one other of Sydney's Victorian police stations.

NEED A
BREAK?

The **Gumnut Café** is more than just an ideal refreshment stop. In this second-oldest (1830) building in the Rocks—originally the residence of blacksmith William Reynolds—a painless history lesson comes with a delicious lunch. The restaurant tucked away in his sandstone cottage serves tasty salads, pasta dishes, and cakes. The best tables are at the back in the shady garden. The Gumnut has a devoted clientele, and reservations are necessary at lunchtime. If you're staying in the area, breakfast in the courtyard is a great start to the day. Prices are moderate. ⊠ *28 Harrington St.,* ☎ *02/9247–9591.*

㉙ Observatory Hill. The city's highest point at 145 ft, this was known originally as Windmill Hill because the first windmill in the colony once stood here—but not for long. Soon after it was built, the canvas sails were stolen, the machinery was damaged in a storm, and the foundations cracked. Before it was 10 years old, the mill was useless. Several other windmills were erected in the area, however, and this part of the Rocks is still known as Millers Point. In 1848 the signal station at the top of the hill was built. This later became an astronomical observatory, and Windmill Hill changed its name to Observatory Hill. Until 1982 the metal ball on the tower of the observatory was cranked up the mast and dropped at precisely 1 PM so that ship captains could set their chronometers.

⑲ Overseas Passenger Terminal. Busy Circular Quay West is dominated by the structure and dock of this maritime station. The terminal was rebuilt in 1987 to accommodate the enormous ships that often call into Sydney as part of their cruise itineraries. There are a couple of excellent waterfront restaurants at the terminal's northern end, and it's worth taking the escalator to the upper deck for a good view of the harbor and Opera House.

㉞ Suez Canal. This narrow alley acquired its name before drains were installed, when rainwater would pour down its funnel-like passageway and gush across George Street. It was a haunt of the notorious Rocks gangs of the late 19th century, when robbery and crime were rife in the area.

㉕ Sydney Harbour Bridge. Known affectionately by Sydneysiders as the "old coat hanger," Harbour Bridge was a monumental engineering feat when it was completed in 1932. The roadway is supported by the arch above, not by the massive stone pylons, which were added for aesthetic rather than structural reasons. The 1,650-ft-long bridge is 160 ft wide and contains two railways tracks, eight road lanes, a cycleway, and a footpath. Actor Paul Hogan worked for several years as a rigger on the bridge, long before he tamed the world's wildlife and lowlife as the star of the film *Crocodile Dundee*.

There are two ways to experience the bridge and its spectacular views. The first, and less expensive, is to follow the walkway from its access point near the **Argyle Stairs** (☞ Argyle Cut, *above*) to the **South East Pylon.** This structure houses a display on the bridge's construction, and you can climb the 200 steps to the lookout and its unbeatable harbor panorama. ⊠ *S. East Pylon, Sydney Harbour Bridge,* ☎ *02/9247–3408.* ⌸ *$2.* ⊙ *Daily 10–5.*

Another more expensive option is the **BridgeClimb** tour, which takes you on a guided walking tour to the very top of the Harbour Bridge.
㉚ (☞ Contacts and Resources *in* Sydney A to Z, *below*). **Sydney Observatory.** No longer used for serious sky-gazing, because few stars can be seen through the glow of Sydney's bright lights, this structure on top of Observatory Hill has become a museum of astronomy. The Observatory features a number of hands-on displays, including constellation charts, talking computers, and games designed to illustrate principles of astronomy. During evening observatory shows, you'll have a close-up view of such wonders as the rings of Saturn, the moons of Jupiter, distant galaxies, and the enormous, multicolor clouds of gas known as nebulae. Reservations are required for the show. ⊠ *Observatory Hill, Watson Rd., Millers Point,* ☎ *02/9217–0485.* ⌸ *Evening show $8.* ⊙ *Observatory daily 10–5; show Nov.–Mar., Thurs.–Tues. at 8:30; Apr.–Oct., Thurs.–Tues. at 6:15 and 8:15.*

㉒ Sydney Visitors Information Centre. Once a sailor's home that provided inexpensive accommodations for mariners, this building now offers insight into the history of the Rocks, with displays of artifacts and a short video. Center staff can answer questions about the area and make travel bookings, and the informative Rocks Walking Tours depart from here. The building also contains a couple of good places to eat—the very popular **Sailor's Thai** (☞ Dining, *below*) restaurant and its less-expensive canteen. ✉ *106 George St.,* ☎ *02/9255–1788.* ⊘ *Mar.–Oct., daily 9–5; Nov.–Feb., daily 9–6.*

Upper George Street. The restored warehouses and Victorian terrace houses that line this part of George Street make this a charming section of the Rocks. The covered Rocks Market is held here on weekends (☞ Shopping, *below*).

㉒ Westpac Banking Museum. On a lane off George Street, the museum will display a collection of medals and souvenir pins relating to the Olympic Games until December 2000. ✉ *6–8 Playfair St.,* ☎ *02/9247–9755.* ⊘ *Weekdays 9–5, weekends 10–4.*

Macquarie Street and the Domain South

This walk will introduce you to two of the most remarkable figures in Australian history—Governor Lachlan Macquarie and his government architect, Francis Greenway. Descended from Scottish clan chieftains, Macquarie was an accomplished soldier and a man of vision—the first governor to foresee a role for New South Wales as a free society rather than an open prison. Macquarie laid the foundations for that society by establishing a plan for the city, constructing significant public buildings, and advocating that reformed convicts be readmitted to society. Francis Greenway was himself a former prisoner.

Macquarie's policies may seem perfectly reasonable today, but in the early 19th century they marked him as a radical. When his vision of a free society threatened to blur distinctions between soldiers, free settlers, and convicts, Macquarie was forced to resign. He was later buried on his Scottish estate, his gravestone inscribed with the words "the Father of Australia."

Macquarie's grand plans for the construction of Sydney might have come to nothing were it not for Francis Greenway. The governor had been continually frustrated by his masters in the Colonial Office in London, who saw no need for an architect in a penal colony. Then, in 1814, fate delivered Greenway into his hands. Greenway had trained as an architect in England, where he was convicted of forgery and sentenced to 14 years in New South Wales. Macquarie seized this opportunity, gave Greenway a ticket of leave that allowed him to work outside the convict system, and set him to work transforming Sydney.

For all his brilliance as an architect, Greenway was a difficult and temperamental man. When his patron Macquarie returned to England in 1822, Greenway quickly fell from favor and retired to his farm north of Sydney. Some years later he was charged with misappropriating this property, but he was able to produce a deed giving him title to the land. It is now believed that the signature on the title deed is a forgery. Greenway was depicted on one side of the old $10 notes, which went out of circulation early in the 1990s.

Only in Australia, perhaps, would a convicted forger be depicted on the currency.

A Good Walk

This historically based walk roughly follows the perimeter of the Royal Botanic Gardens and the Domain south. A shady park bench is never far away.

Begin at Circular Quay. Turn your back on the harbor and cross Alfred Street, which runs parallel to the waterfront. The most notable historic building along Alfred Street is the **Customs House** ㊱. When it was built in the late 1880s, the sandstone structure was surrounded by warehouses storing the fleeces that were the principal source of the colony's prosperity.

Walk up Loftus Street, which runs to the right of the Customs House. In Customs House Lane at the rear you can still see a pulley that was used to lower the wool bales to the dockyard from the top floor of Hinchcliff's Wool Stores.

Follow Loftus Street to the small triangular park on your right, **Macquarie Place** ㊲, which has a number of historical monuments. The southern side of the park is bordered by busy **Bridge Street,** lined with a number of grandiose Victorian buildings. Across Bridge Street, the **Lands Department** ㊳ is one of the finest examples of Victorian public architecture in Sydney. Walk up Bridge Street past the facade of the Department of Education. The **Museum of Sydney** ㊴ is on the next block. Built on the site of the first Government House, the museum chronicles the history of the city between 1788 and 1850.

Continue up Bridge Street to the corner of Macquarie Street. The figure on horseback about to gallop down Bridge Street is Edward VII, successor to Queen Victoria. The castellated building behind him is the **Sydney Conservatorium of Music** ㊵, originally built in 1819 as stables for Government House, which is screened by trees near the Opera House.

Your next stop is the lovely 1850s **History House** ㊶, headquarters of the Royal Australian Historical Society. It's just south of Bridge Street on **Macquarie Street,** Sydney's most elegant street. Opposite the History House are the **Garden Palace Gates** ㊷, an elegant wrought-iron entrance to the Royal Botanic Gardens. A little farther along Macquarie Street (Number 145) is the **Royal Australasian College of Physicians** ㊸. The patrician facade of this building gives some idea of the way Macquarie Street looked in the 1840s, when it was lined with the homes of the colonial elite.

The ponderous brown building ahead and to the left is the **State Library of New South Wales** ㊹. Cross the road toward this building, passing the Light Horse Monument and the Shakespeare Memorial. Australian cavalrymen fought with distinction in several Middle Eastern campaigns during World War I, and the former statue is dedicated to their horses—which were not allowed to return due to Australian quarantine regulations.

Continue along Macquarie Street toward the gates of **State Parliament House** ㊺, a building with an intriguing history. It's the northern wing of the building once known as the Rum Hospital, built with profits from the rum trade. In a stroke of political genius, Governor Macquarie persuaded two merchants to build a hospital for convicts in return for an extremely lucrative three-year monopoly on the importation of rum.

The next building on the left is the Victorian-style **Sydney Hospital** ㊻, constructed to replace the central section of the Rum Hospital, which had begun to fall apart almost as soon as it was completed. Beyond the hospital is the **Sydney Mint Museum** ㊼, originally the Rum Hospital's southern wing. It is devoted to the history of gold in Australia.

Next door is the **Hyde Park Barracks** ④. Before Macquarie arrived, convicts were left to roam freely at night, and there was little regard for the sanctity of life or property on the streets of Sydney after dark. As the new governor, Macquarie was determined to establish law and order, and he commissioned Greenway to design this building to house prisoners. Opposite Hyde Park Barracks is the 1970s high-rise **Law Court** building. This area is the heart of Sydney's legal district.

Cross Queens Square to the other side of the road, where the figure of Queen Victoria presides over Macquarie Street. To Victoria's left is another Greenway building, **St. James Church** ④, originally designed as a court of law.

Return to the other side of Macquarie and walk along College Street to **St. Mary's Cathedral** ⑤ (the main entrance is on Cathedral Street). This is Sydney's Roman Catholic cathedral whose design is based on Lincoln Cathedral in England. As you walk along the side of the cathedral, note the pointed arches above the doors and the flying buttresses—the arches that connect the side of the cathedral to supporting piers—both signatures of Gothic style.

At the rear of the cathedral, cross St. Mary's Road to Art Gallery Road. You are now in the parklands of **the Domain south** ⑤. The once-continuous Domain is divided into north and south sections by the Cahill Expressway. Continue past the statue of **Robert Burns,** the Scottish poet. The large trees on the left with enormous roots and drooping limbs are the widely planted Moreton Bay figs, which bear inedible fruit. Directly ahead is the **Art Gallery of New South Wales** ⑤, housed in a grand Victorian building with modern extensions. It contains the state's largest collection of artwork.

This is where the tour ends. From the Art Gallery, you can return to Macquarie Street by crossing the Domain or wandering for a half mile through the Royal Botanic Gardens. If you have an Explorer bus pass, you can catch the bus back to the city center from the front of the gallery.

TIMING
To walk the outlined itinerary should take no more than a morning or afternoon, even with stops to inspect the Museum of Sydney, Sydney Mint Museum, Hyde Park Barracks, and the Art Gallery of New South Wales. Apart from the initial part of the walk, which climbs from Circular Quay to Macquarie Street, the terrain is flat and easy.

Sights to See

⑤ **Art Gallery of New South Wales.** This gallery permanently exhibits Aboriginal, Asian, and European art, as well as the work of some of the best-known Australian artists. A distinctly Australian style has evolved, from early painters who saw the country through European eyes to such painters as Russell Drysdale, whose strident colors and earthy realism give a very different impression of the Australian landscape.

Twentieth-century art is displayed on the entrance level, where large windows frame their own spectacular view of the harbor. Below ground level, in the gallery's major extensions, the Yiribana Gallery displays one of the nation's most comprehensive collections of Aboriginal and Torres Strait Islander art. If you want a change from the usual postcards of kookaburras, kangaroos, and koalas, the bookshop on the ground floor has an offbeat collection. ⊠ *Art Gallery Rd., the Domain,* ☎ *02/9225-1744.* ☜ *Free, special-exhibition fee varies.* ☉ *Daily 10–5.*

㊱ **Customs House.** Close to the site where the British flag was raised on the First Fleet's arrival in 1788, this impressive 1840s–1890s building was in use until 1990 as the city's customs house and later as offices.

Following a $24 million refurbishment, the Customs House reopened in December 1998. The building now houses the Centre for Contemporary Craft, a retail crafts gallery, and the Djamu Gallery, Australia's largest permanent exhibition of Aboriginal and Pacific Island artifacts. The standout in the clutch of restaurants and cafés in this newly sparkling historic structure is the rooftop Café Sydney, overlooking Sydney Cove. ⊠ *Customs House Sq., Alfred St., Circular Quay,* ☎ *02/9265–2007.*

51 **The Domain south.** Laid out by Governor Macquarie in 1810 as his own personal "domain" and originally including what is now the Royal Botanic Gardens, this large area of parkland is a tranquil haven at the city's eastern edge. Used mainly by office workers for lunchtime recreation, the park is also the venue for free outdoor concerts during the Festival of Sydney, held in January.

42 **Garden Palace Gates.** The gates are all that remains of the Garden Palace, a massive glass pavilion that was erected for the Sydney International Exhibition of 1879 and destroyed by fire three years later. On the arch above the gates is a depiction of the Garden Palace's dome. Stone pillars on either side of the gates are engraved with Australian wildflowers. ⊠ *Macquarie St. between Bridge and Bent Sts.*

41 **History House.** You're welcome to visit the home of the Royal Australian Historical Society and its collection of books and other materials. The society offers its considerable resources to anyone who wishes to delve into Australiana. The building itself is of architectural interest. Note the balconies and the Corinthian columns, all made from iron that was just becoming popular when this building was constructed in 1872. ⊠ *133 Macquarie St.,* ☎ *02/9247–8001.* ⊡ *Library $5.* ⊙ *Weekdays 9:30–4:30.*

Macquarie Street is Sydney's most elegant boulevard. It was masterminded by Governor Macquarie who, from 1810 until he was ousted in 1822, planned the transformation of the cart track leading to Sydney Cove into a stylish street of dwellings and government buildings. Fortunately, many of the 19th-century architectural delights here escaped demolition.

48 **Hyde Park Barracks.** This 1819 building is considered Greenway's architectural masterpiece. Essentially a simple structure, its restrained, classical lines are hallmarks of the Georgian era. The clock on the tower is the oldest functioning public timepiece in New South Wales. Today the Hyde Park Barracks houses a collection of artifacts from the convict era and from later years, when it was used as an asylum for Irish orphans and "unprotected women." A surprising number of relics from this period were preserved by rats, which carried away scraps of clothing for their nests beneath the floorboards—a bizarre detail that is graphically illustrated in the foyer. A room on the top floor is strung with hammocks, exactly as it was when the building housed convicts. Try one out for size. ⊠ *Queens Sq., Macquarie St.,* ☎ *02/9223–8922.* ⊡ *$6.* ⊙ *Daily 9:30–5.*

NEED A BREAK?   On a sunny day, the courtyard tables of the **Hyde Park Barracks Café** provide one of the finest places in the city to enjoy an outdoor lunch. The café serves a selection of light, imaginative meals, salads, and open sandwiches, with a wine list including Australian wines. Prices are moderate. ⊠ *Queens Sq., Macquarie St.,* ☎ *02/9223–1155.*

38 **Lands Department.** The figures occupying the niches at the corners of this 1890 sandstone building are early Australian explorers and politicians. James Barnet's building stands among other fine Victorian structures in the neighborhood. ⊠ *Bridge St., near the intersection of Macquarie Pl.*

㊲ Macquarie Place. This park, once a site of ceremonial and religious importance to Aboriginal people, contains a number of important monuments, including the obelisk once used as the point from which all distances from Sydney were measured. On a stone plinth at the bottom of the park is the anchor of HMS *Sirius,* flagship of the First Fleet, which struck a reef and sank off Norfolk Island in 1790. The bronze statue of the gentleman with his hands on his hips represents Thomas Mort, who more than a century ago became the first person to ship refrigerated cargo. The implications of this shipment were enormous. Mutton suddenly became a valuable export commodity, and for most of the next century the Australian economy rode on sheep's backs.

Bridge Street runs alongside Macquarie Place. This V-shaped street was named for the bridge that once crossed the Tank Stream. Formerly the site of the 1789 Government House and the colony's first bridge, a number of grandiose Victorian architectural specimens line its sidewalks.

㊴ Museum of Sydney. Built on the site of the modest original Government House, this museum documents Sydney's early period of European colonization. One of the most interesting features is outside—the striking "Edge of the Trees" sculpture, with its 29 columns that "speak" and contain remnants of Aboriginal and early European inhabitation. Inside the museum, Aboriginal culture, convict society, and the gradual transformation of the settlement at Sydney Cove are woven into the single most evocative portrayal of life in the early days of the country. Many of the exhibits are very innovative, using ultramodern technology and ingenious display methods. The museum has a popular café, and a shop that stocks unusual gifts and other items. ⊠ *Bridge and Phillip Sts.,* ☏ *02/9251–5988.* ᠌ *$6.* ⊘ *Daily 10–5.*

Also near the intersection of Bridge Street and Phillip Street is an imposing pair of sandstone buildings. The historic **Treasury Building** is now part of the Hotel Inter-Continental. James Barnet's **Colonial Secretary's Office**—he also designed the Lands Department—is opposite. Note the buildings' similarities, right down to the figures in the corner niches.

㊽ Royal Australasian College of Physicians. Once the home of a wealthy Sydney family, the building now houses a different elite—the city's most eminent physicians. ⊠ *Macquarie St. between Bridge and Bent Sts.*

㊾ St. James Church. Begun in 1822, the Colonial Georgian–style St. James is Sydney's oldest surviving church, and another fine Francis Greenway design. The building was to be the colony's first law court, and was half completed when Commissioner Bigge, who had been sent from England to investigate Macquarie's administration, ordered that the structure be converted into a church. Now lost among the skyscrapers, the church's tall spire once served as a landmark for ships entering the harbor.

Enter St. James through the door in the Doric portico. The interior walls of the church are covered with plaques commemorating early Australian explorers and administrators. Inscriptions on the plaques testify to the hardships of those early days, when death either at sea or at the hands of Aborigines seems to have been a common fate. ⊠ *Queens Sq., Macquarie St.,* ☏ *02/9232–3022.* ⊘ *Daily 9–5.*

㊿ St. Mary's Cathedral. The first St. Mary's was built here in 1821, but the chapel was destroyed by fire, and work on the present cathedral began in 1868. The building has not been completed, however—due to a shortage of funds, spires that were planned for the front towers have never been built. St. Mary's has some particularly fine stained-glass windows and a terrazzo floor in the crypt, where exhibitions are often held. The cathedral's large rose window was imported from England.

At the front of the cathedral are **statues of Cardinal Moran and Archbishop Kelly,** two Irishmen who were prominent in the Roman Catholic Church in Australia. Due to the high proportion of Irish men and women in the convict population, the Roman Catholic Church was often the voice of the oppressed in 19th-century Sydney, where anti-Catholic feeling ran high among the Protestant rulers. ⊠ *College and Cathedral Sts.,* ☎ *02/9220–0400.* ◻ *Tour free.* ◷ *Weekdays 6:30–6:30, Sat. 8–7:30, Sun. 6:30 AM–7:30 PM; tour Sun. at noon.*

④④ State Library of New South Wales. This large complex is based around the Mitchell and Dixson libraries, which house the world's largest collection of Australiana. The general reference collection housed in the library's modern extension on Macquarie Street is generally of more interest, however. The extension has an excellent book and gift shop, a café, free films, and changing exhibitions with Australian historical and cultural themes in the upstairs gallery.

The foyer inside the heavy glass doors of the imposing 1910 Mitchell Wing contains one of the earliest maps of Australia. It is a copy in marble mosaic of a map made by Abel Tasman, the Dutch navigator. Tasman was not the first European to set eyes on the Australian coastline, but his voyages established that Australia was not the fabled Great South Land for which the Dutch had been searching, believing it to possess great riches.

Beyond the map and through the glass doors is the vast reading room of the Mitchell Library, but you need a reader's ticket (establishing that you are pursuing legitimate research) to enter. You can, however, take a free escorted tour of either or both of the library's buildings. ⊠ *Macquarie St.,* ☎ *02/9230–1414.* ◷ *Weekdays 9–9, weekends 11–5; General Reference Library tour Tues.–Thurs. at 2:30; Mitchell Library tour Tues. and Thurs. at 11.*

④⑤ State Parliament House. This 1816 Rum Hospital building, with its simple facade and shady verandas, is a classic example of Australian colonial architecture. From 1829, two rooms of the old hospital were used for meetings of the executive and legislative councils, which had been set up to advise the governor. The functions of these advisory bodies grew until New South Wales became self-governing in the 1840s, at which time Parliament occupied the entire building. The Legislative Council Chamber—the upper house of the parliament, identifiable by its red color scheme—is a cast-iron, prefabricated structure that was originally intended to be a church on the goldfields of Victoria.

State Parliament generally sits between mid-February and late May, and again between mid-September and late November. Visitors are welcome to the public gallery to watch the local version of the Westminster system of democracy in action. On weekdays, generally between 9:30 and 4, you can tour the building's public areas, which contain a number of portraits and paintings. You must make reservations. ⊠ *Macquarie St.,* ☎ *02/9230–2111.* ◷ *Weekdays, 9:30–4; hours vary when Parliament is in session.*

④⓪ Sydney Conservatorium of Music. Once the governor's stables, this fortresslike, Gothic Revival, Francis Greenway building presents a marked departure from his normally simple and elegant designs. The cost of constructing the stables caused a storm among Governor Macquarie's superiors in London and eventually helped bring about the downfall of both Macquarie and his architect.

On an irregular basis, this establishment's talented students give free lunchtime (usually Wednesday and Friday) and evening concerts. Call for details. ⊠ *Conservatorium Rd., off Macquarie St.,* ☎ *02/9230–1222.*

46 **Sydney Hospital.** Completed in 1894 as the replacement for the main Rum Hospital building, this institution offered an infinitely better medical option—by all accounts, admission to the Rum Hospital was only slightly preferable to death itself. Convict nurses stole patients' food, and abler patients stole from the weaker. The kitchen sometimes doubled as a mortuary, and the kitchen table was occasionally used to perform operations. ⊠ *Macquarie St. and Martin Pl.*

In front of the hospital is a bronze figure of a boar. This is *Il Porcellino,* a copy of a statue that stands in Florence, Italy. According to the inscription, if you make a donation in the coin box and rub the boar's nose, "you will be endowed with good luck." Sydney citizens seem to be a superstitious bunch, as the boar's nose is very shiny indeed.

47 **Sydney Mint Museum.** The south wing of Greenway's 1816 Rum Hospital became a branch of the Royal Mint after the 1850s Australian gold rushes—a series of events that lured many thousands of gold diggers from around the world. This elegant building has served as a museum focusing on the discovery of gold and its ensuing impact on the nation, but as of December 1998 it has been closed and its future use is to be determined. ⊠ *Macquarie St.,* ☎ *02/9217–0313.* ⊠ *$5.* ☉ *Daily 10–5.*

The Opera House, the RBG, and the Domain North

Bordering Sydney Cove, Farm Cove, and Woolloomooloo Bay, this section of Sydney includes the iconic, symbolic Sydney Opera House, as well as extensive gardens and parkland that create a delightful harborside haven.

The colony's first farming attempt was made here in 1788, and the botanic gardens were initiated in 1816. The most dramatic change to the area occurred in 1959, however, when work began on the site for the Sydney Opera House at Bennelong Point. This promontory was originally a small island, then the site of 1819 Fort Macquarie, and later a tram depot that did little to enhance the cityscape.

A Good Walk

From Circular Quay, walk around Sydney Cove along Circular Quay East. This walkway is also known as **Writers' Walk**; brass plaques embedded into the sidewalk commemorate prominent Australian writers, playwrights, and poets.

Unmistakably ahead, on the Bennelong Point promontory, is the **Sydney Opera House** ㊳. Its distinctive white tiled "sails" and prominent position make this the most widely recognized landmark of urban Australia. The Opera House has fueled controversy and debate among Australians, but whatever its detractors may say, the Opera House leaves no visitor unmoved.

The **Royal Botanic Gardens** ㊴ are behind the Opera House, combining with the rolling parkland of the Domain to form the eastern border of the city. You can either walk around the Farm Cove pathway, or head inland to spend some time exploring the gardens, including a stop at **Government House,** before returning to the waterfront.

The pathway around the cove leads to a peninsula, **Mrs. Macquarie's Point** ⑤, in the northern part of the Domain. It is named for Elizabeth Macquarie, the governor's wife, who planned the road through the parkland. As you round the peninsula and turn toward the naval dockyard at Garden Island, notice the small bench carved into the rock with an inscription identifying it as **Mrs. Macquarie's Chair** ㊱.

Continue through **the Domain north** ㊄ on Mrs. Macquarie's Road to the **Andrew (Boy) Charlton Pool** ㊇, built over Woolloomooloo Bay. It's a great spot for a summer swim. From the pool there are good views of the Garden Island naval base and the suburb of Potts Point, across the bay.

This road eventually takes you to the southern part of the Domain. The once-continuous Domain is divided into north and south sections by the Cahill Expressway, which leads up to the Sydney Harbour Bridge and down into the **Sydney Harbour Tunnel.** The tunnel was completed in the early 1990s and has helped to alleviate traffic congestion on the bridge.

At the end of the walk, you can return to the city and Macquarie Street by reentering the botanic gardens through the Woolloomooloo Gate near the roadway over the Cahill Expressway.

TIMING

A walk around the Sydney Opera House, Royal Botanic Gardens, and the Domain north can easily be accomplished in a morning or afternoon. The walk is highly recommended on a warm summer evening. Allow more time if you wish to explore the gardens more thoroughly— these are delightful at any time of year, though they're especially beautiful in spring.

Sights to See

⑤⑧ Andrew (Boy) Charlton Pool. Named after one of Australia's famous swimmers, this Olympic-size, saltwater pool is extremely popular with locals in summer. It's the perfect place to cool off if you are walking this route on a hot day. ⊠ *The Domain north,* ☎ *02/9358–6686.* ⌨ *$2.* ☉ *Oct.–Apr., weekdays 6 AM–7 PM, weekends 6:30–6.*

⑤⑦ The Domain north. The northern part of the Domain adjoins the Royal Botanic Gardens and extends from Mrs. Macquarie's Point to the Cahill Expressway. Surrounded by Farm Cove and Woolloomooloo Bay, this is a pleasant, harbor-fringed area of parkland that encompasses all sights mentioned in this section, excluding the Opera House on Bennelong Point.

⑤⑥ Mrs. Macquarie's Chair. During the early 1800s, Elizabeth Macquarie often sat on the point in the Domain at the east side of Farm Cove, at the rock where a seat has been hewn in her name. The point is also named for her.

⑤⑤ Mrs. Macquarie's Point. With excellent views of the harbor and north shore, the point and its waterside lawns are a popular place for picnics, especially on warm summer evenings when the sunset makes a spectacular backdrop to the Opera House and Harbour Bridge. This is the classic, postcard view of the Opera House, especially at sunrise and at dusk.

⑤④ Royal Botanic Gardens. Groves of palm trees, duck ponds, a cactus garden, restaurant, greenhouses, and acres of lawns come together in Sydney's finest gardens, where the convicts of the First Fleet established a farm. Their early attempts at agriculture were disastrous, as the soil was poor and few of the convicts came from an agricultural background.

For the first couple of years the prisoners and their guards existed on the verge of starvation. The colony was eventually saved by the arrival of a supply ship in 1790.

The gardens were founded in 1816 and greatly expanded during the 1830s. The wonderful collection of plants and trees are both native Australians and exotics from around the world, and garden highlights include the Sydney Tropical Centre, housed in the Pyramid and Arc glass houses, with a superb collection of tropical plants, and the lush Sydney Fernery. The visitor center is worth a visit, as is the excellent Botanic Gardens Restaurant. The Gardens Shop has unusual souvenirs. Tours leave from the visitor center, near the Art Gallery of New South Wales. ⊠ *The Domain north,* ☎ *02/9231–8125.* 🎟 *Sydney Tropical Centre $5, tour free.* ☉ *Royal Botanic Gardens daily sunrise–sunset; Sydney Tropical Centre and Sydney Fernery daily 10–4; tour daily at 10:30.*

Completed in 1843, the two-story, sandstone, Gothic Revival **Government House** served as the residence of the Governor of New South Wales—who represents the British crown in local matters—until the Labor Party Government handed it back to the public in 1996. The building was designed by the prominent English architect Edward Blore, who completed the plan without ever setting foot in Australia. The house has impressive reception, drawing, and dining rooms on the ground floor. Their prim, almost sterile quality belies their public function. The house's stenciled ceilings, which were repainted in the 1980s, are its most impressive feature. Paintings hanging on the walls bear the signatures of some of Australia's best-known artists, including Roberts, Streeton, and Drysdale. You are free to wander about Government House's gardens, which lie within the Royal Botanic Gardens, on your own, but you must join a guided tour to see the house's interior. ⊠ *Royal Botanic Gardens,* ☎ *02/9931–5200.* 🎟 *Free.* ☉ *House Fri.–Sun. 10–3; gardens daily 10–4.*

❸ **Sydney Opera House.** Considering its long and troubled construction process, it's no minor miracle that the Opera House exists at all. In 1954, the state premier appointed a committee to advise the government on the building of an opera house. The site chosen was Bennelong Point—until that time, the site of a tram depot. The premier's committee launched a competition to find a suitable plan, and a total of 233 submissions came in from architects from all over the world. One of them was a young Dane named Joern Utzon.

His plan was brilliant, but it had all the markings of a monumental disaster. The structure was so narrow that stages would have minuscule wings, and the soaring "sails" that formed the walls and roof could not be built by existing technology.

Nonetheless, Utzon's dazzling, dramatic concept caught the judges' imagination, and construction of the giant podium began in 1958. From the very beginning, the contractors faced a cost blowout—a problem that was to plague the Opera House throughout its construction. The building that was projected to cost $7 million and take four years to erect would eventually require $102 million and 15 years. Construction was financed by an intriguing scheme that appealed to Australian's fondness for gambling. Realizing that citizens might be hostile to the use of public funds for the controversial project, the state government raised the money through the Opera House Lottery. The payout was huge by the standards of the time. For almost a decade, Australians lined up to buy tickets—and the Opera House was built without depriving the state's hospitals or schools of a single cent.

Initially it was thought that the concrete exterior of the building would have to be cast in place, which would have meant building an enormous birdcage of scaffolding at even greater expense. Then, as he was peeling an orange one day, Utzon had a flash of inspiration. Why not construct the shells from segments of a single sphere? The concrete ribs forming the skeleton of the building could be prefabricated in just a few molds, hoisted into position, and joined together. These ribs are clearly visible inside the Opera House, especially in the foyers and staircases of the Concert Hall.

In 1966, Utzon resigned as Opera House architect and left Australia, embittered by his dealings with unions and the government (he has never returned to see his masterpiece). A team of young Australian architects carried on, completing the exterior one year later. Until that time, however, nobody had given much thought to the *interior*. The shells created awkward interior spaces, and conventional performance areas were simply not feasible. It is a tribute to the architectural team's ingenuity that the exterior of the building is matched by the aesthetically pleasing and acoustically sound theaters inside.

In September 1973 the Australian Opera performed *War and Peace* in the Opera Theatre; a month later, Queen Elizabeth II officially opened the building in a ceremony capped by an astonishing fireworks display. Nowadays, the controversies that raged around the building seem moot. Poised majestically on its peninsula, with Circular Quay and Harbour Bridge on one side and the Royal Botanic Gardens on the other, it has become a loved and potent national symbol.

The building is actually far more versatile than its name implies. In reality, it is an entertainment complex allowing a wide range of performances and activities—dance, drama, films, opera, and jazz, as well as four restaurants and cafés, and several bars that cater to the hordes of patrons. Guided one-hour tours of the Opera House depart at frequent intervals from the tour office, on the lower forecourt level, 9:15–4 on most days. All tours can be restricted or suspended due to performances or rehearsals; call in advance. ⊠ *Bennelong Point,* ☎ *02/ 9250-7111.* ☞ *Tour $10.*

Darling Harbour

Until the mid-1980s, this horseshoe-shape bay on the western edge of the city center was a wasteland of disused docks and railway yards. Then, in an explosive burst of activity, the whole area was redeveloped and opened in time for Australia's bicentennial in 1988. Now there's plenty to take in at the Darling Harbour complex: the National Maritime Museum, the large Harbourside shopping and dining center, the Sydney Aquarium, the new in 1998 Cockle Bay waterfront dining complex, and the gleaming Exhibition Centre whose masts and spars recall the square riggers that once berthed here. At the harbor's center is a large park shaded by palm trees, while the Panasonic IMAX Theatre and the Sega World indoor theme park stand at its periphery. The complex is laced together by a series of waterways and fountains.

The Powerhouse Museum is within easy walking distance, and immediately to the south are Chinatown and the Sydney Entertainment Centre. The Star City entertainment complex, with Sydney Casino (☞ Gambling *in* Nightlife and the Arts, *below*) as its centerpiece, is the newest addition to the area—it lies just to the west of Darling Harbour.

Darling Harbour's emphasis is on shopping and entertainment, especially on weekends. This is a particularly good place to bring children—

the area's aquarium and museums should keep most young travelers entertained for hours, and much of the entertainment is free.

A Good Walk

Start at the Market Street end of Pitt Street Mall, Sydney's main pedestrian shopping precinct. Take the monorail—across Market Street and above ground level on the right-hand side of Pitt Street—from here to the next stop (Darling Park), passing the large Queen Victoria Building on your left. Get off at this stop and go down the steps and escalator to **Sydney Aquarium** ⑤⑨—the city's first-class fishbowl full of exotic creatures with fins, flippers, and scales—on your right.

From here, take the escalator back up to historic **Pyrmont Bridge** ⑥⓪ and walk across to the **Australian National Maritime Museum** ⑥①, the large white-roof building on your right. Documenting Australia's vital links with the ocean, the museum features everything from Aboriginal canoes to ships and surfboards.

After visiting the Maritime Museum you can explore the Harbourside center (a good place for a drink or a meal) and then walk through Darling Harbour. On your walk, you'll notice beside the elevated freeway a curved building with a checkerboard pattern on its side. This is the **Panasonic IMAX Theatre** ⑥②, the world's largest movie screen, featuring a series of stunning special-effect presentations. From the theater, cross under the elevated freeway and walk past the carousel. On your left, easily identified by the transparent blue cone on its roof, is Sydney's first indoor theme park, **Sega World** ⑥③.

The intriguing **Powerhouse Museum** ⑥④ is a worthwhile detour from the amusements of Darling Harbour. Walk west to Merino Boulevard, then continue south to William Henry Street and turn right; the museum is just south of the intersection of William Henry and Harris streets. Housed inside an old power station with extensive modern additions, this is by far the city's largest museum, with a vast collection from the Museum of Applied Arts and Sciences.

From the Powerhouse, walk back to William Henry Street and follow it east until it becomes Pier Street. Here you'll find the **Chinese Garden** ⑥⑤.

You can return to the city center by monorail—follow signs to the Haymarket station—or take a short walk around the colorful streets, shops, markets, and restaurants of Chinatown, just south of the Chinese Garden.

TIMING

Although the distance covered on this walk is relatively small, it is full of engrossing and time-consuming places to stop. You'll need at least a half day to see the best of the area. Darling Harbour is very popular with locals and the area is often very crowded on weekends—better to come during the week, if you can.

If you aren't so interested in the museums, a good time to visit is in the evening, when the tall city buildings reflect the sunset and cast their magical images on the water—and you might pop over to Chinatown for dinner. Later, pubs, cafés, and nightclubs turn on lights and music for a party that lasts well past midnight.

Sights to See

🖐 ⑥① **Australian National Maritime Museum.** This soaring, futuristic white building is divided into six galleries that tell the story of Australia and the sea. In addition to figureheads, model ships, and the brassy apparati of nautical enterprise, there are antique racing yachts, and the jet-powered *Spirit of Australia,* current holder of the water speed record. Many displays are interactive. Among the many spectacular exhibits is the fully rigged *Australia II,* the famous 12-m yacht with winged keel that finally broke the Newport Yacht Club's hold on the America's Cup in 1983. An outdoor section features numerous vessels moored at the museum's wharves—including HMAS *Vampire,* a World War II destroyer, a fishing boat that transported Vietnamese "boat people" to Australia in 1977, and a northern Australian pearling lugger. ⊠ *Darling Harbour,* ☎ 02/9552–7777. ⊒ *$9.* ⊙ *Daily 9:30–5.*

65 **Chinese Garden.** The nation's long and enduring links with China—Chinese prospectors came to the Australian goldfields as far back as the 1850s—are symbolized by this tranquil walled enclave. Designed by Chinese landscape architects, the garden includes bridges, lakes, waterfalls, and Cantonese-style pavilions. This is the perfect spot for a break from sightseeing and Darling Harbour's crowds. ⊠ *Darling Harbour,* ☎ 02/9281–6863. ⊒ *$3.* ⊙ *Daily 9:30–5:30.*

62 **Panasonic IMAX Theatre.** Both in size and dramatic impact, this eight-story-tall movie screen is overwhelming. Inside, three one-hour presentations take you on an astonishing wide-angle voyage of discovery—into space, under the sea, or through the human body. Movies are changed every couple of months. ⊠ *Darling Harbour,* ☎ 02/9281–3300. ⊒ *$13.95.* ⊙ *Daily 10–10.*

Ⓒ **64** **Powerhouse Museum.** An architectural amalgam of old and new, this extraordinary museum of applied arts and sciences is housed in the 1890s electricity station that once powered Sydney's trams. Exhibits include costumes and jewelry, a whole floor of working steam engines, a pub, space modules, airplanes suspended from the ceiling, state-of-the-art computer gadgetry, and a 1930s art deco–style movie-theater auditorium. Hands-on displays encourage participation, and older children will be intrigued by the opportunities that these present.

A highlight of the museum is the top-level Powerhouse Garden Restaurant—painted in spectacularly vibrant colors and patterns by famous local artist Ken Done and his team. ⊠ *500 Harris St., Ultimo,* ☎ *02/9217–0444 or 02/9217–0111.* ⊒ *$8.* ⊙ *Daily 10–5.*

60 **Pyrmont Bridge.** Dating from 1902, this is the world's oldest electrically operated swing-span bridge. The structure once carried motor traffic, but it is now a walkway that links Darling Harbour's east and west sides. The monorail runs above the bridge, but the center span still swings open to allow tall-masted ships into Cockle Bay, the landward portion of Darling Harbour.

Ⓒ **63** **Sega World.** Along with such amusement-park favorites as a roller coaster and a haunted house, the attractions at this vast indoor entertainment park include a wraparound theater, a high-tech adventure playground, and VR-1, a virtual reality ride. The park is divided into three theme zones: past, present, and future. Children ages 8 to 15 love this place. ⊠ *1–25 Harbour St., Darling Harbour,* ☎ 02/9273–9273. ⊒ *$25.* ⊙ *Weekdays 11–10, weekends 10–10.*

Ⓒ **59** **Sydney Aquarium.** The city's largest aquarium is a fascinating underwater world, with everything from saltwater crocodiles to giant sea turtles to delicate, multicolor reef fish and corals. Excellent displays illustrate the marine life of the Great Barrier Reef and Australia's largest river system, the Murray-Darling. Children will particularly enjoy the touch pool and the marine mammal sanctuary with its playful seals. The highlights of the aquarium are two transparent tunnels submerged in an oceanarium—a footpath takes you safely through the water while sharks, eels, and stingrays glide overhead. The aquarium is often very crowded on weekends. ☒ *Aquarium Pier, Wheat Rd., Darling Harbour,* ☎ *02/9262–2300.* ☜ *$15.90.* ☉ *Daily 9:30 AM–10 PM.*

Sydney City Center

Most travelers visit Sydney's city center primarily for shopping, but there are several buildings and other places of interest among the myriad office blocks, department stores, and shopping centers.

This walk includes a bird's-eye view of Sydney, several historic buildings, the shopping and architectural delights of the Queen Victoria Building, Hyde Park, and the Australian Museum.

A Good Walk

Begin at the Market Street end of Pitt Street Mall. Turn left into Market Street and walk a few meters to the entrance to **AMP Tower** ⑥⑥. High-speed elevators will whisk you to the top of the city's tallest structure, and the spectacular view will give you an excellent idea of the lay of the land.

Return to Market Street and walk in the other direction to George Street. Turn left and continue to the Sydney Hilton Hotel, on the left-hand side. For a little refreshment now or later in the day, take the steps down below street level to the Marble Bar, an opulent basement watering hole with extraordinary decor and architecture.

Back up on George Street cross the road to enter the **Queen Victoria Building (QVB)** ⑥⑦, a massive Victorian structure that occupies an entire city block. The shops are many and varied, and the meticulous restoration work is impressive.

After browsing in the QVB, exit at the Druitt Street end and cross this road to the rather elaborate **Sydney Town Hall** ⑥⑧, the domain of Sydney City Council and a popular performance space. Next door is **St. Andrew's Cathedral** ⑥⑨, Sydney's foremost Anglican church.

Cut across George Street and walk along Bathurst Street to the southern section of **Hyde Park** ⑦⓪. This is the city center's largest green space and the location of the **Anzac War Memorial**, which commemorates Australians who fought and died in the service of their country.

Continue through the park to College Street, cross the road and walk a few more feet to the **Australian Museum** ⑦①. An excellent natural history museum, it has one of the country's best collections of geological, botanical, and biological specimens from the Australia–Pacific region.

From the museum, cross College Street and then Park Street and follow the shady avenue through the northern half of Hyde Park. This area contains the impressive **Archibald Memorial Fountain**. Continue past the fountain and cross the road to Macquarie Street. As you walk north on Macquarie, you'll pass the **Hyde Park Barracks, Sydney Mint Museum,** and **Sydney Hospital** (☞ Macquarie Street and the Domain south, *above*). In front of the hospital, cross the road to the large pedestrian precinct of **Martin Place** ⑦② and walk the length of the plaza to George Street. Note the impressive Victorian and more recent banks and public buildings, and the cenotaph war memorial near the far end.

From here you can return to the Pitt Street Mall via Pitt Street, or walk north on George Street to Circular Quay.

TIMING

The walk itself should take no longer than a couple hours. Plan more time for an extended tour of the Australian Museum, or for shopping in the Queen Victoria Building. Weekday lunchtimes (generally 1–2) in the city center are elbow-to-elbow affairs, with office workers trying to make the most of their brief break.

Sights to See

66 AMP Tower. Short of taking a scenic flight, a visit to the top of this 1,000-ft golden-minaret-topped spike is the best way to view Sydney's spectacular layout. This is the tallest building in the city, and if you come here on a smog-free day, the views from its indoor observation deck are astounding. The panorama encompasses the entire Sydney metropolitan area of more than 1,560 square km (600 square mi), and you can often see as far as the Blue Mountains, more than 80 km (50 mi) away. ⊠ *100 Market St., between Pitt and Castlereagh Sts.,* ☎ *02/9229–7444.* ☜ *$10.* ☼ *Sun.–Fri. 9 AM–10:30 PM, Sat. 9 AM–11:30 PM.*

71 Australian Museum. The public face of a well-respected academic institution, the strength of this natural history museum is its collection of plants, animals, and geological specimens from the Asia–Pacific region. The museum has a good collection of artifacts from Papua New Guinea in particular, but much of its vast array of Aboriginal artifacts is not on public display. According to Aboriginal belief, some of the objects are considered sacred and should not be seen by uninitiated men and women. The museum has a comprehensive gems and minerals display, an excellent book and gift shop, and a lively café. ⊠ *6 College St., near William St.,* ☎ *02/9320–6000.* ☜ *$5.* ☼ *Daily 9:30–5.*

70 Hyde Park. Declared public land by Governor Phillip in 1792 and used for the colony's earliest cricket matches and horse races, this area was made into a park in 1810. Gardens are formal, with fountains, statuary, and tree-lined walks. The park provides some welcome city-center tranquillity and is popular with office workers at lunchtime. ⊠ *Elizabeth, College, and Park Sts.*

In the southern section of Hyde Park (near Liverpool Street) stands the 1934 Art Deco **Anzac Memorial**. It pays tribute to the Australians who died in the service of their country during the First World War, when the term ANZAC (Australian and New Zealand Army Corps) was coined. The 120,000 gold stars inside the dome represent each man and woman of New South Wales who served in the Great War. The lower level is devoted to an exhibit of war-related photographs. ⊠ *Hyde Park,* ☎ *02/9267–7668.* ☼ *Mon.–Sat. 10–4, Sun. 1–4.*

NEED A BREAK? Stop in the **Marble Bar** for a drink alongside a masterpiece of Victorian extravagance. The 1890 Marble Bar was formerly another hotel bar much favored by gentlemen of the racing fraternity. Threatened with demolition in the 1970s, the whole bar was moved—marble arches, colored glass ceiling, elaborately carved woodwork, paintings of voluptuous nudes, and all—to its present site beneath the Sydney Hilton. By night, it becomes the backdrop for jazz and other live music. ⊠ *Sydney Hilton Hotel, basement level, 259 Pitt St.,* ☎ *02/9266–0610. Closed Sun.*

72 Martin Place. Sydney's largest pedestrian precinct, flanked by banks, offices, and the MLC Shopping Centre, forms the hub of the central business district. There are some grand buildings here—including the beautifully refurbished Commonwealth Bank and the 1870s Venetian Renaissance–style General Post Office building with its 230-ft clocktower. Toward the George Street end of the plaza the simple 1929 cenotaph war memorial commemorates Australians who died in World War I. Every weekday from about 12:30, the amphitheater near Castlereagh Street is the site for well-attended, free lunchtime concerts with sounds from all corners of the music world—from police bands to string quartets to rock-and-rollers. ⊠ *Between Macquarie and George Sts.*

67 **Queen Victoria Building.** Originally the city's produce market, this vast 1898 sandstone structure had become a maze of shabby offices by the time it disappeared under scaffolding in 1981. When the wraps came off five years later, the building was handsomely restored with sweeping staircases, enormous stained-glass windows, and the 1-ton Royal Clock, which is suspended from the glass roof. Other restoration highlights in this 650-ft-long building include the period-style tiling on the ground floor, the central glass dome, and Victorian-era toilets on the Albert Walk level. The QVB is excellent for shopping—the complex includes over 200 boutiques, with those on the upper floors generally more upmarket and exclusive—and the basement level has a variety of inexpensive eating options. ⊠ *George, York, Market, and Druitt Sts.,* ☎ *02/9264–9209.* ☉ *Daily 24 hrs.*

69 **St. Andrew's Cathedral.** Sydney's Gothic Revival Anglican cathedral (the country's oldest) was founded in 1819 and consecrated in 1868. The church was built with local sandstone and designed by Edmund Blacket, Sydney's most famous church architect. Highlights include the ornamental windows illustrating the life of Christ, and the great east window with its images relating to the life of St. Andrew. ⊠ *Sydney Sq., George St., next to Town Hall,* ☎ *02/9265–1661.* ☉ *Mon., Tues., Thurs., and Fri. 7:30–5:30; Wed. 7:30 AM–8 PM; Sat. 9–4; Sun. 7:30 AM–8 PM; tours weekdays at 11 and 1:45, Sun. at noon.*

68 **Sydney Town Hall.** Sydney's most ornate Victorian building—an elaborate, multilayered sandstone structure—is often rather unkindly likened to a wedding cake. The building has some grand interior spaces, especially the vestibule and large Centennial Hall, and performs many functions. The building houses council offices, but is also used as a performance venue for, among others, lunchtime concerts that star the massive Grand Organ, one of the world's most powerful. Tours of the building run from time to time—call ahead for details. ⊠ *George and Druitt Sts.,* ☎ *02/9265–9007; 02/9231–4629 for tour information.* ▣ *Free.* ☉ *Weekdays 9–5.*

Elizabeth Bay and Kings Cross, Darlinghurst, and Paddington

This bus and walking tour takes you into some of the city's inner east suburbs and looks at the people's Sydney—from the mansions of the colonial aristocracy and the humble laborers' cottages of the same period, to the modernized terrace houses of Paddington, one of Sydney's most charming suburbs. You'll also pass through Kings Cross and Darlinghurst, the best-known nightlife district in the country, and visit the acclaimed Sydney Jewish Museum.

A Good Walk

Begin at the bus stop on Alfred Street, just behind Circular Quay, and catch Bus 311, which leaves from the stop at the Harbour Bridge end of the street. This bus carries the sign RAILWAY VIA KINGS CROSS or RAILWAY VIA ELIZABETH BAY. Ask the driver to drop you off at Elizabeth Bay House and take a seat on the left side of the bus.

You'll wind your way through the city streets to Macquarie Street, past the State Library, the New South Wales Parliament, Hyde Park Barracks, and St. Mary's Cathedral. The bus then follows the curve of Woolloomooloo Bay, where it passes **Harry's Café de Wheels,** a unique Sydney institution, and beneath the bows of naval vessels at the Garden Island Dockyard, the main base for the Australian navy. Visiting ships from other Pacific Ocean navies can often be seen along this wharf.

Just before the Garden Island gates, the bus turns right and climbs through the shady streets of Potts Point and **Elizabeth Bay** to **Elizabeth Bay House** ⑦, an aristocratic Regency-style mansion. Built some 150 years ago by Alexander Macleay, the colonial secretary, this is one of Australia's finest historic homes.

After a spin through Elizabeth Bay House, continue north to the **Arthur McElhone Reserve** ⑦ for a pleasant resting spot with harbor glimpses. Take the stone steps leading down from the park to Billyard Avenue. Near the lower end of this street is a walled garden with cypress trees and banana palms reaching above the parapets. Through the black iron gates of the driveway, you can catch a glimpse of Boomerang—a sprawling, Spanish-style villa built by the manufacturer of the harmonica of the same name. Just beyond the house, turn left to **Beare Park** ⑦ overlooking the yachts in Elizabeth Bay.

Return to Billyard Avenue. Wait at the bus stop opposite the first gate of Boomerang for Bus 311, but make sure that you catch one marked RAILWAY, *not* CIRCULAR QUAY. This bus threads its way through the streets of Kings Cross, Sydney's nightlife district, and Darlinghurst. During the day the Cross is only half awake, although the doormen of the various strip clubs are never too sleepy to lure passersby inside to watch non-stop video shows. Ask the driver to deposit you at the stop near the corner of Darlinghurst Road and Burton Street. From here, the moving and thought-provoking **Sydney Jewish Museum** ⑦ is just across the road.

After leaving the museum, walk along the remainder of Darlinghurst Road to Oxford Street. Turn left, and about 300 yards up Oxford Street, on your right, is a long sandstone wall—the perimeter of **Victoria Barracks** ⑦ and its **Army Museum**. These barracks were built in the middle of the last century to house the British regiments stationed in the colony. The troops were withdrawn in 1870 and replaced by Australian soldiers.

Almost opposite the main entrance to the barracks is the start of **Shadforth Street** ⑦, along which you'll see fine examples of terrace houses. These are some of the oldest houses in Paddington. Shadforth Street changes its name to Liverpool Street at the intersection with Glenmore Road.

From Shadforth Street turn right onto Glenmore Road, where the terrace houses are even more elaborate. Follow this road past the intersection with Brown Street to the colorful collection of shops known as Five Ways. The **Royal Hotel** (✉ 237 Glenmore Rd., Paddington, 02/331–2604) on the far corner has a fine Victorian pub with leather couches and stained-glass windows. It's a good place to stop for something cool to drink. On the floor above the pub there is a balconied restaurant that is particularly popular on sunny afternoons.

Walk up Broughton Street to the right of the Royal Hotel. Turn right at Union Street, left into Underwood, and right at William Street. You are now among the boutique shops of Paddington and may want to spend some time browsing here before completing the walk. On the right, **Sweet William** (✉ 4 William St., Paddington, ☎ 02/9331–5468) is a shop for chocolate lovers. If you're in the mood, don't miss Oxford Street's offbeat clothing and curio shops.

Walk toward the city along Oxford Street to the restored colonial mansion of **Juniper Hall** ⑦, which marks the end of this tour.

There are buses back to the city from the other side of Oxford Street. But if the sun is shining, consider heading out to Bondi Beach, a mere 20-minute ride on Bus 380.

TIMING

Allow the better part of a day to make your way through these neighborhoods, especially if you have a good look around Elizabeth Bay House and the Sydney Jewish Museum. If you wish to tour Victoria Barracks, take this trip on a Thursday and get there by 10 AM, which probably means going there first and seeing the preceding places in the afternoon.

The walk around Paddington is not particularly long, but some of the streets are rather steep. This walk can be shortened considerably by continuing along Oxford Street from the Victoria Barracks to Juniper Hall, rather than turning onto Shadforth Street. There is an additional diversion on Saturday, when the famous Paddington Bazaar (☞ Shopping, *below*) brings zest and color to the upper end of Oxford Street.

Sights to See

74 **Arthur McElhone Reserve.** Another of the city's welcome havens, the reserve has tree ferns, a gushing stream, a stone bridge over a carp pond, and excellent views up the harbor. ⊠ *Onslow Ave., Elizabeth Bay.* ☎ *Free.* ◷ *Daily, sunrise–sunset.*

75 **Beare Park.** As a rule, local favorites are worth checking out—so it is with this waterfront park. With its pleasant harbor views, it's a favorite recreation spot with Elizabeth Bay locals. The adjoining wharf is often busy with sailors coming and going to their yachts, moored out in the bay. ⊠ *Off Ithaca Rd., Elizabeth Bay.* ☎ *Free.* ◷ *Daily, sunrise–sunset.*

73 **Elizabeth Bay House.** Regarded in its heyday as the "finest house in the colony," this 1835–39 mansion has retained little of its original furniture, but the rooms have been restored in the style of its early life. The most striking feature is an oval-shape salon, naturally lit through glass panels in a dome roof, with a staircase that winds its way to the upper floor. The colonial secretary Alexander Macleay lived here for only six years before suffering crippling losses in the colonial depression of the 1840s. In return for settling his father's debts, his son William took possession of the house and most of its contents and promptly evicted his father. ⊠ *7 Onslow Ave., Elizabeth Bay,* ☎ *02/ 9356–3022.* ☎ *$6.* ◷ *Tues.–Sun. 10–4:30.*

Much of the densely populated but still-charming harborside suburb of **Elizabeth Bay** was originally part of the extensive Elizabeth Bay House grounds. Wrought-iron balconies and French doors on some of the older apartment blocks give the area a Mediterranean feel. During the 1920s and 1930s this was a fashionably bohemian quarter of the city.

OFF THE
BEATEN PATH

HARRY'S CAFÉ DE WHEELS – The attraction of this dockyard nighttime food stall is not so much the pies and coffee Harry dispenses as the clientele. Harry's is a beloved Sydney institution, and famous opera singers, actors, and international rock-and-roll stars have been spotted here rubbing shoulders with shift workers and taxi drivers. Sampling one of the stall's famous meat pies with peas is a must. ⊠ *1 Cowper Wharf Rd., Woolloomooloo.*

79 **Juniper Hall.** Built in 1824 by a gin distiller, Robert Cooper, this Paddington notable was named for the juniper berries used to make the potent beverage. Cooper did everything on a grand scale—and that included raising and housing his family. He built Juniper Hall for his third wife, Sarah, whom he married when he was 46 (she was a mere teenager) and who bore 14 of his 24 children. The house later became an orphanage. It was renovated at considerable public expense and opened as a museum during the 1980s. Due to lack of funds the house is now closed to the public and contains offices. ⊠ *248 Oxford St., Paddington.*

Paddington. Most of this suburb's elegant two-story houses were built during the 1880s, when the colony experienced a long period of economic growth following the gold rushes of the 1860s. The balconies are trimmed with decorative wrought iron, sometimes known as Paddington lace, that initially came from England and later was produced in Australian foundries. If you look closely at the patterns, you may be able to distinguish between the rose-and-thistle design that came from England and the flannel flower, fern, and lyre-bird feather designs made in Australia.

During the depression of the 1890s, Paddington's boom came to an abrupt end. The advent of the automobile and motorized public transport just a few years later meant that people could live in more distant suburbs, surrounded by gardens and trees. Such inner-city neighborhoods as Paddington became unfashionable. The area declined further during the depression of the 1930s, when many terrace houses were converted into low-rent accommodations and most of the wrought-iron balconies were boarded up to create extra rooms.

In the late 1960s inner-city living became fashionable, and many young couples rushed to buy these quaint but dilapidated houses at bargain prices. Renovated and repainted, the now-stylish Paddington terrace houses give the area its characteristic, villagelike charm. Today you can expect to pay at least $450,000 for a small terrace house.

㉘ Shadforth Street. Built at about the same time as Elizabeth Bay House, the tiny stone houses in this street were assembled to house the workers who built and serviced the ☞ **Victoria Barracks.**

㉖ Sydney Jewish Museum. Combining artifacts with interactive media and audiovisual displays, this museum simultaneously chronicles the history of the Jewish people in Australia and commemorates the 6 million Jews who were killed in the Holocaust. Exhibits are brilliantly arranged on eight levels, which lead upward in chronological order, beginning with the handful of Jews who arrived on the First Fleet in 1788, to the founding of the State of Israel, to survivors of the concentration camps who now live in Australia. ⊠ *Darlinghurst Rd. and Burton St., Darlinghurst,* ☎ *02/9360–7999.* ⊡ *$6.* ☉ *Mon.–Thurs. 10–4, Fri. 10–2, Sun. 11–5.*

㉗ Victoria Barracks. Built by soldiers and convicts from 1841 on to replace the colony's original Wynyard Barracks—and still occupied by the army—this vast building is an excellent example of Regency-style architecture. The 740-ft-long sandstone facade is particularly impressive. Most of the area within the walls is taken up by a parade ground, and an army band performs here from 10 AM every Thursday, when anyone is welcome on a free tour of the complex. Dress uniforms have been abolished in the Australian army, so the soldiers wear their parade-ground dress, which includes the famous slouch hat: The brim is cocked on the left side, allowing soldiers to present arms without knocking off their hats.

The **Army Museum** is on the far side of the parade ground, in the former military prison. Exhibits cover Australia's military history from the early days of the Rum Corps to the Malayan conflict of the 1950s. Its volunteer staff is knowledgeable and enthusiastic, and students of military history will not be disappointed. ⊠ *Oxford St., Paddington,* ☎ *02/9339–3000.* ⊙ *Museum Thurs. 10–noon, Sun. 10–2:30; barracks tour mid-Feb.–early Dec., Thurs. at 10 AM.*

Around Sydney

The Sydney area has numerous activities of interest that are well away from the city center and inner suburbs. These include historic townships, the Sydney 2000 Olympics site, national parks in which to enjoy the Australian bush, and wildlife and theme parks that will appeal particularly to children.

Other points of interest are the beaches of **Bondi** and **Manly,** the historic city of **Parramatta,** founded in 1788 and located 26 km (16 mi) to the west, and the magnificent **Hawkesbury River** that winds its way around the city's western and northern borders. Also within easy reach of the city, the waterside suburb of **Balmain** has an interesting Saturday flea market (☞ Shopping, *below*).

Visiting many of these places by public transport would take a considerable amount of time and effort, so it may be smarter to rent a car or to go with one of the tour operators that offer excursions and day trips (☞ Guided Tours *in* Sydney A to Z, *below*).

TIMING

Each of the sights below could easily fill the best part of a day. For those short on time, some tour companies combine visits within a particular area—for example, a day trip west to the Olympic Games site, Australian Wildlife Park, and the Blue Mountains.

Sights to See

☺ ⑧⑤ **Australian Wildlife Park.** Part of the ☞ **Australia's Wonderland** complex, this park delivers close encounters with the widest array of animals of Sydney area parks, including koalas, kangaroos, and other Australian fauna, as well as the chance to view crocodiles and rain-forest birds. Also in the park is the **Outback Woolshed,** where sheep are rounded up and shorn in a 30-minute demonstration of a time-honored Australian tradition. ⊠ *Wallgrove Rd., Eastern Creek,* ☎ *02/9830–9100.* ⊡ *$9.95; free if you also visit Australia's Wonderland.* ⊙ *Daily 9–5.*

☺ ⑧⑤ **Australia's Wonderland.** The largest amusement park in the Southern Hemisphere is landscaped and choreographed for total fun. Action ranges from a Ferris wheel to a roller coaster to the ☞ **Australian Wildlife Park.** The complex is in the metropolitan region's west. Admission prices cover all rides and entry fees, including the wildlife park and woolshed. ⊠ *Wallgrove Rd., Eastern Creek,* ☎ *02/9830–9100.* ⊡ *$37.* ⊙ *Daily 10–5.*

⑧⓪ **Bondi.** In spite of its glorious beach and sparkling views, the suburb of Bondi has only recently acquired social status. Bondi—an Aboriginal word meaning "place of breaking waters"—was developed during the 1920s and '30s. But the spare, redbrick architecture, lack of trees, and generally flat terrain did their share to reduce the suburb's appeal. Over the years, Bondi acquired a seedy image fostered by low rents and a free-and-easy lifestyle that the suburb afforded. Author Peter Corris—Australia's Raymond Chandler—used Bondi as a tawdry, neon-lit backdrop for his 1980s thriller, *The Empty Beach.*

During the 1990s, Bondi's proximity to the city and affordable real estate attracted young and upwardly mobile residents. Most of the old apartment blocks have been smartly renovated, and Campbell Parade has been populated with a row of glittering cafés and delicatessens.

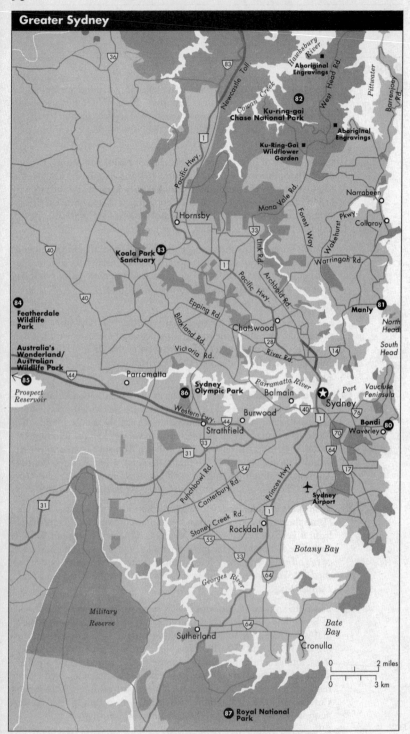

Greater Sydney

Aboriginal Engravings

82 Ku-ring-gai Chase National Park

Ku-Ring-Gai Wildflower Garden

Aboriginal Engravings

Narrabeen

Collaroy

Hornsby

83 Koala Park Sanctuary

Warringah Rd.

Mona Vale Rd.

Forest Way

Wakehurst Pkwy.

84 Featherdale Wildlife Park

Australia's Wonderland/ Australian Wildlife Park

Prospect Reservoir

Epping Rd.

Blaxland Rd.

Victoria Rd.

Chatswood

River Rd.

81 Manly

North Head

South Head

Parramatta

86 Sydney Olympic Park

Balmain

Parramatta River

Port

Vaucluse Peninsula

Sydney

80 Bondi Waverley

Western Fwy.

Burwood

Strathfield

Punchbowl Rd.

Canterbury Rd.

Princes Hwy.

Stoney Creek Rd.

Sydney Airport

Rockdale

Botany Bay

85

Georges River

Military Reserve

Bate Bay

Sutherland

Cronulla

0   2 miles

0   3 km

87 Royal National Park

Pacific Hwy.

Newcastle Toll

Cowan Creek

Hawkesbury River

West Head Rd.

Pittwater

Barrenjoey Rd.

Link Rd.

Archbold Rd.

Apart from a pleasant day at the beach (☞ Beaches, *below*), Bondi's main appeal is sociological. This is where Sydney sheds its clothes and most of its inhibitions. Many of the city's sporting subcultures congregate here—among them cyclists, anglers, surfers, bodybuilders, and skateboarders—as does a crowd of exhibitionists and eccentrics. The promenade along the back of the beach is the best place to take all of this in.

To get to Bondi, take Bus 380 or 382 from Circular Quay via Elizabeth and Oxford streets; or catch a train from the city to Bondi Junction, then board Bus 380 or 382. A higher-cost option is the Bondi & Bay Explorer bus (☞ Guided Tours *in* Sydney A to Z, *below*).

🖐 ❽❹ **Featherdale Wildlife Park.** Northwest of the city, this park is home to a roll call of Australia's extraordinary fauna in their native bush setting—creatures that even most Australians won't ever see in the wild. ✉ *217 Kildare Rd., Doonside,* ☎ *02/9622–1644.* ✆ *$12.* ⊙ *Daily 9–5.*

🖐 ❽❸ **Koala Park Sanctuary.** At this private park on Sydney's northern outskirts, you can feed and photograph a koala. Cuddling Australia's favorite marsupials is prohibited by state law. The sanctuary also houses dingoes, kangaroos, emus, and wallaroos, and there are sheep-shearing and boomerang-throwing demonstrations. Feeding times are 10:20, 11:45, 2, and 3. ✉ *84 Castle Hill Rd., West Pennant Hills,* ☎ *02/9484–3141.* ✆ *$9.50.* ⊙ *Daily 9–5.*

❽❷ **Ku-ring-gai Chase National Park.** Originally inhabited by the Guringai Aboriginal tribe, for which the park is named, this is the site of many ancient Aboriginal rock engravings and paintings. The creation of the park in the 1890s also ensured the survival of large stands of eucalypts, as well as small pockets of rain forest in moist gullies. The wildlife here includes swamp wallabies, possums, and goannas (Australian monitor lizards), as well as a wide range of bird species. The many trails that traverse the park are a delight and are mostly designed for easy-to-moderate hikes. Among them, the 3-km (2-mi) Garigal Aboriginal Heritage Walk at West Head is recommended as it takes in ancient rock-art sites. There are many trails in the Bobbin Head area, and from Mt. Ku-ring-gai train station you can walk the 3-km (2-mi) Ku-ring-gai track to Appletree Bay. Another track, the 30-minute Discovery Trail, is negotiable in a wheelchair and offers an excellent introduction to the region's flora and fauna. Leaflets on all of the walks are available at the park's entry stations and from the Kalkari Visitor Centre and the Wildlife Shop at Bobbin Head.

The park is only 24 km (15 mi) north of Sydney. Railway stations at Mt. Ku-ring-gai, Berowra, and Cowan, close to the park's western border, provide access to walking trails (on Sunday, for example, you can walk from Mt. Ku-ring-gai station to Appletree Bay then Bobbin Head, where a bus can take you to the Turramurra rail station). By car, take the Pacific Highway to Pymble, then turn into Bobbin Head Road, or continue on the highway to Mt. Colah and turn off into the park on Ku-ring-gai Chase Road. Another approach: follow the Pacific Highway to Pymble, then drive along the Mona Vale Road to Terry Hills and take the West Head turnoff.

Camping in the park is permitted only at the Basin in Pittwater. Sites must be booked in advance (☎ 02/9972–7378). Rates are $15 per night for two people during peak periods and $10 in the off-season. Each additional person is $3 during peak periods and $2 at other times; children under 5 are free. Supplies can be purchased in Palm Beach.

For more information, contact **Ku-ring-gai Chase National Park Visitors Centre.** ✉ *Box 834, Hornsby 2077,* ☎ *02/9457–9322 weekdays; 02/9457–9310 weekends.*

㉛ Manly. Until the Sydney Harbour Bridge was built in the 1930s, Manly's air of distant enchantment and ease made it a popular holiday resort. Many Sydneysiders can still recall childhood holidays spent at Manly, embroidered with sandcastles, dribbling ice creams, and visits to the Manly Aquarium and the amusement park on Manly Pier.

A sprawling suburb surrounding the base of North Head, the rearing promontory at the northern approach to Sydney Harbour, Manly has an ocean beach as well as a harbor beach (☞ Beaches, *below*). The area was named by Governor Phillip, the colony's first governor, when he noted the "manly behavior" of the local Aborigines. Two years later in 1790, he might have reconsidered his choice of words when those same Aborigines speared him in the shoulder at Manly Cove.

Manly is more family oriented than Bondi—better mannered, better shaded, and well equipped with cafés—although it does lack its southern sister's sheer entertainment value. If you're thinking about spending the day in Manly, there is also the Quarantine Station (☞ Sydney Harbour, *above*) to visit. To get to Manly, take a ferry or JetCat from Circular Quay; from its landing point the beach is a 10-minute walk.

★ ㉇ **Royal National Park.** Established in 1879 on the coast south of Sydney, the Royal has the distinction of being the first national park in Australia and the second in the world, after Yellowstone National Park in the United States. Originally set aside as a combination botanical and zoological garden for city dwellers, the park remains popular among Sydneysiders on long weekends and holidays. Surprisingly few foreign visitors visit the national park, however; those who do are guaranteed great bird-watching—more than 200 species have been recorded.

Several walking tracks traverse the park, most of which require little or no hiking experience. The Lady Carrington Walk, a 10-km (6-mi) trek, is a self-guided tour that crosses 15 creeks and passes several historic sites. Other tracks take you along the coast past beautiful wildflower displays and through patches of rain forest. You can canoe the Port Hacking River upstream from the Audley Causeway; rent canoes and boats at the Audley boat shed on the Port Hacking River.

Royal National Park is 35 km (22 mi) south of Sydney via the Princes Highway to Farnell Avenue (south of Loftus) or McKell Avenue at Waterfall. The Illawarra–Cronulla train line stops at Loftus, Engadine, Heathcote, Waterfall, and Otford stations, where most of the park's walking tracks begin. The park charges a $7.50 entrance fee per vehicle per day.

Although most visitors stay for only a day, campsites are available. Camping facilities at Bonnie Vale Camping Area generally require reservations and deposits at the park visitor center in Audley, especially during school vacations and long weekends. Camping fees are $10 per night for two people and $2 for each additional person over five years of age. Hot showers, toilets, and laundry facilities are available at the eastern end of Bonnie Vale, 1,650 ft from the campsite. Bush camping is currently forbidden, in order to speed recovery of vegetation affected by the bushfires. Groceries can be purchased in Bundeena, about a mile from the camping area.

Further information is available from the **Royal National Park Visitor Centre** (✉ Box 44, Sutherland 2232, ☎ 02/9542–0648) or from the **National Parks and Wildlife Service** district office (☎ 02/9542–0666).

㉈ **Sydney Olympic Park.** Located 14 km (9 mi) west of the city center, this is the focus of events for the 2000 Olympic and Paralympic Games. Sprawling across 1,900 acres on the shores of Homebush Bay, the site was originally a muddy, mangrove-covered backwater on the Parramatta River. By the 1960s, Homebush Bay had served as a racecourse, brickworks, armaments depot, and a slaughterhouse. During the next decade the bay experienced its ugliest era when it was contaminated through uncontrolled dumping of household and industrial waste—some of it highly toxic.

The transformation has been miraculous. Rising from the shores of the bay is a series of majestic stadiums, arenas, and accommodation complexes. The centerpiece of Olympic Park is the 110,000-seat, $665 million Olympic Stadium. Among the park's vast array of sporting facilities is an aquatic center, archery range, athletic center, tennis center, a velodrome, and parkland. The Olympic Village will provide accommodation for 15,300 athletes and officials, all within a few minutes walk of most sporting events.

The best way to see Sydney Olympic Park is on an Explorer Bus Tour, operated by Sydney Buses. Explorer Buses leave the Visitor Centre every 20 minutes between 9:30 and 3:30 and travel in a circuit around the site. Passengers can leave the bus at any Explorer Bus stop, stroll around the facility and board any following Explorer Bus. A shuttle bus is available between the Centre and Strathfield Station, reached by train from Town Hall or Central stations. ✉ *1 Australia Ave., Homebush Bay,* ☎ *02/9735–4306.* 🎟 *$10.* ⊙ *Daily 9–5.*

BEACHES

Numbers in the margin correspond to beaches on the Sydney Beaches map.

Sydney is tailor-made for beach lovers. Within the metropolitan area there are over 30 ocean beaches, all with golden sand and rolling surf, as well as several more beaches around the harbor with calmer water for safe swimming. If your hotel is on the city side of the harbor, the logical choice for a day at the beach is the southern ocean beaches between Bondi and Coogee. On the north side of the harbor, Manly is easily accessible by ferry, but beaches farther north involve a long trip by car or public transport.

Lifeguards are on duty at most of Sydney's ocean beaches during summer months, and flags indicate whether a beach is being patrolled. "Swim between the flags" is an adage that is drummed into every Australian child, with very good reason: The undertow can be very dangerous. Idyllic as it might appear, Sydney's surf claims a number of lives each year—a high proportion of them visitors who are not familiar with local conditions. The flags indicate that a beach is patrolled by lifeguards. If you get into difficulty, don't fight the current. Breathe evenly, stay calm, and raise one arm above your head to signal the lifeguards.

Some visitors to Sydney are concerned about sharks. Although there is no shortage of sharks both inside and outside the harbor, many Sydney beaches are protected by nets, and the risk of shark attack is very low. A more common hazard is jellyfish, known locally as bluebottles, which inflict a painful sting—with a risk of death if the sting is not treated quickly. Vinegar is the common remedy, and the staff at most beaches will supply it. Many beaches will post warning signs when bluebottles are present, but you can determine the situation for yourself by looking for the telltale blue bladders washed up along the waterline.

A more real beach-related problem is the risk of skin cancer, caused by excessive exposure to sunlight. As a result of their addiction to a powerful sun, Australians suffer from this form of cancer more than any other people on earth, and the depletion of the ozone layer has increased the risk. Precautions are simple and should be followed by every visitor: Wear a hat, as well as sunglasses, sit in the shade between 11 AM and 3 PM, and protect your skin with high-SPF sun block at all times.

Topless sunbathing is common at all Sydney beaches, but full nudity is permitted only at a couple of locations, including Lady Jane Beach, close to Watsons Bay on the south side of the harbor.

Details of how to reach the beaches by bus, train, or ferry are provided below, but some of the city's harbor and southern beaches are also on the **Bondi & Bay Explorer** bus route (☞ Guided Tours *in* Sydney A to Z, *below*). These are Nielsen Park, Camp Cove, Lady Jane, Bondi, Bronte, Clovelly, and Coogee.

Inside the Harbor

★ ⑩ **Balmoral.** This long, peaceful beach—among the best of the inner-harbor beaches—is backed by parkland in one of Sydney's most exclusive northern suburbs. The Esplanade, which runs along the back of the beach, has several snack bars and cafés. You could easily combine a trip to Balmoral with a visit to Taronga Zoo (☞ *above*). To reach Balmoral, take the ferry from Circular Quay to Taronga Zoo, then board Bus 238. ✉ *Raglan St., Balmoral.*

⑫ **Camp Cove.** Just inside South Head, this crescent-shaped beach is where Sydney's fashionable people come to see and be seen. The gentle slope of the beach and the relatively calm water make it a safe playground for young children. A shop at the northern end of the beach sells a variety of salad rolls and fresh fruit juices. The grassy hill at the southern end of the beach has a plaque to commemorate the spot where Captain Arthur Phillip, the commander of the First Fleet, first set foot inside Port Jackson. Parking is limited, and if you arrive by car after 10 AM on weekends, you'll have a long walk to the beach. Take Bus 324 or 325 from Circular Quay. ✉ *Cliff St., Watsons Bay.*

⑪ **Lady Jane.** Lady Jane—officially called Lady Bay—is the most accessible of the nude beaches around Sydney. From Camp Cove, follow the path north then climb down the short steep ladder leading down the cliff face to the beach.

⑬ **Nielsen Park.** This beach at the end of the Vaucluse Peninsula is small by Sydney standards, but behind the sand is a large, shady park that is ideal for picnics. The headlands at either end of the beach are especially popular for their magnificent views across the harbor. Despite the crowds, it is always possible to find a quiet spot on the grass. The beach is protected by a semicircular net, so don't be deterred by the correct name of this beach—Shark Bay. The shop and café behind the beach sell drinks, snacks, and meals. Parking is often difficult on weekends. A 10-minute walk will take you to historic Vaucluse House (☞ Sydney Harbour, *above*) and a very different harborside experience. Take Bus 325 from Circular Quay. ✉ *Greycliffe Ave. off Vaucluse Rd., Vaucluse.*

South of the Harbor

★ ⑭ **Bondi.** Wide, wonderful Bondi (pronounced *bon*-dye) is the most famous and most crowded of all Sydney beaches. It has something for just about everyone, and the droves who flock here on a sunny day give it a bustling, carnival atmosphere unmatched by any other Sydney beach. Facilities include toilets and showers. Cafés, ice cream stands, and restaurants are on Campbell Parade, which runs behind the beach. Families tend to prefer the more sheltered northern end of the beach. Surfing is popular at the south end, where you'll also find

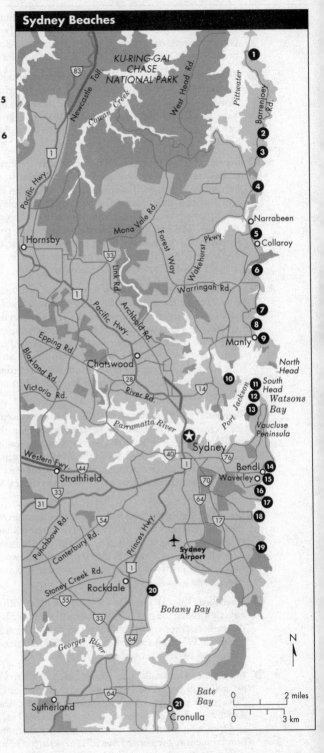

Sydney Beaches

a path that winds along the sea-sculpted cliffs to Tamarama and Bronte beaches. Take Bus 380 or 382 from Circular Quay via Elizabeth and Oxford streets, or take the train from the city to Bondi Junction, then board Bus 380 or 382. ⊠ *Campbell Parade, Bondi.*

⑳ **Botany Bay.** Despite this bay's historical association with Captain James Cook, Lady Robinson's Beach, which stretches for several miles along the bay, is bleak, featureless, and close to a major traffic artery. Take Bus 302 or 303 from Circular Quay, or take the train from the city to Rockdale, then board Bus 478. ⊠ *Grand Parade, Brighton-le-Sands.*

★ ⑯ **Bronte.** If you want an ocean beach close to the city that has good facilities, a choice of sand or parkland, and a terrific setting, this one is hard to beat. Bronte is surrounded by a wooded park of palm trees and Norfolk Island pines. The park includes a playground and sheltered picnic tables, and a couple of excellent cafés are in the immediate area. The breakers can be fierce here, but the sea pool at the southern end of the beach offers safe swimming at any time. Take Bus 378 from Central Station, or take the train from the city to Bondi Junction, then board Bus 378. ⊠ *Bronte Rd., Bronte.*

★ ⑰ **Clovelly.** Swimming is safe here, at the end of a long, keyhole-shaped inlet, even on the roughest day. There are toilet facilities but no snack bars or shops in the immediate area. This is also a popular spot for snorkeling. The semi-enclosed bay provides a sheltered, warm-water habitat for many semi-tropical species, including Bluey, the locally famous giant grouper. Take Bus 339 from Argyle Street, Millers Point (the Rocks), or Wynyard bus station; Bus 341 from Central Station; or a train from the city to Bondi Junction, then board Bus 329. ⊠ *Clovelly Rd., Clovelly.*

⑱ **Coogee.** A reef protects this lively beach (pronounced *kuh*-jee, not *coo*-jee), creating calmer swimming conditions than those found at its neighbors. A grassy headland overlooking the beach has an excellent children's playground. Cafés in the shopping precinct at the back of the beach sell ice cream, pizza, and the ingredients for picnics. Take Bus 373 from Circular Quay or Bus 372 from Central Station. ⊠ *Coogee Bay Rd., Coogee.*

㉑ **Cronulla.** Even on the hottest day you can escape the crowds at Cronulla, the southernmost and largest beach in the metropolitan area. Good surf is usually running at this beach, and the sand is backed by parkland. Cronulla is a long way from the city by train, however, and its attractions don't justify a long trip for anyone not staying nearby. ⊠ *Kingsway, Cronulla.*

⑲ **Maroubra.** This expansive beach is very popular with surfers, although anyone looking for more than waves will probably be unimpressed by the rather scrappy surroundings and the lackluster shopping area. Take Bus 395 from Central Station or Bus 396 from Circular Quay. ⊠ *Marine Parade, Maroubra.*

★ ⑮ **Tamarama.** This small, fashionable beach (it's also known as "Glam-a-rama") is one of Sydney's prettiest, but the rocky headlands that squeeze close to the sand on either side make it less than ideal for swimming. A café at the back of the beach sells open sandwiches, fresh fruit juices, and fruit whips. Surfing is not allowed. Take the train from the city to Bondi Junction, then board Bus 391, or walk for 10 minutes along the cliffs from the south end of Bondi Beach. ⊠ *Tamarama Marine Dr., Tamarama.*

North of the Harbor

❸ Bungan. If you *really* want to get away from it all, this is the beach for you. Very few Sydneysiders have discovered Bungan, and those who have would like to keep it to themselves. As well as being relatively empty, this wide, attractive beach is one of the cleanest, due to the prevailing ocean currents. Access to the beach involves a difficult hike down a wooden staircase, and there are no facilities. Take Bus 184 or 190 from the Wynyard bus station. ⊠ *Beach Rd., off Barrenjoey Rd., Mona Vale.*

❺ Collaroy–Narrabeen. This is actually one beach that passes through two suburbs. Its main attractions are its size—it's almost 3 km (2 mi) long—and the fact that it's always possible to escape the crowds here. The shops are concentrated at the southern end of the beach. Take Bus 155 or 157 from Manly or Bus 182, 184, 189, or 190 from the Wynyard bus station. ⊠ *Pittwater Rd.*

❻ Dee Why–Long Reef. Separated from Dee Why by a narrow channel, Long Reef Beach is remoter and much quieter than its southern neighbor. However, Dee Why has better surfing conditions, a big sea pool, and several take-out shops. Take Bus 136 from Manly. ⊠ *The Strand, Dee Why.*

❼ Freshwater. This small beach is protected by sprawling headlands on either side, making it popular among families. The surf club on the beach has good facilities as well as a small shop that sells light refreshments. Take Bus 139 from Manly. ⊠ *The Esplanade, Harbord.*

★ ❽ Manly. The Bondi Beach of the north shore, Manly caters to everyone except those who want to get away from it all. The beach itself is well equipped with changing and toilet facilities. The nearby shopping area, the Corso, is lined with cafés, souvenir shops, and ice cream parlors. Manly also has several nonbeach attractions (☞ Around Sydney, *above*). Coming from the city, the ferry ride makes a day at Manly feel more like a holiday than just an excursion to the beach. Take a ferry or JetCat from Circular Quay; from the dock at Manly the beach is a 10-minute walk. ⊠ *Steyne St., Manly.*

❷ Newport. With its backdrop of hills and Norfolk Island pines, this broad sweep of sand is one of the finest of the northern beaches. Within easy walking distance is a shopping center offering one of the best selections of cafés and take-out shops of any Sydney beach. Newport is known for its bodysurfing, and the atmosphere is fairly relaxed. Take Bus 189 or 190 from the Wynyard bus station. ⊠ *Barrenjoey Rd., Newport.*

❶ Palm Beach. The wide, golden sands of Palm Beach mark the northern end of Sydney's beaches. The ocean beach runs along one side of a peninsula separating the large inlet of Pittwater from the Pacific Ocean. Bathers can easily cross from the ocean side to Pittwater's calm waters and sailboats, and you can take a circular ferry trip around this waterway from the wharf on the Pittwater side. The view from the lighthouse at the northern end of the beach is well worth the walk; on a windy day, the southern end of the beach affords some protection. Nearby shops and cafés sell light snacks and meals. The suburb of Palm Beach is a favorite with successful filmmakers and with Sydney's wealthy elite, many of whom own weekend houses in the area. Take Bus 190 from Wynyard bus station. ⊠ *Ocean Rd., Palm Beach.*

❾ Shelly. This delightful little beach is protected by a headland rising behind it to form a green, shady park, and it is well endowed with food options. The snack shop and restaurant on the beach sell everything from light refreshments to elaborate meals, and there are a couple of waterfront cafés at nearby Fairy Bower Bay. On weekends the beach is crowded and parking in the area is nearly impossible—it's best to walk along the seafront from Manly. Take a ferry or JetCat from Circular Quay to Manly; from there the beach is a half-mile walk. ⊠ *Marine Parade, Manly.*

❹ Warriewood. Enticing and petite in its cove at the bottom of looming cliffs, Warriewood has excellent conditions for surfers and windsurfers. For swimmers and sunbathers, however, the beach does not justify the difficult journey down the steep cliffs. Anyone traveling by public transport faces a long walk from the nearest bus stop. Basic toilet facilities are available on the beach, but there are no shops nearby. Take Bus 184, 189, or 190 from Wynyard bus station or Bus 155 from Manly. ⊠ *Narrabeen Park Parade, Warriewood.*

DINING

By Terry Durack

Although most Sydney restaurants are licensed to serve alcohol, the few that aren't generally allow you to bring your own bottle (BYOB). Reservations are generally required with a few noticeable exceptions where no bookings at all are taken. Lunch is normally served between noon and 2:30, and dinner is served, usually in a single sitting, between 7 and 10:30. A 10% tip is customary, and there may be a corkage fee in BYOB restaurants, but there is no sales tax or service charge. Some establishments may add a small surcharge on weekends and holidays.

CATEGORY	COST*
$$$$	over $60
$$$	$40–$60
$$	$20–$40
$	under $20

per person, excluding drinks and tip

The Rocks and Circular Quay

French

$$$$ ✕ **Quay.** The much-awarded Bilsons restaurant has changed. It now has a new name, new chairs, new carpet, and smart new uniforms by Sydney designer Jodie Boffa. What have not changed are the mind-boggling views of Circular Quay, the Harbour Bridge, and the Opera house, and chef Guillaume Brahimi's sleek, assured cooking. Inspired by the finest local ingredients, Brahimi's class shines through in dishes such as his basil-infused tuna, whole roasted veal sweetbreads, and chargrilled beef tenderloin with merlot sauce and Paris mash. ⊠ *Overseas Passenger Terminal, Circular Quay West,* ☎ *02/9251–5600. Reservations essential. AE, DC, MC, V. No lunch weekends.*

Italian

$$$$ ✕ **bel mondo.** Some of Sydney's most refined modern Italian cooking is found in a restored 1913 Rocks district warehouse space that also houses the Argyle Department store. With its glamorous big-night-out feel and dramatic, raised, open kitchen, bel mondo is pure theater. But it's the food, prepared by the talented Manfredi family, that keeps the crowds coming back. Flavors are cool and classy, from a quick antipasto and a spaghetti at the low-key bar, to the silky house-made gnocchi with black truffles and delectable preserved ginger panna cotta. ⊠ *Argyle Department Store, 12–24 Argyle St., Level 3, the Rocks,* ☎ *02/9241–3700. Reservations essential. AE, DC, MC, V. No lunch Sat.*

Modern Australian

$$$$ ✕ **Bennelong.** Sydney's favorite sightseeing stop, the Opera House, is also a favorite dining stop. With its dazzling views and heart-stopping Joern Utzon architecture, the Bennelong can sometimes feel intimidating. But forget that you're in the middle of one of the world's truly awesome buildings and try to enjoy yourself. Chef Michael Moore, who previously headed up Sir Terence Conran's Bluebird restaurant in London, clearly wants us to have fun. To this end, he has installed a Conran-inspired crustacea bar and a sultry torch singer. The menu is neither stuffy nor predictable, including a Thai-influenced fish salad, an inventive dish of vine-wrapped ricotta, and a cute passion fruit pavlova. ✉ *Sydney Opera House, Bennelong Point,* ☎ *02/9250–7578 or 02/9250–7548. Reservations essential. AE, DC, MC, V. Closed Sun. No lunch.*

$$$$ ✕ **Rockpool.** A meal at Rockpool is a crash course in what modern
★ Australian cooking is all about, conducted in a brave new world of glamorous chrome and glass. Chefs Neil Perry and Kahn Danis weave Thai, Chinese, Mediterranean, and Middle Eastern influences into their repertoire with effortless flair and originality. Prepare to be amazed by herb- and spice-crusted tuna on braised eggplant salad, stir-fried squid with black-ink noodles, slow-cooked abalone with black fungi and truffle oil, and the magnificent Chinese roast pigeon with shiitake mushroom lasagna. If there's room (there's always room), try the famous date tart. ✉ *107 George St., the Rocks,* ☎ *02/9252–1888. Reservations essential. AE, DC, MC, V. Closed Sun. No lunch Sat.*

$$ ✕ **MCA Café.** Neil Perry, of Rockpool fame, walks across the road to this smart café tucked into the Museum of Contemporary Art. Snare an umbrella-shaded table on the neat terrace (ask when you book), and you'll enjoy picture-postcard views of the Opera House and Circular Quay. That might be Sydney Harbour out there, but the food is full of Mediterranean sunshine, running from simple pasta dishes to the golden, tarragon-roasted chicken breast or the thick, grilled tuna steak Ligurian-style. When you've finished you can always walk off lunch with a leisurely stroll through the adjoining contemporary art gallery. ✉ *Museum of Contemporary Art, 140 George St., the Rocks,* ☎ *02/ 9241–4253. Reservations essential. AE, DC, MC, V. No dinner.*

Thai

$$$ ✕ **Sailor's Thai.** The Darley Street Thai team does it again with this glamorously restored restaurant in the old Sailor's Home in the Rocks district. The three rooms are stepped like rice paddies, creating a warm, glowing space with a sense of history. The food can be very good indeed, including oysters with ginger and kaffir lime; a fragrant banana-blossom salad; and a deliciously complex curry of beef and pumpkin. Upstairs, you'll find a casual noodle bar serving delights like Kanom Jeem noodles, *som dtam* (shredded green papaya salad), and cold Singha beer at a long, stainless steel table. ✉ *106 George St., the Rocks,* ☎ *02/9251–2466. Reservations essential. AE, DC, MC, V. Closed Sun. No lunch Sat.*

City Center Area

Chinese

$$ ✕ **Golden Century.** For two hours—or as long as it takes for you to consume delicately steamed prawns, luscious mud crab with ginger and shallots, and *pipis* (triangular clams) with black bean sauce—you're in Hong Kong. This place is a seafood heaven, with wall-to-wall fish tanks filled with crab, lobster, abalone, and schools of barramundi, parrot fish, and coral trout. You won't have to ask if the food is fresh; most of it is swimming around you as you eat. The atmosphere is no-frills and the noise level can be deafening, but the eating is very good.

Dining

Ampersand, **22**
Banc, **17**
Bayswater Brasserie, **37**
bel mondo, **3**
Bennelong, **2**
bills, **45**
bonne femme, **41**
Buon Ricordo, **46**
Chinta Ria Temple of Love, **20**
Cicada, **32**
Coast, **21**
Darley Street Thai, **38**
Fishface, **42**
Forty-One, **16**
Fu-Manchu, **44**
Golden Century, **25**
Jersey Cow, **51**
Kam Fook, **26**
La Mensa, **48**
Matsukase, **16**
MCA Café, **9**
MG Garage Restaurant, **29**
Paramount, **33**
Pazzo, **30**
Prasit's Northside on Crown, **28**
Quay, **6**
Rockpool, **4**
Sailor's Thai, **5**
Salt, **40**
Star Bar and Grill, **34**
The Summit, **18**
Wockpool, **23**

Central Sydney Dining and Lodging

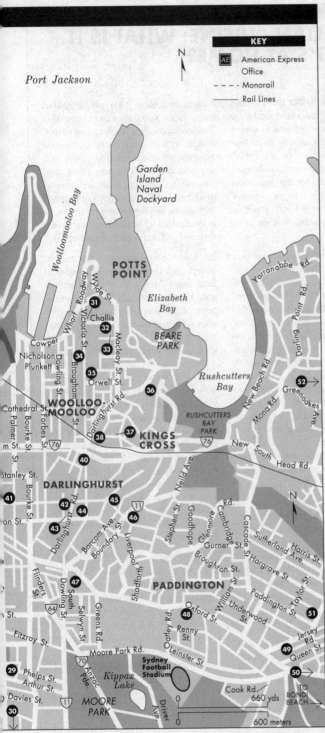

Port Jackson

Garden
Island
Naval
Dockyard

KEY

AE	American Express Office
- - - -	Monorail
——	Rail Lines

N

Woolloomooloo Bay

POTTS
POINT

Elizabeth
Bay

BEARE
PARK

Yarranabbe Rd.

Darling Point Rd.

Rushcutters
Bay

Wylde St.

Hampden Rd.

Victoria St.

Challis

Macleay St.

Cowper Wharf

Dowling St.

Brougham St.

Nicholson
Plunkett

Orwell St.

WOOLLOO-
MOOLOO

Cathedral St.

Bourke St.

Forbes St.

Palmer St.

Darlinghurst Rd.

RUSHCUTTERS
BAY
PARK

KINGS
CROSS

New Beach Rd.

Mona Rd.

Greenoakes Ave.

New South Head Rd.

Stanley St.

DARLINGHURST

Bourke St.

Darlinghurst Rd.

Barcom Ave.

Boundary St.

Liverpool St.

Shadforth

Neill Ave.

Stephen St.

Goodhope

Glenmore Rd.

Cambridge St.

Gurner St.

Broughton St.

Cascade St.

Hargrave St.

Sutherland Ave.

Harris St.

Taylor St.

N

Flinders St.

South Dowling St.

Selwyn St.

Greens Rd.

PADDINGTON

Oxford St.

Ootley Rd.

Renny St.

Leinster St.

William St.

Underwood St.

Paddington St.

Jersey Rd.

Queen St.

Phelps St.

Arthur St.

Moore Park Rd.

Arzac Pde.

Kippax
Lake

Sydney
Football
Stadium

Cook Rd.

TO
BONDI
BEACH →

Fitzroy St.

Davies St.

MOORE
PARK

Driver Ave.

0   660 yds

0   600 meters

31 32 33 34 35 36 37 38 40 41 42 43 44 45 46 47 48 49 50 51 52 29 30 64 70 76 11

Lodging

ANA Hotel, **12**

Brooklyn Bed and
Breakfast, **27**

Double Bay Bed and
Breakfast, **52**

The Grace Hotel, **19**

Harbour Rocks
Hotel, **8**

Hotel Inter-Continental
Sydney, **15**

The Hughenden, **49**

Medusa, **43**

Observatory Hotel, **11**

Park Hyatt Sydney, **1**

Ravesi's on Bondi
Beach, **50**

Regent of
Sydney, **13**

Ritz-Carlton,
Sydney, **14**

The Russell, **10**

Sebel of Sydney, **36**

Simpsons of Potts
Point, **31**

Stafford Apartments
Sydney, **7**

Sullivans Hotel, **47**

Trickett's, **24**

Victoria Court
Sydney, **35**

AUSTRALIAN CUISINE: WHAT IS IT WHEN IT'S AT HOME?

AUSTRALIA SIMPLY DIDN'T HAVE time to sit back and wait for a home-grown cuisine to evolve in the traditional way. By the time the country was settled by the British 200 years ago, the industrial revolution had already made it virtually impossible for any single region to be isolated enough to gradually call upon its own resources, without outside influence or interference.

So we borrowed an Anglo-Saxon way of eating that had little to do with where, what, or whom we happened to be. We learned, of necessity, to include what was in our natural larder. The incredibly vast land mass of Australia means that somewhere in the country is a micro climate that is suitable for producing whatever we feel like eating—from the tropical fruit and sugarcane fields of northern Queensland, to the grazing pastures and citrus groves of the temperate Riverina and Riverland areas, to the cool climate dairy products of Victoria and Tasmania. It also didn't take us too long to realize that a country surrounded by water is a country surrounded by oysters, clams, crabs, lobsters, prawns, and fish.

The next great influence came from the Southern Europeans who came to this country as refugees after the Second World War. Many were Spaniards, Greeks, and Italians, people who had lived with coastal breezes in their veins, and whose lives and foods had been warmed by the Mediterranean sun.

But the emergence of a truly identifiable Australian way of eating came when we finally realized in the late '70s that it was actually Asia's doorstep we were on, and not England's. These Asian and Mediterranean influences, together with a continual drive for superior produce, have shaped and are still shaping the new Australian cuisine. It's a cuisine that has many faces. Key dishes can immortalize indigenous produce, such as rare roasted kangaroo with baby beets, or steamed barramundi (northern rivers fish) with soy and ginger. At the same time, they can totally transform more universal ingredients, like char-grilled Atlantic salmon with preserved lemon and couscous, or a miraculous checkerboard ice cream flavored with aniseed and pineapple.

But Australian cuisine is no slammed-together grab-bag of fusion techniques or East meets West. It's not about ingredients. It's about attitude. It's brash, easygoing, big-flavored, fresh, and thoroughly natural. It's Japanese-born Tetsuya Wakuda's impossibly silky ocean trout confit with trout roe and konbu seaweed at Tetsuya's in Sydney. Or Malaysian-born Cheong Liew's bravely conceived braised chicken with sea scallops, veal sweetbreads, roasted fennel, and black moss at The Grange in Adelaide. Or Sydney-born Neil Perry's adventure trek of mud crab, sweet pork, and green paw paw salad at Rockpool in Sydney. It's also Greg Malouf's larger-than-life veal rump stuffed with merguez sausage on feta-whipped pease pudding at O'Connell's in Melbourne, and Chris Jackman's delicate snow pea custard with fresh morel mushrooms at Mit Zitrone in Hobart.

This is the sort of cooking that has made Australia a modern culinary force, and stamped Sydney as one of the three current food capitals of the world, along with New York and London. Let the academics ponder if it is a true cuisine or just a lifestyle. The rest of us will do the only sensible thing—head off to a great Australian restaurant and make up our own minds.

— Terry Durack

Supper is served from 10 PM until 3 AM. ⊠ *393–399 Sussex St., Haymarket,* ☎ *02/9212–3901. AE, DC, MC, V.*

$$ ✕ **Kam Fook.** If you're looking for an intimate restaurant, Kam Fook is the wrong place. Located in one of Chinatown's bustling, Hong Kong–style shopping malls, Kam Fook has the distinction of being Sydney's largest restaurant. Though it holds a whopping 800 people, there always seem to be a hundred more waiting at lunchtime for Sydney's best *yum cha* (dim sum). At night, things are a little quieter; a fine array of Cantonese banquet dishes include refined shark-fin soups, good roast meats, and excellent seafood from the tanks. ⊠ *Market City, 9–13 Hay St., Haymarket,* ☎ *02/9211–8988. AE, DC, MC, V.*

French

$$$$ ✕ **Ampersand.** The history of modern Sydney dining can be marked out in Tony Bilson restaurants running from Tony's Bon Gout to Berowra Waters, Fine Bouche, Kinsellas, and Bilsons. This swish, beautifully appointed waterside eatery is his most ambitious project yet. The chefs at Ampersand have been culled from the world's finest restaurants including Arpege in Paris and Tokyo's Taillevent Robuchon. The breeding shows in dishes such as abalone à la Provençale, salmon confit with a cabernet glaze, and free-range chicken in *half mourning* (with truffles). ⊠ *Roof Terrace, Cockle Bay Wharf, Darling Park,* ☎ *02/9264–6666. Reservations essential. AE, DC, MC, V. No lunch Sat. No dinner Sun.*

$$$ ✕ **Banc.** Dashing restaurateur-about-town Stan Sarris and British-trained chef Liam Tomlin have joined forces to turn a former bank into the city center's most lavishly appointed dining room, complete with marble columns, high ceilings, and sleek, two-toned banquettes. Throw in a 22-page wine list, a heavily laden cheese trolley, and a legal-eagle lunch crowd, and you have the city's most seductive dining scene. It's made even more seductive by Tomlin's rack of pork, fillet of beef Rossini, vine ripened–tomato terrine, and chocolate and orange tart. ⊠ *53 Martin Pl., Haymarket,* ☎ *02/9233–5300. Reservations essential. AE, DC, MC, V. Closed Sun. No lunch Sat.*

Japanese

$$$$ ✕ **Matsukase.** Inside Chifley Plaza, a sleek, modern shrine to haute shopping, Matsukase is a throwback to quieter, less frantic times. The rock garden setting, winding paths, and rice paper screens recall the soothing lines of a traditional Japanese inn. Matsukase began life as a tempura specialist, but Sydney's "tempurists" no longer have it all to themselves. It is now equally well known for its sushi, sashimi, noodles, and full-on kaiseki banquets that may include streamed bracken with grated taro, snapper grilled with sea urchin, burdock and prawn mince in fish stock, as well as some of the best tempura this side of Tokyo. ⊠ *Level 1, Chifley Plaza, 2 Chifley Square,* ☎ *02/9229–0191. Reservations essential. AE, DC, MC, V. Closed Sun. No lunch weekends.*

Malaysian

$$ ★ ✕ **Chinta Ria Temple of Love.** Part-time jazz DJ Simon Goh puts a unique spin on Malaysian restaurants. His latest effort features a giant laughing buddha, miked-up chefs, and retro furniture salvaged from a car factory canteen. The music is loud and swinging, much like the crowd that flock here. The no-reservations policy means you need to get here early to be sure of a table; waits can be lengthy, even on Monday nights. Still, the coconut-rich curry laksa, fiery blachan spinach, flaky curry puffs, and Hokkien mee noodles are worth the wait. ⊠ *Roof Terrace, Cockle Bay Wharf, Darling Park,* ☎ *02/9264–3211. AE, DC, MC, V.*

Modern Australian

$$$$ ✕ **Forty-One.** The view of Sydney from the 41st floor is glamorous and glorious, the private dining rooms are lush and plush, and Dietmar

Sawyere's Asian-influenced, classical food is full of flair and finesse. Especially recommended are the dramatically presented crown roast of hare with Asian mushrooms, the voluptuous ravioli of goat's cheese and potato with black truffles, and the cruelly delicious Valrhona chocolate tart. Forty-One's decadent Krug Room is a snug little haven for those who still believe a glass of champagne and a dollop of caviar can cure most of the world's ills. ✉ *Chifley Tower, Level 41, 2 Chifley Sq.,* ☎ *02/9221–2500. Reservations essential. AE, DC, MC, V. Closed Sun. No lunch Sat.*

$$$$ ✕ **The Summit.** Fun dining is replacing fine dining in Sydney. Nowhere
★   is this more obvious than the Summit, a thirty-year-old revolving restaurant once famous for its all-you-can-eat buffets. Under culinary visionary Anders Ousback, the Summit has been reborn and is now the darling of the see-and-be-seen black-clad brigade. As Sydney revolves around you at a meter a minute, go retro and order the prawn cocktail followed by duck à l'orange, or stay true to the times with beef carpaccio and black truffles, and fillets of skate with glazed turnips. ✉ *Level 47, Australia Square, 264 George St.,* ☎ *02/9247–9777. Reservations essential. AE, DC, MC, V.*

$$$ ✕ **Coast.** Swish new waterside complexes and good dining don't always go hand in hand, but Coast is just one of several very good eateries that have made Cockle Bay Wharf one of Sydney's most enjoyable eating areas. The place is pure Sydney with its vaguely nautical good looks, sunny outdoor terrace, and sparkling water views. The food is typical Sydney bistro—deep-fried calamari with aïoli; simply grilled reef fish of the day with pink-eye potatoes and lemon oil; and rack of lamb with roast eggplant, tomato, and pesto. ✉ *Roof Terrace, Cockle Bay Wharf, Darling Park,* ☎ *02/9267–6700. AE, DC, MC, V.*

Pan-Asian

$$$ ✕ **Wockpool.** In the heart of tourist-laden Darling Harbour, Wockpool glows and shimmers like a futuristic Pan-Asian space station. Filmy silk hangs from the ceiling, and the whole place has a rakish, Philippe Starck sense of the modern about it. The brainchild of Rockpool's Neil Perry, Wockpool started life as a wired-up, streetwise noodle bar in nearby Potts Point, but soon moved to this large space on the ground floor of the Panasonic Imax Theatre. Chef Claudia Dunlop presents modern Asian cooking at its most glamorous and fluent, such as a seductive stir-fried crab omelet and gloriously sticky caramelized pork. ✉ *Panasonic Imax Theatre, Southern Promenade, Darling Harbour,* ☎ *02/ 9211–9888. Reservations essential. AE, DC, MC, V.*

East Sydney and Darlinghurst

Cafés

$ ✕ **bills.** This sunny, corner café is so addictive, it should come with a
★   health warning. It's a favorite hangout of everyone from local nurses to semi-disguised rock stars, and you never know who you might be sitting next to at the big communal table (isn't that Leonardo DiCaprio?). If you're not interested in the silky creaminess of what have to be Sydney's best scrambled eggs, try the ricotta hot cakes with honeycomb butter. At lunch you'll have to decide between the spring-onion pancakes with gravlax and the most famous steak sandwich in town. Good luck. ✉ *433 Liverpool St., Darlinghurst,* ☎ *02/9360–9631. Reservations not accepted. No credit cards. BYOB. Closed Sun. No dinner.*

Chinese

$ ✕ **Fu-Manchu.** With its bright-red stools, shiny-red chopsticks, stainless-steel communal tables, and light, cutting-edge design, you'd almost expect fiddly, fashionable fusion food. But Fu-Manchu keeps to simple, no-fuss stir-fries, noodle dishes, and Chinese roast meats. The wonton noodle soup with red roasted pork is heaven in a bowl, the Peking duck wraps are hand-held delights, and the northern-style dumplings are the real thing. ⊠ *249 Victoria St., Darlinghurst,* ☎ *02/9360–9424. Reservations not accepted. No credit cards. BYOB.*

Italian

$$ ✕ **Pazzo.** If the food at this neighborly, easygoing Italian eatery tastes just like mama used to make, then it's probably because mama did make it. Many of the daily specials are prepared for the restaurant by the mothers of owners Raffaele Faro and Franco Braico. Signora Braico's famed gnocchi has to be tasted to be believed, while Signora Faro's lasagna could make you homesick for Rome. Chef Blair Davison also keeps his hand in with a show-time antipasto platter, a succulent sage-roasted spatchcock, and gorgeously messy slow-braised veal shanks. ⊠ *583 Crown St., Surry Hills,* ☎ *02/9319–4387. Reservations essential. AE, MC, V. Closed Sun. No lunch.*

Modern Australian

$$$$ ✕ **MG Garage Restaurant.** Surry Hill's MG Garage has Sydney all revved ★ up. As well as a glamorous good-time restaurant, it's also a sports car showroom. High performance chef Janni Kyritsis has wowed 'em at Berowra Waters and the Bennelong. Here, he wows them with an amazing salmon *coulibiac* (with rice, eggs, shallots, and mushrooms and wrapped in a brioche pastry shell); guinea fowl baked in clay with pancetta, mushrooms, and barley pilaf; and mango with sauternes and candied lime. ⊠ *490 Crown St., Surry Hills,* ☎ *02/9383–9383. Reservations essential. AE, DC, MC, V. Closed Sun. No lunch Sat.*

$$$ ✕ **Salt.** Are you wearing black? Is your hand in instant martini posi-★ tion? Do you look like someone groovy and influential? Then you're ready to dine at Salt, the very latest, very hippest, Mod Oz bistro, where everyone looks as if they've stepped out of a Bret Easton Ellis novel. Chef Luke Mangan has worked with three-star chefs in London, and his skills shine in dishes such as the delicate Japanese custard with raw salmon belly smeared with soy, ginger, and shallot or the deliciously crisp tempura of quail. ⊠ *229 Darlinghurst Rd., Darlinghurst,* ☎ *02/9332–2566. Reservations essential. AE, DC, MC, V.*

$$ ✕ **bonne femme.** After cooking alongside some of Sydney's top chefs, ★ and achieving almost cult status during her days at Paddington's Grand National Hotel, it was only a matter of time before Genevieve Copeland opened her very own restaurant. The space is confident, high on detail, and low on fuss, much like Copeland's cooking, which runs from a warm salad of tender veal tongue and tomatoes to a signature dish of salt-baked spatchcock. Already, bonne femme has the air of a stayer with a character that manages to be unique, original, and relevant. ⊠ *191–193 Palmer St., East Sydney,* ☎ *02/9331–4455. Reservations essential. AE, DC, MC, V. Closed Mon. No lunch Sat.–Tues.*

Seafood

$$ ✕ **Fishface.** Don't expect sea views here. In fact, the largest nearby body of water is to be found at the Laundromat a block or two up the road. Nevertheless, Fishface specializes in some of the freshest, best-value seafood in town. It's a cozy, street-smart sort of place full of fashionably thin types who don't mind waiting for one of the six tables. Paul Wrightson's limited menu depends on what didn't get away that morning and might include barbecued blackfish, tempura prawns, and tuna with steamed *pipis* (triangular clams). ⊠ *132 Darlinghurst Rd., Darlinghurst,* ☎ *02/9332–4803. Reservations not accepted. No credit cards. BYOB. No lunch Mon.–Sat.*

Thai

$$ ✕ **Prasit's Northside on Crown.** Owner Prasit Prateeprasen is the pied piper of pork, peppercorns, and pad Thai, opening restaurants about as often as most of us open newspapers. But these days, Sydney's golden-haired boy seems to be settling down. Now in its fourth year, his most ambitious and successful restaurant has a reassuring air of permanence about it. The place is buzzy and loud, with equally loud gold and purple decor to match. The food makes most suburban Thai restaurants look like, well, suburban Thai restaurants. The lamb masaman curry and stuffed blue swimmer crab are heartily recommended. ✉ *413 Crown St., Surry Hills,* ☏ *02/9319–0748. Reservations essential. AE, DC, MC, V. BYOB. Closed Sun. No lunch Mon.– Wed. and Sat.*

Kings Cross

Modern Australian

$$$ ✕ **Bayswater Brasserie.** The Bays, as regulars affectionately call it, has
★   been serving freshly opened oysters, colorful cocktails, and easygoing Mediterranean- and Asian-influenced cuisine since 1982. Though the owners have been busy opening newer, flashier restaurants around town in recent years, the Bays hasn't missed a beat. Start with a drink in the moody back bar, then try for a table in the front room, styled like a French brasserie. The menu changes regularly, but if you're in luck, it might feature lamb prosciutto with eggplant tapenade, mahimahi in cardamom curry, or passion fruit soufflé. ✉ *32 Bayswater Rd., Kings Cross,* ☏ *02/9357–2177. Reservations not accepted. AE, DC, MC, V.*

Thai

$$$$ ✕ **Darley Street Thai.** Seeing well beyond the hit-and-run fixes of
★   sugar-pot green curries, chef David Thompson has pared down his technique to an authentic purity of style that is rare even in Thailand. In such dishes as caramelized beef with harbor prawns, hot-and-sour mussel soup, and a lush curry of partridge, corn, and coconut, this food takes no prisoners. The decor is as dramatic as the food, with hot-pink walls, bright-green cushions, and gold leaf–adorned fixtures. ✉ *28– 30 Bayswater Rd., Kings Cross,* ☏ *02/9358–6530. Reservations essential. AE, DC, MC, V. No lunch.*

Paddington

Italian

$$$ ✕ **Buon Ricordo.** Walking into this happy, bubbly place is like turning
★   up at a private party in the backstreets of Naples. Host, chef, and surrogate uncle Armando Percuoco invests classic Neapolitan and Tuscan techniques with inventive personal touches to produce dishes like warmed figs with Gorgonzola and prosciutto, truffled egg pasta, and scampi with saffron sauce and black ink risotto. Everything comes with Italian style that you can see, feel, smell, and taste. Leaving the restaurant feels like leaving home. ✉ *108 Boundary St., Paddington,* ☏ *02/ 9360–6729. Reservations essential. AE, DC, MC, V. Closed Sun. and Mon. No lunch Tues.–Thurs.*

$$ ✕ **La Mensa.** Steve Manfredi, of the highly fashionable bel mondo, went down-market (but only just) and across town to open this smart, modern café/food shop with celebrity wholesaler Barry McDonald. Its pressed-metal surfaces, park-bench seating, and windows thrown open

to the street give the place an irresistibly chic but informal air. Food runs from filled baguettes and homey soups to generous pastas and inventive salads. And if you think you'll still feel like eating later on, you can always shop for olive oil, jams, pastas, and confectionery to take away. ✉ 257 Oxford St., Paddington, ☎ 02/9332–2963. Reservations not accepted. AE, DC, MC, V.

Modern Australian

$$$ ✕ **The Jersey Cow.** Don't let the old milk cans outside the door, the pasture green carpet, and the rustic cow sketches fool you. The Cow is no hokey theme restaurant. It's an up-to-the-minute Sydney bistro powered by the big-hearted cooking of British-born Darryl Taylor. Trained under London legend Garry Rhodes with stints under some of the finest chefs in Britain and Sydney, Taylor produces big luscious, peasant flavors that practically leap out of dishes. Try his squab and escarole salad; spit-roasted lamb with lavender; and grilled swordfish with bean and boiled lemon salad. ✉ 152 Jersey Rd., Woolhara, ☎ 02/9328–1600. Reservations essential. AE, DC, MC, V. Closed Sun. No lunch.

Potts Point

Modern Australian

$$$$ ✕ **Paramount.** Christine Manfield, the high priestess of Mod Oz cook-
★ ing, has no shortage of believers at her glamorous, softly glowing Potts Point restaurant. It's a cozy space, all curves and swerves and softness, full of bright, good-looking food and bright, good-looking people. You'll love the food, especially the grilled sea scallops with chili salt squid and black-ink noodles; soy-braised, corn-fed chicken; and brandied cherry and coconut trifle. Manfield's natty, curved-edge cookbooks have made her something of a celebrity in Sydney food circles; pick one up while you're here. ✉ 73 Macleay St., Potts Point, ☎ 02/9358–1652. Reservations essential. AE, DC, MC, V. No lunch.

$$$ ✕ **Cicada.** Chef Peter Doyle combines the warm, easy flavors of the Mediterranean with razor-sharp French technique to produce marvels like almond sesame–crusted tuna, spiced pork belly, and roasted squab with thyme-scented gnocchi. Vegetarians will fare well with dishes such as spinach and eggplant curry and salads such as beetroot, chèvre, and leeks. At night the fashionable and the famished scramble for a table in the glamorous main dining room, but at lunch the sun-drenched balcony is a magnet for wearers of the darkest sunglasses in town. ✉ 29 Challis Ave., Potts Point, ☎ 02/9358–1255. Reservations essential. AE, DC, MC, V. Closed Sun. No lunch Sat.–Tues.

$$ ✕ **Star Bar and Grill.** By the time serial restaurateur Neil Perry opens a new eatery, he's already thinking about what's next. Which probably explains why this Perry-owned location has had four different personas in as many years beginning with the Mediterranean-based Rocket, mod-Asian Wockpool, and the humbler Wockpool noodle bar. Now he's gone right back to where he started with simple Mediterranean food supplemented by superbly cooked spit roasts. It's a smart neighborhood choice for a medium night out when you feel like a daiquiri and a great steak and chips or spit-roasted chicken with rosemary potatoes. ✉ 155 Victoria St., Potts Point, ☎ 02/9356–2911. Reservations essential. AE, DC, MC, V.

Sydney Area Dining

Cafés

$$$ ✕ **Sean's Panaroma.** It may look like a cross between a half-finished bomb shelter and a neglected beach house, but this beachside café is home to Sean Moran, one of Sydney's brightest and most innovative young chefs. Weekend breakfasts feature legendary offerings of fruit smoothies and eggs any which way, while lunches are easygoing affairs. At night, things get a little more serious as Moran cooks up memorable dishes including roast guinea fowl with parsnip puree; braised barramundi with olives, lemon, and spinach; and raspberry, blackberry, and blueberry trifle. ⊠ *270 Campbell Parade, Bondi Beach,* ☎ *02/9365–4924. Reservations essential. No credit cards. BYOB. Closed Mon. and Tues. in winter. No lunch weekdays. No dinner Sun.*

Chinese

$$ ✕ **Sea Treasure.** It may be a Chinese restaurant in the suburbs, but a suburban Chinese restaurant it most definitely is not. This is home to some of the most authentic Cantonese cooking you'll find this side of Tsim Sha Tsui. The daily dim sum lunch is one of Sydney's finest (save room for *wor tip* potsticker dumplings), while at night, king crab with pepper butter sauce, chili lobster, and steamed parrot fish all draw raves. If in doubt, put yourself in the capable hands of Ying Tam, the affable restaurant manager. Do whatever he says and you won't go wrong. ⊠ *46 Willoughby Rd., Crows Nest,* ☎ *02/9906–6388. AE, MC, V.*

French

$$$$ ✕ **Claude's.** Chef Tim Pak Poy seems barely old enough to have absorbed all of the craft and technique he exhibits with his startlingly executed and thoughtfully presented food. The restaurant is tiny and unprepossessing, proving that good things really do come in small, plainly wrapped packages. While the cuisine is basically French, Pak Poy allows the best local produce and his own flight of fancy to shine through. Claude's is BYOB, so be sure to bring a bottle worthy of such creations as truffled custard in vegetable broth, slow-roasted loin of veal, and raised quince and pear tart. ⊠ *10 Oxford St., Woollahra,* ☎ *02/9331–2325. Reservations essential. AE, MC, V. Closed Sun. and Mon. No lunch.*

$$$ ✕ **Bistro Deux.** Following the outstanding success of Bistro Moncur in Woollahra, Damien Pignolet and Ron White have repeated their French-bistro-in-a-pub formula at Rozelle's Sackville Hotel. Bistro Deux keeps the same black-and-white murals and regional French menu as the original, but has its own feel thanks to chef George Sinclair, who has cooked just about everywhere worth cooking in this town. Look out for his grilled duck neck sausage with lentils, vegetable antipasto, and old-fashioned crumbed cutlets. ⊠ *Sackville Hotel, 599 Darling St., Rozelle,* ☎ *02/9555–7788. Reservations not accepted. AE, DC, MC, V. Closed Mon.*

$$$ ✕ **Bistro Moncur.** After building Claude's into a gastronomic jewel, Damien Pignolet went around the corner to open a loud and proud bistro that spills over with happy-go-lucky patrons who don't mind waiting a half hour for a table. Here, it is relaxing in itself to watch others enjoying the food. How refreshing—to order salmon and get salmon, to order sausages and get sausages, and to have no disappointments. Even the coffee at the end of the meal is the ultimate coffee. And the bill, though not cheap, is appropriate to the bistro nature of the place. ⊠ *Woollahra Hotel, 116 Queen St., Woollahra,* ☎ *02/9363–2782. Reservations not accepted. AE, DC, MC, V. Closed Mon.*

Japanese

$$ ✕ **Shimbashi Soba.** Yoshi Shibazaki's popular Japanese eatery is always crowded, even though its new location is double the size of the old. Shibazaki is one of only 50 chefs recognized by the Japanese government as a master of *soba* (buckwheat noodles) and *udon* (thick wheat noodles). The cold soba noodles with dipping sauce make a refreshing summertime dish, while Nabeyaki udon hot pot and beef sukiyaki with udon are year-round crowd pleasers. For a special treat, call ahead to order the Shimbashi hot pot of udon, chicken, prawn, eel, salmon, and more. ⊠ *Grosvenor and Young Sts., Neutral Bay,* ☎ *02/ 9908–3820. AE, DC, MC, V. Closed Sun. and Mon.*

Modern Australian

$$$$ ✕ **Catalina Rose Bay.** To experience the essential Sydney in a single meal, head straight for Catalina. Every night here resembles a glittering charity premiere as famous personalities toy with blue swimmer crab with coriander noodles, chicken poached with cassia bark, and hazelnut soufflé. By day, all eyes are on the harbor as boats, sea planes, and the odd pelican drift by. Bright, light, and white, this is a gorgeously modern restaurant bustling with gorgeously modern food. ⊠ *Lyne Park off New South Head Rd., Balmoral,* ☎ *02/9371–0555. Reservations essential. AE, DC, MC, V.*

$$$$ ✕ **Tetsuya's.** Tetsuya Wakuda has won three different awards naming
★ his restaurant the finest in Sydney, so it shouldn't come as any surprise that dinner reservations are booked two months in advance. It's worth getting on the waiting list or coming for lunch to sample Wakuda's unique blend of Western techniques and Japanese flavors. While the dining room is totally unassuming with its plain, sensible good looks, the food is breathtaking. Dishes such as wondrous slow-cooked ocean trout, ostrich carpaccio, and blue cheese *bavarois* leave other chefs gasping. ⊠ *729 Darling St., Rozelle,* ☎ *02/9555–1017. Reservations essential. AE, DC, MC, V. Closed Sun. and Mon. No dinner Sat.*

$$$ ✕ **The Bathers' Pavilion.** Balmoral Beach is blessed. Not only does it
★ possess an inviting sandy beach and great water views, but it also boasts one of the best eating strips north of the Harbour Bridge. Queen of the strip is the completely renovated and rejuvenated Bathers' Pavilion, which includes a restaurant, a café, and a lavish private dining room. Former Regent Hotel executive chef, Serge Dansereau, cooks with one hand on the seasons and the other on the very best local ingredients, producing food that is colorful, light, and thoroughly appropriate to its time and place. ⊠ *4 the Esplanade, Balmoral,* ☎ *02/9969–5050. AE, DC, MC, V.*

$$$ ✕ **Boathouse on Blackwattle Bay.** When Sydneysiders talk about "the bridge," they're not necessarily referring to Sydney Harbour. Almost as loved is very much newer Anzac Bridge, which you can see best from a window table at this waterside eatery. You also get a good view of the fish markets, appropriate since seafood is the focus here, with clams, mussels, crabs, and lobsters all coming from live tanks in the kitchen. Meat eaters can console themselves with roast duck and spiced figs or roast pork belly with sweet potato and apple. ⊠ *End of Ferry Rd., Glebe,* ☎ *02/9518–9011. Reservations essential. AE, MC, V. Closed Mon.*

$$ ✕ **Hugo's.** Snappy leisure wear and "cool dude" dispositions are the order of the day at Hugo's—and that's just the waitstaff. Like Bondi itself, Hugo works effortlessly on many levels, without ever taking itself too seriously. Weekend breakfasts are legendary, especially if you can snag one of the outside bench seats so you can watch the waves as well as the passing parade of gorgeous suntans. At night, things get serious with the justly famous pan-fried prawn and avocado stack, roasted duck breast on bok choy, and spanner crab linguine. ⊠ *70 Campbell Parade, Bondi Beach,* ☎ *02/9300–0900. Reservations essential. AE, DC, MC, V. No lunch weekdays.*

The Bathers'
Pavilion, **2**

Bistro Deux, **12**

Bistro
Moncur, **9**

Boathouse on
Blackwattle
Bay, **11**

Catalina Rose
Bay, **5**

Claude's, **10**

Doyle's on the
Beach, **4**

Hugo's, **7**

Pier, **6**

Sea Treasure, **1**

Sean's
Panaroma, **8**

Shimbashi
Soba, **3**

Tetsuya's, **13**

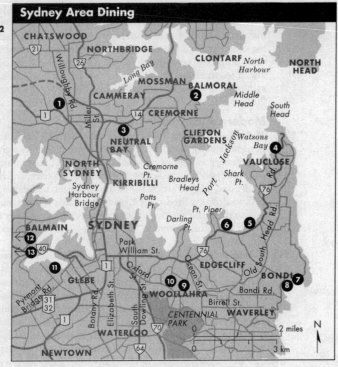

Seafood

$$$ ✕ **Doyle's on the Beach.** After the Harbour Bridge and the Opera House, an alfresco lunch of fish-and-chips at Doyle's ranks as one of Sydney's most popular tourist draws. Views across the harbor are spectacular, people-watching is first-rate, and—on a sunny day—a chilled glass of sauvignon blanc and a dozen oysters is hard to beat. During the weekday lunch hour the restaurant operates its own water taxi. ✉ *11 Marine Parade, Watsons Bay,* ☎ *02/9337–2007. Reservations essential. DC, MC, V.*

$$$ ✕ **Pier.** With its wraparound harbor views and ship-shape good looks, it's hard to think of a more appropriate place to enjoy Australia's finest seafood. Chefs Steve Hodges and Greg Doyle know their fish, and manage to reach beyond the predictable char-grills and fish-and-chips without being gimmicky. The freshness of the produce itself sings in such dishes as tuna in red wine butter sauce, pot-roasted rock lobster with chili and black bean, and peach Melba. ✉ *594 New South Head Rd., Rose Bay,* ☎ *02/9327–6561. Reservations essential. AE, DC, MC, V.*

LODGING

One of the most striking recent developments in Sydney's lodging scene has been the introduction of several bed & breakfast establishments offering rooms at under $180 per night. Of course, the city's big, glamorous, international-style hotels continue to offer impeccable service and convenient location, and they slash rates on weekends when their high-paying corporate customers return home. Weekend discounts of up to 30% are typical. The most desirable hotel location is undoubtedly the Rocks, which combines harbor views, proximity to major historic and cultural attractions, and a tranquil atmosphere. The area around Kings Cross has several hotels and guest houses that offer easy access to the city's raunchy nightlife district. All hotels have already been booked out far in advance for the duration of the 2000 Olympic Games.

If you arrive in Sydney without a hotel reservation, the best place to start looking is the **Tourism New South Wales information counter** at the international airport, which acts as a clearinghouse for hotel rooms. It can usually give you significant savings on published room rates.

CATEGORY	COST*
$$$$	over $300
$$$	$180–$300
$$	$135–$180
$	under $135

All prices are for a standard double room.

The Rocks and Circular Quay

$$$$ 🏨 **ANA Hotel.** Towering above Sydney Harbour from a prime position in the Rocks, this is Sydney's largest hotel, and the place to go for a room with a view. Rooms are opulent and decorated with a subdued Asian theme. Although north-facing rooms have exceptional views across the harbor, views on the other sides—Darling Harbour, the city, or the eastern suburbs—are only marginally less impressive. On the 36th floor, the glass wall of the Horizons Bar provides the best views of Sydney Harbour, especially in the evening. ⊠ *176 Cumberland St., 2000,* ☎ *02/9250–6000,* 📠 *02/9250–6250. 548 rooms, 25 suites. 3 restaurants, 2 bars, no-smoking rooms, indoor pool, sauna, exercise room, laundry service and dry cleaning, concierge, business services. AE, DC, MC, V.*

$$$$ 🏨 **Hotel Inter-Continental Sydney.** This sleek, sophisticated, multistory hotel rises from the honey-colored sandstone facade of the historic Treasury Building, adding a note of warmth and tradition. Opened in 1985, it is near the harbor and within easy walking distance of Circular Quay, the Opera House, and the central business district. The best views are from the rooms facing north, which overlook Harbour Bridge, or from the rooms on the eastern side of the hotel. Three executive floors offer valet and limousine service to and from the airport, and complimentary breakfast and evening cocktails in the private lounges. ⊠ *117 Macquarie St., 2000,* ☎ *02/9230–0200,* 📠 *02/9240–1240. 465 rooms, 33 suites. 4 restaurants, bar, 2 no-smoking floors, indoor pool, sauna, exercise room, laundry service and dry cleaning, concierge, business services. AE, DC, MC, V.*

$$$$ 🏨 **Observatory Hotel.** Located in a quiet back street in the Rocks, this
★   small, elegant hotel is a popular choice for those who prefer a less conspicuous city address. Throughout the hotel, antique reproductions accented by Venetian and Asian mementos create a warm, opulent character that evokes the mood of a gracious Georgian country house. Guest rooms are extremely spacious and decorated in a restrained color scheme with quality fabrics and walnut furnishings; the best are the junior suites, in particular rooms 313 and 310. The health club is the finest of any city hotel. The four-story hotel's single weakness is its lack of views. ⊠ *89–113 Kent St., 2000,* ☎ *02/9256–2222,* 📠 *02/9256–2233. 74 rooms, 22 suites. 2 restaurants, bar, indoor pool, sauna, steam room, exercise room, laundry service and dry cleaning, concierge, business services. AE, DC, MC, V.*

$$$$ 🏨 **Park Hyatt Sydney.** Moored in the shadow of Harbour Bridge, this
★   is the city's most expensive hotel, with the finest location of any in Sydney. Its character is luxurious, cosmopolitan, and distinguished by the extra dash of sophistication (such as butler service) that is the hallmark

of Park Hyatts. The color scheme is dominated by sandstone and earth tones, and the decor combines reproductions of classical statuary with contemporary bronzes and Australian artwork. Most rooms in the four-story hotel overlook Campbell's Cove and the Opera House; most have balconies. The bathrooms are among the biggest and best in town, and all rooms have a walk-in wardrobe. ⊠ *7 Hickson Rd., 2000,* ☎ *02/ 9241–1234,* FAX *02/9256–1555. 122 rooms, 36 suites. 2 restaurants, bar, pool, sauna, spa, exercise room, laundry service and dry cleaning, concierge, business services. AE, DC, MC, V.*

$$$$ 🏨 **Regent of Sydney.** Completed in 1983 and extensively renovated
★ since, this glossy, glamorous harbor-front hotel is a favorite with corporate clients and well-heeled vacationers. Each floor has an attendant who unpacks guests' luggage, handles laundry, and arranges all tour, entertainment, and restaurant bookings. Rooms are luxuriously appointed, and about half have unobstructed views of the Opera House and Harbour Bridge. If you are comfortable with $500-per-night rooms, the junior suites are the best in town. ⊠ *199 George St., 2000,* ☎ *02/9238–0000,* FAX *02/9251–2851. 555 rooms, 39 suites. 3 restaurants, 2 bars, pool, beauty salon, sauna, exercise room, laundry service and dry cleaning, concierge, business services. AE, DC, MC, V.*

$$$$ 🏨 **Ritz-Carlton, Sydney.** This small, unobtrusive establishment is the
★ most sumptuous of the city's deluxe elite hotels. It is in a prime position close to the Opera House, Circular Quay, the Royal Botanic Gardens, and the central business district. Decor throughout is a mixture of marble, antiques, warm-toned fabrics, and soft lighting—an intimate and opulent blend that evokes the European hotel tradition. Rooms are large and luxurious, and most have French doors leading to a small balcony. Rooms on the east side have views of the Botanic Gardens and the Opera House. ⊠ *93 Macquarie St., 2000,* ☎ *02/9252– 4600,* FAX *02/9252–4286. 93 rooms, 13 suites. Restaurant, dining room, bar, pool, sauna, exercise room, laundry service and dry cleaning, concierge. AE, DC, MC, V.*

$$$ 🏨 **Harbour Rocks Hotel.** This converted, historic, Rocks wool store offers reasonable value for location, but limited character. Top-floor rooms on the eastern side of the four-story building afford glimpses of Circular Quay and the Opera House. In order to preserve the character of the building, the hotel is air-conditioned only in the public areas, and there are no guest elevators. ⊠ *34–52 Harrington St., 2000,* ☎ *02/9251–8944,* FAX *02/9251–8900. 54 rooms. Restaurant, bar, laundry service. AE, DC, MC, V.*

$$$ 🏨 **Stafford Apartments Sydney.** Conveniently located, this establishment has self-contained apartments as well as hotel rooms with kitchen facilities. Decor and furnishings are tasteful but spare, with a Scandinavian feel that is both elegant and uncluttered. Rooms on the fourth through sixth floors of the main building have views across Circular Quay to the Opera House. ⊠ *75 Harrington St., 2000,* ☎ *02/9251– 6711,* FAX *02/9251–3458. 54 apartments. Pool, sauna, exercise room, business services. AE, DC, MC, V.*

$$ 🏨 **The Russell.** For charm, character, and a central location, it would be
★ hard to beat this small, century-old hotel on the edge of the Rocks. No two rooms are quite the same, and rates vary considerably depending on room size and facilities. The spacious double rooms at the front have views of Circular Quay; there are also somewhat quieter, standard-size double rooms overlooking Nurses Walk or opening onto an internal courtyard. In keeping with the Victorian character of the hotel, rooms are not air-conditioned but the ceiling fans and windows more than compensate. Breakfast is included. ⊠ *143A George St., 2000,* ☎ *02/9241–3543,* FAX *02/9252–1652. 29 rooms. Restaurant. AE, DC, MC, V.*

City Center Area

$$$ ⊞ **The Grace Hotel.** At the heart of the city's shopping and business district, this hotel has been totally restored and retains traces of the art deco style of its origins. Rooms are well proportioned and uncluttered and furnished in warm, soothing colors. The hotel is especially popular with corporate travelers. During World War II, the building was used as the Sydney headquarters for General Douglas Macarthur's Pacific campaign. Despite the busy location, rooms are quiet; those that overlook the central well of the building are recommended for jet-lagged travelers in search of total silence. ⊠ *77 York St., 2000,* ☎ *02/9272–6888,* FAX *. 382 rooms, 6 suites. 2 restaurants, pool, sauna, exercise room, laundry services and dry cleaning, business services. AE, DC, MC, V.*

Paddington and Woollahra

$$ ⊞ **The Hughenden.** This Victorian mansion has recently been converted to accommodate travelers at a prestigious eastern suburbs address. Rooms are small but prettily decorated, and each has an en-suite bathroom. Rooms 21, 23, 24, and 25 are the largest, although they overlook the moderately busy street below. Near many of Sydney's finest antiques shops and art dealers, the hotel offers easy access to Oxford Street, Centennial Park, and Paddington. The city and the eastern beaches are 10–15 minutes by public transport. A full, cooked breakfast is included. ⊠ *14 Queen St., Woollahra 2025,* ☎ *02/9363–4863,* FAX *02/9362–0398. 37 rooms. Restaurant, bar. AE, DC, MC, V.*

$ ⊞ **Sullivans Hotel.** This small, friendly, family-owned and -operated hotel is an exceptional value. Just a 15-minute walk from the city in fashionable Paddington, the hotel is close to the shops, cafés, restaurants, movie theaters, and nightlife of Oxford Street. The best rooms are those overlooking the central courtyard, pool, and the terrace houses at the rear. Those that overlook the city are more likely to be affected by traffic noise. Bathrooms and desks in most rooms were upgraded in 1998. ⊠ *21 Oxford St., Paddington 2021,* ☎ *02/9361–0211,* FAX *02/9360–3735. 62 rooms. Café, pool, bicycles. AE, DC, MC, V.*

East of the City

$$$$ ⊞ **Sebel of Sydney.** Situated close to the Kings Cross nightlife district, this hotel's clubby atmosphere makes it a favorite with visiting media celebrities and senior executives alike. Rooms are spacious and well equipped. The solid wood furnishings and heavy fabrics used throughout set a comfortable and conservative yet modern tone. Views are not a notable feature of this hotel, although those that face east above the seventh-floor overlook the yacht basin in Rushcutters Bay. ⊠ *23 Elizabeth Bay Rd., Elizabeth Bay 2011,* ☎ *02/9358–3244,* FAX *02/9357–1926. 140 rooms, 26 suites. Restaurant, bar, pool, sauna, health club, business services. AE, DC, MC, V.*

$$$ ⊞ **Medusa.** Housed inside a Victorian terrace house, this small, elegant establishment has broken new ground among Sydney's hotels, and the international style arbiters have applauded long and loud. Staff are dressed by Armani, colors are brash, and furnishings might have come direct from a Milan design gallery. Every room is different, and each features a kitchenette. Behind the glamour is a comfortable, well-run hotel with friendly, attentive staff and exceptional accommodation at this price level. ⊠ *267 Darlinghurst Rd., Darlinghurst 2010,* ☎ *02/9331–1000,* FAX *02/9380–6901. 18 rooms. Bar. AE, DC, MC, V.*

$$$ ⊞ **Simpsons of Potts Point.** On a quiet street just a few minutes' stroll from Kings Cross, this hotel retains many decorative features from its Victorian origins, including stained-glass windows and a grand cedar staircase. Rooms are comfortable and decorated in a modestly opulent period style. The best room is the slightly more expensive Cloud Room, which has a palatial en-suite bathroom. Continental breakfast is included. ⊠ *8 Challis Ave., Potts Point 2011,* ☎ *02/9356–2199,* 𝔽𝔸𝕏 *02/9356–4476. 14 rooms. AE, DC, MC, V.*

$$ 🖭 **Double Bay Bed and Breakfast.** In one of Sydney's most exclusive harborside suburbs, this two-story terrace house run by the affable Bill and Margaret Cox offers a high standard of comfort at an affordable price. The house is richly decorated with antiques, and all of the soft furnishings are made by Margaret, who has a background in fashion design. Breakfast is the full monty: eggs benedict with lemon myrtle, homemade breads, smoked salmon with gumleaf oil, wattleseed pancakes, and, for traditional types, steak, bacon, tomatoes, and eggs. ⊠ *63 Cross St., Double Bay 2028,* ☎ *02/9363–4776,* 𝔽𝔸𝕏 *02/9363–1992. 3 rooms, 2 with bath. AE, DC, MC, V.*

$$ 🖭 **Victoria Court Sydney.** Set on a leafy street near Kings Cross, this small, smart hotel is appealing for more than just its reasonable rates. Hand-painted tiles and etched-glass doors recall its Victorian ancestry, yet the rooms come with the modern blessings of en-suite bathrooms and comfortable beds. ⊠ *122 Victoria St., Potts Point 2011,* ☎ *02/9357–3200,* 𝔽𝔸𝕏 *02/9357–7606. 25 rooms. AE, DC, MC, V.*

Sydney Area Lodging

$$ 🖭 **Ravesi's on Bondi Beach.** This small, boutique hotel looks out on Australia's most famous beach and offers a dash of style at a moderate price. All rooms are spacious, well kept, and uncluttered, decorated in a stylish sand-and-sea color scheme enhanced by art deco touches, in keeping with the building's origins. Oceanfront rooms have the best views, in particular Room 6. For family-size space, the split-level suites, which have their own terrace, are recommended. Least expensive are those double rooms without a sea view. The second-floor restaurant is popular and noisy; request a room on the top floor for peace and privacy. Frequent bus service takes 25 minutes to get to the city. ⊠ *Campbell Parade and Hall St., Bondi Beach 2026,* ☎ *02/9365–4422,* 𝔽𝔸𝕏 *02/9365–1481. 16 rooms. Restaurant, bar. AE, DC, MC, V.*

$$ 🖭 **Trickett's.** The Victorian character of this converted mansion is evident in such features as 13-ft ceilings, a ballroom, and hallways elegantly enhanced with Oriental rugs and porcelain. Guest rooms are vast, although simply furnished, and each has a bathroom with robes supplied. In a quiet neighborhood only a 10-minute bus ride from the city, this hotel is close to a wide variety of dining options; two waterfront parks are within easy walking distance. Continental breakfast is included. ⊠ *270 Glebe Point Rd., Glebe 2037,* ☎ *02/9552–1141,* 𝔽𝔸𝕏 *02/9692–9462. 7 rooms. No credit cards.*

$ 🖭 **Brooklyn Bed and Breakfast.** Tucked away in an inner-west suburb, this late-Victorian guest house offers accommodations with character and exceptional value. Bedrooms are on the upper level, and except for the single room at the rear, all are large and comfortable and equipped to sleep three. The front room with balcony is especially recommended. Breakfasts here include muesli and other cereals, stewed fruits, croissants and toast, orange juice, and tea and coffee. The house is a 15-minute train ride from the city. The cafés and restaurants of Norton Street, Sydney's "little Italy," are within a 10-minute walk. Owner Angela Finnigan is convivial and helpful. ⊠ *25 Railway St., Petersham 2049,* ☎ *02/9564–2312. 5 rooms. AE, DC, MC, V.*

NIGHTLIFE AND THE ARTS

The Arts

The most comprehensive listing of upcoming events is in the "Metro" section of the *Sydney Morning Herald* published on Friday; on other days, browse through the entertainment section of the paper. Tickets for almost all stage presentations can be purchased through **Ticketek** agencies. For credit-card bookings (AE, DC, MC, V) call the **Ticketek Phone Box Office** (☎ 02/9266–4800). Alternatively, you can buy tickets for Opera House performances and the major musical and theatrical shows through **Firstcall** (☎ 02/9320–9000), which also takes credit-card bookings (AE, MC, V). The **Halftix Booth** (☎ 02/9966–1723) sells tickets for each night's performances at half price on a cash-only basis. The booth is in Martin Place near Macquarie Street and opens at noon.

Ballet, Opera, Classical Music

Sydney Opera House. Despite its name, this famous building is actually a showcase for all the performing arts: It has five theaters, only one of which is devoted to opera. The Opera House is the home of the Australian Ballet and the Sydney Dance Company, as well as the Australian Opera Company. The complex also includes two stages for theater and the 2,700-seat Concert Hall, where the Sydney Symphony Orchestra and the Australian Chamber Orchestra perform regularly. ⊠ *Bennelong Point,* ☎ *02/9250–7777.* ☉ *Box office Mon.–Sat. 9–8:30.*

Dance

Aboriginal Islander Dance Theatre. This troupe presents modern interpretations of traditional Aboriginal dances. The company performs in its headquarters near the Rocks. ⊠ *3 Cumberland St., The Rocks,* ☎ *02/9252–0199.*

Sydney Dance Company. Innovative contemporary dance is the specialty of this internationally acclaimed group, who generally perform at the Opera House when they are not touring outside Sydney. ⊠ *Pier 4, Hickson Rd., Walsh Bay,* ☎ *02/9221–4811.*

Theater

Belvoir Street Theatre. The two stages here are often home to innovative and challenging political and social drama. A highlight is "Theatresports," in which competing teams of actors construct highly imaginative and impromptu dramas, held most Sunday nights. The theater is a 10-minute walk from Central Station. ⊠ *25 Belvoir St., Surry Hills,* ☎ *02/9699–3444.*

Capitol Theatre. The 100-year-old Capitol building, which fell into disrepair during the 1980s, has been gloriously renovated and transformed into the city's most elaborate performance space. The 2,000-seat theater presents major mainstream musicals, such as *West Side Story, Miss Saigon,* and *Sweet Charity.* ⊠ *13 Campbell St., Haymarket,* ☎ *02/9320–9122.*

Lyric Theatre. The Star City entertainment complex's 2,000-seat theater is managed by Andrew Lloyd Webber's Really Useful Group. It presents a variety of internationally acclaimed theatrical productions and concerts. ⊠ *20–80 Pyrmont St., Pyrmont,* ☎ *02/9777–9150.*

Stables Theatre. Dedicated to experimental works, this small theater occasionally shines with brilliant displays of young, local talent. ⊠ *10 Nimrod St., Kings Cross,* ☎ *02/9361–3817.*

State Theatre. The architecture alone dazzles, even if the show does not. Built in 1929 and restored to its full-blown opulence in 1980, the theater's Gothic foyer features a vaulted ceiling, mosaic floors, marble columns and statues, and brass and bronze doors. A highlight of the magnificent theater is the 20,000-piece chandelier that is supposedly the world's second largest. The 2,000-seat theater is now used as a venue for touring acts, musicals, and, every June, for the Sydney Film Festival. ⊠ *49 Market St.,* ☎ *02/9373–6537.*

The Wharf Theatre. Located on a redeveloped wharf in the shadow of Harbour Bridge, this is the home of the Sydney Theatre Company, one of the most original and highly regarded companies in Australia. For large-scale productions, the company usually performs in the Opera House. ⊠ *Pier 4, Hickson Rd., Walsh Bay,* ☎ *02/9250–1777.*

Nightlife

"Satan made Sydney," wrote Mark Twain, quoting a citizen of the city, and there can be no doubt that Satan was the principal architect behind **Kings Cross.** This is Australia's most notorious nightlife district. Temptations are varied and openly displayed, and although the area is reasonably safe, it is no place for the fainthearted. Strictly speaking, Kings Cross refers to the intersection of Victoria Street and Darlinghurst Road, although the name "The Cross" applies to a much wider area. Essentially, it is a quarter mile stretch of bars, burlesque shows, cafés, video shows, and massage parlors. The area does not come to life much before 10 PM, and the action runs hot for most of the night (especially weekends).

Sydneysiders in search of late-night action are more likely to head for Oxford Street, between Hyde Park and Taylor Square, where the choice ranges from pubs to the hottest discos in town. Oxford Street is also the nighttime focus for Sydney's large gay population.

The entertainment section published daily in the *Sydney Morning Herald* is the most informative guide to current attractions in the city's pubs and clubs. For inside information on the club scene—who's been seen where and what they were wearing—pick up a free copy of *Beat,* available at just about any Oxford Street café.

Comedy Clubs
Comedy Hotel. Also known as the Harold Park Hotel, the house specialty of this pub/bistro is stand-up comedy and cabaret. ⊠ *115 Wigram Rd., Glebe,* ☎ *02/9552–1791.* 🎫 *$10–$20.* ☉ *Mon.–Sat. from 8:30 PM.*

Gambling
Star City Casino. This glitzy, Las Vegas–style casino opened in 1997 as the centerpiece of the new Star City entertainment complex. It has 200 gaming tables and 1,500 slot machines. Gambling options include roulette, craps, blackjack, baccarat, and the classic Australian game of two-up. ⊠ *20–80 Pyrmont St., Pyrmont,* ☎ *02/9777–9000.* ☉ *Daily 24 hrs.*

Gay Bars and Clubs
Albury Hotel. A longtime anchor to Sydney's gay scene, this popular pub still draws the crowds with its muscle-bound barmen and nightly drag shows. It's usually the first port of call for gay visitors. ⊠ *6 Oxford St., Paddington,* ☎ *02/9361–6555.* ☉ *Daily 2 PM–2 AM.*

Banana Bar. At the heart of Darlinghurst, Australia's gay and lesbian enclave, this stylish bar is the place to go for cocktails, quiet conversation, and soft music, except for late on Friday and Saturday nights, when it succumbs to the feverish contagion of Oxford Street. ⊠ *1–5 Flinders St., Darlinghurst,* ☎ *02/9360–6373.* ☉ *Daily 3 PM–3 AM.*

Club 77. This small basement club attracts a varied crowd with music that ranges from trance to jazz to tribal. ⊠ *77 William St., East Sydney,* ☎ *02/9361–4981.* ▦ *$5–$8.* ⊙ *Fri.–Sun. 9 PM–3 AM.*

DCM. This dance club is one of the hottest on Sydney's gay and lesbian nightclub strip. ⊠ *31–33 Oxford St., Darlinghurst,* ☎ *02/9267–7380.* ▦ *$5–$20.* ⊙ *Thurs.–Fri. 11 PM–7 AM, Sat. 10 PM–10:30 AM, Sun. 9 PM–7 AM.*

Midnight Shift. A perennial favorite with the leather and denim set, this gay nightclub is well known for its throbbing techno-music and its laser light show. Traditionally a bastion for men, the club is now increasingly popular with lesbians. ⊠ *85 Oxford St., Darlinghurst,* ☎ *02/ 9360–4463.* ▦ *$10.* ⊙ *Mon.–Thurs. 9 PM–3 AM, Fri.–Sat. 10 PM–6 AM, Sun. 11 PM–6 AM.*

Jazz Clubs

The Basement. Close to the waterfront at Circular Quay, this subterranean club is the city's premier venue for top Australian and overseas jazz, blues, and funk musicians. Dinner is also available. ⊠ *29 Reiby Pl., Circular Quay,* ☎ *02/9251–2797.* ▦ *$5–$20.* ⊙ *Weekdays 4:30 PM–midnight, weekends 7 PM–midnight.*

Harbourside Brasserie. With the lights of Harbour Bridge twinkling in the background, this nightclub is a popular place to dine while listening to music. The entertainment varies from rock to world music, but the club is best known as a contemporary jazz venue. A wide range of food, from light snacks to steaks with all the trimmings, is available until midnight. ⊠ *Pier 1, Hickson Rd., Walsh Bay,* ☎ *02/9252–3000.* ▦ *$5–$20.* ⊙ *Tues.–Sun. usually 7 PM–3 AM.*

Nightclubs

Blackmarket Nightclub. Blackmarket opens its doors just as the other clubs are closing, revving up the music until well past sunrise. On Friday nights the club hosts Hellfire, Sydney's most prominent S & M club. ⊠ *111 Regent St., Chippendale,* ☎ *02/9283–5555.* ▦ *$15.* ⊙ *Fri. 10 PM–5 AM, weekends 10 PM–7 AM.*

The Cauldron. This disco and its accompanying quality restaurant near Kings Cross is the place where Sydney's well-heeled sophisticates gather. Despite the name, the club is spacious and airy, except on weekends, when it's packed to the rafters. ⊠ *207 Darlinghurst Rd., Darlinghurst,* ☎ *02/9331–1523.* ▦ *$10–$15.* ⊙ *Tues.–Sat. 6 PM–3 AM.*

Ettamogah Bar and Family Restaurant. Based on a famous Australian cartoon series depicting an outback saloon, this theme pub has three bars and an open-air restaurant. The atmosphere varies from family-friendly during the day to nightclub in the evening. ⊠ *225 Harbourside, Darling Harbour,* ☎ *02/9281–3922.* ▦ *Thurs.–Sat. $5–$10.* ⊙ *Weekdays 11 AM–midnight, Sat. 11 AM–3 AM, Sun. 11 AM–11 PM.*

Lizard Lounge. The Exchange Hotel's upstairs cocktail lounge/dance club offers a more refined alternative to the raucous action of the street-level bar. ⊠ *34 Oxford St., Darlinghurst,* ☎ *02/9331–1936.* ▦ *$5 (Sat. only).* ⊙ *Mon.–Thurs. 5 PM–1 AM, Fri.–Sun. 5 PM–3 AM.*

RIVA. The best nightclub in any Sydney hotel, this impressive venue has a variety of very different entertainment experiences, from fashion parades to a disco. Live funk or rhythm and blues are also a staple. The clientele reads like a *Who's Who* of social Sydney. ⊠ *130 Castlereagh St.,* ☎ *02/9286–6666.* ▦ *$12–$20.* ⊙ *Wed.–Sat. 10 PM–5 AM.*

Soho Lounge. The grooviest and most civilized cocktail bar in Kings Cross, the mood on the upper-story is young, hip, and elegant. The adjoining pool room is rated one of the city's finest. ⊠ *171 Victoria St., Potts Point,* ☎ *02/9358–6511.* ▦ *$10.* ⊙ *Daily 6 PM–3 AM.*

Pubs with Music

Mercantile Hotel. In the shadow of Harbour Bridge, this hotel is Irish and very proud of it. You can hear fiddles, drums, and pipes rising above the clamor in the bar, and lilting accents lifted in song, seven nights a week. ⊠ *25 George St., the Rocks,* ☎ *02/9247–3570.* ⊘ *Mon.–Wed. 10 AM–midnight, Thurs.–Sat. 10 AM–1 AM, Sun. 10 AM–midnight.*

Rose, Shamrock and Thistle. Popularly known as the Three Weeds, this friendly, boisterous pub 5 km (3 mi) from the city center is one of the best places to hear live music—generally from Thursday through Saturday. ⊠ *193 Evans St., Rozelle,* ☎ *02/9810–2244.* ⊠ *Music nights $5–$10.* ⊘ *Mon.–Sat. noon–midnight, Sun. noon–10.*

OUTDOOR ACTIVITIES AND SPORTS

Cricket

For Australians, the pinnacle of excitement is The Ashes, when the Australian national cricket team takes the field against their age-old rivals and forebears—the English. It happens every other summer (December–January), and the two nations take turns hosting the event. Cricket season runs from October through March. The Ashes is next scheduled for Australia in 2002–03.

Football

Rugby League, known locally as footie, is Sydney's winter addiction. This is a fast, gutsy, physical game that bears some similarities to North American football, although the action is more constant and the ball cannot be passed forward. The season falls between April and September. The **Sydney Football Stadium** (⊠ Moore Park Rd., Paddington, ☎ 02/9360–6601 for stadium for match information and ticket sales) is the main venue.

Golf

More than 80 golf courses lie within a 40-km (25-mi) radius of the Sydney Harbour Bridge; 35 of them are public courses. Golf clubs and carts are usually available for rent, but caddies are not.

Bondi Golf Club is a nine-hole public course on the cliffs overlooking famous Bondi Beach. While the par-28 course is hardly a challenge for serious golfers, the views are inspiring. The course is open to the public after noon on most days. ⊠ *5 Military Rd., North Bondi,* ☎ *02/ 9130–1981.* ⊠ *Greens fee $12.*

New South Wales Golf Course is a rigorous, challenging, par-72 championship course on the cliffs at La Perouse, overlooking Botany Bay. The course is generally open to nonmembers midweek, but visitors must make advance arrangements with the pro shop. ⊠ *Henry Head, La Perouse,* ☎ *02/ 9661–4455.* ⊠ *Greens fee $100.*

A 90-minute drive northwest of Sydney, **Riverside Oaks Golf Club** is a spectacular course in a classic bush setting on the banks of the Hawkesbury River. ⊠ *O'Brien's Rd., Cattai,* ☎ *02/4560–3299.* ⊠ *Greens fee weekdays $63, weekends $78.*

Running

One of the finest paths in the city is the route from the **Opera House to Mrs. Macquarie's Chair,** along the edge of the harbor, through the Royal Botanic Gardens. At lunchtime on weekdays, this track is crowded with corporate joggers.

In the eastern suburbs, a running track runs south along the cliffs from **Bondi Beach to Tamarama**; it is marked by distance indicators and includes a number of exercise stations.

The **Manly** beachfront is good for running. If you've got legs for it, you can run down to Shelly Beach, or pop over the hill to Freshwater Beach and follow it all the way to check out Curl Curl's huge waves.

Sailing and Boating

At **Eastsail,** near Kings Cross, you can rent, for about $95 per half day, a small boat to sail or motor yourself around the harbor. It's also possible to charter a skippered yacht for a full day's excursion for around $1,500. ⊠ *D'Albora Marine, New Beach Rd., Rushcutters Bay,* ☎ *02/ 9327–1166.*

The **Northside Sailing School** at Middle Harbour rents out small sailboats. Rates start at $20 per hour, and you can also book an instructor to show you the ropes. ⊠ *The Spit, Mosman,* ☎ *02/9969–3972.*

Scuba Diving

Pro Dive offers courses and shore- or boat-diving excursions around the harbor and city beaches. Some of the best dive spots are close to the eastern suburbs' beaches of Clovelly and Coogee, where Pro Dive is based. A full day out with an instructor or dive master costs around $100, including rental equipment. ⊠ *27 Alfreda St., Coogee,* ☎ *02/9665–6333.*

Surfing

What beaches are best for surfing is a matter of personal opinion, but you can usually count on good waves south of Bondi. North of the harbor, stay between Manly and Newport for good waves. In summer, surfing reports are a regular feature of radio news broadcasts—that's Sydney (☞ Beaches, *above*).

Tennis

Cooper Park Tennis Courts is a complex of eight synthetic grass courts in a park surrounded by bush about 5 km (3 mi) east of the city center. ⊠ *Off Suttie Rd., Cooper Park, Double Bay,* ☎ *02/9389–9259.* ▱ *Weekdays 7 AM–5 PM $16 per hr, 5–10 PM $19 per hr; weekends 8 AM–5 PM $18 per hr, 5–10 PM $20 per hr.*

Parklands Sports Centre has nine courts set in a shady park approximately 2½ km (1½ mi) from the city center. ⊠ *Lang Rd. and Anzac Parade, Moore Park,* ☎ *02/9662–7033.* ▱ *Weekdays 8 AM–5 PM $15 per hr, 6–9 PM $17 per hr; weekends 8 AM–6 PM $17 per hr.*

Windsurfing

The bays and inlets of Sydney Harbour afford great windsurfing opportunities, and **Rose Bay Aquatic Hire** rents out windsurfers for $35 per hour. Hobie Cats and Lasers rent for $15 per hour and up. ⊠ *1 Vickery Ave., Rose Bay,* ☎ *02/9371–7036.* ▱ *$15 per hr, high-performance board $20.* ☉ *Oct.–Mar., daily during daylight, weather permitting.*

SHOPPING

Sydney is Australia's shopping capital. Some of the finest souvenirs are to be found in the city's Aboriginal art galleries, opal shops, crafts galleries, or weekend flea markets. If you're concerned about buying genuine Australian products, look carefully at the labels: Stuffed koalas and kangaroos made in Taiwan have become a standing joke in Australia. In the city, shops are generally open on weekdays between 9 and 5:30. Thursday night, most shops stay open until 9, although some close at 7. Saturday shopping hours are from 9 to 4. Most department stores and shops in such tourist areas as the Rocks and Darling Harbour are open Sunday. The most widely accepted credit cards are American Express, MasterCard, and Visa.

Department Stores

David Jones. "Dee Jays," as it's known locally, is the largest department store in the city, with a reputation for excellent service and high-quality goods. Clothing by many of Australia's finest designers is on display here, and the store also markets its own fashion label at reasonable prices. The basement level of the men's store is a food hall with a range of treats from all over the world. ✉ *Women's store,* ✉ *Elizabeth and Market Sts.; men's store,* ✉ *Castlereagh and Market Sts.,* ☎ *02/9266–5544.* ⊙ *Mon.–Wed. and Fri. 9–6, Thurs. 9–9, Sat. 9–5, Sun. 11–5.*

Grace Bros. Opposite the Queen Victoria Building, this is the place to shop for clothing and accessories by Australian and international designers. ✉ *George and Market Sts.,* ☎ *02/9238–9111.* ⊙ *Mon.–Wed. and Fri. 9–6, Thurs. 9–9, Sun. 11–5.*

Duty-Free Shops

Overseas visitors can take advantage of great bargains on electronics, cameras, perfume, and liquor at the many duty-free shops scattered throughout the city. Most of the prices in Sydney's duty-free shops are comparable with those in the duty-free bargain centers of Singapore and Hong Kong. Although you can purchase goods at any time with the display of a ticket to leave Australia and a passport, you have to collect them from the shop only 48 hours before you leave. You must carry the goods, which are sealed in plastic carrier bags, on the plane as hand luggage, and you cannot open the goods until you clear customs, located just beyond the immigration desk at the airport. The range of perfumes, liquor, and electronics at the airport duty-free stores is less extensive than in town.

Allders Duty Free. This Circular Quay store sells a wide selection of jewelry, liquor, electronics, and clothing. ✉ *22 Pitt St.,* ☎ *02/9241–5844.*

Angus and Coote. Sydney's specialist jeweler offers a wide selection of duty-free watches and gemstones. ✉ *496 George St.,* ☎ *02/9267–1363.* ⊙ *Mon.–Sat. 10–6, Sun. 12:30–6.*

Downtown Duty Free. With two city outlets, Downtown is popular among airline flight crews, who are generally a reliable indicator of the best prices. ✉ *Strand Arcade, basement level, off Pitt St. Mall,* ☎ *02/9233–3166;* ✉ *105 Pitt St.,* ☎ *02/9221–4444.* ⊙ *Mon.–Wed. 9–5:30, Thurs. 9–8:30, Sat. 9–5, Sun. 11–4.*

Flea Markets

Balmain Market. This Saturday market, set in a leafy churchyard less than 5 km (3 mi) from the city, has a rustic appeal that is a relaxing change from city-center shopping. The 140-odd stalls display some unusual and high-quality bric-a-brac, craftwork, and jewelry. Inside the church hall you can buy a truly international range of snacks, from Indian samosas to Indonesian satays to Australian meat pies. ✉ *St. Andrew's Church, Darling St., Balmain.* ⊙ *Sat. 8:30–4.*

Paddington Bazaar. Popularly known as Paddington Market, the stalls crammed with essential oils and tribal jewelry give this busy churchyard bazaar a New Age feel, although it's also a great place to shop for children's clothing and T-shirts at bargain prices. The market is also an outlet for a handful of avant-garde but unknown dress designers, whose clothing is still affordable. The market is a lively, entertaining environment that acts as a magnet for buskers and some of the flamboyant characters of the area. While you're in the neighborhood, check out **Oxford Street**'s cafés and clothes boutiques. ✉ *St. John's Church, Oxford St., Paddington.* ⊙ *Sat. 10–4.*

The Rocks Market. Weekends, this sprawling covered bazaar transforms the upper end of George Street into a cultural collage of music, food, arts, crafts, and entertainment. ✉ *Upper George St., near Argyle St., the Rocks.* ⊙ *Weekends 10–5.*

Shopping Centers and Arcades

Harbourside. The shopping area of the Darling Harbour complex contains more than 200 clothing, jewelry, and souvenir shops. However, its attraction as a shopping area is due not so much to the shops themselves as to its striking architecture and spectacular waterside location. The shopping center is open daily and has many cafés, restaurants, and bars that overlook the harbor. ⊠ *Darling Harbour.*

Pitt Street Mall. The pedestrian plaza in the heart of Sydney's shopping area includes the Mid-City Centre, Centrepoint Arcade, Imperial Arcade, Skygarden, Grace Bros, and the charming and historic Strand Arcade—six multilevel shopping plazas crammed with more than 450 shops, most of which sell clothing. ⊠ *Between King and Market Sts.*

Queen Victoria Building. A sprawling example of Victorian architecture near Town Hall, the QVB contains more than 200 boutiques, cafés, and antiques shops. Even if you have no intention of shopping, the meticulously restored 1890s building itself is worth a look. The QVB is open 24 hours a day, although the shops trade at the usual hours. ⊠ *George, York, Market, and Druitt Sts.,* ☎ *02/9264–9209.*

Specialty Stores

ABORIGINAL ART

Aboriginal art includes functional items, such as boomerangs and spears, as well as paintings and ceremonial implements that testify to a rich culture of legends and dreams. Although much of this artwork remains strongly traditional in character, the tools and colors used in Western art have fired the imaginations of many Aboriginal artists. The two outstanding sources of Aboriginal art are Arnhem Land and the Central Desert Region, which are close to Darwin and Alice Springs, respectively. Although there is no shortage of Aboriginal artwork in either place, much of the best finds its way into the galleries of Sydney and Melbourne.

Aboriginal Art Centres. This chain of variously named shops sells Aboriginal work, from large sculpture and bark paintings to such small collectibles as carved emu eggs. ⊠ *Aboriginal and Tribal Art Centre, 117 George St., Level 1, the Rocks,* ☎ *02/9247–9625; Aboriginal Art Shop,* ⊠ *Opera House, Upper Concourse,* ☎ *02/9247–4344.* ⊘ *Aboriginal and Tribal Art Centre daily 10–5, Aboriginal Art Shop daily 10–6.*

Coo-ee Aboriginal Art. A wide selection of wearable Aboriginal artwork includes jewelry and T-shirts painted with abstract designs, sold at moderate prices. ⊠ *98 Oxford St., Paddington,* ☎ *02/9332–1544.* ⊘ *Mon.–Sat. 10–6, Sun. 11–5.*

BOOKS

Ariel Booksellers. This large, bright browser's delight at the lower end of Paddington is the place to go for anything new or avant-garde. It also has the best collection of art books in Sydney. ⊠ *42 Oxford St., Paddington,* ☎ *02/9332–4581.* ⊘ *Daily 10 AM–midnight.*

Dymocks. Big, bustling, and packed to its gallery-level coffee shop, this mid-city bookstore is the place to go for all literary needs. ⊠ *424–430 George St.,* ☎ *02/9235–0155.* ⊘ *Mon.–Wed. and Fri. 9–5:30, Thurs. 9–9, weekends 9–4.*

The Travel Bookshop. Stop in here for Sydney's most extensive range of maps, guides, armchair travel books, and histories. ⊠ *Shop 3, 175 Liverpool St.,* ☎ *02/9261–8200.* ⊘ *Weekdays 9–6, Sat. 10–5, Sun. noon–5.*

BUSH APPAREL AND CAMPING AND OUTDOOR GEAR

Mountain Designs. Located in the middle of Sydney's rugged row of outdoor specialists, this store sells the serious camping and climbing hardware necessary to keep you alive and well in the wilderness. ✉ *499 Kent St.,* ☎ *02/9267–3822.* ⊙ *Mon.–Wed. 9–5:30, Thurs. 9–9, Fri. 9–6, Sat. 9–5, Sun. 10–4.*

Paddy Pallin. For serious bush adventurers heading for the Amazon, Annapurna, or wild Australia, Paddy's should be the first stop. You'll find maps, books, and mounds of gear tailored especially for the Australian outdoors. ✉ *507 Kent St.,* ☎ *02/9264–2685.* ⊙ *Mon.–Wed. 9–5:30, Thurs. 9–9, Fri. 9–6, Sat. 9–5, Sun. 10–4.*

R. M. Williams. This is the place to buy your trendy Australian country wear, including an Akubra hat, Drizabone riding coat, plaited kangaroo-skin belt, and moleskin trousers. ✉ *389 George St.,* ☎ *02/ 9262–2228.* ⊙ *Mon.–Wed. and Fri. 9–5:30, Thurs. 9–9, Sat. 9–4, Sun. 10–4.*

CDS AND TAPES

Folkways. If you're looking for a range of Australian bush, folk, and Aboriginal records, Folkways has an especially impressive selection. ✉ *282 Oxford St., Paddington,* ☎ *02/9361–3980.* ⊙ *Mon. 9–6, Tues.–Wed. and Fri. 9–7, Thurs. 9–9, Sat. 9:30–6:30, Sun. 10–5.*

CRAFTS

Australian Craftworks. Many of the wares here—superb woodwork, ceramics, knitwear, and glassware, as well as small souvenirs made by leading Australian crafts workers—are displayed in the cells of this former police station. ✉ *127 George St., the Rocks,* ☎ *02/9247–7156.* ⊙ *Fri.–Wed. 9–7, Thurs. 9–9.*

Object Stores. The beautiful creations in glass, wood, ceramic, and metal sold in these two waterside stores have been crafted for the connoisseur. ✉ *88 George St., the Rocks,* ☎ *02/9247–7984;* ✉ *31 Alfred St., Customs House,* ☎ *02/9247–7318.* ⊙ *Weekdays 10–5:30, weekends 10–5.*

KNITWEAR

Dorian Scott. A wide range of Australian knitwear for men, women, and children includes bright, bold high-fashion garments as well as sweaters and scarves in natural colors. ✉ *105 George St., the Rocks,* ☎ *02/9247–4090.* ⊙ *Weekdays 9:30–7, Sat. 9:30–6, Sun. 10–6.*

OPALS

Australia has a virtual monopoly on the world's supply of this fiery gemstone. The least expensive stones are doublets, which consist of a thin shaving of opal mounted on a plastic base. Sometimes the opal is covered by a quartz crown, in which case it becomes a triplet. The most expensive stones are solid opals, which cost anything from a few hundred dollars to a few thousand. Opals are sold at souvenir shops all over the city, but anyone who intends to buy a valuable stone should visit an opal specialist.

Flame Opals. Selling nothing but solid opals, set in either sterling silver or 18-karat gold, the shop has a wide selection of black, white, and Queensland boulder opals, which have a distinctive depth and luster. The sales staff is very helpful. ✉ *119 George St., the Rocks,* ☎ *02/ 9247–3446.* ⊙ *Weekdays 9–7, Sat. 10–5, Sun. 11:30–5.*

Gemtec. This is the only Sydney opal retailer with total ownership of its entire production process—mines, workshops, and showroom—making prices very competitive. In the Pitt Street showroom, you can see artisans at work cutting and polishing the stones. ✉ *51 Pitt St.,* ☎ *02/ 9251–1599.* ⊙ *Weekdays 9–5:30, weekends 10–4.*

T-SHIRTS AND BEACHWEAR

Done Art and Design. Prominent artist Ken Done catches the sunny side of Sydney with vivid, vibrant colors and bold brush strokes. His shop sells a variety of practical products carrying his distinctive designs, including bed linens, sunglasses, beach towels, beach and resort wear, and T-shirts. ⊠ *123 George St., the Rocks,* ☎ *02/9251–6099.* ☉ *Weekdays 9–6, weekends 10–6.*

SYDNEY A TO Z

Arriving and Departing

By Bus

Bus service is available to all major cities from Sydney. Purchase tickets for long-distance buses from travel agents, by telephone with a credit card, or at bus terminals. **Greyhound Pioneer Australia** (☎ 13–2030) and **McCafferty's** (☎ 13–1499) operate from the Central Station (Eddy Avenue) terminus just south of the City Center. Lockers are available in the terminal.

By Car

Driving in and out of Sydney has become slightly easier thanks to an improved freeway system. With the assistance of a good road map or street directory, you shouldn't have too many problems.

Remember that distances between major Australian cities are large, and two days would be required to comfortably cover the route to or from Melbourne or Brisbane. These may be called "highways," but most major Australian roads are modest by North American or European standards.

The main roads to and from other state capitals are: the **Pacific Highway** (Hwy. 1) north to Brisbane (982 km/609 mi), the **Hume Highway** (Hwy. 31) southwest to Canberra (335 km/208 mi) and Melbourne (874 km/542 mi), and the **Princes Highway** (Hwy. 1) to the NSW south coast and Melbourne (1,038 km/644 mi). Adelaide is 1,425 km (884 mi) away via the Hume and Sturt (Hwy. 20) highways, and Perth is a long and not particularly recommended 4,132-km (2,562-mi) drive via Adelaide.

By Plane

AIRLINES

International airlines serving Sydney from North America, Europe, and major Southeast Asian cities include **Air New Zealand, Ansett Australia, British Airways, Canadian Airlines International** (connecting with Qantas via Honolulu), **Cathay Pacific Airways, Japan Airlines, Qantas Airways, Singapore Airlines,** and **United Airlines.**

Domestic flights into Sydney include those of **Ansett Australia, Qantas Airways,** and **Hazelton Airlines.**

Qantas flights with numbers from QF1 to QF399 depart from the Kingsford–Smith airport's international terminal, and flights numbered QF400 and higher depart from the domestic terminal.

See Air Travel *in* Smart Travel Tips for airline telephone numbers.

AIRPORTS

Kingsford–Smith is Sydney's main airport, 8 km (5 mi) south of the city. Trolleys are available in the baggage area of the international terminal. You can convert your money to Australian currency at the **Thomas Cook** bureaus, in both the arrivals and departures areas, open from about 5 AM to 10 PM or later, depending on flight arrival or departure times.

Tourism New South Wales has two information counters in the international terminal's arrivals hall. One provides free maps and brochures and handles general inquiries, while the other deals with accommodations bookings. Both counters are open daily from approximately 6 AM to 11 PM.

Kingsford–Smith's **domestic and international terminals** are 3 km (2 mi) apart. To get from one terminal to the other, you can take a taxi for about $9, use the **Airport Shuttle Bus,** or catch the **Airport Express** bus. The latter departs approximately every 10–15 minutes, between about 5 AM and 11 PM and both cost $2.50.

BETWEEN SYDNEY AIRPORT AND CENTER CITY

The green-and-yellow **Airport Express** bus provides a fast, comfortable link between the airport terminals and the city, Kings Cross, Bondi, Coogee, Darling Harbour, and Glebe. For those traveling with fewer than four people, the cost compares favorably with the cost of a taxi. From the international and domestic terminals, Bus 300 stops first at Central Station, then travels along George Street to Circular Quay and the Rocks. Bus 350 stops at Central Station, Elizabeth Street, Liverpool Street, Oxford Street, and Darlinghurst Road, ending its route with a circuit through Kings Cross, Potts Point, and Elizabeth Bay. Bus 351 goes to Coogee Beach and Bondi Beach, and Bus 352 goes to Darling Harbour and Glebe. Buses depart at intervals of between 8 and 30 minutes from the airport, generally from around 6 AM to 11 PM. Refer to timetables outside the airport terminals for full details, or call the State Transit Infoline (☎ 13–1500). A brochure on the service is usually available from the Tourism New South Wales counter at the airport. ✆ One-way $6, round-trip $10.

Taxis are available from the ranks outside the terminal buildings. The fare to city hotels is about $28, about $25 to Kings Cross.

Scheduled for completion early in 2000, the airport **rail link** will be the fastest way to travel between the airport and the city center. At press time, the expected cost of a ticket is $10.

A chauffeured **limousine** to the city hotels costs about $75. Waiting time is charged at the rate of $60 per hour. Operators include **Premier Limousines** (☎ 02/9313–42 77) and **Astra Hire Cars** (☎ 02/9693–5300).

By Ship

Cruise ships call frequently at Sydney as part of their South Pacific itineraries. Passenger ships generally berth at the **Sydney Cove Passenger Terminal** at Circular Quay. The terminal is in the shadow of Harbour Bridge, close to many of the city's major attractions as well as to the bus, ferry, and train networks. Otherwise, passenger ships berth at the **Darling Harbour Passenger Terminal,** which is a short walk from the city center. For information on ship arrivals and departures, call the **Maritime Services Board** (☎ 02/9364–2800; 02/9364–2000 after hrs).

By Train

The main terminal for long-distance and intercity trains is **Central Station** (✉ Eddy Ave.), about a mile south of the city center. Two daily services (morning and evening) between Sydney and Melbourne are available; the trip takes about 10 hours. Three *Explorer* trains make the four-hour trip to Canberra daily. The *Indian-Pacific* leaves Sydney on Monday and Thursday afternoons for Adelaide (26 hours) and Perth (64 hours). The overnight *Brisbane XPT* makes the 15-hour Sydney–Brisbane journey every day. Call the state rail authority, **Countrylink** (☎ 13–2232), between 6:30 AM and 10 PM daily for information about fares and timetables.

Tickets for long-distance train travel can be purchased from **Countrylink Travel Centres** at Central Station, Circular Quay (✉ 1 Alfred St.),

Wynyard Station (✉ 11–31 York St.), and Town Hall Station (✉ Queen Victoria Bldg., lower level, George and Park Sts.).

Getting Around

Despite its vast size, Sydney's primary attractions are packed into a fairly small area, and such areas as the Rocks, Darling Harbour, and the Opera House are best explored on foot. Getting to and from these places is simple on Sydney's buses, ferries, and trains—except during rush hours. Mostly you will find public transport an efficient, economical way to see the city.

A **Travelpass** allows you unlimited travel aboard buses, ferries, and trains—but not trams—within designated areas of the city for a week or more. The most useful is probably the week-long Blue Travelpass ($17.10), which covers the city and eastern suburbs and inner-harbor ferries (ferries to Manly will cost extra). Travelpasses are available from railway and bus stations and from most news agents on bus routes.

If you're planning on spending three days or less in Sydney and taking the Airport Express bus, the guided Sydney Explorer and Bondi & Bay Explorer buses, and any of the three sightseeing cruises operated by the State Transit Authority, **Sydneypass** ($70 for three days, five-and seven-day passes available) will save you money. The pass also allows unlimited travel on any public bus or harbor ferry, and most suburban train services. Purchase passes from the **Tourism New South Wales counter** on the ground floor of the international airport terminal, or from the driver of any Explorer or Airport Express bus.

For the duration of the Olympic Games, access to Olympic Park will be by train and bus only. Private vehicles will not be allowed to enter the site during this period. Olympic Games ticketholders will be provided with free transport to Olympic Park via bus or train from the city center. Information on transportation routes and options will be included in a comprehensive information pack that will be provided along with games tickets.

For route, timetable, and ticket price information on Sydney's buses, ferries, and trains call the **State Transit Infoline** (☎ 13–1500), daily 6 AM–10 PM.

By Bus

On Sydney's well-developed bus system, fares are calculated by the number of city sections traveled. The minimum two-section bus fare ($1.20) applies to trips throughout the inner-city area. You would pay the minimum fare, for example, for a ride from Circular Quay to Kings Cross, or from Park Street to Oxford Street in Paddington. Tickets may be purchased from the driver. Discounted fares are available in several forms, including **Travelten** passes (valid for 10 journeys), which start at $8.80 and are available from bus stations and most news agents.

By Car

Driving a car around Sydney is not particularly recommended. Many roads are poorly marked, and harbor inlets and hilly terrain allow for few straight streets. Parking space is limited; furthermore, Sydney drivers are best known for speed and intolerance. If you do decide to take the plunge and drive, ask your car-rental agency for a street directory, or purchase one from a news agent.

By Ferry

No finer introduction to the city is to be found than aboard one of the commuter ferries that ply Sydney Harbour. The hub of the ferry system is **Circular Quay,** and ferries run to almost 30 spots the length and breadth of the harbor between about 6 AM and 11:30 PM. One of the most popular sightseeing trips is aboard the Manly ferry, a 30-minute journey from Circular Quay that provides glimpses of harborside mansions and the sandstone cliffs and bushland along the north shore. On the return journey from Manly, consider taking the JetCat, which skims the waves in an exhilarating 15-minute trip back to the city.

The one-way Manly ferry fare is $4, and the JetCat costs $5.20; fares for shorter inner harbor journeys start at $2.80. You can also buy economical ferry-and-entrance-fee passes, available from the Circular Quay ticket office, to such attractions as Taronga Zoo and Sydney Aquarium.

By Limousine

Chauffeur-driven limousines are available for trips around Sydney, and at your request, the driver will give a commentary on the major sights. Limousines can be rented for approximately $80 per hour. Operators include **Premier Limousines** (☎ 02/9313–4277) and **Astra Hire Cars** (☎ 02/9693–5300).

By Monorail

The **monorail** (☎ 02/9552–2288) is one of the fastest and most relaxing forms of public transport, but its use is limited to travel between the city center, Darling Harbour, and the Chinatown area. The flat-rate fare is $2.50, but $6 all-day passes are a better value if you intend to use the monorail to explore. The monorail operates every two–six minutes, generally from 7 AM to late evening, but times vary seasonally.

By Taxi

Taxis are a relatively economical way to cover short to medium distances in Sydney. A 3-km (2-mi) trip from Circular Quay to the eastern suburbs costs around $13. Drivers are entitled to charge more than the metered fare if the passenger's baggage exceeds 55 pounds, if the taxi has been booked by telephone, or if the passenger crosses Harbour Bridge, where a toll is levied. Taxis are licensed to carry four passengers. Most drivers will accept payment by American Express, Diners Club, or Mastercard. Taxis can be hailed on the street, hired from a taxi rank, or booked by phone. Taxi ranks can be found outside most bus and railway stations as well as the larger hotels. Complaints should be directed to **Taxi Cab Complaints** (☎ 1800/648–478). On the south side of the harbor, the most efficient telephone booking service is provided by **Taxis Combined Services** (☎ 02/9332–8888). North of the bridge, try **Premier Cabs** (☎ 13–1017).

By Train

For journeys in excess of 7 km (4 mi), Sydney's trains are considerably faster than buses. However, the rail network has been designed primarily for rapid transit between outlying suburbs and the city. Apart from the City Circle line, which includes the Circular Quay and Town Hall stations and the spur line to Kings Cross and Bondi Junction, the system does not serve areas of particular interest to visitors. Travelers using trains should remember the following axioms: All trains pass through Central Station; Town Hall is the "shoppers" station; the bus, ferry, and train systems converge at Circular Quay. Trains generally operate from 4:30 AM to midnight.

As an example of fare prices, a one-way ticket from Town Hall Station to Bondi Junction costs $2. A variety of discounted fares is also available, including **Off-Peak** tickets that apply on weekends and after 9 AM on weekdays.

By Tram

The **Sydney Light Rail** (☏ 02/9660–5288) is a limited system that provides a fast and efficient link between Central Station, Darling Harbour, and the Star City casino and entertainment complex. The modern, air-conditioned tram cars operate at 5- to 11-minute intervals, 24 hours per day. Round-trip tickets cost $3–$4.

By Water Taxi

A fun, fast, but somewhat expensive way to get around is by water taxi. These operate to and from practically anywhere on Sydney Harbour that has wharf or steps access. Contact **Harbour Taxi Boats** (☏ 02/9555–1155) or **Taxis Afloat** (☏ 02/9955–3222) for details and bookings.

Contacts and Resources

Car Rentals

All major rental companies, as well as a number of smaller operators, are represented in Sydney. Generally, the larger companies charge higher prices but offer unrestricted mileage and a greater number of pickup and drop-off facilities. Expect to pay about $80 per day for a medium-size automatic and about $70 for a compact standard model from a major operator, although some companies vary their rates considerably on a day-to-day basis. Small local operators often restrict travel to within a 50-km (30-mi) radius of the city center. Nevertheless, some real bargains are to be found, and a one-year-old model can cost as little as $40 per day. For rentals of one month or more with unrestricted travel, the rate on a new, medium-size sedan is anything from $50–$70 per day.

Major car-rental operators are **Avis** (☏ 02/9353–9000), **Budget** (☏ 13–2727), **Hertz** (☏ 13–3039), and **Thrifty** (☏ 1300/367–227). Smaller companies include **Dollar** (☏ 02/9223–1444) and **Bayswater** (☏ 02/9360–3622).

Consulates

British Consulate General (Gateway Building, 1 Macquarie Pl., Level 16, ☏ 02/9247–7521), **Canadian Consulate General** (111 Harrington St., Level 5, ☏ 02/9364–3000), **New Zealand Consulate General** (1 Alfred St., Level 14, Circular Quay, ☏ 02/9247–1999), and **U.S. Consulate General** (19–29 Martin Pl., Level 59, ☏ 02/9373–9200).

Doctors and Dentists

Doctors and dentists are widely available throughout the city, and there are many medical centers where appointments are not necessary. You can contact any of the services and establishments listed below or, alternatively, ask for recommendations at your hotel.

Dental Emergency Information Service (☏ 02/9369–7050) can provide you with the name and number of a nearby duty dentist, but this service is available only after 7 PM daily. **Royal North Shore Hospital** (Pacific Hwy., St. Leonards, ☏ 02/9926–7111) has an accident and emergency department and is 7 km (4 mi) northwest of the city center. **St. Vincent's Public Hospital** (Victoria and Burton Sts., Darlinghurst, ☏ 02/9339–1111), 2½ km (1½ mi) east of city center, provides emergency treatment.

Emergencies

Dial ☏ 000 for **fire, police, or ambulance** services. You can also make nonemergency police inquiries through the **Sydney Police Centre** (☏ 02/9281–0000).

Guided Tours

Dozens of guided tours operate in Sydney and the surrounding area. Options include everything from a shopping tour to abseiling (rapelling) in the Blue Mountains (☞ Chapter 3). The Sydney Visitors Information Centre (and the other booking and information centers detailed in Visitor Information, *below*) can provide you with many more suggestions and recommendations.

BOAT TOURS AND CRUISES

A replica of Captain Bligh's HMAV *Bounty* is alive and afloat on Sydney Harbour, and **Bounty Cruises** has various harbor excursions. A lunch cruise departs weekdays and travels east along the harbor. Most of the voyage is made under sail, and all on board are encouraged to take a turn with the ropes and the wheel. A commentary is provided, and the cruise focuses as much on square-rigger sailing and the *Bounty*'s history as on the sights of Sydney Harbour. For photographers, the nightly dinner cruise offers spectacular possibilities. Cruises depart from Campbell's Cove, in front of the Park Hyatt Hotel. ☎ 02/9247–1789. ✉ *Lunch cruise $52, weekend lunch $75, dinner cruise $80. ☉ Lunch cruise daily at 12:30, dinner cruise daily at 7.*

Captain Cook Cruises is the largest cruise operator on the harbor. Its best introductory trip is the 2½-hour **Coffee Cruise**, which follows the southern shore of the harbor to Watsons Bay, crosses to the north shore to explore Middle Harbour, and returns to Circular Quay. The **Sydney Harbour Explorer** cruise allows passengers to disembark from the cruise boat at the Opera House, Watsons Bay, Taronga Zoo, or Darling Harbour, explore, and catch any following Captain Cook explorer cruise. Four Explorer cruises depart daily from Circular Quay at two-hour intervals, beginning at 9:30 AM. Coffee cruises depart daily at 10 and 2:15. Dinner, sunset, and show-time cruises are also available. All cruises depart from Wharf 6, Circular Quay. ☎ 02/9206–1111. ✉ *Coffee cruise $32, Explorer cruise $20.*

The **State Transit Authority** runs the following cruises aboard harbor ferries, at lower costs than those of privately operated cruises. Light refreshments are available on board. All cruises depart from Wharf 4 at the Circular Quay terminal.

For those with limited time, the **Morning Harbour Cruise** is a one-hour cruise that takes in the major sights of the harbor to the east of the city. ☎ 13–1500. ✉ *$12. ☉ Daily at 10 and 11:15 AM.*

The **Afternoon Harbour Cruise** is a leisurely 2½-hour tour that takes in the scenic eastern suburbs and affluent Middle Harbour. (For the cruise itinerary, *see* Sydney Harbour *in* Exploring, *above*.) ☎ 13–1500. ✉ *$17. ☉ Weekdays at 1, weekends at 1:30.*

The 1½-hour **Evening Harbour Lights Cruise** takes you into Darling Harbour for a nighttime view of the city from the west, then passes the Garden Island naval base to view the Opera House and Kings Cross. ☎ 13–1500. ✉ *$14. ☉ Departs Mon.–Sat. at 8.*

EXCURSIONS AND DAY TRIPS

Several coach companies run a wide variety of day trips in and around the Sydney region. There are city tours and excursions to such places as the Blue Mountains, the Hunter Valley wine region, Canberra, wildlife parks, and the 2000 Olympics site at Homebush Bay. The following major operators all have a 24-hour inquiry and reservation service. **AAT King's** (☎ 02/9252–2788), **Australian Pacific Tours** (☎ 13–1304), **Murrays Australia** (☎ 02/9252–3590).

NATIONAL PARKS AND THE BUSH

Bush Limousine Tour Company (☏ 02/9418–7826) specializes in small group tours with an emphasis on quality. A choice of off-the-shelf or tailor-made tours is available to places such as the Blue Mountains, the Southern Highlands, the Hunter Valley, and the alpine region of southern New South Wales.

Wild Escapes (☏ 02/9482–2881) specializes in small group ecotour and cultural excursions aboard four-wheel drive vehicles, including trips to the Blue Mountains, the Hawkesbury River, the Hunter Valley, South Coast, and Olympic Park. Charters are available, but standard prices are about $190 for a full-day tour, including lunch with wine and cheese.

Wildframe Eto Tours (☏ 02/9314–0658) operates two one-day hiking and sightseeing trips to the Grand Canyon area, one of the loveliest parts of the Blue Mountains. Groups are limited to a maximum of 16, and all guides have specialist qualifications. The price is $55, or $72 for a slightly less demanding walk, which also includes lunch.

ORIENTATION TOURS

Tickets for either of the following State Transit Authority bus tours cost $25. They are valid for one day and can be purchased on board the buses, or from the **New South Wales Travel Centre.** ✉ *11–31 York St.,* ☏ *13–2077.*

The only guided bus tour of the inner city is the **Sydney Explorer** bus, which makes a 35-km (22-mi) circuit of all the major attractions in the city, including the Rocks, Kings Cross, Darling Harbour, Chinatown, and across Harbour Bridge to Milsons Point. Ticket holders can board or leave the bus at any of the 22 stops along the route and catch any following Explorer bus. The bright-red buses follow one another every 20 minutes, and the service operates from 9 AM daily. The last bus to make the circuit departs Circular Quay at 5:25 PM. If you wish to stay on board, the entire circuit takes around 90 minutes.

The **Bondi & Bay Explorer** bus runs a guided bus tour of the eastern suburbs. The blue bus begins its 35-km (22-mi) journey at Circular Quay and travels through Kings Cross, Double Bay, Vaucluse, and Watsons Bay to the Gap, then returns to the city via Bondi, Bronte, and other beaches; Centennial Park; and Oxford Street. You can leave the bus at any of its 18 stops and catch a following bus, or remain on board for a round-trip of about two hours. Buses follow one another at 30-minute intervals beginning at 9 AM. The last bus departs Circular Quay at 4:20 PM.

SPECIAL-INTEREST TOURS

Australian Special Interest Tours (☏ 02/9973–1673) provide personalized service on their small-group day tours around the Sydney area. You can take an Aboriginal art and culture tour; play golf; go surfing with an instructor; go bird-watching; or take a sightseeing trip to the Northern Beaches. The price for a day tour for two is around $220.

BridgeClimb (☏ 02/9252–0077) is a unique tour that offers the ultimate view of the harbor and city center. Wearing a special suit and harnessed to a static line, climbers ascend the steel arch of the Sydney Harbour Bridge in the company of a guide. The tour lasts for three hours and costs $98 per person. Tours depart from 5 Cumberland Street, the Rocks.

Easyrider Motorbike Tours (☏ 02/9247–2477) is just one of several companies that offer exciting chauffeur-driven (you ride as a passenger) Harley-Davidson tours to such places as the city's beaches, the Blue Mountains, Royal National Park, Hawkesbury River, and the Hunter Valley wineries. A two-hour tour costs $120 per person, and a full-day excursion starts at about $300.

WALKING TOURS

The Rocks Walking Tours offer introductions to the Rocks (the site of Sydney's original settlement by Europeans) with an emphasis on the buildings and personalities of the convict period. The tour, which lasts for 1½ hours, travels at a gentle pace and involves little climbing. ⊠ *106 George St., the Rocks,* ☎ *02/9247–6678.* ☞ *$11.* ☉ *Weekdays at 10:30, 12:30, and 2:30; weekends at 11:30 and 2.*

Sydney Guided Tours with Maureen Fry are an excellent introduction to Sydney. Standard tours cost $15 and cover the colonial buildings along Macquarie Street, a ramble through the historic waterside suburbs of Glebe and Balmain, or Circular Quay and the Rocks. Theme tours include art galleries, food and markets, shops, and a tour of the Opera Centre, where operas are rehearsed before they move to the Sydney Opera House (☎ 02/9660–7157, FAX 02/9660–0805).

Late-Night Pharmacies

Your best bet for a late-night pharmacy is in the major city hotels, or in the Kings Cross and Oxford Street (Darlinghurst) areas. You can also call the **Pharmacy Guild**'s 24-hour number for advice and assistance (☎ 02/9235–0333).

Travel Agencies

Scarcely a shopping plaza or main street in Sydney lacks a travel agency. Both **American Express Travel Service** (⊠ 92 Pitt St., ☎ 02/9239–0666) and **Thomas Cook** (⊠ 175 Pitt St., ☎ 02/9231–2877) are in the heart of the city, as well as in a number of suburbs.

Visitor Information

There are tourist information booths throughout the city, including Circular Quay, Martin Place, Darling Harbour, and the Pitt Street Mall. For all information related to the Sydney 2000 Olympic Games, call 13–6363.

The **Backpacker's Travel Centre** specializes in tours, accommodations, and information for the budget traveler. ⊠ *Shop 33, Imperial Arcade, off Pitt St. near Market St.,* ☎ *02/9231–3699.*

The **Sydney Visitors Information Centre** is the major source of information, brochures, and maps for Sydney and New South Wales. ⊠ *106 George St., the Rocks,* ☎ 02/9255–1788, FAX 02/9241–5010.

Countrylink, the state rail authority, is another source of Sydney and New South Wales travel information. ⊠ *11–31 York St.,* ☎ *02/13–2077.*

The **Sydney Information Line** has useful recorded service and entertainment information. ☎ *02/9265–9007.*

The **Tourist Information Service** (☎ 02/9669–5111) is a free phone-in facility that provides information on accommodations, tours, and shopping. It also provides other tips on what to see and do in Sydney.

2 NEW SOUTH WALES

Although its capital city may be the ultimate urban experience south of Hong Kong, New South Wales plays virtually all of the continent's rural and coastal variations: historic towns, mountain ranges, seductive sands, subtropical rain forest, and some of the finest vineyards in the country. For those looking for sporting opportunities, it provides excellent hiking, scuba diving, fishing, skiing, golf, horseback riding, cave exploring, and white-water rafting.

By Michael
Gebicki

FOR MANY TRAVELERS, SYDNEY is New South Wales, and they look to the other, less-populated states for the wilderness experiences for which Australia is famous. Although there is no substitute for Queensland's Great Barrier Reef or the Northern Territory's Kakadu National Park, anyone with limited time could sample many of Australia's natural wonders within the borders of New South Wales. The state incorporates the World Heritage areas of Lord Howe Island and the subtropical rain forests of the north coast, as well as desert Outback, the highest mountain peaks in the country, moist river valleys, warm seas, and golden beaches—all within easy reach of the country's largest, most glamorous city.

New South Wales was named by Captain James Cook during his voyage of discovery in 1770: The area's low, rounded hills reminded him of southern Wales. It was the first state to be settled by the British, whose plan to establish a penal colony at Botany Bay in 1788 was scrapped in favor of a site a short distance to the north—Sydney Cove. Successive waves of convicts helped swell the state's population, but the discovery in 1850 of gold at Bathurst on the western edge of the Great Dividing Range sparked a population explosion. The state's economic might was bolstered by gold and further strengthened by the discovery of huge coal seams in the Hunter Valley. Timber and wool industries also thrived.

With approximately 6.3 million people, New South Wales is Australia's most populous state. Although this is crowded by Australian standards, it's worth remembering that New South Wales is larger than every U.S. state except Alaska. The state can be divided into four main regions. In the east, a coastal plain reaching north to Queensland varies in width from less than a mile to almost 100 miles. This plain is bordered to the west by a chain of low mountains known as the Great Dividing Range, which tops off at about 7,000 ft in the Snowy Mountains in the state's far south. On the western slopes of this range is a belt of pasture and farmland. Beyond that are the western plains and Outback, an arid, sparsely populated region that takes up two-thirds of the state.

Eighty km (50 mi) west of Sydney in the Great Dividing Range are the Blue Mountains, a domain of tall eucalyptus trees, deep river valleys, and craggy sandstone outcrops that provide the perfect environment for hiking and adventure activities. The mountains are also famous for their charming guest houses and lush, cool-climate gardens. About 100 km (62 mi) south from Sydney, the Southern Highlands form a cool upland region that is geographically similar to the Blue Mountains. The difference here is a more genteel atmosphere, and the added attraction of the nearby temperate South Coast beaches. The wine-growing Hunter Valley region is about 240 km (150 mi) northwest of Sydney. Wine, food, historic towns, and tranquil countryside are the main attractions in this area.

The North Coast stretches almost 600 km (372 mi) up to the Queensland border, its seaside delights contrasting with the rest of the state's rural splendor. With its sandy beaches, surf, and warm climate, the area is a perfect holiday playground. Finally, a tiny, remote speck in the Pacific Ocean, Lord Howe Island is the state's tropical island paradise, ringed with fringing coral, stacked with towering, forested volcanic peaks, and teeming with sea birds and marine life.

Pleasures and Pastimes

Dining

Dining standards vary dramatically throughout New South Wales—from superb city-standard restaurants to average country-town fare. As popular weekend retreats for well-heeled Sydneysiders, the Blue Mountains and Southern Highlands have a number of fine restaurants and cozy tearooms that are perfect for light lunches or afternoon teas. In the Hunter Valley, there are several excellent restaurants to match the fine wines. The Snowy Mountains region is not gastronomically distinguished, though it is famous for its trout.

In spite of the North Coast's excellent seafood and exotic fruits, fine dining is rare away from such major resort centers as Coffs Harbour and Port Macquarie. The small northern town of Byron Bay stands out, however, for its sophisticated choice of cafés and restaurants. Despite its minuscule size and isolation, Lord Howe Island attracts a polished and well-heeled clientele who demand a high standard of dining. At restaurants throughout New South Wales, reservations are always advised.

CATEGORY	COST*
$$$$	over $50
$$$	$35–$50
$$	$20–$35
$	under $20

*per person, excluding drinks

Lodging

The state's accommodation scene includes everything from run-of-the-mill motels to large, glossy seaside resorts and historic guest houses in the Blue Mountains and Southern Highlands. Bear in mind that room rates are often much lower weekdays than weekends, particularly in the areas closest to Sydney (the Blue Mountains, Hunter Valley, and Southern Highlands). In the Snowy Mountains prices are highest during the winter ski season.

CATEGORY	COST*
$$$$	over $250
$$$	$175–$250
$$	$100–$175
$	under $100

*All prices are for a standard double room.

Outdoor Activities and Sports

New South Wales is well-endowed for anyone who enjoys the great outdoors. The mountains and national parks offer inspiring walks, horse riding, and camping. Deep in the south of the state, the Snowy Mountains—Australia's winter playground—offer excellent cross-country skiing in particular. Aquatic sports are another specialty, including fishing, snorkeling, scuba diving, and boating.

Note: *See* Chapter 12 for more information on bicycling, bushwalking, camel trekking, cross-country skiing, four-wheel-driving, horseback riding, and rafting in New South Wales' great outdoors.

Shopping

Locally made crafts are the best buys for the visitor, and there are a few areas that dominate, such as Byron Bay, the Blue Mountains, and Southern Highlands. It would be difficult to visit the Hunter Valley without purchasing some of the excellent wines tasted on your tour, but the area is also full of antiques shops (particularly around Pokolbin

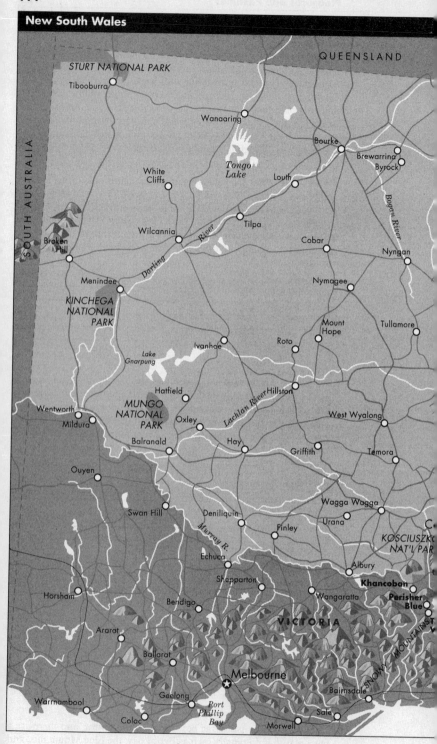

QUEENSLAND

STURT NATIONAL PARK

Tibooburra

Wanaaring

Bourke

Brewarrina
Byrock

Tongo Lake

White Cliffs

Louth

Bogan River

Wilcannia

Tilpa

Darling River

Cobar

Nyngan

Broken Hill

SOUTH AUSTRALIA

Menindee

Nymagee

KINCHEGA NATIONAL PARK

Mount Hope

Tullamore

Ivanhoe

Roto

Lake Gnarpung

Hatfield

Hillston

MUNGO NATIONAL PARK

Oxley

Lachlan River

West Wyalong

Wentworth
Mildura

Balranald

Hay

Griffith

Temora

Ouyen

Wagga Wagga

Swan Hill

Deniliquin

Finley

Urana

KOSCIUSZKO NAT'L PAR

C

Horsham

Murray R.

Echuca

Albury

Khancoban

Shepparton

Wangaratta

Perisher Blue

Bendigo

VICTORIA

SNOWY MOUNTAINS

Ararat

Ballarat

Bairnsdale

Warrnambool

Melbourne

Geelong

Port Phillip Bay

Sale

Colac

Morwell

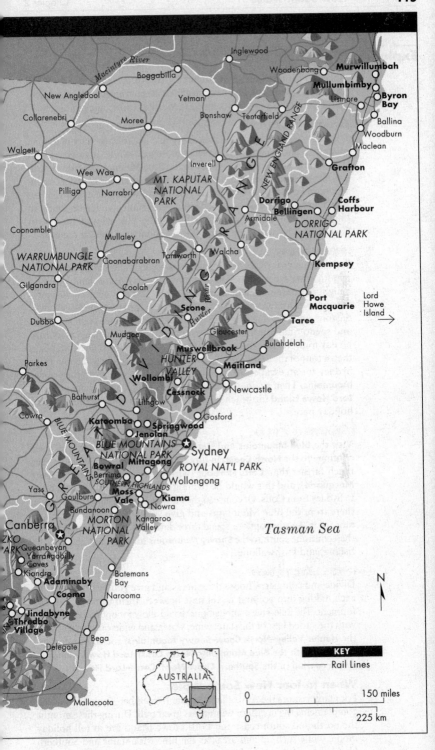

Macintyre River

Inglewood

Woodenbong **Murwillumbah**

Boggabilla **Mullumbimby**

New Angledool Yetman Lismore **Byron Bay**

Collarenebri Bonshaw Tenterfield Ballina

Moree Woodburn

Walgett Maclean

Wee Waa Inverell **Grafton**

Pilliga Narrabri

Coonamble MT. KAPUTAR NATIONAL PARK

Dorrigo **Coffs Harbour**

Bellingen

Armidale DORRIGO NATIONAL PARK

Mullaley

WARRUMBUNGLE NATIONAL PARK Tamworth Walcha

Coonabarabran

Gilgandra Coolah **Kempsey**

Scone **Port Macquarie** Lord Howe Island →

Dubbo Gloucester **Taree**

Mudgee HUNTER VALLEY Bulahdelah

Parkes **Muswellbrook**

Maitland

Wollombi

Cessnock Newcastle

Bathurst Lithgow

Cowra Gosford

Katoomba **Springwood**

Jenolan

BLUE MOUNTAINS NATIONAL PARK ★ Sydney

Bowral **Mittagong** ROYAL NAT'L PARK

Berrima

SOUTHERN HIGHLANDS Wollongong

Yass **Moss Vale** **Kiama**

Goulburn Nowra

Bundanoon

Canberra MORTON NATIONAL PARK Kangaroo Valley

ZKO ARK Queanbeyan

Yarrangobilly Caves

Kiandra Batemans Bay

Adaminaby Narooma

Cooma

Jindabyne Tasman Sea

Thredbo Village

Bega

Delegate

Mallacoota

NEW ENGLAND RANGE

RANGE

GREAT DIVIDING RANGE

Hunter River

BLUE MOUNTAINS

N

AUSTRALIA

KEY
— Rail Lines

0   150 miles

0   225 km

and Wollombi), arts-and-crafts shops, and galleries that display the works of local artists and potters.

Exploring New South Wales

Since New South Wales covers a large area, and it is unlikely that you'll have the time to explore far beyond the eastern fringe, we have selected six of the state's most rewarding, accessible, and scenic regions.

Great Itineraries

It is wise to decide in advance whether you'd like to cover a lot of ground quickly or choose one or two places to linger a while. If you have four days or less, stick close to Sydney in the Blue Mountains or the Southern Highlands, or just hop on a plane to Lord Howe Island as an invigorating contrast to Sydney. In a very busy week you could visit the Blue and Snowy mountains and either the Hunter Valley or Southern Highlands, while two weeks would allow a Blue Mountains–North Coast–Lord Howe circuit or brief stops in most of the six regions.

IF YOU HAVE 4 DAYS

Start with a visit to the **Blue Mountains**—you could cover our round-trip itinerary from Sydney in a fairly hectic day or, preferably, spend a night in **Katoomba, Blackheath,** or **Leura** and make it a two-day excursion. Return to Sydney, then head north to the **Hunter Valley.** A two-day/one-night driving visit here would be enough to see the main sights and spend time touring the wineries before traveling back to Sydney on day four. Alternatives would be a quick visit to the Blue Mountains, then a tour of the **Southern Highlands,** or you could fly to **Cooma** from Sydney for an escape to Australia's highest alpine region, the **Snowy Mountains.** Then again, you might want to chuck all of that and fly to **Lord Howe Island** for beaches, reefs, soaring mountains, and a perfect holiday pace.

IF YOU HAVE 7 DAYS

Visit the **Blue Mountains** and **Hunter Valley** as described above, then continue to the **North Coast.** In three days of driving you wouldn't get much farther than **Coffs Harbour** (with overnights there and in **Port Macquarie**), and this would be rushing it, but it's possible to fly back to Sydney from Coffs. Of course, if the North Coast appeals, head straight there from the Blue Mountains and give yourself a chance to take in more of it. Another option: Spend three days in the **Southern Highlands,** then continue south to the **Snowy Mountains** for some alpine air, trout fishing, and bushwalking.

IF YOU HAVE 14 DAYS

Divide and conquer: Choose three areas and give yourself four days in each, taking into account travel time between them to round out the fortnight. The following combinations would allow for optimal encounters with the varied best of the state: wine, water, and wide-open spaces with the **Hunter Valley–North Coast–Snowy Mountains;** rocks, rain forests, and reefs with the **Blue Mountains–North Coast–Lord Howe Island;** or a watery triad of the **Southern Coast–North Coast–Lord Howe.**

When to Tour New South Wales

For many visitors the Australian summer (December–February), which complements the northern winter, has great pull. During these months the north and south coast and Lord Howe Island are in full holiday mode, while such upland areas as the Blue Mountains and Southern Highlands offer a relief from Sydney's stifling humidity. This is also the ideal season for bushwalking in the cool Snowy Mountains, but be aware that some of the hotels here close from October through May— the off season for skiing. The best times to visit the Hunter Valley are during the February–March grape harvest season and the September Hunter Food and Wine Festival.

Remember that although the North Coast holiday region is at its peak (and its most crowded) in summer, autumn (March–May) and spring (September–November) are also good times to visit—especially the far north, which is usually quite hot and humid in summer.

On Lord Howe Island, February is the driest (and hottest), and August is the windiest month. Many of the island's hotels and restaurants close for at least part of the June-to-August period. Summer is the best bet, especially for swimming, snorkeling, and diving, but from Christmas through the first half of January the island is booked solid months in advance.

There are some wonderful options if you are in New South Wales in winter (officially June, July, and August). The Snowy Mountains ski season runs from early June to early October. And the "Yulefest" season from June through August is a popular time to visit the Blue Mountains, with blazing log fires and Christmas-style celebration packages.

THE BLUE MOUNTAINS

Sydneysiders have been doubly blessed by nature. Not only do they have a magnificent coastline right at their front door, but a 90-minute drive west puts them in the midst of one of the most spectacular wilderness areas in Australia—Blue Mountains National Park. Standing at 3,500-plus ft high, these "mountains" were once the bed of an ancient sea. Gradually the sedimentary rock was uplifted until it formed a high plateau, which was etched by eons of wind and water into the wonderland of cliffs, caves, and canyons that exists today. Now these richly forested hills, crisp mountain air, gardens that blaze with autumn color, vast sandstone chasms, and little towns of timber and stone are supreme examples of Australia's diversity. The mountains' distinctive blue coloring is caused by the evaporation of oil from the dense eucalyptus forests. This disperses light in the blue colors of the spectrum, a phenomenon known as Rayleigh Scattering.

For a quarter of a century after European settlement, these mountains marked the limits of westward expansion. Early attempts to cross them ended at sheer cliff faces or impassable chasms. For convicts, many of whom believed China lay on the far side, the mountains offered a tantalizing possibility of escape. But not until 1813 did explorers finally forge a crossing by hugging the mountain ridges—the route that the Great Western Highway to Bathurst follows today.

When a railway line from Sydney was completed at the end of the 19th century, the mountains suddenly became fashionable, and guest houses and hotels flourished. Wealthy Sydney businesspeople built grand weekend homes here, cultivating cool-climate gardens that are among the area's man-made glories. Mountain walking was popular at the time, and the splendid network of trails that crisscrosses the area was created during this period. Combined with the dramatic natural beauty of the region, the history and charm of local villages make the Blue Mountains one of the highlights of any tour of Australia.

It is possible to see much of the area on a day trip from Sydney, but an overnight stop will reap rich rewards. Our coverage of New South Wales follows the route of the Great Western Highway from its ascent of the mountains to their western edge before leading you back to Sydney by a more northerly route, the scenic Bells Line of Road.

Numbers in the margin correspond to points of interest on the Blue Mountains map.

Springwood and the Lower Blue Mountains

79 km (49 mi) northwest of Sydney.

Such lower Blue Mountains towns as Glenbrook, Blaxland, and Springwood are commuter territory, but it is worth stopping at the useful **Blue Mountains Information Centre** beside the highway at Glenbrook, 66 km (41 mi) from Sydney. The office is open Monday–Saturday 8:30–5 and Sunday 8:30–4:30. Between Springwood and the town of Faulconbridge, a sign points to the right, indicating the way to an intriguing museum.

❶ Dedicated to the Australian artist and writer, the National Trust–listed **Norman Lindsay Gallery and Museum** is one of the cultural highlights of the Blue Mountains. Lindsay is best known for his paintings, etchings, and drawings, but he also built model boats, sculpted, and wrote poetry and children's books, among which *The Magic Pudding* has become an Australian classic. Some of his most famous paintings were inspired by Greek and Roman mythology and depict voluptuous nudes. Lindsay lived in this house during the latter part of his life (he died in 1969), and it contains a representative selection of his superb work (featured in the movie *Sirens* starring another Aussie icon, Elle MacPherson). The landscaped gardens, containing several of Lindsay's sculptures, are delightful, and you can also take a short but scenic bushwalk beyond the garden. ⊠ *14 Norman Lindsay Crescent, Faulconbridge,* ☎ *02/4751–1067.* ☜ *$6.* ☉ *10–4.*

Wentworth Falls

26 km (16 mi) west of Springwood.

This attractive township has numerous crafts and antiques shops, a lake, and a popular golf course. Wentworth Falls straddles both sides of the highway, but most points of interest and views of the Jamison Valley and Blue Mountains National Park are to the south side of the road.

❷ Built largely from New Zealand kauri pine, the 1888 Victorian house of **Yester Grange** has been restored and filled with period antiques and dozens of 19th-century paintings. There are tearooms here, and the veranda at the front of the house overlooks lush green lawns, which contrast with the rugged backdrop of the Jamison Valley. The house is signposted left off the highway just beyond the town of Bullaburra. ⊠ *Yester Rd.,* ☎ *02/4757–1110.* ☜ *$5.* ☉ *Weekdays 10–4, weekends 10–5.*

★ **❸** From a lookout in the **Falls Reserve,** south of the town of Wentworth Falls, there are magnificent views both out across the Jamison Valley to the Kings Tableland and of the 935-ft-high **Wentworth Falls** themselves. The best view of the falls is obtained by following the trail that crosses the stream and zigzags down the sheer cliff face, signposted "National Pass." If you continue, the National Pass cuts back across the base of the falls and along a narrow ledge to the delightful Valley of the Waters, where it ascends to the top of the cliffs, emerging at the Conservation Hut (☞ *below*). The complete circuit is rated as a moderate walk, and at least three hours is required. ⊠ *Falls Rd., 2 km (1¼ mi) along highway from Yester Grange.*

Dining

$ ✕ **Conservation Hut.** In the Blue Mountains National Park on top of the cliffs overlooking the Jamison Valley, this spacious, no-smoking,

The Blue Mountains

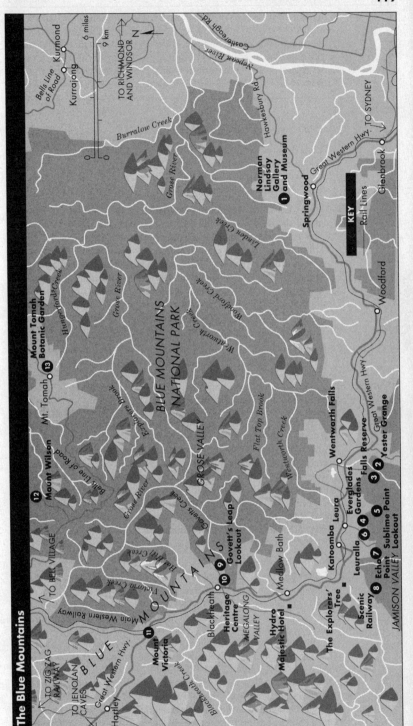

KEY
Rail Lines

Norman Lindsay Gallery and Museum ❶

Springwood

Woodford

Glenbrook

TO SYDNEY

Great Western Hwy.

Hawkesbury Rd.

Castlereagh Rd.

Nepean River

TO RICHMOND AND WINDSOR

Bells Line of Road

Kurmond

Kurrajong

Burralow Creek

Grose River

Grose River

Hungerford Creek

Mount Tomah Botanic Garden ⓭

Mt. Tomah

Mount Wilson

Bells Line of Road

TO BELL VILLAGE

TO ZIG-ZAG RAILWAY

TO JENOLAN CAVES

Great Western Hwy.

Hartley

BLUE MOUNTAINS

Blackheath Creek

Mount Victoria ⑪

Main Western Railway

Blackheath

Heritage Centre ⑩

MEGALONG VALLEY

Hydro Majestic Hotel

Medlow Bath

Govett's Leap Lookout ⑨

Hat Hill Creek

Victoria Creek

Grose River

Govetts Creek

Berghofers Brook

BLUE MOUNTAINS NATIONAL PARK

GROSE VALLEY

Woodford Creek

Wentworth Creek

Flat Top Brook

Leura Creek

Springwood

The Explorers' Tree

Scenic Railway ⑧

Echo Point ⑦

Katoomba

Leuralla ⑥

Leura

Everglades Gardens ③

Wentworth Falls

Falls Reserve

Yester Grange ②

Sublime Point ⑤

④

JAMISON VALLEY LOOKOUT

6 miles

9 km

N

0

0

mud-brick bistro serves simple, savory fare and satisfying cakes to the strains of classical music on weekends. An open balcony is a real delight on warm days, and a fire blazes in the cooler months. A hiking trail from the bistro leads down into the Valley of the Waters, one of the splendors of the mountains—it's a wonderful pre-meal walk. ⊠ *Fletcher St.,* ☎ *02/4757–3827. DC, MC, V. BYOB. No dinner.*

Leura

5 km (3 mi) west of Wentworth Falls.

Leura is one of the prettiest mountain towns, with charming old buildings lining an entire main street that has been classified as an urban conservation area by the National Trust. There are plenty of unusual shops in town, as well as some excellent cafés and restaurants.

❹ Leura's delightful **Everglades Gardens** is one of the best public gardens in the Blue Mountains region. This National Trust–listed, cool-climate arboretum and nature reserve was established in the 1930s. Plantings include native bushland and exotic flora, a rhododendron garden, an alpine plant area, and formal European-style terraces. From the gardens, the views of the Jamison Valley and the rugged escarpment and cliff are magnificent. Everglades also has an interesting art gallery. ⊠ *37 Everglades Ave.,* ☎ *02/4784–1938.* ☜ *$5.* ☉ *Sept.–Feb., daily 10–5; Mar.–Aug., daily 10–4.*

★ **❺** You'll get another great view of the Jamison Valley and the generally spectacular Blue Mountains scenery from the **Sublime Point Lookout,** just outside Leura. This far less crowded vantage point provides a different perspective of the famous **Three Sisters** rock formation at nearby Katoomba. ⊠ *Sublime Point Rd.*

❻ The mansion of **Leuralla** dates from 1911 and still belongs to the family of Dr. H. V. ("Doc") Evatt (1894–1965), the first president of the General Assembly of the United Nations, and later the leader of the Australian Labor Party. The historic house contains a collection of 19th-century Australian art and a small museum dedicated to Dr. Evatt. It is surrounded by pleasant gardens. Within the grounds of Leuralla is the **New South Wales Toy and Railway Museum,** an extensive collection of railway memorabilia that will delight train buffs. The toy display includes tinplate automobiles, ships, and planes, as well as antique dolls and bears. ⊠ *Olympian Parade and Balmoral Rd., Leura,* ☎ *02/ 4784–1169.* ☜ *$6.* ☉ *Daily 10–5.*

Dining and Lodging

$$$ ✕ **Silks Brasserie.** Regarded as one of the finest restaurants in the Blue Mountains, this eatery offers Sydney-standard food, wine, and service. Dishes include fresh fish with Asian-style sauces, osso bucco served with couscous, sautéed tiger prawns in champagne vinaigrette with sesame-seed biscuits, and a seafood medley with lemongrass and cardamom cream sauce—as well as a range of tempting desserts and a cheese plate. The simple but elegant interior is warmed in colder months by a log fire. ⊠ *128 the Mall,* ☎ *02/4784–2534. AE, MC, V.*

$$ ✕ **Cafe Bon Ton.** At the lower end of Leura Mall, this bright, elegant
★ café is a good choice for breakfast, coffee and cake, or a three-course dinner. The food, like the decor, is essentially Italian, with pasta, pizza, and a choice of meat, fish, and vegetarian fare. In winter a log fire burns in the grate, and on warm summer days the shady garden at the front is ideal for lunch. The café serves some of the best coffee in the mountains. ⊠ *192 the Mall,* ☎ *02/4782–4377. AE, MC, V. BYOB. No dinner Tues.*

$$$ ⚃ **Fairmont Resort.** Perched on the edge of the cliffs and surrounded by gardens, the Fairmont might be the largest hotel in the mountains, but it still has the cozy warmth of a traditional Blue Mountains guest house. Rooms are well-equipped and decorated in several soothing color schemes; those facing the valley have better views. A range of facilities and activities are available, and guests have access to the adjoining Leura Golf Course, the finest in the mountains. ✉ *1 Sublime Point Rd., 2780,* ☎ *02/4782–5222,* 𝖥𝖠𝖷 *02/4784–1685. 193 rooms, 17 suites. 2 restaurants, bar, indoor pool, outdoor pool, sauna, spa, 18-hole golf course, 4 tennis courts, exercise room, squash. AE, DC, MC, V.*

$$$ ⚃ **Little Company Retreat.** Built at the turn of the century, this sprawling, single-story guest house has a solid, imposing character befitting its former status as a convent. The house is surrounded by flower-filled gardens and separated from tennis courts by an avenue of conifers. Bedrooms are modest in size, but the living rooms are inviting and each has its own en suite bathroom. A croquet lawn is at the back of the house, and the town is within walking distance. The guest house operates four local four-bedroom homes that are ideal for families or small groups. Bookings are heavy on weekends. Rates include breakfast and dinner. ✉ *2 Eastview Ave. 2781,* ☎ *02/4782–4023,* 𝖥𝖠𝖷 *02/4782–5361. 13 rooms. Pool, putting green, 2 tennis courts. AE, DC, MC, V.*

OFF THE **CLIFF DRIVE –** From Leura, this dazzling 19-km (12-mi) journey leads to
BEATEN PATH Echo Point at Katoomba and beyond. The road skirts the rim of the Jamison Valley, often only yards from the cliff edge, and provides truly spectacular Blue Mountains views. Begin at the southern end of the Mall, Leura's main street.

Katoomba

2 km (1¼ mi) west of Leura.

Easily the largest town in the Blue Mountains, Katoomba developed in the early 1840s as a coal-mining settlement, turning its attention to tourism later in the 19th century. The town center has shops, cafés, and places to stay, but the breathtaking local scenery is the real reason to come.

❼ The best views around Katoomba are from **Echo Point,** which overlooks the densely forested Jamison Valley and soaring sandstone pillars. These formations are named the **Three Sisters,** from an Aboriginal legend that relates how three siblings were turned to stone by their witch-doctor father to save them from the clutches of a mythical monster. This formation also illustrates the geological character of the Blue Mountains. The area was once a sea bed that rose over a long period and subsequently eroded, leaving behind tall formations of sedimentary rock. From Echo Point you can clearly see the horizontal sandstone bedding in the landscape. The Three Sisters formation is floodlit at night. ✉ *Follow Katoomba St. south out of Katoomba to Echo Point Rd., or take Cliff Dr. from Leura.*

Echo Point is also the location for a **Blue Mountains Information Centre,** which can provide useful information on bushwalks from Katoomba. Several walks, varying in duration from ½ hour (an easy stroll to the Three Sisters) to a far more challenging four hours, start from the Echo Point area. ✉ *Echo Point Rd.,* ☎ *02/4739–6266.* ☉ *Daily 9–5.*

❽ Far below Echo Point, the **Scenic Railway** was built into the cliff face during the 1880s to haul coal and shale from the mines in the valley. When the supply of shale was exhausted, the railway was abandoned until the 1930s, when the Katoomba Colliery began using the carts to give tourists the ride of their life on the steep incline. Today the carriages are far more comfortable, but the ride down to the foot of the cliffs is no less exciting. Just a few steps from the railway is the **Scenic Skyway,** a cable car that carries passengers for a short ride across the gorge, with a 1,000-ft drop below. If you're going to pick one, the railway is more spectacular. ⊠ *Cliff Dr. and Violet St.,* ☎ *02/4782–2699.* 🎦 *Round-trip fare for railway and skyway, $5 each.* ⊙ *Daily 9–5.*

A very different Katoomba attraction is the **Edge Maxvision Cinema.** This giant cinema screen is about the height of a six-story building and runs a variety of films. The most worthwhile is *The Edge,* an exciting 40-minute movie on the region's valleys, gorges, cliffs, waterfalls, and other dramatic scenery. The large complex includes a café and gift shop, and at night the cinema screens regular feature films. ⊠ *225–237 Great Western Hwy.,* ☎ *02/4782–8928.* 🎦 *$12.50.* ⊙ *Daily; The Edge begins at 10 AM.*

Dining and Lodging

$ ✕ **Paragon Cafe.** In the center of Katoomba, this 1916 restaurant is one of the traditional favorites of the area. With its chandeliers, gleaming cappuccino machine, and bas-relief figures above the booths, the wood-paneled restaurant recalls the Blue Mountains in their heyday. The menu has all-day fare, including homemade soups, grills, pasta dishes, famous Paragon meat pies, seafood, and substantial cakes and waffles. Nothing is more traditional here than afternoon tea—hot scones with whipped cream, jam, and coffee or tea. The place closes at 5 sharp. ⊠ *65 Katoomba St.,* ☎ *02/4782–2928. AE, MC, V. Closed Mon. No dinner.*

$$$$ ✕🏨 **Lilianfels Blue Mountains.** This elegant hotel incorporates a historic house in its design, giving guests the best of a traditional country hotel combined with all the frills of five-star accommodation. Guest rooms are spacious and plush, with warm fabrics and colors. The majestic views are best appreciated from one of the slightly more expensive valley view rooms. The dining room, Darleys, serves exceptional modern Australian country food to both guests and visitors in refined surroundings; reservations are essential. ⊠ *Lilianfels Ave., Echo Point 2780,* ☎ *02/4780–1200,* ℻ *02/4780–1300. 81 rooms, 5 suites. 2 restaurants, bar, indoor pool, sauna, steam room, spa, tennis court, exercise room, mountain bikes, laundry service and dry cleaning, concierge. AE, DC, MC, V.*

$$$ 🏨 **Echoes.** Perched precipitously above the Jamison Valley, this striking small hotel offers traditional Blue Mountains warmth and comfort and an excellent restaurant. Wentworth, the room on the corner of the top floor, has particularly good views on two sides. The hotel is close to the Three Sisters and the network of trails that lead down into the Jamison Valley. Smoking is not permitted. Rates include breakfast. ⊠ *3 Lilianfels Ave., 2780,* ☎ *02/4782–1966,* ℻ *02/4782–3707. 12 rooms. Restaurant, bar, sauna, spa. AE, DC, MC, V.*

$$$ 🏨 **Mountain Heritage Country House Retreat.** Set on a ridge close to Katoomba and overlooking the Jamison Valley, this elegant country house offers some of the best views in the mountains. The atmosphere is warm and welcoming, and the house is steeped in history. Country-house furnishings make use of Australian motifs in a variety of room styles. The two very private Valley View suites have their own verandas, kitchens, lounge rooms with fireplaces, and Jacuzzis. ⊠ *Apex and Lovel Sts., 2780,* ☎ *02/4782–2155,* ℻ *02/4782–5323. 37 rooms, 4 suites. Restaurant, bar, pool, exercise room, volleyball, mountain bikes, recreation room. AE, DC, MC, V.*

En Route   West of Katoomba, the Cliff Drive changes its name to Narrow Neck Road and returns you to the Great Western Highway. From there, the highway winds along the ridge top, passing a couple of points of interest between Katoomba and the next main town of Blackheath. About ½ mile beyond where Narrow Neck Road joins the highway, the **Explorers' Tree** on the left marks an important historic site. George Blaxland, William Charles Wentworth, and William Lawson, the men who finally pioneered the route across these mountains in 1813, carved their initials into the trunk of this tree, which in time has grown over the traces of their passing.

At the small village of Medlow Bath, 4 km (2½ mi) beyond the Explorers' Tree, it is impossible to miss the enormous **Hydro Majestic Hotel** on the left-hand side of the highway. Originally a European-style spa, this sprawling Art Deco building was a fashionable hotel in the 1930s, especially popular with honeymoon couples. During World War II the U.S. Army used the hotel as a hospital for soldiers wounded in the Pacific. The Hydro subsequently fell on hard times, but extensive restoration has recaptured some of its original Art Deco splendor. The view of Megalong Valley from the Casino Lounge is outstanding, making it a fine place for coffee or a light lunch. The ballroom to the left of the main entrance is worth a look, too. Seekers of atmosphere will be drawn to the hotel's bar, which takes on a slightly Hitchcockian mood after dark—arrive at dusk for a drink on the terrace while the sun is still lighting the valley below. ⊠ *Great Western Hwy., Medlow Bath,* ☎ *02/4788–1002.*

Blackheath

12 km (7½ mi) north of Katoomba.

Blackheath, at the summit of the Blue Mountains (3,495 ft), was visited and named by Governor Macquarie in 1815 after a rough road had been constructed through here to the town of Bathurst, beyond the mountains. The main attractions are the magnificent easterly views over the Grose Valley, which also has outstanding hiking trails. Blackheath has delightful gardens and several antiques shops.

9 Blackheath's most famous view is from the **Govett's Leap Lookout,** with its striking panorama of the Grose Valley and Bridal Veil Falls to the right. Govett was a surveyor who mapped this region extensively in the 1830s. He calculated that the perpendicular drop near the falls is 528 ft. ⊠ *End of Govett's Leap Rd.*

10 A two-minute stroll from Govett's Leap Lookout, the **Heritage Centre,** operated by the National Parks and Wildlife Service, offers useful information on Aboriginal and European historic sites, as well as helpful suggestions for camping, guided walks, and hiking in Blue Mountains National Park. The center also features videos, interactive educational displays, exhibitions, and a nature-oriented gift shop. The adjacent **Blackheath Bakery** is locally famous for its delicious sourdough bread. ⊠ *Govett's Leap Rd.,* ☎ *02/4787–8877.* ☉ *Daily 9–4:30.*

In a deep mountain valley off the Great Western Highway 15 km (9 mi) from Blackheath, the **Megalong Australian Heritage Centre** is a working sheep and cattle property and demonstration farm, with displays of farm animals and pioneer farm skills. Events begin at 10:30 AM and include a cattle show, a Clydesdale horse show, tractor rides, and sheep-shearing—most of which should appeal to children. There is also a baby animal nursery here, and both adults and children can go horseback riding around the farm's 2,000 acres. If you'd like to go farther afield, you can join an overnight muster ride. ⊠ *Megalong Rd., Megalong Valley,* ☎ *02/4787–9165.* ▨ *$9.50.* ☉ *Daily 7:30–5.*

Dining and Lodging

$$$ ✕ **Vulcan's.** The concrete floor and rough redbrick walls of this tiny
Blackheath café belie its reputation for outstanding food. Operated by
Phillip Searle (formerly one of the leading lights of Sydney's dining scene)
and Barry Ross, Vulcan's specializes in slow-roasted dishes, often with
Asian or Middle Eastern spices. The restaurant's checkerboard ice
cream—with star anise, pineapple, licorice, and vanilla flavors—is a
favorite that looks as good as it tastes. There is an outdoor dining area.
The weekend breakfast is highly recommended. Smoking is not per-
mitted. ✉ *33 Govetts Leap Rd.,* ☎ *02/4787–6899. AE, DC, MC, V.
BYOB. Closed Mon.–Thurs.*

$$$$ ✕▦ **Cleopatra.** Tucked away in leafy Blackheath, this charming farm-
★ house evokes the manners of a French country house. The finest ac-
commodations are in the apartment, which has its own private sitting
room. Decor is a stylish mix of arranged wildflowers, botanical prints,
and fine antiques. Surrounding the house is a mature garden. At the
Cleopatra Restaurant chef Dany Chouet conjures up the robust cook-
ing of her native Dordogne with such dishes as sweetbreads with wild
mushrooms or roasted loin of lamb; you must supply your own wine.
The enormous popularity of both the restaurant and the guest house
makes it advisable to book well in advance. All meals are included in
the rates. ✉ *118 Cleopatra St., 2785,* ☎ *02/4787–8456,* ℻ *02/4787–
6092. 5 rooms, 3 with bath. Restaurant, tennis court. MC, V.*

$$–$$$ ▦ **Jemby Rinjah Lodge.** Set in bushland on the edge of Blue Moun-
★ tains National Park, this environmentally sensitive lodge was designed
for the urban escapist in search of a wilderness experience. Each of the
self-contained timber cabins sleeps up to six. Furnishings are of natu-
ral wood, and a picture window in each cabin opens onto a small deck.
Three "tree houses" elevate guests to the same level as the kookabur-
ras. Lodges without kitchens are also available at a lower rate. At the
center of the complex is a comfortable lounge area and Isopogons Restau-
rant, which serves country-style meals. Activities include free guided
walks of the Grose Valley, feeding wild parrots, and spotlighting pos-
sums at night. ✉ *336 Evans Lookout Rd., 2785,* ☎ *02/4787–7622,*
℻ *02/4787–6230. 10 cabins, 15 lodge rooms share 6 baths, 3 tree
houses. Restaurant, hiking, kitchenettes. MC, V.*

Horseback Riding

At the foot of the Blue Mountains, 10 km (6 mi) from Blackheath, **Wer-
riberri Trail Rides** conduct reasonably priced half- to two-hour horse-
back rides through the beautiful Megalong Valley. Everyone is catered
to—with quiet horses for beginners, ponies on leads for young chil-
dren, and frisky mounts for experienced riders. All rides are guided,
and hard hats are supplied. Rides start at $15 for a half hour, to $35
for two hours. ✉ *Megalong Rd., Megalong Valley,* ☎ *02/4787–9171.*

Mount Victoria

⓫ *7 km (4 mi) northwest of Blackheath.*

The settlement of Mount Victoria has a Rip Van Winkle air about it—
drowsy and only just awake in an unfamiliar world. A walk around
the village reveals many atmospheric houses and stores with the patina
of time spelled out in their fading paintwork. Mount Victoria is at the
far side of the mountains at the western limit of this region, and there
are a couple of off-the-beaten-path attractions that are best reached
from this village.

OFF THE
BEATEN PATH

JENOLAN CAVES – A labyrinth of underground rivers and vast limestone chasms, these caves are filled with stalactites, stalagmites, columns, and lace-like rock on multiple levels. Sculpted by underground rivers, there are as many as 300 caves in the Jenolan area.

The first European to set eyes on the caves was James McKeown, an escaped convict who preyed on the stagecoaches traveling across the mountains and who used the caves as a hideout in the 1830s. A search party eventually followed his horse's tracks, and the capture of McKeown made his secret caves suddenly famous. Tours were organized soon thereafter, but the most spectacular caves weren't found for another two decades.

Three caves near the surface can be explored without a guide, but to see the very best formations, you need to take a guided tour. Nine of these caves are open to the public: they are graded according to difficulty, and even the easiest entails climbing a total of 300 stairs interspersed throughout the cave. The Lucas Cave tour in particular is a good aerobic workout. Tours depart every 15 minutes on weekends, approximately every 30 minutes on weekdays, and last from one to two hours. Cave lovers may want to inquire about the caves in Abercrombie and Wombeyan (☞ The Southern Highlands and South Coast, *below*) to the west and south of Jenolan.

To reach the caves, follow the Great Western Highway north out of Mount Victoria as it winds through rural hill country, then turn after Hartley southwest toward Hampton. Jenolan Caves is 59 km (37 mi) from Mount Victoria. ✉ *Jenolan,* ☎ *02/6359–3311.* 🎫 *$12–$20.* ◷ *9:30–5.*

★ The **Zig Zag Railway** will delight train buffs. Dramatic views and the huff-and-puff of a vintage steam engine make this cliff-hugging, 16-km (10-mi) round-trip ride a thriller. Built in 1869, this was the main line across the Blue Mountains until 1910. The track is laid on the cliffs in a giant "Z," and the train climbs the steep incline by chugging backward and then forward along switchbacking sections of the track—hence its name. The steam engine operates on weekends, public holidays, and weekdays during the school holidays. A vintage self-propelled diesel-powered rail car is used at other times. The railway is 19 km (12 mi) northwest of Mount Victoria. Take the Darling Causeway north out of town, then turn northwest on Bells Line of Road in Bell. ✉ *Bells Line of Rd., Clarence,* ☎ *02/6353–1795.* 🎫 *$13.* ◷ *Daily; trains depart Clarence Station weekdays at 11, 1, and 3 and weekends at 10:30, 12:15, 2, and 3:45.*

Dining

$ ✕ **Bay Tree Tea Shop.** This cozy café is delightful at any time, but particularly welcoming on chilly afternoons when a fire is burning in the grate and scones are served piping hot from the kitchen. The menu includes hearty soups, salads, a fantastic "meat pie hotpot," lasagna, and quiches. Almost everything is made on the premises—bread, cakes, and even the jam that is served with afternoon tea. The Bay Tree is open on school holidays. ✉ *26 Station St.,* ☎ *02/4787–1275. No credit cards. Closed Tues. and Wed. No dinner.*

En Route The **Bells Line of Road** route back to Sydney is reached by taking the Darling Causeway north out of Mount Victoria and turning right at the village of Bell. Named after explorer Archibald Bell, who discovered a path over the mountains from Richmond, and built by convicts in 1841, this scenic road runs from Lithgow to Richmond and winds its way along the mountain ridges. Along the way you'll pass gardens, apple orchards, small villages, and roadside fruit stalls.

Mount Wilson

⑫   *30 km (17 mi) northeast of Mount Victoria.*

This enchanting village lies off the Bells Line of Road at the end of Five Mile Road, which snakes along a sandstone ridge. Built more than a century ago by wealthy families seeking a retreat from Sydney's summer heat, the settlement was planted with avenues of elms, beeches, and plane trees that give it a distinctly European air. The town is at its prettiest during spring and autumn, when its many gardens are in full splendor.

A short stroll through the cool, shady woodland of the town's **Cathedral of Ferns** is highly recommended. This pretty glen is on Mount Irvine Road—there is no admission fee, and a jaunt around the circular track takes 15–20 minutes.

Mount Tomah

25 km (16 mi) southeast of Mount Wilson.

Located on the Bells Line of Road, the area around the village of Mount Tomah has strong appeal for garden lovers.

⑬   The cool-climate branch of Sydney's Royal Botanic Gardens, the **Mount Tomah Botanic Garden** provides a spectacular setting for many native and imported plant species. At 3,280 ft above sea level, the moist, cool environment is perfect for rhododendrons, conifers, maples, and a variety of European deciduous trees. The delightful gardens also have a shop, a visitor center, picnic areas, and a restaurant with modern Australian cuisine. Guided walks are available by arrangement. ⊠ *Bells Line of Rd.,* ☎ *02/4567–2154.* ▨ *$5 per car.* ☉ *Mar.–Sept., daily 10–4; Oct.–Feb., daily 10–5.*

En Route   The Bells Line of Road winds past the villages of Bilpin and Kurrajong, with a terrific panorama of the Sydney metropolitan region from the Bellbird Hill Lookout near Kurrajong, and then continues through Richmond and Windsor. These latter settlements were founded in 1810 and contain several historic churches and other buildings from the mid-1800s; if you have time, it's worth having a look around both towns. From Richmond, Sydney is about a 60-minute drive away.

Blue Mountains A to Z

Arriving and Departing

BY CAR

Leave Sydney via Parramatta Road and the M4 Motorway, which leads to Lapstone at the base of the Blue Mountains. From there, continue on the Great Western Highway and follow the signs to Katoomba. The 110-km (68-mi) journey to Katoomba takes between 90 minutes and two hours.

BY TRAIN

The Blue Mountains are served by Sydney's **Cityrail** (☎ 13–1500) commuter trains, with frequent services to and from the city between 5 AM and 11 PM. The round-trip fare on weekdays between Sydney's Central Station and Katoomba, the main station in the Blue Mountains—and the only town where you can rent a car—is $18.80. If you travel on weekends, or begin travel after 9 AM on weekdays, the fare falls to $11.20.

Getting Around

BY BUS

Public buses operate between the Blue Mountains settlements, although the areas of greatest scenic beauty are some distance from the towns. If you want to see the best that the Blue Mountains have to offer, take a guided tour or hire a vehicle and drive from Sydney.

BY CAR

Renting a car is the best plan, and you can do so in either Sydney or Katoomba. Distances between Blue Mountains towns are short, roads are generally in good condition, and there are many scenic routes and lookouts that are accessible only by car.

BY TRAIN

Train services from Sydney stop at most of the many small stations that dot the railway line from the base of the mountains to Mount Victoria. However, if you're traveling by train only, you'll be very limited in the scope of what you can see.

Contacts and Resources

CAR RENTALS

If you plan to rent a car in Katoomba, be sure to reserve one in advance from: **Thrifty** (☎ 02/4784–2888) or **Cales** (☎ 02/4782–2917). If you intend to drive to the Blue Mountains from Sydney, *see* Sydney A to Z *in* Chapter 1.

EMERGENCIES

Ambulance, fire brigade, and police. ☎ *000*.

GUIDED TOURS

One of Sydney's most popular escapes, the Blue Mountains are served by many tour operators. You can day-trip from Sydney with a coach touring company or make your own way to the mountains and then link up with a guided tour. The region is also great for mountain biking, rappelling, rock climbing, hiking, and horseback riding. *See* Chapter 12 for more information on outdoor outfitters in the area.

Adventure Sports. Blue Mountains Adventure Company (⊠ Box 242, Katoomba 2780, ☎ 02/4782–1271, 𝔽𝔸𝕏 02/4782–1277) offers rappelling, canyoning, mountain biking, and caving trips for all levels of ability. The company began as the Blue Mountains Climbing School, and rock climbing remains a specialty. Most outings (from $89 for a one-day trip) are of a one-day duration, and costs include equipment, lunch, and transportation from Katoomba. **Great Australian Walks** (☎ 02/9555–7580, 𝔽𝔸𝕏 02/9810–6429), based in Sydney, offers a three-day guided walk along the historic Six Foot Track from Katoomba to Jenolan Caves (from $370, including wine and all meals). Walkers—typically about a dozen—sleep in a lodge one night and tents the other, and carry only a light day pack. Guides are artists, writers, musicians, or naturalists, and the walks appeal to cultivated tastes. Hikes depart every Friday in spring and autumn, less frequently in other seasons. **Outland Expeditions** (☎ 1800/227–345, 𝔽𝔸𝕏 02/4787–1766; from $80 for a one-day trip) operates canyoning and other guided adventure trips in the Blue Mountains, as well as courses in rappelling, rock climbing, and canyoning. One-, two-, and five-day trips are available, as is transportation from Sydney.

Four-Wheel-Drive Tours. The local Blue Mountains company **Cox's River Escapes** (⊠ Box 81, Leura 2780, ☎ 02/4784–1621 or 015/400–121, 𝔽𝔸𝕏 02/4784–2450; ✉ from $95 for a half-day tour) has off-the-beaten-track half- or full-day four-wheel-drive tours for a maximum of six people in each air-conditioned vehicle. Operator Ted Taylor knows the region and its flora and fauna intimately, and provides a highly personalized service, complete with home-cooked morning or afternoon teas and lunches. Horseback riding, rappelling, and trout fishing are options, and guided bushwalking and camping trips can also be arranged. Reservations are essential. **Wild Escapes** (✉ Box 116, Asquith 2077, ☎ 02/9482–2881, FAX 02/9477–3114; ✆ from $199 for a one-day tour, including meals and wine) has various small-group day trips from Sydney to the Blue Mountains. The most popular trip by this award-winning company is the four-wheel-drive High Country Ecotour, which departs the beaten track near Katoomba and snakes back to Sydney through fire trails in the Jamison Valley, with bushwalks and a champagne picnic en route.

Orientation Tours. Australian Pacific Tours (✉ Circular Quay W, Sydney, ☎ 13–1304) has daily bus tours from Sydney to the Blue Mountains (from $71) and Jenolan Caves (from $89.50). The company also offers daily departures for a two-day Jenolan Caves/Blue Mountains tour, which includes accommodations at Jenolan Caves Guest House (from $215). Buses depart from the Overseas Shipping Terminal, on the Harbour Bridge side of Circular Quay. Free hotel pickup is available upon request. **Fantastic Aussie Tours** (✉ 283 Main St., Katoomba, ☎ 02/4782–1866) can arrange a number of tours. On weekends and public holidays from 9:30 AM to 4:30 PM, the **Blue Mountains Explorer Bus** ($18) meets trains from Sydney at the Katoomba Railway Station. The double-decker makes 18 stops on its 50-minute circuit, including many of the major attractions around Katoomba and Leura. You are free to leave the tour at any point and join a following bus. On weekdays, a half-day **Blue Mountains Highlights Bus** ($34) meets trains from Sydney at the Katoomba Railway Station (train schedules might change, so call ahead; ☞ Arriving and Departing, *above*). At the end of the tour, the buses return to Katoomba Station to reconnect with Sydney-bound trains. Fantastic Aussie Tours has other half- and full-day bus and four-wheel-drive tours around the Blue Mountains region.

VISITOR INFORMATION

Blue Mountains Information Centres are at Echo Point in Katoomba and at the foot of the mountains on the Great Western Highway at Glenbrook. ☎ 02/4739–6266. ◷ *Echo Point, daily 9–5; Glenbrook, weekdays 9–5, weekends 8–4:30.*

Sydney Visitors Information Centre has information on Blue Mountains accommodation, tours, and sights. ✉ *106 George St., the Rocks, Sydney 2000,* ☎ *02/9255–1788,* FAX *02/9241–5010.* ◷ *Daily 9–6.*

THE SOUTHERN HIGHLANDS AND SOUTH COAST

By Anne
Matthews

Updated by
Michael
Gebicki

This fertile upland region just over 100 km (62 mi) southwest of Sydney was first settled during the 1820s by farmers in search of grazing lands. Later during the 19th century, wealthy Sydney folk built grand country houses here, primarily to escape the city's summer heat and humidity. Farming still prevails today, but the area's rolling hills, intricate landscape, and aristocratic airs continue to attract visitors. Although the region is often compared with England, Australia's ruggedness manages to dramatize even this picturesque rural scene with the steep sandstone gorges and impenetrable forests of Morton National Park. As a bonus, the South Coast—with its excellent surfing and swimming beaches—is just a short drive away.

At an altitude of around 2,100 ft above sea level, the Southern Highlands experiences four distinct seasons. It is pleasantly cool here in summer, snow occasionally falls in winter, and the area comes alive with the rich colors of falling leaves in autumn (March–May). The Highlands are famous for their country hotels, guest houses and restaurants, antiques and crafts, and English-style gardens, as well as hiking, golf, horseback riding, and other outdoor activities.

The towns and sights of the Southern Highlands make an ideal two- to four-day round-trip either from Sydney or as a stopover on the way to Canberra or the Snowy Mountains. Distances between towns and villages are so small that you might consider basing yourself in Bowral, one of the most attractive towns that has most of the accommodations, and taking day trips from there. If you are heading back to Sydney after seeing the Highlands, take the South Coast route past beaches and the attractive seaside township of Kiama.

Mittagong

103 km (64 mi) southwest of Sydney.

Although it's known as the gateway to the Southern Highlands, the commercial center of Mittagong holds few attractions except for a selection of crafts and antiques shops. The Tourism Southern Highlands Information Centre on Main Street has maps and local brochures.

OFF THE BEATEN PATH

WOMBEYAN CAVES – From Mittagong, you can take a detour through rugged mountain scenery to these spectacular and delicate limestone formations. Five caves are open to the public, although the Fig Tree Cave is the only one where you can look around on your own. Guided tours to the others take place at regular intervals throughout the day. You can also explore the bushwalking trails and look for wildlife. The caves are just 66 km (41 mi) from Mittagong, but the journey along the narrow, winding, and partly unsealed road takes about 1½ hours each way. ⊠ *Wombeyan Caves Rd., via Mittagong,* ☏ *02/4843–5976.* ⊑ *Self-guided cave tour $10, guided 1-cave tour $12, guided 2-cave tour $20.* ☉ *Daily 8:30–5.*

Berrima

14½ km (9 mi) southwest of Mittagong.

Founded in 1829, Berrima is an outstanding example of an early Georgian colonial town, preserved in almost original condition. The entire English-style settlement is virtually a museum of early colonial sandstone and brick buildings (many of them built by convicts), such as the National Trust–listed Harpers Mansion and the Holy Trinity Church. The 1839 Berrima Gaol is still in use, and the 1834 Surveyor General Inn is Australia's oldest continuously licensed hotel—one of several in the country that make the same claim. In addition to its historic buildings, restaurants, and tea shops, Berrima's stores sell antiques, crafts, and traditional Australian knitwear. To learn more about the town's history, pick up a copy of the self-guided walking tour at the courthouse, or join one of the extremely knowledgeable local guides (☞ Guided Tours *in* Southern Highlands A to Z, *below*).

On weekends, take a $5 village tour by hopping aboard a restored early 1800s **Cobb & Co. stagecoach** pulled by Clydesdale horses.

The 1838 **Berrima Courthouse,** with its grand, classical facade, is the town's architectural highlight. The impressive sandstone complex, now a museum, contains the original courtroom and holding cells. Inside is a reenactment of an infamous murder trial, as well as audiovisual and conventional displays of such items as iron shackles and cat-o'-nine-tails that were once used on recalcitrant convicts. The courthouse also serves as the local information center. ⊠ *Wilshire St.,* ☏ *02/4877–1505.* ⊑ *Museum $3.* ☉ *Daily 10–4.*

Dining

$$ ✕ **White Horse Inn.** This meticulously restored inn is not just a fine example of colonial Australian architecture; the atmospheric 1832 hotel (which is reputed to have a resident ghost) is an ideal spot for lunch and morning or afternoon tea indoors or in the courtyard. The lunch menu features soups, salads, open sandwiches, excellent focaccias, and many desserts. If you are visiting Berrima in the evening, more expensive modern-Australian fare is served in the traditionally decorated formal dining rooms. ✉ *Market Pl.,* ☎ *02/4877–1204. AE, DC, MC, V.*

Shopping

The Bell Gallery. The craftwork at Berrima's classiest gallery includes unusual glassware, pottery, fabrics, and other handmade items. ✉ *10 Jellore St.,* ☎ *02/4877–1267.* ☉ *Fri.–Tues. 10–4 (Wed. and Thurs. by appointment only).*

Peppergreen in Berrima. Among the town's numerous antiques shops, this one is outstanding both for its size and its extraordinary range of old wares. In addition to the more predictable jewelry, silver, glassware, and china items, Peppergreen stocks buttons, books, old lace and linen, and other intriguing collectibles. ✉ *Market Pl.,* ☎ *02/4877–1488.* ☉ *Weekdays 10–5, weekends 9–5:30.*

Bowral

9½ km (6 mi) east of Berrima.

The commercial center for the Southern Highlands, genteel Bowral has been a desirable country address for the wealthy since the 1880s. This is now the region's largest town, and its burgeoning population of around 7,500 includes many city retirees. Bowral is famous for its fine old houses, tree-lined streets, and antiques and crafts shops. The parks and private gardens are the focus of the colorful spring **Tulip Time Festival,** held every September and October. For panoramas of Bowral, Mittagong, and the surrounding countryside, don't miss the scenic drive up 2,830-ft-high **Mount Gibraltar,** which has four short walking trails at the summit.

Bowral's main attraction—at least for cricket fans—is the **Bradman Museum.** Bowral was the childhood home of Australia's legendary cricketer Sir Donald (The Don) Bradman (b. 1908), who played for and captained the Australian team 1928–48. With film footage, photographs, and a great deal of sporting memorabilia, this excellent museum commemorates The Don's remarkable achievements and also pays tribute to the game of cricket, one of Australia's enduring obsessions. Located next to the town's idyllic cricket oval, the museum includes a shop and tearooms. ✉ *Glebe Park, St. Jude St.,* ☎ *02/4862–1247.* ✐ *$7.* ☉ *Daily 10–4.*

Dining and Lodging

$$$ ✕ **Grand Bar and Brasserie.** This lively city-style brasserie is open for lunch and dinner daily, and its modern Australian menu changes seasonally. Pastas, steaks, salads, and Asian dishes are featured on an extensive menu that aims to please just about everyone, although some ingredients in the sauces seem more for visual effect than for any gastronomic reason. Wine is available by the glass. ✉ *The Grand Arcade, 295 Bong Bong St.,* ☎ *02/4861–4783. AE, DC, MC, V.*

$ ✕ **Janeks.** This small, casual café is one of the few eateries in Bowral with outdoor seating. Come for breakfasts, milk shakes, smoothies, cakes, waffles, and an all-day menu that lists toasted sandwiches, soups, focaccias, pastas, and salads. At dinner, look for such Mod Oz dishes as steamed mussels with lemongrass, chili, and coriander;

smoked tuna steak with a salad with wasabi dressing; or a warm salad with wild duck, mesclun, artichokes, and balsamic dressing. ⊠ *Corbett Plaza, Wingecarribee St.,* ☎ *02/4861–4414. Reservations essential for dinner. MC, V. BYOB. No dinner Mon.–Thurs.*

$$$$ ✕⊡ **Milton Park.** Set in expansive English-style gardens on a forested estate 13 km (8 mi) east of Bowral, this modern hotel has as its nucleus the former country retreat of one of Sydney's elite families. Throughout, the hotel is plushly decorated in a warm, patrician, country style. Most guest rooms lead onto an internal courtyard; the six suites have spa baths. Dinner, contemporary Australian fare with European and Asian influences, is served in the elegant Hordern Room. Nonresidents are welcome to dine here. ⊠ *Horderns Rd., 2576,* ☎ *02/4861–1522,* ℻ *02/4861–4716. 34 rooms, 6 suites. 2 restaurants, bar, pool, massage, 3 tennis courts, boccie, croquet, horseback riding, mountain bikes. AE, DC, MC, V.*

$$ ✕⊡ **Links House Small Hotel.** This friendly, stylish hotel, in a quiet location directly opposite the Bowral golf course, has been catering to visitors since 1928. Rooms are small but tastefully appointed, and the suites are ideal for families. If you book well in advance, you may be fortunate enough to secure Number 20—a delightful cottage-style room in the hotel's gardens. The lounge areas are cozy and welcoming, and the hotel has a mild air of eccentricity that has won a faithful clientele. A full, cooked breakfast is included. A modern Australian menu is served in Basil's Restaurant. ⊠ *17 Links Rd., Bowral 2576,* ☎ *02/4861–1977,* ℻ *02/4862–1706. 13 rooms with shower, 4 suites. Restaurant, pool, tennis court, boccie, croquet. AE, DC, MC, V.*

Moss Vale

10 km (6 mi) southeast of Berrima.

Founded as a market center for the surrounding farming districts, which now concentrate on horses, sheep, and dairy and stud cattle, Moss Vale is a pleasant township with abundant antiques and crafts shops. It is a good place to shop and stroll, and the attractive Leighton Gardens in the center of town are particularly attractive in spring and autumn.

On the banks of the Wingecarribee River north of Moss Vale, the lagoon and swamplands of the **Cecil Hoskins Nature Reserve** have been a wildlife sanctuary since the 1930s. This important wetland area is home to more than 80 species of local and migratory waterfowl, including pelicans and black swans. You may even be fortunate enough to see a reclusive platypus here. The reserve has bird-watching blinds, a picnic area, and several easy walking tracks with excellent views of the river and wetlands. ⊠ *Moss Vale–Bowral Rd., Bowral,* ☎ *02/4887–7270.* ◷ *Daily dawn–dusk.*

Golf

With its well-groomed greens and on-course accommodation, the par-71 **Moss Vale Golf Club** (⊠ Arthur St., ☎ 02/4868–1503 or 02/4868–1811) is regarded as one of the best and most challenging in this golf-mad region. Visitors are welcome every day except Saturday, but it is best to phone first. Greens fees are $25 weekdays, $30 weekends.

Sutton Forest and Bundanoon

6–13 km (4–8 mi) south of Moss Vale.

The drive from Moss Vale through the tranquil villages that lie to the south is particularly rewarding—a meandering journey that winds past dairy farms and horse stud farms. Although relatively unimportant today, **Sutton Forest** was the focus of the area's early settlement.

In later years, this small township became the country seat of the governors of New South Wales, who periodically based themselves at the grand country house, Hillview. The village, 6 km (4 mi) from Moss Vale, also contains a few shops and the pleasant Sutton Forest Inn. The nearby hamlet of **Exeter** is where you'll find the 1895 St. Aidans Church, complete with a vaulted timber ceiling and beautiful stained-glass windows.

South of Sutton Forest, **Bundanoon** (Aboriginal for "place of deep gullies") was once an extremely busy weekend getaway for Sydneysiders. Its popularity was due to its location—on the main rail line to Melbourne, at a bracing elevation of 2,230 ft and perched above the northern edge of spectacular Morton National Park (☞ *below*). The tranquil village is still delightful and provides the best access to the park's western section. There are a few antiques and crafts shops, and Bundanoon is also the focus of the annual **Brigadoon Festival,** held in April, a lively event that features pipe bands, highland games, and all things Scottish.

Dining and Lodging

$$$ ✕🏨 **Peppers Manor House Southern Highlands.** Adjoining the Mount Broughton golf course (☞ *below*) and set in 185 acres of gardens and pastureland, this elegant country resort is based around a grand 1920s family home. The old homestead's baronial great hall has a high vaulted ceiling and leaded windows, and there are five traditionally decorated guest rooms in the main building. Other accommodations are in the modern Garden Wing. Three suites are available, and the two-bedroom Elms Cottages are ideal for families. Both guests and non-residents can dine in the hotel's stylish Kater's Restaurant, which serves innovative Australian country cuisine. Rates include a hearty breakfast. ⊠ *Kater Rd., Sutton Forest 2577,* ☎ *02/4868–2355,* 🖷 *02/4868–3257. 40 rooms with bath or shower, 3 suites. Restaurant, bar, saltwater pool, 18-hole golf course, 2 tennis courts, croquet, volleyball, mountain bikes. AE, DC, MC, V.*

Outdoor Activities and Sports

GOLF

The exclusive, Scottish-style **Mount Broughton Golf & Country Club** (⊠ Kater Rd., Sutton Forest, ☎ 02/4869–1597) has a picturesque, par-72, 18-hole championship course that is considered by pros to be among the top 100 in Australia. Facilities are of a very high standard. Visitors are welcome, but call in advance. Greens fees are $35 weekdays, $45 weekends.

HORSEBACK RIDING

The superbly equipped **Highlands Equestrian Centre** (⊠ Sutton Farm, Illawarra Hwy., Sutton Forest, ☎ 02/4868–2584) offers cross-country rides and classes for everyone from beginners to advanced riders who are capable of dressage and show jumping. Pony rides are available for $10; escorted trail rides start at $30. Reservations are essential. The farm also offers accommodation in its historic 1830s homestead.

Morton National Park and Fitzroy Falls

19 km (12 mi) southwest of Moss Vale.

With more than 400,000 acres, rugged **Morton National Park** is one of the state's largest national parks. This superbly scenic region encompasses sheer sandstone cliffs and escarpments, scenic lookouts, waterfalls, and densely forested valleys; it is very popular with bushwalkers and bird-watchers. The Bundanoon area has a variety of walks, many of which can be completed in less than an hour. These include short hikes to the historic Erith Coal Mine, the lookout at Mt. Carnarvon,

Fairy Bower Falls, and Ferntree Gully. You can also walk to Glow Worm Glen, a small sandstone grotto that is home to fungus gnat larvae, who trail a sticky, iridescent filament to attract small insects for their meals. The track to the glen is accessible after dark. Information on all walks is available from the National Parks and Wildlife Service Fitzroy Falls Visitor Centre.

The park's eastern highlight is Fitzroy Falls, where the water tumbles 270 ft from the craggy sandstone escarpment. A boardwalk leads to lookouts with spectacular views of the falls and the heavily forested Yarrunga Valley. Several marked bushwalks of varying lengths along the escarpment's eastern and western edges allow further exploration of the area. Birdlife is prolific—look for kookaburras, parrots, and even the elusive lyrebird. The **Fitzroy Falls Visitor Centre** (⊠ Nowra Rd., ☎ 02/4887–7270), operated by the National Parks and Wildlife Service, is open daily from 8:30 to 5. It includes a shop, information displays, and a pleasant café.

OFF THE
BEATEN PATH

BURRAWANG – From Fitzroy Falls you can take a short scenic drive to the northeast via the sleepy hamlets of Myra Vale and Wildes Meadow. Originally an 1860s timber village, Burrawang has retained much of its original charm in its weatherboard houses and buildings, such as the 1870s **Burrawang General Store.** On weekends pay a visit to the **Old School House,** where you'll find an excellent collection of antiques for sale and a dining room that serves delicious lunches, cakes, teas, and coffees. Burrawang is 11 km (7 mi) from Fitzroy Falls.

The attractive farming area around **Robertson,** 8 km (5 mi) east of Burrawang, provided the setting for the movie *Babe*—yes, all those green, English-looking fields were in fact located in Australia's Southern Highlands. You can also explore the temperate rain forest of **Robertson Nature Reserve** on a short walk, then call in at the rustic local pub for a drink.

Kangaroo Valley

18 km (11 mi) southeast of Fitzroy Falls.

After descending the slopes of Barrengarry Mountain, from which there are wonderful views of the plains and coast below, the Moss Vale Road reaches Kangaroo Valley, a lush dairy farming region first settled during the early 1800s. Many old buildings remain, and the entire charming, verdant region is National Trust–classified. The Kangaroo Valley township has several cafés and crafts shops, and you can hire a canoe, golf, swim in the river, or hike. The entrance to the village is marked by the grand, medieval-style Hampden Bridge, which was erected over the Kangaroo River in 1897.

Next to Hampden Bridge, the **Pioneer Settlement Reserve** has a unique perspective on the valley's history. The site includes Pioneer Farm, a re-creation of a late-19th-century homestead, and a variety of forest and woodland bushwalks. ⊠ *Moss Vale Rd.,* ☎ *02/4465–1306.* 🖃 *$3.* 🕙 *Daily 9:30–4:30.*

En Route After leaving the township, turn left after about 3 ½ km (2 mi) onto the narrow, precipitous Kangaroo Valley Road, which leads to the delightful town of **Berry.** Styling itself as the "Town of Trees," this roadside settlement has carefully preserved its 19th-century heritage and architecture. The town's 1886 bank now serves as the local history museum, and the main street is lined with craft and gift shops housed in attractive old buildings.

From Berry you can either travel to Kiama along the Princes Highway or you can take a more scenic coastal route via the sands and wild surf of spectacular **Seven Mile Beach,** and the quiet seaside villages of **Gerroa** and **Gerringong.** It is 26 km (16 mi) to Kiama along the latter route.

Dining and Lodging

$$$ ✕ ▦ **Woodbyne.** Just off the Pacific Highway south of Berry, this pretty, all-white timber villa radiates a sense of calm and refinement. Five spacious guest rooms, decorated in neutral tones, create a simple, elegant backdrop for the mixed furnishings and fabrics. Each one has a garden view and an en-suite bathroom. The garden is only a few years old, yet the strength of its design harks back to another era that delighted in precise composition. Breakfast is included, and dinner is served in the art gallery on Saturday nights. ⊠ *4 O'Keefe's La., Jaspers Brush 2535,* ☎ *02/4848–6200,* ℻ *02/4448–6211. 5 rooms. Restaurant. AE, MC, V.*

Kiama

47 km (29 mi) northeast of Kangaroo Valley.

First "discovered" by the intrepid explorer George Bass, who sailed here from Sydney in his small whaleboat in 1797, this attractive coastal township of 23,000 began life as a fishing port. Kiama has long been a popular vacation center, however, due to its mild climate, fine beaches, pleasant walks, and easy rail access from Sydney. In 1996 it was proclaimed "Australia's Tidiest Town."

Despite its popularity as a holiday town, Kiama has preserved several significant 19th-century buildings, such as the National Trust–listed weatherboard cottages on Collins Street, the Presbyterian church, and Manning Street's surprisingly grand post office. The Kiama Visitors Centre has a "Heritage Walks" brochure that describes points of interest around the town center.

The town's beaches—including Kendalls, Easts, Surf, and Bombo—are excellent for swimming and surfing. Other popular activities around Kiama are fishing and scuba diving. Several boat operators based in the harbor offer game, sports, and deep-sea fishing trips, and others cater to divers.

Two of Kiama's most visited sights are located at **Blowhole Point.** These are the blowhole itself, through which—given the right conditions—the sea erupts, and the impressive 1887 **Kiama Lighthouse.**

OFF THE **JAMBEROO –** One of the Kiama area's highlights is a short excursion to
BEATEN PATH this delightful old settlement 9 km (5½ mi) inland. Settlers first came to this tranquil farming valley in the 1820s. The village contains some interesting shops and several old stone buildings, including the 1875 National Trust–classified schoolhouse. The old-style Jamberoo Pub is a good spot for an ice-cold beer on a hot day.

Dining and Lodging

$$ ✕ **Chachis.** In one of Collins Street's historic 1880s cottages, this friendly and reasonably priced Italian-style ristorante serves lunch, dinner, and snacks. Meat, seafood, and vegetarian main courses are available, and the penne, spaghetti, fettuccine, and ravioli come with a choice of eight sauces. The dessert menu is extensive and tempting. Dining is either indoors or on the veranda. ⊠ *The Terraces, Collins St.,* ☎ *02/4233–1144. AE, MC, V. BYOB.*

$$$$ ✕ ▦ **Villa Dalmeny l'Hotel Privé.** Among tuned-in Sydneysiders, this
★ handsome Victorian guest house has established a reputation as one of the best reasons to head south for the weekend. In a quiet back street

of Kiama, Villa Dalmeny has four spacious guest rooms, each decorated in a lively style that reflects owner Jacqueline Noss-Ferrero's cosmopolitan tastes and travels. Born in the French-speaking part of Switzerland, Jacqueline learned her culinary techniques on New York's Park Avenue; thus, dinner at Villa Dalmeny is a gourmet affair, served with all the pomp and circumstance that the occasion demands. Rates include breakfast, and dinner is included in the weekend prices. Visitors are welcome for dinner by prior arrangement. Smoking is not permitted indoors, and children are not allowed. ⊠ *72 Shoalhaven St., 2533,* ☎ *02/4233–1911,* FAX *02/4233–1912. 4 rooms with shower. Restaurant. No credit cards.*

En Route Between Kiama and Sydney, the Princes Highway loops inland, skirting Lake Illawarra and the port and major industrial center of Wollongong, the state's third-largest city. Other than beaches, a museum, and an art gallery, there is nothing of interest in Wollongong itself. After Wollongong, the road signposted "Bulli" is a scenic alternative to the main highway, winding past small townships and beaches before it scales the escarpment above **Stanwell Park,** a famous hang-gliding launch point with fantastic views down the coast. From Stanwell Park, it will take about an hour to reach central Sydney.

Southern and South Coast Highlands A to Z

Arriving and Departing

BY BUS

Greyhound Pioneer Australia (☎ 13–2030) and **McCaffertys** (☎ 13–1499) offer daily service between Sydney and Mittagong. The journey takes 2½ hours, and the round-trip fare costs $46–$56. The same companies also run daily buses from Canberra (2 hours) at $40–$48 round-trip.

BY CAR

From central Sydney, head west along Parramatta Road and follow the signs to the Hume Highway (Hwy. 5). Join the Hume Highway at Ashfield and drive southwest until you reach the Mittagong exit. Mittagong is 103 km (64 mi) southwest of Sydney, and the drive should take 1½–2 hours.

BY TRAIN

Sydney's **Cityrail** (☎ 13–1500) commuter line trains have frequent daily service to Mittagong, Bowral, Moss Vale, and Bundanoon. Trains from Sydney also stop daily at Kiama. Round-trip fares are the same to both the Southern Highlands (Bowral) and Kiama: $21.20, or $12.80 for an off-peak ticket.

Getting Around

BY BUS

Local buses run between the main Highlands towns, but these will not take you to the out-of-the-way attractions. Renting a car is the best way to see most of the area.

BY CAR

Distances between towns and attractions are small, and roads are generally in very good condition and scenic—all the more reason to drive them yourself.

Contacts and Resources

CAR RENTALS

To rent a car in Sydney, *see* Sydney A to Z *in* Chapter 1. In the Southern Highlands, you can hire a car from **Avis** (⊠ Shell Service Station, Argyle and Yarrawa Sts., Moss Vale, ☎ 02/4868–1044), **Hertz** (⊠

Highlands Small Business Shop, Unit 4, Sherwood Village, Kirkham Rd., Bowral, ☎ 02/4862–1755), and **Thrifty** (✉ Mobil Service Station, Hume Hwy., Mittagong, ☎ 02/4872–1283). Call ahead to reserve a car.

EMERGENCIES

Ambulance, fire brigade, and police. ☎ 000.

GUIDED TOURS

The best way to see the old buildings and other attractions of Berrima is on an informative stroll with **Historic Berrima Village Guided Walking Tours** (☎ 02/4877–1505). Tours ($5.50) depart from the Berrima Courthouse on Wilshire Street daily at 11:30, 1, and 2:30. **Wild Escapes** (☎ 02/9482–2881) has a full-day tour ($199) from Sydney that includes Kiama, Kangaroo Valley, and the Southern Highlands. Wild Escapes specializes in small-group travel, with an emphasis on the natural environment. Prices include lunch and drinks.

VISITOR INFORMATION

Kiama Visitors Centre has information on the Kiama, Jamberoo, and Minnamurra areas. ✉ *Blowhole Point, Kiama 2533,* ☎ *02/4232–3322 or 1800/80–3897.* ☉ *Daily 9–5.*

Sydney Visitors Information Centre has information on Southern Highlands and South Coast accommodations, tours, and sights. ✉ *106 George St., the Rocks, Sydney 2000,* ☎ *02/9255–1788,* ℻ *02/9241–5010.* ☉ *Daily 9–6.*

Tourism Southern Highlands Information Centre. ✉ *62–70 Main St., Mittagong 2575,* ☎ *02/4871–2888 or 1300/65–7559.* ☉ *Daily 8–5:30.*

THE HUNTER VALLEY

The meandering waterway that gives this valley its name is one of the most extensive river systems in the state. The Hunter Valley covers an area of almost 25,103 square km (9,650 square mi), stretching from the town of Gosford north of Sydney to Taree, 177 km (110 mi) farther north along the coast, and almost 300 km (186 mi) inland. From its source on the rugged slopes of the Mount Royal Range, the Hunter River flows through rich grazing country and past the horse stud farms around Scone in the upper part of the valley, home of some of Australia's wealthiest farming families. In the Lower Hunter region, the river crosses the vast coal deposits of the Greta seam. Coal mining, both open-cut and underground, is an important industry for the Hunter Valley, and the mines in this area provide the fuel for the steel mills of Newcastle, the state's second-largest city, which lies at the mouth of the Hunter River.

To almost everyone in Sydney, however, the Hunter Valley conjures up visions not of coal mines or cows but of wine. The Hunter is the largest grape-growing area in the state, with more than 70 wineries and a reputation for producing excellent wines. Much of it has found a market overseas, and visiting wine lovers might recognize the Hunter Valley labels of Rosemount, Rothbury Estate, or Lindemans.

In recent years the area has become a favorite weekend destination for Sydneysiders. In addition to wine tasting, the Hunter Valley's historic towns, bushland walks, and excellent restaurants draw crowds. During the week you'll find quiet roads, empty picnic grounds, spare tables in restaurants—and less expensive accommodations.

The arrangement of towns and sights below follows a logical order for anyone arriving from Sydney. Start at the Hunter Valley gateway town of Cessnock, then continue to Pokolbin and the main Lower Hunter wineries. Two optional detours are the historic village of Wollombi and the Upper Hunter Valley settlements of Muswellbrook and Scone. The easiest return route to Sydney from the Upper Hunter is via the historic town of Maitland and the Sydney–Newcastle Freeway.

Cessnock

185 km (115 mi) north of Sydney.

The large town of Cessnock is better known as the entrance to the Lower Hunter Valley than for any particular attraction in the town itself. Between 1890 and 1960 this was an important coal-mining area, but when coal production began to decline during the 1950s, the mines gradually gave way to vines.

Any tour of the area's vineyards should begin at Cessnock's **Wine Country Visitor Information Centre** (☞ *Visitor Information in* Hunter Valley A to Z, *below*). The center can provide maps of the vineyards, brochures, and a free, handy visitor's guide.

At **Rusa Park Zoo,** 3 km (2 mi) north of Cessnock, animals from all over the world mingle with such Australian fauna as koalas, wallabies, kangaroos, wombats, snakes, and lizards in a 24-acre bushland park. There are more than 90 species of animals and birds here, including monkeys, deer, and antelope. Visitors can hand-feed the monkeys with food provided at 11 and 2. Barbecue and picnic facilities are provided. ✉ *Lomas La., Nulkaba,* ☎ *02/4990–7714.* ✇ *$7.* ✆ *Daily 9:30–4:30.*

Golf

Cessnock Golf Club (✉ Lindsay St., ☎ 02/4990–1633) is one of the Hunter Valley's more notable courses. The club welcomes visitors on most days, but it's best to check beforehand. Greens fees are $20.

Wollombi

31 km (19 mi) southwest of Cessnock.

Nothing seems to have changed in the atmospheric town of Wollombi since the days when the Cobb & Co. stagecoaches rumbled through town. Founded in 1820, Wollombi was the overnight stop for the coaches on the second day of the journey from Sydney along the convict-built Great Northern Road—at that time the only route north. The town is full of delightful old sandstone buildings and antiques shops. There is also a museum. The local hotel, the **Wollombi Tavern,** serves its own exotic brew, which goes by the name of Dr. Jurd's Jungle Juice. The pub also scores high marks for its friendliness and local color.

Lodging

$$ 🏠 **Avoca House.** Overlooking the Wollombi Brook just outside town,
★ this charming century-old house, with its vine-covered verandas and central courtyard, is a country classic with a layout that guarantees privacy. Rooms are tastefully furnished, and the owners, Russell and Kay Davies, pay great attention to detail to ensure that their guests have a comfortable and memorable stay. The largest of the three rooms is a self-contained suite with a queen-size bedroom and sitting room. Rates include a hearty country-style breakfast. Dinner is available by arrangement. ✉ *Wollombi Rd., 2325,* ☎ *02/4998–3233,* FAX *02/4998–3319. 2 rooms without bath, 1 suite. MC, V.*

Pokolbin

10 km (6 mi) northwest of Cessnock.

The Lower Hunter wine-growing region is centered around the village of Pokolbin, where there are antiques shops, good cafés, and dozens of wineries. Here are a few suggestions of wineries to visit.

In a delightful rural corner of the Mount View region, **Briar Ridge Vineyard** is one of the Hunter Valley's most outstanding small wineries. Established in 1972, it was purchased by winemaker Neil McGuigan—member of a famous Australian wine family—in the mid-1990s. It produces a limited range of sought-after reds, whites, and sparkling wines; the semillon, chardonnay, shiraz, and superbly intense cabernet sauvignon are highly recommended. The vineyard is on the southern periphery of the Lower Hunter vineyards, about a five-minute drive from Pokolbin. ⊠ *Mount View Rd., Mount View,* ☎ *02/4990–3670.* ⊙ *Weekdays 9–5, weekends 10–5.*

On the lower slopes of Mount Bright, one of the loveliest parts of the Lower Hunter region, is **Drayton's Family Wines.** Wine making is a Drayton family tradition dating back to the mid-19th century, when Joseph Drayton first cleared these slopes and planted vines. Today, the chardonnay, semillon, and shiraz made by this winery are some of the most consistent award-winners around, and a full range of wines is available for tasting. ⊠ *Oakey Creek Rd.,* ☎ *02/4998–7513.* ⊙ *Weekdays 8–5, weekends 10–5.*

The **Lindemans Hunter River Winery** is the home of Lindemans, one of the largest and most prestigious wine makers in the country, since the early 1900s. In addition to its Hunter Valley vineyards, the company also owns property in South Australia and Victoria, and a wide range of outstanding wines from these vineyards can be sampled in the tasting room—try the red Burgundy, semillon, or chardonnay. The winery has its own museum, featuring vintage wine-making equipment, as well as two picnic areas, one near the parking lot and the other next to the willow trees around the dam. ⊠ *McDonalds Rd.,* ☎ *02/4998–7684.* ⊙ *Weekdays 9–4:30, weekends 10–4:30.*

The Rothbury Estate, set high on a hill in the heart of Pokolbin, is one of the Lower Hunter Valley's premier wineries, established in 1968 by Australian wine-making legend Len Evans. Rothbury grows grapes in many areas of New South Wales, but grapes grown in the Hunter Valley go into the Brockenback Range wine, its most prestigious. The fine semillon and earthy shiraz wines that make this vineyard famous are available in a delightful tasting room sample. The charming on-site café (☞ *below*) has good food and, of course, a terrific wine list. Guided tours are given on weekends at 11 and 2. ⊠ *Broke Rd.,* ☎ *02/4998–7672.* ⊙ *Daily 9:30–4:30.*

Founded in 1858, **Tyrrell's Wines** is the Hunter Valley's oldest family-owned vineyard. This venerable establishment offers a wide selection of wines and was the first to commercially produce chardonnay in Australia—its famous Vat 47 Chardonnay is still a winner. Enjoy the experience of sampling fine wines in the old-world tasting room, or take a picnic lunch to a site overlooking the valley. Tours of the facilities are given Monday through Saturday at 1:30. ⊠ *Broke Rd.,* ☎ *02/4993–7000.* ⊙ *Mon.–Sat. 8–5.*

The low stone and timber buildings of the **McGuigan Hunter Village** are the heart of the Pokolbin wine-growing district. This large complex includes a resort and convention center, gift shops, restaurants, and two tasting rooms, those of the **McGuigan Brothers Winery** and the underground rooms of **Hunter Cellars**. At the **Hunter Valley Cheese Company**'s shop you can taste superb Australian cheeses before you buy. At the far end of the complex you'll find a large, shady picnic area with barbecues and an adventure playground. ⊠ *Broke and McDonalds Rds.,* ☎ *02/4998–7466.* ☉ *Daily 10–5.*

Dining and Lodging

$$$$ ✕ **Robert's at Pepper Tree.** Built around a century-old pioneer's cottage and surrounded by grapevines, this stunning restaurant is the brainchild of chef Robert Molines. The modern Australian menu draws inspiration from regional French and Italian cooking, which is applied to local hare, scallops, and lamb. In the airy, country-style dining room—complete with antique furniture, bare timber floors, and a big stone fireplace—first courses might include char-grilled quails and a seafood salad of octopus, tuna, prawns, and mussels. Head for the cozy fireside lounge for after-dinner liqueurs. ⊠ *Halls Rd.,* ☎ *02/4998–7330. AE, DC, MC, V.*

★

$$ ✕ **Rothbury Cafe.** Located above the Rothbury Estate's tasting room, this bright, relaxed café provides wonderful views of the vineyards and beyond. The menu specializes in country-style cuisine, changing frequently to utilize locally grown foods. On the menu you might find anything from prime local beef rib with wild Pokolbin peach chutney and parsnip chips to duck pizza or lamb tagine with quince. The estate's own premium wines are sold by the bottle or the glass. Service is friendly and efficient. ⊠ *The Rothbury Estate, Broke Rd.,* ☎ *02/ 4998–7363. AE, DC, MC, V. No dinner.*

$$$$ ✕🏠 **Peppers Guest House Hunter Valley.** In a grove of wild peppercorn trees, this cluster of long, low buildings surrounded by flagstone verandas imitates the architecture of a classic Australian country homestead. The atmosphere extends to the luxurious guest rooms, which are decorated with scrubbed-pine furnishings and floral-print fabrics, and to the Chez Pok restaurant's fine country-style fare with French, Asian, and Italian influences. This hotel has a devoted following and is booked well in advance for weekends. ⊠ *Ekerts Rd. 2320,* ☎ *02/4998–7596,* FAX *02/ 4998–7739. 47 rooms with shower, 1 4-bedroom homestead. Restaurant, bar, indoor pool, sauna, spa, tennis court. AE, DC, MC, V.*

$$$ ✕🏠 **Casuarina Country Inn.** Lapped by a sea of grapevines, there's a powerful whiff of fantasy about this luxurious country resort. Each of the palatial guest suites is furnished according to particular themes, such as the infamous French Bordello suite, with its four-poster canopy bed; the Victorian suite, with its stunning period furnishings; and the Chinese imperial suite, with its opium couch for a bed. The nearby **Casuarina Restaurant** specializes in substantial flambéed dishes, which are theatrically prepared at your table. There is a minimum two-night booking on weekends. ⊠ *Hermitage Rd. 2320,* ☎ *02/4998–7888,* FAX *02/4998–7692. 8 suites, 3 cottages. Restaurant, pool, sauna, tennis court. AE, MC, V.*

$$$$ 🏠 **Convent Pepper Tree.** The most luxurious accommodations in the Hunter Valley, this former convent was transported 605 km (375 mi) from its original home in western New South Wales. There's a maximum of 34 guests at any given time, which creates a friendly, intimate atmosphere despite the imposing two-story timber building. Rooms are cozy, spacious, and elegantly furnished, each with doors that open onto a wide veranda. The house is surrounded by the vineyards of the Pepper Tree Winery and is adjacent to **Robert's at Pepper Tree** (☞ *above*), which has delicious meals. Rates include a full country breakfast plus pre-dinner drinks and canapes. ⊠ *Halls Rd. 2320,* ☎ *02/4998–7764,* FAX *02/4998–7323. 17 rooms. Restaurant, pool, spa, tennis court, bicycles. AE, DC, MC, V.*

$$–$$$ ☷ **The Carriages Guest House.** Set on 36 acres at the end of a quiet country lane is a rustic-looking but winsome guest house. Each of its very private suites features antique country pine furniture and a large sitting area, and many have open fireplaces. The more expensive Gatehouse Suites also have spa baths and full kitchen facilities. Breakfast— a basket of gourmet goodies delivered to your door, or served to guests in the Gatehouse Suites—is included. The owners offer horse-drawn carriage rides and champagne picnics (☞ Somerset Carriages *in* Hunter Valley A to Z, *below*). Children are not allowed. ⊠ *Halls Rd. 2321,* ☎ *02/4998–7591,* ℻ *02/4998–7839. 6 suites with shower, 4 with bath. Saltwater pool, tennis court. AE, MC, V.*

$$ ☷ **Glen Ayr Cottages.** Tucked away in the Pokolbin bushland, these trim, colonial-style timber cottages have fully equipped kitchens, en-suite bathrooms, and marvelous views from their verandas. The cottages are built on a ridge with vineyards on one side and eucalyptus forest on the other. The furnishings are comfortable but simple: no televisions, radios, or telephones are allowed to compete with the songs of birds. Three of the cottages will sleep four comfortably, and both the Morrison and the two-story Ferguson sleep eight. ⊠ *Box 188, Cessnock 2325,* ☎ *02/ 4998–7784,* ℻ *02/4998–7476. 5 cottages. AE, MC, V.*

$ ☷ **Vineyard Hill Country Motel.** This motel sits on a rise in a secluded
★   part of the Hunter Valley with views across the vineyards to the Pokolbin State Forest. Its smart, modern one- and two-bedroom air-conditioned lodgings are an exceptional value. Each pastel-color suite has its own high-ceiling lounge area and a kitchen equipped with a coffeemaker and a choice of microwave or convection oven. French doors open onto a private deck. The reception area has a selection of prepared dishes ready for reheating in your room, as well as meats, salads, pâtés, and cheeses. Full, cooked breakfasts are available. The best views are from Rooms 4 through 8. There is a minimum stay of two nights on weekends. ⊠ *Lovedale Rd. 2320,* ☎ *02/4990–4166,* ℻ *02/ 4991–4431. 8 suites. Kitchenette, pool, spa. AE, MC, V.*

En Route   You can drive around the scenic vineyard countryside between Pokolbin and Rothbury, then take Branxton Road to the village of Branxton on the New England Highway. From Branxton, it is 71 km (44 mi) via the town of Singleton to Muswellbrook and the Upper Hunter Valley.

Muswellbrook

111 km (69 mi) northwest of Pokolbin.

First settled in the 1820s as cattle farming land, the Upper Hunter Valley town of Muswellbrook is an agricultural and coal mining center with few attractions other than tranquil, rolling hills and rich farmlands, some historic buildings, and the Regional Art Gallery. There are numerous wineries around the nearby village of Denman, however, including Arrowfield Wines and the excellent Rosemount Estate.

Scone

26 km (16 mi) north of Muswellbrook.

Noted for its high-quality horse and cattle stud farms and its penchant for playing polo—the town is known as the horse capital of Australia—the charming Upper Hunter farming town of Scone contains some historic mid-19th-century buildings and a local museum, and there are particularly fine accommodations in the area.

Dining and Lodging

$$$$ ✕⊞ **Belltrees Country House.** Located on a working cattle and horse
★ ranch that dates from the 1830s, this outstanding rural retreat offers
its guests a taste of the finer side of Australian country life. You can
also enjoy horseback riding, polo, archery, and clay pigeon shooting;
or, take a four-wheel-drive spin into the surrounding mountains. The
historic property has its own schoolhouse, store, and church. Accommodations are in a modern building surrounded by gardens; two
charming, self-contained cottages; and the secluded, romantic Mountain Retreat, which offers unparalleled views from atop its 5,000-ft mountain perch. Belltrees is a two-hour drive from the Lower Hunter wineries
on sealed roads. ⊠ *Gundy Rd. 2337,* ☎ *02/6545–1668,* FAX *02/6546–
1122. 3 rooms with bath, 5 with shower; 3 cottages. Saltwater pool,
tennis court, archery, horseback riding. AE, MC, V.*

Maitland

121 km (75 mi) southeast of Scone.

On the return trip to Sydney, a visit to this historic town is recommended.
Its history is best absorbed by strolling along High Street, which has
a number of colonial buildings and is classified by the National Trust
as an urban conservation area. Leading off this thoroughfare, Church
Street has several handsome two-story Georgian homes, a couple of
which are open to the public.

In one of Church Street's Georgian houses, the **Maitland City Art
Gallery** contains both a permanent collection and changing exhibitions.
⊠ *Brough House, Church St.,* ☎ *02/4933–1657.* ☉ *Weekdays 1–4,
Sat. 1:30–5, Sun. 10:30–5.*

The National Trust's **Grossman House** adjoins Maitland's art gallery.
The 1870 home reopened in mid-1995 after extensive restoration and
is furnished as a Victorian merchant's town house with an interesting
collection of colonial antiques. ⊠ *Church St.,* ☎ *02/4933–6452.* ⊡
$2. ☉ *Weekends 1:30–4:30; also by appointment.*

OFF THE **MORPETH –** This riverside village is a scenic 5-km (3-mi) country drive
BEATEN PATH from Maitland. Due to the settlement's comparative isolation, its quaint
shop fronts, wharves, and even the hitching posts have survived from the
time when this was an important trading station for the Hunter River
Steam Navigation Company. Today the hamlet is a backwater of the
best possible kind: a place for browsing through crafts shops or just sitting under a tree by the riverbank.

Dining and Lodging

$$$ ✕⊞ **Old George and Dragon.** With its sumptuous color scheme, green
★ baize walls, oil paintings, Asian curios, and plush furnishings, this for-
mer coaching inn–where the stagecoaches of Cobb & Co. once main-
tained stables and rooms for passengers—comes undiluted from the
full-blown opulence of the Victorian era. Four rooms are decorated in
period style, and an enclosed courtyard brimming with greenery. The
Old George and Dragon is one of the shining stars in the state's galaxy
of country dining experiences, and the hotel rate includes dinner. Like
the restaurant's decor, the food is of classic tradition: Roast partridge
with apples and calvados, Tasmanian salmon with sorrel sauce, and
fillet of beef are among the main courses on a menu that changes each
season. The dazzling wine list, which is several pages long, includes a
compendium of Australia's finest. Reservations are essential for the
restaurant, which serves lunch by arrangement Tues.–Sat. and is closed

Sun.–Mon. ⊠ *48 Melbourne St., East Maitland 2323,* ☎ *02/4933–7272,* FAX *02/4934–1481. AE, DC, MC, V.*

Golf

Maitland Golf Club (⊠ Sinclair St., East Maitland, ☎ 02/4933–7512 or 02/4933–4141) is another of the Hunter Valley's notable courses. The club welcomes visitors on most days, but it's best to check beforehand. Greens fees are $20.

The Hunter Valley A to Z

Arriving and Departing

BY BUS

Keans Express Travel (☎ 02/4990–5000 or 1800/04–3339) buses make the 2½-hour journey from Sydney's Central Coach Terminal on Eddy Avenue (near Central Station) to Cessnock daily. The round-trip fare is $44.

BY CAR

Leave Sydney by the Harbour Bridge or Harbour Tunnel and follow the signs for Newcastle. Just before Hornsby this road joins the Sydney–Newcastle Freeway. Take the exit from the freeway signposted "Hunter Valley Vineyards via Cessnock." From Cessnock, the route to the vineyards is clearly marked. Allow 2½ hours for the 185-km (115-mi) journey from Sydney.

Getting Around

BY CAR

If you plan to spend several days exploring the area, you will need a car. Other than taking a guided tour on arrival, this is the most convenient way to visit the wineries and off-the-beaten-path attractions, such as Wollombi and Morpeth.

BY BUS

An excellent alternative to the dangerous combination of driving and sampling too many wines is to hop aboard one of the minibuses operated by Cessnock-based **Vineyard Shuttle Service** (☎ 019/32–7193 or 02/4991–3655). The buses travel between area hotels, wineries, and restaurants. A day pass (good from 9 AM to 5 PM) with unlimited stops is $20, or $28 with evening transportation to and from the restaurant of your choice. The dinnertime shuttle service is $10 without purchase of a day pass.

Contacts and Resources

CAR RENTALS

To rent a car in Sydney, *see* Sydney A to Z *in* Chapter 1. In the Hunter Valley you can rent from **Hertz** (⊠ 191 Wollombi Rd., Cessnock, ☎ 02/4991–2500). Reserve prior to arrival.

EMERGENCIES

Ambulance, fire brigade, and police. ☎ *000.*

GUIDED TOURS

Several Sydney-based bus companies tour the Hunter Valley. Alternate ways to explore the region are by horse-drawn carriage, bicycle, motorbike, or even in a hot-air balloon. Full details are available from the Wine Country Visitor Information Centre (☞ *below*).

Ballooning. Drifting across the valley while the vines are still wet with dew is an unforgettable way to see the Hunter Valley. **Balloon Aloft** offers hour-long flights and serves a champagne breakfast upon your return. ☎ *02/4938–1955 or 1800/02–8568.* ☒ *Weekdays $200, weekends $225.*

Bus Tours. AAT King's operates a one-day bus tour of the Hunter Valley and Wollombi from Sydney on Tuesday, Wednesday, Thursday, and Sunday. Buses depart from the Overseas Passenger Terminal on the Harbour Bridge side of Circular Quay at 8:45, returning at 7:15. Free hotel pickup is available on request. ☎ 02/9252–2788. ⚐ *$95, including lunch and wine tasting.*

Horse-Carriage Tours. Half-day or full-day horse-drawn carriage tours of the wineries are offered by **Somerset Carriages.** The full-day tour includes a champagne gourmet picnic. ⊠ *Pokolbin,* ☎ 02/4998–7591. ⚐ *½-day tour from $160 per couple, full-day tour from $260 per couple.*

VISITOR INFORMATION

Scone (Upper Hunter) Tourist Information Centre. ⊠ *Kelly and Susan Sts., Scone 2337,* ☎ 02/6545–1526. ☉ *Daily 9–5.*

Sydney Visitors Information Centre has information on Hunter Valley accommodations, tours, and sights. ⊠ *106 George St., the Rocks, Sydney 2000,* ☎ 02/9255–1788, ☒ 02/9241–5010. ☉ *Daily 9–6.*

Wine Country Visitor Information Centre. ⊠ *Turner Park, Aberdare Rd., Cessnock 2325,* ☎ 02/4990–4477. ☉ *Weekdays 9–5, Sat. 9:30–5, Sun. 9:30–3:30.*

THE NORTH COAST

The North Coast is one of the most glorious and seductive stretches of terrain in Australia. An almost continuous line of beaches defines the coast, with the Great Dividing Range rising to the west. These natural borders frame a succession of rolling green pasturelands, mossy rain forests, towns dotted by red-roof houses, and waterfalls that tumble in glistening arcs from the escarpment.

A journey along the coast leads through a series of rich agricultural districts, beginning with grazing country in the south and moving into plantations of bananas, sugarcane, mangoes, avocados, and macadamia nuts. Dorrigo National Park outside Bellingen and Muttonbird Island in Coffs Harbour are two parks good for getting your feet on some native soil and for seeing unusual bird life. The North Coast is also a major vacation playground, sprinkled with resort towns that offer varying degrees of sophistication.

The tie that binds the North Coast is the Pacific Highway. Crowded, slow, and deadly dull, this highway rarely affords glimpses of the Pacific Ocean. If you take the time to explore some of the side roads, however, the rewards will more than compensate for the length of the journey. The following description of towns and other sights generally follows the route of the highway as it leads north to the Queensland border. There are several off-highway diversions to particularly attractive or historic stretches of coastline, as well as several inland towns and natural attractions that justify a detour.

In addition to surfing, swimming, and boating, which are popular throughout this region, Coffs Harbour and Byron Bay both have excellent diving and several notable dive operators who provide trips and instruction. White-water rafting is a popular sport in the Coffs Harbour region.

It is feasible to drive the entire length of the North Coast in a single day, but allow at least three—or, better still, a week—to properly sample some of its attractions.

Numbers in the margin correspond to points of interest on the North Coast map.

Taree

⓮ *335 km (208 mi) north of Sydney.*

The first major town along the North Coast, Taree is the commercial center of the Manning River district. Apart from a few fine beaches in the area, or perhaps to make an overnight stop, there is little reason to linger here on the way north.

Lodging

$$–$$$$ 🏠 **Clarendon Forest Retreat.** If you're looking for affordable luxury in a forest setting, this is a fine choice. The resort's six self-contained, self-catering cottages are spread throughout the valley to guarantee privacy. Each is spotlessly kept and equipped with a kitchen, laundry, two bedrooms, and a loft room. The trio of more expensive sandstone cottages have sunken spa pools and antique furnishings. Activities on the 1,000-acre beef-cattle property include horseback riding, swimming, tennis, bushwalking, and wildlife-viewing. The nearest surf beach is a 15-minute drive. Book at least three months in advance; a two-night minimum stay is required. ✉ *Coates Rd., Failford via Taree 2430,* ☎ *02/6554–3162,* 📠 *02/6554–3242. 6 cottages. Kitchenettes, heated pool, tennis court, horseback riding. MC, V.*

Port Macquarie

⓯ *82 km (51 mi) north of Taree.*

Set at the mouth of the Hastings River, Port Macquarie was founded as a convict settlement in 1821. The town was chosen for its isolation to serve as an open jail for prisoners convicted of second offenses in New South Wales. By the 1830s the pace of settlement was so brisk that the town was no longer isolated and its usefulness as a jail had ended. Today's Port Macquarie has few reminders of its convict past and is flourishing as a vacation and retirement area.

Operated by the Koala Preservation Society of New South Wales, the town's **Koala Hospital** is both a worthy cause and a popular attraction. The Port Macquarie region supports many of these extremely appealing but endangered marsupials, and the hospital cares for 150 to 200 sick and injured koalas each year. You can walk around the grounds to view the recuperating animals. Try to time your visit during the afternoon feeding, around 3 PM. ✉ *Macquarie Nature Reserve, Lord St.,* ☎ *02/6584–1522.* 💲 *Donation requested.* ☉ *Daily 9–4:30.*

The **Sea Acres Rainforest Centre** comprises 178 acres of coastal rain forest on the southern side of Port Macquarie. There are more than 170 plant species here, including 300-year-old cabbage tree palms, as well as native mammals, reptiles, and prolific birdlife. An elevated boardwalk allows you to stroll through the lush environment without disturbing the vegetation. The center has informative guided tours, as well as a gift shop and pleasant rain forest café. ✉ *Pacific Dr.,* ☎ *02/6582–3355.* 💲 *$8.50.* ☉ *Daily 9–4:30.*

Housed in a historic two-story shop near the Hastings River is the eclectic **Hastings District Historical Museum,** which displays period costumes, memorabilia from both world wars, farm implements, antique clocks and watches, and relics from the town's convict days. This wide-ranging collection represents the town's social history in an entertaining, enlightening manner. ✉ *22 Clarence St.,* ☎ *02/6583–1108.* 💲 *$4.* ☉ *Mon.–Sat. 9:30–4:30, Sun. 1–4:30.*

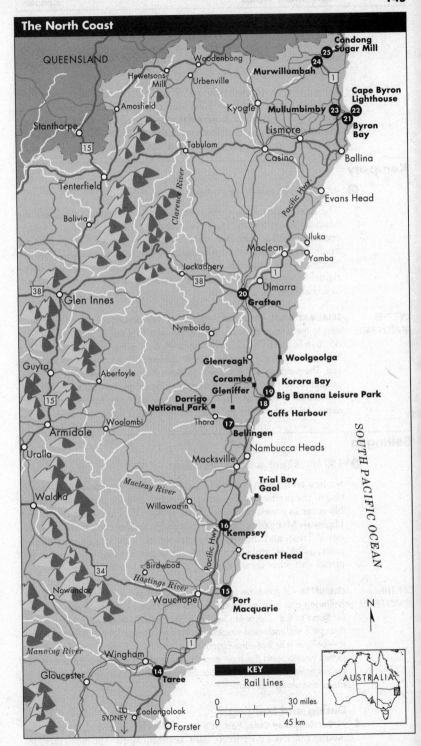

The North Coast

QUEENSLAND

Woodenbong
Hewetsons Mill
Urbenville
Murwillumbah **24**
25 Condong Sugar Mill
Amosfield
Kyogle
Mullumbimby **23** **22** Cape Byron Lighthouse
Stanthorpe
21 Byron Bay
Lismore
15
Tabulam
Casino
Ballina
Tenterfield
Pacific Hwy
Evans Head
Bolivia
Clarence River
Iluka
Maclean
Yamba
Jackadgery
38
1
Glen Innes
38
20 Ulmarra
Grafton
Nymboida
Glenreagh
Woolgoolga
Guyra
Aberfoyle
Coramba
Korora Bay
15
Gleniffer
19 Big Banana Leisure Park
Dorrigo National Park
18 Coffs Harbour
Armidale
Woolombi
Thora
17 Bellingen
Uralla
Macksville
Nambucca Heads
Macleay River
Trial Bay Gaol
Waldha
Willawarrin
16 Kempsey
Crescent Head
Birdwood
Hastings River
15 Port Macquarie
34
Nowendoc
Wauchope
Manning River
1
Wingham
14 Taree
Gloucester
TO SYDNEY
Coolongolook
Forster

SOUTH PACIFIC OCEAN

Pacific Hwy

N

KEY
— Rail Lines

0 ____ 30 miles
0 ____ 45 km

AUSTRALIA

St. Thomas Church is in the same area as the Hastings District Historical Museum. It is the country's third-oldest church, completed in 1828 and built by convicts using local cedar and stone blocks cemented together with powdered seashells. ⊠ *Hay and William Sts.,* ☎ *02/6584–1033.* 🎫 *$2.* ☉ *Weekdays 9:30–noon and 2–4.*

En Route　A rough but scenic alternative to taking the Pacific Highway north from Port Macquarie is the unpaved Maria River Road that runs through forests and farmland to **Crescent Head**—a beach renowned in the surfing world. Take the vehicular ferry across the Hastings River from Port Macquarie to reach the road, then rejoin the highway near Kempsey.

Kempsey

16 *48 km (30 mi) north of Port Macquarie.*

The next major Pacific Highway town is Kempsey, inland on the Macleay River. It is the business center for a large farming and timber region, as well as the place where Australia's famous Akubra hats are made. Of interest in the town itself are several historic buildings, the Macleay River Historical Society Museum and Settlers Cottage, an Aboriginal-themed park, and various arts and crafts shops. The nearby coastline is also worth a look.

OFF THE
BEATEN PATH
TRIAL BAY GAOL – North of Kempsey, a well-marked road leads northeast to the village of South West Rocks and Trial Bay Gaol (☎ 02/6566–6168), 37 km (23 mi) from town. Built in the 1870s and 1880s by convicts, this jail occupies a dramatic position on the cliffs above the sea. The purpose of the jail was to teach prisoners useful skills, but the project proved too expensive and was abandoned in 1903. During World War I, the prison became an internment camp for some 500 Germans. Admission to the jail is $3; hours are 9–5 daily.

Bellingen

17 *100 km (62 mi) north of Kempsey.*

Set in a river valley a few miles off the Pacific Highway, Bellingen is one of the prettiest towns along the coast, and the detour will probably come as a welcome relief if you've been droning along the Pacific Highway. Many of Bellingen's buildings have been classified by the National Trust, and the picturesque town has a museum and plenty of cafés, galleries, and crafts outlets. Bellingen is a favored hangout for artists and other creative types.

OFF THE
BEATEN PATH
GLENIFFER – If you have an hour to spare, cross the Bellinger River at Bellingen and take an 18-km (11-mi) excursion on the Bellingen–Gleniffer Road to the village of Gleniffer. This tranquil, rambling journey leads through farmlands and wooded valleys and across Never Never Creek to—believe it or not—the Promised Land. Author Peter Carey once lived in this vicinity, and the river and its surroundings provided the backdrop for his novel *Oscar and Lucinda*. Several swimming holes and picnic areas are along this road.

Dining and Lodging

$ ✕ **Carriageway Café.** Part of a magnificently restored emporium, this modish café has a selection of light, healthful meals. The menu includes breakfasts, rolls, soups, salads, pasta dishes, cakes, and fresh fruit juices, as well as one of the best cups of coffee on the North Coast. ⊠ *77 Hyde St.,* ☎ *02/6655–1672. AE, MC, V.* ☉ *Mon.–Sat. 8:30–5:30, Sun. 9–3:30.*

$$ ▦ **Koompartoo.** On a hillside overlooking Bellingen, these self-contained, open-plan cottages are superb examples of local craftsmanship, particularly in their use of timbers from surrounding forests. Each has a complete kitchen and family room, and they are very reasonably priced. You can also book a small guest room closer to the main house. Breakfast is available by arrangement. ⊠ *Rawson and Dudley Sts., Bellingen 2454,* ☎ ℻ *02/6655–2326. 4 cottages with shower. Kitchenettes, spa. MC, V.*

En Route   From Bellingen, a meandering and spectacular road circles inland to meet the Pacific Highway close to Coffs Harbour. This scenic route first winds along the river, then climbs more than 1,000 ft up the heavily wooded escarpment to the **Dorrigo Plateau.**

★   At the top of the Dorrigo Plateau is **Dorrigo National Park** (☎ 02/6657–2309), a small but outstanding subtropical rain forest that is included on the World Heritage list. Signposts along the main road indicate walking trails. The Satinbird Stroll is a short rain forest walk, and the 6-km (4-mi) Cedar Falls Walk leads to the most spectacular of the park's many waterfalls. The excellent **Dorrigo Rainforest Centre**, open daily from 9 to 5, offers information, educational displays, and a shop, and from here you can walk out high over the forest canopy along the Skywalk boardwalk. The national park is approximately 31 km (19 mi) from Bellingen.

☾   Beyond Dorrigo township, a gravel road completes the loop to the towns of **Coramba** and Moleton, the latter of which is the location for **George's Gold Mine** (⊠ Bushmans Range Rd., ☎ 02/6654–5355). Perched on a ridge high above the Orara Valley, this 250-acre cattle property still uses the slab huts and mustering yards built in the region's pioneering days. Owner George Robb is one of the legendary old-timers of the area, and his tour of his gold mine is a vivid account of the personalities and events from the days when "gold fever" gripped these hills. In addition to the mine and its historic equipment, the property has its own rain forest, mountain springs, stand of rare red cedars, and a barbecue-picnic area. Admission (which includes a tour) is $9. George's Gold Mine is open Wednesday through Sunday from 10 to 5, daily during school holidays, and the last tour of the property departs at about 3 PM.

Coffs Harbour

⓲   *35 km (22 mi) northeast of Bellingen via the Pacific Highway, 103 km (64 mi) from Bellingen via the inland scenic route along the Dorrigo Plateau.*

The major industry of Coffs Harbour is obvious well before you arrive. This is the state's "banana republic," and the surrounding hillsides are covered with long, neat rows of banana palms. Set at the foot of steep green hills, the town also has great beaches and a mild climate—an idyllic combination that has made it one of the most popular vacation spots along the coast. Coffs is a convenient halfway point in the 1,000-km (620-mi) journey between Sydney and Brisbane.

The town has a lively and attractive harbor in the shelter of **Muttonbird Island,** and a stroll out to this nature reserve is delightful in the evening. To get there follow the signs to the Coffs Harbour Jetty then park near the fish cooperative. A wide path leads out along the breakwater and up the slope of the island. The trail is steep, but the views from the top are worth the effort. The island is named after the muttonbirds (also known as shearwaters) that nest here between September and April, spending their days at sea and returning to their burrows in the evening. In late April, the birds begin their annual migration to New Zealand, the Philippines, and past Japan to the Aleutian Islands between eastern Siberia and Alaska. Between June and September Muttonbird Island is also a good spot from which to view migrating whales.

Near the port in Coffs Harbour, the giant **Pet Porpoise Pool** aquarium includes sharks, colorful reef fish, turtles, seals, and dolphins. A 90-minute sea circus show can be viewed at 10:30 or 2:15. Children may help feed the dolphins and seals. ⊠ *Orlando St.,* ☎ *02/6652–2164.* ☒ *$12.50.* ⊙ *Daily 9–4:30.*

Just north of the city, impossible to miss, is the Big Banana—the symbol of Coffs Harbour. This monumental piece of kitsch is part of the **⑲ Big Banana Leisure Park** complex, which offers a fascinating look at the past, present, and future of horticulture. Three tours are available: one by minibus and another on a 2-km elevated railway. The guided walking tour travels through a hydroponic growing area, packing shed, and plantation filled with an incredible variety of tropical fruits. Other attractions include the toboggan run and an ice-skating rink. At the end of the tour, wander down the hill to the Nut House and the Banana Barn to purchase the park's own gourmet jams, pickles, and fresh tropical fruit. ⊠ *Pacific Hwy.,* ☎ *02/6652–4355.* ☒ *Minibus tours $5 and $6.50, train tour $10.* ⊙ *Daily 9–5.*

OFF THE
BEATEN PATH

GOLDEN DOG – In the tiny village of Glenreagh about 35 km (22 mi) northwest of Coffs Harbour, the Golden Dog is a fine example of an atmospheric bush pub. The place is full of character and old local memorabilia, and it's famous for its eccentricities—you might even see a horse or motorbike in the bar! The bistro is open daily for lunch, as well as dinner on Friday and Saturday, but a particularly good time to visit is for Sunday lunch, when jazz, bush, or folk bands often perform in the beer garden. ⊠ Coramba Rd., Glenreagh, ☎ 02/6649–2162.

Dining and Lodging

$$ ✕ **Avanti.** On the High Street "Strip"—a row of a dozen restaurants near the harbor—this is a very popular place for Italian food. The decor is traditional outside-of-Italy Italian, and the menu includes a range of freshly cooked, homemade pastas. The crab ravioli is particularly recommended, and fish, meat, and chicken dishes are all available. ⊠ *396 High St.,* ☎ *02/6652–4818. AE, MC, V. BYOB. Closed Sun.*

$$ ✕ **Blue Fig Espresso Bar.** Despite its minuscule dimensions and the domestic cooking equipment, this restaurant south of Coffs Harbour has won a devoted clientele for its passionate, innovative food. Parmesan-crusted smoked sardines with eggplant jam, roast quail with roasted pumpkin and verjuice sauce, and ox fillet with a tomato and lime chutney are typical selections from a menu that does nothing by the book. ⊠ *22 1st Ave., Sawtell,* ☎ *02/6658–4334. AE, MC, V. Closed Sun. and Mon. No dinner Tues.–Wed.*

$$$ ☷ **Aanuka Beach Resort.** Clustered in cabanas amid palms, frangipani, ★   and hibiscus, each of the cedar suites at this glamorous resort has its own lounge, kitchen facilities, private laundry, and private two-person spa bath set in a glass-ceiling bathroom. All suites feature teak furniture and antiques collected from Indonesia and the South Pacific. The landscaping is highly imaginative; the pool, for example, is immersed in a miniature rain forest with a waterfall and hot tub. The resort borders a secluded white sandy beach and the blue waters of the Pacific Ocean. Rates include a tropical buffet breakfast. ⊠ *Box 6069, Firman Dr., 2540,* ☎ *02/6652–7555,* ☏ *02/6652–7053. 48 suites. 2 restaurants, 2 bars, kitchenettes, indoor pool, 4 outdoor pools, hot tub, sauna, 3 tennis courts, exercise room. AE, DC, MC, V.*

$$$ 🏨 **Pelican Beach Travelodge Resort.** This terraced beachfront complex is one of the most striking resorts on the North Coast. Spacious guest rooms are decorated in pastel colors, and each has a private balcony or patio that faces either the sea or the mountains to the west. Facilities are stylish and include a huge saltwater swimming pool resembling a tropical lagoon. Children have their own outdoor junior gym and miniature golf course. ✉ *Pacific Hwy., 2450,* ☎ *02/6653–7000,* FAX *02/6653–7066. 112 rooms. Restaurant, bar, saltwater pool, hot tub, sauna, 3 tennis courts, exercise room, children's programs, playground. AE, DC, MC, V.*

Outdoor Activities and Sports

SCUBA DIVING

The warm seas around Coffs Harbour make this particular part of the coast, with its moray eels, manta rays, turtles, and gray nurse sharks, a scuba diver's favorite. Best are the Solitary Islands, 7–21 km (4–13 mi) offshore. **Island Snorkel & Dive** (☎ 02/6654–2860) and **Dive Quest** (☎ 02/6654–1930) have equipment, dive tours, snorkeling trips, and an instruction course for novice scuba divers.

WHITE-WATER RAFTING

The highly regarded local adventure company **Wildwater Adventures** offers one-, two-, and four-day rafting trips down the Nymboida River. This is a genuine white-water river, suitable for novices but wild enough to satisfy even the most adventurous. Between shooting the rapids, the rafts travel through quiet rain forest and steep-sided gorges. Trips begin from Bonville, 14 km (9 mi) south of Coffs Harbour on the Pacific Highway, but pickups from the Coffs Harbour and Bellingen region can be arranged. ✉ *26 Butlers Rd., Bonville,* ☎ *02/6653–4469.* 💲 *1-day trip from $135, including meals.*

Shopping

Hidden by gum trees 16 km (10 mi) north of Coffs Harbour, the four-level **Lake Russell Gallery** houses a first-rate collection of contemporary Australian art and craftwork. Prices are low, and the complex includes pleasant tearooms. ✉ *Smiths Rd. and Pacific Hwy.,* ☎ *02/6656–1092.* ◷ *Daily 10–5.*

En Route   A few miles north of the Big Banana, the Pacific Highway loops through banana plantations toward the sea. A short detour off this road will take you to **Korora Bay,** a small crescent of sand cradled between rocky headlands. About 10 km (6 mi) north of Korora Bay, a wide, shallow lagoon formed by **Moonee Creek** offers safe, sheltered bathing for children. Note that the beaches between Korora Bay and Moonee are often unsafe for swimming because of wild pounding surf and the absence of lifeguards outside of school holiday periods.

About 15 km (9 mi) north is the town of **Woolgoolga**—"Woopi" to locals—known for its large Sikh population, whose ancestors came to Australia from India at the end of the 19th century. The **Guru Nanak Sikh Temple** is the town's main attraction; request entrance at the Temple View Restaurant opposite. Woolgoolga is 58 km (36 mi) from Grafton.

Grafton

②⓪   *84 km (52 mi) north of Coffs Harbour.*

This sizeable city is at the center of the Clarence Valley, a rich agricultural district with a number of sugarcane farms. The highway bypasses Grafton, but it's worth detouring to see some of the notable Victorian buildings on Fitzroy, Victoria, and Prince streets. The **Grafton**

Regional Gallery (✉ 158 Fitzroy St.) museum displays traditional and contemporary Australian arts and crafts.

Grafton is famous for its jacaranda trees, which erupt in a mass of purple flowers in the spring. During the last week of October, when the trees are at their finest, Grafton holds its **Jacaranda Festival.** The celebration includes arts-and-crafts shows, novelty races, children's rides, and a parade.

En Route   Between Grafton and the far north coast, the Pacific Highway enters sugarcane country, where tiny sugarcane trains and thick, drifting smoke from burning cane fields are ever-present. The highway passes the fishing and resort town of **Ballina,** where beaches are the prime feature; the best option is to continue north to Byron Bay.

Byron Bay

㉑ *176 km (109 mi) north of Grafton (exit right from the highway at Bangalow or Ewingsdale).*

Byron Bay is the easternmost point on the Australian mainland and perhaps earns Australia its nickname, the "Lucky Country." Fabulous beaches, storms that spin rainbows across the mountains behind the town, and a sunny, relaxed style cast a spell over practically everyone who visits. For many years Byron Bay was a mecca for surfers lured by abundant sunshine, perfect waves on Wategos Beach, and tolerant locals who allowed them to sleep on the sand. These days Byron Bay has been discovered by a more upscale clientele, but fortunately the beachfront has been spared from high-rise resorts. There are many art galleries and crafts shops to explore, and local folk offer sea kayaking and hang gliding tours. The town is at its liveliest on the first Sunday of each month, when Butler Street becomes a bustling market.

㉒ Byron Bay is dominated by the **Cape Byron Lighthouse,** (✉ Lighthouse Rd., ☎ 02/6685–8565) the most powerful beacon on the Australian coastline. The lighthouse grounds are open daily from 8 to 5:30. The headland above the parking lot near the lighthouse is a launching point for hang-gliders, who soar for hours on the warm thermals. This is also a favorite place for whale-watching between June and September, when migrating humpback whales often come close inshore. The headland is the highlight of the **Cape Byron Walking Track,** which circuits a 150-acre reserve and passes through grasslands and rain forest. There are several vantage points along the track from which you may spot dolphins in the waters below.

Several superb **beaches** lie in the vicinity of Byron Bay. In front of the town, **Main Beach** offers safe swimming, and **Clarks Beach,** closer to the cape, has better surf. The most famous surfing beach, however, is **Wategos,** the only entirely north-facing beach in the state. To the south of the lighthouse, **Tallow Beach** extends for 6 km (4 mi) to a rocky stretch of coastline around Broken Head, which features a number of small sandy coves. Beyond Broken Head is lonely **Seven Mile Beach.**

Dining and Lodging

$$$ ✕ **Fig Tree Restaurant.** In its century-old farmhouse with distant views
★   of Byron Bay and the ocean, the Fig Tree offers creative Mod Oz cuisine in magnificently forested surroundings. Produce fresh from the owners' farm stands out on a regularly changing menu that usually includes pasta dishes, seafood, and salads served with homemade bread. Ask for a table on the splendid veranda. The restaurant is 5 km (3 mi) inland from Byron Bay. ✉ *4 Sunrise La., Ewingsdale,* ☎ *02/6684-7273.*

Reservations essential. AE, DC, MC, V. BYOB. Closed Sun.–Tues. No lunch Wed.

$$$ ✕ **Misaki.** Sushi and sashimi star on a menu that takes the taste buds on a gastronomic tour of Japan. Along the way, there are a few surprising additions, such as macadamia nuts and avocados from the local plantations, and mud crabs and tuna fresh from the surrounding seas. The ambience is relaxed and friendly, and the covered courtyard is a perfect choice for warm evenings. ⊠ *Shops 1 &2, 11 Fletcher St.,* ☎ *02/6685–7966. Reservations essential. AE, DC, MC, V. Closed Sun., Mon. No lunch.*

$ ✕ **Beach Café.** A Byron Bay legend, this outdoor café is a perfect place
★ to sit in the morning sun and watch the waves. The café opens at 7:30 daily, and breakfasts are wholesome and imaginative. The fresh juices and tropical fruits alone are worth the 10-minute stroll along the beach from town. ⊠ *Clarks Beach,* ☎ *02/6685–7598. MC, V. No dinner.*

$$$ ✕🖭 **Taylors Country House.** Hidden in a jungle of strangler figs and cam-
★ phor laurel in the hills behind Byron Bay, this luxurious guest house brings sophistication to the natural charm of the North Coast. Guest rooms are large and sumptuously furnished with antiques, but the self-contained Summer House offers the ultimate luxuries: an emperor-sized bed, a spa bath, and a chef's kitchen. Breakfasts, relying on fresh fruits and eggs from the 15-acre property, are included in the rates. Gourmet dinners are served to house guests most nights. Children are not welcome. ⊠ *McGettigans La., Ewingsdale 2481,* ☎ *02/6684–7436,* 𝖥𝖠𝖷 *02/6684–7526. 5 rooms, 1 house. Saltwater pool. MC, V.*

$$$ 🖭 **On the Bay Beach House.** Overlooking Byron Bay's Main Beach, this large, modern guest house offers an exceptional standard of comfort, style, and facilities. Locally made fabrics and furniture have been used extensively throughout the house, and all guest rooms have ocean views and access to sundecks. The penthouse offers extra space and luxury at a slightly higher price. Children under 15 are not accommodated. Rates include breakfast. ⊠ *44 Lawson St. 2481,* ☎ *02/6685–5125,* 𝖥𝖠𝖷 *02/6685–5198. 5 rooms. Pool. MC, V.*

$ 🖭 **Wheel Resort.** In a secluded bushland setting adjacent to the beach, this delightful resort has facilities especially tailored to wheelchair users, but everyone is welcome here. Wide pathways afford easy access to the 6½-acre surroundings, accommodations have been modified for safety and convenience, and the pool has a gently sloping ramp. Self-contained timber cabins, available with either one or two bedrooms, have cork-tile floors, cool cream and natural wood colors, and exposed rafters. The resort is 2½ km (1½ mi) south of Byron Bay. ⊠ *39–51 Broken Head Rd. 2481,* ☎ *02/6685–6139,* 𝖥𝖠𝖷 *02/6685–8754. 6 cabins with shower. Restaurant, saltwater pool, spa. MC, V.*

Nightlife

With nine main venues, the small town of Byron Bay offers an unusually wide choice of music and entertainment every night of the week. **The Carpark** (⊠ The Plaza, Jonson St., ☎ 02/6685–6170) is a nightclub and restaurant featuring Thai and Mediterranean-style food and live bands. **Cocomangas Bar, Restaurant, and Nightclub** serves up tropical cocktails and live dance music into the wee hours Monday through Saturday. ⊠ 32 Jonson St., ☎ 02/6685–8493.

Scuba Diving

The **Byron Bay Dive Centre** offers snorkeling and scuba-diving trips for all levels of experience, plus gear rental and instruction. The best local diving is at Julian Rocks, some 3 km (2 mi) offshore, where the confluence of warm and cold currents supports a profusion of marine life. ⊠ 111 Jonson St., Byron Bay, ☎ 02/6685–7149.

Shopping

Byron Bay is one of the state's arts and craft centers, with many innovative and high-quality items for sale, such as leather goods, offbeat designer clothing, essential oils, natural cosmetics, and ironware.

Colin Heaney Hot Glass Studio. Exquisite hand-blown glass goblets, wineglasses, paperweights, and sculpture are sold here, but another attraction is watching the glassblowers at work (weekdays 9–4). ⊠ *6 Acacia St., Industrial Estate,* ☎ *02/6685–7044.* ⊙ *Weekdays 9–5, weekends 10–4.*

Mullumbimby

❷❸ *23 km (14 mi) northwest of Byron Bay.*

Affectionately known as "Mullum," Mullumbimby is a peaceful inland town with several historic buildings, interesting arts and crafts shops, and a reputation for attracting alternative-lifestyle types. The town is at the center of a fertile banana and subtropical fruit-growing region, well worth a short detour off the Pacific Highway.

Dining and Lodging

$$$$ ✕☷ **Sakura Farm.** Genzan Kosaka, the owner, is a Zen Buddhist priest, and a stay at his farm is a unique experience of Japanese culture. Guest quarters are pristine and Western-style, either in a three-bedroom house or in a newer, cozier two-bedroom lodge that offers a higher level of privacy. The chance to sample authentic Japanese cooking is a big attraction, but chef Seiko Kosaka also prepares French meals from time to time. Other options include shiatsu massage, instruction in Buddhist meditation, and taking Japanese-style open-air baths. Rates include all meals. ⊠ *Left Bank Rd., Lot 5 2482,* ☎ FAX *02/6684–1724. 2 cottages. Japanese baths, massage, hiking. MC, V.*

Murwillumbah

❷❹ *53 km (33 mi) northwest of Byron Bay.*

Dominated by the towering, cone-shape peak of 3,800-ft Mount Warning, pleasant, rambling Murwillumbah rests amid sugarcane plantations on the banks of the Tweed River. Apart from the seaside resort of Tweed Heads, Murwillumbah is the last town of any size before the Queensland border.

❷❺ At the **Condong Sugar Mill,** on the banks of the Tweed River 5 km (3 mi) north of town, you can take an informative tour during the crushing season, July–November. The one-hour visit includes a video and a hands-on tour of the mill, during which you are invited to sample sugar and some of the other products manufactured at the complex. ⊠ *Pacific Hwy., Murwillumbah,* ☎ *02/6670–1700.* ☐ *$5.* ⊙ *July–Nov., daily 9–3, weather permitting.*

North Coast A to Z

Arriving and Departing

BY BUS

Greyhound Pioneer Australia (☎ 13–2030), **McCafferty's** (☎ 13–1499), and **Pioneer Motor Service** (☎ 02/9281–2233) frequently run between Sydney and Brisbane, with stops at all major North Coast towns. Sydney to Coffs Harbour is a 9-hour ride, Byron Bay takes 12.

BY CAR

From Sydney, head north via the Harbour Bridge or Harbour Tunnel and follow the signs to Hornsby and Newcastle. Join the Sydney–Newcastle Freeway, then continue up the Pacific Highway (Hwy. 1), the main route along the 604-km (375-mi) Taree-to-Queensland coast. Taree is 335 km (208 mi) north of Sydney.

BY PLANE
From Sydney, **Ansett Australia** (☎ 13–1300) and its subsidiaries **Impulse** and **Hazelton** operate frequent services to Port Macquarie, Kempsey, Coffs Harbour, Ballina (close to Byron Bay), and Coolangatta (just over the Queensland border, but convenient for the far north of New South Wales). **Qantas Airways** and its subsidiary **Eastern Australia Airlines** (☎ 13–1313) fly into Taree, Port Macquarie, Kempsey, Coffs Harbour, Grafton, and Coolangatta.

BY TRAIN
Trains stop at Taree, Kempsey, Coffs Harbour, Grafton, Byron Bay, and Murwillumbah, but much of the Sydney–Brisbane railway line runs inland and the service is not particularly useful for seeing the North Coast. Call **Countrylink** (☎ 13–2232), the New South Wales rail operator, for fare and service details.

Getting Around
The long-distance buses mentioned above are more than adequate for travel between the coast's main centers, and all of the larger towns provide local bus services. Bus travel, however, is not recommended for getting off the beaten track or exploring beyond the major towns. A car is essential for touring the North Coast's off-highway attractions and traveling at your own pace.

Contacts and Resources

CAR RENTALS
Car-rental agencies here are: **Avis** (⊠ Ballina, ☎ 02/6686–7650; ⊠ Coffs Harbour, ☎ 02/6651–3600), **Budget** (⊠ Coffs Harbour, ☎ 02/6651–4994), **Hertz** (⊠ Byron Bay, ☎ 02/6685–6522; ⊠ Coffs Harbour, ☎ 02/6651–1899; ⊠ Port Macquarie, ☎ 02/6583–6599). You can also rent a car in Sydney to make the drive up the coast (☞ Sydney A to Z *in* Chapter 1).

EMERGENCIES
Ambulance, fire brigade, and police. ☎ *000.*

GUIDED TOURS
Macquarie Mountain Tours (☎ 02/6585–9242) offers a full-day, four-wheel-drive trip into the rain forest surrounding **Port Macquarie.** The tour costs $80. A barbecue lunch is included. **Mountain Trails 4WD Tours** (☎ 02/6658–3333) offers half- and full-day tours of the rain forests and waterfalls of the Great Dividing Range to the west of **Coffs Harbour** in luxurious transport—a seven-seat Toyota Safari or a 14-seat, Australian-designed four-wheel-drive vehicle. The region is rich in natural and historic attractions, and the award-winning tours have a long-standing reputation for excellence. The half-day tour costs $56 and the full-day tour is $80, including lunch and morning and afternoon snacks.

VISITOR INFORMATION
Byron Bay Visitor Information Centre. ⊠ *Jonson St.,* ☎ *02/6685–8050.* ⊙ *Daily 9–5.*

Coffs Harbour Visitor Information Centre. ⊠ *Rose Ave. and Marcia St.,* ☎ *02/6652–1522 or 1800/02–5650.* ⊙ *Daily 9–5.*

Murwillumbah Visitors Centre. ⊠ *Pacific Hwy. and Alma St.,* ☎ *1800/67–4414 or 02/6672–1340.* ⊙ *Mon.–Sat. 9–4, Sun. 9–3.*

Port Macquarie Visitor Information Centre. ☎ *1800/02–5935 or 02/ 6581–8000.* ⊙ *Weekdays 8:30–5, weekends 9–4.*

Sydney Visitors Information Centre has information on North Coast accommodation, tours, and sights. ✉ *106 George St., the Rocks, Sydney 2000,* ☎ *02/9255–1788,* ℻ *02/9241–5010.* ⊙ *Daily 9–6.*

LORD HOWE ISLAND

By David
McGonigal

Updated by
Michael
Gebicki

A tiny crescent of land 782 km (485 mi) northeast of Sydney, Lord Howe Island is the most remote and arguably the most beautiful part of New South Wales. With the sheer peaks of Mount Gower (2,870 ft) and Mount Lidgbird (2,548 ft) richly clad in palms, ferns, and grasses, its golden sandy beaches, and the clear turquoise waters of the lagoon, this is a remarkably lovely place. Apart from the barren spire of Ball's Pyramid, a stark volcanic outcrop 16 km (10 mi) across the water to the southeast, the Lord Howe Island Group stands alone in the South Pacific. In 1982 the area was placed on UNESCO's World Heritage list as a "natural area of universal value and outstanding beauty." That's a fair assessment of why it is a favorite among certain Australians trying to get away from it all—and why they've been keeping it to themselves for so long.

Not only is the island beautiful, but its history is fascinating. It may be that the first ship to sight it did so in 1788, when it passed by on its way to the Norfolk Island penal settlement farther out in the Pacific. And evidence, or lack of it, suggests that Lord Howe was uninhabited by humans until three Europeans and their Maori wives and children settled it in the 1830s. English and American whaling boats then began calling in for supplies, and by the 1870s the small population included a curious mixture of people from America (including whalers and a former slave), England, Ireland, Australia, South Africa, and the Gilbert Islands. Many of the descendants of these early settlers still live on Lord Howe. In the 1870s, when the importance of whale oil declined, islanders set up an export industry of the seeds of the endemic Kentia (*Howea forsteriana*), the world's most popular indoor palm. It's still a substantial business, but rather than seeds, seedlings are now sold.

Lord Howe is a remarkably safe and relaxed place, where cyclists and walkers far outnumber the few cars, and where locals and visitors alike leave doors unlocked and bags unattended. There are plenty of walks, both flat and rather precipitous, and fine beaches. Among the many bird species is the rare, endangered, flightless Lord Howe woodhen (*Tricholimnas sylvestris*). In the sea below the island's fringing reef is the world's southernmost coral reef, with more than 50 species of hard corals and over 500 fish species. For its size, the island has enough to keep you alternately occupied and unoccupied for at least five days. It even boasts a dining scene of an unexpectedly high quality.

Less than 300 people live here, which is part of the reason that much of the island shows so little impact from its 150-plus years of sustained human habitation. Visitor numbers are limited to 400 at any given time, though at present hotel beds can only accommodate 393 tourists. The allocation of those remaining seven tourists is the subject of local controversy.

Exploring

The first view of Lord Howe Island rising sheer out of the South Pacific is spectacular. The sense of wonder only grows as you set out to explore the island, which, at a total area of 3,220 acres (about 1 mi by 7 mi), is pretty manageable. You don't have to allow much time to see the town; most of the community is scattered along the rolling hills at the northern end of the island. There's a school, a hospital, a few shops, and three churches. Everything else is either a home or lodge.

As one of the very few impediments to winds sweeping across the South Pacific, the mountains of Lord Howe Island create their own weather. Visually, this can be spectacular as you stand in sunshine on the coast watching cap clouds gather around the high peaks. The average annual rainfall of about 62 inches mostly comes down in winter. Note that, except during the period of Australia's summer daylight saving time (when Lord Howe and Sydney are on the same time), island time is a curious half hour ahead of Sydney. It's also important to be aware that many of the lodges, restaurants, and tour operators close in winter—generally from June through August—and accommodation prices are reduced considerably during that period.

Sights to See

In town, a good first stop is the **Lord Howe Museum.** The sign on the door is typical of the island's sense of time—"The museum is staffed entirely by volunteers . . . if there is no one in attendance by 2:15 pm it should be assumed that the museum will not be open on that day." Inside there's an interesting display of historical memorabilia and a less impressive collection of marine life and stuffed land animals. ✉ Lagoon Rd. 💺 $4. ⊙ Daily 2–4.

A very enjoyable way of filling a sunny day is to take a picnic down to **Neds Beach,** on the eastern side of the island, where you'll find green lawns sloping down to a sandy beach and clear blue waters. This is a fantastic place for swimming and snorkeling—fish swim close to the shore, and the coral is just a few yards out.

There are many **walks** around the island: short, moderate, and considerable. The short to moderate category includes a flat, easy walk around forested **Stevens Reserve,** right in the heart of town; trips to surf-pounded **Blinky Beach,** to great views from the **Clear Place** and at **Middle Beach;** and to a good snorkeling spot under the heights of Mount Gower by **Little Island.** The moderate climbs up **Mount Eliza** and **Malabar** at the island's northern end are more strenuous than the other walks, although much less so than Mount Gower, and they afford tremendous views of the island, including its hulking, mountainous southern end and the waters and islets all around.

The ultimate challenge on Lord Howe is the climb up the southernmost peak of **Mt. Gower,** which rises straight out of the ocean to an astonishing 2,870 ft above sea level. National park regulations require that you use a guide when climbing Mt. Gower. Jack Shick (☎ 02/6563–2218) is a highly recommended guide who makes the climb on Monday and Thursday in summer. The cost is $25. Meet at Little Island Gate at 7:30 AM sharp—reservations are not required, but you'll need to bring lunch and drinks, and wear a jacket and sturdy walking shoes. After a scramble along the shore, the ascent into the forest begins. There's time for a break at the Erskine River crossing by some pretty cascades, then it's a solid march to the summit. The views, the lush vegetation, and the chance to see the rare island woodhen all make the hike worthwhile.

Dining and Lodging

$$ ✕ **Aunty Sue's.** This delightful restaurant just beyond the village proper has indoor and outdoor dining. The decor is light and modern, with

polished floorboards and painted timber walls, and the covered deck overlooks lush gardens. Marcia Branson, previously executive chef at an acclaimed Sydney restaurant, creates delicious modern Australian dishes with fresh, island-grown produce. Dine on chili salt squid, roasted de-boned quail with couscous and currant stuffing, or seafood and saffron pie. Desserts might include Greek walnut cake or warm apple tart with ice cream. ⊠ *Anderson Rd.,* ☎ *02/6563–2093. AE, MC, V. Closed Mon., Wed.*

$$ ✗ **Beachcomber Lodge.** If you prefer traditional home-cooked fare, the Beachcomber provides a good-value buffet of hot and cold dishes in its licensed dining room on Thursday evening, as well as a popular "island fish fry" dinner on Sunday. The locally caught fish is cooked in beer batter and accompanied by chips and salads. Main courses are followed by a variety of desserts, a cheese platter, and coffee. ⊠ *Anderson Rd.,* ☎ *02/6563–2032. AE, DC, MC, V.*

$ ✗ **Trader Nick's Lagoon Café.** The meals at this bright, modern, and totally indoor café are generous and well priced, with child-size portions available. Many guests drop in for tea or coffee and cake, but the café serves beer, wine, and cocktails as well. Salads, nachos, pizzas, and antipasto plates are available, as are fish-and-chips, enormous burgers, and chicken tortillas. The café is open daily 9–5. ⊠ *Lagoon Rd.,* ☎ *02/6563–2019. AE, MC, V.*

$$$$ ✗⊞ **Capella Lodge.** Lord Howe's most luxurious accommodation may seem a bit out of the way on the island's south end, but you'll be rewarded by truly dramatic views. The lodge's veranda looks over beaches, the ocean, and the lofty peaks of Mount Lidgbird and Mount Gower. The nine high-ceiling guest suites are tastefully decorated with unique textiles and shuttered doors that let light in while maintaining privacy. The equally stylish **White Gallinule Restaurant**—the best on the island—serves all guest meals. Presentation is excellent, and the menu changes daily. Nonguests can come for dinner, too; call ahead for reservations (☎ 02/6563–2008). The owners also operate the luxurious Capella Apartments at the other end of the island. Rates include breakfast. ⊠ *Lagoon Rd. 2898,* ☎ *Sydney booking office: 02/9290–1922,* ℻ *02/9290–1615. 9 rooms. Restaurant, bar, snorkeling, canoeing, mountain bikes. AE, MC, V.*

$$$ ✗⊞ **Trader Nick's.** This intimate retreat is tucked away at the north end of the island. Set in tropical gardens, the spacious, self-contained suites and one- and two-bedroom apartments are beautifully decorated and feature well-equipped kitchens, separate lounge areas, and private decks—there are no televisions to disturb the tranquillity. Mountain bikes are available for hire, and a complimentary transport service is also available. Guests and nonresidents can dine at the excellent **Williams Restaurant** (☎ 02/6563–2002), which serves fine wine and light modern cuisine nightly. Hydroponic lettuces and herbs are grown on the property, and all cakes, breads, and pastas are made at the restaurant. Rates include a full breakfast. ⊠ *Old Settlement Beach, 2898,* ☎ *Sydney booking office: 02/9299–2211,* ℻ *02/9299–4644. 6 suites, 4 apartments. Restaurant, bar, kitchenettes, snorkeling, fishing. AE, MC, V.*

$$ ✗⊞ **Pinetrees.** Run by descendants of the island's first settlers, this is the largest resort on the island and one of the few that stays open all year. The original 1884 homestead forms part of this centrally located resort, but most accommodations are in undistinguished motel-style units, which have verandas leading into pleasant gardens. Five Garden Cottages are a cut above the other rooms, and two luxury one-bedroom suites were added in 1998. At **Pinetrees Restaurant** (☎ 02/6563–2177), you have a selection from a limited but well-balanced menu at each meal. Dinner, for example, might feature seared local tuna with snow pea and celeriac salad, veal piccata with herb pasta and sweet pepper sauce, or grilled kingfish with roast tomatoes and salsa verde. Nonguests are welcome to dine at Pinetrees. Rates include all meals. Credit cards are accepted for advance reservations only, not for use on the island. ✉ *Lagoon Rd., 2898,* ☎ *02/9262–6585,* ⅣⅩ *02/9262– 6638. 31 rooms with shower, 2 suites. Restaurant, bar, tennis court, billiards. AE, DC, MC, V.*

$$$ ⊡ **Somerset.** Set in subtropical gardens, this self-catering lodge was established by the descendants of whaler Nathan Chase Thompson, who was born in Somerset, Massachusetts, and was one of Lord Howe's early settlers. Although not overly luxurious, the spacious units have televisions, ceiling fans, and kitchenettes, plus separate living rooms and private verandas. The grounds contain pleasant barbecue areas and free laundry facilities. Bikes, helmets, and snorkeling gear are available for rental. The lodge is in an ideal location, close to town and walking distance from excellent beaches. ✉ *Neds Beach Rd., Lord Howe Island 2898,* ☎ *02/6563–2061,* ⅣⅩ *02/6563–2110. 25 apartments. Kitchenettes. AE, MC, V.*

Outdoor Activities and Sports

Fishing
Fishing is a major activity on Lord Howe. There are several well-equipped boats that regularly go out for kingfish, yellowfin tuna, marlin, and wahoo. These include the **Belle Chase** (☎ 02/6563–2032), **MV Barracuda** (☎ 02/6563–2155 or 02/6563–2185), and **TSMV Lulawai** (☎ 02/6563–2010). A half-day trip, including tackle and bait, costs around $65. It's best to arrange an excursion as soon as possible after arriving on the island.

Golf
Visitors are welcome at the spectacularly located nine-hole **Lord Howe Island Golf Club,** and you can rent clubs and carts. ☎ *02/6563–2054 or 02/6563–2195.* ▨ *Greens fee $20 for 9 or 18 holes.*

Scuba Diving
The reefs of Lord Howe Island provide a unique opportunity for diving in coral far from the equator and, unlike many of the Queensland islands, superb diving and snorkeling is literally just offshore, rather than a long boat trip away. Even though the water is warm enough for coral, however, most divers use a 5mm wetsuit. It's all boat diving with good equipment, operated by **Pro Dive** under the expert eye of Jeff Deacon. Although you won't find the Barrier Reef's profusion of coral, you'll still see fine displays of plate coral, black coral trees, and an impressive array of fish—from lion fish and bull rays to leopard fish, box fish, and the ubiquitous parrot fish. Dives can be arranged any day; in mid-summer there are up to four trips daily. Although certified divers are catered to throughout the winter, dive courses are not operated in June and July. If you are going to Lord Howe specifically for diving, contact **Pro Dive Travel** (☎ 02/9232–5733 or 1800/80–6820, ⅣⅩ 02/9232–5788) in Sydney, which has packages that include accommodations, airfares, and diving.

Snorkeling
If you're not interested in diving, snorkeling is also excellent off Lord Howe Island. The best spots are on the reef that fringes the lagoon, at Neds Beach and North Bay, and around the Sylph Hole off Old Settlement Beach—a spot that turtles frequent. Snorkeling gear can be rented from your lodge. A good way to get to the reef, and view the coral en route, is on a glass-bottom boat trip—both the **Blue Petrel** and **Coral Princess** offer two-hour cruises that include snorkeling gear in the $15 charge.

Lord Howe Island A to Z

Arriving and Departing

BY PLANE

Unless you have your own boat, the only practical way of getting to Lord Howe Island is by **Qantas** (☎ 13–1313) from Brisbane or Sydney. In both cases, the flying time is about two hours. Your hosts on Lord Howe Island will pick you up from the airport. There is a $20 Island Service Levy (paid on departure) per adult, and you should note that the baggage allowance is only 31 lbs per person. Special discounts on airfares to the island are often available for overseas visitors if you purchase tickets outside of Australia.

Getting Around

BY BICYCLE

Despite the island's hills and high peaks, much of the terrain is fairly flat, and bicycles are the ideal form of transport. These can be hired at your lodge, or from **Wilson's Hire Service** on Lagoon Road, for approximately $4 per day. By law, helmets must be worn, and they are supplied with the bikes.

BY CAR

There are just six rental cars on the island. Your lodge can arrange one for you (if any are available) for about $50 per day. However, with 24 km (15 mi) of roads on the island, even cutting the 24 kph (15 mph) maximum permissible driving speed in half, you'll soon run out of places to go.

Contacts and Resources

EMERGENCIES

Ambulance, fire brigade, and police. ☎ *000.*

Doctor. ☎ *02/6563–2056.*

Hospital. ⊠ *Lagoon Rd.,* ☎ *02/6563–2000.*

GUIDED TOURS

Ron's Ramble (☎ 02/6563–2010) is a scenic and highly informative three-hour stroll ($12.50) around a small section of the island, with knowledgeable guide Ron Matthews explaining much about Lord Howe's geology, history, and plant and animal life. Groups are limited to 16 people, and the relaxed pace makes the walk suitable for all ages. The rambles take place on Monday, Wednesday, and Friday afternoons. **Islander Cruises** (☎ 02/6563–2021) has several tours around the island, including ferries and cruises to North Bay for snorkeling and, weather permitting, a two-hour sunset cocktail cruise on the lagoon. Prices range from $10 to $20 round-trip, and private charters are also available. **Whitfield's Island Tours** (☎ 02/6563–2115) runs a half-day air-conditioned bus tour ($18) that provides a good overview of the island's history and present-day life. The tours include morning or afternoon tea at the Whitfield home. Tours operate Monday, Wednesday, and Friday.

MONEY MATTERS

Although most major credit cards are accepted, there are no ATMs on the island and visitors should carry adequate cash or traveler's checks in addition to their credit cards.

VISITOR INFORMATION

Contact the **Lord Howe Island Board** (⊠ Lord Howe Island, NSW 2898, ☎ 02/6563–2066, FAX 02/6563–2127) for advance information on the island. Although Lord Howe has a **visitor center** (☎ 02/6563–2114), open weekdays from 9 to 12:30, with general information, most of the tours and activities should be arranged through **Thompson's Store** on Neds Beach Road, the **Lagoon Cafe** on Lagoon Road, or **Joy's Shop** on Middle Beach Road. A notice board outside the visitors center indicates which trips should be booked where.

Sydney Visitors Information Centre. ✉ *106 George St., the Rocks, Sydney 2000,* ☎ *02/9255–1788,* 🆇 *02/9241–5010.* ⊙ *Daily 9–6.*

THE SNOWY MOUNTAINS

Down by Kosciuszko, where the pine-clad ridges raise

Their torn and rugged battlements on high,

Where the air is clear as crystal, and the white stars fairly blaze,

At midnight in the cold and frosty sky . . .

Banjo Paterson's 1890 poem, "The Man from Snowy River," tells of life in the Snowy Mountains—the hard life, to be sure, but with its own beauty and great reward. It's still possible to experience the world that Paterson described, by visiting any of the hundred-odd old settlers' huts scattered throughout the Snowys. Hike the mountains and valleys with camera in hand, and breathe deeply the crystal-clear air.

Reaching north from the border with Victoria, this section of the Great Dividing Range is an alpine wonderland. The entire region is part of Kosciuszko (pronounced "koh-shoosh-ko") National Park, the largest alpine area in Australia, which occupies a 6,764-square-km (2,600-sq-mi) chunk of New South Wales. The national park also contains Australia's highest point in Mt. Kosciuszko, which reaches a modest—on a worldwide scale—7,314 ft. Mountain peaks and streams, high meadows, forests, caves, glacial lakes, and wildflowers provide for a wealth of outdoor activities.

This wilderness area is perfect for cross-country skiing in winter and, in other seasons, for walking and all kinds of adventure activities. The many self-guided walking trails are excellent, especially the popular Mount Kosciuszko summit walk (☞ **Thredbo Village**). In addition, local operators, and others based in Sydney, offer hiking, climbing, mountain biking, white-water rafting, and horseback riding tours and excursions.

A number of lakes—Jindabyne, Eucumbene, Tooma, and Tumut Pond reservoirs—and the Murray River provide excellent trout fishing opportunities. Khancoban's lake is a favorite for anglers, and Adaminaby is another fishing center. Tackle can be rented in a few towns, and a local operator offers excursions and instruction. The trout fishing season extends from the beginning of October to early June.

Although the downhill skiing isn't what Americans and Europeans are used to, the gentle slopes and relatively light snowfalls are perfect for cross-country skiing. Trails from Cabramurra, Kiandra, Perisher Valley, Charlotte Pass, and Thredbo are very good; don't hesitate to ask locals about their favorites. The ski season officially runs from the June holiday weekend (second weekend of the month) to the October holiday weekend (first weekend).

Après-ski action in the Snowys is focused on the hotels in Thredbo, the large Perisher Blue resort, and the subalpine town of Jindabyne. Most hotel bars have live music in the evenings during the ski season, ranging from solo-piano to jazz to rock bands. Thredbo tends toward the cosmopolitan end of the scale, and Jindabyne makes up with energy what it lacks in sophistication. Note, however, that many of the hotels close from October through May (room rates are considerably cheaper during these months in hotels that stay open), and nightlife is much quieter outside of the ski season.

This itinerary loops through the middle of Kosciuszko National Park, beginning and ending at the region's main town of Cooma. Allow at least a few days for the round-trip, part of which follows slower but very scenic gravel roads. Or use Cooma, Jindabyne, or Thredbo as bases for exploring the area. If you plan to see the Yarrangobilly Caves, you may want to drive there straight from Cooma on the Snowy Mountains Highway. Bear in mind that the national park is about 305 km (190 mi) closer to Canberra than to Sydney, and be sure to call ahead to confirm snow conditions if you intend to ski.

Note: For information on local outdoor outfitters, *see* Chapter 12.

Numbers in the margin correspond to points of interest on the North Coast map.

Cooma

㉖ *419 km (260 mi) southwest of Sydney, 114 km (71 mi) south of Canberra.*

The gateway to the Snowy Mountains and the ideal place to gather some information on the region (from the visitors center), Cooma is a relatively attractive town with some interesting, albeit recent, history. Cooma is the headquarters for the **Snowy Mountains Hydroelectric Authority.** Between 1949 and 1974, over 100,000 people from more than 30 different countries were employed in the construction of the Snowy Mountains Hydroelectric Scheme. The 16 major dams, 7 power stations, lakes, tunnels, and pipelines that make up the extensive scheme can generate almost 4 million kilowatts of electricity, which is distributed to Victoria, South Australia, New South Wales, and the Australian Capital Territory.

The Snowy Mountains Hydroelectric Authority's **Snowy Information Centre** offers films and displays that explain the technical workings of this huge, complicated project—one of the world's modern engineering wonders. There are also three power stations in the Snowy Mountains region (including those at Khancoban and Cabramurra; ☞ *below*) that are open for visits and tours; bookings can be made at the center in Cooma. ✉ *Monaro Hwy., Cooma,* ☎ *02/6453–2004 or 1800/62–3776.* ⊙ *Weekdays 8–5, weekends 8–1.*

Fishing
Based in Cooma, the **Alpine Angler** (☎ 02/6452–5538) has trout fly-fishing excursions for novices and advanced anglers throughout the Snowy Mountains region. Lessons, equipment, transportation, and even accommodation are available.

Jindabyne

㉗ *63 km (39 mi) south of Cooma.*

This resort town was built in the 1960s on the shores of Lake Jindabyne, a man-made lake that flooded the original town when the Snowy River was dammed. In summer, there is a variety of outdoor activities centering on the lake, and plenty of hiking, boating, and fishing equipment is available to rent or buy if you need it. For information on park trails and activities, stop in at the **Snowy Region Visitor Centre** (☎ 02/6450–5600), located in the center of Jindabyne on the main Kosciuszko Road. Here you can find information on hikes, flora and fauna, and all that **Kosciuszko National Park** has to offer. In win-

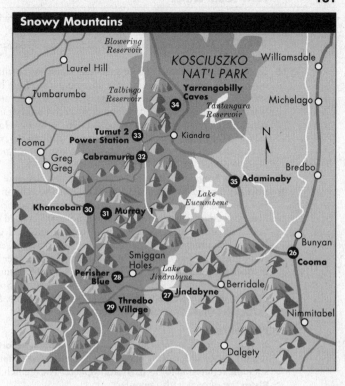

Snowy Mountains

ter, Jindabyne becomes a major base for budget skiers, with plenty of inexpensive local chalets and apartments.

Dining and Lodging

$$ ✗ **Balcony Bistro.** Huge steaks and seafood platters are the house specials at this very popular restaurant—on busy winter nights you'll have to wait in line to grill your selections. The bistro is small, dark, and intimate, and on a balcony above the dining area is a bar with some tables on a covered deck overlooking Lake Jindabyne. During ski season, Balcony Bistro doubles as a nightclub. ⊠ *Old Town Centre, Level 3,* ☎ *02/6456–2144. AE, DC, MC, V. No lunch.*

$$ ✗ **Crackenback Cottage.** On the road to Thredbo on the outskirts of Jindabyne, this stone-and-timber bistro glows with rustic warmth. Expect generous servings of traditional favorites—soup, salad, roasts, pie, and mountain trout—as well as wood-fired pizzas with such innovative toppings as local smoked trout or goat cheese. The restaurant also serves scones and afternoon tea, but it is famous for its *gluhwein* (mulled wine) and Australia's largest selection of schnapps. ⊠ *Alpine Way, Thredbo Valley,* ☎ *02/6456–2198. AE, DC, MC, V. No dinner Sun.–Tues.*

$ ✗ **Brumby Bar and Bistro.** Only the lighting is subdued in this lively bistro, which is as popular for its live entertainment as it is for its food. The menu includes grilled steaks, chicken, beef Stroganoff, panfried trout and other seafood, lasagna, and schnitzels. Help yourself to the salad and vegetable bar. ⊠ *Alpine Gables Motel, Kalkite St. and Kosciuszko Rd.,* ☎ *02/6456–2526. Reservations not accepted. AE, MC, V.*

$$$ 🏨 **Station Resort.** Set on 50 tranquil rural acres and accommodating over 1,400 guests, this is by far the largest resort in the Snowy Mountains. Popular with the under-35s and families, the hotel offers relatively inexpensive lodging, spacious and comfortable rooms, and dining choices of a bistro, a grill, or a pizza station. Guest rooms sleep from two to seven people. A daily shuttle service connects the hotel with the

Skitube Terminal. Rates can include meals and ski lift tickets. The resort is 6 km (4 mi) from Jindabyne. ⊠ *Dalgety Rd., 2627,* ☏ *02/6456–2895,* ℻ *02/6456–2544. 250 rooms with shower. 3 restaurants, 2 bars, nightclub. AE, DC, MC, V.*

$$ 🏨 **Alpine Gables Motel.** These split-level suites in the village of Jindabyne each have a kitchenette, a lounge, and a separate bedroom upstairs. The modern decor makes extensive use of wood and glass, and warm earth tones predominate. Suites can accommodate up to six people. ⊠ *Kalkite St. and Kosciuszko Rd., 2627,* ☏ *02/6456–2555,* ℻ *02/6456–2815. 42 rooms. Restaurant, bar, kitchenettes, room service sauna, spa, ski shop, recreation room, laundry service and dry cleaning, car rental. AE, DC, MC, V.*

$ 🏨 **Eagles Range.** The two cedar lodges on this 300-acre sheep ranch
★ offer perhaps the best combination of comfort and value in the Snowys. For families or small groups, self-catering accommodations are available in a three-bedroom lodge. Other guests are housed on a dinner, bed, and breakfast basis in the two-story Homestead guest house. Both are charmingly rustic, with exposed wood rafters, country-style furniture, and views of the surrounding ranges. The larger building has an open fireplace, and the smaller one has a wood-burning stove. The property is about 12 km (7½ mi) from Jindabyne. ⊠ *Box 298, Dalgety Rd., Jindabyne 2627,* ☏ ℻ *02/6456–2728. 4 rooms, 1 3-bedroom lodge. Spa, horseback riding, mountain bikes. MC, V.*

Nightlife

In winter, the nightclub and bars inside the **Station Resort** (☞ *above*) usually rock until at least 1 AM, and the **Jindabyne Hotel** has a long-standing reputation for its party atmosphere. The nightclub at **Balcony Bistro** (☞ *above*) is also popular.

Outdoor Outfitters

Paddy Pallin is a clothing and equipment specialist for outdoor adventurers. In addition to retail sales, the shop also rents out everything needed for a week in the wilderness, from Gore-Tex jackets to mountain bikes and all kinds of ski gear. The shop also has guided expeditions of all kinds (☞ Guided Tours *in* Snowy Mountains A to Z, *below*). ⊠ *Kosciuszko Rd., Thredbo turnoff,* ☏ *02/6456–2922.*

BP Ski Hire (⊠ BP Service Station, Kosciuszko Rd., Jindabyne, ☏ 02/ 6456–1959) rents snowboards and downhill or cross-country skis and equipment. The same equipment is available in Thredbo Village from **Thredbo Sports** (☞ *below*).

En Route From Jindabyne, divergent roads lead to two major destinations for walking, skiing, and generally exploring magnificent Kosciuszko National Park. One is Kosciuszko Road, which takes you to the northern route and Perisher Blue, and the other is the Alpine Way to the Skitube Terminal and Thredbo Village.

Kosciuszko Road heads north to Sawpit Creek, from which point you need snow chains between June 1 and October 10. Rent chains from gas stations in Cooma and Jindabyne. This road continues to the vast ☞ **Perisher Blue** ski region (including the resorts of Smiggin Holes, Perisher Valley, Mount Blue Cow, and Guthega), as well as the less-commercial skiing area around **Charlotte Pass,** which is at the very end of the road but accessible by over-snow transport during winter. There are several excellent walks from Charlotte Pass, including a particularly scenic 10-km (6-mi) round-trip walk to **Blue Lake**, part of a 21-km (13-mi) loop that connects a number of peaks and a couple of other glacial lakes, and a more strenuous 18-km (11-mi) round-trip walk to the summit of Mount Kosciuszko.

In the other direction from Jindabyne, the **Alpine Way** runs southwest to **Thredbo Village** and past the **Skitube Terminal** at Bullocks Flat, approximately 21 km (13 mi) from Jindabyne. The 8-km (5-mi) **Skitube** (☎ 02/6456–2010) has an underground-overground shuttle train that transports skiers to the terminals at Perisher (10 minutes) and Mount Blue Cow (19 minutes). The service operates 24 hours daily in winter, and is open year-round.

Perisher Blue

㉘ *30 km (19 mi) west of Jindabyne.*

The four adjoining skiing areas of Smiggin Holes, Perisher Valley, Mount Blue Cow, and Guthega have merged to become the megaresort of "Perisher Blue." This is the largest snowfield in Australia, with 50 lifts and T-bars that serve all standards of slopes, as well as over 100 km (62 mi) of cross-country trails. Because it is a snowfield area— at 1,700 m (5,575 ft) above sea level—Perisher Blue virtually closes down between October and May. Some lodges and cafés do stay open, especially around the Christmas holidays.

Dining and Lodging

$$$$ ✗⊞ **Perisher Valley Hotel.** With a location on the slopes of Perisher Blue, this is a true "ski-in and ski-out" hotel. Each of the 31 luxurious suites accommodate between two and six people, and gourmet meals are served in its Snowgums Restaurant, which has stunning views of the mountain scenery. Renowned for its outstanding service and facilities, the hotel is open only during the ski season. Rates include breakfast, dinner, and over-snow transport to the hotel. ⊠ *Mount Kosciuszko Rd., Perisher Valley 2624,* ☎ *02/6459–4455,* ℻ *02/6457–5177. 31 suites. 2 restaurants, 2 bars, sauna, spa, ski shop, ski storage, shops, laundry service and dry cleaning. AE, DC, MC, V. Closed Oct.–May.*

$$–$$$ ⊞ **Perisher Manor.** Rooms at this ski-in, ski-out hotel vary from budget level to stylish, deluxe accommodations with views. All rooms are centrally heated and very comfortable, and the hotel has 24-hour reception, a lobby lounge with an open fireplace, drying rooms, and ski lockers. It is open only in ski season. ⊠ *Perisher Valley Rd., Perisher Valley 2624,* ☎ *02/6457–5291,* ℻ *02/6457–5064. 49 rooms. Restaurant, café, 2 bars, ski storage, children's programs. AE, MC, V. Closed Oct.–May.*

Nightlife

Perisher Manor stages rock bands throughout the ski season. If you want to join the après-ski set, drop in at the cocktail bar of the **Perisher Valley Hotel.**

Skiing

Lift tickets for use at any of the **Perisher Blue** (☎ 02/6459–4495) ski areas are $65 per day, $270 for five days. From the Bullocks Flat Skitube Terminal, combined Skitube and lift tickets are $77 per day. From here, skiers can schuss down the mountain to a choice of four high-speed quad chairlifts and a double chair. **Blue Cow** has a good choice of beginner- and intermediate-level runs, but no accommodations are available.

Thredbo Village

㉙ *32 km (20 mi) southwest of Jindabyne.*

Nestled in a valley at the foot of the Crackenback Ridge, this resort has a European feeling that is unique on the Australian snowfields. In addition to having some of the best skiing in the country, this is an all-seasons resort with bushwalking, fly fishing, canoeing, white-water rafting, tennis courts, mountain-bike trails, a nine-hole golf course, and a 2,300-ft-long alpine slide. The pollution-free, high-country environment is also the home of the Australian Institute of Sport's Thredbo Alpine Training Centre, which was primarily designed for elite athletes but is now open to the public. Facilities include an Olympic-sized swimming pool; a running track; squash, basketball, badminton, volleyball, and netball courts; and a well-equipped gymnasium. The altitude at Thredbo Village is 1,370 m (5,000 ft) above sea level.

The **Crackenback Chairlift** provides easy access to Mount Kosciuszko, Australia's tallest peak, with great views of the Aussie alps. From the upper chairlift terminal at 6,447 ft, the journey to the 7,314-ft summit is a relatively easy 12-km (7½-mi) return hike in beautiful alpine country. You can also take a mile walk to an overlook. Hikers should be prepared for unpredictable and sometimes severe weather.

Dining and Lodging

$$$ ✕🏨 **Bernti's Mountain Inn.** Located in the heart of Thredbo within walking distance of the chairlifts, Bernti's is a unique, boutique-style mountain inn with friendly service and superb food. The rooms have delightful views, and most have king-size beds. The lounge has a welcoming fire, and a bar and pool table. Outside, there are whirlpools and plunge pools overlooking the mountains, as well as a sauna to relax tired muscles. The popular terrace café serves snacks and drinks, and at night the restaurant takes on a romantic atmosphere—and serves an eclectic array of innovative dishes alongside a comprehensive wine list. The inn is open year-round, and rates are considerably cheaper out of ski season. ⊠ *Mowamba Pl., Thredbo 2627,* ☎ *02/6457–6332,* FAX *02/6457–6348. 27 rooms. Restaurant, bar, sauna, spa, ski storage, nightclub, laundry service. AE, DC, MC, V.*

$$$ 🏨 **Novotel Lake Crackenback Resort.** En route to Thredbo and poised on the banks of a lake that mirrors the surrounding peaks of the Crackenback Range, these luxury apartments offer family-size accommodations. Apartments in this all-season resort include one-bedroom-plus lofts, which sleep four, to three-bedroom areas. Each has a modern kitchen, a laundry with drying racks, under-floor heating, a fireplace, and such thoughtful extras as undercover parking and lockable ski racks outside the rooms. ⊠ *Alpine Way, via Jindabyne, 2627,* ☎ *02/6456–2960,* FAX *02/6456–1008. 46 apartments. Restaurant, bar, kitchenettes, indoor pool, sauna, 9-hole golf course, 3 tennis courts, exercise room. AE, DC, MC, V.*

$$ 🏨 **Thredbo Alpine Hotel.** Within easy reach of the ski lifts at Thredbo, the rooms here are spacious and comfortable, decorated in warm autumn colors, and furnished with contemporary wood and glass. The hotel has a choice of restaurants and après-ski facilities. Rates include Continental breakfast. Private apartments available for hire in the village. ⊠ *Box 80, Thredbo Village 2625,* ☎ *02/6459–4200,* FAX *02/6459–4201. 65 rooms. 3 restaurants, 4 bars, indoor pool, sauna, spa, tennis court, ski storage, nightclub. AE, DC, MC, V.*

Nightlife

At the center of the village, and open only in winter, the **Thredbo Alpine Hotel** has a popular nightclub and a choice of three bars.

Skiing

Among downhill resorts of the area, **Thredbo** has the most challenging runs—with the only Australian giant-slalom course approved for World Cup events—and the most extensive snowmaking in the country. ☎ *02/6459–4100.* 🎫 *Lift tickets $60 per day, $250 for 5 days.*

Thredbo Sports rents downhill and cross-country skis and snowboards. ⊠ *Ski-lift terminal, Thredbo Village,* ☎ *02/6459–4100.*

En Route Between Thredbo and Khancoban, the Alpine Way turns south and then west as it skirts the flanks of **Mount Kosciuszko.** This 40-km (25-mi) gravel section of the highway, often impassable in winter but reasonable at other times, leads through heavily forested terrain, with pleasant views to the south. Nineteen kilometers (12 miles) past Dead Horse Gap is the turnoff to **Tom Groggin,** the highest point of the Murray River accessible by road. Australia's longest river travels west for another 2,515 km (1,560 mi) before it meets the sea south of Adelaide.

Khancoban

30 *81 km (50 mi) northwest of Thredbo.*

Once a dormitory town for workers on the Snowy Mountains Hydroelectric Scheme—it's close to a dam and two of the project's power stations—Khancoban is now a favorite with anglers who try their luck in the lake created by the damming of the Swampy Plain River.

31 In a picturesque valley outside Khancoban is the Snowy Mountains Hydroelectric Authority's **Murray 1 "Inflowmation Station."** Interactive displays demonstrate the importance of water in Australia, the driest inhabited continent. From here you can see the power station's 10 turbine generators. ⊠ *Alpine Way, via Khancoban,* ☎ *02/6453–2004 or 1800/62–3776.* ☉ *Daily 9–4.*

32 The road north from Khancoban leads past the Tooma and Tumut Pond reservoirs and Round Mountain to **Cabramurra.** At 1,490 m (4,890 ft) this is the highest town in Australia. The scenic **Goldseekers Track** is a pleasant 3 km (2 mi) return walk that starts at Three Mile Dam, approximately 8 km (5 mi) north of Cabramurra on Link Road.

33 Just north of Cabramurra there is another major component of the Snowy Mountains Hydroelectric Scheme—the **Tumut 2 Power Station.** You can tour the station, read informative displays about the Snowy Scheme's construction, and go inside the mountain to explore some of the scheme's workings. ⊠ *Elliot Way, via Cabramurra,* ☎ *02/6453–2004; 1800/62-3776 for reservations. Reservations essential.*

This is the long, but very scenic, way back around to Adaminaby and Cooma. Before you get there you'll pass through **Kiandra,** a small, now-tranquil village that was the site of a frantic early 1860s gold rush. Kiandra is 81 km (50 mi) from Khancoban.

34 **Yarrangobilly Caves** (☎ *02/6454–9597*) is a network of limestone grottoes full of stalactites, stalagmites, and other rock formations. A few of the caves are open to the public; one of them, South Glory Cave, has a self-guided tour. Four other caves must be toured with a guide. You can also bathe in 80°F thermal pools, an enjoyable complement to the 53°F chill inside the passages. The caves are within Kosciuszko National Park and the area contains pristine wilderness, including the spectacular Yarrangobilly Gorge. The caves are about 21 km (13 mi) north of Kiandra. The self-guided tour costs $8 and the guided tour is $10. The caves are open daily from 9 to 5 (subject to winter road conditions).

Adaminaby

35 *40 km (25 mi) southeast of Kiandra, 50 km (31 mi) northwest of Cooma.*

Halfway between Kiandra and Cooma, this is the town closest to **Lake Eucumbene,** the main storage dam for the Snowy Mountains Hydroelectric Scheme. The lake holds eight times as much water as Sydney Harbour. Adaminaby was moved to its present site in the 1950s, when the lake was created, and the area is now best known for its horseback holidays (☞ Reynella, *below*) and recreational fishing—the town's most famous structure is an 18-yd-long fiberglass trout.

Lodging

$$
★

🏠 **Reynella.** Set in undulating country near the highest point in Australia, this sheep and cattle property offers guests a chance to saddle up and head off into "The Man from Snowy River" country. Reynella has been in operation since the early 1970s, and it is renowned for its multiday horseback safaris into Kosciuszko National Park—all levels of riding ability are welcome. The homestead provides a relaxing atmosphere and basic but comfortable lodge-style accommodations with shared facilities. In winter, the property is a perfect base for both downhill and cross-country skiing. It is 9 km (5½ mi) south of Adaminaby. Rates include all meals. ⊠ *Bolaro Rd., Adaminaby 2630,* ☎ *02/6454–2386,* 𝔽𝔸𝕏 *02/6454–2530. 20 rooms without bath. Horseback riding, tennis court, fishing. MC, V.*

Snowy Mountains A to Z

Arriving and Departing

BY BUS

During ski season, **Greyhound Pioneer Australia** (☎ 13–2030) makes daily runs between Sydney and the Snowy Mountains via Canberra. The bus stops at Cooma, Berridale, Jindabyne, Thredbo, the Skitube Terminal, and Perisher Blue. It is a seven-hour ride to Thredbo from Sydney, three hours from Canberra.

BY CAR

Take Parramatta Road from Sydney to the juncture with the Hume Highway at Ashfield, about 8 km (5 mi) from the city center. Follow the highway to just south of Goulburn and then turn onto the Federal Highway to Canberra. The Monaro Highway runs south from Canberra to Cooma. The 419-km (260-mi) journey takes at least five hours.

BY PLANE

Impulse Airlines (reservations through Ansett Australia, ☎ 13–1300) operates daily flights between Sydney and Cooma. From Cooma's airport, it is a half-hour drive to Jindabyne.

Getting Around

BY BUS

In winter, shuttle buses connect the regional towns with the ski fields. At other times of the year, the only practical way to explore the area is by rental car or on a guided tour.

BY CAR

To visit anything beyond the main ski resort areas, a car is a necessity. Be aware, however, that driving these often steep and winding mountain roads in winter can be hazardous, and you must carry snow chains from June through October.

BY SKITUBE

The Skitube shuttle train (running from the Alpine Way, between Jindabyne and Thredbo, to the Perisher Blue area) operates year-round and is a useful means of reaching either of these resorts. For full details of services and fares, contact the **Skitube information office** (☎ 02/6456–2010).

Contacts and Resources

CAR RENTALS

Rent cars in Cooma from **Thrifty Car Rental** (⊠ Sharpe St., ☎ 02/6452–5300), which also has an office at the airport.

EMERGENCIES

Ambulance, fire brigade, and police. ☎ *000*.

Cooma District Hospital. ⊠ *Bent St., Cooma,* ☎ *02/6252–1333.*

GUIDED TOURS

Adventure Sports. In addition to joining up with one of the tour operators listed here, you could also, if you are an experienced walker, undertake one of the area's many fine walks without a guide. Talk to staff at the Snowy Region Visitor Centre in Jindabyne (☞ *below*) for suggestions and trail maps.

Local operator **Morrell Adventure Travel** (⊠ 57 Oliver St., Berridale 2628, ☎ 02/6456–3681) has various guided hiking and mountain-biking trips in the Snowy Mountains between November and April. Trips range from three to 15 days, starting at $375 including all meals. Jindabyne's **Paddy Pallin** (⊠ Kosciuszko Rd., Thredbo turnoff, Jindabyne 2627, ☎ 02/6456–2922 or 1800/62–3459) offers bushwalking, mountain biking, white-water rafting and canoeing, and horseback riding. An outstanding choice of cross-country ski programs is also available, from introductory weekends to snow-camping trips.

Bus Tours. Murrays Australia (☎ 13–2251 or 02/6295–3611) operates both skiing/accommodation packages and a transportation service (during the ski season only) to the Snowy Mountains from Canberra. These depart from the Jolimont Tourist Centre, Alinga Street and Northbourne Avenue.

VISITOR INFORMATION

Cooma Visitors Centre. ⊠ *119 Sharpe St., Cooma,* ☎ *02/6450–1742 or 02/6450–1740.* ⊙ *June–Sept., daily 7–6; Oct.–May, daily 9–5.*

Snowy Region Visitor Centre. ⊠ *Kosciuszko Rd., Jindabyne,* ☎ *02/ 6450–5600.* ⊙ *Daily 8–6.*

Sydney Visitors Information Centre. ⊠ *106 George St., the Rocks, Sydney 2000,* ☎ *02/9255–1788,* FAX *02/9241–5010.* ⊙ *Daily 9–6.*

3 CANBERRA AND THE A.C.T.

Surrounded by rugged mountain ranges between Sydney and Melbourne, Canberra is the nation's airy, spacious, immaculately groomed capital, and the urban heart of the Australian Capital Territory. A showcase for Australia's artistic, technological, and sporting excellence, it is also a city that revels in the great outdoors.

THE NATIONAL CAPITAL is the city that Australians most like to dislike. In the national consciousness, "Canberra" stands for politicians and bureaucrats who spend and sometimes squander the national wealth, conceive grandiose projects for their own personal embellishment, make unreasonable decisions, and ride around in taxpayer-funded cars while the rest of the country rolls up its sleeves and works. In fact the reality is vastly different. Canberra is typically Australian through and through. Those who live there will tell you that "to know Canberra is to love it," although a significant proportion of its residents seem to flee their home city at every opportunity, to judge by the number of vehicles with Canberra registration plates seen on Sydney's streets every weekend.

By Michael Gebicki

The need for a national capital arose only in 1901, when the Australian states—which had previously operated separate and often conflicting administrations—were united in a federation. An area of about 2,330 square km (900 square mi) of undulating, sheep-grazing country in southeastern New South Wales was set aside and designated the Australian Capital Territory (A.C.T.). The inland site was chosen partly for reasons of national security and partly to end the bickering between Sydney and Melbourne, both of which claimed to be the country's legitimate capital. The name Canberry—an Aboriginal word meaning "meeting place" that had been previously applied to this area—was changed to Canberra for the new city. Like everything else about it, the name was controversial, and debate has raged ever since over which syllable should be stressed. These days, "*Can*-bra" is more common than "Can-*ber*-ra."

From the very beginning this was to be a totally planned city. An international design competition was won by Walter Burley Griffin, a Chicago architect and associate of Frank Lloyd Wright. Griffin arrived in Canberra in 1913 to supervise construction, but progress was slowed by two world wars and the Great Depression. By 1947 Canberra was little more than a country town with only 15,000 inhabitants.

Development increased during the 1950s, and the current population of more than 300,000 makes it by far the largest inland city in Australia. Griffin's original plan has largely been fulfilled in the wide, tree-lined avenues and spacious parkland of present-day Canberra. The major public buildings are arranged on low knolls on either side of man-made Lake Burley Griffin, the focus of the city. Satellite communities—using the same radial design of crescents and cul-de-sacs employed in Canberra, but with a shopping center at their nucleus—have been created to house the city's growing population.

Canberra's overall impression is one of spaciousness, serenity, and an almost unnatural order. There are no advertising billboards, no strident colors, and very few buildings more than a dozen stories high. Canberra verges on being a one-company town: almost 50% of the workforce is employed in government, giving the city a peculiar homogeneity. It is paradoxically unlike anywhere else in Australia—the product of a brave attempt to create an urban utopia—and its success or failure has fueled many a pub debate.

Pleasures and Pastimes

In its academies, museums, galleries, and public buildings, Canberra is an eloquent symbol of the modern, sophisticated, technologically advanced nation that it leads. Yet the visitor is never allowed to forget that it also a uniquely Australian experience. Buried among tall, forested hills that ring with the sounds of wild Australia, Canberra can frustrate the best intentions. The pristine lawns that lap against the brick villas of suburbia are still singed when the Australian summer turns on its blast-furnace heat and water restrictions come into force. The most likely source of the summer haze that hangs over Canberra is bushfires, and the greatest danger in Australia's political capital comes not from terrorists' bombs but from nesting magpies, which jealously guard their territory by swooping silently from their perches and pecking unwary trespassers smartly on the head. Canberra makes the most of its situation with parks, cycle paths, easy access to surrounding national parks, sporting facilities that are the envy of the rest of the nation, and an addiction to the great outdoors.

Dining

Despite its modest size, Canberra's dining scene has been spurred to the culinary heights by the youth, affluence, and sophisticated tastes of its inhabitants. Canberra now claims to have more restaurants per person than any other city in Australia, and the very best would fare well against restaurants in Sydney or Melbourne.

CATEGORY	COST*
$$$$	over $50
$$$	$35–$50
$$	$20–$35
$	under $20

per person, excluding drinks and service

Galleries, Museums, and Public Buildings

With over 30 national institutions, Canberra has an impressive array of museums, art galleries, and public buildings to visit. Completed in 1988, the vast, modern Parliament House is the most famous of these, but the National Gallery of Australia, the National Science and Technology Centre (Questacon), the Australian Institute of Sport, and the Australian War Memorial provide no less fascinating glimpses into the nation's history, character, and aspirations.

Lodging

Most hotels in the city have sprung up since the 1960s, and few offer more than modern, utilitarian facilities. Exceptions are the country homesteads tucked away in the surrounding mountain ranges. These expansive country dwellings give you a chance to experience life on working sheep and cattle farms, often in magnificently rugged surroundings, without sacrificing creature comforts. Generally, these lodgings are too distant from Canberra to serve as a practical base for exploring the national capital.

CATEGORY	COST*
$$$$	over $250
$$$	$150–$250
$$	$80–$150
$	under $80

All prices are for a standard double room.

Parks, Reserves, and the Great Outdoors

Canberra's surrounding mountain ranges and river valleys, combined with the crisp spring and autumn weather, give the city a wide repertoire of invigorating outdoor pursuits. Within the A.C.T. itself lie a national park, a nature reserve, and vast areas of bush and parkland that are great for walks. Lake Burley Griffin and its environs provide a scenic backdrop for walking and cycling. Kosciuszko National Park and the New South Wales snowfields are also within easy reach of the capital—far closer than they are to Sydney.

EXPLORING CANBERRA AND THE A.C.T.

Canberra's most important public buildings are located within the Parliamentary Triangle, formed by the lake on the north side and two long avenues, Commonwealth and Kings, which radiate from Capital Hill, the city's political and geographical epicenter. The triangle itself can be explored comfortably on foot, but you'll need transportation for the rest of your stay in the city.

Although locals maintain otherwise, with its radial roads, erratic signage, and often large distances between suburbs, Canberra can be difficult to negotiate by car. The best solution is to buy a good street map, and try to relax about missing turnoffs and ending up on the wrong radial road. Maps featuring clearly marked scenic drives are available from the Canberra Visitor Centre. If you don't rent a car, Canberra's ACTION buses and the Murrays Canberra Explorer (☞ Central Canberra *and* Canberra and the A.C.T. A to Z, *below*) can get you around town comfortably and without stress.

Numbers in the text correspond to numbers in the margin and on the Canberra map.

Great Itineraries

Most of Canberra's galleries, museums, and public buildings can be seen in a couple of days, while the capital's parks and gardens, and Namadgi National Park to the south, can easily delay you for another day or so. There are also several lesser-known attractions, such as Lanyon Homestead, that warrant a visit.

IF YOU HAVE 2 DAYS

In two busy days you will be able to see most of the main city attractions. You could start day one with the spectacular view from the **Telstra Tower** ⑯, then visit the **National Capital Exhibition** ③ for a good look into Canberra's planning and history. Next stop should be the **Parliamentary Triangle,** where you can easily spend the remainder of the day visiting the National Gallery of Australia, Questacon, Old Parliament House, and Parliament House. Fill in the city center gaps on the second day with the **Australian National Botanic Gardens** ⑮, **Australian War Memorial** ⑭, and the **National Film and Sound Archive** ①.

IF YOU HAVE 4 DAYS

After seeing all of the above, spend days three and four visiting the **Australian Institute of Sport, St. John the Baptist Church and the Schoolhouse Museum** ⑬, and the **Royal Australian Mint,** and then take a drive around the pleasant suburb of Yarralumla and the **Yarralumla Diplomatic Missions** ⑩ en route to the **National Aquarium and Australian Wildlife Sanctuary** ⑰. You should also be able to fit in a visit to **Lanyon Homestead** and **Tidbinbilla Nature Reserve,** to the city's south. Or, take a day and head to **Namadgi National Park** for a walk or hike.

IF YOU HAVE 6 DAYS

Within six days your itinerary could easily cover the above suggestions, with time to spare for a gentle bicycle ride around **Lake Burley Griffin,** a day hike in **Namadgi National Park,** and perhaps a visit to the **Deep Space Communications Complex** at Tidbinbilla. You could also take a trip a few miles north of the city to **Cockington Green,** continuing on to the **Federation Square** shopping complex at Gold Creek Village. Or spend a couple of days in **Kosciuszko National Park** 200 km (125 mi) away in southern New South Wales. The main summer activities are hiking, fishing, and horse riding, while in winter (June–October) both cross-country and downhill skiing are options.

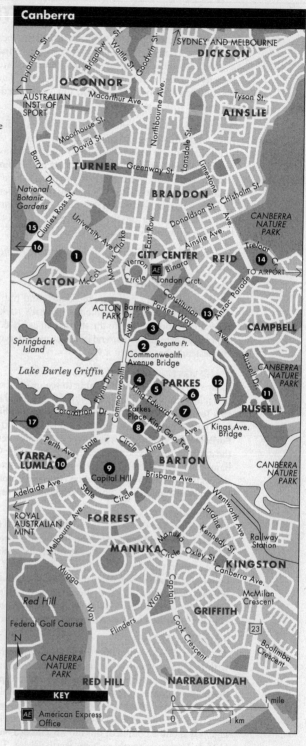

Canberra

When to Tour Canberra and the A.C.T.

One particularly good time to visit the national capital is in March and April, when autumn paints the city parks with amber. This also coincides with the theater, dance, musical productions, open-air film festival, and jazz and rock concerts of the March Canberra Festival. This festival now incorporates the colorful international Hot Air Balloon Fiesta. The spring flower celebration, Floriade, takes place in September and October.

Central Canberra

The first part of this self-drive tour takes in virtually all of central Canberra's major attractions, including the Parliamentary Triangle buildings, the lakeside sights, and the Australian War Memorial. Bus tours, which depart every two hours daily, also visit most of the sites on this itinerary.

For full details on guided city tours, *see* Canberra and the A.C.T. A to Z, *below*.

A Good Tour

From the city center, Murrays Canberra Explorer bus first heads to the **Australian War Memorial** ⑭, at the top of Anzac Parade, one of the nation's most popular attractions. The bus then stops at Regatta Point, where there are excellent views of **Lake Burley Griffin** and the **Captain Cook Memorial Jet** ②, a spectacular fountain that rockets a plume of water far above the lake. This is also the location for the **National Capital Exhibition** ③, which explains how the city was planned and built, and reveals the civic secrets of Canberra's present and future with videos, models, and audiovisual displays.

There is plenty to see at the next stop, over Commonwealth Avenue Bridge to the lake's southern shore and the Parliamentary Triangle: the **National Library of Australia** ④, the interactive **Questacon–The National Science and Technology Centre** ⑤, the **High Court of Australia** ⑥, and the **National Gallery of Australia** ⑦, the nation's premier art gallery. It would be easy to spend an entire morning or afternoon exploring Questacon and the National Gallery, but for most visitors, the library and High Court deserve only a quick glance.

Nearby, **Old Parliament House** ⑧ was once the hub of national politics, but this gracious old building now houses the National Portrait Gallery. Farther up Capital Hill, sprawling **Parliament House** ⑨ is a striking contrast to its humble predecessor and deserves an extended visit.

Back on the bus, you'll circle the **Yarralumla Diplomatic Missions** ⑩ before stopping at the Royal Australian Mint. Next stop is the **National Aquarium and Australian Wildlife Sanctuary** ⑰, a must-see if you have not yet experienced Australia's unique indigenous birds, animals, and marine life.

The bus then climbs to the summit of Black Mountain, capped by the 600-ft-high **Telstra Tower** ⑯, which commands spectacular views of the city, lake, and surrounding countryside. At the foot of the mountain is the **Australian National Botanic Gardens** ⑮, which contains superb displays of native flora.

The bus then skirts the city to visit the Australian Institute of Sport, where Australia's elite athletes are trained, and Cockington Green, an English village in miniature, before returning to the city center.

TIMING
You could squeeze this entire tour into one very busy day, but it would not do justice to Parliament House or any of the major museums or

galleries. To accommodate these, split the first part of the tour into two parts—take a break after the National Gallery of Australia, and resume your sightseeing on the following day at Old Parliament House.

The major galleries and museums (particularly the Australian War Memorial, National Gallery, and Questacon) become crowded on weekends, so explore these on a weekday if you can.

Sights to See

⑪ **Australian–American Memorial.** For Americans, this slender memorial with an eagle at its summit will have particular significance. It was unveiled in 1954 to commemorate the role of American forces in the defense of Australia during World War II. The monument is located near the northern side of Kings Avenue Bridge, surrounded by the government departments in charge of Australia's armed services. ⊠ *Russell Dr., Russell.*

⑮ **Australian National Botanic Gardens.** Australian plants and trees have evolved in isolation from the rest of the world, and these delightful gardens on the lower slopes of Black Mountain display the world's best collection of the continent's unique flora. The rain forest, rockery, Tasmanian alpine garden, and the eucalyptus lawn—with more than 600 species of eucalyptus—are the 125-acre site's highlights. Two self-guided nature trails start from the rain forest gully, and free guided tours depart from the visitor center at 11 on weekdays, 11 and 2 on weekends. ⊠ *Clunies Ross St., Black Mountain, Acton,* ☎ *02/6250–9540.* ⊡ *Free.* ☉ *Gardens daily 9–5 (until 8 in Jan.), visitor center daily 9:30–4:30.*

⑭ **Australian War Memorial.** Both as a memorial to Australians who served their country in war time and as a military museum, this is a shrine of great national importance. Built roughly in the shape of a Byzantine church, it is also the most popular tourist attraction in the national capital. Exhibits cover the period from the Sudan campaign of the late 19th century to the Vietnam War. Displays include a Lancaster bomber, a Spitfire, tanks, landing barges, the giant German Amiens gun, and sections of two of the Japanese midget submarines that infiltrated Sydney Harbour during World War II. The memorial is the focus of the powerful Anzac Day ceremony in Canberra, held on April 25. Free guided tours are available daily at 10, 10:30, 11, 1:30, and 2. ⊠ *Anzac Parade at Limestone Ave., Campbell,* ☎ *02/6243–4261.* ⊡ *Free.* ☉ *Daily 10–5.*

The impressive facade of the War Memorial is best appreciated from the broad avenue of **Anzac Parade.** Anzac is an acronym for the Australian and New Zealand Army Corps, formed during World War I. The avenue is flanked by several memorials commemorating the army, navy, and air force, as well as some of the campaigns in which Australian troops have fought, including one of the most recent—the Vietnam War. The red gravel used on Anzac Parade symbolizes the blood spilled by Australians in war.

❷ **Captain Cook Memorial Jet.** Located in Lake Burley Griffin, off Commonwealth Park's Regatta Point, this water jet commemorates James Cook's discovery of the east coast of Australia in 1770. On windless days the jet spurts a six-ton plume of water 490 ft into the sky—making this one of the world's highest fountains.

Lake Burley Griffin. At the very heart of the city, this large lake is one of Canberra's most captivating features. The parks that surround the lake are ideal for walking and cycling, and you can hire catamarans, canoes, or a variety of boats from Acton Park on the northern shore.

❻ **High Court of Australia.** As its name implies, this gleaming concrete-and-glass structure is the ultimate court of law in the nation's judicial system. The court of seven justices convenes only to determine constitutional matters or major principles of law. Inside the main entrance of the building, the public hall contains a number of murals depicting various constitutional and geographic themes. Each of the three courtrooms over which the justices preside has a public gallery, and you can observe the proceedings when the court is in session. ⊠ *King Edward Terr., Parkes,* ☎ *02/6270–6850.* 🖃 *Free.* 🕒 *Daily 9:45–4:30.*

👆 🕗 **National Aquarium and Australian Wildlife Sanctuary.** Although rather small and not really worthy of a "National" title (except that it is in the A.C.T.), this complex nonetheless brings the sensations of the Great Barrier Reef and Australia's river lands to the shores of Lake Burley Griffin. A submerged walk-through tunnel gives fish-eye views of the underwater world, and there are two dozen display tanks alive with corals, marine animals, and exotic fish. The adjoining 15-acre wildlife sanctuary is a bushland park that provides a habitat for the more remarkable species of Australia's fauna: emus, koalas, penguins, dingoes, kangaroos, and Tasmanian devils. ⊠ *Lady Denman Dr., Scrivener Dam, Yarralumla,* ☎ *02/6287–1211.* 🖃 *$10.* 🕒 *Daily 9–5:30.*

❸ **National Capital Exhibition.** Photographs, models, plans, audiovisual displays, and a laser model inside this lakeside pavilion illustrate the past, present, and future development of the national capital. Cyclops, a remote-control video camera mounted on top of Mt. Ainslie, gives a bird's-eye view of the city. From the pavilion's terrace there are sweeping views of the Parliamentary Triangle across the lake: The National Library on the right and the National Gallery on the left form the base of the Parliamentary Triangle, which rises toward its apex at Parliament House on Capital Hill. The terrace is a great spot from which to photograph the lakeside buildings, and the **Captain Cook Memorial Jet.** The restaurant and kiosk on the terrace serve full meals and light snacks, and if the sun is shining, sit down at a table, relax, and enjoy the scenery. ⊠ *Regatta Point, Commonwealth Park,* ☎ *02/ 6257–1068.* 🖃 *Free.* 🕒 *Apr.–Oct., daily 9–5; Nov.–Mar., daily 9–6.*

⓬ **National Carillon.** The tall, elegant bell tower on Lake Burley Griffin's Aspen Island was a gift from the British government to mark Canberra's 50th anniversary in 1963. The carillon consists of 53 bells, and 45-minute recitals are played daily at 12:45 every weekday in summer (Wednesday only in winter), 2:45 weekends and public holidays, and 5:45 Thursdays during summer. The music ranges from popular songs to hymns and special carillon compositions. ⊠ *Aspen Island, off Wendouree Dr., Parkes,* ☎ *02/6257–1068.*

❶ **National Film and Sound Archive.** Australia's movie industry was booming during the early years of this century but ultimately it could not compete with the sophistication and volume of imported films. Concern that film stock and sound recordings of national importance would be lost prompted the construction of this edifice to preserve Australia's movie and musical heritage. The archive contains an impressive display of Australian moviemaking skills, including a short film that was shot on Melbourne Cup Day in 1896—the oldest in the collection. Special exhibitions, changing twice yearly, focus on aspects of the industry ranging from rock music to historic newsreels. ⊠ *McCoy Circuit, Acton,* ☎ *02/6209–3111.* 🖃 *$5.50.* 🕒 *Daily 9–5.*

❼ **National Gallery of Australia.** The nation's premier art gallery contains a sprinkling of works by the masters, including Rodin, Picasso, Pollock, and Warhol, but its real strength lies in its Australian artwork. The gallery houses the most comprehensive exhibition of Australian art in the country, with superlative collections of Aboriginal art as well as paintings by such famous native sons as Arthur Streeton, Sir Sidney Nolan, Tom Roberts, and Arthur Boyd. There is an excellent bookshop with an extensive selection of Australian art postcards, as well as a restaurant and a brasserie. Free guided tours commence from the foyer at 11 and 2 each day. An additional charge usually applies to special-interest exhibitions, which often feature artwork from around the world. ⊠ *Parkes Pl., Parkes,* ☎ *02/6240–6502.* 🖾 *$3.* ⊙ *Daily 10–5.*

NEED A
BREAK?

The National Gallery has two good spots to catch your breath amid the Parliamentary Triangle's assault of history, culture, and science. The **Mirrabook Outdoor Restaurant,** in the pleasant sculpture garden, serves excellent lunch. The Brasserie is open daily from 10 to 4, and the outdoor eatery serves lunch daily from noon to 2:30 PM. Reservations are essential for Mirrabook. ⊠ *Parkes Pl.,* ☎ *02/6273-2836.*

❹ **National Library of Australia.** Based loosely on the design of the Parthenon in Athens, this treasury of knowledge contains more than 5 million books and 500,000 aerial photographs, maps, drawings, and recordings of oral history. Changing exhibitions are displayed in the mezzanine gallery. Guided one-hour tours of the library take place Tuesday, Wednesday, and Thursday at 2 PM. ⊠ *Parkes Pl., Parkes,* ☎ *02/ 6262–1111.* 🖾 *Free.* ⊙ *Mon.–Thurs. 9–9, Fri.–Sun. 9–5.*

❽ **Old Parliament House.** Built in 1927, this long, white building was meant to serve only as a temporary seat of government, but it was more than 60 years before its much larger successor was finally completed on the hill behind it. Now that the politicians have moved out, the beautifully renovated building is open for public inspection. Guided tours, departing from Kings Hall on the half-hour, take you through the legislative chambers, party rooms, and suites that once belonged to the prime minister and the president of the Senate. Old Parliament House also contains the relatively new and expanding **National Portrait Gallery,** which displays likenesses of important Australians past and present. In the old House of Representatives, you can watch a 45-minute sound and light show entitled, appropriately, *Order! Order!* While you're in the area, take a stroll through the delightful **Senate Rose Gardens.** ⊠ *King George Terr., Parkes,* ☎ *02/6270–8222.* 🖾 *$2, including sound and light show.* ⊙ *Daily 9–4, sound and light show 10:30 and 2:30.*

❾ **Parliament House.** Much of this vast, futuristic structure is submerged, covered by a domed glass roof that follows the contours of Capital Hill. From a distance, the most striking feature of the billion-dollar building is its 250-ft flagpole. Although it might look only as big as a postage stamp, the Australian flag that flies night and day from the top is actually the size of a double-decker bus.

The design for the new Parliament House was chosen in an international contest that attracted more than 300 entries. The contest was won by the New York firm of Mitchell, Guirgola & Thorp, whose design merged structural elegance with the natural environment. Work commenced in 1980, and the building was completed for the Australian Bicentennial in 1988.

You approach the Parliament building across a vast courtyard featuring a central mosaic entitled *Meeting Place,* designed by Aboriginal artist Nelson Tjakamarra. Native timber has been used almost exclusively throughout the building, and the work of some of Australia's finest contemporary artists hangs on the walls.

Parliament generally sits on weekdays (except Friday) between mid-February and late June and mid-August to mid-December. Both chambers have public galleries, but debate in the House of Representatives—where the prime minister sits—is livelier and more newsworthy than in the Senate. The best time to be present in the House of Representatives is during Question Time, starting at 2 PM, when the government and the opposition are most likely to be at each other's throats. To secure a ticket for Question Time, contact the **sergeant-at-arms' office** (☎ 02/6277–4889). Book a week in advance, if possible. Guided tours are available every half hour from 9 AM to 4 PM, and you are free to wander around much of the building at your own leisure. ⊠ *Capital Hill,* ☎ *02/6277–5399.* ☉ *Daily 9–5 (later when Parliament is sitting).*

✺ ❺ **Questacon–The National Science and Technology Centre.** This interactive science facility is the city's most entertaining museum. Built around a central "drum," Questacon entertains and educates with about 200 hands-on exhibits. High-tech computer gadgetry is used along with anything from pendulums to feathers to illustrate principles of mathematics, physics, and human perception. Staff are on hand to explain the scientific principles behind the exhibits, and intriguing science shows are performed regularly. This stimulating, participative environment is highly addictive and great fun—you're likely to have trouble getting out in less than a couple hours. ⊠ *King Edward Terr., Parkes,* ☎ *02/6270–2800.* ☜ *$8.* ☉ *Daily 10–5.*

⓭ **St. John the Baptist Church and the Schoolhouse Museum.** These are the oldest surviving buildings in the Canberra district. When they were constructed in the 1840s, the land was part of a 4,000-acre property that belonged to Robert Campbell, a well-known Sydney merchant. The homestead, Duntroon, remained in the Campbell family until it was purchased by the government as a site for the Royal Military College. The schoolhouse is now a small museum with relics from the early history of the area. ⊠ *Constitution Ave., Reid,* ☎ *02/6249–6839.* ☜ *Museum $1.50; church free.* ☉ *Museum Wed. 10–noon, weekends 2–4; church daily 9–5.*

⓰ **Telstra Tower.** The city's tallest landmark, this 600-ft structure on the top of Black Mountain is one of the best places to begin any tour of the national capital. Three viewing platforms give breathtaking views of the entire city as well as the mountain ranges to the south. The tower houses an exhibition on the history of telecommunications in Australia and a revolving restaurant with a spectacular nighttime panorama. The structure provides a communications link between Canberra and the rest of the country and serves as a broadcasting station for radio and television networks. Its massive scale and futuristic style caused a public outcry when it was built more than a decade ago. Some residents still call it "the needle" for its syringe-like profile, but the focus of architectural debate has since shifted to the buildings within the Parliamentary Triangle. ⊠ *Black Mountain Dr., Acton,* ☎ *02/6248–1911 or 1800–80–6718.* ☜ *$3.* ☉ *Daily 9 AM–10 PM.*

⓵⓪ **Yarralumla Diplomatic Missions.** The expensive, leafy suburb of Yarralumla, west and north of Parliament House, contains many of the the city's 70 or so diplomatic missions. Some of these were established when Canberra was little more than a small country town, and it was only with great reluctance that many ambassadors and their staffs were persuaded to transfer from the temporary capital in Melbourne.

On Coronation Drive you will find the unmistakable **Chinese Embassy,** while the **British High Commission** is on Commonwealth Avenue. The handsome white, neoclassical building of the **South African Embassy** is located on State Circle. Nearby Moonah Place is home to the

Williamsburg-style U.S. Embassy, the Indian High Commission, and the Embassy of the Philippines. Some of these embassies and high commissions open their doors for public inspection on special occasions—for more details, contact the Canberra Visitor Centre (☞ Canberra and the A.C.T. A to Z, *below*).

Around Canberra and the A.C.T.

Canberra's suburbs and the rural regions of the A.C.T. offer a variety of lesser attractions. These include the Australian Institute of Sport, a nature reserve with native animals, two national parks, a historic homestead, and Canberra's important contribution to the space race. You will need a car to reach these attractions, as they are not on any of the sightseeing bus routes.

TIMING

Unless you plan to use the section below as a see-all checklist, choose a few places to visit over the course of a day or two. The Australian Institute of Sport, Cockington Green, and the Royal Australian Mint are within 15 minutes of the city; the Canberra Deep Space Communications Complex and Lanyon Homestead are twice as far. Namadgi National Park and Tidbinbilla Nature Reserve are 45–60 minutes to the south and west, respectively. A trip to Kosciuszko National Park warrants at least a couple days in itself.

Sights to See

Australian Institute of Sport. Established in 1980 to improve the performance of Australia's elite athletes, this 150-acre site north of the city includes athletic fields, a swimming center, an indoor sports stadium, and a sports medicine center. Hour-and-a-half-long tours, some guided by AIS athletes, depart daily at 11:30 and 2:30, with additional tours at 10 and 1 on weekends and public holidays. Half of the tour takes in visits to the various facilities, where you may be able to watch some of the institute's squads in training. The remaining time is spent in the new Ansett Sports Visitors Centre; here, displays and a video wall focus on AIS athletes and the achievements of Australian sporting stars, and there are many fun, hands-on exhibits. You must join a tour to explore the institute, but visitors are welcome to use some of the facilities, including the swimming pool and tennis courts, for a reasonable fee. ⊠ *Leverrier Crescent, Bruce,* ☎ *02/6214–1444 or 02/6214–1010.* ☞ *Guided tour $8.* ☉ *Weekdays 8:30–4:45, weekends 9:45–4:15; tours weekdays 11:30 and 2:30, weekends 10, 11:30, 1, and 2:30.*

Canberra Deep Space Communications Complex. Managed and operated by the Commonwealth Scientific and Industrial Research Organization (CSIRO), this is one of just three tracking stations in the world linked to the Deep Space control center, the long-distance arms of the U.S. National Aeronautics and Space Administration (NASA). The function of the four giant antennae at the site is to relay commands and data between NASA and space vehicles or orbiting satellites. The first pictures of men walking on the moon were transmitted to this tracking station. The station is not open to the public, but the visitor information center houses models, audiovisual displays, and memorabilia from space missions. ⊠ *Off Paddy's River Rd., Tidbinbilla, 40 km (25 mi) southwest of Canberra,* ☎ *02/6201–7838.* ☉ *Daily 9–5 (9–8 in summer).*

☾ **Cockington Green.** Thatch-roof houses, castles, and canals have been reproduced in small scale to create a miniature slice of England on this 5-acre site. The display also has the Heritage Rose Walk, with its splendid display of roses, and the Torquay Restaurant, which serves contemporary cuisine as well as such suitably British dishes as steak-

and-kidney pie and roast beef with Yorkshire pudding. The park is located about 11 km (7 mi) north of the city center, off the Barton Highway. ⊠ *11 Gold Creek Rd., Gold Creek Village, Nicholls,* ☎ *02/6230–2273.* ⊡ *$8.50.* ⊙ *Daily 9:30–4:30.*

Kosciuszko National Park. Kosciuszko (pronounced "koh-*shoosh*-ko") is a wonderful alpine park, and Australia's largest. It is actually located in New South Wales, although a segment of its boundary does touch the A.C.T. The gateway city, Cooma, is only 114 km (71 mi) from Canberra. For more information on Kosciuszko National Park, *see* The Snowy Mountains *in* Chapter 2.

Lanyon Homestead. On the plain beside the Murrumbidgee River, this classic homestead from pioneering days has been magnificently restored. When it was built in 1859, the house was the centerpiece of a self-contained community, and many of the outbuildings and workshops have been preserved. The adjacent **Nolan Gallery** (☎ 02/6237–5192) displays a selection of the well-known Ned Kelly paintings by the famous Australian painter Sir Sidney Nolan. The property is 30 km (19 mi) south of Canberra off the Monaro Highway. ⊠ *Tharwa Dr., Tharwa,* ☎ *02/6237–5136.* ⊡ *Homestead $5, gallery $2.* ⊙ *Tues.–Sun. 10–4.*

Namadgi National Park. Covering almost half the total area of the Australian Capital Territory's southwest, this national park encompasses a well-maintained network of walking trails through mountain ranges, trout streams, and some of the most accessible subalpine forests in the country. The park's boundaries are within 30 km (19 mi) of Canberra, and its former pastures, now empty of sheep and cattle, are grazed by hundreds of eastern grey kangaroos in the early mornings and late afternoons. There are 150 km (93 mi) of marked walking tracks, and at Yankee Hat, off the Naas Boboyan Road, you can visit an Aboriginal rock art site.

If you are an experienced navigator of wild country, the remote parts of the park have superb terrain. The higher altitudes are covered in snow June–September. The **Namadgi Visitors Centre** (open 9–4 weekdays, 9–4:30 weekends) is on the Naas/Boboyan Road, 3 km (2 mi) south of the village of Tharwa. ⊠ *Namadgi National Park, via Tharwa, 2620,* ☎ *02/6207–2900.*

Royal Australian Mint. If you really want to know how to make money, this is the place to visit. The observation gallery inside the mint has a series of windows where visitors can watch Australian coins being minted. Blanks are brought from the basement storage level up to the furnaces, where they are softened and finally sent to the presses to be stamped. The foyer has a display of rare coins, and silver and gold commemorative coins are on sale. There is no coin production on weekends and from noon to 12:40 on weekdays. ⊠ *Denison St., Deakin,* ☎ *02/6202–6999.* ⊙ *Weekdays 9–4, weekends 10–3.*

Tidbinbilla Nature Reserve. Set in eucalyptus forests in the mountain ranges 40 km (25 mi) southwest of Canberra, this 12,000-acre reserve has large walk-through enclosures where you can observe kangaroos, wallabies, and koalas in their native environment. The walking trails cross rocky mountaintops, open grassland, and gullies thick with tree ferns. The reserve also has some unusual rock formations, including Hanging Rock, a granite outcrop once used as a shelter by the Aboriginal inhabitants of the area. Bird-watchers should plan to visit during the 2:30 PM feeding time, when many colorful species can be seen and photographed at close quarters. Ranger-guided walks—including evening wildlife-spotlighting tours and strolls in search of koalas and platypuses—are available on weekends and during school holidays. The visitor center features a slide show and nocturnal animals exhibit. ⊠ *Paddy's River Rd., Tidbinbilla,* ☎ *02/6205–1233.* ⌑ *$8 per car.* ☉ *Daily 9–6 (9 PM in summer); visitor center weekdays 10–4, weekends 9–5:30.*

DINING

By Betty Forrest

Updated by
Michael
Gebicki

Central Canberra and Northern Suburbs

ITALIAN

$$$ ✕ **Mezzalira on London.** Sleek and glossy, this city center restaurant has become the fashionable place to be seen among Canberra's smart set. The menu varies from robust Italian pasta dishes and pizzas to char-grilled salmon with rocket and balsamic vinegar, grilled Italian sausages with truffle-oil mash, and grilled vegetables in a red wine sauce. Pizzas from the wood-fired oven are especially recommended for casual dining at a modest price. The espresso enjoys a reputation as Canberra's finest. ⊠ *Melbourne Building, West Row and London Circuit, Canberra City,* ☎ *02/6230–0025. AE, DC, MC, V. Closed Sun.*

$$ ✕ **Tosolini's.** A long-standing favorite with Canberra's café society, this Italian-accented brasserie has a choice of indoor or sidewalk-table eating and a menu that works hard from breakfast through dinner, with fresh fruit juices, fruit shakes, focaccia, and a small selection of main meals featuring pasta, risotto, and pizzas. The coffee is particularly good, and the cakes have an enthusiastic following. Try to plan lunch for before or after the noon–2 crush. ⊠ *East Row and London Circuit, Canberra City,* ☎ *02/6247–4317. AE, DC, MC, V. BYOB (bottled wine only). No dinner Sun. or Mon.*

MODERN AUSTRALIAN

$$$$ ✕ **The Republic.** Canberra's finest brasserie follows a formula that has been tried and tested in Australia's dining capitals, and the result has won the hearts and minds of the locals. The Mod Oz cuisine integrates the flavors of Asia and the Mediterranean and applies them to a menu strong on seafood. The decor—from aluminum water jugs to glass panels on the walls—brings a dash of Sydney style to capital-city dining. ⊠ *20 Allara St., Canberra City,* ☎ *02/6247–1717. AE, DC, MC, V. Closed Sun. No lunch Sat. or Mon.*

$$$ ✕ **Fringe Benefits.** Creative food served in spacious, stylish surroundings is the specialty of this city-fringe restaurant, for several years among Canberra's finest. The menu plunders freely from East and West to come up with dishes such as duck sausages with lentils, deep-fried quail with coriander jam, ginger-cured salmon with saffron risotto, and a decadent chocolate mousse. As well as an impressive wine cellar, wine is also available by the glass. ⊠ *54 Marcus Clarke St., Canberra City,* ☎ *02/6247–4042. AE, DC, MC, V. Closed Sun. No lunch Sat.*

PAN-ASIAN

$$$ ✕ **The Chairman and Yip.** The menu at the Chairman and Yip wins
★   universal praise for its innovative mix of Asian and Western flavors against a backdrop of artifacts from Maoist China. On the menu, you'll find duck pancakes and steamed barramundi with cumquats, ginger, and shallots. Finish with a delicious dessert, such as sticky-rice pudding or fig pudding with brandy sauce. The service, wine list, atmosphere, and decor are all outstanding. ⊠ *108 Bunda St., Canberra City,* ☎ *02/6248–7109. Reservations essential. AE, DC, MC, V. BYOB (bottled wine only). No lunch Sat.*

STEAK

$$$ ✕ **Charcoal Restaurant.** Practically unchanged since it opened for business in the 1960s, this restaurant still serves the capital's best beef. Politi-

Dining

The Chairman and Yip, **6**

Charcoal Restaurant, **4**

The Fig Café, **18**

Fringe Benefits, **2**

Mezzalira on London, **8**

The Oak Room, **12**

Prickly Pear, **16**

The Republic, **11**

Tosolini's, **5**

Lodging

Argyle Executive Apartments, **9**

Avalanche Homestead, **19**

Brindabella Station, **13**

Chifley on Northbourne, **1**

Hyatt Hotel Canberra, **12**

Manuka Park Apartments, **17**

Olims Canberra Hotel, **7**

Parkroyal Canberra, **10**

Quality Inn Downtown, **3**

Rydges Capital Hill, **14**

Telopea Inn on the Park, **15**

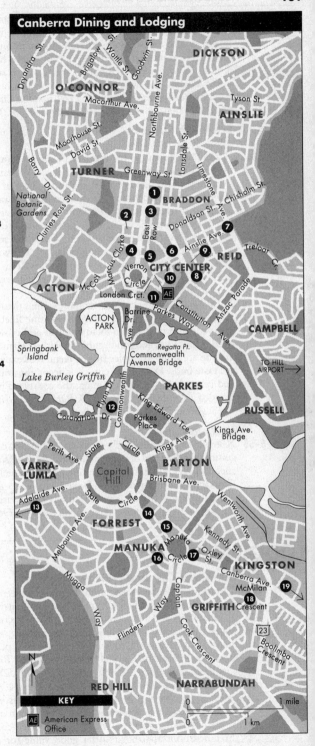

Canberra Dining and Lodging

cians and businesspeople flock here for lunch—it sometimes seems more like a gentlemen's club than a restaurant. Wooden panels and wine racks line the walls, and at night soft lights and maroon upholstery provide a romantic glow. The superb steaks vary from a half-pound sirloin to a monster two-pounder. A limited range of fish and poultry dishes is also available. The wine list has more than 100 varieties of Australian reds, including some local wines. ⊠ *61 London Circuit, Canberra City,* ☎ *02/6248–8015. AE, DC, MC, V. Closed Sun. No lunch Sat.*

Southern Suburbs

MODERN AUSTRALIAN

$$$$ ✕ **The Oak Room.** At the heart of the Hyatt Hotel Canberra, this is
★ the city's most elegant dining experience—a must for a special occasion. In the two dining rooms, an atmosphere of refinement and romance is engineered through the subdued lighting and plush furnishings, accented by the same Art Deco motifs that are used throughout the rest of the hotel. The menu is sumptuous and international in character, with dishes such as veal fillet on woodland mushrooms, or consomme of crustaceans with tapioca pearls. The wine list is extensive. ⊠ *Hyatt Hotel Canberra, Commonwealth Ave., Yarralumla,* ☎ *02/ 6270–8977. Reservations essential. Jacket required. AE, DC, MC, V. Closed Sun. and Mon. No lunch Sat.*

$$ ✕ **The Fig Café.** The prices are far more serious than the café label might
★ suggest, but so is the food. Char-grilled lamb fillet with a pesto crust, rare yellowfin tuna with a salad of olives and snow peas, duck legs in a red curry sauce, and lemon curd tart with a cream and lemonade marmalade are some examples from a menu that experiments freely with the taste buds. Despite the city-slick decor, the atmosphere is friendly and relaxed. If the sun is shining, the courtyard is especially recommended for lunch. ⊠ *Shop 2, 4 Barker St., Griffith,* ☎ *02/6295– 6915. AE, DC, MC, V. Closed Sun. and Mon.*

SOUTHWESTERN

$–$$ ✕ **Prickly Pear.** This lively Manuka restaurant offers southwestern cuisine with flair and draws a predominantly youthful crowd. Specialties such as beef chili and blue corn tortillas are paired with old favorites like corn bread and guacamole. Desserts, such as peach and orange gazpacho with wild berries, can be outrageously lavish. The Prickly Pear has both a bar and outdoor dining area. ⊠ *36–38 Franklin St., Manuka,* ☎ *02/6239–4322. AE, DC, MC, V. BYOB.*

LODGING

Canberra City and Northern Suburbs

$$$ ⌸ **Parkroyal Canberra.** In a prime location between the city center and the National Convention Centre, this modern, atrium-style hotel has good facilities and a moderate level of luxury. Decorated in cream and honey tones, guest rooms are large, comfortable, and well-equipped. Public areas have a cool, contemporary style, with plenty of chrome and glass, giant potted plants, and fresh flowers. ⊠ *1 Binara St., Canberra City 2601,* ☎ *02/6247–8999,* FAX *02/6257–4903. 287 rooms, 6 suites. 2 restaurants, 2 bars, heated pool, sauna, exercise room, laundry service and dry cleaning, concierge, business services. AE, DC, MC, V.*

$$ ⌸ **Argyle Executive Apartments.** Located within a five-minute walk
★ of the city center, these smart, stylish, fully self-contained, two- and three-bedroom apartments offer good value for a family or small group. Each unit has a spacious living and dining area, a separate kitchen with a microwave oven and dishwasher, a secure garage, and free laundry facilities. Set amid gardens, each has either a balcony or a private courtyard. Apartments are serviced daily. ⊠ *Currong and Boolee*

Sts., Reid 2612, ☎ 02/6275–0800, ⅏ 02/6275–0888. 24 apartments. Kitchenettes. AE, DC, MC, V.

$$ 🏨 **Chifley on Northbourne.** The rooms and facilities here rival those in some of Canberra's more expensive hotels. The dark timber furnishings, piano, and open fire create a cozy, clublike atmosphere in the reception area, and the olive-and-cinnamon color scheme and gum-leaf motif in the rooms give them a very Australian feel. The hotel is close to the city center, but it unfortunately overlooks one of the city's major arteries, so light sleepers should request a poolside room at the back of the hotel. ✉ 102 Northbourne Ave., Braddon 2601, ☎ 02/6249–1411, ⅏ 02/6249–6878. 78 rooms. Restaurant, bar, pool, exercise room, laundry service and dry cleaning, business services. AE, DC, MC, V.

$$ 🏨 **Olims Canberra Hotel.** With its original National Heritage–listed building, and a modern addition built around a landscaped courtyard, this former pub has double rooms, split-level suites with kitchens, and two- and three-bedroom suites. Furnishings and decor are contemporary in style, with laminated, pinelike wood finishes, fabrics and carpets tinged with red ocher, and beige walls. Rates are reduced Friday–Sunday. The hotel is about 1 km (½ mi) east of the city center, close to the Australian War Memorial. ✉ Ainslie and Limestone Aves., Braddon 2601, ☎ 02/6248–5511, ⅏ 02/6247–0864. 77 rooms, 49 suites. 2 restaurants, bar, laundry service and dry cleaning. AE, DC, MC, V.

$$ 🏨 **Quality Inn Downtown.** This recently refurbished motel has modern facilities and is an excellent value—both the price and the proximity to the city center make this a good choice for budget travelers. There are three types of rooms, some of which have kitchens, and the place is kept absolutely spotless. ✉ 82 Northbourne Ave., Braddon 2601, ☎ 02/6249–1388, ⅏ 02/6247–2523. 65 rooms. Restaurant, exercise room, coin laundry. AE, DC, MC, V.

Canberra South

$$$ 🏨 **Hyatt Hotel Canberra.** This elegant hotel, the finest in the national
★ capital, occupies a 1924 Heritage building that was restored in its original Art Deco style. Large, luxurious rooms—and 18 spacious suites—are decorated in warm peach and earth tones. Enormous marble bathrooms will appeal to anyone who enjoys a good soak in the tub. The hotel has extensive gardens and is within easy walking distance of the Parliamentary Triangle. Afternoon tea, held daily between 2:30 and 5 in the gracious Tea Lounge, is one of Canberra's most popular traditions. ✉ Commonwealth Ave., Yarralumla 2600, ☎ 02/6270–1234, ⅏ 02/6281–5998. 231 rooms, 18 suites. 3 restaurants, 2 bars, indoor saltwater pool, sauna, spa, tennis court, exercise room, laundry service and dry cleaning, concierge, business services. AE, DC, MC, V.

$$$ 🏨 **Rydges Capital Hill.** One of Canberra's most luxurious hotels, the Rydges attracts a largely business clientele. The atrium ceiling is composed of immense fabric sails. Rooms, large and well-maintained, have recently been refurbished. The 38 Spa Suites and two Premier Suites are particularly sumptuous. The hotel is close to Parliament House, and in the evening its bar always has a stimulating flow of political gossip from parliamentary staff and members of the press, who drop in regularly. ✉ Canberra Ave. and National Circle, Forrest 2603, ☎ 02/6295–3144, ⅏ 02/6295–3325. 146 rooms, 40 suites. Restaurant, bar, indoor pool, sauna, spa, health club, laundry service and dry cleaning, concierge, business services. AE, DC, MC, V.

$$ 🏨 **Manuka Park Apartments.** The comfortable one- or two-bedroom apartments and interconnecting suites in this low-rise building all have cooking facilities, a living room, and a laundry area. Fully carpeted, open-plan rooms have a clean, contemporary feel. Located in a leafy suburb within easy walking distance of the restaurants, boutiques, and

antiques shops of the Manuka shopping district and surrounded by land-scaped gardens, the apartments are serviced daily, and each has a private balcony or courtyard. ⊠ *Manuka Circle and Oxley St., Manuka 2603,* ☎ *02/6285–1175,* FAX *02/6295–7750. 40 apartments. Saltwater pool. AE, DC, MC, V.*

$$ ⊞ **Telopea Inn on the Park.** This motel lies in a tranquil, leafy southern suburb bordered by parklands and close to Parliament House. Its rooms are small but a good value, and the larger ones with kitchenettes will appeal to families. ⊠ *16 New South Wales Crescent, Forrest 2603,* ☎ *02/6295–3722,* FAX *02/6239–6373. 45 rooms. Restaurant, bar, indoor pool, sauna, spa. AE, MC, V.*

Outside Canberra

$$$$ ⊞ **Avalanche Homestead.** Perched on a hillside in the Tinderry Mountains, this large, modern homestead offers its guests a taste of the "real" Australia. Rooms are spacious and comfortable, and communal activities—including dining—take place in an enormous hall-like room. Guest numbers are limited, and hosts Faye and Frank Biddle place a high priority on individual needs. Daily activities include horseback riding, cattle mustering, sheep shearing, trout fishing, and bushwalking. The property is 45 km (28 mi) south of Canberra and adjoins an 80,000 acre nature reserve that abounds with kangaroos, wallabies, wombats, and colorful birds. Rates include all meals, beverages, and activities. ⊠ *Box 544, Burra Creek, Queanbeyan 2620,* ☎ *02/6236–3245,* FAX *02/ 6236–3302. 6 rooms with shower, 1 with bath. Pool. AE, DC, MC, V.*

$$$$ ⊞ **Brindabella Station.** Set beside a trout stream in a cleared valley amid the rugged glories of the Brindabella Ranges, this turn-of-the-century Australian homestead combines a traditional farm holiday with the added attraction of historic surroundings. Guest numbers are limited to a maximum of four couples at a time. Activities include trout fishing, bushwalking, swimming, mountain biking, canoeing, and watching the abundant wildlife. Accommodation is either in the homestead or in an adjacent cottage, prettily decorated in a crisp, country style. The station is 60 km (38 mi) west of Canberra, some of it along a rough mountain road. Rates include all meals, beverages, and activities. Smoking is not permitted in the homestead. ⊠ *Brindabella Valley, Brindabella 2611,* ☎ *02/6236–2121,* FAX *02/6236–2128. 4 rooms. MC, V.*

NIGHTLIFE AND THE ARTS

Canberra after dark has a reputation for being dull. Actually, the city isn't quite as boring as the rest of Australia thinks, nor again as lively as the citizens of Canberra would like to believe. Most venues are clustered in the city center and the fashionable southern suburb of Manuka. Except on weekends, few places offer live music. The Thursday edition of the *Canberra Times* has a "What's On" section.

The Arts

Canberra Theatre Centre. The city's premier arts and theater venue is used by the local opera company, theatrical troupe, and symphony orchestra. Performances by such major national companies as the Australian Ballet are frequently held here. For a listing of current events, check the entertainment pages of the *Canberra Times.* ⊠ *Civic Sq., London Circuit, Canberra City,* ☎ *02/6257–1077.*

Nightlife

Bobby McGee's. The party atmosphere at this flamboyant, American-style restaurant and entertainment lounge complex appeals to a varied group. In the restaurant, Cinderella might seat you, a matador offer you cocktails, and a Roman centurion wait on your table. The music in the entertainment lounge ranges from "Heartbreak Hotel" to this week's pop hits. Service is slick and professional, and the staff are gregarious and spontaneous—it would require effort not to have a good time. ⊠ *Rydges Canberra Hotel, London Circuit, Canberra City,* ☏ *02/6257–7999.* ▦ *$5 Fri. after 8.* ☉ *Weekdays 5 PM–3 AM, Sat. 7 PM–4 AM.*

Casino Canberra. An attempt was made to create a European-style facility by leaving out slot machines in favor of the more sociable games of roulette, blackjack, poker, minibaccarat, pai gow, and keno. There are 40 gaming tables here, and the complex includes two restaurants, two bars, and a nightclub. ⊠ *21 Binara St., Canberra City,* ☏ *02/6257–7074.* ☉ *Daily noon–6 AM.*

La Grange Boutique Bar & Brasserie. In Manuka, this lively bar attracts a young, fashionable crowd. The disco swings Thursday through Saturday, and live jazz is a Sunday afternoon staple. ⊠ *Capitol Cinema Bldg., Franklin St., Manuka,* ☏ *02/6295–8866.* ▦ *Sat. $5.* ☉ *Mon.–Wed. 4 PM–5 AM, Thurs.–Sun. 11:30 AM–5 AM.*

The Private Bin. One of Canberra's longest-running night spots, this large, loud club incorporates a bar, a beer garden, pool tables, and a tri-level disco. The clientele is mostly under 25, but the club's Waffles Piano Bar attracts older, more sophisticated patrons. Comedy nights, held every Wednesday from about 9 PM, are recommended. ⊠ *50 Northbourne Ave., Canberra City,* ☏ *02/6247–3030.* ☉ *Varying hrs for different bars, but generally weekdays noon–about 2 AM, Sat. 6 PM–3 AM, Sun. 7 PM–1 AM.*

OUTDOOR ACTIVITIES AND SPORTS

Bicycling

Canberra has almost 160 km (100 mi) of cycle paths, and the city's relatively flat terrain and dry, mild climate make it a perfect place to explore on two wheels. One of the most popular cycle paths is the 40-km (25-mi) circuit around Lake Burley Griffin.

Mr. Spokes Bike Hire has a wide range of bikes as well as tandems and baby seats. Bikes cost $8 for the first hour, including helmet rental, $20 for a half day, and $30 for a full day. The shop is open on school holidays. ⊠ *Barrine Dr., Acton Park,* ☏ *02/6257–1188. Closed Mon. and Tues.*

Boating

You can rent aquabikes, surf-skis, paddleboats and canoes daily (except during the winter months of June, July, and August) for use on Lake Burley Griffin from **Burley Griffin Boat Hire.** Rates start at $9 for a half hour. ⊠ *Barrine Dr., Acton Park,* ☏ *02/6249–6861.*

Golf

On the lower slopes of Red Hill, the **Federal Golf Course** is regarded as the most challenging of the city's courses. Nonmembers are welcome on most weekdays, provided they make advance bookings. ⊠ *Red Hill Lookout Rd., Red Hill,* ☏ *02/6281–1888.* ▦ *Greens fee $40 for 18 holes.*

An undulating 27-hole course on the edge of the lake, **Royal Canberra** is the city's premier golf club—due not only to the course itself but also to its membership list, which includes leading politicians from both sides of the government. The club welcomes nonmembers who can show evidence of membership in another golf club and who come with a letter of introduction. Open days are generally Monday, Thursday, and

Friday, but call first. ⊠ *Westbourne Woods, Yarralumla,* ☎ *02/6282–7000.* 🖅 *Australian golf club members $110 for 18 holes; $200 for members of overseas clubs.*

Hiking

Namadgi National Park, Tidbinbilla Nature Reserve, and **Kosciuszko National Park** have excellent bushwalking tracks (☞ Around Canberra and the A.C.T., *above*).

Running

A favorite running track is the circuit formed by the lake and its two bridges—Kings Avenue Bridge and Commonwealth Avenue Bridge.

Tennis

The **National Sports Club** offers play on synthetic grass courts. ⊠ *Mouat St., Lyneham,* ☎ *02/6247–0929.* 🖅 *$14.50 per hr during daylight, $16.50 per hr under lights.* ☉ *Daily 9 AM–10 PM.*

At the **Australian Institute of Sport,** you can play on one of the establishment's six outdoor courts. ⊠ *Leverrier Crescent, Bruce,* ☎ *02/6214–1281.* 🖅 *$8 per hr.* ☉ *Weekdays 8 AM–10 PM, weekends 9–8.*

SHOPPING

Canberra is not famed for its shopping, but there are a number of high-quality arts and crafts outlets where you are likely to come across some unusual gifts and souvenirs. The city's markets are excellent, and the galleries and museums are also good for interesting and often innovative items designed and made in Australia. In addition to the following suggestions, there are several malls and shopping centers in Canberra City.

Cuppacumbalong Craft Centre, a pioneering homestead near the Murrumbidgee River, is now a crafts gallery for potters, weavers, painters, and woodworkers, many of whom have their studios in the outbuildings. The quality of the work is universally high and there is an opportunity to meet and talk with the artisans. The center is located about 34 km (21 mi) south of Canberra, off the Monaro Highway. ⊠ *Naas Rd., Tharwa,* ☎ *02/6237–5116.* ☉ *Wed.–Sun. 11–5.*

Federation Square. Located next to Cockington Green (☞ Around Canberra and the A.C.T., *above*) on the city's northern outskirts, this complex of more than 20 specialty shops includes clothes, crafts, pottery, and gift stores. The large shopping center also has a restaurant, coffee shop, children's playground, and walk-in aviary. ⊠ *O'Hanlon Pl., Gold Creek Village, Gungahlin,* ☎ *0411/10–3075.* ☉ *Daily 10–5.*

Gorman House Markets. These central city markets, which are located in and around a heritage building that also serves as an arts center, sell excellent arts and crafts, old books, secondhand clothes, and have live music, puppet shows, and great food. ⊠ *Ainslie Ave., Braddon,* ☎ *02/6249–7377.* ☉ *Sat. 10–4.*

Old Bus Depot Markets. This old bus depot, south of the lake in the suburb of Kingston, is now home to a lively Sunday market. Handmade crafts are the staples here, and exotic, inexpensive food and buskers add to the shopping experience. ⊠ *Wentworth Ave., Kingston Foreshore, Kingston,* ☎ *02/6292–8391.* ☉ *Sun. 10–4; Dec., weekends 10–4.*

CANBERRA AND THE A.C.T. A TO Z

Arriving and Departing

By Bus

The main terminal for intercity coaches is the **Jolimont Tourist Centre** (⊠ 65–67 Northbourne Ave.). Canberra is served by two major coach lines, both of which have at least three daily services to and from Sydney: **Greyhound Pioneer Australia** (☎ 13–2030) and **Murrays Australia** (☎ 13–2251).

By Car

From Sydney, take the Hume Highway to just south of Goulburn and then turn south onto the Federal Highway to Canberra. Allow 3½ to 4 hours for the 300-km (186-mi) journey. From Melbourne, follow the Hume Highway to Yass and turn right beyond the town onto the Barton Highway. The 655-km (406-mi) trip takes around 8 hours.

By Plane

Canberra Airport is located 7 km (4½ mi) east of the city center. *See* Air Travel *in* Smart Travel Tips for information on airlines.

BETWEEN THE AIRPORT AND CITY

Taxis are available from the rank at the front of the terminal. The fare between the airport and the city is about $12. **Canberra City Sights and Tours** (☎ 02/6249–3171 or 0412/625–552), a shuttle company, offers airport service for $6–$10, reservations required.

By Train

The Canberra Railway Station (☎ 02/6239–0111) is located on Wentworth Avenue, Kingston, about 5 km (3 mi) southeast of the city center. EXPLORER trains make the 4-hour trip between Canberra and Sydney three times daily. A daily coach-rail service operates on the 10-hour run between Canberra and Melbourne. Passengers must travel the 60 km (37 mi) between Canberra and Yass Junction by bus.

Getting Around

By Bus

Canberra's public transportation system is the **ACTION** bus network. Buses operate 6:30 AM–11:30 PM weekdays, 7 AM–11:30 PM Saturday, and 8 AM–7 PM Sunday. There is a flat fare of $2 per ride. If you plan to travel extensively on buses, purchase a Day Sightseeing ticket ($6.70), which allows unlimited travel on the entire bus network. A Shopper's Off Peak Daily ticket, which allows travel between 9 AM and 4 PM and after 6 PM on weekdays and all day on weekends, costs $4.

Tickets, maps, and timetables are available from the Canberra Visitor Centre and the **Bus Information Centre** (⊠ East Row and Alinga St., Civic, ☎ 02/6207–7611).

By Car

Canberra is not an easy city to drive in, and you may well find yourself confused by the radial road system and its turnoffs. Still, because sights are scattered about and not easily connected on foot or by public transport, a car is a good way to see the city itself, as well as the sights in the Australian Capital Territory.

Bus tours, which depart every two hours daily, also visit the major city sights. For full details, *see* Guided Tours, *below.*

Maps ($2) featuring clearly marked scenic drives may be purchased at the Canberra Visitor Centre.

By Taxi

Taxis can be summoned by phone or hired from ranks, but you cannot flag them down in the street. **Aerial Taxis** (☎ 02/6285–9222) is the city's only taxi service.

Contacts and Resources

Car Rentals

National car-rental operators with agencies in Canberra include **Avis** (✉ 17 Lonsdale St., Braddon, ☎ 02/6249–6088); **Budget** (✉ Shell Service Station, Girrahween St., Braddon, ☎ 02/6257–1305); **Hertz** (✉ 32 Mort St., Braddon, ☎ 02/6257–4877 or 13–3039); and **Thrifty** (✉ 29 Lonsdale St., Braddon, ☎ 02/6247–7422). A local operator that offers discount car rentals is **Rumbles Rent A Car** (✉ 11 Paragon Mall, Gladstone St., Fyshwick, ☎ 02/6280–7444).

Doctors

Canberra Hospital has a 24-hour emergency department. ✉ *Yamba Dr., Garran,* ☎ *02/6244–2222.*

Embassies and High Commissions

British High Commission (Commonwealth Ave., Yarralumla, ☎ 02/6270–6666, ☉ weekdays 8:45–5), **Canadian High Commission** (Commonwealth Ave., Yarralumla, ☎ 02/6273–3844, ☉ weekdays 8:30–12:30 and 1:30–4:30), **New Zealand High Commission** (Commonwealth Ave., Yarralumla, ☎ 02/6270–4211, ☉ weekdays 8:45–5), and **U.S. Embassy** (Moonah Pl., Yarralumla, ☎ 02/6270–5000, ☉ weekdays 8:30–12:30).

Emergencies

Ambulance, fire brigade, and police. ☎ *000.*

Guided Tours

ORIENTATION TOURS

Murrays Canberra Explorer offers an affordable introduction to Canberra. In its comprehensive circuit of the city, the red Explorer bus stops at most of the major sights, including Parliament House, the National Gallery, the National Botanic Gardens, the embassies, and the Australian War Memorial. A driver provides commentary, and you are free to leave the bus at any of the 18 stops and board any following Explorer bus. You can also take a two-hour nonstop trip—a good orientation. Tours leave from the Jolimont Tourist Centre at 65–67 Northbourne Avenue and from the Canberra Visitor Centre at 330 Northbourne Avenue, Dickson, every two hours from 8:40 to 4:40. Murrays also offers a range of day or half-day sightseeing tours of Canberra and the surrounding area. ☎ *13–2251.* 🖃 *$18 full day, $8 for two hours.*

Travel Agencies

American Express Travel. ✉ *Centrepoint Building, City Walk and Petrie Plaza,* ☎ *02/6247–2333.*

Thomas Cook. ✉ *18–19 Canberra Centre, Bunda St.,* ☎ *02/6257–2222.*

Visitor Information

Canberra Visitor Centre. The city's tourist information bureau is a convenient stop for those entering Canberra by road from Sydney or the north. The staff makes accommodation bookings for Canberra and the Snowy Mountains. ✉ *330 Northbourne Ave., Dickson,* ☎ *02/6205–0044 or 1800–02–6166.* ☉ *Daily 9–6.*

Canberra Centre. The ground floor kiosk in the Canberra Centre is another useful source of information on attractions and shops. ✉ *Bunda and Akuna Sts.* ☉ *During shopping hrs.*

4 MELBOURNE AND VICTORIA

Melbourne (say *mel*-burn) is the urbane, cultivated sister of brassy Sydney. To the extent that culture is synonymous with sophistication—except when it comes to watching Australian-rules football or the Melbourne Cup—some call this city the cultural capital of the continent. Outside the city, watch the sundown race of fairy penguins on Phillip Island, marvel at the sculpted South Ocean coastline, sample some of the country's tasty wine in and around charming Victorian towns, or bushwalk in a splendid variety of national parks.

By Walter
Glaser and
Michael
Gebicki

Updated by
Josie Gibson

SEPARATED FROM NEW SOUTH WALES by the mighty
Murray River and fronted by a rugged and beautiful coastline, Victoria's terrain is as varied as any in
the country. If you're expecting an Australian norm of big sky and vast
desert horizons, you may be surprised by lush farms, vineyards, forests,
and mountain peaks. And though it's younger than its rival, New
South Wales, Victoria possesses a sense of history and continuity often
missing in other Australian states, where humanity's grasp on the land
appears temporary and precarious—even the smallest rural communities in Victoria erect some kind of museum.

If, like its dowager namesake, Victoria is a little stuffy and old-fashioned,
then the state capital of Melbourne is positively Old World. For all the
talk of Australia's egalitarian achievements, Melbourne society displays an almost European obsession with class. The city is the site of
some of the nation's most prestigious schools and universities, and
nowhere is it more important to have attended the right one. In a country whose convict ancestors are the frequent butt of jokes, Melburnians pride themselves on the fact that, unlike Sydney, their city was founded
by free men and women who came to Victoria of their own accord.

Nonetheless, whatever appearances they maintain, Melburnians do love
their sports. The city is sports mad—especially when it comes to the
glorious, freewheeling Melbourne Cup. On the first Tuesday of each
November, everyone heads to Flemington for the horse race that brings
the entire nation to a grinding halt. Gaily dressed in all manner of out-
rageous costume, from Christmas trees to tiaras, blue-collar workers
and society dames converge to sip champagne, picnic, and cheer on
their favorite thoroughbreds before making the rounds of Cup parties.

Perhaps the mania displayed at almost all Melbourne sporting events
is a reawakening of the raucous excitement that blossomed in the city
during the days of the gold rush. When gold was discovered in 1851,
fortune seekers overran Victoria. Before long, the towns of Bendigo,
Castlemaine, and Ballarat were whirlwinds of activity, as miners poured
in from around the country and the world to try their luck in the goldfields. These were wild times, and the diggers who rolled into nearby
Melbourne to blow off steam were a colorful bunch. The lucky ones
had plenty of money to spend, and spend they did. Many of the gracious buildings that line the streets today are products of that gold rush
boom, which saw the population quadruple within 10 years, as those
who came to seek their fortunes in Victoria settled around what was
rapidly becoming a bona fide capital city.

In Australian terms, Victoria is a compact state, astonishing in its contrasts and all the more exciting for them. Beyond the urban sprawl of
Melbourne, which now extends its tentacles as far as the Mornington
Peninsula, the great oceanscapes of the West Coast are among the most
seductive elements of Victoria's beauty. The romantic history of the
gold rushes pervades central Victoria, while paddle wheelers still ply
the waters of the mighty Murray River. The long stretch of the Murray region is also known for its wineries. And from the Grampians in
the west to the sprawling alpine parks in the east, the great Victorian
outdoors is reason enough itself to plan a trip.

Pleasures and Pastimes

The Arts

Melbourne regards itself as the artistic and cultural capital of Australia.
It is home to the Australian Ballet and a range of opera, theater, and

dance companies—from the traditional to the avant garde. Many regional Victorian cities have their own smaller companies, and their own enthusiastic supporters. Art galleries, both formal and eclectic, abound.

Dining

As a food center, Melbourne is blessed. While most cities consider themselves lucky to have one major fresh food market, Melbourne has markets by the dozen. Fine cheeses and palate-pleasing wines are made right on Melbourne's doorstep, while a caring band of butchers, bakers, and wholesalers keep chefs stocked with the latest, the freshest, and the best. In recent years, Melbourne's dining scene has diversified into a vast smorgasbord of cuisines and dining experiences. Chinese restaurants on Little Bourke Street are the equal of anything in Hong Kong. The neighborhood of Richmond's Victoria Street convincingly reincarnates Vietnam. The central business district now boasts so many hole-in-the-wall Italian cafés that you could almost be in Rome. And a stroll down Fitzroy Street in St. Kilda is a racy, cosmopolitan walk on the wild side, where you'll find everything from sushi and Singapore *laksa* (spicy Malaysian noodle soup) to spaghetti and *som tum* (Thai green papaya salad).

Outside Melbourne, one can still eat well, especially in Victoria's wine country, where an exciting form of regional cooking is evolving at restaurants such as Arthurs on the Mornington Peninsula. Some of the best Greek food in the state can be found along the famous Great Ocean Road at Kosta's in Lorne, and city-smart food stops continue to spring up all around the state, as at The Queenscliff Hotel in the seaside village of Queenscliff and at the Lake House in the spa-town of Daylesford.

CATEGORY	COST*
$$$$	over $60
$$$	$45–$60
$$	$30–$45
$	under $30

per person, excluding drinks and tip

Lodging

Melbourne's best hotels are world class, ranging from marble and glass properties to gracious Victorian-era edifices. Throughout the state, bed-and-breakfasts, host farms, and old-fashioned guest houses are welcome alternatives to hotel and motel accommodations.

CATEGORY	COST*
$$$$	over $220
$$$	$150–$220
$$	$100–$150
$	under $100

All prices are for a standard double room.

Nightlife

Many Victorians content themselves with a night at the movies, but nightclubs, live music venues, pubs, and bars are always full of action, especially in Melbourne and larger regional towns. Melbourne's nightlife mecca is King Street, where dozens of clubs and bars jostle for customers.

Outdoor Activities and Sports

Bushwalking, canoeing, fishing, hiking, rafting, and riding are all choices here—it's a great state for getting out into the bush. Victoria has a variety of outstanding national parks; coastal, mountain, rain forest, and riparian environments that are havens for remarkable plant and animal life. Port Campbell, Grampians, Alpine, and Wilson's

Victoria

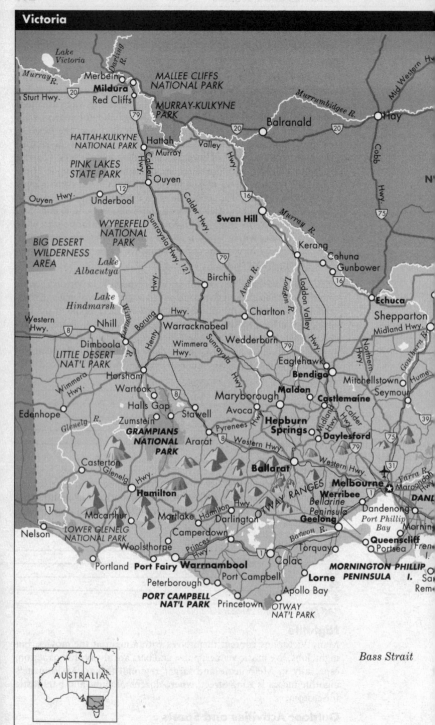

Bass Strait

AUSTRALIA

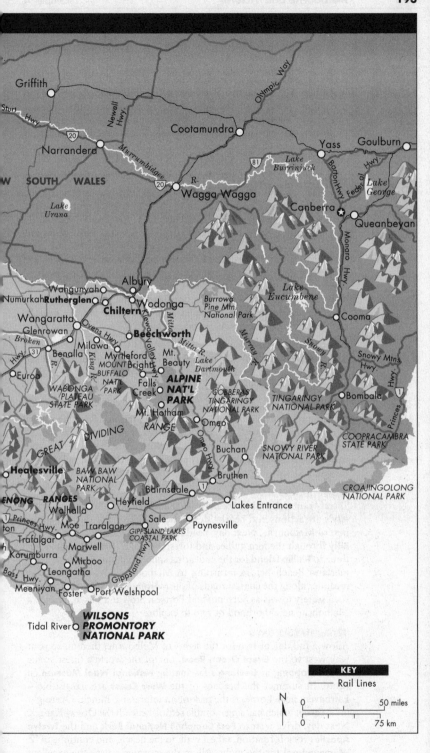

KEY
—— Rail Lines

N

0   50 miles

0   75 km

Promontory national parks can easily be combined with one or two of the tours or side trips in this chapter. For more information on bush-walking, cross-country skiing, horseback riding, and rafting in Victoria's great outdoors, *see* Adventure Vacations *in* Chapter 12.

As for spectator sports, Victorians do love a good match, like Aussies in general. The Melbourne Cup horse race in November brings the entire city to a standstill. The same is true of Australian-rules football, one of a few varieties of "footie." This, the nation's number-one spectator sport, has its stronghold in Melbourne. The season begins in March and reaches its climax at the Grand Final, held in September, when crowds of 100,000 are commonplace.

Exploring Melbourne and Victoria

Victoria has something for almost every traveler, starting with the urban pleasures of Melbourne. Along the West Coast, you'll find rugged, cliff-lined seascapes, dense forests, and charming resort towns. Inland are historic goldfields communities, river towns along the Murray, and Victoria's esteemed vineyards, the smaller boutique variety of which are particularly inviting. But Victoria's contrasting landscape is best represented in its national parks: the weathered offshore rock formations of Port Campbell; the waterfalls, flora, and fauna of the Grampians; the high-country solitude of Alpine National Park; and the densely forested mountains and white-sand beaches of Wilson's Promontory.

Great Itineraries

The state's relatively small size makes Victoria's principal attractions appealingly easy to reach. Another region, another taste of this richly endowed state, is never too far away.

In five days, you can explore the glorious West Coast, particularly the stunning rock formations of Port Campbell National Park, and head into the Gold Country; traveling for a week, you can add the wineries and historic towns of the northeast. With more than 10 days, you can take in remote and less touristy places such as the Wilson's Promontory and Alpine national parks.

IF YOU HAVE 3 DAYS

Spend your nights in ⚄ **Melbourne,** and divide your days between the city's attractions and nearby destinations. Take a full day to see the best of Melbourne. Next day, head for the hills, and a ride on **Puffing Billy** through the fern gullies and forests of the ⚄ **Dandenongs.** Continue to **Phillip Island** for the endearing sunset Penguin Parade at Summerland Beach before returning to Melbourne. On the third day meander along the coastal roads of the **Mornington Peninsula** through such stately towns as Sorrento and Portsea. Stop at a beach, or pick a Melbourne neighborhood or two to explore.

IF YOU HAVE 5 DAYS

Allow a full day or two for the sights of Melbourne, then make your way west to the **Great Ocean Road,** one of the world's finest scenic drives, stopping at **Geelong**'s fascinating **National Wool Museum** en route. In summer the beaches of the **West Coast** are irresistible—Fairhaven, near Lorne, is the pick of an impressive bunch. Overnight in ⚄ **Lorne,** which has a memorable setting beneath the Otway Ranges. Next day, drive west to **Port Campbell National Park** and the **Twelve Apostles** rock formation, take a walk to the beach, and continue to ⚄ **Warrnambool** for the night. Allow the morning to see the excellent Flagstaff Hill Maritime Village before driving northeast to ⚄ **Ballarat,** the center of the goldfields region. Explore the town's 19th-century streetscapes in the evening before viewing the sound-and-light show at Sovereign Hill Historical Park. The following morning, revisit Sovereign Hill and its entertaining re-creation of the 1851 gold diggings, then return to Melbourne.

IF YOU HAVE 10 DAYS

Spend your first two days and nights in Melbourne, with an evening excursion to Phillip Island, then take the West Coast drive, overnighting in ☒ **Lorne** before exploring in detail the delights of **Port Campbell National Park** and ☒ **Warrnambool.** Drive 29 km (18 mi) west of Warrnambool to ☒ **Port Fairy,** one of Victoria's most beautiful towns. Start early the next day for a drive via **Grampians National Park,** where you can pet the tame kangaroos at Zumstein, to ☒ **Ballarat.** Head through **Daylesford** and the spa town of **Hepburn Springs** to ☒ **Bendigo,** where the Golden Dragon Museum examines the history of the Chinese on the goldfields. Next is ☒ **Echuca,** the town that best evokes the vibrancy of life on the Murray River. Then drive via the wineries of the northeast to lovely ☒ **Beechworth** for two nights. Spend a full day in and around the **Alpine National Park**—take a walk among the wildflowers in summer, ski in winter—before making your way back to the capital.

When to Tour Melbourne and Victoria

Melbourne—and, indeed, most of the state—is at its most beautiful in fall, March–May. Days are crisp, sunny, and clear, and the foliage in parks and gardens is glorious. Melbourne winters can be gloomy, but by September the weather clears up, the football finals are on, and spirits begin to soar. Book early if you want to spend time in Melbourne in late October or early November when the Spring Racing Carnival and the Melbourne International Festival are in full swing; likewise in early March when the city hosts a Formula 1 motor racing grand prix.

The West Coast is a busy summer retreat for Melburnians and accommodation can be hard to find between Christmas and New Year's. By the same token, some would argue that the wild seas and leaden skies of winter provide the most suitable ambience for this dramatic scenery. Northeast winters are dry and sunny, thanks to the cloud-blocking bulk of the Great Dividing Range, and perfect for touring. Summer is extremely hot there and in gold country, where spring and fall are often perfect.

MELBOURNE

When she came to Melbourne in 1956 to make the film *On the Beach,* Ava Gardner was credited with quipping that the city *would* be a great place to make a movie about the end of the world. As it turns out, an enterprising journalist invented the comment, but these days Melburnians recall the alleged remark with wry amusement rather than rancor, which shows how far this city of 3.5 million has come. And, considering that Melbourne is consistently rated among the "world's most livable cities" in quality-of-life surveys, Melburnians seem to have opinion on their side.

The symbol of Melbourne's civility, as in turn-of-the-century Budapest or in Boston, is the streetcar. Solid, dependable, going about their business with a minimum of fuss, trams are an essential part of the city. For a definitive Melbourne experience, climb aboard a tram and proceed silently and smoothly up the "Paris end" of Collins Street.

As escapes from the rigors of urban life, the parks and gardens in and around Melbourne are among the most impressive features of the capital of the Garden State. More than one-quarter of the inner city has been set aside as recreational space. The profusion of trees, plants, and flowers creates a feeling of rural tranquillity within the thriving city.

Exploring Melbourne

Melbourne is built on a coastal plain at the top of the giant horseshoe of Port Phillip Bay. The **city center** is an orderly grid of streets on the north bank of the Yarra River, where the state parliament, banks, multinational corporations, and splendid Victorian buildings that sprang up in the wake of the gold rush now stand. This is Melbourne's heart, which you can explore at a leisurely pace in a couple of days. In **South Melbourne,** one of the "neighborhoods" (suburbs) outside of the city center, the Southgate development has refocused Melbourne's vision on the Yarra River. Once a blighted stretch of factories and run-down warehouses, the southern bank of the river is now a vibrant, exciting part of the city, and the river itself is finally taking its rightful place in Melbourne's psyche. Stroll along the Esplanade in the suburb of **St. Kilda,** amble past the elegant houses of **East Melbourne,** enjoy the shops and cafés in **Fitzroy** or **Carlton,** rub shoulders with locals at the Victoria Market, nip into the Windsor for afternoon tea, or hire a canoe at Studley Park to paddle along one of the prettiest stretches of the Yarra—and you will discover Melbourne's soul as well as its heart.

Numbers in the text correspond to numbers in the margin and on the Melbourne City Center and Melbourne Suburbs maps.

City Center

Melbourne's center is an orderly grid of wide streets, framed by the Yarra River to the south and a string of parks to the east. On the river's southern bank, the Southgate development, the arts precinct around the National Gallery, and the King's Domain–Royal Botanic Gardens areas also merit attention (☞ South Melbourne and Richmond, *below*).

A GOOD WALK

One of the finest vistas of the city is from Southbank Promenade, looking across the Yarra River and its busy water traffic to the city's sparkling towers. Start with a stroll around the shops, bars, cafés, and buskers of **Southgate** ① and a visit to the **Victorian Arts Center** ② (☞ South Melbourne, *below*) before crossing the ornate Princes Bridge to the city proper. Take a look to the east from the bridge; the Melbourne Cricket Ground and the Melbourne Park tennis center dominate the scene. On the green banks of the Yarra, boathouses edge toward the water and rowers glide across the river's surface.

At the corner of Swanston and Flinders streets are three major landmarks: **Flinders Street Station** ③, with its famous clocks, **Young and Jackson's Hotel** and its infamous *Chloe,* and **St. Paul's Cathedral** ④. This corner also marks the beginning of **Swanston Street,** a pedestrian roadway intended to bring people off the sidewalks and onto the street. Ironically, though, once there, you have to dodge trams, tour buses, and even service and emergency vehicles—so it's better to keep to the sidewalk after all. The once-gray **City Square** ⑤ was recently renovated into a greener, brighter, and more people-friendly public space. The witty statues along this stretch of road are worth examining in some detail. Fifty yards up the Collins Street hill on the City Square side is the **Regent Theatre,** a fabulous 1930s picture palace transformed into a live theater and the latest in a series of rebirths in Melbourne's classic theater life. Go west on the north side of Collins Street to the **Block Arcade** ⑥, the finest example of the many arcades that Melbourne planners built to defy the strictness of the grid pattern. Turn right between the Hunt Leather and Weiss clothing shops, cross Little

Melbourne City Center

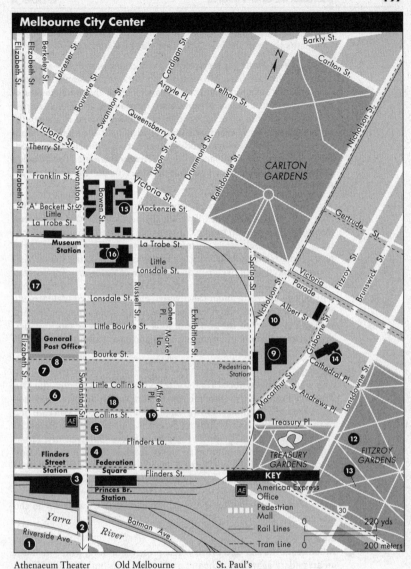

Collins Street, and bear right to enter the airy, graceful **Royal Arcade** ⑦. Standing guard over the shops are Gog and Magog, the mythical giants that toll the hour on either side of Gaunt's Clock.

Bourke Street Mall ⑧ is a cluttered, lively pedestrian zone—although trams run through here, too—busy with buskers and sidewalk artists. Climb the Bourke Street hill to the east to reach the **State Houses of Parliament** ⑨ and adjacent **Parliament Gardens** ⑩ at the end. Across the street from the gardens is the **Princess Theatre,** and to the southeast is the venerable **Windsor Hotel,** an ideal spot for high tea. Walk south to the **Old Treasury Building** ⑪ and its Melbourne Exhibition, then cross the Treasury Gardens to the **Fitzroy Gardens** ⑫ and **Cook's Cottage** ⑬. Head along Landsdowne Street to see the towering **St. Patrick's Cathedral** ⑭.

Walk west along Albert Street, which feeds into Lonsdale Street, then turn right at Russell Street. Two blocks north is the **Old Melbourne Gaol** ⑮, where you can briefly consort with assorted scoundrels. Backtrack down Russell Street, turning right into La Trobe Street; at the next corner is the **State Library** ⑯. This was once also the site of Melbourne's excellent (if overcrowded) **Museum of Victoria,** now relocated to controversial new premises in the Carlton Gardens. End your tour with a little shopping under the inverted glass cone of Lonsdale Street's **Melbourne Central** complex. If you're there on the hour, make your way to the center of the cone and look for the massive clock, which turns into a tableaux of twittering birds and native animals to the tune of "Waltzing Matilda."

TIMING

The walk itself—without time for the Victorian Arts Center, the Old Treasury Building, the State Houses of Parliament, or refreshments—takes around 90 minutes. However, plan a longer stroll if you can; one of the Arts Center exhibitions might catch your eye, or you might decide to take in the Melbourne Exhibition at the Old Treasury. Pleasant weather might tempt you to sit for a while in the lovely Fitzroy Gardens, or you might choose to descend to the grassy riverbanks east of Princes Bridge for a stress-free interlude. If shopping takes your fancy—Southgate, Melbourne's city arcades and Melbourne Central have some of the city's finest outlets—you could while away a day in the city center.

SIGHTS TO SEE

⑱ **Athenaeum Theater and Library.** The present building, which includes an art gallery as well as a theater and library, was built in 1886. These days, the Athenaeum is used mainly for live theatrical performances, yet it is also remembered as the venue for the first talking picture show ever screened in Australia. If you don't make it to a show, take a peek inside 8:30–5 weekdays or 8:30–noon Saturday. ⊠ *180 Collins St.,* ☏ *03/9650–3100.*

⑥ **Block Arcade.** Melbourne's most elegant 19th-century shopping arcade was restored in 1988 when 100 years of grime was scraped back to reveal a magnificent mosaic floor. The arcade was built during the 1880s, when the city was flushed with the prosperity of the gold rushes, a period recalled as "Marvelous Melbourne." ⊠ *282 Collins St. and 100 Elizabeth St.,* ☏ *03/9654–5244.*

NEED A
BREAK?

The **Hopetoun Tea Room** (⊠ Block Arcade, ☏ 03/9650–2777) has been serving delicate sandwiches, refined cakes, and perfectly poured cups of tea for a century. It's a slice of 1890s Melbourne time-warped into the present without too many modern intrusions.

⑧ Bourke Street Mall. Once the busiest east–west thoroughfare in the city, Bourke is now a pedestrian zone (but watch out for those trams!). Two of the city's biggest department stores are here, Myer (Number 314) and David Jones (Number 310). An essential part of growing up in Melbourne is being taken to Myer's at Christmas to see the window displays. ⊠ *Bourke St. between Elizabeth St. and Swanston Walk.*

Carlton Gardens. The 40 acres of tree-lined paths, artificial lakes, and flower beds in this English-style 19th-century park form a backdrop for the **Exhibition Buildings** that were erected in 1880 and are still used for trade shows. The gardens are on the northeast edge of the city center, bounded by Victoria Parade and Nicholson, Carlton, and Rathdowne streets. The outstanding Museum of Victoria was relocated here from its former home next to the State Library and will reopen in mid-2000. The new museum building, a blend of classical and modern architecture, created quite a stir among city aesthetes.

⑰ Church of St. Francis. This Roman Catholic church was constructed in 1845, when the city was barely a decade old. The simple, frugal design starkly contrasts with the Gothic exuberance of St. Paul's, built 40 years later. The difference illustrates just what the gold rush did for Melbourne. ⊠ *Elizabeth and Lonsdale Sts.*

⑤ City Square. Once a messy, dismal open space where Melbourne came to eat lunch, listen to bands, and assemble for protest marches, City Square underwent yet another redevelopment in 1998–99, which incorporated a new hotel and more welcome greenery. Shoppers are sometimes startled by the lifelike bronze statues that emerge from the crowd—a series of tall, thin men striding across the mall, or a growly dog reaching for some unfortunate's ankles. The square also features the statue of Robert Burke and William Wills, whose 1860–61 expedition was the first to cross Australia from south to north. In bronze as in life, their fate is to wander, as this statue has already been relocated several times. The redevelopment of City Square ties in with the radical development of **Federation Square**, located across Flinders Lane on the other side of St Paul's Cathedral. The aggressively modernist redesign of Federation Square, which will officially reopen on its centenary, January 1, 2001, has been a source of local controversy. ⊠ *Swanston St. between Collins St. and Flinders La.*

⑬ Cook's Cottage. Once the property of the Pacific navigator Captain James Cook, this modest cottage was transported stone by stone from Great Ayton in Yorkshire and reerected in the lush Fitzroy Gardens in 1934. It is believed that Cook lived in the cottage between voyages. The interior is simple and sparsely furnished, a suitable domestic realm for a man who spent much of his life in cramped quarters aboard small ships. ⊠ *Fitzroy Gardens, near Lansdowne St. and Wellington Parade.* 🎫 *$3.* ⊙ *Apr.–Oct., daily 9–5; Nov.–Mar., daily 9–5:30.*

Crown Casino. Melbourne's first casino opened in 1994 in the World Trade Centre, and in 1997 moved to its permanent site on the south bank of the Yarra. This is Australia's largest casino (and some say its most crass)—the associated development of hotels, restaurants, bars, entertainment outlets, and boutiques spreads over four city blocks. In any case, there's plenty to do. ⊠ *Riverside Ave.,* ☎ *03/9292–8888.*

⑫ Fitzroy Gardens. This 65-acre expanse of European trees, manicured lawns, garden beds, statuary, and sweeping walks is Melbourne's most popular central park. Among its highlights is the **Avenue of Elms,** a majestic stand of 130-year-old trees that is one of the few in the world that have not been devastated by Dutch elm disease. ⊠ *Lansdowne St. and Wellington Parade.* 🎫 *Free.* ⊙ *Daily sunrise–sunset.*

❸ Flinders Street Station. The clocks on the front of this grand Edwardian hub of Melbourne's suburban rail network are a favorite meeting place for Melburnians. When it was proposed to replace them with television screens there was an uproar. Today, you will find both clocks and screens. ⊠ *Flinders St. and St. Kilda Rd.*

⓯ Old Melbourne Gaol. The city's first jail is now a museum run by the Victorian branch of the National Trust. The jail has three tiers of cells with catwalks around the upper levels. Its most famous inmate was Ned Kelly, who was hanged here in 1880. His death mask and one of the four suits of armor used by his gang are displayed in a ground-floor cell. Evening candlelight tours are a popular, if macabre, facet of Melbourne nightlife. ⊠ *Russell St.,* ☎ *03/9663–7228.* ☞ *$8; $17 for candlelight tours.* ☉ *Daily 9:30–4:30.*

⓫ Old Treasury Building. The neoclassical brick and bluestone facade of the Old Treasury dominates the eastern end of Collins Street. It was built in 1857 to hold the gold that was pouring into Melbourne from mines in Ballarat and Bendigo—architect J.J. Clark designed the building when he was only 19—with subterranean vaults protected by iron bars and foot-thick walls. The **Melbourne Exhibition**, occupying the entire ground floor, takes you from Aboriginal times to the present with relics from Melbourne's past borrowed from public and private collections. Not to be missed is the "Built on Gold" show staged in the vaults themselves. ⊠ *Treasury Pl. and Spring St.,* ☎ *03/9651–2233.* ☞ *$5.* ☉ *Weekdays 9–5, weekends 10–4.*

⓭ Paris End. Beyond the cream and red Romanesque facade of St. Michael's Uniting Church, the eastern end of Collins Street takes on a name coined by Melburnians to identify the elegance of its fashionable shops as well as its general hauteur. Alas, modern development has stolen some of the area's architectural appeal, but shoppers will still find the venerable **Le Louvre** salon (Number 74), favored by Melbourne's high society, and the trendy new incarnation of an old favorite, **Georges** (Number 162).

⓾ Parliament Gardens. Stop here for a breath of cool green air in the center of the city. The gardens have a modern fountain and an excellent view of the handsome yellow ☞ **Princess Theatre** across Spring Street. The gardens are also home to the lovely ☞ **St. Peter's Church.** ⊠ *Parliament, Spring, and Nicholson Sts.* ☉ *Gardens: daily sunrise–sunset.*

NEED A
BREAK?

Pellegrini's Espresso Bar (⊠ 66 Bourke St., ☎ 03/9662–1885) serves industrial-strength coffee and bargain-priced cakes, sandwiches, and pasta dishes. At lunchtime, the narrow bar draws a mixed crowd of students, shoppers, and business executives.

Princess Theatre. The ornate, 1886 wedding cake–style edifice was refurbished in the late 1980s for a production of *Phantom of the Opera*, which was a blockbuster success. The theater, across from Parliament Gardens, is one of Melbourne's Broadway-style venues, along with the Regent Theatre on Collins Street. ⊠ *163 Spring St.,* ☎ *03/9299–9800.*

OFF THE
BEATEN PATH

RIALTO TOWERS OBSERVATION DECK – If you want a bird's-eye view of Melbourne, there's no better—or more popular—place than from the 55th floor of the city's tallest building. The 360-degree panorama is superb, with views on a clear day extending to the Dandenong Ranges and far out into Port Phillip Bay. ⊠ *476 Flinders La.,* ☎ *03/9629–8222.* ☞ *Observation deck $7.50.* ☉ *Daily 10–10.*

❼ Royal Arcade. Built in 1869, this is the city's oldest shopping arcade and, despite alterations, it retains an airy, graceful elegance notably lacking in more modern shopping centers. Walk about 30 paces into the arcade, turn around, and look up to see the statues of Gog and Magog, the mythical monsters that toll the hour on either side of **Gaunt's Clock.** At the far end is a wrought-iron portico from the same period, one of the few remaining examples of the verandas that used to grace the city center. ⌧ *355 Bourke St.,* ☎ *03/9629–8888.*

⓮ St. Patrick's Cathedral. Begun in 1858, construction of Melbourne's Roman Catholic cathedral took 82 years to finish. Another Gothic Revival building, St. Pat's lacks the exuberant decoration of St. Paul's, Melbourne's Anglican cathedral. Ireland supplied Australia with many of its early immigrants, especially during the Irish potato famine in the middle of the 19th century, and the church is closely associated with Irish Catholicism in Australia. A statue of the Irish patriot Daniel O'-Connell stands in the courtyard. ⌧ *Cathedral Pl.,* ☎ *03/9667–0377.* ☉ *Weekdays 6:30–6, weekends 7:15 AM–7:30 PM.*

❹ St. Paul's Cathedral. This headquarters of Melbourne's Anglican faith (completed in 1892) is regarded as one of the most important works of William Butterfield, a leader of the Gothic Revival style in England. The interior is highly decorative, right down to the patterned floor tiles. The English organ is particularly noteworthy. Outside the cathedral is the **Statue of Matthew Flinders,** the first seaman to circumnavigate the Australian coastline, between 1801 and 1803. ⌧ *Flinders and Swanston Sts.,* ☎ *03/9650–3791.* ☉ *Daily 7–7.*

St. Peter's Church. Two years after St. Peter's was built in 1846, Melbourne was proclaimed a city from its steps. You'll find the church, one of Melbourne's oldest buildings, at the top end of Parliament Gardens. ⌧ *Albert and Nicholson Sts.*

❾ State Houses of Parliament. Begun in 1856, this building was used as the National Parliament from the time of federation in 1900 until 1927, when the first Parliament House was completed in Canberra. Today, this commanding building houses the Victorian Parliament. When the state body is in session, you can watch the political process at work from the public gallery. At other times the Upper and Lower House chambers are open to the public. The Upper House, and the Legislative Council chamber in particular, is a study in Victorian opulence. To view these chambers, simply ask at the reception desk inside the front door. Parliament usually sits on Tuesday afternoon and all day Wednesday and Thursday March–July and again August–November. The view down Bourke Street from the front steps is spectacular at night. Plans to extend the building, adding the ornate dome that was in the original design but never built, were announced in 1996, but later scrapped amid political bickering. ⌧ *Spring St.,* ☎ *03/9651–8911.* ▣ *Free.* ☉ *Weekdays 9–4; guided tour at 10, 11, noon, 2, 3, and 3:45 when parliament is not in session.*

⓰ State Library. On a rise behind lawns and heroic statuary, this handsome 1853 building was constructed during the gold-rush boom. It's currently undergoing a major phased renovation, due to finish in 2005. The library houses more than 1.5 million volumes, one of Australia's finest collections of manuscripts, and a vast number of maps, prints, and paintings. If you just want to take a quick look around, be sure to inspect the 115-ft dome of the Reading Room, the largest reinforced concrete dome in the world when it was built in 1913. The library's records of the Burke and Wills Expedition (whose statues are in City Square) are a highlight of its holdings. ⌧ *328 Swanston St.,* ☎ *03/9669–9888.* ▣ *Free.* ☉ *Mon. and Wed. 10–9, other days 10–6.*

OFF THE
BEATEN PATH

VICTORIA MARKET – North of the city center there are bargains galore, but you don't have to be a shopper to enjoy this sprawling, spirited bazaar. Built on the site of the city's first graveyard, the century-old market is the prime produce outlet, and it seems that most of inner-city Melbourne comes here to buy its strawberries, fresh flowers, and imported cheeses. On Sunday, jeans, T-shirts, bric-a-brac, and secondhand goods are the order of the day. ⊠ *Queen and Victoria Sts.,* ☎ *03/9320–5822.* ☉ *Tues. and Thurs. 6–2, Fri. 6–6, Sat. 6–3, Sun. 9–4.*

Windsor Hotel. Not just a grand hotel, the Windsor is home to one of Melbourne's proudest institutions—the ritual of afternoon tea, served daily 3–5 PM. Changes during the past several years have significantly altered the hotel's interiors. The Grand Dining Room, a Belle Époque extravaganza with a gilded ceiling set with seven glass cupolas through which streams tinted sunlight, is now open only to private functions (try to steal a look at the wonder anyway); the former lounge is now the restaurant, renamed 101 Spring Street; and a Hard Rock Café has emerged where a bar once existed. But afternoon tea lives on. Far more than a genteel graze, afternoon tea at the Windsor has long been an integral part of the Melbourne experience—a lesson in the city's manners and mores in what is probably the grandest hotel in the country. Ask about special deals like the Chocolate Indulgence, offered June–September for $39.50 per person. ⊠ *103 Spring St., 3000,* ☎ *03/9633–6000.* 🍴 *Tea weekdays $25, Sat. $28; Sun. afternoon buffet tea $35 per person.*

Young and Jackson's Hotel. Pubs are not generally known for their artwork, but if you climb the steps to the bar you will find *Chloe*, a painting that has scandalized and titillated Melburnians for many decades. The larger-than-life nude, painted by George Lefebvre in Paris in 1875, has hung on the walls of Young and Jackson's Hotel for most of this century. In a more prudish era, *Chloe* was a great drawing card for the pub, although nowadays magazine covers on the newsstand outside are far more provocative. ⊠ *Swanston and Flinders Sts.,* ☎ *03/9650–3884.*

South Melbourne and Richmond

These two riverside neighborhoods are home to the Southgate complex, King's Domain Gardens, which includes the Royal Botanic Gardens and a number of other interesting sights, the Victoria Arts Centre complex, some great restaurants, and, for lovers of sport, the Melbourne Cricket Ground.

SIGHTS TO SEE

King's Domain Gardens. This expansive stretch of parkland includes Queen Victoria Gardens, Alexandra Gardens, the ☞ **Shrine of Remembrance**, Pioneer Women's Garden, the Sidney Myer Music Bowl, and the ☞ **Royal Botanic Gardens**. The floral clock in Queen Victoria Gardens talks and tells time, providing a brief recorded history of the gardens in and around Melbourne. It is situated opposite the Victorian Arts Centre on St. Kilda Road in one of the Domain's many informal gardens. ⊠ *Between St. Kilda and Domain Rds., Anderson St., and Yarra River.*

OFF THE
BEATEN PATH

MELBOURNE CRICKET GROUND – A visit here to tour its outstanding museums is essential for an understanding of Melbourne's sporting obsession. Tours cover the Australian Gallery of Sport and Olympic Museum; the famous Long Room, usually accessible only through membership of the Melbourne Cricket Club (for which there is a *20-year* waiting list); the MCC Cricket Museum and Library; the Great Southern Grandstand; and

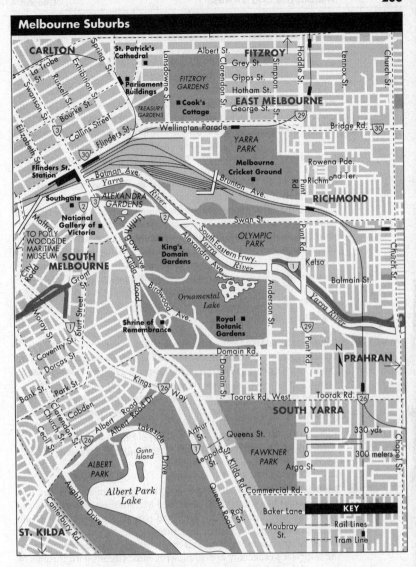

Melbourne Suburbs

pictorial walkways. The memorabilia, especially the cricket-related bits, is some of the best in the world. And although Sydney looks forward to the 2000 Olympics, Melbourne proudly remembers the 1956 Games, for which the MCG was the main stadium. The ground is a pleasant 10-minute walk from the city center or a tram ride to Jolimont Station. ⊠ *Jolimont Terr., Jolimont,* ☎ *03/9657–8879.* ▣ *$9.50.* ☉ *Tours daily on the hour 10–3 (except on event days).*

National Gallery of Victoria. This massive, moat-encircled, bluestone and concrete edifice closed in mid-1999 for major renovations. But don't despair: while most of its impressive collection has been put in moth-balls until a grand reopening in 2001, a selection of works is on show at a temporary gallery in the former Museum of Victoria building on Russell Street in the city. ⊠ *180 St. Kilda Rd.,* ☎ *03/9208–0222.*

OFF THE
BEATEN PATH

POLLY WOODSIDE MARITIME MUSEUM – This site includes both the *Polly Woodside*, a commercial square-rigged sailing ship, and a museum devoted to maritime history. Displays cover the voyages of Captain James Cook, the First Fleet, sailors' crafts, and Victorian shipwrecks. ⊠ *Lorimer St. E, Southbank,* ☎ *03/9699–9760.* ☞ *$7.* ⊙ *Daily 10–4.*

Royal Botanic Gardens. The present design and layout were the brainchild of W. R. Guilfoyle, curator and director of the gardens from 1873 to 1910. Within its 100 acres are 12,000 species of native and imported plants and trees, sweeping lawns, and ornamental lakes populated with ducks and swans that love to be fed. The oldest section of the gardens is Tennyson Lawn, where four English elm trees are more than 120 years old. A fern gully built around an old billabong (pond) contains American swamp cypress, the tallest tree in the gardens. You can discover the park on your own or by joining the free guided walks that leave from the Herbarium. The main entrance to the gardens is on Birdwood Avenue, opposite the Shrine of Remembrance (☞ *below*). During summer there are al fresco performances of classic plays, usually Shakespeare, along with children's classics such as *Wind in the Willows* and the highly popular *Moonlight Cinema* series. The garden setting guarantees an enchanting evening. ⊠ *King's Domain S, Birdwood Ave.,* ☎ *03/9252–2300.* ☞ *Free.* ⊙ *Nov.–Mar., daily 7:30 AM–8:30 PM; Apr.–Oct., daily 7:30–5:30.*

OFF THE
BEATEN PATH

SHRINE OF REMEMBRANCE – Melbourne's War Memorial, in the King's Domain Gardens, was dedicated in 1934 to commemorate the fallen in World War I and has since grown to recognize service in World War II, Korea, Malaya, Borneo, Vietnam, and the Gulf War. The temple-style structure is designed so that at 11 AM on Remembrance Day—the 11th day of the 11th month, when in 1918 armistice for World War I was declared—a beam of sunlight passes over the Stone of Remembrance in the Inner Shrine. In the forecourt is an Eternal Flame. ⊠ *St. Kilda Rd., South Melbourne,* ☎ *03/9654–8415.* ☞ *Donations accepted.* ⊙ *Daily 10–5.*

① **Southgate.** On the river's edge next to the Victorian Arts Center, this development has successfully refocused Melbourne's attention on the Yarra and revitalized a sadly neglected part of the city. It is a prime spot for a promenade and for lingering in general. There are designer shops, classy restaurants, bars, and casual eating places for whiling away the hours. It's especially appealing weekends, vibrant with throngs of people doing whatever they're doing. The Southgate promenade links with the forecourt of Crown Casino. ⊠ *Maffra St. and City Rd.* ☎ *03/9699–4311.*

② **Victorian Arts Centre.** This Southbank arts precinct encompasses the Melbourne Concert Hall, Arts Complex, and National Gallery (☞ *above*). Although it lacks the architectural grandeur of Sydney's Opera House, the Arts Centre is Melbourne's most important cultural landmark and the venue for performances by the Australian Ballet, Australian Opera, and the Melbourne Symphony Orchestra. One-hour tours of the complex leave at noon and 2:30 on weekdays, 10:30 and noon on Saturday, from the Arts Centre shop. On Sunday, a 90-minute backstage tour begins at 12:15. At night, look for the center's spire—lit with brilliant fiber-optic cables, it creates a magical spectacle. ⊠ *100 St. Kilda Rd.,* ☎ *03/9281–8000.* ☞ *Tour $9, backstage tour (no children) $12.* ⊙ *Mon.–Sat. 9–5, Sun. 10–5.*

St. Kilda

The cosmopolitan bayside suburb of **St. Kilda,** 6 km (4 mi) south of the city center, is to Melbourne what Bondi is to Sydney. Whatever St. Kilda lacks in surf, it more than makes up for with its culinary offerings. It is at its best on Sunday afternoon, when half of Melbourne comes here to promenade, eat ice cream, and watch the world go by. The St. Kilda experience begins at the pier—a fine place to stroll and watch sailboats.

The **Esplanade,** which parallels the beach, is the scene of a lively and entertaining Sunday market crowded with arts-and-crafts stalls, which form a backdrop for performances by buskers and street-theater troupes. To the south, the Esplanade curves around the **Luna Park** amusement area. **Acland Street** is St. Kilda's restaurant row—an alphabet soup of restaurants and cuisines, including Chinese, Lebanese, Italian, French, and Jewish. St. Kilda is the center for Melbourne's Jewish population, and the best-known nook to nosh in is **Scheherezade** (⊠ 99 Acland St., ☎ 03/9534–2722), opened in 1958 by Polish émigrés Masha and Avram Zeliznikow. Those with an eye for fashion prefer **Café di Stasio** (⊠ 31 Fitzroy St., ☎ 03/9525–3999), a small Italian café with personality and a gutsy menu (☞ Dining, *below*). Both Acland and **Barkly** streets have interesting and alternative shops.

By night, St. Kilda becomes Melbourne's red-light district, although it pales in comparison with Sydney's Kings Cross. To reach the suburb from the city, take Trams 16, 96, or 12.

OFF THE BEATEN PATH

LUNA PARK – The main attraction of this faded amusement park, modeled after New York's Coney Island, is the Big Dipper roller coaster. The park also has a Ferris wheel, bumper cars, and a ghost train. ⊠ *Lower Esplanade, St. Kilda,* ☎ *03/1902–240112.* ⊠ *Park admission free, major rides $3.* ☉ *Sun.–Thurs. 1–5, Fri.–Sat. 1–11.*

Fitzroy

Two km (1¼ mi) north of the city center, **Fitzroy** is Melbourne's bohemian quarter. What was once a drab, deprived part of the city is now prized by upwardly mobile white-collar workers looking for affordable housing within easy reach of city jobs. There are no inspiring monuments or grand municipal buildings to be seen here, but if you're looking for an Afghan camel bag or a secondhand paperback, or yearn for a café where you can sit over a plate of tapas and watch Melbourne go by, Fitzroy is the place.

The main drag is **Brunswick Street.** Roar Studios (Number 115) and the **Woman's Gallery** (Number 375) specialize in the work of up-and-coming Australian artists. **On Shore** (Number 267) sells only Australian-made arts and crafts, which make excellent souvenirs. **Port Jackson Press** (Number 397) publishes and sells prints by Australian artists. The **Brunswick Street Bookstore** (Number 305) has a good range of modern Australian literature.

Along with Lygon Street in nearby **Carlton** (☞ *below*), Brunswick is also one of Melbourne's favorite eat streets. **The Black Cat Café** (⊠ 252 Brunswick St., ☎ 03/9419–6230) is a delightful throwback to the 1950s coffee lounge. Across the street, **Guernica** (⊠ 257 Brunswick St., ☎ 03/9416–0969) is a smart, highly regarded modern Australian restaurant. **The Provincial Hotel** (⊠ 299 Brunswick St., ☎ 03/9417–2228) is a born-again pub serving pizzas cooked in a wood-fired oven and gargantuan dishes of pasta. A little farther up, **Rhumbarella's** (⊠ 342 Brunswick St., ☎ 03/9417–5652), is a hot scene, forever dispensing coffee and cocktails to the hip and hungry. And **Babka Bak-**

ery Café (⊠ 358 Brunswick St., ☎ 03/9416–0091) serves everything from great breads and cheesecake to Russian breakfast blintzes.

Carlton

Some of inner Melbourne's finest residential streets are found in this suburb, especially in its northern reaches. It is also one of the liveliest parts of the city, with the Lygon Street restaurant row as its focus. Lygon Street is the city's Little Italy, with countless Italian restaurants and cafés, although most of them, sadly, are undistinguished. But the area has great color, particularly at night when the sidewalks are thronged with diners and strollers and a procession of high-revving muscle cars rumbling along the strip.

To see the best of Carlton's **Victorian-era architecture,** venture north of Princes Street, paying particular attention to Drummond Street, with its rows of gracious terrace houses, and Canning Street, which has a mix of workers' cottages and grander properties. The streetscapes, accented by mature trees, have gone largely unaltered since the end of the last century. The whole area repays gentle rambling.

Lygon Street also beckons, a perfect example of Melbourne's multiculturalism—where once you'd have found only Italian restaurants, you now discover Thai, Afghan, Malay, Caribbean, and Greek eateries. Walking north from Queensberry Street you'll find the monolithic **Toto's Pizza House** (⊠ 101 Lygon St., ☎ 03/9347–1640), which claims to be Australia's first pizzeria. Whether or not the boast is true, Toto's has served cheap pizza for more than 45 years. For Caribbean island cooking, try the curries of **Jamaica House** (⊠ 106 Lygon St., ☎ 03/9663–5715), a local haunt of many years. At **Casa del Gelato** (⊠ 161 Lygon St.) you can enjoy some of the city's best ice cream. For Southeast Asian fare, **Lemongrass Restaurant** (⊠ 189 Lygon St., ☎ 03/9347–5204) serves a more sophisticated and understated strain of Thai food than the boisterous curries of other Thai restaurants, and **Nyonya Malaysian Restaurant** (⊠ 191 Lygon St., ☎ 03/9347–8511) is good for reasonably priced, well-prepared dishes.

Across Grattan Street is a local institution, the **University Café** (⊠ 257 Lygon St., ☎ 03/9347–2142). The **Lygon Food Store** (No. 263) is the place for Italian cheeses and cured meats—just eyeing the windows' piles of *parmigiano* and pendant *prosciutto* guarantees weight gain (but go ahead and pick up a picnic anyway). **Tiamo** (⊠ 303 Lygon St., ☎ 03/9347–5759) has been a trysting place for generations of Melbourne lovers, who come for the cozy atmosphere, wholesome food, and good coffee. The legendary **Jimmy Watson's Wine Bar** (⊠ 333 Lygon St., ☎ 03/9347–3985) is the spot for a convivial glass or two downstairs, or a more formal meal upstairs.

East Melbourne

Another historic enclave of Victorian houses that dates from the boom following the gold rushes of the 1850s, **East Melbourne** is less than 1 km (½ mi) from the city center. For a concise tour of the neighborhood, whose harmonious streetscapes are a great excuse for a stroll, start at the southeast corner of Fitzroy Gardens and head north on Clarendon to George Street. Turn right and take in the procession of superb terrace houses and mature European trees as you walk down the gentle slope of the street. Two blocks ahead, turn left on Simpson, then again on wide, gracious Hotham Street. On either side of the grassy median that divides the roadway, the mix of terrace houses and freestanding mansions includes some of the suburb's finest architecture. Back at Clarendon, turn north. Bishopscourt, the bluestone residence of the Anglican Archbishop of Melbourne, occupies the next block. Wind right again down Gipps Street and make your way to pretty Darling Square. For different scenery on the way back, take Simpson Street south and turn right on Wellington Parade.

South Yarra/Prahran

One of the coolest spots to be on any given night is in South Yarra and Prahran. The heart of this trendy area is Chapel Street, a long road packed with pubs, bars, notable restaurants, upmarket boutiques, cinemas, and even army disposal stores and pawn shops. One of the classiest places to stop for a bite, if you can get in, is **Caffe e Cucina** (⊠ 581 Chapel St., ☎ 03/9827–4139). **Kasbah** (⊠ 481 Chapel St., ☎ 03/9826–6442) is a more casual option. Farther down is the spruced-up **Chapel Street Bazaar** (⊠ 217–223 Chapel St., ☎ 03/9529–1727), a series of wooden stalls selling everything from stylish secondhand clothes to sunglasses and knickknacks. Of course, if you're after a real market, it's difficult to find one better than the renovated **Prahran Market** (⊠ off Chapel near Commercial Rd., ☎ 03/9522–3301), where committed foodies will find everything from starfruit and lemongrass to emu eggs and homemade relishes. If you're feeling alternative rather than trendy, head for **Greville Street**, which runs off Chapel near the former Prahran Town Hall and is home to more bars and eateries, groovy clothes, and music shops. The revered live music venue here is the **Continental Cafe** (⊠ 132A Greville St., Prahran, ☎ 03/9510–2788; ☞ Nightlife, *below*).

Around Melbourne

Como House. A splendid white Victorian mansion overlooking the Yarra, Como is Melbourne's finest example of an early colonial house. The main part of the mansion was built around 1855, and the kitchen wing predates that by 15-odd years. The gardens slope down toward the Yarra River, demonstrating the landscaping finesse of Baron von Mueller, who was also responsible for planning the city's Royal Botanic Gardens. ⊠ *Lechlade Ave. and Williams Rd., South Yarra,* ☎ *03/9827–2500.* ☒ *$9.* ⊙ *Daily 10–5.*

☺ **Melbourne Zoological Gardens.** Recognized as one of the finest zoos in the world, the Melbourne Zoo continues to make improvements. The grounds have been transformed into gardens, and most of the animal enclosures have been renovated into "open-environment settings." Of particular interest are animals unique to Australia, such as the koala, kangaroo, wombat, emu, and echidna. A lion park, reptile house, and butterfly pavilion are also on site, as is a simulated African rain forest where the only group of gorillas in the country resides. Jazz bands occasionally serenade visitors and animals on summer evenings. The zoo is 4 km (2½ mi) north of Melbourne city center. ⊠ *Elliot Ave., Parkville,* ☎ *03/9285–9300.* ☒ *$14.* ⊙ *Jan.–Mar., daily 9 AM–9:30 PM; Apr.–Dec., daily 9–5.*

Rippon Lea. Begun in the late 1860s, Rippon Lea is a sprawling polychrome brick mansion built in the Romanesque style. By the time of its completion in 1903 the original 15-room house had swollen into a 33-room mansion. The gardens were inspired by romantic Victorian concepts of landscape gardening that were fashionable in England at the time. Notable features include a grotto, a tower that overlooks the lake, a fernery, and humpback bridges. In summer plays are performed on the grounds. A recent drama of choice was an adaptation of Henry James's *Turn of the Screw.* ⊠ *192 Hotham St., Elsternwick,* ☎ *03/9523–6095.* ☒ *$9.* ⊙ *Tues.–Sun. 10–5.*

☺ **Scienceworks Museum.** A former sewage-pumping station in suburban Spotswood has been transformed into a much more glamorous place.

This hands-on museum entertains while it educates—kids will have a ball. There are permanent and changing exhibits and regular programs of science-related activities. A perennially popular permanent exhibit is Sportsworks, where you can test your speed against an Olympic sprinter and perform other sporting feats. ⊠ *2 Booker St., Spotswood,* ☎ *03/9392–4800.* ☒ *$8.* ☉ *Daily 10–4:30.*

Dining

Updated by
Terry Durack

Reservations are generally advised in the city, and although most restaurants are licensed to sell alcohol, the few that aren't will usually allow you to bring your own. Wine lists range from encyclopedic to small and selective, featuring Australian wines, which show unequaled freshness and fruit. Lunch is served noon–2:30, and dinner—usually a single seating—is 7–10:30. A 10% tip is customary, and there may be a corkage fee in BYOB restaurants. Expect neither sales tax nor service charge.

City Center

CHINESE

$$$$ ✕ **Flower Drum.** Under meticulous owner Gilbert Lau, Flower Drum
★ has blossomed as one of the country's truly great Chinese restaurants, serving superb Cantonese and Sichuan cuisine. The restrained elegance of the decor, deftness of the service, and intelligence of the wine list puts most other restaurants to shame. Simply ask your waiter for the day's special and prepare yourself for a feast: perhaps crisp-skinned Cantonese roast duck served with plum gravy, succulent dumplings of prawn and flying fish roe, a perfectly steamed Murray cod, or huge Pacific oysters daubed with black bean sauce. ⊠ *17 Market La.,* ☎ *03/9662–3655. Reservations essential. AE, DC, MC, V. No lunch Sun.*

$$$ ✕ **Mask of China.** Though it hardly seems fair, Melbourne has the country's finest Chinese restaurants all to itself. Mask of China is quietly elegant, the food refined and refreshingly subtle. The focus is on little-known flavors of Chiu Chow, a type of Cantonese cooking. Seafood is a real treat, especially the abalone, sweet and salty prawns, and perfectly steamed whole fish. For an authentic Chiu Chow experience, try the *chin jew* chicken (chicken with deep-fried pearl leaves) or the soyed goose with vinegar dipping sauce. ⊠ *115–117 Little Bourke St.,* ☎ *03/9662–2116. AE, DC, MC, V. No lunch Sat.*

FRENCH

$$$ ✕ **Langton's.** Chef Philippe Mouchel has taken up residence in this elegant subterranean city space, along with his precious $180,000 Bonnet stove. Both the more upmarket restaurant and easygoing wine bar offer excellent values, considering Mouchel's three-star pedigree and wine man Stewart Langton's epic wine list. In the wine bar, tuck into a sensational chicken and avocado salad, or a substantial spit-roasted veal rib. In the restaurant, choose between the exotic *tagine* (a Moroccan stew) of farmed rabbit, the gorgeously sticky *daube* (a French casserole of braised meat, red wine, and vegetables) of pig's feet, and the harmonious duck medley platter. ⊠ *Sargood House, 61 Flinders La.,* ☎ *03/9663–0222. Reservations essential. AE, DC, MC, V. Closed Sun. No lunch weekends.*

ITALIAN

$$$ ✕ **Marchetti's Latin.** Though the Latin has been a Melbourne institution since 1919, its reputation has never been as formidable, nor its following as devoted, as under the irrepressible current chef and owner, Bill Marchetti. With the stage presence of an opera singer, Marchetti has made this a favorite of visiting Hollywood types as well as devoted locals. All rave about innovative dishes like tortellini filled with Queens-

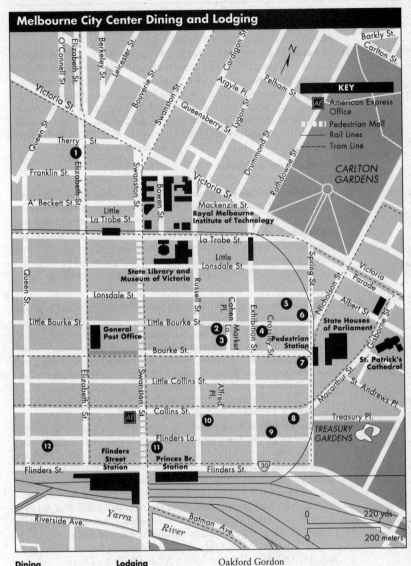

Melbourne City Center Dining and Lodging

KEY

AE American Express Office

Pedestrian Mall

Rail Lines

Tram Line

Dining

Becco, **4**

Flower Drum, **3**

Langton's, **9**

Marchetti's Latin, **5**

Mask of China, **2**

Lodging

The Adelphi, **11**

Grand Hyatt, **10**

Grand Mercure Hotel Melbourne, **12**

Hotel Sofitel Melbourne, **8**

Oakford Gordon Place, **6**

Windsor Hotel, **7**

Hotel Y, **1**

land mud crab, sensational pumpkin-filled ravioli, and suckling pig with Sardinian mint. ⊠ *55 Lonsdale St.,* ☎ *03/9662–1985. Reservations essential. AE, DC, MC, V. No lunch Sat.*

$$ ✕ **Becco.** Every city center needs a place like Becco, with its drop-in bar, lively dining room, and attached gourmet food store full of great cheeses, imported pastas, and preserves. At lunchtime, no-time-to-dawdle business types tuck into white-bait fritters, tagliolini with fresh tuna, risotto pescatora, and ricotta cake. Things get a little moodier at night, when a Campari and soda at the bar is an almost compulsory precursor to dinner. ⊠ *11–12 Crossley St.,* ☎ *03/9663–3000. Reservations essential. AE, DC, MC, V. No lunch weekends.*

Melbourne Suburbs

CAFÉS

$$ ✕ **Richmond Hill Café and Larder.** Leading chef and food writer Stephanie Alexander and cheese master Will Studd are the forces behind this bright and buzzy café-cum-produce store. The bistro fare brims with wonderful flavors, from the chicken, almond, and mushroom pie to an old-fashioned steak sandwich. After you've eaten, pick up some marvelous cheese and country-style bread from the adjoining store. ⊠ *48–50 Bridge Rd., Richmond,* ☎ *03/9421–2808. AE, DC, MC, V. No dinner Sun.*

FRENCH

$$$$ ✕ **Pomme.** Jeremy Strode—one of a band of young English chefs who
★ have redefined the Melbourne dining scene—makes good use here of the skills he learned at top London restaurants. The wine list is intelligent, the service is caring, and the food is often revolutionary. There isn't a bad dish on the menu, but the pot-roasted pigeon with potatoes and the roasted John Dory with chicken and thyme juices are especially recommended. The restaurant is stylish and intimate. ⊠ *37 Toorak Rd., South Yarra,* ☎ *03/9820–9606. Reservations essential. AE, DC, MC, V. Closed Sun. No lunch Sat. and Mon.*

$$$ ✕ **Circa, the Prince.** If the recently reinvented Prince hotel is the crowning glory of the St. Kilda strip, then Circa is the jewel in the crown. Here is a restaurant that glows with a knowing, inner-urban, Philippe Starck flair. It's hard not to feel glamorous while sitting on a white leatherette banquette, sipping pinot noir and eating the highly crafted food of chef Michael Lambie. Start with the luscious foie gras and pressed–ham hock terrine, then move on to the deftly rolled rabbit saddle with *pommes fondant* (small egg-shaped potatoes simmered in butter). Finish with a pyramid of passion fruit sorbet and hazelnut parfait. ⊠ *2 Acland St., St. Kilda,* ☎ *03/9534–5033. Reservations essential. AE, DC, MC, V. Closed Mon. No lunch Tues.–Thurs.*

$$ ✕ **France-Soir.** Suddenly, you're not south of the Yarra River anymore;
★ you're on the Left Bank of the Seine, in a world of crisp paper tablecloths, waiters clad in long black aprons, and patrons drinking aristocratic burgundies and Kronenbourg beer. Diners sit elbow to elbow, praising each other's food and listening to the conversations around them. Onion soup here is the genuine article, oysters are shucked strictly to order, *pommes frites* (french fries) are *fantastique,* and *andouillette*

raises the humble sausage to dizzy heights. Do leave room for the *tarte Tatin* (upside-down apple pie), a work of art. ⊠ *11 Toorak Rd., South Yarra,* ☎ *03/9866–8569. Reservations essential. AE, DC, MC, V.*

$$ ✕ **Luxe.** Just as top-flight Parisian restaurants open cheaper bistros,
★ Melbourne's est est est restaurant (☞ *below*) has established this low-key eatery with spectacular results. Luxe looks great in a postmodern, bomb-shelter way, and the crowd is extremely groovy. However, the real attractions are chefs Karen White and Rita Macali and their take on French bistro fare: ham hock, lentil, and parsley terrine; navarin of lamb; and the *choucroute* (a French variation on sauerkraut) of cabbage and frankfurters; all of which would be at home in a fine hotel's dining room. ⊠ *13 Inkerman St., St. Kilda,* ☎ *02/9534–0255. Reservations not accepted. AE, DC, MC, V. No lunch Mon.–Thurs.*

ITALIAN

$$$ ✕ **Café di Stasio.** This café treads a very fine line between mannered
★ elegance and decadence. A sleek marble bar and modishly ravaged walls contribute to the sense that you've stepped into a scene from *La Dolce Vita*. Happily, Café di Stasio is as serious about its food as its sense of style. Crisply roasted duck is now a local legend, char-grilled baby squid is a sheer delight, and the pasta is always al dente. If the amazingly delicate lobster omelette is on the menu, do yourself a favor and order it. ⊠ *31 Fitzroy St., St. Kilda,* ☎ *03/9525–3999. Reservations essential. AE, DC, MC, V.*

$$ ✕ **Caffe e Cucina.** Close your eyes and think of Italy. This always-packed café set the standards for Melbourne's many atmospheric espresso stops. It draws the fashionable, look-at-me crowd for a quick coffee and pastry downstairs, or for a more leisurely meal upstairs in the warm, woody dining room. Order melt-in-the-mouth gnocchi, calamari *San Andrea* (lightly floured and deep fried), prosciutto with figs, and a glass of Victorian pinot noir. For dessert, the tiramisu is even better looking than the crowd. ⊠ *581 Chapel St., South Yarra,* ☎ *03/9827–4139. Reservations essential upstairs, not accepted downstairs. AE, DC, MC, V.*

$$ ✕ **Melbourne Wine Room Restaurant.** While the Wine Room itself buzzes
★ day and night with young, black-clad types clinging to glasses of local pinot noir and snacky finger food, the adjoining restaurant is far less frenetic. Elegantly whitewashed, with a moody glow that turns dinner for two into a romantic tête-à-tête, it possesses a gloriously down-at-the-heels sense of glamour. Chef Karen Martini-King's Italianate fare is at once confident and determinedly single-minded, running from powerful risottos to solid, forceful pastas, and no-nonsense grills that make you sit up and take notice. ⊠ *125 Fitzroy St., St. Kilda,* ☎ *03/9525–5599. Reservations essential. AE, DC, MC, V. No lunch.*

$ ✕ **Café a Taglio.** Rarely has pizza been this delicious, or this groovy. While there is a blackboard menu of very good pastas and other Italian dishes, regulars prefer to cruise the counter, choosing from the giant squares of pizza on display. Pizza toppings include bright-orange pumpkin, strikingly pretty rosemary and potato, tangy anchovy and olives, beautifully bitter radicchio, pancetta, tomato, and more. Grab a glass of house red, and don't be surprised if someone wants to take your photograph. ⊠ *157 Fitzroy St., St. Kilda,* ☎ *03/9534–1344. Reservations not accepted. No credit cards. Closed Mon.*

JAPANESE

$$ ✕ **Akita.** Melbourne has plenty of Japanese restaurants with beautiful
★ decor, dazzling tatami rooms, and a glitzy clientele. This isn't one of them. Here the fancy footwork is confined to the menu. The handwritten specials list could serve as a seasonal calendar: In summer it's awash with clams in butter and sake or vinegared crabs, while winter brings braised root vegetables and savory egg custards. There's no better Japanese restaurant in town. ⊠ *Courtney and Blackwood Sts., North Melbourne,* ☎ *03/9326–5766. AE, DC, MC, V. Closed Sun. No lunch Sat.*

MALAYSIAN

$ ✕ **Chinta Blues.** This is a curious, beckoning sort of place that manages
★ to combine both the charms of a Malaysian-style coffeehouse with the vibe and cool of a modern street-smart café, with barely a seam showing. Tables are simple plywood, seating is by way of communal benches, and the walls are covered in dark wooden shelves stocked with Asian groceries. Curry laksa—a bathtub of noodles, chicken, and prawns in a spicy broth—is heaven in a bowl, and spinach *blachan* (with fermented, dried shrimp paste) and spicy wok-fried noodles will soothe most hotheads. ⊠ *6 Acland St., St. Kilda,* ☎ *03/9534–9233. AE, MC, V.*

MODERN AUSTRALIAN

$$$$ ✕ **est est est.** Tables are double-clothed, the wine list is encyclopedic,
★ and the food is as balanced as a tightrope walker. Chefs Donovan Cooke and Philipa Sibley-Cooke have cooked their way through the three stars of France and the rising stars of Britain, and their skills show in blue swimmer crab tortellini, roast saddle of rabbit, and fingers of John Dory with roasted salsify, an endearingly old-fashioned root vegetable. Also memorable are scallops and roasted calamari sauced with squid ink, and a glossy chocolate pyramid filled with Valrhona chocolate. ⊠ *440 Clarendon St., South Melbourne,* ☎ *03/9682–5688. Reservations essential. AE, DC, MC, V. Closed Sun. No lunch.*

$$$$ ✕ **Jacques Reymond's.** French discipline and an Asian palette delightfully intertwine in this glamorous Victorian mansion with open fireplaces, soft candlelight, and a secret garden. The wine list is the stuff an oenophile dreams of, and service is intelligent, intuitive, and informed. The Burgundian-born chef uses the finest Australian produce to create such classics as roasted white rabbit with tandoori spices, and glazed pigeon with Sichuan pepper sauce. ⊠ *78 Williams Rd., Windsor,* ☎ *03/9525–2178. Reservations essential. AE, DC, MC, V. Closed Sun. and Mon. No lunch Sat.*

$$$ ✕ **Donovan's.** This bay-side hot spot has all the allure of a smart beach house that's straight out of *Martha Stewart Living* magazine. Get a window table and enjoy wide-open views of St. Kilda beach and its passing parade of rollerbladers, skateboarders, dog walkers, and ice-cream lickers. Owners Kevin and Gail Donovan are such natural hosts you'll feel like bunking down overnight, while chef Robert Castellani serves up lemon vodka risotto, swordfish with onion relish, and veal scallopine. ⊠ *40 Jacka Blvd., St. Kilda,* ☎ *03/9534–8221. Reservations essential. AE, DC, MC, V.*

$$$ ✕ **Mecca.** Most attempts at modern Australian cooking are based either on the Mediterranean flavors of Italy and southern France or the distinctive influences of Southeast Asia. In her new, smart riverside restaurant, chef Cath Claringbold has added a detour through the Middle East, as a result of working with Lebanese-born Greg Malouf at O'Connells (☞ *below*) in South Melbourne. Among the usual Mediterranean offerings

Melbourne Suburbs Dining and Lodging

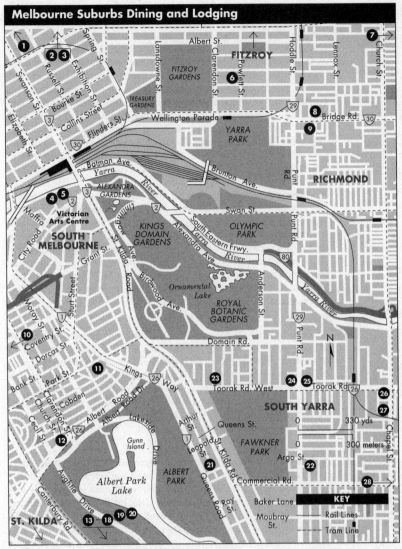

Dining

Akita, **1**

Café a Taglio, **17**

Café di Stasio, **16**

Caffe e Cucina, **27**

Chinta Blues, **15**

Circa, the Prince, **20**

Donovan's, **13**

est est est, **12**

France-Soir, **24**

Jacques Reymond's, **28**

Luxe, **19**

Mecca, **4**

Melbourne Wine Room Restaurant, **14**

O'Connell's, **10**

Pomme, **25**

Richmond Hill Café and Larder, **9**

Toofey's, **2**

Vlado's, **8**

Walter's Wine Bar, **5**

Lodging

City Park Motel, **11**

Country Comfort Old Melbourne Hotel, **4**

Hotel Como, **26**

Lygon Lodge Carlton, **3**

Magnolia Court Boutique Hotel, **6**

Oakford Apartments, **22**

Oakford Fairways, **21**

Pathfinder Motel, **7**

Robinson's by the Sea, **18**

The Tilba, **23**

is more exotic fare, including rack of lamb crusted with *dukkha* (an Egyptian spice mixture) and duck flavored with *ras el hanout* (a Moroccan mixture of berries, pods, and roots). ⊠ *Mid Level, Southgate, Southbank,* ☏ *03/9682–2999. Reservations essential. AE, DC, MC, V.*

$$ ✕ **O'Connell's.** Combine classic French training with a Lebanese background and you'll have some of the most intriguing food in Melbourne, served in the no-frills dining room of this reborn suburban pub. Fortunately, the wine list is comprehensive enough to take on whatever chef Greg Malouf serves up, including mushroom ravioli with haloumi cheese, couscous with seven vegetables, and grilled black pudding with Egyptian fried egg. Finish with a layered coffee cream pot, a creamy custard flavored with coffee. ⊠ *Montague and Coventry Sts., South Melbourne,* ☏ *03/9699–9600. Reservations essential. AE, DC, MC, V. Closed Sun. No lunch Sat.*

$$ ✕ **Walter's Wine Bar.** Smack in the middle of Melbourne's lively Southgate complex, this is one nonstop party. Nibble on a classy platter of local cheeses, sip a lively Mornington Peninsula pinot or a well-raised Yarra Valley chardonnay, and dine on simple grills and other bistro-style dishes such as duck confit, smoked salmon, and upmarket burgers. Whether you sit outside on the balcony overlooking the river or inside with the milling throng, it is an essential Melbourne experience. ⊠ *Southgate Complex, Level 3, South Melbourne,* ☏ *03/9690–9211. Reservations essential. AE, DC, MC, V.*

SEAFOOD

$$$ ✕ **Toofey's.** Michael Bacash's Middle Eastern background and Italian training combine to form a refreshing Mediterranean approach to Australian seafood. Toofey's has the good looks of a trendy bistro and the good sense to serve only what's best at fish markets that day. It's here that you'll find Melbourne's definitive spaghetti marinara, as well as sardines *Zahle* (served with eggplant dip), and a bountiful seafood risotto. ⊠ *162 Elgin St., Carlton,* ☏ *03/9347–9838. AE, DC, MC, V. No lunch weekends.*

STEAK HOUSE

$$$ ✕ **Vlado's.** Vlado Gregurek snaps on a fresh pair of pristine white gloves every time he picks up a new cut of beef and tenderly inspects it. If you love a good steak, you'll love Vlado's. His restaurant is amazingly single-minded: Pictures of grazing cattle hang on the walls above business people grazing on set menus of liver, sausage, and perfectly grilled meat. Salads may be so-so, mustards and horseradish uninspired, and strawberry pancake desserts undistinguished—just remember that you have come here for the steak of your life. ⊠ *61 Bridge Rd., Richmond,* ☏ *03/9428–5833. Reservations essential. AE, DC, MC, V. Closed Sun. No lunch Sat.*

Lodging

City Center

$$$$ ★ 🏨 **Grand Hyatt.** Melbourne's top hotel for glitz, glamour, and service is at the Paris End of Collins Street. Soft tones infuse the decor throughout, with a luxurious lobby in roseate marble and oak paneling. A separate atrium includes two floors of elegant shops and a vast international food court that supplements the hotel's dining rooms. Top floors have attractive views, and all rooms are graced with marble bathrooms, king-size beds, and small sitting areas. Four Regency Club floors have their own check-in facility and lounge and provide complimentary Conti-

nental breakfasts and refreshments throughout the day. ✉ *123 Collins St., 3000,* ☎ *03/9657–1234,* ᴵᴬˣ *03/9650–3491. 547 rooms, 48 suites. 2 restaurants, 2 bars, food court, pool, tennis court, health club, nightclub, business services. AE, DC, MC, V.*

$$$$ 🏨 **Grand Mercure Hotel Melbourne.** Formerly the Sebel of Melbourne, the Grand Mercure is the smallest of the city's upscale hotels, with only 58 one- and two-bedroom suites. Rooms are tastefully decorated in apricot, burgundy, lemon, and pale green, and are beautifully furnished. All have kitchenettes with a microwave oven and a refrigerator. Guests have use of a small private courtyard, inspired by the Renaissance gardens of Italy. The central location is a bonus. ✉ *321 Flinders La., 3000,* ☎ *03/9629–4088,* ᴵᴬˣ *03/9629–4066. 58 suites. Restaurant, bar, health club. AE, DC, MC, V.*

$$$$ 🏨 **Hotel Sofitel Melbourne.** The glossy hotel half of this twin-towered Collins Place complex was designed by architect I. M. Pei, and it combines glamour and excellent facilities with a prime location. Guest rooms, which begin on the 35th floor of the 50-story building, are built around a mirrored central atrium, and views are exceptional. The hotel's rooms and views are the best in town, although service standards are not as high as they might be. ✉ *25 Collins St., 3000,* ☎ *03/9653–0000,* ᴵᴬˣ *03/9650–4261. 310 rooms, 52 suites. 2 restaurants, bar, room service, health club, business services. AE, DC, MC, V.*

$$$$ 🏨 **Windsor Hotel.** The aristocrat of Melbourne hotels, the century-old
★ Windsor combines the character of the Victorian era with the modern blessings of first-rate food and comfortable beds. Guest rooms are plushly decorated with Laura Ashley–style wall coverings and rosewood furnishings; the marble bathrooms are, however, modest in size compared with those in modern hotel rooms of the same price. Standard rooms are rather small, but the two-room executive suites provide good value, and the Victorian suites are vast. The hotel commands a position opposite the Parliament House, close to theaters, parks, and fine shops. ✉ *103 Spring St., 3000,* ☎ *03/9633–6000,* ᴵᴬˣ *03/9633-6001. 160 rooms, 20 suites. Restaurant, 2 bars, business services. AE, DC, MC, V.*

$$$ 🏨 **The Adelphi.** This design-driven boutique hotel breaks new ground with its contemporary style. The functionalist maple-and-matte-finish metal surfaces and clean, cool aesthetics might be a little brittle for some tastes, but it's a one-minute walk from City Square, as central as you can get. The Adelphi's pièce de résistance is an 80-ft lap pool on the top floor, which has a glass bottom that juts out from the edge of the building—bathers literally swim into space. The view from the bar on the same floor, framed by the Gothic Revival spires of St. Paul's, is heavenly. The best rooms are those at the front, whose numbers end in "01." ✉ *187 Flinders La., 3000,* ☎ *03/9650–7555,* ᴵᴬˣ *03/9650–2710. 26 rooms with shower, 8 with bath. Restaurant, 2 bars, pool. AE, DC, MC, V.*

$$$ 🏨 **Oakford Gordon Place.** This historic 1883 structure is one of the
★ most interesting and comfortable apartment hotels in the city. It's just a stone's throw from the Parliament Building and is surrounded by excellent restaurants and theaters. It is also a good value, considering its city-center setting. Modern, comfortable apartments contain washing machines, dryers, and dishwashers. Breakfast is served on a covered terrace. The studio and one- and two-bedroom apartments face a vine-covered courtyard with a 60-ft saltwater pool and a century-old palm tree. ✉ *24 Little Bourke St., 3000,* ☎ *03/9663–2888,* ᴵᴬˣ *03/9639–1537. 82 apartments. Restaurant, pool, sauna, spa. AE, DC, MC, V.*

$ ▣ **Hotel Y.** Built in 1975 for budget travelers, this motel provides clean, comfortable, no-frills accommodations. It's picked up several tourism awards in recognition of its excellent value. Rooms are simply furnished, each with its own bathroom. There is a central television lounge in the building, along with a pool. The city center and Victoria Market are within walking distance. ⊠ *489 Elizabeth St., 3000,* ☎ *03/9329–5188,* FAX *03/9329–1469. 60 rooms. Cafeteria. AE, DC, MC, V.*

Melbourne Suburbs

$$$$ ▣ **Hotel Como.** Close to the restaurants and shops of South Yarra, one
  ★   of Melbourne's most prestigious suburbs, this luxury hotel is as popular with business travelers as it is with visiting artists and musicians. Gray marble and chrome are prominent throughout the smart art deco interior. Rooms have king-size beds, bathrobes, and Jacuzzis. Some suites on the third and sixth floors have access to private Japanese gardens, and select suites have fully equipped kitchenettes. The Como enjoys a reputation for outstanding service. ⊠ *630 Chapel St., South Yarra 3141,* ☎ *03/9825–2222,* FAX *03/9824–1263. 30 rooms, 77 suites. Indoor pool, sauna, health club. AE, DC, MC, V.*

$$$ ▣ **Country Comfort Old Melbourne Hotel.** A few minutes north of the central business district by car or tram, this hotel mimics New Orleans architecture, with wrought-iron balconies and a cobblestone central courtyard. There is a small reception area instead of a traditional lobby, and the comfortable, spacious Victorian-style guest rooms are decorated with warm colors and brass beds. ⊠ *5–17 Flemington Rd., Carlton 3053,* ☎ *03/9329–9344,* FAX *03/9328–4870. 225 rooms, 8 suites. 2 restaurants, bar, pool. AE, DC, MC, V.*

$$–$$$ ▣ **The Tilba.** Built as a grand residence at the turn of the century, The
  ★   Tilba became a hotel in 1920, and staying here feels like a sojourn in a luxurious private house. During World War II it was occupied by Ladies for the Armed Services and later fell on hard times until it was renovated in the mid-1980s. Now you'll find a small hotel with genuine charm, filled with antiques and eclectic pieces of furniture. In one room, for example, a bedstead was once the gate on a Queensland cattle ranch. The hotel overlooks Fawkner Park and is a short stroll from the Toorak Road shops and restaurants. ⊠ *30 Toorak Rd. W, South Yarra 3141,* ☎ *03/9867–8844,* FAX *03/9867–6567. 2 rooms with bath, 15 rooms with shower. AE, DC, MC, V.*

$$ ▣ **City Park Motel.** Close to the parks on the south side of the city, this ultramodern, four-story motel is ideal for travelers on limited budgets. Rooms have coffee makers and small refrigerators, and those in the front of the redbrick building have balconies. The executive–honeymoon suite has a spa bath and sauna. There are relatively few amenities, but the city is about 1½ km (1 mi) away and frequent tram service is available on St. Kilda Road, a two-minute walk from the hotel. ⊠ *308 Kings Way, South Melbourne 3205,* ☎ *03/9699–9811,* FAX *03/9699–9224. 44 rooms, 6 suites. Restaurant, bar. AE, DC, MC, V.*

$$ ▣ **Oakford Apartments.** If you prefer private apartments to hotel rooms, consider staying at these all-suite town houses at four various locations in elegant South Yarra. The studios and two- or three-bedroom apartments are bright and comfortable, and all have washing machines, dryers, dishwashers, and Jacuzzis. ⊠ *23 Argo St.;* ⊠ *631 Punt Rd.;* ⊠ *19 Kensington Rd.;* ⊠ *26 Davis Ave., South Yarra 3141;* ☎ *03/9820–8544,* FAX *03/9820–8517. 20 apartments per property. Pool, tennis court. AE, DC, MC, V.*

$$ ▣ **Oakford Fairways.** Opposite the Albert Park Lake and golf course and just 2 km (1 mi) south of the central business district, this is another favorite with those who prefer lodging in apartments. The 1930s-style property consists of luxurious one- and two-bedroom apartments surrounded by private lawns and manicured flower beds. Avoid the east wing, because it faces heavily trafficked Queens Road. The St. Kilda Road tram provides easy access to the city. ☒ *32 Queens Rd., Albert Park 3206,* ☎ *03/9820–8544,* fax *03/9820–8517. 48 apartments. Pool, tennis court, business services. AE, DC, MC, V.*

$$ ⊞ **Robinson's by the Sea.** This lovely terrace house overlooks Port Phillip
★ Bay, a five-minute stroll from the nightlife of Fitzroy Street, St. Kilda. The sitting room is warm, inviting and furnished with excellent antiques and objets d'art. The prize front bedroom has a large balcony, a king-size bed, and its own sitting area. Other rooms are smaller but quieter. This, one of Melbourne's best bed-and-breakfasts, is run by Wendy Robinson, a virtual one-woman B&B industry: she also writes guides to inns and B&Bs around the country and conducts hospitality-training courses. Mrs. Robinson's famous breakfasts are included in the rate. ☒ *335 Beaconsfield Parade, St. Kilda West 3182,* ☎ *03/9534–2683,* fax *03/9534–2683. 5 rooms share 3 baths. AE, DC, MC, V.*

$ ⊞ **Lygon Lodge Carlton.** In the heart of Melbourne's Little Italy and just a short tram ride from the city center, this motel is close to some of the city's best ethnic restaurants—the perfect place for the budget-conscious traveler who appreciates a colorful, lively neighborhood. Some deluxe rooms have kitchenettes, only a few dollars more than standard rooms. ☒ *220 Lygon St., Carlton,* ☎ *03/9663–6633,* fax *03/9663–7297. 42 rooms. Restaurant. AE, DC, MC, V.*

$ ⊞ **Magnolia Court Boutique Hotel.** This small, friendly hotel in the historic suburb of East Melbourne profits from the area's serenity and accessibility. Rooms and furnishings are simple and spotless. Standard rooms are modest in size, but the honeymoon suite and the cottage offer more space and comfort at a moderately higher rate. A family room with a kitchen and space for six is also available. The hotel is separated from the city center by Fitzroy Gardens and is about a 12-minute walk from Spring Street. ☒ *101 Powlett St., East Melbourne 3002,* ☎ *03/9419–4222,* fax *03/9416–0841. 23 rooms, 3 suites. Café. AE, DC, MC, V.*

$ ⊞ **Pathfinder Motel.** Built in the early 1960s in quiet, residential Kew, this relaxed, comfortable motel is on a direct tram line to the city, 7 km (4 mi) away. The reception area and lobby, furnished with antiques, face a courtyard with a small waterfall and fish pond. Rooms are cream-color brick, with polished wood furniture and floral fabrics. ☒ *Burke and Cotham Rds., Kew 3101,* ☎ *03/9817–4551,* fax *03/9817–5680. 21 rooms, 3 apartments. Restaurant, room service, pool. AE, DC, MC, V.*

Nightlife and the Arts

The Arts

Melbourne Events, available from all tourism outlets, is a comprehensive monthly guide to what's happening in town. For a complete listing of performing arts events, galleries, and film, consult the "EG" (Entertainment Guide) supplement in the Friday edition of the *Melbourne Age.*

DANCE

In the 2,000-seat State Theatre at the Arts Centre, the **Australian Ballet** (☎ 03/9684–8600) stages five programs annually and frequently presents visiting celebrity dancers from around the world. For information, telephone Ticketmaster (☎ 03/13–6166 for credit-card reservations).

MUSIC

Big-name, crowd-drawing contemporary artists perform at **Melbourne Park** (☒ Batman Ave., ☎ 03/9286–1234). The **Melbourne Sports and**

Entertainment Centre (✉ Swan St., ☎ 03/9429–6288) hosts major Australian and international artists. The **Melbourne Concert Hall** (✉ Arts Centre, 100 St. Kilda Rd., ☎ 03/9281–8000) stages concerts in a classy atmosphere.

Open-air summertime (Dec.–Mar.) concerts can be seen at the **Sidney Myer Music Bowl** (✉ King's Domain near Swan St. bridge, Melbourne). Call Ticketmaster (☎ 03/13–6166) for ticket information.

The **Melbourne Symphony Orchestra** performs virtually year-round in the 2,600-seat Melbourne Concert Hall in the Arts Centre (✉ 100 St. Kilda Rd., ☎ 03/13–6166).

OPERA

The **Australian Opera** has regular seasons, often with performances by world-renowned stars. The length and time of seasons vary (best to call when you arrive), but all performances take place in **Melbourne Concert Hall** (✉ 100 St. Kilda Rd., ☎ 03/9684–8198. Direct further inquiries to Ticketmaster (☎ 03/13–6166).

THEATER

The **Half-Tix** ticket booth in the Bourke Street Mall sells tickets to theater attractions at half price on performance days. ☎ 03/9650–9420. ☉ Mon. 10–2, Tues.–Thurs. 11–6, Fri. 11–6:30, Sat. 10–2.

The **Melbourne Theatre Company** (☎ 03/13–6166), Melbourne's first and most successful theater company, has two seasons yearly, during which classical, international, and Australian works are performed at the Russell Street Theatre (✉ 19 Russell St.).

The city's second-largest company, the **Playbox at the CUB Malthouse Company** (✉ 113 Sturt St., South Melbourne, ☎ 03/9685–5111) stages about 10 new or contemporary productions a year. The theater, the CUB Malthouse, is a flexible space designed for a range of drama, dance, and circus companies.

The equivalent of Off Broadway in the United States, the **Universal Theatre (UT)** (✉ 13 Victoria St., Fitzroy, ☎ 03/9419–3777) is home to daring, avant-garde productions. The UT is an atmospheric, moody, oddly shaped theater that seats 300 on three sides of its stage. A smaller theater is on the upper floor.

The **Princess Theatre** (✉ 163 Spring St., ☎ 03/9299–9800) is the home of Broadway-style blockbusters. The refurbished **Regent Theatre** (✉ 191 Collins St., ☎ 03/9299–9500) also presents mainstream productions. **Her Majesty's Theatre** (✉ 219 Exhibition St., ☎ 03/9663–3211) sees a range of musicals. Intimate revues and plays are staged at the **Comedy Theatre** (✉ 240 Exhibition St., ☎ 03/9209–9000). **La Mama** (✉ 205 Faraday St., Carlton, ☎ 03/9347–6142) puts on innovative, intimate, and contemporary productions in a bohemian setting. **Theatreworks** (✉ 14 Acland St., St. Kilda, ☎ 03/9534–3388) concentrates on contemporary Australian plays.

Nightlife

BARS

The 35th-floor cocktail bar at the **Hotel Sofitel** (✉ 25 Collins St., ☎ 03/9653–0000) has spectacular views. The **Grand Hyatt** (✉ 123 Collins St., ☎ 03/9657–1234) is a sophisticated place. Find Old World charm at the **Windsor Hotel** (✉ 103 Spring St., ☎ 03/9653–0653). The **Hilton on the Park** (✉ 192 Wellington Parade, ☎ 03/9419–2000) is perfect for drinks before or after the football or cricket game at the Melbourne Cricket Ground. **Sheraton Towers** (✉ 1 Southgate Ave., Southgate, ☎ 03/9696–3100) is a good place for a drink at Southgate. **Rockman's Regency** (✉ Exhibition and Lonsdale Sts., ☎ 03/9662–3900) has an excellent location close to Chinatown.

Live music is often played at the following spots; bars not located in major hotels tend to be more casual. **Hairy Canary** (✉ 212 Little Collins St., ☎ 03/9654–2471) is currently one of the hottest places in the city. **The George Hotel** (✉ Fitzroy and Grey Sts., St. Kilda, ☎ 03/9525–5599) is in a superbly renovated 19th-century building. **Cha Cha's** (✉ 20 Chapel St., Windsor, ☎ 03/9525–1077) caters to the pre-dinner crowd of busy Chapel Street. **Dog's Bar** (✉ 54 Acland St., St. Kilda, ☎ 03/9525–3599) attracts a hip, young clientele.

COMEDY CLUBS

The **Comedy Club and Last Laugh** (✉ 380 Lygon St., Carlton, ☎ 03/9348–1622) is a popular place to see top-class Australian and international acts.

The Esplanade Hotel (✉ 11 Upper Esplanade, St. Kilda, ☎ 03/9534–0211) is a testing ground for local comedians as well as a hallowed live music venue ☞ Music, *below*.

DANCING

Most of the central city's dance clubs are along the **King Street** strip. Popularity is a fickle thing—follow the crowds if you want the latest and hippest. Take note that King Street has a reputation for late-night violence. Authorities and club owners have recently improved the situation, but be cautious.

Chasers. One of the city's most enduring night spots, this is a good bet for anyone under 35. Music varies from night to night. Call ahead for the latest lineup. ✉ *386 Chapel St., Prahran,* ☎ *03/9827–6615.* ☜ *$5–$10.* ☼ *Wed.–Sun. 10 PM–7 AM.*

Metro. This multilevel, high-tech nightclub has eight bars, a glass-enclosed café, and three dance floors, where the action ranges from fast to furious. Metro is one of the hottest clubs in town with Melbourne's twentysomethings. ✉ *20–30 Bourke St.,* ☎ *03/9663–4288.* ☜ *$10.* ☼ *Thurs.–Sat. 9 PM–5 AM.*

MUSIC

Continental Cafe. This classy spot on funky Greville Street attracts top-name Australian and international performers. ✉ *132A Greville St., Prahran,* ☎ *03/9510–2788.* ☜ *$10–$25, dinner and show $36–$65.*
At the Crown Casino, the **Crown Showroom** and the **Mercury Lounge** attract international and Australian highlighters. ✉ *Crown Entertainment Complex, Level 3, Southbank,* ☎ *03/9292–8888.* ☜ *$11.50–$30.*
Bell's Hotel (✉ Moray and Coventry Sts., South Melbourne, ☎ 03/9690–4511) is one of Melbourne's famed jazz haunts. **Ruby Reds** (✉ 11 Drury La., ☎ 03/9662–1544) is the city center's jazz mainstay. The **Limerick Arms Hotel** (✉ 364 Clarendon St., South Melbourne, ☎ 03/9690–0995) is probably the best-known jazz venue in the country. For rock-and-roll, punk, and grunge, the **Esplanade Hotel** (✉ Upper Esplanade, St. Kilda, ☎ 03/9534–0211) is one of Melbourne's established spots for high-quality live rock and pop; dress down.

Outdoor Activities and Sports

Australian-Rules Football

This is Melbourne's choice for winter football. The two most important venues for national-league games are the **Melbourne Cricket Ground** (✉ Brunton Ave., Yarra Park, ☎ 03/9657–8867) and **Waverley Park** (✉ Wellington Rd., Mulgrave, ☎ 03/9560–6166). Tickets are available through **Ticketmaster** (☎ 03/13–6122 for credit-card reservations) or at the playing field.

Close-Up

AUSTRALIAN-RULES FOOTBALL

DESPITE ITS NAME, NOVICE observers frequently ask the question: "What rules?" This fast, vigorous game, played between teams of 18, is one of four kinds of football down under. Aussies also play Rugby League, Rugby Union, and soccer, but Aussie Rules, widely known as "footie," is the one to which Victoria, South Australia, the Top End, and Western Australia subscribe. It's the country's most popular spectator sport.

Because it is gaining an international television audience, the intricacies of Aussie Rules football are no longer the complete mystery they once were to the uninitiated: The ball can be kicked or punched in any direction, but never thrown. You'll see players make spectacular leaps vying to catch a kicked ball before it touches the ground, for which they earn a free kick. The game is said to be at its finest in Melbourne, and any defeat of a Melbourne team—particularly in a grand final, as happened a few years ago—is widely interpreted as a sign of moral lassitude in the state of Victoria.

New South Wales and Queensland devote themselves to two versions of rugby. Rugby League, the professional game, is a faster, more exciting version of Rugby Union, the choice of purists.

Bicycling

Melbourne and its environs contain more than 100 km (62 mi) of bike paths, including scenic routes along the Yarra River and Port Phillip Bay. Bikes can be rented at one of the mobile rental shops in trailers alongside the bike paths. For information, contact **Bicycle Victoria** (⊠ 19 O'Connell St., ☎ 03/9328–3000).

Boating

At the **Studley Park Boathouse,** canoes, kayaks, and rowboats are available for hire on a peaceful, delightful stretch of the Lower Yarra River, about 7 km (4 mi) east of the city center. Rentals cost from $18 per hour for a two-person kayak or rowboat to $24 per hour for a four-person rowboat. ⊠ *Studley Park, Kew,* ☎ *03/9853–1972.* ☉ *Daily 9–sunset.*

Cricket

All big international and interstate cricket matches in Victoria are played at the **Melbourne Cricket Ground** October–March. The stadium has lights for night games and can accommodate 100,000 people. Tickets are available at the gate or through **Ticketmaster** (☎ 03/13–6122 for credit-card reservations). ⊠ *Brunton Ave., Yarra Park,* ☎ *03/9657–8867.*

Golf

Melbourne has the largest number of championship golf courses in Australia, and some of the private courses, such as Metropolitan, Royal Melbourne, and Kingston-Heath, are world-class. Area courses include: **Albert Park Golf Course** (⊠ Queens Rd., Melbourne, ☎ 03/9510–5588), **Brighton Golf Links** (⊠ Dendy St., Brighton, ☎ 03/9592–1388), **Ivanhoe Public Golf Course** (⊠ Vasey St., East Ivanhoe, ☎ 03/9499–7001), **Sandringham Golf Links** (⊠ Cheltenham Rd., Cheltenham, ☎ 03/9598–3590), and **Yarra Bend Golf Course** (⊠ Yarra Bend Park Rd., Fairfield, ☎ 03/9481–3729).

Horse Racing

Melbourne is the only city in the world to declare a public holiday for a horse race—the **Melbourne Cup**—held on the first Tuesday in November since 1861. The Cup is also a fashion parade, and most of Melbourne society turns out in full regalia. The rest of the country comes to a standstill, with schools, shops, offices, and factories tuning in to the action.

The city has four top-class race tracks. **Flemington Race Course** (✉ Epsom Rd., Flemington, ☎ 03/9371–7171), 3 km (2 mi) outside the city, is Australia's premier race course and home of the Melbourne Cup. **Moonee Valley Race Course** (✉ McPherson St., Moonee Ponds, ☎ 03/9373–2222) is 6 km (4 mi) from town and holds the Cox Plate race in October. **Caulfield Race Course** (✉ Station St., Caulfield, ☎ 03/9257–7200), 10 km (6 mi) from the city, runs the Blue Diamond in March and the Caulfield Cup in October. Finally, **Sandown Race Course** (✉ Racecourse Dr., Springvale, ☎ 03/9518–1300), 25 km (16 mi) from the city, runs the Sandown Cup in November.

Motor Racing

Somewhat controversially, Melbourne snatched the right to host the **Australian Formula 1 Grand Prix** from the city of Adelaide. Melbourne's first GP was held in March 1996, and was a major success despite the threat of protests and disruption by local residents and others outraged by the destruction of parkland to build the racing circuit at Albert Park, 3 km (2 mi) from the city center. The race was awarded the title of best GP of the year 1996 and 1997 by the international GP organizing committee.

Running

Some of the more popular local courses include the 4-km (2½-mi) **Tan,** beginning at Anderson Street and Alexandra Avenue and looping around the perimeter of the Royal Botanic Gardens; the 5-km (3-mi) **Albert Park Lake Run** in Albert Park; and the **Bay Run,** an 18-km (11-mi) round-trip run along Port Phillip Bay, starting at Kerford Road and Beaconsfield Parade in Albert Park and continuing on to Bay Street in Brighton.

Soccer

The sport is played almost year-round in **Olympic Park** (✉ Ovals 1 and 2, Swan St., Melbourne, ☎ 03/9429–6288).

Tennis

The **Australian Open** (☎ 03/9286–1234), held in January at the Melbourne Park National Tennis Centre, is one of the world's four Grand Slam events.

If you wish to play tennis during your stay, plan to do so on weekdays, since most courts are booked solid at night and on weekends. Public courts for hire in and around the city include **Melbourne Park National Tennis Centre** (✉ Batman Ave., Melbourne, ☎ 03/9286–1244), with 15 outdoor and five indoor Rebound Ace courts; **Fawkner Park Tennis Center** (✉ Fawkner Park, Toorak Rd. W, South Yarra, ☎ 03/9820–1551), with six outdoor courts; **East Melbourne Tennis Centre** (✉ Powlett Reserve, Albert St., East Melbourne, ☎ 03/9417–6511), with four outdoor courts; and **Collingwood Indoor Tennis Centre** (✉ 100 Wellington St., Collingwood, ☎ 03/9419–8911), with five indoor synthetic grass courts.

Shopping

From the haute couture of upper Collins Street's Paris End to the shops of suburban Toorak Village, Melbourne has firmly established itself as the nation's fashion capital. Australian designer labels are available on High Street in Armadale, on Toorak Road and Chapel Street in South Yarra, and on Carlton's Lygon Street. High-quality vintage clothing abounds on Greville Street in Prahran. Most shops are open Monday–Thursday, 9–5:30, Friday until 9, and Saturday until 5. Major city stores are open Sunday until 5.

Department Stores

Daimaru (✉ 211 LaTrobe St., Melbourne, ☎ 03/9660–6666), a multilevel department store that is part of the 200-store Melbourne Central shopping complex, brings the world's smartest fashions to the heart of the city.

David Jones (✉ 310 Bourke St., Melbourne, ☎ 03/9643–2222) in the Bourke Street Mall is one of the city's finer department stores.

Myer Melbourne (✉ 314 Bourke St., Melbourne, ☎ 03/9661–1111) is a vast department store with a long-standing reputation for quality merchandise.

Markets

Metro! Craft Center. The imposing Victorian building of the city's former meat market houses a vast collection of work by leading jewelers, woodworkers, printers, and ceramic artists. ✉ *42 Courtney St., North Melbourne,* ☎ *03/9329–9966.* ☉ *Tues.–Sun. 10–5.*

Prahran Market. This stylish suburb's market sells nothing but food—a fantastic, mouthwatering array imported from all over the world. ✉ *177 Commercial Rd., Prahran,* ☎ *03/9522–3301.* ☉ *Tues. and Thurs. dawn–5, Fri. dawn–6, Sat. dawn–5.*

Shopping Centers, Arcades, and Malls

Australia on Collins (✉ 260 Collins St., ☎ 03/9650–4355) is the latest downtown shopping-center entrant, with one of its floors devoted to gifts and housewares. **Aero Design, R.G. Madden,** and **Made in Japan** sell particularly striking goods.

Block Arcade (✉ 282 Collins St. and 100 Elizabeth St., ☎ 03/9654–5244), the elegant 19th-century shopping arcade, contains the venerable **Hopetoun Tea Tooms, Melee Jewellers'** estate jewelry, **Orrefors Kosta Boda,** the **Porcelain Doll Co.,** and the **National Trust Gift Shop.**

Crown Entertainment Complex (✉ Southbank, ☎ 03/9292–8888), adjacent to the casino, offers Versace, Donna Karan, Gucci, Armani, and Prada shops, among others.

High Street between the suburbs of Prahran and Armadale, to the east of Chapel Street, is where you are most likely to find the best collection of antiques shops in Australia.

The Jam Factory (✉ 500 Chapel St., South Yarra, ☎ 03/9826–0537) is made up of a group of historic bluestone buildings that house cinemas, fashion, food, and gift shops, as well as a branch of the giant Borders book and music store.

Melbourne Central (✉ 300 Lonsdale St., ☎ 03/9665–0000), a dizzying complex whose biggest tenant is **Daimaru** department store, is huge enough to enclose a 100-year-old shot tower (used to make bullets) in its atrium.

Royal Arcade (✉ 355 Bourke St., ☎ 03/9629–8888), built in 1846, is Melbourne's oldest shopping arcade. It remains a lovely place to shop, and it is home to splendid **Gaunt's Clock,** which tolls away the hours.

Southgate (✉ 4 Southbank Promenade, South Melbourne, ☎ 03/9699–4311), directly opposite Flinders Street Station on the other bank of the Yarra, shelters an excellent combination of shops and eateries. The spectacular riverside location is a short walk both from the city center across Princes Bridge and from the Victorian Arts Center, making it an excellent choice for lunch; there's outdoor seating next to the Southbank promenade.

Sportsgirl Centre (✉ 234 Collins St., ☎ 03/9650–6755) sells some of Melbourne's most popular young women's clothing labels, particularly leisurewear. You'll find food as well as fashion in the four-level shopping mall.

Chapel Street in South Yarra between Toorak and Dandenong Roads is where you'll find some of the ritziest boutiques in Melbourne, as well as cafés, art galleries, and several fine restaurants.

Specialty Stores

BOOKS

Brunswick Street Bookstore. This Fitzroy favorite sells modern Australian literature, some of which you won't find outside the country. ✉ 305 Brunswick St., Fitzroy, ☎ 03/9416–1030.

Hill of Content. Knowledgeable staff and an excellent selection of titles make this a Melbourne favorite. ✉ 86 Bourke St., ☎ 03/9662–9472.

CLOTHING

Sam Bear. This Melbourne institution sells everything from Aussie outerwear to Swiss Army knives. ✉ 225 Russell St., ☎ 03/9663–2191.

JEWELRY

Altmann and Cherny is a leading jeweler that specializes in opals and offers tax-free prices to overseas tourists. ✉ 120 Exhibition St., ☎ 03/9650–9685.

Makers Mark Gallery showcases the work of some of the country's finest jewelers. ✉ Shop 9, 101 Collins St., ☎ 03/9654–8488.

MUSIC

Discurio has an excellent range of music, with a good selection of traditional and contemporary Australian artists represented. ✉ 105 Elizabeth St., ☎ 03/9600–1488.

SOUVENIRS

You can shop for Australian-made goods at the **Australiana General Store** outlets (✉ 1227 High St., Armadale, ☎ 03/9822–2324; ✉ Shop 20/45, Collins St., Melbourne, ☎ 03/9650–2075) and **Aboriginal Handcrafts** (✉ 125–133 Swanston St., 9th Floor, Melbourne, ☎ 03/9650–4717). You might also try the **National Trust Gift Shop** (✉ 38 Jackson St., Toorak, ☎ 03/9827–9385).

Tours

Professional shoppers might want to take advantage of **Shopping Spree Tours** (☎ 03/9596–6600), which offers lunch and escorted shopping tours to some of Melbourne's best manufacturers and importers. Tours depart at Monday–Saturday at 8:30. The cost is $50 per person.

Melbourne A to Z

Arriving and Departing

BY BUS

Greyhound/Pioneer (☎ 13–2030) links the city with all Australian capital cities and with major towns and cities throughout Victoria. The terminal for both is on the corner of Swanston and Franklin streets.

BY CAR

The major route into Melbourne is Hume Highway, which runs northeast to Canberra, 646 km (400 mi) distant, and Sydney, which is 868 km (538 mi) away. Princes Highway follows the coast to Sydney in one direction and to Adelaide, 728 km (451 mi) northwest of Melbourne, in the other. The Western Highway runs northwest 111 km (69 mi) to Ballarat, and the Calder Highway travels north to Bendigo, a journey of 149 km (92 mi).

BY PLANE

Melbourne Airport is 22 km (14 mi) northwest of the central business district and can be reached easily from the city on the Tullamarine Freeway. The international terminal is in the center of the airport complex; domestic terminals are found on either side. International airlines flying into Melbourne include **Air New Zealand, Ansett Australia, British Airways, Qantas,** and **United.** Domestic carriers serving Melbourne are **Ansett Australia/Kendell** and **Qantas.** ☞ Air Travel *in* Smart Travel Tips for airline telephone numbers.

Between the Airport and City center. Skybus (☎ 03/9335–3066) is a private bus service that operates between the airport terminals and the city, but for three or more people traveling together, a taxi to the city is a better value. En route from the airport, the bus makes a loop through the city before terminating at Spencer Street Station. The shuttle departs from the airport every half hour from 6:40 AM to 11:40 PM, then every hour. Airport-bound buses depart from Spencer Street at half-hourly then hourly intervals from 5 AM to 10:45 PM. From 1:10 AM to 4:10 AM, airport-bound shuttles depart from Town Hall on Swanston Street. 🚌 *$10.*

Taxis are widely available. The cost of a taxi into town is approximately $40. **Limousines** to the city cost about $60. Larger limousine companies include **Australian National Limousine** (☎ 03/13–1908) and **Limousines Australia** (☎ 1800/678–596).

BY TRAIN

Spencer Street Railway Station is at Spencer and Little Collins streets. Public transportation is available here, but cumbersome luggage would be better served by a taxi at the queue outside the station.

Getting Around

BY CAR

Melbourne's regimented layout makes it easy to negotiate by car, but two unusual rules apply because of the tram traffic on the city's major roads. Trams should be passed on the *left,* and when a tram stops, the cars behind it also must stop, unless there is a railed safety zone for tram passengers.

At various intersections within the city, drivers wishing to turn *right* must stay in the *left* lane as they enter the intersection, then wait for the traffic signals to change before proceeding with the turn. The rule is intended to prevent traffic from impeding tram service. For complete directions, look for the black-and-white traffic signs suspended overhead as you enter each intersection where this rule applies. All other right-hand turns are made from the center. It is far easier to understand this rule by seeing it in action rather than reading about it.

The **Royal Automobile Club of Victoria (RACV)** (☎ 03/13–1955) is the major source of information on all aspects of road travel in Victoria.

BY PUBLIC TRANSPORTATION

The city's public transport system includes buses, trains, and trams (streetcars). In fact, Melbourne has one of the world's largest tram networks, with 365 km (226 mi) of track in the inner city and suburbs. By and large, the system is a delight—fast, convenient, and cheap.

The city's public transport system is operated by **Metropolitan Transit** (☎ 13–1638), which divides Melbourne into three zones. Zone 1 is the urban core, where you will spend most of your time. The **basic ticket** is the one-zone ticket, which can be purchased on board or pre-purchased from news agents and other outlets for $2.30 and is valid for travel within that zone on any tram, bus, or train for a period of two hours after purchase. For travelers, the **most useful ticket** is probably the Zone 1 day ticket, which costs $4.40 and is available on board any tram. For anyone intending to make extensive use of Melbourne's public transport system, a **free route map** is available from the Victoria Tourist Information Centre (☞ Visitor Information, *below*). **Trams** run until midnight and can be hailed wherever you see a green and gold tram-stop sign. A free City Circle tram operates daily 10–6 on the fringe of the Central Business District, with stops in Flinders, Spencer, La Trobe, Victoria, and Spring streets. Look for the burgundy-and-cream color scheme.

BY TAXI

Taxis are metered, and empty taxis can be hailed on the street and at taxi stands or ordered by phone. Melbourne's taxis are gradually adopting a yellow color scheme, and drivers are required to wear uniforms. Major taxi companies include **Silver Top** (☎ 03/13–1008), **North Suburban** (☎ 03/13–1008), **Embassy** (☎ 03/9320–0320), and **Black Cabs Combined** (☎ 13–2227).

Contacts and Resources

B&B RESERVATION AGENCIES

Call or write for a brochure from **Bed & Breakfast Australia** (⊠ Box 727, Newport Beach, NSW 2106, ☎ 02/9999–0366). **Tourism Victoria** produces a brochure, "Victorian Bed & Breakfast Getaways," available from the Victoria Tourist Information Centre (☞ Visitor Information, *below*). Another leaflet, "Melbourne's B & Bs," lists 20 of the best properties in the city and suburbs. It is also available from the Tourist Information Centre.

CAR RENTALS

Avis (☎ 1800/22–5533), **Budget** (☎ 13–2727), and **Hertz** (☎ 03/13–3039) all have offices at Melbourne Airport as well as downtown. If you hire from a major car-rental company, expect to pay between $80 and $95 per day for an automatic sedan and about $70 per day for a compact standard model. If you don't mind an older model and can return the car to the pick-up point, the smaller local rental agencies offer vehicles at rates far below those of the major companies. Some of these smaller agencies are **Cheapa** (☎ 03/9878–9882), **Delta** (☎ 13–1390), and **Rent-a-Bomb** (☎ 03/9428–0088).

EMERGENCIES

Ambulance, fire brigade, and police. ☎ *000.*

Alfred Hospital (⊠ Commercial Rd., Prahran, ☎ 03/9276–2000). **Royal Dental Hospital** (⊠ Elizabeth St. and Flemington Rd., ☎ 03/9341–0222). **Royal Women's Hospital** (⊠ 132 Grattan St., Carlton, ☎ 03/9344–2000). **St. Vincent's Hospital** (⊠ Victoria Parade, Fitzroy, ☎ 03/9288–2211).

GUIDED TOURS

Bay Cruises. The *Wattle* is a restored steam tug that cruises Port Phillip Bay. The highlight of the one-hour voyage is a visit to a seal colony. The boat runs from Melbourne mid-October–late June, except for summer holidays, when cruises depart from Rye on the Mornington Peninsula. ⊠ *Station Pier, Port Melbourne,* ☎ *03/9328–2739.* ☜ *$10.* ☺ *Boats depart summer, daily; fall–spring, Sun.*

Cycling Tours. Melbourne's excellent bicycle path network and flat terrain makes cycling pleasurable. **City Cycle Tours** (☎ 03/9585–5343; ☜ $30 morning tour, $20 afternoon tours) has two "afternoon appetizer" tours focusing on inner-Melbourne and St. Kilda, and a three-hour morning trip that visits Albert Park for a spin around the Formula 1 Grand Prix track before returning to the city via parks and bicycle paths. For more information about cycling around Melbourne—with or without help—contact **Bicycle Victoria** (☎ 03/9328–3000, 𝖥𝖠𝖷 03/9328–2288).

Orientation Tours. Gray Line has several guided tours of Melbourne and its surroundings by coach and boat. The Melbourne Experience is a basic three-hour tour that visits the city center's main attractions and some of the surrounding parks. The tour departs daily at 9 AM from the company's headquarters. ⊠ *184 Swanston St.,* ☎ *03/9663–4455.* ▧ *$40.*

Australian Pacific Tours (☎ 13–1304), **AAT Kings** (☎ 03/9663–3377), **Great Sights** (☎ 03/9639–2211), and **Melbourne Sightseeing** (☎ 03/9663–3388) all offer similar general trips and prices.

City Explorer has a do-it-yourself tour of the city on a bus that circles past major attractions, including the zoo and the parks to the east. The tour ticket is valid for 16 stops along the circuit, and it allows you to leave the double-decker bus at any of the route's stops and board any following City Explorer bus. The tour begins at Flinders Street Station. ☎ *03/9563–9788.* ▧ *$22 for a one-day pass.*

Sports Tours. Journey Corporation (⊠ 245 Cardigan St., ☎ 03/9348–1344, FAX 03/9348–1011) specializes in sporting tours of Melbourne. Headed by AFL football star Paul Salmon, the company organizes packages for major sporting events including Aussie Rules football games, tennis, golf, cricket, and the Formula 1 Grand Prix. Tours include accommodations and admission.

Yarra River Cruises. The modern, glass-enclosed boats of the **Melbourne River Cruises** fleet take one- and two-hour cruises daily, either west through the commercial heart of the city or east through the parks and gardens, or a combination of the two. The boat departs from Berth 1, Princes Walk, on the opposite side of Princes Bridge from Flinders Street Station. ⊠ *Vault 18, Banana Alley, Queensbridge St.,* ☎ *03/9614–1215.* ▧ *1-hr cruise $13, 2-hr cruise $25.* ☉ *Daily 10–4 every ½ hr.*

Yarra Yarra Water Taxis (☎ 0411/255–179) offers a 1950s speedboat as an alternative to the larger cruise boats. The size of the boat makes it possible to follow the Yarra as far as Dight's Falls, passing some of Melbourne's wealthiest suburbs on the way. It rents for $75 per hour and can carry up to six passengers. Picnic baskets are available. There's also a private barbecue tour for $100 an hour.

Walking Tours. Melbourne Heritage Walks and Tours (☎ 03/9827–1085, FAX 03/9827–4263) runs a 90-minute stroll that takes its cues from the city's architecture to portray the social and political history of Melbourne. Tour guide Maxine Wood is lively and entertaining, and her contacts allow her entry to such places as the backstage chambers of Parliament House and the corridors of Government House. The tours, on Wednesday morning and Sunday afternoon, cost $20 per person. Private tours for groups also can be arranged.

LATE-NIGHT PHARMACY

Leonard Long Pharmacy (⊠ Williams Rd. and High St., Prahran, ☎ 03/9510–3977) is open 9 AM–midnight.

VISITOR INFORMATION

Melbourne Information Center. In addition to the tourist information center at Town Hall, there are information booths at Bourke Street Mall and Flinders Street Station. The Bourke Street Mall booth is open Monday–Thursday 9–5, Friday 9–7, weekends 10–4. The Flinders Street Station booth operates Monday–Thursday 9–5, Friday 9–6, Saturday 10–4, and Sunday 11–4. ⊠ *Town Hall, Swanston and Little Collins Sts., 3000,* ☎ *03/9658–9955.* ☉ *Weekdays 9–6, weekends 9–5.*

City Experience Center. This interactive orientation facility in Melbourne Town Hall provides information in six languages with large-screen videos, touch screens, permanent displays, and daily newspapers, and there is access to the Melbourne Web site as well. The free Melbourne Greeters service pairs you with a local volunteer who shares your interests. You can spend two to four hours with the volunteer touring relevant parts of the city and talking about subjects such as Aboriginal culture, Australian film, parks and gardens, shopping, gay culture, history, theater, and sports. To book a **Melbourne Greeter** (☎ 03/9658–9955, FAX 03/9654–1054) you must give at least three days' notice, preferably more. ✉ *Swanston and Little Collins Sts.,* ☎ *03/9658–9955.* ⊙ *Weekdays 9–6, weekends 9–5.*

The **Victorian Tourism Information Service** (☎ 03/13–2842; ⊙ daily 8–6) provides tourism information about Victoria for the cost of a local call.

The **AusRes Booking Service** adjoining the Melbourne Information Center (☞ *above*) can help if you're looking for accommodation. ☎ *03/9650–1522.* ⊙ *Weekdays 9–6, weekends 9–5.*

Royal Automobile Club of Victoria (RACV) (☎ 03/13–1955) can assist with booking accommodation, car rental, and holiday packages.

Department of Natural Resources and Environment provides information on Victoria's national parks. ✉ *240 Victoria Parade, East Melbourne 3002,* ☎ *03/9412–4011.*

SIDE TRIPS FROM MELBOURNE

Taking day trips around Melbourne is one of the pleasures of visiting the city. To the east, in the **Dandenong Ranges,** a narrow, winding road will take you on a scenic journey through rain forests and flower-filled towns of timber houses. South of Melbourne, the Bellarine Peninsula to the west and the **Mornington Peninsula** to the east form a horseshoe around Port Phillip Bay. Of the two, the Mornington Peninsula is more picturesque. **Phillip Island** has gloriously rugged coastline and koalas, seals, and thousands of fairy penguins. Every evening, the seabirds push themselves out of the sea and flop back *en masse* to their burrows—this amusing procession is Victoria's number-one tourist attraction.

The Dandenongs/Yarra Valley

Melbourne comes to the Dandenong Ranges for a breath of fresh air, especially in summer, when the cool, moist hills provide a welcome relief from the heat of the city. And it heads for the lush Yarra Valley—home of many top-class wines—when the thirst strikes. Both areas are an hour's drive east of the city.

Healesville
About 60 km northeast of Melbourne

A drive through the verdant Yarra Valley to the hills, taking in wineries such as **Domaine Chandon** (✉ Green Point, Maroondah Hwy., ☎ 03/9739–1110) or **De Bortoli** (✉ Pinnacle Ln., Dixon's Creek, ☎ 03/5965–2271), can easily be combined with a visit to the nationally recognized haven, the **Healesville Sanctuary.** Coming face to face with wildlife ranging from majestic, wedge-tailed eagles to grumpy wombats is a fascinating experience, especially in the tranquil bush setting. ✉ *Badger Creek Rd., Healesville,* ☎ *03/5957–2800.* 🎫 *$14.* ⊙ *Daily 9–5.*

Belgrave
43 km (27 mi) southeast of Melbourne.

Sherbrooke Forest is a remnant of the woodlands that once covered the ranges. Belgrave is an unexceptional town at its heart, but a place with one of Melbourne's favorite attractions. At the turn of the century, the government carved four narrow-gauge railway tracks through the forests of the Dandenongs to assist pioneers.

Side Trips from Melbourne

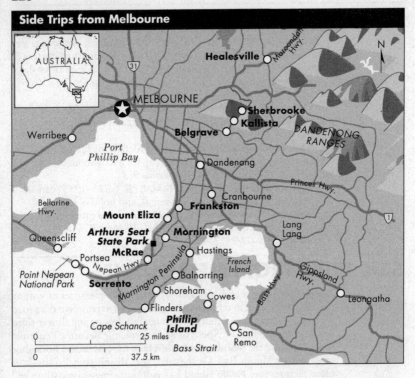

🐛 **Puffing Billy** is the sole survivor from the narrow-gauge era, a gleaming little steam engine that hauls passenger wagons from Belgrave to Emerald Lake. It's the perfect way to take in the picture-book scenery of forests and trestle bridges. The 13-km (8-mi) trip takes almost one hour each way. ✉ *Old Monbulk Rd.,* ☎ *03/9754–6800.* 💳 *$18.*

Sherbrooke
47 km (29 mi) southeast of Melbourne, 8 km (5 mi) north of Belgrave.

Deep in the lush expanse of the Dandenong Ranges National Park, the 6-acre **George Tindale Memorial Garden** hosts azaleas, camellias, and hydrangeas that spill down the hillside. ✉ *Sherbrooke Rd.,* ☎ *03/9755–2413.* 💳 *$4.* ☺ *Mon.–Sat. 10–5.*

The mountain roads near the little settlement of Sherbrooke loop through towering forests of mountain ash and giant tree ferns. If you stop and listen for a minute, you will probably hear the tinkling calls of bellbirds and perhaps the cry of a whipbird, a piercing, drawn-out note that ends, as you might guess, with a sharp whip-crack sound. Another bird common to this area is the flightless lyrebird, an accomplished mimic that has even been known to imitate the sound of a distant chain saw.

Kallista
48 km (30 mi) southeast of Melbourne, 5 km (3 mi) northeast of Belgrave.

The **Alfred Nicholas Memorial Garden** is named for its founder, who made a fortune selling aspirin. The sprawling Art Deco mansion of the Nicholas family, which can be seen through the trees at the top of the hill, has a somewhat checkered history as a luxury hotel. The garden is particularly notable for its fuchsias and rhododendrons. Don't miss the waterfall and ornamental lake, at their best when surrounding trees

are wearing their autumn colors. ⊠ *Sherbrooke Rd.,* ☎ *03/9755–2726.*
☞ *$3.* ⊙ *Daily noon–5.*

Dining

$$$$ ✕ **Cotswold House.** One of the gastronomic gems of country Victoria,
this rustic charmer sets out epicurean food in a dazzling hillside setting. The dining room overlooks trees and gardens that are illuminated
at night. Dishes include a light soufflé of King Island blue cheese served
with a fig brioche, and snapper roasted with a coriander crust. The
weekday lunch menu is simpler and less expensive. ⊠ *Blackhill Rd.,
Menzies Creek,* ☎ *03/9754–7884. AE, DC, MC, V. Mon.–Wed. No
dinner Sun.*

$$$ ✕ **Sacrebleu.** For something a bit different than scones and cream, head
for this new restaurant hidden in a small shopping center opposite the
Mt. Dandenong Hotel. Sacrebleu—the name is a mild 14th-century ex-
pletive—opened in 1998 and serves up an interesting combination of
bistro and traditional French food. Entrées range from light fare, such
as spicy king prawn salad, to favorites like fillet of beef in red wine
sauce. The wine list is a mix of Australian and French labels, perfect
for sipping outside on a summer's day. ⊠ *Shop 5, 1526 Mt. Dande-
nong Tourist Rd., Olinda,* ☎ *03/9751–2520. AE, DC, MC, V.*

$$ ✕ **Kenloch.** In an old mansion with sweeping gardens studded with tall
trees, fern gullies, and rhododendrons, this stately and somewhat old-
fashioned restaurant serves such appropriately traditional meals as beef
fillet with peppercorn sauce. In the afternoon the emphasis is on Devonshire teas, sandwiches, and small savory dishes. ⊠ *Mt. Dandenong
Tourist Rd., Olinda,* ☎ *03/9751–1008. AE, DC, MC, V. Closed Mon.
and Tues.*

Mornington Peninsula

Mornington Peninsula rings the southeastern half of Port Phillip Bay.
If you choose to set aside a sunny day for a drive down the peninsula,
you'll be treated to a glimpse of life in one of Melbourne's favorite weekend and holiday retreats. Mornington has long been a favorite with
moneyed Melburnians, and the tip of the peninsular boot is shod with
Gatsbyesque weekend houses and a scattering of stylish restaurants.
If you are visiting the peninsula in summer, pack your swimsuit to take
advantage of the area's wonderful beaches.

There are two things to look for as you drive down the peninsula. For
one, you'll notice the timber beach huts appearing near Dromana and
suddenly increasing in number around Rye. These are bathing boxes;
privately leased beach huts that are one of the peculiarities of Victorian
life. At some beaches they form an almost continuous line along the shore,
identical in every way—size, shape, proximity to each other, and the little balconies that jut out above the sea—except color. A peek inside says
volumes about their owners. Some are like aquatic sports stores, stocked
with fishing tackle; water skis, masks, and flippers; and even dinghies.

The low, scrubby trees growing along the shoreline from McRae south
are tea-trees, which appeared in the 19th century as the original
banksias and she-oaks were burned as fuel in limestone kilns that supplied Melbourne with much of its building mortar. A species of
melaleuca, tea-trees were actually used to supply a substitute tea in the
early days of the colony.

Frankston

42 km (26 mi) south of Melbourne.

A bustling outer Melbourne suburb at the base of picturesque Olivers
Hill, Frankston proper has a pleasant beach, but just 3 km (2 mi) south

you'll find two secret local beaches where residents come to swim and picnic. To reach **Pelican Point** and **Davey's Bay Yacht Club,** turn right on Old Mornington Road; follow it to the end of Marathon Drive, then turn right again onto Davey's Bay Road.

Mount Eliza

48 km (30 mi) south of Melbourne, 6 km (4 mi) south of Frankston.

A commuter suburb of Melbourne, Mount Eliza is relatively well-to-do and tree-filled, just inland from Port Phillip Bay. The **Omell Manyung Gallery,** one of the Melbourne area's most popular galleries, exhibits the work of up-and-coming Australian artists. ✉ *1408 Nepean Hwy.,* ☎ *03/9787–2953.* ▣ *Free.* ☉ *Mon., Thurs., and Fri. 11–4; weekends 11–5.*

Canadian Bay Reserve, Mount Eliza's beach is popular for its boat club and excellent picnic facilities. ✉ *Canadian Bay Rd. off Mount Eliza Way.*

Mornington

8 km (5 mi) south of Mount Eliza, 56 km (35 mi) south of Melbourne.

The **Mornington Peninsula Regional Gallery** is one of Victoria's 16 regional art centers. Names to look for among its outstanding collection of works by Australian artists include Fred Williams, Sam Fullbrook, William Dobell, Sir Russell Drysdale, and John Passmore. ✉ *4 Vancouver St.,* ☎ *03/5975–4395.* ▣ *$3.* ☉ *Tues.–Fri. 10–4:30, weekends 11–4:30.*

Arthurs Seat

20 km (12 mi) south of Mornington; follow the Esplanade from Mornington through Mount Martha. 76 km (47 mi) south of Melbourne.

Arthurs Seat State Park has walking tracks, a public garden, and a scenic drive or ride on a chairlift to a 1,000-ft summit, which provides a sweeping view of the surrounding countryside. ✉ *Arthurs Seat Rd., at Mornington Peninsula Hwy.,* ☎ *03/5987–2565.* ▣ *Chairlift $7.50.* ☉ *Sept.–June, daily 11–5; July–Aug., weekends 11–5.*

McRae

2 km (1¼ mi) west of Arthurs Seat, 76 km (47 mi) south of Melbourne.

Built in 1844, the **McRae Homestead** was one of the first houses erected in this area, which is why the National Trust has it listed as a historic monument. The original furniture is on display, and guides give half-hour tours of the property. Even when the house is closed, the caretaker may offer to show you around. ✉ *8 Charles St.,* ☎ *03/5986–6244.* ▣ *$5.* ☉ *Daily noon–4:30; groups by appointment.*

Sorrento

93 km (58 mi) southwest of Melbourne, 17 km (10 mi) from McRae.

Sorrento, with its evocative Italian name, is appropriately one of the prettiest of the bayside beach towns. Lawns are backed by shade trees, a trim white gazebo, and a fish-and-chips shop out over the water that leads to a tumbledown jetty—a picturesque roost for pelicans. Sorrento developed as a fashionable resort more than a century ago when George Coppin formed a company named the Sorrento Ocean Amphitheatre Company, which built tramways through the town and linked it with Melbourne by paddle steamer. More recently, Sorrento has become the arts-and-crafts center for the peninsula, and the stretch of highway between Sorrento and Blairgowrie has no fewer than eight galleries.

Aside from extremely popular seal exhibits, you'll find more than 200 fish species swimming about at **Sorrento Marine Aquarium.** ⊠ *St. Aubin's Way,* ☎ *03/5984–4478.* ☐ *$5.* ☉ *Daily 9–5; seal feeding daily at noon except Tues.*

En Route At the end of the Nepean Highway, in Portsea, turn left into Back Beach Road and make a right to **London Bridge,** a fantastic natural span carved by the ocean. After some time on the beach by the arch, the sole of the Mornington Peninsula boot runs in a straight line for 28 km (17 mi), forming a long, narrow coastal park that ends at Cape Schanck, where you can visit the **Cape Schanck Lighthouse and Museum.** The sea can be violent along this coastline—in 1967, Australian prime minister Harold Holt drowned at Cheviot Beach just west of London Bridge—and swimming is advisable only where the beach is patrolled by lifeguards.

Dining

$$ ✕ **Arthurs.** Considered the Mornington Peninsula's best dining expe-
★ rience, Arthurs has three eateries, all with fine views of Port Phillip Bay: the formal Peak, the informal and cheaper Vineyard Bistro, and an ice cream and snack kiosk. In the restaurant, the herbed ricotta gnocchi is delicious, or try the poached peaches in champagne syrup. Simpler lunches include eggplant slices rolled around a ricotta filling. ⊠ *Arthurs Seat Scenic Rd., Arthurs Seat,* ☎ *03/5981–4444. AE, DC, MC, V. Closed Mon. and Tues.*

$$ ✕ **Licciardo's.** This noisy, bustling storefront trattoria relies on the quality of its food, not its decor or its casual service, to keep the crowds coming. Daily specials are listed on large blackboards on the walls. Dishes include seafood risotto with spicy tomato sauce, barbecued mussels with herb bread, and rabbit fillets on a bed of noodles with basil. Seafood salads are highly recommended, and pasta and antipasto dishes are generally excellent. The exquisite chocolate soufflé is often available even when it does not appear on the menu. ⊠ *84 Mount Eliza Way, Mount Eliza,* ☎ *03/9787–7710. AE, DC, MC, V. No lunch Mon., Tues., or Sat.*

$$ ✕ **Poff's.** On a hillside with views across a vineyard to the valley
below, this modern restaurant has rapidly acquired a solid reputation. The menu is small and dishes are described with an austerity that downplays their caliber. Main courses include ocean trout, lamb kebab, roast duckling, and steak Diane—all simple and all delightful. Russian dishes, such as meat dumplings in broth flavored with soy sauce, garlic, and chili and topped with sour cream, are a specialty. The Crème caramel is fantastic. ⊠ *Red Hill Rd., Red Hill, 7 km (4 mi) from McRae,* ☎ *03/5989–2566. AE, DC, MC, V. Closed Mon.–Wed. No dinner Thurs.*

Phillip Island

★ *125 km (78 mi) south of Melbourne.*

This is the home of the greatly popular fairy penguins, whose nightly waddle from the sea to their burrows in nearby dunes draws throngs of onlookers, particularly on summer weekends and holidays. Be prepared for wet and windy conditions at any time of the year.

The penguin spectacle is interesting, but the island's changing coastline may ultimately be more appealing. At the end of the Summerland Peninsula, out past the Penguin Parade, two rock formations are particularly captivating. At low tide, you can walk across a basalt causeway to the **Nobbies** and take in the splendid views along the wild northern coast of Phillip Island. Wildlife here is abundant—with thousands of shearwaters (muttonbirds) in residence September–April. After their breeding season, they return north to the Bering Straight in the Arctic.

Farther out to sea, **Seal Rocks** are home to the largest colony of Australian fur seals. In midsummer there may be 5,000 seals basking on rocky platforms and capering in the sea. Get a bird's-eye view from the new **Seal Rocks Sea Life Center** (☎ 03/5952–9333). Opened in 1998, the center focuses on educating visitors about nature in an entertaining way. You can exhaust yourself on the Voyage of Discovery, learning about seals, sealers, scientists, and explorers.

Unlike the large and stately emperor penguins of the Antarctic, **fairy penguins** rarely grow much bigger than a large duck. Seeing them on Phillip Island, however, is hardly a back-to-nature experience. The penguins emerge from the surf onto a floodlit beach, while a commentator in a tower describes their progress over a public address system. Spectators, who watch from concrete bleachers, may number several thousand on a busy night. For many people, the most memorable part of the experience is the sight of the fluffy young penguins, who stand outside their burrows waiting for their parents to return with food. Camera flashbulbs are forbidden, which effectively prevents still photography. For anyone interested in seeing the animals in a less touristy setting, fairy penguins are common to most of the southern Victorian coastline, and the locals in most coastal towns will point out places where they can be seen. ⊠ *Summerland Beach,* ☎ *03/5956–8300 or 03/5956–8691.* ✇ *$9.50.*

Lodging

$$$ ⊡ **Rothsaye on Lovers Walk.** Whether for the fine beach on the doorstep or the outstanding accommodations, these seaside cottages have great appeal. The bedrooms, which have room for up to seven guests, are beautifully appointed, with thoughtful touches such as breakfast baskets, beach chairs and umbrellas, fishing lines, and even sunscreen. Fresh flowers, antiques, king-size beds, and an array of magazines festoon the rooms. There is always the floodlit delight of Lovers Walk, which you can follow into the center of the town of Cowes from the front door. Children are not accommodated. ⊠ *2 Roy Ct., Cowes 3922,* ☎ FAX *03/5952–2057. 3 cottages. Beach, fishing. MC, V.*

Side Trips from Melbourne A to Z

Car Rentals

Renting a car in Melbourne and driving south is the most practical way of seeing the Mornington Peninsula. Agencies include **Avis** (☎ 1800/22–5533), **Budget** (☎ 13–2727), **Hertz** (☎ 03/13–3039), **Cheapa** (☎ 03/9878–9882), **Delta** (☎ 03/13–1390), and **Rent-a-Bomb** (☎ 03/9428–0088).

Emergencies

Ambulance, fire brigade, and police. ☎ *000.*

Guided Tours

Day trips from Melbourne are offered by local tour operators, including **Australian Pacific Tours** (☎ 13–1304), **Gray Line** (☎ 03/9663–4455), and **AAT Kings** (☎ 03/9663–3377). All three depart from 184 Swanston Street. Dandenongs tours cost about $42, Penguin Parade tours around $80.

Visitor Information

Victoria Visitor Information Centre. ⊠ *Town Hall, Swanston and Little Collins Sts., 3000,* ☎ *03/9658–9955.* ☉ *Weekdays 9–6, weekends 9–5.*

Phillip Island Information Centre. ⊠ *Phillip Island Tourism Rd., Newhaven 3925,* ☎ *03/5956–7447,* FAX *03/5956–7905.*

WEST COAST REGION

Victoria's Great Ocean Road is arguably the country's most dramatic and spectacular coastal drive, heading west from Melbourne along rugged, windswept beaches. The road, built during the Great Depression atop majestic cliffs, occasionally dips down to sea level. Here in championship surfing country, some of the world's finest waves pound mile after mile of uninhabited golden sandy beaches. As you explore the coastline, don't miss Bell's Beach, site of the Easter Surfing Classic, one of the premier events of the surfing world. But be careful! Only the most competent swimmers should take a dip here, and then only at a lifeguard-patrolled beach with other swimmers. The fierce undertow along this coastline can be deadly.

The West Coast provides access to two of Victoria's major parks. Port Campbell National Park lies along the ocean and includes in its 30-km (19-mi) span some of Australia's most haunting coastline. And northeast of Hamilton, you can head into the mountains of Grampians National Park that begin to rise out of the plains about 80 km (50 mi) inland from the Southern Ocean.

Although this region is actually on the southeast coast of the Australian mainland, it lies to the west of Melbourne, and to Melburnians is therefore known as the "West Coast." From the city, you should allow two or more days for a West Coast sojourn.

Werribee

32 km (20 mi) southwest of Melbourne.

Once a country town, now a generally undistinguished outer suburb of Melbourne, Werribee is notable for the glorious Werribee Park Mansion and its attendant safari-style zoo.

The 60-room Italianate **Werribee Park Mansion,** dating from 1877, is furnished with period furniture and set on more than 10 hectares (25 acres) of formal gardens. This was one of the grandest homes in the colony, built by wealthy pastoralists Thomas and Andrew Chirnside. ⊠ *K Rd.,* ☎ *03/9741-2444.* ☞ *$10.* ☉ *Daily 10–4:45.*

☾ **Victoria's Open Range Zoo,** part of the original Werribee Park property, is a safari-style zoo of the highest caliber. Safari buses travel through a landscape that replicates southern Africa, passing among giraffe, rhinoceros, zebra, and hippopotamus. Australian animals also live in the park. A walk-through section houses cheetahs, apes, meerkats, and other African animals in natural conditions. The zoo is closely aligned with the Melbourne Zoo. ⊠ *K Rd.,* ☎ *03/9731-9600.* ☞ *$14.* ☉ *Daily 9–5; tours depart frequently 10–3:40.*

Geelong

72 km (45 mi) southwest of Melbourne, 40 km (25 mi) west of Werribee.

Victoria's second-largest city, Geelong relies on heavy industry, notably automobile construction, for its prosperity. Its proximity to the great surf beaches of the West Coast is its greatest appeal. There is little reason to linger.

The **National Wool Museum** tells the story of this major Australian industry. There are three galleries highlighting the harvesting of wool, its manufacture into textiles, and the methods by which it is sold. Exhibits include a reconstructed shearers' hut and 1920s mill workers' cottage. Audiovisual displays tell the story in an entertaining and informative manner. ⊠ *Mooroobool and Brougham Sts.,* ☎ *03/5227–0701.* ⊠ *$7.* ⊘ *Daily 9:30–5.*

Queenscliff

103 km (64 mi) southwest of Melbourne, 31 km (19 mi) south of Geelong.

The lovely coastal village of Queenscliff makes for a worthy—and well-signposted—detour on the drive between Geelong and Lorne. During the late 19th century this was a favorite weekend destination for well-to-do Melburnians, who traveled on steam ferries to stay at the area's grand hotels. Some, like The Queenscliff Hotel, draw tourists to this day.

Dining and Lodging

$$$ ✕⊞ **The Queenscliff Hotel.** Gloriously restored to its original state, the Queenscliff offers fine dining in either a small formal room, a leafy conservatory, or an outdoor courtyard. Fish and game are favored, with main-dish choices including kangaroo with Asian flavors and star-anise sauce. A separate list is available for vegetarians. Rooms are simply furnished and decorated in 19th-century style. ⊠ *16 Gellibrand St., 3225,* ☎ *03/5258–1066. 22 rooms without bath. Restaurant. AE, DC, MC, V.*

En Route   From Queenscliff, heed signs to the Great Ocean Road. Follow it for 45 km (28 mi) to **Torquay,** Australia's premier surfing and windsurfing resort. Here is Bell's Beach, famous for its Easter surfing contests and its October international windsurfing competitions. Continue to the **Great Ocean Road,** a positively magnificent coastal drive that officially begins at Eastern View, 10 km (6 mi) east of Lorne.

Lorne

140 km (87 mi) southwest of Melbourne, 95 km (59 mi) southwest of Queenscliff, and 50 km (30 mi) southwest of Torquay.

A little town at the edge of the Otway Range, Lorne is the site of both a wild celebration every New Year's Eve and the popular Pier-to-Pub Swim held shortly thereafter. Some people make their reservations a year in advance for these events. It's the site of the Great Otway Classic, a footrace held annually on the second weekend in June.

Just before the road enters Lorne, it crosses the Erskine River. From a campsite near the bridge, an 8-km (5-mi) trail winds up the **Erskine River valley.** This lush, green haven of eucalyptus, tree ferns, waterfalls, and rustic bridges is delightful, but keep an eye out for leeches if you're bare-legged. The track passes the Sanctuary, a rock amphitheater where early pioneers gathered for religious services. If you're not in the mood for a walk, Erskine Road, which exits Lorne to the north, passes close to Erskine Falls.

Dining and Lodging

$$ ✕ **Kosta's.** Lively, bright, informal, and noisy, especially in peak sea-
★   son, this gaily decorated taverna and wine bar specializes in Greek food and international dishes, such as Moroccan lamb stew, homemade *tsatziki* (a yogurt, cucumber, and garlic dip), and char-grilled lamb. Fresh local specialties include char-grilled fish and lobster. ⊠ *42 Mountjoy Parade,* ☎ *03/5289–1883. AE, MC, V.*

$ ⊞ **Erskine House.** The 1868 Erskine House was built in a 12-acre garden and fully restored in 1930. This charming, spotless guest house, in 1930s style, is perfect if you want a relaxed, Art Deco hotel without phones, televisions, or radios. Rates include breakfast. ⊠ *Mount-*

joy Parade, 3232, ☎ *03/5289–1209. 67 rooms, 13 suites. 8 tennis courts, putting, croquet, and lawn bowls greens. AE, DC, MC, V.*

En Route Forty-five km (28 mi) after Lorne, the Great Ocean Road passes the charming, historic fishing town of **Apollo Bay**. The highway then weaves in and out of the rain forest until it reaches the coastal town of Wattle Hill, where a dead-end side road will lead you to the shore at **Moonlight Head,** part of **Otway National Park** (☎ 03/5235–9303). The coastal formation was named by Matthew Flinders, the first circumnavigator of Australia, who saw the headland during a fierce storm when the moon broke through the clouds for a moment; several other ships, not his, have foundered here. The cliffs are among the highest in the country.

The Great Ocean Road heads inland again slightly, coming back to the coast at **Princetown.** This is the beginning of Port Campbell National Park, the most dazzling section of the drive. For the next 32 km (20 mi), the road snakes along the cliff tops for a heart-stopping, roller-coaster ride.

Port Campbell National Park

★ *225 km (140 mi) west of Melbourne, 66 km (41 mi) east of Warrnambool.*

Stretching some 30 km (19 mi) along the southern Victoria coastline, **Port Campbell National Park** is the site of some of the most famous geological formations in Australia. Along this coast the ferocious Southern Ocean has gnawed at limestone cliffs for ages, creating a sort of badlands-by-the-sea, where columns of resilient rock stand 165–330 ft offshore. There are several scenic lookouts along the way, and each one seems more spectacular than the last. The most famous formation is the **Twelve Apostles**, as much a symbol for Victoria as the Sydney Opera House is for New South Wales. Despite the name, only eight pillars are visible—the rest have been claimed by the waves. Equally dramatic are the formations at **Bay of Martyrs** and **Bay of Islands Coastal Reserve**. Both are less crowded with tour buses than the Twelve Apostles, and at Bay of Islands you can watch new rock stacks taking shape.

The level of the sea was much higher 25 million years ago, and as the water receded, towering sediments of sand, mud, limestone, and seashells were left standing to face the waves. The ocean is continuously carving these massive towers into strange shapes, even as they slowly crumble into the sea.

The best time to visit the park is January–April, when you can also witness events on nearby **Muttonbird Island**. Toward nightfall, hundreds of hawks and kites circle the island in search of hungry, impatient baby muttonbirds emerging from their protective burrows. The hawks and kites beat a hasty retreat at the sight of thousands of adult shearwaters approaching with food for their chicks as the last light fades from the sky.

Generally speaking, you don't come to Port Campbell to bushwalk, but if you want to explore the area on foot, pick up a pamphlet for the self-guided Discovery Walk at the **Port Campbell Visitors Centre** (✉ Morris St., Port Campbell,, ☎ no phone), open daily 9 to 5. The walk begins near Port Campbell Beach and takes about 1½ hours to complete. It is safe to swim only at this beach—the pounding surf and undertow are treacherous at other nearby beaches. Swimmers should opt instead for the few isolated pools found in sheltered coves along the coastline.

Lodging

Campsites at the **Port Campbell Recreation Reserve** (☎ 03/5598–6369), in the town of Port Campbell, start at $12 per day for a site without electricity, $15 for a site with power. En-suite cabins are available from $55 a day. The campground has hot water and showers. Advance reservations are suggested.

Arriving and Departing

Port Campbell is 250 km (155 mi) southwest of Melbourne via Geelong. The area is accessible by car along the Great Ocean Road between Princetown and Peterborough.

Visitor Information

Port Campbell National Park. ⊠ *Tregea St., Port Campbell, 3269,* ☎ *03/5598–6382.*

Department of Natural Resources and Environment. ⊠ *240 Victoria Parade, East Melbourne 3002,* ☎ *03/9412–4011.*

Warrnambool

262 km (162 mi) west of Melbourne, 122 km (76 mi) west of Lorne, and 66 km (41 mi) west of Port Campbell.

The nearest major population center to Port Campbell National Park, Warrnambool is in the midst of wool and dairy-farm country. It's a friendly city of robust, hardy people who live off the land and sea. Held in February, the town's **Wunta Fiesta** includes whale-boat races, a seafood and wine carnival, and children's activities.

★ The sheltered bay at **Logan's Beach,** 3 km (2 mi) from the center of Warrnambool, is a nice place for a stroll. Winter offers the added fascination of watching **southern right whales** close to the shore, where they give birth to their calves. They take up residence here for a considerable stretch of time and are easily observed from the shore, where there is a cliffside viewing platform. The **Warrnambool Visitor Information Center** (☎ 03/5564–7837) can advise you of their presence and direct you to the best observation points.

☾ A highlight in Warrnambool is **Flagstaff Hill Maritime Village,** a re-created 19th-century village built around a fort constructed in 1887, during one of the Russian scares that intermittently terrified the colony. In the village, visit an 1853 lighthouse that's still in use, wander through the old fort, or board the *Reginald M,* a trading ship from the South Australian Gulf. ⊠ *Merri and Banyan Sts.,* ☎ *03/5564–7841.* ☏ *$9.50.* ☾ *Daily 9–5.*

☾ **Lake Pertobe Adventure Playground** is an 86-acre children's paradise. Facilities include lakes with children's powerboats, paddleboats, kayaks, canoes, pleasure boats, and junior sailing craft, as well as a playground, barbecue facilities, and walking tracks. ⊠ *Pertobe Rd.,* ☎ *03/5564–7800.* ☏ *Free.* ☾ *Daily.*

☾ Collect your **Kid's Country Treasure Hunt Guide** kit at the **Warrnambool Visitor Information Centre** (⊠ 600 Raglan Parade, ☎ 03/5564–7837). Children who answer the questions on the "treasure map" (designed to introduce them to Warrnambool and its surroundings) get a free badge, book, or decal from the information center.

Hopkins Falls, 13 km (8 mi) northeast of Warrnambool on Wangoom Road, makes for a pleasant side trip. After parking your car, you can inspect the waterfalls comfortably on foot.

Tower Hill State Game Reserve, on an extinct volcano now green with vegetation, is a half-hour drive northwest of Warrnambool. The reserve is an attempt to return part of the land to a native state by introducing local flora and fauna. Spend some time at the park's natural history center and then walk around the trails. ⊠ *Princes Hwy., Koroit,* ☎ *03/5565–9202.* ⊠ *Free.* ⊘ *Reserve daily 8–5; natural history center daily 9:30–4:30.*

Dining and Lodging

$$ ✕ **Mahogany Ship.** Decorated in a loosely nautical theme, this restaurant above the Flagstaff Hill Maritime Village has splendid views of Lady Bay harbor and the ocean beyond. Local crayfish (spiny lobsters) are a specialty; steak and poultry dishes are also available. Children are served from a separate menu, which includes that Australian favorite, fish-and-chips. The tavern next door serves less expensive meals. ⊠ *Flagstaff Hill Maritime Village, Merri St.,* ☎ *03/5561–1833. AE, DC, MC, V.*

$$ ✕ꗠ **Quamby Homestead.** This magnificent century-old homestead is
★ furnished with Australian antiques and is an ideal base from which to explore the Warrnambool area. Modern rooms have en-suite facilities in former staff quarters, which are set apart from the homestead and surrounded by an English-style garden, where native birdcalls compete with the shrieks of resident peacocks. The dining room, in the homestead, serves fine country meals, which are available to nonresident guests on weekends. Rates include breakfast and dinner. Children under 12 are not accommodated. ⊠ *Caramut Rd., Woolsthorpe, 26 km (16 mi) north of Warrnambool,* ☎ *03/5569–2395,* ☒ *03/5569–2244. 7 rooms. Dining room. AE, DC, MC, V.*

$ ꗠ **Central Court Motel.** On Princes Highway opposite the Warrnambool Tourist Information Centre, this neat, contemporary two-story motel is a 10-minute walk from the main shopping center. ⊠ *581 Raglan Parade, 3280,* ☎ *03/5562–8555,* ☒ *03/5561–1313. 36 rooms, 2 suites. Restaurant, pool, baby-sitting. AE, DC, MC, V.*

$ ꗠ **Sundowner Mid City Motor Inn.** This modern, two-story motel, on Princes Highway, is set in a neatly manicured garden a short distance from the town center. Dinner dances are held on Saturday night. ⊠ *525 Raglan Parade, 3280,* ☎ *03/5562–3866,* ☒ *03/5562–0923. 61 rooms, 9 suites. Restaurant, bar, room service, pool, baby-sitting. AE, DC, MC, V.*

Outdoor Activities and Sports

BICYCLING

The **Melbourne to Warrnambool Road Race** is a cycling classic held annually on the second Saturday in October. The race starts at 7:15 AM at Port Melbourne and finishes at Raglan Parade in Warrnambool at approximately 2:30 PM.

CAR RACING

The **Grand Annual Sprintcar Classic** (☎ 03/5562–8229) is held at Premier Speedway in Allansford east of Warrnambool during the last weekend in January.

FISHING

Warrnambool and the surrounding district offer great river and surf fishing. A 28-day fishing license costs $10 and is required for fishing the rivers and streams of Victoria. Contact **Warrnambool Shooters and Anglers Shop** (⊠ Liebig St., ☎ 03/5562–3502) for information.

GOLF

The **Warrnambool Golf Course** (☎ 03/5562–2108) is a first-class 18-hole course off Younger Street. Greens fees are $18; club rental is $6 and a motorized cart for 18 holes costs $30.

Shopping

For crafts and home-grown produce, visit the **Warrnambool Town and Country Crafts Community Market** (⊠ Swan Reserve, Raglan Parade), which is held on the second Saturday morning of each month. The Warrnambool **Saturday Market** is held on the first Saturday of each month in the Safeway parking lot.

Port Fairy

291 km (180 mi) west of Melbourne, 29 km (18 mi) west of Warrnambool.

Port Fairy wins the vote of many a Victorian as the state's prettiest village. The second-oldest town in Victoria, it was originally known as Belfast, and there are indeed echoes of Ireland in the landscape and architecture. Founded during the whaling heyday in the 19th century, Port Fairy was once a whaling station with one of the largest ports in Victoria. The town still thrives as the base for a fishing fleet, and as host to one of Australia's most famous folk festivals every March. More than 50 of the cottages and sturdy bluestone buildings that line the banks of the River Moyne have been classified as landmarks by the National Trust, and few towns repay a leisurely stroll so richly.

The **Historical Society Museum** contains relics from whaling days and from the many ships that have foundered along this coast. ⊠ *Old Courthouse, Gipps St.,* ☎ *no phone.* 🖃 *$2.* ☾ *Wed. and weekends 2–5.*

Mott's Cottage is a restored limestone-and-timber cottage built by Sam Mott, a member of the whaling crew that discovered the town in the cutter *Fairy.* ⊠ *5 Sackville St.,* ☎ *03/9654–4711. Admission $2.* ☾ *Wed. and weekends 1–4, or by appointment.*

Dining and Lodging

$ ✕ **Lunch.** Lunch is open for, well, lunch—and dinner, brunch, and morning and afternoon tea. Snack on scrambled eggs with smoked salmon, a ploughman's lunch, focaccia with a variety of fillings, or sample more exotic fare such as falafel and *baba ghanoush* (a Middle Eastern eggplant appetizer). With notice, picnic baskets can be prepared. ⊠ *20 Bank St.,* ☎ *03/5568–2642. MC, V. BYOB. Closed Mon. and Tues.*

$$ ✕🖃 **Dublin House Inn.** This solid stone building dates from 1855 and is furnished in period style. Chef Glenn Perkins uses the freshest local produce, creating dishes that incorporate everything from seafood to free-range chicken, duckling, and local beef. Lobster is available, but call ahead. The 32-seat dining room opens for dinner daily during summer. Dublin House Inn also has rooms for an overnight stay—functional rather than luxurious, but no less pleasant for their period style. ⊠ *57 Bank St., Port Fairy 3284,* ☎ *03/5568–2022,* 🖷 *03/5568–2158. 3 rooms, 1 apartment. AE, MC, V. No lunch.*

$ 🖃 **Goble's Mill House.** An imaginative refurbishment of an 1865 flour mill on the banks of the Moyne River transformed its various levels into six guest rooms and a spacious sitting area, all furnished with antiques. The upper-story loft bedroom is especially appealing, with a balcony overlooking the ever-active river. You can also enjoy fishing off the Mill House's private jetty. Breakfast is included. ⊠ *75 Gipps St., Port Fairy 3284,* ☎ *03/5568–1118,* 🖷 *03/5568–1178. 6 rooms. MC, V.*

Hamilton

290 km (180 mi) west of Melbourne, 82 km (51 mi) north of Port Fairy, 97 km (60 mi) southeast of Halls Gap at Grampians National Park.

One of western Victoria's principal inland cities, Hamilton is set in rich grazing country. It has a lovely botanical garden and a lake made from damming the Grange Burn. There is a beach on the lake, and the water is full of trout. The town is the original seat of the Ansett family (of Down Under airline fame), and there is evidence of their fortune in and around town. Consider heeding the call of the Grampians Mountains, visible along the skyline north of Hamilton, and heading the 100-odd km (60-odd mi) into forested, craggy **Grampians National Park** (☞ *below*).

The **Hamilton Art Gallery**'s highly respected collection of watercolors, engravings, pottery, antique silver, and porcelain from the Mediterranean is well worth a visit. ⊠ *Brown St.,* ☎ *03/5573–0460.* ⊙ *Weekdays 10–5, Sat. 10–noon and 2–5, Sun. 2–5.*

Lodging

$$ 🏠 **Arrandoovong Homestead.** Amid the tranquillity of a 1,235-acre grazing property, this 1850s bluestone homestead is home to 5,000 sheep as well as an increasingly popular bed-and-breakfast. Owners Jeanie and Bill Sharp, who bought Arrandoovong in 1952, lead guests upstairs to spacious, lovingly maintained, antiques-furnished rooms. Dinner is available on request at $35 per person. The homestead is 20 minutes from Hamilton, ideally located for day trips to South Australia's famed Coonawarra wine region, the Shipwreck Coast, and the Grampians. ⊠ *Chrome Road, Branxholme 3302,* ☎ *03/5578–6221,* FAX *03/5578–6249. 3 rooms, 2 with bath. AE, MC, V.*

West Coast Region A to Z

Arriving and Departing

BY CAR

Take the Princes Highway west from Melbourne to Geelong. From there, follow signs to Queenscliff and Torquay, where you will connect with the Great Ocean Road. For an alternative inland route to Warrnambool, much quicker but vastly less interesting, take the Princes Highway.

BY TRAIN

The West Coast **railway** (☎ 03/5226–6500) operates daily services between Melbourne and Warrnambool.

Getting Around

BY CAR

Driving is the most convenient way to see the region, and the only way to really enjoy the Great Ocean Road. Distances are considerable, and the going may be slow on the most scenic routes, especially during the summer holiday period.

BY TRAIN

Geelong is fed by small, fast, and frequent Sprinter trains from Melbourne. The West Coast Railway, a newly formed private company, serves points farther west. Although the trains provide restful means of getting to main centers, they run inland and don't provide the extraordinary views you can see by car.

Contacts and Resources

EMERGENCIES

Ambulance, fire brigade, and police. ☎ *000.*

GUIDED TOURS

AAT Kings (☎ 03/9663–3377) has a choice of one- or two-night tours of the Great Ocean Road from Melbourne. The one-day tour costs $88. A choice of accommodations is available on the two-day tour, which runs $232–$248.

The Wayward Bus (☎ 1800/88–2823) is a minibus that takes three days to meander from Melbourne to Adelaide via the Great Ocean Road, Mount Gambier, and the Coorong, with overnight stops at Port Fairy and Beachport. Aimed primarily at backpackers, the tour is enjoyable, informative, inexpensive, and highly recommended. Passengers can leave the bus at either overnight stop and catch the following bus. The tours depart Melbourne on Wednesday and Saturday, more frequently in summer. The cost is $180 per person, including picnic lunches, but excluding accommodations.

VISITOR INFORMATION

Geelong Great Ocean Road Visitor Information Centre. ⊠ *Stead Park, Princes Hwy., Geelong,* ☎ *03/5275–5797.* ⊙ *Daily 9–5.*
Port Fairy Tourist Information Centre. ⊠ *Bank St., Port Fairy,* ☎ *03/5568–2682.* ⊙ *Daily 9–5.*
Warrnambool Visitor Information Centre. ⊠ *600 Raglan Parade, Warrnambool,* ☎ *03/5564–7837.* ⊙ *Weekdays 9–5, weekends 10–4.*

GRAMPIANS NATIONAL PARK

★ The Grampians combine stunning mountain scenery, abundant native wildlife, and a variety of invigorating outdoor activities. Close to the western border of Victoria, this 412,000-acre region of sharp sandstone peaks was forced up from an ancient seabed, sculpted by eons of wind and rain, then carpeted with a fantastic array of wildflowers. More than 900 wildflower species, 200 species of birds, and 35 species of native mammals populate the park.

"Gariwerd" is the Aboriginal name for this area. The abundant food supply made these ranges a natural refuge for Aboriginal groups. More than 100 caves have been found daubed with their paintings, which are simpler than the complex iconography of the Arnhem Land or Western Desert Aboriginal people.

The park has more than 160 km (99 mi) of walking trails, from short, easy tracks to challenging overnight expeditions through rugged terrain. For anything more than a short stroll, warm, waterproof clothing is a must. Some of the best short walks are the 2½-hour climb to the summit of Mt. William; the 2½-hour hike to the Pinnacle from the Wonderland Turntable, which leads past fantastic rock formations to a magnificent view; and the two-hour walk to MacKenzie Falls from Zumstein. Grampians National Park is also popular with rock climbers, who focus their activities on Mount Arapiles.

There are also spectacular drives through the park. The circuit of the Wonderland Range from Halls Gap, the 15-km (8-mi) drive from Halls Gap to Zumstein via the Mt. Victory Road, and the drive between Halls Gap and Dunkeld, at the southern entrance to the park, are highly recommended.

The gateway to the Grampians is Halls Gap, a small, busy town where koalas are sometimes found snoozing in the trees and kangaroos graze on the outskirts in the evening. The best time to visit the park is October–December, when wildflowers are in bloom, the weather is mild, and summer crowds have yet to arrive.

Don't miss the **Brambuk Cultural Centre** (⊠ Dunkeld Rd., Halls Gap, ☎ 03/5356–4452). Owned and operated by Aboriginal people, it provides a unique living history of Aboriginal culture in this part of Victoria. Don't miss the new *Dreaming Theatre,* which illustrates local legends.

Dining and Lodging

The national park base is Halls Gap, which offers a choice of motels, guest houses, host farms, and caravan parks. Eleven campgrounds exist within the national park. The fee is $8.60 per site for up to six people, and the rule is first come, first served. Pick up a permit at the park's visitor center (☞ Visitor Information, *below*) or at the campground.

$–$$ ✕ **Kookaburra.** This is the best local bet for food. Try the venison in steak, sausage, or pie. Or, choose duckling, milk-fed veal, or pork fillet smoked over cherrywood embers. Finish with a traditional sago plum pudding. ⊠ *Grampians Rd., Halls Gap,* ☎ *03/5356–4222. AE, MC, V.*

$$ 🏠 **Glenisla Homestead.** For an atmospheric alternative to motel accommodation, this 1842 B&B on the western side of the national park is highly recommended. ⊠ *Off Hamilton-Horsham Rd., Cavendish 3314,* ☎ *03/5380–1532,* 🆅🆇 *03/5380–1566. AE, MC, V.*

Arriving and Departing

BY CAR

Halls Gap is reached via Ballarat and Ararat on the Western Highway (Hwy. 8). The town is 260 km (160 mi) northwest of Melbourne, 97 km (61 mi) northeast of Hamilton, 146 km (91 mi) west of Ballarat.

Guided Tours

Gray Line (☎ 03/9663–4455) operates a one-day tour of the Grampians ($85) that departs Melbourne on Monday and Saturday.

Visitor Information

Grampians National Park Visitor Centre. ⊠ *Dunkeld Rd., Halls Gap 3381,* ☎ *03/5356–4381.*

Department of Natural Resources and Environment. ⊠ *240 Victoria Parade, East Melbourne 3002,* ☎ *03/9412–4011.*

GOLD COUNTRY

Victoria was changed forever in the mid-1850s by the discovery of gold in the center of the state. Fantastic news of gold deposits caused immigrants from every corner of the world to pour into Victoria to seek their fortunes as "diggers"—a name that has become synonymous with Australians ever since. Few miners became wealthy from their searches, however; the real money was made by those supplying goods and services to the thousands who had succumbed to gold fever.

Gold towns that sprang up like mushrooms to accommodate these fortune seekers prospered until the gold rush receded, when they became ghost towns or turned to agriculture to survive. Today, Victoria's gold is again being mined in limited quantities, while these historic old towns remain interesting relics of Australia's past.

If you are planning to go to Grampians National Park (☞ *above*), its principal service town of Halls Gap is some 150 km (93 mi) west of Ballarat. From Bendigo at the end of this section, Echuca on the Murray River (☞ *below*) is an easy 90-km (56-mi) drive north.

Ballarat

106 km (66 mi) northwest of Melbourne, 146 km (91 mi) east of Grampians National Park.

In the local Aboriginal language, the name Ballarat means "resting place," since a plentiful supply of food was to be found around Lake Wendouree, to the north of the present township. The town flourished when gold was discovered here in 1851, but it was not Australia's first major gold strike—that honor belongs to Bathurst, in western New South Wales. However, Victoria in 1851 *was* El Dorado; 90% of the gold mined in Australia during the boom years of the 19th century came from the state. The biggest finds were at Ballarat and then Bendigo, and the Ballarat diggings proved to be among the richest alluvial goldfields in the world. In 1854, Ballarat was the scene of the battle of the Eureka Stockade, a skirmish that took place between miners and authorities, primarily over the extortionate gold license fees that miners were forced to pay. More than 20 men died in the battle, the only time that Australians have taken up arms in open rebellion against their government.

Montrose Cottage and Eureka Museum of Social History. Built in 1856 by a Scottish miner, Montrose Cottage was the first bluestone house in Ballarat. Inside you can see furniture and handwork of the period. Adjoining the cottage is a museum with an impressive display of artifacts from Ballarat's gold-mining days and an excellent display on the women of Eureka. The tours conducted by Laurel Johnson, the owner of the museum, are lively and informative. ⊠ *111 Eureka St.,* ☎ *03/ 5332–2554.* ⌑ *$5.50.* ⊘ *Daily 9–5.*

The prosperity of the gold rush left Ballarat well-endowed with handsome buildings, and the short stretch of **Lydiard Street** around Sturt Street has a number of notable examples.

One of the historic edifices of Lydiard Street is the **Ballarat Fine Arts Gallery,** which contains works by several famous Australian painters, including Russell Drysdale, Sidney Nolan, and Fred Williams. Its most impressive exhibit is the tattered remains of the original Southern Cross flag that was flown defiantly by the rebels at the Eureka Stockade. Many Australians advocate the adoption of the Southern Cross in preference to the present Australian flag, which features the Union Jack, regarded as an anachronistic symbol of the country's link with Great Britain. ⊠ *40 Lydiard St.,* ☎ *03/5331–5622.* ⌑ *$4.* ⊘ *Daily 9–5.*

On the shores of Lake Wendouree, Ballarat's **Botanic Gardens** are identifiable by the brilliant blooms and classical statuary. At the rear of the gardens, the Begonia House is the focus of events during the town's **Begonia Festival**, held annually in February or March. Many of the garden's trees are on the National Trust's Register of Significant Trees, including swamp cypress, California redwood, and a druid's oak. Busts on the Avenue of the Prime Ministers and 19th-century Italian marble sculpture provide interesting statuary. ⊠ *Wendouree Parade,* ☎ *no phone.* ⌑ *Free.* ⊘ *Daily sunrise–sunset.*

☾ **Sovereign Hill Historical Park** is built on the site of the Sovereign Hill Quartz Mining Company's mines. This is an authentic re-creation of life, work, and play on the gold diggings at Ballarat following the discovery of gold here in 1851. On the lowest part of the site are the tent camp and diggings, which were built in the first months of the gold rush, when gold was panned from creeks or dug from the earth with picks and shovels. On Main Street, running uphill from the diggings, are the shops, workshops, and public buildings from 1854 to 1861. Notice the New York Hotel and the T. Murphy California Tentmaker shop, reminders that many of the miners came from the United States. At the top of the hill lies the third stage of Sovereign Hill—the mine and the pithead equipment. When the surface gold gave out, miners were forced to dig along the ancient watercourses that lay deep underground, and this was where the real treasure lay. It was in such a mine on the Ballarat goldfields that the Welcome Nugget was discovered in 1858 by a group of Cornish miners. At today's prices, it would be worth just over a million dollars.

Near the entrance to the complex is the **Voyage to Discovery,** an indoor museum designed to provide an overview of society and the world at large at the time of the gold rush. The museum is excellent, with imaginative dioramas and computer terminals that encourage you to become an active participant in the gold-discovery process.

Across Bradshaw Street from the historical park is the **Gold Museum,** which displays an extensive collection of nuggets from the Ballarat diggings as well as some examples of finished gold in the form of jewelry. The museum houses an excellent souvenir shop.

Sovereign Hill is the backdrop for **Blood on the Southern Cross,** a 90-minute sound-and-light spectacular that focuses on the Eureka uprising. The story is told with passion and dramatic technical effects, although the sheer wealth of historical detail clouds the story line. The climax of the show is the battle of the Eureka Stockade. Be prepared for chilly nights, even in midsummer. Numbers are limited and advance bookings are recommended. ⊠ *Sovereign Hill Park, Bradshaw St.,* ☎ *03/5331–1944.* ⌕ *$18.50, including Gold Museum; Blood on the Southern Cross $18.50; Sovereign Hill and Blood on the Southern Cross $37.* ☼ *Park daily 10–5; Gold Museum Sun.–Fri. 10–5:30, Sat. 12:30–5:30. Sometimes closed for maintenance Aug. and Dec. No sound-and-light show Sun.*

♻ **Ballarat Wildlife and Reptile Park.** This bushland park is home to native Australian wildlife from a wide range of habitats. Animals include saltwater crocodiles, snakes, lizards, wombats, echidnas, and kangaroos. A koala tour takes place daily at 11. The park also has a café, and barbecue and picnic areas. ⊠ *Fussel and York Sts., East Ballarat,* ☎ *03/5333–5933.* ⌕ *$10.50.* ☼ *Daily 9–5:30.*

Dining and Lodging

$$$ × **Gill's.** This boat-shed restaurant has lovely views of Lake Wen-
★   douree and a light, airy environment ideal for a leisurely brunch, afternoon tea, or a romantic interlude. The Caesar salad is tasty, as is the homegrown borscht. Breakfast is served weekends and public holidays. ⊠ *View Point, Lake Wendouree, Ballarat,* ☎ *03/5333–3333. AE, DC, MC, V. Closed Sun. and Mon.*

$$ × **Dyer's Steak Stable.** Set in a former hotel stable, this restaurant relies on a simple formula of robust food, fine wine, and a welcoming atmosphere. Game dishes and a range of steaks with various sauces are the house specialties. *Little Bridge St., Ballarat,* ☎ *03/5331–2850. AE, DC, MC, V. Closed Sun. No lunch Sat.*

$$–$$$ ×⌂ **The Ansonia.** Built in the 1870s as professional offices—rescued
★   from oblivion by the current owners, who refurbished a derelict shell—the Ansonia is now an excellent boutique hotel and restaurant. Open from 7 AM–late, the restaurant features a sumptuous breakfast, plus lunch and dinner. The fare is eclectic; for example, Moroccan lamb sits alongside Caesar salad and steaks. There are four different styles of accommodation, from two-room apartments to studios, all of which are beautifully furnished and appointed. ⊠ *32 Lydiard St. S, Ballarat 3350,* ☎ *03/5332–4678,* ℻ *03/5332–4698. 20 rooms. Restaurant. AE, DC, MC, V.*

$–$$ ⌂ **Ravenswood.** Tucked behind a garden brimming with peach trees, pussy willows, fuchsias, and climbing roses, this three-bedroom timber cottage is ideal for anyone looking for family-size accommodation with kitchen facilities. The house has been decorated with contemporary furniture and carpeting to a high standard of comfort. The cottage is a little less than 1½ km (1 mi) from the center of Ballarat. Break-fast supplies are provided. ⊠ *Box 1360, Ballarat Mail Center 3354,* ☎ *03/5332–8296,* FAX *03/5331–3358. 1 cottage. AE, DC, MC, V.*

Golf

Ballarat Golf Club (⊠ Sturt St., West Ballarat, ☎ 03/5334–1023 or 053/34–1573). Greens fees are $13 for 18 holes, and clubs are available for rent. Call the pro shop for bookings.

Daylesford and Hepburn Springs

109 km (68 mi) northwest of Melbourne, 45 km (28 mi) northeast of Ballarat.

Nestled in the slopes of the Great Dividing Range, Daylesford and its nearby twin, Hepburn Springs, constitute the spa capital of Australia. The water table here is naturally aerated with carbon dioxide and rich in soluble mineral salts. This concentration of natural springs was first noted during the gold rush and a spa was established at Hepburn Springs in 1875, when spa resorts were fashionable in Europe. After a long decline, this spa has been revived in a '90s, health-conscious style.

The main attraction is the **Hepburn Springs Spa Centre.** This bright, modern complex offers a variety of mineral baths and treatments, in-cluding communal spa pools, private aerospa baths, massages, facials, saunas, and float tanks. Treatments run $8–$77; rates are slightly higher on weekends. ⊠ *Main Rd., Mineral Springs Reserve,* ☎ *03/5348–2034.* ⊙ *Daily 10–8.*

Above the Hepburn Springs Spa Centre, a path winds through the **Mineral Springs Reserve** past a series of mineral springs, each with a slightly different chemical composition—and a significantly different taste. Any empty bottles you have can be filled free with the mineral water of your choice.

Perched on a hillside overlooking Daylesford, the **Convent Gallery** is a former nunnery that has been restored to its lovely Victorian state. It displays contemporary Australian pottery, glassware, jewelry, sculp-ture, and prints, all for sale. At the front of the gallery is **Bad Habits,** a sunny café that serves light lunches and snacks. ⊠ *Daly St.,* ☎ *03/5348–3211.* ▨ *$3.* ⊙ *Daily 10–6.*

Dining and Lodging

$$–$$$ ✕▥ **Lake House Restaurant.** Consistently rated one of central Victo-
    ★   ria's best restaurants, this rambling lakeside pavilion brings glamour to spa country. The seasonal menu utilizes local produce and features dishes such as smoked-trout tortellini and kangaroo tenderloin and a selection of imaginative Asian-accented and vegetarian dishes—all presented with style and imagination. Tables on the deck are perfect for lunch on a warm day. The wine list features some of the finest vin-tages of the surrounding vineyards. Guest rooms in the lodge have a breezy, contemporary feel: Those at the front offer better views, but slightly less privacy, than those at the back, which are screened by rose-entwined trellises. Children are not accommodated on weekends. Breakfast is included in the rate. ⊠ *King St., Daylesford 3460,* ☎ *03/5348–3329,* FAX *03/5448–3995. 12 rooms. Restaurant, bar, pool. AE, DC, MC, V.*

$$ ▥ **Dudley House.** On Hepburn Springs's main street, it's hard to miss this timber Federation classic—similar to the Queen Anne style in En-gland and the United States—behind a neat hedge and picket gate. The house was painstakingly restored and, with antique furnishings and cozy atmosphere, offers comfort and romance. The white room at the

front and the blue room at the rear are the ones to request. The town's spa baths are within walking distance. Neither smoking nor children under 16 are allowed. Rates include breakfast; dinner is available by arrangement. ⊠ *101 Main St., Hepburn Springs 3460,* ☎ *03/5348–3033. 4 rooms. Dining room. AE, MC, V.*

$$ ⊞ **Holcombe Homestead.** This is country living at its aristocratic best: a century-old farmhouse that is one of the architectural glories of rural Victoria, complete with kangaroos, kookaburras, and a trout stream. The house has been furnished in keeping with its Victorian character, and to preserve its architectural integrity, guests share one bathroom. Those who arrive midweek often have the entire house to themselves. Guests can arrange to cook their own meals, and the owners, who live in a neighboring house, will prepare box lunches and dinner on request. Breakfast is included. ⊠ *Holcombe Rd., Glenlyon 3461, 15 km (9 mi) from Daylesford,* ☎ *03/5348–7514,* ⅎ̶Ⱥ̶X̶ *03/5348–7742. 3 rooms without bath. Tennis court, fishing, mountain bikes. AE, DC, MC, V.*

Castlemaine

119 km (74 mi) northwest of Melbourne, 38 km (24 mi) north of Daylesford.

Castlemaine is another gold-mining town, yet the gold here was mostly found on the surface. Lacking the deeper reef gold where the real riches lay, the town never reached the prosperity of Ballarat or Bendigo, as is evidenced by its comparatively modest public buildings.

Castlemaine Market, built in 1862 to resemble an ancient Roman basilica, is an exception among the town's generally unadorned public buildings. The statue on top of the building is Ceres, Roman goddess of the harvest.

Buda House is a tribute to the diversity of talents drawn to Australia's gold rush. Built in 1861, the house was purchased two years later by Ernest Liviny, a Hungarian jeweler who established a business on the Castlemaine goldfields. It was the last of his six daughters, Hilda, who left the house and its contents to the state when she died in 1981.

Buda House is essentially simple, yet it shows an Eastern European love of culture. Twentieth-century woodcuts in the hall are especially fine, and the work of several important artists is displayed. Look for prints by Margaret Preston, whose native flowers of the 1920s show a strong, stylized design sense. The house contains a number of Ernest Leviny's own designs, as well as photographs, paintings, sculptures, and embroidery created by his industrious and talented daughters. The gardens are delightful, with a fresh discovery at every turn. ⊠ *42 Hunter St.,* ☎ *03/5472–1032.* ▭ *$7.* ⊙ *Daily 9–5.*

Maldon

137 km (85 mi) northwest of Melbourne, 16 km (10 mi) northwest of Castlemaine.

Relative isolation has preserved Maldon, a former mining town, almost intact, and today the entire main street is a magnificent example of vernacular goldfields architecture; look for bull-nose roofing over the verandas, a feature now back in architectural vogue. Maldon's charm has become a marketable commodity—now the town is busy with tourists and thick with tea shops and antiques sellers. Its atmosphere is best absorbed in a short stroll along the main street.

Three km (2 mi) south of Maldon is **Carman's Tunnel,** a gold mine that has remained unaltered since it closed in 1884. The mine, which can be seen only on a candlelight tour, offers fascinating insight into the ingenious techniques used by early gold miners. The 1,870-ft tunnel is dry, clean, and spacious, and the tour is suitable for all ages. Tours are given weekends 1:30–4. ⊠ *Parkin's Reef Rd.,* ☎ *03/5475–2453.* 🎫 *$4.*

☺ **Castlemaine & Maldon Railway.** This 45-minute loop aboard a historic steam train winds through forests of eucalyptus and wattle, which are spectacular in spring. Check for specials, such as the lovers' fling on Valentine's Day. ☎ *03/5475–2966.* 🎫 *$10.* ☉ *Departs Maldon Station Wed. at 11:30 and 1, Sun. at 11:30, 1, and 2:30.*

Bendigo

150 km (93 mi) northwest of Melbourne, 36 km (22 mi) northeast of Maldon, 92 km (57 mi) south of Echuca on the Murray River.

Gold was discovered in Bendigo district in 1851, and the boom lasted well into the 1880s. The city's magnificent public buildings bear witness to the richness of its mines. Today Bendigo is a bustling, enterprising small city—not as relaxing as other goldfields towns, but its architecture is noteworthy. Most of Bendigo's distinguished buildings are arranged on either side of **Pall Mall** in the city center. These include the **Shamrock Hotel, General Post Office,** and **Law Courts,** all majestic examples of late-Victorian architecture.

Despite its unprepossessing exterior, the **Bendigo Art Gallery** houses a notable collection of contemporary Australian painting, including the work of Jeffrey Smart, Lloyd Rees, and Clifton Pugh. Pugh once owned a remote outback pub infamous for its walls daubed with his own pornographic cartoons. The gallery also houses some significant 19th-century French Realist and Impressionist works, bequeathed by a local surgeon. ⊠ *42 View St.,* ☎ *03/5443–4991.* 🎫 *Free.* ☉ *Daily 10–5.*

The 1,665-ft mine shaft of the **Central Deborah Gold-Mine** yielded almost a ton of gold before it closed in 1954. To experience life underground, take a guided tour of the mine. An elevator descends 200 ft below ground level. ⊠ *Violet St.,* ☎ *03/5443–8322.* 🎫 *$15.50; combined entry with Vintage Talking Tram $21.* ☉ *Daily 9–5; last tour at 4:05.*

Joss House (Temple of Worship) was built in gold rush days by Chinese miners on the outskirts of the city. Constructed of handmade bricks and painted a brilliant red, the temple is no longer used for sacred purposes. Joss House is a reminder of the Chinese presence in the Victorian goldfields; at the height of the boom in the 1850s and '60s, about a quarter of the miners were Chinese. These men were usually dispatched from villages on the Chinese mainland, and they were expected to work hard and return as quickly as possible to their villages with their fortunes intact. Very few Chinese women ever accompanied the men, and apart from their graveyards and temples, there is little evidence of any Chinese presence in the goldfields. The Chinese were scrupulously law-abiding and hard-working—qualities that did not always endear them to other miners—and anti-Chinese riots were common. In some areas, an Office of the Chinese Protector was established to safeguard their interests. ⊠ *Finn St., Emu Point,* ☎ *03/5442–1685.* 🎫 *$3.* ☉ *Daily 10–5.*

The superb **Golden Dragon Museum** evokes the Chinese community's role in Bendigo life, past and present. Its centerpieces are the century-old Loong imperial ceremonial dragon and the Sun Loong dragon, which, at more than 106 yards in length, is said to be the world's longest. When carried in procession, it requires 52 carriers and 52 relievers—the head alone weighs 64 pounds. Also on display are other ceremonial objects, costumes, and historic artifacts. ⊠ *5–9 Bridge St.,* ☎ *03/5441–5044.* ☜ *$6.* ⊘ *Daily 9:30–5.*

A good introduction to Bendigo is a tour aboard the **Vintage Talking Tram,** which includes a taped commentary on the town's history. The tram departs on its 8-km (5-mi) circuit every hour on the half hour between 9:30 and 3:30 from the ☞ **Central Deborah Gold-Mine.** You can step off and on at any stop. ⊠ *Violet St.,* ☜ *$8, combined tram ride and Central Deborah Gold-Mine $21.* ⊘ *Daily 9–5.*

Dining and Lodging

$$ ✕ **Bazzani.** This restaurant fuses a mainly Italian menu with Asian influences. Try the lemon-olive spiced chicken with wonton crisps, or poached tiger prawns with a soba noodle salad, finishing with the orange and Cointreau crème brûlée, or several other very tempting desserts. A good selection of local and Pyrenées wines are all very well priced. Lighter alternatives fill the lunch menu, plus coffee and snacks. ⊠ *Howard Place,* ☎ *03/5441–3777. AE, DC, MC, V.*

$$ ✕ **Metropolitan.** In a classic Australian country pub with wide verandas and distinctive stained-glass windows, this restaurant offers a choice of all-day dining in the brasserie against a background of unobtrusive rock music, or in the more refined atmosphere of the Grillroom. Both have an identical menu that features pasta dishes, sandwiches, salads, steaks, and seafood. Children have their own special menu. ⊠ *224 Hargreaves St.,* ☎ *03/5443–4916. Reservations not accepted. AE, DC, MC, V.*

$$ ☷ **Nanga Gnulle.** On a hillside on the outskirts of Bendigo, Rob and Peg Green have created a haven in mud brick and timber, surrounded by a superb garden. Pronounced "nanga nully," the name means "small stream" in the local Aboriginal language. The atmosphere is extremely relaxing and friendly, and the decor is warm, with lots of wood furniture and natural fabrics. The larger of the two rooms is on the lower part of the contemporary split-level house. Smoking and children under 16 are not allowed inside. Breakfast is included. ⊠ *40 Harley St., 3550,* ☎ *03/5443–7891,* FAX *03/5442–3133. 2 rooms. MC, V.*

$$ ☷ **Shamrock Hotel.** This landmark Victorian hotel at the city center offers a choice of accommodation, from simple, traditional guest rooms with shared facilities to large suites. If you're looking for reasonably priced luxury, ask for the Amy Castles Suite. Rooms are spacious and well maintained, but furnishings are dowdy and strictly functional. The hotel's location and character are the real draws. ⊠ *Pall Mall and Williamson St., 3550,* ☎ *03/5443–0333,* FAX *03/5442–4494. 24 rooms, 20 with bath. 2 restaurants, 3 bars. AE, DC, MC, V.*

Shopping

Bendigo Mohair Farm (⊠ Maryborough Rd., Lockwood, ☎ 03/5435–3400) is a working Angora-goat stud farm. The showroom displays hand-knit sweaters, mohair rugs, scarves, hats, ties, and toys for purchase. The farm also has barbecue and picnic facilities.

Sports

GOLF

Bendigo Golf Club (⊠ Golf Links Rd., Epsom, ☎ 03/5448–4206). Greens fees are $13; you can rent clubs for $10 per round.

TENNIS

Bendigo Indoor Grass Tennis. Five artificial grass courts are open daily. ⊠ *Edwards Rd.,* ☎ *03/5442–2411.* ☜ *$12 per hr 9–6, $16 per hr 6–midnight.* ⊘ *Daily 9 AM–midnight.*

En Route From Bendigo, Echuca and the Murray River region are just under 100 km (62 mi) away. ☞ **Northeast Wineries and Murray River,** *below.*

Gold Country A to Z

Arriving and Departing

BY CAR

To reach Bendigo, take the Calder Highway northwest from Melbourne; for Ballarat, take the Western Highway. The mineral springs region and Maldon lie neatly between the two main cities.

BY TRAIN

Rail service to Ballarat or Bendigo is available. For timetables and rates, contact **V-Line** (☎ 03/13–2232) or the **Royal Automobile Club of Victoria (RACV)** (☎ 03/13–1955).

Getting Around

BY CAR

For leisurely exploration of the Gold Country, a car is essential. Although public transport adequately serves the main centers, access to smaller towns is less assured, and even in the bigger towns, attractions tend to be widely dispersed.

Contacts and Resources

EMERGENCIES

Ambulance, fire brigade, and police. ☎ *000.*

GUIDED TOURS

Operators who cover this area include **Gray Line** (☎ 03/9663–4455), **Australian Pacific Tours** (☎ 13–1304), and **AAT Kings** (☎ 03/9663–3377); all three depart from 184 Swanston Street in Melbourne.

VISITOR INFORMATION

Ballarat Tourist Information Centre. ⊠ *39 Sturt St., Ballarat,* ☎ *03/5332–2694.* ◷ *Weekdays 9–5, weekends 10–4.*
Bendigo Tourist Information Centre. ⊠ *Old Post Office, Pall Mall, Bendigo,* ☎ *03/5444–4445.* ◷ *Daily 9–5.*
Daylesford Tourist Information Centre. ⊠ *49 Vincent St., Daylesford,* ☎ *03/5348–1339.* ◷ *Daily 10–4.*

MURRAY RIVER REGION

From its birthplace on the slopes of the Great Dividing Range in southern New South Wales, the Mighty Murray winds 2,574 km (1,596 mi) in a southwesterly course before it empties into Lake Alexandrina, south of Adelaide. On the driest inhabited continent on earth, such a river, the country's largest, assumes great importance. Irrigation schemes that tap the river water have transformed its thirsty surroundings into a garden of grapevines and citrus fruits.

Once prone to flooding and droughts, the river has been laddered with dams that control the floodwaters and form reservoirs for irrigation. The lakes created in the process have become sanctuaries for native birds. In the pre-railroad age of canals, the Murray was an artery for inland cargoes of wool and wheat, and old wharves in such ports as Echuca bear witness to the bustling and colorful riverboat era.

Victoria, Tasmania, New South Wales, and Western Australia were planted with vines during the 1830s, fixing roots for an industry that has earned its international repute. One of the earliest sponsors of Victorian viticulture was Charles LaTrobe, the first Victorian governor. LaTrobe had lived at Neuchâtel in Switzerland and married the daughter of the Swiss Counsellor of State. As a result of his contacts, several

Swiss wine makers emigrated to Australia and developed some of the earliest Victorian vineyards in the Yarra Valley, east of Melbourne.

Digging for gold was a thirst-producing business, and the gold rushes stimulated the birth of an industry. By 1890 well over half the total Australian production of wine came from Victoria. But just as it devastated the vineyards of France, the strain of tiny plant lice, phylloxera, arrived from Europe and wreaked havoc in Victoria. In the absence of wine, Australians turned to beer, and not until the 1960s did wine regain national interest. Although most wine specialists predict that Victoria will never recover its preeminence in the Australian viticulture, high-quality grapes are grown in several parts of the state, best known for muscat, tokay, and port. The Rutherglen area produces the finest fortified wine in the country, and anyone who enjoys the after-dinner "stickies" is in for a treat when touring there.

All wineries in this region have tasting rooms where you are welcome to sample before you buy. However, each of them produces a dizzying array of wines—before you begin, indicate your general preference to the sales staff and allow them to guide you.

Southeast of Rutherglen, the town of Beechworth is a fine example of a goldfields town. In addition to enjoying historical credentials, Beechworth has a choice of charming guest houses. The town is also a logical point from which to detour to Alpine National Park (☞ *below*), where days' worth of bush-walking trails wind through Victoria's highest peaks.

The Murray River region covered in this section stretches some 460 km (290 mi) between Rutherglen in the northeast to Mildura in the northwest. So, short of devoting a week or more to the area, it's best to pick one or two sections to explore. A tour of the Rutherglen wineries and the Beechworth locale makes a convenient break on the drive between Sydney and Melbourne on the Hume Freeway (Rte. 31). You could take this all in in a single day, though more time would be rewarded. If you'd rather start in Echuca, Melbourne and the Gold Country town of Bendigo are good jumping-off points. West of Echuca, long stretches of open country separate interesting locales—the way to go if you're headed on to Adelaide. Although the Murray River Valley Highway parallels the course of the river, it is only by making a detour that you will actually glimpse the brown river, lined with river red gums.

Beechworth

271 km (168 mi) northeast of Melbourne, 96 km (60 mi) from Alpine National Park.

One of the prettiest towns in Victoria, Beechworth flourished during the gold rush. When gold ran out, Beechworth was left with all the apparatus of prosperity—fine Victorian banks, imposing public buildings, breweries, parks, prisons, and hotels wrapped in wrought iron—but with scarcely two nuggets to rub together. However, poverty preserved the town from such modern amenities as aluminum window frames, and many historic treasures that might have been destroyed in the name of progress have been restored and brought back to life.

A stroll along **Ford Street** is the best way to absorb the character of the town. You pass several distinguished buildings, among them **Tanswell's Commercial Hotel** and the **government buildings.** Note the jail—antiques shops, and the sequoia trees in **Town Hall Gardens.** Much of Beechworth's architecture is made of the honey-color granite found outside of town.

NED KELLY: AN EXTRAORDINARY LIFE

SUCH IS LIFE." With those words Ned Kelly plunged to his death, hanged for murder at the age of 24.

Although it's been more than a century since his hanging, Ned Kelly continues to provoke controversy. Many Australians revere him, although his critics consider him a common criminal. But thanks to a mere two-year reign as a bushranger, he has been immortalized in film, art, through countless works of song, poetry, and prose.

The English had Robin Hood, the Americans Jesse James. People love a hero, and Ned Kelly was a natural: a tall, tough, idealistic youth who came to symbolize the struggle against an uncaring ruling class. Like many other lads from Irish working-class families, Ned got to know the police at a young age. He was convicted of assault and indecent behavior at 16 then served a three-year stint in Melbourne's notorious Pentridge Prison for allegedly receiving a stolen horse. However, it was matriarch Ellen Kelly's arrest—on what some claim were trumped-up charges—that was the turning point in the story. Warrants were issued for sons Ned and Dan, and a subsequent shoot-out left three policemen dead.

The heat was soon on the Kelly boys and their friends Joe Byrne and Steve Hart, whose occasional group raids worked the police into a frenzy. The gang's reputation was reinforced by their spectacular crimes, which were executed with humanity and humor. In 1878 they held scores of settlers hostage on a farm near Euroa en route to robbing the local bank, but they kept the folks entertained with demonstrations of horsemanship. The following year they took control of the town of Jerilderie for three days, dressing in police uniforms and captivating the women. According to one account, Joe Byrne took the gang's horses to the local blacksmith and charged the work to the NSW Police Department.

The final showdown was ignited by the murder of a police informer and former friend, Aaron Sherritt. The gang fled to Glenrowan, where Ned ordered a portion of the train line derailed to delay the police. Meanwhile, the gang holed up in a local pub, where they played cards and danced. Unfortunately for the Kelly gang, the police were warned of the plan by a captive who had managed to escape, and the scene for a bloody confrontation was set.

Although the gang had heavy body suits made from thick boards, all were shot except Ned, who took a bullet in his unprotected legs and was eventually captured. In hastily arranged proceedings in Melbourne, Judge Redmond Barry ordered Ned Kelly hung, a sentence carried out on November 11, 1880—despite a petition of 60,000 signatures attempting to spare him. As the judge asked the Lord to have mercy on Ned's soul, the bushranger defiantly replied that he would meet him there.

Twelve days after Ned Kelly's death, Judge Redmond Barry died.

— Josie Gibson

This is also Kelly country. Australia's favorite outlaw, Ned Kelly, once rode these hills, and Beechworth's most conspicuous public building is the handsome sandstone jail where Kelly was held before he was taken to Melbourne to be tried and hanged.

The **Burke Museum** takes its name from Robert Burke, who, with William Wills, became one of the first white explorers to cross Australia from south to north in 1861. Burke was superintendent of police in Beechworth, 1856–59. Paradoxically, but not surprisingly, the small area and few mementos dedicated to Burke are overshadowed by the **Ned Kelly** exhibits, which include letters, photographs, and memorabilia that give genuine insight into the man and his misdeeds. Following the shooting of the police at Stringybark Creek, Kelly and his gang were seen in the hills 5 km (3 mi) from Beechworth. The man who set out to report their whereabouts had to pass six pubs along the way, and he arrived at Beechworth so drunk that the police refused to believe his story and locked him up. A day later, the man sobered up, and the police realized their mistake and mounted a raid—but too late. The museum also displays a reconstructed streetscape of Beechworth in the 1880s. ⊠ *Loch St.,* ☎ *03/5728–1420.* ⊡ *$5.* ☾ *Daily 10:30–3:30.*

The **Carriage Museum** is in a corrugated-iron building that was once a stable. Displays range from simple farm carts and buggies to Cobb & Co. stagecoaches, some of which were modeled on U.S. designs. ⊠ *Railway Ave.* ⊡ *$1.50.* ☾ *Daily 10:30–12:30 and 1:30–4:30.*

OFF THE BEATEN PATH

MT. BUFFALO NATIONAL PARK – If you don't want to go all the way to Alpine National Park, visit this beautiful, much-loved corner of the Victorian alps about 50 km (31 mi) south of Beechworth. Anderson Peak and the Horn both top 5,000 ft, and the park is full of interesting granite formations, waterfalls, animal and plant life, and more miles of walking tracks than you're likely to cover. The gorge walk is particularly scenic. Lake Catani has swimming and a camping area. Primary access to the park is from Myrtleford and Porepunkah. Both towns have hotels and motels.

Dining and Lodging

$$$$ ★ ✕▥ **Howqua Dale Gourmet Retreat.** This is a true gem of rural Victoria, and its owners Marieke Brugman and Sarah Stegley fully pampers their guests. Marieke's cooking is wonderful, and Sarah has an encyclopedic knowledge of wine, especially Victorian vintages. Accommodations are luxurious, with splendid views. Each room is decorated and furnished in a particular theme, such as Asian, Victorian, modern and Balinese, with appropriate art, and each has its own access to the garden. Horseback-riding, boating on nearby Lake Eildon, or fishing can be arranged. Prices include meals, which vary seasonally. Brugman also conducts cooking schools on-site. The drive takes about two hours but is worth it for arguably the best gourmet getaway in the state. ⊠ *Howqua River Rd., 140 km (88 mi) southwest from Beechworth, Howqua 3722,* ☎ *03/5777–3503,* ℻ *03/5777–3896. 6 rooms. Restaurant, bar, pool, tennis court. AE, DC, MC, V.*

$$ ✕▥ **The Bank.** This restaurant's refined, dignified ambience befits its status as a former Bank of Australasia. The food, based on local produce like high-country beef and quail, is proficiently prepared and presented with style. Monday–Saturday is reserved for semi-formal, à la carte dining; a family-style carvery is available Sunday. Four luxurious garden suites are in the original carriage house and stables. Rates include breakfast. ⊠ *86 Ford St.,* ☎ *03/5728–2223,* ℻ *03/5728–2883. 4 suites. AE, DC, MC, V. No lunch Mon.–Sat.*

$$ ✕🍴 **Kinross.** A two-minute walk from the center of Beechworth, this
★ atmospheric former manse hosts a wealth of creature comforts. Rooms
are decorated with chintz fabrics and furnished with dark-wood an-
tiques. Sink into one of the plush armchairs and enjoy the fireplace.
Each room has one, as well as electric blankets and eiderdown pillows
on the beds. Room 2, at the front of the house, is the largest. Rates in-
clude breakfast, and hosts Christine and Bill Pearse prepare dinner by
arrangement. ⊠ *34 Loch St., 3747,* ☎ *03/5728–2351,* 🆀🆇 *03/5728–*
5333. 5 rooms. Dining room. AE, MC, V.

$ 🍴 **Country Rose.** In a quiet back street about 1 km (½ mi) from the
center of Beechworth, this converted garage adjoining a family home
is large and an extremely good value for anyone looking for comfort,
privacy, and tranquillity. The decor is frilly, with antique iron bedsteads,
and there's a fully equipped kitchen. The house is surrounded by a com-
mercial rose garden, through which guests are welcome to wander. Rates
include breakfast. ⊠ *Malakoff St., 3747,* ☎ *03/5728–1107. 2 rooms.*
No credit cards.

$ 🍴 **Rose Cottage.** Tucked behind a pretty garden close to the center of
town, this small timber guest house oozes country charm. Guest rooms
are comfortable, with French doors that open onto the garden. The
house is filled with antiques, accented with Tiffany-style stained-glass
lamps, and draped with lace—which might be a bit overpowering for
some. Children are accommodated by prior arrangement. Rooms are
often booked far in advance. Rates include breakfast. ⊠ *42 Camp St.,*
3747, ☎ *03/5728–1069. 4 rooms. AE, DC, MC, V.*

Hot-Air Ballooning

Balloon Flights Victoria (☎ 03/5798–5417, 🆀🆇 03/5798–5457) offers
hot-air balloon flights over farmland near Strathbogie Ranges. A one-
hour flight costs $185 per person, including a champagne breakfast
upon touchdown. Flights are available year-round and depart from a
Longwood farm near Euroa, on the Hume Highway, a 90-minute
drive from Melbourne.

Shopping

Buckland Gallery sells Australian crafts and souvenirs that are far su-
perior to the average, including soft toys, hats, woolen and leather items,
edible Australiana, turned-wood candlesticks, pottery, and children's
wear. ⊠ *Ford and Church Sts.,* ☎ *03/5728–1432.* ☉ *Daily 9–5:30.*

Chiltern

274 km (170 mi) northeast of Melbourne, 31 km (19 mi) north of Beech-
worth.

Originally known as Black Dog Creek, Chiltern is another gold-rush
town that fell into a coma when gold ran out. The main street of this
tiny village is an almost perfectly preserved example of a 19th-century
rural Australian streetscape, a fact not unnoticed by contemporary film-
makers. Notable buildings include the **Athenaeum Library and Museum,**
the **Pharmacy,** the **Federal Standard Office,** and the **Star Hotel,** which
has in its courtyard the largest grapevine in the country, with a girth
of almost 6 ft at its base.

Lake View House is the childhood home of Henry Handel Richard-
son, the pen name of noted 19th-century novelist Ethel Florence, whose
best-known works are *The Getting of Wisdom* and *The Fortunes of*
Richard Mahony. In *Ultima Thule,* one of Richardson's characters re-
flects on Chiltern, which the author fictionalized as Barambogie: "Of
all the dead-and-alive holes she had ever been in, this was the dead-
est." Among the memorabilia on display is a Ouija board the author

used for seances. ⌗ *Victoria St.,* ☎ *03/5726–1317.* ⌗ *$2.* ⏾ *Weekends 10:30–noon and 1–4.*

OFF THE BEATEN PATH	**YACKANDANDAH –** From Chiltern, you might find the 40-km (25-mi) drive southeast, through hilly countryside to the picturesque gold mining town of Yackandandah, worth a two-hour detour. The town has interesting old buildings, a variety of new shops, a couple of pubs, and places to have Devonshire teas.

Rutherglen

274 km (170 mi) northeast of Melbourne, 18 km (11 mi) northwest of Chiltern.

Rutherglen itself has little to delay the traveler—it's an agricultural area producing fine grapes. The surrounding red loam soil signifies the beginning of the Rutherglen wine district, the source of Australia's finest fortified wines. If the term conjures up visions of cloying ports, you're in for a surprise. "Like Narcissus drowning in his own reflection, one can lose oneself in the aroma of a great old muscat"—is the verdict of James Halliday in his authoritative *Australian Wine Compendium.*

All Saints Vineyards & Cellars. This castellated winery has been in business since 1864, and although it was taken over by another wine maker from northeast Victoria, Brown Brothers, in 1991, the All Saints traditions and label remain. Pay particular attention to the Lyrebird Liqueur Muscat, a big complex wine full of rich berry flavors. ⌗ *All Saints Rd., Wahgunyah, 9 km (5 mi) from Rutherglen,* ☎ *02/6033–1922.* ⏾ *Daily 9–5.*

Another long-established winery, **Buller's Calliope Vineyard** was recently modernized, and many of its vintage stocks of muscat and fine sherry were distributed through the cellar outlet. Also on the winery's grounds is **Buller Bird Park**, an aviary. ⌗ *Three Chain Rd. and Murray Valley Hwy.,* ☎ *02/6032–9660.* ⏾ *Mon.–Sat. 9–5, Sun. 10–5.*

Despite the slick image proffered by **Campbell's Rutherglen Winery,** this is a family business that dates back more than 120 years. You can wander freely through the winery on a self-guided tour. Campbell's Merchant Prince Brown Muscat, Second Edition, is highly regarded by connoisseurs; Campbell Family Vintage Reserve is available only at the cellar door. ⌗ *Murray Valley Hwy.,* ☎ *02/6032–9458.* ⏾ *Mon.–Sat. 9–5, Sun. 10–5.*

Chambers Rosewood Winery was established in the 1850s and is one of the heavyweight producers of fortified wines. Bill Chambers's muscats are legendary, with blending stocks that go back more than a century; don't miss the chance to sample the vast tasting range. ⌗ *Off Corowa Rd.,* ☎ *02/6032–8641.* ⏾ *Mon.–Sat. 9–5, Sun. 10–5.*

Pfeiffer Wines. Along with exceptional fortified wine, the establishment claims fine varietal wine—like its Pfeiffer chardonnay. It also boasts one of the few Australian plantings of gamay, the classic French grape used to make beaujolais. At this small, rustic winery, you can order a picnic basket stuffed with crusty bread, pâté, cheese, fresh fruit, wine, and smoked salmon, but be sure to reserve in advance. Wine maker Chris Pfeiffer sets up tables on the old wooden bridge that spans Sunday Creek, just down from the winery. Phone ahead to book a table on the bridge. ⌗ *Distillery Rd., Wahgunyah, 9 km (5 mi) from Rutherglen,* ☎ *02/6033–2805.* ⏾ *Mon.–Sat. 9–5, Sun. 11–4.*

Dining and Lodging

$$ ✕ **Terrace Restaurant.** Part of the All Saints estate, the restaurant is a welcome place to rest after a heavy wine-tasting itinerary. The menu offers light fare such as Mediterranean eggplant or more exotic choices like emu osso buco. Desserts are excellent, especially when combined with a formidable northeast fortified wine. ⊠ *All Saints Rd., Wahgunyah,* ☎ *02/6033–1922. AE, DC, MC, V. No dinner.*

$ ✕ **Mrs. Mouse's Teahouse.** Decorated from top to toe with toy mice, this quaint country tea house north of Rutherglen sells traditional scones and tea by day and wholesome country meals at night. The food relies on local produce, including the delicious berries and stone fruits of the Warby Ranges. If you're planning a picnic, inquire about the legendary Mouse hamper. Next door is a food shop. ⊠ *12 Foord St., Wahgunyah, 9 km (5 mi) north of Rutherglen,* ☎ *02/6033–1102. Reservations not accepted. MC, V. No dinner Sun.–Wed.*

$ 🛏 **Wine Village Motor Inn.** In the heart of Rutherglen, this motel has a pool for relaxing during hot northeastern summer days. ⊠ *217 Main St., 3685,* ☎ *02/6032–9900,* FAX *02/6032–8125. 16 rooms. Pool. AE, DC, MC, V.*

Festivals

The main event in the region is the **Rutherglen Wine Festival,** held during Labor Day weekend in March. The festival is a celebration of food, wine, and music—in particular jazz, folk, and country. Events are held in town and at all surrounding wineries. For more information contact the **Rutherglen Tourist Information Centre** (☎ 02/6032–9166).

Echuca

206 km (128 mi) north of Melbourne, 194 km (120 mi) west of Rutherglen, 92 km (57 mi) north of Bendigo.

Echuca's name derives from a local Aboriginal word meaning "meeting of the waters," a reference to the town's setting at the confluence of the Murray, Campaspe, and Goulburn rivers. In colonial times these rivers conveyed products from the interior. When the railway from Melbourne reached Echuca in 1864, the town became the junction at which wool and wheat cargo were transferred to railroad cars from barges on the Darling River in western New South Wales. During the second half of the 19th century, Echuca was Australia's largest inland port. River trade languished when the railway network extended into the interior, but reminders of Echuca's colorful heyday remain in the restored riverboats, barges, historic hotels, and the Red Gum Works, the town's sawmill, now a working museum. Echuca's importance was recognized in the 1960s, when the National Trust declared the port a historic area. Nowadays it is a busy town of almost 10,000, the closest of the river towns to Melbourne.

If you're starting out on foot, it may help to know that **High Street,** the main street of shops and cafés, will take you to the river.

A tour of the historic river precincts begins in the **Port of Echuca** office, where you can purchase a "passport" that gives admission to the Star and Bridge Hotels and the Historic Wharf area. The Star Hotel displays a collection of machinery and equipment associated with the riverboat trade. Tours cost $8, or $12 with a river cruise. ⊠ *Murray Esplanade,* ☎ *03/5482–4248.*

In the **Historic Wharf,** the heavy-duty side of the river trade business is on view, including a warehouse, old railroad tracks, and riverboats. Unlike those of the Mississippi or the Danube, the small, squat, utilitarian workhorses of the Murray are no beauties. Among the vessels docked at the wharf, all original, is the **PS** *Adelaide,* Australia's oldest operating paddle steamer. The Adelaide cannot be boarded, but it occasionally is stoked up, with the requisite puff-puffs, chug-chugs, and toot-toots.

The **Bridge Hotel** (☞ Dining and Lodging, *below*) was built by Henry Hopwood, ex-convict father of Echuca, who had the foresight to establish a punt and later to build a bridge at this commercially strategic point on the river. The hotel is sparsely furnished, however, and it takes great imagination to re-create what must have been a roistering, rollicking pub frequented by river men, railway workers, and drovers.

Red Gum Works. Timber from the giant river red gums that flourish along the Murray was once a major industry in Echuca. Stop and watch the wood turners, whose work is for sale in the gallery next door. ✉ *Murray Esplanade,* ☎ *03/5480–6407.* ☞ *Free.* ☉ *Daily 9–5.*

Sharp's Movie House and Penny Arcade is a nostalgic journey back to the days of the penny arcades. Have your fortune told; test your strength, dexterity, and lovability; or watch a peep show that was once banned in Australia. There are 34 machines here, the largest collection of operating penny arcade machines in the country. The movie house shows edited highlights of Australian movies that date back to 1896. A visit is highly recommended. ✉ *Bond Store, Murray Esplanade,* ☎ *03/5482–2361.* ☞ *$10.* ☉ *Daily 9–5.*

Life-size wax effigies of U.S. presidents may be the last thing you would expect to find in Echuca, but the **World in Wax Museum** has a Washington, Lincoln, and Kennedy—along with Fidel Castro, T. E. Lawrence (of Arabia), Queen Elizabeth II, and Australian celebrities and native sons. ✉ *630 High St.,* ☎ *03/5482–3630.* ☞ *$7.* ☉ *Daily 9–5:30.*

Riverboat trips along the Murray are especially relaxing if you've been following a hectic touring schedule. Several riverboats make short, one-hour excursions along the river, including the **PS** *Pevensey* and the **PS** *Canberra.* River traffic is limited to a few speedboats, small fishing skiffs, and an occasional kayak. The banks are thickly forested with river red gums, which each require as much as half a ton of water per day. *PS Pevensey tickets,* ✉ *Port of Echuca, Murray Esplanade,* ☎ *03/5482–4248.* ☞ *$12.* ☉ *Departs five times daily. PS Canberra tickets,* ✉ *Bond Store, Murray Esplanade,* ☎ *03/5482–2711.* ☞ *$10.* ☉ *Departs daily at 10, 11:30, 12:45, 2, and 3:15.*

Dining and Lodging

$$ ✕ **Bridge Hotel Restaurant.** On the ground floor of a historic hotel, this popular riverside restaurant offers generous country meals making the most of regional produce. Dishes feature local yabbies (crayfish) and beef; try the rib-eye steak teamed with fresh Murray yabbies in a mustard chardonnay cream. The restaurant occupies three rooms decorated in Victorian style and furnished with period antiques. Adjoining the restaurant is a bistro that serves simpler, less expensive fare. When the sun shines, request a table in the garden. ✉ *1 Hopwood Pl.,* ☎ *03/5482–2247. AE, DC, MC, V.*

$$
★ 🛏 **Murray House.** As soon as you step inside Murray House you know that you're entering a much-loved home. Since superb host-owners Len Keeper and Doug Hall moved in, they have transformed their 1920s building with unique pieces that they have gathered over the years from around the world. Rooms are tastefully and individually decorated, and there is a self-contained two-bedroom cottage in the grounds. The sitting room and the lovely cottage garden are ideal places to while away

the hours. Rates include breakfast. ⊠ *55 Francis St., 3564,* ☎ *03/5482–4944,* 𝕱𝕬𝕏 *03/5480–6432. 5 rooms, 1 cottage. MC, V.*

$$ 🏨 **River Gallery Inn.** In a renovated 19th-century building, this hotel consists of large rooms that provide a high standard of comfort at a reasonable price. Each is decorated and furnished according to a different theme, such as the pretty French provincial room, the opulent Victorian suite, or the mock-rustic early Australia suite. Accommodations are above an arts-and-crafts gallery. Although four rooms overlook the street, none are affected by street noise. Four rooms have whirlpool baths; the larger rooms can sleep four. Rates include breakfast. ⊠ *578 High St., 3564,* ☎ *03/5480–6902. 6 rooms, 2 suites. AE, MC, V.*

Outdoor Activities and Sports

BOATING

Echuca Boat and Canoe Hire (⊠ Victoria Park Boat Ramp, ☎ 03/5480–6208; ☉ Daily 8–6) rents one-person kayaks, canoes, and motorboats. Combination camping/canoeing trips are also available. A canoe costs $15 per hour, $50 per day; a kayak is $12 per hour, $25 per day.

FISHING

No license is required to fish the Murray River on the Victorian side. Rods and bait are available from **Echuca Boat and Canoe Hire** (☞ *above*).

GOLF

Rich River Golf Club (⊠ West of Moama, across Murray River from Echuca, ☎ 03/5482–2444), a superb 36-hole championship course, charges $27 greens fees for 18 holes and $12 for clubs and cart rental.

WATERSKIING

The **Southern 80 Water-Ski Race,** held during the first weekend in February, is best viewed from the Echuca Boat Ramp. The race consists of high-power boats that pull two skiers apiece for 80 km (50 mi) through the twists and turns of the Murray River.

Swan Hill

97 km (60 mi) northwest of Echuca, 251 km (156 mi) southeast of Mildura.

Named in 1836 by the explorer Major Thomas Mitchell for the swans that kept him awake at night, Swan Hill is a prosperous town surrounded by rich citrus groves and vineyards.

The 12-acre **Swan Hill Pioneer Settlement** evokes life in a 19th-century Victorian river port with its displays of replicas of pioneer homes, stores, machinery, and the landlocked paddle wheeler *Gem,* once the largest cargo-passenger boat on the Murray. Today it houses a restaurant, art gallery, and souvenir shop. At night, the settlement becomes the backdrop for a sound-and-light show, which uses state-of-the-art lighting effects to bring the history of Swan Hill to life. ⊠ *Horseshoe Bend,* ☎ *03/5032–1093.* 🎟 *$13; sound-and-light show $8.50.* ☉ *Daily 9–5, show begins about 1 hr after sunset.*

Dining and Lodging

$$ ✕ **Gem Restaurant.** Stroll on board the vintage paddle steamer PS *Gem,* extensively restored in 1999 and moored high and dry in Pioneer Settlement, for an evening meal. The menu includes some unusual Australian bush tucker—including witchetty grubs and kangaroo tail soup—but its real strengths are the excellent local yabbies, Murray cod, beef, and lamb dishes. ⊠ *Pioneer Settlement,* ☎ *03/5032–1093. AE, DC, MC, V. No lunch.*

$ ▦ **Lady Augusta Motor Inn.** Completed in 1991, this two-story motel is a short stroll from the town center. It surrounds a tree-lined courtyard and allows a choice of moderately large double rooms, two-bedroom suites, and spa suites. All are well maintained. ✉ *375 Campbell St., 3585,* ☎ *03/5032–9677,* ℻ *03/5032–9573. 24 rooms. Restaurant, bar, pool. AE, DC, MC, V.*

En Route   From Swan Hill, the Murray Valley Highway traverses farm country that has seen many years of irrigation—the only green in this rust-color semidesert is that of the citrus crops and vineyards. Unfortunately, in some cases the land has been spoiled by excess salinity, one of the side effects of irrigation. Experiments are underway to plant salt-tolerant native trees in affected areas. After passing the south end of Hattah-Kulkyne National Park, which is full of kangaroos and interesting bird life, turn right onto the Calder Highway (Hwy. 79) and proceed north through Red Cliffs, which has a Sunday market, into Mildura.

Mildura

251 km (156 mi) northwest of Swan Hill, 557 km (345 mi) northwest of Melbourne.

Claiming more hours of sunshine per year than Queensland's Gold Coast, Mildura is also known for dried fruit, wine, citrus, and avocados, as well as its hydroponic vegetable-growing industry. The town was developed in 1885 by two Canadians, George and William Chaffey, who were persuaded to emigrate by Victorian premier Alfred Deakin. The Chaffey brothers were world pioneers in irrigation. The irrigated vineyards of the Riverland region are enormously productive, and provide Australians with much of their inexpensive cask wines—although rarely does a premium table wine bear a Riverland label.

At the **Pioneer Cottage,** you can get a good idea of what life was like in the days when Mildura was one antipodean frontier of European settlement. ✉ *3 Hunter St.,* ☎ *03/5023–3742.* ▨ *$2.50.* ☉ *Daily 10–4.*

It's worth a peek into the **Workingman's Club** (✉ Deakin Ave., ☎ 03/5023–0531) just to see the bar: At 300 ft, it's one of the world's longest. All of Mildura turns out to drink at its 27 taps.

On the banks of the Murray, the **Golden River Zoo** has an extensive collection of native and exotic birds in walk-through aviaries, as well as daily shows featuring pumas, dingoes, and monkeys. Spanish dancing horses perform at noon. Camel and train rides along the river are available during school holidays. ✉ *Flora Ave.,* ☎ *03/5023–5540.* ▨ *$12.* ☉ *Daily 10–4.*

Among Mildura's paddle steamers, the **PS Avoca** is one of the oldest still operating on the river. Built in 1877, this steamer has been immaculately restored and now carries more than 200 passengers on a variety of daytime sightseeing cruises that include lunch and live entertainment—and bands or shows on evening dinner cruises. ✉ *Mildura Wharf,* ☎ *03/5021–1166.* ▨ *Lunch cruise $16 plus meals; dinner cruise $35–$40.* ☉ *Lunch cruise Tues. and Sat. at noon; dinner cruise Wed., Thurs. and Sat. at 7. Check schedules for additional cruises.*

Lindemans Karadoc Winery is one of the largest and most sophisticated facilities in Victoria. This winery produces much of Lindemans' bulk wines, which end up being drained from "Château Cardboard" dispensers in Ozzie households, but the entire range of Lindemans' respected wines can be sampled here. ✉ *Karadoc Rd., Karadoc, 10 km (6 mi) from Mildura,* ☎ *03/5024–0357.* ☉ *Weekdays 9–5, weekends 10–4:30.*

Trentham Estate Winery is worth visiting for its delightful vistas as much as its medal-winning wines. Located on a picturesque bend of the Murray River, the restaurant serves local produce like yabbies and kangaroo, which team admirably with the prize-winning wines available for tasting. In fine weather, guests can eat on the veranda or under towering gums overlooking the river. To find Trentham, head across the Murray and follow the Sturt Highway through Buronga until you see the Trentham Estate sign on the right. ✉ *Sturt Hwy., Trentham Cliffs, 15 km (9 mi) from Mildura,* ☎ *03/5024–8888.* ☉ *Winery daily 9–5, lunch Tues.–Sun. 11–3.*

☾ A popular option for kids, the **Aquacoaster** is a big complex of pools that includes an enormous water slide. ✉ *18 Orange Ave.,* ☎ *03/5023– 6955.* ☷ *$9.* ☉ *Weekdays 2:30–6, weekends 1:30–6:30, school holidays 10–9.*

Dining and Lodging

$$ ✕ **Stefano's.** For good food and a lively atmosphere, head for Stefano's in the old cellars of the historic Grand Hotel. The northern Italian cuisine is tasty and prepared primarily from the Riverland's bountiful local produce. The extensive menu includes mud-crab on pasta salad, chicken and prosciutto tortellini, fresh vegetarian fettucine, and sumptuous European selection of desserts and cakes. This is a terrific place for families. ✉ *Grand Hotel, 7th St. (enter from Langtree Ave.), Mildura,* ☎ *03/5023–0511. AE, DC, MC, V. No dinner Sun.*

$ ⛉ **Chaffey International Motor Inn.** Rooms and facilities at this modern, centrally located motel are well above average for country Victoria—and certainly better than those at any other motel in town. Rates drop by more than $20 Friday–Sunday. ✉ *244 Deakin Ave., 3500,* ☎ *03/5023–5833,* ☷ *03/5021–1972. 32 rooms. Restaurant, bar, pool, spa. AE, DC, MC, V.*

$ ⛉ **Mildura Country Club Resort.** This modern motel has spacious grounds, a large swimming pool, pleasantly decorated rooms, and a resort atmosphere, but what really sets it apart is the surrounding golf course. All rooms are open to the 18-hole course. ✉ *12th St. Ext., 3500,* ☎ *03/5023–3966,* ☷ *03/5021–1751. 40 rooms. Restaurant, bar, pool, exercise room. AE, DC, MC, V.*

Murray River Region A to Z

Arriving and Departing

BY CAR

Beechworth and Rutherglen are on opposite sides of the Hume Freeway, the main Sydney–Melbourne artery. Allow four hours for the journey from Melbourne, twice that from Sydney. Echuca is a three-hour drive from Melbourne, reached most directly by the Northern Highway (Hwy. 75).

BY TRAIN

Trains run to most of the major towns in the region, including Echuca, Rutherglen, Swan Hill, and Mildura—but not Beechworth. This reasonable access is most useful if you do not have a car or want to avoid the long-distance drives.

Getting Around

BY CAR

The wide-open spaces of the northeast wineries and Murray River districts make driving the most sensible and feasible means of exploration. There is enough scenic interest along the way to make the long drives bearable, especially if you trace the river route. The direct run from Melbourne to Mildura is quite daunting (557 km/345 mi); however, those towns accessed by the Hume Highway are easily reached from the capital city.

BY TRAIN

As with most country Victorian areas, direct train access from Melbourne to the main centers is reasonable, but getting between towns isn't as easy. The train to Swan Hill or Mildura may be an appealing option for those utterly discouraged by the long drive.

Contacts and Resources

EMERGENCIES

Ambulance, fire brigade, and police. ☎ *000.*

GUIDED TOURS

The **Gray Line** (☎ 03/9663–4455) operates one-day tours of Echuca, departing Melbourne on Wednesday and Sunday at 8:45 AM. The cost is $83.

VISITOR INFORMATION

Beechworth Tourist Information Centre. ⊠ *Ford and Camp Sts.,* ☎ *03/ 5728–1374.* ⊙ *Daily 9–5:30.*
Echuca Tourist Information Centre. ⊠ *Leslie St. and Murray Esplanade,* ☎ *03/5480–7555.* ⊙ *Daily 9–5.*
Mildura Tourist Information Centre. ⊠ *Langtree Mall,* ☎ *03/5023–3619.* ⊙ *Weekdays 9–12:30 and 1–4, weekends 10–4.*
Rutherglen Tourist Information Centre. ⊠ *Walkabout Cellars, 84 Main St.,* ☎ *02/6032–9166.* ⊙ *Daily 9–5.*
Swan Hill Regional Information Office. ⊠ *306 Campbell St., Swan Hill,* ☎ *03/5032–3033.* ⊙ *Daily 9–5.*

ALPINE NATIONAL PARK

The name Alpine National Park actually applies to three loosely connected areas in eastern Victoria that follow the peaks of the Great Dividing Range. This section covers the area, formerly called Bogong National Park, that contains the highest of the Victorian Alps. Its many outdoor activities include excellent walking trails among the peaks, fishing (license required), horseback riding, mountaineering, and skiing.

The land around here is rich in history. *Bogong* is an Aboriginal word for "big moth," and it was to Mount Bogong that Aborigines came each year after the winter thaw in search of bogong moths, considered a delicacy. Aborigines were eventually displaced by cattlemen who brought their cattle here to graze. Since the creation of the park in the mid-1980s, grazing has become more limited.

Stately snow gums grace the hills throughout the year, complemented by alpine wildflowers in bloom October–March. There are half- and full-day trails for bushwalkers, many of them in the Falls Creek area south of Mount Beauty. The popular Bogong High Plains Circuit is a tough trail ascending Mount Bogong. You could easily spend a week or more hiking the park's trails.

In winter the area is completely covered in snow, and bushwalkers put on cross-country skis, especially at Falls Creek and Mount Hotham. Cross-country skiing is the best way to take in the Down-Under snowscape, enhanced by the exotic shapes of the gum trees.

Dining and Lodging

The town of Bright is reasonably well supplied with dining possibilities. **Simone's** (⊠ Ovens Valley Motel Inn, Ovens Highway, Bright, ☎ 03/5755–2022) is a remarkable find with its classic osso buco, gnocchi, panna cotta, and tempting daily specials. **Poplars** (⊠ Star Rd., Bright,

☎ 03/5755–1655) is a more upmarket spot specializing in regional produce such as rainbow trout and veal.

For places to stay, old cattlemen's huts are scattered throughout the park and may be used by hikers free of charge. These, however, are often occupied, and shelter is never guaranteed. Bush camping is permitted throughout the park, and there is a basic campground at Raspberry Hill.

Hotels, motels, commercial camping, and caravan parks are in the major towns around the park, including Bright, Mount Beauty, Harrietville, Anglers Rest, Glen Valley, and Tawonga, as well as in the ski resorts of Falls Creek, Mount Buller, and Mount Hotham year-round.

Skiing
Ski resorts are open at Falls Creek, Mount Buller, Mount Buffalo, and Mount Hotham in winter.

Arriving and Departing
BY BUS
Bus services operate from Albury on the New South Wales border in the north. During ski season, buses depart from Mount Beauty for Falls Creek and Mount Hotham, and depart from Melbourne for Falls Creek.

BY CAR
Alpine National Park is 323 km (200 mi) northeast of Melbourne, and you can reach it two ways. If you want to go to the park taking a short detour through the historic town of Beechworth (☞ The Murray River Region, *above*), take the Hume Freeway (Rte. 31) north out of Melbourne and turn southeast onto the Ovens Highway at Wangaratta. Beechworth is about a 30-km (19-mi) detour off the Hume. You can also follow the Princes Highway east from Melbourne through Sale and Bairnsdale. Pick up the Omeo Highway north from here to Omeo, and then head west to Cobungra and Mount Hotham. The turnoff for Falls Creek is another 39 km (24 mi) north of Omeo.

Visitor Information
Alpine National Park. The ranger station for the park is on Mount Beauty, and there are information centers in Bright, Omeo, and Falls Creek. The station at Mount Beauty offers ranger-led programs. ⊠ *Box 180, Mount Beauty, 3699,* ☎ *03/5754–4693.*

Department of Natural Resources and Environment. ⊠ *240 Victoria Parade, East Melbourne 3002,* ☎ *03/9412–4011.*

WILSON'S PROMONTORY NATIONAL PARK

★ This southernmost granite peninsula once connected Tasmania with mainland Australia, and you'll find botanical and geological odds and ends common both to the mainland and the wayward island. **Wilson's Promontory** is well-endowed with wildlife. More than 180 species of bird have been sighted here, and Corner Inlet, along Five Mile Beach, is a seabird sanctuary. Near the visitor center at Tidal River, you'll probably sight tame marsupials, including kangaroos, wombats, and koalas. Wilson's "Prom" is Victoria's most popular national park because it has most of everything, from remarkable granite outcroppings and upcroppings (tors) to wonderfully secluded beaches.

There are more than 20 well-marked trails here, some meandering past pristine beaches and secluded coves excellent for swimming, others more strenuous. One tough but popular trail is the 9½-km (6-mi) Sealer's Cove Walk, which traverses the slopes of Mount Wilson Range before descending through Sealer's Swamp to the tranquil Sealer's Cove. The Lilly Pilly Gully nature walk, a 5-km (3-mi) trip among tree ferns and giant mountain ash, gives a good introduction to the park's plant and animal life with the aid of informative signs posted along the way. And from the top of Mount Oberon on a good day, you'll be able to see across the Bass Straight all the way to Tasmania.

Dining and Lodging

There's not much to be said about food in the area, unless you catch and cook it yourself. In Foster, north of the national park, try **Black Cherry** (☎ 03/5682–2110), which is open for lunch daily and dinner on Saturday only. The **Foster Motel** (☎ 03/5682–2022) has a dining room while the **Exchange Hotel** (☎ 03/5682–2377) puts on a good pub dinner.

With 480 campsites, the well-known **Tidal River campground** is among Australia's largest. Reservations at this popular spot during peak periods (December–February and holiday weekends) are hard to come by and should be made well in advance. During peak season, sites cost $15 per night for up to three persons, $3.20 for each additional person. Off-season rates are $8 per night for up to three persons, $3.20 per night for each additional person. Stiff cancellation fees apply. Also at Tidal River are single-room motor trailers, known as "huts," which contain two double bunk beds, a hot plate, heaters, and running cold water. Blankets and linen are not provided. Toilets and showers are available at the campground. Cost is $42 for four-berth and $63 for six-berth trailers. Reserve campsites or trailers with the **Tidal River park office** (☎ 03/5680–9555).

Heated cabins and units accommodating two–six people are available at Tidal River. Rates are $660 per week for a cabin for two people, and $390 per week for two in a lodge. Cabins and units may be reserved up to 12 months in advance by calling the **Tidal River park office** (☎ 03/5680–9500) or through the **Melbourne Information Center** (✉ Town Hall, Swanston and Little Collins Sts., 3000, ☎ 03/9658–9955), open weekdays 9–6, weekends 9–5.

Arriving and Departing

BY CAR

To get to Wilson's Prom, 231 km (143 mi) south of Melbourne, take the Princes Highway to Dandenong, and then the South Gippsland Highway south to Meeniyan or Foster. Tidal River is another 70 km (43 mi) from there. There is no public transportation to the park.

Visitor Information

Wilson's Promontory National Park headquarters sells a variety of guidebooks. ✉ *Tidal River 3960,* ☎ *03/5680–9555.*
Department of Natural Resources and Environment. ✉ *240 Victoria Parade, East Melbourne 3002,* ☎ *03/9412–4011.*

5 TASMANIA

Separated from the mainland by the rough
Bass Strait, the island of Tasmania holds a
bounty of natural diversity and old-fashioned
hospitality. It's a hiker's dream, rich with
untracked wilderness along its southwest
and west coasts. Elegant English settlements
with vast gardens fringe the east and north
edges. Remnants of the island's volatile days
as a penal colony await exploration in the
abundance of small museums and historic
sites which preserve the lore of this
fascinating piece of Australia.

ABOUT THE SIZE of Ohio, and with a population of less than a half million, the island of Tasmania is an unspoiled reminder of a simpler, slower lifestyle. It has been called the England of the south, as it, too, is richly cloaked in mists and rain, glows with russet and gold shades in the fall, and has the chance of an evening chill year-round. Where the English tradition of a Christmas roast may strike visitors as strange during a steamy Sydney summer, such rites appear natural amid Tasmania's lush quilt of lowland farms and villages. Many towns retain an English ambience, with their profusion of Georgian cottages and commercial buildings, the preservation of which attests to Tasmanians' attachment to their past.

Updated by Bev Malzard

Aborigines, who crossed a temporary land bridge from Australia, first settled the island some 23,000 years ago. Europeans discovered it in 1642, when Dutch explorer Abel Tasman arrived at its southwest coast, but not until 1798 was Tasmania (then called Van Diemen's Land, after the Governor of the Dutch East Indies) thought to be an island. Much of Tasmania's subsequent history is violent, however, and there are episodes that many residents may wish to forget. The entire population of full-blooded Aborigines was wiped out by English troops and settlers, and the establishment in 1830 of a penal settlement at Port Arthur for the colony's worst offenders ushered in a new age of cruelty. Tragically, in April 1996, a lone gunman brought that brutality back when he randomly shot dozens of people, killing 35, most of them in the penal settlement's café. That murderer is now serving a sentence of life imprisonment without parole.

Today, walking through the lovely park in Port Arthur or the personable streets of Hobart, it's difficult to picture Tasmania as a land of turmoil and tragedy. But that is the great dichotomy of this island, for, in many ways, Tasmania is still untamed. One of the most mountainous islands in the world, tracts of its southwest remain unexplored, their access barred by impenetrable rain forests. Of all Australia's states, Tasmania has set aside the greatest percentage of land as national parks, and the island's extreme southern position results in a wild climate that's often influenced by Antarctica. Thus, if you're planning a trip into the wilderness, be prepared for sudden and severe weather changes—a snowstorm in summer isn't unusual.

Pleasures and Pastimes

Dining

Tasmania's clean air, unpolluted waters, and temperate climate provide a pristine environment in which fresh seafood, beef, dairy goods, fruit and vegetables, and wine are produced year-round. In particular, the island's culinary fame is based on its superb, bounteous seafood. Tasmanian dairy products are worth the indulgence, notably King Island's cheeses and thick double cream. With more than 100 vineyards, Tasmania is establishing itself as a force in Australian wine-making, and the quality reds and whites from small producers are gaining accolades locally and overseas.

CATEGORY	COST*
$$$$	over $40
$$$	$25–$40
$$	$10–$25
$	under $10

per person, excluding drinks and service

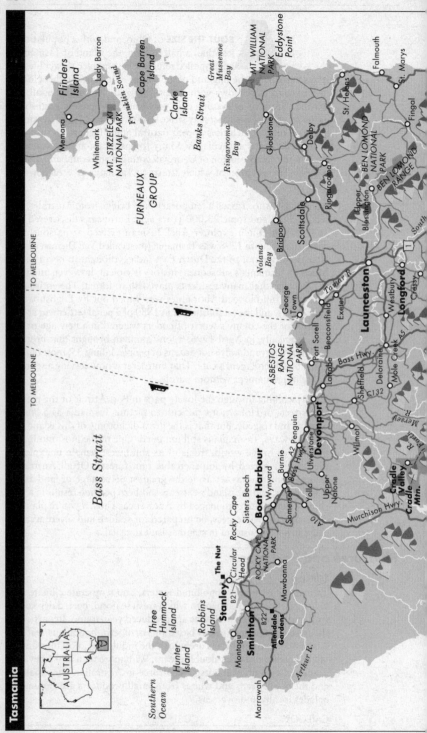

Tasmania

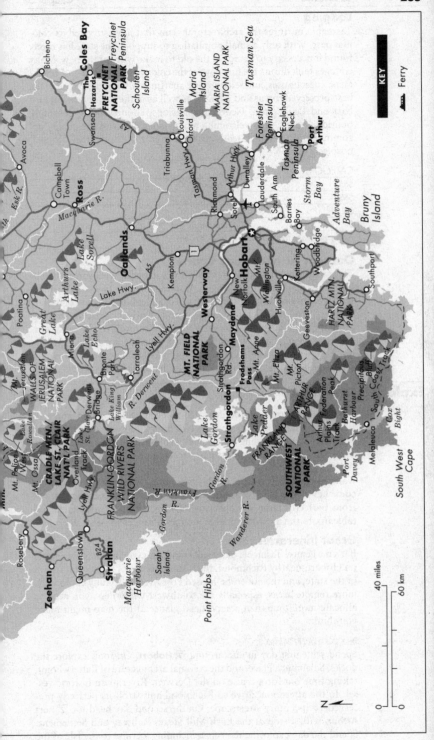

Tasman Sea

Bicheno

Coles Bay

The
Hazards Freycinet
FREYCINET Peninsula
NATIONAL
PARK

Avoca

Schouten
Island

Maria
Island

MARIA ISLAND
NATIONAL PARK

Forestier
Peninsula Eaglehawk
Neck

Louisville **Port**
Orford Tasman **Arthur**
Triabunna Peninsula

Dunalley
Campbell
Town Lauderdale *Storm*
Ross Richmond Arthur Hwy. South Arm *Bay*

Macquarie R. Sorell Barnes *Adventure*
Bay *Bay*

Bruny
Island

Esk R. Woodbridge

Poatina **Oatlands** Kempton Kettering Southport
Westerway New
Arthurs **Hobart** Norfolk Geeveston
Lake Lake Hwy. **Maydena** Huonville *HARTZ MTN.*
Great Lake *Sorell* Mt. *NATIONAL*
Lake Miena Echo Frodshams Mt. Wellington *PARK*
Tarraleah Strathgordon Pass Anne
Mt. Rd. Mt. Field
Jerusalem Bronte Mt. **MT. FIELD** Mt. Elisa
WALLS OF Park **NATIONAL** ARTHUR
JERUSALEM Derwent **PARK** RANGE
Mt. *NATIONAL* Bridge Lake
Rowallan *PARK* R. Derwent Arthur
Mt. Lake King Lake Federation Precipitous
Jerusalem St. Clair William Gordon Pedder Plains Peak Bluff
Mt. Ossa Overland **Strathgordon** FRANKLIN Bathurst South Coast Track
CRADLE MTN./ Track RANGE Harbour
Mt. Pelion **LAKE ST. CLAIR** Lake **SOUTHWEST** *Cox*
West **NAT'L PARK** Gordon **NATIONAL** *Bight*
FRANKLIN-GORDON Port **PARK**
WILD RIVERS Davey
Roseberry NATIONAL PARK Franklin Melaleuca *South West*
Gordon R. *Cape*
Queenstown Lyell Hwy. R. Wanderer R.
Zeehan Sarah
Strahan Island
Macquarie Harbour

Point Hibbs

40 miles

60 km

N

0
0

Lodging

Tasmania nurtures the architectural gems that have survived its colonial past. With only a small population to support, the state has rarely found it necessary to demolish the old to make way for the new. Many cottages built during the first days of the colony are now bed-and-breakfasts, guest houses, and self-catering apartments. They are found in the best-preserved towns and villages, as well as in the major cities of Hobart and Launceston. Georgian mansions, country pubs, charming boutique hotels, and welcoming motels are all part of the quality accommodation network ready to invite you in for some real "Tassie" hospitality.

CATEGORY	COST*
$$$$	over $200
$$$	$130–$200
$$	$75–$130
$	under $75

All prices are for a standard double room.

Outdoor Activities and Sports

Tasmania is an outdoor adventurer's playground, with some of Australia's best and most challenging walking terrain. The state's southwest wilderness is still virtually untouched, and it is the domain of serious trekkers. You'll find less strenuous and relatively pristine walking around Cradle Mountain and the Freycinet Peninsula on the east coast. The island is also great for cycling, diving, bushwalking (hiking), rafting, sea kayaking, game and trout fishing, and jet-skiing. For information on activities in the great outdoors, *see* Chapter 12.

Exploring Tasmania

Tasmania is compact—the drive from southern Hobart to northern Launceston takes little more than two hours. However, although the hilly terrain and winding roads make exploration of some areas more time-consuming, the scenes usually are more breathtaking as well. In the great, untrammelled southwest, there are no roads and few bushwalking trails, so even the wild, fast-running rivers of the region become key elements in transportation. Elsewhere, the landscape ranges from perfectly tame to entirely wild—from classic rural farmland tableaux to the most formidable mountain ranges in Australia.

Great Itineraries

If it's the genteel Tasmania of colonial times that you're after, concentrate on Hobart, nearby Richmond, the historic towns of the central region of the state, and the not-to-be-missed Port Arthur. To fully explore the more remote areas, especially the southwest wilderness, you need to allocate more time than a superficial glance at the map might make you think.

IF YOU HAVE 3 DAYS

Spend your first day in and around ☒ **Hobart.** On foot, explore the docks, Salamanca Place, and the colonial architecture of Battery Point, taking time out for a cruise on the Derwent River in an historic vessel. In the afternoon, drive to Richmond and stroll its perfectly preserved 19th-century streetscape. On the second day head for ☒ **Port Arthur,** with a stop at the Bush Mill Steam Railway and Settlement. Spend the day exploring the ruins, including a cruise to the Isle of the Dead convict burial ground. On your final day, return slowly to Hobart, taking in some of the other sights of the Tasman Peninsula en route. Don't miss the drive to the summit of Mt. Wellington, where a panorama of the city in its lovely seaside setting awaits.

See ⊞ **Hobart** on day one, with an excursion to Richmond—or, if you have a sweet tooth, to the Cadbury chocolate factory. On your second day, drive to ⊞ **Port Arthur,** spending time taking in the beauty of the Tasman Peninsula on the way. The gorgeous setting of the penal settlement makes the horrors of the past seem all the more dramatic. Hikers and lovers of exquisite scenery should leave early on the third day and drive to ⊞ **Coles Bay** on the **Freycinet Peninsula.** Climb the steep path to the outlook over impossibly perfect Wineglass Bay, then descend to the pure white sands for a swim in the ocean. The following day, drive slowly back to Hobart through the historic villages of ⊞ **Ross** and **Oatlands,** topping off the day by taking in the panoramic view from Mt. Wellington.

Extra time gives you the chance to see the wonders of the west coast. Explore ⊞ **Hobart** and Richmond before heading south to the Tasman Peninsula and ⊞ **Port Arthur.** Return to Hobart on day three, with an ascent of Mt. Wellington. Depart early the next morning for ⊞ **Strahan,** on the west coast via the peculiarly appealing moonscape of Queenstown, where mining has scarified the once-green mountainsides. Spend two nights at Strahan, with time for a leisurely cruise on the Gordon River, before driving north to ⊞ **Stanley,** a lovely village set beneath the rocky majesty of the Nut. Continue east to ⊞ **Launceston** before turning inland to ⊞ **Cradle Mountain** and its fantastic bushwalking and superb scenery. After two nights, circle back to Hobart along the historic central route.

When to Tour Tasmania

Winter can draw freezing blasts from the Antarctic; this is not the time of year for the highlands or wilderness areas. It's better in the colder months to enjoy the cozy interiors of colonial cottages and open fireplaces of welcoming pubs. The east coast is generally mild and more protected from the weather than the west, which is struck by the "roaring 40s," weather-bearing winds that blow across the southern 40s latitudes, unobstructed by land masses for thousands of miles. Summer can be surprisingly hot—bushfires are common—but temperatures are generally lower than on the Australian mainland. Early autumn is beautiful, with deciduous trees in full color. Spring, with its wildflowers, is a splash of pastel hues.

HOBART

Straddling the Derwent River at the foot of Mt. Wellington's forested slopes, Hobart may rival Sydney as Australia's most beautiful state capital. Founded as a penal settlement in 1803, Hobart is the second-oldest city in the country after Sydney, even though it feels as as though it's the oldest. Many of the colonial brick and sandstone, convict-built structures have been restored and now define the atmosphere of this small city of 185,000.

As in Sydney, life here revolves around the port. The Derwent River has one of the deepest harbors in the world, its broad estuary making it a sporting paradise. It was the Derwent that attracted the original settlers, who quickly capitalized on the natural treasure. Many of the converted warehouses that still line the wharf were formerly used to store Hobart's major exports—fruit, wool, and corn—as well as the products of the whaling fleet that used the city as a base.

Hobart comes alive between Christmas and the New Year, when it's summer Down Under, during the annual Sydney-to-Hobart yacht race. The competition dominates conversations among Hobart's citizens, who descend on Constitution Dock for a three-day fete (what they call a "quiet little drink"). Otherwise, Hobart *is* a quiet city whose nightlife is largely confined to the action at the Wrest Point Casino in Sandy Bay.

Exploring Hobart

Numbers in the text correspond to numbers in the margin and on the Downtown Hobart map.

A Good Walk

Begin by the city's focal point at the docks, the old warehouses of **Macquarie Wharf**. Spend a couple of hours at the **Tasmanian Museum and Art Gallery** ③, opposite **Constitution Dock** ④, before following the line of the wharves to **Salamanca Place** ⑦. This is Hobart's most vibrant shopping district and gathering place, where the colorful Salamanca morning market opens on Saturday. The new **Antarctic Adventure** ⑧ museum is here and deserves a visit of at least two hours. At the end of Salamanca Place, follow Castray Esplanade south, turn left into Clarke Avenue and then right into Secheron Road, where you'll find the **Maritime Museum of Tasmania** ⑨. After your visit, stroll farther along Secheron Road to Mona Street and turn right. Follow Mona Street onto Hampden Road, which leads to the **Narryna Van Diemen's Land Memorial Folk Museum** ⑩ and an array of antiques shops, charming cottages, and other historic buildings. Head back toward Castray Esplanade, but this time turn left into Runnymede Street and the delightful **Arthur's Circus** ⑪ around the green before returning to Salamanca Place.

TIMING

The dock and wharf areas are always busy, on weekdays with fishing vessels and commuter boats and on weekends with pleasure craft and sightseeing ferries. Saturday is the optimum time for Salamanca Place, when the area's morning market is set up, although the craft and art galleries are more pleasant on weekdays, when crowds are smaller.

Sights to See

⑧ **Antarctic Adventure.** Hobart is Australia's Antarctic capital, home to the Australian Antarctic Division and the Office of Antarctic Affairs, and Antarctic Adventure is Tasmania's most exciting new attraction. Exhibits at this new museum cover Antarctica's wildlife, explorers, and weather; however, this is no dry, sober museum. Guests visit a re-created authentic Antarctic field camp, experience sub-zero temperatures in the cold room (warm-weather gear provided), and take a snow ski or toboggan slide on the "Blizzard" simulator ride. ⊠ *2 Salamanca Sq.,* ☎ *03/6220–8220 or 1800/35–0028.* ⊡ *$16.* ☉ *Sun.–Fri. 10–5, Sat. 9–5.*

⑪ **Arthur's Circus.** Hobart's best-preserved suburb is an enchanting collection of tiny houses and cottages set in a circle around a village green on Runnymede Street, in the heart of historic Battery Point. Built in the 1840s and 1850s, most of these houses have been nicely restored.

⑤ **Brooke Street Pier.** The busy waterfront at Brooke Street Pier is the departure point for harbor cruises. ⊠ *Franklin Wharf.*

Cadbury-Schweppes chocolate factory. Very few children (or adults!) can resist a tour of the best chocolate and cocoa factory in Australia. Book well in advance through the visitor information center (☎ 03/6249–0111). ⊠ *Claremont, 12 km (7½ mi) north of Hobart.* ⊡ *$10.* ☉ *Tours weekdays 9, 9:30, 10:30, and 1.*

② **Cat and Fiddle Arcade.** Kitschy but entertaining, the arcade has a giant clock that reenacts the nursery rhyme every hour. It's worth a stop if

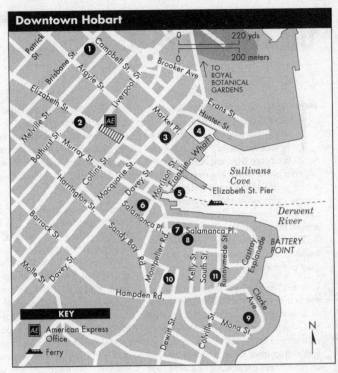

Downtown Hobart

you're in the area at the right time. ⊠ *Elizabeth St., between Liverpool and Bathurst Sts.*

❹ **Constitution Dock.** Yachts competing in the annual Sydney-to-Hobart race moor at this colorful marina dock during the first week of January. Buildings fronting the dock are century-old reminders of Hobart's trading history. ⊠ *Hunter and Davey Sts.*

❾ **Maritime Museum of Tasmania.** Located in the 1831 Secheron House, the museum is a fine example of Georgian architecture and houses one of the best maritime collections in Australia, including figureheads, whaling implements, models, and photographs dating as far back as 1804. ⊠ *21 Secheron Rd.,* ☎ *03/6223–5082.* ⌨ *$4.* ☉ *Daily 10–4:30.*

❿ **Narryna Van Diemen's Land Memorial Folk Museum.** Museum exhibits depict the life of Tasmania's pioneers in a gracious old town house. A collection of colonial relics is displayed. ⊠ *103 Hampden Rd.,* ☎ *03/6234–2791.* ⌨ *$5.* ☉ *Weekdays 10:30–5, weekends 2–5.*

❻ **Parliament House.** Built by convicts in 1840 as a customs house, this building did not acquire its present function until 1856. Contact the Clerk of the House if you want to watch a session of parliament from the viewing gallery. The grounds of Parliament House are maintained by the Royal Botanic Gardens. ⊠ *Morrison St., between Murray St. and Salamanca Pl.,* ☎ *03/6233–2374.*

❶ **Penitentiary Chapel and Criminal Courts.** Built and used during the early convict days, these buildings vividly portray Tasmania's penal, judicial, and religious heritage in their courtrooms, old cells, and underground tunnels. If you want to get spooked, come for the nighttime ghost tour (reservations recommended). ⊠ *Brisbane and Campbell Sts.,* ☎ *03/6231–0911.* ⌨ *$6; ghost tour $7.* ☉ *Tour weekdays 10–3; ghost tour daily at 7:45 PM.*

THE CONVICT PAST

THE PHYSICAL RUINS OF Tasmania's dark, convict past lay bare the misery that give it the nickname "Hellhole of the Pacific." This was a center for hard-core criminals banished to the island's brutal penal stations, the first of which was established at Hobart's Macquarie Harbour in 1821. By the time Lt. Colonel Governor George Arthur assumed his post in Van Diemen's Land in 1824, 50% of the island's population—some 6,000 prisoners—were already part of the colony.

Convicts were divided into seven classes, the first of which could work for wages or to own property. Half the criminals were in Class 2—settlers' servants who received food and clothing in exchange for their employment. Class 3 convicts worked on government projects; Class 4 were road gangs; and Class 5 were sentenced to hard labor in chains. Classes 6 and 7 were punished for offenses committed within the colony, but although the former endured severe labor, the latter served their time in chains.

In 1830, the Port Arthur penal settlement opened with 68 prisoners and became Australia's main convict center. With the closure of the Maria Island colony in 1832 and Macquarie Harbour a year later, numbers at Port Arthur quickly increased to 675 prisoners in 1833. More buildings were assembled to hold the growing population, as was a semaphore system linking Port Arthur with Hobart via numerous hill-top stations. However, convict banishment to Van Diemen's Land ceased in 1853; insane convicts were incarcerated in the old wooden barracks until a special asylum was finished in 1868.

The Isle of the Dead lay offshore of the Port Arthur colony, a burial ground for those who perished in the early settlement years. Originally called Opossum Island, half was reserved for the burial of soldiers, officers, and their families, whose graves were marked by elaborate headstones; the other half was for convicts, whose plots were unmarked. Records indicate that 1,769 prisoners and 180 others were buried on this lonely island.

One of the most fascinating—and feared—buildings of the colony was the Model Prison, where punishments, including floggings, took place. Completed in 1852, the goal of this pinwheel-shaped prison was penance with reform. Thus, some criminals were isolated from all human contact, where they could contemplate their misdeeds and embark on the road to reformation. By 1840, floggings at the Model Prison had mostly been replaced with punishment by this solitary confinement, the treadmill, and work in the coal mines.

The penal colony soon became a self-sufficient industrial center where prisoners sawed timber, built ships, laid bricks, cut stone, and made tiles, shoes, iron castings, and clothing. In its heyday, the prison town had a population of 1,200 convicts and some 1,000 free people. But while the officers and their families lived comfortably, playing chess, painting, and joining in musical evenings, barracks life was sparse for the common soldiers and convicts.

Port Arthur has mellowed into the present, its natural beauty and colonial architecture highlighting the positive side of its history. The convict ruins and ghost tales that speak of the less savory legacies, though, serve to remind both visitors and citizens that this is where much of the country's current attitudes toward friendship, freedom, and authority began.

— Bev Malzard

★ ❼ **Salamanca Place.** Old whaling ships used to dock at Salamanca Place. Today many of the warehouses that were once used by whalers along this street have been converted into crafts shops, art galleries, and restaurants. On Saturday, a boisterous morning market takes place, where dealers of Tasmanian arts and crafts, antiques, old records, and books display their wares. Keep an eye open for items made from beautiful Tasmanian timber, particularly Huon pine.

NEED A BREAK?

Retro Cafe. The Retro is among the most stylish and coolly casual of Salamanca Place's busy cafés with sidewalk tables. ☒ *Salamanca Pl. and Montpelier Retreat,* ☎ *03/6223–3073. AE, DC, MC, V.*

❸ **Tasmanian Museum and Art Gallery.** Overlooking Constitution Dock, the museum and gallery have many exhibits on Tasmania's history. It is the best place in Hobart to learn about the island's Aborigines and unique wildlife. ☒ *40 Macquarie St.,* ☎ *03/6223–1422.* ☞ *Free.* ☉ *Daily 10–5.*

☾ **Tudor Court.** This cutesy replica of an English Tudor village is very well put together, but kids are more likely to find it memorable than adults. ☒ *827 Sandy Bay Rd.,* ☎ *03/6225–1194.* ☞ *$3.* ☉ *Daily 9–5:30.*

OFF THE BEATEN PATH

Royal Tasmanian Botanical Gardens – The well-tended gardens—the largest area of open land in Hobart—are rarely crowded and are a welcome relief from the city. Exotic plants represent the English horticultural tradition, and there are interesting native Tasmanian species as well. One section has been specially designed for wheelchairs. The Japanese Garden is dominated by a miniature Mt. Fuji. Children love the flowered clock. A museum and education center is open daily noon–4. ☒ *Tasman Bridge, adjacent to Government House,* ☎ *03/6234–6299.* ☞ *Free.* ☉ *Daily 8–4:45.*

AROUND HOBART

Richmond. A half-hour's drive northeast from Hobart and 100 years behind the big city, this colonial village is a major tourist magnet. On weekends you might struggle to find a place to park the car or jostle with crowds on the town's long main street, which is lined with craft, antiques, and souvenir shops, cafés, and restaurants. To get the best sense of Richmond's character and historic importance, wander off the main drag a little. **Richmond Bridge,** Australia's oldest and a picturesque counterpoint to the town's church-spired skyline, is a convict-built stone structure dating from 1823. **Richmond Jail** (☒ 37 Bathurst St., ☎ 03/6260–2127) is well preserved and full of evocative historical interpretive materials. Built in 1825, five years before the city's settlement, the jail has eerie displays of chain manacles, domestic utensils, and a variety of instruments of torture. The jail is open daily 10–5; admission is $5.

Dining

$$$ ✕ **Alexander's Restaurant.** Located at the historic Lenna of Hobart
★ hotel, Alexander's offers some of Tasmania's finest cuisine. Start your meal with, say, local mussels, leek and mushroom terrine, homemade ravioli, or cerviche. Beautifully presented main dishes include prime beef fillet, aged local venison, marinated field mushrooms, and Atlantic salmon rolled through Moroccan spices and served on a warm salad of beans with new potatoes, tomatoes, quail eggs, and capers. For dessert, try the pears poached in red wine and cinnamon, the summer pudding, or, if you dare, the orange-scented chocolate tart. ☒ *20 Runnymede St., Battery Point,* ☎ *03/6223–2911. Reservations essential. Jacket required. AE, DC, MC, V.*

$$$ ✕ **Dear Friends.** One of the most elegant restaurants in Tasmania, this
★   converted flour mill by the wharf is famous for contemporary cuisine,
       and each meal is carefully and artistically arranged. Tables are gener-
       ously spaced among old-world furniture and antique bric-a-brac. Game
       dishes, such as roasted venison, are a specialty, as are Atlantic salmon
       and lamb cutlets. The wine list features Tasmania's finest. ⊠ *18 Brook
       St.,* ☎ *03/6223–2646. Reservations essential. Jacket required. AE,
       DC, MC, V. Closed Sun.*

$$$ ✕ **Meehan's.** Plan to splurge for a big night out at the Grand Chan-
       cellor Hotel's signature restaurant, which has superb views of Hobart's
       bustling waterfront. The menu is seasonal and highlights local produce;
       options might include aged King Island porterhouse steak with arti-
       choke mash, grilled onion, and red wine au jus; or barbecued, boned
       quail marinated in lemon, garlic, herbs, and wine and served with cous-
       cous and Mediterranean vegetables. The wine list is excellent. ⊠ *1 Davey
       St.,* ☎ *03/6235–4535 or 1800/22–2229. Reservations essential. Jacket
       and tie. AE, DC, MC, V.*

$$$ ✕ **Wrest Point Revolving Restaurant.** Breathtaking views of the city eas-
       ily justify a visit to this revolving restaurant atop one of Hobart's
       tallest buildings. Luckily, the food is equally rewarding. Tables are widely
       spaced around a mirrored central column and all have views. Special-
       ties include the City Lights dinner ($48 per person), a three-course meal
       based on seasonal produce, and prawns flambéed at the table with flair.
       Don't miss the smoked Tasmanian salmon appetizer. ⊠ *Wrest Point
       Hotel, 410 Sandy Bay Rd.,* ☎ *03/6225–0112. Reservations essential.
       Jacket required. AE, DC, MC, V.*

$$ ✕ **Drunken Admiral.** The log-fire ambience here is raucous and the walls
       are cluttered with seafaring paraphernalia. With all this naval kitsch,
       you might expect the food to be second-rate, but each nautically named
       dish is well prepared. Try the Sydney-to-Hobart seafood platter, a
       combination of hot and cold delicacies; or, at $29.90 per person, you
       can sample the seafood extravaganza of the Drunken Admiral set din-
       ner. Afterward, if you're up to it, indulge in freshly baked sticky al-
       mond pudding. ⊠ *17–19 Hunter St., Old Hobart Town,* ☎ *03/6234–
       1903. Reservations essential. AE, MC, V.*

$$ ✕ **Mures Upper Deck Restaurant.** Situated on the top floor of the Mures
★   Fish House complex on the wharf, the Upper Deck has superb indoor
       and alfresco views of the harbor and lively Salamanca Place. Because
       the interior, made of Tasmanian wood, amplified diners' chatter, huge
       stuffed fishes were suspended from the ceiling to absorb the noise—the
       restaurant is now famous for them. Try the flathead, the house version
       of a local fish, trevalla—panfried with smoked trout pâté and Brie. Down-
       stairs, **Mures Lower Deck** (☎ 03/6231–2121) is a less expensive alter-
       native: You order, take a number, pick up your food, and eat it at tables
       outside. Also in the complex, **Orizuru** (☎ 03/6231–1790) has Hobart's
       best and freshest sushi and sashimi. ⊠ *Victoria Dock,* ☎ *03/6231–1999.
       AE, DC, MC, V; no credit cards at Mures Lower Deck.*

$$ ✕ **Prossers Fine Seafood Restaurant.** Situated in Hobart's charming
       beach-side suburb of Sandy Bay, this seafood restaurant serves local
       fare, with plenty "catch-of-the-day" specials. Grain-fed beef, fresh
       fish and shellfish, and Mod Oz cuisine highlight the seasonal menus.
       The $25, four-course, fixed-price meal is a great value and changes
       monthly. ⊠ *Long Point, Sandy Bay,* ☎ *03/6225–2276. Reservations
       essential. Jacket and tie. AE, DC, MC, V.*

$$ ✕ **Sisco's on the Pier.** Relocated from its plush city center premises,
★   Sisco's has undergone a transformation in everything except the qual-
       ity of its Catalonian and Mediterranean cuisine. It remains one of the
       best Spanish restaurants in Australia, renowned for its air-dried ham,
       homemade pork sausages, stuffed squid, and river trout. The light, fresh

decor includes bright outdoor areas, and strolling guitar players provide plenty of fun, romance, and atmosphere. ⊠ *The Pier, Murray St.,* ☎ *03/6223–2059. AE, DC, MC, V. Closed Sun.*

$$ ✕ **Aegean Restaurant.** Don't go to this lively Greek restaurant looking for romance. This is the place to bring a large group—the larger the better—for a meal interspersed with belly dancing, plate throwing, and traditional Greek dancing. During lulls, enjoy moussaka, vegetarian platters, marinated chicken livers, or grilled chicken. The restaurant doesn't have a license for alcohol, but patrons may bring their own wine, beer, and spirits. ⊠ *121 Collins St.,* ☎ *03/6231–1000. AE, DC, MC, V. Closed Sun.–Mon.*

$ ✕ **Ali Akbar.** A roaring fire and Lebanese music welcome you to this
★ traditional restaurant in northern Hobart. White tablecloths and fresh flowers add to the appealing atmosphere. Here you'll find modern interpretations of traditional dishes—and superb use of local produce. Typical Lebanese dishes include *maqlubat-al-qarnabeet* (a mixture of cauliflower, pine kernels, and spiced rice) and *sambousek* (yeast pastry filled with feta cheese, egg, and parsley). After 9 PM you can order the banquet plate, a combination of hot and cold dishes. ⊠ *321 Elizabeth St.,* ☎ *03/6231–1770. Reservations essential. AE, DC, MC, V. BYOB. Closed Mon.*

$ ✕ **Riviera Ristorante.** On the wharf across the street from the Grand Chancellor Hotel, this simply decorated restaurant is always busy and noisy. You can expect to stand in line for tables packed together on the restaurant's bare floor, but the wait is worthwhile. All the food, including the pasta, is very tasty. Seven choices of pizza and 10 different sauces accompany four types of pasta. The exuberant seafood marinara is a classic. ⊠ *15 Hunter St., Sullivans Cove,* ☎ *03/6234–3230. Reservations essential. AE, MC, V.*

Lodging

$$$$ 🏨 **Grand Chancellor Hotel.** Across the street from the old wharf and
★ steps from some of the best restaurants in Hobart, this monolith seems a bit out of place amid Hobart's quaint colonialism. What it lacks in period charm, however, it more than makes up for in luxury. All rooms have a large wooden desk and thick white guest bathrobes—no detail, it seems, has been forgotten. Some rooms overlook the harbor. ⊠ *Box 1601, 1 Davey St., 7001,* ☎ *03/6235–4535 or 1800/22–2229,* ℻ *03/6223–8175. 212 rooms, 12 suites. 2 restaurants, bar, indoor pool, beauty salon, massage, sauna, health club, laundry service, airport shuttle, car rental. AE, DC, MC, V.*

$$$$ 🏨 **Salamanca Inn.** Close to the Salamanca Place market, these elegant self-contained units are built from Tasmanian timber and incorporate the latest energy-saving devices. The inn was built in 1988, but its architectural design blends in well with this historic district. Queen-size sofa beds, modern kitchens, and free laundry facilities make these apartments perfect for families. Ask for a room on the sunny western side, but don't expect great views from a three-story building. All apartments are serviced by housekeepers. ⊠ *10 Gladstone St., 7000,* ☎ *03/6223–3300 or 1800/03–0944,* ℻ *03/6223–7167. 60 rooms. Restaurant, pool, spa. AE, DC, MC, V.*

$$$–$$$$ 🏨 **Wrest Point Hotel and Casino.** Built in 1940, this 17-floor luxury hotel earned its fame in 1973, when it opened the first legalized gambling casino in Australia. Lodgings include the more expensive tower and the moderately priced motor inn. In the tower, higher floors offer enjoyable views of either Mt. Wellington or the Derwent River. Regine's Videoteque and the nightclub are major entertainment spots in Hobart. ⊠ *410 Sandy Bay Rd., Sandy Bay, 7005,* ☎ *03/6225–0112 or 1800/*

03–0611, FAX 03/6225–2424. *184 rooms and 13 suites in tower; 81 rooms in motor inn. 2 restaurants, room service, indoor pool, beauty salon, tennis court, health club, cabaret, casino, nightclub. AE, DC, MC, V.*

$$$ ⊞ **Islington Elegant Private Hotel.** A converted 1845 mansion, this guest
★   house exudes good taste from the moment you enter its spacious, black-and-white tiled entrance hall. Rooms are decorated in colonial style with antiques and matching Colefax & Fowler curtains and bedspreads. Although minutes from the city center, the hotel seems comfortably isolated, with a lush garden, outdoor pool, and stunning view of Mt. Wellington. Ask for a room with garden access. Personal service is stressed, with your comfort and whims taken care of by your friendly hosts. A large complimentary Continental breakfast is served in a sunny conservatory. ⊠ *321 Davey St., 7000,* ☎ *03/6223–3900,* FAX *03/6224–3167. 8 suites. Pool. AE, DC, MC, V.*

$$$ ⊞ **Lenna of Hobart.** A short stroll from Battery Point and Salamanca
★   Place, this 19th-century hotel is an eclectic mix of Old World charm and Australian colonial furnishing. Inside this 1874 Italianate mansion, soft lights glow through stained-glass walkways that are lined with urns and Greek statuary. Rooms are furnished with flower-upholstered wicker chairs, canopy beds, and antique-style telephones. Alexander's Restaurant serves some of the best cooking in the state (☞ *Dining, above*). ⊠ *20 Runnymede St., 7000,* ☎ *03/6232–3900 or 1800/03–0633,* FAX *03/6224–0112. 45 rooms, 4 suites. Restaurant. AE, DC, MC, V.*

$$ ⊞ **Westside Hotel.** Well-positioned in the city center, the modern Westside has functional, rather than stylish, rooms, most of which have city skyline or harbor views. Four executive suites with Jacuzzis are decorated in styles from modern to Japanese, and two double rooms are specifically designed for guests with disabilities. ⊠ *156 Bathurst St., 7000,* ☎ *03/6234–6255,* FAX *03/6234–7884. 139 rooms, 4 suites. Restaurant, room service. AE, DC, MC, V.*

Cottages and Guest Houses

$$ ⊞ **Barton Cottage.** Built in 1837, this Battery Point lodge has been com-
★   pletely refurbished but still maintains its colonial grace while offering modern conveniences. Rooms with such names as Footman, Pantrymaid, and Chambermaid are simply decorated with antiques, and all have private baths. The old coachhouse has been restored into a private hideaway. ⊠ *72 Hampden Rd., 7000,* ☎ *03/6224–1606,* FAX *03/ 6224–1724. 6 rooms. AE, DC, MC, V.*

$$ ⊞ **Colville Cottage.** From the moment you pass through the white picket fence into the garden surrounding this cottage, you can't help but feel relaxed. The interior exudes warmth and welcome with hardwood floors, fireplaces, and antique furniture. Fresh flowers and bay windows trimmed with iron lace add to the cozy atmosphere, where attention to detail is a top priority. Rates include breakfast. ⊠ *32 Mona St., 7000,* ☎ *03/6223–6968,* FAX *03/6224–0500. 6 rooms. MC, V.*

$$ ⊞ **Cromwell Cottage.** Built in 1873, this simple guest house is remarkable for its colorful rooms, including all-red, all-yellow (the sunniest), or all-blue quarters; otherwise, ask for the garden room. Wonderful old brass beds and antique furnishings complete the decor. Some rooms have a view of the Derwent River. Rates include breakfast. ⊠ *6 Cromwell St., 7000,* ☎ *03/6223–6734,* FAX *03/6223–6605. 5 rooms. No credit cards.*

$$ ⊞ **Elms of Hobart.** Classified by the National Trust, this immaculately restored mansion in North Hobart offers colonial-style accommodations. Built in 1917 in a mesh of architectural styles that range from Edwardian to California bungalow, this former private home retains its hospitable ambience. Six suites on two floors have fireplaces, elec-

tric blankets, telephones, and tea makers. ⊠ *452 Elizabeth St., North Hobart 7000,* ☎ *03/6231–3277. 6 suites. Laundry. AE, MC, V.*

$$ 🔝 **Warwick Cottages.** Annie's Room and Pandora's Box are identical cottages built by convicts in 1854. Now they're filled with an assortment of colonial bric-a-brac that lends individual charm. Pandora's Box, for example, has an antique meat grinder and old-style carriage lanterns. A winding staircase in each cottage leads to a double bed upstairs, and the ground floor has two single beds. ⊠ *119–121 Warwick St., 7000,* ☎ *018/12–5049,* 𝔽𝔸𝕏 *03/6254–1527. 2 cottages. V.*

Nightlife and the Arts

Hobart's nightlife is tame. Consult the Friday or Saturday editions of the local newspaper, the *Mercury,* for the latest in evening entertainment. *This Week in Tasmania,* available at most hotels, is a comprehensive guide to current performances and rock and jazz concerts.

Casino

Located in the Wrest Point Hotel, the **Wrest Point Casino** has blackjack, American roulette, minibaccarat, keno, minidice, craps, federal wheel, federal poker and stud poker, and two-up. Maximum stakes are $500 (a special suite on the ground floor caters to high rollers). The Wrest Point also offers late-night comedy and cabaret. ⊠ *410 Sandy Bay Rd., Sandy Bay,* ☎ *03/6225–0112 or 008/03–0611.* ☉ *Mon.–Thurs. 1 PM–3 AM, Fri. and Sat. 1 PM–4 AM, Sun. noon–3 AM.*

Music

Every second Saturday night, the **Carlysle Hotel** (⊠ 232 Main Rd., Derwent Park, ☎ 03/6272–0299) hosts '60s–'90s night with local radio DJ Brett Marley. For something more sedate, try the piano bar at the **Grand Chancellor** (⊠ 1 Davey St., ☎ 03/6235–4535). For the serious bop-till-you-drop set, try **Round Midnight** (⊠ 39 Salamanca Pl., ☎ 03/6223–2491) and **Stoppy's Waterfront Tavern** (⊠ 21 Salamanca Pl., ☎ 03/6223–3799).

The **ABC Odeon** (⊠ 167 Liverpool St., ☎ 03/6235–3634) hosts concerts of the Tasmanian Symphony Orchestra. The ABC and the Conservatorium of Music stage regular lunchtime concerts in the State Library Auditorium on Murray Street.

Theater

Theatre Royal (⊠ 29 Campbell St., ☎ 03/6234–6266) is an architectural gem that dates back to 1834; notice the portraits of composers painted on the magnificent dome. Other performances can be seen at the **Playhouse Theatre** (⊠ 106 Bathurst St., ☎ 03/6234–1536). Both feature classic and contemporary plays by Australian and international playwrights, but you are likely to see more cutting-edge work at the Playhouse.

Wine Bar

Oenophiles should try Tasmanian wine, some of which is exceptional. Look for Pipers Brook, Heemskerk, Freycinet, and Moorilla Estate labels at **Nickelby's Wine Bar** (⊠ 217 Sandy Bay Rd., Sandy Bay, ☎ 03/6223–6030).

Outdoor Activities and Sports

Bicycling

For rentals, try **Peregrine Adventures** (⊠ 5/13 Beechworth Rd., Sandy Bay, ☎ 03/6225–0944).

Bushwalking

A variety of hiking trails are within easy reach of Hobart, including several routes around Mt. Wellington, which you'll need a car to reach. Stop in at the Tasmanian Travel and Information Centre (☞ Hobart A to Z, *below*) for more information.

Fishing

Tasmania's well-stocked lakes and streams are among the best places in the world for trout fishing. The season runs from August through May, and licensed trips can be arranged through the **Tasmanian Travel and Information Centre** (☞ Hobart A to Z, *below*).

Skiing

Tasmanian snowfields are only an hour's drive from Hobart. The main ski area is at Mt. Field, 81 km (50 mi) northwest of Hobart. Contact the **Tasmanian Travel and Information Centre** (☞ Hobart A to Z, *below*) for information on conditions, accommodations, and equipment rental.

Spectator Sports

You'll be able to watch cricket, soccer, and Australian-rules football in Hobart. Cricket matches take place November–March at the **Bellerive Oval** (☎ 03/6244–7099) in the Queens Domain; football matches are Saturday afternoons in winter (April–August) at **North Hobart Sports Ground** (☎ 03/6234–3203). You can buy tickets ($10–$40) at the gates.

Swimming

The **Hobart Olympic Pool** (⊠ Domain Rd., ☎ 03/6234–4232) and **Clarence Swimming Centre** (⊠ Riawena Rd., Montagu Bay, ☎ 03/6244–2294) both welcome visitors.

Shopping

Tasmania is noted for its artisans and craftspeople, who use local timber—Huon pine, sassafras, and myrtle—to fashion such items as letter racks and salad bowls. Stores worth a visit include **Aspect Design** (⊠ 79 Salamanca Pl., ☎ 03/6223–2642), which stocks blown glass, wooden products, pottery, jewelry, and postcards; **Handmark Gallery** (⊠ 77 Salamanca Pl., ☎ 03/6223–7895), which sells Hobart's best wooden jewelry boxes as well as art deco–style jewelry, pottery, painting, and sculpture; the **National Trust Gift Shop** (⊠ Galleria, 33 Salamanca Pl., ☎ 03/6223–7371), crowded with smaller items, such as lacework and Tasmanian-motif tea towels; and **Sullivan's Cove** (⊠ 47 Salamanca Pl., ☎ 03/6223–7262), in an 1860s building, which carries crafts, prints, and women's clothing.

Hobart A to Z

Arriving and Departing

BY BUS

Tasmanian Redline Coaches (☎ 03/6231–3233 or 1300/30–0520) run daily to towns and cities across the state. Buses also meet the ferry from Victoria that comes into Tasmania's northern port city, Devonport (☞ Northwest Coast A to Z, *below* for ferry information). Tassie Wilderness Passes, five-day tickets (to be used in seven days) for unlimited travel around Tasmania, cost $99; 14-day tickets cost $149; and 30-day tickets cost $220.

BY CAR

If you're arriving in Devonport on the *Spirit of Tasmania* ferry from Melbourne, Hobart is about four hours south by car.

BY PLANE

Hobart International Airport is one hour by air from Melbourne or two hours from Sydney. On the island, **Airlines of Tasmania** flies between Hobart, Launceston, and the northwest and west coasts. Tickets can also be booked through **Tasmanian Travel and Information Centres** (☞ Visitor Information, *below*) in cities around the island. *See* Air Travel *in* Smart Travel Tips for information on airlines.

Between the Airport and Downtown. Hobart International Airport is 22 km (14 mi) east of Hobart. The trip along the Eastern Outlet Road should take no more than 20 minutes by car. **Tasmanian Redline Coaches** (☞ *above*) has regular shuttle service for $7 per person between the airport and its downtown depot at 199 Collins Street. For small groups, **taxis** are an economical way to travel to the city. Metered taxis are available at the taxi stand in front of the terminal. The fare to downtown Hobart is approximately $25.

Getting Around

BY BUS

The **Metropolitan Transport Trust** (MTT) operates a bus system from downtown Hobart to the surrounding suburbs daily from 6 AM to midnight. Special "Day Rover" tickets for $3.10 permit unlimited use of buses for a day. Tickets may be used 9 AM–4:30 PM and after 6 PM. For inquiries, try Metroshop ⊠ *18 Elizabeth St.,* ☎ *03/6233–4222.*

BY CAR

Unlike mainland Australia, most places in Tasmania are within easy driving distance, rarely more than three or four hours in a stretch. Hobart itself is extremely compact—most sights are easily visited on a walking tour. If you do drive in the city, watch the one-way street system in the city center, which takes some getting used to.

BY TAXI

You can hail metered taxis in the street or find them at designated stands and major hotels. Cabs for hire have lighted signs on their roofs. Contact **City Cabs** (☎ 03/6234–3633) or **Taxi Combined** (☎ 03/6234–8444).

Contacts and Resources

B&B RESERVATION AGENCIES

Homehost Tasmania (⊠ Box 780, Sandy Bay 7005, ☎ 03/6224–1612, FAX 03/6224–0472) arranges for visitors to stay in Tasmanian homes, many of which are farms, cottages, and Federation-style houses. The latter dwellings—popular at the turn of the century, when the Australian states became a Federation—are one-level buildings with surrounding verandas, often with iron lace decorating the outer posts. Prices are generally inexpensive to moderate, and breakfast is included. Dinners often can be arranged as well.

CAR RENTALS

Cars, campers, caravans, and minibuses are available for hire. The largest companies are **Avis** (☎ 03/6234–4222 or 1800/03–0008), **Budget** (☎ 03/6234–5222 or 03/6213–2727), **Autorent Hertz** (☎ 03/6234–5555 or 13–6039), and **Colonial Thrifty** (☎ 03/6234–1341 or 1800/22–6434). Some lower-priced rental companies include **Lo-Cost Auto Rent** (☎ 03/6231–0550 or 1800/03–0023) and **Range Rent-a-Bug** (☎ 03/6231–0300).

EMERGENCIES

Ambulance, fire brigade, and police: ☎ 000. **Hospitals: St. Helen's Private Hospital** (⊠ 186 Macquarie St., ☎ 03/6221–6444); **Royal Hobart Hospital** (⊠ 48 Liverpool St., ☎ 03/6238–8308).

Bicycling. Brake Out Cycling Tours (403 Sandy Bay Rd., ☎ 03/6278–2966) leads tours from Mt. Wellington, Mt. Nelson, and other neighboring scenic areas. The company provides all equipment, and a guide and support vehicle accompany you on the road. Lunch and morning and afternoon teas are included on most tours.

Flightseeing. Par Avion Tours (☎ 03/6248–5390) offers some of the most exciting ways to see Hobart and its surroundings. One flight goes to Melaleuca Inlet on the west coast and includes a boat trip with **Wilderness Tours** around Bathurst Harbour, with stops for bushwalking. The cost is all-inclusive, and lunch and afternoon tea are provided.

Harbor Tours. Transderwent (⊠ Franklin Wharf Ferry Pier, ☎ 03/6223–5893) runs the MV *Emmalisa,* an old-fashioned ferry, daily around Derwent Harbour. Cruises (1¼ hours) include an excellent commentary on Hobart and its environs, and the lunchtime trip includes a hot meal. Fare is $10 ($18 for the lunch cruise).

The **MV *Cartela*** (⊠ Franklin Wharf Ferry Pier, ☎ 03/6223–1914), built in 1912, plies the harbor and D'Entrecasteaux Channel in the morning, at lunch, and in the afternoon. Fares start at $14. The ***Rhona H*** sailing ship (⊠ Franklin Wharf Ferry Pier, ☎ 018/13–3396) takes to the harbor four times daily. The $25 cost includes refreshments.

Orientation Tours. Hobart Sightseeing (⊠ 199 Collins St., ☎ 03/6231–3511) runs half-day city sightseeing tours on Tuesday, Thursday, and Saturday mornings, including visits to Battery Point and Salamanca Place. The cost is $23. **TigerLine–Gray Line** (⊠ 4 Liverpool St., ☎ 03/6234–4077) buses operate full-day tours every Saturday that take in Salamanca Place, nearby Russell Falls National Park, and Richmond. Fare is $47.

Walking Tours. Walks led by the **National Trust** (☎ 03/6223–7570) provide an excellent overview of Battery Point, including visits to mansions and 19th-century houses. Tours leave the wishing well (near the post office in Franklin Square) at Battery Point every Saturday at 9:30 AM, and the $8 cost includes morning tea. The National Trust also conducts daily tours (hourly 10–2) of the old penitentiary, courthouse, and chapel on Campbell Street. ⊠ *National Trust, 6 Brisbane St.,* ☎ 03/6223–5200.

Contact the **Tasmanian Travel and Information Centre** (⊠ 20 Davey St., at Elizabeth St., Hobart 7000, ☎ 03/6230–8233).

PORT ARTHUR

102 km (63 mi) southeast of Hobart.

When Governor Arthur was looking for a site to dump his worst convict offenders in 1830, the Tasman Peninsula was a natural choice. Joined to the rest of Tasmania only by the narrow Eaglehawk Neck, the spit was easy to isolate and guard. And so Port Arthur was born, a penal colony whose name became a byword for vicious horror and cruelty. Between 1830 and 1877, nearly 13,000 convicts served sentences in Britain's equivalent of Devil's Island, and nearly 2,000 of them died here. Few men escaped: Dogs were used to patrol the narrow causeway and sharks were reputed to infest the waters. Reminders of those dark days remain in some of the names—Dauntless Point, Stinking Point, Isle of the Dead. But today, this once-foreboding peninsula has become Tasmania's major tourist attraction, filled with beautiful scenery and historic sites that recapture Australia's difficult beginnings. Although many visitors come here on a day trip from Hobart, consider at least an overnight stay. There is more than enough to do here to occupy a couple of days, and watching afternoon shadows lengthen over the ruins creates a mood much more in keeping with the settlement's doleful past.

Walking these grounds at dawn is magical, especially when taking in the view from the knoll behind the church.

Following the bloody rampage of gunman Martin Bryant, Port Arthur's eerie atmosphere has taken on a more poignant air. In April 1996, Bryant shot 35 people at the historic site and in a nearby village; this was Australia's single worst killing. He was tried, pleaded guilty, and sentenced to life in jail without remission. The café that was a scene of slaughter has been demolished, save for a portion retained as a memorial to the dead. At press time, a visitor center and restaurant complex were in the works, although the state was divided on the architectural style and how the building's physical presence would affect the landscape.

Exploring Port Arthur

The former **Port Arthur Penal Settlement** grounds now comprise one of the nicest parks in Tasmania—but be prepared to do a lot of walking among widely scattered sites. When you stand by scenic Carnarvon Bay, it is hard to imagine the bloodshed and misery that once existed here. But when you walk into the solitary confinement cells or the main penitentiary, it's hard to fight off the unsettling feeling. Most of the original buildings were damaged by bush fires in 1877, shortly after the settlement was abandoned, but you can still see the beautiful church, round guard house, commandant's residence, model prison, hospital, and government cottages.

The old **lunatic asylum** is now an excellent museum featuring a scale model of the Port Arthur settlement, a video history, and a collection of tools, leg irons, and chains. Along with a walking tour of the grounds and entrance to the museum, admission includes a harbor cruise, of which there are eight daily in summer. There is a separate twice-daily cruise to and tour of the **Isle of the Dead**, which sits in the middle of the bay. It is estimated that 1,769 convicts and 180 others are buried here, mostly in communal pits. No headstones were used to mark the sites; bodies were simply bundled in sailcloth, thrown in a hole, and sprinkled with quicklime. ⊠ *Arthur Hwy.,* ☎ *03/6250–2539 or 1800/659–101.* 🎟 *Penal Settlement Tour $13, Isle of the Dead tour $5; admission valid for multiple entries over 24-hr period.* ☉ *Site open daily 9–5; Isle of the Dead tour daily at noon and 3.*

☾ **Bush Mill Steam Railway and Settlement** is a great place to learn about a miller's life at the turn of the century. Highlights are a replica steam-powered bush sawmill, with a working steam engine, and a narrow-gauge steam railway that was once used to transport timber. The train runs at least three times daily for rides. ⊠ *Arthur Hwy.,* ☎ *03/6250–2221.* 🎟 *$12.50.* ☉ *Daily 9–5.*

The **Tasmanian Devil Park** is a wildlife refuge for injured animals of many species. It's probably the best place in the state to see Tasmanian devils (burrowing carnivorous marsupials about the size of a dog), as well as quolls, boobooks, masked owls, eagles, and other native fauna. At the adjacent and co-managed **World Tiger Snake Center**, learn about the use of venomous tiger snakes in medical research. ⊠ *Arthur Hwy., 11 km (7 mi) north of Port Arthur, Taranna,* ☎ *03/6250–3203.* 🎟 *Tasmanian Devil Park $10, snake center $7, joint ticket $16.* ☉ *Daily 9–5:30.*

Dining and Lodging

$ ✕ **Tracks.** This small colonial-style restaurant at the Bush Mill specializes in salads and delicious home-baked scones. Other treats include vegetable stockpot and marinated Scotch fillet, called bushman's steak.

Try apple crumble and ice cream for dessert. ⊠ *Arthur Hwy., Port Arthur,* ☎ *03/6250–2221. Reservations not accepted. AE, DC, MC, V.*

$$　🏨 **Cascades Colonial Accommodation.** Part of a onetime convict outstation that dates to 1841, these cottages are comfortable and full of character. Each has kitchen facilities, and breakfast provisions are included in the room rate. A small museum related to the property is also on site. ⊠ *Nubeena Rd., 20 km (12 mi) north of Port Arthur, Koonya 7187,* ☎ FAX *03/6250–3121. 4 cottages. No credit cards.*

$$　🏨 **Port Arthur Motor Inn.** Situated on a ridge behind an old church,
★　this motel overlooks the entire historic Penal Settlement site. The comfortable but somewhat old-fashioned guest rooms sport 1960s decor, with small bathrooms. Although none of the accommodations has good views, the hotel's main restaurant, the Commandant's Table, overlooks the prison ruins and has a particularly lovely vista at sunset. The food, sadly, is unworthy of the setting—you would do better to eat in the much cheaper (but viewless) pub restaurant adjacent. ⊠ *Arthur Hwy., Port Arthur 7182,* ☎ *03/6250–2101 or 1800/03–0747,* FAX *03/6250–2417. 35 rooms. Bar. AE, DC, MC, V.*

$$　🏨 **Port Arthur Villas.** A 10-minute walk from the penal colony site, these modern apartments have design elements that follow Port Arthur style, such as verandas, old-fashioned brickwork, and pleasant cottage gardens. Studio and two-bedroom apartments are well appointed and have fully equipped kitchens. Barbecue facilities and a playground are also on site. ⊠ *Safety Cove Rd., Port Arthur 7182,* ☎ *03/6250–2239,* FAX *03/6250–2589. 9 apartments. Kitchenettes, playground. AE, DC, MC, V.*

Port Arthur A to Z

Arriving and Departing

BY CAR

Port Arthur is an easy 90-minute drive from Hobart via the Lyell and the Arthur highways, but it is worth pausing at such places as Eaglehawk Neck, where tethered guard dogs once dissuaded escaped convicts from heading farther north. Nearby is the Tessellated Pavement, an interesting geological formation; the Blowhole, spectacular in wild weather; and Tasman Arch, a naturally formed archway.

Getting Around

BY CAR

A private vehicle is essential if you want to explore parts of the Tasman Peninsula beyond the historic settlement.

Contacts and Resources

GUIDED TOURS

The **Port Arthur Penal Settlement** (☎ 03/6250–2539 or 1800/65–9101) conducts a variety of daily tours around Port Arthur (☞ *above*). A self-guided audiocassette tour gives visitors a running commentary on the sites for $3. In the popular nightly **ghost tours** ($10), guides recount stories of apparitions and supposed hauntings at the site while walking its darkened attractions by torchlight. Depending on the season, between two and 10 ghost tours depart nightly.

Hobart Sightseeing (⊠ 199 Collins St., Hobart, ☎ 03/6231–3511) has full-day tours, $49, of the penal settlement and Bush Mill. **Remarkable Tours** (☎ 03/6250–2359; 03/6250–2539 to book through Port Arthur Information Office) offers minibus tours from the Port Arthur Penal Settlement to such nearby scenic sites as Remarkable Cave and observation points along the coast. **Tasman Peninsula Detours** (☎ 03/6250–3355), based in Port Arthur, gives daily four-wheel-drive tours of rain forests, beaches, and the convict ruins. The all-day tour includes morning and afternoon tea, as well as a barbecue lunch with wine. The **Tasmanian Travel and Information Centre** (✉ 20 Davey St., at Elizabeth St., ☎ 03/6230–8233) organizes day trips from Hobart to Port Arthur by bus.

FREYCINET NATIONAL PARK

It took the early European explorers of Van Diemen's Land four voyages and 161 years to realize that the Freycinet Peninsula, a thickly forested wedge of granite jutting east into the Southern Ocean, was not an island.

In 1642 Abel Tasman saw it through fierce squalls and, thinking it separate from the mainland, named it van der Lyn's Island, after a member of the Dutch East India Company's council of governors. In 1773, Tobias Furneaux of the HMS *Adventure,* part of Captain Cook's second world expedition, passed by far enough out to sea to believe Tasman's theory. Twenty-five years later, explorer Matthew Flinders—who at age 25 circumnavigated the island of Tasmania with his cat in a little boat, the *Tom Thumb*—agreed. It was not until 1803, when Nicolas Baudin's hydrographer, Pierre Faure, took a longboat and crew into what is now Great Oyster Bay, that van der Lyn's island was proven to be attached to the island. It was named the Freycinet Peninsula after the expedition's chief cartographer.

It is ironic that this piece of Tasmania's east coast was so misunderstood because of foul weather when the climate here is as benign as anywhere on the island. And this climate, especially in summer, is one reason why the wild Freycinet Peninsula is prime walking terrain.

The road onto the peninsula halts just beyond the township of **Coles Bay.** The carpark is always busy with serious hikers strapping on backpacks, as well as day trippers deciding whether they're up to the steep 30-minute climb to the lookout platform above the precise half-moon shape of **Wineglass Bay.** Many stop here, but others plunge down the rocky, precipitous slope to the bay, where talcum-soft white sand meets turquoise water. With the hulking granite bluffs of **Mt. Graham** and **Mt. Freycinet** looming in the background above a mantle of trees, it couldn't be more spectacular. The walk to the end of Wineglass Bay and back to the carpark takes about 2½ hours.

The park's many walking trails are well signposted. On a day trip, you can walk across the peninsula at its narrowest point, along the **Isthmus Track** past swamps and myriad waterbirds, to Hazards Beach, which is more protected for swimming than Wineglass Bay. You can then return on the **Hazards Beach Track,** beneath the mighty bulk of the snaggle-toothed Hazards, the daunting granite towers that glower over the national park. This walk takes about 4½ hours.

A longer walk of about six hours takes you along the length of lovely **Hazards Beach,** along which there is evidence of Aboriginal occupation in the numerous shell middens (old refuse heaps) that dot the dunes. A more strenuous walk climbs from the end of Wineglass Bay over the summit of **Mt. Graham,** and then to **Cook's Beach,** returning along Hazards Beach. This walk will take at least seven hours. Daily entry to the park costs $2.50, $8 for vehicles.

Dining and Lodging

Camping is permitted in the park, and there is a campground inland of Cook's Beach. Walkers should register at the booth in the carpark. Water is scarce, particularly in summer, so overnighting is advised for experienced campers only. Walkers can also spend the night inside Cook's

Hut, the granite and tin homestead of the 19th-century grazier who attempted to make a living on this marginal land.

$$$ ✕⌷ **Freycinet Lodge.** The lodge's wooden one- and two-bedroom cabins are unobtrusively situated in a densely treed setting overlooking Great Oyster Bay. Simple but comfortable rooms and furnishings are enriched with handsome Tasmanian timber. Secluded balconies are ideal for drinking in the views. Local seafood on the menu is particularly good; meals are not included in room rates. ⊠ *Freycinet National Park, Coles Bay 7215,* ☏ *03/6257–0101,* ℻ *03/6257–0278. 36 rooms. Restaurant, tennis court, recreation room. AE, DC, MC, V.*

Arriving and Departing

BY BUS

Tasmanian Redline Coaches (☏ 03/6231–3233 or 1300 360–000) runs between Hobart and Bicheno, where you can connect with a local bus that runs twice daily on weekdays, and once on Saturday, to Coles Bay. A shuttle bus runs from Coles Bay to the carpark within the national park.

BY CAR

Freycinet National Park is 206 km (128 mi) northeast of Hobart and 214 km (133 mi) southwest of Launceston. From either city, it is about a three-hour drive.

Contacts and Resources

GUIDED TOURS

Freycinet Experience (⊠ 22 Brisbane St., Box 1879, Launceston 7250, ☏ 03/6334–4615, ℻ 03/6334–5525) runs excellent four-day walks in the park. Accommodation is in high-quality tent camps and an architectural award–winning timber lodge overlooking the stunning sands of Friendly Beaches. You have the choice on the second day of traversing Mt. Graham or taking the easier option of following the beach and bush track. Food is outstanding—you'll taste plenty of Tasmanian seafood, wine, and produce. Cost is $1,095 per person, including round-trip transportation from Hobart.

VISITOR INFORMATION

Freycinet National Park (☏ 03/6257–0107).

THE MIDLANDS

Folklore about the isolated Midlands often borders on the bizarre— but most of the stories, mind you, are told by non-Midlanders. Due to the lack of a good road and the distance from civilization, legends say that families couldn't even get their deceased to town to register them as dead until weeks after they had departed. The first real road appeared two centuries ago, blazed by brave explorers who linked Hobart with Launceston, near Tasmania's north coast. Journeys back then stretched to eight days, but later coach trips took just 15 hours along an improved road, considered Australia's most modern. Today, you can speed between the cities on the 200-km (124-mi) Midlands Highway (or Heritage Highway) in less than three hours. To do so, however, would mean bypassing many of Tasmania's appealing historic sites and English-style villages.

The Great Western Tiers mountains on the Midlands' horizon are a backdrop to verdant, undulating pastures that are strongly reminiscent of England. Off the beaten trail you'll discover trout-filled streams and lakes, snow-skiing slopes, grand Georgian mansions, and small towns redolent with colonial character.

Oatlands

85 km (53 mi) north of Hobart.

Situated alongside Lake Dulverton, Oatlands is a Georgian gem built during the 1820s to serve the newly arrived local farming community as a garrison town and to house convicts building the highway. It was named in June 1821 by Governor Macquarie for what he predicted would be the best use for the surrounding fertile plains. The whole town of Oatlands resembles an open-air museum, with buildings sporting informative plaques and a main street straight out of the 19th century.

The most outstanding structure in Oatlands is the sandstone **Council Chambers and Town Hall,** erected in 1880. The building is not open to the public. Oatlands has the greatest concentration of such sandstone buildings in Australia—more than 150 are within a 2-km (1-mi) radius.

The oldest building here is the **Court House.** The large room at its core was reputedly built in 1829 by two convicts in four months. A charming row of workers' cottages is at the end of High Street.

Callington Mill (☎ 03/6254–1525), open weekdays 9–5, was completed in 1837 and used wind power to grind grain. With the surrounding mill buildings, it gives a glimpse into early Tasmanian industry.

Of Oatlands' churches, Georgian **St. Peter's Anglican** was built in 1838 from a design by John Lee Archer, the colony's civil engineer, who also designed the bridge at Ross. **St. Paul's Catholic** was built in 1848, again of the mellow golden sandstone prevalent in Oatlands. The **Presbyterian Campbell Memorial Church** was erected in 1856 and rebuilt in 1859 after the original steeple collapsed.

Dining and Lodging

$ ✕ **Blossom's of Oatlands.** Unlike most buildings in town, this convict-built structure is made of brick, not sandstone, and it retains the original wooden floors and open fireplaces. The menu changes each week but invariably features rainbow trout and Tasmanian-apple pie topped with rich King Island cream. ⊠ *116–118 High St.,* ☎ *03/6254–1516.*

$$ ▤ **Amelia Cottage.** Convict-built in 1838, this cottage contains many of its original features, including shutters, a fuel stove, a baker's oven, and a flagstone kitchen floor, with modern amenities cleverly concealed. A claw-foot bath, an antique high chair and crib, and children's toys are highlights. The nursery, which can sleep 12, is a special feature of the cottage. ⊠ *104 High St., 7120,* ☎ *03/6254–1264. 4 cottages. AE, DC, MC, V.*

$–$$ ▤ **Wilmot Arms Inn.** Built in 1843, Wilmot Arms' term as a tavern inn was interrupted 100 years ago when its proprietor took up religion, turned his back on the demon of alcohol, and changed his place of business into a private residence. It is furnished with antiques, a vintage piano, and an open fireplace and is exclusively for nonsmokers. All meals are available, and there's a guest laundry facility. ⊠ *Main Rd., Kempton 7030, 32 km (20 mi) south of Oatlands,* ☎ *03/6259–1272. 5 rooms without bath. Dining room. AE, MC, V.*

$ ▤ **Oatlands Lodge.** The two-story guest house has one of the prettiest interiors in Tasmania, with convict-split sandstone walls complemented by attractive and comfortable country furnishings and quilts. This building is right in the middle of Oatlands, but as the village is no longer on the highway, it's a blessedly tranquil place. Built in 1837, Oatlands Lodge once served as a shop and a girls' school. A complete English-style breakfast is included. ⊠ *92 High St., 7120,* ☎ *03/6254–1444. 4 rooms. AE, MC, V.*

Ross

55 km (34 mi) north of Oatlands, 140 km (87 mi) north of Hobart.

This pretty village of some 500 residents is Tasmania's most historic town.

Ross Bridge (1836) is architect John Lee Archer's best-loved work. Graceful arches are highlighted by local sandstone and the decorative carvings of a convicted highwayman, Daniel Herbert, who was given freedom for his efforts. Herbert's work can also be seen throughout the graveyard where he's buried. ⊠ *Bridge St.*

The buildings at the intersection of **Church Street** (the main road) and Bridge Street are often said to summarize life neatly. They include the **Man-O-Ross Hotel** (temptation), the **Town Hall** (re-creation), the **Catholic Church** (salvation), and the **Old Gaol** (damnation). Other historic buildings in Ross include the **Macquarie Store,** the **Old Ross General Store,** and the old **Scotch Thistle Inn,** built around 1840. The Man-O-Ross is the town's best option for food of the basic counter meal variety.

The **Tasmanian Wool Centre** was built in 1988 as a bicentennial project to provide information about the wool industry. It's fitting that it should be here: The area produces some of Australia's best superfine wool, which is among the best fine wool in the world (New Zealand, on the other hand, excels at producing coarse wool). The chance to see and feel the difference between various wools and their divergent thicknesses (and leave with hands soft from lanoline) is worth the admission. In 1989, the state-record price paid for wool was set for a local bale, which fetched more than $300,000 ($3,008.50 per kilo) and was made into prestige suit lengths. An excellent crafts shop with a selection of high-quality goods is at the front of the building. ⊠ *Church St.,* ☎ *03/6381–5466.* ⊞ *$4.* ☉ *Nov.–mid-Apr., daily 9–5:30; mid-Apr.–Oct., daily 10–4.*

Lodging

$$ ▦ **Colonial Cottages of Ross.** Four self-contained cottages, built between 1830 and 1880, provide charming and historic accommodation. Apple Dumpling Cottage (circa 1880) and Hudson Cottage (circa 1850) sleep four adults; Church Mouse Cottage (circa 1840) is just for two; and Captain Samuel's Cottage (circa 1830) accommodates six or more people. Bathroom and kitchen facilities are modern. ⊠ *Church St.,* ☎ *03/6381–5354,* FAX *03/6381–5408. 4 cottages. AE, MC, V.*

$ ▦ **Ross Bakery Inn.** Right next to St. John's Church of England, this colonial sandstone building was erected in 1832 and served as the Sherwood Castle Hotel. It is now a very comfortable four-room guest house with a bakery on the premises. At breakfast you get to taste the daily bread straight from the wood-fired oven. ⊠ *Church St.,* ☎ *03/ 6381–5246,* FAX *03/6381–5360. 4 rooms. AE, MC, V.*

En Route   North of Ross, **Campbell Town** has two notable firsts. In 1877, Alfred Barret Biggs, a local schoolteacher who had read of Alexander Graham Bell's invention of the telephone in 1876, built his own telephone, partly out of Huon pine. Using the telegram line at Campbell Town railway station, Biggs called Launceston. That may have been the first telephone call in Australia—or in the Southern Hemisphere. Some of his prototype telephones are in Launceston's Queen Victoria Museum. The facts about Mr. Biggs are nebulous (he also developed telescopes) and, as he died in 1900, unlikely ever to be resolved.

In 1931, Harold Gatty, a local lad, joined American flyer Wiley Post on his record-breaking world circumnavigation (8 days, 15 hrs, 51 min, and a distance of 27,360 km, or 16,963 mi). In so doing, Gatty became the first navigator on a round-the-world flight. A metal globe in the park on the western side of the road, at the northern end of Campbell Town, commemorates his achievement.

Longford

72 km (45 mi) northwest of Ross, 212 km (131 mi) north of Hobart.

It's worth taking a short detour from the highway to visit another National Trust–designated historic site. Settled in 1813, Longford was one of northern Tasmania's first towns. Between the 1950s and the 1970s, Longford attracted interest with its auto racing road circuit, which no longer exists.

The Archer family name is all over Longford, and their legacy is in the town's buildings. Of particular early historic interest is **Christ Church,** built in 1839 and set on spacious grounds. William Archer, the first Australian-born architect (of European descent), designed the west window of the church, which is regarded as one of the country's finest. **Panshanger,** a historic, neoclassical villa, belonged to William Archer's uncle Joseph. **Brickendon** was William's father's.

Thomas Archer originally owned **Woolmers,** now one of the best preserved (and least altered) of the area's homesteads. Surprisingly, though, there are several historic country estates around Longford not built by Archers. ⊠ *Pateena Rd.,* ☎ *03/6391–1251.* 🎟 *$6.* 🕓 *Wed.–Sun. 9–5:30.*

Longford Wildlife Park is set in natural bushland, with a man-made lake, and is home to free-ranging animals, including deer. ⊠ *Pateena Rd.,* ☎ *03/6391–1630.* 🎟 *$4.* 🕓 *Tues.–Sun. 9–5.*

Lodging

$$ 🏨 **Racecourse Private Hotel.** Built in 1840 as the grand Railway Hotel in anticipation of the railway line—which took 35 years to be built and ended up bypassing Longford—this establishment catered to itinerants and elderly ladies until the 1930s. Over the years it became seedy, until a guest in the attic built himself a fire and burned down most of the house. In 1978 a couple purchased the property and spent three years rebuilding the hotel with materials from condemned buildings around town. Today, in addition to its National Trust classification and National Estate listing, the hotel also holds a World Heritage listing for its architectural and community value. The pleasant guest house has four rooms in upstairs attics and a fifth on ground level. There's a log fire in the parlor and an array of photographs depicting the hotel's checkered past. ⊠ *114 Marlborough St., 7301,* ☎ *03/6391–2352,* 𝔽𝔸𝕏 *03/6391–2430. 5 rooms. AE, DC, MC, V.*

Midlands A to Z

Arriving and Departing

BY CAR

The Midland Highway bypasses Oatlands, Ross, and Longford, which is one reason they've kept their old-fashioned characters. Oatlands is only an hour's drive from Hobart. These towns can be seen as part of a day trip from the capital or as stops along the drive between Hobart and Launceston.

Contacts and Resources

GUIDED TOURS

Fielding's Historic Tours (⊠ Oatlands, ☎ 03/6254–1135) has a daytime Convict Tour ($6), available by appointment, and an atmospheric

Ghost Tour at 9 PM ($8), which inspects Oatlands' jails and other historic buildings by lamplight.

Specialty Tours of Ross (⊠ Church St., Ross, ☎ 03/6381–5354) is operated by the informative and genial Tim Johnson, a local history buff who also runs Colonial Cottages of Ross. His Ross Historic Tour has a minimum rate of $25 for up to five people. Reservations are essential.

LAUNCESTON

Nestled in a fertile agricultural basin where the South and North Esk rivers join to form the Tamar, the city of Launceston (pronounced lon-*sess*-tun) is the commercial center of Tasmania's northern region. Its abundance of unusual markets and shops is concentrated downtown, unlike Hobart's gathering of shops in its historic center, set apart from the commercial district. Launceston is far from bustling, and is remarkable for its pleasant parks, turn-of-the-century homes, historic mansions, and private gardens. Perhaps its most compelling asset is the magnificent scenery on which it verges: rolling farmland and the rich loam of English-looking landscapes powerfully set off by the South Esk meandering through towering gorges.

Exploring Launceston

Aside from its parks and gardens, Launceston's main appeal is the sumptuous surrounding countryside.

Almost in the heart of the city, **Cataract Gorge** is one of the most spectacular sights in Australia. The South Esk River flows through the gorge on its way toward the Tamar River. A 1½-km (1-mi) path leads along the face of the precipices to the Cliff Grounds Reserve, where picnic tables, a pool, and a restaurant are located. The park itself looks like a botanic garden, with peacocks strutting through the open lawns and ornate gazebos. Take the chairlift in the first basin for a thrilling aerial view of the gorge. Just over 1,000 ft, it is the longest single chairlift span in the world. Several self-guided nature trails wind through the park as well. ⊠ *Paterson St., at Kings Bridge,* ☎ *03/6331–5915.* 🎫 *Chairlift $5.* ☉ *Daily 9–4:40.*

Trevallyn Dam, on the western outskirts of Launceston, is in a stunning wildlife preserve. Boating down the South Esk River is common here, but for a unique adventure, try **cable hang gliding**—a 650-ft flight from the edge of a 60-ft cliff. Strapped into a harness and hooked onto a cable, you'll have the thrill of hang gliding with none of the risks. An 85-year-old woman has taken the ride, as has the owner's dog! ⊠ *Trevallyn Dam Rd.,* ☎ *03/6330–1567.* 🎫 *$9.* ☉ *Dec.–Apr., daily 10–5; May–Nov., weekends and holidays 10–4.*

The **Queen Victoria Museum,** opened in 1891 in honor of Queen Victoria's Golden Jubilee, combines items of Tasmanian historical interest with natural history. The museum has a large collection of stuffed birds and animals (including the now-extinct thylacine, or Tasmanian wolf), as well as a Chinese Joss House and a display of coins. ⊠ *Wellington and Paterson Sts.,* ☎ *03/6331–6777.* 🎫 *Free.* ☉ *Mon.–Sat. 10–5, Sun. 2–5.*

☺ The **Penny Royal World and Gunpowder Mill** is the closest thing to a large amusement park in Tasmania, and families can easily spend an entire day here. Rides in sailboats, barges, and trams are included in the ticket price, as are exhibits in the various buildings. Inspect the foundry, museum, and historic gunpowder mills, where cannons are periodically fired. Admission includes a ride on the quaint paddle steamer MV *Lady Stelfox* (☎ 03/6331–6699), which cruises up the Cataract Gorge and into the River Tamar. A licensed bar and other refreshments are on board; departures are every hour daily, 10:10–3:10. ✉ *Paterson St.*, ☎ *03/6331–6699*. 🎟 *$19.50; $6.50 for steamer ride only.* ⊙ *Daily 9–4:30.*

OFF THE BEATEN PATH	**WAVERLY WOOLLEN MILLS –** These mills on the North Esk River are still powered by a waterwheel. Opened in 1874, they take pride in using only the finest Tasmanian wool. A store on the premises sells products made in the mills. ✉ *Tasman Hwy. and Waverly Rd.*, ☎ *03/6339–1106.* 🎟 *$4.* ⊙ *Weekdays 9–5.*

Dining

$$$ ✕ **Fee and Me.** One of Tasmania's top dining venues, Fee and Me has
★ won more culinary accolades than you could poke a mixing spoon at. "Fee" is the talented chef, Fiona Hoskin, who creates the wonderful food served here. You might begin with Tasmanian Pacific oysters or chicken dumplings in a fragrant broth. Delectable mains include steamed mussels in a rich tomato broth, roasted quail on potato straws with honeyed chili sauce, and roasted loin of Tasmanian venison. Finally, sink your teeth into a chocolate globe filled with chocolate and banana mousse and rum sauce. The licensed restaurant serves wine from Australia's top vineyards; note the fine selection of local and nationally acclaimed wines. Over the years the stately colonial structure has housed a hospital, a doctor's office, a guest house, a ladies' school, and Red Cross quarters. ✉ *190 Charles St.*, ☎ *03/6331–3195. Reservations essential. Jacket required. AE, MC, V. Closed Sun.*

$$$ ✕ **The Terrace.** The Country Club Casino's spacious restaurant was designed for the privacy of its diners. Tables, each with a silver champagne bucket, are separated by low walls. Specialties include smoked duck breast, local scallops, and Atlantic salmon. Steaks are served panfried or au poivre. Special fixed-price dinners include tickets to the evening's cabaret show. ✉ *Country Club Ave., Prospect Vale*, ☎ *03/6344–8855. Jacket and tie. AE, DC, MC, V. Closed Sun.–Mon.*

$$ ✕ **Shrimps.** For the best selection of seafood in Launceston, this is the place. This brick convict-built 1824 building was formerly a candy shop and then a private home. The tables are small and widely spaced, and the blackboard menu might feature oysters, trevalla, whitebait (a minnow-sized delicacy), mussels, and abalone fresh from the restaurant's tank. ✉ *72 George St.*, ☎ *03/6334–0584. AE, DC, MC, V. Closed Sun.*

$ ✕ **Posh Nosh.** This noisy, aromatic deli has some of the best and cheap-
★ est food in Launceston. Everything is served fresh or made on premises. A delightful place for lunch, specialties include King Island Brie with smoked beef and a gourmet ploughman's lunch of sea trout. Try the fresh salads and the sumptuous focaccia filled with local produce. You can request a selection of goodies to take away for a picnic in one of Launceston's beautiful parks—the perfect way to spend an afternoon. Although the restaurant doesn't have a liquor license, patrons may bring their own beer, wine, and spirits. ✉ *127 St. John St.*, ☎ *03/6331–9180. AE, MC, V. BYOB. Open until 5:30. Closed weekends.*

$ ✕ **Ripples.** Part of Ritchie's Mill Arts Centre and directly across from the Penny Royal World, this tiny tearoom is a pleasant lunch or afternoon stopover. It serves the best pancakes and crepes in town and fine coffee. ✉ *Paterson St.*, ☎ *03/6331–4153. No credit cards. No dinner.*

Lodging

$$$$ ⊞ **Country Club Casino.** This luxury property on the outskirts of Launceston is decorated in soft pastels of gray, blue, and pink. The curved driveway to the club is lined with flowers and manicured gardens, and the championship golf course is one of the best in Australia. The club offers gambling, dancing, and cabaret shows at night. ⊠ *Country Club Ave., Prospect Vale, 7250,* ☎ *03/6344–8855 or 1800/03–0211,* FAX *03/6343–1880. 88 rooms, 16 suites. Restaurant, room service, indoor pool, sauna, spa, 18-hole golf course, tennis court, horseback riding, squash, casino, dance club. AE, DC, MC, V.*

$$$ ⊞ **Launceston Novotel.** This six-story building in the heart of Launceston was designed with elegance in mind. When empty, however, the soaring marble foyer can appear quite daunting. Guest rooms are comfortable, decorated in pastels with light-color furniture. Lower floors can be noisy from street activity, so ask for a room on a higher floor— but don't expect a view. Adjacent is Yorktown Mall, Launceston's major shopping zone. ⊠ *29 Cameron St., 7250,* ☎ *03/6334–3434 or 1800/ 03–0123,* FAX *03/6331–7347. 165 rooms, 7 suites. 3 restaurants, bar, room service, laundry service. AE, DC, MC, V.*

$$ ⊞ **Alice's Place.** Constructed from the remains of three buildings erected during the 1840s, this delightful cottage is best known for its whimsical touches. The drawers of the antique furniture might contain old-fashioned eyeglasses or books; an old turtle shell and a deer's head hang on the wall; and an old Victrola and a four-poster canopy bed lend colonial charm. Modern conveniences are cleverly tucked away among the period furnishings—take a bath in a huge old tub and then dry your hair with an electric dryer. ⊠ *17 York St., 7250,* ☎ *03/6334– 2231,* FAX *03/6334–2696. 1 unit sleeps 4. AE, MC, V.*

$$ ⊞ **O'Hara's Resort Hotel.** A stone's throw from the Country Club Casino, this moderately priced complex contains holiday villas with fully equipped kitchens. Perfect for families, each wood- and brick-lined unit has unobtrusive furnishings with simple bedding, matching curtains, and large picture windows. Guests can play golf on the country club's course and use its other facilities. ⊠ *10 Casino Rise, 7250,* ☎ *03/6343– 1744,* FAX *03/6344–9943. 55 villas. Restaurant, kitchenettes, pool, tennis court. AE, DC, MC, V.*

$$ ★   ⊞ **Old Bakery Inn.** Guests in this colonial complex can choose from three areas: a converted stable, the former baker's cottage, or the old bakery. A loft above the stables is also available. All rooms are decorated in colonial style, with antique furniture and lace curtains. One room in the old bakery was actually the oven—its walls are 2 ft thick. ⊠ *York and Margaret Sts., 7250,* ☎ *03/6331–7900,* FAX *03/6331– 7756. 24 rooms. Restaurant. AE, MC, V.*

$$ ★   ⊞ **Prince Albert Inn.** First opened in 1855, the inn shines like a gem in the lackluster downtown. Crossing the threshold of an Italianate facade, you'll enter a Victorian time warp, where wall-to-wall portraits of British royalty hang in the plush dining room. Renovations in seven of the guest rooms have not broken the spell; lace curtains, velvet drapery, and fluffy comforters maintain the atmosphere and maximize comfort. Smoking is not allowed. ⊠ *Tamar and William Sts., 7250,* ☎ *03/6331–1931,* FAX *03/6334–1579. 22 rooms. AE, DC, MC, V.*

Nightlife and the Arts

The **Country Club Casino** has blackjack, American roulette, minibaccarat, keno, minidice, federal and stud poker, federal wheel, and two-up. There is also late-night dancing. ⊠ *Country Club Ave., Prospect Vale 7250,* ☎ *03/6344–8855.* ☉ *Mon.–Thurs. 1 PM–3 AM, Fri. and Sat. 1 PM–4 AM, Sun. noon–3 AM.*

There is no cover charge at **Regine's Discotheque,** also at the casino. ⊙ *Wed., Thurs., and Sun.* 9 PM–4 AM, *Fri. and Sat.* 10 PM–5 AM.

The **Silverdome** (⊠ Bass Hwy., ☎ 03/6344–9988) holds regular concerts—everything from classical to heavy metal. The **Princess Theatre** (⊠ Brisbane St., ☎ 03/6337–1270 or 03/6326–3384) features local and imported stage productions.

Shopping

Launceston is a convenient place for a little shopping, with most stores centrally located on George Street and in nearby Yorktown Mall. Some of the better arts-and-crafts stores include **National Trust Old Umbrella Shop** (⊠ 60 George St., ☎ 03/6331–9248), **Design Centre of Tasmania** (⊠ Brisbane and Tamar Sts., ☎ 03/6331–5506), **Emma's Arts** (⊠ 78 George St., ☎ 03/6331–5630), and **Gallery Two at Ritchie's Mill Arts Centre** (⊠ 2 Bridge Rd., ☎ 03/6331–2339). **The Sheep's Back** (⊠ 53 George St., ☎ 03/6331–2539) sells woolen products exclusively.

Sports

Details about upcoming sporting events, including cricket and Australian-rules football, can be found in the Friday *Examiner.*

Launceston A to Z

Arriving and Departing

BY BUS

Hobart Coaches (☎ 03/6334–3600) and **Tasmanian Redline Coaches** (⊠ 112 George St., ☎ 03/6331–3233 or 1300/30–0520) serve Launceston from Devonport, Burnie, and Hobart.

BY CAR

Highway 1 connects Launceston with Hobart three hours to the south and with Devonport 1½ hours to the northwest.

BY PLANE

The Launceston airport is served by several domestic airlines, including **Airlines of Tasmania, Ansett Australia,** and **Qantas.** *See* Air Travel *in* Smart Travel Tips for information on airlines.

Getting Around

BY BICYCLE

Rent bicycles from the **Youth Hostel** (⊠ 36 Thistle St., ☎ 03/6344–9779) for $11 per day for a touring bike, or $18 per day for a mountain bike. Costs per week are respectively $65 and $95.

BY TAXI

Central Cabs (☎ 03/6331–3555) and **Taxi Combined** (☎ 03/6331–5555) can be hailed in the street or booked by phone.

Contacts and Resources

CAR RENTAL

Cars, campers, caravans, and minibuses are available for hire at several agencies in Launceston: **Avis** (☎ 03/6391–8314 or 1800/22–5533), **Autorent Hertz** (☎ 03/6335–1111), **Budget** (☎ 03/6334–0099), and **Colonial Thrifty** (☎ 03/6391–8105).

EMERGENCIES

Ambulance, police, and fire brigade: ☎ 000. **Hospitals: Launceston General** (⊠ Charles St., ☎ 03/6332–7111), **St. Luke's Hospital** (⊠ 24 Lyttleton St., ☎ 03/6331–3255, and **St. Vincent's Hospital** (⊠ 5 Frederick St., ☎ 03/6331–4444).

Orientation Tours. A **City Sights** (✉ St. John and Paterson Sts., ☎ 03/
6336–3122; 🎫 $19, 🕐 Nov.–Apr., twice daily) tour of Launceston by
replica tram may be booked through the Tasmanian Travel and Information Centre (☞ *below*). **Launceston Historic Walks** (☎ 03/6331–
3679) conducts a leisurely stroll ($10) through the historic heart of the
city. Walks leave from the Tasmanian Travel and Information Centre
(☞ *below*) weekdays at 9:45.

Outdoor Adventure Tours. Tasmanian Wilderness Travel (☎ 03/6334–
4442) leads day tours to Cradle Mountain and the Tamar Valley, from
$39.

The **Tasmanian Travel and Information Centre.** (✉ St. John and Paterson Sts., ☎ 03/6336–3122) is open weekdays 9–5 and Saturday 9–
noon.

NORTHWEST COAST

The Northwest Coast of Tasmania is one of the most exciting and least
known areas of the state. Most of the local inhabitants are farmers,
anglers, or lumberjacks—they're a hardy bunch, but they're also some
of the friendliest folk in Tasmania. The rugged coastline here has long
been the solitary haunt of abalone hunters, and from the area's lush
grazing land comes some of Australia's best beef and cheese. Tasmanian farmers are the only legal growers of opium poppies (for medic-
inal use) in the Southern Hemisphere, and fields in the northwest are
blanketed with their striking red flowers.

Devonport

*89 km (55 mi) northwest of Launceston, 289 km (179 mi) northwest
of Hobart.*

In the middle of the north coast, Devonport is a sleepy town that's more
used to serving local farmers than tourists. In today's world, you might
find that this is just what you're looking for. It is also the Tasmanian
port where the ferry from Melbourne docks (☞ Northwest Coast A
to Z, *below*).

Stop at the **Tiagarra Aboriginal Cultural and Art Centre** to see remnants
of Tasmania's Aboriginal past, including more than 250 images of rock
engravings. ✉ *Mersey Bluff*, ☎ *03/6424–8250.* 🎫 *$3.* 🕐 *Daily 9–5.*

Dining and Lodging
$ ✕ **Rialto Gallery.** Simple pasta dishes are the orders of the day at this
Venetian-style Italian restaurant. Cream-based sauces are favored.
Other entrées include such classics as veal scaloppine. ✉ *159 Rooke
St.,* ☎ *03/6424–6793. AE, DC, MC, V. No lunch weekends.*

$$ ✕🏨 **Lighthouse Hotel.** This contemporary, salmon-pink building with
★ an enclosed garden atrium is an unexpected delight in the small coastal
town of Ulverstone. Predominantly blue guest rooms are furnished with
blond-wood pieces. The international cuisine at the Atrium Restaurant
($$), the resident bistro, features provincial produce in a changing menu.
✉ *33 Victoria St., at Reiby St., 21 km (13 mi) from Devonport, Ul-
verstone 7315,* ☎ *03/6425–1197,* 📠 *03/6425–5973. 28 rooms. Restaurant, sauna, spa, exercise room. AE, MC, V.*

Shopping
For a large selection of Australian colonial, English, and country cot-
tage furniture and antiques, go to **Thomsons of Devonport** (✉ 13
Formby Rd., ☎ 03/6424–8360).

En Route Head west on Bass Highway toward Burnie. If you have time, stop in at **Penguin,** a charming little town with little penguin statues for litter baskets on its sidewalks. It's a quintessential small town where the milk bar is larger than the nearest pub. From Penguin the road leads through the Table Cape region to Wynyard, passing through rich farm country and gentle, rolling hills.

Boat Harbour

180 km (112 mi) northwest of Launceston, 342 km (212 mi) northwest of Hobart.

Continue west on the Bass Highway past Wynyard to **Boat Harbour.** This secluded area, popular with summer vacationers, rarely gets cold, even in winter.

OFF THE BEATEN PATH — Beyond Boat Harbour near Sisters Beach is the 10-acre **Birdland Native Gardens,** where you can see native Tasmanian birds flying in open aviaries. The picnic grounds here are a fine spot for lunch and afternoon barbecues. ⊠ *Wattle Ave.,* ☎ *03/6445–1270.* ⌨ *$2.* ☉ *Daily 9–5.*

Dining

$ ✕ **Jacobs Restaurant.** For a tiny settlement, this establishment is a remarkable find with exceptional fare. Local seafood, including oysters and crayfish, are specialties—as are unusual game dishes such as emu. ⊠ *Bass Hwy.,* ☎ *03/6445–1107. AE, MC, V.*

Stanley

140 km (87 mi) west of Devonport, 430 km (267 mi) northwest of Hobart.

★ The famous **Nut**—Tasmania's version of Uluru (Ayers Rock)—is in Stanley. Perched at the northernmost point of mainland Tasmania, the Nut, a sheer volcanic plug some 12½ million years old, is almost totally surrounded by the sea. Visitors can either tackle the steep 20-minute climb or take a chairlift ($4 one way, $6 round-trip) to the summit. From the top, walking trails lead in all directions. Contact **Nut Chairlifts** (⊠ Box 43, 7331, ☎ 03/6458–1286) for information.

Stanley, the town at the foot of the Nut, is one of the prettiest villages in Tasmania and a must for anyone traveling in the northwest. It is filled with historic cottages, friendly tearooms, unique shops, and country inns.

Dining

$ ✕ **Hursey Seafoods.** Some say the best fish and chips in Tasmania are found at this place, which comprises a casual downstairs café, a more formal upstairs space, and a takeout counter. You can choose your fish and shellfish from tanks at the shop. You might try muttonbird (shearwater), a local specialty, but not everyone appreciates its oily, gamey taste. ⊠ *2 Alexander Terr.,* ☎ *03/6458–1103. MC, V.*

Lodging

$ ▥ **Touchwood Cottage.** Built in 1840, this is one of Stanley's oldest homes, and it's furnished with plenty of period pieces. The product of an architect's whimsy (or incompetence), the cottage is known for its doorways of different sizes and oddly shaped living room. The hosts are welcoming and afternoon tea is served on arrival. The cottage is ideally located near the Nut and the popular Touchwood crafts shop, where guests receive a discount. ⊠ *33 Church St., 7331,* ☎ *03/6458–1348. 3 rooms without bath. MC, V.*

Shopping

The **Plough Inn** (⊠ 35 Church St., ☎ 03/6458–1226) has a collection of handicrafts and antiques. **Touchwood Quality Crafts** (⊠ Church St., ☎ 03/6458–1348) has one of the finest selections of Tasmanian crafts in the state.

Smithton

140 km (87 mi) west of Devonport, 510 km (316 mi) northwest of Hobart.

You're climbing out on a limb for natural beauty when you go to Smithton, because the town itself has few attractions. Travelers come here to get away, to venture outdoors in remote places, and to explore the rugged Northwest Coast. Two nature reserves in the area, **Julius River** and **Milkshakes Hills,** are worth visiting.

Dining and Lodging

$$–$$$ ✕🖭 **Tall Timbers.** This lodge is one of the finest establishments in the
★   northwest. Built with Tasmanian wood, the main house has a cozy bar and two restaurants, one for formal dining and the other a huge bistro. In a separate Tasmanian-wood building, rooms are simply decorated and equipped with the latest energy-saving devices. The staff is young, energetic, and friendly. The restaurant, **Grey's Fine Dining,** has high ceilings, plank walls, and rafters made from Tasmanian timber. Specialties include rock crayfish, chicken breast, rabbit hot pot, Atlantic salmon, and crêpes suzette for dessert. ⊠ *Scotchtown Rd., Box 304, Smithton 7330,* ☎ *03/6452–2755 or 1800/03–0300,* ℻ *03/6452–2742. 32 units. 2 restaurants, bar. AE, DC, MC, V.*

En Route   **Allendale Gardens,** south of Smithton, were cultivated as a hobby and have come to rival the Royal Botanic Gardens in Hobart. Around each corner of these private gardens is a surprise: a cluster of native Tasmanian ferns or a thicket of shrubs and flowers. Forest walks of 10–25 minutes' duration take you past trees more than 500 years old. The gardens are filled with more birds than you're likely to see in other areas of Tasmania. ⊠ *Eurebia, Edith Creek, 14 km (9 mi) from Smithton,* ☎ *03/6456–4216.* 🎟 *$5.* ☉ *Sept.–May, daily 9–6.*

Northwest Coast A to Z

Arriving and Departing

BY BUS

Hobart Coaches has offices in Devonport (⊠ King St., Devonport, ☎ 03/6424–6599) and Burnie (⊠ 54 Cattley St., Burnie, ☎ 03/6431–1971).

Tasmanian Redline Coaches has offices in Devonport (⊠ 9 Edward St., Devonport, ☎ 03/6424–5100); Burnie (⊠ 117 Wilson St., Burnie, ☎ 03/6431–3233); Smithton (⊠ 19 Smith St., Smithton, ☎ 03/6452–1262); and Queenstown (⊠ Orr St., Queenstown, ☎ 03/6471–1011).

BY FERRY

The *Spirit of Tasmania* makes the 14-hour trip from Melbourne to Devonport three times a week. The ferry carries 1,278 passengers and up to 490 cars. Cabin rates range from $550 to $190 each way, with suites from $225, in low season (April 18–September 24). Ferrying a car costs between $30 and $40 each way. Facilities include children's playrooms, gift shops, and several restaurants and bars. Advance bookings are essential. The company's new catamaran, the *Devil Cat,* cuts the crossing time in half. Cost is $179 per adult, $40 per car in high season, and $160 per adult, $30 per car in shoulder season. The "Cat" only runs between December 12 and April 14. ⊠ *Box 323, Port Mel-*

bourne, VIC 3207; ⊠ *Box 168E, East Devonport, TAS 7310,* ☎ *13–2010;* FAX *1800/63–6110.*

BY PLANE

Devonport and Wynyard are served by several domestic airlines, including **Airlines of Tasmania** and **Kendell Airlines.** *See* Air Travel *in* Smart Travel Tips for information on airlines.

Getting Around

BY BICYCLE

Rent bicycles in Devonport at **Hire a Bike** (⊠ 51 Raymond Ave., ☎ 03/6424–3889).

BY CAR

Many of the northwest roads are twisty and even unpaved in the more remote areas. A few may require four-wheel-drive vehicles; however, two-wheel-drive is sufficient for most touring. Be prepared for sudden weather changes—this is one of the colder parts of Tasmania, and snow in the summertime is not uncommon.

Contacts and Resources

CAR RENTALS

Cars, campers, and minibuses are available for rent in Devonport, Burnie, and Wynyard. The numbers of the following companies are for their offices in Devonport: **Autorent Hertz** (☎ 03/6424–1013), **Avis** (☎ 03/6427–9797), **Budget** (☎ 03/6424–7088), **Colonial Thrifty** (☎ 03/6427–9119).

EMERGENCIES

Ambulance, fire brigade, and police: ☎ 000.

GUIDED TOURS

Bass Flight Services conducts scenic flights that depart from both Cradle Valley and Devonport. Tours take visitors over the valley and across to Barn Bluff, Mt. Ossa, the Acropolis, Lake St. Clair, Mt. Olympus, and other sights in the area. Doors on the planes are removable for photography. Thirty- to 90-minute flights are available. ⊠ *Cradle Valley,* ☎ *03/6492–1132;* ⊠ *East Devonport Airport, Devonport,* ☎ *03/6427–9777.*

VISITOR INFORMATION

Tasmanian Travel and Information Centre has offices in Devonport (⊠ 5 Best St., Devonport, ☎ 03/6424–4466) and Burnie (⊠ 48 Civic Sq., off Little Alexander St., Burnie, ☎ 03/6434–6111).

WEST COAST

The wildest and least explored countryside in Australia lies on Tasmania's west coast. Much of the land is national park, and most has been protected only after fierce battles between conservationists, loggers, and the state and federal governments. Strahan is the only town of any size on the west coast, and it is the center for cruises on the pristine Gordon River to Macquarie Harbor, where the cruel, remote Sarah Island penal settlement was established in 1821 and closed in 1834. Convicts worked in hellish conditions here to log valuable Huon pine for ships and furniture.

Strahan

305 km (189 mi) northwest of Hobart.

This lovely, lazy fishing port has one of the deepest harbors in the world and a population under 500. It used to be a major port for mining companies, and its waters are still brown from the effect of ore mixing with tannin from surrounding vegetation. The town sits on the edge of Macquarie Harbor, and mixes a still-active fishing industry with tourism. The foreshore walking track gives an excellent view of Strahan's delightful setting. Cruises along the Gordon River to the ravishingly beautiful World Heritage Site of **Franklin-Gordon Wild Rivers National Park** constitute the main tourist activity here.

Strahan Wharf Centre is both a visitors center and a museum that concentrates on local subjects and is not afraid to tackle such controversial issues as past conservation battles over the Gordon River and the fate of Tasmania's Aborigines. ✉ *Strahan Rd.,* ☎ *03/6471–7488.* 🖭 *Museum $4.50.* ⊙ *Daily 10–6.*

Gordon River Cruises has two half-day trips daily that travel 24 km (15 mi) up Macquarie Harbour and the Gordon River, and a daily, summer-only, full-day tour that includes lunch. An informative commentary accompanies the trip past historic Sarah Island and clusters of tea, melaleuca, sassafrass, and Huon pine trees. You can disembark at Heritage Landing and take a half-hour walk through the vegetation. Reservations are essential. ✉ *Box 40, 7468,* ☎ *03/6471–7187.* 🖭 *Full-day $62, half-day $44.*

West Coast Yacht Charters has daily twilight cruises on Macquarie Harbour aboard the 60-ft ketch *Stormbreaker,* that include a dinner of the famed local crayfish ($45). The company also operates a two-day sailing excursion ($290), a morning fishing trip (a negotiable $35, including gear, bait, and morning tea), and overnight cruises on the Gordon River ($80, all meals included). The latter sail to Sir John Falls, a trip designed to pick up white-water rafters from the Franklin River, but on which passengers from Strahan are welcome. ✉ *Esplanade, 7468,* ☎ *03/6471–7422.*

World Heritage Cruises's MV *Heritage Wanderer* sails daily from mid-August until June, leaving Strahan Wharf at 9 AM and returning at 4:30 PM. Meals and drinks are available on board. The leisurely journey pauses at Sarah Island, Heritage Landing, and the Saphia Ocean Trout Farm on Macquarie Harbour. ✉ *Box 93, 7468,* ☎ *03/6471–7174,* 🅵🅰🆇 *03/ 6471–7431.* 🖭 *$42.*

Dining and Lodging

$$ ✕ **Hamers Hotel.** The crayfish salad at this hotel is legendary ($27 for a half cray, $45 for a whole). However, if you prefer other seafood and steak, the food is better than most pub counter meals for about the same price. Dessert includes a choice of fresh cakes. ✉ *Esplanade,* ☎ *03/6471–7191. MC, V.*

$$$ 🏨 **Franklin Manor.** When it was converted in 1990 from a private home into a guest house, the Manor immediately became *the* place to stay in Strahan. Set in gardens near the harbor, it has open fires and a relaxing lounge. Rooms have TVs, phones, and heated towel rails. The restaurant is known for its refined, comfortable ambience. An à la carte menu includes lobster, oysters, pot-roasted quail, and sea trout. ✉ *Esplanade, 7468,* ☎ *03/6471–7311. 13 rooms. Restaurant, bar, spa. AE, DC, MC, V.*

$$ 🏨 **Strahan Motor Inn.** The most popular hotel in Strahan is only 1,800 ft from the Gordon River cruise dock and includes an annex. Ask for rooms in the main building overlooking the harbor; those in the annex have limited views and are noisier. Colonial furniture and beds with quilt coverings create a welcoming ambience. ✉ *Jolly St., Strahan 7468,* ☎ *03/6471–7160. 61 rooms. Restaurant. AE, DC, MC, V.*

Zeehan

72 km (45 mi) north of Strahan, 375 km (233 mi) northwest of Hobart.

During the past century, silver-lode discoveries transformed Zeehan into one of the state's largest towns—it once had 26 hotels—but some 25 years later deposits started to run out, and Zeehan went the way of many failed mining towns.

A drive along Main Street takes you past the transient splendor of the Grand Hotel and the Gaiety Theatre; both buildings now belong to the **West Coast Pioneers' Memorial Museum** and stand empty, awaiting renovation. The museum itself, in the historic old School of Mines Building, has an excellent mineral exhibit among its collections. ⊠ *Main St.,* ☎ *03/6471–6225.* ☉ *Apr.–Oct., daily 8:30–5; Nov.–Mar., daily 8:30–6.*

For pub food, the **Cecil Hotel** (Main St., ☎ 03/6471–6221) serves hearty fare at reasonable prices.

En Route   A brief detour from the highway route between Strahan and Zeehan takes you to **Queenstown,** set amid one of the most shocking landscapes on earth. Decades of mining have stripped the earth of all vegetation (although some replanting is going on), leaving a stark, unearthly scene.

West Coast A to Z

Arriving and Departing

BY CAR

The West Coast is a long way from everywhere. The road from Hobart winds from the lowlands into the high country, with excellent views of Lake St. Clair and the distant mountains of central Tasmania. From the north, the highway snakes down to Zeehan, with an alternative sandy track (usually passable with a conventional vehicle) between Zeehan and Strahan.

Getting Around

BY BOAT

Cruises are the only way for most people to get a taste of the west coast's stunning wilderness. Exploration along the Gordon River is deliberately slow, so as not to erode the fragile riverbanks and damage the ecosystem conservationists fought so hard to preserve.

BY CAR

A vehicle is absolutely essential for moving from place to place on the west coast.

Contacts and Resources

EMERGENCIES

Ambulance, fire brigade, and police: ☎ 000.

GUIDED TOURS

Wilderness Air (☎ 03/6471–7280) flies seaplanes from Strahan Wharf over Frenchman's Cap, the Franklin and Gordon rivers, Lake Pedder, and Hells Gates, with a landing at Sir John Falls. It's a great way to see the area's peaks, lakes, coast, and rivers.

CENTRAL TASMANIAN NATIONAL PARKS

Cradle Mountain–Lake St. Clair National Park

★ Cradle Mountain–Lake St. Clair National Park contains the most spectacular alpine scenery in Tasmania and the top mountain trails in Australia. Popular with hikers of all levels of ability, the park has several high peaks, including Mt. Ossa, the highest in Tasmania (more than 5,300 ft). The Cradle Mountain section of the park lies in the north, where the Waldheim Chalet, built by the park's founder, Gustav Weindorfer, stands guard over the valley below.

The southern section of the park, Lake St. Clair, is popular not only for boat trips but also for trails that circumnavigate the lake. Trout fishing is permitted with a license, and boat trips can be arranged from Cynthia Bay.

It is impossible to visit the park without hearing of the **Overland Track**: One of the most famous trails in Australia, it traverses 85 km (53 mi) between the park's north and south boundaries. More than 200 people per week hike the trail, which has several basic sleeping huts that are available on a first-come, first-served basis. Because space in the huts is limited, hikers are advised to bring their own tents. If you prefer to do the walk in comfort, there are also well-equipped, heated private structures managed by Cradle Mountain Huts (☞ Chapter 12).

The toughest part of the Overland is in the northern section of the park where most hikers begin the moderately steep climb of Cradle Mountain that must be made on the first day. The climbing is not nearly as difficult to bear as the weather, however. Even in summer, frequent storms are guaranteed to douse hikers. The trail, which takes between 5 and 10 days to traverse, passes over and around many of the mountains and lakes in the park as well as through temperate rain forest. The park also contains many rewarding shorter trails.

Dining and Lodging

Caravan, car, and bus campgrounds are 2 km (1 mi) north of the park and provide showers, toilets, laundry facilities, and cooking shelters with electric barbecues. Usage is free. Tent sites cost $5–$8 per person, per night. Bunkhouse accommodations are $16–$20 per person, per night. Sites with electrical hookup are $8–$10 per person, per night. Advance booking is essential (☎ 03/6492–1395).

$$$ ✕☎ **Cradle Mountain Lodge.** This wilderness lodge gave birth to a genre
★ in Australia, and it is the most comfortable place to stay at Cradle Mountain. Accommodations are not luxurious, but they are homey. The high-ceiling guest rooms, two per cabin, each have their own kitchenette and are cheerfully decorated. The environment is what counts here, and it is magnificent—many walking trails begin at the lodge door. After a good meal in the dining room, you can walk outside to watch a gathering of Tasmania's wildlife dine on the lodge's leftovers. Meals are not included in room rates. ✉ *Box 153, Sheffield 7306,* ☎ *03/6492–1303,* ℻ *03/6492–1309. 77 rooms. Dining room, kitchenettes. MC, V.*

Arriving and Departing

BY BUS

Tasmanian Wilderness Transport & Tours (☎ 03/6334–4442) runs to Cradle Mountain from Devonport, Strahan, and Launceston. It also serves Lake St. Clair from Launceston, Devonport, and Hobart. **Tasmanian Redline Coaches** (☎ 03/6234–4577) operates buses daily (except Sunday) from Hobart and Queenstown to Derwent Bridge, near the park entrance.

BY CAR

Lake St. Clair is 173 km (107 mi) from Hobart and can be reached via the Lyell Highway, or from Launceston via Deloraine or Poatina. **Cradle Mountain** is 85 km (53 mi) south of Devonport and can be reached by car via Claude Road from Sheffield or via Wilmot. Both lead 30 km (19 mi) along Route C132 to Cradle Valley. The last 10 km (6 mi) are unpaved.

Visitor Information

For more information, contact **Cradle Mountain National Park** (✉ Box 20, Sheffield 7306, ☎ 03/6492–1133) or **Lake St. Clair National Park** (✉ Derwent Bridge 7465, ☎ 03/6289–1172).

Mt. Field National Park

The first national park created in Tasmania, Mt. Field still ranks as the most popular among Tasmanians and visitors alike. The park's easily navigable trails, picnic areas, and well-maintained campsites are ideal for family outings. Animals, including wallabies and Tasmanian devils, are often out and about around dusk.

Some 80 km (50 mi) northwest of Hobart, the park contains the most popular ski area in southern Tasmania. Located on Mt. Mawson, it has challenging trails for cross-country skiers and some downhill skiing. For walkers, however, summer is the best time to visit. The most popular trail is the **Russell Falls Nature Walk**. This 1-km (½-mi) path is paved part of the way and is suitable for wheelchairs. Numbered pegs inform walkers about vegetation along the route. The path leads bushwalkers from eucalyptus forest into temperate rain forest and ends at Russell Falls. Along the way, the trail passes the tallest hardwood trees in the world, a variety of eucalyptus known as mountain ash (locally as swamp gum), some of which tower more than 325 ft.

Lodging

A campground and a caravan park, equipped with toilets, hot water, showers, and laundry facilities, are near the entrance to Mt. Field. Firewood is provided free of charge. Fees are $10 for a campsite and $12 for a powered site for two. Minimal grocery supplies may be purchased at the kiosk near the caravan park. Wilderness huts are on certain trails throughout the park. They cost $20 for two adults.

Arriving and Departing

From Hobart, drive north on the Lyell Highway and then west on Maydena Road. Scheduled buses leave Hobart for the park weekdays, except public holidays.

Visitor Information

You can contact **Mt. Field National Park** (✉ Box 41, Westerway 7140, ☎ 03/6288–1149).

SOUTHWEST NATIONAL PARK

The largest park in Tasmania, Southwest encompasses the entire southwestern portion of the state, connecting with Franklin-Gordon Wild Rivers, Cradle Mountain–Lake St. Clair, and the Walls of Jerusalem national parks to create an unsurpassed wilderness area. One of the few virgin land tracts in Australia unaffected by human tampering, the Southwest National Park has trees topping 300 ft in a dense, temperate rain forest. Indeed, its five mountain ranges and more than 50 lakes were unknown to all but the most avid bushwalkers until the park gained notoriety in 1974 with the drowning of Lake Pedder. The lake was flooded to boost the power of a nearby hydroelectric dam, and it is now about 25 times the size of the original. Conservationists still argue for the lake's draining and restoration, but it seems a forlorn hope.

The only vehicle route into the park passes through the towns of Maydena and Strathgordon before plunging into rain forest and past rock formations dating back more than 500 million years.

Southwest is a park for the hardiest of travelers. Only one trail, the seven- to nine-day **Western Arthurs Transverse,** is well marked. Parts of it require short ascents, best made with ropes, up steep gullies and cliff faces. The hike should not be attempted by anyone who minds being wet and cold, because the park is often hit with violent storms, even in summer. Do not embark on walks in the park without registering (and logging out) with the **Tasmanian Police** (☎ 03/6230–2111) in Hobart. Admission is $2 per car.

Lodging
Free campsites are available at Lake Pedder, Scott's Peak Dam, and Edgar Dam. Gas, food, and accommodations are available in Strathgordon.

Arriving and Departing
BY BUS
A regularly scheduled minibus is available from **Tasmanian Wilderness Transport and Tours** (☎ 03/6334–4442 or 1800/03–0505) in Hobart on Tuesday, Thursday, and weekends from December through March. The cost is $35 one way or $65 round-trip.

BY CAR
Southwest National Park is 174 km (108 mi) from Hobart and only can be reached by car from the north via Strathgordon Road. The route passes through Maydena to Frodshams Pass, where a left turn leads to Scott's Peak Road and the park.

BY PLANE
Two companies provide air service into the park at Cox Bight and Melaleuca: **Par Avion** (☎ 03/6248–5390) and **TASAIR** (☎ 03/6248–5088).

Visitor Information
Try contacting **Southwest National Park** (✉ Box 41, Westerway 7140, ☎ 03/6233–6191) for more information.

6 QUEENSLAND

A fusion of Florida, Las Vegas, and the Caribbean, Queensland is a mecca for crowd lovers and escapists alike, whether you wish to be awash in the Coral Sea, to stroll from cabana to casino with your favorite cocktail, or to cruise rivers and rain forests with crocs and other fascinating creatures of the tropics.

Updated by
Jane Carstens

QUEENSLAND is a state of enormous geographic variety—the sheer size of it defies homogeneity. Queensland occupies 1,727,999 square km (667,180 square mi)—more than four times the size of California. Its eastern seaboard stretches 5,200 km (3,224 mi)—about the distance from Rome to Cairo—from the subtropical Gold Coast to the wild and steamy rain forests of the far north. Only in recent years has the northern tip, the Cape York Peninsula, been fully explored, and crocodiles still claim a human victim once in a while. Away from the coastal sugar and banana plantations, west of the Great Dividing Range, Queensland looks as arid and dust-blown as any other part of Australia's interior. Few paved roads cross this semidesert, and, as in the Red Centre, communication with remote farms is mostly by radio and air. Not surprisingly, most of the state's 3.4 million inhabitants reside on the coast.

The Queensland license plate calls this the "Sunshine State," a sort-of Australian Florida—a laid-back stretch of beaches and sun where many Australians head for their vacations. The state has actively promoted tourism, and such areas as the Gold Coast in the south and Cairns in the north have exploded into mini-Miamis, complete with high-rise buildings, casinos, and beachfront amusements.

At the same time, Queenslanders have been called intensely parochial. This was especially true during the reign of the conservative Sir Joh Bjelke-Petersen, whose 20-year span as premier ended in 1989 when the National Party elected a new leader following an inquiry that revealed corruption in the government and police force. The now famous Fitzgerald Inquiry tarnished Queensland's image, but even Bjelke-Petersen's detractors admired his legacy of a balanced budget and a fiscally sound low-tax economy.

This is the only Australian state that didn't adopt daylight saving time, which means that summertime airline schedules can get confusing. Detractors have smirked that this is because Queenslanders don't like change, but the reality is based on practical concerns: People living in the far reaches of the northwest would have been severely affected. Unless the state were divided in half, its residents would reject the time change because it wasn't advantageous for everyone.

The major attraction for Australians and foreign tourists alike is the Great Barrier Reef. This 1,900-km (1,200-mi) ecological masterpiece supports thousands of animal species. With such an abundance of marine life, it's not surprising that Queensland is a fishing mecca. Cairns and Lizard Island in the far north are renowned for big-game fishing—black marlin can weigh in at more than a half ton. The reef, an integral part of any trip to the state, is discussed separately in Chapter 7.

Queensland was thrust into the spotlight with the Commonwealth Games in 1982 and World Expo '88. These two events exposed Brisbane (pronounced "*briz*-bin") to the wider world and helped bring the city, along with other provincial capitals, to full-fledged social and cultural maturity. Consequently, Queensland is a vibrant place to visit, and Sunshine Staters are far more likely to be city kids who work in modern offices than stereotypical bushies—people with the lack of sophistication characteristic of living in the bush—who work the land. Whatever their background, Queenslanders are known for their friendliness and hospitality. Typical of lands blessed with hot weather and plenty of sunshine, the pace of life is relaxed.

Pleasures and Pastimes

Dining

After only a few days in Queensland, you'll find that the concept of specialized rural cuisines is virtually unknown here. Steak and seafood predominate once you leave city limits behind. There are a few exceptions to that rule, however. Brisbane has its share of new, Mediterranean–Asian–influenced menus, and in Noosa people argue about dishes and spices and the merits of the special local ingredients of "Noosa Cuisine" with a fervor that others reserve for the horse races or football. The state is a great source of produce from land and sea. Cairns and the coast up to Mossman have some fine restaurants. Above that, cooking is decidedly more basic.

CATEGORY	COST*
$$$$	over $50
$$$	$40–$50
$$	$30–$40
$	under $30

*per person, excluding drinks and service

Diving

Cairns is a great base for divers. The cognoscenti may argue whether the Great Barrier Reef or the Red Sea offers better diving, but the fact remains that the reef is one of the certified wonders of the world.

Fishing

If you're a serious deep-sea angler, Cairns is your mecca. Scores of charter boats leave the city in pursuit of black marlin, tuna, and reef fish.

Lodging

Queensland accommodations range from rain-forest lodges, outback pubs, and backpacker hostels to five-star beachside resorts and big-city hotels. The luxury resorts are clustered around the major tourist areas of Cairns, the islands, and the Gold Coast. In the smaller coastal towns, accommodation is mostly in motels.

CATEGORY	COST*
$$$$	over $280
$$$	$140–$280
$$	$80–$140
$	under $80

*All prices are for a standard double room.

Queensland's Great Outdoors

From the varied ecosystems of Lamington National Park on the New South Wales Border, to the gorges and Aboriginal rock paintings of Carnarvon northwest of Brisbane, to the rain forests of Daintree National Park north of Cairns, Queensland has one of the most extensive and organized park systems in Australia. Along the east coast, there seems to be a marine park or tiny, island park every few miles.

If you have the time, an explorer's curiosity, or just wish to see one of the world's last wild jungles, take a trip north from Cairns. The remaining pockets of ancient, untouched wilderness that warrant the area's listing as a World Heritage site provide one of the most archetypal Australian adventures that you'll have.

Reef Visits

Snorkeling, scuba diving, and glass-bottom boat trips on the Great Barrier Reef (☞ Chapter 7) are essential parts of any trip to Queensland.

Queensland

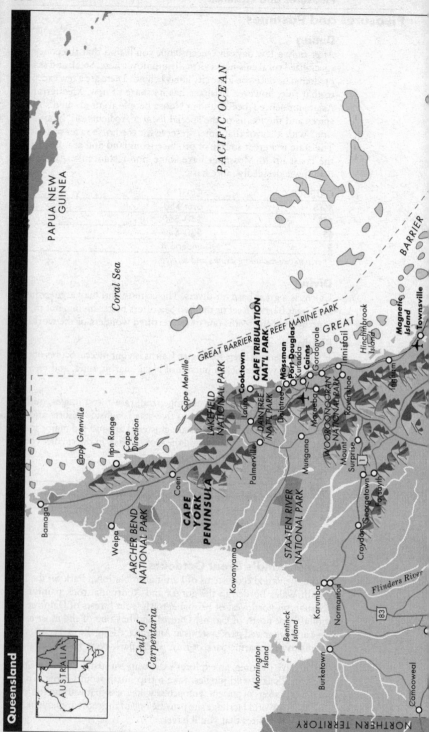

KEY
— Rail Lines
◯ Reef

Exploring Queensland

At the south end of the state, bordering New South Wales, the Gold Coast is much like Miami Beach or Waikiki. The Sunshine Coast north of Brisbane is somewhat quieter and less touristy, with long, almost deserted beaches and beautiful rain forest. If you really want to get away from it all to the pulsing tropical heart of nature, head north of Cairns to Cape Tribulation and Daintree National Parks.

If you do have a few weeks and would like to cover a lot of the state, don't drive up the coast. It's a boring road, and you hardly ever see the water. Fly instead. Keep in mind that the state's great distances mean additional transit time. If you want to drive from the Gold or Sunshine coasts near Brisbane up to the Great Barrier Reef, it will take a half day or more en route.

Great Itineraries

IF YOU HAVE 3 DAYS

Fly into ⌐ **Cairns** and take a boat out to one of the reef islands (☞ chapter 7) for a day, then head up to ⌐ **Cape Tribulation** for the next two days to take in the sights and sounds of the rain forest. If you'd rather have a Miami Beach–style trip, fly into ⌐ **Brisbane** and head straight for the glitzy **Gold Coast,** overnighting in ⌐ **Surfers Paradise.** You could end that spree with a final night and day in ⌐ **Lamington National Park** for its subtropical wilderness and bird life.

IF YOU HAVE 5 DAYS

Spend three days on shore and two days on the reef. Take the first night in ⌐ **Brisbane,** then head up the **Sunshine Coast** for a hike up one of the **Glass House Mountains** on the way to ⌐ **Noosa Heads.** Apart from beach- and surf-time, take in the Sunshine Coast's monument to kitsch, **Big Pineapple,** and indulge in one of their famous ice-cream sundaes. Then make your way back to Brisbane for a flight to ⌐ **Cairns** and either a boat to the reef or a drive to the **rain forest** north of Cairns for cruising the rivers, listening to the jungle, relaxing on the beach, and looking into the maw of a crocodile.

IF YOU HAVE 7 OR MORE DAYS

Unless you're keen on seeing everything, limit yourself to a couple of areas, such as **Brisbane, the Sunshine Coast,** and the rain forests **North from Cairns,** and take three to four days in each—Queensland's climate is conducive to slowing down. Extended stays will also allow you to take a four-wheel-drive trip all the way to the top of **Cape York Peninsula** from **Cairns,** go for overnight bush walks in national parks, spend a few days on a **dive boat** exploring islands and reefs north of Cairns, trek inland to the Outback's **Carnarvon National Park** and **Undarra lava tubes,** or just lie back and soak in the heat.

When to Tour Queensland

Down Under, the farther north you go, the hotter it gets. Summer is normally sweltering, and the north is plenty warm in winter for ocean swimming. North of Cairns, the best time for visiting is between May and September, when the daily maximum temperature averages around 80°F and the water is comfortably warm. During the wet season up there, from about December through March, expect monsoon conditions. Elsewhere in the state, fall and spring are nicest, in part because the tropical coast is besieged from October through April by deadly box jellyfish that make ocean swimming impossible. The jellies don't drift out to the reef or south of the Tropic of Capricorn, however. Because of school holidays, sea- and reef-side Queensland tend to fill up around Christmas and into January.

BRISBANE

Until the mid-1970s this city, Australia's third largest in population and one of the world's largest in area, still had a country feeling and attitude. During the 1980s, Brisbane underwent an impressive spurt of growth and modernization that culminated in today's pleasantly contemporary cityscape of pedestrian plazas, riverside vistas, and café culture. Much of this occurred as a response to Brisbane's hosting the 1982 Commonwealth Games and Expo '88, events that put the city on the world map.

Brisbane was founded as a penal colony for prisoners who had committed crimes after their arrival in Australia. The waterway across which the city sprawls was discovered by two escaped convicts in 1823, and the penal settlement was established on its banks the following year, 32 km (20 mi) from Moreton Bay.

Few historic buildings have survived the wrecker's ball, and today's city is very much a product of recent development. Far surpassing the architecture are the open spaces: Brisbane is beautifully landscaped, brimming with jacarandas, tulip trees, flame trees, oleanders, frangipani, and the ever-stunning bougainvillea. In summer the city broils, and although the climate is pleasant at other times of the year, there is never any doubt that this is a subtropical region.

Exploring Brisbane

Numbers in the text correspond to numbers in the margin and on the Brisbane map.

City Center

Brisbane's inner-city landmarks—a combination of Victorian, Edwardian, and slick high-tech architecture—are best explored on foot. Most of them lie within the triangle formed by Ann Street and the bends of the Brisbane River.

A GOOD WALK

Start at **St. John's Anglican Cathedral** ①, near the corner of Wharf and Ann streets. Like so many other grand edifices in Australia, this building was never completed—although work has resumed on the unfinished western end. Inside the cathedral grounds, the **Deanery** has been finished, in fact long before the first stone for the cathedral was laid. This house, originally built as a doctor's residence, became a temporary government house when Queensland was proclaimed a separate colony from New South Wales in 1859. The proclamation of separation was read from its veranda.

Walk southeast along Wharf Street, across Queen Street, down Eagle Street, and southwest on Elizabeth Street to **Old St. Stephen's Church** ②, which stands in the shadow of St. Stephen's Catholic Cathedral. Both buildings are in Gothic Revival style. The church is believed to have been designed by Augustus Pugin, a noted English architect who designed much of London's Houses of Parliament.

One block northwest of the church, and worlds away in terms of style, is the **National Bank Building** ③. Don't miss a look at the doors and interior of this Classical palazzo if you're at all interested in architecture. Continue southwest along Queen Street for one block to **MacArthur Chambers** ④, General Douglas MacArthur's main Pacific office during World War II and one of Brisbane's earliest office blocks.

Head northwest along Edward Street and turn right into Adelaide Street. On the left look for **Anzac Square and the Shrine of Remem-**

Brisbane

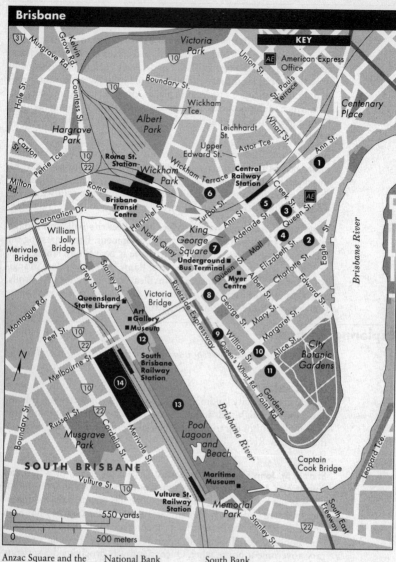

KEY

AE American Express Office

Anzac Square and the Shrine of Remembrance, **5**

Brisbane City Hall, **7**

Brisbane Convention and Exhibition Centre, **14**

MacArthur Chambers, **4**

Mansions in George Street, **10**

National Bank Building, **3**

Old Commissariat Store, **9**

Old St. Stephen's Church, **2**

Old Windmill, **6**

Parliament House, **11**

Queensland Cultural Centre, **12**

St. John's Anglican Cathedral, **1**

South Bank Parklands, **13**

Treasury Building, **8**

brance ⑤, built in memory of Australian casualties in World War I. The circular Doric Greek Revival Cenotaph is particularly handsome, and there are lawns around the memorial if you'd like to take a break. On April 25, Anzac Day, a moving dawn service is held here in remembrance of Australia's fallen soldiers.

Return to Edward Street and head northwest to Wickham Terrace. Turn left and follow the street as it curves to the **Old Windmill** ⑥, also known as the Observatory. This is one of only two remaining convict-built buildings from the days when Brisbane was a penal settlement, called Moreton Bay, which was set up to take Sydney's particularly recalcitrant convicts.

Back on Edward Street, walk two blocks southeast and turn right into Adelaide Street. Past David Jones department store and abutting King George Square is the classical, temple-fronted, bell-towered **Brisbane City Hall** ⑦, one of Australia's largest city halls. Consider taking the lift to the bell tower for great views of the city—when the bells aren't ringing.

From City Hall, walk over to the Queen Street Mall between George and Edward streets for a choice of places to wet your whistle or have a bite of lunch. There is often free entertainment at lunch hour (noon–1).

Head south to George Street and the **Treasury Building** ⑧, alias the Conrad Treasury Casino. Continue southeast on William Street, which runs behind the Treasury Building, to the **Old Commissariat Store** ⑨, which is the city's other surviving convict-built structure. Today it houses the Royal Historical Society of Queensland along with its museum and library. Farther along William Street, turn left into Margaret Street and then right into George Street. The **Mansions in George Street** ⑩, built of brick and sandstone just before the turn of this century, are former town houses now occupied by offices, a restaurant, a book shop, and the National Trust gift shop.

For a break from the city streets, cross Alice Street and step into the **City Botanic Gardens** that stretch over to the river. There are some venerable trees in the garden that are well worth extending your walk to see, as well as a charming restaurant-cum-café tucked away at the back of the gardens. Back out on Alice Street, at the end of William Street amid tropical palms, is the splendid French Renaissance **Parliament House** ⑪, which earned its colonial designer a meager 200-guinea salary. If Queensland's Parliament is in session, you can look in on the proceedings from a visitor's gallery.

Return to Queen Street along George Street and walk over Victoria Bridge. Across the Brisbane River, the sleek **Queensland Cultural Centre** ⑫ extends for a block on either side of Melbourne Street. Plan to spend time here exploring the expansive rooms of the Queensland Art Gallery (⊙ daily 10–5) or the Queensland Museum natural history exhibits (⊙ daily 9–5), perhaps picking up a reminder of your visit at the complex's shops.

Just south of the cultural center along the river is **South Bank Parklands** ⑬. An enormously popular destination for Brisbane folk and visitors alike, it contains a sprawling beach lagoon, popular for swimming (and complete with lifeguard), markets on Friday night and all weekend, cafés and restaurants, along with plenty of places to sit and relax. At the northwest corner of the park is the **Brisbane Convention and Exhibition Centre** ⑭.

TIMING

Without pausing at any of the attractions, this walk takes almost two hours and includes a hike up a small hill to get to the Old Windmill. South Bank Parklands will require the most exploring, especially if you are there when the markets are operating. During Brisbane's blistering summer it's a good idea to carry water, as the humidity can be draining. Winter is quite pleasant. The boardwalk along the river at South Bank is a great place to enjoy the city views.

SIGHTS TO SEE

⑤ Anzac Square and the Shrine of Remembrance. Walking paths through Anzac Square stretch across green lawns, directing all eyes toward the shrine, which is constructed of Queensland sandstone; an eternal flame burns within for Australian soldiers who died in World War I. Equally spine-tingling is the **Shrine of Memories**, a crypt below the flame, which stores soil samples labeled "forever Australian" that were collected from battlefields on which Australian soldiers perished. ⊠ *Adelaide St. between Edward and Creek Sts.* ✆ *Free.* ☉ *Shrine weekdays 11–3.*

⑦ Brisbane City Hall. Once referred to as the "million pound town hall" because of the massive funds poured into its construction, this community center built in 1930 has been a major symbol of Brisbane's civic pride. The substantial Italianate city hall is one of Australia's largest. Visitors and locals "ooh" and "aah" at the grand pipe organ and circular concert hall. Other features include an observation platform affording superb city views and a ground-floor museum and art gallery. You can tour both the building and its huge clock tower, home to one of Australia's largest civic clocks. ⊠ *King George Sq., Adelaide St.,* ✆ *07/3403–4048.* ✉ *Free.* ☉ *Mon.–Sat. 10:30–4.*

NEED A
BREAK?

The **Queen Street Mall** is a two-block pedestrian boulevard stretching from George Street to Edward Street. It features a wide selection of places to eat, ranging from take-out food to elegant restaurants. The **David Jones** department store (on the mall) has a well-stocked food hall, where you can assemble your own picnic to eat in nearby King George Square.

⑭ Brisbane Convention and Exhibition Centre. This imposing building covers 4½ acres and is equipped with four exhibition halls, a 4,000-seat Great Hall, and a Grand Ballroom. ⊠ *Glenelg and Merivale Sts.,* ✆ *1800/03–6308.*

④ MacArthur Chambers. As commander-in-chief of the Allied Forces fighting in the Pacific, General Douglas MacArthur came to Australia from the Philippines, leaving the Japanese in control there with his notorious vow, "I shall return." This present-day office building was MacArthur's World War II headquarters. ⊠ *Queen St., entrance at 201 Edward St.*

⑩ Mansions in George Street. Constructed in 1890, these were originally six fashionable town houses—worth a detour even if they're out of your way. These splendid Victorian terrace houses with elegant wrought-iron lace trim house the National Trust gift shop, restaurants, bookshops, and professional offices. ⊠ *40 George St.*

③ National Bank Building. Brisbane's National Bank went up in 1885 and is one of the country's finest Italian Renaissance–style structures. Aside from the majestic entrance hall with its ornate ceilings and eye-catching dome, the most interesting features are the front doors, which were crafted from a single cedar trunk. ⊠ *308 Queen St.* ☉ *Weekdays 9–4.*

⑨ Old Commissariat Store. Convict-built in 1829, this was the first stone building in Brisbane. It has served variously as a customs house, storehouse, and immigrants' shelter. Currently the headquarters of the Royal Historical Society of Queensland, it is built on the spot where Brisbane's original timber wharf was located. ⊠ *115 William St.,* ☎ *07/3221–4198.* ⊡ *Donations accepted.* ☉ *Tues.–Fri. 11–2.*

❷ Old St. Stephen's Church. The tiny old church that adjoins St. Stephen's Catholic Cathedral opened in May 1850. This is Brisbane's oldest house of worship, a particularly fine example of Gothic Revival architecture. The church is not open to the public. ⊠ *Elizabeth St. near Creek St.*

⑥ Old Windmill. From the streets below, the view of the windmill at the top of Edward Street is almost obscured by trees. It is the oldest of the few remaining convict buildings in Brisbane. The poorly designed 1828 windmill never worked very well; whenever the wind died down, convicts were forced to power a treadmill to crush grain for the colony's bread, thus tagging this landmark the "Tower of Torture." When fire erupted across the city in 1864, scorching almost everything in its path, the windmill survived with only minimal damage. Stripped of its blades, the tower now looks a lot like a lighthouse. The large copper ball on top of the building used to drop at 1 PM every day so people could set their watches accurately. As early as 1930, experimental television broadcasts were beamed from here to Ipswich, 33 km (20 mi) away. Entering the building isn't allowed. ⊠ *Wickham Park, Wickham Terr.*

⑪ Parliament House. Opened in 1868, this stone-clad building, with a Mount Isa copper roof, had a legislative annex added in the late 1970s. The interior is fitted with polished timber, brass, and frosted and engraved glass. If State Parliament is sitting, you can observe the action from the visitors' gallery. On weekdays, building tours are available. Afterward, wander through the adjacent **City Botanic Gardens.** ⊠ *George and Alice Sts.,* ☎ *07/3226–7111.* ⊡ *Free.* ☉ *Tour weekdays at 9:30, 10:30, 11:15, 2:30, 3:15, and 4.*

⑫ Queensland Cultural Centre. The Queensland Art Gallery, Queensland Museum, State Library, Performing Arts Complex, and a host of restaurants, cafés, and shops are all here. On weekdays at noon there are free tours of the Performing Arts Complex; backstage peeks at the 2,000-seat Concert Hall and Cremorne Theatre are often included. The cultural center is on the west side of the Brisbane River near Victoria Bridge. ⊠ *Melbourne St.,* ☎ *07/3840–7303 art gallery; 07/3840–7555 museum; 07/3840–7810 library; 07/3840–7444 or 13–6246 performing arts complex.* ⊡ *Free.* ☉ *Gallery daily 10–5; museum daily 9:30–5; library Mon.–Thurs. 10–8 and Fri.–Sun. 10–5.*

❶ St. John's Anglican Cathedral. Built in 1901 with porphyry rock, this is a fine example of Gothic Revival architecture. Services are held on Sunday at 7:30 AM, 9:30 AM, and 5 PM, with evensong at 6 PM. Inside the cathedral grounds is the **Deanery,** which predates the construction of the cathedral by almost 50 years. The proclamation declaring Queensland separate from New South Wales was read from the building's east balcony on June 6, 1859. The building served as Government House for Queensland for three years after the declaration. The interior of the Deanery isn't open to the public. ⊠ *373 Ann St.,* ☎ *no phone.* ☉ *Guided cathedral tours on request, weekdays 10–4.*

⑬ South Bank Parklands. One of the most appealing urban parks in Australia, Brisbane's World Expo '88 site reopened with its current identity in 1992. Major changes to the park, including the building of a tree-lined arbor walk, an IMAX theater, and the transformation of Grey Street into a pedestrian precinct, were started in 1997 and completed in 1999. Aside from shops, restaurants, and a maritime museum, the 40-acre complex includes gardens, foot- and cycling paths, and a Nepalese-style carved-wood pagoda, and provides excellent views of the city. The park's Wildlife Sanctuary is a critter repository with almost 850 varieties of butterflies as well as many of the weird and wonderful insects and animals that inhabit Australia. The parklands, which feature Friday night Lantern Markets and a weekend Crafts Village, lie alongside the river just south of the Queensland Cultural Centre. ✉ *Grey St.*, ☎ *07/3867–2000; 07/3867–2051 entertainment information.* ✇ *Butterfly and Insect House Wildlife Sanctuary $8, Maritime Museum $5.* ☉ *Parklands daily 5 AM–midnight, Lantern Markets Fri. 5–10 PM, Crafts Village Sat. 10–5, Sun. 9–5.*

⑧ **Treasury Building.** Overlooking the river and surrounded by bronze figurative statuary, this massive Italian Renaissance edifice stands on the site of the officers' quarters and military barracks from the original penal settlement. In 1995, the building reopened as **Conrad Treasury Casino.** It aims for a dignified, European style of gambling rather than Las Vegas glitz. ✉ *William and Elizabeth Sts.*

Around Brisbane

☾ **Australian Woolshed.** The woolshed presents a slice of Australiana that is fascinating for both children and adults. In a one-hour stage show, eight rams from the major sheep breeds found in Australia perform. This is not a circus, but an opportunity to gain insight into the dramatically different appearances—and personalities—of sheep. There is also a koala sanctuary, where, for a fee of $12, you can be photographed holding a koala. Barbecue lunches are available, and there is an extensive crafts shop. Australian Woolshed can be reached by train to Ferny Grove Station (about a 10 minute walk from the station) or by taxi (about a $20 return ride). ✉ *148 Samford Rd., Ferny Hills,* ☎ *07/3351–5366.* ✇ *$12.* ☉ *9:30–5, shows daily at 9:30, 11, 1, 2:30.*

★ **Lone Pine Koala Sanctuary.** Queensland's most famous fauna park, founded in 1927, claims to be the oldest animal sanctuary in the world. The real attraction for most visitors is the koalas, although there are also emus, wombats, and kangaroos. Some of the animals can be petted, and for $8 visitors can have a quick cuddle and a photo with a koala. One way to get to the park is by **cruise boat** (☞ *below*). ✉ *Jesmond Rd., Fig Tree Pocket,* ☎ *07/3378–1366.* ✇ *$12.50.* ☉ *Daily 7:30–4:45.*

The **MV *Mirimar,*** a historic 1930s ferry, travels daily to the Lone Pine Koala Sanctuary from North Quay at the Victoria Bridge in Brisbane proper. Your *Mirimar* ticket is good for a discount on the Lone Pine entrance fee. ☎ *07/3221–0300.* ✇ *$15 round-trip.*

Dining

By Jacki Passmore

Updated by Jane Carstens

Australian

✕ **The Shingle Inn.** Nothing's changed here since the 1930s, and that's part of the appeal. Homemade cakes and pastries are displayed in the front window. Dark-wood tables, old-style fans, and the soft glow of lanterns fill the dining room. The waitstaff wear scarves in their hair and vintage uniforms, and many of the patrons have been lunching here for decades. Old-fashioned favorites like pavlova, lemon meringue pie, and lime mint juleps are available. ✉ *254 Edward St.,* ☎ *07/3221–9039. No credit cards. Closed Sun.*

$

Brisbane Dining and Lodging

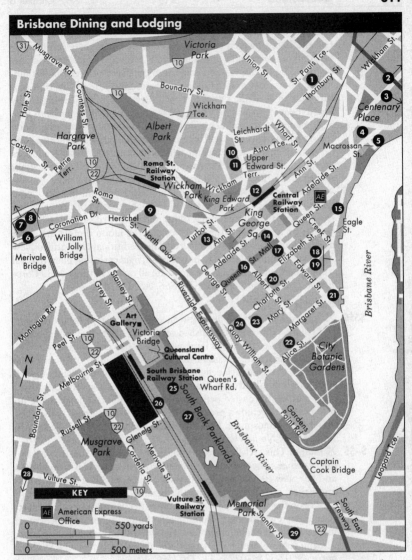

Dining

E'cco Bistro, **4**

Grape Wine & Food Bar, **2**

Il Centro, **18**

Indigo, **3**

Jameson's, **5**

Jimmy's on the Mall, **16**

Kim Thanh Chinese & Vietnamese Restaurant, **28**

Malaysian Experience, **7**

Michael's Riverside Restaurant, **15**

New York Latin, **25**

Oriental Bangkok Restaurant, **11**

Oxley's on the River, **6**

Pier 9 Oyster Bar and Seafood Grill, **19**

The Shingle Inn, **14**

Siggi's at the Heritage, **21**

Sirocco Mediterranean Café, **27**

Summit Restaurant, **8**

Lodging

Annie's Shandon Inn, **10**

Bellevue Hotel, **23**

Brisbane City Travelodge, **9**

Carlton Crest Hotel, **13**

Conrad Treasury Brisbane, **24**

The Heritage, **21**

Hillcrest Central Apartments, **29**

Hilton Brisbane, **17**

Quay West, **22**

Royal Albert Boutique Hotel, **20**

Rydges South Bank, **26**

Sheraton Brisbane Hotel & Towers, **12**

Thornbury House, **1**

Contemporary

$$$$ ✕ **Siggi's at The Heritage.** Socialites rub shoulders with visiting celebrities and high-powered businesspeople at this supremely comfortable no-smoking restaurant in the luxurious **Heritage** hotel (☞ Lodging, *below*). The service is impeccable, and the decor of the adjacent dining and bar areas makes full use of the architecture of the 19th-century Port of Brisbane Office in which they are placed. The classically based menu changes frequently and is supplemented each month with a set menu based on a theme such as seafood or Greek cooking. Look for asparagus and crab salad with caviar crème fraîche, and spring lamb on roasted marinated eggplant with a pinot jus. Desserts are just as worthy. ⊠ *Edward and Margaret Sts.,* ☎ *07/3221–4555. Reservations essential. AE, DC, MC, V. Closed Sun. and Mon. No lunch.*

$$ ✕ **Oxley's on the River.** A five-minute taxi ride from the city center takes you to the only restaurant in Brisbane that's built right on the river. By day the dining room is sunny and has a bird's-eye view of river traffic; by night, light from the city and the moon dimple the water and lend an intimate, romantic feel. The traditional char-grilled New York–cut sirloin, Queensland barramundi, mud crab, and fillets of coral trout stuffed with a ragout of seafood are all rightly famed. ⊠ *330 Coronation Dr., Milton,* ☎ *07/3368–1866. AE, DC, MC, V.*

Eclectic

$$$$ ✕ **Jameson's.** Set in a warehouse once used as storage for the old port of Brisbane, this simply furnished restaurant offers fine dining with a view of the river through a large window at one end of the room. The changing menu features cuisine that draws on a number of international influences to create such delights as ravioli of rabbit and orange topped with Kangaroo Island crayfish and baby leeks, or saffron vermicelli tossed with mud crab, roasted pepper, and macadamia rouille. The bar offers a chance to enjoy a predinner drink or a game of pool in the same warehouse atmosphere. ⊠ *473 Adelaide St.,* ☎ *07/3831–7633. AE, DC, MC, V. No lunch weekends.*

$–$$ ✕ **Indigo.** This stylish bistro produces sophisticated meals, with frequent menu changes accompanied by a solid wine list. An open kitchen and bar, as well as a small pantry shop outside selling bottled goods and cakes, complement the establishment's intimate atmosphere. If they're on the menu when you visit, try butterfly wings of pickled beetroot under a warm potato cake, or, after dinner, arborio-rice ice cream in layered sheets of almond wafers. The wood-fired pizzas are also good. A menu for kids ages 4–12 is also offered. ⊠ *695 Brunswick St., New Farm,* ☎ *07/3254–0275. AE, DC, MC, V.*

$–$$ ✕ **Jimmy's on the Mall.** On the Queen Street Mall, Jimmy's puts diners in the middle of the city's action. The black-and-white decor and potted plants give this brasserie an elegant air, and food is cooked to order in a big open kitchen. Whether you're looking for nachos or prime sirloin, you'll probably find it on the extensive menu. Under the same ownership are Jimmy's Uptown and Jimmy's Downtown; there's one at each end of the Queen Street Mall. ⊠ *Queen Street Mall,* ☎ *07/ 3229–9999. AE, DC, MC, V.*

Italian

$$$ ✕ **Il Centro.** No expense has been spared in fitting this handsome Eagle
★ Street Pier eatery with gleaming wood floors, terra-cotta and dark-blue tiles, enormous windows that take advantage of the river view, and undercover outdoor seating. Wondrous aromas spill out of an open kitchen into the stylish dining room. On the seasonal menu watch for quail ravioli with Italian parsley, crab lasagna, or panfried chicken saltimbocca on a warm salad of pumpkin, asparagus, and arugula. Then throw your diet out the window and try semifreddo with vanilla, butterscotch,

and honeycomb. There is also an excellent wine list. ✉ *Eagle Street Pier, 1 Eagle St.,* ☎ *07/3221–6090. AE, DC, MC, V. No lunch Sat.*

Latin

$$ ✕ **New York Latin.** Restaurateur Peter Hackworth has transformed the old South Bank Information Centre into a spacious, colorful dining establishment with a large bar and open kitchen. Latin costumes adorn the walls; most nights, live music from a small stage further enhances the festive atmosphere. Cuban roast chicken wrapped in banana leaves and rib eye steak glazed with dark rum sugar are like mambo music for the mouth. ✉ *South Bank Parklands, Grey St.,* ☎ *07/3844–0088. AE, DC, MC, V.*

Malaysian

$ ✕ **Malaysian Experience.** Unfortunately situated beside the Legal and General building carpark, this authentic restaurant produces very good Malaysian cuisine. Tuck into noodles, *laksa* (Malaysian curry soup), claypot chicken, and curries that come straight from the Malay peninsula. ✉ *80 Jephson St., Toowong,* ☎ *07/3870–2624. Reservations essential. AE, DC, MC, V. No lunch Sun.*

Mediterranean

$$ ✕ **Sirocco Mediterranean Café.** No article of Mediterranean kitsch has been left out of this South Bank Parklands eatery. Nonetheless, the place to be seen is in the more nautical outdoor area. Nosh on slivers of pita dipped into *melitzanosaláta* (eggplant dip). Heartier options include souvlaki and large seafood platters for four to share. ✉ *South Bank Parklands, Grey St.,* ☎ *07/3846–1803. AE, DC, MC, V.*

$ ✕ **Grape Wine & Food Bar.** Located in the historic Wickham Hotel, this smallish bistro shares its space with a wine bar, art gallery, wobbly staircase, and alarmingly slanted verandas. Its creative fare has people coming back again and again. Try sesame-crusted tuna, wasabi roe, soy-soaked shiitake, and aged lime dressing alongside something from the superb wine list, which has plenty of varieties by the glass. Exotic cheeses are also available. ✉ *308 Wickham St., Fortitude Valley,* ☎ *07/3852–1301. AE, DC, MC, V. Closed Sun. No lunch Sat.–Wed.*

Modern Australian

$$$ ✕ **E'cco Bistro.** The excellent food in this petite dining place has earned it a loyal following. The white-columned entry leads into a maroon and black dining room with an open bar and kitchen. The minimalist menu offers a carefully chosen selection of dishes such as Atlantic salmon with shaved fennel, olives, peppers, and pancetta followed by custard tart with caramelized mango. ✉ *100 Boundary St.,* ☎ *07/3831–8344. Reservations essential. AE, DC, MC, V. Closed Sun. and for 3 wks from Dec. 24. No lunch Sat.*

$$$ ✕ **Summit Restaurant.** Perched beside the lookout on the slopes of Mount Coot-tha, this restaurant offers unbeatable views of the city, especially at night when lights shimmer around it. The original building dates from 1925 and has been patronized by such lights and dignitaries as Katharine Hepburn, Princess Alexandra, and King Peter of Yugoslavia. Treat yourself to cream of macadamia nut soup followed by char-grilled lamb medallions, then end with a tropical fruit ice cream served in a coconut shell. Taxi fare to the Summit from the city is about $15. ✉ *Mount Coot-tha Lookout, Sir Samuel Griffith Dr.,* ☎ *07/3369–9922,* FAX *07/3369–8937. AE, DC, MC, V.*

Pan-Asian

$ ✕ **Kim Thanh Chinese & Vietnamese Restaurant.** Great food at bargain prices has made this restaurant an institution among Brisbane diners. It's famous for its kitsch decorations—like the large bamboo shrimps perched on the wall. The menu features a huge variety of Vietnamese and Chinese dishes, but choices from other Asian cultures are also available. After tasting the Mongolian lamb on a hot plate, *goi cuon* (transparent spring rolls), and barbecued prawns wrapped in sugarcane, you may want to change the rest of your itinerary to stay here and trawl the rest of the menu. Take-out is also available. ⊠ *99 Hardgrave Rd., West End,* ☎ *07/3844–4954. AE, DC, MC, V.*

Seafood

$$$$ ✕ **Michael's Riverside Restaurant.** Michael Platsis owns four very different restaurants, all in the Riverside Centre, and the jewel of the bunch is this silver-service establishment. You'll encounter sweeping views of the Brisbane River while you enjoy the Queensland seafood followed by the raspberry drambuie crème brûlée. No worries about BYOB here: Michael's has what might be the best wine cellar in town. ⊠ *Riverside Centre, 123 Eagle St.,* ☎ *07/3832–5522. Reservations essential. AE, DC, MC, V. No lunch Sat., no dinner Sun.*

$$–$$$ ✕ **Pier 9 Oyster Bar and Seafood Grill.** The city's most stylish seafood
★ place prepares a host of fish dishes, from fish-and-chips to lobsters. The dining room's glass walls admit plenty of sunshine and have fine river views. Only the best of the catch from the Northern Territory to Tasmania is served here, and several types of fresh oysters are delivered daily and shucked to order. Try the wok-seared king prawns or the barbecued Moreton Bay bugs if they're available. There is a sizable Australian wine list, with a selection available by the glass. ⊠ *Eagle Street Pier, 1 Eagle St.,* ☎ *07/3229–2194. AE, DC, MC, V.*

Thai

$$ ✕ **Oriental Bangkok Restaurant.** A pleasant 20-minute walk from the central business district, this Thai restaurant—tucked behind a small office and shopping complex—serves meals as good as any in Bangkok. Begin with hot-and-sour soup or creamy chicken soup with Thai ginger, then sample one of the curries or salads. The seafood salad, with fresh prawns, is a sensation of complementary citrus flavors. Roast duck curry and whole coral trout Thai-style are unforgettable entrées. The staff recommends a slightly sweet and fruity wine, such as gewürztraminer, to suit hot and spicy curries. ⊠ *454 Upper Edward St.,* ☎ *07/3832–6010. AE, DC, MC, V. Closed Sun. No lunch.*

Lodging

$$$$ 🏨 **Conrad Treasury Brisbane.** Like the Conrad Treasury Casino one
★ block to the north, Brisbane's newest top hotel finds itself within a beautiful, sandstone example of Edwardian Baroque architecture. The rooms are equipped with modern amenities—luxurious bathrooms, coffeemakers, individually controlled air-conditioning, and a wide range of movies to watch. All rooms have antique furnishings and the hotel has five very different restaurants (Marco Polo's east-west fusion cuisine is notable), to suit all budgets and tastes. ⊠ *William St., 4000,* ☎ *07/3306–8888,* FAX *07/3306–8880. 81 rooms, 16 suites. 5 restaurants, 4 bars, health club, casino, laundry service. AE, DC, MC, V.*

$$$$ 🏨 **The Heritage.** On the riverfront next to the City Botanic Gardens,
★ this is arguably Brisbane's finest hotel. Its soaring lobby, full of artwork, flower arrangements, and an expanse of natural woods, is warm and inviting, and it is a popular gathering spot. Guest rooms are decorated in neoclassical style in muted yellow and beige. They enjoy clear views over the river. There are five no-smoking floors. The staff's attention to detail is legendary; if you require a fax machine in your room, your fax number will be the same on subsequent visits. The hotel offers a butler service, and the signature restaurant, Siggi's (☞ Dining,

above), has one of Queensland's best wine cellars. ✉ *Edward and Margaret Sts., 4000,* ☎ *07/3221–1999 or 1800/77–3700,* FAX *07/3221–6895 or 1800/77–3900. 232 rooms, 20 suites. 3 restaurants, 3 bars, no-smoking floor, pool, sauna, spa, exercise room. AE, DC, MC, V.*

$$$$ 🏨 **Sheraton Brisbane Hotel & Towers.** Despite its position directly above the city's main commuter rail station, this high-rise hotel is a quiet and extremely pleasant place to stay. The travertine marble floor of the mezzanine lobby is complemented by plenty of brass and natural timber, and there is a spectacular skylit atrium. Floors 27 through 29 constitute the pricier Sheraton Towers, where service and comfort are extended to include personalized registration and use of the exclusive Towers Club lounge on the 27th floor as well as facilities on the lower floors. Decorated in soft pastels, the rooms in both sections of the hotel are spacious and elegant, with marble bathrooms and small sitting areas. ✉ *249 Turbot St., 4000,* ☎ *07/3835–3535,* FAX *07/3835–4960. 392 rooms, 26 suites. 3 restaurants, pool, beauty salon, exercise room. AE, DC, MC, V.*

$$$–$$$$ 🏨 **Hilton Brisbane.** Designed by Australian architect Harry Seidler, this eye-catching, curved 25-story building has an imposing atrium that ranks among the largest in the Southern Hemisphere. All of the spacious and well-appointed rooms open onto the atrium; they feature small sitting areas. The Queen Street Mall is at the hotel's back door, and the Wintergarden shopping center is housed on the first three floors of the hotel. ✉ *190 Elizabeth St., 4000,* ☎ *07/3231–3131,* FAX *07/3231–3199. 322 rooms. 2 restaurants, 5 bars, pool, tennis court, health club, dance club. AE, DC, MC, V.*

$$$ 🏨 **Carlton Crest Hotel.** Opposite the City Hall, close to the center of
★ town, this hotel is an ideal stopping point. The hotel consists of two towers and a central lobby that is elegantly furnished with French-style sofas and carpets. The Crest Tower rooms are on the small side, but the bathrooms are spacious; the Carlton Tower executive rooms are furnished in earthy tones and are (understandably) quite spacious. Oliver's Restaurant, which has a large glass-enclosed balcony adjacent to the sidewalk, is worth patronizing both for its international fare and for the people-watching potential of its balcony. ✉ *Ann and Roma Sts., 4000,* ☎ *07/3229–9111 or 1800/77–7123,* FAX *07/3229–9618. 432 rooms, 6 suites. 3 restaurants, 3 bars, pool, sauna, exercise room. AE, DC, MC, V.*

$$$ 🏨 **Quay West.** Opposite Brisbane's Botanic Gardens, this modern hotel exudes a sense of taste with pressed-metal ceilings, sandstone floors and columns, hammered-iron decorations, and white louvered shutters. The warm, earthy tones and soft pastels of the decor complement the sandstone, and the suites are fitted with plantation teak furniture and raw silk drapes. They include fully equipped kitchens and laundries. The first floor of the hotel has a tropically landscaped area surrounding the heated pool, which has five sandstone carvings of merino rams that form an interesting waterfall. A poolside pergola is supported by intricately carved early 19th-century teak columns from South Africa. ✉ *132 Alice St., 4000,* ☎ *07/3853–6000,* FAX *07/3853–6060. 134 suites. Restaurant, bar, pool, sauna, spa, exercise room. AE, DC, MC, V.*

$$$ 🏨 **Royal Albert Boutique Hotel.** This Heritage-listed building is situated right in the heart of Brisbane and offers more than you would expect from a standard hotel. The larger-than-average rooms all have a self-contained kitchen and laundry. The reproduction antique furniture and cream-and-plum plush carpets add elegant finishing touches. This is a small hotel where the staff are very friendly and take pride in greeting guests by name. There is a licensed brasserie on the ground floor. ✉ *Elizabeth and Albert Sts., 4000,* ☎ *07/3291–8888,* FAX *07/3229–7705. 27 rooms, 28 suites, 4 apartments. Restaurant. AE, DC, MC, V.*

$$$ 🏨 **Rydges South Bank.** Sandwiched between the Brisbane Convention and Exhibition Centre and South Bank Parklands, the Rydges is an excellent choice for business or holiday travelers. The rooms are predominantly olive green and pale yellow, and have modern furnishings and computer work stations. The in-house Chinese restaurant, Peking House, has earned a reputation for fine food. Although there is no pool in the complex, Kodak Beach at South Bank is very close, and it's a fine place to swim. ✉ 9 Glenelg St., 4101, ☎ 07/3255–0822, 𝐅𝐀𝐗 07/3255–0899. 238 rooms, 65 suites. 2 restaurants, 2 bars, spa, sauna, exercise room. AE, DC, MC, V.

$$–$$$ 🏨 **Brisbane City Travelodge.** In the Brisbane Transit Centre—a short walk from the business district—this 18-story hotel caters to businesspeople. The dark glass exterior is lackluster, but the use of wicker in the lounge area gives the lobby a distinctive Queensland flavor. Furnished in shades of beige and blue, rooms are unusually large and comfortable. Standard double rooms have queen-size beds; king studios have king-size beds. The hotel's Verandah Café is open and airy; the Drawing Room Restaurant is formal and elegant; and the Jazz 'n' Blues Club is a casual, locally popular spot for drinks and live music. ✉ Roma and Hershel Sts., 4000, ☎ 07/3238–2222, 𝐅𝐀𝐗 07/3238–2288. 191 rooms, 2 suites. 2 restaurants, 3 bars, sauna, laundry service. AE, DC, MC, V.

$$–$$$ 🏨 **Hillcrest Central Apartments.** With the ongoing construction of apartments in front of this nine-story complex, some of its river and city views have been interrupted—but not all. Hillcrest is located close to the South Bank Parklands and next to a private hospital. Its apartments have modern Italian decor in pale shades of yellow and blue-gray, with sliding glass doors leading onto private balconies. Each apartment has a fully equipped kitchen and color TV. Large family units with two bedrooms are available, as are studios and one-bedrooms. ✉ 311 Vulture St., South Brisbane, 4000, ☎ 07/3846–3000 or 1800/67–8659, 𝐅𝐀𝐗 07/3846–3578. 16 rooms, 64 apartments. Restaurant, pool, sauna, tennis court, laundry service. AE, DC, MC, V.

$$ 🏨 **Bellevue Hotel.** Rooms in this modern hotel are rather plain, but the heart of Brisbane location is hard to beat. Modern amenities such as minibars and cable television compensate for lack of character. ✉ 103 George St., 4000, ☎ 07/3221–6044, 𝐅𝐀𝐗 07/3221–7474. 100 rooms. Restaurant, coffee shop, pool, laundry service. AE, DC, MC, V.

$$ 🏨 **Thornbury House.** At first glance this historic B&B looks tiny, but
★ looks are deceiving—the 19th-century merchant's house has three levels. Inside, buttermilk-color walls, polished floors, thick carpets, and wooden furniture give it old-world charm. And where that charm translates into sharing bathrooms (one room has its own bath), the waffle-weave bathrobes supplied for guests are a thoughtful comfort. The tariff includes a full breakfast, which you can enjoy in the garden courtyard. A more formal sitting room, where you'll find complimentary port on a sideboard, is provided for quiet evenings. ✉ 1 Thornbury St., 4000, ☎ 07/3832–5985, 𝐅𝐀𝐗 07/3832–7255. 9 rooms, 1 with bath. AE, MC, V.

$ 🏨 **Annie's Shandon Inn.** A five-minute walk from the railway station, this small, modern, B&B-style lodge has pleasant rooms decorated with Laura Ashley–style wallpaper. The pink and blue exterior and homey additions inside, such as lots of large dolls lining the central corridor, make it almost kitschy. The property is clean and well managed. Continental breakfast is included in room rates, and local tour buses conveniently stop outside. Payment is required on arrival. ✉ 405 Upper Edward St., 4000, ☎ 07/3831–8684, 𝐅𝐀𝐗 07/3831–3073. 19 rooms, 4 with bath. AE, MC, V.

Nightlife and the Arts

The Arts

Concerts, ballet, opera, theater, jazz, and other events are listed in the Saturday edition of *The Courier–Mail* newspaper. Thursday's paper includes a free What's On magazine, which is a comprehensive entertainment guide for Brisbane.

The **Performing Arts Complex** (✉ Melbourne St., ☎ 07/3840–7444 or 13–6246) at the city's cultural heart, hosts both international and Australian entertainers and performing troupes. The **Art Gallery** (✉ Melbourne St., ☎ 07/3840–7303) hangs an interesting range of permanent and visiting exhibitions. It's open daily 10 to 5.

Nightlife

Adrenalin Sports Bar. This night spot replaced the popular Hogie's Pool Bar and Nightclub, but has lost none of the its predecessor's taste for large American-style haunts with pool tables, 40 television screens broadcasting sporting events, and a large open bar surrounded by tables and chairs. ✉ *127 Charlotte St.,* ☎ *07/3229–1515.* 💲 *Free.* ☼ *Daily 11:30 AM–3 AM.*

Breakfast Creek Hotel. This classic old Australian pub has hardly changed during the last century. Popular with blue-collar workers, the bar serves pub food and steaks. There is a restaurant in the garden outside. ✉ *2 Kingsford-Smith Dr., Breakfast Creek,* ☎ *07/3262–5988.* ☼ *Daily 10–10.*

★ **Conrad Treasury Casino.** With a dress code that prohibits collarless shirts, shorts, and sporting footwear, this *is* a European-style casino. The Conrad Treasury has three levels of gaming, with a total of 104 tables and more than 1,000 machines. Games include roulette, blackjack, baccarat, minibaccarat, craps, big six, keno, and two-up. For high rollers there is the exclusive Club Conrad (reserved for members), and there are three restaurants and four bars in the complex. ✉ *Queen St.,* ☎ *07/3306–8888.* ☼ *24 hrs.*

Rosie's Tavern, a café, bar, club, and tavern in the historic Rowes Arcade, caters to a sophisticated clientele of thritysomethings. ✉ *235 Edward St.,* ☎ *07/3229–4916.* 💲 *5–7 PM $1, after 7 PM $15.* ☼ *Mon.–Sat. 10 AM–5 AM, Sun. 10 AM–3 AM.*

Outdoor Activities and Sports

Cricket

Queensland Cricketer's Club provides playing schedules and ticket information for the nation's favorite sport, which is played over the Australian summer. ✉ *Vulture St., East Brisbane,* ☎ *07/3896–4555.*

Fishing

Anne's Sportfishing Charters can arrange any local on-water activity. Anne Donaldson, the proprietor, is also helpful in dispensing advice to visitors about fishing trips and local regulations. ✉ *24 Grattan Terr., Wynnum,* ☎ *07/3396–2149,* FAX *07/3393–0558.*

Golf

To play a round of golf at one of the city's premier courses contact **Indooroopilly Golf Club** (✉ Meiers Rd., Indooroopilly, ☎ 07/3870–3728). There are two courses here, the West and the East; however, only the East—a 36-hole, par-72 course—is open to visitors. You could also try **St. Lucia Golf Club** (✉ Cnr. or Indooroopilly Rd. and Carawa St., ☎ 07/3870–3938).

Rugby

Rugby League, a professional variation of rugby, is played in winter in Australia. For match programs and information call **Queensland Rugby Football League Limited** (☎ 1900/93–4212). Rugby Union, the more familiar international game, is also popular. Call **Queensland Rugby Union Limited** (☎ 07/3214–3333).

Tennis

For information about playing at Brisbane's municipal or private courts or for details of upcoming tournaments, contact **Queensland Tennis.** ⊠ *83 Castlemaine St., Milton,* ☎ *07/3368–2433.*

Walking

The National Trust publishes an informative **Historic Walks** brochure that is available from the Queensland Government Travel Centre and some hotels. ⊠ *Edward and Adelaide Sts.,* ☎ *13–1801.*

Shopping

Department Stores

The famous **David Jones** and **Myer** department stores are downtown on the Queen Street Mall.

Discount Stores

Stones Corner, a business and residential area about 10 km (6 mi) south of the city center, is a popular shopping area where a variety of shops have opened discount outlets selling goods that are either seconds or end-of-season styles. Country Road, Sportsgirl, and Table Eight are a few of the brands available. Houseware stores are also represented. ⊠ *Logan and Old Cleveland Rds., Stones Corner.*

Malls and Arcades

The **Queen Street Mall** is considered the best downtown shopping area, with numerous buskers, flower stalls, and a generally festive atmosphere. **Myer Centre** (⊠ Queen, Elizabeth, and Albert Sts.) houses the national department store of the same name, as well as boutiques, specialty shops, delis, restaurants, cinemas, and an upstairs amusement park. The historic and aesthetically pleasing **Brisbane Arcade** joins Queen Street Mall and Adelaide Street and features elegant designer boutiques and jewelry shops. **Rowes Arcade** (⊠ 235 Edward St.) is a renovated 1920s ballroom and banquet hall. **Wintergarden Complex** (Queen Street Mall) was recently renovated and has a range of boutiques and specialty shops, as well as a food court. **Broadway on the Mall** connects via a walkway to David Jones, and it has a very good food center on the lower ground floor. **The Pavilion** (⊠ Queen and Albert Sts.) has two levels of exclusive shops. **Tattersalls Arcade** (⊠ Queen and Edward Sts.) also caters to discerning shoppers. **Savoir Faire** (⊠ 20 Park Rd., Milton) is an upscale shopping and dining complex 10 minutes from the business district. **Chopstix** (⊠ 249 Brunswick St., Fortitude Valley) is a collection of 20 Asian shops and restaurants in the heart of Chinatown.

Markets

The Riverside Centre (⊠ 123 Eagle St.) is home to the **Cat's Tango Riverside Markets,** an upscale arts-and-crafts market, which is open Sunday 8–4. **South Bank Parklands** has a Friday night Lantern Market that is open 5–10, and a Crafts Village that sells good-quality homemade clothing and arts and crafts on Saturday 10–5, Sunday 9–5.

Specialty Stores

ABORIGINAL CRAFTS

Queensland Aboriginal Creations sells genuine Aboriginal hunting paraphernalia and boomerangs, woomeras, didgeridoos, bark paintings, pottery, and carvings. ⊠ *199 Elizabeth St.,* ☎ *07/3224–5730.*

ANTIQUES

Brisbane Antique Market, near the airport, collects more than 40 dealers' antiques, collectibles, and jewelry under one roof. ⊠ *791 Sandgate Rd., Clayfield,* ☎ *07/3262–1444.*

Cordelia Street Antique and Art Centre, housed inside an old church, purveys an interesting range of antiques and jewelry. ⊠ *Cordelia and Glenelg Sts.,* ☎ *07/3844–8514.*

Paddington Antique Centre is a converted picture theater filled with antiques and bric-a-brac. ⊠ *167 Latrobe Terr., Paddington* ☎ *07/3369–8088*

AUSTRALIAN PRODUCTS

Greg Grant Country Clothing specializes in the legendary Drizabone oilskin coats, Akubra and leather hats, whips, R. M. Williams boots, and moleskins. ⊠ *Myer Centre, Queen St.,* ☎ *07/3221–4233.*

My Country sells country-style clothing for the whole family, plus stockwhips, moleskins, and steerhide belts, all made in Australia. ⊠ *Broadway on the Mall, Level 1, Queen Street Mall,* ☎ *07/3221–2858.*

OPALS

Quilpie Opals has a large selection of Queensland boulder opals as well as high-grade opals, available as individual stones or already set. ⊠ *Lennons Plaza Building, 68 Queen St. Mall,* ☎ *07/3221–7369.*

SOUVENIRS

The National Trust Gift Shop sells quality Australian-made handicrafts, plus postcards, books, and novelty items. ⊠ *The Mansions, 40 George St.,* ☎ *07/3221–1887.*

Brisbane A to Z

Arriving and Departing

BY BUS

Long-distance bus companies serving Brisbane include **Greyhound Pioneer Australia** (⊠ Brisbane Transit Centre, Roma St., ☎ 07/3258–1670 or 13–2030) and **McCafferty's** Express Coaches (⊠ Brisbane Transit Centre, Roma St., ☎ 07/3236–3035 or 13–1499).

BY CAR

Brisbane is 1,002 km (621 mi) from Sydney along coastal Highway 1. An inland route from Sydney follows Highway 1 to Newcastle and then heads inland on Highway 15. Either drive can be made in a day; however, two days are recommended for ample time to sightsee along the way.

BY PLANE

Brisbane International Airport is served by a multitude of international airlines. *See* Air Travel *in* Smart Travel Tips for information on international as well as domestic carriers.

Between the airport and the city center. Brisbane International Airport is 9 km (6 mi) from the city center. **Coachtrans** (☎ 07/3236–1000) provides a daily bus service, called SkyTrans Shuttle, to and from city hotels every 30 minutes between 5 AM and 8:30 PM. The fare is $6.50 per person one way, $12 round-trip.

Taxis to downtown Brisbane cost approximately $30.

BY TRAIN

Railways of Australia run nightly service between Sydney and Brisbane (14 hours). There is regular service from 5:30 AM until 12 midnight between Brisbane and the Gold Coast. The *Sunlander* and the luxurious *Queenslander* trains make a total of four runs a week between Brisbane and Cairns in the north. Other long-distance passenger trains are the *Spirit of the Tropics* (twice per week) between Brisbane and Townsville, the *Spirit of Capricorn* (once per week) between Brisbane and Rockhampton, the new high-tech *Tilt Train* between Brisbane and Rockhampton (six times per week), the *Inlander* between Townsville and Mount Isa (twice per week), the *Westlander* between Brisbane and Charleville (twice per week), and the *Spirit of the Outback* between Brisbane and Longreach (twice per week). Packages, such as Reef and Rail or Outback Aussies Adventures, are also available. Trains depart from the Roma Street Station. For details contact **Queensland Rail** (⊠ 305 Edward St., ☎ 07/3235–2222) or the **City Booking Office** (☎ 13–2232).

The Great South Pacific Express (☎ 1800/62–7655) offers first-class "Orient Express" type luxury rail service among Sydney, Brisbane, and Cairns. The train runs twice weekly each way and can be combined with numerous sightseeing tours, such as an air excursion to a coral cay on the Great Barrier Reef to snorkel and enjoy a picnic lunch.

Getting Around

BY BUS

Buses are a good way for vacationers to get around, as stops are well signposted and the buses mostly run to schedule. For routes, schedules, and fares, call **Trans Info** (☎ 13–1230).

BY CAR

All major car-rental agencies have offices in Brisbane, including **Avis** (☎ 07/3252–7111), **Thrifty** (☎ 07/3252–5994), **Hertz** (☎ 13–3039), and **Budget** (☎ 13–2727). Four-wheel-drive vehicles are available.

BY FERRY

Speedy **CityCat ferries** (☎ 13–1230), run by the Brisbane City Council, call at 13 points along the Brisbane River, from Bretts Wharf to the University of Queensland. They run daily 6 AM–10:30 PM about every half hour. The CityCat ferries are terrific for taking a leisurely look at Brisbane river life. From the city skyline to the homes of the well-heeled, there's usually something of interest to see.

BY TAXI

Taxis are metered and relatively inexpensive. They are available at designated taxi stands outside hotels, downtown, and at the railway station, although it is usually best to phone for one. The best taxi companies in Brisbane are **Yellow Cabs** (☎ 13–1924) and **Black and White Cabs** (☎ 13–1008).

Contacts and Resources

EMERGENCIES

Ambulance, fire brigade, and police. ☎ *000.*

Royal Brisbane Hospital. ☎ *07/3253–8111.*

GUIDED TOURS

Australian Day Tours offers a range of half- or full-day tours of Brisbane, as well as trips to the Gold Coast, Noosa Heads, and the Sunshine Coast. ⊠ *Brisbane Transit Centre, Roma St., Level 3,* ☎ *07/3236–4155 or 1800/36–1788.*

City Sights open tram-style buses, run by the Brisbane City Council, make half-hourly circuits of city landmarks and other points of inter-

In case you want to see the world.

At American Express, we're here to make your journey
a smooth one. So we have over 1,700 travel service locations in over 130 countries ready to help. What else
would you expect from the world's largest travel agency?

do more

Travel

Call 1 800 AXP-3429 or visit
www.americanexpress.com/travel

In case you want to be welcomed there.

We're here to see that you're always welcomed at establishments everywhere. That's why millions of people carry the American Express® Card – for peace of mind, confidence, and security, around the world or just around the corner.

do more

Cards

In case you're running low.

We're here to help with more than 190,000 Express Cash locations around the world. In order to enroll, just call American Express at 1 800 CASH-NOW before you start your vacation.

do more AMERICAN EXPRESS

Express Cash

And in case you'd rather be safe than sorry.

We're here with American Express® Travelers Cheques. They're the safe way to carry money on your vacation, because if they're ever lost or stolen you can get a refund, practically anywhere or anytime. To find the nearest place to buy Travelers Cheques, call 1 800 495-1153. Another way we help you do more.

do more

Travelers Cheques

est. They leave from Post Office Square every 40 minutes, starting at 9 AM, with a break from 12:20 to 1:40. You can buy tickets on the bus, and you can get on or off at any of the 19 stops. ✉ *Brisbane City Council, 69 Ann St.,* ☎ *13–1230.* 🚌 *$15.*

City Nights tours depart daily from the Brisbane City Hall, City Sights Bus Stop 2 (Adelaide St.), at 6 PM for a trip up scenic Mount Coot-tha. After enjoying the city's lights you are taken on a CityCat ferry ride down the Brisbane River before joining the bus for a ride back to town through the historic Valley precinct. The tour finishes at City Hall at 8:30 PM. ✉ *Brisbane City Council, 69 Ann St.,* ☎ *13–1230.* 🚌 *$15.*

Club Crocodile River Queen, a paddle wheeler formally called the Kook-aburra Queen, runs daily morning tea and buffet cruises, plus seafood lunch and dinner cruises along the Brisbane River. They also have af-ternoon tea on Sunday. The cruises often feature live entertainment. ✉ *Eagle Street Pier, 1 Eagle St.,* ☎ *07/3221–1300.* 🚌 *$20–$55 per person.*

VISITOR INFORMATION

Brisbane Tourism. ✉ *Elizabeth St., Box 12260, 4001;* ✉ *Brisbane City Hall, Adelaide St.,* ☎ *07/3221–8411;* ✉ *Queen St. Mall,* ☎ *07/3229–5918.*

Queensland Government Travel Centre provides information about all of Queensland. ✉ *Edward and Adelaide Sts., GPO Box 9958, 4001,* ☎ *13–1801.*

CARNARVON NATIONAL PARK

Despite its remote location 700 km (434 mi) northwest of Brisbane—*way* off the beaten path—Carnarvon National Park (☎ 07/4984–4505) is one of the most popular parks in central Queensland. Its 21 km (13 mi) of walking tracks are suitable for the whole family, with only a few side tracks that involve difficult ascents. Even on hot days, the park's shady gorges are cool and refreshing.

Carnarvon is famous for its ancient Aboriginal paintings, particularly those in the Art Gallery and Cathedral Cave. Both galleries span more than 165 ft of sheer sandstone walls covered with red ochre stencils of ancient Aboriginal life—among them weapons and hands. An ex-tensive boardwalk system with informational plaques allows easy ac-cess to the fragile paintings.

Several popular walking trails wind through the park, most of them branching off the main trail, which begins near the main campground. The 18½-km (11½-mi) round-trip trail to Cathedral Cave leapfrogs back and forth across the Carnarvon Creek at well-placed, round boulders. Except at stream crossings, the trail is flat and well marked. Side trips off the main trail lead to the popular Moss Garden, a collection of sand-stone walls blanketed in green moss, and the Amphitheater, an enclosed gorge accessible by a 30-ft steel ladder. Take water with you when hik-ing, because creek water is not potable. Carnarvon is best visited dur-ing the dry season, April through October, when most roads to the park are passable.

Lodging

The **main campground** is at the end of the only road into the park. Fees are $3.50 per person per night or $14 for a family. The facilities in-clude cold-water showers and toilets. Bookings are essential; if you plan to visit during school holiday periods, call up to nine months in ad-vance. The park offers several remote hike-in camping areas in addition to the main campground. Rates for the 23 cabins at **Carnarvon Gorge Oasis Lodge** (✉ Park Entrance, Warego Hwy., ☎ 07/4984–4503) are $165 per person, including full board and activities. The lodge also has a general store that sells food staples as well as fuel, gas, and ice.

Arriving and Departing

A four-wheel-drive vehicle is recommended for travel to Carnarvon, especially right after the wet season (January–late April), when many roads may still be flooded. Two-wheel-drive vehicles are adequate during the height of dry season. From Brisbane, take the Warego Highway 486 km (301 mi) west to Roma, then 271 km (168 mi) north toward Injune and Carnarvon. The final 70 km (43 mi) are rather rough. Be sure to bring food for at least two extra days in case of road flooding.

GOLD COAST AND LAMINGTON NATIONAL PARK

For many years this was the fastest-growing playground in Australia. As a result, skyscraper condominiums jostle for waterfront positions, while the streets below are lined with souvenir shops, fast-food stalls, and restaurants. The area can be garish, glitzy, and even crass—but it is never, *never* dull. Don't come here if you want to get away from it all. Life on the Gold Coast is a nonstop party.

An hour south of Brisbane, the Gold Coast officially comprises the 32 km (20 mi) from Southport to Coolangatta, but it has sprawled almost as far inland as Nerang. It is the most developed tourist destination in Australia, its popularity ensured by 300 days of sunshine a year and an average temperature of 75°F. Christmas and June through August are peak seasons.

Away from the Gold Coast scene, **Lamington National Park** is an interesting tropical–subtropical–temperate ecological border zone. That makes for a complex abundance of plant and animal life that's astounding. The park is on the Queensland–New South Wales border, about a three-hour trip from Brisbane, or about an hour from Surfers Paradise.

For the sake of putting some form on the twisting ribbon of development that is the Gold Coast, this section is arranged as if you were approaching the area by road from Brisbane and following the coast from north to south, down as far as the New South Wales border.

Coomera

48 km (30 mi) south of Brisbane.

☺ **Dreamworld.** In just one day at this family theme park, you can thrill on the fastest, tallest ride in the world, The Tower of Terror, then take a free fall from 39 stories on the Giant Drop. You can also watch Bengal tigers play and swim with their handlers on Tiger Island, cuddle a koala in Koala Country, or journey into a fragile world on the Creature Cruise. There are entertaining shows, costumed characters roaming the park, and an amazing six-story IMAX screen theater. The park is 40 minutes outside Brisbane and 20 minutes from Surfers Paradise along the Pacific Highway. ✉ *Dreamworld Pkwy.,* ☎ *07/5588–1111 or 1800/07–3300.* ☞ *$44.* ◷ *Daily 10–5; Main St., Plaza Restaurant, and Koala Country daily 9–5.*

Oxenford

2 km (1 mi) south of Coomera.

○ **Warner Bros. Movie World** is one of the most popular tourist attractions in Australia and one of the few movie theme parks outside the United States. The park incorporates Warner Roadshow Movie World Studios, where you can see the actual Riddler's Lair set from *Batman Forever,* and learn how the special effects for the movie were produced. The park is also home to the Lethal Weapon ride, which is the only suspended looping coaster in Australia as well as the Wild West Adventure ride, which pushes thrill seekers over the edge of a 60-ft waterfall at 70 kph (45 mph). There is a good children's section and plenty of shops selling Warner Bros. souvenirs. ⊠ *Pacific Hwy.,* ☎ 07/5573–3999 or 07/5573–8485. ▦ *$44.* ☉ *Daily 9:30–5:30. Closed Dec. 25 and Apr. 25.*

○ When you're looking for **Wet 'n' Wild Water Park,** keep your eyes out for Matilda, the giant kangaroo mascot of the 1982 Brisbane Commonwealth Games. The park has magnificent water slides, as well as a wave pool with a 3-ft-high surf. One favorite attraction is the Dive-in-Movies, where a giant screen at the back of the wave pool shows recent releases Saturday night from September through April and every night in January. And of course there's Calypso Beach, a tropical island fringed with white sandy beaches, surrounded by a slow-moving river where guests can laze about in brightly colored tubes. ⊠ *Pacific Hwy.,* ☎ 07/5573–2277. ▦ *$25.* ☉ *Sun.–Fri. 10–5, Sat. 10–9.*

Hope Island

6 km (4 mi) east of Oxenford.

Home to a Hyatt Regency hotel, **Sanctuary Cove** is a huge resort area with two golf courses, an outstanding marina, and a shopping center filled with boutiques, restaurants, a cinema, health club, and a small brewery. It is the result of a 1980s experiment in forming a very exclusive, secure community. Most residents travel around the village in golf carts, saving their cars for the times when they have to venture out into the wider world. It's reached by turning north off the highway at Oxenford.

Crafts enthusiasts should stop at **Village Square** (near Sanctuary Cove) to soak up 9 acres of Australian arts and crafts. Opened in late 1998, Village Square is a theme village of 300 studio shops where such treasures as an Australian boomerang, locally made pottery, and homemade children's clothes can be bought. There are also artisans at work to watch, street entertainers, cafés, and restaurants. Buses depart Brisbane's Roma Street Transit Centre at 8:30 and 9:30 for the park, and the Gold Coast train leaves Central station at 8:26 and 9:26 for Coomera where a bus will transfer you to the park. *Southport–Oxenford Rd.,* ☎ 07/5530–1885. ▦ *$2.* ☉ *Daily 9–5.*

Lodging

$$$$ 🏨 **Hyatt Regency Sanctuary Cove.** Set in landscaped tropical gardens,
★ this opulent low-rise hotel resembles a monumental Australian colonial mansion. Five three-story guest courts are luxuriously appointed, each with its own large, private balcony. The main lobby building, known as the Great House, leads past a cascading waterfall to the courtyard and swimming pool–spa area. There's also a sandy beach lagoon fed with filtered saltwater next to the resort's main harbor. A walkway from the hotel leads directly into the village. ⊠ *Manor Circle, Casey Rd.,* ☎ 07/5530–1234, ℻ 07/5530–8056. *223 rooms, 24 suites. 2 restaurants, 2 bars, 2 pools, health club, sauna, spa, 2 18-hole golf courses,*

9 tennis courts, bowling, squash, deep-sea fishing, baby-sitting, children's programs. AE, DC, MC, V.

South Stradbroke Island

1 km (½ mi) east of the Gold Coast.

South Stradbroke Island is about 20 km (12 mi) long and 2 km (1 mi) wide. The first white settlers—cane farmers—arrived on the island during the 1870s, followed by oysterers in the 1880s. Old oyster beds can still be seen in the waters on the boat ride to Couran Cove Resort.

Lodging

$$$–$$$$ ☒ **Couran Cove Resort.** Fifteen minutes by boat from the glitz of the Gold Coast, Couran Cove Resort offers a haven of peace and harmony. The vision of Olympic athlete Ron Clarke, this eco-tourism resort opened in 1998 and offers an amazing array of sporting facilities: Biking, swimming, tennis, rock climbing, baseball, basketball, and more. There's also an innovative covered 180-m (594-ft), three-lane running track opened by sprinter Carl Lewis. Many Olympic teams will be training here before the Sydney Games, including the American track and field team. The resort includes spacious self-contained rooms, an onsite store with basic groceries, and a restaurant and two cafés. Every accommodation has a view over the beach, bush, or lagoon; many are built over the water so you can fish off the balcony. Couran Cove has its own patrolled surf beach, and a variety of water sports are offered. Packages are available for day-trippers. ☒ *South Stradbroke Island, Box 224, Runaway Bay, Gold Coast 4216,* ☎ *07/5597–9000 or 1800/ 63–2211,* ℻ *07/5597–9090. 192 apartments, 50 lagoon lodges, 25 villas, 127 cabins, 3 wilderness lodges, 100 tents. Restaurant, bar, 2 cafés, kitchenettes, 2 pools, health club, 4 driving ranges, tennis courts, beach, snorkeling, windsurfing, boating, jet skiing, parasailing, waterskiing, boating, camping, fishing, bicycles, children's programs ages 5–12, chapel, business services, convention center. AE, DC, MC, V.*

Southport

16 km (10 mi) southeast of Oxenford.

In Southport, look for the turnoff to the **Spit,** a natural peninsula pointing north. This is where you'll find fine dining, exclusive shops, and the town's top attraction.

☺ **Seaworld** is Australia's largest marine park. Six daily shows feature whales, dolphins, sea lions, and waterskiing. There is also a Pirates 3-D Adventure show, starring Eric Idle and Leslie Nielsen, with fantastic special effects. Rides include a monorail, a corkscrew roller coaster, and water slides. Dolphin Cove, the largest natural dolphin lagoon in the world, opened in 1996. Limited numbers of visitors, age 14 years or more, can swim with the dolphins. Early bookings are recommended. All rides except helicopter and parasailing flights and swimming with the dolphins are included in the ticket price. ☒ *Seaworld Dr., The Spit,* ☎ *07/5588–2222.* ☒ *$44.* ☺ *Daily 9:30–5.*

Dining and Lodging

$$–$$$ ✗ **Cafe Romas.** At this stylish café overlooking the Southport Marina, diners may sit under a black-and-white awning on the boardwalk, or one level up on the café's verandah, or inside the café itself, decorated in European style and lit by Parisian lamps. The seaside setting dovetails nicely with a menu that draws on the ocean's bounty, including mussels al fresco and tempura prawns. ☒ *Marina Mirage Shopping Center, the Spit,* ☎ *07/5331–2488. AE, DC, MC, V.*

$$$$ 🏨 **Sheraton Mirage.** A low-rise building nestled amid lush gardens and
★ fronting a secluded beach, this resort has a distinctly Australian look.
Rooms are tastefully furnished in soft colors and overlook gardens, the
Pacific Ocean, or vast saltwater lagoons. A suspension bridge over the
road links the resort with the elegant Marina Mirage Shopping Center, although you would be wise to sample the excellent fare at the resort's own restaurants first. Don't miss the weekly poolside barbecue
in summer. ⊠ *Seaworld Dr., the Spit, 4217,* ☎ *07/5591–1488,* ℻ *07/
5591–2299. 303 rooms, 40 suites. 3 restaurants, coffee shop, no-
smoking rooms, pool, health club, 4 tennis courts, nightclub, children's
programs ages 6–14, laundry service. AE, DC, MC, V.*

Boating

You can rent yachts and cabin cruisers from **Popeye's Boat Hire.** ⊠
Mariner's Cove, 212 Seaworld Dr., the Spit, ☎ *07/5591–2553 or 07/
5532–5822.*

Fishing

Gold Coast Fishing Tackle can provide tackle and advice about the best
local fishing spots. ⊠ *15 Nind St.,* ☎ *07/5531–0755.*

Nightlife and the Arts

For the most elegant disco on the Gold Coast, head for **Rolls** nightclub
at the Sheraton Mirage. The decor is built around a single glorious vintage Rolls-Royce fitted with a small table, which may be booked (for
a fee) by patrons who wish to enjoy snacks and drinks in its ultimate
luxury. This is the place to come for champagne, cocktails, light supper, and live music. ⊠ *Seaworld Dr., the Spit,* ☎ *07/5591–1488.* 🎵
Free. ☉ *Fri. and Sat. 9 PM–5 AM.*

Shopping

One of the most elegant shopping centers on the Gold Coast is the **Marina Mirage,** where you'll find such designer boutiques as Yves Saint
Laurent, Aigner, Louis Vuitton, and Hermès, along with fine antiques,
beach and leisure wear, perfume, and duty-free goods. There are fine
restaurants, a medical center, and marina facilities as well. ⊠ *Seaworld
Dr., the Spit,* ☎ *07/5577–0088.*

Main Beach

6 km (4 mi) south of Southport.

Along with being a residential area full of high-rise apartments and
houses, Main Beach is a popular swimming spot for Brisbane residents
who are looking for good surf without the crowds of Surfers Paradise.
Tedder Avenue at Main Beach is one of the local haunts. It has a strip
of elegant coffee shops and cafés separate from the tourist areas, which
makes it the spot to get the measure of real-time Gold Coast life.

Surfers Paradise

8 km (5 mi) south of Southport; 72 km (45 mi) south of Brisbane.

The heart of town is an eclectic collection of high-rises overlooking the
beach, where bodies bake in the sand under signs warning of the risks
of skin cancer. Park as close to Cavill Avenue as possible.

If your thirst for the bizarre isn't satisfied by the crowds in Surfers Paradise, the displays at **Ripley's Believe It or Not! Museum** will give you
that extra thrill. This is the home of the famous African Fertility statues—more than 500 women have said they became pregnant soon after
rubbing them. ⊠ *Raptis Plaza, Cavill Ave.,* ☎ *07/5592–0040.* 🎟
$9.95. ☉ *Daily 9 AM–11 PM.*

Surfers Paradise hosts the annual **Indy Car Race.** The date changes each year, but when it occurs it's a big event, with streets blocked off to create a challenging course for the world's top speed demons. For more information contact the Gold Coast Indy Office (☎ 07/5588–6800).

Dining and Lodging

$$$ × **Danny's.** In a spacious and elegant room overlooking the river,
★ guests are seated in comfortable booths while a trio plays Continental and Latin American music. The menu includes memorable international and Italian dishes, such as the Mona Lisa salad of fresh prawns, smoked salmon, and avocado with an orange–sour cream dressing. Danny's also serves the pasta that well-fed tenor Luciano Pavarotti says is his favorite: spinach spaghetti with Moreton Bay bugs (a type of lobster). For dessert, have Mamma's homemade gelato. ⊠ *Tiki Village, Cavill Ave.,* ☎ *07/5538–2818. AE, DC, MC, V. No lunch.*

$$$ × **Mango's.** This Nerang River–front restaurant features a mix of Santa Fe and tropical decor, including a thatched roof, exposed beams, palm trees, and a waterfall. Even though the restaurant seats 400, the candlelit tables and clever layout make dinners as intimate as you want them to be. The menu is swimming with seafood dishes. Try grilled springwater barramundi or grilled lobster with brandy butter. ⊠ *Tiki Village, Cavill Ave.,* ☎ *07/5531–6177. AE, DC, MC, V. No lunch Mon.–Thurs.*

$$–$$$ × **Omeros Bros. Seafood Restaurant.** This restaurant has retained a loyal
★ following from its Brisbane days; the chefs took their seafood skills with them when the establishment relocated to the Gold Coast in 1998. Housed in a magnificent Inca-style bungalow, the setting is pure resort elegance with cast-iron chairs, blue and yellow walls, and crisp white tablecloths. The menu ranges from simple dishes, such as grilled fish with salad, to the more exotic, such as mussels poached in bouillabaisse and red wine sauce. A small children's menu is also offered. ⊠ *Ocean Ave. and Gold Coast Hwy.,* ☎ *07/5584–6060. AE, DC, MC, V*

$–$$ × **Hard Rock Café Surfers.** Packed with the usual rock memorabilia, this has been one of the hottest spots on the coast since it opened in 1996. You'll walk into the Pray for Surf bar and Hard Rock Shop on the ground floor; the Skyhooks café—named for the Australian rock band of the '70s—is on the second floor. The menu is full of American favorites like burgers, grilled sandwiches, and french fries. ⊠ *Cavill Ave. and Gold Coast Hwy.,* ☎ *07/5539–9377. AE, DC, MC, V.*

$$$ ⌸ **Marriott Surfers Paradise Resort.** The lobby's giant columns and grand
★ circular staircase—cooled by a colorful Indian punkah—showcase this hotel's opulent style. The large guest rooms, decorated in gentle hues of beige, light plum, and moss green, have walk-in closets, marble bathrooms, safes, balconies, and ocean views. The hotel is close to both the Nerang River and the main beach. The hotel's own beach, on a saltwater lagoon stocked with brilliantly colored fish, is deep enough for scuba lessons. The freshwater outdoor pool is surrounded by gardens. There are dive and water-sports shops on premises; you can rent boardsailing equipment, water skis, and catamarans on the river. ⊠ *158 Ferny Ave., 4217,* ☎ *07/5592–9800,* ℻ *07/5592–9888. 330 rooms, 13 suites. 2 restaurants, 2 bars, in-room VCRs, pool, sauna, spa, steam room, 2 tennis courts, exercise room, baby-sitting. AE, DC, MC, V.*

$$–$$$ ⌸ **Moroccan Beach Resort.** Opposite a patrolled section of the beach, these white Mediterranean-style apartments offer a stark contrast to the blue skies and water. The pick of the development's three towers is the Esplanade, which has absolute beach frontage. The hotel-style rooms are quite small—but comfortable—and the one- and two-bedroom apartments are spacious and luxuriously appointed. Apartments come with a well-equipped kitchen and laundry facilities. Outside, there is a common barbecue area. ⊠ *9 Elkhorn Ave.,* ☎ *07/5526–9400,* ℻

07/5526–9700. 30 rooms, 150 apartments. 3 pools, wading pool, 3 hot tubs AE, DC, MC, V.

$$ 🎑 **ANA Hotel Gold Coast.** This 22-story hotel is only a short walk from the beach and Cavill Avenue. It's the perfect spot if you like being in the center of the action during the annual Indy Car Race. Bookings for that time are advised well in advance. Rooms have soft pastel decor with blond-wood furniture and balconies with views over central Surfers Paradise. Service is impeccable. ⊠ *22 View Ave., 4217,* ☎ *07/5579–1000,* 📠 *07/5570–1260. 404 rooms, 17 suites. 2 restaurants, 2 bars, pool, sauna, 2 tennis courts, exercise room. AE, DC, MC, V.*

Nightlife and the Arts

New nightspots spring up in Surfers Paradise all the time. Some of the long-running favorites are **Melba's on the Park** (⊠ Cavill Ave., ☎ 07/5538–7411), the **Penthouse Nightclub** (⊠ Orchid Ave., ☎ 07/5538–1388), and **Bensons Nightclub** (⊠ Orchid Ave., ☎ 07/5538–7600).

Shopping

Raptis Plaza (⊠ Between Cavill Mall and the Esplanade, ☎ 07/5592–2123) is filled with enticing boutiques and cafés, while **Elkhorn Avenue**, parallel to Cavill Avenue, is where you'll find luxe shops like Cartier, Prada, and Hermès. The **Paradise Centre** (⊠ Cavill Ave., ☎ 07/5592–0155) has 120 shops and restaurants, as well as an extensive amusement arcade and a Woolworth's variety store. **Surfers Paradise Beach Front Markets** (☎ 07/5581–7500) sell locally made arts and crafts every Friday night (5:30–10) on the boardwalk at the beach end of Cavill Mall.

Ashmore

7 km (4½ mi) west of Surfers Paradise.

Lodging

$$$–$$$$ 🎑 **Royal Pines Resort.** Nestled beside the Nerang River, this resort offers the best of everything: 500 acres of manicured gardens, two championship golf courses, a PGA Golf Academy, two tennis courts, small lakes, a native wildlife sanctuary, and a marina that has access to the Nerang River and the ocean. The resort hosts major golf events, including the Australian Ladies Masters, which is held in late February or early March. It even has its own church, which is popular for weddings. The rooms are nicely decorated with pastel colors and natural-wood furnishings. Junior suites, which have hot tubs overlooking the golf courses, are the ones to reserve. ⊠ *Ross St.,* ☎ *07/5597–1111 or 1800/07–4999,* 📠 *07/5597–2277. 285 rooms, 45 suites. 6 restaurants, 2 bars, 3 pools, 2 18-hole golf courses, 27-hole putting green, 7 tennis courts, health club, marina, kids club, church. AE, DC, MC, V.*

Broadbeach

8 km (5 mi) south of Southport.

Dining and Lodging

$$$ ✕🎑 **Hotel Conrad and Jupiters Casino.** This hotel-casino always seems to be bustling, especially in the sprawling lobby, where people meet to head for a restaurant, bar, or into the main gambling rooms. The casino offers 100 gaming tables and more than 100 gaming machines; high rollers should steer straight for the lavishly appointed Club Conrad. There are six restaurants in the complex, including the buffet-style Food Fantasy, which is a Gold Coast favorite for families, and Andiamo, a local Italian star. ⊠ *Broadbeach Island, Gold Coast Hwy., 4218,* ☎ *07/5592–1133 or 1800/07–4344,* 📠 *07/5592–8219. 609 rooms, 29 suites, 2 penthouses. 6 restaurants, 9 bars, coffee shop, pool, whirlpool, sauna, 4 tennis courts, squash, casino. AE, DC, MC, V.*

Nightlife

Jupiter's Casino in Broadbeach provides flamboyant around-the-clock entertainment. The Casino features 100 gaming tables on two levels, and includes blackjack, baccarat, craps, sic-bo, pai gow, keno, plus more than 100 gaming machines, which are open 24 hours a day, 7 days a week. Fortunes Nightclub, on the top level of the complex, is open nightly, and the 950-seat showroom often features glitzy Las Vegas–style productions. ⊠ *Gold Coast Hwy.,* ☎ *07/5592–1133.*

Shopping

Oasis Shopping Centre. This development is the retail heart of beach-side Broadbeach, with over 100 retailers as well as an attractive mall where open-air coffee shops stand umbrella-to-umbrella along the edge. A monorail runs from the center to Conrad Jupiters and the Pan Pacific Hotel. ⊠ *Victoria Ave.,* ☎ *07/5592–3900.*

Pacific Fair. This sprawling outdoor shopping center is Queensland's largest, and its major retailers and 260 specialty shops should be enough to satisfy even die-hard shoppers. There are also undercover malls, landscaped grounds with three small lakes, a children's park, and a village green. The shopping center is adjacent to Jupiter's Casino. ⊠ *Hooker Blvd.,* ☎ *07/5539–8766.*

Burleigh Heads

9 km (6 mi) south of Surfers Paradise.

Presented to the National Parks and Wildlife Association by wildlife naturalist David Fleay, **David Fleay's Wildlife Park** consists of wet-lands and rain forests in their natural states and 4 km (2½ mi) of magnificent bushwalks. You'll see koalas, swamp wallabies, brolgas, ibises, platypuses, swans, and crocodiles. The park is west of town. ⊠ *W. Burleigh Rd.,* ☎ *07/5576–2411 or 07/5576–2767.* ☞ *$9.50.* ⊙ *Daily 9–5.*

Dining

$$$ ✕ **Oskars on Burleigh.** Perched on the beachfront, the magnificent view clear to Surfers Paradise makes this restaurant worth a visit. Prawns in coconut, macadamia nuts, and curry mayonnaise followed by glazed mango and coconut tart with double cream are some of the tropically inspired delights on the menu. You can enjoy these dishes from inside the restaurant (where glass walls ensure an unhindered view of the coastline) or from the very large open deck on the surf side. Terra-cotta tiles, blue and green trim, and simple wooden furniture complete the experience. ⊠ *43 Goodwin Terr.,* ☎ *07/5576–3722,* 🖷 *07/5576–3788. AE, DC, MC, V.*

Currumbin

6 km (4 mi) south of Burleigh Heads.

Across the creek from Palm Beach on the Gold Coast Highway is the community of Currumbin and the **Currumbin Sanctuary.** What started off as a bird park in 1947 is now a 70-acre National Trust Reserve that is home to huge flocks of Australian lorikeets, as well as other exotic birds, bilbies, kangaroos, and koalas. Aboriginal dancers also perform daily. Try to be on hand between 8 AM and 9 AM or 4 PM and 5 PM when the lorikeets are fed. The park's lovely grounds are ideal for picnics, and there is a café/restaurant on site. ⊠ *28 Tomewin St., off Gold Coast Hwy.,* ☎ *07/5534–1266.* ☞ *$16.* ⊙ *Daily 8–5.*

Coolangatta

> *25 km (16 mi) south of Surfers Paradise; 97 km (60 mi) south of Brisbane.*

This southernmost Gold Coast border town blends into its New South Wales neighbor, Tweed Heads. It's a pleasant town, with a state-line lookout at the Captain Cook memorial at Point Danger.

Gold Coast Hinterland–Lamington National Park

A visit to the Gold Coast wouldn't be complete without a short journey to nearby **Lamington National Park.** Be forewarned, however, that this can induce culture shock: The natural grandeur of the national park contrasts dramatically with the man-made excesses of the coastal strip. The valleys and peaks of Lamington are home to two types of dense rain forest: the warm tropical variety common in Queensland, and remnants of the cooler subtropical rain forest that blanketed Australia when it was still part of the ancient, Southern Hemisphere supercontinent of Gondwanaland between 50 and 100 million years ago. There is a third forest culture in the park as well, as this is the northernmost point in Australia where the Antarctic beech grows. You'll find it only at higher elevations.

Bushwalkers are well served here, with 160 km (100 mi) of walking tracks that lead to streams, cascades, and waterfalls, through eroded caves, along cliffs, and into fern-filled gullies. The park is a bird-watcher's delight, with more than 200 species identified, including 14 parrot, 16 honeyeater, and 5 owl species. Flashy crimson rosellas are particularly noticeable—the park is home to thousands of these birds, which are not shy about eating out of people's hands. Campers shouldn't be surprised to see brushtail and ringtail possums lurking around the campground at night.

Only two roads lead into the park, one ending at Binna Burra in the northeast, and the other at Green Mountains Lodge (O'Reilly's Mountain Resort) in the south. Several trails wind through the park from these two privately run facilities. The Border Track is a 43-km (27-mi) round-trip walk that connects the two lodges and takes two days to complete. Other trails branch off this one and lead to some of the more than 500 waterfalls in the park. The Senses Track at Binna Burra is a short loop of either 1,300 or 2,300 ft. Designed for the blind, ropes guide walkers to Braille informational signs that dot the trail (parts of the trail have been in disrepair, so check in advance if the ropes are intact). A tape-recorded commentary is also available. Both resorts include introductory walks through the rain forest in their rates.

Rain is likely to fall at any time of the year, but April through October is usually the driest period. The park is 2,805 ft above sea level, so evenings are generally cool. Bring appropriate hiking boots for solid footing on park trails.

Dining and Lodging

There are two lodges to choose from in the Lamington area. Both have budget as well as higher-price accommodations. Binna Burra also has a campground that charges $9 per person per night, and a group of on-site tents that cost $36 per night for two people, $54 per night for four. Bring your own linens or rent them at the Binna Burra lodge for an additional charge.

$$$–$$$$ ✕🏨 **Binna Burra Mountain Lodge.** Founded in 1933, Binna Burra Mountain Lodge has three levels of cabins, offering varying degrees of privacy; most expensive are the cabins with private baths. Tariffs include all meals and guided activities, such as guided bushwalks and mountain biking. To reach Binna Burra, 98 km (61 mi) south of Brisbane, take Route 1 to Nerang, then follow back roads through Beechmont to the lodge; or turn off of Route 1 at Oxenford and drive past Canungra. The lodge also operates a Binna Burra bus that makes a daily return trip to the Surfers Paradise Transit Centre. ✉ *Binna Burra, Beechmont,* ☎ *07/5533–3622. 41 cabins. Restaurant, bar, pool. AE, DC, MC, V.*

$$$–$$$$ ✕▥ **O'Reilly's Rain Forest Guesthouse.** This guest house has three styles of cabins, ranging from a 1930s-style house with shared bathroom up to a mountain-style unit with private bathroom. Rates include all meals and activities, such as guided forest walks. The resort is 109 km (68 mi) from Brisbane via Route 1 through Oxenford and Canungra. The road is twisting and steep, and too narrow for RVs. ✉ *Green Mountains, via Canungra 4275,* ☎ *07/5544–0644. 45 rooms. Restaurant, bar. AE, DC, MC, V.*

Arriving and Departing

Access to O'Reilly's Mountain Resort from Brisbane is via Route 13 through Tamborine and Canungra. The road is twisting and steep, and too narrow for RVs—four-wheel-drive vehicles are recommended. To reach Binna Burra, drive south on Route 13 and turn off at Beaudesert to Nerang and the park.

Buses leave Brisbane for O'Reilly's ($35 round-trip) Sunday through Friday at 9:30 AM from the **Transit Centre** (✉ Roma St., Brisbane, ☎ 07/3285–1777).

Visitor Information

Naturally Queensland Information Centre. ✉ *160 Ann St., Brisbane 4000,* ☎ *07/3227–8187.*

Gold Coast A to Z

Arriving and Departing

BY BUS

Long-distance buses traveling between Sydney and Brisbane stop at Coolangatta and Surfers Paradise. **McCafferty's** (☎ 07/5538–2700 or 13–1499) and **Murrays Coaches** (☎ 07/5526–3822 or 13–2251) operate between Brisbane's Roma Street transit center and the Gold Coast. **Greyhound Pioneer Australia** (✉ 6 Beach Rd., Surfers Paradise, ☎ 13–2030) runs an express coach from the Gold Coast to Brisbane International Airport and Coolangatta Airport, as well as day trips that cover southeast Queensland with daily connections to Sydney and Melbourne.

BY CAR

The Gold Coast begins 65 km (40 mi) south of Brisbane. Take the Pacific Highway (Hwy. 1) south to the Gold Coast Highway, which runs through the towns of Southport, Surfers Paradise, and Coolangatta. From Brisbane International Airport take the Toll Road over the Gateway Bridge to avoid having to drive through Brisbane, then follow the signs to the Gold Coast.

BY PLANE

See Air Travel *in* Smart Travel Tips for information on airlines serving **Coolangatta Airport.**

BY TRAIN

There is a regular service from 5:30 AM until 12 midnight between Brisbane and the Gold Coast. Contact **Queensland Rail** (✉ 305 Edward St., ☎ 07/3235–2222 or 13–2232).

Getting Around

BY BUS

The **Surfside Buslines** (☎ 13–1230) runs an excellent bus service every 15 minutes between Gold Coast attractions, along the strip between Tweed Heads and Southport.

BY CAR

All major car-rental agencies have offices in Brisbane and at the Coolangatta Airport. On the Gold Coast itself, hire cars from **Avis** (⊠ Ferny and Cypress Aves., Surfers Paradise, ☎ 07/5539–9388), **Budget** (⊠ Coolangatta Airport, ☎ 07/5536–5377), and **Thrifty** (⊠ 3006 Gold Coast Hwy., Surfers Paradise, ☎ 07/5538–6511; ⊠ Coolangatta Airport, ☎ 07/5536–6955). Four-wheel-drive vehicles are available.

Contacts and Resources

EMERGENCIES

Ambulance, fire brigade, and police. ☎ *000.*

Gold Coast Hospital. ☎ *07/5571–8211.*

GUIDED TOURS

Terranora Coach Tours (⊠ 85 Anne St., Southport, ☎ 07/5538–7113) and **Coachtrans** (⊠ 552 Reserve Rd., Coomera, ☎ 07/5588–8700) have a variety of day tours of the Gold Coast. Coachtrans also offers theme park transfers.

VISITOR INFORMATION

Gold Coast Information Centres. ⊠ *Beach House Plaza, Marine Parade, Coolangatta,* ☎ *07/5536–7765;* ⊠ *Cavill Mall Kiosk, Surfers Paradise,* ☎ *07/5538–4419.*

Gold Coast Tourism Bureau. ⊠ *64 Ferny Ave., Level 2, Surfers Paradise 4217,* ☎ *07/5592–2699.*

SUNSHINE COAST

One hour from Brisbane by car to its southernmost point, the Sunshine Coast is a 60-km (37-mi) stretch of white-sand beaches, inlets, lakes, and mountains. It begins at the Glass House Mountains in the south and extends to Rainbow Beach in the north. Kenilworth is its inland extent, 40 km (25 mi) west of the ocean. Except for a few touristy eyesores, it has avoided the high-rise glitz of its southern cousin, the Gold Coast. You'll find a quieter, more relaxing pace here, with abundant national parks, secluded coves, and magnificent rain forests spilling down to the ocean.

The Sunshine Coast is for the physically active—swimming and surfing are superb, and sports facilities are every bit as good as those on the Gold Coast. It's also the place to find some monumental Aussie kitsch, like the Ettamogah Pub, Big Pineapple, and the House of Bottles.

Our coverage follows the inland Bruce Highway north, then turns seaward to Noosa Heads, returning south along the ocean shore.

Numbers in the margin correspond to points of interest on the Sunshine Coast map.

En Route   The Bruce Highway runs north from Brisbane through flat eucalyptus country and past large stands of pine, which are slowly retreating as Brisbane housing sprawls northwards. Shortly after the Caboolture turnoff, 44 km (27 mi) north of Brisbane, you will come to a region that was once home to a large Aboriginal population but is now a prosperous dairy center. Here also is the turnoff to **Bribie Island,** 25 km

(16 mi) to the east, which has magnificent beaches, some with glass-calm waters and others with rolling Pacific surf.

Glass House Mountains

⑮ *65 km (40 mi) north of Brisbane.*

More than 20 million years old, the Glass House Mountains consist of nine dramatic, conical outcrops. Pick a peak and go for a climb. Some are gently sloped, while others are serious enough to attract intrepid rock climbers. The mountains are also a favorite destination for experienced hang-glider pilots. The cones lie along the old main road about a half hour outside Brisbane to the west of the Bruce Highway.

The **Australia Zoo,** formally called Queensland Reptile and Fauna Park, has Australian animals, including pythons, taipans, adders, kangaroos, crocodiles, eagles, and wallabies. Animal demonstrations and feeding occur throughout the day, and it's even possible to have your photo taken with a giant python. There are also plenty of walking paths to explore by yourself. ⊠ *Glass House Mountains Rd., 5 km (3 mi) north of Glass House Mountains, Beerwah,* ☎ *07/5494–1134.* ☒ *$13.* ⊙ *Daily 8:30–4.*

Palmview

21 km (13 mi) north of Glass House Mountains, 82 km (51 mi) north of Brisbane.

There's a large, red-roof parody of a classic Australian pub on the left side of the Bruce Highway a few kilometers north of Palmview. A vintage car is perched precariously on the roof, and the whole building appears on the verge of collapse. This is the **Ettamogah Pub,** whose name and design are based on the famous pub featured for decades in the work of Australian cartoonist Ken Maynard. It has an upstairs bistro, a beer garden, and bar. Next door, the **Ettamogah Bakery** sells excellent pies.

⑯

The **Aussie World** amusement area adjacent to Ettamogah Pub has a large shed with pool tables as well as long wooden tables that form the pub's beer garden. There are also camel and pony rides, a Ferris wheel, a minilake with motorized boats, an extensive souvenir outlet that sells Ettamogah-brand beverages, and an opal shop. The **Aboriginal Cultural Centre** displays Aboriginal art. An Aboriginal artist is usually on hand demonstrating indigenous art making, and the Ettamogah Dance Troupe gives twice-daily performances. ⊠ *Bruce Hwy.,* ☎ *07/ 5494–5444.* ⊙ *Mon.–Sat. 9 AM–10 PM, Sun. 9–9.* ☒ *Free.*

Forest Glen

10 km (6 mi) northwest of Palmview.

⑰ The expansive **Forest Glen Sanctuary** is a drive-through park that covers 52 acres of forest and pastureland where rusa, fallow, chital, and red deer will come right up to your car, especially if you have purchased a 50¢ feed bag. The park is also home to emus and other bird life. A nocturnal house has a wide variety of Australian night animals, such as possums and gliders. Koala shows are given daily at 11 and 2; a wombat show is featured at 12:30. ⊠ *Bruce Hwy.,* ☎ *07/5445–1274.* ☒ *$10.90.* ⊙ *Daily 9–5.*

⑱ The **Moonshine Valley Winery** produces surprisingly good wines made from locally grown fruit. Tastings are offered of its fortified ginger wine, Mulberry Rose, and Tom Cobb, a genuine Australian spirit that tastes like strong bourbon.

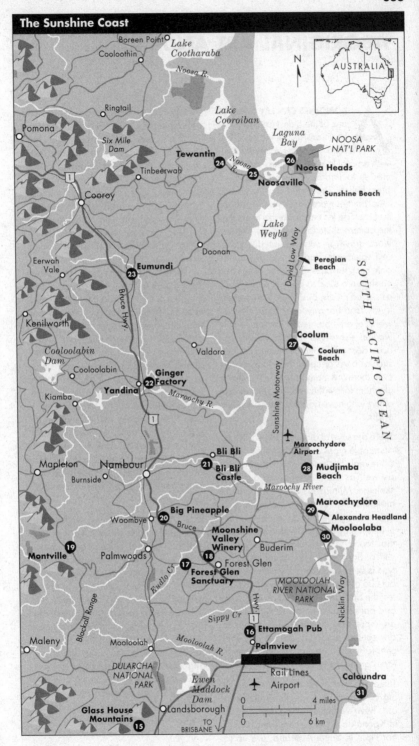

The Sunshine Coast

N

AUSTRALIA

Boreen Point
Cooloothin
Lake Cootharaba
Noosa R.

Ringtail

Pomona

Six Mile Dam

Lake Cooroiban

Tewantin 24

Noosa R.

25 **Noosaville**

26 **Noosa Heads**

Laguna Bay

NOOSA NAT'L PARK

Tinbeerwah

Cooroy

Sunshine Beach

Lake Weyba

Eerwah Vale

Eumundi 23

Doonan

Peregian Beach

Kenilworth

Cooloolabin Dam

Cooloolabin

Valdora

Coolum 27

Coolum Beach

S O U T H   P A C I F I C   O C E A N

Kiamba

22 **Ginger Factory**

Yandina

Maroochy R.

1

Mapleton

Nambour

Burnside

Bli Bli 21

Bli Bli Castle

Maroochydore Airport

28 **Mudjimba Beach**

Maroochy River

Woombye

20 **Big Pineapple**

Bruce

Maroochydore 29

Alexandra Headland

Mooloolaba

30

Montville 19

Palmwoods

17

18

Moonshine Valley Winery

Buderim

Forest Glen

Forest Glen Sanctuary

Eudlo Cr

MOOLOOLAH RIVER NATIONAL PARK

Blackall Range

Maleny

Mooloolah

Sippy Cr

16 **Ettamogah Pub**

Palmview

Mooloolah R.

Nicklin Way

Hwy. 1

Rail Lines

✈ Airport

0 ———— 4 miles

0 ———— 6 km

DULARCHA NATIONAL PARK

Ewen Maddock Dam

Landsborough

TO BRISBANE

Caloundra

31

Glass House Mountains 15

Close-Up

ABORIGINAL ART AND MUSIC

ABORIGINES CAN LAY CLAIM TO one of the oldest art and music traditions in the world. Traditionally a hunter-gatherer society with an oral lore, Aborigines used these modes to impart knowledge and express beliefs. The underlying sacred and ritual themes were based primarily upon the Dreaming (an oral history that established the pattern of life for each clan). Pictures were drawn in sand, painted on trees or implements, and carved or painted onto rock surfaces. Similarly, songs and music were used to portray events such as sacred rituals, bush fires, or successful hunts. Traditionally only men created works of art—painted or carved—while women expressed themselves through body decoration and by making artifacts such as bags or necklaces. Today, however, there are many female artists, some of whom follow the traditional styles and others who have adapted their own style of art.

There are several different and easily recognizable types of Aboriginal art. X-ray art reveals the exterior of the creatures as well as their internal organs and skeleton. Mimi art is a myriad of small matchlike figures of men, women, and animals engaged in some obvious activity such as a hunt. This art resembles that found in many Pacific Islands as well as South Africa and Spain. Another type is stenciling, especially of the hands, but also of feet and sometimes entire bodies; the body part is placed on a surface and paint is sprayed around it to leave an impression on the object. Symbolic art features diagonal, parallel, or concentric lines painted or carved onto surfaces of the body art.

The oldest form of Aboriginal art is painting or engraving on rocks. Archaeologists have evidence that the marks made in Koonalda cave, beneath the Nullarbor Plain in South Australia, are up to 20,000 years old. Rock art is predominately magical-cum-religious expression in haunting red or white figures. It often testifies to successful hunts or evokes the likeness of ancestral spirits. Like art, music also had a purpose and followed regional or song lines. For example, a clan might sing about a bushfire in different ways according to their song line—how and where the fire started, how it spread, and how it eventually died down. Other differences might be in the song words or in the place names, marking off the territory of that group as distinct from others as the song traveled along the path of the fire. Music was also used to recount stories of travels made by animal or human ancestors, often in minute detail describing each place and event, to define tribal lands and boundaries. The didgeridoo is possibly the world's oldest musical instrument, originally found in Northern Australia. It is made from tree trunks hollowed out by termites and is used to accompany chants and songs. In most tribal groups, men, women, and children can play the instrument. It is played by sealing your mouth at one end and vibrating your lips. The didgeridoo acts as an amplifier to produce a haunting, hollow sound.

Today there is not only a resurgence of Aboriginal art and music, but also an acceptance of it in contemporary mainstream Australian art. Young Aborigines who may not have had a strong religious or tribal upbringing are learning about their ancestors through art and music. An example of this are the Aborigines who formed Tjapukai Cultural Park near Cairns. Through the park, the local Aborigines were able to resurrect their tribal language and culture and then present it to the public through music and art. They can present contemporary art works that are connected with their Dreaming, and keep their ancestral connection alive to pass on to future generations.

— Jane Carstens

Montville

⑲ *16 km (10 mi) northwest of Forest Glen.*

Settled in 1887, this quaint mountain village is called the creative heart of the Sunshine Coast. There are panoramic views of the coast from the main street, which was built with a blend of Tudor, Irish, and English cottages of log or stone; Bavarian and Swiss houses; and old Queenslanders. Shops in town are filled with a browser's delight of curiosities and locally made crafts.

Dining and Lodging

$$–$$$ ✕ **Mirabelle.** The much-loved Mirabelle always appeals with its wooden floors, exposed beams, and a partial wall of glass windows that afford spectacular coastal views. The food is a pleasure, with favorites that include eggplant wafers with smoked ham and mozzarella. ⊠ *96 Main St.,* ☎ *07/5442–9489. AE, MC, V. Closed Mon.–Tues. No dinner Wed., Thurs., or Sun.*

$$–$$$ 🏠 **Montville Country Cabins.** Built from local timber, all ten of these cabins are perched on a gentle hill that slopes down to a pond. The cottage furniture and quaint touches, such as cane baskets and log fires, or hot tubs with bush views, make for the perfect romantic getaway. The property, which is 5 km (3 mi) from Montville's main street, adjoins the Obi Obi National Park and attracts a prolific range of birdlife. Cabins come with a fully equipped kitchen. ⊠ *396 Western Ave.,* ☎ *07/5442–9484,* 🖷 *07/5442–9213. 10 cabins. AE, DC, MC, V.*

Shopping

The small, ivy-covered **Herb Garden** cottage shop is packed with such goods as natural skin care products, books, aromatherapy supplies, candles, decorator pieces, and handcrafted jewelry. ⊠ *Main St.,* ☎ *07/5442–9190.*

Natures Image Photography sells beautiful photographs of Australian animals and landscapes. Photographers Andrew Goodall and Monica Krueger have been traveling Australia for many years capturing its changing moods and unique charms on film. All photographs can be bought framed or unframed for easier transportation. An ever-expanding range of greeting cards featuring many of their most popular images is also available. *Main St.,* ☎ 🖷 *07/5442–9564.*

Nambour

9 km (6 mi) north of Forest Glen, 101 km (63 mi) north of Brisbane.

☺ ⑳ Sunshine Plantation is home of the impossible-to-miss **Big Pineapple.** The 50-ft fiberglass monster towers over the highway, and you can climb inside to learn how pineapples are grown. The plantation is a tourist-oriented operation, incorporating a large souvenir shop, jewelry store, arts and crafts shop, restaurants, flume rides, train rides, and an animal nursery. It is also a good place to see how macadamia nuts and other tropical fruits are cultivated. If that's not enough, take a ride on the Nutmobile for a trip to the Magic Macadamia Nut. Other rides include Tomorrow's Harvest, a boat ride through an undercover hydroponic garden, and a cane train ride through a sugar cane plantation. ⊠ *Bruce Hwy., 6 km (4 mi) south of Nambour,* ☎ *07/5442–1333.* 🎟 *Entry free, rides, $7–$8 each or $15.50 for all three rides.* ☉ *Daily 9–5.*

☺ ㉑ At the north end of Nambour, opposite a Toyota dealership, is the turnoff for Bli Bli. Children love the **Bli Bli Castle,** a surprisingly realistic 1973 replica of a Norman castle. It is starting to show its age but still has everything necessary for a rousing game of make-believe, including dungeons and a torture chamber. ⊠ *David Low Way, Bli Bli,* ☎ *07/5448–5373.* ⌦ *$9.* ⊙ *Daily 9–4:30.*

Yandina

9 km (6 mi) north of Nambour.

㉒ The **Ginger Factory** is one of the legendary establishments of Queensland tourism, and it now goes far beyond its original factory-door sale of ginger. Of course, there's a café and a large shop area selling ginger in all forms—from crystallized to various incorporated into jams, marmalades, and chocolates. There's also a miniature train ride ($4) and the Bunya Park Wildlife Sanctuary ($6). A viewing deck overlooks the ginger factory itself, as well as a theaterette, where demonstrations on ginger cultivation and production are given. ⊠ *50 Pioneer Rd. (Coolum Rd.), 1 km (½ mi) east of Bruce Hwy.,* ☎ *07/5446–7100.* ⌦ *Free.* ⊙ *Daily 9–5.*

Dining

$$$ ✕ **Spirit House.** The owners here, who lived for five years in Thailand, have done a remarkable job rendering Thai cuisine on Queensland soil. The restaurant is set in a beautiful rain forest garden, with a nursery and cooking school on site. Try the deep-fried sweet potato and prawn dumplings, then move on to grilled swordfish steaks with a mild coconut curry sauce. ⊠ *4 Ninderry Rd.,* ☎ *07/5446–8994. AE, DC, MC, V. No dinner Sun.–Tues.*

Eumundi

㉓ *18 km (11 mi) north of Nambour, 21 km (13 mi) southwest of Noosa Heads.*

One of the best **street markets** on the Sunshine Coast is held on Saturday from 6:30 AM to 12:30 PM on Memorial Drive in Eumundi. You'll find colorful wares by local craftspeople.

Lodging

$$ ☷ **Taylor's Damn Fine Bed & Breakfast.** Damn fine indeed. The main house is a gracious old Queenslander filled with an eclectic but harmonious blend of retro and country furnishings. The spacious guest rooms have private baths—four have double beds, one has twins. Two are adjacent to the main house in a restored railway carriage. The house overlooks 4 acres of lush paddock that borders the North Maroochy River, where you can take a short rain forest walk. There is also a pool and a 190-yard golf-driving range. Taylor's is a short stroll from Eumundi's main street, and a 15-minute drive to Noosa. Dinner is available by prior arrangement. ⊠ *15 Eumundi–Noosa Rd.,* ☎ *07/5442–8685,* ⅻ *07/5442–8168. 5 rooms. AE, DC, MC, V.*

Tewantin

㉔ *18 km (11 mi) northeast of Eumundi, 7 km (4 mi) west of Noosa Heads.*

Dining

$$$ ✕ **Jetty Licensed Restaurant.** For a romantic lunch, take a boat from
★ Tewantin to the Jetty, upriver from town on the edge of Lake Cootharaba. The restaurant may also be reached by road. Simple fare, based on seafood and local produce, is served on a glassed-in veranda overlooking the lake. The menu changes continually, but always uses local produce. Typical dishes include grilled barramundi, Moreton Bay bugs, and grilled prawns. This spot, a favorite with locals, is licensed with a range of reasonably priced wines. ⊠ *Boreen Parade, 21 km (13 mi) north of Tewantin, Boreen Point,* ☎ *07/5485–3167. MC, V. No dinner Sun.–Thurs.*

Boating

You can rent catamarans, windsurfers, paddle skis, and motorboats at **Everglades Caravan Park and Boat Hire** (☎ 07/5485–3213) in Boreen Point, north of Tewantin on the western side of Lake Cootharaba.

River Cruises

Everglades Water Bus Co. conducts combined boat–and–four-wheel-drive tours from Harbour Town Jetty in Tewantin to the Everglades, Cooloola National Park, Cherry Venture, Bubbling Springs, and Coloured Sands. Another boat takes you to the Jetty Restaurant in Boreen Point. ⊠ *Harbour Town Marina,* ☎ *07/5447–1838.*

Noosaville

❷❺ *4 km (2½ mi) east of Tewantin, 3 km (2 mi) west of Noosa Heads.*

A snug little town dotted with small hotels and apartment complexes, Noosaville is the access point for trips to the **Teewah Coloured Sands,** an area of multicolored sands that were created by natural chemicals in the soil. Dating from the Ice Age, some of the 72 different hues of sand form cliffs rising to 600 ft.

Dining

$$
★
✕ **Chilli Jam Cafe.** For its delicious food and festive atmosphere, Chilli Jam has earned a large and loyal following. The decor—bright purple walls with green trim and terra-cotta tiling, and wooden tables with simple cotton-throw place settings—is guaranteed to impress you the way the food will. Everything on the menu is intended to be shared family style, from the salad of caramelized pork, fresh licorice root, and Asian greens to the crispy fried whiting fillets with roasted ginger and garlic chips. ⊠ *195 Weyba Rd., at Swan St.,* ☎ *07/5449–9755. MC, V. BYOB. Closed Sun and Mon. No lunch.*

Golf

The **Noosa Valley Country Club** accepts visiting players. A 9-hole course is open daily, but tee-off times must be booked in advance. ⊠ *92 Valley Dr., Doonan,* ☎ *07/5449–1411.*

River Cruises

Cooloola Cruises takes in the Everglades and the Noosa River and Lakes. The Cooloola Safari is the most comprehensive and adventurous tour, combining a cruise with a four-wheel-drive trip to Coloured Sands, Cherry Venture, and the rain forest, and including barbecue lunch and morning and afternoon teas. ⊠ *Gympie Terr.,* ☎ *07/5449–9177.*

Noosa Heads

❷❻ *39 km (24 mi) northeast of Nambour, 17 km (11 mi) north of Coolum, 140 km (87 mi) north of Brisbane.*

Noosa Heads is one of the most stylish resort areas in Australia. Although the country's new money tends to head for the glitter of the Gold Coast's Surfers Paradise, the old money retreats to Noosa. Set beside the calm waters of Laguna Bay at the northern tip of the Sunshine Coast, the town consisted of nothing more than a few shacks in the early to mid-1980s. Surfers discovered it first, lured by the spectacular waves that curl around the sheltering headland of Noosa National Park. Today, Noosa Heads is a charming mix of surf, sand, and sophistication. Elegant boutiques and restaurants lure you in from the streets. Lovely trails wind through nearby Noosa National Park's rain forest, leading to beautiful coves with white-sand beaches and crashing surf. Views along the trail from Laguna Lookout to the top of the headland take in miles of magnificent beaches, ocean, and dense vegetation.

Dining and Lodging

$$$–$$$$ ✕ **Lindoni's Ristorante Italiano.** The decor in this stylish restaurant is stunning with a black and cream tile floor, crisp white table cloths, inset arches with large vases of flowers, and a lovely street-front courtyard lit with large candelabras. The food is also magnificent. Try the *pollo faraglioni* (chicken cooked with ham, tomatoes, and mushrooms) or a simple seafood lasagna baked to perfection. ⊠ *Hastings St.,* ☎ *07/ 5447–5111. AE, DC, MC, V. No lunch.*

$$$–$$$$ ✕ **Season.** This innovative establishment serves Mediterranean cuisine indoors and out. Try the crispy-skin salmon with green papaya salad topped with chili-lime dressing, or the veal with white wine and wild mushroom risotto, broad beans, and truffle oil. ⊠ *30 Hastings St.,* ☎ *07/5447–3747. Reservations not accepted. BYOB. AE, DC, MC, V. No lunch.*

$$–$$$ ✕ **Saltwater.** Upstairs and down, at café-style tables inside or on a plant-fringed balcony overlooking Hastings Street, the seafood here is consistently delectable. Try Tasmanian roe on scallops that are flame grilled and served with a sun-dried-tomato bread crust, or fillets of Noosa River mullet marinated in mild, pink tandoori spices and yogurt and served over fragrant jasmine rice. Proprietor Steve Cross also owns a winery in Victoria, which accounts for Saltwater's own brand wine. Take-out raw and cooked seafood is also available if you want to picnic on the beach. ⊠ *8 Hastings St.,* ☎ *07/5447–2234. AE, DC, MC, V.*

$–$$ ✕ **Cato's Restaurant and Bar.** With large windows thrown wide to bustling Hastings Street, Cato's is nothing if not awake and alive. For a more relaxed atmosphere, head to the upstairs dining section. Light, tropical fare—such as fish fillets with glazed mango, watercress, and figs, or prawn-and-avocado salad with vinaigrette dressing—predominates. ⊠ *Sheraton Noosa Resort, Hastings St.,* ☎ *07/5449–4787. AE, DC, MC, V.*

$ ✕ **Aromas.** Part of a successful chain of cafés that was started in Brisbane in the early '80s, this one has a loyal clientele who come for the film-noir ambience and great people-watching. Come for breakfast, a good selection of cakes, biscuits, and light meals, and an excellent selection of coffees and alcoholic beverages. ⊠ *32 Hastings St.,* ☎ *07/ 5474–9788. AE, DC, MC, V.* ☉ *Weekdays 7 AM–midnight, weekends 7 AM–1 AM.*

$$$$ ⌂ **Sheraton Noosa Resort.** This six-story, horseshoe-shape complex faces
★ fashionable Hastings Street on one side and the river on the other. There are various themes at play here, from the hard-to-miss pink and blue exterior to the luxury poolside villas. It is hard to find fault with the rooms; each has a kitchenette, balcony, and Jacuzzi. ⊠ *Hastings St., 4567,* ☎ *07/5449–4888,* FAX *07/5449–2230. 149 rooms, 8 villas, 2 penthouses. Pool, sauna, health club. AE, DC, MC, V.*

$$$–$$$$ ⌂ **Netyana Noosa.** This low-rise beachfront complex of suites is popular among Australian managerial types. Guests are pampered with soft bathrobes and English toiletries. Most suites have verandas large enough for room-service dining. The Presidential suite has a private terrace with an outdoor Jacuzzi, and a magnificent dining room in which a local chef will serve specially prepared dinners on request. ⊠ *75 Hastings St., 4567,* ☎ *07/5447–4722 or 1800/07–2072,* FAX *07/5447–3914. 48 suites. Pool, sauna, spa, exercise room, laundry service. AE, DC, MC, V.*

$ ⌂ **Halse Lodge.** If you are looking for cheap accommodation in the heart of Noosa, aim here. This 1880 heritage-listed building is the last timber structure in Noosa, and it is southeast Queensland's longest-serving guest house. The rooms are clean, the shared baths modern, and the large utility rooms are dotted with pictures of Noosa from yesteryear. There are several choices of accommodation: two double rooms, each with a double bed; three twin rooms, each with two single beds; and a dormitory. Next to the main building is Bishop's Cottage, a converted church that is being renovated to accommodate more double rooms. There are also free weekly movies, free use of boogie boards and surf boards, and a licensed bar. The whole complex is a long stone's throw from Hastings Street, set in 2 acres of garden and rain forest overlooking town. ✉ *Halse La., 4567,* ☎ *07/5447–3377 or 1800/24–2567,* FAX *07/5447–2929. 16 bunk rooms with shared bath. Bar. MC, V.*

Shopping

Hastings Street has the best shopping in Noosa Heads, with chic boutiques, basic beach shops, bookshops, housewares and gift shops, and a jewelry store.

Water Sports

Sea Wind Charters and Holiday Tours rents a variety of yachts and Jet Skis. The company also has a half-day cruise ($65) with stops for snorkeling. ✉ *10 Cooloosa St., Sunshine Beach,* ☎ *07/5447–3042.*

Coolum

27 *17 km (11 mi) south of Noosa Heads, 25 km (16 mi) northeast of Nambour.*

At the center of the Sunshine Coast, Coolum makes an ideal base for exploring the surrounding countryside. The easygoing town also has what is probably the finest beach along the Sunshine Coast.

Dining and Lodging

$$$ ✕▨ **Hyatt Regency Resort.** Spread out at the foot of Mt. Coolum, this
★ is one of the best health spa–resorts in Australia. The spa has everything a fitness fanatic could want—pools, an aerobics room, a supervised gym, Jacuzzis, a hair and beauty salon, and over 130 beauty, pampering, and health treatments. The resort also has a championship 18-hole golf course designed by Robert Trent Jones, Jr., lighted tennis courts, a beach club, and a mile of ocean surf. Accommodations consist of one-bedroom suites and two-bedroom villas. Continental breakfast is included. The Ambassadors Club offers two-bedroom luxury villas and three-bedroom residences. A boutique, wine shop, and restaurants are arranged around the complex's village square. Transport around the 370-acre resort is via the resort shuttle. ✉ *Warran Rd., Coolum Beach, 4573,* ☎ *07/5446–1234,* FAX *07/5446–2957. 324 apartments. 8 restaurants, 9 pools, spa, 18-hole golf course, 9 tennis courts, health club, beach, dance club, baby-sitting, children's programs ages 2 weeks–12 years. AE, DC, MC, V.*

Mudjimba Beach

28 *9 km (5½ mi) north of Maroochydore.*

Lodging

$$$ ▨ **Novotel Twin Waters Resort.** Nestled amid 660 private acres, this hotel was built around a 15-acre saltwater lagoon bordering both the Maroochy River and Mudjimba Beach (a boardwalk joins the resort and the beach). The resort, more of a family place than the glitzier Hyatt in Coolum Beach, is well spread out over this area, and features a separate golf club that offers an 18-hole championship course—one of Queensland's finest—that is home to kangaroos and ducks. There are resident golfing, surfing, and tennis pros. The saltwater lagoon is the site of much water-based activity, such as catamaran sailing, windsurfing, and canoeing, all of which are free of charge to guests. The excellent restaurant, Lily's-on-the-Lagoon, is perched over one section of the lake. ⊠ *Ocean Dr.,* ☎ *07/5448–8000,* FAX *07/5448–8001. 244 rooms, 128 suites. 3 restaurants, 4 bars, pool, whirlpool, driving range, 18-hole golf course, 6 tennis courts, paddle tennis, volleyball, beach, windsurfing, boating, baby-sitting, children's programs ages 6–12 years. AE, DC, MC, V.*

Maroochydore

㉙ *18 km (11 mi) south of Coolum, 21 km (13 mi) north of Caloundra, 18 km (11 mi) east of Nambour.*

Maroochydore has been a popular beach resort for several years and suffers its fair share of high-rise towers. Nevertheless, with its location at the mouth of the Maroochy River, the town has excellent surfing and swimming beaches.

Dining and Lodging

$$$–$$$$ ✕ **Portraits Restaurant.** Formally called Signatures, this establishment can be hard to find: You have to go through a parking lot just off First Avenue. However, the food is well worth the effort, as is the setting. A deck overlooks the Maroochy River and the surf beyond. There's a New Orleans feel to the decor, with its dark-wood posts, painted wooden walls, crystal glasses, and low hanging fringed lamps. There are large pictures of celebrities on the walls, and each dish is named after a Hollywood or television star. The Mel Gibson is lime-cured salmon salad topped with a chive and pumpkin vinaigrette, while the Marilyn Monroe is—what else?—the special of the day. ⊠ *6 Duporth Ave.,* ☎ *07/5443–6401. AE, MC, V. Closed Sun. No lunch Mon.*

$$–$$$$ ▥ **Catalina Resort.** One block from the beach, this high-rise complex offers lovely sea views. Each apartment is furnished differently, and beach views start on the sixth floor. All apartments are self-contained with kitchen and laundry and are serviced weekly. ⊠ *6th Ave.,* ☎ *07/5443–8666,* FAX *07/5443–7942. 51 apartments. Pool, whirlpool, sauna, tennis court, recreation room. AE, DC, MC, V.*

Outdoor Activities and Sports

FISHING
Rods and reels are available at **Maroochydore Fishing World.** ⊠ *22 1st Ave.,* ☎ *07/5443–2714.*

GOLF
The **Headland Golf Club,** an 18-hole course only a few kilometers inland from Maroochydore, is open to visitors on Sunday, Monday, and Friday. ⊠ *Golf Links Rd., Buderim,* ☎ *07/5444–5800.*

TENNIS
Courts and coaching are available at **Alinga Tennis Centre.** ⊠ *121 Sugar Rd.,* ☎ *07/5443–4584.*

Shopping

One of the best shopping centers on the Sunshine Coast is **Sunshine Plaza** (⊠ Aerodrome Rd.), in Maroochydore, with several major department stores.

En Route For superb surfing in the southern part of the Sunshine Coast, head for the beach at **Alexandra Headland,** 5 km (3 mi) south of Maroochydore.

Mooloolaba

㉚ *5 km (3 mi) south of Maroochydore.*

Mooloolaba—the port for the local prawning and fishing fleets, as well as deep-sea charter boats—has one particularly notable attraction:

Underwater World, with its walk-through aquarium. In a clear acrylic underwater tunnel you'll stare face-to-face with giant sharks, stingrays, and other local marine species. The marine complex, one of the best in Australia, has a shark feeding, a crocodile lagoon, a seal show, an Oceanarium, Ocean Discover Centre, and Theatre of the Sea. If marine life interests you, plan to spend time here. ⊠ *Parkyn Parade,* ☎ *07/5444–8488.* ⊠ *$18.90.* ☉ *Daily 9–6.*

Boating

You can hire canopied motorboats from **Swan Boat Hire.** ⊠ *59 Bradman Ave., Maroochydore,* ☎ *07/5443–7225.*

Fishing

Deep-sea fishing charters can be arranged through **Mooloolaba Reef and Game Charters.** ⊠ *33 Jessica Blvd.,* ☎ *07/5444–3735.*

Nightlife

Friday's On the Wharf is a popular nightspot. ⊠ *Parkyn Parade and River Esplanade,* ☎ *07/5444–8383.*

Rock On Nightclub is the scene for younger revelers. ⊠ *Esplanade,* ☎ *07/5478–3422.*

Shopping

The **Wharf Shopping Centre** (⊠ Parkyn Parade) is a re-creation of a 19th-century fishing village with boutiques, souvenir shops, food outlets, a games arcade, and a tourist information center. It is adjacent to Underwater World.

Caloundra

㉛ *21 km (13 mi) south of Maroochydore, 56 km (35 mi) south of Noosa Heads, 91 km (56 mi) north of Brisbane.*

It's not just excellent beaches that makes Caloundra so popular. The town is also free of the glitz of the more touristy Queensland resorts. Retirees have been moving here for some time now, and it is also popular with Brisbanites, many of whom have Caloundra weekend houses or apartments.

Sunshine Coast A to Z

Arriving and Departing

BY BUS

Coachtrans (☎ 07/3236–1000) offers daily bus service from Brisbane Airport and the Roma Street Transit Centre in Brisbane to Caloundra, Mooloolaba, Maroochydore, Noosa, and Tewantin.

BY PLANE

See Air Travel *in* the Gold Guide for information on airlines serving Maroochydore Airport. Note that it is almost as convenient to fly into Brisbane, which is only an hour's drive away.

BY TRAIN

Trains, including the new high tech *Tilt Train,* leave regularly from **Roma Street Transit Centre** (⊠ Roma St., ☎ 07/3235–2222) in Brisbane en route to Nambour, the business hub of the Sunshine Coast. Once in Nambour you will need a car, so it makes more sense to drive from Brisbane or to take a bus.

Getting Around

BY CAR

A car is a necessity on the Sunshine Coast. The traditional route to the coast has been along the Bruce Highway (Hwy. 1) to the Glass House

Mountains, and turn off at Cooroy—this makes for about a two-hour drive from Brisbane to Noosa, the heart of the area. However, the motorway may be marginally faster—turn off the Bruce Highway at Tanawah (toward Mooloolaba) and follow the signs. The most scenic route is to turn off the Bruce Highway to Caloundra and follow the coast to Noosa Heads.

Contacts and Resources

CAR RENTAL

All major companies have offices in Brisbane (☞ Brisbane A to Z, *above*). The following international companies have local offices: **Avis** (⊠ Maroochydore and airport, ☎ 07/5443–5055; ⊠ Noosa Heads, ☎ 07/5447–4933), **Budget** (⊠ Maroochydore, ☎ 07/5443–6555), **Hertz** (⊠ Noosa Heads, ☎ 07/5447–2253; ⊠ airport, ☎ 07/5448–9731), and **Thrifty** (⊠ airport, ☎ 1300/36–7227).

EMERGENCIES

Ambulance, fire brigade, and police. ☎ *000.*

Caloundra Hospital. ☎ *07/5491–1888.*

Nambour General Hospital. ☎ *07/5470–6600.*

GUIDED TOURS

Adventures Sunshine Coast has one-day trips from **Noosa Heads** and **Caloundra** that take you walking or canoeing in rain forests and mountains. ⊠ *69 Alfriston Dr., Buderim,* ☎ *07/5444–8824.*

Breakfast in Bed. If you don't feel like cooking or going out for breakfast, have breakfast come to you. Breakfast in Bed will deliver a breakfast hamper, suitable for two to three people, to your door. Choices range from basic to gourmet and include goodies such as King Island cream, smoked salmon, and tropical fruit. ⊠ ☎ *07/5448–0024 or 0408/73–4821.*

Black Thunder Ballooning (☎ 07/5493–0699) floats over the Sunshine Coast from **Caboolture** for three-quarters of an hour, including the traditional champagne celebration.

Southern Cross Motorcycle Tours (☎ 07/5445–0022) is one of the best ways to get a feel for the Sunshine Coast. Ride a Harley Davidson motorcycle from the beach to the Blackall Range. Southern Cross Motorcycle Tours has a team of experienced guides who know the area and will take you on a quick joy ride or a whole day's excursion.

Tropical Coast Tours runs regular tours to attractions around the Sunshine Coast, Brisbane, and the Gold Coast. ⊠ *54 Newfield St., Sunrise Beach,* ☎ *07/5449–0822.*

VISITOR INFORMATION

Caloundra Tourist Information Centre. ⊠ *7 Caloundra Rd., Caloundra,* ☎ *07/5491–0202.*

Maroochy Information Centre. ⊠ *6th Ave., Maroochydore,* ☎ *07/5479–1566.*

Noosa Tourist Information Centre. ⊠ *Hastings St., Noosa Heads,* ☎ *07/5447–4988.*

FRASER ISLAND

Some 200 km (124 mi) north of Brisbane, Fraser Island is both the largest of Queensland's islands and the most unusual. Instead of coral reefs and coconut palms, it has wildflower-dotted meadows, freshwater lakes, a teeming and exotic bird population, dense stands of rain forest, towering sand dunes, and sculpted, multicolor sand cliffs along its east coast—a lineup that has won the island a place on UNESCO's World Heritage list. The surf fishing is legendary, and humpback whales and their calves can be seen wintering in Hervey Bay between May and September. The island also has interesting Aboriginal sites dating back a millennia.

Once you've seen Fraser's 140-km (87-mi) east coast—nearly one continuous beach—it will come as no surprise that this is the world's largest sand island. But these are beaches like few others anywhere else. Colors stray from the typical beige to deep rust and sugar white, and shapes range from sensuous drifts to huge dunes.

Fraser's east coast marks the intersection of two serious Australian passions: an addiction to the beach and a love affair with the motor vehicle. Unrestricted vehicle access means that this coast has become a giant sandbox for four-wheelers. All vehicles entering the island must have a Vehicle Access Permit ($30) fixed to the windshield. There are a number of places in southeast Queensland where you can obtain these and camping permits for the island. For the name of the closest center contact **Hervey Bay City Council** (✉ 77 Tavistock St., Torquay, ☎ 07/4125–0222). If you prefer your wilderness *sans* dune-buggying, head for the unspoiled interior of the island.

Exploring Fraser Island

Highlights of a drive north along the east coast include the rusting hulk of the *Maheno,* lying half buried in the sand, a roost for seagulls and a prime hunting ground for anglers when the tailor are running. North of the *Maheno* wreck are the **Pinnacles**—also known as the Cathedrals—a stretch of dramatic, deep-red cliffs.

Great Sandy National Park (☎ 07/4123–7100 or 07/4127–9191) covers the top third of the island. The park's beaches around Indian Head are known for their shell middens—basically attractive rubbish heaps that were left behind after Aboriginal feasting. The head's name is another kind of relic: Captain James Cook saw Aborigines standing on the headland as he sailed past, and he therefore named the area after inhabitants he believed to be "Indians." Farther north, past Waddy Point, is one of Fraser Island's most magnificent variations on sand. Wind and time have created enormous dunes, which are constantly swept clean of footprints by a breeze that blows off Hervey Bay. The southern border of the park is just past the Cathedral Beach Resort.

The center of the island is a quiet, natural garden of paperbark swamps, giant satinay and brush box forests, wildflower heaths, and 40 freshwater lakes—including the spectacularly clear **Lake McKenzie,** which is ringed by a beach of incandescent whiteness.

The island's excellent network of walking trails converges at **Central Station,** a former logging camp at the center of the island. Services here are limited to a map board, parking lot, and campground. It's a promising place for spotting dingo, however. Comparative isolation has meant that Fraser Island's dingoes are the most purebred on the east coast of Australia; to ensure the future of the breed, domestic dogs are not permitted on the island. The dingoes here are unfazed by human contact, but they are still wild animals. Don't feed them, and keep a close eye on children.

Two noteworthy walking tracks lead from Central Station: A boardwalk heads south to **Wanggoolba Creek,** a favorite spot of photographers; this little stream snakes through a green palm forest, trickling over a bed of white sand between clumps of the rare angiopteris fern. A slightly longer trail leads north to **Pile Valley,** where you'll find a stand of giant satinay trees. This timber is so dense and durable that it was shipped to Egypt to be used as pilings for the Suez Canal.

Lodging

You must have a permit ($3.50 per person per night) to camp on Fraser Island, except in private campsites. The island is managed by the **Department of Environment and Heritage,** and you can obtain a permit from a number of places in southeast Queensland. For the name of the closest center, contact **Hervey Bay City Council** (⊠ 77 Tavistock St., Torquay, ☎ 07/4125–0222).

$$$ 🏨 **Fraser Island Retreat.** This is the pick of the east coast accommodations. Formally known as Happy Valley Resort, it is in fact more of a retreat than a resort, with its breezy one- and two-bedroom bungalows with polished timber floors and bamboo furnishings. The on-site restaurant has a pleasant atmosphere, but the food is nothing to write home about. A small store sells groceries and fishing supplies, as well as gas and diesel. ☎ 07/4127–9144, FAX 07/4127–9131. *9 rooms with shower. Restaurant, bar, grocery. AE, MC, V.*

$$$ 🏨 **Kingfisher Bay Resort & Village.** Wrapped around a bay on the island's west coast, this is a stylish, high-tech marriage of glass, stainless steel, dark timber, and corrugated iron. Although the two-story structures are by no means inconspicuous, developers have succeeded in attractively integrating the resort with the environment. There are 152 hotel rooms, 109 self-contained villas, a 112-bed wilderness lodge for groups, and a team of highly skilled rangers who conduct a variety of four-wheel-drive guided tours. Rangers also offer free nature walks and activities daily, and children can join in a free junior ranger program on weekends and during Australian school holiday periods. Three-day guided wilderness adventures ($225) include a stay in the resort's wilderness lodge. Four-wheel-drive vehicles are available for individual hire. Meals are not included in room rates, but they are reasonably priced. ⊠ *Box 913, Brisbane 4001,* ☎ *07/4120–3333 or 1800/07–2555,* FAX *07/3221–3270. 152 rooms, 109 villas, 112-bed lodge. 3 restaurants, bar, 4 pools, spa, 2 tennis courts. AE, DC, MC, V.*

Fraser Island A to Z

Arriving and Departing

Hervey Bay is the name given to the expanse of water between Fraser Island and the Queensland coast. It is also the generic name given to a conglomeration of four nearby coastal towns—Urangan, Pialba, Scarness, and Torquay—that have grown into a single settlement. This township is the jumping-off point for most excursions to Fraser Island. Travelers should be aware that maps and road signs usually refer to individual town names, not Hervey Bay.

BY BUS

McCafferty's Express Coaches (☎ 13–1499) and **Greyhound Pioneer** (☎ 13–2030) run between Brisbane and Hervey Bay, where the bus terminal is near the Fraser Island ferry dock.

BY CAR

Although the southernmost tip of Fraser Island is 200 km (124 mi) north of Brisbane, the best access to the island is from the Hervey Bay area, another 90 km (56 mi) away. Take the Bruce Highway to Maryborough, then follow signs to Urangan.

Vehicle ferries (☎ 07/4125–5155) run to Fraser Island from Mary River Heads (12 km, or 7 mi, south of Urangan). Fare is $37.50 one way or $65 return including the driver, plus $4 for each additional passenger.

Sunstate Airlines (☎ 13–1313) has several flights daily between Brisbane and Hervey Bay Airport on the mainland.

Getting Around

Despite the island's free-range feeling, the rules of the road still apply. Wear seat belts, drive on the left, and obey the speed limit—the island has a serious accident rate of about one per week. Watch out for creek crossings, which are often deeper than they look and can be quite dangerous, and keep an eye on the tide. Tide tables are available from ranger stations or from any shop on the island. It is generally advised to keep your vehicle off the beach for three hours before high tide and four hours after.

Contacts and Resources

Four-wheel-drive rentals may be cheaper on the mainland, but factoring in the ferry ticket makes it less expensive to get your rental on-island. Rent four-wheel-drives at **Kingfisher Bay Resort & Village** (☎ 07/4120–3333), **Eurong Beach Resort** (☎ 07/4127–9122), and **Happy Valley** (☎ 07/4127–9145).

Air Fraser Island operates whale-watching flights of 45 minutes or more across Hervey Bay between July and October. Aircraft seat six people. ☎ 07/4125–3600. ▣ *Prices start at $40 per person, minimum 4 people.*

Fraser Island Discovery Tours has three-day safaris to Fraser Island from Brisbane, departing each Friday. A maximum of 20 passengers tour the island by four-wheel-drive vehicle and spend two nights in a Wilderness Lodge at Kingfisher Bay Resort & Village. ☎ 07/3821–1694. ▣ *$365.*

The **Kingfisher** passenger ferry runs between Urangan and North White Cliffs, near Kingfisher Bay Resort. Fare includes morning tea, lunch, and a ranger-led walking tour. ☎ 07/4125–5155. ▣ *$30.*

Mimi MacPherson's Whale-Watching Expeditions. Supermodel Elle's sister has been running this successful operation from Hervey Bay since 1989. Tours depart daily from Urangan Boat Harbour at Hervey Bay from July through October. ☎ 07/4124–7247. ▣ *$62–$65.*

Fraser Coast Tour Booking Office and Whale Watch Centre is a good source of information, maps, and brochures. The center will also help you with tour and accommodations bookings. ✉ *Buccaneer Ave., Urangan,* ☎ 07/4128–9800.

Hervey Bay Tourist Office. ✉ *46 Main St., Shop 4, Pialba,* ☎ 07/4124–4050.

TOWNSVILLE AND MAGNETIC ISLAND

By Jane Carstens and David McGonigal

Updated by Jane Carstens

Townsville is Australia's largest tropical city, with a population of 140,000. Unlike tourist-filled Cairns to the north, it relies on its deepwater port from which sugar, beef, wool, and the mineral wealth of Mount Isa are exported. The city is the commercial capital of the north and a major center for education, scientific research, and defense. Townsville is built around the pink granite outcrop of Castle Hill, the first feature one notices about the place, which rises from otherwise featureless coastal plains to just under 1,000 ft. On the banks of the boat-filled Ross Creek, Townsville is a pleasant city, an urban sprawl of palm-fringed malls, white lattice verandas on historic colonial buildings, and lots of parkland and gardens. If you want to get into the *real* Australian tropical life, this is the place to visit. It isn't fancy, but there is a fair amount to see, including the Reef Zoo. Townsville is also the stepping off point for Magnetic Island, one of the largest Queensland islands.

Magnetic Island is essentially an island suburb, where the sounds of birds and other wildlife replace the sounds of the city. Captain James Cook bestowed the title Magnetic on the island in the erroneous belief that the ironstone deposits caused his compass to err. He was wrong, but the name stuck, and today 2,500 people call the island home.

The terrain of Magnetic Island is well suited for bushwalking—it's hilly rather than mountainous—and 75% of it is national park. There are some great jungle walks and a serrated coastline of rocky headlands sheltering palm-shaded beaches. Wallabies, koalas, possums, and a great variety of birds make up the wild population of the island. Reefs protect the shoreline, but, unlike islands farther offshore, marine stingers can infest the beaches between October and April.

Townsville

Townsville's focal point was until recently the **Flinders Mall,** a tropically landscaped pedestrian mall in the heart of the city center. However, its popularity has declined with locals more inclined to shop in large suburban malls. On Sunday morning it is the venue for the **Cotters Market,** an arts and crafts offering of locally made items, as well as food and entertainment.

Most visitors head for the top of **Castle Hill,** 1 km (½ mi) from the city center on foot, or about 4 km (2½ mi) by car, on a steep walking track that doubles as one of the most scenic jogging routes in Queensland. If you're game, branch off onto one of several goat tracks that lead up the pink granite hill. However you get to the top, the summit provides great views of the city as well as the islands of the Great Barrier Reef. While you're perched on top, think about the proud local resident who, along with various scout troops, spent years in the 1970s piling rubble onto the peak to try to add the 23 ft that would officially make it Castle Mountain. Technically speaking, a rise has to exceed 1,000 ft to be called a mountain—and this one tops out at just 977 ft.

Great Barrier Reef Wonderland is on the waterfront, only a few minutes' walk from the city center. It includes three attractions, which are separate operations. The **Reef Zoo** (☎ 07/4750–0800) boasts the largest natural-coral aquarium in the world—a living slice of the Great Barrier Reef. There are more than 100 species of hard coral, 30 soft corals, and hundreds of fish species. It also features an enclosed underwater walkway, which makes it seem as if you're strolling along the bottom of the sea. The **Museum of Tropical Queensland** (☎ 07/4721–2399) was completely overhauled in 1998 and 1999 and is scheduled to reopen in June 2000. A feature of the new museum will be a high-tech presentation of HMS *Pandora* artifacts and an extensive interpretation of the Great Barrier Reef. The **Omnimax Theatre** (☎ 07/4721–1481) screens eight shows daily; a movie about the Great Barrier Reef is the feature film. Other films cover subjects such as marine studies, Aboriginal studies, and geography. ⊠ *Flinders St. E,* ☎ *07/4721–2411.* 🎫 *Reef Zoo $14.80; Omnimax Theatre $9.* ☉ *Daily 9–5.*

Take a walk along **Flinders Street** to look at some of Townsville's turn-of-the-century colonial architecture. **Magnetic House** still has a hitching rail. **Queens Building** is in Classical Revival style. The apparently immovable **masonry clock tower** (⊠ Flinders and Denham Sts.) of the post office was erected in 1889 but taken down during World War II so it wouldn't be a target for air raids. It was put up again in 1964.

The National Trust has placed three very different dwellings alongside each other at the **Castling Street Heritage Centre.** The 1884 worker's dwelling is a simple cottage that has been refurnished. The 1921 farmhouse is a typical example of the house occupied by early Queensland farmers. Currajong is a grand residence that was built in 1888 and has been completely restored and furnished. Hurricane Sid caused considerable damage to the properties in 1998, but the restoration work has been mostly completed. ⊠ *5 Castling St., West End,* ☎ *07/4772–5195.* 🎫 *$5.* ☉ *Wed. 10–2, weekends 1–4. Closed most of Dec.–Jan.*

Townsville Common, also known as the Townsville Environment Park, is an important bird sanctuary. One may doubt the wisdom of encouraging birds to live at the seaward end of the airport runway, but they don't seem to mind. It's hard not to be impressed by the profusion of spoonbills, jabiru storks, pied geese, herons, and ibis, plus the occasional wallabies, goannas, and even an echidna. Children will be fascinated by the sight of large brolgas performing their elegant dances. The best time to visit is either at dawn or dusk. Most of the birds leave these swamplands from May through August, the dry months, but they're all back by October. To get to the Common, take a taxi past the airport. Access is free.

OFF THE BEATEN PATH

BILLABONG SANCTUARY – This 22-acre nature park is inhabited by crocodiles, koalas, wombats, dingoes, and wallabies, as well as a range of bird life, including cassowaries, kookaburras, and beautiful red-tailed black cockatoos. Educational shows throughout the day give you the chance to learn more about native animals and their habits and include koala feeding, crocodile feeding, and handling snakes. ⊠ *Bruce Hwy., Nome, 17 km (10 mi) south of Townsville,* ☎ *07/4778–8344.* 🎫 *$18.* ☉ *Daily 8–5.*

Dining

$$$ ✕ **Flutes.** This popular local eatery makes up for its plain decor with good service and excellent fare. Try such starters as prawns tempura in chili plum sauce, and such main courses as Spanish mackerel fillets slowly cooked in a tomato and olive sauce with herbs, or a combination of king prawns and lobster sautéed in rich garlic and cheese sauce served with wild rice pilaf. ⊠ *Townsville Reef International, 63 the Strand,* ☎ *07/4721–1777. AE, DC, MC, V. No lunch.*

$$ ✕ **Pinocchio's on Flinders.** Warm terra-cotta and moss green accents
★   create an inviting ambience in this intimate restaurant. In the upstairs section, original local art provides a charming touch. Among a good selection of seafood, steak, and pasta dishes, panfried calamari with a

light salad is a favorite, as is the Reef and Beef: top-grade eye fillet served with Australian lobster, prawns, scallops, and béarnaise sauce. ⊠ *223 Flinders St. E,* ☎ *07/4771–2209. Reservations essential. AE, DC, MC, V. Closed Sun. No lunch Sat.*

$–$$ ✕ **One Palmer.** Situated on Townsville's "eat street," this eclectic
★ restaurant/bar/café provides a relaxed setting for chicken tikka focaccia with char-grilled eggplant, pepper, and avocado or a selection of tapas such as onion *bhaji* (spiced onion fritters) and *nori* (seaweed) rolls from the Naughty Beagle Tapas and Wine Bar. The open bar, cane furnishings, and iron trim help create a relaxed ambiance. ⊠ *1 Palmer St.,* ☎ *07/4772–3435. AE, DC, MC, V.*

Lodging

$$$$ 🏨 **Sheraton Townsville Hotel & Casino.** When it opened in the 1980s, this Sheraton forever changed the tourism profile of what was at the time a rather sleepy town. It dominates Townsville's waterfront vista and, although it has a rather bland, block-shaped architectural design, it manages to look sophisticated against the adjacent marina. This waterfront location translates into great views across to Magnetic Island from all 11 floors. Rooms are decorated in bright tropical reds, blues, and greens and are larger than standard hotel rooms. This is a busy hotel—with North Queensland's first casino—but rooms are pleasantly quiet. ⊠ *Box 1223, Sir Leslie Thiess Dr., 4810,* ☎ *07/4722–2333. 176 rooms, 16 suites. 3 restaurants, 5 bars, in-room VCRs, pool, sauna, spa, 2 tennis courts, exercise room, casino. AE, DC, MC, V.*

$$ 🏨 **Centra Townsville.** This cylindrical 20-story building is a Townsville landmark, its salt-shaker design a tribute to one of the city's industries. Its prime advantage is its location in the heart of the city center. The decor reflects its tropical location with vibrant reef colors and cane furniture. Rooms have good views of the city and waterfront. Popular among business travelers, the hotel is a favorite for functions and conferences. ⊠ *Flinders Mall, 4810,* ☎ *07/4772–2477. 149 rooms, 40 suites. Restaurant, 2 bars, pool, laundry service. AE, DC, MC, V.*

$$ 🏨 **Townsville Reef International.** This four-story beachfront hotel over-
★ looking Cleveland Bay is a pleasant modern property with a high standard of service. It has typical Queensland decor, with lots of lattice, tropical prints, and muted grays and greens. From Flutes restaurant (☞ Dining, *above*) and the palm trees shading the pool, to private balconies overlooking the bay and Magnetic Island, this is a fine place to stay. ⊠ *63 the Strand, 4810,* ☎ *07/4721–1777. 45 rooms. Restaurant, in-room VCRs, pool, hot tub, laundry service. AE, DC, MC, V.*

$–$$ 🏨 **Seagull's Resort on the Seafront.** This very pleasant, two-story
★ brick complex is set in three acres of palm tree–studded tropical gardens. The hotel rooms are spacious and have cane furniture and a tropical color scheme. Self-contained apartments and suites with kitchenettes are also available. Seagull's restaurant serves generous portions of a variety of local seafood. The resort is 2½ km (1½ mi) from the city center and about a ten-minute walk to the beach. ⊠ *74 the Esplanade,* ☎ *07/4721–3111. 55 rooms with shower, 11 suites, 4 apartments. Restaurant, bar, in-room VCRs, 2 pools, tennis court, playground, laundry service, tour desk. AE, DC, MC, V.*

Nightlife and the Arts

The **Civic Theatre** (⊠ Boundary St., ☎ 07/4727–9797) hosts some of the state's finest performing artists, and the **Breakwater Entertainment Centre** (⊠ Entertainment Dr., ☎ 07/4771–4000), which can seat 4,000, has hosted such international acts as Tom Jones and Tina Turner. The center is also the home of the Townsville Suns National Basketball League team.

For gamblers, the main attraction in Townsville is the **Sheraton Townsville Hotel & Casino** (☞ Lodging, *above*), which has a full range of gaming opportunities including minibaccarat, sic bo, blackjack, roulette, keno, and slot machines, as well as the Australian game of two-up.

Outdoor Activities and Sports

BEACHES

Townsville is blessed with a long golden strand of beach along the northern edge of the city. There is no surf, as the beach is sheltered by the reef and Magnetic Island.

DIVING

Surrounded by tropical islands and warm waters, Townsville is an important diving center. Diving courses and excursions here are not as crowded as in the hot spots of Cairns or the Whitsunday Islands.

The wreck of the *Yongala,* a steamship that sank just south of Townsville in 1911 lies in 99 ft of water about 16 km (11 mi) offshore, 60 km (37 mi) from Townsville. Now the abode of a vast variety of marine life, it is one of Australia's best dive sites and can be approached as either a one- or two-day trip. All local dive operators offer trips out to the site.

The world-renowned **Mike Ball Dive Expeditions** (⊠ 252 Walker St., ☎ 07/4772–3022) has three-day trips (from $406) to the *Yongala* every Tuesday which include on-board meals, linens, tanks, and weight belts. Gear can also be rented.

Other major dive operators are **Pro-Dive** (⊠ Great Barrier Reef Wonderland, Flinders St. E, ☎ 07/4721–1760) and **Sun City Watersports** (⊠ 121 Flinders St., ☎ 07/4771–6527).

FISHING

Cleveland Bay Sport Fishing Charters (⊠ 26 Whitsunday Dr., Kirwan, ☎ 015/635–758) will organize fishing trips along coastal estuaries.

GOLF

Rowes Bay Golf Course has an 18-hole and a newer par-3, nine-hole course. ⊠ *Cape Pallarenda Rd., Pallarenda,* ☎ *07/4774–1188.*

Willows Golf Club is an 18-hole championship course. ⊠ *19th Ave., Kirwan,* ☎ *07/4773–4777.*

Shopping

Flinders Street Mall, a bright and sunny street closed to vehicular traffic, has been the main shopping area of Townsville in years past. Recently, locals have all headed for the suburban centers. **Castletown Shoppingworld** (⊠ 35 Kings Rd., Pimlico ☎ 07/4772–1699) offers a variety of shops including Lloma Jewellers (a well-established Townsville jeweler), Woolworths supermarket, Discount Jeans, a post office, and a medical center.

Magnetic Island

The bulk of Magnetic Island's 52 square km (20 square mi) is national parkland, laced with miles of walking trails and rising to a height of 1,640 ft on Mount Cook. The terrain is punctuated with huge granite boulders and softened by tall hoop pines, eucalypt forest, and small patches of rain forest. The park is a haven for wildlife, including rock wallabies, koalas, and an abundance of bird life.

The 2,500-odd year-round residents live on the eastern shore, where you'll also stay while on holiday. The main settlements are Picnic Bay, Arcadia, Nelly Bay, and Horseshoe Bay. But don't look for the high-rises of the Gold Coast or the luxurious resorts of the Whitsundays. Magnetic Islanders live here for the relaxed lifestyle and natural surroundings.

One way to get an overview of Magnetic Island is to ride the **Magnetic Island Bus Service,** whose drivers provide commentary. Your $9 ticket allows unlimited travel for one day, enabling you to return to the places you like most. A three-hour guided tour is also offered with a driver, commentary, and morning or afternoon tea for $26. Reservations for the guided tour are essential; they depart at 9 and 1 daily. ⊠ *44 Mandalay Ave., Nelly Bay,* ☎ *07/4778–5130.*

The beaches all around the island are another reason to visit. Alma Bay's beach near Arcadia is good for swimming and snorkeling. Near the northeastern corner of the island, Radical Bay has a small, idyllic beach surrounded by tree-covered rock outcrops. Horseshoe Bay has the largest beach, with boat rentals as well. There is good snorkeling at Nelly Bay, and Geoffrey Bay has a well-marked snorkel trail. Free self-guiding trail cards that identify various corals and sea life are available from the information center adjacent to the Picnic Bay Jetty.

Hiking trails on the island are relatively easy. A track to West Point from Picnic Bay leads through interesting terrain to good birding spots (3 hrs round-trip). The most popular walk is to World War II gun emplacements overlooking Horseshoe and Florence bays. This trip takes 45 minutes each way at a leisurely pace. The best views are on the Nelly Bay to Arcadia walk and are rewarding if you take the higher ground. There are 24 km (16 mi) of tracks on the island.

The walking trails of the island run under gum trees that are home to many koalas. The **Koala Park Oasis** in Horseshoe Bay is North Queensland's largest koala sanctuary, where you can see and touch koalas. ⊠ *Horseshoe Bay,* ☎ *07/4778–5260.* ☑ *$10.* ☉ *Daily 9–5.*

Dining and Lodging

Magnetic Island's lodgings are geared largely to the needs of Australians on holiday rather than to those of international visitors. As a result they tend to be less expensive.

$$ ✕☷ **Magnetic Island International Hotel.** This comfortable resort is nestled amid 11 acres of lush gardens 2 km (1 mi) from the beach. Rooms follow a pastel-yellow color scheme, with kitchenettes, tiled floors, and cane furniture. At the resort's terrace restaurant, MacArthur's, beef and seafood are the mainstays; try grilled coral trout on a bed of crisp snow peas topped with tiger prawns and finished with a lemon and chive *beurre blanc.* As for activities, hiking trails into the national parkland are nearby, and the energetic can take advantage of floodlit tennis courts in the cool evenings. Courtesy arrival and departure coach transfers from Picnic Bay to the resort are available. ⊠ *Mandalay Ave., Nelly Bay,* ☎ *07/4778–5200 or 1800/07–9902. 80 rooms with shower, 16 suites. Restaurant, bar, pool, 2 tennis courts, exercise room, recreation room, playground, laundry service. AE, DC, MC, V.*

$ ✕☷ **Arcadia Resort.** This pleasant resort is opposite both Geoffrey and Alma bays. The original single-story wooden building stands adjacent to one of two pools, and 1980 saw the addition of the motel-style terrace rooms. Owner Gary McGill has embarked upon replacing the unfortunate mission brown, red, and green colors with pastels, but progress (by his own admission) is slow. The bar-restaurant area is next to a pool and is open to the public. Dining here is a casual affair and the food—predominantly steak, seafood, and salads—is good value for the money. The resort also has a shopping arcade with a dive center, and other shops and restaurants are close by. ⊠ *7 Marine Parade, Arcadia 4819,* ☎

07/4778–5177, FAX 07/4778–5939. *27 rooms with shower. Restaurant, brasserie, in-room VCRs, 2 pools, laundry service. MC, V.*

Horseback Riding

The pace of life on Magnetic Island is perfectly suited to riding. With **Bluey's Horseshoe Ranch Trail Rides** you can take a one-hour bush ride, or a more extensive two-hour bush and beach ride with a chance to take the horses swimming. Half-day rides are also offered. Bring your swimwear and wear good covered shoes. All other equipment—including riding trousers if you don't have anything suitable—is supplied. ⊠ *38 Gifford St., Horseshoe Bay,* ☎ *07/4778–5109.*

Water Sports

Horseshoe Bay Watersports offers sailing, parasailing, waterskiing, aquabikes, and canoes for hire. ⊠ *97 Horsehoe Bay Rd.,* ☎ *07/4758–1336.*

Townsville and Magnetic Island A to Z

Arriving and Departing

TOWNSVILLE

By Bus. Greyhound Pioneer (☎ 13–2030), **McCafferty's** (☎ 13–1499), and **Bus Australia** (☎ 13–2323) all run regularly from the **Townsville Transit Centre** (⊠ Palmer and Plume Sts., South Townsville, ☎ 07/4721–2322) to Cairns and Brisbane and to points farther south.

By Car. Townsville is 1,400 km (870 mi) by road from Brisbane—a colossal, dull drive. The 370 km (230 mi) journey from Townsville to Cairns, with occasional Hinchinbrook Island views, is more appealing.

By Plane. Ansett Australia and **Qantas** fly frequently to Brisbane, Cairns, interstate cities, and overseas destinations. **Flight West** (☎ 13–2392) has a comprehensive flight network throughout Queensland.

Airport Shuttle Service (☎ 07/4775–5544) runs shuttle buses that meet each flight. The cost of the transfer to the city is $5 one-way or $8 return. **Standard White Cabs** (⊠ 11 Yeatman St., Hyde Park, ☎ 07/4772–1555 or 13–1008) are available from a stand at the airport. If there are none there, there is a free phone to the dispatch radio room. The average cost of the journey to a city hotel is $14.

By Train. The *Queenslander* travels between Brisbane and Townsville once weekly, the *Sunlander* travels the route three times weekly, and the *Spirit of the Tropics* travels twice weekly. For more information call the Railways Booking Office (☎ 13–2232) in Brisbane.

MAGNETIC ISLAND

By Boat. Sun Ferries (☎ 07/4771–3855) has fast catamaran service every day from Townsville (leaving from 168–192 Flinders St. E and from the Breakwater Terminal) to Picnic Bay on the island. Bus and island transfers meet the ferry during daylight hours. There are at least nine departures daily; the 20-minute trip costs $13. **Capricorn Barge Company** (☎ 07/4772–5422) runs a car and passenger ferry service to Magnetic Island with three to five departures daily.

Getting Around

TOWNSVILLE

By Bicycle. Townsville's flat terrain is well suited to cycling. Pick up a rental at **City Cycles** (⊠ 251A Charters Towers Rd., Hermit Park, ☎ 015/968–469).

By Car. Avis (☎ 07/4721–2688), **Budget** (☎ 07/4725–2344), **Hertz** (☎ 07/4775–5950), and **Thrifty** (☎ 1800/65–8959) all have rental cars available in Townsville.

By Taxi. You can flag a **Standard White Cab** (✉ 11 Yeatman St., Hyde Park, ☎ 07/4772–1555 or 13–1008) on the street or find one at stands or hotels.

By Bicycle and Scooter. Magnetic Island Bike and Snorkel Hire (✉ The Esplanade, Picnic Bay, ☎ 07/4778–5411) rents bicycles for $12 a day. They also rent snorkeling equipment. **Road Runner Scooter Hire** (✉ The Esplanade, Picnic Bay, ☎ 07/4778–5222) rents scooters and trail bikes, and also conducts Harley Davidson tours.

By Bus. Magnetic Island Bus Service (☎ 07/4778–5130) meets each boat at Picnic Bay in the south and travels across to Horseshoe Bay in the north of the island. An unlimited day pass costs $9.

By Mini Moke. A Mini Moke is a soft-top version of the tiny Minor Mini car. They are ideal if you want to explore the island but don't feel comfortable on two wheels. **Magnetic Island Rent-A-Moke** (✉ The Esplanade, Picnic Bay, ☎ 07/4778–5377) rents Mini Mokes for $35 plus 30¢ per km. Rates include fuel and insurance for one driver over 25 years of age; drivers under 25 pay a bit more.

By Taxi. Magnetic Island Taxi (☎ 13–1008 or 07/4772–1555) has a stand at the ferry terminal at Picnic Point.

Contacts and Resources

EMERGENCIES

Ambulance, fire brigade, and police. ☎ *000.*

Townsville General Hospital. ✉ *Eyre St.,* ☎ *07/4781–9211.*

DOCTORS

24 hour Medical Centre (✉ 301 Ross River Rd., Aitkenvale, ☎ 07/4725–3324) can provide nonurgent medical assistance.

GUIDED TOURS

Pure Pleasure Cruises runs from the Great Barrier Reef Wonderland wharf out to its pontoon at Kelso Reef on the outer edge of the Great Barrier Reef. The trip out takes 2½ hours by high-speed wave piercer. Once there, you have the choice of fishing, snorkeling, diving (for experienced divers; beginners can take an introductory dive), or viewing the coral through the floor of a glass-bottom boat. Morning and afternoon tea and a tropical buffet lunch are included in the cost ($124). The boat departs daily (except Mon. and Thurs.) at 9 AM, returning at 5:30 PM. Hotel pick-ups are available. ✉ *Wonderland Terminal, Flinders St.,* ☎ *07/4721–3555.*

Coral Princess has a four-day cruise from Townsville to Cairns or one-way or return. The ship carries 54 passengers in great comfort. There are plenty of stops for snorkeling, fishing, and exploring such resort islands as Dunk and Orpheus. The crew includes marine biologists who give lectures and accompany you on excursions. If you are a diver, you can rent equipment on board; if you wish to learn, lessons are available. ✉ *Coral Princess, Breakwater Marina, Townsville 4810,* ☎ *07/ 4721–1673 or 1800/07–9545.* 🛏 *From $1,045 per person.*

VISITOR INFORMATION

Magnetic Island Tourist Bureau is the island's primary oracle. ✉ *26 the Grove, Nelly Bay 4819,* ☎ *07/4778–5596.*

National Parks and Wildlife Service (☎ 07/4778–5378) has an office in Picnic Bay on Magnetic Island with information on walking trails.

Townsville Enterprise has the widest range of material and information on all local attractions. ⊠ *Enterprise House, the Strand, Box 1043, Townsville 4810,* ☎ *07/4771–3061.* ☉ *Weekdays 8:30–5.*

Flinders Mall Information Centre has a kiosk in Flinders Mall. ☎ 07/4721–3660.

CAIRNS

Cairns is the capital of the region known as Far North Queensland. The city is closer to Papua New Guinea than it is to most of Australia, although its sense of isolation has decreased with its role as an international gateway. Nevertheless, it still feels like a sleepy tropical town. Many older homes are built on stilts to catch ocean breezes, and overhead fans are ubiquitous. The city itself is totally flat, surrounded by rain forest, and macadamia, sugarcane, and pineapple plantations. The Coral Sea forms the town's eastern boundary, and to the west are the slopes of the dividing range leading up to the Atherton Tableland.

In many respects, the city is nothing more than a staging post—high-rise hotels, motels, and cheap hostels abound, but most people use the town as a base for exploring the surrounding ocean and rain forest. If you want to immerse yourself in Queensland's natural wonders, Cairns is the place to start.

Exploring Cairns

The **Esplanade** and the waterfront are the focal points of life in Cairns. Fronting Trinity Bay, the Esplanade is the site of many of the town's best stores and hotels. It is also where many of the backpackers who throng to Cairns like to gather, giving it a lively, slightly bohemian feel. Trinity Bay is a shallow stretch of hundreds of yards of mangrove flats, uncovered at low tide, that attract interesting bird life. In the late 1980s, some of the waterfront was filled in, and **Pier Market Place,** a shopping-hotel complex, was constructed.

Cairns can trace its beginnings to the point where the Esplanade turns into **Wharf Street.** In 1876 this small area was a port for the gold and tin mined inland. The area later became known as the Barbary Coast because of its criminal element. Today, it's once again a thriving port. Wander over to **Marlin Marina** where the charter fishing boats are moored. Big-game fishing is a major industry, and fish weighing more than 1,000 pounds have been caught in the waters off the reef. The docks for the catamarans that conduct Great Barrier Reef tours (☞ Cairns A to Z, *below*) are found here at Marlin Marina and at nearby **Trinity Wharf.**

The actual center of Cairns is **City Place,** a quaint pedestrian mall where you can watch the passing parade. Some of the town's few authentic pubs, as well as the major shopping area, are around the square.

The **Cairns Museum** houses a collection of artifacts and photographs of the city's history, including a fascinating exhibit on the life of Aborigines in the rain forest. The museum is next to City Place on Shields Street. ⊠ *Lake and Shields Sts.,* ☎ *07/4051–5582.* ☒ *$4.* ☉ *Mon.–Sat. 10–3.*

Attend one of the informative and entertaining lectures presented by **Reef Teach** (☎ 07/4051–6882) at the City Library. Six nights a week, a marine biologist uses slides and samples of coral to inform prospective divers and general sightseers about the Great Barrier Reef's evolution and the unique inhabitants of this delicate marine ecosystem. ⊠ *Cairns City Library, Bolands Centre, 14 Spence St.* ☒ *$10.* ☉ *Lecture Mon.–Sat. 6:15 PM–8:30 PM.*

Around Cairns

The **Tjapukai Aboriginal Cultural Park** features three theaters, one of which draws on state-of-the-art holographic technology. A surrounding encampment vignettes aspects of tribal life, including fire-making, didgeridoo playing, preparation of bush foods and medicines, and instruction on how to throw a boomerang and spear. Development of the Cultural Park was overseen by Aboriginal elders. A good range of Aboriginal artworks are on display and for sale. The park moved to its present location at the base of the **Skyrail Rain Forest Cableway** (☞ Guided Tours *in* Cairns A to Z, *below*) from a previous home in Kuranda. ⊠ *Kamerunga Rd., Caravonica Lakes, Smithfield, 15 km (9 mi) north of Cairns,* ☎ *07/4042–9999.* 🎟 *$24.* ⊙ *Daily 9–5.*

Wooroonooran National Park, which extends from just south of Gordonvale and stretches to the Palmerston Highway between Innisfail and Milla Milla, is one of the most densely vegetated areas in Australia. This park is the result of combining a few separate parks, including Bellenden Ker. Rain forest dominates Wooroonooran from lowland tropical rain forest to the stunted growth on Mount Bartle Frere, at 5,287 ft the highest point in Queensland, where you'll find Australia's largest remaining area of upland rain forest. Encompassing both the eastern and western slopes of the Bellenden Ker range, the park is largely undeveloped.

The park has a variety of trails, including a short (2,624 ft) paved path that leads from the parking area to Josephine Falls, which is a fine place to swim. Picnic facilities and toilets are there as well. For the more adventurous, a 15-km (9 mi) return trail leads from the parking area to the summit of Mount Bartle Frere. The two-day hike has some rough patches along the way, including steep climbs and rock scrambling, but it is well worth the effort for the spectacular view of the surrounding rain forest—unless the mountain is shrouded in fog. Avoid the gympie stinging tree: Its large, round leaves are covered with sharp barbs that inflict a painful sting.

To reach the park, look for signs south of Cairns along the Bruce Highway. Bush camping is allowed, with ranger permission, throughout the park, except at Josephine Falls. Permits cost $3.50 per person per night. Take supplies with you. ⊠ *Department of Environment and Heritage, McLeod St., Cairns 4870,* ☎ *07/4052–3096.*

OFF THE BEATEN PATH

UNDARA VOLCANIC NATIONAL PARK – The lava tubes here are a fascinating geological oddity in the Outback, and they are attracting an ever-increasing number of visitors for day visits and overnight trips. The hollow basalt tubes were created by a volcanic outpouring 190,000 years ago. There are several places where it is possible to walk into the tubes; leaving the ferns, vines, and wallabies at the entrance, you'll step onto the smooth, dry tunnel floor. Above, horseshoe bats twitter and flitter in the crannies. Patterns etched in the ceiling by water seepage create an incongruous cathedral effect.

Undara lies on the western side of the ranges, 400 km (248 mi) from Cairns. Day tours to Undara from the city are operated by **Australian Pacific Tours** (⊠ Orchid Plaza, Lake St., ☎ 07/4051–9299), departing daily from April through November, and from December through March on Tuesday, Wednesday, Saturday, and Sunday. The cost of the tour is $99, lunch included. There are accommodations at the **Undara Lava Lodge** (⊠ Kennedy Hwy., ☎ 07/4097–1411, FAX 07/4097–1450), which consists of interesting old railway cars converted to comfortable (if compact) motel rooms.

Dining

$$-$$$$ ✕ **Tawny's On The Jetty.** This waterfront restaurant has been owned and managed by Klaus and Junelle Urban since it opened in 1977. The menu is extensive and features local seafood and fresh produce from the nearby Atherton Tablelands. It includes surprises such as crocodile with Kakadu plums (native bush tucker), as well as more traditional seafood offerings. Desserts, such as banana and macadamia nut pudding, are tropically inspired. ⊠ *Marlin Parade,* ☎ *07/4051–1722. AE, DC, MC, V. No lunch.*

$$$ ✕ **Sirocco Restaurant.** On the waterfront in the Radisson Plaza Hotel at the pier (☞ Lodging, *below*), this restaurant serves innovative modern Australian cuisine. The decor is gracious and elegant, and tables are set with silver cutlery. Many of the dishes have tropical undertones, such as char-grilled fresh reef fish with sweet potato mash and wok-fried tableland vegetables, lemongrass, and coriander butter; or lightly smoked duck breast with arugula leaves and mango accompanied by King Island cream. Make sure you save room for something sweet—the dessert tray has to be seen to be believed. ⊠ *Radisson Plaza Hotel at the Pier, Pierpoint Rd.,* ☎ *07/4031–1411. AE, DC, MC, V. Closed Sun. and Mon.*

$$ ✕ **Breezes Brasserie.** Ceiling-to-floor windows overlooking Trinity
★ Inlet and the distant mountains set the mood in this attractive restaurant in the Hilton Cairns (☞ Lodging, *below*). The decor is bright, with tropical greenery, white tablecloths, and candles. You can feast on everything from quick sandwiches to full-course dinners. The modern Australian fare includes delights such as smoked Tasmanian salmon served with a bug mush (Australian lobster mixed with mashed potato), accompanied by red wine jus. The specialty, however, is seafood, and a spectacular seafood and Mediterranean buffet is available nightly. ⊠ *Hilton Cairns, Wharf St.,* ☎ *07/4052–6786. AE, DC, MC, V. No lunch.*

$ ✕ **Red Ochre Grill.** This restaurant uses about 40 different native foods to create modern Australian cuisine. Try the Australian antipasto platter of emu paté profiterole, crocodile spring roll, and kangaroo carpaccio with wild basil and parmesan for starters. Move on to lemon myrtle–cured salmon with native violet salad. The decor is warm red and terra-cotta, with a large freshwater tank in the middle displaying local red claw yabbies and rainbow fish. There is a good Australian wine list available by the glass or bottle. ⊠ *43 Shields St.,* ☎ *07/4051–0100. AE, DC, MC, V. No lunch Sun.*

$ ✕ **Roma Roulette.** Popular with locals and visitors alike, this Italian restaurant has an easygoing, informal atmosphere, and smiling chef Antonio often personally advises customers on what to order. Two long-running Roma favorites are *pasta tricolore* and *scaloppine al vino bianco.* Seafood is also recommended. ⊠ *48A Aplin St.,* ☎ *07/4051–1076. AE, DC, V. BYOB. Closed Mon.–Tues.*

Lodging

$$$$ ⊞ **Hilton Cairns.** The seven-story Hilton curves along the shoreline and
★ offers wonderful sea views; it's near the business district and a famous game-fishing club. The lobby, which looks out past lush gardens to the ocean, is distinctly tropical, with ceramic floor tiles and an atrium filled with rain-forest palms and ferns. Plants from a rooftop garden dangle in the long external walkways, and rooms on the lowest level open onto a palm forest that grows on the lobby roof. Rooms are tastefully appointed and furnished. ⊠ *Wharf St., 4870,* ☎ *07/4050–2000,* ☎ *07/4050–2001. 159 rooms, 5 suites. 2 restaurants, pool, hot tub, sauna, laundry service. AE, DC, MC, V.*

$$$$ 🏨 **Radisson Plaza Hotel at the Pier.** The Radisson's nautical look is appropriate, as it overlooks Trinity Wharf and Marlin Marina, the main Cairns terminals for cruises to the Barrier Reef. The hotel's conservative, low-rise design is typical of northern Queensland, but its lobby atrium is so spectacular—a replica of a rain forest with real and artificial plants and a boardwalk—that it's a tourist attraction in its own right. All rooms are spacious, and some are designed for guests with disabilities. Pier Marketplace, with numerous shops and restaurants, adjoins. ✉ *Pierpoint Rd., 4870,* ☎ *07/4031–1411,* FAX *07/4031–3226. 198 rooms, 21 suites. 2 restaurants, pool, hot tub, sauna, business services. AE, DC, MC, V.*

$$$$ 🏨 **Reef Hotel Casino.** The Reef is part of an entertainment complex in
★ the heart of Cairns. A rooftop conservatory is a tropical hothouse by day, at night turning into a candlelit dinner theater within a rain forest. Along with a coffee shop, nightclub, and several bars, you'll also find a very good Chinese restaurant, Pacific Flavours Brasserie, and the more dignified Anthias Restaurant. If you arrive before your room is ready or need to check out well before your flight, the Transit Lounge has the facilities of a first-class airport lounge. ✉ *35–41 Wharf St., 4870,* ☎ *07/4030–8888 or 1800/80–8883,* FAX *07/4030–8788. 127 suites. 4 restaurants, 4 bars, pool, exercise room, casino. AE, DC, MC, V.*

$$$ 🏨 **Holiday Inn Cairns.** This seven-story hotel offers views of Trinity Bay and the Coral Sea. Decorated with a marble floor, luxurious rugs, and cane sofas, the glass-wall lobby overlooks the hotel gardens. Guest rooms feature bright tropical colors, cane chairs, and wood tables. The hotel is within walking distance of shops, restaurants, and the business district. ✉ *Esplanade and Florence St., 4870,* ☎ *07/4050–6070,* FAX *07/4031–3710. 228 rooms, 6 suites. Restaurant, bar, room service, laundry service. AE, DC, MC, V.*

$$$ 🏨 **Il Palazzo Boutique Hotel.** This boutique hotel is close to the city and offers luxury in a smaller package. A 6½-ft Italian marble replica of Michelangelo's David greets you in the foyer, and other intriguing *objets* appear throughout the hotel. The suites are spacious, with a soft-green color scheme, forged-iron and glass tables, and cane furniture. They all have fully equipped kitchens and laundry machines. The hotel even offers a grocery service where you pick the items and they will be delivered to the hotel for you. ✉ *62 Abbott St., 4870,* ☎ *07/4031– 1055 or 1800/81–3222. 38 suites. Restaurant, pool, beauty salon. AE, DC, MC, V.*

$$$ 🏨 **Pacific International.** A soaring three-story lobby makes for an im-
★ pressive entrance to this hotel facing the waterfront and the marina. Guest rooms are furnished with cane and rattan chairs, soft pastels, tropical plants, and Gauguin-style prints. All have private balconies, tea and coffee makers, and color TVs. Rooms for guests with disabilities are available. ✉ *The Esplanade and Spence St., 4870,* ☎ *07/4051– 7888 or 1800/07–9001,* FAX *07/4051–0210. 163 rooms, 13 suites. 2 restaurants, 2 bars, pool, coffee shop. AE, DC, MC, V.*

$$ 🏨 **Cairns Colonial Club Resort.** Set in 10½ acres of lush tropical gardens, this two-story, colonial-style complex won the Beautiful Garden Award for the Cairns area for several years in a row. The resort is built around three lagoon-style swimming pools, and the public areas and rooms are simply furnished with cane furniture, ceiling fans, and vivid tropical cushions. Apartments with cooking facilities are available. Two rooms offer special facilities for guests with disabilities. A free shuttle makes the 7-km (4-mi) run to the city center hourly, and courtesy airport transfers are provided. ✉ *18–26 Cannon St., Manunda, 4870,* ☎ *07/4053–5111,* FAX *07/4053–7072. 264 rooms, 82 apartments. 2 restaurants, 3 bars, 3 pools, spa, sauna, tennis court, exercise room, laundry service, playground. AE, DC, MC, V.*

$ ⊞ **Hides of Cairns.** Within a heartbeat of the city center, this circa-1890 structure, with its breezy verandas, is a superb example of colonial outback architecture. An adjoining motel section has modern rooms with tropical decor. Rates include Continental breakfast. ⊠ *Lake and Shields Sts., 4870,* ☎ *07/4051–1266,* FAX *07/4031–2276. 72 rooms. Restaurant, 5 bars, pool, hot tub. AE, DC, MC, V.*

Nightlife

1936. This blend of retro and modern isn't exactly the place to go for a quiet chat, but the live nightly shows and "underworld" feel of Manhattan in the 1930s actually work quite well. ⊠ *Reef Hotel Casino, 35–41 Wharf St.,* ☎ *07/4030–8715.* ⊡ *$5 (free to hotel guests).* ☉ *Weekends 9:30 PM–3 AM.*

The Pier Tavern. Overlooking the waterfront, this lively, upmarket watering hole is a good place to meet locals. ⊠ *The Pier Marketplace, Pierpoint Rd.,* ☎ *07/4031–4677.*

Outdoor Activities and Sports

Adventure Trips

Raging Thunder offers adventure packages that take in the Great Barrier Reef, white-water rafting through the rain forest, the Tjapukai Aboriginal Cultural Park, Kuranda Scenic Railway or Skyrail, and hot air ballooning over the Atherton tablelands—the best of Cairns in one package. ⊠ *52–54 Fearnley St.,* ☎ *07/4030–7990.*

RNR Rafting runs very exciting one-, two-, and five-day white-water expeditions that are suitable only for the physically fit. ⊠ *4 Shields St.,* ☎ *07/4051–7777.*

Beaches

Cairns has no beaches of its own; most visitors head out to the reef to swim and snorkel. Just north of the airport, however, are **Machans Beach, Holloways Beach, Yorkey's Knob, Trinity Beach,** and **Clifton Beach.** Do not swim in these waters from October through May, when deadly box jellyfish, called marine stingers, float in the water along the coast. Some beaches have small netted areas, but it is advisable to stick to hotel pools at that time. Stingers stay closer to shore and are usually not found around the Great Barrier Reef or any nearby islands.

Diving

A large number of diving schools in Cairns offer everything from beginner's lessons to equipment rentals and expeditions for experienced divers. Contact **Deep Sea Divers Den** (⊠ 319 Draper St., ☎ 07/4031–2223), **Reef Magic Cruises** (⊠ 13 Shields St., ☎ 07/4031–1588), **Pro Dive** (⊠ Marlin Parade, ☎ 07/4031–5255), **Quicksilver Diving Services** (⊠ Marina Mirage, Port Douglas, ☎ 07/4099–5050), and **Sunlover Cruises** (⊠ Trinity Wharf, ☎ 07/4031–1055 or 1800/81–0512).

Shopping

Malls

Orchid Plaza (⊠ 79–87 Abbott St., ☎ 07/4051–7788) has clothing stores, cafés, record stores, a pearl emporium, dreamtime art gallery, and post office. **Palm Court** (⊠ 34–42 Lake St.) offers a variety of specialty shops. On the waterfront, **Trinity Wharf** (⊠ Wharf St., ☎ 07/4031–1519) has everything from designer clothes and souvenirs to resort wear, hairdressers, restaurants, and a coach terminal. Shoppers can request complimentary transportation from their hotels. On the Esplanade, the **Pier Marketplace** (⊠ Pierpoint Rd., ☎ 07/4051–7244) houses such international chains as Brian Rochford and Country Road, and the offices of yacht brokers and tour operators. Many of the cafés, bars, and restaurants open onto verandas on the waterside.

Markets

Held Friday afternoon, Saturday all day, and Sunday morning, **Rusty's Bazaar** is the best street market in Cairns. Everything from homegrown fruit and vegetables to secondhand items and antiques is on sale. ⊠ *Grafton and Sheridan Sts.*

Cairns Night Markets, held nightly, are also popular. Here you'll find souvenir items, arts and crafts, and T-shirts. ⊠ *The Esplanade, at Alpin St.*

Specialty Stores

The well-respected **Original Dreamtime Gallery of Alice Springs** (⊠ Orchid Plaza, 7/8 Palm Ct., Lake St., ☎ 07/4051–3222) sells top-quality artwork created by the Aborigines of the Northern Territory. **Gallery Primitive** (⊠ 26 Abbott St., ☎ 07/4031–1641) has Aboriginal and New Guinean arts and artifacts on display and for sale. **Reef Gallery** (⊠ The Pier Marketplace, ☎ 07/4051–0992) sells paintings by leading local artists. **Australian Craftworks** (⊠ Shop 20, Village La., Lake St., ☎ 07/4051–0725) has one of the city's finest collections of local crafts.

Cairns A to Z

Arriving and Departing

BY BUS

Greyhound Pioneer Australia (☎ 13–2030), **Murrays Coaches** (☎ 07/4035–2622), and **McCafferty's** (☎ 07/4051–5899 or 13–1499) operate daily express buses from major southern cities.

BY CAR

The 1,712-km (1,061-mi) route from Brisbane to Cairns runs along the Bruce Highway (Hwy. 1), which later becomes the Captain Cook Highway. Although the entire route is paved, there are many tortuous sections that make driving difficult. Throughout its length, the road rarely touches the coast. Unless you crave endless fields of sugarcane, it's not even picturesque. It's best to fly to Cairns and rent a car instead.

BY PLANE

See Air Travel *in* the Gold Guide for information on airlines.

BY TRAIN

Trains arrive at the **Cairns Railway Station** on Bunda Street (☎ 07/4052–6249). The *Sunlander* and *Queenslander* trains make the 32-hour journey between Brisbane and Cairns. The *Sunlander* runs three times a week to Cairns. The *Queenslander* has been refurbished to the level of most luxury cruise ships, making the journey equal in comfort to that of the world's great deluxe trains. It runs once a week.

The Great South Pacific Express (☎ 1800/62–7655) offers first class "Orient Express" type luxury among Sydney, Brisbane, and Cairns. The train runs twice weekly each way and includes many extra sightseeing tours during the journey.

Getting Around

BY TAXI

Black and White Taxis (☎ 13–1008).

Contacts and Resources

CAR RENTAL

Avis (☎ 07/4035–9100), **Budget** (☎ 07/4051–9222), **Hertz** (☎ 13–3039), and **Thrifty** (☎ 07/4051–8099) have airport and/or city locations. Four-wheel-drive vehicles are available.

EMERGENCIES

Ambulance, fire brigade, and police. ☎ *000*.

Cairns Base Hospital. ☎ *07/4050–6333.*

GUIDED TOURS

★ **Cableway Tours:** The remarkable **Skyrail Rain Forest Cableway** was built in the mid-1990s to the tune of $35 million. The base station is 15 km (9 mi) north of Cairns; from there six-person cable cars carry you on a 7½-km (5-mi) journey across the top of the rain forest canopy to the tiny highland village of Kuranda. (There's a market here Wednesday through Friday and Sunday.) There are two stops along the way where you can walk to Barron Falls or into the rain forest. Despite the protests of some conservationists—some of whom glued their hands together around a tree only to discover they had picked a tree that was not to be removed—the Skyrail does provide a unique perspective on this astonishingly rich area. ⊠ *Caravonica Lakes, Kamerunga Rd. and Cook Hwy., Smithfield,* ☎ *07/4038–1555.* ⊡ *One-way $27, round-trip $45.* ⊘ *8–3:45 daily; 2:30 is the last time to board for a round-trip.*

Great Barrier Reef Tours: Coral Princess (⊠ Breakwater Marina, Townsville, 4810, ☎ 07/4721–1673 or 1800/079–545) conducts a four-day trip from Cairns to Townsville, vice versa, or round-trip aboard a cruise ship that carries 54 passengers in great comfort. There are plenty of stops for snorkeling, fishing, and exploring Dunk and Orpheus islands. The crew includes marine biologists who lecture on board and on excursions from the boat. Diving gear can be rented, and lessons are available.

Great Adventures Outer Barrier Reef and Island Cruises (⊠ Wharf St., ☎ 07/4051–0455 or 1800/07–9080) runs a fast catamaran daily to Green and Fitzroy islands, Norman Reef, and Moore Reef (where diving and snorkeling, and helicopter overflights are available). Some trips include barbecue luncheon and coral viewing from an underwater observatory and a semi-submersible.

Ocean Spirit Cruises (⊠ 33 Lake St., ☎ 07/4031–2920) has a full-day tour aboard the *Ocean Spirit,* the largest sailing vessel of its type in the world, and the smaller *Ocean Spirit II.* A daily trip to Michaelmas or Upollo Cay includes four hours at the Great Barrier Reef, coral viewing from a semi-submersible or a glass bottom boat at Upolo Cay, swimming and snorkeling, and a fresh seafood lunch. Introductory diving lessons are available.

Four-Wheel-Drive Tours: Wild Track Adventure Safaris (⊠ Box 2397, Cairns 4870, ☎ 07/4055–2247, ⅍ 07/4058–1930) runs trips to the top of the Cape York Peninsula from June through November. For more information, *see* Four-Wheel-Drive Tours *in* Chapter 12.

Nature Tours: Daintree Wildlife Safari (☎ 07/4098–6125) runs 1½-hour tours down the Daintree River. **Daintree Rain Forest River Trains** (☎ 07/4090–7676) run full-day and half-day tours through mangrove swamps and thick rain forest to see native orchids, birds, and crocodiles.

Tropic Wings Coach Tours offers a variety of trips in the Cairns area, including tours to Atherton Tablelands, waterfalls, Kuranda, Port Douglas, Daintree Rain Forest, the Outback, and the Gulf of Carpentaria west and north of Cairns. ⊠ *278 Hartley St.,* ☎ *07/4035–3555.*

Train Tours: Kuranda Scenic Railway from Cairns to Kuranda is one of the most scenic rail journeys of the world. Kuranda is the gateway to the Atherton Tableland, an elevated area of rich volcanic soil that produces some of Australia's finest beef, dairy, and produce. Between this tableland and the narrow coastal strip is a rugged dividing range filled with waterfalls, lakes, caves, and gorges. The train makes the 40-minute ascent through the rain forest via the Barron River Gorge and 15 hand-hewn tunnels. A wide range of tours is available, from full-day rain forest safaris to simple round-trip train and bus rides. ✉ *Cairns Railway Station, Bunda St.,* ☎ *07/4031–3636 for reservations.* *$25 one-way, $40 round-trip.*

VISITOR INFORMATION

Far North Queensland Promotion Bureau. ✉ *51 The Esplanade, Cairns,* ☎ *07/4051–3588.*

NORTH FROM CAIRNS

The Captain Cook Highway runs from Cairns to Mossman, a relatively civilized stretch known mostly for the resort town of Port Douglas. Past the Daintree River, wildlife parks and sunny coastal villages fade into one of the most sensationally wild corners of the continent. If you came to Australia in search of high-octane sun, empty beaches and coral cays, steamy jungles filled with exotic bird noises and rioting vegetation, and a languid, beachcomber lifestyle, then head straight for the coast between Daintree and Cooktown.

The southern half of this coastline lies within Cape Tribulation National Park, part of the Greater Daintree Wilderness Area, a region named to UNESCO's World Heritage list because of its unique ecology. If you want to get a peek at the natural splendor of the area, there's no need to go past Cape Tribulation. However, the Bloomfield Track does continue on to Cooktown, a destination that will tack two days onto your itinerary. This wild, rugged country breeds some notoriously maverick personalities and can add a whole other dimension to the Far North Queensland experience.

It is not advisable to tackle the wilderness of the Far North alone. By its very nature, the national park requires an expert interpreter. To untrained eyes, the rain forest can look like nothing more than giant roots underfoot and palm trees overhead. But there is so much within the forest to see, and a guide can help you train your eyes on all that's weird and wonderful. Many tour operators offer day trips across the Daintree River from either Cairns or Port Douglas. After a day with a guide, you'll be prepared to do a little more on your own. Better still, stay a couple of days at Cape Tribulation, leaving your footprints on empty beaches, snorkeling off the coral reefs, and drifting off to sleep while the jungle croaks, drips, and squeaks around you.

Prime time for visiting the area is from May through September, when the daily maximum temperature averages around 80°F and the water is comfortably warm. During the wet season, which lasts from about December through March, expect monsoon conditions. Toxic box jellyfish make the coastline unsafe for swimming during the Wet, but the jellies don't drift out as far as the reefs, so you're safe there.

Numbers in the margin correspond to points of interest on the Far North Queensland Coast map.

Palm Cove

32 *23 km (14 mi) north of Cairns.*

Palm Cove, a mere 20-minute drive north of Cairns, is one of the jewels of Queensland and an ideal base for exploring the far north. It is an oasis of quietude that those in the know seek out for its magnificent trees, calm waters, and excellent restaurants. The loudest noises

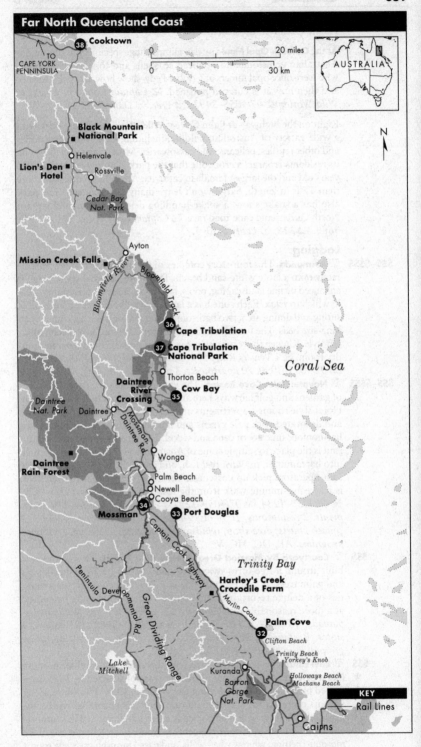

Far North Queensland Coast

you are likely to hear are the singing of birds and the lapping of the Pacific Ocean on the beach.

At the **Outback Opal Mine** you can glimpse huge specimens of this unique Australian gemstone and opalized seashells and fossils. The owners, who were once opal miners at Coober Pedy, show how an opal is formed and then how it is cut and polished. ⊠ *Captain Cook Hwy. next to Wild World,* ☎ *07/4055–3492.* 🎟 *Free.* ☉ *Daily 9–5.*

Right on the highway at Palm Cove is **Wild World,** a 10-acre park with a wide variety of Australian wildlife, including kangaroos, crocodiles and other reptiles, pelicans, and cassowaries. Most distinguished among its residents is Sarge, a crocodile that the park claims is more than 100 years old and the largest female in captivity. At 1,540 pounds and more than 17 ft in length, Sarge won't leave many unconvinced. The park also has a snake show, a snake-handling demonstration, and a giant North Queensland cane-toad race. ⊠ *Captain Cook Hwy.,* ☎ *07/4055–3669.* 🎟 *$18.* ☉ *Daily 8:30–5.*

Lodging

$$$–$$$$ 🏨 **Alamanda.** This four-story complex of vacation apartments opens directly onto a large white-sand beach. The white, colonial-style design is enhanced by fine landscaping, pools, barbecues, and plenty of sunny areas in which to relax. Each suite has a large, private veranda, a comfortable sitting and dining area, two bathrooms, and two or three bedrooms with king-size beds. The furnishings are all custom designed in a cheery, modern style. Kitchens have granite-top counters, and there is a separate laundry room. ⊠ *1 Veivers Rd., 4879,* ☎ *07/4055–3000 or 1800/67–2236,* FAX *07/4055–3090. 70 apartments. 3 pools, spa. AE, DC, MC, V.*

$$$–$$$$ 🏨 **Novotel Palm Cove Resort.** The villagelike buildings and 100 acres of gardens and golf fairways here are a five-minute walk from the beach. Hotel-style rooms—apartments are also available—are average in size and decorated with pale greens and muted yellows. The furniture is a harmonious mixture of cane and wood. The resort's Paperbark Restaurant is the place to sample some of Australia's prime beef fillets, or tuck into barramundi, prawns, reef fish, and crabs. Palm Cove jetty, where tour operators pick up passengers for trips to the Great Barrier Reef, is just a five-minute walk from the resort. ⊠ *Coral Coast Dr., 4879,* ☎ *07/4059–1234,* FAX *07/4059–1297. 152 rooms, 72 suites, 119 apartments. 2 restaurants, 10 pools, 9-hole golf course, 3 tennis courts, 2 squash courts, dive shop, windsurfing, boating, jet skiing, children's programs. AE, DC, MC, V.*

$$$ 🏨 **Courtyard By Marriott Great Barrier Reef Resort.** This complex is built around a free-form swimming pool shaded by giant melaleucas and palm trees. It's an escapist's delight. You can enjoy all the amenities of a deluxe resort, including plush rooms with private balconies, at a more reasonable rate. ⊠ *Box 122, Vievers Rd. and Williams Esplanade, 4879,* ☎ *07/4055–3999,* FAX *07/4055–3902. 185 rooms, 4 suites. Restaurant, bar, pool, spa, tennis court, baby-sitting, playground, laundry service. AE, DC, MC, V.*

$$$ 🏨 **Reef House.** Set amid lovely gardens, this charming hotel seems more
★ like a private club. The main building was constructed in 1885 by a retired politician, and a new wing was added in 1986. The lobby, along with its mural of the Queensland rain forest, is decorated with a superb collection of New Guinea Sepik River handicrafts. The comfortable rooms have a turn-of-the-century atmosphere characterized by mosquito netting, whitewashed walls, and pastel furnishings. Some rooms have bars and refrigerators. ⊠ *99 Williams Esplanade,* ☎ *07/4055–3633,* FAX *07/4055–3305. 63 rooms, 7 suites. 3 pools, laundry service. AE, DC, MC, V.*

En Route North of Palm Cove, where the Captain Cook Highway swoops toward
★ the sea, a sign announces the beginning of the **Marlin Coast,** and for
the next 30 km (19 mi) the road plays hide-and-seek with a glorious
stretch of shoreline, ducking inland through tunnels of coconut palm
and curving back to the surf.

On Cook Highway, **Hartley's Creek Crocodile Farm** is the home of the
renowned Charlie, a saltwater crocodile that is the crocodile held
longest in captivity—he's been a "pet" for about 65 years. Apart from
Charlie and his hundreds of crocodile mates, visitors can look at many
native animals, such as koalas, kangaroos, dingoes, snakes, lizards, and
such native birds as the rare cassowary, which is a large and colorful
bird found only in New Guinea and parts of northern Australia. All
of these animals can be enjoyed in the park's rain forest setting. ⊠ *Cook
Hwy., 40 km (25 mi) north of Cairns,* ☎ *07/4055–3576.* ☎ *$15.50.*
☉ *Daily 8–5, crocodile show at 11 and 3, crocodile photos at 4, koalas
and dingoes at 1, snake show at 2.*

Port Douglas

③③ *61 km (38 mi) north of Cairns.*

In the early '80s Port Douglas was a sleepy little fishing village, but
today it's one of the "in" places to go in Australia. The road into town
passes through sugarcane fields then widens and is flanked by palm
trees that were planted elsewhere during World War II for palm oil,
then moved here to create this avenue. Known simply as the "Port"
to locals, the town has an indefinable mystique. Enough of the old
Queensland colonial buildings remain to give it an authentic feel, despite the growing presence of modern resorts and hotels. High-speed
cruises leave the Port for the Outer Reef (☞ Guided Tours *in* North
from Cairns A to Z, *below*).

Dining and Lodging

$$$$ ✕ **Macrossans.** This modern, glass-walled restaurant in the Sheraton
Mirage Port Douglas (☞ *below*) is a study in opulence. High-quality
antiques, floor-length white tablecloths, and elegant silver settings
complement the cuisine. French dishes prepared with fresh seafood and
local produce are appropriately lightened to suit the tropics. The food
is beautifully presented, usually with a garnish of exotic fruit. Try Mossman prawns if they are available, and save some room for dessert. Choco-
late-laden black-and-white terrine is the chef's specialty. ⊠ *Davidson
St.,* ☎ *07/4098–5888. AE, DC, MC, V. No lunch.*

$$$–$$$$ ✕ **Nautilus Restaurant.** Pull up one of the high-back cane chairs out-
★ side under a canopy of magnificent tropical palms. The modern Aus-
tralian cuisine is fresh and original, with plenty of seafood on the
menu, and all dishes are beautifully presented. The Nautilus is famous
for its mud crabs cooked to order. Try the mille-feuille wonton of mar-
inated barramundi, or leeks and sweet peppers with coconut and
lemon dressing, or Thai chicken curry with steamed rice. For dessert,
you can't go wrong ordering poached peach with passion fruit sabayon.
⊠ *17 Murphy St.,* ☎ *07/4099–5330. AE, DC, MC, V. No lunch.*

$$$$ ▦ **Sheraton Mirage Port Douglas.** This is unquestionably the far north's
★ best resort in the deluxe bracket. If you go for glitz, polished marble,
exotic foliage, and lagoon-size pools, then look no further. Elegant guest
rooms are decorated with cane furniture upholstered in blues and
greens, and tropical-print bedspreads. Rooms overlook the hotel gar-
dens, golf course, or lagoons that surround the resort. Valets are avail-
able 24 hours a day to assist with everything from replenishing ice buckets
to arranging special candlelight dinners in the room. Guests are free
to use the gym and tennis courts at the neighboring Mirage Club. ⊠

Davidson St., 4871, ☎ *07/4099–5888,* FAX *07/4099–4424. 294 rooms, 3 suites. 4 restaurants, 3 bars, coffee shop, pool, exercise room, laundry service. AE, DC, MC, V.*

$$$ 🏨 **Thala Beach Lodge.** This locally owned and operated hotel sits amid
★ 145 private acres and has over a mile of private beach frontage between Cairns and Port Douglas. The ambience is unspoiled wilderness; the buildings are built high on timber poles to peer out through a canopy of trees. The natural rock pool area is a stunning place to while away a few hours gliding between the several levels of pools canopied by tree cover above. The main building is built out from a rocky ridge on high timber poles; the wonderful restaurant here enjoys 180-degree views from the rain forests in the north down to Cairns in the south. Tour operators pick up at the front door. ⊠ *Private Rd., Oak Beach, 4871,* ☎ *07/4057–5300,* FAX *07/4057–5333. 85 suites. Restaurant, bar, no-smoking rooms, pool, beach, tour desk. AE, DC, MC, V.*

Shopping

Unquestionably the best and most elegant shopping complex in northern Queensland, the **Marina Mirage** contains 40 fashion and specialty shops for souvenirs, jewelry, accessories, resort wear, and designer clothing. ⊠ *Wharf St.,* ☎ *07/4099–5775.*

Mossman

③④ *14 km (9 mi) northwest of Port Douglas, 75 km (47 mi) north of Cairns.*

Mossman is a sugar town with a population of less than 2,000. Its appeal lies not in the village itself but 5 km (3 mi) out of town where you find the beautiful waterfalls and river at Mossman Gorge.

Dining and Lodging

$$$$ ✕🏨 **Silky Oaks Lodge and Restaurant.** Situated on a hillside sur-
★ rounded by national parkland, this hotel is reminiscent of the best African safari lodges. Air-conditioned villas on stilts overlook either the rain forest and the river below or a natural rock swimming pool. The villas have tropically inspired decor, and some have spa baths. Views from the verandas are stunning. Dining in the open-side timber Tree House Restaurant is nothing short of idyllic. Dishes range from classical to nouvelle, such as baked barramundi fillet served on steamed asparagus with a macadamia nut and lime butter sauce, or rack of lamb marinated in an herb yogurt. The restaurant has an excellent selection of Australian wine. The lodge is the starting point for four-wheel-drive, cycling, and canoeing trips into otherwise inaccessible national park rain forest. ⊠ *Finlayvale Rd., Mossman Gorge, 4873,* ☎ *07/4098–1666,* FAX *07/4098–1983. 60 rooms. Restaurant, bar, pool, tennis court, library. AE, DC, MC, V.*

En Route New species of fauna and flora are still being discovered in the **Daintree Rain Forest,** and the tropical vegetation is as impressive as anything found in the Amazon Basin. Collect information and maps for exploring from park rangers, since you'll need to detour off the main road to find the best areas for walking. You'll want to explore part of the area in a four-wheel-drive vehicle—some of the rain forest tracks are unpaved and muddy, and it is often necessary to ford streams. There are also guided four-wheel-drive tours, which include walking within the rain forest. Or at least enjoy a ride on a river boat (☞ *North from Cairns A to Z, below*). The national park is 35 km (22 mi) northwest of Mossman.

The intrepid will follow the Mossman–Daintree Road as it winds through sugarcane plantations and towering green hills to the **Daintree River crossing.** The Daintree is a relatively short river, yet it's fed by heavy monsoonal rains that make it wide, glossy, and brown—and a favorite inland haunt for saltwater crocodiles.

The relationship between the area's reptile and human inhabitants is not always harmonious: During a 1985 New Year's Eve party, a local resident was snatched from the bank of the river, and her enraged companions took their revenge on every crocodile they could find. To dramatize the resulting decline in the crocodile population, local tour operator Brian Strike swam across the river at the ferry crossing—with nary a nibble. Although the waters right at the ferry may have been thinned, during most times of the year you won't have to travel far to spot a croc. ☎ 07/4098–7536. 🖃 $7 per car, $1 per walk-on passenger. ☺ Ferry crossings every 20 min daily 6 AM–midnight.

On the north bank of the Daintree River, a sign announces the beginning of **Cape Tribulation National Park** (☞ Cape Tribulation, below). The road beyond the ferry crossing is paved.

Cow Bay

③⑤ 17 km (11 mi) northeast of the Daintree River crossing, 47 km (29 mi) north of Mossman.

The sweep of sand at Cow Bay is fairly typical of the beaches north of the Daintree, with the advantage that the fig trees at the back of the beach offer welcome shade. Follow Buchanans Creek Road north from the Daintree River crossing, which after about 10 km (6 mi) turns toward the sea and Cow Bay.

Dining and Lodging

$ ✕🏨 **Crocodylus Village.** Set in a rain forest clearing about 3 km (2 mi) from Cow Bay, the Village is highly recommended for adventurous and budget-conscious travelers. Guests are accommodated in large, fixed-site tents, which are more like cabins since they are raised off the ground and enclosed by a waterproof fabric and insect-proof mesh. Some tents are set up as dormitories with bunk beds, others are private with showers. Both styles are basic, but the entire village is neat and well maintained, and it offers an excellent activities program. Restaurant prices are low, and the atmosphere is friendly and relaxed. Reserve ahead, especially in peak season between June and August. ✉ Buchanan Creek Rd., ☎ 07/4098–9166, ☏ 07/4098–9131. 5 dormitory tents, 10 private tents. Restaurant, bar, pool. MC, V.

Cape Tribulation

③⑥ 27 km (17 mi) north of Cow Bay, 34 km (21 mi) north of the Daintree River crossing, 139 km (86 mi) north of Cairns.

Cape Tribulation was named by Captain James Cook, who was understandably peeved after a nearby reef inflicted a gaping wound in the side of his ship, HMS Endeavour, forcing him to seek refuge at the present-day site of Cooktown. To reach the tiny settlement, set dramatically at the base of Mount Sorrow, proceed north from Cow Bay along a road that plays a game of hide-and-seek with the sea, climbing high over the Noah Range before reaching town.

In many ways, Cape Tribulation is a microcosm of Queensland's diverse climates and terrain. Along this undeveloped coastal strip, rain forest, mangroves, coral, and sea all come together, and the waters have their dangerous appeal, with saltwater crocodiles lurking in larger local streams.

The Cape Tribulation settlement, small enough to shoot past in a blink, is the activities and accommodations base for the surrounding national park. You'll find a shop, a couple of lodges, and that's about it. The cape's natural credentials are impeccable, however. Nowhere else on the Australian coastline do coral reef and rain forest exist in such unspoiled proximity. Until recently, the only tourists who came this way were backpackers who holed up in lodges here for a few dollars a night, and tourism in the area still has a casual, back-to-nature feeling. All of the regional tours—including rain forest walks, reef trips, horseback riding, and fishing—can be booked through the village shop. If you'd rather loaf on the beach, the one nearest to town is about a five-minute stroll along a boardwalk that cuts through a mangrove swamp. The beach to the north of Cape Tribulation is more scenic. Keep in mind that swimming in the ocean from October through April is perilous because of marine stingers.

③⑦ **Cape Tribulation National Park** is an ecological wonderland, a remnant of the forests in which flowering plants first appeared on earth—an evolutionary leap that took advantage of insects for pollination and provided an energy-rich food supply for the early marsupials that were replacing the dinosaurs. Experts can readily identify species of angiosperms, the most primitive flowering plant, many of which are found nowhere else on the planet. If you were searching for the most ancient roots of humankind, sooner or later you would find yourself here, in this very forest.

The park stretches along the coast and west into the jungle from Cow Bay to Aytor. The beach is usually empty, except for the tiny soldier crabs that move about by the hundreds and scatter when approached. Hikers exploring the mangroves are likely to see an incredible assortment of small creatures that depend on the trees for survival. Most evident are mudskippers and mangrove crabs, but keen observers may spot green-backed herons crouched among mangrove roots.

The best time to see the rain forest is in the dry season, May through September. Walking along dry creek beds is the best way to explore. Bring plenty of insect repellent.

Several tour companies in Cairns offer day trips to the rain forest in four-wheel-drive buses and vans. Contact the **Department of Environment** (✉ 10–12 McLeod St., Cairns 4870, ☎ 07/4052–3096).

Dining and Lodging

Camping is permitted at **Noah's Beach,** about 8 km (5 mi) south of Cape Tribulation, for a nominal fee. Privately run campgrounds and small resorts can be found along the Daintree Road at Myall Creek and Cape Tribulation.

$$$–$$$$ ✕🏨 **Coconut Beach Rainforest Resort.** The most dignified of accommodations at Cape Tribulation sits swathed in a jungle of fan palms, staghorn ferns, giant melaleucas, and strangler figs, about 2 km (1 mi) south of the cape itself. The centerpiece of the resort is the Long House, a striking, pole-frame building that overlooks the main swimming pool. Stay in individual villas or in less-expensive, older-style rooms, which are clustered in blocks of three. The resort makes much of its eco-awareness, so the rooms are fan-cooled rather than air-conditioned. The beach is only a two-minute walk away, or you can take advantage of an elevated walkway set into the nearby rain forest canopy, habitat of local birds. ✉ Box 334H, Edge Hill 4870, ☎ 07/4098–0033 or 1800/81–6525, FAX 07/4098–0047. 27 rooms and 40 villas. Restaurant, bar, 3 pools, mountain bikes. AE, DC, MC, V.

$$$-$$$$ ✕⊞ **Ferntree Rainforest Resort.** This very comfortable resort has large, split-level villas and bungalows that are hunkered in the rain forest, close to the beach. They both make the most of the natural environment. ✉ *Box 334H, Edge Hill 4870,* ☎ *07/4098–0000,* ℻ *07/4098– 0011. 22 bungalows, 20 villas, 8 suites. Restaurant, pool, laundry service. AE, DC, MC, V.*

En Route The **Bloomfield Track** leads north from Cape Tribulation. Less than 30 km (19 mi) long, it is one of the most controversial strips of roadway in Australia, and it still generates powerful passions. The decision in the early '80s to carve a road through the Daintree wilderness provoked one of the most bitter conservation battles of recent memory. The road went through, but the ruckus was instrumental in securing a World Heritage listing for the Daintree, thereby effectively shutting out logging operations. At Cape Tribulation a sign warns that the track is open only to four-wheel-drive vehicles, and although no one will stop you from driving through in a conventional vehicle, the rough passage over the Cowie Range essentially closes the road to all but the most rugged machines.

Bloomfield River

22 km (14 mi) north of Cape Tribulation.

The Bloomfield River is subject to tides at the ford, and you must cross the river only when the water level has dropped sufficiently to allow safe crossing. Extreme care is needed because the submerged causeway can be difficult to follow, and it is fairly common for vehicles to topple off.

Dining and Lodging

$$$$ ✕⊞ **Bloomfield Wilderness Lodge.** This lodge sits in rugged surroundings near the mouth of the Bloomfield River and consists of timber bungalows, each of which has a balcony at the front, lots of open latticework, and a ceiling fan. Activities include guided walks, fishing, beachcombing along small but deserted beaches, and croc-spotting cruises on the Bloomfield River. The most convenient access is by plane from Cairns, with the final trip by boat from the Bloomfield River (arranged by the lodge). Rates include all meals and flight transfers from Cairns. Children under 12 are not accommodated. ✉ *Box 966, Cairns 4870,* ☎ *07/4035–9166,* ℻ *07/4035–9180. 17 rooms. Restaurant, bar, pool. AE, DC, MC, V.*

En Route At the Aboriginal settlement of Wujal Wujal on the north bank of the river, make the short detour inland to **Mission Creek Falls,** where the river is safe for swimming. Some 20 minutes' drive north of the Bloomfield River is a great swimming spot: Pull over to the left where a sign identifies the Cedar Bay National Park and walk down the steep gully to a creek; at the bottom of a small cascade is one of the most perfect swimming holes you're ever likely to find.

About 33 km (20 mi) north of Wujal Wujal at the junction of the rain forest and an area of open woodland is the **Lion's Den Hotel** (☎ 07/ 4060–3911), a pub whose corrugated-iron walls and tree-stump chairs ooze un-self-conscious character. The walls are covered in graffiti, from the simple KILROY WAS HERE variety to the totally scandalous, and for the price of a donation to the Royal Flying Doctor Service, you can add your own wit to the collection. It's easy to pass a pleasant afternoon here just observing who and what wanders in the door.

At the junction of Northern Road—you'll see it called the Bicentennial National Trail on some maps—and the Cooktown Development

Road, jumbled piles of rock beside the road identify **Black Mountain National Park.** The distinctive coloration of these granite boulders is caused by a black algae. Climbing the rocks is difficult and dangerous, and there are stinging trees in the area. For the nonadventurous, the formations are best appreciated from the roadside.

Cooktown

38 *96 km (60 mi) north of Cape Tribulation, 235 km (146 mi) north of Cairns.*

Cooktown is the last major settlement on the east coast of the continent. It is a frontier town on the edge of a difficult wilderness, its wide main street consisting mainly of two-story pubs with four-wheelers parked out front. Despite the temporary air, Cooktown has a long and impressive history. It was here in 1770 that Captain James Cook beached HMS *Endeavour* to repair her hull. Any tour of Cooktown should begin at the waterfront, where a statue of Captain Cook gazes out to sea, overlooking the spot where he landed.

A town was established a hundred years after Cook's landfall when gold was discovered on the Palmer River. Cooktown mushroomed and quickly became the largest settlement in Queensland after Brisbane, but as in many other mining boomtowns, life was hard and often violent. Chinese miners flooded into the goldfields and anti-Chinese sentiment flared into race riots, echoing events that had occurred at every other goldfield in the country. Further conflict arose between miners and local Aborigines, who resented what they saw as a territorial invasion and the rape of the region's natural resources; such place names as Battle Camp and Hell's Gate testify to the pattern of ambush and revenge.

Cooktown is a sleepy shadow of those dangerous days—when it had 64 pubs on a main street 3 km (2 mi) long—but a significant slice of history has been preserved at the **James Cook Historical Museum,** formerly a convent of the Sisters of Mercy. The museum houses relics of the gold-mining era, Chinese settlement, both world wars, Aboriginal artifacts, canoes, and a notable collection of seashells—not to mention artifacts relating to the intriguing story of Mrs. Watson, who escaped from a party of hostile Aborigines on Lizard Island with her son and a Chinese servant in a huge cooking pot, only to perish of thirst on another island. The museum also contains mementos of Cook's voyage, including the anchor and one of the cannons that were jettisoned when the HMS *Endeavour* ran aground. ⊠ *Helen and Furneaux Sts.,* ☎ *07/ 4069–5386.* ⊞ *$5.* ☉ *Daily 9:30–4.*

Lodging

$$ 🏨 **Sovereign Resort.** This attractive, colonial-style hotel in the heart of town is the best bet in Cooktown. The two-story timber-and-brick affair with verandas across the front, terra-cotta tiles, and soft-color decor gives the air of a plantation house. Appealing guest rooms trimmed with rustic wooden doors, terra-cotta floor tiles, and bright blues and reds overlook tropical gardens at the rear of the building. ⊠ *Charlotte St.,* ☎ *07/4069–5400. 24 rooms, 5 suites. Restaurant, bar, pool. AE, MC, V.*

En Route   From Cooktown, the northern tip of the Australian mainland is still some 800 km (500 mi) distant via the road that runs along the middle of Cape York. Access to the **Cape York Peninsula** used to be granted to only a lucky (or crazy) few, but new roads now make it relatively easy to travel in a four-wheel-drive vehicle from Cairns right to the tip of the Cape.

North from Cairns A to Z

Arriving and Departing

BY BUS

Coral Coaches (☎ 07/4031–7577) runs buses between Cairns, Port Douglas, and Cape Tribulation.

Coral Coaches (☎ 07/4031–7577) operates an air-conditioned bus service between Cairns and Cooktown along the inland route.

BY CAR

To head north by car from Cairns, take Florence Street from the Esplanade for four blocks and then turn right into Sheridan Street, which is the beginning of northbound Highway 1. Highway 1 leads past the airport and forks 12 km (7 mi) north of Cairns; take the right fork for Cook Highway, which goes as far as Mossman. From Mossman, the turnoff for the Daintree River crossing is 29 km (18 mi) north on the Daintree–Mossman Road. Except for four-wheel-drive vehicles, rental cars are not permitted on the narrow, twisting road north of the Daintree River.

BY PLANE

Hinterland Aviation (☎ 07/4035–9323) links Cairns with Cow Bay—the airport for Cape Tribulation—and the Bloomfield River. The flight to Cow Bay costs $85 per person each way, with a minimum of two people required. To Bloomfield, the cost is $75. Both airfields are isolated dirt strips, and passengers must arrange onward transport to their destination in advance. In-flight coastal views are spectacular.

Getting Around

The **Coral Coaches** bus (☎ 07/4031–7577) travels between the Daintree Ferry crossing and Cape Tribulation twice daily in each direction.

Contacts and Resources

CAR RENTAL

Avis (☎ 07/4035–9100) has four-wheel-drive Toyota Landcruisers for rent from Cairns; the cost varies daily depending on availability of vehicles. For other car rental information, *see* Cairns A to Z, *above*.

EMERGENCIES

Be advised that doctors, ambulances, firefighters, and police are scarce to nonexistent between the Daintree River and Cooktown.

Ambulance, fire brigade, and police. ☎ 000.

Mossman Police (☎ 07/4098–1200), **Port Douglas Police** (☎ 07/4099–5220), **Mossman District Hospital.** (☎ 07/4098–2444), and **Cooktown Hospital** (☎ 07/4069–5433).

GUIDED TOURS

Australian Wilderness Safari has a one-day wildlife and wilderness trip into Cape Tribulation National Park—as well as tours of the Daintree Rain Forest—aboard air-conditioned four-wheel-drive vehicles. All tours depart from Port Douglas, are led by naturalists, and include use of binoculars and reference books. Lunch and afternoon tea is included, and groups are limited to 12 people or less. This is one of the longest-established rain forest tours and one of the best. ☎ 07/4098–1766. ✉ $115.

Crocodile Express is a flat-bottom boat, which cruises the Daintree River on crocodile-spotting excursions. The boat departs from the Daintree River crossing at 9:30, 10:30, and 2:30 for a one-hour cruise. Trips also depart from the Daintree Village regularly from 10 to 4 for a 1½-hour cruise. ☎ 07/4098–6120. ✉ *1-hr cruise $15, 1½-hr cruise $18.*

Kuku-Yalanji Dreamtime Tours. Kuku-Yalanji Aborigines are the indigenous inhabitants of the land between Cooktown in the north,
Chillagoe in the west, and Port Douglas in the south. Guides from this
tribe will take you on a one-hour walk through stunning rain forest
and point out such significant features as cave paintings and special
Aboriginal sites. They also tell you about traditional bush tucker and
medicine. Afterward, tea and damper are served under a bark warun
(shelter), where you can chat with your guide and ask questions. ⊠
Gorge Rd., 24 km (15 mi) northwest of Port Douglas, ☎ *07/4098–*
1305. ⊡ *$15.* ⊙ *Weekdays 8:30–5; walks at 10, 11:30, 1, and 2:30.*

Native Guide Safari Tours is operated by Hazel Douglas, an Aboriginal woman whose knowledge and passion for her ancestral homeland—
which extends from Port Douglas to Cape Tribulation—set this one-day
tour apart. After departing from Port Douglas, you'll sample some of
the edible flora of the Daintree region, learn how Aboriginal people
maintained the balance of the rain forest ecosystem, and hear legends
that have been passed down over thousands of years. Be sure to pack
swimwear, insect repellent, and good walking shoes. A maximum of
11 passengers is allowed on each tour. Half-day tours (minimum 3 people) or private charters (minimum 4 people) are also available by consultation. The price includes pickup in Port Douglas, Quicksilver
Catamaran ride from Cairns to Port Douglas (for Cairns passengers),
picnic lunch and Daintree River Ferry crossing. ⊠ *58 Pringle St.,*
Mossman, 4873. ☎ *07/4098–2206,* ℻ *07/4098–1008.* ⊡ *$105 ($115*
from Cairns).

Strikies Safaris operates a two-day, four-wheel-drive safari along the
coast from Cairns to Cooktown. ☎ *07/4099–5599.* ⊡ *$220, exclud-*
ing accommodations.

VISITOR INFORMATION

Cape Tribulation Tourist Information Centre. ⊠ *Cape Tribulation Rd.,*
☎ *07/4098–0070.*

Cooktown Travel. ⊠ *Charlotte St., Cooktown,* ☎ *07/4069–5446.*

7 THE GREAT BARRIER REEF

There's an island here for every paradise-seeker. Besides the world's best diving and snorkeling, the Great Barrier Reef's island resorts offer unspoiled white sandy beaches, lush rain forests, and plenty of pampering. Champagne flows on Bedarra Island, a super-private resort that permits only a handful of visitors. Dunk Island offers some of Australia's most beautiful gardens, and Lady Elliot is a diver's heaven. South Molle and Hamilton islands are for families, while singles flock to Great Keppel.

Updated by
Jane Carstens

MORE THAN 2,000 km (1,200 mi) long and as much as 80 km (50 mi) wide, the Great Barrier Reef parallels the Queensland seaboard from the Sunshine Coast near Brisbane as far north as Papua New Guinea. It is the world's largest living organism, composed of billions of coral polyps whose bony skeletons knit together to form one large structure that shelters countless plants and animals. The Great Barrier Reef is the richest marine resource in the world—and you won't find more remarkable diving and snorkeling anywhere on earth. Much of the reef has been incorporated into the Great Barrier Reef Marine Park, and strict laws govern its preservation. At the same time, the reef is attracting more and more vacationers, to whom a host of island resorts now cater. Although the islands that these resorts occupy are billed as Great Barrier islands, most are not on the reef at all but close to shore. Hamilton Island, for instance, is more than 70 km (43 mi) from the reef. Still, they do have fringing coral, the variety that grows in the islands' sheltered coves, and can be every bit as fascinating as the main reef.

This chapter is arranged in three geographical sections covering islands off the mid-Queensland coast from south to north. The sections group together islands that share a common port or jumping-off point. Addresses for resorts often include the word "via" to indicate which port town to use to reach the island.

Pleasures and Pastimes

Dining

Food is an important part of any vacation. On the Barrier Reef it's likely to be a highlight. Australia's wide-open spaces and benign climate produce a remarkable range of fresh produce. The seas and shoals that surround these islands deliver an equally munificent bounty of seafood: crayfish, scallops, shrimp, and countless fish are featured on most menus.

At many resorts, rates include all meals, which are served in the dining room, although outdoor barbecues and seafood buffets are also commonplace. Some resorts offer more than one choice of restaurant, as well as a premium restaurant for which you pay extra. Keep in mind that special package rates are generally available.

CATEGORY	COST*
$$$$	over $50
$$$	$40–$50
$$	$30–$40
$	under $30

per person, excluding drinks and service

Island Time

Life in and around the reefs may be the reason that most people visit Queensland's island chain, but flora and fauna on the islands themselves can be fascinating. Some islands have rain forests, or hills and rocky areas, or those postcard-perfect beaches. In other words there is more to do on land than just relax—the choice is yours.

Lodging

You can't exactly pick and choose among different hotels on a Great Barrier Reef island—a resort and its island are basically one entity. So choose an island based on your taste and budget. Many islands cater to those wanting peace and tranquillity, whereas others attract a crowd wanting just the opposite. An island generally has only one resort, although the resort may offer a variety of accommodations.

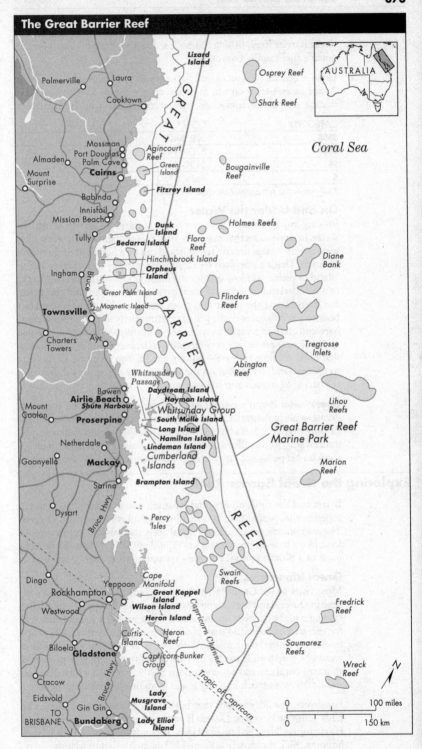

The Great Barrier Reef

Lizard
Island

GREAT

Osprey Reef

Shark Reef

AUSTRALIA

Coral Sea

Palmerville

Laura

Cooktown

Mossman
Port Douglas
Palm Cove

Almaden

Cairns

Agincourt
Reef

*Green
Island*

Bougainville
Reef

Mount
Surprise

Babinda

Fitzroy Island

Innisfail
Mission Beach

Holmes Reefs

Tully

**Dunk
Island**

Flora
Reef

Diane
Bank

Bedarra Island

Hinchinbrook Island

Ingham

**Orpheus
Island**

Flinders
Reef

BARRIER

Great Palm Island

Magnetic Island

Townsville

Tregrosse
Inlets

Charters
Towers

Ayr

Abington
Reef

*Whitsunday
Passage*

Daydream Island

Lihou
Reefs

Bowen

Airlie Beach
Shute Harbour

Hayman Island

Whitsunday Group

Mount
Coolon

Proserpine

South Molle Island

Long Island

Great Barrier Reef
Marine Park

Netherdale

Hamilton Island

Lindeman Island

Goonyella

Mackay

*Cumberland
Islands*

Marion
Reef

Sarina

Brampton Island

REEF

Dysart

*Percy
Isles*

Dingo

Cape
Manifold

*Swain
Reefs*

Yeppoon

**Great Keppel
Island**

Rockhampton

Wilson Island

Fredrick
Reef

Westwood

Heron Island

Curtis
Island

*Heron
Reef*

Biloela

Gladstone

*Capricorn-Bunker
Group*

Saumarez
Reefs

Cracow

Wreck
Reef

Eidsvold

**Lady
Musgrave
Island**

Tropic of Capricorn

TO
BRISBANE

Gin Gin

Bundaberg

**Lady Elliot
Island**

0   100 miles

0   150 km

Bruce Hwy.

Bruce Hwy.

Bruce Hwy

Capricorn Channel

N

With some exceptions, such sporting activities as sailing, snorkeling, and tennis are normally included in basic rates. However, trips to the Great Barrier Reef, fishing charters, scuba diving, and other sports requiring fuel usually cost extra.

Dress in general is resort casual, the next step up from T-shirts and jeans. As for amenities, rooms in most resorts are equipped with air-conditioning, telephones, televisions, tea and coffeemakers, and refrigerators.

CATEGORY	COST*
$$$$	over $400
$$$	$300–$400
$$	$150–$300
$	under $150

All prices are for a standard double room.

On and Under the Water

Visiting any of these islands obviously requires a journey across the water. In some cases that may be a ferry ride or flight of just a few minutes; in other cases the trip to the island can be a highlight of the whole vacation. That's particularly true if you elect to fly by helicopter to Heron Island or pick a window seat for the flight to Lizard Island: you'll take in a wonderland of reefs and coral cays layered in blue and turquoise. But even taking the water taxi from Hamilton Island or Shute Harbour to a Whitsunday resort will demonstrate why so many people come here and charter a yacht to cruise the Whitsunday Passage. Once you arrive at your resort, it's very tempting to let inertia set in and stay settled until it's time to leave—but try not to. You've come all the way to Queensland, so get out on the water to see the variety that makes this string of islands and islets so special.

Divers' note: If you are certified or plan to get certification for scuba diving while in Australia, bring a physician's statement from home confirming that you don't have any conditions that would endanger you underwater. Resort diving, where you are paired off with an instructor who keeps an eye on you, does not require medical certification.

Exploring the Great Barrier Reef

If you had the time, money, and patience, you could string a holiday together that would take you to all the island resorts of this chapter. The map linking these various coastal ports and offshore resorts would look like a lace-up boot 1,600 km (1,000 mi) long. It would also take most of a month to do if you only spent a night in each place.

Great Itineraries

Most visits to the Great Barrier Reef combine time on an island with time in Queensland's mainland towns and parks. But keep in mind that staying a night or more on any island will give you a much better feel for this part of the world than you'll get from any number of day trips to the reef from the mainland. With a week or more on your hands, it would be worthwhile to stay on two very different islands: perhaps a southern coral cay and a mountainous northern one, in which case you should allow as much as a day to get from one island to the next.

For divers, consider islands that have fringing reef around them, like Lady Elliot or Heron or Lizard. If you're after the good life, look into Hayman, Bedarra, or Lizard islands. If you want to do a little island-hopping, pick the closely arranged Whitsunday Group islands.

IF YOU HAVE 1 DAY

Take an early boat from **Cairns** to **Fitzroy Island,** or from **Shute Harbour** to **Daydream Island.** Spend a couple of hours snorkeling, take a walk around the island to get a look at its wilds, then find a quiet beach for a daydream afternoon. Or take a boat to a pontoon on the outer reef for a day on and in the water. A helicopter flight back will provide an astounding view of the reef and islands from above.

IF YOU HAVE 3 DAYS

Pick one island that has the water sports and on-land activities you appreciate—flora and fauna, beaches and pools, or resort nightlife—and give yourself a taste of everything. Carefully choosing an island will allow you to enjoy every moment while you're there.

IF YOU HAVE 7 OR MORE DAYS

Planning a full week on an island means that you're probably a serious diver, a serious lounger, or both. So pick an island that has fringing coral, such as **Lady Elliot, Heron,** or **Lizard,** plan to spend a day or two out on the reef itself, and you'll have the diving experience of a lifetime. If you take more time on an island, choose one that has great beaches and terrain to explore.

When to Tour the Great Barrier Reef

The majority of Barrier Reef islands lie north of the Tropic of Capricorn and have a distinctly monsoonal climate. In summer, expect some tropical downpours during your trip, but they are unlikely to last more than a few hours. And count on it being hot everywhere—hotter the farther north you go. If you're aiming for a northern island, you'll find that the warm days, clear skies, and balmy nights of winter are ideal. If you choose an island on the southern end of the chain, keep in mind that some winter days are too cool for swimming, and summertime is deliciously hot, with no lack of the attendant thunderstorms of a subtropical climate.

Remember that Australian seasons are the reverse of the northern hemisphere: summer runs from December through February, winter from June through August. North of the Tropic of Capricorn, daytime temperatures in winter rarely fall below 81°F (27°C).

MACKAY–CAPRICORN ISLANDS

Lady Elliot Island

★ Lady Elliot Island is a 100-acre coral cay on the southern tip of the Great Barrier Reef, positioned within easy reach of Bundaberg on the Queensland coast. Fringed on all sides by the reef and graced with a white coral beach, this oval isle is diving heaven. Its clear, calm waters afford superb views of schools of mantas, turtles, morays, sharks, and millions of tropical fish. If you want to get away from it all, wildlife easily outnumbers the 140 guests on this vacation spot. Even the top-level lodgings pale in comparison to those on other islands. And Lady Elliot is one of the few islands in the area where camping (modified) is part of the resort's offering. There are no televisions, only one guest telephone, and social activities revolve around diving, reef walking, and the island's lively bar and restaurant. Between October and April, Lady Elliot becomes a busy breeding ground for birds, while green and loggerhead turtles begin to emerge from the water to lay their eggs between November and January, with hatching taking place between January and April.

Dining and Lodging

$$ ✕🏨 **Lady Elliot Island Resort.** Don't go to Lady Elliot if you're looking for luxury. You'll stay in simple waterfront cabins with polished wood floors. The cabins are sparsely decorated with plastic chairs and pine fur-

niture and are serviced at least twice weekly. Campers stay in permanent oceanfront safari tents and share facilities. Dinner and breakfast are included in the basic price and served in the dining room; they tend to be simple, with an emphasis on grilled dishes, salads, and seafood, and served buffet style. ⊠ *Box 206, Torquay, Queensland 4655,* ☎ *07/4125–5344 or 1800/07–2200,* FAX *07/4125–5778. 24 rooms with shower, 5 suites, 14 tent-cabins, 6 lodge cabins. Pool, 2 bars, driving range, dive shop, baby-sitting, playground, coin laundry. AE, DC, MC, V.*

Outdoor Activities and Sports

Certified divers can rent equipment at the resort's dive shop. Scuba-diving lessons can be arranged through Lady Elliot's excellent dive school for $440 per person. Visitors coming for this five-day program must plan to stay from Sunday through Saturday and bring a medical report and two passport photos. In addition, the resort offers reef walks, glass-bottom boat rides ($10), and island walks.

Arriving and Departing

BY PLANE

Lady Elliot is the only coral cay with its own airstrip. Small aircraft make the 80-km (50-mi) flight from Hervey Bay, Bundaberg, and Gladstone, coastal towns about 320 km (200 mi) north of Brisbane. Daily flights run from Bundaberg, Hervey Bay, and Brisbane. A round-trip fare for the 30-minute flight from Bundaberg or the 35-minute flight from Hervey Bay to Lady Elliot on Whitaker Air (☎ 07/4125–5344 or 1800/07–2200) costs $130. There are strict limitations on luggage—only 22 pounds per person are allowed.

Day Trips

You can arrange a day trip to Lady Elliot through the resort (☎ 07/4125–5344 or 1800/07–2200). It will include the scenic flight, buffet lunch, a glass-bottom boat ride, a reef walk (if tides are appropriate), and a free snorkeling lesson. The cost is $185 per person from Bundaberg or Hervey Bay for the flight, lunch, and use of snorkeling gear.

Lady Musgrave Island

Lady Musgrave Island sits at the southern end of the Great Barrier Reef Marine Park about 40 km (25 mi) north of Lady Elliot Island. The island is a true coral cay of 35 acres—just 500 yards wide—and it is surrounded by 5 km (3 mi) of coral reef and a massive yet calm 3,000-acre lagoon. When day-trippers, yachties, divers, and campers converge, traffic on Lady Musgrave gets heavy, but the island has some of the best diving and snorkeling in Queensland. In quiet times, campers have a chance to view a variety of sea life surrounding this tiny speck of land in the Pacific.

In summer (November through March), the island is a bird and turtle rookery. You can expect to find such species as white-capped noddies, wedge-tailed shearwaters, and green and loggerhead turtles. There is also an abundance of flora, including casuarina and pisonia trees.

Camping

The island is uninhabited and has only basic facilities (one toilet block and emergency radio equipment) for campers. Camping permits are available from the **Queensland Department of Environment** (☎ 07/4976–0766) for $3.50 per person per night, or a maximum of $14 per family. Because numbers are restricted to 50 people, early bookings are advisable. Commercial tour operators will transport all camping equipment (including a small dinghy) and deliver fresh water, ice, milk, and bread on their regular trips.

Arriving and Departing

You can reach the island on the catamaran MV *Lady Musgrave,* or the trimaran MV *Spirit of Musgrave.* Both depart from **Port Bundaberg,** 20 minutes northeast of Bundaberg, Monday–Thursday and Saturday at 8:30 AM, returning at 5:45 PM. The trip takes 2½ hours in each direction and costs $112 for day-trippers, $216 for campers (to secure return passage). Scuba diving (including equipment) is an extra $50 for one dive, $70 for two dives for certified divers, or $60 for an introductory lesson. Coach pickup from accommodations in Bundaberg is available for $8 per person. For more information on either boat call 07/4159–4519 or 1800/07–2110.

Heron Island

★ Whereas most resort islands lie well inside the shelter of the distant reef, Heron Island, the most famous of the Queensland islands, is actually part of the reef. Seventy km (43 mi) northwest of the mainland port of Gladstone, Heron is a national park and bird sanctuary, which makes it the ideal place to learn about indigenous life on a coral island.

From November through March, hundreds of migrating green turtles and a number of loggerhead turtles arrive to mate and lay their eggs on the sandy foreshores, mere steps away from Heron's beachside suites. Each turtle returns three or four times during the nesting season to lay clutches of up to 120 eggs, and thousands of tiny hatchlings emerge from the nests from December through April. Between July and October (September is best), humpback whales pass here on their journey from the Antarctic.

The waters are spectacular, teeming with fish and coral, and ideal for snorkeling and scuba diving. The water is clearest in June and July and cloudiest during the rainy season, January and February.

Heron Island is also home to thousands of birds, including noddy terns, grey and white herons (hence the island's name), silver eyes, and rails. From September through March the indigenous birdlife is joined by large numbers of migrating birds—some from as far away as the Arctic.

You won't find a wide range of activities and entertainment on Heron, as on some other islands. The maximum housed by Heron Island Resort, the island's only accommodation, is a cozy 250 people; there are no day-trippers. But these might be reasons why you decide to come here.

You can visit uninhabited **Wilson Island,** a Great Barrier Reef Marine Park coral cay, on a day trip from Heron Island. Ten km (6 mi) to the south, it's an attractive adjunct of the Heron Island Resort, which controls access to it. In January and February, Wilson Island becomes the breeding ground for roseate terns and green and loggerhead turtles.

Dining and Lodging

$$$–$$$$ ✕🏨 **Heron Island Resort.** Set among palm trees and connected by sand paths, the accommodations here range from simple cabins with shared bathrooms to large, comfortable suites. With private balconies, cane furniture, and pastel or vibrant reef-inspired decor, the modern suites are worth the extra expense. There are no telephones or TVs in guest rooms. The Pandanus Lounge, with a seaward side made primarily of glass, houses a coffee shop and bar that opens onto wide terraces and the main pool; this is the best spot to wind down after a day outdoors. Organized entertainment is sparse, although the resort does have live music each night and shows excellent movies about the reef and diving. Meals, included in the resort's basic rate, are of a high standard. Breakfast and lunch are served buffet style with hot dishes and

a variety of salads and tropical fruits. Dinner is à la carte, and there's a once-weekly seafood smorgasbord. ⊠ *P&O Australian Resorts, Box 478, Sydney, NSW 2001,* ☎ *13–2469; 800/225–9849 in the U.S. 1 beach house, 86 suites, 30 cabins with shared bath. Restaurant, bar, coffee shop, 2 pools, paddle tennis, tennis court, dive shop, snorkeling, recreation room. AE, DC, MC, V.*

Outdoor Activities and Sports

Snorkeling, scuba diving, and fishing excursions are booked through the dive shop. Open-water diving courses are available for $395 and resort diving is $120 for one day. Excursions for experienced divers range from one to five days, starting at $44 for a single dive.

Nondivers who want to explore the reef's underwater world can board a semisubmersible sub that offers tours from Heron Island twice daily. Or they may opt for a guided reef walk, a turtle-watching tour, or a visit to the island's Marine Research Station. There are also a swimming lagoon, outdoor pools, table tennis, a tennis court, and a game room. (Note that beach fishing and spear fishing are prohibited.)

Arriving and Departing

BY BOAT

A high-speed catamaran (☎ 13–2469 or 07/4972–5166) has a two-hour run to Heron Island from Gladstone, a town on the Queensland coast, for $78 one way or $156 round-trip. The journey can be rough, and some visitors have problems with gas fumes and seasickness.

BY HELICOPTER

Marine Helicopters (☎ 07/4978–1177) has a 25-minute helicopter flight to Heron Island from Gladstone for $240 one way or $395 round-trip. The baggage restriction is 15 kg (33 lb) per person and one piece of hand luggage. Lockup facilities for excess baggage are free.

Great Keppel Island

Over the years the Great Keppel Island Resort has garnered a reputation similar to Fort Lauderdale's at spring break. Crowds are smaller, but it is a party place. Guests tend to be young singles, although the resort does draw its share of families. Only 13 km (8 mi) off the coast and 48 km (30 mi) northeast of Rockhampton, the island was originally a sheep station, and the old homestead remains on the hill that overlooks the island. Great Keppel is large—8 km (5 mi) wide and 11 km (7 mi) long—and there are several private residences in addition to the resort. Unfortunately, it's 40 km (25 mi) from the Great Barrier Reef, which makes any trip out there lengthy. It does have a fair amount to offer, though, both on shore and off: many walking trails, 17 stunning beaches with dozens of sports activities, and excellent coral growth in many sheltered coves. An underwater observatory at nearby Middle Island allows you to watch marine life without getting wet. A confiscated Taiwanese fishing boat has been sunk alongside the observatory to provide shelter for tropical fish.

Dining and Lodging

$–$$ ✕🏨 **Great Keppel Island Resort.** The villas and two-story accommodations of Great Keppel stand among gardens (adjacent to the airstrip) and extend up the island's hills. Rooms are comfortable and decorated in cheery pinks and greens, with natural timber and spacious balconies. The Hillside Villas are air-conditioned and have wonderful views but are some distance from the beach. The Admiral Keppel restaurant, set in a large, open room overlooking the beach and the bay, has both smorgasbord and à la carte dining. The menu is a mélange of Continental and island cooking and changes daily according to the availability of fresh ingredients. Barbecues and buffets predominate, and there are occasional theme dinners. ✉ *PMB 8001, North Rockhampton, Queensland 4702,* ☎ *07/4939–5044 or 1800/24–5658; 800/227–4411 in the U.S. 60 villas, 132 rooms with shower. 3 restaurants, 5 bars, coffee shop, 5 pools, beauty salon, 7-hole golf course, 3 tennis courts, aerobics, archery, badminton, basketball, paddle tennis, racquetball, softball, squash, snorkeling, windsurfing, boating, jet skiing, parasailing, waterskiing, nightclub, children's programs. AE, DC, MC, V.*

Outdoor Activities and Sports

Great Keppel Island offers almost every conceivable sport. Included in the basic rate are snorkeling, fishing, sailing, windsurfing, tennis, squash, golf, archery, basketball, baseball, volleyball, and badminton. You'll pay an extra fee for any activity that requires fuel, including island cruises, Barrier Reef cruises, motor boating, and parasailing. Camel rides along the beach, tandem skydiving, and scuba-diving lessons are also available.

Arriving and Departing

BY BOAT

Keppel Tourist Services (☎ 07/4933–6744) has two vessels that serve the island from **Rosslyn Harbour**, near Rockhampton and Yeppoon. It also operates a round-trip coach pickup ($14) between Rockhampton hotels and Rosslyn Harbour. The *Spirit of Keppel* departs at 11:30 and 3:30 and costs $20 each way or $27 round-trip. The larger *Reefcat* departs at 9:15 and stops near the island at the company's own pontoon for snorkeling and swimming. A tour of the underwater observatory costs $10 for guests and nonguests alike.

BY PLANE

Great Keppel Island Resort has its own plane (☎ 1800/24–5658) to bring visitors to the island. Fare is $109 return from **Rockhampton** or $145 return from **Gladstone**.

Brampton Island

Actually part of the Cumberland Islands near the southern entrance to the Whitsunday Passage, 195-acre Brampton Island is one of the prettiest in the area. Seven coral-and-white sandy beaches encircle the island, and the hilly interior's rain forests are populated by kangaroos, colorful rainbow lorikeets, and butterflies. Most of the island is a designated national park. The resort has a loyal clientele that returns annually, attracted by a vacation style far less structured than on other resort isles. There is live entertainment every evening and a variety of theme nights, dancing, and floor shows. The biggest attraction, of course, is the water—especially snorkeling over the reef between Brampton and adjoining Carlisle islands.

Dining and Lodging

$–$$ ✕🔲 **Brampton Island Resort.** Popular with overseas visitors in the 30-to-50 age group, this resort offers comfort and quiet. Rooms were refurbished in 1998 and are in large, Polynesian-style buildings, many of which face the beach. High ceilings and verandas give them an airy atmosphere, which is enhanced by rattan furniture, ceiling fans, and soft blue-and-coral decor. Some rooms are as high as 10 ft off the ground, allowing ocean breezes to waft underneath. The restaurant at Brampton Island serves a buffet breakfast, smorgasbord lunch, and an à la carte dinner featuring local seafood. Three meals a day are included in the basic price. An "Island Night" is held every Saturday, during which the chefs prepare a huge seafood dinner. The dining room is part of the entertainment complex, which overlooks the main beach to magnificent views of the Whitsunday Passage. Keep in mind that you can also arrange beach picnics. ⊠ *P&O Australian Resorts, Box 478, Sydney 2001,* ☏ *13–2469; 800/225–9849 in the U.S. 108 rooms with shower. 2 bars, 2 pools, 6-hole golf course, 3 tennis courts, badminton, basketball, boccie, snorkeling, waterskiing. AE, DC, MC, V.*

Outdoor Activities and Sports

Brampton Island's extensive facilities and numerous activities include free tennis courts, a six-hole golf course, archery, table tennis, beach volleyball, snorkeling, sailing, and windsurfing. For an extra charge, the resort also has fishing trips, waterskiing, and tube rides.

Arriving and Departing

BY BOAT

The **Heron II** (☏ 13–2469), a high-speed modern monohull, leaves **Mackay Outer Harbour** Thursday through Monday at 11:30. Fare is $30 one way and $60 round-trip. Complimentary coach transfers from Mackay airport are available.

BY PLANE

Transtate Airlines (☏ 13–2469) flies to Brampton from the coastal town of **Mackay** in a nine-seat Britton islander plane. Prices start at $80 round-trip.

Guided Tours

Brampton Island is 50 km (31 mi) from the Great Barrier Reef. Outer reef day trips aboard the high-speed catamaran *Spirit of Roylen* depart on Wednesday at 10:15 and return at 4:30, depending on the weather and a minimum of 22 people booking the trip. The cost is $130 per person. The **Hardy Reef** tour involves catching a seaplane to the outer reef, landing on the water, then snorkeling over the coral. This tour can be chartered for $225 per person. A two- to three-hour fishing trip also departs twice weekly. The cost is $50 per person, which includes bait, tackle, and, in the evening, a chef's preparation of your own catch.

CENTRAL ISLANDS

Lindeman Island

Lindeman Island is one of the largest bits of land (2,000 acres) in the Whitsunday Group. More than half of the island is national park, with 20 km (12 mi) of walking trails that wind through tropical growth and up hills that reward a climb with fantastic views. Bird-watching is excellent here, and, yet, the blue tiger butterflies that you can see in Butterfly Valley may be even more impressive than the birds. Seven secluded beaches are added attractions. The island is 40 km (25 mi) northeast of Mackay at the southern entrance to the Whitsunday Passage.

☾ The **Club Med Village** runs a Petit Club for children ages 2 to 3, a Mini-Club for children ages 4 to 7, and a Kids' Club for those 8 to 12; however, there are no care facilities for children under 1 year. Swimming, tennis, and archery are among the planned events, as are hikes into the national park and boat trips around the island.

Dining and Lodging

$$$ ✕▥ **Club Med Lindeman Island.** This three-story resort filled with rain forest palm trees sits on the southern end of the island. Rooms overlook the sea and have a balcony or patio, and all border the beach and pool. Away from the main village are the golf clubhouse, sports center, disco, and restaurant. Entertainment includes cabaret shows in the theater. The price includes meals, activities, and entertainment. ⊠ *Lin-*

deman Island via Mackay, Queensland 4741, ☎ *07/4946–9333,* FAX *07/4946–9598. 224 rooms with shower or shower and bath. Restaurant, 4 bars, 2 pools, 9-hole golf course, 5 tennis courts, aerobics, archery, badminton, basketball, hiking, snorkeling, windsurfing, children's programs, coin laundry. AE, DC, MC, V.*

Outdoor Activities and Sports

Club Med's basic price includes use of its five lighted tennis courts, paddle skis, catamarans, and snorkeling and windsurfing equipment, as well as archery, cricket, volleyball, basketball, football, badminton, hiking, aerobics, and even a circus school that teaches the basics of swinging from a trapeze.

Lindeman has one of the most picturesque nine-hole golf courses anywhere. For an additional fee, resort and refresher scuba diving courses are provided, and there are diving excursions to the outer reef by air (30 minutes each way) and boat (two hours each way).

Arriving and Departing

BY BOAT

Boats regularly serve the island from the small port at **Shute Harbour** (36 km/22 mi east of Proserpine), which is the major coastal access point for all the resorts in the Whitsunday region. The trip takes about an hour and costs $23 one way or $46 round-trip. There are also direct half-hour water-taxi transfers from **Hamilton Island Airport** (☎ 07/4946–9499).

BY PLANE

Island Air Taxis (☎ 07/4946–9933) planes fly to the Lindeman airstrip upon demand. The one-way cost is $75 from Proserpine, $60 from Shute Harbour, $45 from Hamilton Island, and $105 from Mackay.

Long Island

This aptly named narrow island lies just off the coast south of Shute Harbour. Although it's 40 km (25 mi) long, it's a mere 655 ft wide at the Palm Bay resort. It has walking trails through large areas of thick, undisturbed rain forest, which is protected as national parkland. Over the years the island has seen several resort styles; the most dramatic conclusion of which came when the original Palm Bay, opened in 1933, was leveled by a cyclone in 1970. Today there are two very different resorts here.

Dining and Lodging

$$ ✕▥ **Club Crocodile Long Island Resort.** A constant stream of guests flies into the Hamilton Island airport, then takes the transfer boat to this resort. Previously known as Whitsunday Long Island Resort, it is geared to families, and has child-care facilities available. It's not the place to go for a quiet time communing with nature, because the focus here is on outdoor activities, particularly on water sports. ✉ *PMB 26, via Mackay, Queensland 4740,* ☎ *07/4946–9400 or 1800/07–5125,* FAX *079/46–9555. 160 units with shower. Restaurant, café, grill, 2 pools, sauna, spa, tennis court, exercise room, snorkeling, windsurfing, boating, jet-skiing, waterskiing, baby-sitting, children's programs, coin laundry. AE, DC, MC, V.*

$$ ✕▥ **Palm Bay.** Much smaller than the Club Crocodile resort, Palm Bay is also much quieter. The six raised, thatch-roof bures and eight cabins stand along a sandy beach near a large bay. Accommodations packages include meals in the restaurant (more home-style than haute); or, you can pay a room-only rate and purchase individual meals, or buy supplies at the resort's Island Trader store and cook for yourself. The store has reasonable prices and a fair selection of goods, but if you crave special items, you'd better bring them along. All nonmotorized activities, such as canoeing, paddle skiing, and windsurfing, are included in the rate. ⊠ *Palm Bay Hideaway, PMB 28, via Mackay, Queensland 4740,* ☎ *07/4946–9233,* FAX *07/4946–9309. 14 units with shower. Restaurant, kitchenettes, pool, spa, windsurfing, coin laundry. AE, DC, MC, V.*

Arriving and Departing

BY BOAT

Reach Long Island by **Whitsunday All Over and Water Taxi** (☎ 07/4946–9499) from either Shute Harbour or Hamilton Island. Boats leave Shute Harbour at 7:15, 9:15, 1:30, 4, and 5:15, and the 15-minute journey costs $24 round-trip. A water taxi meets each flight into Hamilton Island, and the 30- to 45-minute transfer to either resort costs $44 one way for adults.

Hamilton Island

The construction of this resort island was surrounded with controversy. The original developer paid scant attention to conservationists and proceeded to dynamite the top off one of the hills to make a helipad, build a seawall to prevent the tides from draining the swimming area, dredge a boat marina, erect a high-rise apartment tower, and then remove the side of another hill to accommodate a runway for what would be the Whitsundays' major airport. Despite this aggressive development, over 80% of this Whitsunday-group island has been carefully preserved in its natural state, which translates into beautiful beaches, native bush trails, and spectacular lookouts.

The island has the greatest range of activities and amenities of any Queensland resort. In addition to an extensive sports complex and Barrier Reef excursions, there are six different types of accommodation, nine restaurants, a full range of shops and boutiques, and a 200-acre fauna park. The nightlife ranges from Bohemes Dance Club, which swings into the wee hours three nights a week, to the resort's mellow Mantaray Café, perfect for quiet conversation.

Hamilton Island is divided into two distinct areas: the resort, a combination of high-rise and cottage accommodations overlooking Catseye Beach, and the boat harbor, which is flanked by restaurants, shops, an ice cream parlor, a fish-and-chips carryout, and the best bakery in the Whitsundays. The whole complex was given a $40 million makeover in 1997.

🌣 The **Clownfish Club** (☎ 07/4946–9999, ext. 8546) caters to children of three age groups: 4 years and younger, 5 to 9 years, and 10 to 14 years. Each has age-appropriate organized activities, such as sandcastle-making, snorkeling, water polo, and beach olympics. Programs are included in the rates, but are subject to availability.

Dining

$$$ ✕ **The Beach House.** At Hamilton Island's signature restaurant, chef Geoff Nocher is famous for encouraging his guests to make requests. Should you wish, Nocher will design a menu of delicious modern Australian dishes around your choice of wines. The Beach House is true to its name, with timbered walls and terra-cotta tiled floors, colorful rugs, and comfortable wicker chairs. Best of all, it's right on Catseye Beach. ⊠ *Main resort complex,* ☎ *07/4946–8580. AE, DC, MC, V. Closed Mon.*

$$$ ✕ **Romanos Italiano Restaurant.** With polished wood floors and a balcony overlooking the harbor, Romanos is the place to come for a quiet meal. The kitchen produces such dishes as Moreton Bay Bugs Provençale, bugs in a tomato and herb sauce, and rigatoni *Amatriciana* (with tomato, bacon, onion, and chili). ⊠ *Marina Village, Harbourside,* ☎ *07/4946–9999. AE, DC, MC, V.*

$ ✕ **Toucan Tango Café and Bar.** Overlooking the waters of both Cats-eye Beach and the main resort, this restaurant features vibrant summer colors, high ceilings, timber furniture, an Italian terrazzo floor, and potted palms in a cool, tropical theme. It is the relaxed all-day dining option, with a large menu of snacks and a nightly seafood buffet. The cocktail bar, with live entertainment nightly, makes the Toucan Tango the hub of activity until late. ✉ *Main resort complex,* ☎ *07/4946–9999. AE, DC, MC, V.*

Lodging

Make reservations for all accommodations on Hamilton Island with the **Hamilton Island Resort** (☎ 1800/07–5110).

$$$$ ▥ **Beach Club Resort.** The island's flagship property, this 24-room two-story resort has uninterrupted beachfront views. Special touches include airport pickup, exclusive butler service, and personal hosts to arrange everything from restaurant and tour bookings to flight tickets, room service, and specific housekeeping needs. Each room is named after a Whitsunday beach and features a painting of that beach, commissioned from a local artist. Many rooms overlook the private pool. *24 rooms. Restaurant, pool, laundry service. AE, DC, MC, V.*

$$$$ ▥ **Reef View Hotel.** Famous for its breathtaking views of the sea, this hotel has a choice of Garden View and Coral Sea vistas. Each room has its oven private balcony, and no-smoking floors are available. *370 rooms, 16 suites. Restaurant, pool, spa, coin laundry. AE, DC, MC, V.*

$$$ ▥ **Coconut Palm Bungalows.** The steeply sloping roofs and small balconies of this complex resemble Polynesian huts. The decor is also Polynesian, with grass mattings and bright floral bedspreads. Each of these small, individual units contains a king-size bed, a small bar, and a furnished patio. *50 bungalows. Pool, spa. AE, DC, MC, V.*

$$ ▥ **Whitsunday Holiday Apartments.** Looking out over the Coral Sea toward Whitsunday Island, these twin 13-story towers consist of the only self-contained apartments on Hamilton Island. The one- and two-bedroom apartments are complete with large balconies, fully equipped kitchens, and dining and sitting areas. *165 one-bedroom apartments, 30 two-bedroom apartments. 2 pools, spa, coin laundry. AE, DC, MC, V.*

Outdoor Activities and Sports

Hamilton Island Resort has a variety of free activities; fees apply only to motorized water sports. A Health and Racquet Club, mini-golf course, golf driving range, go-karts, target shooting range, four large swimming pools, flood-lit tennis courts, and a Wire Flyer hang glider are on the island, as are a catamarans, jet skis, paddle skis, waterskis, speed boats, and parasailers. Reserve ahead through the **Tour Booking Desk** (☎ 07/4946–8535).

FISHING

The island's deep-sea game fishing boat, *Renegade,* will take you in search of marlin, sailfish, Spanish mackerel, and tuna, which thrive in the waters of the Whitsundays during November. Charters for six people can be arranged through Hamilton Island's **Tour Booking Desk** (☎ 07/4946–8535) year-round. Private charters are $1,750 for a full day, $920 for a half day. Shared tours, requiring a minimum of six people and a maximum of 12, are $225 per person full day, $120 per person half day.

SCUBA DIVING

If you've never dived before, Hamilton has a complimentary introductory scuba course, which includes pool instruction, equipment rental, and a dive with a qualified instructor. If you are already qualified, all equipment can be rented and a variety of diving trips arranged.

Shopping

Hamilton Island's Marina Village has many shops with ladies' and men's resort wear, children's clothes, souvenirs, and gifts. An art gallery, art studio, butcher, florist, pharmacy, realtor, medical center, video store, and beauty salon are also on the premises.

Arriving and Departing

BY BOAT

Fantasea Cruises' catamaran *Fantasea 1* (☎ 07/4946–5111) makes the 35-minute journey from Shute Harbour six times daily for $38 round-trip.

BY PLANE

Hamilton is the only Queensland island with an airport large enough to accommodate commercial jets. **Ansett Australia** (☎ 13–1344) operates 43 direct flights to the island each week from Sydney (2 hours), Cairns, and Brisbane (1½ hours). **Qantas** (☎ 13–1313) also has direct daily service to the island from Sydney. Flight connections from other interstate capitals are also available. Boat transfers to all other Whitsunday resort islands can be made from the wharf adjoining the airport.

Guided Tours

Hamilton Island Aviation (☎ Tour Booking Desk 07/4946–5111) has scenic flights to the reef and over the Whitsundays, as well as convenient transfers to the other islands. They also operate a number of picnic flights to Whitehaven Beach and other getaways.

Fantasea Cruises runs reef trips daily from Hamilton and other islands, as well as from all mainland Whitsunday resorts. From Hamilton it's a 75-km (47-mi) trip to the company's own pontoon on magnificent Hardy Reef Lagoon. Every tour gives you four hours on the reef to swim, snorkel, ride in a semisubmersible, or simply relax. Cost is $125 with a buffet lunch. For reservations contact the resort's **Tour Booking Desk** (☎ 07/4946–5111).

A high-speed catamaran sails daily to **Whitehaven Beach,** a 6½-km (4-mi) stretch of glistening sand. The catamaran, run by Fantasea Cruises, leaves the harbor at noon for the 30-minute trip to the beach, returning to Hamilton about 4:15 PM. Cost is $49 with lunch. For reservations contact the resort's **Tour Booking Desk** (☎ 07/4946–5111).

A large number of vessels at Hamilton Island are available for **charter** and group trips. Call **Sun Sail** (☎ 07/4946–9900) or **Moorings** (☎ 02/9693–5401; 800/535–7289 in the U.S.) for information.

South Molle Island

A relatively large island (1,040 acres) not far from Shute Harbour, South Molle was originally inhabited by Aborigines, who collected basalt here to use for their axes. Much later, it became the first of the Whitsundays to be used for grazing; hence its extensive grassy tracts. Now the island is a national park with a single, family-oriented resort settled on sheltered Bauer Bay in the north. Protected between two headlands, the bay often remains calm when wind rips through the rest of the Whitsundays.

Dining and Lodging

$$ ✕🏨 **South Molle Island Resort.** From the water it doesn't look very large; only when you explore the complex do you realize that there are 200 guest rooms. Nestled in a bay at the northern end of the island, only the resort's long jetty reaches out into deep water beyond the fringing reef. The well-maintained property appeals to young couples, families (there is full child-care service), and retirees alike. Every room has a balcony, and several standards of accommodation are available. All dining room meals and most activities are included in the rate; only sports requiring fuel cost extra. Corals is the resort's signature restaurant, while the Island Restaurant and Bar is the casual dining option. South Molle's self-promotion is understated, but it's one of the most pleasant resorts in the Whitsundays. ⊠ *South Molle Island, via Shute Harbour, Queensland 4741,* ☎ *07/4946–9433. 200 units with shower. 2 restaurants, pool, spa, 9-hole golf course, 2 tennis courts, exercise room, dive shop, jet skiing, parasailing, waterskiing, windsurfing, children's programs, coin laundry. AE, DC, MC, V.*

Arriving and Departing

BY BOAT

The island's own boats will bring you from Shute Harbour, or take **Whitsunday All Over and Water Taxi** (☎ 07/4946–9499) from Hamilton Island (☞ *above*). The former leave Shute Harbour at 9, 12:30, and 5. The 30-minute trip costs $24 round-trip for adults, $14 for children 4–14, and is free for children 3 and younger. A water taxi meets each flight into Hamilton Island; the 30-minute ride costs $44 each way for adults.

Daydream Island

Every part of this island in the heart of the Whitsundays is incorporated into the resort, yet somehow it manages to keep the original feel of a tropical paradise—much of the rain forest is intact and there are lush gardens everywhere. The island is divided, with 301 guest accommodations at the northern end and a day-visitor center in the south. The nightly entertainment and daily activities keep guests returning year after year.

Blinky Bill's Kids Club provides free, fully licensed child care and a range of activities daily. Open nightly, the Rascal Kids' Dinner Restaurant has fun, appealing meals.

Dining and Lodging

$$ ✕🏨 **Daydream Island Resort.** In spite of the difference in price and size, the three types of accommodations offered are all well appointed by Barrier Reef island standards. The Garden Rooms do not have ocean views, but they make up for this with their pool and tropical garden vistas. The Ocean View and larger Sunlover rooms have panoramic views of the Whitsundays, as does the Great Ocean suite, a self-contained, three-bedroom, condo-style apartment. All rooms have modern, light-color furnishings. Food is not included in the basic price of the resort, but guests can dine at the Waterfall Café Restaurant, the Tavern restaurant bar, the coffee shop, or the elegant Sunlover Restaurant, where seafood is the specialty. ⊠ *Daydream Island, PMB 22, via Mackay, Queensland 4740,* ☎ *07/4948–8488 or 1800/07–5040. 300 rooms, 1 suite. 3 restaurants, coffee shop, 2 pools, 2 whirlpools, sauna, 2 tennis courts, badminton, boccie, exercise room, dive shop snorkeling, windsurfing, jet-skiing, waterskiing. AE, DC, MC, V.*

Outdoor Activities and Sports

Most sports are included in room rates, such as tennis, badminton, volleyball, windsurfing, parasailing, fishing, snorkeling, and waterskiing. Daily resort activities are centered around the swimming pool and bar.

A day trip to the reef for scuba diving costs $80; $100 for two dives. If you have no experience, a $60 two-hour introductory course qualifies you to dive on the reef with supervision from an instructor the next day.

THE REEF

T'S HARD TO IMAGINE THAT the Great Barrier Reef, which covers an area about half the size of Texas, is so fragile that even human sweat can cause damage. However, despite its size, the Reef is a finely balanced ecosystem sustaining zillions of tiny polyps, which have been building on top of each other for thousands of years. So industrious are these critters that the reef is over 1,640 ft thick in some places. These polyps are also fussy about their living conditions and only survive in clear, salty water around 17.5ĕC (63.5ĕF) and less than 98 ft deep.

Marine polyps are primitive, sacklike animals with a mouth surrounded by tentacles, and they are closely related to anemones and jellyfish. Coral can consist of just one polyp (solitary) or many hundreds (colonial), which form a colony when joined together. These polyps create a hard surface by producing lime; as they die, their coral "skeletons" remain, which form the reef's white substructure. The living polyps give the coral its colorful appearance.

The Great Barrier Reef begins south of the Tropic of Capricorn around Gladstone and ends in the Torres Strait below Papua New Guinea, making it about 2,000 km (1,240 mi) long and 356,000 sq km (137,288 sq mi) in area. Declared a World Heritage Site in 1981, it is managed by the Great Barrier Reef Marine Park Authority, which was itself established in 1976. Consequently, detailed observations and measurements of coral reef environments only date back to around this time. Thus, annual density bands in coral skeletons, similar to rings formed in trees, are important potential storehouses of information about past marine environmental conditions.

The reef is a living animal, although early scientists thought it was a plant, which is forgivable. Soft corals have a plant-like growth and a horny skeleton that runs along the inside of the stem. In contrast, the hard, calcareous skeletons of stony corals are the main building blocks of the reef.

Like any living creature, corals must reproduce to survive. They can bud or split from the original polyp, fertilize their eggs internally before releasing them, or shed eggs and sperm into the water for external fertilization. To ensure a better-than-average reproduction rate for the latter method, many corals spawn together on one night of the year, about five days after the full moon in late spring (October–November).

The Great Barrier Reef is a diver's heaven that attracts thousands of visitors every year. Apart from the coral, divers can swim with 2,000 species of fish, dolphins, dugongs, sea urchins, starfish, and turtles. Dive sites are unlimited, with about 3,000 individual reefs, 300 coral cays, 890 fringing reefs, and 600 islands from which to choose. However, although many islands are developed with resorts, freshwater is nonexistent; self-sufficiency is a must for explorers and campers. Removing or damaging any part of the reef is a crime, so divers and tourists are asked to take home only photographs and memories of one of the world's great natural wonders.

— Jane Carstens

Arriving and Departing

BY BOAT

Whitsunday All Over and Water Taxi (☎ 07/4946–9499) runs regularly to Daydream from Shute Harbour ($24 round-trip). The company also offers transit from Hamilton Island (☞ Hamilton Island, *above*) for $44 each way.

BY PLANE

Although most people come by boat from Hamilton Airport, an alternative is to use **Flight West** (☎ 13–2392) or **Qantas** (☎ 13–1313) to Proserpine on the mainland. Then catch a bus to Shute Harbour with **Whitsunday Shuttle Service** (☎ 07/4946–1515) and a boat from Shute Harbour to the island.

Day Trips

Only 15 minutes by boat from Shute Harbour, Daydream is one of the few islands where day visits are not merely allowed but actively encouraged. Day visitors aren't permitted to use resort facilities, but there is a separate visitor center and a miniresort with a pool, cash bar, and disco. Water sports are available for a fee. In addition, there are many boutiques and shops.

You can take a trip to the outer reef from either Shute Harbor or the island itself, as the Daydream Island Resort boats pick up at both locations on its way out to the reef.

Hayman Island

★ Quite simply, Hayman Island is one of the finest resorts in the world. Situated in the northern Whitsunday Passage, it caters to people for whom luxury is a priority. The architecture of the hotel is first-class, with reflecting pools, sandstone walkways, manicured tropical gardens, and sparkling waterfalls. The atmosphere is closer to an exclusive club than a resort.

Swimming pools at Hayman are delights. One wing of the hotel has a huge seawater lagoon with walkways leading across to a central island, which, in turn, encircles a large, pentagon-shape freshwater pool. Deck chairs are arranged under the shelter of palms and umbrellas. The hotel's other wing features another freshwater pool partly surrounded by tropical gardens and a vast fish pond across which white swans glide.

Hayman Island is a 900-acre crescent with a series of hills along its spine. The area around the resort is arid, but beautiful walking trails crisscross the island. The view of the Whitsunday Passage from the hills is unbeatable. The main beach is right in front of the hotel, but more secluded beaches, as well as fringing coral, can be reached by boat.

Hayman has its own marina with a sheltered anchorage for the island's diving and cruise boats, charter vessels, and yachts. The resort also has a nightclub. Several boutiques selling clothing, perfume, cosmetics, and jewelry are in the hotel's shopping arcade, and there is an organized children's activity center.

Dining

The base rate at the Hayman Island Resort includes a full hot and cold buffet breakfast. Otherwise, you sign for meals, and the charges are added to your hotel bill. Reservations are recommended for all restaurants and can be booked through the resort's concierge.

$$$$ ✕ **La Fontaine.** With Waterford chandeliers and Louis XVI decor, this elegant French restaurant is the resort's culinary showpiece. The cuisine rivals the finest restaurants on the mainland and features such innovative dishes as *suprême de volaille et langouste en crème d'algues* (chicken breast and wing stuffed with lobster in cream sauce) and *noisettes d'agneau rôties à la compote d'échalote* (roast medallions of lamb with compote of shallots and red capsicum coulis). Dinner is usually accompanied by live music. A private dining room is available. *Jacket required. No lunch.*

$$$$ ✕ **Oriental Seafood Restaurant.** This Asian establishment overlooks one of the most authentic Japanese gardens in Australia. Black lacquer chairs, shoji screens, and such superb Japanese artifacts as Buddhist statues give this outstanding restaurant a comfortably exotic ambience. Try *hoi man poo* (Thai-style mussels in black bean sauce), shark-fin soup, or jellyfish vinaigrette. Long pants are required for men. *No lunch.*

$$ ✕ **Beach Pavilion.** Popular with guests coming directly from the beach or the pool for lunch or sunset cocktails, this restaurant serves snacks, hamburgers, steaks, and other simple dishes in a pleasantly informal atmosphere.

$$ ✕ **Coffee House.** Serving dishes that range from simple sandwiches and cakes baked in the hotel's kitchens to full meals, this coffee shop offers a choice between indoor seating and breezy, sunlit outdoor tables.

$$ ✕ **La Trattoria.** With its red-and-white-checkered tablecloths and casual furnishings, this classic provincial Italian restaurant could easily be in Sorrento or Portofino. Seated either inside or outdoors, diners can choose from an extensive list of pastas and traditional Italian dishes. Prices are very reasonable. *No lunch.*

$$ ✕ **Planters.** This Australian restaurant uses rattan furniture, ceiling fans, and hibiscus artwork to create a relaxed local mood. You can feast on seafood or Australian delicacies such as kangaroo and emu. *No lunch.*

Lodging

$$$$ ⊡ **Hayman Island Resort.** It seems that money can buy almost everything. Asian artifacts, European tapestries, Persian rugs, and exquisite objets d'art enliven the lobby, restaurants, and rooms, where footsteps and voices echo between the marble walls and floor. Set in tropical gardens next to the pool and lagoon areas, Palm Garden Rooms have garden views and private terraces, while Beachfront Rooms allow you to walk from your patio straight onto the coral-sand beach. For utter luxury, nothing could top the 11 Penthouse Suites, each of which is decorated in a different style, ranging from Californian and Moroccan to French and North Queensland. ⊠ *Hayman Island, Queensland 4801,* ☎ *07/ 4940–1234 or 1800/07–5175,* ℻ *07/4940–1567. 270 rooms, 33 suites, 11 penthouses. 4 restaurants, bar, 3 pools, beauty salon, sauna, spa, putting green, 5 tennis courts, badminton, snorkeling, windsurfing, parasailing, waterskiing, baby-sitting, laundry service. AE, DC, MC, V.*

Outdoor Activities and Sports

All nonmotorized water sports on Hayman Island—such as catamarans, Windsurfers, and paddle skis—as well as use of the putting green, table tennis, basketball, and badminton facilities are included in guests' rates. Squash, tennis, golf, windsurfing and catamarans are also complementary. The resort's water-sports center has a training tank for diving lessons, and a dive shop sells everything from snorkels to complete wet suits and sports clothing. The marina organizes parasailing, waterskiing, sailing, boating, fishing, coral-viewing, windsurfing, and snorkeling. Contact the hotel's **Recreation Information Centre** (☎ 07/ 4940–1723) for reservations and information.

Arriving and Departing

Hayman does not have an airstrip of its own. Take **Ansett Australia** (☎ 13–1344) or **Qantas** (☎ 13–1313) to Hamilton Island, where you'll board one of Hayman's three luxury motor yachts, *Sun Eagle,*

Sun Goddess, or *Sun Paradise.* Australian sparkling wine is served during the 60-minute trip to the island. On arrival at the wharf, guests are driven to the resort about 1 km (½ mi) away. Make sure you are ticketed all the way to Hayman Island including the motor yacht leg, or the luxury motor yacht will cost $320 for the round-trip journey to Hayman from Hamilton Island.

Guided Tours

The Hayman Island Resort's **Recreation Information Centre** (☎ 07/4940–1723) provides information on all guided tours from or around the island.

A coral-viewing trip aboard the **Reef Dancer** ($60 per person) departs three to four times daily. A Whitehaven Beach Cruise ($130) departs Tuesday and Friday at 9:45.

Reef Goddess, Hayman Island's own boat, makes Great Barrier Reef excursions Monday, Wednesday, Friday, and Saturday from 9:15 to 4. The $160-per-person charge includes snorkeling, some drinks, and a light lunch. There is a dive master on board, and the day-trip cost for divers is $185 (plus $45 for gear hire). On Tuesday and Friday it goes to Whitehaven Beach for $130, including lunch, and on Sunday there is a half-day morning trip costing $120 for snorkelers and $145 (plus $45 gear hire) for divers.

The $348 **Heli Reef** helicopter tour includes an aerial sweep of the Great Barrier Reef, snorkeling (equipment supplied), lunch, and coral viewing at Hardy Reef aboard a submarine. Certified divers can dive for an additional $95. Flights take off daily. Reserve at the concierge desk.

The Hayman Island **Coral Air Whitsunday** seaplanes also fly over the reef. After an aerial tour over Hook and Hardy reefs, the plane lands in the sheltered waters of Blue Lagoon (within Hardy Reef Lagoon). Here you board a semisubmersible boat for a tour of the reef. More adventurous passengers can snorkel with on-board gear. The cost of the two-and-a-half-hour tour is $240 for adults; reserve at the concierge desk.

CAIRNS ISLANDS

Orpheus Island

Volcanic in origin, this narrow island—11 km (6 mi) long and 1 km (½ mi) wide—uncoils like a snake in the waters between Halifax Bay and the Barrier Reef. Although patches of rain forest exist in the island's deeper gullies and around the sheltered bays, Orpheus is a true Barrier Reef island, ringed by seven unspoiled sandy beaches and superb coral. Incredibly, 340 of the known 350 species of coral grace Orpheus's waters. James Cook University has a Marine Research Station on the island.

Dining and Lodging

$$$$ ╳▥ **Orpheus Island Resort.** If you are looking for glitzy accommodation surrounded by restaurants, bars, and boutiques, then this is *not* the place to go. Orpheus is for people who want to get away from it all. It offers privacy, sophistication, and total relaxation in an unspoiled environment.

On the west coast of the island right on the beach, the resort itself is a cross between a South Seas island and an elegant Italian hotel, with terra-cotta floors, Persian rugs, and comfortable rattan furniture. Choose between beachfront terrace rooms, grouped four to a building; studio units in five groups of three; or two freestanding bungalows, which have queen-size beds, sitting areas, and whirlpool baths. All are beachfront rooms. Six luxury Mediterranean-style villas, on the hill behind the resort, are available from $590 per person per night. There are no nightclubs, and rooms are TV- and telephone-free. Instead, a recreation room with TV, video games, gym equipment, and a billiard table is provided. Guests can also go bushwalking.

Although a full array of activities and water sports is offered, you might find yourself content to laze about, waiting for the next culinary offering. All à la carte meals and snacks are included in the price, and the cuisine at Orpheus is superior. The resort's chefs create dishes that emphasize seafood from the nearby reef. Given enough time, the kitchen will also accommodate special orders. Much of the cuisine reflects both European and tropical Queensland influences, and you can choose from such dishes as deviled king prawns, sautéed scallops with ginger and broccoli, and broiled barramundi with capers, beets, and ginger. The restaurant also has an extensive list of Australian wine, and because the resort houses a maximum of 74 guests, dinners tend to be friendly and intimate. Even buffet breakfasts are sumptuous and, on request, the kitchen will prepare gourmet picnic hampers. Potted plants, large palms, and blond wicker and wood give the open-sided dining room a distinctly tropical feel.

The resort has various value-for-money packages that are worth looking into. Day visitors are not permitted, and the resort does not cater to children under 15. ⊠ *Orpheus Island, PMB 15, Townsville Mail Centre, Queensland 4810,* ☎ *07/4777–7377 or 1800/07–7167,* 䕬 *07/ 4777–7533. 31 rooms, 2 bungalows, 6 villas. Restaurant, 2 pools, tennis court. AE, DC, MC, V.*

Outdoor Activities and Sports

The resort has two freshwater swimming pools, a Jacuzzi, a tennis court, and a host of walking trails that wind through the national park. Snorkeling and diving from the island's beaches are spectacular, and at low tide the coral around the resort is exposed so you can actually go reef walking. Most activities, such as waterskiing, windsurfing, sailing, canoeing, boating, and rides in a glass-bottom boat, are included in the room rate.

For an additional fee, outer-reef fishing charters can be arranged. Trips are subject to weather conditions; a minimum of six passengers is required.

Arriving and Departing
BY PLANE

Orpheus Island is 24 km (15 mi) offshore opposite the town of Ingham, about 80 km (50 mi) northeast of Townsville. The 25-minute flight from **Townsville** to Orpheus aboard a Nautilus Aviation seaplane costs $290 per person round-trip; from **Cairns** an hour-long round-trip costs $460 per person. Book flights when you make your reservation with Orpheus Island Resort.

Guided Tours

The coral around Orpheus is some of the best in the area, and cruises to the outer reef can be arranged through the resort. Whereas most of the islands are more than 50 km (31 mi) from the reef, Orpheus is just 15 km (9 mi) away.

Dunk Island

Dunk Island, which provided the setting for E. J. Banfield's 1908 escapist classic *Confessions of a Beachcomber,* is divided by a hilly spine that runs its entire length. The eastern side is mostly national park, with dense rain forest and secluded beaches accessible only by boat. Beautiful paths have been tunneled through the rain forest, along which you might see the large blue Ulysses butterfly, whose wingspan can reach 6 inches. Dunk Island Resort's prize-winning gardens are some of the best maintained in Australia, and the cascading series of swimming pools is a delight. The atmosphere is informal—guests are not required to change for dinner—and light entertainment is offered every night in the main lounge. The resort is on the western side of the island overlooking the mainland. Owned by P&O Australian Resorts, it's particularly popular with middle-income Australians and families. Situated 5 km (3 mi) off the coast of Queensland's tropical north, Dunk is, at 3,000 acres, the largest of the Family Group islands.

Dining and Lodging

$$ ✕🏨 **Dunk Island Resort.** Set among coconut palms, flowering hibiscus, and frangipani, the resort overlooks the waters of Brammo Bay. Guests have a choice of four types of accommodation. The Bayview suites are the island's newest and best. At the end of each block, they have grand beach views. Each has a single and a queen bed. Only slightly less expensive than the villas, the Beachfront Units offer the best value and the most privacy. These spacious rooms were refurbished in 1998 and have latticed balconies, cool tile floors, modern wicker furniture, and blue, coral, and cream decor. The Garden Cabanas do not have beach views but are among tropical gardens. High ceilings and large sliding-glass doors create a sense of airiness, augmented by a simple style that relies on light colors, woven mats, and basic tiling. Housed in two-story buildings, the least-expensive Banfield Units also have balconies overlooking the resort's gardens, and some rooms are available for families. Keep in mind that in this very wet climate, some of the garden accommodations can feel very damp. Rooms are serviced daily. The Beachcomber Restaurant is the resort's main dining spot. Overlooking lovely gardens and a shoreline lit by gas flares at night, this restaurant has a resort atmosphere enhanced by wood beams, cane furniture, and plentiful potted plants. EJ's on the Deck offers casual brasserie meals and snacks for lunch and dinner from 10 AM to 10 PM. BB's on the Beach has a casual Australian beach atmosphere and is open from 11 AM until 7 PM. Breakfast is included in the price. ✉ *P&O Australian Resorts, Box 478, Sydney NSW, 2001,* ☎ *13–2469; 800/225–9849 in the U.S., 88 units, 24 suites, 36 cabanas. 2 restaurants, 2 pools, spa, 6-hole golf course, 3 tennis courts, aerobics, archery, badminton, basketball, boccie, croquet, horseback riding, jogging, squash, volleyball, boating, jet skiing, parasailing, waterskiing, children's programs. AE, DC, MC, V.*

Outdoor Activities and Sports

In addition to reef cruises and fishing charters, the resort has a full range of water sports, including snorkeling, sailing, windsurfing, waterskiing, and parasailing. Dunk Island also has a 6-hole golf course, horseback riding, archery, two squash courts, four tennis courts, and freshwater swimming in two huge cascading pools. Resort rates include all sports except horseback riding, scuba diving, and activities requiring fuel.

You also can wander throughout the island along well-maintained trails with the help of a map provided by the resort. All walks are graded according to difficulty. Some of the harder ones, particularly to the top of Mount Koo-ta-loo, have beautiful views.

Arriving and Departing

BY BOAT

The catamaran **MV Quickcat** (☎ 07/4068–7289) departs Clump Point Jetty in Mission Beach daily at 10 for the 30-minute ride to Dunk Island, returning at 4:45. Round-trip fare is $22.

BY PLANE

Dunk Island has its own sealed landing strip. **Transtate Airlines** (☎ 07/ 4035–9663) serves the island three times daily from Cairns for $160 round-trip.

Guided Tours

The **MV Quickcat** (☎ 07/4068–7289), a large passenger catamaran, runs daily to the reef some 35 km (22 mi) away, leaving Dunk Island at 11:30 and returning at 4:30. The trip includes snorkeling, a glass-bottom boat ride, morning and afternoon tea, and a buffet lunch. Round-trip fare is $117.

Bedarra Island

Within the confines of this tiny, 247-acre island 5 km (3 mi) off the northern Queensland coast you'll come across natural springs, a dense rain forest, and eight separate beaches. This is also the site of one of the Barrier Reef's smallest and finest resorts: Bedarra Island Resort. Owned by P&O Australian Resorts, this tranquil getaway was extensively refurbished in 1998 and has remained popular with affluent executives who want complete escape. It's the only Great Barrier Reef resort with an open bar, and the liquor (especially champagne) flows freely. Bedarra accommodates only 30 people, and guests stay in freestanding villas hidden amid thick vegetation but still just steps from golden beaches. This is not a place to look for organized activity. Privacy and quiet are what Bedarra is all about: No children under 16.

Dining and Lodging

$$$$ ✕▥ **Bedarra Island Resort.** This establishment vies with Lizard, Hay-
★ man, and Orpheus islands to attract wealthy travelers seeking a discreet retreat or a quiet, luxurious holiday. Elevated on stilts, two-story, open-plan, tropical-style villas blend into the island's dense vegetation. Polished wood floors, ceiling fans, and exposed beams set the tone for bright, airy accommodations that bear little resemblance to standard hotel rooms. Each villa has a balcony with a view of the ocean, and a queen-size bed.

All meals and drinks are included in the price. The resort is limited to 30 guests, which means that food preparation is free of the institutional blandness sometimes found at larger resorts. Despite the full à la carte menu, you are urged to request whatever dishes you like. The emphasis is on seafood and tropical fruit, including such dishes as fresh pasta with skewered lobster, prawns, and chicken. Breakfast includes such morning treats as thick muesli and eggs Benedict. The restaurant is modern and airy, set in a round timber building with tile floors and plenty of natural wood, and it flows onto a deck that overlooks the pool. The outdoor bar is well stocked. ⊠ *P&O Australian Resorts, Box 478, Sydney NSW, 2001,* ☎ *13–2469; 800/225–9849 in the U.S. 16 villas. Restaurant, bar, pool, 2 tennis courts, snorkeling, laundry service. AE, DC, MC, V.*

Outdoor Activities and Sports

Snorkeling around the island is good, although the water can get cloudy during the rainy season (January and February). In addition, you can windsurf, sail, fish, or boat. A swimming pool and floodlit tennis courts are on site. Fishing charters can be organized.

Arriving and Departing

Bedarra Island is just a few minutes by boat from **Dunk Island** (☞ *above*), at which you arrive before transferring to a small boat for the 20-minute ride to Bedarra. The cost is $90 round-trip, booked through the resort.

Guided Tours

To get to the Barrier Reef from Bedarra you have to return to Dunk Island, from which all reef excursions depart.

Fitzroy Island

This rugged, heavily forested national park has an extensive fringing reef, which is excellent for snorkeling and diving. On-island, the principal walking trail is a two-hour loop which takes you past a lighthouse to a lookout almost 900 ft above the surrounding waters. Although it's a mere 45-minute cruise from the tourist center of Cairns, Fitzroy has remained distinctly low-key.

Overall, Fitzroy is an option for those who prefer an affordable island. Camping facilities are available and can be booked through the **Department of Environment and Heritage** (⊠ 10–12 McLeod St, Cairns 4870, ☎ 07/4052–3096). The resort opened in the early 1980s, and the island is most popular as a day trip from Cairns (☞ Great Barrier Reef A to Z, *below*).

Dining and Lodging

$–$$$ ✕🏠 **Fitzroy Island Resort.** Casual, two-bedroom cabins are furnished in natural woods and bright prints. A bunkhouse for backpackers is also on-site, and the Rainforest Restaurant serves well-presented meals. The tariff includes three meals a day. ⊠ *Fitzroy Island, Box 2120, Cairns, Queensland 4870,* ☎ *07/4051–9588,* ℻ *07/4052–1335. 8 units with shower, 1 bunkhouse. Restaurant, 2 bars, pool, dive shop, coin laundry. AE, DC, MC, V.*

Arriving and Departing

The boat for Fitzroy departs daily at 8:30 and 10:30 from **Great Adventures** (⊠ Wharf St., ☎ 07/4051–0455 or 1800/07–9080) in Cairns. Round-trip fare is $30.

Lizard Island

The farthest north of any of the Barrier Reef resorts, Lizard Island Lodge is small, secluded, and very upmarket. This is a place to relax and unwind, safely protected from business pressures and prying eyes.

At 2,500 acres, the island is larger and quite different from the others in the Barrier Reef. Composed mostly of granite, Lizard has a remarkable diversity of vegetation and terrain, and grassy hills give way to rocky slabs interspersed with valleys of rain forest. The whole island is a national park ringed by miles of white-sand beaches, and it may have the best examples of fringing coral of any of the resort islands. Excellent walking tracks lead to key lookouts with spectacular views of the coast. The highest point, Cooks Look (1,180 ft), is the historic spot from which, in August 1770, Captain James Cook of the *Endeavour* finally spied a passage through the reef that had held him captive for a thousand miles. Lizards, for which he named the island, often bask on the lodge's front lawn.

Diving and snorkeling in the crystal-clear waters off Lizard Island are a dream. Twenty kilometers (12 mi) from Lizard, Cod Hole is rated by divers as one of the best sites in the world. Here you will find giant potato cod that swim up to be fed and petted—an awesome experience, considering these fish weigh more than 250 pounds and are more than 6 ft long! In the latter part of the year, when black marlin are running, Lizard Island becomes the focal point for big-game anglers worldwide.

Dining and Lodging

$$$$ ✕🏨 **Lizard Island Lodge.** Queensland's most idyllic resort, the Lizard Island Lodge offers sumptuous villas with sail-shaded decks and views of the turquoise bay. Forty large, comfortable rooms are decorated in pastel blue, green, and white, each with its own veranda, polished wood floors and blinds, and soft furnishings with Balarinji Aboriginal motifs. The two Anchor Bay suites, separate from the other units, have living rooms and are closer to the beach. All rooms have king- or queen-size beds. To keep the sense of isolation, there are no televisions.

Meals (but not drinks) are included in the base rate. In recent years the quality of the cooking, always high, has been elevated further by a team of talented chefs. The resort has a spacious dining room with a modern tropical decor accented by cane-back chairs and ceiling fans. To let in the ocean breeze, the restaurant is open to a veranda, where guests dine over splendid views across the gardens and palms to the water. Seafood is the foundation for the restaurant's cuisine. Although the menu changes daily, diners can expect such dishes as New Zealand green-lipped mussels poached in white wine and served with a light cream and garlic sauce, fresh coral trout panfried and served with a passion-fruit sauce, or tournedos of Northern Territory buffalo on a bed of mushrooms accompanied by a tomato sauce. Vegetarian dishes are also available. The menu is complemented by an excellent wine list. Upon request, the chef will prepare picnic baskets with a bottle of chilled wine. ⊠ *Lizard Island, PMB 40, via Cairns, 4871,* ☎ *07/4060–3999 32 rooms, 2 suites, 8 villas. Restaurant, bar, pool, tennis court, snorkeling, windsurfing, boating, waterskiing, laundry service. AE, DC, MC, V.*

Outdoor Activities and Sports

The lodge has an outdoor pool, a tennis court, catamarans, outboard dinghies, windsurfers, and fishing supplies. There is superb snorkeling around the island's fringing coral.

DEEP-SEA GAME FISHING

Lizard Island is one of the big-game fishing centers in Australia: Several world records were set here in 1991, 1992, 1993, and 1995. Fishing is best between August and December, and a marlin weighing more than 1,200 pounds is no rarity here. A day's fishing on the outer reef, including use of tackle, costs $1,775. Inner reef and night fishing are also available. One day's inner reef fishing with light tackle costs $1,025.

SCUBA DIVING

The resort will arrange supervised scuba diving trips to both the inner and outer reef, as well as local dives and night dives. Introductory and refresher courses are available. A four-day full-certification scuba course costs $900, including all equipment and local dives.

Arriving and Departing

Lizard Island has its own small airstrip served by **Eastland Airlines** (☎ 07/4060–3999). Daily one-hour flights from **Cairns** cost $404 round-trip.

Guided Tours

The reefs around the island have some of the best marine life and coral anywhere. The 16-km (10-mi) trip to the outer Reef ($160) will take you to snorkeling and diving locations, including the world-famous Cod Hole, where crew feed the giant potato cod and the Maori wrasse. Inner reef trips are available for $115. Glass-bottom boat and snorkeling trips and the use of motorized dinghies are included in guests' rates.

GREAT BARRIER REEF A TO Z

Arriving and Departing

Regular boat and air services are available to most of the Great Barrier Reef resorts, but because all of the destinations are islands, they require extra travel time, sometimes as much as a day. Plan on scheduling the last leg of your trip for the early morning, when most charters and launches depart. In some cases travel is limited to certain days of the week, so coordinate international and domestic flights, as well as helicopters and launches, accordingly. It may be necessary to stay overnight at a mainland city before taking the last leg to the island. For information about reaching the various islands, *see* Arriving and Departing *in* individual island headings.

The Queensland towns that serve as jumping-off points for the reef islands covered in this chapter include Townsville, Bundaberg, Gladstone, Rockhampton, Yeppoon, Mackay, Proserpine, Shute Harbour, and Cairns. Information on some of these towns appears in Chapter 7.

Getting Around

By Chartered Boat

Sailing around the Great Barrier Reef islands in your own boat has become very popular in recent years, and there are a number of charter companies that rent out yachts and cabin cruisers.

For uncrewed charters, contact **Australian Bareboat Charters** (⊠ Box 357, Airlie Beach, Queensland 4802, ☎ 07/4946–9381 or 1800/07–5000), **Club Seafarer** (⊠ 5/5–11 Hollywood Ave., Bondi Junction, NSW 2020, ☎ 02/9693–5899 or 1300/65–6484), **Cumberland Charter Yachts** (⊠ Box 49, Airlie Beach, Queensland 4802, ☎ 07/4946–7500 or 1800/07–5101), **Queensland Yacht Charters** (⊠ Box 293, Airlie Beach, Queensland 4802, ☎ 07/4946–7400 or 1800/07–5013), and **Whitsunday Rent a Yacht** (⊠ PMB 25, via Mackay, Queensland 4741, ☎ 07/4946–9232 or 1800/07–5111).

Crewed charters are available from **Club Seafarer** (☞ *above*) or **Sunsail Australia** (⊠ Box 65, Hamilton Island, Queensland 4803, ☎ 07/4946–9900 or 1800/80–3988).

Camping

Brochures and guides to the Queensland coast often leave the impression that you have the choice of staying either on the mainland or at an island resort, but for the adventurous there is a third option. On many uninhabited islands lying within national parks, you are allowed to camp, as long as you have permission from the **National Parks and Wildlife Service.** For details, or to find out which regional office looks after a particular island, contact the service's head office in Brisbane. ⊠ *Naturally Queensland Information Centre, Dept. of Environment, 160 Ann St., Brisbane, Queensland 4002,* ☎ *07/3227–8187.* ☉ *Weekdays 8:30–5.*

The myriad islands of the Whitsunday Group are especially popular with young campers. For more information, contact the **Whitsunday Information Centre of the Department of Environment.** It is 3 km (2 mi) from Airlie Beach toward Shute Harbour. ⊠ *Box 332, Airlie Beach, Queensland 4802,* ☎ *07/4946–7022,* FAX *07/4946–7023.* ☉ *Weekdays 8–5, Sat. 9–1.*

Contacts and Resources

Emergencies

Emergencies are handled by the front desk of the resort on each island. Each resort can summon aerial ambulances or doctors. Hamilton Island has its own doctor.

Guided Tours

FROM CAIRNS

Coral Princess has a four-day cruise from Townsville to Cairns or one way or return on a comfortable 54-passenger minicruise ship. There are plenty of stops for snorkeling, fishing, and exploring at such resort islands as Dunk and Orpheus. The crew includes marine biologists who give lectures and accompany you on excursions. Divers can rent equipment on board; lessons are also available. ⊠ *Coral Princess, Breakwater Marina, Townsville 4810,* ☎ *07/4721–1673 or 1800/07–9545.* ☎ *From $1,045 per person.*

Great Adventures (⊠ Trinity Wharf, Wharf St., Cairns, ☎ 07/4051–0455 or 1800/07–9080) operates fast catamaran service daily to Green and Fitzroy islands, Norman Reef, and Moore Reef, where diving, snorkeling, and helicopter overflights are available. Some trips include barbecue luncheon and coral viewing from an underwater observatory and a semisubmersible.

Ocean Spirit Cruises (⊠ 33 Lake St., ☎ 07/4031–2920) has a full-day tour aboard the *Ocean Spirit,* the largest sailing vessel of its type in the world, and the smaller *Ocean Spirit II.* A daily trip to Michaelmas or Upollo Cay includes four hours at the Great Barrier Reef, coral viewing in a semisubmersible or a glass-bottom boat at Upolo Cay only, swimming and snorkeling, and a fresh seafood lunch. Introductory diving lessons are available.

Quicksilver Connections operates tours to the reef from Cairns, Palm Cove, and Port Douglas (☞ From Port Douglas, *below*).

FROM MACKAY

Roylen Cruises (⊠ Box 169, Mackay 4740, ☎ 1800/07–5032) has cruises to the Great Barrier Reef on Sunday, Wednesday, and Friday. Trips include coral viewing at the underwater observatory; snorkeling and scuba-diving gear are available for hire.

FROM MISSION BEACH

The **Quick Cat Cruise** (☎ 1800/65–4242) catamaran travels to Dunk Island and continues on to the Great Barrier Reef for snorkeling and coral viewing. Cruises leave at 10 AM Monday through Saturday.

FROM PORT DOUGLAS

Quicksilver Connections (⊠ Marina Mirage, Port Douglas, ☎ 07/4099–5500) runs day trips aboard their high-speed catamaran MV *Quicksilver* to their large floating dual-level pontoon on Agincourt Reef. Once there, guests can swim, snorkel, or scuba dive around the reef or board the *Quicksilver Sub,* a semisubmersible with superb underwater views through its keel windows. Ten-minute helicopter flights over the reef are also available from a landing platform on the pontoon for $89 per person.

FROM TOWNSVILLE

Coral Princess operates cruises to Cairns (☞ From Cairns, *above*).

Pure Pleasure Cruises (☎ 07/4721–3555) runs from the Great Barrier Reef Wonderland wharf to its pontoon at Kelso Reef on the outer edge of the Great Barrier Reef. The trip takes 2½ hours by high-speed catamaran. Once there, you have the choice of fishing, snorkeling, introductory and experienced diving, or viewing the coral through the floor of a glass-bottom boat. Morning and afternoon tea and a tropical buffet lunch are included in the $124 cost. The boat departs daily (except Mon. and Thurs.) at 9 AM, returning at 5:30 PM. Hotel pickups are available.

Visitor Information

Contact the **Queensland Tourist and Travel Corporation** (✉ Government Travel Centre, Adelaide and Edward Sts., Brisbane, Queensland 4000, ☎ 13–1801).

8 ADELAIDE AND SOUTH AUSTRALIA

Come to park-blanketed Adelaide for its biennial Festival of the Arts or simply for a calmer urban experience. Elsewhere in the state, step back in time on quiet, relaxing Kangaroo Island; explore some of Australia's most celebrated wineries, an hour or two from the capital; unwind on a Murray River cruise, as your own pilot if you choose; gaze at the great variety of Australian wildlife; live underground with opal miners; or trek through one of the Outback national parks.

OFTEN CALLED the city of churches or the Festival City—a reference to the biennial Adelaide Festival of the Arts—Adelaide is easy to explore. We have William Light, the first surveyor-general of the colony, to thank for that. In 1836, on a flat saucer of land between the Mount Lofty Ranges and the sea, Light laid out the city center—one square mile divided into a grid of broad streets running north to south and east to west—and surrounded it with parks. He put a large square at the center and other squares in each quarter of the city.

By Michael Gebicki

Updated by Tony Baker

Today Light's plan is recognized as a work that was far ahead of its time. Largely due to his foresight, this city of a million people moves at a leisurely pace, free of the typical urban menace of traffic jams and glass canyons. The rest of South Australia gives even more reason to cherish this poise and gentility, for Adelaide stands on the very doorstep of the harshest, driest land in the most arid of the earth's populated continents.

Nearly 90% of South Australia's residents live in the fertile south around Adelaide. Hugging the shoreline—wary of moving too close to the barren, jagged hills and stony deserts of the parched interior—they've left the northern half of the state virtually unchanged since the first settlers arrived. Heat and desolate desert terrain have thwarted all but the most determined efforts to conquer the land. Indeed, "conquer" is too strong a word for what is often little better than subsistence. In Coober Pedy, an opal mining town in the far north, residents live underground to avoid temperatures that top 118°F (48°C).

The scorched hills of the ruggedly beautiful Flinders Ranges north of Adelaide hold Aboriginal cave paintings and fossil remains from the ages when the area was an ancient seabed. Beyond that is Lake Eyre, a great salt lake that in 1989 filled with water for only the third time in its recorded history. The Nullarbor ("treeless") Plain stretches west across state lines in its tirelessly flat, ruthlessly arid march into Western Australia.

By comparison, Adelaide is an Eden, but reminders of the harsh, desiccated land on which the city verges abound. Poles supporting electric wires are made from steel and cement rather than wood: Timber is precious. Toward the end of summer it is common to find trees in the city parks crowded with brilliantly colored parrots, which have fled to these oases from the desert. For many residents, the most urgent concern is not rising crime or property taxes but bushfire. The city is still haunted by the memory of the Ash Wednesday bushfires that devastated the Adelaide Hills at the end of the long, hot summer of 1983 and cast a pall of smoke over the city that blotted out the sun.

Yet South Australia is, perhaps ironically, well equipped for the good life. It produces most of the country's wine, and the sea ensures a plentiful supply of lobster and tuna. Cottages and guest houses tucked away in the countryside around Adelaide are among the most charming and relaxing in the country. Although the state doesn't have attractions on the scale of Sydney Harbour or the Great Barrier Reef, and it draws far fewer visitors than the eastern states, you're likely to come away from here with the feeling that you've discovered one of Australia's best-kept secrets.

South Australia

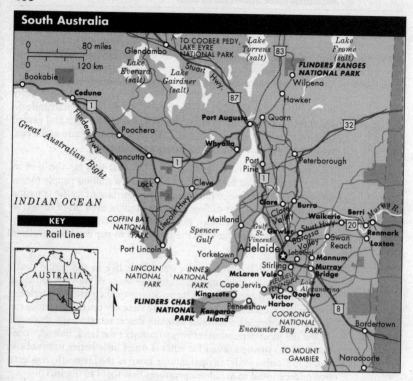

Pleasures and Pastimes

The Arts

Adelaide's Festival Centre is the focus of the city's cultural life. Its name hints at the highlight of South Australia's arts calendar—the biennial Adelaide Festival of the Arts, a tremendously successful festival that was the forerunner to other artistic celebrations throughout Australia. In off-festival years, Adelaide hosts the Womadelaide celebration of world music. Country towns and regions have their own festivals, the most notable of which are the annual Barossa Music Festival and the biennial Barossa Vintage (wine) Festival, which alternates with the Adelaide Festival.

Dining

South Australia, along with the Northern Territory, led the way in educating the Australian palate in the pleasures of bush tucker—the wild foods found in the Australian countryside that have been used for millennia by the Aboriginal people. Kangaroo, crocodile, emu, and other exotic fare was introduced to a skeptical public who now embrace it and seek ever more inventive preparations of native ingredients—although some question the ethics of using native animals for food. Local seafood is featured on many menus, especially tuna caught in the waters of Spencer Gulf and the Great Australian Bight.

CATEGORY	COST*
$$$$	over $40
$$$	$30–$40
$$	$20–$30
$	under $20

*per person, excluding drinks and service

Lodging

Adelaide's accommodations are bargains compared with those in any other Australian capital city. Even so, you might consider staying outside the city in the Adelaide Hills, which offer the best of both worlds: easy access to the pleasures of the city as well as to the vineyards, orchards, and rustic villages that are tucked away in this idyllic, rolling landscape. Wonderfully restored historic homes and guest houses are plentiful in Adelaide and throughout the state.

CATEGORY	COST*
$$$$	over $175
$$$	$100–$175
$$	$60–$100
$	under $60

All prices are for a standard double room.

Outdoor Activities

Kangaroo Island's Flinders Chase and the Outback's Flinders Ranges national parks are great places to take in the geographical variety of South Australia, from coastal land and seascapes to rugged Outback mountain terrain. Cleland Wildlife Park is one of the best ways to see the full spectrum of native wildlife. Wherever you're traveling, though, you should always carry water in this dry state and drink often.

Wine

South Australia is considered Australia's premium wine region and produces more than half the total Australian vintage. The premier wines of the Barossa Valley, Clare Valley, McLaren Vale, and Coonawarra are treasured by connoisseurs worldwide, and many South Australian producers and wines have been awarded international honors. Whether or not you make it to any vineyard tasting rooms, you'll have plenty of opportunities in restaurants to sample both.

Exploring Adelaide and South Australia

South Australia might neatly be partitioned into two areas: the dry, hot north and the greener, more temperate south. The green belt includes Adelaide and its surrounding hills and orchards, the Barossa and Clare valleys' vineyards, the beautiful Fleurieu Peninsula, and the Murray River's cliffs and lakes. Offshore, residents of Kangaroo Island live in a delightfully cocooned way. Heading up to the almost extraterrestrial Coober Pedy is one way to get a glimpse of life in the Outback.

Great Itineraries

The majority of the state's attractions are within an easy half-day's journey of Adelaide. The nearby Adelaide Hills capture the essence of South Australia's character, while an Outback journey provides an intense contrast—wide horizons, trackless deserts, and barren, starkly beautiful mountains.

IF YOU HAVE 3 DAYS

Spend a leisurely day in the countrylike atmosphere of ⊞ **Adelaide,** with a tram-car excursion to the beach suburb of Glenelg. Spend the next day in the ⊞ **Adelaide Hills,** strolling the historic streets of Hahndorf, and taking in the panorama from atop Mount Lofty, before tasting the great wines of the Barossa Valley.

IF YOU HAVE 5 DAYS

The pleasures of ⊞ **Adelaide** and its suburbs, including a walk around the 19th-century streets of North Adelaide, will fill a day. On days two and three, make for the ⊞ **Adelaide Hills,** followed by a visit the ⊞ **Barossa Valley** wineries and historic villages, perhaps with a night on a vineyard estate. Then drive, take the fast ferry, or fly to ▦ **Kangaroo Island** and savor its wildlife and fierce beauty.

IF YOU HAVE 7 DAYS

Spend a day in ▦ **Adelaide,** nosing through museums and perhaps picnicking on the banks of the Torrens River. Next morning, head into the leafy ▦ **Adelaide Hills,** where car buffs will love the National Motor Museum. On day three, descend to the ▦ **Barossa Valley,** where the German influence is strong and the free tastings at dozens of wineries are a temptation you needn't resist. Then take the ferry south of Adelaide to ▦ **Kangaroo Island,** where two days and nights will give you time to explore its remote corners and provide a verdant respite before plunging into the Outback at extraordinary ▦ **Coober Pedy** (consider flying to maximize your time). There you can live, eat, and shop underground as the locals do and *fossick* (rummage) for opal gemstones. If you're a hiker, consider spending a couple of days at **Flinders Ranges National Park,** one of the country's finest Outback parks.

When to Tour South Australia

The Adelaide Festival of the Arts and Womadelaide are held in March, when the fiercest summer heat has abated. Adelaide has the least rainfall of all Australian capital cities, so you are likely to encounter dry weather at any time of the year. In high summer the midday heat should be avoided throughout the state, when the Outback in particular is too hot for comfortable touring. If exploring the interior, wait for winter, which is pleasantly warm. For photographs, the brilliant late afternoon Outback light is magical. Summers can be hot and dry in South Australia, and winters can be cold. The best times to visit national parks here are spring and autumn.

ADELAIDE

Central Adelaide's eminently sensible, thoroughly regimented grid pattern of streets makes for easy exploration, and the lovely streetscapes have an appeal that transcends their attractions. The entire city center is an island surrounded by parks, with the meandering Torrens River flowing through the heart of the green belt—at its finest passing the Festival Centre and the picturesque Adelaide Oval.

Exploring Adelaide

City Center

Numbers in the text correspond to numbers in the margin and on the Adelaide map.

A GOOD WALK

Victoria Square ① is Adelaide's geographical heart and a perfectly appropriate place to begin a walking tour. Head north along King William Street, with the **General Post Office** ② on your left. Directly opposite is the **Old Treasury Building Museum** ③, parts of which date from 1839. The **Town Hall** ④, built from designs by Edmund Wright, mayor of Adelaide in 1859, is next door.

Turn right into Grenfell Street. Two blocks beyond Hindmarsh Square on the right is the **Tandanya Aboriginal Cultural Institute** ⑤, which showcases the work of Australia's indigenous people. Turn left down East Terrace and left again into Rundle Street, which is lined with restaurant and bars, most with pavement tables and chairs. This becomes Rundle Mall, Adelaide's main shopping strip. At King William Street, turn right and walk a block to North Terrace.

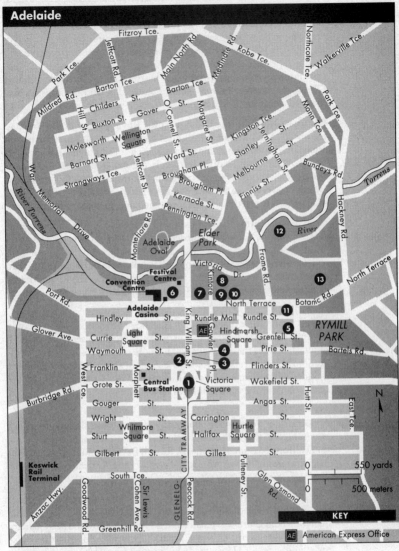

Adelaide

Art Gallery of South Australia, **10**

Ayers House, **11**

Botanic Gardens, **13**

General Post Office, **2**

Migration Museum, **8**

Old Treasury Building Museum, **3**

Parliament House, **6**

South African War Memorial, **7**

South Australian Museum, **9**

Tandanya Aboriginal Cultural Institute, **5**

Town Hall, **4**

Victoria Square, **1**

Zoological Gardens, **12**

Dominating this busy corner is the formidable Greco-Roman facade of **Parliament House** ⑥. To its left is Old Parliament House, the historic rooms of which used to house a museum (it is no longer open to the public). The **South African War Memorial** ⑦, a bronze statue of a mounted trooper commemorating the Boer War, stands opposite. Walk up Kintore Avenue, past the white marble **City of Adelaide Lending Library** to the **Migration Museum** ⑧, one of Australia's most evocative and affecting museums.

Return to North Terrace, walk past the **Royal Society of the Arts** and the library, and turn left at the grassy courtyard to the **South Australian Museum** ⑨, which holds a particularly rich collection of Aboriginal artifacts. Next along North Terrace is the **Art Gallery of South Australia** ⑩, with its neoclassical exterior. Continue on North Terrace and cross to **Ayers House** ⑪, once the scene for the highlights of Adelaide's social calendar and the home of seven-time state premier Sir Henry Ayers.

Cross North Terrace and walk along Frome Road, the shady avenue that leads to the **Zoological Gardens** ⑫. The zoo conducts breeding programs for threatened species such as the red panda and the Persian leopard. South of the zoo are the magnificent **Botanic Gardens** ⑬. You can return to the city either by the footpath that follows the River Torrens or aboard one of the Festival Centre launches.

TIMING

A walk past, rather than through, Adelaide's attractions will take only a couple of hours. The South Australian Museum deserves at least 90 minutes, as does the Art Gallery. The more eclectic contents of the Migration Museum repay detailed viewing. In summer, time your visits to indoor attractions such as museums and the art gallery so you are under cover at the hottest time of day.

SIGHTS TO SEE

⑩ **Art Gallery of South Australia.** Many famous Australian painters are represented in this collection, including Tom Roberts, Margaret Preston, Clifford Possum Tjapaltjarri, Russell Drysdale, and Sidney Nolan. A separate wing houses Aboriginal artifacts and Australiana. ⊠ *North Terr.,* ☎ *08/8207–7000.* ▨ *Free.* ⊙ *Daily 10–5.*

⑪ **Ayers House.** Between 1855 and 1897, this sprawling colonial structure was the home of Sir Henry Ayers, the premier of the state and the man for whom Uluru was renamed Ayers Rock. It's now the headquarters of the National Trust of South Australia, caretaker of the state's historic buildings. Sir Henry made his fortune in the copper mines at Burra, which enabled him to build this 41-room mansion. Most of the rooms have been restored with period furnishings, although few of the pieces actually belonged to the Ayers family. The admission price includes a one-hour tour. The elegant, café-style Conservatory restaurant is located inside Ayers House. ⊠ *288 North Terr.,* ☎ *08/8223–1234.* ▨ *$5.* ⊙ *Tues.–Fri. 10–4, weekends 1–4.*

⑬ **Botanic Gardens.** These magnificent formal gardens include roses, giant water lilies, an avenue of Moreton Bay figs, an Italianate garden, acres of green lawns, and duck ponds. The latest additions to the gardens are a palm house and the Bicentennial Conservatory, an enormous glass dome that provides a high-humidity, high-temperature environment for rain-forest species. Guided tours leave from the Simpson Kiosk in the center of the gardens Tuesday and Friday at 10:30. The **Botanic Gardens Restaurant** (☞ *Dining, below*) has one of the prettiest views of any city restaurant. ⊠ *North Terr.,* ☎ *08/8228–2311.* ⊙ *Gardens: weekdays 7–sunset, weekends 9–sunset.*

2 General Post Office. Constructed in 1867, this is one of a series of historic Victorian-era buildings on King William Street. ✉ *Franklin and King William Sts.*

NEED A
BREAK?

PIE FLOATER CARTS – The "floater," a meat pie submerged in pea soup is South Australia's contribution to the culinary arts. Many locals insist that you have not really been to Adelaide unless you've tasted this dish, and the traditional place to try one is from the pie cart found at Adelaide Casino between 6 PM and 1 AM. Other nocturnal stands can be found on Grote Street just off Victoria Square and outside the General Post Office in Franklin Street.

8 Migration Museum. This fine facility chronicles the origins, hopes, and fates of some of the millions of immigrants who settled in Australia over the past two centuries. The museum is starkly realistic, and the bleak welcome that awaited many migrants as recently as the 1970s is graphically illustrated in the reconstructed quarters of a migrant hostel. The museum is housed in the historic buildings of the Destitute Asylum, where many found themselves when the realities of Australian life failed to match their expectations. ✉ *82 Kintore Ave.,* ☎ *08/8207–7570.* 🖼 *Free.* ☉ *Weekdays 10–5, weekends 1–5.*

3 Old Treasury Building Museum. The exploration and survey of South Australia is a story of quiet heroism, and this museum is dedicated to the memory of such trailblazers as Charles Sturt, whose explorations of the Murray and Darling rivers contributed to the understanding of Australia's greatest river system, and Edward Eyre, who in 1840–1841 walked the desert from Adelaide to Perth. Included in the display of gleaming brass surveying equipment is Light's theodolite, which was used in the planning of Adelaide. ✉ *Flinders and King William Sts.,* ☎ *08/8226–4130.* 🖼 *Free.* ☉ *Weekdays 10–4.*

6 Parliament House. This parliament building was completed in two stages, 50 years apart, the west wing in 1889 and the east wing in 1939. Ten Corinthian columns are the most striking features of its classical design. Alongside is **Old Parliament House,** which dates from 1843. ✉ *North Terr. between King William and Montefiore Sts.*

St. Cyprian's Anglican Church. This ivy-draped house of worship was built in the late 1800s as part of a mission that ministered to the working classes in Lower North Adelaide. Architect Daniel Garlick gave it a simple Gothic-revival style that works well with the architecture in the surrounding neighborhood. The foundation stone was laid by Lady Jervois, the governor's wife, in 1883, and the porch was added that same year. The limestone structure is set over a bluestone plinth with brick dressings. The sandstone sanctuary at the back was added in 1910. Most of the original interior is intact, including the vaulted ceiling and the organ. ✉ *70–72 Melbourne St.,* ☎ *08/8305–9350.*

7 South African War Memorial. This statue was unveiled in 1904 to commemorate the volunteers of the South Australian Bushmen's Corps who fought with the British in the Boer War. Through the gates behind the statue you can catch a glimpse of **Government House,** the official residence of the state governor, which was completed in 1878. ✉ *King William St. and North Terr.*

9 South Australian Museum. Don't be put off by the dusty, jumbled, and old-fashioned displays in this extensive collection of Melanesian artifacts—the objects deserve careful inspection. Unfortunately, the museum lacks the space to display more than a fraction of its outstanding Aboriginal anthropological collection. ✉ *North Terr.,* ☎ *08/8207–7500.* 🖼 *Free.* ☉ *Daily 10–5.*

⑤ Tandanya Aboriginal Cultural Institute. The first major Aboriginal cultural facility of its kind in Australia, Tandanya houses a high-quality changing exhibition of works by Aboriginal artists, a theater for dance and music performances, and an excellent gift shop. ⊠ *253 Grenfell St.,* ☎ *08/8223–2467.* ⊡ *$4.* ☉ *Daily 10–5.*

④ Town Hall. This imposing building was constructed in 1863 in Renaissance style, modeled after buildings in Genoa and Florence. ⊠ *King William St.,* ☎ *08/8203–7777.*

. . . .

NEED A
BREAK?

The **Bull and Bear Ale House**'s specialty is Two Dogs alcoholic lemonade served cold, refreshing, and straight from the tap. It's best not to inquire about the source of the distinctive name unless you are prepared for a ribald joke about Native Americans. ⊠ *91 King William St.,* ☎ *08/ 8231–5795.*

. . . .

❶ Victoria Square. This is the very heart of Adelaide. The fountain in the square uses the Torrens, Onkaparinga, and Murray rivers as its theme. Surrounding the square are a few stone colonial buildings. One is the three-story **Torrens Building** on the east side of the square.

⑫ Zoological Gardens. Adelaide's zoo is small, but the landscaping and lack of crowds make this a pleasant place to see Australian fauna. You might particularly enjoy the aviary of Australian birds. ⊠ *Frome Rd.,* ☎ *08/ 8267–3255.* ⊡ *$10.* ☉ *Daily 9:30–5 (until 8 Wed. and Sun. in Jan.).*

From the zoo you can return to the city either by the footpath that follows the river Torrens through a pretty park or aboard one of the **Pop-Eye launches.** The boats travel between the front gate of the zoo and Elder Park, in front of the Festival Centre (☞ Nightlife and the Arts, *below*). ⊡ *$2.* ☉ *Boats depart weekdays hourly 11:25–3:25, weekends every 20 min 11–5.*

Around Adelaide

Cleland Wildlife Park. Just a half-hour drive from Adelaide, Cleland is one of the most unusual parks in Australia. It has only a few bushwalking trails, but its main attraction is the Native Wildlife Park. Developed in the 1960s, the park is divided into five separate environments through which animals roam freely, and this is one of the few places where you are guaranteed to see wombats, emus, and kangaroos. Swampy billabongs harbor waterfowl difficult to spot elsewhere, and enclosures protect endangered species such as yellow-footed rock wallabies and Cape Barren geese. Two major walking tracks lead outside the Native Wildlife Park. Both are steep climbs offering panoramic views of neighboring Adelaide. Contact **Adelaide Sightseeing** (☎ 08/8231–4144) for information on tours to the park. ⊠ *From Adelaide follow Greenhill Rd. and turn right at Summit Rd., or take Southeastern Fwy. and turn left through Crafers to Summit Rd.,* ☎ *08/8339–2444.* ⊡ *Native Wildlife Park admission $7.50.* ☉ *Daily 9–5 (Fri. and Sat. 9–7 during daylight savings time); closed fire-ban days.*

☾ Magic Mountain. This beachside amusement park in Glenelg has video games, a huge water slide, and assorted amusement park rides. A tram ($2.70) runs from Victoria Square to Glenelg. ⊠ *Colley Reserve, Glenelg,* ☎ *08/8294–8199.* ⊡ *Rides $2–$4 each.* ☉ *Late Sept.–Easter, weekdays 10–10 or later, weekends 10–midnight.*

Port Dock Station. Steam buffs will delight in the historic collection of locomotive engines and rolling stock located in the former Port Adelaide railway yard. The finest of its kind in Australia, the collection includes enormous "Mountain"-class engines and the historic "Tea and

Sugar" train, once the lifeline for camps scattered across the deserts of South and Western Australia. ⊠ *Lipson St., Port Adelaide,* ☎ *08/8341–1690.* ⊡ *$6.* ⊙ *Daily 10–5.*

Ⅽ **South Australian Maritime Museum.** Located inside a restored stone warehouse, the museum brings maritime history vividly to life with ships' figureheads, relics from shipwrecks, intricate scale models, slot machines from a beachside amusement park, and a full-size sailing coaster. In addition to the main display in the warehouse, the museum also includes a lighthouse, a collection of historic sailing vessels, and a steam tug tied up at the wharf nearby. ⊠ *126 Lipson St., Port Adelaide,* ☎ *08/8341–1690.* ⊡ *$8.50.* ⊙ *Daily 10–5.*

Dining

By Jacquie van Santen

Updated by Tony Baker

Australian

✕ **Charlick's Feed Store.** Nationally celebrated chef-author Maggie Beer is one of the creative forces behind this establishment near the Rundle Street restaurant strip in the city's east end. Special attention is given to native Australian foods, including the ubiquitous kangaroo, succulent yabbies (crayfish), and Murray River carp. Start with Mrs. Beer's brilliant pâté, and take your time over the formidable wine list. ⊠ *Ebenezer Pl.,* ☎ *08/8223–7566. AE, DC, MC, V. No lunch Sat.*

$$
★

Cafés

$$ ✕ **Boltz Café.** With semi-industrial decor—dull blue-green paint, exposed ducts, metal and vinyl chairs—medium-volume rock music, and a midnight closing time, this café targets the young and hip. The menu lists a choice of salad, pizza, focaccia, and such crowd pleasers as fish-and-chips, chicken curry, and ribs. You'll also find dishes like warm chicken salad with pickled pears, roasted walnuts, mixed greens, and blue cheese dressing. There is live entertainment some nights, when a cover charge of $12–$15 per person may apply. The coffee is great. ⊠ *286 Rundle St.,* ☎ *08/8232–5234. Reservations not accepted. AE, DC, MC, V. No dinner Sun.*

$$ ✕ **Ruby's Café.** Sunday brunch is an institution at this chrome-and-vinyl, 1950s-diner-style café. Lemon-scented chicken, kangaroo fillet with fresh egg noodles, and ham, potato, and pea soup are offered. Desserts include traditional vanilla, banana, and toffee pudding. ⊠ *255B Rundle St.,* ☎ *08/8224–0365. AE, DC, MC, V. BYOB. No lunch Mon.–Sat.*

$$ ✕ **Universal Wine Bar.** This high-gloss, split-level bar-café with giant mirrors and exposed wine racks along one wall remains a favorite of Adelaide's fashionable café society. Main meals include char-grilled quail and radicchio, grilled goat cheese salad, and several duck entrées, but grazing is the name of the game here. The bar plate, an antipasto platter that features such exotic treats as witloof with balsamic dressing and kangaroo pastrami, is a meal for two. A wide and interesting selection of wines is sold by the glass. ⊠ *285 Rundle St.,* ☎ *08/8232–5000. AE, DC, MC, V. Closed Sun.*

★

Continental

$$$ ✕ **Jarmer's.** In this elegantly converted villa in the eastern suburbs, Austrian-born Peter Jarmer creates a perfect marriage of classic and nouvelle cuisine techniques with the best local ingredients. Jarmer is a no-shortcuts perfectionist and one of the most original chefs in Australia. His exceptionally well priced wine list complements the food. ⊠ *297 Kensington Rd., Kensington Park,* ☎ *08/8332–2080. Reservations essential. AE, DC, MC, V.*

Adelaide Dining and Lodging

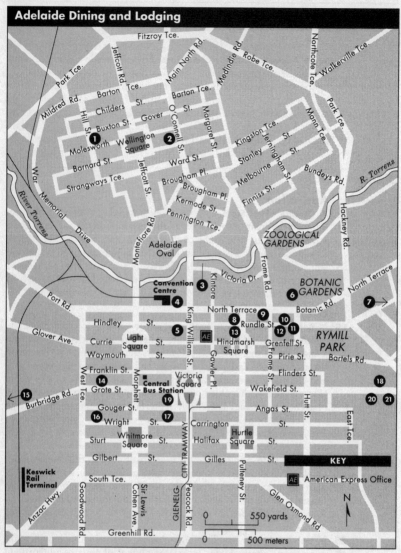

Dining

Amalfi Pizzeria Ristorante, **9**
Blake's, **4**
Boltz Café, **10**
Botanic Gardens Restaurant, **6**
Charlick's Feed Store, **18**
Chloe's, **7**
Grange Jetty Kiosk, **15**

Grange Restaurant, **19**
Jarmer's, **20**
Jasmin, **13**
Jolley's Boathouse, **3**
Magill Estate, **21**
The Oxford, **2**
Ruby's Café, **12**
Shiki, **4**
Universal Wine Bar, **11**
Le Zinc, **17**

Lodging

Adelaide's Bed and Breakfast, **14**
Directors Studios and Suites, **16**
Hilton International Adelaide, **19**
Hindley Parkroyal, **5**
Hyatt Regency Adelaide, **4**

The Mansions, **8**
North Adelaide Heritage Apartments, **1**

Eclectic

$$$$ **✕ Blake's.** This sophisticated spot, the Hyatt Regency Adelaide's (☞
★ Lodging, *below*) finest, is perfect for a big night out. Rough timber and
small, cozy spaces create a relaxed, intimate atmosphere. Highlights
of the main-course menu are poached, herb-wrapped lamb loin with
lentils and shallots, or seafood risotto with coconut milk and lemongrass. The impressive wine list includes some of the finest labels in the
country. ⊠ *Hyatt Regency Adelaide, North Terr.,* ☎ *08/8238–2381.
Reservations essential. AE, DC, MC, V. Closed Sun. No lunch.*

$$$ **✕ Magill Estate.** Near the city vineyards where Australia's most famous
wine, Penfolds Grange, was created, this pavilion-style building looks
across the gnarled vines to the city skyline and coast. The menu is a
showcase of modern Australian cooking, and the wine list is a museum
of Penfolds finest, including Grange by the glass. An experience as well
as a meal. ⊠ *78 Penfolds Rd., Magill,* ☎ *08/8301–5551. AE, DC, MC,
V. No lunch Mon.–Thurs. and Sat. No dinner Sun.–Mon.*

$ **✕ The Oxford.** One of Adelaide's best-value restaurants is in the midst
of a burgeoning café scene in North Adelaide. The Oxford specializes
in such inventive dishes as spatchcock (young chicken) with chili-
lemon butter, red Thai-style braised-duck-leg curry, and oxtail Lyon-
naise with salsa verde. At the same time, the Caesar salad served in a
whole lettuce is as good as any you will find. ⊠ *101 O'Connell St.,
North Adelaide,* ☎ *08/8267–2652. AE, DC, MC, V. No lunch Sat. or
dinner Sun.*

French

$$$ **✕ Chloe's.** Grand dining, a modern French menu, and the all-seeing
★ owner and maître d' Nick Papazahariakis define this glamorous and
polished yet unpretentious restaurant. The dining-room appointments—Georgian chairs, crystal decanters, Lalique chandeliers, and
gleaming silver—give every meal a sense of occasion, and prices are
surprisingly modest. Panfried duck breast with game wonton, and
fresh date tart with lemon glaze are signature dishes on a menu that
draws its inspiration from European and Eastern cuisine. The 20,000-
bottle cellar—a must-see for patrons—showcases Australia's best labels, plus some top-notch French favorites. ⊠ *36 College Rd., Kent
Town,* ☎ *08/8363–1001. AE, DC, MC, V. Closed Sun. No lunch Sat.*

$$ **✕ Le Zinc.** Opposite the central market, this city restaurant takes its
name from the zinc-topped bar. From the onion soup to the *tarte aux
pommes* (apple tart), the aperitifs may be French, but the wines are
emphatically Australian. A café and bar are also on the premises. ⊠
41 Gouger St., ☎ *08/8212–2345. Reservations recommended. AE, DC,
MC, V. Closed Sun.–Mon.*

Indian

$$ **✕ Jasmin.** Traditional Indian prints and artifacts give an authentic ambience to this celebrated restaurant. Jasmin specializes in Punjabi cook-
ing and offers more than 200 wines from some of Australia's smaller
vineyards. The Tandoori fish and chicken are highly recommended. ⊠
31 Hindmarsh Sq., ☎ *08/8223–7837. AE, DC, MC, V. Closed Sun.
and Mon. No lunch Sat.*

Italian

$$ **✕ Amalfi Pizzeria Ristorante.** Along with the low prices, bustle, no-
frills atmosphere, and menu of Italian favorites, this mid-city bistro serves
up a few surprises. The flavors here speak of sunlight: The specials board
might list linguine with fresh blue swimmer crab, chicken breast stuffed
with cheese and wrapped in prosciutto, or barbecued chili-infused
squid with char-grilled vegetables. Pasta dishes are large and the pizza
is some of the best in town. ⊠ *29 Frome St.,* ☎ *08/8223–1948. Reser-*

vations not accepted. AE, DC, MC, V. Closed Sun. No lunch Sat. or Mon.

Japanese

$$$ ✕ **Shiki.** The Hyatt Regency Adelaide's (☞ Lodging, *below*) elegant Japanese restaurant is decorated with authentic Japanese sculptures and elaborate floral arrangements. In keeping with the name, which means "four seasons," four set menus are offered in addition to à la carte dining. Unusual dishes include smoked and seared kangaroo fillet served with ponsu sauce, and tempura of barramundi—but you will also find sushi, sashimi, and teriyaki dishes. At five *teppanyaki* tables, chefs put on a show as they cook—the grill plate on which they prepare the food is part of the table itself. ⊠ *Hyatt Regency Adelaide, North Terr.,* ☎ *08/8238–2381. Reservations essential. AE, DC, MC, V. Closed Sun. and Mon. No lunch.*

Modern Australian

$$$$ ✕ **Grange Restaurant.** The best in-house restaurant of any hotel in town,
★   the Hilton's (☞ Lodging, *below*) upbeat brasserie has a casual, contemporary flair that's right for any time of day. Mediterranean and Asian cooking styles fuse on a modern Australian menu that lists ragout of possum with root vegetables and basil noodles, and red roasted snapper with green chili, coriander snow-pea shoots, and calamari shavings. Executive chef Cheong Liew, nationally praised, also cooks such exotica as braised shark lips, mughlai-style pigeon, and saltwater duck. ⊠ *Hilton International Adelaide, 233 Victoria Sq.,* ☎ *08/8217–0711. AE, DC, MC, V. No dinner Sun.*

$$$ ✕ **Grange Jetty Kiosk.** Overlooking the sand, sea, and sunset on a sub-
★   urban beach 20 minutes from town, the renovated kiosk highlights local seafood treated with modern Australian fusion techniques. Entrées include King George whiting fillets with prawns in tempura batter, and Kangaroo Island marron baked with bourbon and lime—and this is just the place to discover the joy of South Australian oysters. ⊠ *Esplanade and Jetty Rd., Grange,* ☎ *08/8235–0822. Reservations essential. MC, V. Closed some days in winter.*

$$ ✕ **Botanic Gardens Restaurant.** In the heart of the idyllic Adelaide Botanic Gardens, this delightful place serves modern Australian cuisine with Asian and southern European influences, along with some of the finest vintages from South Australia's smaller wineries. Main dishes include soy- and lime-braised oxtail with crispy spiced polenta, and pork fillet with a steamed ginger bun and chili black bean sauce. In addition to daily lunch, a traditional afternoon tea of scones, jam, and cream is served. ⊠ *North Terr.,* ☎ *08/8223–3526. Reservations essential. AE, DC, MC, V. No dinner.*

$$ ✕ **Jolley's Boathouse.** Blue canvas deck chairs and white-painted timber create a relaxed, nautical air, befitting the restaurant's position overlooking the river Torrens. The menu emphasizes such grilled delicacies as yearling sirloin with sage and parsnip cake, and braised venison shank tart with caramelized onions and seeded mustard. The restaurant is very popular for Sunday lunch, and it's quite romantic on a warm evening. ⊠ *Jolley's La.,* ☎ *08/8223–2891. AE, DC, MC, V. No dinner Sun.–Tues.*

Lodging

$$$$ 🏠 **Hilton International Adelaide.** Overlooking Victoria Square in the heart of the city, this Hilton has extensive facilities and a highly professional staff. Guest rooms are large, comfortable, and well-maintained. Corner rooms are slightly larger than standard rooms. The best views, of the Adelaide Hills, are from rooms on the east side of the hotel above the 10th floor. The superb Grange Restaurant (☞ Dining, *above*) is on site. ⊠ *233 Victoria Sq., Box 1871, 5001,* ☎ *08/8217–0711,* FAX *08/8231–0158. 380 rooms, 15 suites. 3 restaurants, 2 bars, pool, spa, tennis court, exercise room, nightclub. AE, DC, MC, V.*

$$$$ ⊞ **Hyatt Regency Adelaide.** Adelaide's premier hotel, this statuesque
★ atrium-style building has a luxurious and convenient blend of service, comfort, facilities, and location. The hotel's octagonal towers create unusual room shapes—a welcome change from the uniformity of most other accommodations. The best view is from the riverside rooms above the eighth floor. Four Regency Club floors have extra facilities, including separate concierge service as well as complimentary Continental breakfast and evening aperitifs and hors d'oeuvres. The hotel also includes three first-rate restaurants, Blake's and Shiki (☞ Dining, *above*), and Riverside. ⊠ *North Terr., 5000,* ☎ *08/8231–1234,* FAX *08/ 8231–1120. 367 rooms, 21 suites. 3 restaurants, room service, sauna, spa, exercise room, nightclub. AE, DC, MC, V.*

$$ ⊞ **Adelaide's Bed and Breakfast.** An intimate alternative to the big hotels, this stone guest house evokes its Victorian ancestry with bold colors and big brass beds. Of the four upstairs bedrooms, those at the front are larger but more affected by traffic noise during the daytime. For a small surcharge, you can have the ground-floor bedroom with its own bathroom. The house is a 10-minute walk from the city center and about ¾ km (½ mi) from the main attractions in North Terrace. ⊠ *239 Franklin St., 5000,* ☎ *08/8231–3124,* FAX *08/8212–7974. 5 rooms, 1 with bath. Restaurant. AE, DC, MC, V.*

$$ ⊞ **Directors Studios and Suites.** The rooms in this smart, modern hotel
★ rival those in many of the city's luxury hotels. The absence of expansive public areas, however, means the room rate is about half that of the others. The functional but stylish layout features corridors enclosed by a glass roof and miniature tropical gardens. Apart from standard hotel-style rooms, studio apartments include kitchenettes and baths as well as showers, which easily justify their marginally higher price. Of these, numbers 301 and 302 are more spacious and have city views. Traveling executives form a large part of the clientele. A pub with a dining room, open for all meals, adjoins the hotel. ⊠ *259 Gouger St., 5000,* ☎ *08/8231–3572,* FAX *08/8231–5989. 22 rooms, 36 studios. Kitchenettes. AE, DC, MC, V.*

$$ ⊞ **The Mansions.** These self-catering accommodations combine a central location with good value. Studio and one-bedroom serviced apartments are spacious, comfortable, and equipped with complete kitchen facilities, although furnishings and decor are totally lacking in personality. If you intend to do your own cooking, pay the slightly higher cost for a one-bedroom apartment. The hotel has no dining facilities, but the Hindley Street restaurant district is within easy walking distance, and Rundle Mall, the main shopping area, is less than 50 yards from the front door. ⊠ *21 Pulteney St., 5000,* ☎ *08/8232–0033,* FAX *08/8223– 4559. 40 apartments. Sauna, spa. AE, DC, MC, V.*

$$ ⊞ **North Adelaide Heritage Apartments.** Tucked away in a leafy cor-
★ ner of the city, these apartments and cottages have character, a dash of luxury, and a reasonable price tag. The creation of antiques dealers Rodney and Regina Twiss, the Heritage Apartments vary in size, but each has a bath, sitting room, kitchen, and from one to three bedrooms. Furnishings are in opulent late-Victorian style. The most intriguing of the cottages is the Friendly Meeting Chapel, a former Forresters Lodge meeting hall turned into an open-plan apartment. The city is about 2 km (1 mi) away, and none of the apartments is more than a 10-minute walk from a bus stop. Breakfast is available at a minimal charge. ⊠ *109 Glen Osmond Rd., Eastwood 5061,* ☎ *08/8272–1355,* FAX *08/8272– 6261. 6 cottages, 5 apartments. AE, DC, MC, V.*

$ ☷ **Hindley Parkroyal.** The Parkroyal is an oasis in the heart of Adelaide's nightlife precinct and within walking distance of most other attractions. Facilities include two restaurants, Oli's and Cafe Mo. ⊠ *65 Hindley St., 5000,* ☎ *08/8231–5552,* ℻ *08/8223–5552. 131 rooms, 47 suites. 2 restaurants, room service, pool. AE, DC, MC, V.*

Nightlife and the Arts

The Arts

For a listing of performances and exhibitions, look to the entertainment pages of the *Advertiser.* Tickets for concerts and plays can be purchased from Bass ticket agencies, which are located at the Festival Centre, Myer Center Point, Hindley Street, Rundle Street, and Her Majesty's Theatre. For credit card bookings, call **Bass Dial 'n' Charge.** ☎ 08/8413–1246. ⊘ *Mon.–Sat. 9–6. AE, DC, MC, V.*

The biggest arts festival in the country, the three-week **Adelaide Festival of the Arts,** takes place in March of even-numbered years. It's a cultural smorgasbord of outdoor opera, classical music, jazz, art exhibitions, comedy, and cabaret presented by some of the world's top artists. In past years musicians and writers have included Dublin's Abbey Theatre, Kiri Te Kanawa, Placido Domingo, Billy Connolly, Muddy Waters, and Salman Rushdie. For information on festival events, contact the South Australian Government Travel Centre (☞ Adelaide A to Z, *below*).

The **Adelaide Festival Centre** is the city's major venue for the performing arts. The **State Opera,** the **South Australian Theatre Company,** and the **Adelaide Symphony Orchestra** perform here regularly. On the lighter side, the center also hosts champagne brunches on Sunday morning in its **bistro** (☎ 08/8216–8744), and outdoor rock-and-roll, jazz, and country music concerts in its amphitheater. The complex also includes **Lyrics** restaurant (☎ 08/8216–8600). ⊠ *King William Rd.,* ☎ *08/8216–8600.* ⊘ *Box office Mon.–Sat. 9:30–8:30.*

In odd-numbered years the three-day **Womadelaide Festival** of world music takes place in late February or early March, with stages erected in the Botanic Gardens and crowds of 60,000 plus. Performers have included Peter Gabriel and the late Pakistani devotional singer Nusrat Fateh Ali Khan.

Nightlife

CASINO

Compared with Las Vegas the action inside the **Adelaide Casino** is sedate, but this stately sandstone building is undoubtedly one of Adelaide's main draws. All the major casino games are played here, as well as a highly animated Australian two-up, in which you bet against the house on the fall of two coins. The casino complex includes five bars and a restaurant. ⊠ *North Terr.,* ☎ *08/8212–2811.* ⊘ *Daily 10–4.*

CLUBS

In nightclubs, cover charges vary according to the night and the time of evening. A listing of nightlife for the coming week can be found in *The Guide,* a pull-out section of the Thursday edition of the *Advertiser.* The daily edition lists attractions for that day.

Adelaide's bright young things can generally be found nightclubbing along **Hindley Street** or relaxing in the trendy cafés of **Rundle Street.**

Margaux's on the Square is a plush, elegant nightclub and a regular haunt for the city's sophisticates. ⊠ *Hilton International Adelaide Hotel, Victoria Sq.,* ☎ *08/8217–0711.* ▨ *$5–$15.* ⊘ *Thurs.–Sat. 9 PM–3 AM.*

Cargo Club attracts a stylish clientele with live funk, jazz, and soul music. ✉ *213 Hindley St.,* ☎ *08/8231–2327.* ⊘ *Tues.–Sat. 10 PM–dawn.*

Mystics, dark, stylish, and intimate, attracts a sleek, over-25 crowd with disco and live music. ✉ *Stamford Plaza Hotel, 150 North Terr.,* ☎ *08/ 8217–7552.* ⊘ *Fri. and Sat. 8 PM–3 AM.*

Outdoor Activities and Sports

Beaches
Adelaide's 25-km (15-mi) coastline from North Haven to Brighton is practically one long beach. There is no surf, but the sand is clean. The most popular spots are those to the west of the city, including **Henley Beach** and **West Beach.** Farther south, **Glenelg** has a carnival atmosphere that makes it a favorite with families.

Cricket
The main venue for interstate and international competition is the **Adelaide Oval.** ✉ *War Memorial Dr. and King William St.,* ☎ *08/8231– 3759.*

Football
Australian Rules football is the most popular winter sport in South Australia. Games are generally played on weekends at **Football Park** (✉ Turner Dr., West Lakes, ☎ 08/8268–2088). The Adelaide Crows team plays in the national AFL competition, generally every second Sunday at Football Park. The Port Adelaide Power joined the league in 1997, which ensures a national league game virtually every week in Adelaide. Games are popular, particularly since the Crows scored back-to-back national championships in 1997 and 1998: thus, tickets for AFL matches are very hard to come by. The season runs from the beginning of April to the end of August. Finals are held in September, and local teams will play a match or two then if they qualify.

Golf
The **City of Adelaide Golf Links** has two short (par-3) 18-hole courses and a championship course. You can hire clubs and carts from the pro shop. ✉ *War Memorial Dr., North Adelaide,* ☎ *08/8267–2171.* ✉ *Greens fee for par-3 courses $8 daily; championship course $14 weekdays, $17 weekends.*

Running
The parks north of the city have excellent running routes, especially the track beside the river Torrens.

Tennis
Located just across the Torrens from the city, the **Memorial Drive Tennis Courts** has hard and grass courts. ✉ *War Memorial Dr., North Adelaide,* ☎ *08/8231–4371.* ✉ *$12 per hr until 5 PM, $18 until 10 PM.* ⊘ *Weekdays 9 AM–10 PM, Sun. 9–5.*

Shopping

Jewelry and Gems
South Australia is the world's largest source of opals. Excellent selections of opals and other gems can be found at **Opal Field Gems** (✉ 29 King William St., 3rd floor, ☎ 08/8212–5300) and the **Opal Mine** (✉ 30 Gawler Pl., ☎ 08/8223–4023). For high-quality antique jewelry try the **Adelaide Exchange** (✉ 10 Stephens Pl., behind David Jones department store, ☎ 08/8212–2496) and **Megaw and Hogg Antiques** (✉ 26 Leigh St., off Hindley St., ☎ 08/8231–0101).

Malls

Adelaide's main shopping area is **Rundle Mall** (⊠ Rundle St. between King Williams and Pulteney Sts.), a pedestrian plaza lined with boutiques and department stores. Shops in this area are open Monday–Thursday 9–5:30, Friday 9–9, Saturday 9–5. Sunday hours are irregular. For information on specific shops in this area, visit the Rundle Mall Information Centre in the booth near the corner of King William Street. The center is open weekdays 9–5 and weekends 10–1.

Markets

Central Market is one of the largest produce markets in the Southern Hemisphere. The stalls in this sprawling complex also sell T-shirts, records, and electrical goods. ⊠ *Victoria Sq.* ⊙ *Tues. 7–5:30, Thurs. 11–5:30, Fri. 7 AM–9 PM, Sat. 7–1.*

Market Adventures is a behind-the-scenes guided tour of the central market led by respected food authority Graeme Andrews. You can meet stall holders, share their knowledge, and taste the wares. ☎ *018/842–242.* ⌨ *$20.* ⊙ *Tues. and Thurs. at 10:30 and 1:30, Fri. at 10 and 2.*

Adelaide A to Z

Arriving and Departing

BY BUS

The **Central Bus Station** (☎ 08/8415–5533), open 6 AM to 10 PM, is near the city center at 101 Franklin Street. It is the terminal for all intercity bus companies: **Greyhound/Pioneer** (☎ 13–2030), **Premier** (☎ 08/8233–2744), and **Stateliner** (☎ 08/8415–5555).

BY CAR

Adelaide has excellent road connections with other states. Highway 1 links the city with Melbourne, 728 km (451 mi) southeast, and with Perth, 2,724 km (1,689 mi) to the west, via the vast and bleak Nullarbor Plain. The Stuart Highway provides sealed road access to the Red Centre. Alice Springs is 1,542 km (956 mi) north of Adelaide.

BY PLANE

Adelaide Airport is 6 km (4 mi) west of the city center. The international and domestic terminals are about ¼ mi apart. International airlines serving Adelaide are **British Airways, Singapore Airlines, Malaysia Airlines, Garuda Indonesia, Cathay Pacific,** and **Qantas.** Domestic airlines flying into Adelaide include **Ansett Australia, Air Kangaroo Island, Augusta Airways, Kendell,** and **Qantas.** *See* Air Travel *in* Smart Travel Tips for airline telephone numbers.

The **Transit Bus** (☎ 08/8381–5311) costs $6 and links the airport terminals with the city hotels and the rail and bus stations. On weekdays the bus leaves the terminals at 30-minute intervals between 7:30 AM and 1:30 PM and 4:30 PM and 9 PM. Between 1:30 and 4:30, the bus departs at one-hour intervals. On weekends the bus departs every hour between 7:30 AM and 8:30 PM. **Taxis** are available from the stands outside the air terminal buildings. The fare to the city is about $15.

BY TRAIN

The station for interstate and country trains is the **Keswick Rail Terminal** west of the city center. The terminal has a small café and snack bar, and taxis are available from the rank outside (☎ 08/8217–4111). The *Overland* makes daily 12-hour runs between Melbourne and Adelaide. The *Ghan* (Rail Australia, ☎ 13–2232 or 1800/88–8480) makes the 20-hour journey to Alice Springs weekly November–April and at least twice weekly May–October. The *Indian Pacific* links Adelaide with Perth (37½ hours) and Sydney (28 hours) twice a week.

Getting Around

BY BICYCLE

Adelaide's parks, flat terrain, and wide, uncluttered streets make it a perfect city for two-wheel exploring. **Linear Park Mountain Bike Hire** rents 21-speed mountain bikes by the hour or for $20 per day and $80 per week, including a helmet, lock, and maps. ⊠ *Elder Park, adjacent Adelaide Festival Centre,* ☎ *018/844–588.* ⊙ *By appointment only.*

BY BUS AND TRAIN

Fares on the public transportation network are based on peak (9 AM–3 PM) and off-peak travel. There are discounts for seniors and students. A single-trip peak ticket is $2.80, off-peak $1.60. Tickets are available from most railway stations and from the TransAdelaide Information Centre (☞ *below*). Anyone who expects to travel frequently can economize with a **Multitrip Ticket** ($19), which allows 10 rides throughout the three bus zones. Off-peak Multitrip tickets are $10.60. Another economical way to travel is with the **Daytrip Ticket,** which allows unlimited bus, train, and tram travel throughout Adelaide and most of its surroundings after 9 AM. It costs $5.40 for adults.

The free **City Loop Bus** makes almost 30 stops in downtown Adelaide, including Hindley Street, Victoria Square, and Rundle Mall. The bus runs on the half-hour in both directions Monday–Thursday 8:30–6, Friday 8:30 AM–9 PM, and Saturday 9–5. Buses have ramp access for wheelchairs and baby carriages.

If you think you'll make extensive use of Adelaide's public buses, purchase a copy of the Public Transport map for 30¢, also available from the **TransAdelaide Information Centre.** ⊠ *Currie and King William Sts.,* ☎ *08/8210–1000.* ⊙ *Daily 7 AM–8 PM.*

BY TAXI

Taxis can be hailed on the street, booked by phone, or collected from a rank. It is often difficult to find a cruising taxi beyond the central business district. Some taxis will accept credit cards. **Suburban Taxi Service** (☎ 08/8211–8888) offers reliable booking service.

BY TRAM

One of the city's last surviving trams runs between Victoria Square and the lively beachside suburb of Glenelg. Ticketing is identical to that of city buses.

Contacts and Resources

CAR RENTALS

The following have offices both at the airport and downtown: **Avis** (⊠ 136 North Terr., ☎ 08/8410–5727 or 1800/22–5533), **Budget** (⊠ 274 North Terr., ☎ 13–2727), **Thrifty** (⊠ 100 Franklin St., ☎ 08/8211–8788 or 800/65–2008).

EMERGENCIES

Police, fire, or ambulance (☎ 000). **Royal Adelaide Hospital** (⊠ North Terr. and Frome Rd., ☎ 08/8223–0230).

GUIDED TOURS

Orientation Tours. The **Adelaide Explorer** is a replica tram that takes passengers on a two-hour tour of the highlights of the city and Glenelg, Adelaide's seaside suburb. Passengers may leave the vehicle at any of the attractions along the way and join a following tour. Tours depart every half hour. ⊠ *14 King William St.,* ☎ *08/8364–1933.* ☞ *$22.*

Adelaide Sightseeing operates a morning city sights tour. The company also has trips to ☞ Cleland Wildlife Park outside of Adelaide. ⊠ *101 Franklin St.,* ☎ *08/8231–4144.* ☞ *$27.*

Festival Tours operates a morning city tour that takes in all the highlights, including the view from Light's Vision lookout and a visit to St. Peter's Cathedral. ✉ *18 King William St.,* ☎ *08/8374–1270.* 🖭 *$25.*

American Express Travel (✉ 13 Grenfell St., ☎ 08/8212–7099).

Thomas Cook (✉ 45 Grenfell St., ☎ 08/8212–3354).

South Australian Government Travel Centre. ✉ *1 King William St., 5000,* ☎ *08/8212–1505.*

State Information Centre has travel books and brochures on South Australia and an especially good range of hiking and cycling maps. ✉ *1 King William St., 5000,* ☎ *08/8303–2033.*

What's On in Adelaide (☎ *08/8411–699*) is a recorded information service that covers current events and attractions in both the city and the Adelaide Hills.

THE ADELAIDE HILLS

The green slopes, wooded valleys, and gardens brimming with flowers of the Adelaide Hills are a pastoral oasis in this desert state. The combination of orchards, vineyards, avenues of tall conifers, and town buildings of rough-hewn stone gives this region a distinctly European feel and makes the hills one of the best reasons to visit Adelaide. During the steamy summer months these hills, barely 15 km (10 mi) from the heart of Adelaide, are consistently cooler than the city.

To reach the Hills, follow Payneham Road northeast from Adelaide to Gorge Road, which leads to Torrens Gorge. This delightful drive leads through a succession of orchards, vineyards, and historic towns, with the Torrens river flashing through the trees.

Birdwood

44 km (27 mi) east of Adelaide.

Birdwood was originally named Blumberg (Hill of Flowers), but it was renamed during the First World War in honor of the commander of the Australian military forces. The town's historic flour mill, built in 1852, now has a role as the home of Australia's best motoring museum.

The **National Motor Museum** is a must for automobile enthusiasts and has enough general interest to captivate those usually unmoved by motor vehicles. This outstanding collection includes the first vehicle to cross Australia (1908); the first Holden, Australia's indigenous automobile, off the production line (1948); and hundreds of other historic autos and motorcycles. ✉ *Main St., Birdwood,* ☎ *08/8568–5006.* 🖭 *$8.50.* ⏱ *Daily 9–5.*

Mt. Lofty

30 km (19 mi) southwest of Birdwood, via Mount Torrens and Lobethal; 16 km (10 mi) southeast of Adelaide.

There are splendid views of Adelaide from the lookout at the 2,300-ft peak of **Mt. Lofty.** Much of the surrounding area was devastated during the Ash Wednesday bush fires of 1983; you can see the skeletal remains of some historic mansions behind the television antennas just below the summit.

Dining and Lodging

$$$$ ✕ **Hardy's.** The formal dining room inside Mt. Lofty Country House is one of the highlights of this elegant country-house hotel. Although it reflects the opulence of the restaurant, the international menu is also stylishly modern. Try locally farmed venison fillet served on beetroot, Spanish onion, and chili risotto with butternut squash mousseline and sweet pepper sauce. The wine list includes South Australia's finest. ⊠ *74 Summit Rd., Crafers,* ☎ *08/8339–6777. Reservations essential. Jacket required. AE, DC, MC, V.*

$$ ✕ **Summit.** The new building atop Mt. Lofty has spectacular views of
★ the hills, city, and coast across to Yorke Peninsula. Chef Patrice Ricourt draws on the surrounding market gardens, farms, and bakeries for his ingredients. The wine list does the same for the Hills wineries. Try the smoked salmon, the peak product of an uncommon and successful Hills enterprise. ⊠ *Summit Rd., off South Eastern Fwy., Mt. Lofty,* ☎ *08/ 8339–2600. MC, V. No dinner Mon.–Tues.*

$$$$ 🏨 **Mercure Grand Hotel Mount Lofty House.** This is country living at its finest. Enjoy the sophisticated pleasures of gourmet dining and thoughtful service at this refined country house against a backdrop of rolling hills and crisp mountain air. The house sits in a commanding position just below the summit of Mt. Lofty, overlooking the patchwork of vineyards, farms, and bushland in the Piccadilly Valley. The house itself is surrounded by informal gardens and shaded by giant sequoias. Guest rooms are large and well furnished. ⊠ *74 Summit Rd., Crafers 5152,* ☎ *08/8339–6777,* 𝐅𝐀𝐗 *08/8339–5656. 28 rooms, 2 suites. Restaurant, bar, pool. AE, DC, MC, V.*

Mylor

10 km (6 mi) south of Mt. Lofty via the town of Crafers, the South Eastern Freeway, and Stirling; 25 km (16 mi) southeast of Adelaide.

Mylor is a picturesque little village, merely a speck on the map. It's worth visiting for the role that a wildlife sanctuary in its midst plays in the preservation of native animals.

At **Warrawong Sanctuary** there are no koalas to cuddle, but this is one of the few chances you will have to see kangaroos, wallabies, bandicoots, and platypuses in their native habitat. There are morning and evening guided walks around this protected 35-acre property of rain forest, gurgling streams, and black-water ponds; because most of the animals are nocturnal, the evening walk is the most rewarding. There is also a walk-and-dinner package available. Reservations for walks are essential. ⊠ *Stock Rd.,* ☎ *08/8370–9422.* 🚶 *Dawn and evening walks $15, walk and dinner $28.50 including drinks.*

Bridgewater

6 km (4 mi) north of Mylor, 22 km (14 mi) southeast of Adelaide.

Bridgewater came into existence in 1841 as a place of refreshment for bullock teams fording Cock's Creek. It was officially planned in 1859 by the builder of the first Bridgewater mill.

It would be difficult to miss the handsome 130-year-old **stone flour mill** with its churning waterwheel that stands at the entrance to the town. These days the mill houses the first-class Granary Restaurant (☞ Dining and Lodging, *below*) and serves as the shopfront for Petaluma Wines, one of the finest labels in Australia. The prestigious Croser champagne is matured on the lower level of the building, and you can tour the cellars by appointment. ⊠ *Mt. Barker Rd.,* ☎ *08/8339–3422.* ☺ *Wine tasting daily 10–5.*

Dining and Lodging

$$ ✕ **Granary Restaurant.** More commonly known as Bridgewater Mill,
★ this stylish restaurant inside a converted flour mill is one of the best
in the state. The modern Australian menu is small and limited to lunch,
but the food is as fresh, original, and as well presented as the sur-
roundings. Imaginative use is made of local produce in such dishes as
goat cheese baked with eggplant and roasted capsicum pepper, and minia-
ture oyster pie served with mushrooms and chervil cream. In summer,
book ahead to get a table on the deck beside the waterwheel. If you're
feeling flush, ask to see the special wine list. ⊠ *Mt. Barker Rd.*, ☎ *08/
8339–3422. AE, DC, MC, V. Closed Tues. No dinner.*

$ ✕ **Aldgate Pump.** This friendly country pub has a lengthy menu that
ranges from a hearty moussaka to Thai curries and salad dishes. The
restaurant, with eucalyptus log fires in winter, overlooks a shady beer
garden. The welcome is warm whatever the weather. ⊠ *1 Strathalbyn
Rd., 2 km (1 mi) from Bridgewater, Aldgate,* ☎ *08/8339–2015. Reser-
vations not accepted. AE, DC, MC, V.*

$$ ▥ **Aldgate Village Inn.** Formerly the Aldgate general store, this rustic, century-old stone building provides atmospheric lodgings in the pretty
village of Aldgate. Guest rooms are simply but neatly furnished, and
breakfast is included in the tariff. An apartment offers more spacious
accommodation at a higher price. Its greatest asset is its tranquil location, surrounded by wooded hills, just a 20-minute drive from the
city of Adelaide. ⊠ *30 Kingsland Rd., Aldgate 5154,* ☎ *08/8370–8144.
5 rooms. AE, DC, MC, V.*

Hahndorf

7 km (4 mi) east of Bridgewater, 29 km (18 mi) southeast of Adelaide.

Hahndorf is a picture-perfect village that might have sprung to life from
the cover of a chocolate box. Founded 150 years ago by German settlers, Hahndorf consists of a single shady main street lined with stone-
and-timber shops and cottages. Most old shops have become
arts-and-crafts galleries and antiques stores, although German traditions survive in cake shops and a butcher's shop. The village is extremely
crowded on Sunday.

The **Hahndorf Academy** contains several works by Sir Hans Heysen, a
famous Australian landscape painter who lived in this area at the turn
of the century. ⊠ *68 Main St.,* ☎ *08/8388–7250.* ▤ *$2.* ⊙ *Daily
10:15–5.*

Lodging

$$$ ▥ **Apple Tree Cottage and Gum Tree Cottage.** This is your chance to
★ escape to your own country cottage in idyllic surroundings. Set in rolling
countryside on a cattle stud farm near the historic village of Hahn-
dorf, cottages come with antique furnishings, open log fires, well-
equipped kitchens, and air-conditioning. Apple Tree Cottage is a
two-story Georgian farmhouse surrounded by a lake and gardens
close to an orchard. Gum Tree Cottage was built only a few years ago,
but the stonework, red-gum beams, and post-and-rail fence suggest
a pioneer's house of the last century. During your stay, you can row
to the large dam next to the house or stretch out in a hammock slung
underneath a walnut tree. Adelaide is about 40 minutes away by car.
Rates include supplies for a full breakfast. ⊠ *Box 100, Oakbank 5243,
10 km (6 mi) northeast of Hahndorf,* ☎ *08/8388–4193. 2 cottages.
No credit cards.*

Adelaide Hills A to Z

Getting Around

The Adelaide Hills are served by the Adelaide suburban network, but buses, particularly to some of the more remote attractions, are limited. *See* Arriving and Departing *in* Adelaide A to Z, *above.*

The best way to explore the area is by car, which gives you the freedom to discover the country lanes and villages that are an essential part of the hills experience. *See* Car Rentals *in* Adelaide A to Z, *above.*

Contacts and Resources

Adelaide Sightseeing (☎ 08/8231–4144) runs a daily afternoon coach tour of the Adelaide Hills and historic Hahndorf village ($28 adults). The tour departs from the Central Bus Station at 101 Franklin Street.

Adelaide Hills Tourist Information Centre. ⊠ *64 Main St., Hahndorf 5243,* ☎ *08/8388–1185.*

THE BAROSSA VALLEY

Some of Australia's most famous vineyards are found in the Barossa Valley, less than an hour's drive northeast of Adelaide. The wide, shallow valley's 50 wineries produce a huge array of wine, including aromatic Rhine riesling, which sells for $6 a bottle; Seppelts unique, century-old Para Port, which goes for up to $3,000; and Penfold's Grange, Australia's most celebrated wine.

What sets the Barossa apart is not so much the quality of its wine as its cultural roots. The area was settled by Silesian immigrants who left the German-Polish border region to escape religious persecution. These conservative, hardworking farmers brought traditions that you can't miss in the solid bluestone architecture, the tall, slender spires of the Lutheran churches, and the Black Forest cake that has taken the place of Devonshire tea. All of this gives the Barossa a character and identity that no other wine-growing area of Australia possesses. Its scenery, history, architecture, and distinctive cuisine can appeal to anyone.

The Barossa lives, thinks, and breathes wine, and any tour of the area will usher you into the mysterious world of wine tasting. The haze of jargon enshrouding this rite might seem obscure and intimidating at first, but keep in mind that the heady passion uniting wine lovers could take you by surprise. If you are new to the process, relax and let your sense of taste guide you.

Every winery in the Barossa operates sale rooms, which will usually have 6–12 varieties of wine available for tasting. Generally, you will begin with a light, aromatic white, such as Riesling, move on through heavier white, and then repeat the process with red wine. Sweet and fortified wine should be left until last. You are not expected to sample the entire range; to do so would overpower your taste buds. It's far better to give the tasting-room staff some idea of your personal preferences and let them suggest wine for you to taste.

Numbers in the margin correspond to points of interest on The Barossa Valley map.

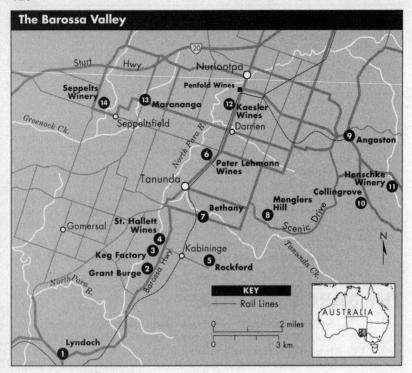

The Barossa Valley

KEY

— Rail Lines

AUSTRALIA

Lyndoch

❶ *58 km (36 mi) northeast of Adelaide.*

This pleasant little town, surrounded by vineyards, as most are in the Barossa Valley, owes the spelling of its name to a draftsman's error. It was meant to be named Lynedoch, after the British soldier Lord Lynedoch.

Dining and Lodging

$$ ✕🏠 **Miners Cottage.** It would be hard to imagine a more romantic hideaway than this peaceful country charmer. Set among giant gum trees above a billabong, the small, century-old stone cottage consists of a slate-floor kitchen sitting room, a bedroom, and a bath. The decor is delightful—lace, antiques, tiny windows, thick stone walls, and a veranda at the back that overlooks a swimming pool in the garden below. The cottage is situated on a 66-acre farm in rolling country with a number of fine walks close by. Dinner is available by prior arrangement. ✉ *Box 28, Cockatoo Valley 5351, 10 km (6 mi) from Lyndoch,* ☎ *08/8524–6213,* FAX *08/8524–6650. 1 cottage. Dining room, pool. MC, V.*

$$ 🏠 **Christabelle Cottage.** Self-contained, private, and romantic, this 1849 cottage offers classic Australian accommodations. The space includes a bedroom, sitting room, kitchen, bathroom, and garden. This is a fine base for exploring the Barossa Valley from the quiet hamlet of Lyndoch. ✉ *8 King St., Lyndoch 5351,* ☎ FAX *08/8524–4825. MC, V.*

Tanunda

13 km (8 mi) north of Lyndoch, 70 km (43 mi) north of Adelaide.

The cultural heart of the Barossa, Tanunda is its most German settlement. The four Lutheran churches in the town testify to its German heritage, which is reinforced by the proliferation of shops offering German pastries, breads, and wursts—not to mention the wine—on Tanunda's main street. Many of the valley's best wineries are close by.

❷ The **Grant Burge** winery is one of the most successful labels of the young, independent winegrowers of the Barossa. Grant Burge produces mainly white wine, and his semillon and Rhine riesling in particular are highly regarded by wine judges. ⊠ *Jacobs Creek, 5 km (3 mi) from Tanunda,* ☎ *08/8563–3700.* ⊙ *Daily 10–5.*

❸ The **Keg Factory** uses traditional methods to make oak casks for Barossa wineries. You can watch coopers (barrel makers) working the American and French oak staves inside the iron hoops. The small port kegs make a wonderful souvenir of the Barossa. ⊠ *St. Halletts Rd.,* ☎ *08/8563–3012.* ⊙ *Mon.–Sat. 8–5.*

❹ **St. Hallett Wines** uses 100-year-old vines for its signature Old Block shiraz, a classic and fantastic Australian red. This is one of the area's best wineries. Tastings are in the comfortable Old Block Cellar, where a log fire encourages wintertime lingering. Poacher's Blend Semillon and Barossa Valley Shiraz are also good choices. ⊠ *St. Halletts Rd.,* ☎ *08/8563–2319.* ⊙ *Oct.–June, daily 10–5; July–Sept., Sun. 11–5.*

❺ **Rockford** is a small wine maker with a tasting room to match in a small, dark-stone barn. The specialty here is heavy, rich wine made from some of the oldest vines in the Barossa. These vines bear small quantities of fruit with intense flavor and often survive only in areas as small as a single acre, which makes them costly for anyone but a dedicated, small-scale winery to produce. A range of notable wine has appeared under the Rockford label; don't miss the opportunity to taste the cabernet sauvignon and Basket Press Shiraz, an outstanding example of this most traditional of Australian varieties. Call in advance to arrange a tasting. ⊠ *Krondorf Rd.,* ☎ *08/8563–2720.*

❻ **Peter Lehmann Wines.** Peter Lehmann is a larger-than-life Barossa character whose wine consistently wins awards and medals. The tasting room is among the most pleasant in the valley, and staff are friendly and informative. Look for semillons, shiraz, cabernet malbec, and Cellar Collection wines. ⊠ *Para Rd.,* ☎ *08/8563–2500.* ⊙ *Weekdays 9:30–5, weekends 10:30–4:30.*

Dining and Lodging

$$ ✕ **1918 Bistro and Grill.** Housed in a restored villa, this pretty, rustic restaurant makes exemplary use of the distinctive regional produce of the Barossa Valley, which ranges from olive oil to almonds to sausages. Dishes might include leek risotto with lemon parsley and Parmesan or char-grilled snapper with leek, mint, and pea vinaigrette. Don't miss the clean-skin (unlabeled) local house wines. ⊠ *94 Murray St.,* ☎ *08/8563–0405. AE, DC, MC, V.*

$ ✕ **Lanzerac Cafe.** On the main street of Tanunda, the largest of the Barossa's tiny towns, Wyndham and Patricia House's restaurant and gallery provide Australian country cooking at its most relaxed and its creative best. Try the gloriously elaborate antipasto plate, or a pizza topped with local smoked meats and wursts. ⊠ *109 Murray St.,* ☎ *08/8563–00322. AE, DC, MC, V.*

$$$ 🔲 **Lawley Farm.** Built around a courtyard shaded by peppercorn trees, ★ the charming stone cottages here were assembled from the remains of barns that date from the pioneering days of the Barossa. Their rustic character is enhanced by antique furnishings and a family of peacocks that struts the grounds. The Lyndoch Suite, with massive ceiling beams from local wineries, and the sunny Bethany suite are particularly appealing. The Krondorf Suite is the original 1852 cottage, with a wood-

THE SHOCKING TRUTH ABOUT AUSTRALIAN WINE

PREPARE TO BE THOROUGHLY taken aback, or at least a touch startled, as the new breeds from Australia's wine makers rise up to meet the challenge of an exciting new generation of chefs who need wines to work magic with the feisty, spice- and herb-laden flavors of Asia and the Mediterranean in their cooking. Today's lighter, more refreshing wine styles have left traditional wine-and-food–pairing theories dragging their heels in the dust.

The search for a truly Australian wine style is loaded with surprises. From the wineries of Northeast Victoria, an area known for its full-bodied reds, come some truly remarkable fortified tokays and muscats, all with a delicious, wild, untamed quality that is so rich and sticky you don't know whether to drink them—or spread them. Among the more notable varieties are the All Saints Classic Release Tokay, Campbell's Liquid Gold, and Tokay Bailey's Old Muscat. Believe it or not, these are perfect with Australia's distinctive farmhouse cheeses, such as Milawa Gold (North East Victoria), Yarra Valley Persian Fetta, and Meredith Blue (from Victoria's Western District).

Practically unknown beyond these shores is what was once affectionately but euphemistically known as sparkling burgundy, an effervescent red made mainly from shiraz grapes using the traditional méthode champenoise. A dense yet lively wine with fresh, fruity tones, it is particularly suited to game and turkey and is now an integral part of a festive Australian Christmas dinner. Look for labels such as Seppelts Harpers Range, Yalumba Cuvée Two, and Hugh Hamilton Sparkling Shiraz.

Then there are the classic rieslings of the Barossa and Clare valleys of South Australia, first introduced by German and Silesian settlers last century. Today, wines such as Heggies Riesling, Petaluma Riesling, and Wirra Wirra Hand Picked Riesling are just as much at home with Middle Eastern merguez sausage and couscous as they are with knockwurst and sauerkraut.

Also very Australian in style are the big, oaky semillons of the Hunter Valley (try Tyrrell's Vat 1 Semillon and Lindeman's Hunter River Semillon) and the powerful steak-and-braised-meat–loving cabernets from the rich, red "terra rossa" soil of the Coonawarra district in South Australia. These wines, including Petaluma Coonawarra, Lindeman's Pyrus, and Hollick Coonawarra, have a habit of knocking first-timers' socks off.

As a breed, the Australian shiraz style is well worth getting to know. It has delicious pepper-berry characteristics and food-friendly companionability. Fortunately, not all Australian shiraz carries the now astronomic Grangelike price tags. In fact, other Schubert-inspired wines, such as Penfold's bins 128 and 389, are far more accessible, as are a clutch of worthy labels that includes Elderton Shiraz from the Barossa Valley, Brokenwood Graveyard Vineyard from the Hunter Valley, and Seppelt Great Western Shiraz from the Grampians in Victoria.

For an old-world variety, shiraz is very much at home with modern Australian cooking, working beautifully with a Moroccan-inspired lamb tagine, Mediterranean-style roasted goat, pasta, and yes, even kangaroo with beetroot.

So there you have it. If you are about to embark on your own personal discovery of Australian wines, you have been warned. Australian wines have been stopping people in their tracks ever since the first grapes were grown in the first governor's garden back in 1788. Now get ready to be amazed, astonished, and shocked—into having another glass.

— Terry Durack

burning stove and low-beam doors. ⊠ *Box 103, Krondorf Rd., 5352,* ☎ ℻ *08/8563–2141. 7 suites. Spa, recreation room. AE, DC, MC, V.*

$ 🏨 **Blickinstal.** These motel-style units are set on a farm on the lower slopes of the Barossa Ranges. The name means "look into the valley," which perfectly describes the view of almond trees and vineyards. Guest rooms have a contemporary, functional design. ⊠ *Box 17, Rifle Range Rd., 5352,* ☎ ℻ *08/8563–2716. 4 rooms. Kitchenettes. MC, V.*

Bethany

❼ *4 km (2½ mi) southeast of Tanunda, 70 km (43 mi) northeast of Adelaide.*

The village of Bethany was the original German settlement in the Barossa. Those who established the town in 1842 divided the land exactly as they did in their Silesian homeland—with the farmhouses side by side at the front of long, narrow strips of land that run down to Bethany Creek. Today Bethany is a Sleepy Hollow, its appearance and character frozen in a past century, and its size and importance eclipsed by the nearby towns. Its one shop, the Bethany Art and Craft Gallery, is set in a garden brimming with flowers.

❽ **Menglers Hill** is the best spot from which to view a panorama of the Barossa. The parking lot near the summit overlooks the patchwork of vineyards in the valley below. Like so much of South Australia, the Barossa suffers from a shortage of rain; in summer the landscape is scorched brown. Only the vineyards, most of which are irrigated, stand out as bright-green rectangles.

Angaston

❾ *17 km (11 mi) north of Bethany, 86 km (53 mi) northeast of Adelaide.*

This part of the Barossa was settled largely by immigrants from the British Isles, and the architecture of Angaston differs noticeably from the low stone buildings of the German towns.

❿ **Collingrove.** Until 1975, this patrician country house was the ancestral home of the Angas family, the descendants of George Fife Angas, one of the founders of modern South Australia. The family carved a pastoral empire from the colony and at the height of their fortunes controlled 14.5 million acres from this house. Today the house is administered by the National Trust, and you can inspect the Angas family portraits and memorabilia, including Dresden china, a hand-painted Louis XV cabinet, and Chippendale chairs. The veranda at the front of the house overlooks formal gardens. You can also overnight at Collingrove (☞ *below*). ⊠ *Eden Valley Rd.,* ☎ *08/8564–2061.* 🎫 *$3.* ⏱ *Oct.–June, weekdays 1–4:30, weekends 11–4:30; July–Sept., Mon.–Thurs. 1–4:30, weekends 11–4:30.*

⓫ Stephen and Prue Henschke, the wine makers of **Henschke Winery,** were named International Red Wine Makers of the Year (1994–95) at London's International Wine Challenge. Taste the magnificent Hill of Grace, a superb wine by any standards, and you will understand why Henschke is the Barossa's premium winery. Other great reds include Cyril Henschke Cabernet Sauvignon and Mount Edelstone Shiraz. Their semillon is also excellent. The winery is 4 km (2½ mi) from Keyneton on a passable dirt road. ⊠ *Valley Rd., 11 km (7 mi) south of Angaston, Keyneton,* ☎ *08/8564–8223.* ⏱ *Weekdays 9–4:30, Sat. 9–noon.*

OFF THE BEATEN PATH
BAROSSA DELIGHTS –From Henschke Winery, turn right into the dirt road and left at the second road, Gnadenberg Road, along which you will

see the **Hill of Grace** vineyard opposite the pretty 1860 **Gnadenberg Zion Church.** Turn left into Lindsay Park Road, passing the famous **Lindsay Park horse stud farm,** and return to Angaston.

Dining and Lodging

$$$$ ✕ **Vintners.** This relaxed, sophisticated restaurant combines French
★   and Asian techniques in preparing local trout, lamb, kangaroo, and homemade sausage, with seasonings that span the world from Paris to Penang. Beef cheeks on kipfler potato are served with a watercress garnish and wines that are made two minutes from the restaurant. This is the Barossa Valley at its confident best. ⊠ *Nuriootpa Rd.,* ☎ *08/8564–2488. AE, DC, MC, V. Closed Tues. No lunch Sat. or dinner Sun.*

$$ 🏠 **Collingrove.** This stately country house surrounded by undulating
★   pastures was built more than a century ago by the Angas family, one of South Australia's pioneer-era dynasties. Guests stay in the former servants' quarters at the back of the house, where large, comfortable rooms are furnished in a rustic style with antique iron bedsteads, cane chairs, and pine wardrobes. The house operates under the auspices of the National Trust and is open during the day. When it is closed, guests can look around and use the former library as a lounge. Dinner is available by prior arrangement. ⊠ *Eden Valley Rd., 5353,* ☎ FAX *08/8564–2061. 4 rooms without bath. Spa. AE, DC, MC, V.*

Shopping

Bethany Art and Craft Gallery is housed in Angaston's Old Police Station and Courthouse, an 1855 building with stone walls 20 ft thick. The former prisoners' exercise yard, now covered with translucent roofing, is used to exhibit the work of some of Australia's finest artisans. ⊠ *12 Washington St., Angaston,* ☎ *08/8564–3344.* ☉ *Daily 10–5.*

Nuriootpa

6 km (4 mi) northwest of Angaston, 74 km (46 mi) northeast of Adelaide.

Long before it was the Barossa's commercial center, Nuriootpa was used as a place of bartering by local Aboriginal tribes, hence its name: Nuriootpa means "meeting place."

⑫ **Kaesler Wines.** One of the area's boutique wineries, the cellar door (tasting room) was originally a farm stable. Century-old vines underpin the establishment's shiraz and sparkling shiraz. This remarkable little enterprise also has a restaurant and cottage accommodations. ⊠ *Barossa Valley Way,* ☎ *08/8562–2711.* ☉ *Daily 10–5.*

Marananga

⑬ *6 km (4 mi) west of Nuriootpa, 68 km (42 mi) northeast of Adelaide.*

The tiny hamlet of Marananga inhabits one of the prettiest corners of the Barossa. The original name for this area was Gnadenfrei, which means "Freed by the Grace of God"—a reference to the religious persecution the German settlers suffered under the Prussian kings before they emigrated to Australia. Marananga, the Aboriginal name, was adopted in 1918, when a wave of anti-German sentiment spurred many name changes in the closing days of World War I. The barn at the lower end of the parking lot is one of the most photogenic in the Barossa.

Marananga marks the beginning of a 3-km (2-mi) avenue of date palms planted during the depression of the 1930s as a work-creation scheme devised by the Seppelts, a wine-making family. Look for the Doric temple on the hillside to the right—it's the Seppelt family mausoleum.

⑭ The avenue of date palm trees ends at **Seppelts Winery,** one of the most magnificent in the Barossa. Joseph Seppelt was a Silesian farmer who purchased land in the Barossa after arriving in Australia in 1849. Under the control of his son, Benno, the wine-making business flourished, and today the winery and its splendid grounds are a tribute to the family's industry and enthusiasm. Fortified wine is a Seppelts specialty: This is the only winery in the world that has vintage ports for every year as far back as 1878. The sauvignon blanc, chardonnay, and cabernet are also worth tasting. Seppelts runs an excellent tour of the winery, including the carriage museum, which houses some of the finest horse-drawn vehicles in the country. ⊠ *Seppeltsfield Rd., 3 km (2 mi) south of Marananga, Seppeltsfield,* ☎ *08/8562–8028.* ☜ *Tour $3.* ☉ *Weekdays 8:30–5, Sat. 10:30–4:30, Sun. 11–4; tour weekdays at 11, 1, 2, and 3 and weekends at 11:30, 1:30, and 2:30.*

Dining and Lodging

$ ✕ **Barossa Picnic Baskets.** These baskets come stuffed with all the meat, pâté, cheese, salad, and fruit needed for a perfect lunch outdoors. Three feasts are available, including a vegetarian basket, and each comes with a bottle of wine and a map directing you to picnic spots. ⊠ *Gnadenfrei Estate,* ☎ *08/8562–2522. AE, DC, MC, V.*

$$$$ ✕▥ **The Lodge.** This rambling, aristocratic bluestone homestead was
★ built in 1903 for one of the 13 children of Joseph Seppelt, the founder of the showpiece winery across the road. Its lawns, rose garden, native woodland, and orchards of plum, peach, pear, almond, and apple trees are lovely. Inside, the house has a library, wine cellar, formal dining room, and a sitting room furnished with big, comfortable sofas. Located off a lounge room at the rear of the house, four guest bedrooms are large, luxuriously equipped, and furnished in period style. Meals make good use of local produce. Due to its quiet setting, families with children are discouraged. ⊠ *Seppeltsfield Rd., 3 km (2 mi) south of Marananga, Seppeltsfield 5355,* ☎ *08/8562–8277,* 𝔽𝔸𝕏 *08/8562–8344. 4 rooms. Restaurant, pool, tennis court. MC, V. Closed Tues. and Wed. except by appointment.*

$$$ ✕▥ **Hermitage of Marananga.** Located on a quiet back road, this hilltop inn has large, modern guest rooms furnished with a sense of style that sets them apart from standard motel accommodations. ⊠ *Seppeltsfield Rd., at Stonewell Rd., Marananga 5352,* ☎ *08/8562–2722,* 𝔽𝔸𝕏 *08/8562–3133. 10 rooms. Restaurant, pool, spa. AE, DC, MC, V.*

Shopping

Pooters Old Wares, situated in a charming corrugated-iron building, houses a fascinating treasury of handmade furniture and farm implements—much of it unearthed from the cellars of the local German community. ⊠ *Seppeltsfield Rd.,* ☎ *08/8562–2538.* ☉ *Tues.–Thurs. and weekends 11–5.*

Barossa Valley A to Z

Arriving and Departing

BY CAR

The most direct route from Adelaide to the Barossa Valley is via the town of Gawler. From Adelaide, drive north on King William Road. About 1 km (½ mi) past the Torrens River Bridge, take the right fork onto the Main North Road. After 6 km (3 mi) this road forks to the right—follow signs to the Sturt Highway and the town of Gawler. At Gawler, leave the highway and follow the signs to Lyndoch on the southern border of the Barossa. The 50-km (31-mi) journey should take about an hour. A more attractive, if circuitous, route travels through the Adelaide Hills' Chain of Ponds and Williamstown to Lyndoch.

Getting Around

BY CAR

The widespread nature of the Barossa wineries means a car is by far the best way of getting around. But remember, if you intend to taste wines at a number of vineyards, that there are stiff penalties for driving under the influence of alcohol, and random breath testing occurs throughout the state. *See* Car Rentals *in* Adelaide A to Z, *above.*

Contacts and Resources

EMERGENCIES

Police, fire, or ambulance. ☎ *000.*

GUIDED TOURS

Festival Tours (☎ 08/8374–1270) operates a full-day tour of the Barossa from Adelaide for $54, including lunch. Tours depart from 18 King William Street. **Barossa Valley Tours** (☎ 08/8562–1524) operates a six-hour coach tour of the wineries and churches of the Barossa for $30, lunch included, with pickup in Lyndoch, Tanunda, Angaston, and Nuriootpa.

VISITOR INFORMATION

Barossa Wine and Tourism Association. ✉ *66–68 Murray St., Tanunda 5352,* ☎ *08/8563–0600.*

THE CLARE VALLEY

The Clare is the "other" South Australia grape-growing valley. Smaller and less well known than the Barossa, the Clare Valley nonetheless holds its own. Its robust reds and delicate whites are among the country's finest, and the Clare is generally regarded as the best area in Australia for fragrant, flavorsome rieslings. Almost on the fringe of the vast inland deserts, the Clare is a narrow sliver of fertile soil about 30 km (19 mi) long and 5 km (3 mi) wide, with a micro-climate that makes it ideal for premium wine making.

The first vines were planted here as early as 1842, but it is only in the last decade that the Clare Valley's viticultural reputation has taken its place on the national stage. The mix of small family wineries and large-scale producers, historic settlements and grand country houses, snug valleys and dense native forest has rare charm. And beyond the northern edge of the valley, where the desert takes hold, there is the fascinating copper mining town of Burra, which makes for a natural adjunct to any Clare Valley sojourn.

Auburn

110 km (68 mi) north of Adelaide.

Auburn, the southern gateway to the Clare Valley, initially developed as an overnight halt for wagon trains carting the copper ore of Burra down to Port Wakefield. The historic buildings of the St. Vincent Street and Main North Road precinct are worth a look for their superb stonework. Auburn was the birthplace of Australian poet C. J. Dennis—the town's heritage walk includes the home in which he was born.

The **Kollektakan Memorabilia Museum** is the first in Australia dedicated to Coca-Cola products. There are three rooms filled with Coca-Cola bottles and cans, advertisements, packaging and history, plus a gift shop. ✉ *36 Main North Rd.,* ☎ *08/8849–2373.* ☞ *$2.* ☼ *Weekdays 9:30–5, weekends 9:30–5:30.*

Jeffrey Grosset established his small, highly regarded **Grosset Wines** in 1981 in an old butter factory. His wines include Polish Hill and Watervale rieslings, a late-harvest riesling, and Gaia, a blend of cabernet sauvignon, cabernet franc, and merlot grapes. The vineyard, at 1,870 ft elevation, is the highest in the Clare Valley. Tours are available by appointment. ⊠ *King St.,* ☎ *08/8849–2175.* ☉ *Sept. (until vintage is sold out), Wed.–Sun. 10–5.*

Watervale

8 km (5 mi) north of Auburn, 118 km (73 mi) north of Adelaide.

This tiny hamlet amid acres of vines is fitted with a number of heritage-listed buildings in a very pretty setting.

Crabtree of Watervale winery, perhaps uniquely among Australian wineries, welcomes children, who are encouraged to explore the property and make friends with its many animals while adults enjoy tasting the vineyard's produce. Tastings and sales are in the original cellars (1870s). The riesling is especially good, as are the shiraz and cabernet sauvignon. ⊠ *North Terr.,* ☎ *08/8843–0069.* ☉ *Daily 9–5, vineyard tour by appointment.*

The cellar buildings of historic **Quelltaler Estate** date from 1863. There is a lovely picnic area in front of the cellar. Of greatest interest is the small wine museum, which includes early wine-making equipment. Try the fruity riesling and full-flavored reds. ⊠ *Quelltaler Rd.,* ☎ *08/8843–0003.* 🎟 *Free.* ☉ *Weekdays 9–5, Sat. 11–4, Sun. noon–4.*

Sevenhill

8 km (5 mi) north of Watervale, 126 km (78 mi) north of Adelaide.

Sevenhill is the geographic center of the Clare Valley, and the location of the first winery in the region, established by Jesuit priests in 1851 to produce altar wine. The area had been settled by Austrian Jesuits three years earlier, who named their seminary after the seven hills of Rome. They also, rather optimistically, named a local creek the Tiber.

If you have the inclination or opportunity to visit only one Clare winery, make it **Sevenhill Cellars.** This was the creation of the Jesuits, and they still run the show. In the 1940s the winery branched into commercial production, which today accounts for 75% of its business. By appointment, you can receive a guided tour from the charming wine maker Brother John May (it may be the only winery tour in the world where the farewell is "God bless you"). Otherwise you are free to roam the cellars and winery. The original cellars, musty and cool even in midsummer, are reached by a stepladder. Visit St. Aloysius Church, built of stone quarried on the property, and its crypt, in which Jesuits have been interred since 1865. ⊠ *College Rd.,* ☎ *08/8843–4222.* ☉ *Weekdays 8:30–4:30, Sat. 9–4.*

Skillogalee Winery is not only known for its excellent wines—its restaurant is the Clare Valley's number-one dining experience (☞ Dining and Lodging, *below*). Wine tasting takes place in a small room of a 140-year-old cottage (the restaurant occupies the others). Try the excellent shiraz, cabernet, and riesling. ⊠ *Hughes Park Rd.,* ☎ *08/8843–4311.* ☉ *Daily 10–5.*

Jeanneret Wines is one of the youngest producers in the valley—its first sales were in 1994. Nestled in a heavily treed area on the edge of the Spring Gully Conservation Park, it is worth visiting for the setting alone. There is a charming picnic spot beneath gum trees, which is a perfect place to enjoy a newly purchased bottle of riesling or shiraz. ⊠ *Jean-neret Rd.,* ☎ *08/8843–4308.* ⊘ *Daily 11–5.*

Dining and Lodging

$–$$$ ✕ **Skillogalee Winery.** This Clare Valley darling fills the rooms of a
★ 140-year-old cottage and spills onto a beautiful veranda overlooking the vineyard. For a light meal, try the vine pruner's lunch, chef Diana Palmer's spin on the British ploughman's lunch. More substantial fare includes braised oxtail and a fragrant chicken curry. Sticky toffee pudding is a dessert favorite. ⊠ *Hughes Park Rd.,* ☎ *08/8843–4311. AE, DC, MC, V. No dinner.*

$$$$ ▨ **Thorn Park Country House.** Saved from ruin by owners David Hay
★ and Michael Speers, Thorn Park is one of Australia's finest bed-and-breakfasts. The lovely 135-year-old house is furnished with the finest antiques. A sitting room and small library are particularly charming, and the grounds, filled with hawthorns, elms, and heritage roses, are equally impressive. House guests can enjoy a superb dinner and an incredible cooked breakfast; David also runs occasional cooking schools. ⊠ *College Rd.,* ☎ *08/8843–4304. 5 rooms. Dining room, library. AE, DC, MC, V.*

Mintaro

10 km (6 mi) southeast of Sevenhill, 126 km (78 mi) north of Adelaide.

Originally a stop on the Burra–Port Wakefield copper ore route, Mintaro later became known for its enormous slate deposit, which was used internationally for pool tables and locally for building. The tiny town is beautifully preserved; its one street, lined with shops and houses, is Heritage-listed.

More grand than the cottages of Mintaro hamlet is **Martindale Hall.** This gracious manor house, which dates from 1879, was built by Edmund Bowman in an attempt to lure his fiancée to move from England to the colonies. He failed. Bowman subsequently spent his time buying property and enjoying sport and society, but his fortune dwindled because of debt and drought, and he was forced to sell the hall in 1891. Decades later, in 1965, Martindale Hall was willed to the University of Adelaide. Today it is furnished in period style and doubles as an upscale bed-and-breakfast. The building featured in director Peter Weir's first film, *Picnic at Hanging Rock.* ⊠ *Mintaro Rd.,* ☎ *08/8843–9088.* ▨ *$5.* ⊘ *Weekdays 11–4, weekends noon–4.*

Clare

20 km (12 mi) northeast of Mintaro, 136 km (84 mi) north of Adelaide.

The bustling town of Clare is the commercial center for the Clare Valley. Unusual for ultra-English South Australia, many of its early settlers were Irish. Thus we have the valley's name, after the Irish county Clare, as well as place names such as Armagh and Donnybrook.

The **Old Police Station Museum** has an interesting collection of memorabilia from Clare's early days, as well as Victorian furniture and clothing, horse-drawn vehicles, and agricultural machinery. The 1850 stone building was Clare's first courthouse and police station. ⊠ *West Terr.,* ☎ *08/8842–3656.* ▨ *$2.* ⊘ *Sat. 10–noon and 2–4, Sun. 10–noon.*

The 1895 **Wendouree Cellars** is one of the smallest wineries in the Clare, but it is also one of its most historic and, thus, is treasured. Renowned for producing big wines from very old vines—its shiraz is particularly worthy—Wendouree also makes a fine cabernet sauvignon and an exceptional cabernet malbec blend. ⊠ *Wendouree Rd.,* ☎ *08/8842–2896.* ⊙ *Mon.–Sat. 10–4:30.*

On the fringe of Clare is **Leasingham Wines,** among the biggest producers in the valley. The winery began operation in 1893, which makes it one of the oldest vineyards. The tasting room is in an attractive old still house. Leasingham's reputation of late has been forged by its red wines, particularly the peppery shiraz. ⊠ *7 Dominic St.,* ☎ *08/8842–2555.* ⊙ *Weekdays 8:30–5, weekends 10–4.*

Burra

44 km (27 mi) northeast of Clare, 156 km (97 mi) north of Adelaide.

Burra isn't strictly part of the Clare Valley, but it's an important adjunct to any visit to the Clare. Burra, like many Australian towns, developed because of mineral wealth. In this case it was copper, which for a time in the early 1850s made Burra Australia's largest inland town, and its seventh-largest settlement overall. The ore ran out quickly, however—the biggest mine closed just 32 years after it opened—and Burra settled into a comfortable existence as a service town.

The innovative **"Burra Passport"** makes touring Burra's 11-km (7-mi) Heritage Trail simple and enjoyable. The passport ($20 per car) includes a guidebook, map, and key, the latter of which gives visitors access to several historic sites along the Heritage Trail. Passport holders also receive a discount on admission at two museums. Purchase the passport at the tourist office in Market Square; open daily 9–4.

The Burra Passport key allows half-price admission to the Enginehouse Museum and access to the **Burra Mine Site.** The open cut, so-called Monster Mine contains many relics of the early days, including a powder magazine, machinery, and chimneys. ⊠ *West and Linkston Sts.,* ☎ *08/ 8892–2056.* 🎫 *Museum $3.* ⊙ *Weekdays 12:30–2:30, weekends 12:30–3:30.*

The **Bon Accord Mine** (⊠ Linkston St.), unlike the phenomenally successful Monster Mine, was a failure. However, the canny Scottish owners made the best of a bad lot by selling the mine shaft, which hit the water table, to the town as a water supply. The old mine is now an interesting museum. Admission is $3, or $1.50 with the Burra Passport.

Redruth Gaol (⊠ Tregony St.), a colonial prison that later served as a girls' reformatory, houses an informative display on its checkered history. The jail appeared in the Australian film *Breaker Morant.* The **Unicorn Brewery Cellars** (⊠ Bridge Terr.) are cool and inviting in the desert heat of a Burra summer, even though there's no longer any beer in the house. The 1873 brewery lasted for 30 years and was regarded as one of Australia's best producers.

Another Burra attraction is **Hampton,** which was built as an English mining village, with separate Cornish, Scottish, Welsh, and colonial settlements. The ruins of the village, mainly the foundations of homes, are a stark reminder of the transitory nature of colonial industry, and, in a way, of life. To get here, drive north on Tregony Street from Redruth Gaol and take the first right turn. At the T-junction, turn left into the Hampton carpark.

Malowen Lowarth is one of several dozen cottages at Paxton Square built between 1849 and 1852 as housing for miners who had moved from the creek dugouts. It is now owned by the National Trust and operates as a museum featuring period furniture and fittings. Entry is additional to the Burra passport. ⊠ *Paxton Sq.*, ☎ *08/8892–2154.* ☜ *$2.* ☉ *Sat. 1–3, Sun. 10:30–2:30, or by appointment.*

Clare Valley A to Z

Arriving and Departing

BY CAR

The Clare Valley is about a 90-minute drive from Adelaide via the Main North Road. From the center of Adelaide, head north on King William Street through the heart of North Adelaide. King William becomes O'-Connell Street. After crossing Barton Terrace, look for the Main North Road signs on the right. The road passes through the satellite town of Elizabeth, bypasses the center of Gawler, and then runs due north to Auburn, the first town of the Clare Valley when approaching from the capital. Main North Road continues down the middle of the valley to Clare. From Clare town, follow signs to Burra, on the Barrier Highway.

Getting Around

BY CAR

As with the Barossa, a car is essential for exploring the Clare Valley in any depth. Taste wine in moderation if you'll be at the wheel later; penalties are severe for drunk driving. *See* Car Rentals *in* Adelaide A to Z, *above.*

Contacts and Resources

EMERGENCIES

Police, fire, or ambulance. ☎ *000.*

VISITOR INFORMATION

Clare Valley Tourist Information Center. ⊠ *Town Hall, 229 Main North Rd., Clare,* ☎ *08/8842–2131.* ☉ *Daily 9–4.*

FLEURIEU PENINSULA

The Fleurieu has traditionally been seen as Adelaide's backyard. Generations of Adelaide families have vacationed in the string of beachside resorts between Victor Harbor and Goolwa, near the mouth of the Murray River. It is so close to Adelaide and so easy to get to that its appeal has been somewhat overlooked in the recent past. No longer. The wineries of the McLaren Vale attract connoisseurs, the beaches and bays bring in surfers, swimmers, and sun seekers, and towns like Victor Harbor are being rediscovered by new generations of tourists.

You can easily combine a day trip to the Fleurieu with one or more nights on Kangaroo Island. The ferry from Cape Jervis, at the end of the peninsula, takes one hour to reach Penneshaw on the island. During Australian holiday periods reserve space on the ferry in advance.

McLaren Vale

39 km (24 mi) south of Adelaide.

There are more than 50 wineries in and around this town. The first vines were planted at northern Reynella in 1838 by Englishman John Reynell, who had collected them en route from the Cape of Good Hope. The McLaren Vale has always been known for its big reds, shiraz notably, but in recent years more white varietals have been planted and softer reds developed.

Chapel Hill Winery is a small, somewhat exclusive vineyard, with the tasting room set in an old, hilltop chapel. Wine maker Pam Dunsford was the queen of the district's first bushing festival in 1991, a celebration of the new vintage. Wines include rich shiraz and cabernet sauvignon, as well as for memorably powerful chardonnay. ⊠ *Chapel Hill Rd.,* ☎ *08/8323–8429.* ⊙ *Weekdays 9–5, weekends 11–5.*

At **d'Arenberg Wines,** family-run since 1912, excellent wine is complemented by a fine restaurant. The splendidly named Chester d'Arenberg Osborn is the wine maker who is known for his quality whites, including a Noble Riesling (botrytis affected)—a luscious dessert wine—and a wide range of powerful reds and fortified wines. d'Arry's Verandah Restaurant overlooks the vineyards, the valley, and the sea. The menu, which changes daily, may include roasted pigeon or venison, loin of goat, deep-fried fish, or saltbush hogget. ⊠ *Osborn Rd.,* ☎ *08/8323–8206.* ⊙ *Winery daily 10–5; lunch weekends only.*

The most historic of McLaren Vale's wineries is **Seaview,** which was established in 1850. The large tasting room is particularly impressive, lined with old carved wine vats. You can look around the winery and its historic buildings, but there are no organized tours. A delicious array of whites, including fantastic sparkling wines, and a couple of reds are produced here. ⊠ *Chaffey's Rd.,* ☎ *08/8323–8250.* ⊙ *Weekdays 9–4:30, Sat. 10–5, Sun. 11–4.*

The restored cellars of **Wirra Wirra Vineyards** were built in 1894, and they couldn't be more appealing than in winter, when a roaring fire is burning. Try riesling, cabernet sauvignon, shiraz, the good-value Church Block Dry Red, and a méthode champenoise white. ⊠ *McMurtrie Rd.,* ☎ *08/8323–8414.* ⊙ *Mon.–Sat. 10–5, Sun. 11–5.*

Goolwa

44 km (27 mi) southeast of McLaren Vale, 83 km (51 mi) south of Adelaide.

Beautifully situated near the mouth of the mighty Murray River, Goolwa grew fat on the river paddle steamer trade last century. At one point it boasted 88 pubs. Today its envious position close to the sea, Lake Alexandrina, and the lovely Coorong National Park has seen tourist business replace river trade as the main source of income. South Australia's first railway line was built to Port Elliott, Goolwa's sea port in 1854.

Signal Point is an excellent interpretive center on Goolwa Wharf that uses audiovisual techniques to tell stories of the indigenous Ngarrindjeri people and the river trade. Other displays include artifacts, charts, paintings, and models. ⊠ *Goolwa Wharf,* ☎ *08/8555–3488.* ⊠ *$5.* ⊙ *Daily 10–5.*

Goolwa Wharf is the launch for daily cruises on the **PS** *Mundoo,* a replica paddle steamer that makes half- and full-day trips to Currency Creek, Narnu Bay, the Mundoo Channel, and Goose and Goat Islands. The **MV** *Aroona* cruises past the Murray mouth to the wild Coorong Peninsula, where you can step ashore and cross to the ocean. The *Coorong Pirate,* a replica pirate ship, has 45-minute cruises around the mouth of the Murray River, while the *Coorong Explorer,* a modern, shallow-draft boat, has an all-day cruise to Coorong National Park, with lunch and morning and afternoon teas included in the price. ⊠ *Goolwa Wharf,* ☎ *08/8555–3488.* ⊠ *PS Mundoo cruise $15, with lunch $30; MV Aroona cruise $18, with lunch $28; MV Aroona pelican-feeding cruise $12; Coorong Pirate cruise $6; Coorong Explorer cruise $59.*

Coorong National Park, a sliver of land stretching southeast of the Fleurieu Peninsula and completely separate from it, hugs the South Australian coast for more than 150 km (93 mi). Most Australians became aware of the Coorong's beauty from the 1970s film *Storm Boy,* which told the story of a boy's friendship with a pelican. These curious birds are one reason why the Coorong is a wetland area of world standing. Even if you aren't interested in birdlife the Coorong's beaches and dunes have plenty of appeal: The area was also a major habitation for Aborigines, and shell middens give abundant evidence of their life here. The mainland side of the park, which you would reach driving straight from Adelaide, is off of Princes Highway south of the fishing town of Meningie.

Victor Harbor

16 km (10 mi) west of Goolwa, 83 km (51 mi) south of Adelaide.

In some ways, Victor Harbor has come full circle. In the 1830s the town was a major whaling center, from which whalers set out to hunt the southern right whale. The species was so named because it was considered the "right" whale to kill—it was slow, easy to target, and its flesh had a high oil content that caused the whale to float after being harpooned. The leviathans came to Encounter Bay, named for the meeting here in 1802 of English and French explorers Matthew Flinders and Nicholas Baudin, to breed in the winter and early spring. Their great numbers made whaling a profitable trade, but the last whale was killed in the bay in 1878. Within that 50-year period the southern right was nearly hunted to extinction. Now the majestic creatures are back— as many as 40 at a time—and Victor Harbor is again capitalizing on their presence.

The **South Australian Whale Center** tells the often graphic story of the whaling industry along the SA coast, particularly in Encounter Bay. The interpretive displays are excellent, spread over three floors, and deal with dolphins, seals, and penguins—all of which can be seen in these waters—as well as whales. In whale-watching season (June–September), the center has information on sightings. ⊠ *Railway Terr.,* ☎ *08/8552–5644.* ☎ *$6.* ☉ *Daily 9–5.*

Visit the **Bluff,** a few kilometers west of Victor Harbor, to see where whalers once stood lookout for their prey. Today the granite outcrop, also known as Rosetta Head, serves the same purpose in very difference circumstances. To enjoy views from the Bluff, it's a steep climb to the top.

Granite Island is linked to the mainland by a causeway, along which a double-decker tram pulled by Clydesdale horses trundles. The large, native colony of fairy penguins is best seen at dusk. You can walk to the summit of the island, or take a chairlift if you're flagging. ☎ *08/8552–1777.* ☎ *Return tram trip $3, including chairlift.*

The steam-powered **Cockle Train** travels the original route of South Australia's first railway line on its journey to Goolwa. Extended from Port Elliot to Victor Harbor in 1864, the line traces the lovely Southern Ocean beaches on its 16 km (10 mi) route. The train runs over Easter, during school holidays, and on selected Sundays. ⊠ *Railway Terr.,* ☎ *08/8391–1223.* ☎ *Round-trip fare $12.*

Head to **Urimbirra Wildlife Park** if you feel like gawking at a menagerie of native Ozzie animals and birds, more than 70 species in all. Among the collection at this open-range zoo are kangaroos, saltwater and freshwater crocodiles, Cape Barren Geese, and pelicans, which you can see in the wild in Coorong National Park to the south. ⊠ *Adelaide Rd.,* ☎ *08/8554–6554.* ☎ *$6.50.* ☉ *Daily 9–6.*

Fleurieu Peninsula A to Z

Arriving and Departing

BY CAR

The Fleurieu is an easy drive south from Adelaide; McLaren Vale itself is little more than an hour away. Leave central Adelaide along South Terrace or West Terrace, linking with the Anzac Highway, which heads toward Glenelg. At the intersection with the Main South Road, turn left. This road will take you almost to McLaren Vale. After a detour to visit the wineries, watch for signs for Victor Harbor Road. About 20 km (12 mi) south, the highway splits, one road heads for Victor Harbor, the other for Goolwa. Those two places are connected by a major road that follows the coastline. Drivers heading to Cape Jervis and the Kangaroo Island ferry should stay on Main South Road.

Getting Around

BY CAR

A car is the best means to visit the Fleurieu Peninsula, especially if you wish to visit any wineries, which are not served by public transport. *See* Car Rentals *in* Adelaide A to Z, *above.*

Contacts and Resources

EMERGENCIES

Police, fire, or ambulance. ☎ *000.*

VISITOR INFORMATION

Goolwa Tourist Information Center. ✉ *Old Library Bldg., Cadell St. and Goolwa Terr.,* ☎ *08/8555–1144.* ☉ *Daily 10–4.*

Victor Harbor Tourist Information Center. ✉ *10 Railway Terr.,* ☎ *08/ 8552–4255.* ☉ *Daily 10–4.*

KANGAROO ISLAND

Kangaroo Island, Australia's third-largest island, is barely 16 km (10 mi) from the Australian mainland. Yet the island belongs to another age—a folksy, friendly, less sophisticated time when you'd leave your car unlocked and wave to other drivers as they passed.

The island's interior is stark and barren for the most part, but the coastline is sculpted into a series of bays and inlets teeming with bird and marine life. In fact, wildlife is probably the island's greatest attraction. In a single day you can stroll along a beach crowded with sea lions and watch kangaroos, koalas, pelicans, sea eagles, and fairy penguins in their native environment.

At the beginning of the 19th century Kangaroo Island was a haven for escaped convicts and sailors who had deserted their whaling ships, some of them from North American ports. These castaways preyed on the coastal Aborigines and made a living from trading sealskin. Eventually their raids became too bold, and the colonial government sent an armed expedition to the island in 1827. Most of the renegades were dragged away to Sydney in chains, and the island was left with a population of less than a dozen.

Many people treasure Kangaroo Island for what it lacks. Although it's just a two- to three-hour trip from Adelaide, there are no resorts and virtually no nightlife, and its only luxuries are salty sea breezes, sparkling clear water, and solitude.

Exploring Kangaroo Island

The towns and most of the accommodations are located in the eastern third of the island. The most interesting sights are on the southern coast, so it's advisable to tour the island in a clockwise direction, leaving the beaches of the north coast for later in the day. You can take in a fair amount in a single day, but allow three days at least to truly explore the island. Except in the main towns, gas stations and shops are scarce. Before heading out for the day, you should have a full tank of gas and a picnic lunch. Many of the roads are loose gravel, so take care when driving.

At the start of your journey, it is advisable to purchase a national parks **Island Pass** ($15), available from any national park ranger station or from the **Department of Environment and Natural Resources office** (✉ 27 Dauncey St., Kingscote 5223, ☎ 08/8552–2381). The pass covers all national park entry fees, vehicle fees, ranger-guided tours, and camping fees for 14 nights, and it is valid from July 1 to June 30 of the following year.

Kingscote

121 km (75 mi) southwest of Adelaide.

Ferries from Port Adelaide and Glenelg arrive in Kingscote, the largest town on Kangaroo Island. It has a more substantial character than its sister towns Penneshaw and American River. Reeves Point, at the northern end of town, marks the beginning of South Australia's colonial history. Settlers landed here in 1836 and established the first official town in the new colony, but you'll have to use your imagination to appreciate this. Little remains of the original settlement, which was abandoned barely three years after it began, due to poor soil and a lack of fresh water. The town comes alive in mid-February for a weekend of horse races.

☙ Throughout January, rangers from the **Department of Environment and Natural Resources** run an extensive activities program designed to introduce children to the nature and history of the island. Events include lighthouse tours, tidal-pool walks, and evenings on the beach to watch fairy penguins waddle ashore. ✉ *27 Dauncey St., Kingscote, ☎ 08/8552–2381.*

Dining and Lodging

$$ ✕ **Cygnet Cafe.** Kangaroo Island's first-quality dining experience is a classy café transformed from a former gas station. The cuisine, which draws its influences from such places as Asia and North Africa, is as innovative as the interior design with its dazzling use of color. The menu changes fortnightly, but you will always find spicy Malay chicken curry and wonderful, rich, brandy chocolate prune cake on the list. Local products are used extensively: Kangaroo Island cream, sheep's milk yogurt, mutton, turkey, and corn-fed chicken. ✉ *Playford Hwy., Cygnet River, 13 km (8 mi) west of Kingscote, ☎ 08/8553–9187. AE, DC, MC, V. No dinner Mon. or Tues.*

$$$$ ☷ **Correa Corner.** In rambling native gardens on the shores of Nepean Bay, and named after an indigenous plant, this luxurious bed-and-breakfast makes an ideal base for exploring the island. You can enjoy the company of the wallabies in the garden, but not the pitter-patter of little feet; children under 16 are not welcome. ✉ *The Parade and 2nd St., Brownlow 5223, 2 km (1 mi) from Kingscote, ☎ 08/8553–2498, FAX 08/8553–2355. 3 rooms. No credit cards.*

$$$ ⊞ **Sorrento Resort.** Overlooking a beach that is home to a colony of fairy penguins, Sorrento offers motel rooms and one-, two-, or three-bedroom units with their own cooking facilities. Village rooms are less expensive and are not serviced daily, but they have a garden setting that is preferable to the neat, clean, but rather charmless motel rooms. ⊠ *North Terr. (Box 352), Penneshaw 5222, 59 km (37 mi) east of Kingscote,* ☎ *08/8553–1028,* ℻ *08/8553–1024. 18 rooms, 9 apartments. Restaurant, bar, pool, sauna, spa, tennis court. AE, DC, MC, V.*

$$ ⊞ **Wanderers Rest.** This country inn with 19th-century colonial charm is nestled among native trees on an American River hillside. The size, furnishings, and stylish decor of the motel rooms make this one of the best bargains on the island. ⊠ *Box 34, Bayview Rd., American River 5221, 39 km (24 mi) west of Kingscote,* ☎ *08/8553–3140,* ℻ *08/8553–3282. 8 rooms. Restaurant, bar, pool, spa. AE, DC, MC, V.*

$ ⊞ **The Kings.** A sense of style and the natural beauty of American River characterize this boutique bed-and-breakfast. Facilities include a heated swimming pool. For something different, try the American River whiting for breakfast in the conservatory dining room. ⊠ *Bayview Rd. (Box 33), American River 5221, 39 km (24 mi) west of Kingscote,* ☎ *08/ 8553–7003. Pool. No credit cards.*

Seal Bay Conservation Park

60 km (37 mi) southwest of Kingscote via the Playford Hwy.

The sea lion colony at Seal Bay Conservation Park is one of the most accessible anywhere—and the sight of these animals lazing on the beach, suckling their young, and bodysurfing in the waves is the highlight of any trip to Kangaroo Island. Australian sea lions, which recover here from their long and strenuous fishing trips, allow humans to approach within about 15 ft. The colony numbers approximately 500; about 100 sea lions can usually be found on the beach, except on stormy days, when they take shelter in the sand dunes. You can visit the beach only in a tour party led by a park ranger, but apart from the busy summer holiday period, you are usually allowed to wander freely—albeit under the watchful eye of the ranger. The slope from the ranger station to the beach is moderately steep. ⊠ *Seal Bay,* ☎ *08/8552–8233.* ▦ *Tour $7.50.* ☉ *Tour Dec.–Jan., daily every 15–30 min 9–4:30; Feb.–Nov., daily every 45 min 9–4:30.*

Little Sahara

7 km (4½) west of Seal Bay Conservation Park, 67 km (42 mi) southwest of Kingscote.

Towering white-sand dunes cover several square miles here, and a short walk is hard to resist. To get here from Seal Bay Road, turn left onto the South Coast Highway and continue until just before a one-lane bridge. Turn left onto the rough track that leads to Little Sahara.

Vivonne Bay

60 km (37 mi) southwest of Kingscote, 181 km (112 mi) southwest of Adelaide.

There isn't much here besides a jetty, a few crayfish boats, and a beach that disappears into the distance, but if you continue to **Point Ellen,** views of the bay and Vivonne Bay Conservation Park are superb.

Hanson Bay

20 km (12 mi) west of Vivonne Bay, 80 km (50 mi) southwest of Kingscote.

A narrow, winding road ends at Hanson Bay, a perfect little sandy cove. The gentle slope of the beach and the rocky headlands on either side provide safe swimming. On the far side of the headland to the east are several secluded beaches, although these are more exposed and riptides make swimming dangerous. You can catch salmon from these beaches. The limestone caves of Kelly Hill are also nearby.

Lodging

$$ ⚏ **Hanson Bay Cabins.** These neat, self-contained log cabins are set in coastal heath near Flinders Chase National Park, one of the most isolated spots on the island. A pristine white-sand beach, where swimming is safe for children, is 50 yards away. ⊠ *10 McKenna St., Hanson Bay, Kensington Park 5068,* ☎ *08/8353–2603,* ℻ *08/8553–2673. Six 2-bedroom cabins. No credit cards.*

Fishing

Fishing is excellent on the island's beaches, bays, and rivers. Crayfish can be caught from the rocks, sea salmon and mullet from the beaches, and bream in the rivers. The island's deep-sea fishing fleet holds several world records for tuna. No permit is required, although restrictions do apply to the size and quantity of fish you can keep. Rent boats and fishing tackle from the **Tacklebox Boat Hire** (⊠ American River Wharf, ☎ 08/8553–3150).

Flinders Chase National Park

80 km (50 mi) west of Kingscote, 200 km (124 mi) southwest of Adelaide.

Some of the most beautiful coastal scenery in Australia is on the western end of Kangaroo Island at Flinders Chase National Park. The rest of the island is widely cultivated and grazed, but the park has maintained much of its original vegetation since it was declared a national treasure in 1919.

The seas crashing onto the southern coast of Australia are merciless, and their effects are visible in the oddly shaped rocks off the coast of Kangaroo Island. For instance, a limestone promontory was carved from underneath at Cape du Couedic on the island's southwestern shore, producing what is now known as **Admiral's Arch.** About 4 km (2½ mi) east along the coast are **Remarkable Rocks,** huge boulders balanced precariously on the promontory of Kirkpatrick Point.

Starting in the 1920s, animals from the mainland were introduced to the island. Today a large population of koalas and Cape Barren geese live in the park. Much of the wildlife is so tame that a barricade had to be constructed at the Rocky River Campground to keep humans in and kangaroos and geese out.

Flinders Chase has several 3- to 7-km (2- to 4-mi) **walking trails,** which take one–three hours to complete. The trails meander along the rivers to the coast, passing mallee scrub and sugar gum forests. The 3-km (2-mi) Rocky River Walking Trail leads to a powerful waterfall before ending on a quiet sandy beach.

The park is on the western end of the island, bounded by the Playford and West End highways.

Lodging

All accommodations within the national park are controlled by the Department of Environment and Natural Resources (☞ Visitor Information, *below*). Camping is allowed only at designated sites for $2 per tent site at Rocky River and at bush campground, plus $2 for each adult and $1 for each child. Cottages are simply but comfortably furnished with rustic sofas, chairs, and tables. Except for Hartley Hut, all have cooking facilities. Prices listed below apply per adult, per night.

🏠 **Old Homestead and Mays Cottage.** Built by the Mays family for their family and their mailman, these can be rented on a nightly basis. The Homestead, which sleeps six, rents for $25 a night. Mays Cottage, which sleeps four, rents for $10.

🏠 **Karatta, Parndana and Troubridge Cottages.** Located at Cape du Couedic, 20 km (12 mi) from the Rocky River Headquarters, each sleeps six and costs $27.40.

🏠 **Flinders Light Cottage.** The lodge at Cape Borda sleeps six and rents for $25.

🏠 **Hartley Hut.** This hut at Cape Borda sleeps four and rents for $15.

🏠 **Seymour and Thomas Cottages.** These lighthouse cottages at Cape Willoughby sleep 8 and rent for $25.

Visitor Information

Department of Environment and Natural Resources. ⊠ *27 Dauncey St., Kingscote 5223,* ☎ *08/8552–2381.*

Snellings Beach

50 km (31 mi) west of Kingscote.

Surrounded by high, rolling pastures, Snellings is broad and sandy, one of the best beaches on the island. Swimming is safe, but there are no facilities. ⊠ *N. Coast Rd.*

Kangaroo Island A to Z

Arriving and Departing

BY CAR FERRY

Vehicular ferries allow access for cars through either Kingscote or Penneshaw. The most popular option is the ferry from Cape Jervis at the tip of the Fleurieu Peninsula, a 90-minute drive from Adelaide.

The **MV *Philanderer III* and MV *Island Navigator*** (☎ 13–1301) make the one-hour crossing between Cape Jervis and Penneshaw. There are three sailings per day between March and December, and up to 10 per day in summer months. These ferries are by far the most popular means of transport between the island and the mainland, and reservations are advisable during the summer holidays. The one-way crossing costs $60 per vehicle, $30 per person. The **MV *Island Seaway*** (☎ 08/8447–5577), another ferry, makes the seven-hour journey between Port Adelaide and Kingscote. The fare is $62 per vehicle, and $25.50 for each adult.

BY PASSENGER FERRY

Fast Ferries (☎ 08/295–2688) operates daily cruiser trips from Glenelg (accessible from Adelaide by tram) to Kingscote, taking just over two hours. The one-way fare is $43, return is $86.

BY PLANE

Kendell Airlines flies daily between Adelaide and Kingscote, the island's main airport. The return fare is $140. Ask about the availability of 14-

day advance purchase fares, which cost $110 return. Flights to the island take about 40 minutes. *See* Air Travel *in* Smart Travel Tips for airline telephone numbers.

Getting Around

Apart from a bus service that connects Kingscote, American River, and Penneshaw, there is no public transport on the island. The main attractions are widely scattered and the most practical way to see them is either on a guided tour or by car.

Contacts and Resources

CAR RENTALS

Budget Rent-a-Car. ⊠ *76 Dauncey St., Kingscote 5223,* ☎ *08/8552–3133.*

GUIDED TOURS

Adventure Charters of Kangaroo Island (☎ 08/8552–9119, FAX 08/8552–9122) offers island tours ranging from one to three days, as well as a three-day trip that combines walking and four-wheel-driving. Sea fishing, cliff climbing, kayaking, and diving tours can also be arranged. **Australian Odysseys** (⊠ Box 494, Penneshaw 5222, ☎ 08/8553–1294) operates four-wheel-drive tours. **The Island Travel Centre** (⊠ 27 Gresham St., Adelaide 5000, ☎ 08/8212–4550) is an Adelaide travel agent specializing in tours and transport to Kangaroo Island as well as accommodations there. **Kangaroo Island Sealink** (⊠ Box 570, Penneshaw 5222, ☎ 13–1301 or 08/8552–2274) operates a one-day coach tour of the island in conjunction with the ferry service from Cape Jervis. It costs $135.

Kendell Airlines (☞ Arriving and Departing, *above*) also packages its air services in conjunction with the tours offered by various travel operators on the island. Choices include a standard one-day island bus tour or a four-wheel-drive tour with the emphasis on adventure. The coach tour costs $69, the four-wheel-drive tour $160. Airfare is additional. You can also construct individual itineraries.

VISITOR INFORMATION

Dudley Council Office. ⊠ *Middle Terr., Penneshaw 5222,* ☎ *08/8553–1011.*

THE MURRAY RIVER

The "Mighty Murray" is the longest river in Australia and among the longest rivers on the planet. From its source in the Snowy Mountains of New South Wales, it travels some 2,415 km (1,500 mi) through 11 locks before it enters the ocean southeast of Adelaide. As European pioneers settled the interior, the river became a major artery for their cargoes of wool and livestock. During the second half of the 19th century, the river reverberated with the churning wheels and shrieking whistles of paddle steamers. This colorful period ended when railways shrank the continent at the turn of the century, easing the difficulty of overland transport and reducing dependence on the river. Today the Murray is a sporting paradise for water-skiers, boaters, and anglers.

The Murray's role as an industrial waterway may be over, but it remains a vital part of the economy and life of South Australia. It provides water for the vast irrigation schemes that have turned the desert into a fruit bowl, and it supplies Adelaide with its domestic water. The Riverland region is one of the country's largest producers of citrus fruits and supplies more than 40% of the nation's wine—although the quality of Riverland wine doesn't compare with the wine of the Barossa.

In spite of what the railroads did to river traffic, or perhaps because of it, the only way to see the river properly is to spend a few days on a boat. At this stretch of the Murray, a car is a less efficient and less appealing way to travel through the countryside. A trip down the broad brown river is still an adventure; the history of the little towns on its banks, along with river culture and its importance to South Australia, merits some study. Most rewarding, however, is the area's natural beauty. Couched within high ocher cliffs, the Murray is home to river red gums, still lagoons, and abundant bird life.

There are two ways to take a trip up or down river. You can either ride on a riverboat and let someone else do the driving and the cooking, or choose to pilot a houseboat yourself. *See* Murray River A to Z, *below,* for information on both options.

Renmark

256 km (159 mi) east of Adelaide.

Heading upstream from Renmark toward Wentworth in Victoria, the Murray River is at its tranquil best, gliding between tall cliffs and spilling out across broad lakes filled with bird life. No towns lie along this section of the river, so this is the route to take for peace and quiet. Downstream from Renmark the river is more populated, although only during peak summer periods does the Murray become even remotely crowded.

On a willow-lined bend in the river, Renmark is a busy town, one of the most important on the Murray—a center for the fruit industry, the mainstay of the Riverland region. Fruit growing began here in 1887, when the Canadian Chaffey brothers were granted 250,000 acres to test their irrigation plan. One of the original wood-burning water pumps they devised can still be seen on Renmark Avenue.

Olivewood, the original homestead of Charles Chaffey, is run by the National Trust and is open to visitors. ⊠ *21st St.,* ☎ *08/8586–6175.* ☑ *$3.50.* ☉ *Thurs.–Mon. 10–4.*

Dining is less than spectacular in Renmark. However, the **Renmark Golf and Country Club Restaurant** and the buffet dinners at the **Renmark Club** have decent fare.

Berri

52 km (32 mi) downstream from Renmark, 236 km (146 mi) northeast of Adelaide.

Berri was once a refueling station for the river steamers and today is the economic heart of the Riverland. Wine production is the major industry—the town's Berri Estates is one of the largest single wineries in the southern hemisphere.

For anyone who wants to see what the Riverland is all about, the **Berrivale Orchards** showroom has a 15-minute video on various stages of the fruit-growing process. ⊠ *Sturt Hwy.,* ☎ *08/8582–1455.* ☉ *Weekdays 8:30–4:30, Sat. 9–noon.*

The **Riverland Display Centre** has an exhibition of classic cars and motorcycles. ⊠ *Sturt Hwy.,* ☎ *08/8582–2325.* ☑ *$2.* ☉ *Daily 10–4.*

Loxton

43 km (27 mi) downstream from Berri, 255 km (158 mi) east of Adelaide.

Loxton is a hard-working town, one of the most attractive on the river, surrounded by orchards and the vineyards of the Penfold Winery, one of Australia's premier producers.

In Loxton's **historical village,** many of the town's 19th-century buildings have been reconstructed beside the river. ✉ *East Terr.,* ☎ *08/8584–7194.* ⊠ *$5.* ☉ *Weekdays 10–4, weekends 10–5.*

In East Terrace, the **Loxton Hotel-Motel** serves reasonable counter meals, and the **Loxton Palace** is a standard Chinese restaurant.

Waikerie

120 km (74 mi) downstream of Loxton, 177 km (110 mi) northeast of Adelaide.

The teeming bird life in this part of the river gave the town of Waikerie its name—the Aboriginal word means "many wings." Surrounded by irrigated citrus orchards and vineyards overlooking the river red gums and cliffs of the far bank, the town is also a center for airplane gliding.

Waikerie International Soaring Centre's scenic flights in light aircraft are a great way to see the river and the rich farmland along its banks. ✉ *Box 320, Sturt Hwy., 5330,* ☎ *08/8541–2644.* ⊠ *20-min flight $45.*

En Route Cruising downstream between Waikerie and Swan Reach you approach the tiny settlement of **Morgan.** When you round the bend in the river and catch a glimpse of this sleepy little backwater, it's hard to believe that it was once the state's second-busiest port. In Morgan's heyday at the end of the last century, freight from the upper reaches of the Murray was unloaded here and sent by train to Port Adelaide. The demise of river traffic put an end to its prosperity. Fortunately the towering wharves, railway station, and the shops and hotels along Railway Terrace have been preserved largely in their original state.

Swan Reach, not surprisingly named for its bird population, lies 51 km (32 mi) downstream from Morgan. This quiet town overlooks some of the prettiest scenery on the Murray. Below town, the river makes a huge curve—known as the Big Bend—before flowing onward.

Mannum

195 km (121 mi) downstream from Waikerie, 84 km (52 mi) east of Adelaide.

Murray River paddle steamers had their origins in Mannum when the first riverboat, the *Mary Ann,* was launched in 1853. The town has a number of reminders of its past, including the paddle steamer **Marion,** now a floating museum. ✉ *William Randell's Wharf.* ⊠ *$2.* ☉ *Daily 10–4.*

Mannum Club, on Randell Street, has river views from its dining room; **Captain Randell's Restaurant** has a fine position on the wharf overlooking the river and the ferry traffic.

Murray Bridge

35 km (22 mi) downstream from Mannum, 78 km (48 mi) east of Adelaide.

Murray Bridge is the largest town on the South Australian section of the river, and its proximity to Adelaide makes it a popular spot for fishing, waterskiing, and picnicking. Crowds get heavy on weekends.

Dining alternatives are reasonably extensive in Murray Bridge. The **Amorosa** in Bridge Street serves good Italian food. The **Oriental Garden,** in Adelaide Road, and the **Happy Gathering,** in First Street, are the town's Chinese offerings.

Murray River A to Z

Arriving and Departing

BY BUS

Stateliner Coaches (⊠ 111 Franklin St., Adelaide, ☎ 08/8415–5555) operates a daily service between Adelaide and the towns of Berri and Renmark. The one-way fare from Adelaide to Renmark–Berri is $28. The trip takes 3½ hours to Berri, 4 to Renmark.

BY CAR

Leave Adelaide by Main North Road and follow signs to the Sturt Highway and the town of Gawler. This highway continues east to Renmark. Allow 3½ hours for the 295-km (183-mi) trip to Renmark.

Getting Around

BY BOAT

Cruise vacations on the river are available aboard large riverboats or in rented houseboats. The latter sleep 4–10 people and range in quality from basic to luxurious.

BY CAR

Although the Sturt Highway crosses the river several times between Waikerie and Renmark, and smaller roads link more isolated towns along the river, the most impressive sections of the Murray can be seen only from the water. If you've rented a car, drive to Mannum, Berri, or Renmark and hook up with a river cruise or rent a houseboat to drive yourself along the river.

Contacts and Resources

BOAT RENTALS

During peak summer holiday season, a deluxe eight-berth houseboat costs about $1,200 per week, and a four-berth boat starts at around $540. Off-peak prices drop by as much as 20%. Water and power for lights and cooking are carried on board. No previous boating experience is necessary—the only requirement is a driver's license.

Houseboats are supplied with basic safety equipment, such as life preservers, with which you should familiarize yourself before departure. Treat your houseboat as your home, and safeguard personal effects by locking all doors and windows before going out.

Liba-Liba has a fleet of 30 houseboats for rent and is based in both Renmark and Wentworth, at the junction of the Murray and Darling rivers in southwestern New South Wales. ⊠ *Jane Eliza Landing, Box 805, Renmark 5341,* ☎ *1800/81–0252.*

Swan Houseboats are among the most comfortable, well-equipped, and luxurious accommodations on the river. ⊠ *Box 345, Murray River, Berri 5343,* ☎ *1800/08–3183.*

GUIDED TOURS

PS *Murray Princess* is a copy of a Mississippi River paddle wheeler that makes five-day and weekend cruises from Mannum. All cabins are air-conditioned and include en suite bathrooms. Passengers have access to a spa and sauna. For reservations, contact Captain Cook Cruises. ⊠ *96 Randell St., Mannum 5238,* ☎ *1800/80–4843 or 08/8569–2511.*

Proud Mary offers two- to five-night cruises upstream from Murray
Bridge, which is only a 45-minute drive from Adelaide. You travel in
comfortable, air-conditioned cabins. The cost is from $550 per person
on a twin-share basis. For reservations, contact Proud Australia Holidays. ⊠ *23 Leigh St., Level 2, Adelaide 5000,* ☎ *08/8231–9472.*

VISITOR INFORMATION
Berri Tourist and Travel Centre. ⊠ *24 Vaughan Terr.,* ☎ *08/8582–1655.*
☉ *Weekdays 9–5, Sat. 9–noon.*

Renmark Information Centre. ⊠ *Murray Ave.,* ☎ *08/8586–6703.* ☉
Weekdays 9–5, Sat. 9–4, Sun. noon–4.

THE OUTBACK

South Australia is the country's driest state, and its Outback is a largely
featureless expanse of desert, the only vegetation being scrubby salt-
bush and hardy eucalyptus trees holding on in the normally dried-up
water courses. The landscape is marked by geological uplifts, abrupt
transitions between plateaus broken at the edges of ancient, long-in-
active fault lines. These uplifts are all the more dramatic for their un-
expectedness when you come across them. Few roads track through
this desert wilderness—the main highway is the Stuart, which runs all
the way to Alice Springs in the Northern Territory.

The people of the Outback are as hardy as the terrain. They are also
often eccentric, colorful characters who will happily bend a visitor's
ear over a drink in the local pub. These remote, isolated communities
attract loners, adventurers, fortune-seekers, and people simply on the
run. In this unyielding country of big sky and vast distances, you must
be tough to survive.

Coober Pedy

850 km (527 mi) northwest of Adelaide.

Known as much for the troglodytic lifestyle of its inhabitants—all
2,500 of them, most of whom live underground in dugouts gouged into
the hills—as for its opal riches, Coober Pedy is arguably Australia's
most singular place. The town is ringed by mullock heaps, pyramidal
piles of rock and sand left over after mining shafts are dug. Opals are
Coober Pedy's reason for existence; this is the world's richest opal field.

Opal was discovered here in 1915, and miners returning from World War
I introduced the first dugout homes when they were forced underground
by the searing heat. In midsummer, temperatures can reach 48°C (118°F),
but inside the dugouts the air remains a constant 22°–24°C (72°–75°F).
Australia has 95% of the world's opal deposits, and Coober Pedy has
the bulk of that wealth. Mining is controlled so that small operators,
not large conglomerates, do the digging and discover the riches.

Big finds are big news, but it is not only licensed miners who strike it
rich—dugout home extension has been particularly popular since one
local found a $40,000 seam of opal while hacking out a new room.
Working mines are off-limits to visitors, although if you befriend a miner
in the pub chances are you'll be invited for an off-the-record tour.

Coober Pedy is a brick and corrugated-iron settlement propped un-
ceremoniously on a scarred desert landscape. It is not pretty in any conventional sense; it's a town built for efficiency, not beauty. However,
its ugliness has a kind of bizarre appeal.

Keep in mind that this is a "macho" town, and single women are generally advised to use common sense in dealings with men in the Outback.

Exploring

Noodling—fossicking (rummaging) for opal gemstones—is encouraged and requires no permit, provided you are not on a pegged claim and use no digging devices. However, care must be taken, as disused shafts are unmarked and not filled in. The Jeweler's Shop mining area on the edge of town is the most popular area for noodling. Don't expect to make your fortune there, however.

Although most of Coober Pedy's underground devotions are decidedly secular in nature, the town does have five underground churches. **St. Peter and St. Paul's** Catholic Church is a heritage-listed building, and the **Catacomb** Anglican Church is notable for its altar fashioned from a windlass (a winch) and lectern made from a log of mulga wood. The newest church, the **Serbian Orthodox,** is perhaps the most striking, with its scalloped ceiling, rock-carved icons, and brilliant stained-glass windows.

Aboriginal-owned **Umoona Opal Mine and Museum** is an enormous underground complex with a mine and display home as well as opal sales and souvenirs. ⊠ *Hutchinson St.,* ☎ *08/8672–5288.* ✑ *Free, mine tour $5.* ⊘ *Daily 8–7; mine tour daily at 10, noon, 2, and 4.*

The **Old Timers Mine** is an original opal mine turned into a museum. Two underground houses, furnished in 1920s and 1980s styles, are part of the complex, which exhibits mining equipment and memorabilia in a network of hand-dug tunnels and shafts. ⊠ *Crowders Gully,* ☎ *08/ 8672–5555.* ✑ *$5.* ⊘ *Daily 9–5.*

Outside of Town

Breakaways. This striking series of rock formations, known locally as the Moon Plain, is reminiscent of the American West, with its buttes and jagged hills. There are fossils and patches of petrified forest in this strange landscape, which has appealed to filmmakers of apocalyptic films. *Mad Max 3—Beyond Thunderdome* was filmed around here, as was *Ground Zero,* the Australian film about the dawn of the nuclear age. The scenery is especially evocative early in the morning. The Breakaways area is 30 km (19 mi) northeast of Coober Pedy.

Dog Fence. An extraordinary measure designed to protect the valuable sheep-grazing land to the south from marauding dingoes, this fence runs 5,600 km (3,500 mi)—9,600 km (6,000 mi) by some people's reckoning—from far away Queensland. It is a simple wire fence, and its arrow-straight run across this barren country gives it a sad, lonely grandeur. You'll find it in the Breakaways area, 30 km (19 mi) northeast of Coober Pedy.

Dining and Lodging

$$ ✕ **Umberto's.** Perched atop the monolithic Desert Cave Hotel, this restaurant oddly fails to take advantage of its prime position—there are no views from the tables—but the food compensates. Try kangaroo fillet with a port wine and red currant glaze, or crocodile fried in tempura batter with a light honey, soy, and ginger dipping sauce. It's uncommonly good food for an Outback town. ⊠ *Desert Cave Hotel, Hutchinson St.,* ☎ *08/8672–5688. AE, DC, MC, V.*

$ ✕ **Last Resort Café.** This is the place for great cakes, ice cream, and wonderful breakfasts—the "hangover" breakfast is highly recommended by locals in the know. The ambience is friendly and casual. ⊠ *Post Office Hill Rd.,* ☎ *08/8672–5072. AE, DC, MC, V. No dinner.*

$ ✕ **Old Miner's Dugout Café.** Run by an American ex-pat, the café is renowned for its kangaroo with potato and salad, and Anne's Ambrosia chocolate cake. Most dishes are home-style productions. ⊠ *Hutchinson St.,* ☏ *08/8672–5541. AE, MC, V. Closed Sun. No lunch.*

$$$ ⊞ **Desert Cave Hotel.** Most visitors to Coober Pedy want the chance to live underground, so here's your opportunity. Nineteen spacious and well-appointed subsurface rooms have red striated rock walls. There is no natural light, so the rooms may be a little dark for some tastes, while others may find the atmosphere claustrophobic. Aboveground rooms are also available. ⊠ *Hutchinson St., 5723,* ☏ *08/8672–5688,* 𝖥𝖠𝖷 *08/8672–5198. 50 rooms. Restaurant, pool, shops. AE, DC, MC, V.*

$$ ⊞ **Coober Pedy Opal Fields Motel.** No underground rooms here, but another form of construction uses nature for insulation. Rammed earth is the building method, and the decor of the guest rooms carries through the earthy feel using desert colors. Two-bedroom apartments are available, complete with cooking facilities. ⊠ *St. Nicholas St., 5723,* ☏ *086/72–3003,* 𝖥𝖠𝖷 *08/8672–3004. 50 rooms. Restaurant, sauna, spa, gym. AE, DC, MC, V.*

$$ ⊞ **Underground Motel.** A little way out of the center, this motel has excellent views of the Breakaways rock formations from its underground rooms. Each is uniquely shaped and simply but comfortably furnished. A kitchen is provided, as are breakfast fixings. ⊠ *Catacomb Rd., 5723,* ☏ *08/8672–5324,* 𝖥𝖠𝖷 *08/8672–5911. 8 rooms. AE, DC, MC, V.*

Shopping

You will find more than 30 shops selling opals in Coober Pedy. One of the best is the **Opal Cutter** (⊠ Post Office Hill Rd., ☏ 08/8672–3086), where stones valued from $7 to $25,000 are for sale. Owners Piet and Barbara Lamont are very helpful and informative. Stop by for a daily display of opal cutting at 5 PM. Another good option is the **Opal Factory** (⊠ Hutchison St., ☏ 08/8672–5300), where you can see the world's largest opal matrix.

Underground Books (⊠ Post Office Hill Rd., ☏ 08/8672–5558) has an excellent selection of reading material, but the best buy is one of proprietor Peter Caust's superb photo postcards, which capture the essence of the desert landscape.

Flinders Ranges National Park

Extending from the northern end of Gulf St.Vincent, the Flinders Ranges, a chain of desert mountains, make up one of the most impressive outback parks in the country. These dry, craggy mountain peaks, once the bed of an ancient sea, have been cracked, folded, and sculpted by millions of years of rain and sun. This furrowed landscape of deep valleys is covered with cypress pine and casuarina, which slope into creeks lined with river red gums. The area is utterly fascinating—both for geologists and for anyone else who revels in wild, raw scenery and exotic plant and animal life.

The scenic center of the Flinders Ranges is **Wilpena Pound,** an 80-sq-km (31-sq-mi) bowl ringed by red hills that curve gently upward, only to fall off in the rims of sheer cliffs. The only entrance to the Pound is a narrow cleft through which the Wilpena Creek sometimes trickles.

The numerous steep trails of Flinders Ranges make them a **bushwalking** mecca, even though the park has few amenities. Water in this region is scarce and should be carried at all times. The best time for walking in the area is during the relatively cool months between April and October. This is also the wettest time of year, so you should be prepared for rain. Between September and late October, wildflowers bring a flush of color to the hillsides.

The most spectacular of the park's walking trails leads to the summit of 3,840-ft **St. Mary's Peak,** the highest point in the Pound's rim and the second-tallest peak in South Australia. The more scenic of the two routes to the summit is the outside trail; give yourself a full day to get up and back. The final ascent is difficult, but views from the top—including the distant white glitter of the salt flats on Lake Frome—make the climb worthwhile.

Arriving and Departing

Flinders Ranges National Park is 460 km (285 mi) north of Adelaide via the Princes Highway to Port Augusta, and then east toward Quorn and Hawker. A four-wheel-drive vehicle is highly recommended for traveling on the many gravel roads in the area.

Dining and Lodging

⚠ **Cooinda Campsite** is the only bush campsite within the Pound, although camping with a permit is allowed throughout the rest of the park. A small rock hole about 2,790 ft from Cooinda is usually filled with fresh water. Otherwise, you must carry water into the campsite.

$$ 🏨 **Wilpena Pound Holiday Resort.** High season at Wilpena Pound is between April and the end of November, when rates rise as the temperatures fall. Stays of three nights or more are rewarded with a 20% discount. Rooms are sizeable and pleasantly furnished, and a licensed restaurant serves fair breakfasts, lunches, and dinners. A campground operated by the motel has powered campsites for $16 per night for two people, plus $2 for each additional person. The resort operates a general store and gas pumps. ⊠ *Flinders Ranges Rd., Wilpena Pound,* ☎ *08/8648–0004,* ℻ *08/8648–0028. 60 rooms. Restaurant, pool, camping.*

Visitor Information

Flinders Ranges National Park. ☎ *08/8648–0048.*

National Parks and Wildlife Service. ⊠ *55 Grenfell St., Adelaide 5000,* ☎ *08/8207–2000.*

The Outback A to Z

Arriving and Departing

BY BUS

Buses leave Adelaide's Central Bus Terminal for **Flinders Ranges National Park** on Thursday and Friday, returning on Thursday and Sunday. *See* Arriving and Departing *in* Adelaide A to Z, *above.*

BY CAR

The main road to **Coober Pedy** is the Stuart Highway from Adelaide, 850 km (527 mi) to the south. Alice Springs is 700 km (434 mi) north of Coober Pedy. The drive from Adelaide to Coober Pedy takes about nine hours on a very good-quality road. To the Alice, it is about seven hours.

BY PLANE

Kendell Airlines flies daily between Coober Pedy and Adelaide via the township of Olympic Dam, which serves the uranium mine at Roxby Downs. *See* Air Travel *in* Smart Travel Tips for airline telephone numbers.

Getting Around

BY CAR

A rental car is the best way to see Coober Pedy and its outlying attractions. Rental vehicles are in extremely short supply in town, so hire elsewhere. Although some of the roads are unsealed—those to the Breakaways and the Dog Fence, for example—surfaces are generally suitable for conventional vehicles. Check on road conditions with the police if there has been substantial rain.

Contacts and Resources

EMERGENCIES

Police, fire, or ambulance. ☎ *000*.

GUIDED TOURS

★ The **Coober Pedy–Oodnadatta Mail Run** tour is a bona fide Australian classic. You'll join the Outback postman in town in his four-wheel-drive vehicle for a 600-km (372-mi) odyssey to tiny Outback settlements and cattle stations. The route passes historic ruins and monuments, such as part of the Overland Telegraph Line and the original line of the Ghan railway. You visit South Australia's smallest town (William Creek, pop. 10) and its biggest cattle station, Anna Creek. This is a trip not to be missed. ☎ *800/06–9911 or 086/72–5558.* ☎ *$60, $89 with lunch (less expensive lunch options are available en route).*

Perentie Outback Tours operates three-day camping tours to the Painted Desert, Oodnadatta, and the Ghan railway ruins. ☎ *08/8672–5558.* ☎ *$385.*

VISITOR INFORMATION

Tourist Information Office. ⊠ *Hutchinson St., Coober Pedy,* ☎ *08/8672–5298.* ☉ *Weekdays 9–5.*

THE RED CENTRE

The luminescent light of the Red Centre—named for the deep color of its desert soils—has a purity and vitality that photographs only begin to approach. For tens of thousands of years, this vast desert territory has been home to Australia's indigenous Aboriginal people. Uluru, also known as Ayers Rock, is a great symbol in Aboriginal traditions, as are so many sacred sites among the Centre's mountain ranges, gorges, dry riverbeds, and spinifex plains. At the center of all this lies Alice Springs, Australia's only desert city.

Updated by
Bev Malzard

AUSTRALIA'S RED CENTRE APPEARS at first sight to be harsh and unforgiving—it is, after all, at the heart of some of the world's largest deserts in the middle of the driest continent in the world. The apparent desolation of the spinifex plains conceals a richness and beauty of plant and animal life that has adapted over millennia to survive and thrive in an environment of extremes. Nights in winter can reach the freezing point, and summer days can soar above 110°F. And with little rain, the pockets of water to be found in isolated gorges and saltpans are precious indicators of surprisingly varied life-forms. Like so many deserts, when you stop to look at the Red Centre closely, you'll find that it is full of beauty and tremendous vitality.

The essence of this land of contrasts is epitomized in the paintings of the renowned Aboriginal landscape artist Albert Namatjirra and his followers. Viewed away from the desert, their images of the MacDonnell Ranges appear at first to be garish and unreal in their depiction of mountain ranges of purples and reds and stark-white ghost gum trees. To see the real thing makes it difficult to imagine them painted in any other way.

Uluru—pronounced *oo-*loo-*roo*—what Anglos have dubbed Ayers Rock, that magnificent stone monolith that rises above the surrounding plains, is but one focus in the Red Centre. The rounded forms of Kata Tjuta (*ka*-ta *tchoo*-ta) are another. The cliffs, gorges, and mountain chains of the MacDonnell Ranges that straddle the desert and Watarrka National Park, or Kings Canyon, are other worlds to explore as well.

Pleasures and Pastimes

Camping
Under a full moon and the Milky Way, camping out in the desert is an experience that you will carry with you for the rest of your life: There are far more stars visible in the southern hemisphere than there are in the north, like the fascinating Magellanic clouds. Nights can be very cold in winter, but happily the native mulga wood supplies the best fire in the world, burning hot and long for cooking and for curling up next to in your sleeping bag—a tent is an unnecessary accoutrement. Pick dry, sandy riverbeds to avoid ants and tall ghost gums for shade in the daytime.

Dining
Although restaurants in Alice Springs and at Ayers Rock Resort are unlikely to surprise visitors with innovative cuisine, they do serve unusual Australian dishes like crocodile, kangaroo, and camel.

CATEGORY	COST*
$$$$	over $45
$$$	$35–$45
$$	$25–$35
$	under $25

per person, excluding drinks

Lodging
The tourism boom of the 1980s resulted in the rapid growth of accommodations in Alice Springs and at Ayers Resort. Newer and better hotels are often out of walking distance from the downtown.

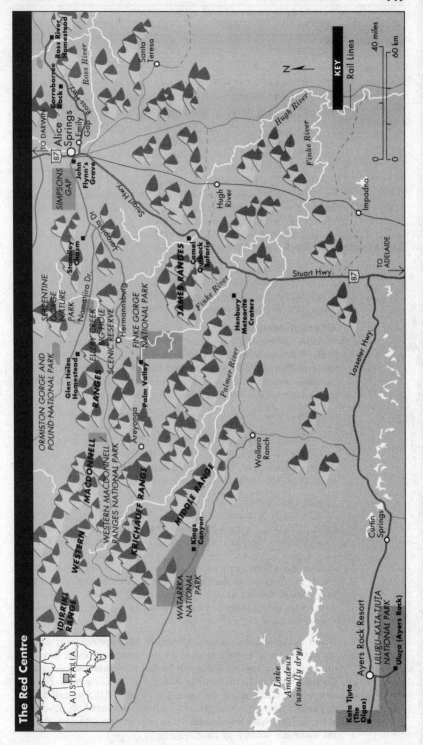

The Red Centre

KEY
Rail Lines

N

40 miles
60 km

Ross River Homestead
Corroboree Rock
Santa Teresa
Alice Springs
TO DARWIN
87
Emily Gap
John Flynn's Grave
SIMPSONS GAP
Stanley Chasm
SERPENTINE GORGE NATURE PARK
Hermannsburg
Namatjira Dr.
ELLERY CREEK BIG HOLE
FINKE GORGE NATIONAL PARK
Glen Helen Homestead
ORMISTON GORGE AND POUND NATIONAL PARK
Palm Valley
Areyonga
WESTERN MACDONNELL RANGES
WESTERN MACDONNELL RANGES NATIONAL PARK
KRICHAUFF RANGE
MIDDLE RANGE
IDIRRIKI RANGE
Kings Canyon
WATARRKA NATIONAL PARK

Hugh River
Finke River
Ross River
Larapinta Dr.
Stuart Hwy.
Hugh River
Impadna
TO ADELAIDE
87
Stuart Hwy.
JAMES RANGES
Camel Outback Safaris
Finke River
Henbury Meteorite Craters
Palmer River
Wallara Ranch
Lasseter Hwy.
Curtin Springs
ULURU-KATA-TJUTA NATIONAL PARK
Ayers Rock Resort
Uluru (Ayers Rock)
Kata Tjuta (The Olgas)
Lake Amadeus (usually dry)

AUSTRALIA

CATEGORY	COST*
$$$$	over $200
$$$	$140–$200
$$	$80–$140
$	under $80

All prices are for a standard double room, excluding the Northern Territory Tourism Marketing Levy of 5%.

Photography, Video, and Filming

Landscape photography in the Red Centre is challenging and rewarding. Amazing light and intense colors change through the day, and your efforts will yield far more meaningful memories of your travels than store-bought souvenirs. Sunset at Uluṟu is but one of hundreds of panoramic sights that will inspire you to pick up your camera. Heat and dust can be a problem, so be sure to take insulated, dust-proof bags for your cameras and film stock. Also take a good UV filter to deflect the fierce light of midday.

Exploring the Red Centre

The primary areas of interest are Alice Springs, which is flanked by the intriguing eastern and western MacDonnell Ranges, and Ayers Rock Resort and Uluṟu–Kata Tjuṯa National Park. Unless you have more than three days, focus on only one of these areas.

Great Itineraries

It doesn't take long for the beauty of the desert to capture your heart. Still, allow yourself enough time in the Red Centre to really let it soak in. If you don't fly right into the Ayers Rock Resort, you'll start in Alice Springs, around which you'll find some spectacular scenery. Poke around town for a day, then head out to the nearby hills.

To get a grip on Australia's notorious "tyranny of distance" and absorb yourself in the unique cultural experience of roadhouse Outback pubs, consider driving from the Alice to Uluṟu. Take in all of the open space and the interesting sights along the way. And when you get to the great Rock, don't forget that the other otherworldly landscape of Kata Tjuṯa (the Olgas) is just down the road.

IF YOU HAVE 3 DAYS

You can hardly ignore one of Australia's great icons: Uluṟu. Drive straight down from Alice Springs to ▦ **Ayers Rock Resort** for lunch, followed by a circuit of the Rock and a look at the **Uluṟu–Kata Tjuṯa Cultural Centre** near its base. On the next day it's worth an early start to catch dawn at **Kata Tjuṯa** for an exploration of its extraordinary domes. End the day with **sunset at the Rock.** Return to Alice Springs via the **Henbury Meteor Craters.** If you fly in and out of Ayers Resort and have more time, take a **Mala or Uluṟu Experience walk** and a **flightseeing** tour of the area.

If you opt to spend your days around ▦ **Alice Springs,** stay in town the first morning to walk around the city center and shop, then head out to the **Alice Springs Telegraph Station Historical Reserve** or **MacDonnell Siding** in the afternoon to look at the Old Ghan train. The next day drive out into either the eastern or western MacDonnell Ranges to explore the gorges and gaps and dip into a water hole. Overnight at the ▦ **Glen Helen Homestead.** Make your way back to town through the mountain scenery on the third day.

IF YOU HAVE 5 DAYS

Combine the two itineraries above, taking in the best of Alice Springs and the MacDonnell Ranges before heading down to the Rock. If you want to take in more of the desert, start out in Uluṟu as above but head west at **Wallara Ranch** for the ⊞ **Watarrka National Park** for a day and two nights exploring **Kings Canyon** by yourself or with one of the Aboriginal guided tours available. Surprisingly little-visited, Kings Canyon is one of the hidden wonders of central Australia.

IF YOU HAVE 7 DAYS

Start with two days in and around ⊞ **Alice Springs,** then two days and a night in ⊞ **Watarrka National Park.** For the remaining three days, knock around ⊞ **Uluṟu–Kata Tjuṯa National Park,** leaving yourself at least a few hours for absorbing the majesty of the desert. Fly out from the resort to your next location.

When to Tour the Red Centre

Winter, May through August, is the best time to visit—nights are crisp and cold, and days are pleasantly warm. High summer temperatures may be too much to cope with for most people, despite extensive air-conditioning at resorts.

Hiking or climbing in the desert carries certain dangers, among them dehydration. Carry plenty of water, even for short trips, and let park rangers, police, or cattle-station owners know where you're going when you undertake long walks. For safety reasons the climb at Uluṟu and Valley of the Winds walk at Kata Tjuṯa are closed when temperatures rise above 97°F.

ALICE SPRINGS

Once a ramshackle collection of dusty streets and buildings, Alice Springs—known colloquially as 'The Alice'—has been transformed in recent decades into an incongruously suburban tourist center in the middle of the desert. A focus of ceremonial activities for the Arrernte Aboriginal tribe, its ancient sites lie cheek by jowl with air-conditioned shops and hotels. Dominated by the MacDonnell Ranges, which change color according to time of day from brick red to purple, the other striking feature of the town is the Todd River. Water rarely runs in the desert, and the deep sandy beds of the Todd, fringed by majestic ghost gum trees, suggest a timelessness far different from the bustle of the nearby town. The Todd's dry riverbed is the scene for one of the Alice's more bizarre celebrations: September's Henley-on-Todd Regatta. A lighthearted send-up of England's staid boating classic, entrants must grab their bottomless homemade boats and run to the finishing line. Twice in the last quarter-century, in 1994 and 1997, this event was cancelled when unexpected rains filled the river!

Until the 1970s the Alice was a frontier town servicing the region's pastoral industry, and life was tough. During World War II it was one of the few (barely) inhabited stops on the 3,024-km (1,875-mi) supply lines between Adelaide and the front line of Darwin. First established at the Old Telegraph Station as the town of Stuart, it was moved and renamed Alice Springs in 1933 after the wife of the telegraph boss, Charles Todd. The town's position in the center of the continent as a communications link has always been important. Today the town hosts both the U.S. secret-communications base of Pine Gap, just out of town, and the only Aboriginal-owned satellite television network, which broadcasts across nearly half of Australia.

Numbers in the margin correspond to points of interest on the Alice Springs map.

Exploring Alice Springs

City Center

❸ Adelaide House. This was the first hospital in Alice Springs, designed by the Reverend John Flynn and run by the Australian Inland Mission (which Flynn established) from 1926 to 1939. In hot weather, the hospital used an ingenious system of air tunnels and wet burlap bags to cool the rooms. The building is now a museum devoted to the mission and pioneering days in Alice Springs. As for John Flynn, who was affectionately known as "Flynn of the Inland," it would be difficult to overstate his contribution to the settlement of inland Australia. The stone hut at the rear of Adelaide House was the site of the first field radio transmission in 1926, which made viable his concept of a flying doctor. The Royal Flying Doctor Service continues to maintain its "mantle of safety" all over Australia's remote settlements. ⊠ *Todd Mall,* ☎ *08/8952–1856.* 🎫 *$3.* ⊘ *Mar.–Nov., weekdays 10–4, weekends 10–noon.*

❶ Anzac Hill. Just north of downtown, Anzac Hill has an excellent view of Alice Springs and the surrounding area, including the MacDonnell Range south of town. From atop the hill, note that **Todd Mall** is one block west of the Todd River, which at best flows only a few days a year. The hill is a good place from which to begin a walking tour. To reach the top, head up Lions Walk, which starts opposite the Catholic church on Wills Terrace downtown.

❷ Museum of Central Australia. The Alice Plaza Building contains the art and natural history collections of the Museum of Central Australia. The museum's animal and mineral specimens are very interesting. ⊠ *Todd Mall, between Wills Terr. and Parsons St.,* ☎ *08/8951–5335.* 🎫 *$2.* ⊘ *Weekdays 9–5, weekends 10–5.*

❹ Old Court House. The wide, simple roof lines of this government building are typical of the Pioneering style of architecture. The building now houses the National Women's Hall of Fame. ⊠ *Parsons and Hartley Sts.* ⊘ *Weekdays 9–4, weekends 10–4.*

❼ Old Hartley Street School. Alas, there is little at the school that recalls the blackboards and lift-top desks in use in 1929, when Miss Pearl Burton was its first teacher—but it's worth a peek anyway. The school is also the headquarters of the Alice Springs National Trust branch, and brochures on local sights are available. ⊠ *Hartley St.,* ☎ *08/8952–4516.* 🎫 *Free.* ⊘ *Weekdays 10:30–2:30.*

❽ Panorama Guth. Artist Henk Guth found canvases too restrictive for his vision of central Australia, so he painted his panoramic, unstintingly realistic work in the round. Panorama Guth, inside an unusual crenellated building, has a circumference of 200 ft and stands 20 ft high. There is also an odd collection of Aboriginal artifacts downstairs. ⊠ *65 Hartley St.,* ☎ *08/8952–2013.* 🎫 *$3.* ⊘ *Mon.–Sat. 9–5, Sun. noon–5.*

❺ The Residency. The high white picket fence on the corner of Parsons and Hartley marks the Residency. Built in 1927 for John Cawood, the first government resident to be appointed to central Australia, it is now a museum with displays depicting the social and economic history of the area. ⊠ *Parsons and Hartley Sts.* 🎫 *Donations accepted.* ⊘ *Weekdays 9–4, weekends 10–4.*

❾ Royal Flying Doctor Service (RFDS). Directed from the RFDS radio base, doctors use aircraft to make house calls on settlements and homes hundreds of miles apart. There is a display of historical material, an audiovisual show, and tours every half hour during the midyear season (April–November). Like the School of the Air (☞ *below*), the

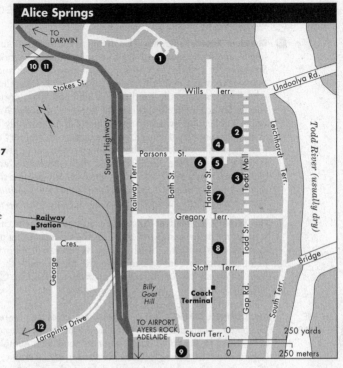

RFDS is still a vital part of life in the Outback. ⊠ *Stuart Terr.,* ☎ *08/
8952–1129.* ☑ *$3.* ⊙ *Mon.–Sat. 9–4, Sun. 1–4.*

⑥ Stuart Town Gaol. The 1908 jail is the oldest surviving building in Alice
Springs—and it looks it. With almost no air coming through its tiny
barred windows, imprisonment here on a long, hot summer day was
punishment indeed. ⊠ *Parsons St.* ☑ *$2.* ⊙ *Weekdays 10–12:30, Sat.
9:30–noon.*

Todd Mall. The Todd Mall pedestrian area is the heart of Alice Springs,
lined with cafés, galleries, banks, and tourist shops. ⊠ *Todd St. between Wills and Gregory Terrs.*

Around Alice

⑩ Alice Springs Telegraph Station Historical Reserve. Just north of town,
the reserve is the site of the first white settlement in the area: the original Alice Springs and the spring itself. The telegraph station buildings
have been restored and are now evocative reminders of the Red Centre as it existed at the turn of the century. Within the buildings, exhibits of life at the station and a display of early photographs chronicle
its history from 1872. There are pleasant picnic areas on the grassy
banks of the river. To reach the reserve on foot, follow the riverside
walk 3 km (2 mi) north from Wills Terrace. ⊠ *Stuart Hwy., 3 km (2
mi) north of Alice Springs,* ☎ *08/8952–1013.* ☑ *$4.* ⊙ *Apr.–Sept.,
daily 8–7; Oct.–Mar., daily 8 AM–9 PM.*

⑪ School of the Air. Operating in many remote areas of Australia, the School
of the Air has an ingenious way of teaching students separated by hundreds of miles. Children take their classes by correspondence course,
supplemented by lessons over the Royal Flying Doctor radio network.
Observing the teacher-student relationship by way of radio is fascinating.

✉ *Head St.,* ☎ *08/8951–6800.* ✉ *Donations accepted.* ⊙ *Weekdays 8:30–4:30, Sat. 8:30–4:30, Sun. 1:30–4:30.*

⑫ **Strehlow Research Centre.** This distinctive, multiroof building with a huge, curved, rammed-earth wall, commemorates the work of Theodor Strehlow (b. 1908). The anthropologist grew up with and later spent many years studying the Aranda people, central Australia Aborigines who have traditionally lived on the land extending north to central Mount Stuart and south beyond the border with South Australia. The center's collection, which consists chiefly of "men's-only" ceremonial artifacts, cannot be displayed because of its contemporary religious significance. Still, the exhibits that are open to the public give rare insight into the beliefs of the Aranda people, their homelands, and their special association with Dr. Strehlow, who actually became their *ingkata,* or ceremonial chief. ✉ *Larapinta Dr., 2 km (1 mi) southwest of town,* ☎ *08/8951–8000.* ✉ *$4.* ⊙ *Daily 10–5, last admission 4:30.*

The Winery. At central Australia's only winery you can enjoy the fruits of the desert and experience a tasting or a restaurant meal. There's the inside restaurant, a brush shelter, or you can drink in the glorious night sky with your favorite tipple on the lawns outside the main building. ✉ *Petrick Rd., off Stuart Hwy.,* ☎ *08/8955–5133.* ⊙ *Feb.–Dec., daily 9–5.*

OFF THE BEATEN PATH

MACDONNELL SIDING – This is the resting place of the now-restored *Old Ghan* train. Named after the Afghans who led camel trains on the route from Adelaide, the train began passenger service on August 6, 1929. Over the next 51 years the *Ghan* provided a vital, if erratic, link with the south. In times of flood it could take up to three months to complete the journey. Service on the new *Ghan* began in 1980 (☞ Arriving and Departing *in* Alice Springs A to Z, *below*).

Between April and November you can take a trip on the *Old Ghan,* 6 km (10 mi) along the original track to Mt. Ertiva. There are morning rides Wednesday at 10 ($12 per person) and evening dinner rides. One of the dinner rides takes you to a bush setting for a camp-oven roasted meal with entertainment ($49); another is a round-trip back to MacDonnell Siding for a more formal dinner ($90). Reservations are advised (☎ 08/8955–5047).The Road Transport Hall of Fame is another feature of the MacDonnell Siding. It is a monument to the unsung heroes and pioneers of Australia's Trucking Industry, which has been vital in opening up the country. ✉ *MacDonnell Siding, Stuart Hwy., 10 km (6 mi) south of town,* ☎ *08/8952–7161.* ✉ *Old Ghan $3, Hall of Fame $3.* ⊙ *Old Ghan daily 9–5, Hall of Fame daily 8:30–5.*

Dining

$$$ ✕ **Overlander Steakhouse.** When local residents take out-of-town guests to a restaurant, this is often the one they choose. The atmosphere is clearly Outback, with an abundance of old saddles, lamps, and equipment from local cattle stations, plus live nightly Australian folk singing. Overall, the Overlander *is* a folkloric experience that maintains a satisfactory standard of cooking. It has a full range of Northern Territory specialties, including an appetizer of vol-au-vent filled with crocodile that lets the unusual chicken-fish flavor come through. For nonresidents, one inevitable main course is the mixed grill of buffalo, kangaroo, camel, and barramundi. Drover's Blowout is a set menu with a taste of everything for $35. ✉ *72 Hartley St.,* ☎ *08/8952–2159. AE, DC, MC, V.*

$$ ✕ **Balloons.** This relaxing bistro in the Plaza Hotel is enhanced by a serene view of the hotel lawns, bounded by the impressive MacDon-

nell Range. The menu has a strong French flair but utilizes some distinctly local ingredients. There is also a buffet lunch and, on Sunday, a champagne brunch. ⊠ *Plaza Hotel, Barrett Dr.,* ☎ *08/8950–8000. AE, DC, MC, V.*

$$ ✕ **Ristorante Puccini.** Dark-wood paneling, subdued lighting, and
★ friendly service are complemented by first-rate Italian cuisine, which, in the middle of the Outback, is nothing short of a revelation. For starters, try carpaccio with pine nuts, or fettuccine *Calabrese* (tossed with hot chilies, spices, tomatoes, and black pepper). Barramundi baked in lemon, garlic, and vermouth is good, too. ⊠ *Todd Mall and Parsons St.,* ☎ *08/8953–0935. AE, DC, MC, V. Closed Sun. No lunch.*

$ ✕ **Oriental Gourmet.** The best Chinese food in the Red Centre is found here. There are no surprises on the menu—honey prawns, beef with black bean sauce, duck with lemon sauce, and the like—but all the dishes are fresh, simple, and soundly prepared. ⊠ *80 Hartley St.,* ☎ *08/8953–0888. AE, MC, V. No lunch.*

Lodging

Hotels and Motels

$$$$ 🏨 **Rydges Plaza Hotel Alice Springs.** With pastel hues and landscaped
★ lawns, this hotel is by far the best in Alice Springs, even if it is a mile walk or a $6 cab ride from town. The rooms are appointed with bleached wood and enhanced by views overlooking the pool and the low, barren mountains behind the hotel. The Plaza also offers an eclectic menu at Balloons (☞ Dining, *above*). ⊠ *Barrett Dr., 0870,* ☎ *08/ 8952–8000,* 𝔽𝔸𝕏 *08/8950–3822. 235 rooms, 7 suites. 2 restaurants, 2 bars, pool, sauna, 2 tennis courts, health club. AE, DC, MC, V.*

$$$ 🏨 **Alice Springs Resort.** On the east bank of the Todd River across from the main downtown area, this hotel has spacious and airy reception and restaurant areas that are graced with high ceilings and filled with potted palms. Many of the rooms open directly onto a large lawn; all are plainly furnished in cane with green carpeting. ⊠ *34 Stott Terr., 0870,* ☎ *08/8952–6699 or 1800/80–5055,* 𝔽𝔸𝕏 *08/8953–0995. 108 rooms. 2 bars, pool, laundry service. AE, DC, MC, V.*

$$ 🏨 **Desert Rose Inn.** This motel provides the best value for families stay-
★ ing in Alice Springs. Budget rooms are cramped and standard rooms are unexceptional, but the deluxe family rooms are spacious and well furnished. Exposed brick walls set the tone for deluxe rooms, which contain a double bed, two single beds, balcony, and kitchenette with sink, microwave, and breakfast table. ⊠ *15–17 Railway Terr., 0870,* ☎ *08/ 8952–1411 or 1800/89–6116,* 𝔽𝔸𝕏 *08/8952–3232. 73 rooms, most with bath or shower. Restaurant, pool, laundry service. AE, DC, MC, V.*

$$ 🏨 **Diplomat Hotel Alice Springs.** The location of the Diplomat is ideal,
★ especially if you don't have a car. It's only 300 ft from the town center, just far enough away to be quiet in the evening. All 90 rooms are comfortable: carpeted, decorated with dark bedspreads and drapes, and air-conditioned. Avoid ground-floor rooms if you want privacy—their full glass doors open onto the central pool and car park area. The staff is friendly. ⊠ *Gregory Terr. and Hartley St., 0870,* ☎ *08/8952–8977 or 1800/80–4885,* 𝔽𝔸𝕏 *08/8953–0225. 90 rooms. Bar, pool, laundry service. AE, DC, MC, V.*

$$ 🏨 **Outback Motor Lodge.** This motel offers simple, clean accommodations. The only public areas are the lawn around a small pool and the office. There is no dining room, but all rooms have kitchen facilities. A Continental breakfast is included. ⊠ *South Terr., 0870,* ☎ *08/ 8952–3888 or 1800/89–6133,* 𝔽𝔸𝕏 *08/8953–2166. 42 rooms with shower. Kitchenettes, pool. AE, DC, MC, V.*

$$ ⊡ **Vista Alice Springs.** Built in 1987, the Vista is shadowed by the mountain range that forms the southern periphery of the town. Apart from the pool and barbecue area at the back of the hotel, there are few public areas. Rooms have bare brick walls, comfortable modern furnishings, and molded fiberglass bathrooms. The downtown area is 2½ km (1½ mi) away, but the hotel provides courtesy transport. ⊠ *Stephens Rd., 0870,* ☎ *08/8952–6100 or 1800/81–0664,* ℻ *08/8952–1988. 140 rooms. Restaurant, bar, pool, spa, tennis court, laundry service. AE, DC, MC, V.*

$ ⊡ **Melanka Lodge.** Just south of the main shopping area, Melanka offers a range of accommodations, including dormitories and double rooms for backpackers, standard rooms, and 60 deluxe rooms with private bathrooms. ⊠ *94 Todd St., 0870,* ☎ *08/8952–2233 or 1800/89–6110,* ℻ *08/8952–2890. 112 rooms, 49 with shower. Restaurant, bar, 2 pools, laundry service. AE, DC, MC, V.*

$ ⊡ **YHA Hostel.** This facility in the center of town has a six-bed dormitory, 13 rooms that sleep four, and one room that sleeps two on twin beds. ⊠ *Leichhardt Terr. and Parsons St., 0870,* ☎ *08/8952–8855,* ℻ *08/8952–4144. 1 double room and 14 dormitory rooms, all with shared bath. Pool, recreation room. MC, V.*

Caravan, Trailer, RV Park

$ ⚠ **MacDonnell Range Holiday Park.** Tucked behind the ranges 5 km
★ (3 mi) south of town, this is an extensive, well-planned park. There is little shade, however. Most of the sites have electrical hookup, and about one-third have a private shower and toilet. ⊠ *Palm Pl. off Ross Hwy.,* ☎ *08/8952–6111 or 1800/80–8373,* ℻ *08/8952–5236. 260 sites, 48 with bath. 2 pools, coin laundry. MC, V.*

Nightlife and the Arts

Lasseters Hotel Casino operates from midday into the wee hours with the full range of games: blackjack, roulette, slot machines, keno, and the Australian game of two-up. ⊠ *Barrett Dr.,* ☎ *08/8950–7777.*

Stars of Starlight, affiliated with the Original Dreamtime Art Gallery (☞ Shopping, *below*), is the place to enjoy Outback theater performances. ⊠ *63 Todd Mall,* ☎ *08/8953–2803.*

Outdoor Activities and Sports

Hot-Air Ballooning

At dawn on most mornings, hot-air balloons can be seen in the sky around Alice Springs. **Outback Ballooning** will pick you up from your hotel about one hour before dawn and return you between 9 AM and 10 AM. The $140 fee covers 30 minutes of flying time and a champagne breakfast. ⊠ *35 Kennett Ct.,* ☎ *1800/80–9790.*

Golf

Alice Springs Golf Club welcomes visitors. Clubs and motorized buggies are available for hire. Greens fees are $17.50 for 9 holes, $30 for 18. ⊠ *Cromwell Dr.,* ☎ *08/8952–5440.*

Tennis

The public tennis courts in **Traeger Park** (⊠ Traeger Ave.) can be rented from the caretaker at the courts. The **Vista** and **Plaza** hotels have tennis courts for guests' use (☞ Lodging, *above*).

Shopping

Apart from the ubiquitous souvenir shops, whose T-shirt designs have reached the level of an art form, the main focus of shopping in Alice Springs is Aboriginal art and artifacts. Central Australian Aboriginal art is characterized by intricate patterns of dots, commonly called sand paintings because they were originally drawn on sand as ceremonial devices. Prices for paintings on canvas range from less than a hundred dollars to several thousand, but these prices are considerably lower than elsewhere in Australia. Two of the better galleries are the **Aboriginal Desert Art Gallery** (⊠ 87 Todd St., ☎ 08/8953–1005) and the **Aboriginal Dreamtime Art Gallery** (⊠ 63 Todd Mall, ☎ 08/8952–8861). The latter is particularly impressive for the number of important Aboriginal artists it represents.

Alice Springs A to Z

Arriving and Departing

BY BUS

Interstate buses operated by **Greyhound** (☎ 08/8952–7888) arrive and depart from outside **Melanka Lodge** (⊠ 94 Todd St.). The **AAT Kings** terminal is just up the road at (⊠ 74 Todd St., ☎ 08/8952–1700). The **McCafferty's Buses** (☎ 08/8952–3952) office and terminal are at 91 Gregory Terrace.

BY CAR

There is only one road into Alice Springs, and it runs north to south: the Stuart Highway, commonly called the Track. The town center lies east of the highway. The 1,610-km (1,000-mi) drive from Adelaide takes about 24 hours; from Darwin the 1,515 km (940 mi) is about 100 km (62 mi) shorter than from the south.

BY PLANE

Alice Springs Airport is 15 km (9 mi) southeast of the center of town. The bright, cool passenger terminal is a welcome relief for anyone who sweated through the shedlike structure it replaced. The local airport is currently served by **Ansett Australia** and **Qantas.** The flight from either Sydney or Melbourne takes 2¾ hours; from Brisbane, three hours; from Adelaide, two hours. *See* Air Travel *in* Smart Travel Tips for airline telephone numbers.

Alice Springs Airport Shuttle Service has a shuttle bus that meets every flight. The ride to your hotel costs $9 each way. On request, the bus will also pick you up at your hotel and take you to the airport. ⊠ *Shop 6, Capricornia Centre, Gregory Terr.,* ☎ *08/8953–0310.*

Alice Springs Taxis (☎ 08/8952–1877) maintains a taxi stand at the airport. The fare to most parts of town is $18–$20.

BY TRAIN

It's impossible to miss your stop at Alice Springs—it's the end of the line. The new *Ghan* (Rail Australia, ☎ 13–2232 or 1800/88–8480), named after the Afghan camel-train drivers who traveled the route before the railway, provides one of the world's classic rail journeys. It's comfortable and well run, although the food does tend toward standard fare. The train leaves Adelaide at 2 PM each Thursday, arriving in Alice Springs at 10 AM Friday. The return train leaves Alice Springs at 2 PM Friday, arriving in Adelaide at 11:45 AM Saturday. Between April and December there is an additional departure from both Adelaide (each Monday) and from Alice Springs (each Tuesday), and departure and arrival times are the same as those of the regular service. Alice Springs's railway station is 2½ km (1½ mi) west of Todd Mall.

Getting Around

BY CAR

If you want to get into the desert, renting a car is a smart idea. Looking farther down the road, it's 440 km (273 mi) from Alice Springs to

Ayers Rock Resort. The trip takes about five hours (☞ On the Way to Uluru, *below*). The road is scenic, paved, and in very good condition.

When traveling off the few paved roads, be sure to carry survival rations, water, and spares. Rental cars cannot be driven out of the Northern Territory except by special arrangement. Your car rental company can help with the details. Some companies allow cross-state driving and others forbid it, so check first if you're planning a road trip beyond the Northern Territory.

Contacts and Resources

CAR RENTAL

Several rental-car companies have offices in Alice Springs: **Avis** (☎ 08/8953–5533), **Budget** (☎ 08/8952–8899), **Hertz** (☎ 08/8952–2644), **Territory Rent-a-Car** (☎ 08/8952–9999), and **Thrifty** (☎ 08/8952–2400).

Road Assistance: The **Road Conditions Information** (☎ 22–32–32) provides the latest information about conditions on the many unpaved roads in the area. In the event of a breakdown, contact the **Automobile Association of N.T.** (☎ 08/8953–1322 or 1800/246–199) in Alice Springs. Its Alice Springs agent for vehicle recovery is at 58 Sargent Street.

EMERGENCIES

Ambulance, fire brigade, and police: ☎ 000. **Dentists: Department of Health Dental Clinic** (✉ Flynn Dr., ☎ 08/8951–6713). **Doctors: Central Clinic** (✉ 76 Todd St., ☎ 08/8952–1088).

Hospital: Alice Springs Hospital (✉ Gap Rd., ☎ 08/8951–7777). **Pharmacies: Alice Springs Pharmacy** (✉ Shop 19, Hartley St., ☎ 08/8952–1554) or **Plaza Amcal Chemist** (✉ Alice Plaza, Todd Mall, ☎ 08/8953–0089).

GUIDED TOURS

The narrated **Alice Wanderer** (☎ 08/8952–2111) completes an hourly circuit of most tourist attractions in and around Alice Springs between 9 and 5 daily. You can leave and rejoin the bus whenever you like for a flat daily rate of $20.

Several companies offer half-day tours of Alice Springs. All trips include visits to the Royal Flying Doctor Service Base, the School of the Air, the Old Telegraph Station, and the Anzac Hill scenic lookout. **AAT Kings** (✉ 74 Todd St., ☎ 08/8952–1700 or 1800/33–4009) runs three-hour tours to the above and Strehlow Centre. There is also a half-day Aboriginal Dreamtime tour to a bush site outside town, where local Aborigines explain their way of life, show how to find bush foods, and demonstrate how their weapons, including boomerangs, are made and used. Courtesy hotel pickup is provided ($45 for town tours, $69 for Dreamtime tour; the two can be combined for $104). **Tailormade Tours & Airport Limousines** (✉ 23 Gosse St., ☎ 08/8952–1731 or 1800/80–6641) offers a three-hour coach tour ($45) that covers most of the same sights as the AAT Kings tour. The company also has a chauffeur-driven, air-conditioned car for city sightseeing at $62 per hour.

VISITOR INFORMATION

The **Central Australian Tourism Industry Association** dispenses information, advice, and maps. ✉ *Gregory Terr. and Hartley St., 0870,* ☎ *08/8952–5199.*

For additional information on buildings of historical significance in and around Alice Springs, contact the **National Trust.** ✉ *Old Hartley Street School, Hartley St.,* ☎ *08/8952–4516.* ☉ *Weekdays 10:30–2:30.*

SIDE TRIPS FROM ALICE SPRINGS

Eastern MacDonnell Ranges–Ross Highway

★ East of the Alice, spectacular scenery and Aboriginal rock art found in the MacDonnell Ranges are well worth a day or more of exploring, and many sights are closer to town than those in the western ranges. Emily Gap (a sacred site), Jessie Gap, Undoolya Gap, and Corroboree Rock (a particularly interesting formation of clustered rocks, which is said to be an ancient storage house for sacred objects) are all within the first 44 km (27 mi) east of Alice Springs. Beyond that, Trephina Gorge and John Hayes Rockhole (both with very good walks), N'D-hala Gorge Nature Park (with numerous hide-and-seek Aboriginal rock carvings), and Ross River Homestead (with overnight lodging; ☞ *below*), are 76 km (47 mi) and farther out.

Dining and Lodging

$$ ✕⛭ **Ross River Homestead Resort.** Situated among rugged ranges next to the river after which it is named, this resort is a place to experience the remote Outback in relative comfort, and with plenty to keep you occupied. Accommodations are basic redwood cabins, each with its own bathroom. A bar and restaurant are on the premises, and horse and camel riding and camping facilities are available. ⊠ *Ross River Hwy., 85 km (53 mi) east of Alice Springs,* ☎ *08/8956–9711,* ⅉ *08/ 8956–9823. 30 cabins. Restaurant, pool, spa. MC, V.*

Western MacDonnell Ranges

★ The MacDonnell Ranges west of Alice Springs are, like the eastern ranges, broken by a series of chasms and gorges, many of which can be visited in a single day, depending on your stamina. To reach them, drive out of town on Larapinta Drive, the western continuation of Stott Terrace.

On the way out to the ranges, **Alice Springs Desert Park** provides an informative way to understand the ecology of 70% of the Australian landmass; that is, the desert. The park opened in 1997, and its core exhibit area of 75 acres presents 120 animal and 320 plant species in the range of Australian ecosystems and includes the largest nocturnal house in the southern hemisphere. The park is also one of the leading research centers on desert ecologies. ⊠ *Larapinta Dr., 6½ km (4 mi) west of Alice Springs,* ☎ *08/8951–8788.* ⅉ *$12.* ⊙ *Daily 7:30–6.*

John Flynn's Grave is on a rise with the stark ranges behind, and the setting is memorable. The grave is unmistakable, too: a rock cairn with a large round stone, one of the Devil's Marbles from near Tennant Creek, on top. ⊠ *Larapinta Dr., 6 km (4 mi) west of Alice Springs.*

Simpsons Gap National Park isn't dramatic, but it is the closest gorge to town. Stark-white ghost gums, red rocks, and the purple-hazed mountains give visitors a taste of the scenery to be seen farther into the ranges. The gap itself can be crowded, but it's only 200 yards from the car park. ⊠ *Larapinta Dr., 24 km (15 mi) west of Alice Springs, then 5⅕ km (3½ mi) on side road,* ☎ *no phone.* ⅉ *Free.* ⊙ *Daily 8–8.*

Standley Chasm is one of the most impressive canyons. At midday, when the sun is directly overhead, the 10-yard-wide canyon glows red from the reflected light. The walk from the car park takes about 20 minutes and is rocky toward the end. There is a kiosk at the park entrance. ⊠ *Larapinta Dr., 48 km (30 mi) west of Alice Springs, then 9 km (5½ mi) on Standley Chasm Rd.,* ☎ *08/8956–7440.* ⅉ *$4.* ⊙ *Daily 7:30–6.*

THE HEARTLAND

FOR MOST AUSTRALIANS, the Red Centre is the mystical and legendary core of the continent. Whether they have been there or not, it symbolizes a steady pulse that radiates deep through the heartland all the way to the coasts.

Little more than a thumbprint within the vast Australian continent, the Red Centre is barren and isolated. Its hard, relentless topography and lack of the conveniences found in most areas of civilization make this one of the most difficult areas of the country in which to explore, much less survive. But the early pioneers—some foolish, some hardy—managed to set up bases that thrived. They created cattle stations, introduced electricity, and implemented telegraph services, enabling them to maintain a lifestyle that, if not luxurious, was at least reasonably comfortable.

The people who now sparsely populate the Red Centre are a breed of their own. Many were born and grew up here, but many others were "blow-ins," immigrants who took up the challenge to make a life in the desert and stayed on as they succeeded. Either way, folks out here have at least a few common characteristics: They're laconic and down-to-earth, canny and astute, and very likely to try to pull your leg when you least expect it. Quite the opposite of fast-talking city-slickers, there's a fortitude to them that is rare today.

And no one could survive the isolation without a good sense of humor: Where else in the world would you hold a bottomless boat race in a dry riverbed? The Henley-on-Todd, as it is known, is a sight to behold, with dozens of would-be skippers bumbling along within the bottomless boat frames. A traditional German Octoberfest also takes place every year, another unlikely event in this dry, desolate place. Like the Henley-on-Todd, the event is marked by hilarity, and includes such competitions as tug-of-war, spitting at the dummy, and stein-lifting championships—plus a requisite amount of beer-drinking.

As the small towns grew and businesses quietly prospered in the mid-1800s, a rail link between Alice Springs and Adelaide was planned. However, the undercurrent of challenge and humor that touches all life here ran through this project as well. Construction began in 1877, but things went wrong from the start. No one had seen rain for ages, and no one expected it; hence, the track was laid right across a flood plain. It wasn't long before locals realized their mistake, when intermittent, heavy floods regularly washed the tracks away. The railway is still in operation today and all works well, but its history is one of many local jokes here.

The Red Centre is the real Australia, a special place where you will meet people whose generous and sincere hospitality will move you. The land and all its riches offer some of the most spectacular and unique sights on the planet. Take time out to shade your eyes from the sun and pick up on the subtleties that nature has carefully camouflaged here, and you will soon discover that the Red Center is not the dead center.

— Bev Malzard

Namatjira Drive

Beyond **Standley Chasm** (☞ *above*) the mileage starts adding up, and be prepared for rough road conditions.

Ellery Creek Big Hole Scenic Reserve is believed to have the coolest swimming hole in the Red Centre. ⊠ *Namatjira Dr., 48 km (30 mi) west of Alice Springs.*

Serpentine Gorge requires a refreshing swim through the gorge to get the best perspective on the place. ⊠ *Namtjira Dr., 106 km (66 mi) west of Alice Springs, then 4 km (2½ mi) on rough track.*

Ormiston Gorge and Pound National Park is one of the few really breathtaking sights of the western ranges. Unfortunately, it can be crowded at times. There are several walks, including the Pound Walk, in the park. ⊠ *Namatjira Dr., 135 km (84 mi) west of Alice Springs.*

Glen Helen Gorge National Park has the most substantial gorge of all, a water hole, and the rather sporadic coursing of the Finke River. ⊠ *Namatjira Dr., 140 km (87 mi) west of Alice Springs.*

DINING AND LODGING

$–$$ ✕⯐ **Glen Helen Homestead.** A variety of accommodations are available at the homestead, from motel and lodge rooms to hostel and camping facilities. Considering its distance from civilization, **Cloudy's** restaurant on site comes well recommended. ⊠ *Namatjira Dr., 135 km (84 mi) west of Alice Springs,* ☎ *08/8956–7489,* ⅻ *08/8956–7495.*

Hermannsburg and Beyond

Another alternative after passing **Standley Chasm** (☞ *above*) is to continue on Larapinta Drive in the direction of **Hermannsburg,** which has tearooms, a supermarket, and a service station. The buildings of the early **Lutheran Mission** have been restored, and the mission is open Tuesday–Sunday; admission is free. ⊠ *Larapinta Dr., 132 km (82 mi) from Alice Springs.*

You need a four-wheel-drive vehicle to continue past Hermannsburg to **Palm Valley** in **Finke Gorge National Park.** The valley is a remnant of a time when Australia had a wetter climate and supported palm trees over large areas. The foliage here includes *Livistonia mariae,* an ancient variety of cabbage palm. Palm Valley is like a slice of the tropical north dropped into the middle of the Red Centre.

ULUṞU AND KATA TJUṮA

It isn't too difficult to see why the Aborigines attach spiritual significance to Uluṟu (Ayers Rock). Rising more than 1,100 ft from the flat surrounding plain, it is one of the world's largest monoliths. More impressive than its size, however, is its color—a glowing red that changes hues constantly throughout the day. Kata Tjuṯa (the Olgas), 53 km (33 mi) west, is a series of 36 gigantic rock domes that hide a maze of fascinating gorges and crevasses. The names Ayers Rock and the Olgas are used to describe these two wonders out of familiarity alone; at the sites themselves, you'll find that the Aboriginal Uluṟu and Kata Tjuṯa are the respective names of preference.

Uluṟu and Kata Tjuṯa have very different compositions: The great monolith is a type of sandstone called arkose, while the rock domes are composed of conglomerate. It was once thought that they rest upon the sandy terrain like pebbles; however, both formations are in fact the tips of tilted rock strata that extend into the earth for thousands of meters. Perhaps two-thirds of each formation extends below the surface, tilted during a period of intense geological activity more than 300 million years ago—the arkose by nearly 90° and the conglomerate only about 15°. The rock surrounding the formations was fractured and quickly eroded away about 40 million years ago, leaving the present structures standing as separate entities.

Both of these intriguing sights lie within Uluṟu–Kata Tjuṯa National Park, which is protected as a World Heritage Site. As such, it is one of only two parks in the world recognized in this way for both its landscape and cultural values. Tourist facilities are outside of the national park at the Ayers Rock Resort. The whole experience is a bit like seeing the Grand Canyon turned inside out, and you'll remember a visit here for a lifetime.

On the Way to Uluṟu

The 440-km (273-mi) drive to Uluṟu from Alice Springs along the Stuart and Lasseter highways takes about five hours, but there are interesting sights along the way if you're prepared to make a few detours.

Camel Outback Safaris is owned by Michelle Gargan and her husband Critin. Michelle is the daughter of local legend Noel Fullerton, who raised and trained his own camels for tourist expeditions, and Michelle has now taken the reins. Day rides, available from 8:30 AM to 4 PM, vary from one hour to 14 days. Half-day rides include a light lunch. Book all rides at least a day in advance. ⊠ *Stuart Hwy., 93 km (58 mi) south of Alice Springs,* ☎ *08/8956–0925,* 🖷 *08/8956–0909.* ✉ *$25 for a one-hour ride.*

The **Henbury Meteorite Craters,** a group of 12 depressions between 6 and 600 ft across, were probably formed by a meteorite shower about 5,000 years ago. One is 60 ft deep. ⊠ *Kings Canyon Rd., 134 km (83 mi) south of Alice Springs and 13 km (8 mi) west of Stuart Hwy.*

★   **Kings Canyon,** in Watarrka (formerly Kings Canyon) National Park, is one of the finest sights in Central Australia. Sheltered within the sheer cliff walls of the canyon is a world of ferns and rock pools, permanent springs, and woodlands. Several walking tracks wind through the gorge and along the ridge tops. The main path is the 6-km (4-mi) **Canyon Walk,** which starts with a fairly steep climb to the top of the escarpment and leads to a delightful water hole in the so-called Garden of Eden halfway through the four-hour walk.

Watarrka National Park is now accessible by car on the **Mereenie Track** from Glen Helen. To make this loop around the Western MacDonnell Ranges, you'll need an Aboriginal Land Entry Permit, which is free from the **Central Australian Tourism Industry Association** (☎ 08/8952–5800 or 1800/645–199) in Alice Springs. ⊠ *Kings Canyon Rd., 134 km (83 mi) south of Alice Springs and 200 km (124 mi) west of Stuart Hwy.*

Dining and Lodging

$$$$ ✕🏨 **Kings Canyon Resort.** Only 6 km (4 mi) from the canyon, this is the only place to stay within Watarrka National Park. All rooms are air-conditioned, with satellite TV, refrigerators, and direct-dial phones. There are souvenir and provision shops. **Carmichael's ($$)** is the premier restaurant, with seating for 180 and a feature wall of Aboriginal art that provides a counterpoint to the sweeping desert views through the large windows. Two- and four-bed backpacker rooms are available, as is a large, well-equipped campground. ⊠ *Ernest Giles Rd., Wattarka National Park. Mailing address:* ⊠ *PMB 136, Alice Springs, NT 0871,* ☎ *08/8956–7442 or 1800/81–7622,* 🖷 *08/8956–7410. 96 rooms with shower, 4 suites, 36 4-bed rooms. Restaurant, 2 bars, café, pool, camping. AE, DC, MC, V.*

Uluru and Kata Tjuta

Allow about 20 minutes to drive to Uluru from the Ayers Rock Resort area; Kata Tjuta will take another 30 minutes. The park entrance fee of $15 is valid for a week. The sunset-viewing area is 13 km (8 mi) from the resort on the way to Uluru.

Uluru

★ There is an inevitable sensation of excitement as you approach the great rock—Uluru just keeps looming larger and larger. After entering the park through a toll gate, you'll come upon the serpentine shape of the **Uluru–Kata Tjuta Cultural Centre,** two buildings that reflect the Kuniya and Liru stories of two ancestral snakes who fought a battle on the southern side of Uluru. Located on the right-hand side of the road just before you reach the rock, the Cultural Centre displays Aboriginal history, along with information on the return of the park to Aboriginal ownership in 1985. Comprehensive explanatory material is available at the Centre, as are descriptions of local plant and animal life. The Centre opened in 1995, and it incorporates the park's ranger station.

As you work your way around Uluru, you'll notice that your perspective of the great rock changes significantly. Four hours will allow you to walk the 10 km (6 mi) around the rock with time to explore the several deep crevices along the way; or you can drive around it on the paved road. Be aware that some places are Aboriginal sacred sites and cannot be entered. These are clearly signposted. Aboriginal art can be found in caves at the base of the rock. If you're comparing notes on native rock art, the work here is neither as extensive nor as impressive as those in Kakadu National Park at the top of the Northern Territory (☞ Chapter 11). It is nonetheless interesting to look at.

Only one trail leads to the top of the rock, and the Aboriginal owners of Uluru don't encourage people to climb it. They don't prohibit it either, but the ranger station displays a well-reasoned argument why you should reconsider your intentions to ascend.

If you decide to climb, it's about 1½ km (1 mi) from the base; the round-trip walk takes about two hours. Be careful: The ascent is very steep. Climbers have fallen to their deaths or had heart attacks; even experienced hikers should use the safety chain on the steep initial incline. Don't attempt the climb if you aren't in good condition. You'll also need to wear solid hiking boots, a hat, sunscreen, and bring drinking water. Once you are on top of the rock, the trail is much easier. You can sign a guest book at the summit. The climb is prohibited when temperatures rise above 97°F.

The other popular way of experiencing Uluru is far less taxing but no less intense: watching the sun sink against it from one of the two sunset-viewing areas. As the last rays of daylight strike, the rock seems lit from within and it positively glows. Just as quickly, the light is extinguished, then the color changes to a somber mauve and finally to black.

SHOPPING

The **Cultural centre** (☎ 08/8956–3139) houses the **Ininti Store** (☎ 08/8956–2437), which sells a range of souvenirs, and the adjoining **Maruku Arts and Crafts Centre** (☎ 08/8956–2558), which is owned by Aborigines and sells Aboriginal painting and handicrafts. There is also a display of traditional huts and shelters.

Kata Tjuta

★ In many ways, Kata Tjuta is more satisfying to explore than Uluru. The latter rock is one immense block, so you feel as if you're always on the outside looking in—but you can really come to grips with Kata

Tjuṯa. As the Aboriginal name, *Kata Tjuṯa* (many heads), suggests, this is a jumble of huge rocks containing numerous hidden gorges and chasms. There are three main walks, the first from the car park into **Olga Gorge**, the deepest valley between the rocks. This is a mile walk, and the round-trip journey takes about one hour. From the parking lot, the walk to *Kata Tjuṯa* **Lookout** is about a mile round-trip and takes about an hour. More rewarding but also more difficult is a walk that continues through the major cleft between the Olgas known as the **Valley of the Winds**. Experienced walkers can complete this 6-km (4-mi) walk in about four hours. Remember to carry at least a quart of water for each hour of walking and to avoid activity during the hottest part of the day. For safety reasons, the Valley of the Winds walk is closed when temperatures rise above 97°F.

Ayers Rock Resort

Dining and Lodging

This is a planned resort where guests choose from among five types of accommodation priced on a descending scale, from the luxurious Sails in the Desert rooms to sites in the Ayers Rock Campground. All reservations can be made through Southern Pacific Hotels' **Travelex** (☎ 1300/363–300 in Australia), or through the resort's **central reservations service** in Sydney (☎ 02/9360–9099).

Dining is limited to hotel restaurants and the less expensive **Gecko's Cafe** (☎ 08/8956–2562), which serves Continental lunch and dinner with gourmet wood-fired pizza and pasta, coffee, and cakes. It's open from 8 AM to 10 AM for coffee and pastries, then from 10 AM to midnight for full service. If you eat outside of your hotel, you can have the meals billed to your room. Not to be missed is the "Sounds of Silence" **Dinner in the Desert** for $90, where you dine under the open sky, surrounded by the vastness of central Australia. This can be one of the most memorable nights on an Outback trip. Book well in advance, perhaps even before you get to Ayers Rock. Don't be surprised by the number of insects attracted to the candlelight; they may be a bit alarming to city-slickers, but they're part of the desert experience.

CATEGORY	COST*
$$$$	over $200
$$$	$140–$200
$$	$80–$140
$	under $80

All prices are for a standard double room, excluding the Northern Territory Tourism Marketing Levy of 5%.

HOTELS AND MOTELS

Because of the transient nature of the staff at this resort-only area, you might find an uneven quality of service at the following establishments.

$$$$ ⊞ **Sails in the Desert.** With architectural shade sails for sun protection,
★   manicured lawns, Aboriginal artwork, and numerous facilities, this three-story hotel aspires to be the resort's best. Open-air stairways and passages contribute to the sense of space and light. Rooms are decorated in ochre shades and have balconies overlooking lawns and gardens; a viewing tower looks out toward Uluṟu in the distance. Deluxe rooms have whirlpool baths. Sails in the Desert also has the best restaurant, the **Kuniya**, which serves such specialties as barramundi, buffalo, and kangaroo. The **Winkiku** restaurant and the **Rock Pool Café** are also on the property. ⊠ *Yulara Dr., Ayers Rock Resort 0872,* ☎ *08/8956–2200, 08/8956–2494, or 1800/08–9622,* ☒ *08/8956–2018. 234 rooms,*

2 suites. 3 restaurants, 3 bars, piano bar, pool, spa, putting green, tennis court, travel services. AE, DC, MC, V.

$$$ 🏨 **Desert Gardens.** If you prefer a smaller hotel, consider the two-story Desert Garden, which has impeccable style and service. Like Sails in the Desert, it is built around a lawn, pool, and extensive gardens with native flora. The modern rooms are small but comfortable and well kept. The hotel is near the visitor center. The **Whitegums** is open for breakfast and dinner, serving light salads of local fruits, nuts, and berries. The **Bunya Bar** serves light snacks for lunch, with an emphasis on fresh, healthy, affordable meals and a relaxed atmosphere. The **Palya Bar** serves snacks and drinks poolside. ⊠ *Yulara Dr., Ayers Rock Resort 0872,* ☎ *08/8956–2100,* FAX *08/8956–2156. 160 rooms. Restaurant, bar, pool, 2 tennis courts, coin laundry. AE, DC, MC, V.*

$$ 🏨 **Outback Pioneer Hotel and Lodge.** Although the theme is the Out-
★ back of the 1860s, complete with rustic decor and bush games in the evening, you won't be roughing it here. The lodge is served by a shuttle bus that runs to the other properties every 15 minutes. Guests at the adjoining **Outback Pioneer Lodge,** an air-conditioned budget accommodation, have access to the hotel's facilities. The **Bough House,** open daily for breakfast, lunch, and dinner, offers hearty central Australian dishes as well as lighter food. The **Pioneer Self-Cook Barbecue** has a fully equipped kitchen that opens at 6:30 PM. As the name suggests, you buy a cut of meat and cook it yourself; alcoholic drinks are available with the barbecue facility. There is also a kiosk where you can buy light meals, snacks, and soft drinks. ⊠ *Yulara Dr., Ayers Rock Resort 0872,* ☎ *08/8956–2170,* FAX *08/8956–2320. 125 rooms, 224 dormitory beds with shared bath, 12 cabins. Pool, coin laundry. AE, DC, MC, V.*

$ 🏨 **Emu Walk Apartments.** These one- and two-bedroom apartments have fully equipped kitchens (down to champagne glasses), living rooms, and daily maid service. Each unit has a sofa bed, so one-bedrooms can sleep four, and the balconied two-bedrooms can accommodate six or eight. There's no restaurant on site, but you are welcome to dine in any of the resort's eateries. ⊠ *Yulara Dr., Ayers Rock Resort 0872,* ☎ *08/8956–2000,* FAX *08/8956–2328. 56 apartments. Coin laundry. AE, DC, MC, V.*

$ 🏨 **Spinifex Lodge.** Originally used to house resort-area staff, most of the rooms in this lodge have two single beds or two bunk beds and most of the amenities you would expect in a good hotel, plus kitchenettes and daily maid service. Bathrooms are shared. ⊠ *Yulara Dr., Ayers Rock Resort 0872,* ☎ *08/8956–2131,* FAX *08/8956–2163. 68 rooms with shared baths. Coin laundry. AE, DC, MC, V.*

CARAVAN, TRAILER, RV PARK

$ ⚠ **Ayers Rock Campground.** This large campground has 220 sites for campers, 500 tent sites, and 14 air-conditioned cabins. The area has rolling green lawns, refrigerators, tables and chairs, and an Outback-style barbecue shelter. ⊠ *Yulara Dr., Ayers Rock Resort 0872,* ☎ *08/ 8956–2055,* FAX *08/8956–2260. 240 sites. Pool, coin laundry. MC, V.*

Child Care

�﾿ The resort's hotels have joined to form a free **Kids Only Club** for 5- to 12-year-olds, which operates daily from 8 AM to 5:30 PM during peak holiday seasons. Activities include sports, excursions to the rock, and forays for bush tucker (native foodstuffs). Reservations should be made the evening before through reception at your hotel. The **Child Care Centre** will look after children between the ages of three months and eight years on weekdays between 8 AM and 5:30 PM. Baby-sitting is available outside these times by arrangement with the center. ⊠ *Next to Community Hall,* ☎ *08/8956–2097.*

Shopping

Ayers Rock Resort has a news agency, a very reasonably priced supermarket (open 8 AM–9 PM), and a couple of souvenir shops. Each of the hotels has an Ayers Rock Logo Shop selling Australian-made garments and leather goods. The **Mulgara Gallery and Craft Works Gallery** (☎ 08/8956–2460) in the foyer of the Sails in the Desert Hotel specializes in high-quality Australian arts and crafts, including Aboriginal works and opal jewelry. A lack of competition ensures that the art is likely to cost more here than in Alice Springs.

Uluru and Kata Tjuta A to Z

Arriving and Departing

BY BUS

Bus companies traveling to Ayers Rock Resort from Alice Springs include **AAT Kings** (☎ 08/8952–1700 or 1800/334–009) and **Greyhound Pioneer** (Todd St., ☎ 08/8952–7888).

BY CAR

It is 440 km (273 mi) from Alice Springs to Ayers Rock Resort; the trip takes about five hours. The road, Lasseter Highway, is paved and in fine condition.

BY PLANE

Connellan Airport is 5 km (3 mi) north of the resort complex. It is served by Ansett Australia and Qantas. Kendall Airlines has a Saturday service to the Rock from Adelaide via Coober Pedy. *See* Air Travel *in* Smart Travel Tips for airline telephone numbers.

BETWEEN THE AIRPORT AND YULARA

AAT Kings (☎ 08/8952–1700) has a complimentary shuttle bus that meets every flight.

Getting Around

BY BUS

AAT Kings (☎ 08/8952–1700) offers a range of daily local tours.

BY CAR

From the resort it's 19 km (12 mi) to Uluru or 53 km (33 mi) to Kata Tjuta. The road to Kata Tjuta is sealed. Routes between hotels and sights are clearly marked, and because prices are competitive with those for the bus tours—especially for larger parties—renting a car may be your best option. There are several car-rental companies at the resort: **Avis** (☎ 08/8956–2266), **Territory Rent-a-Car** (☎ 08/8956–2030), and **Hertz** (☎ 08/8956–2244).

BY TAXI

For a chauffeur-driven limousine, contact **V.I.P. Chauffeur Cars** (☎ 08/ 8956–2283). **Sunworth Transport Service** (☎ 08/8956–2152) can whisk you from the resorts to the sights for much less than the cost of a guided bus tour—plus, you can go at your own convenience.

Guided Tours and Programs

FLIGHTSEEING TOURS

An ideal view of Uluru and Kata Tjuta is from the air. Several light-plane tours are offered, from half-hour flights over Ayers Rock and the Olgas to 110-minute flights over Kings Canyon—with courtesy pickup from your hotel included. Prices range from $65 to $175 per person. Contact **Airnorth Safaris** (☎ 08/8952–6666) or **RockAyer** (☎ 08/8956–2345). Helicopter flights are more expensive: $75 per person for 15 minutes over Ayers Rock or $100 for 20 minutes over the Olgas. A flight over both sights costs $145 per seat. The local operators are **Jayrow** (☎ 08/8956–2077 or 1800/65–0057, ℻ 08/8956–2060) and **RockAyer** (☎ 08/8956–2345).

GENERAL TOURS

Anangu Tours (☎ 08/8956–2123, ℻ 08/8956–3136) owned and operated by Anangu of the Mutitjulu community, offers excellent tours such as the Uluṟu Breakfast Tour ($78), which includes breakfast and an Aboriginal guide, the Kuniya Sunset Tour ($65), the Anangu Culture Pass ($120), the self-drive Liru Tour ($39), and the self-drive Kuniya Tour ($39). Guides are Aboriginal people who work with interpreters.

MOTORCYCLE TOUR

The normally fine climate of the desert makes **Uluṟu Motorcycle Tours** (☎ 08/8956–2019, ℻ 08/8956–2196) enjoyable (and popular) and provides the chance for some very different vacation photographs. Guides communicate with their passengers by helmet intercoms. Prices range from $70 for the Uluṟu Cruise to $85 for sunrise over the Rock and $145 for a three-hour tour to the Olgas.

SLIDE SHOWS

Several free slide shows about local wildlife and flora are given at the auditorium near the resort's visitor center next to the Desert Gardens Hotel on Yulara Drive.

STARGAZING

Central Australia has some of the clearest and cleanest air in the world—just look up into the night sky. A small observatory with a telescope is set up on the resort grounds for just this purpose. Viewing times vary with the seasons; sessions last for about an hour, and can be booked through **Uluṟu Experience** (☎ 1800/80–3174) for $20.

WALKING TOURS

The **Mala Walk** (☎ 08/8956–2299) is free and led by Aboriginal rangers who show you the land from their perspective. The walk starts from the base of the climbing trail. **Uluṟu Experience** (☎ 1800/80–3174) specializes in small group tours of Uluṟu with guides who have extensive local knowledge. The Uluṟu Walk, a 10-km (6-mi) hike around the base of Uluṟu, gives fascinating insight into the significance of the area to the Aboriginal people. It departs daily, includes breakfast, and costs $69. Book at least a day in advance.

Contacts and Resources

EMERGENCIES

Ambulance: ☎ 08/8956–2286. **Ambulance, fire brigade, and police:** ☎ 000. **Doctors:** The **medical clinic** (✉ Flying Doctor Base, near police station, ☎ 08/8956–2286 emergencies is open weekdays 9–noon and 2–5 and weekends 10–11. **Police:** ☎ 08/8956–2166.

VISITOR INFORMATION

The **Uluṟu–Kata Tjuṯa Cultural Centre** (☎ 08/8956–2299) is on the park road just before you reach the rock. It also contains the park's ranger station. The cultural center is open daily 8–5.

A **visitor center** (☎ 08/8957–7377) is next to the Desert Gardens Hotel on Yulara Drive.

10 DARWIN, THE TOP END, AND THE KIMBERLEY

From Darwin Harbour to the rocky domes and towers of Purnululu, the Top End and the Kimberley are regions of great natural beauty. For thousands of years, this area of Northern Australia has been home to Aboriginal people, and stunning examples of ancient Aboriginal rock art remain—on cliffs, in hidden valleys, and in Darwin art galleries. Darwin and Broome—closer to the cities of Asia than to any Australian counterparts—host the nation's most racially diverse populations: Aborigines, Anglos, and Asians sharing a tropical lifestyle.

By David
McGonigal
and Chips
Mackinolty

Updated by
Tony Baker

THE TOP END IS A geographic description—but it is also a state of mind. Isolated from the rest of Australia by thousands of miles of desert and lonely scrubland, Top Enders are different and proud of it. From the remote wetlands and stone country of Arnhem Land—home to thousands of Aboriginal people—to the lush tropical city of Darwin, the Top End is a gateway to a region where people from 50 different national and cultural backgrounds live in what they regard as the real Australia. It's an isolation that contributes to strong feelings of independence from the rest of the country—Southerners are regarded with a mixture of pity and ridicule.

It is also a region of geographical and climatic extremes. The people of the Top End spend more time than other Australians enjoying the outdoors, through sport, a wide variety of community celebrations and, simply, "going bush" for weekends of fishing, hiking, and exploring the many national parks.

Although Aboriginal people recognize up to six different seasons, for most people the year is divided into the Wet and the Dry. The Dry is a period of idyllic weather with warm days and cool nights. So, to make up for those eight months of the year where there is barely a cloud in the sky, the Wet season brings monsoonal storms that dump an average 65 inches of rain in a few short months—and even the rain is warm! Heralded by the notorious heat and humidity of the buildup, the Wet is a time of year when roads are washed out, rivers become impassable for months at a time, and the region faces the ever-present threat of cyclones.

It was during the Wet of 1974–75 that Cyclone Tracy ripped through Darwin with winds of 136 mph, killing 66 people and destroying or damaging more than 80% of its buildings. In this time of year, spectacular electrical storms light up the skies; the region between Darwin and Kakadu National Park has the world's highest recorded rate of lightning strikes—up to 1,000 during a single storm.

The starkness of the isolation of the Top End and Western Australia's Kimberley is reflected in its tiny population. While the Northern Territory occupies one sixth of Australia's landmass, its population of 170,000 makes up less than one hundredth of the continent's citizenry—an average density of one person per 8 square km (3 square mi). In many areas kangaroos and cattle vastly outnumber the locals: The Kimberley, an area of land larger than the state of Kansas, is home to only 30,000 people. Traveling by road from Darwin to Broome is the best way to see the Kimberley, but you'll pass through only nine communities in 2,016 km (1,250 mi), from such tiny settlements as Timber Creek to the big towns, such as Katherine.

The Kimberley possesses some of the most spectacular landscapes in Australia. A land of rugged ranges, tropical wetlands, and desert, of vast cattle stations and wonderful national parks, including the bizarre red-and-black-striped sandstone domes and towers of Purnululu National Park that are among Australia's most beautiful sights, the Kimberley still has the feel of the frontier about it. Like Top Enders, the people of the Kimberley region see themselves as living in a land apart from the rest of the nation, and it's easy to see why—landscape and distance combine to make the Kimberley one of the world's few uniquely open spaces.

Note: *See* Chapter 12 for more information on four-wheel-driving in the Top End and the Kimberley's great outdoors.

INDONESIA

Timor Sea

INDIAN OCEAN

Cape
Londonderry

Admiralty
Gulf

Kalumburu

*Bigge
Island*

*Cambridge
Gulf*

*Joseph
Bonaparte
Gulf*

DRYSDALE
RIVER
NATIONAL
PARK

*Augustus
Island*

**HIDDEN
VALLEY
NATIONAL
PARK**

Wyndham

Buccaneer Archipelago

Kuri Bay

KIMBERLEY
PLATEAU

El Questro ■
Cattle Station

Kununurra

*Collier
Bay*

Charnley R.

Newry

Cockatoo I.

Gibb River

Lake
Argyle

Turkey Creek
(Warmum)

Cape
Leveque

Lombadina

Gibb River Rd.

**PURNULULU
(BUNGLE BUNGLE)
NATIONAL PARK**

*King
Sound*

Beagle Bay

**TUNNEL CREEK
NATIONAL PARK**

Inverway

Lennard R.

Derby

Fitzroy R.

Great Northern Hwy.

Nicholson

**WINDJANA
GORGE
NATIONAL
PARK**

Yeeda

Broome

**GEIKIE GORGE
NATIONAL PARK**

**Fitzroy
Crossing**

**Halls
Creek**

WESTERN AUSTRALIA

Christmas
Creek

N

*WOLFE CREEK
CRATER
NATIONAL PARK*

GREAT SANDY DESERT

0   200 miles
0   300 km

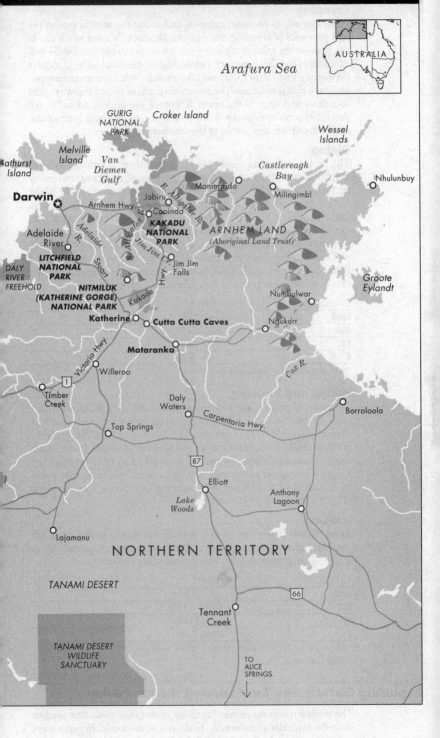

Arafura Sea

AUSTRALIA

GURIG NATIONAL PARK

Croker Island

Wessel Islands

Melville Island

Van Diemen Gulf

Castlereagh Bay

Nhulunbuy

Bathurst Island

Maningrida

Milingimbl

Darwin

Jabiru

E. Alligator R.

Arnhem Hwy

Cooinda

Alligator R.

KAKADU NATIONAL PARK

Adelaide River

Adelaide R.

Jim Jim Cr.

ARNHEM LAND
(Aboriginal Land Trust)

Groote Eylandt

LITCHFIELD NATIONAL PARK

Stuart

Jim Jim Falls

DALY RIVER FREEHOLD

Kakadu Hwy

Numbulwar

NITMILUK (KATHERINE GORGE) NATIONAL PARK

Katherine

Cutta Cutta Caves

Ngukurr

Mataranka

Cox R.

Victoria Hwy

Willeroo

Timber Creek

Daly Waters

Carpentaria Hwy.

Borroloola

1

Top Springs

87

Elliott

Anthony Lagoon

Lajamanu

Lake Woods

NORTHERN TERRITORY

TANAMI DESERT

66

TANAMI DESERT WILDLIFE SANCTUARY

Tennant Creek

TO ALICE SPRINGS

Pleasures and Pastimes

Camping

From Darwin to Broome, camping out under the stars is one of the real pleasures of traveling through the Outback. It's not much fun in the Wet—if the rains don't carry you away, the mosquitoes will—but camping in the Dry is perfect. Depending on personal taste, you don't even need a tent. Most locals just take a swag—a heavy canvas wrapped around a rolled mattress. The region abounds in out-of-the-way spots to pull up and sleep in the open. Wherever you go, ask a local to tell you the best place to throw down your swag, brew a billy (pot) of tea, and contemplate the glories of the southern night skies.

Dining

The menus in Darwin seem to indicate that there is little the average Territorian won't eat—buffalo, crocodile, camel, and kangaroo are all frequently featured. Another local favorite, barramundi, is one of the tastiest fish in the world. Buffalo can be tough, but a tender piece is like a gamey piece of beef. Opinion is divided about crocodile; it, too, can be tough, but (like every other reptile, it seems) a good piece tastes like chicken. Since 1996 a new eating precinct has developed in Darwin's Cullen Bay. Only five minutes from the city, near where Darwin Harbour cruises embark, this cluster of restaurants overlooking the marina provides a range of indoor and outdoor eating venues.

CATEGORY	COST*
$$$$	over $45
$$$	$30–$45
$$	$20–$30
$	under $20

per person, excluding drinks and service

Hiking and Walking

The national parks of the Top End and the Kimberley are ideal for hiking—Australians call it bushwalking—and the parks suit a variety of fitness levels. Major rock-art sites in Kakadu, for example, incorporate bushwalks from an hour or so to a half-day in length. Park rangers supply maps and route information for walks that last overnight and longer. The rugged adventures require care and planning, but you'll be rewarded with unforgettable memories of trekking through some of the most remote places on earth.

Lodging

Apart from Darwin hotels and Top End resorts, accommodations fall into the more basic category. With the local scenery as spectacular as it is, however, these shouldn't be discouraging words.

CATEGORY	COST*
$$$$	over $160
$$$	$100–$160
$$	$60–$100
$	under $60

All prices are for a standard double room, excluding the NT Tourism Marketing Levy of 2.5%.

Exploring Darwin, the Top End, and the Kimberley

The telltale recurring phrase "tyranny of distance" was first used to describe Australia's relationship to the rest of the world. In many ways it still describes the Top End and the Kimberley, with vast distances setting this region apart from the rest of the nation. This is not an area that you can justly contemplate—nor travel, for that matter—in a few days. And especially if you plan to get out to the Kimberley, you should consider seeing it over a couple of weeks and combining it with a visit to the Red Centre for full effect. There are a number of organized tours of varying lengths that may suit the time you have available, but for independent travelers the following are suggested.

Great Itineraries

IF YOU HAVE 3 DAYS

Limit your time to the Top End and **Kakadu** and **Litchfield National Parks**. Start from **Darwin** just after dawn and head east on the Arnhem Highway to **Fogg Dam** to view the birdlife. Continue into the park and picnic at the rock art site at **Ubirr**. Take a **scenic flight** in the afternoon, then a trip to the **Bowali Visitor's Centre**, and overnight at **Jabiru**. On the second day, head to **Nourlangie Rock** and **Anbangbang Billabong**, then continue to the **Yellow Water** cruise at **Cooinda** and stay there for the night. A visit to the **Aboriginal Cultural Centre** is a must on the third day, followed by a drive to **Litchfield National Park** via Batchelor. Depending on your time, a visit to any one of **Florence, Tjaynera,** or **Wangi Falls** for a picnic lunch followed by a stop at **Tolmer Falls** before returning to Darwin will conclude a somewhat hectic but rewarding survey of the Top End.

IF YOU HAVE 5 DAYS

Darwin should still be your starting point. To get straight into the Outback, start with a leisurely visit to **Litchfield National Park**, entering through the town of Batchelor. Don't miss a swim at the **Florence Falls** plunge pool and a picnic at **Petherick's Rain Forest**. Leave Litchfield on the back road to visit the **Territory Wildlife Park** at Berry Springs and move on to stay at the **South Alligator Holiday Village**. An early start on day two will allow you to reach the Kakadu rock art site at **Ubirr** not too long after dawn, if you're ambitious. After Ubirr, stop at **Bowali Visitors Centre** before continuing to **Nourlangie Rock** and **Anbangbang Billabong** for lunch. In the early afternoon visit the **Aboriginal Cultural Centre**, then take the evening **Yellow Water** cruise at **Cooinda**, where you can overnight. On the third day head down the Kakadu Highway to the less-visited southern half of Kakadu National Park, swim at Gumlom Falls and lunch across the South Alligator at Bukbukluk. After lunch drop into the old gold mining town of **Pine Creek** before continuing to **Edith Falls**. Camp there in **Nitmiluk (Katherine Gorge) National Park** or head into **Katherine** for the night. Next morning hire a canoe or take a cruise up Katherine Gorge in Nitmiluk National Park; after lunch head south to **Cutta Cutta Caves** and the thermal pools at **Mataranka** and stay the night at the **Mataranka Homestead**. The return trip to Darwin will give you a chance to explore some of the small roads down "the Track," as the Stuart Highway is called. A diversion from **Hayes Creek** along the path of the old highway to Adelaide River is a beautiful alternative way back to the city.

IF YOU HAVE 10 DAYS

With 10 days, you have a chance to break off from the shorter itineraries and head west to the Kimberley. From Mataranka or Litchfield National Park, go to **Katherine** and take the Victoria Highway for lunch at the Highway Inn in the spectacular gorge country at the Victoria River Crossing, passing then through mesa formations and **Timber Creek** to **Kununurra** for the night. On the sixth day, take in the spectacular landscapes of **Purnululu National Park** by four-wheel-drive or with a guided tour, and spend the night in **Halls Creek**. It'll be a long haul west the seventh day on the Great Northern Highway, but you can make it to **Geikie Gorge National Park** for an afternoon boat tour, a welcome and interesting respite before heading off to camp the night at **Wind-jana Gorge.** Another early start will get you to **Broome** to poke around in the old pearling town. Slow down and take a fishing charter the next day. The return trip through **Derby** and back along the Gibb River Road with an overnight camp at the **El Questro Cattle Station** reveals the Kimberley at its most remote and spectacular. Continue back to Darwin from El Questro. A couple of alternatives: Spend more time at Purnululu National Park and stop your westward trip through the Kimberley at El Questro. Or go ahead and trek all the way to Broome, and fly back to Darwin from there.

When to Tour the Top End

Unless you are used to extreme heat and humidity, the best time to tour is in the Dry, roughly May through August, with inland nights in July becoming quite chilly. On the road, early starts beat the heat and get you to swimming holes in the middle of the day—the crucial time for cooling off. Most boat tours in the region run throughout the day, but morning and evening cruises are best for several reasons: to avoid the heat, to see animals when they are out feeding, to catch sunrises and sunsets, and to take advantage of the ideal light for photography (by noon the light is often harsh and flat).

DARWIN

There is no other city in Australia that dates its history by a single cataclysmic event. For the people of Darwin—including the vast majority who weren't here at the time—everything is dated as before Tracy or after Tracy. It wasn't just the death toll; officially 66 people died on that terrible Christmas Eve, compared to the 243 who died on 1942's first day of Japanese bombing raids. It was the immensity of the destruction wrought by Cyclone Tracy that has marked Australia's northern capital. Casualties of war are one terrible thing; but the helplessness of an entire population faced with natural disaster is something else again. Within a week of Tracy, Australia's biggest peacetime airlift reduced the population from 47,000 people to 12,000, with many refusing to return to a city that, for them, had died.

It's a tribute to those who stayed and those who have come to live here after Tracy that the rebuilt city now thrives as an administrative and commercial center for northern Australia. Old Darwin has been replaced by something of an edifice complex—such buildings as Parliament House and the Supreme Court seem all a bit too grand for such a small city, especially one that prides itself on its relaxed atmosphere. Here Aborigines, Asians, and Anglos live together in an alluring combination of Outback openness and cosmopolitan multiculturalism.

The seductiveness of contemporary Darwin lifestyles belies a Top End history of failed attempts by Europeans dating back to 1824 to establish an enclave in a climate that was harsh and unyielding to new arrivals. The original 1869 settlement, called Palmerston, was built on a parcel of mangrove wetlands and rain forest that had changed little in 15 million years. It was not until 1911, after it had already weathered the disastrous cylones of 1878, 1882, and 1897, that the town was named after the scientist who had visited these shores aboard the *Beagle* in 1839.

Today Darwin is the best place from which to explore the beauty and diversity of Australia's Top End, as well as the wonders of Kakadu, Nitmiluk (Katherine Gorge), and the mighty Kimberley region.

Exploring Darwin

The orientation point for visitors is the Mall at Smith Street. Normally crowded with locals in shorts and T-shirts, groups of Aborigines, and well-dressed office workers, this is a place where cowboy meets croissant. The downtown grid of streets around the Mall is at the very tip of a peninsula; most of the suburbs and outlying attractions are out beyond the airport.

Numbers in the text correspond to numbers in the margin and on the Darwin map.

A Good Walk

From the Smith Street Mall head southwest down Knuckey Street across Mitchell Street. On the right, at the intersection with the Esplanade, is the 1925 **Lyons Cottage** ① museum, which focuses on local history, including early settlement, pearling, and relations with Indonesian and Chinese groups. On the other side of Knuckey Street, the **Old Admiralty House** ② is elevated on columns, once a common architectural feature of Darwin. Farther southeast on the Esplanade, the 1936 **Hotel Darwin** ③ also has an old-time look that will take you back to Darwin's early days.

The Esplanade winds around the hotel to a cairn known as the **Overland Telegraph Memorial** ④, the site of Australia's first telegraph connection with the rest of the world in 1871. Facing the memorial is **Government House** ⑤, which has remarkably withstood the ravages of cyclones and Japanese bombing in World War II.

On the opposite side of the Esplanade, between Mitchell and Smith streets, are the **Old Police Station and Court House** ⑥, which date to 1884, with their long veranda and old stone facades. They currently function as governmental offices. **Survivor's Lookout** ⑦, a memorial to the victims of Japan's first bombing of Australia in 1942, is across the road.

To get to the wharf area, take the stairs down the cliff face. Directly at the bottom of the stairs is the entrance to Darwin's **World War II Storage Tunnels** ⑧, which secured fuel stores in World War II. Inside there are photographs of Darwin during wartime.

A walk of 435 ft to the east leads to **Stokes Hill Wharf** ⑨. The wharf now has a dual function: serving ships and serving locals with restaurants, weekend markets, and a good fishing spot. For a different perspective on fish, stop in at the wharf's **Indo Pacific Marine** ⑩. Inside you'll find a vast tank in which a coral-reef ecosystem and its astonishing collection of fish reside. In the same building, the **Australian Pearling Exhibition** ⑪ has a lively presentation of northern Australia's history of hunting and cultivating pearls.

Returning up the cliff to Smith Street, look to your right for **Christ Church Cathedral** ⑫. **Browns Mart** ⑬, a theater, is on the same side of Smith Street farther down.

Stop in at the **Victoria Hotel,** across Bennett Street on the left-hand side of Smith Street, and proceed to the balcony for a drink—a fine way to conclude a walking tour of Darwin.

City Center

⑪ **Australian Pearling Exhibition.** Since the early 19th century, fortune seekers have hunted for pearls in Australia's northern waters. Exhibits at this museum cover everything from pearl farming to pearl jewelry settings. ⊠ *Stokes Hill Wharf,* ☎ *08/8999–6573.* ▭ *$6.* ☉ *Daily 10–5.*

476

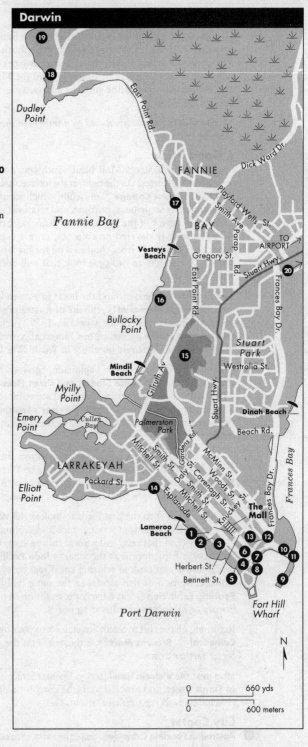

⑬ Browns Mart. Erected in 1885, this building has seen duty as an emporium, a mining exchange, and currently as a theater. ⊠ *Smith St. and Harry Chan Ave.*

NEED A
BREAK? The balcony of the **Victoria Hotel** is a good place for a little refreshment. A Darwin institution since its construction in 1894, the Vic has been hit by every cyclone and rebuilt afterward—most recently in 1978. ⊠ *Bennett and Smith Sts.*

⑫ Christ Church Cathedral. Darwin's Anglican church was largely destroyed by Cyclone Tracy, and the remains of the original 1902 structure have been incorporated into the new building. ⊠ *Smith St. and Esplanade S.*

❺ Government House. Darwin's oldest building, Government House has been the home of the administrator for the area since 1870. The grounds are not open to the public, but most of the building can be seen over the picket fence. Despite being bombed by Japanese aircraft in 1942 and damaged by the cyclones of 1897, 1937, and 1974, it looks much as it did in 1879 when it was first completed. The house faces the ☞ Overland Telegraph Memorial.

❸ Hotel Darwin. When the hotel opened in 1883, it set new standards for lodging in Darwin, including "accommodation suitable for ladies." The present building, erected in 1936, takes up most of a block. It still has period charm, with plenty of wicker, cane, and potted palms (☞ Lodging, *below*). ⊠ *10 Herbert St., at Esplanade,* ☎ *08/8981–9211.*

❿ Indo Pacific Marine. If you'd rather ogle fish than eat them, visit this aquarium at ☞ **Stokes Hill Wharf.** Housed in a huge, glass-sided tank is one of the few self-contained coral-reef ecosystems in the southern hemisphere. Special night tours that reveal fluorescent reef plants and animals include talks and a buffet dinner. ⊠ *Stokes Hill Wharf,* ☎ *08/ 8981–1294.* ▣ *$12, night tours $45.* ◷ *Daily 10–5.*

❶ Lyons Cottage. One of several buildings dating back to the early settlement of northern Australia in downtown Darwin, Lyons Cottage was built in 1925 for executives of the British-Australian Telegraph Company (B.A.T.). The stone building is now a historical museum with exhibits on life in Darwin, the Macassans, the Chinese, pearl diving, the early explorers, and the operation of the telegraph. ⊠ *74 Esplanade,* ☎ *08/8981–1750.* ▣ *Free.* ◷ *Daily 10–5.*

❷ Old Admiralty House. In Darwin's steamy climate the most suitable design for a house is to elevate it on columns. This style of building was once common in Darwin, but the Old Admiralty House is one of only a few of its kind to survive Cyclone Tracy in 1974. The house was built in 1937 to provide lodging for the naval officer commanding northern Australia. ⊠ *Knuckey St. and Esplanade.*

❻ Old Police Station and Court House. These side-by-side 1884 buildings were reconstructed after Cyclone Tracy to serve as offices for the Northern Territory administrator. Their long verandas and stone facades are typical of buildings from the period. ⊠ *Esplanade S between Mitchell and Smith Sts.*

❹ Overland Telegraph Memorial. On the harbor side of the Esplanade— near where it zigzags around the Hotel Darwin—is a cairn that marks the place where the first international telegraph cable came ashore from Java in 1871. A monumental event in Australia's history, this provided the first direct link with the mother country, England. Before that, information and orders from "home" took months to arrive by ship.

❾ Stokes Hill Wharf. The wharf has a number of restaurants and outdoor performance areas where concerts and arts-and-crafts markets are held most weekends during the Dry. It's also a favorite spot for Darwinites to fish: When the mackerel are running, you can join scores of locals over a few beers in late-night fishing parties. The wharf is a working pier as well with berths for cargo ships, trawlers, and defense vessels.

❼ Survivor's Lookout. On the site of World War II's first Japanese bombing raid on Australia, this memorial commemorates those who died, including sailors of the USS *Peary*. The shaded viewing platform holds a panoramic illustrated map describing the events of that fateful day. The lookout is also the gateway, via stairs down the cliff face, to the wharf precinct. ⊠ *Esplanade S.*

❽ World War II Storage Tunnels. Darwin's storage tunnels were built during World War II to store and protect fuel from Japanese bombing raids on the city. Carved into solid rock, the main tunnel is 22 ft high and 210 ft deep. There is a self-guided tour of the dimly lit tunnels, which now house photographic records of the war period. The entrance to the tunnels is at the bottom of the stairs below Survivor's Lookout. ⊠ *Esplanade,* ☎ *018/89–5982.* 🖭 *$4.*

Around Darwin

⓮ Aquascene. Visitors have the chance to hand-feed thousands of fish at Aquascene, on the northwestern end of the Esplanade. Starting with a few mullet over 30 years ago, fish have been coming here to be hand-fed. At high tide, people wade into the water with buckets of bread to feed the schools of batfish, bream, catfish, milkfish, and mullet that now come inshore in a feeding frenzy. ⊠ *Doctors Gully, Esplanade,* ☎ *08/8981–7837.* 🖭 *$4.50.* ☉ *Daily at high tide.*

⓴ Australian Aviation Heritage Centre. Due to its isolation and sparse population, the Northern Territory played an important role in the expansion of aviation in Australia, and this impressive museum traces the history of flight Down Under. Planes on exhibition include a massive B-52 bomber on permanent loan from the United States—one of very few not on U.S. soil—as well as a Japanese Zero shot down on the first day of bombing raids in 1942. ⊠ *557 Stuart Hwy., 8 km (5 mi) northeast of Darwin, Winnellie,* ☎ *08/8947–2145.* 🖭 *$8.* ☉ *Apr.–Sept., daily 8:30–5; Oct.–Mar., daily 10–4.*

☾ The Crocodile Farm. More than just a tourist park, this farm supplies much of the crocodile meat you'll find on menus around the Territory. It is also a research station studying both fresh- and saltwater crocodiles. The best time to visit is during the daily feeding and tour at 2 PM when the generally immobile reptiles become very active. There is an extra feeding session at noon on weekends. ⊠ *Stuart Hwy., 40 km (25 mi) south of Darwin,* ☎ *08/8988–1450.* 🖭 *$9.50.* ☉ *Daily 7:50–5, tour daily on the hr.*

⓯ Darwin's Botanic Gardens. Darwin's gardens make an ideal spot in which to escape the tropical heat. First planted in 1879, they were, like so much else, largely destroyed by Cyclone Tracy. They have been replanted with 400 species of figs and palms, as well as a wetland flora area, a rain forest, and a waterfall. The greenhouse displays ferns and orchids. ⊠ *Gardens Rd.,* ☎ *08/8981–1958.*

⓲ East Point Reserve. East Point Road leads past the beaches of Fannie Bay onto the headland occupied by the East Point Reserve. This is a pleasant expanse of small beaches, cliffs, lawns, and forest, where wallabies can be seen grazing at dawn and dusk.

⑰ Fannie Bay Gaol. If the sordid stuff of prison life stirs your blood, take a trip out to the gaol (pronounced "jail"), which served as a prison from 1883 to 1979. It is now a museum where you can look into the former gaol's living conditions and even the gallows where the last execution in the Northern Territory was performed in 1952. ⊠ *E. Point Rd., Fannie Bay,* ☎ *08/8999–8290.* 🎟 *Free.* ☉ *Daily 10–5.*

⑲ Military Museum. The museum at East Point has an interesting collection of artillery and vehicles. ⊠ *E. Point Rd., East Point,* ☎ *08/8981–9702.* 🎟 *$6.* ☉ *Daily 9:30–5.*

⑯ Museum and Art Gallery of the Northern Territory. Exhibits on natural history, Pacific Island cultures, and visual arts fill this interesting regional museum. One room is devoted to Cyclone Tracy, while the Gallery of Aboriginal Man has displays of Aboriginal art and culture that provide solid insight into the lives of the most ancient inhabitants of the Top End. Also on display are an exceptional collection of bark paintings and the stuffed remains of Sweetheart, a 17-ft crocodile taken from a Top End water hole. ⊠ *Conacher St., Bullocky Point, Fannie Bay,* ☎ *08/8999–8201.* 🎟 *Free except for some traveling exhibits.* ☉ *Weekdays 9–5, weekends 10–5.*

Ⓒ Territory Wildlife Park. In addition to its water buffalo, dingoes, and water birds, this large park has an underwater viewing area from which to observe freshwater fish and a nocturnal house kept dark for viewing animals that are active only at night. Visitors ride around the 960-acre park on a train. Allow at least two hours to tour the park. ⊠ *Stuart Hwy., 47 km (29 mi) south of Darwin, Berry Springs,* ☎ *08/ 8988–6000.* 🎟 *$12.* ☉ *Daily 8:30–4.*

OFF THE
BEATEN PATH

Fogg Dam – Built as a water supply for the ill-fated rice-growing project of Humpty Doo in the late 1950s, Fogg Dam has remained untouched by commercialism in its remote location 68 km (42 mi) east of Darwin. The project failed largely because the birds of the region regarded the rice crop as a rather tasty smorgasbord. The birds have remained, and they provide an unforgettable sight at sunrise and sunset during the Dry. Exercise care driving through this swampland, however, and wear clothes that you don't mind getting dirty.

To get to the Dam from Darwin, take the Stuart Highway to the Arnhem Highway. After 24 km (15 mi) turn left and continue for another 6 km (4 mi); then turn right and drive the last ¾ km (½ mi) to the dam.

Dining

City Center

$$$$ ✗ **The Boardroom.** Located atop the MGM Grand Hotel Casino (☞ Lodging, *below*), this intimate restaurant serves delectable modern Australian cuisine. The somewhat nondescript decor belies an excitingly varied menu with French undertones, and the chefs do wonders with barramundi. It has a very good Australian wine list and a heavenly dessert trolley. ⊠ *MGM Grand Casino, Gilruth Ave., Mindil Beach,* ☎ *08/8943–8888. Reservations essential. AE, DC, MC, V. No lunch Sat.–Wed.*

$$–$$$ ✗ **Christo's on the Wharf.** Part of the Wharf Precinct, Christo's has Darwin's most unusual setting. Situated at the end of a commercial wharf in a renovated corrugated-iron storage shed, this large restaurant is dominated by a traditional Macassarese fishing prau seized by Australian customs in 1990. Open to sea breezes, it is an ideal place to escape from Darwin's summer heat. Seafood takes the foreground, and such Greek dips as *taramasalata* can be followed by chili bugs (small lobsters), lightly

cooked calamari, or garlic prawns, a specialty of the house. ⊠ *Stokes Hill Wharf,* ☎ *08/8981–8658. AE, DC, MC, V.*

\$\$–\$\$\$ ✕ **Hanuman Thai and Nonya Restaurant.** Hanuman sets a standard
★ for dining in Darwin. Dark furniture and deep peacock-blue walls with touches of gold provide atmosphere for fine food and a wine list that includes the best from every grape-growing region in Australia. By drawing on Thai and Nonya (Malaysian) culinary traditions, Hanuman's chefs turn locally produced herbs, vegetables, and seafood into a wide range of innovative dishes. Of special note are Hanuman oysters, lightly cooked in a spicy coriander-and-lemongrass sauce; barramundi baked with ginger flower; *tom yum* soups; and any of the many curries. ⊠ *28 Mitchell St.,* ☎ *08/8941–3500. AE, DC, MC, V.*

\$\$ ✕ **Twilight On Lindsay.** Lush tropical gardens surround this old-style,
★ elevated house. The café serves some of Darwin's more exotic cuisine, adaptations of Asian and European food to tropical climes. The menu is regularly updated, but some perennial customer favorites include rice pancakes with paw-paw salad, shallots, and oyster mushrooms, and grilled escallope of kangaroo with lemongrass–and–red wine sauce, cracked coriander, and sweet pickled mango slices. ⊠ *2 Lindsay St.,* ☎ *08/8981–8631. AE, DC, MC, V. Closed Sun. No lunch Sat., Mon.– Wed.*

\$\$ ✕ **Tonkris Restaurant.** Next to the Plaza Hotel, the Tonkris has a homey atmosphere, plus traditional northern Italian country cooking and an excellent selection of wine. Dine outdoors or in air-conditioned comfort. Along with a range of pastas—the marinara makes best use of local produce—meat dishes are superbly cooked and presented. The lamb cacciatore, topped with anchovy, garlic, and herbs, is highly recommended. ⊠ *Mitchell Plaza,* ☎ *08/8981–0778. AE, DC, MC, V.*

\$ ✕ **Roma Bar.** The decorative theme of the Roma Bar seems only accidentally Italian, and the clientele is similarly eclectic: Office workers, lawyers, and magistrates from the business district mingle with artists, entertainers, and students. Visitors enjoy the good coffee and somewhat rowdy hubbub of business-suited and barefoot Darwinites in their natural habitat. The menu is full of straightforward fare—fresh green salads, pasta, and focaccia. ⊠ *30 Cavenagh St.,* ☎ *08/8981–6729. No credit cards.*

Cullen Bay

\$\$ ✕ **Poseidon.** A statue of the Greek god presides over this waterside restau-
★ rant on the Cullen Bay waterfront and the owners provide authentic Greek cuisine. Ask for the local calamari, char-grilled prawns, and fish of the day basted with oregano, or the steak, marinated Greek-style in lemon, garlic, oregano, and olive oil. ⊠ *62 Marina Blvd, Cullen Bay,* ☎ *08/8981–6788. AE, DC, MC, V.*

Lodging

City Center

\$\$\$\$ 🏨 **Carlton** (formerly Beaufort). With its colorful, round exterior, this
★ five-story hotel is the most striking and unusual in Darwin, as well as the most expensive. The rooms, arranged around a central foyer, are decorated in subtle greens and pinks and accented by natural wood. Most rooms have city or harbor views. ⊠ *Esplanade, 0800,* ☎ *08/8980– 0800 or 1800/89–1119,* 🖷 *08/8980–0888. 196 rooms, 32 suites. 2 restaurants, 3 bars, pool, 2 saunas, exercise room, shops, nightclub, laundry service. AE, DC, MC, V.*

\$\$\$\$ 🏨 **MGM Grand Hotel Casino.** Shaped like pyramids with square tops, this casino and the smaller adjoining hotel are two of the most distinctive structures in the city. Set amid lush lawns and gardens, the three-story hotel is *the* luxury resort in Darwin, with the city's only beachfront accommodations. Well-appointed rooms combine a tropical feeling with dark marble, cherry-wood furniture, and Italian designer lighting fixtures. ⊠ *Gilruth Ave., Mindil Beach, 0800,* ☎ *08/8943–8888,* 𝔽𝔸𝕏 *08/ 8943–8999. 84 rooms, 12 suites. 3 restaurants, 2 bars, pool, sauna, spa, tennis court, exercise room, casino. AE, DC, MC, V.*

$$$$ 🏨 **Rydges Plaza Hotel.** Central to the business district, this 12-story hotel is the tallest in Darwin. Rooms have a pleasant mixture of art deco–style lamps and cool pastel furnishings. With its piano bar and elegant armchairs, the high-ceiling lobby can seem a bit formal if you're coming straight from a fishing trip or the mud pools of Kakadu. Equally posh, if improbably named, is the hotel's restaurant, Igunana. ⊠ *32 Mitchell St., 0800,* ☎ *08/8982–0000 or 1800/89–1107,* 𝔽𝔸𝕏 *08/ 8981–1765. 233 rooms, 12 suites. 2 restaurants, 2 bars, pool, sauna, exercise room. AE, DC, MC, V.*

$$$ 🏨 **Holiday Inn Darwin.** Spectacular views of Darwin Harbour and the city are the highlight of this nine-story hotel. Rooms are light, airy, and equipped with kitchen facilities. Flexible room configurations in the both executive and premier suites make these ideal for larger groups and families. ⊠ *88 Esplanade, 0800,* ☎ *08/8943–4333 or 1800/681– 686,* 𝔽𝔸𝕏 *08/8943–4388. 64 rooms, 140 suites. Restaurant, bar, pool, beauty salon, spa, laundry service. AE, DC, MC, V.*

$$$ 🏨 **Novotel Atrium.** Vying for the title of Darwin's prettiest hotel, the ★ Atrium's seven floors are served by glass elevators opening onto a central, vine-hung atrium. The hotel's bars and restaurants are set around a tiny artificial stream amid palm trees and ferns. Guest rooms are attractive and airy, decorated in pastel blues, and each has its own kitchenette. ⊠ *Peel St. and Esplanade, 0800,* ☎ *08/8941–0755,* 𝔽𝔸𝕏 *08/8981– 9025. 138 rooms, 4 suites. 2 restaurants, 2 bars, pool, laundry service. AE, DC, MC, V.*

$$ 🏨 **All Seasons Premier Darwin Central Hotel.** Darwin's architectural obsession with corrugated iron finds new outlet in this unusual-looking modern hotel. As the name implies, it is the city's most central accommodation, overlooking the Smith Street Mall. All rooms have city views and cool color schemes, and are located around a delightful eight-story atrium. ⊠ *Smith and Knuckey Sts., 0800,* ☎ *08/8944–9000 or 1300/364–263,* 𝔽𝔸𝕏 *08/8944–9100. 102 rooms, 30 suites. Restaurant, bar, pool, laundry service. AE, DC, MC, V.*

$$ 🏨 **Hotel Darwin.** Once the grande dame of Darwin, this two-story colonial hotel has faded with time. The Green Room—the bar where much of the city's business has been discussed over the years—is still a pleasant indoor-outdoor area next to the pool. The rooms belong to an earlier era and their carpets are worn, but they have views over the garden or pool. Despite its slightly run-down look, the hotel maintains its colonial character, including ample use of wicker and cane. ⊠ *10 Herbert St., 0800,* ☎ *08/8981–9211,* 𝔽𝔸𝕏 *08/8981–9575. 66 rooms with shower, 7 with bath. Restaurant, bar, pool, nightclub, laundry service. AE, DC, MC, V.*

$ 🏨 **YHA Hostel.** The hostel provides the cheapest accommodations in town, but for Youth Hostel Association members only. Sleeping areas are basic but clean, bright, and airy. You need to supply or rent sheets, but you'll have all of the other basics, including cooking facilities. ⊠ *69A Mitchell St., 0800,* ☎ *08/8981–3995,* 𝔽𝔸𝕏 *08/8981–6674. 292 beds in 96 rooms with shared baths. Coin laundry. AE, MC, V.*

Gurig National Park

$$$$ ✕🏨 **Seven Spirit Bay.** A couple hundred miles northeast of Darwin on ★ the pristine Cobourg Peninsula is an international resort accessible only by a one-hour light-plane flight. The resort occupies several acres in Gurig National Park and consists of groups of individual hexagonal huts linked to the main complex by winding paths. Each hut contains a single spacious room and has its own fenced outdoor bathroom. The main building, with polished timbers and high ceilings, leads out to the deck and pool and the ocean beyond. There is a resident naturalist, and excursions include photographic tours and bushwalks to see wildlife such as dingo dogs, wallabies, goannas (large lizards), crocodiles, feral water buffalo, and Timorese ponies. The dining room serves light, modern Australian dishes—some of the Territory's best meals—using seafood from the surrounding waters and herbs from resort's gardens. Meals are included in the rate. ⊠ *Box 4721, Darwin 0801,* ☎ *08/8979–0277 or 1800/89–1189,* FAX *08/8979–0284. 24 rooms. Dining room, bar, pool.*

Nightlife and the Arts

Bars and Lounges

For a quiet beer, visit the **Top End Best Western** (⊠ Daly and Mitchell Sts., ☎ 08/8981–6511). If you feel like having a Guinness, **Shenannigans Hotel** (⊠ 69 Mitchell St., ☎ 08/8981–2100) has it on tap. It's also the only place in town where you can get those other two famous Irish beers, Kilkenny and Harp. A bar alternately called the **World Travellers Bar** or Herbie's (⊠ Mitchell and Herbert Sts., ☎ 08/8981–9211), attached to the Hotel Darwin, is a well-known haunt for world-weary travelers on a tight budget. If you're after a late night and a friendly (albeit very smoky) game of pool, try **Squire's Tavern** (⊠ 3E Edmund St., ☎ 08/8981–9761). For the young and hip, step next door to the **Time** (⊠ 3E Edmund St., ☎ 08/8981–9761) nightclub, where you can dance the night away to techno and funk. For a more sedate evening, visit **Petty Sessions** (⊠ Shop 2, Northern Territory House, Mitchell St., ☎ 08/8941–2000).

Casino

MGM Grand Hotel Casino is Darwin's most popular source of evening entertainment. ⊠ *Gilruth Ave.,* ☎ *08/8946–2666.*

Theaters and Concerts

The **Darwin Entertainment Centre** (⊠ 93 Mitchell St., ☎ 08/8981–1222), next door to the Beaufort Hotel, has a large theater that regularly stages concerts, dance, and drama. It also doubles as booking office for other touring concerts in town—especially those at the **Amphitheatre,** Australia's best outdoor concert venue (entrance next to Botanical Gardens on Gardens Road). Check the *Northern Territory News* or the *Sunday Territorian* for current shows, or call the center.

Outdoor Activities and Sports

Bicycling

Darwin is fairly flat, so cycling is a good way to get around—except during the Wet, when you are pretty likely to get soaked. Rent bicycles from **Darwin Bike Hire,** next door to Shenannigans Hotel on Mitchell Street.

Fishing

Barrimundi, the best-known fish of the Top End, can weigh up to 110 pounds and are excellent fighting fish that taste great on the barbie afterward. Fishing safaris can be arranged through **Big Barra** (☎ 08/8932–1473, FAX 08/8932–1473) and **NT Barra Fishing Trips** (☎ 08/8945–1841). For ocean game-fishing contact **Predator Charters** (☎ 0419/41–8800).

Golf

The only 18-hole course in Darwin is **Darwin Golf Club** (⊠ Links Rd., Marrara, ☎ 08/8927–1322); greens fees are $16 for 9 holes and $25 for 18, and the club has motorized carts for hire at $15 and $20. The **Gardens Park Golf Links** (⊠ Botanic Gardens, ☏ 08/8981–6365) is a 9-hole course; fees are $10 for adults. **Palmerston Golf and Country Club** (⊠ Dwyer Crescent, Palmerston, ☏ 08/8932–1324) also has 9 holes; however, with different tees you can play 18. Greens fees are $10 for 9 holes and $15 for 18. You can rent clubs at all three courses.

Health and Fitness Clubs

The most central commercial gym is **Time Out Fitness Centre.** ⊠ 5-2798 *Dashwood Pl.,* ☏ 08/8941–8711. ⊙ *Weekdays 6:30 AM–8 PM, Sat. 9–6, Sun. 10–2.*

Motorscooting

If you don't want to hire a car, a small motorbike is the next best thing. It's a cheap way to get around, although not advisable during the Wet for obvious reasons. **Freedom Cycles** hires small motor scooters for reasonable rates. ⊠ *90 Mitchell St.,* ☏ 08/8981–9995.

Running

The waterfront park parallel to the Esplanade is a good area for running within the city. For a longer run, the beachfront parks along the shores of Fannie Bay to East Point provide generally flat terrain and a great view.

Tennis

The **Darwin Tennis Centre** has four courts. ⊠ *Gilruth Ave., Botanic Gardens,* ☏ 08/8985–2844.

Water Sports

Marine stingers (jellyfish) and other hazards restrict water activities around Darwin. The **beaches** of Fannie Bay, such as Mindil and Vesteys, and those of Nightcliff are no less popular, however, especially on weekends.

For diving, contact **Cullen Bay Dive** (⊠ 66 Marine Blvd., Cullen Bay, ☏ 08/8981–3049) or **Sand Pebbles Dive Shop** (⊠ De Latour St., Coconut Grove, ☏ 08/8948–0444).

To rent sailboats, contact **Darwin Sailing Club** (☏ 08/8981–1700 or 015/61–0753).

Shopping

Aboriginal Art

As in Alice Springs, the best buys in Darwin are Aboriginal paintings and artifacts. A visit to the **Museum and Art Gallery of the Northern Territory** (☞ Around Darwin, *above*) will give you a good idea of the highest standards attainable.The extensive Aboriginal art collection on public display at the **Supreme Court** (⊠ State Sq., Mitchell St.) is complemented by a spectacular floor mosaic of an Aboriginal desert "dot" painting. The best commercial galleries in Darwin are the **Raintree Aboriginal Art Gallery** (⊠ Shop 3, 20 Knuckey St., ☏ 08/8981–2732), and **Framed Gallery** (⊠ 55 Stuart Hwy., ☏ 08/8981–2994).

Markets

For Darwin locals, markets have become as much a form of popular entertainment as they are a shopping venue. Up to a fifth of the city's population may show up for the **Mindil Beach Sunset Markets** (⊠ Mindil Beach, ☏ 08/8981–3454), an extravaganza that takes place every Thursday evening during the Dry (Apr.–Oct.). After the hard work of snacking at hundreds of food stalls, shopping at artisans' booths, and watching singers, dancers, and musicians, Darwinites unpack tables, chairs, and bottles of wine and then watch the sun plunge into the harbor.

Other markets for food, secondhand items, and crafts stands include the **Big Flea Market** (⊠ Rapid Creek Shopping Centre, Trower Rd., Rapid Creek, ☎ 08/8985–5806), which specializes in Asian-influenced produce and cuisine. Hours are Sunday 8–1. The **Parap Market** (⊠ Parap Sq., Parap) is open Saturday 8–2. The **Palmerston Night Market** (⊠ Frances Mall, ☎ 08/8932–2623) is open Friday 5:30–9:30.

Darwin A to Z

Arriving and Departing

BY BUS

Greyhound Pioneer (☎ 08/8981–8700) terminates at the Mitchell Street Shopping Precinct, which is the old **Darwin Transit Centre** (⊠ 69 Mitchell St.), and **McCafferty's** (☎ 08/8941–0911) terminates at 71 Smith Street in the middle of town.

BY CAR

The Stuart Highway is Darwin's land connection with the rest of Australia, and anyone arriving by car will enter the city on this road. Darwin is 1,706 km (1,058 mi) by road from Alice Springs and 4,095 km (2,539 mi) from Sydney.

BY PLANE

Darwin's International Airport is serviced from overseas by **Ansett Australia, Qantas, Singapore Airlines,** and **Malaysia Airlines.** Domestic carriers flying into Darwin are **Qantas Australian** and **Ansett Australia.** *See* Air Travel *in* Smart Travel Tips for airline telephone numbers.

Between the Airport and Downtown. Airport Transfers (☎ 08/8945–1000) has regular bus service between the airport and the downtown area. The cost is $8 per person or $12 for two people traveling together.

The airport is 15 km (9 mi) northeast of the city **by car.** After leaving the terminal, turn left into McMillans Road and left again into Bagot Road. Continue until you cross the overpass that merges into the Stuart Highway, which later becomes Daly Street. Turn left into Smith Street to reach the Smith Street Mall in the heart of the city.

Taxis are available from the taxi rank at the airport. The journey downtown costs about $15.

Getting Around

BY BUS

The bus network in Darwin links the city with its far-flung suburbs. The main **bus terminal** (Buslink, ☎ 08/8947–0577) for city buses is on Harry Chan Avenue, near the Bennett Street end of Smith Street Mall.

BY CAR

The best way to get around Darwin is by car. Rental car companies include **Avis** (⊠ Airport, and 145 Stuart Hwy., Stuart Park, ☎ 08/8981–9922); **Britz-Rentals** (⊠ 44–46 Stuart Hwy., Stuart Park, ☎ 08/8981–2081); **Budget** (⊠ Airport, and 108 Mitchell St., ☎ 08/8981–9800); **Hertz** (⊠ Airport, and Smith and Daly Sts. Darwin, ☎ 08/8941–0944); **Territory Rent-a-Car** (⊠ Airport, and 64 Stuart Hwy., Stuart Park, ☎ 08/8981–8400); and **Thrifty** (⊠ Airport, and 64 Stuart Hwy., Stuart Park, ☎ 08/8981–8555). Four-wheel-drive vehicles are available.

BY TAXI

Contact **Darwin Radio Taxis** (☎ 08/8981–8777), **Darwin Combined Taxis** (☎ 13–1008), or **Taxinet North** (☎ 08/8943–8008).

Contacts and Resources

EMERGENCIES

Ambulance, fire brigade, and police. ☎ *000.*

Royal Darwin Hospital (☎ 08/8922–8888) has a 24-hour emergency room.

Night & Day Medical & Dental Surgery. ✉ *Casuarina Shopping Centre,* ☎ *08/8927–1899.*

Trower Road A/H Medical Service. ✉ *Trower Rd.,* ☎ *08/8927–6905.*

GUIDED TOURS

Every day but Sunday, **Darwin Day Tours** (☎ 08/8981–8696) conducts half-day tours ($29) morning and afternoon. For $7 more you can extend the afternoon tour to take in the sunset with a glass of champagne. Tours include historic buildings, the main harbor, the Botanic Gardens, the Museum and Art Gallery of the Northern Territory, the East Point Military Reserve, and the Fannie Bay Gaol Museum. Fish feeding at Aquascene is sometimes included, depending on the tides.

Daytime and sunset cruises around one of the most beautiful and unspoiled harbors in the world are available on **Darwin Harbour Tours**' *Darwin Duchess.* There's a licensed bar on board. ✉ *Stokes Hill Wharf,* ☎ *08/8978–5094.* 🚢 $25.

VISITOR INFORMATION

Darwin Region Tourism Association. ✉ *Beagle House, Mitchell and Knuckey Sts., Darwin 0800,* ☎ *08/8981–4300.*

KAKADU NATIONAL PARK

Kakadu National Park is a jewel in the array of Top End parks, and many visitors come to the Top End just to experience this tropical wilderness. Located 256 km (159 mi) east of Darwin, the park covers 20,082 square km (7,720 square mi) and protects a large system of unspoiled rivers and creeks, as well as a rich Aboriginal heritage that extends back to the earliest days of humankind. The superb gathering of Aboriginal rock art may be Kakadu's highlight.

Two major types of **Aboriginal artwork** are found here. The Mimi style, which is the oldest, is believed to be up to 20,000 years old. Aborigines believe that Mimi spirits created the red-ochre stick figures to depict hunting scenes and other pictures of life at the time. The more recent artwork, known as X-ray painting, dates back less than 9,000 years and depicts freshwater animals—especially fish, turtles, and geese—living in floodplains created after the last ice age. The animals are drawn complete with heart, spinal cord, lungs, and intestines.

Most of the region is virtually inaccessible during the Wet, so it is strongly advisable to visit the park between May and September. As the dry season progresses, water holes (billabongs) become increasingly important to the more than 280 species of birds that inhabit the park: Huge flocks can be found at Yellow Water, South Alligator River, and Magela Creek. If you do visit during the Wet, scenic flights over the wetlands and Arnhem Land escarpment provide unforgettable moments.

Most of the park is the property of Aboriginal traditional owners and managed by a board with an Aboriginal majority membership. Visitor access is restricted to certain areas.

Orientation

The **Bowali Visitors Centre's** state-of-the-art audiovisual displays and traditional exhibits give an introduction to the park's ecosystems and its bird population, the world's most diverse. The park's Aboriginal owners contribute to the flora and fauna information and provide insight into their culture's traditional hunting practices, land-management techniques, and use of raw materials. ✉ *Arnhem and Kakadu Hwys.*, ☎ *08/8938–1100.* 🎫 *Free.* 🕐 *Daily 8–5.*

Warradjan Aboriginal Cultural Centre. Opened in 1995 at Yellow Water near Cooinda, the cultural center—named after the pig-nose turtle unique to the Top End—is an excellent experience of local native culture. Displays take you through the Aboriginal Creation period, following the path of the creation ancestor Rainbow Serpent through the ancient landscape of Kakadu. Other displays illustrate important stories associated with the park and the activities of the Nayuhyunggi (first people), who created the land, plants, and animals and who gave people laws to live by. ✉ *Kakadu Hwy., Cooinda,* ☎ *08/8979–0051.* 🎫 *Free.* 🕐 *Daily 9–5.*

Exploring

★ Like the main Kakadu escarpment, **Nourlangie Rock** is a remnant of an ancient plateau that is slowly eroding away, leaving sheer cliffs rising high above the floodplains. The main attraction at Nourlangie Rock is the **Anbangbang Gallery,** an excellent frieze of Aboriginal rock paintings. To reach the paintings, drive 19 km (12 mi) from the park headquarters down the Kakadu Highway to the left-hand turnoff to Nourlangie Rock, then follow this paved road (accessible year-round) about 11 km (7 mi) to the parking area and paintings.

Ubirr has an even more impressive array of Aboriginal paintings scattered through six shelters in the rock. The main gallery contains a 49-ft frieze of X-ray paintings depicting animals, birds, and fish. A half-mile path around the rock leads to all the galleries. Ubirr is 43 km (27 mi) north of the park headquarters along a paved road.

The best way to gain a true appreciation of the natural beauty of Kakadu is to visit the **waterfalls** running off the escarpment. Some 39 km (24 mi) south of the park headquarters along the Kakadu Highway, a track leads off to the left toward Jim Jim and Twin falls. This unpaved road is suitable only for four-wheel-drive vehicles and is closed in the Wet. Even in good conditions, the 60-km (37-mi) ride to Jim Jim takes about two hours. The Twin Falls car park is 10 km (6 mi) farther on.

In the Dry you can continue down the Jim Jim and Twin falls road to Pine Creek, a worthwhile shortcut if you are traveling between Kakadu and Katherine.

★ From the parking area at **Jim Jim Falls,** you have to walk a half mile over boulders to reach the falls and the plunge pool it has created at the base of the escarpment. On the right side before the main pool is a beautiful sandy beach shelving to a pleasant, shallow swimming area. After May, the waterflow over the falls may cease but the pools remain well worth visiting.

★ **Twin Falls** is more difficult to reach, but the trip is rewarding. After a short walk from the parking lot, you must swim along a small creek for a few hundred yards to reach the falls—many people use inflatable air beds as rafts to transport their lunch and towels. As you approach, the ravine opens up dramatically to reveal a beautiful sandy beach scattered with palm trees, as well as the crystal waters of the falls spilling onto the end of the beach. If you are feeling energetic, swim across the large pool to a track leading up to the top of the falls. On top, the river has worn the rocks smooth, creating fantastic stone sculpture.

Dining and Lodging

🏕 **Campgrounds** at Merl, Muirella Park, Mardugal, and Gunlom have toilets, showers, and water. Tents are $7 per night. Privately operated campgrounds are available at Frontier Kakadu Village and the Gagudju Lodge Cooinda.

$$$$ ✕🏨 **All Seasons Frontier Kakadu Village.** This 138-room hotel has two room sizes: doubles with one queen-size and one single bed, and family rooms with a queen and two single beds. Room rates are significantly higher during the Dry. ✉ *2½ km (1½ mi) before Arnhem Hwy. crosses South Alligator River,* ☎ *08/8979–0166 or 1800/81–8845,* FAX *08/8979–2254. 138 rooms. Restaurant, café, pool, spa, tennis court, laundry service. AE, DC, MC, V.*

$$$$ 🏨 **Gagudju Crocodile Hotel.** Shaped like a crocodile, this unusual hotel's spacious rooms are the best of the area's three accommodation options. The reception is through the mouth, the swimming pool is in the open courtyard in the belly, and the gardener's shed is at the end of the tail. ✉ *Flinders St., Jabiru,* ☎ *08/8979–2800. 110 rooms. Restaurant, tavern, pool. AE, DC, MC, V.*

$$$ 🏨 **Gagudju Lodge Cooinda.** Conveniently located near Yellow Water, this 48-room facility has light, airy rooms looking out to tropical gardens. ☎ *08/8979–0145 or 800/50–0401,* FAX *08/8979–0148. 48 rooms. Restaurant, bar, pool. AE, MC, V.*

Kakadu A to Z

Arriving and Departing

From Darwin take the Arnhem Highway east to Jabiru. Although four-wheel-drive vehicles are not necessary to travel to the park, they are required for many of the unpaved roads within, including the track to Jim Jim Falls. The entrance fee is $15 per person.

Guided Tours

AERIAL TOURS

Kakadu Air Services (☎ 08/8979–2731, 08/8979–2411, or 1800/08–9113) flies out of Jabiru and Darwin.

BOAT TOURS

★ The **Gagudju Lodge Cooinda** arranges boat tours of **Yellow Water**, the major water hole during the Dry, where innumerable birds and crocodiles gather. There are six tours throughout the day; the first (6:45 AM) is the coolest. ☎ *08/8979–0111.* 🎫 *$26.50.*

GENERAL TOURS

During the Dry, **park rangers** conduct free walks and tours at several popular locations. You can pick up a program at the entry station or at either of the visitor centers. **Billy Can Tours** (✉ Box 4407, Darwin 0801, ☎ 08/8981–9813 or 1800/81–3484, FAX 08/8941–0803) provides a range of two- and three-day camping and accommodation tours in Kakadu, including special wet-season tours and trips that combine excursions to Kakadu with ☞ **Litchfield** and ☞ **Nitmiluk** (Katherine Gorge) national parks. **Odyssey Safaris** (✉ Box 3012, Darwin 0801, ☎ 08/8948–0091 or 1800/89–1190, FAX 08/8948–0646) offers quality deluxe four-wheel-drive tours into Kakadu as well as other areas of northern Australia including the ☞ **Kimberley**, and Litchfield and Nitmiluk national parks.

Visitor Information

Darwin Region Tourism Association. ✉ *Beagle House, Mitchell and Knuckey Sts., Darwin 5744,* ☎ *08/8981–4300.*

Kakadu National Park. ✉ *Box 71, Jabiru 0886,* ☎ *08/8938–1100.*

LITCHFIELD NATIONAL PARK

Litchfield, one of the Northern Territory's newest parks, is also one of the most accessible from Darwin. Convenience hasn't spoiled the park's beauty, however: Almost all of the park's 1,340 square km (515 square mi) are covered by an untouched wilderness of monsoonal rain forests, rivers, and escarpment—cliffs formed by erosion. The highlights of this dramatic landscape are four separate spectacular waterfalls supplied by natural springs year-round from aquifers deep under the plateau. And the park is crocodile free.

Exploring

Lovely trails lead to **Florence, Tjaynera,** and **Wangi Falls,** all of which have secluded plunge pools. **Tolmer Falls** looks out over a natural rock arch and is within a short walk of the parking lot. Near Tolmer Falls—accessible only by four-wheel-drive vehicles—is a series of large, free-standing sandstone pillars known as the **Lost City.** The living landscape is no less unusual: Look for groves of extremely slow-growing **cycad palms,** an ancient plant species that is unique to the area, the larger specimens of which are thought to be hundreds of years old.

Magnetic Termite Mounds, which have an eerie resemblance to eroded grave markers, dot the black-soil plains of the park's northern area. To avoid being crisped by the hot tropical sun, termites orient their mounds so that they face north–south, leaving only a thin edge exposed to direct light.

Dining and Lodging

If you want to stay in Litchfield National Park, you'll have to camp. Sites are available at Florence Falls, Wangi Falls, Buley Rockhole, and Sandy Creek. These ⚠ **campgrounds** are basic—Buley has no shower facilities and Sandy Creek is accessible only by four-wheel-drive vehicles—but the price can't be beat. You'll never pay more than $5 per person per night. Contact the **Parks and Wildlife Commission** (☎ 08/ 8976–0282) for more information.

In Batchelor, you'll find a couple of restaurants and a number of caravan parks, as well as the moderately priced **Rum Jungle Motor Inn.** ✉ 220 Rum Jungle Rd., Batchelor 0845, ☎ 08/8976–0123, ☎ 08/8976–0230. 22 rooms. Restaurant, pool. MC, V.

Arriving and Departing

Litchfield is an easy 122 km (76 mi) from Darwin. Take the Stuart Highway 85 km (53 mi) south to the turnoff for the town of **Batchelor,** and continue on the Batchelor Road to the park's northern border. As you enter the park you will see a sign telling you to tune your radio to 88 on the FM dial. This station provides up-to-date information on the park, such as current road and campsite conditions, and how to get to the park's main areas of interest. Most of the park is accessible by conventional vehicles; four-wheel-drive vehicles are advised after the rains and are necessary to enter the park from **Berry Springs** or Adelaide River. You can make a loop through the park by connecting the Batchelor and Berry Springs entrances.

Guided Tours

Billy Can Tours provides a number of tours to Litchfield, along with those that combine Litchfield with Kakadu and Nitmiluk (Katherine Gorge) national parks. ✉ Box 4407, Darwin 0801, ☎ 08/8981–9813 or 1800/81–3484, ☎ 08/8941–0803.

Visitor Information

Parks and Wildlife Commission of the Northern Territory. ⊠ *Box 45, Batchelor 0845,* ☎ *08/8976–0282.*

KATHERINE

327 km (203 mi) southeast of Darwin.

If you're heading west to the Kimberley or south to the Red Centre, Katherine River is the last permanently flowing water till you get to Adelaide—2,741 km (1,700 mi) to the south! A veritable oasis, Katherine is the crossroads of the region, making it the second-largest town in the Top End with a booming population of 10,500. Named in 1862 by the European explorer John McDouall Stuart after the daughter of his patron, the town was first established to service the Overland Telegraph that linked the south with Asia and Europe. It was the site of the first cattle and sheep runs in the Top End, and the Springvale Homestead 8 km (5 mi) west of town is the oldest still standing in the Northern Territory.

Katherine is now a regional administrative and supply center for the cattle industry, as well as being the site for the largest military air base in northern Australia. The focus of the town is on the Katherine River, which is popular for its fishing, swimming, and canoeing. In a region best known for the spectacular 13 gorges of Nitmiluk National Park, Katherine also is a base for exploring Cutta Cutta Caves and the town of Mataranka.

Among other things, Katherine is home to the world's largest school classroom, the **Katherine School of the Air,** which broadcasts to about 100 students over 301,000 square km (115,700 square mi) of isolated cattle country. Tours are available on weekdays from April through October. ⊠ *Giles St.,* ☎ *08/8972–1833.*

OFF THE
BEATEN PATH

Manyallaluk – The region is a focus for Aboriginal cultures quite different from those of the rest of the Top End and the Red Centre—and an increasing number of tours are available that are owned and operated by Aboriginal people themselves. The community of Manyallaluk is on Aboriginal-owned land 110 km (68 mi) east of Katherine by road. Manyallaluk Tours (☎ 08/8975–4727 or 1800/64–4727, FAX 08/8975–4724) hosts a series of half- to four-day tours with Aboriginal guides that focus on bush tucker (food), art and artifact manufacture, and extensive rock-art sites. You can take the tour in a conventional vehicle or in one of the community four-wheel-drive buses.

Dining and Lodging

$$–$$$ ✕🏨 **Knotts Crossing Resort.** Consistently the best accommodation in Katherine, Knotts Crossing has well-designed rooms in low-slung cabins and a pool and outside bar that are a welcome oasis after a hot day. Katie's bistro serves by far the best local fish around. ⊠ *Cameron and Giles Sts., Katherine 0850,* ☎ *08/8972–2511,* FAX *08/8972–2628. 95 rooms. Restaurant, bar, pool. AE, DC, MC, V.*

Nitmiluk (Katherine Gorge) National Park

31 km (19 mi) north of Katherine.

One of the Territory's most famous parks, Nitmiluk—named after a *cicada* dreaming site at the mouth of the first gorge—is owned by the local Jawoyn Aboriginal tribe and leased back to the Parks and Wildlife Commission. Katherine Gorge, the park's European name, is derived from the area's most striking feature: The power of the Katherine

River in flood during the Wet has created an enormous system of gorges—13 in all—connected by the river. Rapids separate the gorges, much to the delight of experienced canoeists, and there really is no better way to see the gorges than by boat. Regularly scheduled flat-bottom tour boats take visitors on all-day safaris to the fifth gorge, a trip that requires hiking to circumnavigate each rapid. During the Wet, jet boats provide access into the flooded gorges. In general the best time to visit is during the Dry, from May through early November.

For more adventurous travelers, the park offers some of the best **bushwalking trails** in the Top End. Ten well-marked walking tracks, ranging from one hour to five days, lead hikers on trails parallel to the Katherine River and north toward Edith Falls at the edge of the park. Some of the longer, overnight walks lead past Aboriginal paintings and through swamps, heathlands, and small patches of rain forest. Hikers out for the day may want to carry inflatable rafts with them so they can float downstream back to the campground.

The park's **Nitmiluk Centre** (☎ 08/8972–3604) is a beautiful ochre-colored building crouching in the bush near the mouth of the gorge. It houses an interpretive center, an open-air children's playground, and souvenir and restaurant facilities.

Camping

⚠ **Campsites** located near the Katherine River cost $8 per person per night. Bush camping along the river past the second set of rapids is allowed with the ranger's permission.

Outdoor Activities

Canoes can be rented from Nitmiluk Centre or at the gorge boat ramp for $36 per half day for a single canoe or $49 per day for a two-person canoe. A $20 deposit is required; that becomes $60 if you are going on a longer overnight trip up the gorge. Fishing is permitted at Katherine, but be sure to check with the ranger about license and size requirements.

Cutta Cutta Caves

29 km (18 mi) south of Katherine via the Stuart Highway.

The Cutta Cutta Caves, a series of limestone caverns, are home to the rare Ghost and Orange Horseshoe bats. Ranger-led tours take place during the Dry, and the caves are closed in the wettest of the Wet. ☎ 08/8972–1940.

Mataranka

105 km (65 mi) southeast of Katherine.

The tiny township of Mataranka is the original center of Australia's literary expression for the Outback of the "never never"—as in Aeneus Gunn's novel, *We of the Never Never,* about turn-of-the-century life in the area. West of the upper reaches of the Roper River, Mataranka was a major army base during World War II and its most famous attraction, the **Mataranka Thermal Pool,** was first developed as a recreation site by American troops during that period.

Katherine A to Z

Arriving and Departing

BY BUS

Greyhound Pioneer (☎ 08/8981–8700) runs between Darwin and Alice Springs with a stop at Katherine.

Katherine is 327 km (203 mi) southeast of Darwin via the Stuart Highway. Driving to Katherine will allow you to stop along the way at ☞ **Litchfield National Park** and get around easily to Nitmiluk and other sights nearby. And you may want to continue on to Kununurra, 564 km (350 mi) west, or to Alice Springs, 1,145 km (710 mi) to the south.

Air North Regional (☏ 08/8945–2866) serves Katherine, and **Ansett** offers weekday morning and evening flights to Katherine on local commuter airlines. The airport is 10 minutes south of town.

Contacts and Resources

CAR RENTAL

Avis, Budget, Hertz, and **Territory Rent-a-Car** all have offices at the airport. *See* Darwin A to Z, *above,* for telephone numbers.

EMERGENCIES

Katherine Hospital. ☏ *08/8973–9211.*

Police. ☏ *08/8972–0111.*

GUIDED TOURS

Nitmiluk Tours (☏ 08/8972–1044) offers tours of two hours ($27), four hours ($41), and eight hours ($71) up the Katherine River aboard a flat-bottom boat. The fit and adventurous may wish to consider the dry-season-only **Manyallaluk Four-Day Trekking Adventure** (☏ 08/8975–4727 or 1800/64–4727, ℻ 08/8975–4724). Led by Aboriginal guides, this 31-km (19-mi) trek starts from Eva Valley Station, east of the park, and travels by boat down the gorge system to the entrance of Nitmiluk National Park. **Billy Can Tours** (☏ 08/8981–9813 or 1800/81–3484, ℻ 08/8941–0803) has tours that combine excursions to Nitmiluk with Litchfield and Kakadu national parks.

VISITOR INFORMATION

Katherine Visitors Information Centre. ⊠ *Lindsay St. and Stuart Hwy.,* ☏ *08/8972–2650.* ⊙ *Weekdays 9–5, Sat. 9–noon.*

Parks and Wildlife Commission of the Northern Territory can provide information on Nitmiluk National Park. ⊠ *Box 344, 0851,* ☏ *08/8973–8888 or 08/8973–8899.*

THE KIMBERLEY

Perched on the northwestern hump of the loneliest Australian state, only half as far from Indonesia as it is from Sydney, the Kimberley remains a frontier of sorts. The first European explorers, dubbed by one of their descendants as "cattle kings in grass castles," ventured into the heart of the region in 1879 to establish cattle runs. They subsequently became embroiled in one of the country's longest-lasting guerilla wars between white settlers and Aboriginal people, who were led by Jandamarra of the Bunuba people.

The Kimberley remains sparsely populated, with only 30,000 people living in an area of 351,200 square km (135,000 square mi)—that's 12 square km (4½ square mi) per person. The region is dotted with cattle stations and raked with desert ranges, rivers, tropical forests, and towering cliffs. Several of the country's most spectacular national parks are here, including Purnululu (Bungle Bungle) National Park, a vast area of bizarrely shaped and colored rock formations that became widely known to white Australians only in 1983. Facilities in this remote region are few, but if you're looking for a genuine bush experience, the Kimberley represents the opportunity of a lifetime.

This section begins in Kununurra, just over the northwestern border of the Northern Territory, in Western Australia.

Kununurra

376 km (233 mi) west of Katherine, 710 km (440 mi) southwest of Darwin.

Population 2,000, Kununurra is the eastern gateway to the Kimberley. It is a modern planned town with little of historical interest, developed in the 1960s for the nearby Lake Argyle and Ord River irrigation scheme. The town is the base for adventure activities (☞ Four-Wheel-Drive Tours *in* Chapter 12).

Dining and Lodging

$$$ ✕ **George Room in Gulliver's Tavern.** Lots of dark jarrah timber gives the George Room an old English atmosphere. Although the tavern alongside offers simple counter meals, the George aims for greater things. The Continental-style food is good, but service can be erratic. Menu highlights include northern Australian specialties of beef à la Ord, locally fattened grilled beef served with fresh mushrooms and onions, and the favorite fish dish, barramundi brushed with butter and wine, coated in bread crumbs, then topped with cheese and grilled. ⌧ *196 Cottontree Ave.,* ☎ *08/9168–1666. AE, DC, MC, V. Closed Sun. No lunch.*

$$ ✕ **Chopsticks Chinese Restaurant at Country Club Hotel.** The most
★ pleasant dining surprise in the Kimberley, the Aussie-style Chinese cuisine is uniformly excellent. All tables are outdoors, with pleasant views over gardens illuminated by colored lights. Chopsticks' spicier dishes and Szechuan specialties include honey chili king prawns and excellent chili mussels served on a sizzling platter with vegetables. The lightly battered barramundi served with lemon is memorable. ⌧ *Country Club Hotel, 76 Coolibah Dr.,* ☎ *08/9168–1024. AE, DC, MC, V.*

$$ ☷ **Kimberley Court.** Separated from Kununurra's shopping center by
★ a wide park, this small hotel feels like a home away from home. Every room opens onto a cool veranda, and the central courtyard is filled with tropical plants, a pond, and a small aviary. Deluxe rooms are twice as large as standard rooms and come with a kitchenette and whirlpool bath. The swimming pool is a nice place to relax at the end of a hot day. The Kimberley Court may not be the place for a high-powered holiday, but this hotel succeeds where the vast majority fail. ⌧ *Box 384, Erythrina St., Kununurra 6743,* ☎ *08/9168–1411,* ℻ *08/9168–1055. 33 rooms. Restaurant, pool, coin laundry. AE, DC, MC, V.*

$ ☷ **Country Club Hotel.** Kununurra's newest accommodation is in the center of town, encircled by tropical gardens around its own little rain forest. Besides Chopsticks restaurant, a grill room and bar are on the premises. ⌧ *47 Coolibah Drive, Kununurra 6743,* ☎ *08/9168–1024,* ℻ *08/9168–1189. 90 rooms, 2 suites. Restaurant, bar, grill room, 2 pools. MC, V.*

Shopping

Waringarri Gallery (⌧ Speargrass Rd., ☎ 08/9168–1528) has a large selection of Aboriginal art.

Gibb River Road and El Questro

Gibb River Road, the cattle-carrying route through the heart of the Kimberley, provides an alternative to the Great Northern Highway between Kununurra–Wyndham and Derby. The unpaved 700-km (434-mi) road runs through a remote area, and the trip should be done only with a great deal of caution. The road is passable by conventional vehicles only after it's been recently graded. At other times you need a four-wheeler, and in the Wet it's impassable.

Should you decide to take the Gibb River Road, consider stopping for some R&R at **El Questro Cattle Station and Wilderness Park** (☞ Lodging, *below*), a working ranch in some of the most rugged country in Australia. Besides providing an opportunity to see Outback station life, El Questro has a full complement of such recreational activities as fishing and swimming, and horse, camel, and helicopter rides. On individually tailored walking and four-wheel-drive tours through the bush, you can bird-watch or look at ancient spirit figures depicted in the unique *wandjina* style of Kimberley Aboriginal rock painting—one of the world's most striking forms of spiritual art. The turnoff for El Questro is 27 km (17 mi) down the Gibb River Road as you head west from Kununurra.

Dining and Lodging

$–$$$$ 🏨 **El Questro Cattle Station.** Accommodations on the station run the
★ gamut from luxury to bare bones. Staying at the Homestead can be very expensive—but its location at the top of a cliff face above the Chamberlain River rates as one of the most spectacular in Australia, and the price includes all drinks and food, room service, laundry, most activities, and transportation to and from Kununurra, about 50 km (31 mi) away. Nearby are the considerably less expensive bungalows and the campground, which is a great deal—30 secluded sites are right on the river, and barbecue and bathroom facilities are available. At the **Emma Gorge Resort**, which is in a different section of the station, has a licensed restaurant and family cabins that sleep four. ✉ *Box 909, Banksia St., Kununurra 6743; main facility* ☎ *08/9169–1777 or 08/9161–4318,* 🖷 *08/9169–1383 or 08/9161–4355; bungalows and campground,* ☎ *08/9169–1777 or 08/9161–4318,* 🖷 *08/9169–1383 or 08/9161–4355; Emma Gorge Resort,* ☎ 🖷 *08/9161–4388.*

Wyndham

103 km (64 mi) northwest of Kununurra.

The small, historic port on the Cambridge Gulf was established in 1886 to service the Halls Creek goldfields, and it looks as if nothing much has happened in Wyndham in the century since. The wharf is the best location in the Kimberley for spotting saltwater crocodiles as they bask on the mud flats below.

Purnululu (Bungle Bungle) National Park

★ *202 km (125 mi) south and southwest of Wyndham and Kununurra.*

Purnululu (Bungle Bungle) National Park covers nearly 3,120 square km (1,200 square mi) in the southeast corner of the Kimberley. Australians of European descent first "discovered" its great beehive-shaped domes—their English name is the Bungle Bungles—in 1983, proving how much about this vast continent remains outside of "white" experience. The local Kidja Aboriginal tribe knew about these scenic wonders long ago, of course, and called the area Purnululu.

The park's orange silica- and black lichen-striped mounds bubble up on the landscape. Climbing is not permitted because the sandstone layer beneath the thin crust of lichen and silica is fragile and would quickly erode without protection. Walking tracks follow rocky, dry creek beds. One popular walk leads hikers along the **Piccaninny Creek** to **Piccaninny Gorge**, passing through gorges with towering 328-ft cliffs to which slender fan palms cling.

The Bungle Bungles are best seen from April through October and are closed from January through March. Anyone who has the time and a sense of adventure should spend a few days at Purnululu National Park. Facilities are primitive, but the setting and experience are incomparable.

Lodging

Camping is permitted only at two designated campgrounds in Purnululu National Park. None of the campsites has facilities—both the Bellbyrn Creek and Walardi campgrounds have simple pit toilets—and fresh drinking water is available only at the Belburn Creek. The nearest accommodations are in Kununurra (☞ *above*), and most visitors fly in from there.

Arriving and Departing

BY CAR

The Bungle Bungles are 252 km (156 mi) south of Kununurra along the Great Northern Highway. A rough, 55-km (34-mi) unpaved road, negotiable only in a four-wheel-drive vehicle, is the last stretch of road leading to the park from the turnoff at Turkey Creek–Warmum Community. That part of the ride takes about 2½ hours.

BY PLANE

The ideal way to see the park is to arrive by air. There is an airstrip at Purnululu National Park suitable for light aircraft, where tour operators fly clients in from Kununurra, Broome, and Halls Creek to be collected by guides with four-wheel-drive vehicles. April through December, the most popular of these fly-drive tours includes one night of camping in the park. The two companies operating these trips are **East Kimberley Tours** (✉ Box 537, Kununurra, WA 6743, ☎ 08/9168–2213) and **Halls Creek and Bungle Bungle Tours** (✉ Box 2615, Broome, WA 6725, ☎ 08/9168–6217; 015/99–3509 mobile).

Guided Tours

AERIAL TOURS

Alligator Airways (☎ 08/9168–1575) operates both fixed-wing float planes from Lake Kununurra and land-based flights from Kununurra airport. **Slingair Tours** (☎ 08/9169–1300) conducts two-hour flights over the Bungle Bungles for $150 for adults. A more expensive alternative is to take a helicopter flight with **Slingsby Helicopters** (☎ 08/9168–1811).

FOUR-WHEEL-DRIVE TOURS

East Kimberley Tours (☞ *above*) runs from Kununurra into the Bungle Bungle massif. Based to the south in Halls Creek (☞ *below*), **Halls Creek and Bungle Bungle Tours** also has a range of tours to the park.

Visitor Information

Department of Conservation and Land Management. ✉ *Box 942, Kununurra, WA 6743,* ☎ *08/9168–0200.*

Halls Creek

363 km (225 mi) southwest of Kununurra.

Old Halls Creek is the site of the short-lived Kimberley gold rush of 1885. Set on the edge of the Great Sandy Desert, the town has been a crumbling shell since its citizens decided in 1948 to move 15 km (9 mi) away to the site of the present Halls Creek, which has a better water supply. The old town is a fascinating place to explore, however, and small gold nuggets are still found in the surrounding gullies.

Halls Creek is the closest town to the **Wolfe Creek Meteorite Crater,** the world's second largest. The crater is a half mile wide, and its shape has been well preserved in the dry desert air.

Dining and Lodging

$$ ✕⌷ **Kimberley Hotel.** If you arrive by aircraft, you'll practically bump
★ into the Kimberley Hotel—it's located right at the end of the runway! Fortunately for the hotel's guests, the airstrip is used irregularly and only by light planes, so noise isn't a problem. Originally a simple Outback pub with a few rooms, the hotel today sports green lawns, airy rooms, and a swimming pool, making it an oasis in this dusty desert town. The old, cheaper rooms are disappointing, but the newer ones, with their pine furnishings, tile floors, and peach decor, are among the best in the region. The high-ceiling restaurant, which overlooks the lawns and pool, has an excellent wine list and serves some of the best meals in town. ⌷ *Box 244, Roberta Ave., Halls Creek 6770,* ☎ *08/9168–6101,* ⌷⌷ *08/9168– 6071. 42 rooms with shower. Restaurant, pool, spa. AE, DC, MC, V.*

Fitzroy Crossing

290 km (180 mi) west of Halls Creek, 381 km (236 mi) east of Broome.

The main attraction of Fitzroy Crossing is **Geikie Gorge National Park,** which cuts through one of the best-preserved fossilized coral reefs in the world. The town has a couple of basic motels and restaurants.

Geikie Gorge National Park

16 km (10 mi) north of Fitzroy Crossing.

Geikie Gorge is part of a 350-million-year-old reef system formed from fossilized layers of algae—evolutionary precursors of coral reefs— when this area was still part of the Indian Ocean. The limestone walls you see now were cut and shaped by the mighty Fitzroy River; during the Wet, the normally placid waters roar through the region. The walls of the gorge are stained red from iron oxide, except where they have been leached to their original white by the floods, which have washed as high as 52 ft from the bottom of the gorge.

When the Indian Ocean receded, it stranded a number of sea creatures, which managed to adapt to their new conditions. Geikie is one of the few places in the world where freshwater barramundi, mussels, stingrays, and prawns are found. The park is also home to the freshwater archer- fish, which can spit water as far as a yard to knock insects out of the air. Aborigines call this place Kangu, meaning "big fishing hole."

Because both sides of the gorge are wildlife sanctuaries that are off- limits to visitors, the only way to see the gorge is aboard one of the daily boat tours led by park rangers, at 8, 11, and 3. The 1½-hour flat- bottom boat trip costs $15. Rangers are extremely knowledgeable and helpful in pointing out the vegetation, strange limestone formations, and the many freshwater crocodiles along the way. Tourists get to see only a part of the noisy fruit bat colony—estimated at 600,000—that inhabits the region.

Arriving and Departing

BY CAR

From Broome, follow the Great Northern Highway east 381 km (236 mi) to Fitzroy Crossing, then 16 km (10 mi) north on a paved side road to the park. Camping is not permitted at the gorge, so you must stay in Fitzroy Crossing.

Visitor Information

National Park Ranger. ⊠ *Box 37, Fitzroy Crossing, WA 6765,* ☎ *08/ 9191–5121.*

Tunnel Creek and Windjana Gorge National Parks

Tunnel Creek is 111 km (69 mi) north of Fitzroy Crossing; Windjana Gorge is 145 km (90 mi) northwest of Fitzroy Crossing.

On the back road between Fitzroy Crossing and the coastal town of Derby are two geological oddities. **Tunnel Creek** was created when a stream cut an underground course through a fault line in a formation of limestone. You can follow the tunnel's path on foot for a half mile, with the only natural light coming from those areas where the tunnel roof has collapsed. Flying foxes and other types of bats inhabit the tunnel. About 100 years ago, a band of outlaws and their Aborigine leader Jandamarra—nicknamed "Pigeon"—used the caves as a hideout.

Windjana Gorge has cliffs nearly 325 ft high, which were carved out by the flooding of the Lennard River. During the Wet, the Lennard is a roaring torrent, but it dwindles to just a few still pools in the Dry.

Derby

242 km (150 mi) west of Fitzroy Crossing, 226 km (140 mi) northeast of Broome, 921 km (571 mi) west of Kununurra via Halls Creek, 758 km (470 mi) west of Kununurra via the Gibb River Road.

With its port, Derby has long been the main administrative and economic center of the western Kimberley, as well as a convenient base from which to explore **Geikie Gorge, Windjana Gorge,** and **Tunnel Creek.** Without much else to recommend it, the town is known for its giant boab trees—kin to Africa's baobab trees—which have enormously fat trunks. The hollow trunk of one of these trees was reputedly used as a prison at one time. Known as the Prison Tree, this boab has a circumference of 45 ft and is 6 km (4 mi) south of town.

Dining and Lodging

$$ ✕🏠 **Spinifex Hotel.** You'll find basic accommodation here, with the friendliness that typifies an Outback pub. The bar serves solid if uninspired food known as a "counter meal." It's a good place to be on Thursday night for the Smorgasbord or on Friday night for live music. Standard motel-style rooms and hostel-style beds are available. ⊠ *Clarendon St., Derby 6728,* ☎ *08/9191–1233,* ℻ *08/9191–1576. 19 rooms, 12 beds with shared bath. Restaurant, bar. AE, DC, MC, V.*

$$$$ 🏠 **Cockatoo Island Resort.** This exclusive resort in the Buccaneer Archipelago was once a mining camp, its elegant facilities now refurbished into luxurious quarters. Spacious rooms are available in the main lodge, and villas are fitted with polished jarrah-wood flooring, interesting pottery and antiques, and private balconies that overlook the sea. The highlight of the resort, however, is its swimming pool, which is perched on a cliff above the ocean, with views of the entire island. Meals are included in room rates, and many activities can be arranged, including bushwalking, fishing, visits to isolated islands and beaches, and whale-watching. The resort is a 25-minute flight over the King Sound from Derby, 65 minutes from Broome. ⊠ *Mailing address: Box 444, Darwin, 0801,* ☎ *08/8946–4455,* ℻ *08/8941–2134. 14 rooms, 18 villas. Restaurant, bar, pool, tennis court, hiking, boating, fishing, billiards, laundry service. AE, DC, MC, V.*

Broome

216 km (134 mi) southwest of Derby, 1,048 km (650 mi) southwest of Kununurra via Halls Creek, 1,610 km (1,000 mi) southwest of Katherine, 1,935 km (1,200 mi) southwest of Darwin.

Broome is the holiday capital of the Kimberley. It's the only town in the region with sandy beaches, so it has seen the growth of several resorts, a crocodile farm, and a large, if sparsely populated, zoo. Long ago, Broome depended on pearling for its livelihood: Early in the century, 300 to 400 sailing boats employing 3,000 men provided most of the world's mother-of-pearl shell. Many of the pearlers were Japanese, Malay, and Filipino, and the town is still multiracial today. Each August during the famous Shinju Matsuri (Pearl Festival), Broome looks back to the good old days. All but a few of the traditional old wooden luggers have disappeared, and Broome cultivates most of its pearls at nearby Kuri Bay. The town itself retains an air of its boisterous shantytown days, with wooden sidewalks and a charming Chinatown.

Although there are no scheduled boat cruises, there are several boat charter operations in Broome and Derby for single-day or extended **fishing expeditions.** The myriad deserted islands and coastal beaches and the 35-ft tides that surge through here creating waterfalls and whirlpools in the narrows make the Kimberley coast an adventurer's delight. Broome marks the end of the Kimberley.

From here it's another 2,212 km (1,371 mi) south to Perth, or 2,000 km (1,240 mi) back to Darwin.

Dining and Lodging

$$ ★ ✕ **Conti Bar and Bistro.** This sparkling bistro at the Mercure Inn Continental Hotel gets its brightness from terra-cotta tiles and tables and its view of palms and the hotel pool through the plate-glass windows. The blackboard menu changes regularly, but the cuisine is Continental with an emphasis on seafood. ✉ *Mercure Inn Continental Hotel, Weld St.,* ☎ *08/9192–1002. AE, DC, MC, V.*

$$$$ ★ 🏨 **Cable Beach Inter-Continental Resort.** Just a few minutes out of town opposite the broad, beautiful Cable Beach—the only sandy beach near any Kimberley town—this resort is the area's most luxurious accommodation. Seven double and 77 single bungalows are spread through tropical gardens; 176 studio rooms and three suites are also available. The decor is colonial with a hint of Asia. ✉ *Box 1544, Cable Beach Rd., Broome 6725,* ☎ *08/9192–2505 or 1800/09–5508,* 🗠 *08/9192–2249. 258 rooms, 3 suites. 5 restaurants, 5 bars, 2 pools, spa, 12 tennis courts, children's programs, laundry service. AE, DC, MC, V.*

$$$ 🏨 **Mangrove Hotel.** Overlooking Roebuck Bay, this highly regarded hotel has the best location of any accommodations in Broome. All the spacious rooms have private balconies, many with bay views. The pool is surrounded by palms. ✉ *Box 84, Carnarvon St., Broome 6725,* ☎ *08/9192–1303 or 1800/09–4818,* 🗠 *08/9193–5169. 68 rooms with shower. Restaurant, bar, pool. AE, DC, MC, V.*

Shopping

Aboriginal Art

Prices for Aboriginal art in the Kimberley are generally well below those in Darwin or Alice Springs. **Matso's Gallery and Coffee House** (✉ 60 Hammersley St., ☎ 08/9193–5811) specializes in Kimberley arts and crafts, displaying works by the region's most talented Aboriginal artists.

Jewelry

The number of jewelry stores in Broome is completely out of proportion to the size of the town. All of the following shops specialize in high-quality, very expensive pearls and jewelry: **Paspaley Pearling** (✉ 2 Short St., Chinatown, ☎ 08/9192–2203); **Linneys** (✉ Dampier Terr., ☎ 08/9192–2430); the **Pearl Emporium** (✉ Dampier Terr., ☎ 08/9192–1531); and **Broome Pearls** (✉ Dampier Terr., ☎ 08/9192–1295).

The Kimberley A to Z

Arriving and Departing

BY BUS

Greyhound Pioneer (☎ 08/8981–8700) runs the 2,000 km (1,240 mi) between Darwin and Broome.

BY CAR

Distances in this part of the continent are colossal. If you're planning to drive, be prepared for this. From Darwin to Kununurra and the eastern extent of the Kimberley is 903 km (560 mi). From Darwin to Broome on the far side of the Kimberley is 2,000 km (1,240 mi). The route runs from Darwin to Katherine along the Stuart Highway, and then along the Victoria Highway to Kununurra. The entire road is paved but quite narrow in parts—especially so, it may seem, when a road train (an extremely long truck) is coming the other way—so drive with care. Fuel and supplies can be bought at small settlements along the way, but you should always keep supplies in abundance.

BY PLANE

Ansett flies from Darwin to Kununurra, Derby, and Broome.

Contacts and Resources

EMERGENCIES

Ambulance, fire brigade, and police. ☎ *000*.

For emergency assistance, go to the casualty section of a local hospital or call the **Royal Flying Doctor Service** (✉ Derby, ☎ 08/9191–1211). **Broome District Hospital** (✉ Anne St., ☎ 08/9192–1401). **Derby Regional Hospital** (✉ Loch St., ☎ 08/9193–3333). **Kununurra District Hospital** (✉ Coolibah Dr., ☎ 08/9168–1522).

GUIDED TOURS

Amesz Tours (✉ Box 1060, Midlands, WA 6936, ☎ 08/9250–2577 or 1800/99–9204, FAX 09/9250–2634) runs 13- or 18-day safaris from Broome to Darwin, traveling right across the Kimberley and the Top End to Kakadu. A 13-day tour in a four-wheel-drive vehicle covers the region in more detail with a smaller group. **Belray Diamond Tours** (✉ Box 10, Kununurra 6743, ☎ 08/9168–1014, FAX 08/9168–2704) offers a daily air tour (subject to numbers) from Kununurra to the Argyle Diamond Mine, the world's largest, which produces about 6½ tons of diamonds a year.

VISITOR INFORMATION

Broome Tourist Bureau. ✉ *Box 352, Great Northern Hwy., Broome 6725,* ☎ *08/9192–2222,* FAX *08/9192–2063.*

Derby Tourist Bureau. ✉ *2 Clarendon St., Derby 6728,* ☎ *08/9191–1426,* FAX *08/9191–1609.*

Kununurra Tourist Bureau. ✉ *Coolibah Dr., Kununurra 6743,* ☎ *08/9168–1177,* FAX *08/9168–2598.*

Western Australian Tourism Commission. ✉ *16 St. Georges Terr., Perth 6000,* ☎ *08/9220–1700 or 1800/99–3333,* FAX *08/9220–1702.*

11 PERTH AND WESTERN AUSTRALIA

Despite the tyranny of distance, those who make it to the "undiscovered state" are stunned by the diversity of places to go and things to do. Relax on far-flung beaches; go snorkeling around the numerous islands; overnight for an idle wander around Fremantle; hop a train to Kalgoorlie for a weekend on the goldfields; explore the historic towns, wineries, and seaside national parks of the Southwest; wonder at coastal limestone formations in Nambung National Park; or swim with dolphins, manta rays, and whale sharks at Monkey Mia or Ningaloo Reef.

By Helen Ayers
and Lorraine
Ironside

Updated by
Graham
Simmons

ALTHOUGH the existence of the south land—*terra australis*—was known long before Dutch seafarer Dirk Hartog first landed on the coast of "New Holland" in 1616 in today's Shark Bay, the panorama was so bleak he didn't even bother to plant his flag and claim it for the Dutch crown. It took an intrepid English seaman, William Dampier, to see past the daunting prospect of endless beaches, rugged cliffs, heat, flies, and sparse scrubby plains to claim the land for Britain, a nation 12,000 mi away.

Still, nothing can quite prepare you for what lies beyond the city of Perth. The scenery is magnificent, from the awesome, rugged north to the green sweep of the southern plains. But the sheer emptiness—the utter silence broken only by the mournful cry of the crow circling high overhead wherever you wander throughout this vast state—begs description.

Western Australia is a state blessed by wealth and cursed by distance—in every direction Perth is 2,000 mi from any other major city in the world. And the place itself is *huge.* Its million square miles (twice the size of Texas) make up 33% of the Australian continent, yet it is home to just 1.8 million people. Sheep stations here can be the size of Kentucky. And, although it is the dawn of the 21st century, denizens of the state often feel theirs remains an undiscovered country.

Perched as it is on the edge of the continent, Perth is much closer to Indonesia than to its overland Australian cousins; indeed, many Perthsiders take their vacations in Bali rather than in eastern Australia. Such social isolation would ordinarily doom a community to life as a backwater, and for most of its existence Perth has been just that. The gold rush of the 1890s brought a boom to the city, but it did little to change Perth's insularity. The discovery of vast mineral deposits in the 1970s, however, jump-started the state into catching up with the rest of the country. Perth is a young city, the destination of a new breed of hopefuls from the east coast and abroad, lured by the city's energy and uninhibited lifestyle.

The city has fantastic beaches, a beautiful river, and a Mediterreanlike climate that averages eight hours of sunshine a day—although in January and February, the heat becomes oppressive when temperatures climb above the century mark. It is then that the Southwest region, with its lush farmland, vineyards, hillsides profuse with wildflowers, and spectacular coastline, provide a cool escape from the city.

It is to the hot, dry north and to the east, though, that the city looks for its wealth, out in the fly-blown desert that constitutes the majority of Western Australia. In the 1890s it was the goldfields verging on the treeless wastes of the Nullarbor Plain; today it is the Pilbara, the richest source of iron ore in the world. Here, huge machines capable of lifting 5 tons at a time gouge 24,000 tons of rock out of the earth each day. The air conditioner is the most precious possession in the Pilbara, where the mercury frequently hits 120°F. Wages are high, but there is little for employees to buy in the small, company-operated towns. No one thinks twice about driving 1,000 mi round-trip for a long weekend.

For many, work on Western Australia's strip mines or natural gas wells is a necessary hardship to endure before scuttling back to easy living in Perth. The basic tenet of Western Australian life remains the same: To make money, you have to dig!

The Kimberley region in Western Australia's tropical north is closer geographically and in character to the Northern Territory city of Dar-

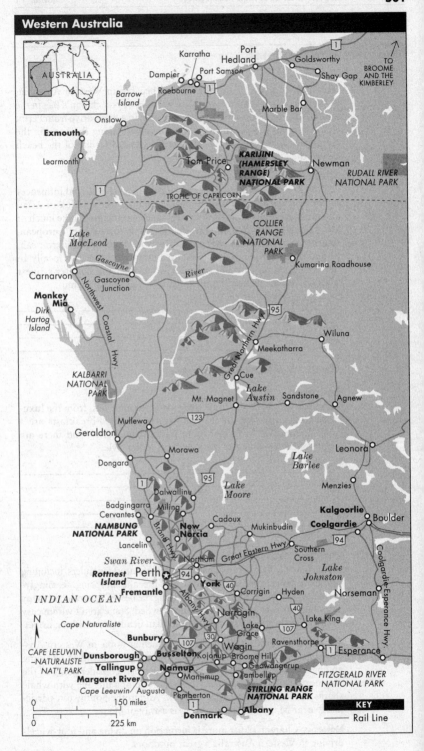

Western Australia

AUSTRALIA

Karratha
Port Hedland
Dampier
Port Samson
Goldsworthy
Shay Gap
TO BROOME AND THE KIMBERLEY
Roebourne
Barrow Island
Marble Bar
Onslow

Exmouth
Learmonth

TROPIC OF CAPRICORN

Tom Price
KARIJINI (HAMERSLEY RANGE) NATIONAL PARK
Newman
RUDALL RIVER NATIONAL PARK

COLLIER RANGE NATIONAL PARK

Lake MacLeod
Gascoyne River
Kumarina Roadhouse

Carnarvon
Gascoyne Junction

Monkey Mia
Dirk Hartog Island

Northwest Coastal Hwy.

95

Wiluna

Meekatharra

KALBARRI NATIONAL PARK

Cue
Lake Austin
Sandstone
Agnew

Mt. Magnet

Mullewa
123

Geraldton

Morawa
Lake Barlee
Leonora

Dongara
95
Lake Moore
Menzies

Dalwallinu
Kalgoorlie
Boulder
Badgingarra
Cervantes
Miling
Cadoux
Mukinbudin
Coolgardie

NAMBUNG NATIONAL PARK
New Norcia
Lancelin
1
Brand Hwy.
Northam
Great Eastern Hwy.
Southern Cross
94
Lake Johnston

Swan River
Perth
94
York
Coolgardie-Esperance Hwy.

Rottnest Island
Fremantle
40
Corrigin
Hyden
Norseman

INDIAN OCEAN
Albany Hwy.
Narrogin
N
Cape Naturaliste
Lake Grace
107
Lake King
Bunbury
107
30
Wagin
Ravensthorpe
CAPE LEEUWIN–NATURALISTE NAT'L PARK
Dunsborough
Busselton
Kojonup
Broome Hill
Esperance
1
Yallingup
Nannup
Gnawangerup
FITZGERALD RIVER NATIONAL PARK
Margaret River
Manjimup
Tambellup
Cape Leeuwin
Augusta
Pemberton
STIRLING RANGE NATIONAL PARK
1
Denmark
Albany

0   150 miles
0   225 km

KEY
— Rail Line

win than it is to Perth. For this reason, information about Broome and the Kimberley is included in Chapter 10.

Pleasures and Pastimes

Beaches

You'll find some of Australia's finest beaches in Western Australia, stretching from the snow-white salt beaches of Frenchman's Bay in the south to beyond Port Hedland in the north. In a day's drive from Perth, you can enjoy a sojourn just about anywhere along the coast in the Southwest, or escape to the life-size chessboard feeling of the beach where the Pinnacles stand watch.

Dining

Although Perth's cuisine has been shaped by such external influences as the postwar European immigration and the recent influx of Asian migrants, an indigenous West Coast cuisine is emerging. Like much of the innovative cooking in Australia, this style fuses Asian, European, and native Australian herbs and spices with French, Mediterranean, and Asian techniques to bring out the best in what is grown locally. In Western Australia's case, this means some of the country's finest seafood, as well as beef, lamb, kangaroo, venison, and emu.

CATEGORY	COST*
$$$$	over $60
$$$	$45–$60
$$	$25–$45
$	under $25

*per person, excluding drinks and service

Lodging

Perth has experienced a hotel trade boom at all levels, from the luxurious to the frill-free. In the countryside, bed-and-breakfasts are a great alternative. In farther-flung parts of the state—and there are plenty of these—much of the lodging is motel style.

CATEGORY	COST*
$$$$	over $125
$$$	$90–$125
$$	$50–$90
$	under $50

*All prices are for a standard double room.

Outdoor Activities and Sports

Western Australia's national parks are full of natural wonders, including fascinating rock formations, exotic bird life, and, in spring, seemingly-surreal wildflowers. The parks are among the best in Australia, in many cases because they are remote and uncrowded. Some aren't within easy reach of Perth, though, so you should plan in advance for long drives.

Water-sports enthusiasts will be very much at home in Western Australia. For wind-in-your-hair types, you can get your fill of jet skiing and parasailing in Perth. Divers should seriously consider going all the way north to Exmouth to take the scuba trip of a lifetime with whale sharks at Ningaloo Reef Marine Park. And in the Southwest, particularly near Margaret River, surfing is a way of life.

Note: See Chapter 12 for more information on diving and four-wheel-driving in Western Australia's great outdoors.

Exploring Perth and Western Australia

Most trips to Western Australia begin in Perth. Apart from its own points of interest, there are a few great day trips to take from the city: to Rottnest Island, to the historic towns of New Norcia or York, and north to the coastal Nambung National Park. The port city of Fremantle is a good place to unwind, and, if you have the time, a tour of the Southwest, with its history, seashore, parks, wildflowers, and first-rate wineries, is highly recommended. The old goldfields towns east of Perth are a slice of the dust-blown Australia of yore. There are also a few long-distance forays worth your while: to the meetings of land and sea creatures at Monkey Mia and Ningaloo Reef Marine Park, and to the ancient rock formations inland at Karijini National Park.

Great Itineraries

Planning your time out west is a matter of focusing on a couple of areas—it's unlikely you'll cover the whole state, even if you decide to permanently relocate. There are a few questions that will help narrow down your choices. Do you have only a few days to spend in and around Perth and Fremantle? Does the thought of cooler air and the coastal scenery of the Southwest appeal to you, or would you rather get in a car and drive to far reaches east or north? Or, do you want to trek north along the coast to Monkey Mia or Exmouth to frolic in and under the waves with amazing sea creatures? Those are your basic options; here are a few possible combinations.

IF YOU HAVE 3 DAYS

Spend most of the first day knocking around **Perth**'s city center, or take the train to pleasantly restored **Fremantle** and stroll through the streets and stop for breaks at sidewalk cafés. In the evening in either city, have dinner overlooking the water. Over the next two days, take a ferry to **Rottnest Island** and cycle around, walk on the beach, fish, or try to spot the small local marsupials called quokkas, then either stay the night or come back to town. If you're feeling ambitious, you could drive a couple of hours north to **Nambung National Park** to see the Pinnacles, captivating coastal rock formations that look like anything from tombstones to trance-state druids moving en masse to the sea, depending on your mood. The historic towns of **York** and **New Norcia** are also good day trips from Perth.

IF YOU HAVE 5 DAYS

This in-between-length trip allows you to take on some of the larger distances in Western Australia, provided that you have the right mode of transportation. Fly north to **Monkey Mia** to learn about and interact with dolphins or to **Exmouth** to dive with whale sharks and watch the annual coral spawning. Or, fly to the **Southwest** coastal area and pick up a car, then drive to see spring wildflowers, wineries, and national parks, and to generally enjoy the good life. You'll have enough time for a day or two around Perth before getting in a car and heading east to the old goldfield towns of **Kalgoorlie** and **Coolgardie.** They may remind you of America's Wild West—except that camel teams rather than stagecoaches used to pull into town—but this is pure Oz all the way.

IF YOU HAVE 7 OR MORE DAYS

Now you can consider all options, mixing a few of the three- and five-day activities. Of course, you could opt to spend the entire week leisurely making your way along the coast of the **Southwest,** tasting the wine at the vineyards of **Margaret River** and around **Albany**, checking out the caves and seashore of **Cape Leeuwin–Naturaliste National Park,** or heading inland to tramp around the fascinating landscape and outstanding spring wildflowers of **Stirling Range National Park.** If you plan to go as far north as **Karijini (Hamersley Range) National Park** for its stunning gorges and rock-scapes, taking a plane will save days compared to getting there by road. From here, you may want to continue to the Western Australian city of Broome and the Kimberley region, or even beyond them to Darwin (☞ Chapter 10).

When to Tour Perth and Western Australia

Generally speaking, it's best to avoid summer travel in Western Australia. Only the Southwest is even slightly bearable. This is no news when you know that the mercury can hover above 100°F for weeks at a time. It's always cooler at the coast, but spring and fall are the ideal months for touring in the south. Spring wildflowers in the Southwest are well worth seeing if you're in the state September–November. If you're going north, the best times to visit are May–August, during the dry season. Nights inland in July can be chilly.

PERTH

Orbiting Earth in 1962, John Glenn was surprised to see a beacon of light shining up from the black void of a Western Australian night. That beacon was Perth, whose residents had turned on every light in the city as a greeting, prompting Glenn to dub it the City of Lights. In many ways Perth remains Australia's city of lights, for just as its citizens reached out to the future then, so do they now.

In its early days Perth was a poor country cousin. The gold rush at the turn of the century changed that for a time, and the more recent minerals boom of the '70s has utterly transformed the city. Buoyed by its mineral wealth and foreign investment, Perth continues to grow steadily. High-rise buildings dot the skyline, and an influx of immigrants has given the city a healthy diversity. And despite the expansion, the city has maintained its relaxed pace of living. Residents live for the water: Half of Perth is always heading for its boats, the old joke goes, while the other half is already on them. And who can blame them? Some of the finest beaches, sailing, and fishing in the world are on the city's doorstep.

For all its modernity, Perth is not a driver's town, and traveling around downtown in the funky "restaurant-belt" of Northbridge is easiest on foot. The main thoroughfare is St. George's Terrace, an elegant street along which many of the most intriguing sights are located. Perth's literal highlight is King's Park, a 1,000-acre garden atop Mount Eliza that affords a panoramic view of the city.

Exploring Perth

Because of its relative colonial youth, Perth has an advantage over most other capital cities. Where others grew into being along with civilization, Perth was laid out with elegance and foresight. Streets were planned so that pedestrian traffic could flow smoothly from one avenue to the next. Most of the points of interest are in the downtown area close to the banks of the Swan River.

City Center

Perth's major business thoroughfare is St. George's Terrace. A pleasant blend of old and new, the city center is located along this street as well as on parallel Hay and Murray streets.

Numbers in the text correspond to numbers in the margin and on the Perth map.

A GOOD WALK

Home to 1.8 million people, Perth is a compact city best explored on foot. Though it was carefully planned and its streets follow a grid system, Perth has managed to avoid the sterile orderliness of Canberra. Its public buildings, however, are not nearly as grand as those in Melbourne. Today it's a pleasant, easily negotiated blend of old and new. Begin your tour in the major downtown area, on the north bank of the Swan River.

Our walking tour begins on Forrest Place at the **General Post Office** ①, a solid sandstone edifice facing **Citiplace** ②, one of the city's bustling pedestrian malls. Head east along Murray Street, passing the **Forrest Chase Shopping Plaza** ③. Beyond this, near the corner at Irwin Street, three blocks away, is the great **Old Fire Station** ④, which is now full of historic fire-fighting artifacts.

Continue east on Murray Street to Victoria Square, one of Perth's finest plazas, which is dominated by **St. Mary's Cathedral** ⑤. Turn right into Victoria Avenue for a block, then right again on Hay Street, passing two of Perth's newer buildings—the **Central Fire Station** ⑥ on your right and the **Law Courts** ⑦ on your left. Turn left into Pier Street and head toward St. George's Terrace. On the corner, adjacent to **St. George's Cathedral** ⑧, is the Deanery, one of Perth's oldest houses.

Look across St. George's Terrace for the Gothic Revival turrets of **Government House** ⑨, then stroll south to **Supreme Court Gardens** ⑩, where you'll see stately Moreton Bay fig trees, some of the finest in Perth. At the western end of the gardens is the charming Georgian **Francis Burt Law Education Centre** ⑪. Across Barrack Street, the glass pyramid of **Alan Green Conservatory** ⑫ has been plunked down on the Esplanade's lawns.

Return to Howard Street and turn left into St. George's Terrace for a walk past many of Perth's newest and most impressive office buildings, including the notable **Bankwest Tower** ⑬ on the corner of William Street. Continuing on St. George's Terrace, you will pass the **Cloisters** ⑭ on your right, built as a boys' high school in 1858. At the top of the terrace is the lone remnant of the former Pensioner Forces headquarters, the **Barracks Arch** ⑮, which stands in front of **Parliament House** ⑯.

For a detour into the greener reaches of Perth, head down Harvest Terrace to Malcolm Street, then circle the roundabout to get to **King's Park** ⑰. The huge botanic garden within its bounds is a great place for an introduction to Western Australia's flora and natural bushland; in spring, the native wildflowers are well worth the trip. You can return to the city on the No. 33 bus.

From Barracks Arch, turn around and walk back along St. George's Terrace to Milligan Street and turn left. When you reach Hay Street, turn right and walk toward the opulent Edwardian exterior of **His Majesty's Theatre** ⑱ at the corner of King and Hay streets. Continue to the Hay Street Mall, one of many city streets closed to traffic, where you'll find **London Court** ⑲, a shopping arcade running north to south between Hay Street and St. George's Terrace. The mechanical clock with three-dimensional animated figures chimes every quarter-hour. Finally, at the intersection of Hay and Barrack streets, **Town Hall** ⑳ is another of Perth's handsome, convict-built structures.

TIMING

It will take 90-some minutes to merely pace off the above route, and you can lengthen this by stopping in shops, gardens, and museums, or by taking a detour down Barracks Street to the river. Temperatures from December through February make all but early morning or evening strolls very uncomfortable.

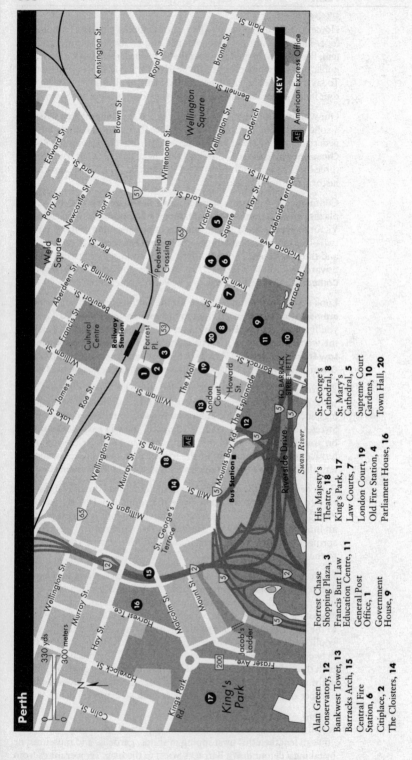

Perth

KEY

AE American Express Office

330 yds

300 meters

N

Alan Green
Conservatory, 12
Bankwest Tower, 13
Barracks Arch, 15
Central Fire
Station, 6
Cityplace, 2
The Cloisters, 14

Forrest Chase
Shopping Plaza, 3
Francis Burt Law
Education Centre, 11
General Post
Office, 1
Government
House, 9

His Majesty's
Theatre, 18
King's Park, 17
Law Courts, 7
London Court, 19
Old Fire Station, 4
Parliament House, 16

St. George's
Cathedral, 8
St. Mary's
Cathedral, 5
Supreme Court
Gardens, 10
Town Hall, 20

Sights to See

⑫ Alan Green Conservatory. A glass pyramid that dominates the neat Esplanade lawns, the conservatory houses a variety of rare and remarkable exotic plants in a carefully controlled environment. ✉ *William St. and Esplanade,* ☎ *08/9265–3153.* ✆ *Free.* ☉ *Mon.–Sat. 10–4, Sun. noon–4.*

⑬ Bankwest Tower. The 1988 tower wraps around the historic 1895 **Palace Hotel,** now used for bank offices. The hotel is a fine example of the ornate architecture that dominated the city during the late 19th century. ✉ *108 St. George's Terr., at William St.*

⑮ Barracks Arch. The city's oddest architectural curiosity stands more or less in front of the seat of government—the highway actually comes between them. This brick monument is all that remains of the headquarters of the Pensioner Forces, which was demolished in 1966. The Tudor-style edifice, built in the 1860s with Flemish bond brickwork, is a memorial to the earliest settlers. ✉ *St. George's Terr. and Malcolm St.*

❻ Central Fire Station. A relatively new building, the Central Fire Station provides a distinctive landmark for the odd visitor who might get disoriented. ✉ *480 Hay St., between Twin and Victoria Sts.*

❷ Citiplace. This bustling pedestrian mall is the stage for a wide variety of street theater and free outdoor concerts. ✉ *Forrest Pl. at Murray St.*

⑭ The Cloisters. Erected in 1858 to serve as the city's first boys' high school, the Cloisters is now only a fragment of its former self. All that remains is its facade, preserved as the front for a multistory shop and office complex. Care has been taken to blend old and new structures without compromising The Cloisters' heritage value. ✉ *200 St. George's Terr.*

❸ Forrest Chase Shopping Plaza. This shop-plex, with its myriad merchants and Myer department store (☞ Shopping, *below*), was considered important enough to warrant a royal opening by Queen Elizabeth II during her 1988 state visit to Australia. ✉ *Murray St. between Forrest Pl. and Barrack St.*

⑪ Francis Burt Law Education Centre. A former courthouse and Perth's oldest public building, this charming 1836 Georgian structure sits amidst the **Supreme Court Gardens** (☞ *below*). The building now contains the **W. A. Law Museum,** with memorabilia and an audiovisual presentation. ✉ *Supreme Court Gardens,* ☎ *08/9325–4787.* ✆ *Free.* ☉ *Feb.–Dec., Tues. and Thurs. 10–2.*

❶ General Post Office. The handsome, colonnaded sandstone building forms an impressive backdrop to the city's major public square, ☞ **Citiplace.** ✉ *Forrest Pl. between Murray and Wellington Sts.*

❾ Government House. Built between 1859 and 1864, this is the official residence of the governor and home to members of the royal family during visits to Perth. It was constructed in Gothic Revival style, with arches and turrets reminiscent of the Tower of London. ✉ *Supreme Court Gardens.*

⑱ His Majesty's Theatre at the corner of King and Hay streets is among Perth's most gracious buildings, and restoration has transformed it into a handsome home for the Western Australian opera and ballet companies. Tours are usually available; call ahead. ✉ *825 Hay St.,* ☎ *08/9265–0999.* ☉ *Weekdays 10–4.*

♺ It's a Small World. A wonderland for children and their parents, this museum of toys and miniatures from around the world displays dollhouses, train stations, and a working Formula 1 racing car that's just

6½ ft long. ⊠ *12 Parliament Pl.,* ☎ *08/9322–2020.* 🎫 *Adults $5, children 3–14 $4.* ☉ *Sun.–Fri. 10–5, Sat. 2–5.*

⑰ King's Park. King's Park encompasses 400 acres of natural bushland, and its many overlooks offer fine views of downtown Perth. Originally this area was important as a gathering place for aboriginal people. It was established as a public park in 1890 and given its present title to mark the accession of Edward VII in 1901. In springtime the park is ablaze with orchids, kangaroo paw, banksias, and other wildflowers. A highlight is the park's 17-acre botanic garden, featuring flora from all over Australia. ⊠ *Fraser Ave. and Kings Park Rd.* 🎫 *Free.* ☉ *8 AM–sunset.*

❼ Law Courts. During this decade, some of the nation's no longer wealthy entrepreneurs, along with two of the state's premiers (one a former ambassador to Ireland) and a deputy-premier, have been brought to trial at the Law Courts. They have been sentenced to terms of imprisonment for mismanaging their own and the public's financial affairs. This debacle has become known under the collective title of *W.A. (Western Australia) Inc.,* and it took a Royal Commission (the equivalent of a United States Senate Inquiry) to winkle out why the public purse had gone from prosperity to poverty in less than 10 years. Repercussions continue to echo in the corridors of power at both state and federal levels. ⊠ *30 St. George's Terr.*

⑲ London Court. A magnet for buskers and anyone with a camera, this outdoor shopping arcade was built in 1937 by gold-mining entrepreneur Claude de Bernales. Along its length you'll find statues of Sir Walter Raleigh and Dick Whittington, the legendary lord mayor of London. Costumed mechanical knights joust with one another when the clock strikes the quarter hour. The arcade's mock-Tudor facade is considered less than attractive by many visitors, but Western Australians stoutly defend it. The row of shops runs north to south between Hay Street Mall and St. George's Terrace, one block west of Barrack Street.

❹ Old Fire Station. The old limestone fire station is a fine colonial structure. No longer operational, it is now a museum housing a photographic exhibit of the history of the fire brigade—from its beginnings, when horses and carts were used, to the present day—as well as a splendid display of old vehicles and equipment. ⊠ *Murray and Irwin Sts.,* ☎ *08/9323–9468.* 🎫 *Free.* ☉ *Weekdays 10–3.*

⑯ Parliament House. From its position on the hill at the top of St. George's Terrace, Parliament House dominates Perth's skyline and serves as a respectable backdrop for the ☞ **Barracks Arch.** Shady old Moreton Bay fig trees and landscaped gardens make the lodge of Western Australian government one of the most pleasant places in the city. Yet because of its location atop the main thoroughfare, and because the freeway comes between it and the city proper, Parliament House doesn't get much pedestrian traffic. Call the Parliamentary Information Officer to arrange a weekday tour. ⊠ *Harvest Terr.,* ☎ *08/9222–7222.* 🎫 *Free.* ☉ *By appointment on weekdays only.*

Perth Concert Hall. When it was built in the 1960s, this small concert hall was considered both elegant and architecturally impressive. Although its architectural merit may now seem questionable to some, its acoustics are still clean and clear. The hall serves as the city's main arts venue. ⊠ *5 St. George's Terr.,* ☎ *08/9321–9900.*

❽ St. George's Cathedral. The church and its **Deanery** form one of the city's most distinctive Old World complexes. Built during the late 1850s as a home for the first dean of Perth, the Deanery is one of the few remaining houses in Western Australia from this period. It is now used as offices for the Anglican Church. ⊠ *Pier St. and St. George's Terr.*

❺ St. Mary's Cathedral. One of Perth's most appealing plazas, **Victoria Square**, is the happy home of St. Mary's. Its environs house the headquarters for the Roman Catholic Church. ⊠ *Victoria Sq.*

Scitech Discovery Centre offers interactive displays of science and technology that educate and entertain children of all ages. ⊠ *City West, West Perth,* ☎ *08/9481–6295.* ☜ *$11.* ⊙ *Daily 10–5.*

❿ Supreme Court Gardens. This favorite lunch spot for hundreds of office workers is also home to some of the finest Moreton Bay fig trees in the state. A band shell in the rear of the gardens is used for summer concerts. ⊠ *Barrack St. and Adelaide Terr.*

⓴ Town Hall. During the 1860s, convict labor built this hall in the style of a Jacobean English market. ⊠ *Hay and Barrack Sts.*

Around Perth

Cohunu Wildlife Park. Come to Cohunu (pronounced co-*hu*-na) for a cuddle session with a live koala (daily 10–4). But take time to view other native animals in their natural surroundings, too—Cohunu has a walk-through aviary that's the largest in the Southern Hemisphere. Kids will love the park's miniature railway. ⊠ *Mills Rd., Martin,* ☎ *08/9390–6090. Railway Station: Gosnells.* ☜ *$14.* ⊙ *Weekdays 10–5, weekends 10–5:30.*

Museum of Childhood. Recognized internationally as a pioneer in the conservation of childhood heritage in Australia, the museum is an enchanting hands-on journey for both children and parents. Among its most prized exhibits is an original alphabet manuscript written, illustrated, and bound by William Makepeace Thackeray in 1833. There are displays of dolls from around the world. ⊠ *Edith Cowan University Campus, Bay Rd., Claremont,* ☎ *08/9442–1373.* ☜ *$3.* ⊙ *Tues.–Fri. and Sun. 10–4. Mid-Dec.–mid-Jan.*

Underwater World. Ride a moving walkway through a submerged acrylic tunnel to view some 2,500 swimming examples of 200 marine species, including sharks and stingrays. A dolphin pool allows you to see these friendly marine mammals up close. Feeding times for the dolphins are 10:30, 1:30, and 4. ⊠ *Hillary's Boat Harbour, 16 km (10 mi) southwest of Perth on West Coast Hwy.,* ☎ *08/9447–7500.* ☜ *Adults $16.50, children over 2 $9.* ⊙ *Daily 9–5.*

Whiteman Park. This enormous recreation area has barbecue facilities, picnic spots, cycle trails, vintage trains and electric trams, and historic wagons and tractors. In an arts-and-crafts section of the park, you can watch potters, blacksmiths, leather workers, toy makers, printers, and stained-glass artists at work. Naturally, wildlife includes kangaroos. ⊠ *Lord St.,* ☎ *08/9249–2446.* ☜ *$5 per car up to 6 people.* ⊙ *Daily 9–6; longer hrs summer weekends and public holidays.*

Dining

New restaurants, snack bars, and food halls spring up constantly in Perth, providing a huge range of culinary choices. Northbridge, northwest of the railway station, is *the* new dining and nightclubbing center of Perth, where reasonably priced restaurants proliferate.

Chinese

$$$ ✕ Genting Palace. The recipient of a Gold Plate award in 1998, the elegant Genting Palace at Burswood International Resort Casino (☞ Lodging, *below*) serves some of the best Chinese food in Perth. Cantonese cuisine predominates, with a few outstanding Szechuan, Shanghai, and Chiu Chow dishes as well. Fresh seafood is a specialty—watch for Chinese delicacies of eel, jellyfish, fresh green lip abalone, and lobster. Other standouts are double boiled black chicken soup with herbs and whole chicken stuffed with shark's fin soup. Dim sum is served weekends until 2:30 PM. ⊠ *Burswood International Resort Casino, Great Eastern Hwy., Burswood,* ☎ *08/9362–7551. AE, DC, MC, V.*

$ ✕ **Uncle Billy's.** When Billy Lee first came to Australia from China as a student in 1951, genuine Chinese restaurants were hard to find. Lee's first restaurant, in the provincial city of Albany, won accolades almost overnight. Since then, the name "Billy Lee" has become a Perth institution. Known for its excellent selection of seafood and traditional Chinese dishes, Uncle Billy's is a traditional haunt for Perth chefs after a long shift, as it stays open until 4 AM. ⊠ *Chung Wah La., off 66 Roe St., Northbridge,* ☎ *08/9228–9388. MC, V.*

Contemporary

$$ ✕ **CBD.** The inner city finally has an excellent casual-dining option. On the ground floor of the Rydges Hotel, this spacious restaurant has chrome and jarrah furniture, linen napery, and quality silver. From the confident kitchen staff comes an imaginative menu with tantalizing twists, with items such as asparagus salad with pecorino cheese and lemon aïoli, and five-spiced chicken with bok choy, sweet potato, and shiitake mushrooms. Twenty-four varieties of table wine and "stickies" (dessert wine) are available by the glass. ⊠ *Hay and King Sts., Northbridge,* ☎ *08/9263–1859. AE, DC, MC, V.*

Eclectic

$$ ✕ **Harrietts of James.** The hottest restaurant on the block is Harrietts, in the fashionable dining/clubbing precinct of Northbridge. With its big cantilever windows, which can be raised during summer to provide seamless indoor/outdoor dining, Harrietts has redefined the term *al fresco.* The green Thai chili mussels are a sensational starter, after which you can choose from an extensive menu of pasta, salads, seafood, and grills, all typical of the new pan-Australasian cuisine. ⊠ *153 James St., Northbridge,* ☎ *08/9227–1184. AE, DC, MC, V.*

$$ ✕ **Oriel.** Ten minutes from the city center lies the quintessential Perth brasserie: Both the dimly lit interior and the outdoor areas are crowded with tables and overflow with people and noise Wednesday to Sunday, when the restaurant is open 24 hours (breakfast is served 1 AM–noon). The imaginative, tasty fare changes seasonally. For breakfast, try the Karri Valley smoked ham and Gruyère croissants, or the banana and macadamia-nut muffins with passion fruit curd. Lunch and dinner entrées are equally tantalizing, offering gravlax of Atlantic salmon with fresh witlof (a Dutch vegetable resembling chicory) and a snow pea salad with vermouth mayonnaise. The impressive wine list offers more than 20 varieties by the glass. ⊠ *483 Hay St., Subiaco,* ☎ *08/9382–1886. Reservations not accepted. AE, MC, DC, V.*

French

$$$ ✕ **Chanterelle.** A Scottish couple, the Peastons, serve high-quality food without pretension at this popular BYOB restaurant in a converted house in Subiaco. The elegant dining area offers a happy blend of formality and friendliness. The menu offers rich dishes from the traditional French repertoire, such as a trio of cream soups, as well as lighter, more contemporary fare. The grilled duck breast and leg confit with green peppercorns, roast pigeon with mushroom ravioli and a thyme jus, and grilled emu fillet with sautéed beet and deep-fried celery are all noteworthy. ⊠ *210 Rokeby Rd., Subiaco,* ☎ *08/9381–4637. Reservations essential. AE, DC, MC, V. BYOB. Closed Sun. and Mon. No lunch Sat.*

Perth Dining and Lodging

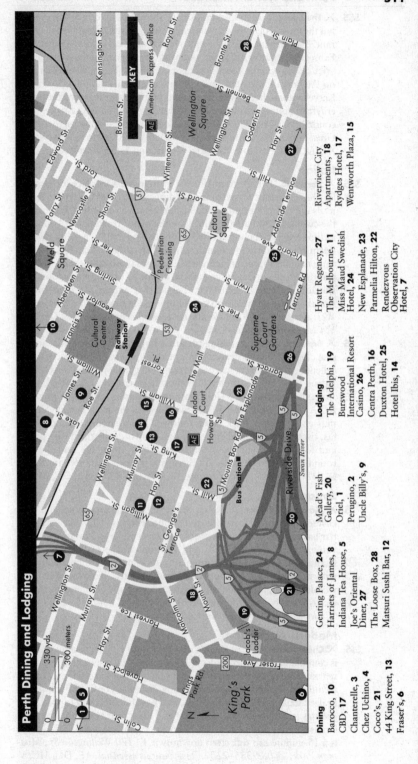

KEY

AE American Express Office

Dining
Barocco, 10
CBD, 17
Chanterelle, 3
Chez Uchino, 4
Coco's, 21
44 King Street, 13
Fraser's, 6

Genting Palace, 24
Harriets of James, 8
Indiana Tea House, 5
Joe's Oriental
Diner, 27
The Loose Box, 28
Matsuri Sushi Bar, 12

Mead's Fish
Gallery, 20
Oriel, 1
Perugino, 2
Uncle Billy's, 9

Lodging
The Adelphi, 19
Burswood
International Resort
Casino, 26
Centra Perth, 16
Duxton Hotel, 25
Hotel Ibis, 14

Hyatt Regency, 27
The Melbourne, 11
Miss Maud Swedish
Hotel, 24
New Esplanade, 23
Parmelia Hilton, 22
Rendezvous
Observation City
Hotel, 7

Riverview City
Apartments, 18
Rydges Hotel, 17
Wentworth Plaza, 15

\$\$\$ ✕ **The Loose Box.** A 45-minute drive from the city center will deter all but the most ardent food lovers from visiting Perth's finest French restaurant. This elegant establishment owes its ongoing success to chef Alain Fabregues, a native of France who was the recipient of the Meilleur Ouvrier de France, the country's highest culinary honor. The menu relies on Australia's seasonal bounty, with highlights including terrine of Kervella goat cheese with lentils and truffles, and marron (freshwater crayfish) and roasted vegetables with fettuccine. The fixed-price, three-course Friday lunch (\$29.50) is remarkable. Service is impeccable. ✉ *6825 Great Eastern Hwy., Mundaring,* ☎ *08/9295–1787. Reservations essential. AE, DC, MC, V. No lunch Mon.–Thurs. and Sat. No dinner Sun.–Tues.*

Italian

\$\$\$ ✕ **Perugino.** This Perth institution is an impressive place for business
★   lunches, romantic trysts, or formal dinners, and chef Giuseppe Pagliaricci's use of fresh produce and his imaginative yet simple approach to the cuisine of his native Umbria are the major reasons. Look for *scottadito* (baby goat chops grilled with olive oil and herbs) and *coniglio* (farm-raised rabbit in a tomato sauce with garlic and chilies). The à la carte menu is supplemented with numerous seasonal specials—usually several excellent risotto and pasta dishes in tasty combination with spinach, ricotta, and chicken. The staff is among the most professional, knowledgeable, and good-humored in town. ✉ *77 Outram St., West Perth,* ☎ *08/9321–5420. Reservations essential. AE, DC, MC, V. Closed Sun. No lunch Sat.*

\$\$ ✕ **Barocco.** Those searching for great Italian and Mediterranean cuisine close to the city center won't be disappointed by Barocco, an excellent new restaurant in a converted 1903 corner pub in Northbridge. Patron Lorenzo Crucitti has already won several awards, including the American Express 1998 Gold Plate award for Brasserie Dining and the RCIA 1998 "Best New Restaurant" award. Starters include Sicilian mussels and warm duck salad, followed by an extensive menu of pastas, risotto, and seafood dishes, including swordfish grilled with potato and leek mash. The views of Northbridge street life and the surrounding city, from tables on the upstairs terrace, are extraordinary. ✉ *318 William St., Northbridge,* ☎ *08/9228–3888. AE, DC, MC, V.*

Japanese

\$ ✕ **Matsuri Sushi Bar.** Stark and clean, with smart black tables and vinyl cushioned chairs, Matsuri is quite unpretentious. This excellent sushi bar has two of Perth's most spectacular fish tanks and some of its best-value Japanese food. Sushi and sashimi can be ordered as small, medium, or large combination plates, or as part of a dinner complete with steamed rice, miso soup, salad, and green tea. Tempura, made with wonderfully light and delicate batter, is especially recommended. Service is friendly and efficient. ✉ *903 Hay St.,* ☎ *08/9324 –2420. MC, V. Closed Sun. No lunch Sat.*

Modern Australian

\$\$\$ ✕ **Chez Uchino.** One of Perth's most innovative chefs, Osamu Uchino, is continuing to gain accolades at his spacious new restaurant. The menu remains focused on Uchino's skilled fusion of Japanese cuisine and French technique, producing such interesting dishes as confit of duck set on braised daikon served with cèpes, and beef fillet teriyaki topped with *yabbies* (small freshwater lobsters) and lotus root tempura. The minimalist dining room is one of the most elegant around. Chez Uchino is a 15-minute cab ride from downtown. ✉ *120 Wellington St., Mosman Park,* ☎ *08/9385–2202. Reservations essential. AE, DC, MC, V. No smoking. Closed mid-Jan.–late Jan. and Sun. and Mon. No lunch.*

$$$ ✕ **Coco's.** A great location on the river in South Perth, trendy patrons, and fine food have made this one of the city's most popular restaurants. It is often packed and noisy, but the floor-to-ceiling windows show off fabulous views of the Perth skyline, the food is excellent, and the service is speedy and efficient. The huge menu changes daily—most items are available in either appetizer or main-course portions. The beef, aged in the restaurant's own cool room, has a formidable reputation. Seafood dishes are always fresh and simply, yet imaginatively, presented. Try, for example, the fresh Mandurah whitebait dusted in Japanese spices, fried crisp, and served on Udon noodles. ⊠ *Southshore Centre, 85 the Esplanade, South Perth,* ☎ *08/9474–3030. Reservations essential. AE, DC, MC, V.*

$$$ ✕ **Fraser's.** This elegant, bilevel restaurant in King's Park has vistas of the city and Swan River and is an excellent choice for breakfast (served daily from 7 AM). When the weather is fair—most of the time in Perth—the large outdoor area fills with happy diners. Chefs Chris Taylor and Brad Ford are passionate about the freshness and quality produce; local seafood is a specialty. Recent standouts include char-grilled squid with sweet red peppers and balsamic vinegar dressing; panfried fillet of red emperor with sweet potato mash and lime nut butter; and char-grilled veal liver and smoked bacon with liqueur muscat sauce and caramelized onions. The menu changes daily. ⊠ *Fraser Ave., King's Park,* ☎ *08/ 9481–7100. Reservations essential. AE, DC, MC, V.*

$$$ ✕ **Indiana Tea House.** Overlooking the beach at Cottesloe is an opulent restaurant where the food is as good as the ocean views. The imperial days of Somerset Maugham are lovingly re-created at the Indiana, which dates from 1903. Asian dishes are favored, particularly those of Indian, Thai, Chinese, Malaysian, and Japanese cuisines. There is, however, a boldness and a sense of re-invention in the dishes, which is characteristic of modern Australian food. Tom yum soup, seared tuna sashimi with pickled cabbage and lotus root crisps, and tandoori chicken with hokkien noodles and aromatic Asian vegetables are all highly recommended. The restaurant's air of casual elegance is perfectly in keeping with the breezy, Western Australia lifestyle. ⊠ *99 Marine Parade, Cottesloe,* ☎ *08/9385–5005. AE, DC, MC, V.*

$$ ✕ **44 King Street.** For several years now, 44 King Street has been garnering accolades for its cutting-edge interpretations of modern Australian cuisine. The menu changes weekly, retaining favorites like the Caesar's salad and the pizza with tomato, chèvre, roasted pepper, and black olives. In winter, soups and slow-cooked dishes are worth trying, while summer brings outstanding seafood salads. Excellent coffee and cakes are available. The service in this no-smoking establishment is fast, friendly, and super-efficient. ⊠ *44 King St.,* ☎ *08/9321–4476. AE, DC, MC, V.*

Pan-Asian

$ ✕ **Joe's Oriental Diner.** At this theme restaurant in the Hyatt Regency, wood, natural brick, terra-cotta, and teak antiques reinforce the theme, and Thai, Indonesian, Malaysian, and Singaporean dishes fill the menu. Hearty soups are complemented by a range of such delicious noodle dishes as *kway teow* (noodles with bean sprouts, prawn, and chicken), or *laksa* (rice noodles in a rich, spicy, coconut-milk soup with chicken, bean curd, and prawns). "Joe's favorite selections" include stir-fried seafood with ginger and oyster sauce, and yabbies (freshwater lobster) with chili bean sauce. This place is great value for money and highly recommended. ⊠ *99 Adelaide Terr.,* ☎ *08/9225–1268. AE, DC, MC, V. Closed Sun. No lunch Sat.*

Seafood

$$$ ✕ **Mead's Fish Gallery.** Visitors to Mead's, a 15-minute cab ride from
★ town, are frequently divided about whether the setting, on the Swan River
surrounded by yachts and mansions of W.A.'s elite, or the seafood is more
spectacular. Feast on the likes of sashimi of Tasmanian salmon, Thai par-
cel of king prawns and snapper served with fresh mango, or char-grilled
baby squid in chili, while gazing at a squadron of pelicans gliding lazily
over the shallow water of the river. The service, overseen by owners War-
ren and Linda Mead, is as outstanding as the wine list. Valet parking
and boat docking services are provided. ⊠ *15 Johnson Parade, Mos-
man Park,* ☏ *08/9383–3388. AE, DC, MC, V. Closed Mon. and Tues.*

Lodging

$$$$ 🏨 **Burswood International Resort Casino.** From the top of its 10-story
★ glass atrium to its 18-hole golf course, Burswood is a distinctive lux-
ury resort. Rooms are as lush as the public spaces, each featuring a
Japanese-fashioned bathroom and a view of either the river or the city.
Suites have Jacuzzis. The adjoining casino is one of the largest in the
southern hemisphere, open around the clock for roulette, blackjack,
baccarat, keno, craps, and two-up. ⊠ *Private Bag 456, Great Eastern
Hwy., Burswood 6100,* ☏ *08/9362–7777,* 🗏 *08/9470–2553. 414
rooms, 16 suites. 6 restaurants, 7 bars, pool, sauna, spa, 18-hole golf
course, 4 tennis courts, health club, casino. AE, DC, MC, V.*

$$$$ 🏨 **Centra Perth.** Within a stone's throw of the central business district,
major shopping areas, cinemas, and restaurants, the Centra's location
is hard to beat. The bar and brasserie, with warm terra-cotta tiles and
wrought-iron furniture, have a Mediterranean feel. An added bonus is
the only indoor heated hotel pool in Perth. ⊠ *778 Hay St., 6000,* ☏
08/9261–7200, 🗏 *08/9261–7277. 181 rooms, 1 suite. Restaurant, bar,
indoor pool, sauna, spa, health club, laundry service. AE, DC, MC, V.*

$$$$ 🏨 **Duxton Hotel.** Opened in 1996, this is within easy walking distance
of the central business district and right next to the Perth Concert Hall.
The comfortable rooms are decorated in soothing autumn tones and
outfitted with furniture made of Australian timber. On the walls of each
room are works by local artists. Be sure to request a room with a view
of the Swan River. ⊠ *1 St. George's Terr., 6000,* ☏ *08/9261–8000,*
🗏 *08/9261–8020. 291 rooms, 15 suites. Restaurant, bar, pool, sauna,
spa, steam room, exercise room, business services. AE, DC, MC, V.*

$$$$ 🏨 **Hyatt Regency.** With a setting on the banks of the Swan River, the
★ Hyatt is within walking distance of Perth's central business district. The
Conservatory, with tasteful cane furniture under a large domed atrium,
is a great place to relax. Rooms are tasteful and spacious. The hotel
offers two floors of the Regency Club, in which room rates include a
complimentary Continental breakfast and evening drinks and canapés.
Regency Club rooms and suites have a private elevator and stunning
views of either Perth or the Swan River. ⊠ *99 Adelaide Terr., 6000,*
☏ *08/9225–1234,* 🗏 *08/9325–8899 or 08/9325–8785. 367 rooms.
3 restaurants, 2 bars, pool, health club, business services, meeting
rooms. AE, DC, MC, V.*

$$$$ 🏨 **Parmelia Hilton.** One of Perth's top hotels, the Parmelia is full of
antiques, and you'll gaze upon a Chinese silk tapestry or Mussolini's
mirror as you await the elevator. Most rooms are furnished in a clas-
sic style, with blue carpets, cream walls, and rosewood reproduction
Queen Anne furniture. Ten of the suites are appointed with crystal chan-
deliers, gilt mirrors, antique furniture, and deep-pile carpeting, and have
luxurious marble bathrooms. All of the suites enjoy river views; other
rooms overlook the hotel pool and cityscape. The hotel began a major
renovation program in 1998 that is expected to last several years. ⊠

Mill St., 6000, ☎ *08/9322–3622,* ⨍Ⓐ𝕏 *08/9481–0857. 222 rooms, 52 suites. Restaurant, bar, pool, sauna, health club, business services. AE, DC, MC, V.*

$$$$ ⊞ **Rendezvous Observation City Hotel.** Watching the sun sink into the
★ Indian Ocean from this luxury beachside resort is a memorable experience. Rooms are stylishly decorated in elegant blues, golds, and mauves, with marble bathrooms and mirrored wardrobes adding just the right touch of luxury. Rooms all have superb ocean views. Dine at the epicurean Savannahs Restaurant, or enjoy alfresco beachside fare at the new Café Estrada. Just 10 minutes by freeway from the city center, the Rendezvous is a great alternative to downtown hotels. ✉ *11 the Esplanade, Scarborough 6019,* ☎ *08/9245–1000,* ⨍Ⓐ𝕏 *08/9245–1345. 333 rooms, 6 suites. 4 restaurants, 3 bars, pool, sauna, spa, 2 tennis courts, exercise room. AE, DC, MC, V.*

$$$$ ⊞ **Rydges Hotel.** Women are especially welcomed at the 16-story Rydges Hotel, a fine addition to Perth's central business district. Rooms are decorated in soothing earth tones, with ultramodern furnishings of chrome, glass, black leather, and velveteen, and those above the 12th floor have commanding views of the river and city. Two women-only floors have additional security and special amenities such as women's magazines, vanity packs, and a "ladies' mini-bar" with stockings, hair pins, and nail polish. King Executive suites, designed for corporate travelers, boast floor-to-ceiling windows and goldfish tanks. Spa suites have separate lounge and dining areas. All guests receive complimentary membership passes for a private fitness center, located nearby. ✉ *Hay and King Sts., Northbridge, 6000,* ☎ *08/9263–1800,* ⨍Ⓐ𝕏 *08/9263–1801. 243 rooms, 6 suites. Restaurant, bar, business services. AE, DC, MC, V.*

$$$ ⊞ **The Melbourne.** Billing itself as "Perth's Boutique Hotel," this stylish new establishment is housed in a restored 1890s building listed on the National Heritage Register. The Perth landmark features all the original design elements of the era, including a grand staircase and elevator. In New Orleans style, The Melbourne offers fine dining in the elegant Louisiana's Restaurant, while the Mississippi Bar and Orleans Bar carry on the theme. ✉ *Hay St., at Milligan St., 6000,* ☎ *08/9320–3333,* ⨍Ⓐ𝕏 *08/9320–3344. 32 rooms, 3 suites. Restaurant, bar, brasserie, room service, laundry service and dry cleaning, convention center. AE, DC, MC, V.*

$–$$$ ⊞ **Wentworth Plaza.** A Federation-era hotel, the Wentworth was merged with the equally old Royal on Wellington Street to form one large, grand hotel. The new rooms recapture period ambience, with accommodations ranging from two-room apartments to single rooms with a private bath to traditional rooms on the Royal Hotel side that share facilities. Downstairs, the Garage Bar, Horsefeathers, Bobby Dazzler, and Moon and Sixpence are popular watering holes where you can rub shoulders with locals. ✉ *300 Murray St., 6000,* ☎ *08/9481–1000,* ⨍Ⓐ𝕏 *08/9321–2443. 96 rooms. Restaurant, 4 bars, room service, coin laundry, free parking. AE, DC, MC, V.*

$$ ⊞ **The Adelphi.** One of the most delightful aspects of this property is
★ its location. Although the main thoroughfare running alongside it can be noisy, the hotel sits at the bottom of King's Park bluff opposite the duck-filled lakes of the freeway parklands. The neat and airy rooms of this enormously popular self-catering facility are decorated with chintz sofas, jarrah coffee tables, and gray and pink furnishings. All face the city skyline, but rooms on the higher floors have views of the river. ✉ *130A Mounts Bay Rd., 6000,* ☎ *08/9322–4666,* ⨍Ⓐ𝕏 *08/9322–4580. 61 rooms. Laundry. AE, DC, MC, V.*

$$ ⊞ **Hotel Ibis.** Closer to the shopping and nightclub action than many central city hotels, the Ibis—a member of the French Accor chain—is efficient and pleasant, a firm favorite with visiting U.S. military personnel. Rooms are compact but cheerful, with light, modern furniture, and are decorated in pink and blue. ⊠ *334 Murray St., 6000,* ☎ *08/ 9322–2844,* 𝔽𝔸𝕏 *08/9321–6314. 152 rooms, 20 suites. Restaurant, bar. AE, DC, MC, V.*

$$ 🖭 **Miss Maud Swedish Hotel.** Old World charm and a delicious Nordic
★ breakfast are two things that make this a Perth favorite. In a centrally located 1911 building, the Miss Maud has the Scandinavian feeling you would expect, with pine furniture and a blue-and-gold color scheme. At the Miss Maud Restaurant and Coffee Shop, famous smorgasbord delicacies bring customers back time and again. Another branch of the restaurant is in Fremantle (☞ *below*). ⊠ *97 Murray St., 6000,* ☎ *08/ 9325–3900,* 𝔽𝔸𝕏 *08/9221–3225. 51 rooms. Restaurant, café, coffee shop, room service. AE, DC, MC, V.*

$$ 🖭 **New Esplanade.** Ideally situated on the Esplanade, this hotel enjoys the same million-dollar view of the Swan River for which flamboyant mining tycoons have forked over fortunes. And it is just a chopstick's toss from the Grand Palace, one of the more popular Chinese restaurants in town. Rooms are comfortable, decorated in shades of green and cream, with contrasting teak woodwork. ⊠ *18 the Esplanade, 6000,* ☎ *08/9325–2000,* 𝔽𝔸𝕏 *08/9221–2190. 85 rooms. Restaurant, bar. AE, DC, MC, V.*

$ 🖭 **Riverview City Apartments.** In one of the city's most prestigious residential areas, these units are a short stroll from the city and King's Park. Rooms are clean and adequate, although the furnishings and decor are somewhat dated, and they are equipped with cooking facilities. ⊠ *42 Mount St., 6000,* ☎ *08/9321–8963,* 𝔽𝔸𝕏 *08/9322–5956. 50 rooms. Kitchenettes. AE, MC, V.*

Nightlife and the Arts

The arts scene in Perth is dominated by local talent, although the acclaimed **Festival of Perth,** held in February and March in venues throughout the city, attracts world-class names in music, dance, and theater. Further information is available from the Festival of Perth office (⊠ University of Western Australia, Mounts Bay Rd., Crawley 6009, ☎ 08/9386–7977).

Full details on all cultural events in Perth are contained in a comprehensive guide in every Saturday edition of the **West Australian.** A free weekly, **X-Press Magazine,** lists music, concerts, movies, entertainment reviews, and who's playing at pubs, clubs, and hotels. **Scoop Magazine,** published quarterly, is an excellent guide to "the essential Western Australian lifestyle." Its big, glossy format includes more than 160 pages of the latest restaurant offerings, arts and sporting events, and club details, as well as interviews and articles on Western Australia's food, travel, and fashion.

Ballet

The **West Australian Ballet Company,** (☎ 08/9481–0707) at His Majesty's Theatre (☞ *below*), runs four short seasons annually, including traditional ballets, modern dance (such as Balanchine), and new experimental and contemporary dance. Performances are in February, May, June, and October.

Bars

Recently architect Michael Patroni has transformed a number of Perth's dilapidated bars into stylish, popular spots, like the **Brass Monkey Pub and Brasserie** (⊠ 209 William St., Northbridge, ☎ 08/9227–9596), the **Queen's Tavern** (⊠ 520 Beaufort St., Highgate, ☎ 08/9328–7267), with an excellent outdoor beer garden, and the **Oriel Cafe and Brasserie** (⊠ 483 Hay St., Subiaco, ☎ 08/9382–1886). The **Greenwood** (⊠ 349

Warwick Rd., Greenwood, ☎ 08/9246–9711) is a stylish pub-brasserie. The Sports Bar, part of the Greenwood, is decorated with an impressive collection of memorabilia. The **Astoria** (⊠ 37 Bay View Terr., Claremont, ☎ 08/9384–1372) is *the* place to go, at any hour, for Perth's young socialites. It's the last word in West Coast chic.

Concerts

Regular recitals by the excellent West Australian Symphony Orchestra, as well as Australian and international artists, are held at the **Perth Concert Hall** (⊠ 5 St. George's Terr., ☎ 08/9321–9900), a modern building overlooking the Swan River.

Nightclubs and Music

Most luxury hotels in Perth have upscale nightclubs that appeal to the over-30 crowd. The **Burswood International Resort Casino** (⊠ Great Eastern Hwy., Burswood, ☎ 08/9362–7777) has its Las Vegas–style cabaret, with national and international performers. **Margeaux's** at the Parmelia Hilton (⊠ Mill St., ☎ 08/9322–3622) and **Player's** at the Sheraton (⊠ 207 Adelaide Terr., ☎ 08/9325–4747) have discos for a more sophisticated crowd. Along more sedate lines, the **Piano Bar** at the Sheraton and the **Millstrasse** at the Parmelia Hilton accompany drinks with piano music.

Jazz and blues lovers can slake their thirst at three popular places. The **Hyde Park Hotel** (⊠ 331 Bulwer St., North Perth, ☎ 08/9328–6166), a no-nonsense Aussie pub, has contemporary jazz Monday night and Dixieland Tuesday night. For blues Tuesday night, try the **Charles Hotel** (⊠ 509 Charles St., North Perth, ☎ 08/9444–1051) and the **Grosvenor Hotel** (⊠ 339 Hay St., ☎ 08/9325–3799). **The Hip-e Club** (⊠ 663 Newcastle St., Leederville, ☎ 08/9227–8899) is a Perth legend that capitalizes on its hippy-era image. **Excapade** (⊠ 187 Stirling St., ☎ 08/9227–8200), one of the most popular spots in the Northbridge area, draws the 18–25 age group with Top-40 hits. Midway between Perth and Fremantle is **Club Bay View** (⊠ 20 St. Quentin's Ave., Claremont, ☎ 08/9385–1331), an upmarket cocktail bar-cum-nightclub, which caters to the well-heeled stockbroker set.

Opera

The **West Australian Opera Company** (☎ 08/9321–5869) presents three seasons annually—in April, August, and November—at His Majesty's Theatre (☞ *below*). The company's repertoire includes classical opera, Gilbert and Sullivan operettas, and occasional musicals.

Theater

His Majesty's Theatre (⊠ 825 Hay St., ☎ 08/9265–0999) opened in 1904, was restored in 1980, and is loved by all who step inside. It is the home of most theatrical productions in Perth. The **Playhouse** (⊠ Pier St., ☎ 08/9325–3344), the **Regal Theatre** (⊠ 474 Hay St., Subiaco, ☎ 08/9381–5522), and the **Hole in the Wall** (⊠ 180 Hamersley Rd., Subiaco, ☎ 08/9381–3694) also feature regular productions. A more casual venue is the **Effie Crump Theatre,** upstairs in the Brisbane Hotel (⊠ Brisbane St., at William St., Northbridge, ☎ 08/9227–7226, which features light comedies and musicals.

Outdoor Activities and Sports

Australian Rules Football

Legend has it this unique blend of soccer and Gaelic football first came to life in Melbourne (Victoria) as an off-season activity for the Australian cricket team, and until quite recently the Victorian Football League (VFL) dominated the game. Now a national game with teams competing from every state, the Australian Football League (AFL) plays every weekend throughout the winter (March–September) at

Subiaco Oval and at the Western Australia Cricket Association (WACA) grounds (☞ Cricket, *below*). The local league, Westar, plays every Saturday around the metropolitan area. For details contact the **Western Australia Football Commission Inc.** (☎ 08/9381–5599).

Beaches

Perth's beaches and waterways are among its greatest attractions; plan to make an excursion to the seaside during your stay.

Traveling north from the Swan River estuary, the first beach you come to is **Leighton** beach, for windsurfers and the astonishing wave jumpers—who ride Windsurfers against the surf to hurl themselves airborne. Then comes **Scarborough,** the beach favored by teenagers and young adults, and then **City Beach,** just 11½ km (7 mi) outside Perth, which is more sedate than Scarborough. **Cottesloe** now attracts a younger set and family groups, while **North Cottesloe** draws young matrons and well-heeled stock exchange executives. **Trigg,** Perth's best beach, is a top surf beach overlooking an emerald-green bay in front of the ocean-view Trigg Island Beach Café-Restaurant.

Bicycling

The vast network of trails in and around the city, particularly in King's Park, makes cycling a pleasure in Perth. Details on trails and free brochures are available from the **Western Australia Tourist Centre** (✉ Forrest Pl. and Wellington St., ☎ 08/9483–1111).

Cricket

The national summer game is played professionally at the **Western Australia Cricket Association** (WACA) grounds in Nelson Crescent, East Perth. For further information, contact the WACA (☎ 08/9265–7222).

Golf

Perth is home to numerous public golf courses: each rents out clubs. The 18-hole course at **Burswood International Resort Casino** (✉ Great Eastern Hwy., Burwood, ☎ 08/9362–7576) is closest to the city. The finest new golfing venue is the **Joondalup Resort** (✉ Country Club Blvd., Joondalup, ☎ 08/9400–8888), 25 minutes north of Perth, which offers three challenging nine-hole courses. Call the **Western Australia Golf Association** (☎ 08/9474–1005) for further details on golf courses in Western Australia. **Golf Escort** (☎ 08/9357–5758)—which offers limousine service, quality clubs, a motorized buggy, greens fees, and golfing partners—is for those who wish to play on Perth's most exclusive courses, most of which are not normally open to the public.

Health Clubs

Health clubs with spas, saunas, and exercise equipment are available to guests at most luxury hotels.

Lords Sports Club features fitness equipment, aerobics, a heated indoor pool, indoor tennis and squash courts, sauna, and spa. ✉ *588 Hay St., Subiaco,* ☎ *08/9381–4777.* 🎟 *$20.* ☉ *Weekdays 6 AM–9 PM, weekends 8–6.*

Motorcycling

A perfect way to enjoy Perth's Mediterranean climate comes from **Deluxe Trike Tours** (☎ 08/9354–9354), which offers one- to eight-hour excursions on a trike (three-wheeled motorcycle that seats three people) or aboard the more familiar Harley Davidson two-wheeled motorcycles.

Running

A number of jogging tracks lead along the Swan River and through King's Park.

Swimming

Aside from Perth's glorious beaches, there are three Olympic-size pools at **Challenge Stadium.** ⊠ *Stephenson Ave., Mt. Claremont,* ☎ *08/ 9441–8222.* ☒ *$3.* ☉ *Weekdays 5:30 AM–9:30 PM, Sat. 5:30 AM–6 PM, Sun. 8–6.*

Tennis

Tennis West (☎ 08/9361–1112) provides details on a variety of tennis courts in the metropolitan area.

Water Sports

Parasailing is available on the South Perth foreshore every weekend, weather and winds permitting. Rent through **Flying High Parasailing** (⊠ Narrows Bridge, ☎ 08/9313–3897). Jet Skis allow for a flight across Perth's waters for speed lovers. **Jet Ski** (☎ 018/91–8810) rents the vehicles, vests, and fuel at an hourly rate.

If you want to enjoy the Swan River at a more leisurely pace, hire a catamaran or a sailboard from **Funcats** at the **Coode Street jetty.** Advance reservations are essential on weekends. ⊠ *South Perth,* ☎ *018/ 92–6003.* ☉ *Daily 9–7:30.*

Shopping

Most centrally located stores are open Monday–Saturday 8–6, though some specialty shops have extended hours. Late-night trading, until 9, is available in the city on Friday, in the suburbs on Thursday. Perth's larger shops generally open 10–5 on Sunday and public holidays, except Christmas, Easter, and Anzac Day (April 25). Your hotel can provide more details about Sunday shopping.

Australiana

Australian souvenirs and knickknacks are on sale at small shops throughout the city. **Purely Australian** (☎ 08/9321–4679) carries the most comprehensive range of Oz-abilia in London Court, Hay Street Mall, and City Arcade. **Carillon Arcade** (⊠ Hay St. Mall, ☎ 08/9322– 1977), in the city center, houses a distinctively Australian store: **R. M. Williams** (☎ 08/9321–7786) sells everything for the Australian bushman, including moleskin trousers, hand-tooled leather boots, and Akubra hats.

Crafts

You can find authentic Aboriginal artifacts at **Creative Native** (⊠ 32 King St., ☎ 08/9322–3398). Out of town, in Subiaco, a former car dealer's workshop has been transformed into an Outback setting. This is the backdrop for **Indigenart** (⊠ 115 Hay St., Subiaco, ☎ 08/9388– 2899), an art gallery–cum–Aboriginal culture center, where visitors can view artwork and talk with the Aboriginal creators. Contemporary and traditional works are complemented by jewelry, fabrics, and clothing. It's a unique journey into the Aboriginal Dreamtime.

Gems

Broome, in the far north of the state, has been regarded as the pearl capital of the world for decades. **Linneys** (⊠ 37 Rokeby Rd., Subiaco, ☎ 08/9382–4077), whose designers and craftsmen have won national awards, has an excellent selection of Broome pearls and will set them in the design of your choice. Opals from South Australia's Coober Pedy are available at **Costello's** (⊠ 5–6 London Ct., ☎ 08/9325–8588). Prized pink diamonds from the Argyle diamond mines are incorporated in stunning pieces by **Charles Edward Jewellers** (⊠ 45 King St., ☎ 08/9321– 5111).

Malls

Citiplace, flanked by the post office and the **Forrest Chase** shopping complex, form the largest mall area. **Myer** (☎ 08/9221–3444) and **Aherns** (☎ 08/9323–0101) department stores both open onto the Murray Street pedestrian mall.

Perth A to Z

Arriving and Departing

BY BUS

Greyhound Pioneer Australia (☎ 13–2030) buses are routed through the **Westrail Centre** (✉ Summer St., ☎ 08/9328–6677) in East Perth.

BY CAR

The **Eyre Highway** crosses the continent from Port Augusta in South Australia to Western Australia's transportation gateway, Norseman. From there, take the Coolgardie–Esperance Highway north to Coolgardie, and the Great Eastern Highway on to Perth. Driving to Perth— 2,580 km (1,600 mi) from Adelaide and 4,032 km (2,500 mi) from Sydney—is an arduous journey, which should be undertaken only with a car (and mental faculties) in top condition. A supply of spare tires and drinking water are essential. Service stations and motels are situated at regular intervals along the route.

BY PLANE

Perth International Airport is 16 km (10 mi) from the city center. It is the international gateway to Australia for visitors from Europe, Africa, and Southeast Asia traveling on Ansett, Qantas, British Airways, Singapore Airlines, Air New Zealand, and Japan Airlines, among others.

Perth's **domestic terminal,** 11½ km (7 mi) from the city, is served by Ansett and Qantas. **Ansett W.A., Airlink** (the regional subsidiary of Qantas, ☎ 13 13 13), and **Skywest** (☎ 08/9334–2288) connect Perth with other towns within the state. *See* Air Travel *in* Smart Travel Tips, *above,* for additional airline telephone numbers.

Taxis between the airports and the city cost approximately $25. Shuttle buses offer regular service to the major hotels and city center and cost $7.

BY TRAIN

Crossing the Nullarbor Desert from the eastern states on **Westrail** (✉ East Perth Terminal, West Parade, ☎ 08/9326–2244 or 13–1053) is one of the great rail journeys of the world. The *Indian Pacific* makes three-day runs from Sydney on Monday and Thursday and two-day runs from Adelaide on Tuesday and Friday.

Getting Around

BY BICYCLE

Perth's climate and its network of excellent trails make cycling a safe and enjoyable way to discover the city—but beware: the summer temperature can exceed 100°F in the shade. Cycling in the heat of the day is not advisable. Wearing a bicycle helmet is required by law, and carrying water is prudent any time. You can rent a bicycle for about $23 a day from **About Bike Hire** (☎ 08/9221–2665) at the southeastern end of Riverside Drive. Free brochures detailing a variety of trails, including stops at historical spots, are available from the **Western Australia Tourist Centre** (☞ *below*).

BY BUS

The Perth central business district and suburban areas are well connected by the **Metrobus** bus line (☎ 13–2213). Tickets are valid for two hours and can be used on Metrobus trains and ferries. The main terminal is at the Perth Central Bus Station on Mounts Bay Road. Buses run daily between 6 AM and 11:30 PM, with reduced service on weekends and holidays.

Rides within the city center are free. **Cat** buses circle the city center, running approximately every 10 minutes on weekdays from 7 AM to 6 PM, Saturday 9 AM to 5 PM. Routes and timetables are available from **Transperth** (☎ 13–2213).

BY CAR

All major car-rental companies, including **Hertz** (☎ 08/9321–7777 or 1800/550–067)and **Avis** (☎ 08/9325–7677 or 1800/225–533), have depots at both the international and domestic airports. "Self-Drive Tours within WA," a free 72-page booklet that suggests itineraries around Perth, Fremantle, and the state, is available from the Western Australia Tourist Centre (☞ *below*) and major car-rental companies.

BY FERRY

Perth Water Transport (☎ 13–2213) ferries make daily runs from 6:50 AM to 7:15 PM between Barrack Street Jetty in Perth to Mends Street, across the Swan River in South Perth. Reduced service runs on weekends and public holidays.

BY TAXI

Cab fare between 6 AM and 6 PM weekdays is an initial $2.50 plus $1 every 1 km (½ mi). From 6 PM to 6 AM and on weekends the rate rises to $3.60 plus $1 per kilometer. Try **Swan Taxis** (☎ 08/9322–3411) or **Black and White** (☎ 08/9333–3322).

BY TRAIN

Fastrack trains run from Perth to Fremantle, Midland, Armadale, Joondalup, and en route stations weekdays from 5:30 AM to 11:30 PM, with reduced service on weekends and public holidays. Suburban and Bunbury trains depart from the city station on Wellington Street.

Contacts and Resources

DENTISTS

The **Perth Dental Hospital** (✉ 196 Goderich St., ☎ 08/9220–5777; 08/9325–3452 after business hours) will give details of private practitioners who provide an emergency service.

EMERGENCIES

Ambulance, fire brigade, and police. ☎ *000*.

Hospitals. The emergency room is open all night at the **Royal Perth Hospital** (✉ Victoria Sq., ☎ 08/9224–2244).

Police. ☎ *08/9222–1111*.

GUIDED TOURS

Boat Tours. Captain Cook Cruises (☎ 08/9325–3341) offers a variety of cruises on the Swan River, traveling from Perth to the Indian Ocean at Fremantle. Cruises cost $12 to $60 and may include meals. **Classic Boat Charters** (☎ 08/9472–4247) has sunset and dinner cruises on the Swan River aboard a handsome jarrah-and-teak motorboat, built in the '50s and restored and relaunched in 1995. The 39-ft vessel accommodates up to 18 passengers, and Western Australian wine and seafood are emphasized. **Boat Torque** (✉ Barrack Street Ferry Terminal, ☎ 08/9221–5844 and 1300/368–686, FAX 08/9325–3717) runs daily excursions to Rottnest Island and has whale-watching and wine cruises as well (☞ *below*).

Wildflower Tours. Springtime in Western Australia (August–November) is synonymous with wildflowers, as 8,000 species blanket an area that stretches 645 km (400 mi) north and 403 km (250 mi) south of Perth. Tours of these areas are popular, and early reservations are essential with **Westrail** (☎ 08/9326–2159), **Feature Tours** (☞ *below*), or **Great Western Tours** (☞ *below*).

Orientation Tours. Australian Pacific (☎ 08/9221–4000), **Great Western Tours** (☎ 08/9421–1411), and **Feature Tours** (☎ 08/9479–4131) run day tours of Perth and its major attractions. Most include visits to major sights and beaches near the city as well.

Walking Tours. Guntrip's Walking Tours (☎ 08/9293–1132) offers a two-hour historical walking tour of the city. **King's Park** (☎ 08/9480–3600) is the heart of Perth's bushland, and a walking tour through the area provides an excellent orientation for visitors. Free walking tours are available daily.

Whale-watching. From September to late November, **Boat Torque** (☞ *above*) heads out to sea for whale-watching off the coast, following the migratory route of humpback whales.

Wine. For a trip upriver to the famous Swan River wineries, the ferry *Mystique,* another craft in the Boat Torque (☞ *above*) fleet, makes daily trips from the Barrack Street Jetty, serving wine coming and going and lunch at one of the wineries.

VISITOR INFORMATION
Western Australian Tourist Centre. ⊠ *Forrest Pl. and Wellington St., Perth, 6000,* ☎ *08/9483–1111.*

SIDE TRIPS FROM PERTH

Rottnest Island

A pleasant cruise down the Swan River or across from Fremantle, Sunny Rottnest Island is an ideal day trip from Perth. It's easy to fall in love with its bleached beaches, rocky coves, blue-green waters, and particularly its unique wallabylike inhabitants called quokkas.

The most convenient way to get around Rottnest is by bicycle, as cars are not allowed on the island and bus service is infrequent. A bicycle tour of the island covers 26 km (16 mi) and can take as little as three hours, though you really need an entire day to enjoy the beautiful surroundings. It's impossible to get lost, since the one main road circles the island and will always bring you back to your starting point. Look for rentals at **Rottnest Bike Hire** (☎ 08/9292–5105 or 08/9221–1828, ⊙ daily 8:30–5) in the main settlement at Thomson Bay.

Heading south from Thomson Bay, between Government House and Herschell lakes, you'll encounter a **quokka colony.** Another colony lies down the road east, near the amphitheater at the civic center in sparkling **Geordie Bay.** Here, tame quokkas will come and eat right out of your hand. Quokkas are marsupials, small wallabies that are easily mistaken for rats; in fact, the island's name means "rat's nest" in Dutch. Well-fed by visitors, the quokkas are quite tame—feeding them is discouraged, however.

Past the quokka colony you'll find **gun emplacements** from World War II. As you continue south to **Bickley Bay,** you can spot the wreckage of ships that came to rest on Rottnest's rocky coastline.

Follow the main road past Porpoise, Salmon, Strickland, and Wilson bays to **West End,** the westernmost point on the island and another graveyard for unfortunate vessels. If you've brought a fishing rod, now is the time to unpack it. As you head back to Thomson Bay, you'll pass a dozen rocky inlets and bays; **Parakeet Bay,** the prettiest, is situated at the northernmost tip of the island.

Back at the Thomson Bay settlement, visit the **Rottnest Museum** (☎ 08/9372–9753), which provides an intriguing account of the island's convict history.

Information is available from the **Rottnest Island Visitors' Centre** (☞ *below*).

Dining

$$ ✕ **The Rottnest Hotel.** The Rottnest Hotel (affectionately known as the Quokka Arms, after the island's small marsupials) offers extraordinary bay views from the popular beer garden. Dining options include one fine restaurant and one that is more casual. The former has a more typical à la carte menu, while at the latter, patrons barbecue their own steaks or seafood before helping themselves to the salad bar. ⊠ *Main Rd., Thomson Bay,* ☎ *08/9292–5011. Reservations essential. AE, MC, V.*

$$ ✕ **Rottnest Island Lodge.** The kitchen at the award-winning Vincentís Restaurant has an excellent buffet breakfast. Seafood is the highlight of the lunches and dinners, which include baby octopus salad served in chili and red wine, with papaya chunks and bean sprouts. Other imaginative dishes are the Thai-style chicken batons on toasted sprouts with cilantro, finished with a roasted peanut dressing, and the "Parakeet's Delight"—wok-fried snow peas, baby corn, bamboo shoots, and sesame-soaked tofu in honey soy sauce. ⊠ *Main Rd., Thomson Bay,* ☎ *08/9292–5161. Reservations essential. AE, DC, MC, V.*

Rottnest A to Z

ARRIVING AND DEPARTING

Boat Torque Cruises (☎ 08/9221–5844 or 1300/368–686) runs ferries to Rottnest Island from both Perth's Barrack Street Jetty and from Fremantle. Speedy air service to the island is available on the **Rottnest Airlines** (☎ 08/9478–1322).

EMERGENCIES

Ambulance, fire brigade, and police. ☎ *000.*

Rottnest Nursing Post (☎ 08/9292–5030). Dial **000** to request emergency assistance from an operator.

GUIDED TOURS

The **Rottnest Island Authority** (⊠ Thomson Bay, ☎ 08/9372–9752) runs a daily two-hour coach tour of the island's highlights, including convict-built cottages, World War II gun emplacements, and salt lakes. The **Oliver Hill Railway** made its debut in late 1994, utilizing 6 km (4 mi) of reconstructed railway line to reach the island's gun batteries. Information is available from the Rottnest Island Visitors' Centre (☞ *below*).

VISITOR INFORMATION

Rottnest Island Visitors' Centre (⊠ Thomson Bay, ☎ 08/9372–9752).

York

90 km (56 mi) east of Perth.

Founded in the 1830s, this town stands as an excellent example of historic restoration. It sits in the lovely Avon Valley east of Perth, and its restored main street, Avon Terrace, evokes the days of the 1890s gold rush. The tiny town is easy to explore on foot and contains attractive edifices made of local sandstone. The **York Motor Museum** (⊠ Avon Terr., ☎ 08/9641–1288) is open daily and houses more than 100 classic and vintage cars, motorcycles, and even some horse-drawn vehicles. Motorcoach rides are available. If you plan to spend the night, consider the colonial **Settler's House** (⊠ Avon Terr., ☎ 08/9641–1503), a romantic hostelry with four-poster beds ($$$).

If you don't have a car, **Westrail** (☎ 08/9326–2244 or 13–1053) provides bus service to York from Perth.

New Norcia

129 km (80 mi) north of Perth.

In 1846 a small band of Benedictine monks arrived in Australia to establish a mission for Aborigines. They settled in New Norcia and eventually built boarding schools and orphanages. Today the brothers in the monastic community continue to live a life of prayer and work—their devotion and labor produce the best olive oil in the state, pressed from the fruit of century-old trees. The original schools have developed into a Catholic college attended by about 200 students. Follow the New Norcia Heritage Trail to explore the monastery, church, old mill, hotel, and jail, in addition to the museum and art gallery, which house unique collections of European and Australian paintings.

The small **Monastery Guest House** (⊠ New Norcia, WA 6509, ☎ 08/9654–8002 for the guesthouse or 08/9654–8018 for community information) gives overnight visitors an idea of the life led by the Benedictine monks. Rooms are simple and inexpensive, although there is a suggested contribution of $40 per day including meals. The monastery bakery makes marvelous nut cake. To reach New Norcia from Perth, take the Great Northern Highway (Route 95).

Nambung National Park

245 km (152 mi) north of Perth.

Located on the Swan coastal plain, Nambung National Park is best known for the Pinnacles Desert situated in the center of the park. Over the years, wind and drifting sand have sculpted forms that loom as high as 15 ft, or merely poke out of the sand three or four inches. These eerie limestone forms, which look like African anthills, are the fossilized roots of ancient coastal plants fused with sand.

You can walk among the pinnacles on a 1,650-ft-long trail from the parking area or drive the scenic, one-way, 3-km (2-mi) Pinnacles Desert Loop (not suitable for large RVs or buses). If you have more time, look for some of the 100-plus species of birds that live around the park's coastal dunes and splendid beaches. Fishing is permitted at Hangover Bay and Kangaroo Point. The best time to visit the park is August–October, when the heath is ablaze with wildflowers. Entrance fees are $3 per car or $2 per bus passenger.

Lodging

Accommodations are available in Cervantes at the **Cervantes Pinnacles Motel** (⊠ Cervantes, WA 6511, ☎ 08/9652–7145) or the **Cervantes Caravan Park** (⊠ Cervantes, WA 6511, ☎ 08/9652–7060). There are toilets near the Pinnacles, but camping is not permitted in the park.

Arriving and Departing

From Perth, travel north about 193 km (120 mi) on the Brand Highway toward Badgingarra, then turn west toward Cervantes and south into the park.

Tours of the park can be arranged in Perth through the **Western Australian Tourist Centre** (⊠ Forrest Pl. and Wellington St., Perth 6000,

☎ 08/9483–1111) or in Cervantes through the **Cervantes Caravan Park** (☞ *above*).

Visitor Information

Contact the **Department of Conservation and Land Management** (✉ Box 62, Cervantes 6511, ☎ 08/9652–7043).

FREMANTLE

Fremantle is the jewel in Western Australia's crown. Located about 19 km (12 mi) southwest of Perth, it is a city busy reinventing itself—though it retains its identity as a place where locals know each other and smile and say hello as they pass in the street.

Modern Fremantle is a far cry from the barren sandy plain that greeted the first wave of English settlers back in 1829, at the newly constituted Swan River Colony. Most were city dwellers, and after five months at sea in sailing ships, the salt-marsh flats where they landed sorely tested their fortitude. Living in tents, with packing cases for chairs, they found no edible crops, and the nearest fresh water was 51 km (32 mi)—and a tortuous trip up the salty waters of the Swan—away. As a result they soon moved the settlement upriver to the vicinity of present-day Perth. Fremantle remained the location of the seaport, however, and it is to this day Western Australia's premier port.

World War II saw the first major stirring in Fremantle, when the slumbering colonial port city provided a welcome landfall for American servicemen assigned to the Antipodes. Postwar immigration then added a new impetus. The last major change was wrought in 1983 when the city's *Australia II* snatched the America's Cup from Newport.

Though Western Australia's hold on the "Auld Mug" trophy was short-lived, there was no stopping Fremantle's comeback once it began. Today "Freo" is a city of gurus and greens, truckies and dockers, yuppies and workers, academics and dropouts. It has a multicultural mix of people living amicably side by side. And local architects have brought about a stunning transformation of the town without defacing the colonial streetscape or its fine limestone buildings. In the leafy suburbs, every other house is a restored 19th-century gem.

Exploring Fremantle

An ideal place to start a leisurely stroll around town is **South Terrace,** known as the Fremantle cappuccino strip. Soak up the ambience as you wander alongside locals through sidewalk cafés or browse in bookstores, art galleries, and souvenir shops. No matter how aimlessly you meander, you'll invariably end up where you began, along the broad sidewalk of the cappuccino strip.

Between Phillimore Street and Marine Terrace in the **West End,** you'll find a collection of some of the best-preserved heritage buildings in the state. The Fremantle Railway Station on Elder Place is a good place to start a walk.

Fremantle also has plenty to entertain children, from pools to a puppet theater to a clutch of museums that are informative and fun. South Beach and Port Beach provide sun, sand, and surf, and numerous parks around the city are stocked with playground equipment. The Esplanade Park is the venue for numerous outdoor activities, including the January Sardine Festival regular weekend funfairs.

Sights to See

Outside the port gates on the western end of town is **Arthur's Head,** with its row of cottages built to house employees of the Customs Department. Nearby **J-Shed** houses the workshop of perhaps the nation's foremost exponent of public art, the sculptor Greg James. His extraordinarily lifelike figures grace a number of Perth and metropolitan sites, including King's Square.

At the end of Marine Terrace, visit the **Kidogo Arthouse,** a gallery and arts center that still displays some works by its former owner, potter Joan Campbell. Or, pause for fresh fish-and-chips, a legacy of British immigration, or the ubiquitous hamburger as you watch the tide roll in from the old sea wall. Try dangling your feet from the wooden jetty that was rebuilt on the spot where it stood in the days of tall ships.

Like most of Fremantle, the fine, Gothic Revival **Fremantle Museum** was built by convicts in the nineteenth century. First used as a lunatic asylum (the ghosts of one or two demented souls are said to haunt the halls), by 1900 it was overcrowded and was nearly shut down. It eventually became a home for elderly women until 1942, when the U.S. Navy made it into their local headquarters. Artifacts trace the early days of Fremantle's settlement in one wing, while another houses the **Fremantle Arts Centre.** The complex contains a restaurant and gift shop, and Sunday afternoon courtyard concerts are a regular feature. ⊠ *Ord and Finnerty Sts.,* ☎ *08/9430–7966.* ⊙ *Mon.–Wed. 10:30–5, Thurs.–Sun. 1–5.*

The 1855 **Fremantle Prison** was decommissioned in 1991 and opened to unshackled visitors the following year. Guided tours provide a fascinating glimpse of the state's oldest prison, including its famous classic-art cell, a superb collection of drawings made by an unknown convict to decorate his quarters. His work has been the inspiration for a new generation of artists, and the iron doors that once slammed shut on convicts at nightfall now slam shut on the work of artists and craftspeople who use the cells as studios by day. Reservations for candlelight tours on Wednesday and Friday are essential. ⊠ *1 The Terrace,* ☎ *08/9430–7177.* ⊡ *$10.* ⊙ *Tours every ½ hr 10–5.*

In **Fremantle Market** you can browse in the Victorian building for everything from potatoes to paintings, incense to antiques, sausages to Chinese take-away. On weekends and public holidays the Market can get super-crowded, but a small café and bar make it a wonderful place to refresh yourself while musicians entertain. Note the sign warning, "Buskers 45 minutes only," which theoretically restricts street entertainers to 45-minute sessions. ⊠ *South Terr. and Henderson St.,* ☎ *08/ 9335–2515.* ⊙ *Fri. 9–9, Sat. 9–5, Sun. 10–5.*

In the center of the business district, **High Street Mall** is the haunt of retired Italian fishermen whiling away their days in conversation. They're a part of the local color in the mall. ⊠ *High, Market, William, and Adelaide Sts.*

One of the oldest commercial heritage-listed structures in Western Australia is **Moores' Building.** It is currently an exhibition and performance space. ⊠ *46 Henry St., Fremantle,* ☎ *08/9335–8366.* ⊙ *Daily 10–5.*

A landmark of early Fremantle atop the limestone cliff known as Arthur's Head, the **Round House** was built in 1831 by convicts to house other convicts. This curious, 12-sided building is the state's oldest surviving structure. From its ramparts, there are great vistas of High Street out to the Indian Ocean. Underneath, a tunnel was carved through the cliffs in the mid-1800s to give ships lying at anchor offshore easy access from town. No longer needed for commercial traffic, the tunnel is still open to Bather Beach patrons. ⊠ *West end of High St.*

Bounded by High, Queen, and William streets, **King's Square** is at the heart of the central business district. Shaded as it is by the spreading branches of 100-year-old Moreton Bay fig trees, it makes a perfect place for a rest. Medieval-style benches complete the picture of Old World elegance. Bordering the square are **St. John's Anglican Church** and the **town hall.**

☼ **Spare Parts Puppet Theatre.** This imaginative children's theater stages productions several times a year. Spare Parts has built up an international reputation and regularly tours abroad. The foyer is a showplace for its puppetry. ⊠ *1 Short St., opposite the railway station,* ☎ *08/ 9335–5044.* ☼ *Daily 10–5.*

Perhaps no city sight is more enchanting than the row of perfectly preserved **Warders Quarters** cottages on **Henderson Street**—and yet they are a grim reminder of the colonial past. Here, convicts hued blocks from the limestone cliffs so that they could build houses for the warders standing guard over them. The courthouse, the police station, and the grim walls of the former prison, much of which the convicts also built, stand alongside the rows of terraced-limestone cottages.

The **Western Australia Maritime Museum** offers a fascinating glimpse into the state's nautical past. A replica of the 17th-century Dutch ship *Duyfken,* lovingly re-created in a workshop adjacent to the Museum, was launched in 1999. The Museum also displays relics from the Dutch and colonial ships that crashed on Western Australia's rocky coastline. A changing gallery of prints and photographs complements the exhibition. ⊠ *1 Cliff St.,* ☎ *08/9431–8444.* ▨ *Donation accepted.* ☼ *Daily 10:30–5.*

NEED A BREAK?	**Culley's Tea Rooms** is the only remaining old-fashioned cake and pie shop serving its daily-baked fare accompanied by a pot of freshly brewed tea or coffee. Tasty lunches, served over the counter or at tables, are from $4.50, and the ambience is just what you would expect from a family business that has succeeded for more than 60 years. ⊠ *116 High St. Mall,* ☎ *08/9335–1286.* ☼ *Mon.–Sat. 8.30–5:30, Sun. 10–5.*

Dining

$$$ ✕ **Chunagon.** This spacious Japanese restaurant, universally recognized as the best in Western Australia, has superb views of the Fremantle boat harbor and the ocean. Choose from *teppanyaki* (Japanese barbecue) items, which include the house special of grilled crayfish, or from the à la carte menu of tempura, teriyaki, sashimi, and sushi. A special teppanyaki area allows you to watch as your meal is barbecued with great theatrics. Try the extraordinary *Akebono* 10-course fixed-price menu, named after the legendary Hawaiian Sumo wrestler. A "VIP Diners' Card" offers discounts to regular customers. ⊠ *46 Mews Rd.,* ☎ *08/ 9336–1000. AE, DC, MC, V. Closed Mon.*

$$$ ✕ **Granita's.** Take an old biscuit factory and mix it with a sprinkle of creativity, and suddenly what was considered the wrong end of South Terrace becomes the *in* place. Seafood and pasta are house specialties— try Italian dishes with an Australian signature, such as *sardine di Fremantle,* grilled sardines served with garlic butter and balsamic vinegar, or *farfalle dockers,* butterfly-shape pasta with caviar, chili peppers, garlic, parsley, and olive oil. Granita's has an excellent cellar of mostly Australian wine and beer. ⊠ *330 South Terr., at Jenkins St.,* ☎ *08/9336– 4660. AE, MC, V.*

$$ ✕ **Joe's Fish Shack.** Fremantle's newest and quirkiest restaurant looks like everyone's vision of a run-down, weather-beaten Maine diner. With uninterrupted harbor views, authentic nautical decor, and great food, you can't go wrong. Recommendations include the salt-and-pepper squid, stuffed tiger prawns, and the chili mussels. ✉ *42 Mews Road,* ☎ *08/9336–7161. AE, DC, MC, V.*

$ ✕ **Istanbul.** The Istanbul is a bright, breezy street-front venue that offers specialties from the Turkish cities of Samsun, Adana, and Iskendar. A secret of this restaurant's success is the fresh-baked Turkish flatbread that accompanies every meal. Start with one of the traditional dips—hummus, eggplant, or potato—then move on to delicacies like grilled lamb and burek (meat- or vegetable-stuffed pastries). Save room for sweet, sticky baklava dessert. Traditional music and belly dancing take place Friday and Saturday nights. ✉ *19-B Essex St.,* ☎ *08/9335–6068. MC, V. BYOB.*

Lodging

$$$$ 🏨 **Esplanade Hotel.** Part of an original colonial hotel, this establishment has provided seafront accommodation and spectacular ocean views to West Australians for over a century. Rooms are appealing, pleasantly furnished, and feature bright pastel colors. Studios are also available. Café Panache, right on the Esplanade, draws crowds all day. ✉ *Marine Terr. and Essex St., Box 1102, 6160,* ☎ *08/9432–4000,* FAX *08/9430–4539. 256 rooms, 3 suites. 2 restaurants, café, 2 pools. AE, DC, MC, V.*

$$$$ 🏨 **South Beach Apartment Hotel.** These modern, two-story, apartments, most with sea views, contain everything for a short- or long-term stay. All apartments are nicely furnished and offer a choice of one, two, or three bedrooms. Each fully equipped living area includes a remote control television, a VCR, and a stereo; kitchens come with ovens, dishwashers, and microwaves. Laundry facilities are available, and there is intercom security to each room. ✉ *330 South Terr., South Fremantle 6162,* ☎ *08/9430–5255,* FAX *08/9430–5266. Kitchenettes, coin laundry. AE, DC, MC, V.*

$$$ 🏨 **Fothergills.** Built in 1892, this two-story limestone terrace furnished with antiques and Italian pottery stands opposite the old Fremantle prison, just a few-minutes' walk from the heart of town. Service and food are wonderful at this B&B, and the house's balconies afford stunning views of the harbor. Breakfast is included. ✉ *20–22 Ord St., 6160,* ☎ *08/9335–6784,* FAX *08/9430–7789. 6 rooms, 4 with bath. Refrigerators, laundry service. AE, DC, MC, V.*

$$$ 🏨 **Moonrakers.** Proprietors Marie and Rob Wuillemin welcome you into their elegant, single-story Victorian abode. Tuck yourself into one of the four-poster beds and wake to the fragrance of a cottage garden. There is also a poolside cottage with its own bath. This B&B is within easy walking distance of the cappuccino strip. The room rate includes breakfast. ✉ *79 South St., South Fremantle 6162,* ☎ *08/9336–2266.* FAX *08/9336–2204. Pool. AE, DC, MC, V.*

Nightlife

The cappuccino strip opens at 7 AM and closes around 3 AM. There is nothing more pleasant after a day when the temperature has topped 100°F than to relax at the sidewalk tables of **Old Papas** (☎ 08/9335–4665), **Ginos** (☎ 08/9336–1464), **Marconi** (☎ 08/9335–3215), **The Dôme** (☎ 08/9336–3040), **Rossini's** (☎ 08/9430–7133), or the totally over-the-top **Miss Maud's** (☎ 08/9336–1599), where everything from breakfast to a late-night glass of wine is served seven days a week.

Bars

In its 19th-century heyday Fremantle had as many as 17 pubs to service weary commercial travelers and workers looking to slake a burning thirst after a day on the docks, in the tanneries, or any of the myriad factories with which the town hummed. Many pubs remain, as much a part of the fabric of Fremantle life as they ever were.

National Hotel. Describing itself as "Friends of the Guinness," the National has live Irish music on Friday and Sunday. ⊠ *98 High St.,* ☎ *08/9335–1786.*

Rosie O'Grady's. This was once the Federal, a fine old Australian hotel, but times have changed the old Australian ambience into a newer Irish pub. ⊠ *William St. opposite town hall,* ☎ *08/9335–1645.*

Sail and Anchor Pub–Brewery. Thanks to its range of home-brewed beers, this remains a popular watering hole. A shady courtyard beer-garden is the fair-weather gathering place. ⊠ *64 South Terr.,* ☎ *08/9335–8433.*

Music

Fly By Night Musicians Club. Many local bands and soloists owe their big breaks to the smoke-free Fly By Night. ⊠ *Parry St.,* ☎ *08/9430–5976.*

Metropolis Concert Club Fremantle. In the heart of Fremantle's cappuccino strip, this nonstop techno and funk dance venue is the place to be on Saturday night. ⊠ *58 South Terr.,* ☎ *08/9336–1609.*

Shopping

Most shops are open Monday–Saturday 9–5:30 and Sunday noon–5, with late-night shopping on Thursday. Some shops can send your purchases overseas.

Bannister Street Craftworks. In a restored 19th-century warehouse a group of craftspeople have gathered in their own workshops to turn out everything from screen printing to woodworks, hand-blown glass, leather goods, and souvenirs. The artists, working as a cooperative, invite you to come in and watch as they demonstrate their skills, or just to browse among the exhibits. ⊠ *8–12 Bannister St.,* ☎ *08/9336–2035.*

Into Camelot. This medieval-style dress shop sells romantic wedding gowns and cloaks, street and evening wear, and peasant smocks for all occasions. Period boots, classic Saxon and Celtic jewelry, masks (feathered and plain), are all available at affordable prices. ⊠ *Shop 9, South Terrace Piazza,* ☎ FAX *08/9335–4698.*

☺ **The Pickled Fairy & Other Myths.** The first shop of its kind in the world, and still only one of two, this is a children's paradise. The fairy theme is everywhere, and Celtic jewelry is sold along with books on magic and mythology. ⊠ *Shop 7B, South Terrace Piazza,* ☎ *08/9430–5827.*

Kakulas Sisters. This unique produce shop overflows with fragrances and sacks of goodies from across the globe, including Costa Rican coffee beans, Colorado black-eyed beans, Brazilian quince and guava pasties, and Japanese teas. ⊠ *High St.,* ☎ *08/9430–4445.*

Fremantle A to Z

Arriving and Departing

Fremantle is served by both train and bus from Perth. Trains bound for Fremantle depart approximately every 20–30 minutes from the **Perth Central Station** on Wellington Street. Bus information is available from **Transperth** (☎ 13–2213).

Contacts and Resources

Ambulance, fire brigade, and police. ☎ *000.*

Fremantle Hospital. ⊠ *Alma St.,* ☎ *08/9431–3400.*

GUIDED TOURS
Fremantle Trams (⊠ William St., ☎ 08/9339–8719) provides a number of tours, including sightseeing trips along the harbor, a fish-and-chip tour, and a history trail. Trams leave from the Town Hall on the hour. **Pride of the West Stagecoach** (⊠ Marine Terr., ☎ 08/9417–5523) offers tours around town in replica Cobb & Co. horse-drawn carriages.

VISITOR INFORMATION
Fremantle Town Hall Information Centre. ⊠ *William St.,* ☎ *08/9431–7878.*

THE SOUTHWEST

Western Australia is famous for its farm, station, and country retreats in a variety of rural settings, from the lush farmlands of the Southwest's Denmark to the 2,500-acre cattle stations in the forbidding Northwest. Considering the contrast, it's not surprising that the Southwest continues to be the state's most popular rural getaway. The combination of fine vineyards, rugged coastal cliffs, rolling green fields, majestic forests, and a Mediterranean climate is truly delightful. Cape Leeuwin–Naturaliste and Stirling Range national parks, located on the coast near Margaret River and inland north of Albany, respectively, are also worth visiting.

Mandurah

75 km (47 mi) south of Perth, 109 km (68 mi) north of Bunbury.

Set on the shores of the perfect horseshoe-shaped **Peel Inlet, Mandurah** is Australia's fastest-growing city—and it's easy to see why. Take a stroll along the scenic boardwalk, fronted by fine civic buildings and shaded by mangrove trees, or dine at one of the many stylish cafés opposite, including **Caffe Pronto, Ristorante Firenze,** or the **Choice café.** Cruise over 150 square km (60 square mi) of inland waterways, or take in the views along the **Estuary Scenic Drive.** The nearby San Marco Quays (Keys) are a prototype for the new, laid-back Western Australia Lifestyle.

$$$–$$$$ 🏨 **All Seasons Atrium Resort.** This classy and breezy hotel, on a hill overlooking the ornamental lake that adjoins Peel Inlet, is a restful retreat, built around a palm tree–lined indoor swimming pool. ⊠ *65 Ormsby Terr., 6210,* ☎ *08/9535–6633,* 𝔽𝔸𝕏 *08/9581–4151. 116 rooms. Restaurant, bar, lobby lounge, indoor lap pool, wading pool, outdoor pool, sauna, spa, tennis court, video games, convention center. AE, DC, MC, V.*

VISITOR INFORMATION
Mandurah Tourist Bureau. At this excellent Tourist office, pick up the free "Mandurah Heartwalks" brochure, which details local walking trails. Adjoining the Bureau is the award-winning **Peel Discovery Centre.** ⊠ *Mandurah Terr., Boardwalk,* ☎ *08/9550–3999.*

En Route   En route from Mandurah to Bunbury, follow Route 10 through the only natural **tuart forest** in the world. These magnificent tuart trees, types of eucalypt, or gum trees, that thrive in arid conditions, have been standing on this land for 400 years.

Bunbury

184 km (114 mi) south of Perth, 53 km (33 mi) north of Busselton.

Bunbury is the major seaport of the Southwest, with a spectacular mangrove boardwalk along the Leschenault Inlet. An excellent new attraction is the **Dolphin Discovery Center** (Koombana Dr., ☎ 08/9791–3088, FAX 08/9791–3420) on Koombana Bay. Around 90 bottle-nosed dolphins visit regularly—their favorite time is 8 AM–noon—and visitors are encouraged to swim or snorkel with them. Bunbury City, with its own "cappuccino strip" and entertainment precinct, is surprisingly sophisticated.

Dining

$$ ✕ **Louisa's.** Regarded as one of the best country restaurants in West-
★ ern Australia, under the direction of owner-chef Darryl Willmott, the casual, brasserie-style fare here is paired with a strong local wine list. Excellent entrées include Thai snapper and lobster curry with coconut rice. Service is top-notch in the comfortable, elegant dining room. ⊠ *15 Clifton St.,* ☎ *08/9721–9959. AE, DC, MC, V. Closed Sun. No lunch Mon.–Thurs. and Sat.*

Busselton

53 km (33 mi) south of Bunbury.

Busselton was settled by the Bussell family in 1834, and it is among the state's oldest towns. Its history and that of the Southwest dairy industry's early years are recorded in the **Old Butter Factory,** a small museum. ⊠ *Peel Terr.,* ☎ *08/9754–2166.* ☜ *$4.* ☉ *Wed.–Mon. 2–5.*

While in Busselton, don't miss taking a walk along the 2-km- (1-mi-) long **Old Jetty.** A train runs along the jetty every half hour from 10 AM to 4 PM.

Dining and Lodging

$$ ✕ **Newton House.** The finest restaurant in the region is housed in a
★ charming, whitewashed 1851 colonial cottage with polished wooden floors and open fireplaces. Master chef Stephen Reagan (who claims ancestry from the Reggio clan of Italy, not the U.S. former president), has a string of culinary awards to back up his reputation. Magic is made from fine regional produce, and the exciting menu changes regularly. If it's available, don't pass up the Pemberton trout. Also, take a look at the Old Barn Gallery attached to the restaurant. ⊠ *Bussell Hwy., Vasse 6280,* ☎ *08/9755–4485. MC, V. BYOB. No dinner Sun.–Wed.*

$$$$ ☷ **Geographe Bayview Resort.** This low-key resort, 6 km (4 mi) south of Busselton, is a restful hangout on the bay. Rooms are light and airy, each with an ocean view. Facilities include a tennis court and two swimming pools. Spinnakers Café and the more elegant Tuart Restaurant provide fine dining that showcases local venison and features a range of vegetarian dishes. ⊠ *Bussell Hwy., 6280,* ☎ *08/9755–4166 or 08/ 9755–4075. 27 rooms, 58 self-contained villas. Restaurant, café, picnic area, refrigerator, pool, putting green, tennis court, beach, windsurfing. AE, DC, MC, V.*

$$–$$$ ☷ **Prospect Villa.** This two-story 1850s house is close to town but a fair walk from the Geographe Bay beaches. Laura Ashley fabrics decorate the rooms and Victorian bric-a-brac provides an atmospheric backdrop for a comfortable B&B. Rates include Continental breakfast. ⊠ *1 Pries Ave., 6280,* ☎ *08/9752–1509; 08/9752–2273 after 7 PM. 4 rooms. AE, MC, V.*

Dunsborough

21 km (13 mi) west of Busselton, 8 km (5 mi) east of Yallingup.

The attractive seaside town of Dunsborough is a booming holiday resort and retirement center. It's perfect for a few days of swimming, sunning, and fishing, and conveniently close to the wineries of Margaret River. If you like ice cream, don't miss **Simmo's.**

Dining and Lodging

$$ ✕ **Ibis Café.** This simple café's philosophy is reflected in its surroundings—don't mind the decor; concentrate on the food. Contained within a small shop in the village center, the Ibis has garnered a reputation for excellent fare at reasonable prices. Its menu of pastas, salads, and grilled seafood, meat, and vegetables changes with the seasons, always featuring local produce. Dessert cakes and tarts are delicious, and the cheese board presents the region's finest. ⊠ *Dunsborough Shopping Village,* ☎ *08/9755–3381. MC, V. BYOB. No dinner Sun. during winter.*

$$ 🏠 **Windmill Cottages.** Rammed-earth construction, verandas, and the colonial styling of these cottages makes them appealing. Tucked into the bushland not far from Geographe Bay, these one- and two-story self-contained cottages sleep from four to eight people and allow you to prepare your own meals in fully equipped kitchens. Linens are serviced daily, and shops are just a five-minute walk away. There is a minimum two-night stay, and special weekly rates are available. ⊠ *Yungarra Dr.,* ☎ *08/9755–3258,* FAX *08/9756–8173. 4 cottages. Kitchenettes. MC, V.*

Cape Leeuwin—Naturaliste National Park

The northernmost part of the park is 266 km (165 mi) south of Perth.

Located on the southwest tip of the continent, this 150-km (93-mi) stretch of coastline is one of Australia's most fascinating areas. The limestone Leeuwin-Naturaliste Ridge directly below the park contains more than 360 known caves. Evidence dates both human and animal habitation here to beyond 40,000 years ago.

At the northern end of the park stands **Cape Naturaliste Lighthouse,** open to visitors 10–4 daily. A mile-long trail leads from Cape Naturaliste to Canal Rocks, passing rugged cliffs, quiet bays, and curving beaches. This is also the start of the 120-km (75-mi) *Cape to Cape Walk.*

The coastal scenery changes drastically from north to south: rocks at some points, calm sandy beaches at others, all interspersed with heathlands, eucalyptus forests, and swamps. It would take days to explore all the intricacies of this park.

Four major cave systems are easily accessible: **Ngilgi,** near Yallingup (☎ 08/9755–2152), open daily 9:30–3:30; **Mammoth** (☎ 08/9757–7411), open daily 8:30–4:30; **Lake** (☎ 08/9757–7411), open daily 9–5; and **Jewel** (☎ 08/9757–7411), open daily 9:30–3:30. Admission is $9–$12 per cave and includes a guided tour. Ngilgi is notable for its massive stalagmites, stalactites, delicate straws, and shawl formations, while Mammoth and Lake caves contain pools of water that offer eerie reflections of stalagmites and stalactites. All four caves are located on Caves Road inside Cape Leeuwin–Naturaliste National Park. The new **CaveWorks** display center at Lake Cave is a recommended introduction to the whole cave system (☎ 08/9757–7411).

Caves Road leads to several lookout points, including Boranup Lookout, a 1,980-ft trail overlooking Hamelin Bay. At Boranup Forest, karri, one of the largest trees in the world, have naturally regenerated following many years of logging.

The view from the top of the lighthouse at Cape Leeuwin allows you to witness the meeting of the Southern and the Indian oceans. In some places, this alliance results in giant swells that crash against the rocks. In others, small coves are blessed with calm waters ideal for swimming and fishing.

Lodging

If you don't plan to camp, there is plenty of lodging available in the area, at Dunsborough (☞ *above*) and Margaret River (☞ *below*).

⚠ **Campgrounds** with toilets, showers, and an information center are located north in Injidup. Campsites cost $5 for two adults, $3 for each additional adult.

Visitor Information

District manager (✉ Queen St., Busselton 6280, ☎ 08/9752–1255).

Margaret River

181 km (112 mi) south of Perth, 39 km (24 mi) south of Busselton, 39 km (24 mi) north of Augusta, 377 km (234 mi) west of Albany.

Some of Australia's finest wines are grown by the numerous wineries here, most of which are open for tastings and sales. **Cape Mentelle** (✉ Wallcliffe Rd., ☎ 08/9757–3266) was one of the first and is still one of the most notable wineries in the area. The rammed-earth winery and tasting rooms, so typical of the buildings in the Margaret River district, are as handsome and memorable as the wine. Wine maker Vanya Cullen produces one of Australia's best chardonnays and an outstanding cabernet merlot at **Cullen Wines** (✉ Caves Rd., Willyabrup, ☎ 08/9755–5277), a family-run business. **Leeuwin Estate** (✉ Stevens Rd., ☎ 08/9757–6253) is a fine winery, where the grounds provide a magical setting for annual concerts of such international artists as George Benson, Dionne Warwick, and Diana Ross. **Vasse Felix** (✉ Harmans Rd. S, Cowaramup, ☎ 08/9755–5242) has an excellent upstairs restaurant and a basement cellar within picturesque grounds. To the south, **Hamelin Bay** (✉ McDonald Road, Karridale, ☎ 08/9389–6020) won several awards in 1997 with its very first vintage.

A brochure with details on individual cellars is available from the **Augusta/Margaret River Tourist Bureau.** ✉ *Bussell Hwy.,* ☎ *08/9757–2911.* ☉ *Daily 9–5.*

A few minutes' walk from the center of Margaret River is the **Old Settlement Museum,** which includes a house, farm buildings, and machinery from the 1920s. This and other "group settlement" farms were built by English veterans of World War I recruited by the Australian government to establish a dairy industry in the then-virgin bush of the Southwest. Although their efforts met with varying success, the industry has survived to the present day. A blacksmith gives craft demonstrations five days a week, and high-quality items are available from the crafts and souvenir shop. The museum's Heritage Tea Rooms serve English-style Devonshire Teas. ✉ *Bussell Hwy.,* ☎ *08/9757–9335.* 🎫 *$5.* ☉ *Summer, daily 10–5; winter, daily 10–2.*

Also in Margaret River, **Eagle's Heritage** is a rehabilitation center for sick and injured birds of prey. ✉ *Boodijup Rd.,* ☎ *08/9757–2960.* 🎫 *$4.* ☉ *Daily 10–5.*

Dining and Lodging

$$$ ✕ **Flutes Café.** The pastoral setting here—over the dammed waters of
★ the Willyabrup Brook and encircled by olive groves in the midst of the Brookland Valley Vineyard—is almost as compelling as the food. The

modern Australian cooking at Flutes is consistently rated among the best in the region and features prime local produce. Margaret River venison, Capel marron (freshwater crayfish), and Vasse asparagus are all excellent, prepared simply yet with flair. ⊠ *Caves Rd., Willyabrup,* ☎ *08/9755–6250. Reservations essential. AE, DC, MC, V.*

$$$ ✕ **Valley Café.** Simon West and Ronnie Dunk have made this one of ★ Western Australia's most popular new restaurants. Try the lime chicken with Kashmiri spices, or the crispy squid. The valley views from the café balcony are sensational. ⊠ *Carters Rd., at Caves Rd., Margaret River,* ☎ *08/9757–3225. AE, DC, MC, V.*

$$ ✕ **Gunyulgup.** Premium local produce is the hallmark of the modern, brasserie-style menu at Gunyulgup: Watch for Cloverdene organic lamb from Karridale, Margaret River venison, and Karri smoked lamb fillet. Start the day with a pancake stack topped by berry syrup and double cream, or try fresh Mandurah crab cakes or *gado-gado* (Indonesian salad with peanut dressing) for lunch. The dining room is stylishly modern and spacious, full of light without losing touch with its earthy, country roots. ⊠ *Gunyulgup Valley Dr., Yallingup,* ☎ *08/9755–2434. AE, DC, MC, V. BYOB. No dinner Tues. and Wed. in winter.*

$$$$ ▦ **Basildene Manor.** This grand, two-story house on the outskirts of Margaret River has long been regarded as one of the region's finest inns. The proud new owners, Garry Nielsen and Julie Whittingham, have lovingly refurbished each of the guest rooms in the circa 1912 house and soon plan to remodel the breakfast conservatory. Rooms are individually decorated in rich lilac, gold, and red colors. A full breakfast is included. ⊠ *Wallcliffe Rd., 6285,* ☎ *08/9757–3140,* ℻ *08/9757–3383. 10 rooms. Dining room, library. AE, DC, MC, V.*

$$$$ ▦ **Cape Lodge.** Early morning calls come from a chorus of kook-★ aburras, and evening is heralded by caroling magpies at this lovely, award-winning property. The decor has a Cape Dutch theme with colonial furniture, captain's chairs, and rattan settees. Guests can be found canoeing on the lake, napping in front of the gargantuan, marble open fire, relaxing in the extensive gardens or snacking on a sumptuous breakfast, which is included. Dinner is available most nights courtesy of executive chef Tony Howell. Because the setting caters more to adults, families with children under 12 are discouraged. ⊠ *Caves Rd., Yallingup 6282,* ☎ *08/9755–6311,* ℻ *08/9755–6322. 18 rooms. Pool, tennis court. AE, DC, MC, V.*

$$$$ ▦ **Gilgara Homestead.** This 1987 replica of an 1870 station homestead on 23 gently rolling acres provides a bucolic atmosphere for a maximum of 14 guests. The award-winning property has romantic rooms furnished with antiques and lace, so it's no surprise that honeymooners choose to stay here. A rose-covered veranda, open fireplaces, and a cozy lounge add to the charm. Because owner Pamela Kimmel fosters local fauna, you might breakfast surrounded by spectacular blue wrens or catch a few kangaroos lounging at the front door. Rates include a gourmet Mediterranean-style breakfast. Due to the inn's romantic ambience, families with children are discouraged. ⊠ *Caves Rd., 6285,* ☎ *08/9757–2705,* ℻ *08/9757–3259. 6 rooms. Breakfast room, horseback riding. AE, DC, MC, V.*

$$$ ▦ **Heritage Trail Lodge.** This hotel has drawn accolades for its unique architecture—the cabin-style accommodations deliberately recall the old tents erected by settler immigrants, as displayed at the adjacent Old Settlement Museum ((☞ *above*)). All furniture has been handcrafted from a single giant karri tree on the property. Slide back the Japanese screen dividing the bath from the living area in each cabin and you get a clear view from the spa into the forest. Continental breakfast, with fresh-baked bread and local cheeses, is included. ⊠ *31 Bussell Hwy.,*

6285, ☎ *08/9757–9595,* FAX *08/9757–9596. 10 timber suites (cabins). Breakfast room, spa. AE, DC, MC, V.*

Nannup

100 km (62 mi) east of Margaret River, 71 km (44 mi) southeast of Busselton, 219 km (136 mi) northwest of Denmark.

Nannup is a small, beautiful town with quaint timber cottages and many heritage buildings. Activities include canoeing the Blackwood River and wandering through the Blythe Gardens. There are a number of scenic drives in the area, including the Blackwood River Tourist Drive, a 10-km (6-mi) scenic drive by the Blackwood River, surrounded by rolling hills with kari and jarrah forests.

Dining and Lodging

$$ ✚ **The Lodge.** Built from century-old materials, the Lodge at Nannup has garnered its share of awards. The charming colonial building, with its exposed beams, stone fireplaces, and elegant lounge, is set amid 10 timbered acres overlooking the Blackwood Valley, 282 km (175 mi) south of Perth. Nearby you'll find tennis, golf, and horseback riding. Rates include a full, home-cooked breakfast. The Lodge doesn't permit smoking indoors, and due to the quiet, adult-oriented setting, families with children are discouraged. ✉ *Grange Rd., 6275,* ☎ *08/9756–1276,* FAX *08/9756–1394. 7 rooms. Restaurant, pool. MC, V.*

En Route Southeast of Nannup on Route 10, **Pemberton** is a great place for a stop on the way to Denmark and Albany. It is known for the karri forests in which stand some of the tallest trees in the world. Many retreat-style lodgings are available; contact the very helpful **Pemberton Tourist Centre** (Box 63, Pemberton 6260, ☎ 08/9776–1133). A few miles outside this timber town, rejoin Highway 1 and drive along through the "Rainbow Coast's" rolling green countryside.

Denmark

197 km (122 mi) east of Pemberton, 55 km (34 mi) west of Albany.

Denmark is a quaint old town nestling on a river—"where forest meets the sea" as the town motto goes. It's an ideal place to pause for a day or two to enjoy such places as the historic butter factory or the artists' studios tucked away on hillside farms.

Have a picnic alongside the river, or follow its course to the sparkling white beaches and clear waters of Wilson's Inlet, where the swimming is superb. Popular ecological tours include one by the government-run **Landcare** to local farms and the river catchment area. Tours and farm stays and motel or chalet accommodations can be arranged through the **Denmark Tourist Bureau** (✉ *Strickland St.,* ☎ *08/9848–2055*).

The **Old Butter Factory** sells the work of local craftspeople and artists as well as antiques and collectibles from southern France. Adjoining is the popular Mary Rose Restaurant. ✉ *11 North St.,* ☎ *08/9848–2525.* ☉ *Mon.–Sat. 10–4:30, Sun. 11–4:30.*

Lodging

$$$$ ✚ **Karri Mia Lodge.** You'll find no more comfortable place to stay in Denmark than at Karri Mia, a resort consisting of a Lodge and separate bungalows. Owners Kane and Michelle Randle have developed a stylish retreat on a secluded 60-acre property. All rooms are decorated in cream and deep sage colors, with cedar wooden blinds and a mix of modern furniture and intricately carved Indonesian antiques. Three rooms have queen-size beds and views of the garden and bushland. Five spacious suites feature king-size beds, spas, and views of the ocean. The lodge also offers two multilevel tower suites with vaulted ceilings, king-size beds, spas, sitting areas, and commanding views of the ocean. Rates include a gourmet breakfast, and a restaurant is currently under construction. ⊠ *Mt. Shadforth Rd., 6333,* ☎ *08/9848–2255,* FAX *08/ 9848–2277. 3 rooms, 7 suites. Breakfast room, minibars, in-room VCRs, hiking, laundry service. AE, DC, MC, V.*

$–$$ 🏠 **Rannoch West Holiday Farm.** A classic 1945 farm stay owned and operated by George and Dorothy Brenton, Rannoch West tends live-stock close to the famed Valley of the Giants forest. Natural attractions abound in the area, as do wineries. Choose to lodge in the homestead on a bed-and-breakfast basis (with dinner available on request), or take one of two self-catering pioneer cottages within the picturesque grounds. ⊠ *South Coast Hwy.,* ☎ *08/9840–8032. 3 rooms, 2 with bath; 2 cottages. Breakfast room, horseback riding. No credit cards.*

Albany

410 km (254 mi) south of Perth via Rte. 30, 55 km (34 mi) east of Denmark, 377 km (234 mi) east of Margaret River.

Lying on the southernmost tip of Western Australia's rugged coastline, this funky yet sophisticated port city is a surprising find. It was the earliest settlement in Western Australia, founded in 1826 as a penal outpost, but was granted city status only in July 1998. Originally named Frederickstown after Frederick, Duke of York and Albany, in 1831 it was proclaimed a part of the Swan River Colony and renamed Albany by Governor James Stirling. With the establishment of the whaling fleet in the 1840s it soon became a boomtown. The main street (Stirling) has changed very little in the last 100 years.

To Albany's fine harbor, whalers brought in up to 850 sperm whales every season until the practice was stopped in 1978. In 1994 whales were seen in King George Sound for the first time since that cessation. The old whaling station has been converted to a museum, **Whaleworld.** ⊠ *Cheynes Beach,* ☎ *08/9844–4021.* 🎫 *$7.* ☉ *Daily 9–5, ½-hr tours on the hr 10–4.*

The Old Gaol on Stirling Terrace was built in 1851 and served as the district jail from 1872 until it was closed in the '30s. Restored by the Albany Historical Society in 1968, it now contains a collection of social and historical artifacts. Ticket holders may also visit **Patrick Taylor Cottage,** a wattle-and-daub (twig-and-mud) dwelling built on Duke Street in 1832 and believed to be the oldest in the district. It contains more than 2,000 items, including period costumes, old clocks, silverware, and kitchenware. ⊠ *Stirling Terr.,* ☎ *08/9841–1401.* 🎫 *$3.50.* ☉ *Daily 10–4.*

The **Residency Museum,** one of the finest small museums in Australia and a focal point for both the social and natural history of the Albany region, is housed in the former offices of the government resident. The lovely sandstone building has sweeping views of the harbor. The Museum includes exhibits devoted to the local Noongar Aboriginal peoples, as well as displays of local geology, flora, and fauna. The saddlery and artisans' gallery adjoining the museum are also worth exploring. ⊠ *Residency Rd.,* ☎ *08/9841–4844.* 🎫 *Free.* ☉ *Daily 10–5.*

Adjacent to the Residency Museum is a faithful replica of the brig **Amity,** on which Albany's original settlers arrived. The replica was built in 1975 by local artisans using timber from the surrounding forest. If you board the ship, climb below deck and try to imagine how 45 men, plus livestock, could fit into such a small craft. ⊠ *Port Rd.,* ☎ *08/9841– 6885.* 🎫 *$2.* ☉ *Daily 9–5.*

The coastline around Albany is spectacular. Be sure to spend some time in the peninsular **Torndirrup National Park.** About 39 km (24 mi) north of Albany, **Porongurup National Park**'s ancient granite formations are also worth a visit. Farther up the highway, **Stirling Range National Park** (☞ *below*) is a mountainous haven for wildflowers and orchids. Albany is also the southern trackhead for the new 930-km (577-mi) **Bibbulman Walking Trail,** which leads through scenic forest country all the way from Perth to Albany.

Dining and Lodging

$$ ✕ **Genevieves.** The restaurant takes its name from a veteran English motorcar made famous by a witty British movie of 1953. Come for delicious bistro-style breakfasts and à la carte dining. All produce is local, and the seafood is caught daily in King George Sound. Among other entrées, the Thai chili squid and the crispy Mount Barker duck are superb. ⊠ *Esplanade Hotel, the Esplanade, Middleton Beach,* ☎ *08/9842–1711. AE, D, MC, V.*

$$ ✕ **Kooka's.** This engaging colonial cottage, under the management of Peter Skinner and Peta Gorton, is frequented by kookaburras (Australian kingfishers) of every description—on lamp shades, trays, saltshakers, teapots, and ornaments. There's even a live bird in the back garden. The wholesome country fare, prepared with flair and expertise, incorporates local produce. Recommendations include shrimp and chicken kebabs, and orange perfumed duck panfried with beansprouts and snow peas, served with wild jasmine rice. ⊠ *204 Stirling Terr.,* ☎ *08/9841–5889. AE, DC, MC, V. BYOB. Closed Sun. and Mon. No lunch Sat.*

$$ ✕ **Nonna's Brasseria.** The Delli-Benedetti family's new and very fashionable eatery, in a lovingly restored old terrace house, attracts crowds morning through night. The menu changes seasonally and specializes in local seafood. Try the lamb fillets or the baked lemon barramundi. ⊠ *131 Lower York St., Stirling Terr.,* ☎ *08/9841–4626. AE, DC, MC, V.*

$ ✕ **Dylan's.** Consistently good food and excellent value are two hallmarks of this casual and extremely popular establishment, and the fine coffee is either a bonus or another reason for calling in. Go for a full breakfast or lighter fare, such as croissants or pancakes. At lunch Dylan's makes some of the best hamburgers in town, while the dinner menu offers slightly more sophisticated selections. ⊠ *84 Stirling Terr.,* ☎ *08/9841–8720. Reservations not accepted. AE, DC, MC, V.*

$$$$ 🏨 **Balneaire Seaside Resort.** This luxury accommodation, "The south of France in the south of the State," was built in 1995 on a prime swath of Middleton Beach. The 17 two- and three-bedroom villa-style apartments overlook lush gardens and a central courtyard designed to resemble a Provencal village square. Each fully equipped villa is decorated in soft pastels, blues, yellows, and soft aquas. The friendly hosts, Martin and Trish Brock, chose Balneaire as a retirement project—but now joke that they've never worked harder in their lives. Their aim is to make each guest's visit as carefree as possible. No meals are provided, but several restaurants are within easy walking distance. ⊠ *27 Adelaide Crescent, Middleton Beach, 6330,* ☎ *08/9842–2877,* ℻ *08/ 9842–2899. 17 apartments. Picnic area, kitchenettes, beach, laundry service. AE, DC, MC, V.*

$$$ 🏨 **Esplanade Hotel.** Perhaps the last surviving example of a traditional Australian family hotel, this colonial-style boutique establishment is reminiscent of Albany's first Esplanade, a grand turn-of-the-century building now under the management of the Joondalup Resort Group (☞ *above*). Guest rooms and suites are immaculate and well appointed. The new Flinders Mews apartments are attached to the hotel. Request a Middleton Beach view, and in winter

be sure to spend some time before a roaring log fire in the lounge reading room. ⊠ *The Esplanade, 6330,* ☎ *08/9842–1711,* FAX *08/9841–7527. 40 rooms, 8 suites. Restaurant, 2 bars, pool, sauna, tennis court, health club, coin laundry. AE, DC, MC, V.*

Nightlife and the Arts

The **Town Hall** served as the center for local government for several decades until it was no longer needed. In 1983 it became a performing arts theater. ⊠ *York St.,* ☎ *08/9841–1661.*

Outdoor Activities and Sports

Grove Park Golf Course. The 18-hole course is about 10 km (6 mi) from Albany. Clubs, bags, and caddies can be hired. ☎ *08/9844–4277.*

Middleton Beach Park has a playground at either end, one for 8–12-year-olds and one for toddlers–7-year-olds. The park is conveniently located just across the road from the popular Beachside Café Restaurant.

Stirling Range National Park

403 km (250 mi) south of Perth, 71 km (44 mi) north of Albany.

During the height of the wildflower season (September and October), the Stirling Ranges, north of Albany, rival any botanical park in the world. Rising from the flat countryside, the ranges fill the horizon with a kaleidoscope of color. The Stirlings are considered the only true mountain range in southwest Australia. They were formed by the uplifting and buckling of sediments laid down by a now-dry ancient sea. More than 1,000 wildflower species have been identified, including 69 species of orchid. This profusion of flowers attracts equal numbers of insects, reptiles, and birds, as well as a host of nocturnal honey possums. Emus and kangaroos are frequent visitors as well.

An extensive road system, including the super-scenic Stirling Range Drive, makes travel from peak to peak easy. Treks begin at designated parking areas. Don't be fooled by apparently short distances—a 3-km (2-mi) walk up 3,541-ft Bluff Knoll takes about three hours round-trip. Take plenty of water and wet-weather gear—the park's location near the south coast makes Stirling subject to sudden storms. Before attempting longer hikes, register your intended routes in the ranger's log book, and log out upon return.

Lodging

Albany is close enough to serve as a base for day hikes (☞ Dining and Lodging *in* Albany, *above*).

The only camping within the park is at ⚠ **Moingup Springs,** which has toilets, water, and barbecues. Campfires are prohibited. Fees are $8 per night for two adults, $4 for additional adults. The **Stirling Range Retreat** (⊠ Chester Pass Rd., Borden 6333, ☎ 08/9827–9229) is just north of the park's boundary opposite Bluff Knoll. Hot and cold showers, laundry facilities, swimming pool, powered and unpowered sites, chalets, and cabins are available. Campfires are permitted. Camping fees are $12 for two adults; other accommodations start at $25 per night. The **Bluff Knoll café** (☎ 08/9827–9293), opposite the Retreat, has a liquor license and is open every day except Christmas. North of the Retreat, **The Lily** (Chester Pass Rd., Amelup 6338, ☎ 08/9827–9205) is a café-vineyard featuring lunch and candlelight dinners in a full-scale replica of a windmill in Puttershoek, Holland.

Arriving and Departing

From Perth, the park can be reached by traveling along the Albany Highway to Kojonup, proceeding east via Broome Hill and Gnowangerup, and then veering south through Borden onto the Albany Road. For a more scenic route, head south from Kojounup, then proceed east along the Stirling Range Drive.

Visitor Information

Stirling Range National Park. ⊠ *Amelup via Borden 6338,* ☎ *08/9827–9230.*

Southwest A to Z

Getting Around

BY CAR

A comprehensive network of highways makes exploring the Southwest practical and easy. Take Highway 1 down the coast from Perth to Bunbury, switch to Route 10 through Busselton and Margaret River, Karridale, and finally Bridgetown, where you rejoin Highway 1 south to Albany via Nannup and Pemberton.

BY PLANE

Skywest (☎ 08/9334–2288) provides daily service to the southern coastal town of Albany. **Flight West Airlines** (☎ 08/9334–2288) runs a service from Perth to Busselton several times per week, as does **Maroomba Airlines** (☎ 08/9478–3850 or 1800/677–747).

Contacts and Resources

EMERGENCIES

Ambulance, fire brigade, and police. ☎ *000.*

Regional hospitals: Bunbury Regional Hospital (⊠ Blair St., Bunbury, ☎ 08/9721–4911), **Margaret River Regional Hospital** (⊠ Farrelly St., Margaret River, ☎ 08/9757–2000), and **Albany Regional Hospital** (⊠ Warden Ave., Albany, ☎ 08/9841–2955).

GUIDED TOURS

Gourmet Tours of Australia (☎ 03/5777–3503, FAX 03/5777–3896) has a six-day cycling tour of the Southwest during wildflower season (Sept.–Oct.) with stops at Margaret River's vineyards and restaurants. **Skywest** (☎ 08/9334–2288 or 13–1300) provides a variety of three- to five-day packages throughout the Southwest that incorporate coaches and hotels or four-wheel-driving and camping. **Westcoast Rail and Coach** (☎ 08/9221–9522) runs regular tours of the Southwest, with departures from Perth railway stations.

VISITOR INFORMATION

The Western Australia Tourist Centre (⊠ Forrest Pl. and Wellington St., Perth 6000, ☎ 1300/361–351, FAX 08/9481–0190) has an excellent library of free information for visitors, including bed-and-breakfast and farm-stay accommodations throughout the region.

Farm and Country Homestay Association of Western Australia (⊠ Brett Pollack, c/o Wooleen Station, Mullewa 6630, ☎ 08/9963–7973, FAX 08/9963–7684) has extensive details of farm-stay accommodations throughout the state, from small holdings with rustic cottages to sheep stations of more than 654,000 acres where guests stay in sheep shearers' quarters and participate in station activities.

THE GOLDFIELDS

Since the day Paddy Hannan stumbled over a sizeable gold nugget on the site of what is now Kalgoorlie, Western Australia's goldfields have ranked among the richest in the world. In their heyday, more than 100,000 men and women were scattered throughout the area, all hoping to make their fortunes. It's still an astonishingly productive area, and the population of Kalgoorlie-Boulder is rapidly increasing rapidly after falling to 30,000 in the 1980s. Sadly, many nearby communities are now nothing more than ghost towns.

The goldfields still appeal to Australians, however. A major new project for Kalgoorlie is the construction of the **Australian Miners' Hall of Fame,** scheduled to open for the centenary of Australian Federation on January 1, 2001.

Comprising the twin cities of Kalgoorlie and Boulder—locals call the conurbation KB, or just Kal—Kalgoorlie-Boulder retains the rough-and-ready atmosphere of a frontier town, with streets wide enough to accommodate the camel teams that were once a common sight here. Open-cut mines gouge the earth everywhere, and a nugget or two might still be found if you have time, patience, and a reliable metal detector.

Kalgoorlie

602 km (373 mi) east of Perth, 39 km (24 mi) east of Coolgardie.

Built from local pink stone, Kalgoorlie's **Post Office** has dominated Hannan Street since it was constructed in 1899. Opposite the post office is the **York Hotel,** one of the few hotels in Kalgoorlie to remain untouched by time. Take a look at its fine staircase and intricate cupola.

On Hannan Street a block south of the post office is the stamped-tin ceiling of **Kalgoorlie Town Hall.** Built in 1908, it is an excellent example of a common style used around the goldfields. The cast-iron Victorian seats in the balcony were imported from England at the turn of the century.

Outside Kalgoorlie Town Hall sits **Paddy Hannan,** arguably the most photographed statue in the nation. This life-size bronze of the town's founder is a replica; the original, which had suffered the vagaries of wind, weather, and the occasional vandal, has been moved inside the Town Hall. However, another bronze statue, this time of a miner wielding a modern "widow-maker" drill, can be found outside the Boulder Town Hall.

☼ The **Museum of the Goldfields** is housed partly within the historic British Arms—once the narrowest pub in the southern hemisphere. This outstanding small museum paints a colorful portrait of life in this boisterous town. The hands-on exhibits are a hit with children. ⊠ *17 Hannan St.,* ☎ *08/9021–8533.* ⊞ *Donation accepted.* ☉ *Daily 10–4:30.*

Not to be missed is the rustic **Bush Two-up Ring** (☎ No phone), about 5 km out of town, one of the few places in Australia where this popular gambling game may legally be played. Also worth seeing are the heritage brothels of Hay Street.

Hannan's North Tourist Mine provides a comprehensive look at the century-old goldfields, with audiovisual displays, a reconstructed prospector's camp, heritage buildings, and opportunities to go underground or to witness a real gold-pour. ⊠ *Eastern Bypass Rd.,* ☎ *08/9091–4074.* ⊞ *$15.* ☉ *Daily 9:30–4:30.*

Dining and Lodging

$$$ ✕ **Amalfi.** Set in the Midas Hotel, the Amalfi serves modern Australian brasserie food. The menu is extensive and super-eclectic, with Asian dishes and pasta placed alongside Cajun chicken, fillet of beef, and char-grilled squid. Don't miss the salmon naan (Indian bread) with pesto. ⊠ *409 Hannan St.,* ☎ *08/9021–3088. Reservations essential. AE, DC, MC, V.*

$$ ✕ **Basil's on Hannan.** This pretty café in the heart of town owes its
★ Mediterranean feel to terra-cotta, wrought-iron, indoor-garden decor
and its goldfields authenticity to the corrugated-metal ceiling. In ad-
dition to terrific coffee, the restaurant offers casual fare that includes
veal dishes and a variety of pastas. The popular Sunday brunch fea-
tures something different for Kalgoorlie—namely focaccia, seafood fet-
tuccine, and a renowned Caesar salad. ⊠ *168 Hannan St.,* ☎ *08/9021–
7832. AE, MC, V. BYOB. No dinner Sun.*

$ ✕ **Exchange Hotel.** The miners in Kalgoorlie favored slaking their thirst
before filling their bellies, but here you can do both at once. A superb
example of a goldfields pub, the redecorated Exchange is replete with
exquisite stained-glass and pressed-tin ceilings. This is probably the only
place in the world where the current gold price is flashed up in neon lights
above the pub facade. The best counter meals (grills and salads) in the
area are served here. The public bar gives an idea of the rough-and-ready
goldfields of old, though the scantily clad bar girls are very young. ⊠
Hannan and Maritana Sts., ☎ *08/9021–2833. AE, DC, MC, V.*

$$$$ ☷ **Mercure Hotel Plaza.** This modern hotel complex—part of the
Novotel/Ibis chain—has a quiet location on a tree-lined street, just a
stone's throw from busy Hannan Street. In 1998, the ground-floor restau-
rant and all guest rooms underwent extensive refurbishment. Rooms
in the four-story building have balconies. The higher floors enjoy views
over the low-rise town. ⊠ *45 Egan St., 6430,* ☎ *08/9021–4544,* FAX
*08/9091–2195. 100 rooms. Restaurant, bar, refrigerator, room service,
pool, spa, free parking. AE, DC, MC, V.*

$$ ☷ **York Hotel.** The historic York, dating from 1901, once contained a
47- by 20-ft billiards room. That is long gone, but the hotel has re-
tained its lovely stained-glass windows and pressed-tin ceilings. Its staircase and dining room are a historian's dream. Rooms are small but
functional, and rates include breakfast. ⊠ *259 Hannan St., 6430,* ☎
08/9021–2337. 16 rooms without bath. Restaurant. AE, MC, V.

Coolgardie

561 km (348 mi) east of Perth, 39 km (24 mi) west of Kalgoorlie.

Tiny Coolgardie is probably the best-maintained ghost town in Australia. A great deal of effort has gone into preserving this historic community—there are some 150 historical markers placed around the town.

The Coolgardie Railway Station operated until 1971 and is now home
to the **Railway Station Museum**'s display on the history of rail transport. The museum also includes a display of photographs, books, and
artifacts that together offer a gripping portrayal of a famous mining
rescue that was once carried out in these goldfields. ⊠ *Woodward St.,*
☎ *08/9026–6388.* ☷ *Donations accepted.* ☉ *Sat.–Thurs. 8:30–4:30.*

One of the most unusual museums in Australia, **Ben Prior's Open Air
Museum** features the machinery, boilers, and other equipment used to
mine the region at the turn of the century, as well as a variety of other
relics from Coolgardie's boom years. If you didn't know it was a museum, you would think this this was a private junkyard. Items include
large covered wagons, old cars, and statues of explorers. ⊠ *Bayley St.,*
☎ *no phone.* ☷ *Free.* ☉ *Daily 9 AM–dusk.*

The stark, weathered headstones in the **Coolgardie Cemetery,** on the
Great Eastern Highway about a half mile east of town, recall stories
of tragedy and the grim struggle for survival in a harsh, unrelenting
environment. Many of the graves remain unmarked because the iden-
tities of their occupants were lost during the wild rush to the eastern

goldfields. Look for the graves of several Afghan camel drivers at the rear of the cemetery.

Also on the Great Eastern Highway, 4 km (2 mi) west of Coolgardie, is the **Coolgardie Camel Farm,** which offers a look at the animals that played a vital role in opening inland Australia. If the roads in town seem overly wide, you'll realize that such dimensions were necessary to accommodate these great beasts. A variety of camel rides are offered, including trips around the yard and one-hour, day-long, or overnight treks. Longer treks allow the chance to hunt for gems and gold. ⊠ *Great Eastern Hwy.,* ☎ *08/9026–6159.* ☎ *$2. Reservations essential for multiday camel treks.* ⊙ *Daily 9–5.*

Goldfields A to Z

Arriving and Departing

BY BUS

Greyhound Pioneer Australia (☎ 08/9481–7066 or 13–2030) departs Perth daily at 6:30 AM for the 330-mi run out to the goldfields.

BY PLANE

Ansett W.A. and **Airlink,** the Qantas regional subsidiary, operate a daily service to Kalgoorlie. The flight takes an hour. *See* Air Travel *in* Smart Travel Tips for airline telephone numbers.

BY TRAIN

The *Prospector* has an appropriate name for the train that runs a daily 7-hour service between Perth and Kalgoorlie. Clean and efficient, it departs from the East Perth Railway Terminal (☎ 08/9326–2244).

Getting Around

The center of Kalgoorlie is compact enough to explore on foot. Hannan Street, named after the man who discovered gold here, is the main thoroughfare and contains the bulk of the hotels and places of interest. **Taxis** (☎ 08/9021–2177) are available around the clock.

Contacts and Resources

EMERGENCIES

Ambulance, fire brigade, and police. ☎ *000.*

Kalgoorlie Regional Hospital. ⊠ *Piccadilly St.,* ☎ *08/9080–5888.*

GUIDED TOURS

All-inclusive package tours from Perth are available by plane, rail, and bus with the companies mentioned under Arriving and Departing, *above.*

Goldfields Air Services (☎ 08/9093–2116) offers an air tour that gives you a bird's-eye view of the open-cut mining technique now used instead of more traditional shaft mining. **Goldrush Tours** (☎ 08/9021–2954) runs an excellent series of tours on the goldfields' history and ghost towns, the profusion of wildflowers in the area, and the ghost town of Coolgardie. South of Kalgoorlie, Boulder is home to the **Loop Line Railroad,** whose train the *Rattler* offers tours of the Golden Mile by rail. The train leaves from the Boulder Railway Station (⊠ Burt St., ☎ 08/9093–13055).

VISITOR INFORMATION

The **Kalgoorlie/Boulder Tourist Bureau** (⊠ 250 Hannan St., ☎ 08/9021–1966) has a staff as enthusiastic and welcoming as they are knowledgeable.

KARIJINI NATIONAL PARK

1,411 km (875 mi) northwest of Perth, 285 km (177 mi) south of Port Hedland.

The huge rocks, crags, and gorges that make up the Hamersley Range in the northwestern corner of the state are among the most ancient land surfaces in the world. Sediments deposited by an inland sea more than 2½ billion years ago were forced up by movements in the earth's crust and slowly weathered by natural elements through succeeding centuries. Much of the 320-km (200-mi) range is being mined for its rich iron deposits, but a small section is incorporated into the national park. Towering cliffs, lush fern-filled gullies, and richly colored stone make this one of the most beautiful parks in Australia.

Karijini's trails are rated easy, moderate, and difficult; all require sturdy shoes, and you should carry plenty of drinking water to avoid dehydration. Gorges can be reached only on foot from parking areas. Dales Gorge is the most popular and easily accessible. The walk is a one-hour return trip from the parking area and ends at the only year-round waterfall in the park, Fortescue Falls. Ferns and mosses line the gorge walls, providing a stunning contrast with the arid landscape outside the park. This walk can be lengthened by hiking downstream to Circular Pool. Other gorges in the park are far more challenging and should be undertaken only by experienced hikers, who must brave freezing water, cling to rock ledges, and scramble over boulders through the Joffre, Knox, and Hancock gorges. Notify a ranger before hiking into any of these gorges.

Because summer temperatures often top 110°F, it's best to visit during the cooler months, from April through early November.

Lodging

⚠ **Camping** is permitted only in designated sites at Yampire Gorge, Circular Pool, Joffre Turnoff, and Weano. Campsites have no facilities except toilets, but gas barbecues are free. The burning of wood is prohibited. Nightly fees are $5, plus $3 for each additional adult.

Food and supplies can be purchased in Wittenoom, where hotel and motel accommodations can be arranged as well. Drinking water is available at Yampire and Joffre roads.

Arriving and Departing

This remote park is best reached by flying from Perth to Port Hedland and renting a car from there, or by flying to Broome (☞ Chapter 10) and driving 551 km (342 mi) on the Great Northern Highway to Port Hedland. Turn south from Port Hedland to the park.

Organized tours start from Perth; contact the **Western Australian Tourist Centre** (✉ Forrest Pl. and Wellington St., Perth 6000, ☎ 08/9483–1111) for details.

Visitor Information

Contact the **Department of Conservation and Land Management** (✉ Box 835, Karratha, 6714, ☎ 08/9143–1488).

MONKEY MIA AND NINGALOO REEF

Monkey Mia

985 km (611 mi) north of Perth.

Monkey Mia is a designated World Heritage Site and the setting for one of the world's most extraordinary natural wonders; nowhere else do wild dolphins interact so freely with human beings. In 1964 a woman from one of the makeshift fishing camps in the area hand-fed one of the dolphins that regularly followed the fishing boats home. Other dolphins followed that lead, and an extensive family of wild dolphins now comes of their own accord to be fed. For many, standing in the shallow waters of Shark Bay to hand-feed a dolphin is the experience of a lifetime. There are no set feeding times—dolphins show up at any hour of the day at the public beach, where park rangers feed them. Rangers will share their food with visitors who want to get close to the sea creatures. There is also a Dolphin Information Centre, which has videos and information. ⊠ *Follow Hwy. 1 north from Perth for 806 km (500 mi) to Denham/Hamelin Rd., then follow signs,* ☎ *08/ 9948–1366.* ⊘ *Information center daily 7:30–4 (sometimes until 6).*

Arriving and Departing

Skywest (☎ 08/9334–2288) offers four flights a week to Shark Bay airport, which serves Monkey Mia. **Greyhound Pioneer Australia** (☎ 08/9481–7066) departs Perth Mondays, Thursdays, and Saturdays at 10:30 AM, arriving at Monkey Mia at 11:10 PM, and Wednesdays, Fridays, and Sundays at 9 PM, arriving at Monkey Mia at 9:15 AM the next day.

Ningaloo Reef Marine Park

1,512 km (938 mi) north of Perth.

Some of Australia's most pristine coral reef runs 251 km (156 mi) along the coast of the Exmouth Peninsula, very far north of Perth. A happy conjunction of migratory routes and accessibility make it one of the best places on earth to see huge manta rays, giant whale sharks, humpback whales, nesting turtles, and the annual coral spawning. **Exmouth Diving Centre** (⊠ Box 573, Exmouth 6707, ☎ 08/9949–1201, ✉ 08/ 9949–1680) offers complete diving packages. A unique tour allows a handful of travelers to assist in the tagging of the giant loggerhead and hawksbill turtles that come ashore to nest in December and January. This hands-on opportunity, organized by officers of the Department of Conservation and Land Management, is available nowhere else in the country. For more information, contact **Coate's Wildlife Tours** (☎ 08/9455–6611, ✉ 08/9455–6621). Also worth seeing near Exmouth is the **Cape Range National Park,** including the Yardie Creek Gorge. ⊠ *Follow North West Coastal Hwy. north 1,170 km (725 mi) to Minilya turnoff; Exmouth is 374 km (232 mi) farther north.*

12 ADVENTURE VACATIONS

By David
McGonigal

Updated by
Michael
Gebicki

YOU'LL MISS AN IMPORTANT ELEMENT of Australia if you don't get away from the cities to explore "the bush" that is so deeply ingrained in the Down Under character. Australians pride themselves on their ability to cope in the great outdoors even if, in many cases, this has never been tested beyond lighting the backyard barbecue. Nevertheless, the heroes of modern Australia are those men and women who opened this vast, unforgiving land to European settlement—like Ludwig Leichhardt, who pioneered the 4,800-km (2,976-mi) route between Brisbane and Port Essington (Darwin) in 1844, only to vanish without a trace during a transcontinental trek in 1848, or Robert O'Hara Burke, who died in 1861 after completing a south–north transcontinental trip with camels.

Many of the adventure vacations today were journeys of exploration only a generation ago. Even now, the four-wheel-drive vehicle is a necessity, not a plaything, in the great heart of Australia. Indeed, the country retains a raw element that makes it ideally suited to adventure vacationing. You can still travel for hours or days in many places without seeing another person or any sign of human habitation. From the tropical jungles of the north to the deserts of the Red Centre to the snowfields of New South Wales and Victoria, one is constantly reminded of how ancient this country is. The mountains you walk or ride through are rounded with age, and the unusual animals and flora you encounter are themselves reason enough to travel to Australia.

You can always choose to travel without a guide, and you can get into some of the activities listed below on your own. The advantage of using a guide in such cases is often educational. You'll learn more about where you are by having a knowledgeable local by your side than you could traveling on your own. If you go out with a guide early in your trip, you can get an introduction to a part of Australia that you might apply to later parts of your trip when you are on your own in the bush.

Adventure vacations are commonly split into soft and hard adventures. A hard adventure requires a substantial degree of physical participation. You may not have to be perfectly fit, but in a few cases, prior experience is a prerequisite. In soft adventures the destination rather than the means of travel is often what makes it an adventure. With most companies, the adventure guides' knowledge of flora and fauna—and love of the bush—is matched by a level of competence that ensures your safety even in dangerous situations. The safety record of Australian adventure operators is very good. Visitors should be aware, however, that most adventure-tour operators require you to sign waiver forms absolving the company of responsibility in the event of an accident or a problem. Australian courts normally uphold such waivers except in cases of significant negligence.

Tour Operators

There are far more adventure-tour operators in Australia than we can include in this chapter. Most are small and receive little publicity outside their local areas, so contact the relevant state tourist office if you have a specific adventure interest. Here are the addresses of the major adventure-tour operators mentioned in the following pages. U.S. addresses are given when available.

Adventure Associates. ⊠ *Box 612, Bondi Junction, NSW 2022,* ☎ *02/ 9389–7466,* ℻ *02/9369–1853.*
Adventure Center. ⊠ *1311 63rd St., Suite 200, Emeryville, CA 94608 U.S.A.,* ☎ *800/227–8747 or 510/654–1879,* ℻ *510/654–4200.*

Adventure Charters of Kangaroo Island. ⊠ *Box 169, Kingscote, Kangaroo Island, SA,* ☎ *08/8553–9119,* FAX *08/8553–9122.*

Alice Springs Camel Outback Safaris. ⊠ *PMB 74, via Alice Springs, NT 0872,* ☎ *08/8956–0925,* FAX *08/8956–0909.*

Bicheno Dive Centre. ⊠ *2 Scuba Ct., Bicheno, TAS 7215,* ☎ *03/6375–1138,* FAX *03/6375–1504.*

Blue Mountains Adventure Company. ⊠ *Box 242, Katoomba, NSW 2780,* ☎ *02/4782–1271.*

Bogong Horseback Adventures. ⊠ *Box 230, Mt. Beauty, VIC 3699,* ☎ *03/5754–4849,* FAX *03/5754–4181.*

Boomerang Bicycle Tours. ⊠ *Box 267, Forestville, NSW 2087,* ☎ *02/9975–4251,* FAX *02/9975–6082.*

Brake Out Cycling Tours. ⊠ *Box 427, Kingston, TAS 7050,* ☎ *03/6229–1999,* FAX *03/6229–8019.*

Cradle Mountain Huts. ⊠ *Box 1879, Launceston, TAS 7250,* ☎ *03/6331–2006,* FAX *03/6331–5525.*

Croydon Travel. ⊠ *34 Main St., Croydon, VIC 3136,* ☎ *03/9725–8555,* FAX *03/9723–9560.*

Dive Adventures. ⊠ *9th level, 32 York St., Sydney, NSW 2000,* ☎ *02/9299–4633,* FAX *02/9299–4644.*

Dive Travel Australia. ⊠ *Shop 3, 50 Kalang Rd., Elanora Heights, NSW 2101,* ☎ *02/9970–6311,* FAX *02/9970–6197.*

East Kimberley Tours. ⊠ *Box 537, Kununurra, WA 6743,* ☎ *08/9168–2213,* FAX *08/9168–2544.*

Ecotrek Bogong Jack Adventures. ⊠ *Box 4, Kangarilla, SA 5157,* ☎ *08/8383–7198,* FAX *08/8383–7377.*

Equitrek Australia. ⊠ *5 King Rd., Ingleside, NSW 2101,* ☎ *02/9913–9408,* FAX *02/9970–6303.*

Exmouth Diving Centre. ⊠ *Payne St., Exmouth, WA 6707,* ☎ *08/9949–1201,* FAX *08/9949–1680.*

Freycinet Experience. ⊠ *Box 43, Battery Point, TAS 7004,* ☎ *1800/50–6003 or 03/6223–7565,* FAX *03/6224–1315.*

Frontier Camel Tours. ⊠ *Box 2836, Alice Springs, NT 0871,* ☎ *08/8953–0444,* FAX *08/8955–5015.*

Great Aussie Pub Crawls on Horseback. ⊠ *Box 379, Glen Innes, NSW 2370,* ☎ *02/6732–1599,* FAX *02/6732–3538.*

Intrepid Tours. ⊠ *17 Sixth St., Quorn, SA 5433,* ☎ *08/8648–6277,* FAX *08/8648–6357.*

Kangaroo Island Odysseys. ⊠ *Box 497, Penneshaw, Kangaroo Island, SA 5222,* ☎ *08/8553–1294,* FAX *08/8553–1294.*

King Island Dive Charters. ⊠ *Box 1, Currie, King Island, TAS 7256,* ☎ *03/6461–1133,* FAX *03/6461–1293.*

Morrell Adventure Travel. ⊠ *57 Oliver St., Berridale, NSW 2628,* ☎ *02/6456–3681,* FAX *02/6465–3679.*

Outback Camel Company. ⊠ *PMB 53, Waikerie, SA 5330,* ☎ *08/8543–2280.*

Packsaddlers. ⊠ *Megalong Rd., Megalong Valley, NSW 2785,* ☎ *02/4787–9150,* FAX *02/4787–5950.*

Paddy Pallin Jindabyne. ⊠ *PMB 5, Jindabyne, NSW 2627,* ☎ *02/6456–2922,* FAX *02/6456–2836.*

Peregrine Adventures. ⊠ *258 Lonsdale St., Melbourne, VIC 3000,* ☎ *03/9662–2700,* FAX *03/9662–2422.*

Pro Dive Travel. ⊠ *Dymocks Building, Suite 1–5, Level 7, 428 George St., Sydney, NSW 2000,* ☎ *02/9232–5733,* FAX *02/9232–5788.*

Reynella Rides/Kosciuszko Trails. ⊠ *Bolaro Rd., Adaminaby, NSW 2630,* ☎ *02/6454–2386,* FAX *02/6454–2530.*

Stoneys' Bluff & Beyond Trailrides. ⊠ *Box 287, Mansfield, VIC 3722,* ☎ *03/5775–2954,* FAX *03/5775–2598.*

Tasmanian Expeditions. ✉ *110 George St., Launceston, TAS 7250,* ☎ *1800/03–0230 or 03/6334–3477,* 𝔽𝔸𝕏 *03/6334–3463.*

Tourism New South Wales Australia (Tourism Commission). ✉ *13737 Fiji Way, Suite C10, Marina del Rey, CA 90292, U.S.A.,* ☎ *310/301– 1903,* 𝔽𝔸𝕏 *310/301–0913.*

Walkabout Gourmet Adventures. ✉ *Box 52, Dinner Plain, VIC 3898,* ☎ *03/5159–6556,* 𝔽𝔸𝕏 *03/5159–6508.*

White Water Rafting Professionals. ✉ *Box 133, Coffs Harbour, NSW 2450,* ☎ *02/6651–4066,* 𝔽𝔸𝕏 *02/6651–5699.*

Wild Escapes. ✉ *Box 116, Asquith, NSW 2077,* ☎ *02/9482–2881,* 𝔽𝔸𝕏 *02/9477–3114.*

Wild Track Adventure Safaris. ✉ *Box 2397, Cairns, QLD 4870,* ☎ *07/4055–2247,* 𝔽𝔸𝕏 *07/4058–1930.*

Wildwater Adventures. ✉ *26 Butlers Rd., Bonville, NSW 2441,* ☎ *02/ 6653–4469,* 𝔽𝔸𝕏 *02/6653–4404.*

World Expeditions. ✉ *441 Kent St., 3rd floor, Sydney, NSW 2000,* ☎ *02/9264–3366,* 𝔽𝔸𝕏 *02/9261–1974.*

Antarctica

Australia is perfectly located as a stepping-off point for trips to Antarctica. Indeed, Australia claims the largest share of Antarctica for administrative purposes, with the Australian Antarctic Territory comprising 42% of the continent. Passenger ships specially adapted for the frozen continent regularly depart from the Tasmanian port of Hobart for the Ross Sea where, besides the regular Antarctic wonders of penguins and icebergs, they visit the historic huts of Scott and Shackleton, looking just as they did the day the explorers left. They also call into the wildlife-rich sub-Antarctic Macquarie, Campbell, and Aucklands islands. Contact Adventure Associates, Peregrine Adventures, or World Expeditions for more information—and do so early as every voyage fills up quickly.

A faster and cheaper, if less satisfying, option is to take a one-day Qantas over-flight of Antarctica organized by Croydon Travel. Taking off from Sydney, Melbourne, or Perth, you fly directly to the ice continent. There are a variety of flight plans, but all fly low so you have good views of the mountains and ice. You're still too high to see animals, however. It's worthwhile paying extra for a window seat not over the wing. Although the experience does not compare with the close-up view, it usually satisfies those who cannot afford the two to three weeks required for the voyage.

Season: November–March.
Locations: Cruises from Hobart; flights from Sydney, Melbourne, and Perth, with connections from other Australian cities.
Cost: From $875 for one day to $15,000 for three weeks.
Tour Operators: Adventure Associates, Croydon Travel, Peregrine Adventures, World Expeditions.

Bicycling

Cycling is an excellent way to explore a small region, allowing you to cover more ground than on foot and to observe far more than you could from the window of a car or bus. Riding down quiet country lanes is a great way to relax and get fit at the same time. Cycling rates as a hard adventure because of the amount of exercise involved.

New South Wales

Morrell Adventure Travel has several tours that include all meals, a support vehicle, guides, mountain bikes, group camping gear, and national park entry fees (where applicable). Its main cycling region is the Snowy Mountains, but it also operates a day ride on the state's South Coast, a weekend ride exploring the Southern Highlands (an area of large manor houses, spectacular formal gardens, and rolling farmland), and a seven-day trip from Canberra to Kosciuszko National Park. Blue Mountains Adventure Company offers several one-day rides on mountain bikes through these plunging walled valleys that border Sydney, actually ridges left from an eroded plateau rather than mountains. The trips include a spectacular ride along Narrow Neck and a ride through a glowworm tunnel. Boomerang Bicycle Tours offers tours from three to six days in length of the Hunter Valley, Snowy Mountains, and Southern Highlands. Tours of the Hunter Valley offers plenty of time to stop and visit the region's boutique wineries. All Boomerang tours include air-conditioned support vehicle, high-quality touring bikes, all meals, and lodging at fine inns, guest houses, and motels.

Season: Year-round.
Locations: Blue Mountains, Snowy Mountains, Southern Highlands.
Cost: From $45 for a half day and $80 for one day to about $1,200 for seven days.
Tour Operators: Blue Mountains Adventure Company, Boomerang Bicycle Tours, Morrell Adventure Travel.

Tasmania

Tasmania is small enough to make cycling a pleasant option. The classic tour is Tasmanian Expeditions' Cycle Tasmania, a seven-day trip from Launceston that leads through pastoral lands down to the fishing villages of the east coast. Terrain includes undulating hills, coastal plains, and dense, temperate rain forests. Tasmanian Expeditions also has a very similar 13-day tour, Tasmanian Panorama, which includes cycling, bushwalking, and rafting. Intended for beginners, the trip covers some of the best adventures Tasmania has to offer: walking in the Cradle Mountain area and the Walls of Jerusalem National Park, cycling down the east coast, and rafting on the relatively peaceful Picton River. All of these tours are sold also by World Expeditions. For a shorter ride, join Brake Out for its half-day ride down Mt. Wellington, which looms behind Hobart.

Season: November–March.
Locations: Central Tasmania and the north and east coasts.
Cost: From $50 for a half-day tour to $1,000 for eight days or $1,650 for 13 days, including camping equipment, support vehicle, bicycles, and all meals.
Tour Operators: Adventure Center, Brake Out Cycling Tours, Ecotrek Bogong Jack Adventures, Tasmanian Expeditions, World Expeditions.

Queensland

Spreading inland from the coastal city of Cairns, The Atherton Tableland is a mixture of tropical rain forests and sleepy towns—an area to be savored rather than rushed through—reached on board a steam train that labors up the steep gradient from Cairns onto the escarpment. The tablelands themselves are relatively level and ideal for cycling. Staying overnight in quaint old wooden pubs, swimming in cool highland ponds, exploring a huge curtain fig tree, and then heading off for the next pub are all great ways to attain a Queensland frame of mind. Peregrine Adventures also includes this mountain biking excursion as a part of a more extensive seven-day adventure trip, with walking, canoeing, and reef excursions.

Season: Year-round.
Location: Atherton Tableland.
Cost: $335 for three days, $1,050 for the seven-day combination trip.
Tour Operator: Peregrine Adventures.

South Australia

South Australia offers gentle cycling on quiet country roads, particularly on Kangaroo Island and around the famous wine regions of the Barossa and Clare valleys, as well as more challenging mountain bike expeditions into the rugged Flinders Ranges, far to the north of Adelaide. Ecotrek Bogong Jack Adventures has a range of such cycling trips— varying from weekends in the wine areas to longer rides on Kangaroo Island and in the Flinders Ranges.

Season: April–October.
Locations: Barossa Valley, Clare Valley, Flinders Ranges, Kangaroo Island.
Cost: From $250 for a weekend to around $1,000 for a seven-day Kangaroo Island cycle safari.
Tour Operator: Ecotrek Bogong Jack Adventures.

Bushwalking (Hiking)

The Australian bush is unique. The olive-green foliage of the eucalypts seems drab at first, but when you walk into a clearing carpeted with thick grass and surrounded by stately blue gums, its special appeal jumps out at you. The bush is a bright and noisy place, too—crimson- and harlequin-hue parrots screech from the canopy overhead, and kookaburras cackle hysterically from the treetops. Chances are good that you will cross paths with kangaroos, wallabies, goannas, and even echidnas (spiny anteaters). This is a land of a million oddities that is best appreciated on foot. An easy ramble with a picnic lunch through the Blue Mountains of New South Wales can be every bit as rewarding as a challenging 21-km (13-mi) hike to a muddy camp in the Tasmanian wilderness. Depending on the type of walk, therefore, bushwalking can be a soft or hard adventure. Associated high-adrenaline hard adventures are *abseiling* (rappelling) and canyoning—forms of vertical bushwalking well suited to some parts of Australia, notably the Blue Mountains of New South Wales.

New South Wales

The scope for casual bushwalking in New South Wales is extensive. The best one-day walk in the Blue Mountains originates in Blackheath and winds through Grand Canyon. The National Pass to Wentworth Falls is also stunning. The Snowy Mountains beyond Perisher are excellent for walking, as are the national parks to the north—especially Barrington Tops, a basalt-capped plateau with rushing streams that have carved deep chasms in the extensive rain forest. The same areas are ideal for longer treks, too. The advantage of joining an adventure tour is the experience and knowledge of the guides, who identify the animals and plants that you encounter along the way and who show you places of interest off the main trails. The camping equipment provided by tour operators is a welcome alternative to buying it in Australia (where prices for outdoor gear are high) or bringing it from home.

Morrell Adventure Travel operates four-day to one-week camping and lodge-based walking tours in the Snowy Mountains between November and April, as does Paddy Pallin, an excellent locally based adventure company. Wild Escapes specializes in small-group tours (two-person minimum), which makes their trips slightly more expensive.

The deeply eroded sandstone canyons of the Blue Mountains are perfect for abseiling down sheer vertical crags and through deep, clean canyons. There is intense competition between tour operators in this area, so a full day of canyoning in the spectacular Grand Canyon or the sublime Claustral Canyon costs less than $100, including lunch. Blue Mountains Adventure Company has more than a dozen different canyoning, climbing, and abseiling programs around this area.

Season: Year-round.
Locations: Blue Mountains, Snowy Mountains, Barrington Tops.
Cost: Rates start at $45 for a half day. Longer trips cost on average about $100 per day, including packs, camping equipment, guide, and food.
Tour Operators: Wild Escapes, Blue Mountains Adventure Company, Morrell Adventure Travel, Paddy Pallin Jindabyne.

Victoria

Victoria's alpine region offers a range of bushwalking vacations to suit every taste. Ecotrek Bogong Jack Adventures has various guided walks in the region, often focusing on the abundant wildflowers of the region. Tours are based in a comfortable lodge in the alpine village of Dinner Plain. Optional activities include trout fishing and nocturnal tours. Walkabout Gourmet Adventures has an epicurean five-day bushwalking experience, during which you'll stay in a country resort and eat good food and drink fine wine while seeing wildlife and relaxing. These gourmet adventures are designed for healthy, active people, and the number of walkers in any group is kept under 16.

Season: October–May.
Locations: Alpine National Park and the Victorian Alps.
Cost: From $65 for a day walk to $850 for six days.
Tour Operators: Adventure Center, Ecotrek Bogong Jack Adventures, Walkabout Gourmet Adventures.

Tasmania

Until recently, some of the best overnight walks in Tasmania were major expeditions suitable only for the highly experienced and very fit. Plenty of these treks are still available, including the nine-day South Coast Track Expedition operated by Tasmanian Expeditions. The trail includes some easy stretches along pristine, secluded beaches, as well as difficult legs through rugged coastal mountains. You must fly into this remote area—it's the combination of difficult trails and extreme isolation that gives this walk spice.

A much easier walk is conducted on the Freycinet Peninsula, about a two-hour drive north of Hobart on the east coast. Much of it can be explored only on foot: The road ends at the pink granite domes of the Hazards, which form a rampart across the top of the peninsula. If you take the time to venture beyond them, you will discover a world of pristine bush where wallabies loll, and white-sand beaches fringe crystal-clear water. The only guided hike is the four-day walk offered by Freycinet Experience. The optional 18-km (11-mi) hike over Mount Graham on the second day is recommended only for experienced trekkers. Hikers carry very light packs and spend the first two nights in comfortable standing camps, complete with wooden platforms, beds, and pillows. The final night is in a Tasmanian hardwood lodge that is situated to take advantage of the best views. The cost is $1,095.

The best-known walk in Tasmania is the trail from Cradle Mountain to Lake St. Clair. It's so popular that boardwalks have been placed along some sections to prevent the path from turning into a quagmire. The walk starts and finishes in dense forest, but much of it runs along exposed highland ridges. The construction of the Cradle Mountain Huts several years ago made this trail far more accessible. However, these huts are available only to hikers on one of Cradle Mountain Huts' escorted walks. The huts are basic, but they provide a level of comfort unimaginable to anyone forced to camp in the mud of the area's mountain ranges. Huts are well heated and extensively supplied; there are even warm showers. Other operators continue to conduct camping tours along the trail as well as elsewhere in Tasmania. The rapid weather changes typical of this area present an extra challenge, but the spectacular mountain scenery makes any discomfort that the cold or wet causes worthwhile.

Season: November–May.
Locations: Central highlands; south, east, and west coasts.
Cost: From about $130 per day, including camping equipment and meals, to $890 for the eight-day Cradle Mountain Huts walk or $1,650 for a comprehensive 13-day tour of the island.
Tour Operators: Cradle Mountain Huts, Freycinet Experience, Peregrine Adventures, Tasmanian Expeditions, World Expeditions.

South Australia

There is a wide range of walking opportunities in South Australia, including spectacular coastal walks and the remarkable Heysen Trail, which traverses nearly 2,000 km (1,240 mi) of the semiarid Flinders Ranges and the more gentle Mount Lofty Ranges. In addition to their Heysen Trail itineraries, Ecotrek Bogong Jack Adventures operates walks on Kangaroo Island and in the rugged Gammon Ranges.

Season: April–October.
Locations: Flinders Ranges, Gammon Ranges, Kangaroo Island.
Cost: From $410 for four days to $670 for seven days.
Tour Operator: Ecotrek Bogong Jack Adventures.

Camel Trekking

Riding a camel is rather like riding two horses strapped together at right angles. Surprisingly, though, sitting astride a wide, padded, camel saddle is more comfortable than riding horseback, and the animals aren't nearly as aggressive as many people believe. In fact, they can be quite endearing, although they do have revolting personal habits. The night silence of your desert campsite will regularly be broken by the sound of camels regurgitating, followed by their dawn screams as they object to waking from their dreams of desert oases. Strange as it may seem, a camel trek is an extremely pleasant way to spend a week or two, and it beautifully recaptures the experience of desert travel as it was in the past. Australian camels come from Afghan stock (hence the name of the *Ghan* train, which follows the old desert route of the Afghan camel trains from Adelaide to Alice Springs), and many now roam wild in the Outback. Camel treks rate as soft adventure.

South Australia

The major camel-tour operator in South Australia, Rex Ellis, has a fascination with the Outback that led him to make the only north–south boat crossing of normally dry Lake Eyre. Between April and October, his camel farm in the Flinders Ranges operates rides from a few hours to eight days. For the more adventurous traveler, he operates a series of camel expeditions over the winter months that strike deep into the desert. These include three weeks in the remote Simpson Desert, 16 days in Sturts Stony Desert and Coongie Lakes, and three weeks along the banks of Coopers Creek. The success of these trips relies on the spirit of adventure of the expedition members, to say nothing of the camels' unique ability to cope with arid conditions.

AUSTRALIA'S ANIMALS

AUSTRALIA'S ANIMALS ARE among nature's oddest creations. So weird are the creatures that hop, burrow, slither, and amble across the Australian landmass that, until this century, it was believed that the continent's fauna had a different evolutionary starting point from the rest of the earth's species.

One of the most fascinating groups of all Australian animals is the monotremes. Classified as mammals, they also exhibit some of the characteristics of reptiles, who preceded them on the evolutionary scale. Monotremes lay eggs, as reptiles do; however, they are warm-blooded and suckle their young with milk, mammalian adaptations that considerably increase their chances of survival. Only three species of monotremes survive: the platypus, a reclusive crustacean-eater found in freshwater streams in eastern Australia, and two species of echidna, a small, furry termite-eater.

Australia's animal life was shaped by its plants, and they, in turn, were determined by the climate, which dramatically changed around 15 million years ago. Moist, rain-bearing winds that once irrigated the heart of the continent died, the great inland sea dried up, and the inland rain forests vanished—flamingos and freshwater dolphins along with them. As forests gave way to grassland, the marsupials thrived.

The kangaroo is a superb example of adaptation. In the parched, semi-desert that covers most of central Australia, kangaroos must forage for food over a wide area. Their powerful hind legs act as springs, enabling them to travel long distances while using relatively little energy.

Young kangaroos are born underdeveloped, when they are barely an inch long. The mother then enters estrous again within days of giving birth. The second embryo develops for just a week and stays dormant until its older sibling leaves the pouch, at which time it enters a 30-day gestation period before being born.

Kangaroos, wallabies, and their midsize relations range enormously in size, habitat, and location. In Australia, you'll find everything from rat-size specimens to the six-ft, 200-pound red kangaroos—and you'll find them everywhere from the cool, misty forests of Tasmania to the northern tip of Cape York.

Best loved of all Australia's animals is the koala. A tree-dwelling herbivore, its diet consists entirely of eucalyptus leaves, which are low in nutrients and high in toxins. As a result, koalas must restrict their energy level; their characteristic pose is propped sleepily in the branch of a tree. Even the koala's brain has adapted to its harsh regimen. A human brain uses about 17% of the body's energy, but the koala overcomes its diet by starting out with a brain the size of a small walnut.

However deficient in the cerebellum it may be, though, one thing that the koala will not tolerate is being called a bear. Cute and cuddly as it is—and despite its resemblance to every child's favorite bed mate—the koala is a marsupial, not a bear.

— Michael Gebicki

Season: Year-round.
Location: Flinders Ranges.
Cost: From $1,450 to $3,990 for 40 days.
Tour Operator: Outback Camel Company.

Northern Territory–The Red Centre

With his long white beard and collection of outback yarns, Noel Fuller-ton of Alice Springs Camel Outback Safaris is one of the Northern Ter-ritory's most colorful characters. He obtained his first camel in 1969, and his company now conducts camel rides of an hour or a day along with a series of camel safaris through the Red Centre from his farm outside Alice Springs (☞ Chapter 9). After a riding accident a few years ago, Noel now leads only occasional trips himself—others are led by his family and staff. Among the places these treks visit is Rainbow Val-ley, remote gorge country that includes the oldest watercourse in the world and an ancient stand of palms.

Frontier Camel Tours offers popular "Take A Camel Out To Dinner" and "Take A Camel Out To Breakfast" tours from their headquarters near Alice Springs, as well as one-hour camel rides that operate every morning and afternoon. In 1998 the company opened a Camel Depot near Uluṟu (Ayers Rock) that offers sunrise and sunset camel rides away from the tourist crowds.

Season: April–September (weekly departures), October–March (every two weeks).
Location: Alice Springs, Uluṟu (Ayers Rock).
Cost: From $65 for a one-hour ride to about $330 for three days or $750–$900 for a week.
Tour Operators: Adventure Center, Alice Springs Camel Outback Sa-faris, Frontier Camel Tours, World Expeditions.

Cross-Country Skiing

Unlike the jagged peaks of alpine regions elsewhere in the world, the ancient Australian Alps have rounded summits, making them ideal for cross-country skiing. Although cross-country doesn't offer the same adrenaline rush as downhill skiing, there are no expensive lift tickets to buy—your legs do all the work. In stark contrast to the crowded slopes, cross-country skiers have a chance to get away from the hordes and experience the unforgettable sensation of skiing through forests of eucalyptus trees, with their spreading branches, pale leaves, and im-pressionistic bark patterns. Cross-country skiing is hard adventure, even though many tours are arranged so that skiers stay in lodges every night. The joy of leaving the first tracks across new snow and the pleasure afforded by the unique scenery of the Australian snowfields is tempered by the remarkable fatigue that your arms and legs feel at the end of the day—an exhilarating combination.

New South Wales

Some 450 km (279 mi) south of Sydney, Jindabyne is the major gate-way to the Snowy Mountains. Paddy Pallin Jindabyne is an offshoot of Australia's most respected outdoor-equipment retail store. It has a complete range of ski tours and cross-country instructional programs. Most of the courses are based out of a lodge, but there are also two-and five-day camping tours across the snow trails of the Main Range.

Season: July–September.
Location: Snowy Mountains.
Cost: From $54 for a full day of instruction to $899 for a five-day tour.
Tour Operators: Paddy Pallin Jindabyne.

Victoria

Ecotrek Bogong Jack Adventures offers a comprehensive program of lodge-based trips, camping expeditions, skiing instruction, and snow-craft courses. Groups are kept small (fewer than 15 people), and there are enough instructors to ensure that you learn quickly. Building snow caves and mastering the art of survival in the snow are excellent skills—even if Australia seems like a strange place to learn them. In reality, however, the open, gentle slopes here are ideal for learning how to ski cross-country. The scenery of the Victorian Alps is dramatic, with the valley sides rising steeply to high-country plains. A major advantage of skiing in Victoria is that the lodges where skiers stay are close to the snowfields. These comfortable lodges are located below the snow-line, and evenings by the fire and the inevitable camaraderie of the group make these stays most enjoyable.

Season: July–September.
Locations: Mansfield, Mt. Beauty, Falls Creek, Mt. Hotham.
Cost: From $250 for two days to $850 for seven days.
Tour Operator: Ecotrek Bogong Jack Adventures.

Diving

Australia is one of the world's premier diving destinations. Much of the attention centers on Queensland's Great Barrier Reef, but there is very good diving elsewhere as well—including Tasmania and Western Australia (☞ *below*) and Lord Howe Island (☞ Chapter 2). Australian diving operations are generally well run and regulated, and equipment is modern and well maintained. Because it's a competitive industry, most instructors are good at their jobs. Of course, although this competition (especially in Queensland) creates lower prices, it also reduces service. Anyone planning on learning to dive in Australia should closely examine what operators provide as part of the package (especially equipment rental and the number of open-water dives) rather than basing a decision solely on cost.

Tasmania

Australia's most southern state is not the obvious place to go diving. However, Tasmania's east coast has a remarkably sunny climate and some exceptional kelp forests, magnificent sponge gardens, anemone, basket stars, squid octopus, and butterfly perch. In winter there's a chance that you will dive with the dolphins and whales that call in here on their migration from Antarctica. And King Island in Bass Strait, off the north coast, has some very good wreck diving. Overall, Tasmania possesses Australia's most wreck-strewn coastline—there are more than 20 sites to choose from, including the wreck of the *Cataraqui,* the country's worst maritime disaster.

Season: Mainly summer, but the best east coast conditions are during winter.
Locations: Bicheno, King Island.
Cost: From $105 per boat dive, including equipment.
Tour Operators: Bicheno Dive Centre, King Island Dive Charters.

Queensland

The main diving centers in Queensland are the island resorts: Cairns (☞ Chapter 6) and the Whitsunday Islands and Port Douglas (☞ Chapter 7). For further details on dive operators there, refer to those chapters.

Season: Year-round.
Locations: All along the coast and Great Barrier Reef islands.

Cost: From $50 for a single dive and $120 for a day trip that includes a boat cruise and two dives. Five-day certification courses start at around $400.

Tour Operators: Dive Adventures, Dive Travel Australia, Pro Dive Travel.

Western Australia

Whale sharks are the world's largest fish. A large one weighs 40 tons and is 50 ft long. It *is* in the shark family, but it is also completely harmless. Like many whales, whale sharks live on tiny krill—not fish, seals, or people. From about March through May each year, more than 100 whale sharks can be found along the Western Australian coast near Exmouth. The exact season varies—depending on the time of the spawning of the coral of Ningaloo Reef. Exmouth is the only place in the world where you can be sure of encountering whale sharks.

If you decide to swim with them, it's as if you have adopted a puppy the size of a truck—or have your own pet submarine. Government regulations prohibit touching them or swimming closer to them than a meter (about a yard). It's an expensive day of diving because you need a large boat to take you out to the sharks, a spotter plane to find them, and a runabout to drop you in their path. Although most of the day is spent with whale sharks, it begins with a dive on Ningaloo Reef. The diversity of coral and marine life here isn't as remarkable as at the Great Barrier Reef, but there is a spectacular juxtaposition of large open-water fish and huge schools of bait fish. Outside of whale-shark season you can encounter a passing parade of humpback whales (from July through Sept.) and nesting turtles (from Nov. through Feb.). Nondivers who wish to go snorkeling may join the expedition for a slightly reduced fee.

Season: March–May.
Location: Exmouth.
Cost: $250 (including all equipment, transfer to the boat, an optional dive on Ningaloo Reef, a salad lunch, and soft drinks. The cost also includes the cost of the spotter aircraft, the runabout to keep you in contact with the whale shark, and the whale shark interaction license fee.)

Tour Operator: Exmouth Diving Centre.

Four-Wheel-Drive Tours

Australia is a vast land with a small population, so many Outback roads are merely clearings through the bush. Black soil that turns into skid pans after rain, the ubiquitous red dust of the center, and the continent's great sandy deserts make a four-wheel-drive vehicle a necessity for exploring the more remote countryside. Outback motoring possesses a real element of adventure—on some roads it's standard practice to call in at the few homesteads along the way so they can initiate search procedures if you fail to turn up at the next farm down the track. At the same time, the laconic Aussies you meet in such places are a different breed from urban Australians, and time spent with them is often memorable. Despite the rugged nature of many of the bush tracks that pass for roads in Australia, four-wheel-drive tours are definitely soft adventure.

Queensland

The most northerly point of the Australian mainland, Cape York is the destination sought by every four-wheel-drive enthusiast in Australia. After passing through the rain forest north of Port Douglas, the track travels through relatively dry vegetation the rest of the way. Several galleries of spectacular Aboriginal rock paintings are here, as are a historic telegraph station and the notorious Jardine River, whose shifting bottom made fording very tricky in the past. Until a few years ago, reaching the Cape was a major achievement; now a ferry service across the Jardine makes it easier, but Cape York is still frontier territory—a land of mining camps, Aboriginal settlements, and enormous cattle stations. For all intents and purposes, civilization stops at Cooktown, some 700 km (434 mi) from the tip of Cape York. From their base in Cairns, Wild Track offers several four-wheel-drive experiences in the region, from a one-day fly-drive trip to Cooktown to a 14-day journey to the tip of Cape York and back.

Season: Mainly May–November.
Location: North of Cairns.
Cost: From $199 for one day and $1,550 for seven days to $1,999 for a two-week return trip.
Tour Operator: Wild Track Adventure Safaris.

South Australia

Unless you have the time to walk, the rugged areas of South Australia are best explored by four-wheel-drive vehicle. Kangaroo Island supports a huge variety of animals, including kangaroos, koalas, fur seals, penguins, and sea lions, as well as such bizarre natural features as huge limestone arches and weather-worn rocks that resemble Henry Moore sculptures. Adventure Charters of Kangaroo Island operates a series of tours, the most comprehensive being a three-day, two-night package.

Alternatively, if you head north, the desert starts relatively near Adelaide. The Flinders Ranges are a low finger of mountains stretching into the desert. Their most notable feature is Wilpena Pound, a huge natural amphitheater filled with small trees and grasses overlooking the barren plains below. Intrepid Tours offers a series of one-day and overnight tours throughout this region.

Season: Year-round.
Locations: Kangaroo Island, Flinders Ranges.
Cost: From $48 for a half-day tour, about $830 for three days on Kangaroo Island (including airfare), and from $600 for a four-day tour through the Outback.
Tour Operators: Adventure Charters of Kangaroo Island, Australian Odysseys, Intrepid Tours.

Northern Territory

Although the number of tourists at Kakadu National Park has risen dramatically each year, some sites can still be reached only by four-wheel-drive vehicle, including Jim Jim Falls and Twin Falls—two of Australia's most scenic attractions. At both of these falls, the water plunges over the escarpment to the flood plains beneath. Below the picturesque falls are deep, cool pools and beautiful palm-shaded beaches. The Adventure Center has comprehensive tours of this remarkable area. World Expeditions has a one-week adventure safari into the wilderness of Kakadu and the remote Cobourg Peninsula.

The **Darwin Region Tourism Association** (✉ 38 Mitchell St., Darwin, NT 0800, ☎ 08/8981–4300, 🖷 08/8981–0653) can provide more information about the numerous tour operators based in Darwin.

Season: April–October.
Locations: Throughout the Northern Territory, but mainly in Kakadu.
Cost: From about $600 for six days to $1,250 for 14 days.
Tour Operators: Adventure Center, World Expeditions.

Western Australia–The Kimberley

Most of the four-wheel-drive adventures in Western Australia take place in the Kimberley region in the far north (☞ Chapter 10). The only practical time to visit the Kimberley is during the Dry, May through November, because roads are very often flooded during the Wet.

The Kimberley boasts some of Australia's richest Aboriginal cultural heritage, and the extraordinary rock art here can be explored in World Expeditions' four-wheel-drive trip to the Bungle Bungles and to the remote, little-explored Keep River National Park on the Northern Territory–Western Australian border. This company also offers an exciting trip from Broome into the Kimberley and Mitchell Plateau area.

East Kimberley Tours has a range of expeditions into the Bungle Bungles, some of which involve flying into the area, then continuing on a one- or two-day exploration of the massif. If you stay overnight, accommodations are at the operators' permanent camp. At least three days are required if you wish to take a four-wheel-drive driving tour into Bungle Bungle from Kununurra. Alternatively, you can take a one-day drive starting at Turkey Creek.

Season: May–November.
Location: The Kimberley.
Cost: From $136 for one day to $1,650 for 11 days; with airfare, from $345 for one day to $620 for three days.
Tour Operators: East Kimberley Tours, World Expeditions.

Horseback Riding

Trail bikes and four-wheel-drive vehicles have slowly been replacing horses on Australian farms and stations over the past 20 years. On the plains and coastal lowlands the transformation is complete, but horses are still part of rural life in the highlands, and it is here that the best horseback adventures are to be found. On a horse trek you come closer to the life of the pioneer Australian bushmen than in any other adventure pursuit. Indeed, the majority of treks are led by Australians with close links to the traditions of bush life.

Riding through alpine meadows and along mountain trails, and sleeping under the stars is an excellent way to see the Australian bush. A typical horseback vacation lasts several days, and the food and equipment for each night's camp is brought in by packhorse or four-wheel-drive vehicle. Although a cook, a guide, and all specialist equipment are provided, participants are expected to help look after the horses. An Australian saddle is a cross between the high Western saddle and the almost flat English one. The horses are normally real workhorses, not riding hacks, and they are used to rough bush work. These trips are essentially soft adventures, for most of the work is done by the horses—it's just hard to convince your cramping leg muscles of this after a long day in the saddle.

New South Wales

The Great Dividing Range, which extends right through New South Wales, has some excellent trails for horseback riding. Almost every country town has a riding school with horses for hire, but a few long rides are particularly outstanding. In the Snowy Mountains high country, a six-day summer ride from Reynella homestead through Kosciuszko National Park covers terrain ranging from open plains to alpine forests. Riders camp out in some of the most beautiful valleys in the park—valleys not easily accessible except by horse. A hundred years ago this was the stuff of pioneer legend.

One of the best stables in the Blue Mountains is Packsaddlers in the Megalong Valley, which conduct regular one-, two-, and three-day rides through the rugged countryside to Cox's River. Leaving the farmlands behind and descending through the forest into the river valley, you enter a part of the country that has changed little since European settlers first arrived in Australia. Two options are available—either with food supplied ($100 per day) or self-catering ($75 per day). Although you're only a few hours due west of Sydney, eating a lunch from a saddlebag by the river while the horses graze nearby is a memorable bush experience.

One of the most unusual rides in Australia is the "Pub Crawl on Horseback," a 150-km (93-mi) ride through the New England Ranges to Sydney's north, with nights spent at old bush pubs along the early stagecoach routes. The tour emphasizes the bush experience, not drinking, because riding into a tiny village and booking into a historic pub is thrill enough. All the communities en route could fairly be described as one-horse towns—at least until your posse checks in.

In addition to its variety of New South Wales riding trips, Equitrek Australia offers riding in South Australia, Queensland, Western Australia, and the Northern Territory.

Season: All year, but mainly November–April.
Locations: Blue Mountains, Snowy Mountains, New England Highlands.
Cost: From $75 to $100 for a day ride to $200 for a weekend and $1,000 for a week.
Tour Operators: Equitrek Australia, Great Aussie Pub Crawls on Horseback, Packsaddlers, Paddy Pallin Jindabyne, Reynella Rides.

Victoria

An important part of the Australian rural mythology is an A. B. (Banjo) Paterson 1895 poem entitled "The Man from Snowy River," based on the equestrian feats of riders in the Victorian high plains who rounded up stock and horses from seemingly inaccessible valleys. For those who wish to emulate the hero of that work, several operators have rides of two to 12 days in the area. Part of the journey is spent above the tree line, where, as Banjo Paterson said, "the horses' hooves strike firelight from the flintstones every stride." Accommodations are either in tents or in the original bushmen's huts that dot the high country.

Season: October–May.
Location: Victorian high plains.
Cost: $290 for two days, $1590 for 12 days.
Tour Operators: Bogong Horseback Adventures, Stoneys' Bluff & Beyond Trailrides.

Rafting

The exhilaration of sweeping down into the foam-filled jaws of a rapid is always tinged with fear—white-water rafting is, after all, much like being tossed into a super-sized washing machine. Although this sort of excitement appeals to many people, the attraction of rafting in Australia involves much more. As you drift downriver during the lulls between the white water, it's wonderful to sit back and watch the wilderness unfold, whether it's stately river gums overhanging the stream, towering cliffs, or forests of eucalyptus on the surrounding slopes. Rafting means camping by the river at night, drinking billy tea brewed over the campfire, going to sleep with the sound of the stream in the background, or sighting an elusive platypus at dawn. The juxtaposition of action and serenity gives rafting an enduring appeal that leads most who try it to seek out more rivers with more challenges. Rivers here are smaller and trickier than the ones used for commercial rafting in North America, and rafts usually hold only four to six people. Rafting companies provide all rafting and camping equipment—you only need clothing that won't be damaged by water (cameras are carried in waterproof barrels), a sleeping bag (in some cases), and sun-screen. Rafting qualifies as hard adventure.

New South Wales

The upper reaches of Australia's longest waterway, the Murray River, are open for rafting between September and November, when the stream is fed by melting snow. The river is cold, but the rapids are challenging, and the Australian Alps are dressed in all their spring glory.

The Gwydir River is fed by a large dam, and the scenery downriver is mainly pastoral, but the river has a series of challenging rapids.

The Nymboida River flows through beautiful subtropical rain forest near Coffs Harbour and is the warmest river with white water in the state. World Expeditions runs all of these rivers, Whitewater Rafting Professionals only operate on the Nymboida.

Season: Generally September–May.
Locations: The Murray River in the southern part of New South Wales, the Gwydir River in the center, and the Nymboida River in the north.
Cost: From $135 for a one-day Nymboida trip to about $260–$300 for a weekend. All camping and rafting equipment is supplied.
Tour Operators: White Water Rafting Professionals, Wildwater Adventures, World Expeditions.

Victoria

The driving time from Melbourne to Victoria's rafting rivers is generally less than from Sydney to the main New South Wales rafting locations. Nevertheless, you need to budget at least a weekend for the trip and be prepared to camp out. The scenery ranges from the rugged Alps of the north to the pastoral areas of eastern Victoria. The Mitta Mitta River is invariably rafted as a two-day trip.

Season: Mainly July–December.
Locations: Mitta Mitta, Thomson, Murray, and Snowy rivers.
Cost: From $270 for a weekend.
Tour Operators: Peregrine Adventures, World Expeditions.

Tasmania

The most exciting white-water rafting gives an instant adrenaline rush. Fortunately, most rivers provide plenty of quiet reaches where you can regain your breath and appreciate the scenery. Nowhere is this more true than on the Franklin River, which has the most spectacular and rewarding rafting in Australia. Deep rocky chasms, grand forested valleys, beautiful sandy beaches, and miles of untouched wilderness make the Franklin something special. The river leads through a truly remote area of Tasmania—there are few places where you can join or leave the river. You have the choice of exploring either the lower or upper parts of the Franklin, or the entire navigable length. By far the most rewarding option is covering the entire river. The combination of isolation, beauty, difficult rapids, and strenuous portages ensures that rafters finish the trip with a real feeling of achievement. It's a difficult and challenging journey that should be tackled only by people who are reasonably fit and comfortable in the bush.

Season: November–March.
Locations: Franklin River, west coast.
Cost: From about $1,000 for six days to $1,900 for 12 days.
Tour Operators: Peregrine Adventures, World Expeditions.

13 BACKGROUND AND ESSENTIALS

Map of Australia

Map of Distances and Flying Times

Portraits of Australia

Books and Videos

Smart Travel Tips A to Z

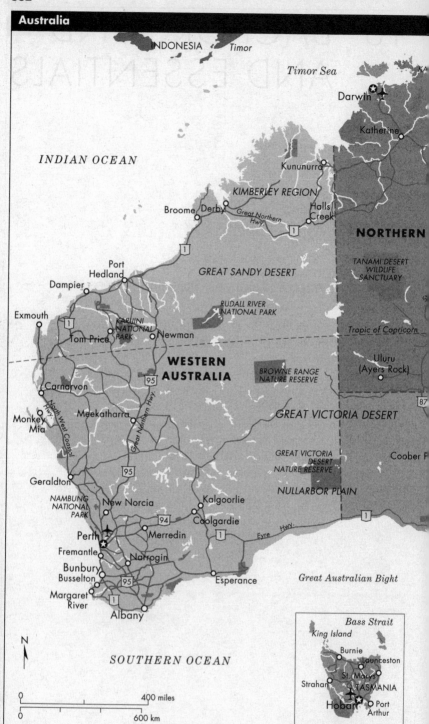

INDONESIA

Timor

Timor Sea

Darwin

Katherine

INDIAN OCEAN

Kununurra

KIMBERLEY REGION

Broome

Derby

Great Northern Hwy.

Halls Creek

NORTHERN

Port Hedland

Dampier

GREAT SANDY DESERT

TANAMI DESERT WILDLIFE SANCTUARY

RUDALL RIVER NATIONAL PARK

Exmouth

KARIJINI NATIONAL PARK

Tom Price

Newman

Tropic of Capricorn

WESTERN AUSTRALIA

BROWNE RANGE NATURE RESERVE

Uluru (Ayers Rock)

Carnarvon

87

Monkey Mia

North West Coastal Hwy.

Meekatharra

Great Northern Hwy.

GREAT VICTORIA DESERT

Geraldton

GREAT VICTORIA DESERT NATURE RESERVE

Coober P

95

NAMBUNG NATIONAL PARK

New Norcia

Kalgoorlie

NULLARBOR PLAIN

94

Coolgardie

Perth

Merredin

1

Eyre Hwy.

1

Fremantle

Narrogin

Bunbury

Busselton

95

Esperance

Great Australian Bight

Margaret River

1

Albany

N

SOUTHERN OCEAN

0   400 miles
0   600 km

Bass Strait

King Island

Burnie

Launceston

St Marys

Strahan

TASMANIA

Hobart

Port Arthur

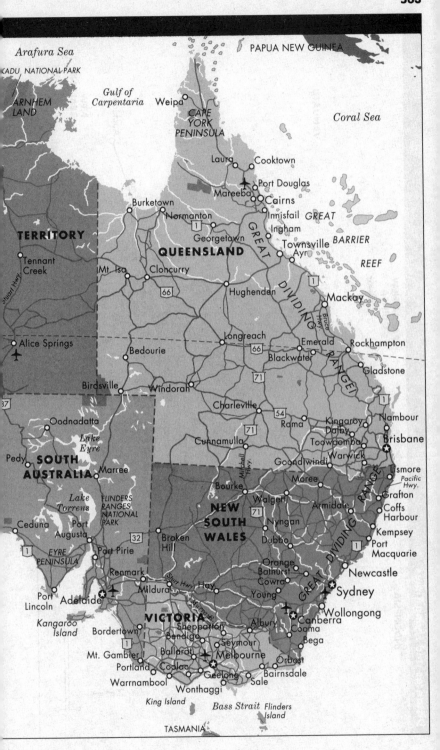

Arafura Sea

KADU NATIONAL PARK

ARNHEM LAND

PAPUA NEW GUINEA

Gulf of Carpentaria Weipa

Coral Sea

CAPE YORK PENINSULA

Laura • Cooktown

Burketown

Port Douglas

Mareeba ✈ Cairns

Normanton

Innisfail

Georgetown Ingham

GREAT

QUEENSLAND Townsville

Ayr

BARRIER

TERRITORY

Tennant Creek

Mt. Isa Cloncurry

Hughenden

REEF

66

GREAT

Mackay

Stuart Hwy

Alice Springs ✈

Longreach

66

Emerald

Rockhampton

Bedourie

Blackwater

DIVIDING

Birdsville

Windorah

Gladstone

Oodnadatta

Lake Eyre

Charleville

54

Rama

Kingaroy

Nambour

RANGE

1

71

Bruce Hwy

SOUTH

Pedy

AUSTRALIA Marree

71

Cunnamulla

Dalby

Toowoomba

Brisbane

Warwick

Goondiwindi

Lismore

Pacific Hwy.

Lake Torrens

FLINDERS RANGES NATIONAL PARK

Mitchell Hwy

Bourke

Moree

Grafton

Ceduna

Port Augusta

32

Broken Hill

NEW SOUTH WALES

Walgett

71

Nyngan

Armidale

Coffs Harbour

Kempsey

EYRE PENINSULA

Port Pirie

1

Dubbo

Port Macquarie

Renmark

Orange

Bathurst

Cowra

Newcastle

Port Lincoln

Adelaide

Mildura

Hay

Young

Sydney

Kangaroo Island

Bordertown

VICTORIA

Shepparton

Albury

Wollongong

Canberra

Cooma

Bendigo

Seymour

Bega

Mt. Gambier

Ballarat

Melbourne

Orbost

Portland

Colac

Geelong

Bairnsdale

Warrnambool

Wonthaggi

Sale

King Island

Bass Strait *Flinders Island*

TASMANIA

Distances and Flying Times

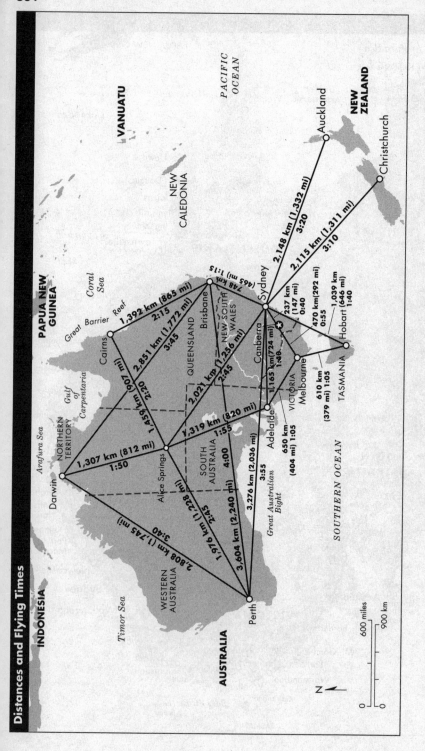

INDONESIA

Timor Sea

Arafura Sea

PAPUA NEW GUINEA

Coral Sea

VANUATU

NEW CALEDONIA

PACIFIC OCEAN

Darwin

NORTHERN TERRITORY

Gulf of Carpentaria

Great Barrier Reef

Cairns

QUEENSLAND

Brisbane

Auckland

NEW ZEALAND

Christchurch

WESTERN AUSTRALIA

Alice Springs

SOUTH AUSTRALIA

NEW SOUTH WALES

Sydney

Perth

Adelaide

Great Australian Bight

Canberra

VICTORIA

Melbourne

Hobart

TASMANIA

SOUTHERN OCEAN

AUSTRALIA

1,307 km (812 mi) 1:50

1,976 km (1,228 mi) 2:45

2,808 km (1,745 mi) 3:40

3,604 km (2,240 mi) 3:55

3,276 km (2,036 mi) 3:55

1,459 km (907 mi) 2:20

2,851 km (1,772 mi) 3:45

1,392 km (865 mi) 2:15

1,319 km (820 mi) 1:55

2,021 km (1,256 mi) 2:45

748 km (465 mi) 1:15

650 km (404 mi) 1:05

1,165 km (724 mi) 1:40

610 km (379 mi) 1:05

237 km (147 mi) 0:40

470 km (292 mi) 0:55

1,039 km (646 mi) 1:40

2,148 km (1,332 mi) 3:20

2,115 km (1,311 mi) 3:10

N

0   600 miles

0   900 km

FIVE THOUSAND MILES
FROM ANYWHERE

Start with the light. Everything starts with the light here.

In the hour before nightfall, what Hollywood calls the "magic hour," the buildings in Australia start to glow with an unearthly light, and the gold-touched clouds look like something Blake might have imagined in his highest moments. The sky becomes a canvas on which absent gods are doodling: over here, patches of tropical blue; over there, shafts of silver slanting through the slate-gray clouds; everywhere, double rainbows arcing over gray Victorian monuments and avenues of palms. Yet this is hardly a warming scene. Rather, the Australian twilight has the same chilly strangeness, the same otherworldly calm—the same off-the-edge-of-the-earthliness—as Iceland in midsummer: a cold and science-fictive beauty. And as the night begins to descend, it seems as if the land is reclaiming itself, and Australia is more than ever a place emptied out of people, some dark, elemental presences awakened behind the placid surfaces of its newborn world.

The light in Australia is like nothing else on earth—as befits, perhaps, a country that feels as if it has fallen off the planet. "Australia's like an open door with the blue beyond," wrote D. H. Lawrence. "You just walk out of the world and into Australia." And the startled intensity of the heavens hints at all the weird paradoxes of this young old land of sunny ironists, a British California caught between a world it has abandoned and one it has yet to colonize. In the vast open blueness of Australia, the only presiding authority, it often seems, is the light.

Australia is, of course, the definitive—perhaps the ultimate—*terra incognita,* its very name derived from the Latin phrase *terra australis incognita,* or unknown land of the south. Captain Cook first bumped into the land of anomalies while trying to observe a transit of the planet Venus. And even today the world's largest island seems to occupy a huge open space in the mind, beyond the reach of our sights. Australia, for one thing, borders nothing and is on the way to nowhere. It feels, in every sense, like the last place on earth. Colonized originally by the British as a place for posthumous lives—a kind of Alcatraz on an epic scale—Australia has always seemed the natural setting for post-apocalyptic imaginings, from Lawrence's utopian visions to Nevil Shute's nuclear wasteland to the haunted deathscape of Mad Max.

What little we know of this tabula rasa, moreover, has generally sounded like fiction. "In Australia alone," as Marcus Clarke wrote, "is to be found the Grotesque, the Weird, the strange scribblings of Nature learning to write." The flattest and driest of the continents defies all the laws of probability with its natural—or unnatural—wonders: not just the world's only egg-laying mammals (the echidna and the duckbill platypus) but the wombat and the wallaby, the koala, the kangaroo, the kookaburra, and the quokka. A land of extremes, it is also one of inversions, an antipodean place where Christmas is celebrated in midsummer and the water goes the wrong way down the drain, a looking-glass world in which trees lose their bark but not their leaves, and crows, it is said, fly backwards (to keep the dust from their eyes). Even the country's social origins are the stuff of Restoration comedy, a

---

This article was written for the Australian bicentennial in 1988. In the time that's elapsed since then, some of the names have changed, but the spirit of *terra australis* as Iyer described it lives on.

down-underworld in which convicts were known as "government men" and thieves were appointed as magistrates—less the Promised than the Threatened Land.

Yet it is in the nature of Lonely Places to attract people, in large part because of their loneliness, and the greatest reason of all for Australia's appeal is, in the end, the very thing that has outlawed it for so long: the tyranny of distance. People are realizing that Australia is so far from the world that it is the ideal place for people who wish to get away from the world, do nothing, and watch others do the same. The quietness, and unhurried spaciousness, of the Empty Continent can make one feel as if one has all the time in the world—indeed, as if time and the world have both been annulled: "rush hour" is not a term in common currency here. And though irreverence is an Australian article of faith, the most urbanized society on earth (70% of Aussies live in eight major cities) is increasingly endowed with all the gentrified accoutrements of a brunch culture: hotels so untouched they feel like resorts, towns that are drawing-board models of clean lines and open spaces, people who are devoted to life, liberty, and the pursuit of happiness. Not the least of the ironies governing a nation whose founding fathers were convicts is, in fact, that it is now most noted for its air of freedom, safety, and civic order.

In Australia's laid-back sense of come-as-you-are palliness, many foreign observers have found a model of democracy in action, a natural kind of Whitmanesque fraternalism free of ideological baggage. Calling a spade a spade is a national habit, after all, and nothing seems to anger the Australian but pretension. Though Lawrence may have been merely being Lawrence when he claimed that Australians were such natural democrats that they did not even like to go upstairs, it is certainly true that a visitor is more likely to be called "mate" than "sir."

Yet if Australians' customs are often as unbuttoned as those of the Amer-

ican West, their manners are generally a little more reserved; touched with *le vice anglais* of self-containment, theirs is still a place of semidetached men in semidetached houses. And even though its feeling of space and ease, like its gold rush past and its sense of limitless future, gives Australia a somewhat Californian air, it feels more provisional, more pressureless than the frontier states of America, less troubled by introspection or ambition. Here, in fact, is a world that makes California seem positively frantic by comparison. In his novel *Bliss,* a typically Australian compound of irony, fancy, and profanity, Peter Carey shrewdly depicts his homeland as a mythic Eden "on the outposts of the American Empire . . . [with] business more or less done in the American style, although without quite the degree of seriousness the Americans liked."

Australia, moreover, still holds to its fondness for the piratical, a sense that distinction lies not in the flaunting but in the flouting of refinement. The country delights in the marginal, glories in its freedom from convention, is determined to be different. There is a store in Sydney (as in London) exclusively for left-handers, and the sign in a Melbourne bookshop canvasses members for a Lost in Space club. And Australia's traditional images of rowdy nonconformity are still in constant evidence. The larrikin lives on in the 11-year-old busker in earrings and rattail haircut who plays drinking songs in front of Sydney harbor while his Fagin looks on from the shadows; the convict and prospector are remembered in the dark humor of the names that overbrood the landscape—Lake Disappointment, Cape Grim, Double Crossing Creek; and the ocker asserts his skeptical down-to-earthiness with the bumper sticker EVERYBODY NEEDS TO BELIEVE IN SOMETHING. I BELIEVE I'LL HAVE ANOTHER BEER. In this seriously macho culture, you see more men in earrings than anywhere else—less a statement of fashion, one senses, than a badge of defiant rebelliousness.

To some extent, too, the myths of frontier still animate the culture.

Many young Australians continue to take off around the world, treating jobs as way stations and anywhere as home, while many retirement couples take to their mobile homes and circumnavigate the land. And though the country feels less restless than America, it is surely just as mobile. Everywhere there are dreams of long horizons: a concierge is studying Chinese to expand his prospects; a cabbie is working 60 hours a week in the hope of visiting South America; a waiter at an exclusive French restaurant simply picks up his camera and guitar and heads off for a new life in the Outback.

Mike, a rugged, long-breeched man who runs a riding stable outside Melbourne, recalls how he came here alone on a boat at the age of 14, propelled by grand dreams awakened by Zane Grey. "There was a feeling that I could do nothing in England; and no matter how well I did at school, I could never go to university. That was just something that people like me didn't do. But over here, anything is possible. No way I could start up a place like this in England."

Besides, with its reverence for unorthodoxy and its sense of being away from it all, Australia remains an ideal retreat for odd men and women out. At times, in fact, one has the impression that it is less a culture than an aggregation of subcultures, a society of fringes—of surfers, cowboys, boozers, and hippies. Alternative lifestyles are the norm in many places, and the prospect of starting a new life has natural appeal for those committed to Rebirthing. The lush rolling hills known as the Rainbow Region, an hour west of the Gold Coast, have become a perfect haven for back-to-the-land purists and hypnotherapists, and the local bulletin board offers all the Oriental arts, from tai chi to tae kwon do. (The Breath of Life Relaxation and Healing Centre promises "Reiki healing" and "Lazaris videos"—all of this next to Woolworth's!) Still, mellowness here takes on a decidedly Aussie twang: "Shoplifting gives you bad karma!" advises a trendy Asian boutique in Sydney. "And if I catch you, I'll make sure you get it in this life—you Rat Fink! Sincerely, Sandi."

At the same time, Australia, like many a colony, has never entirely left behind the country that abandoned it here. As the relentlessly clever Tasmanian-born critic Peter Conrad points out in his half-autobiography, *Down Home,* Australians wistfully tried to assuage their homesickness by reinventing the motherland here—Tasmania alone has "a cliffless Dover, a beachless Brighton, an unindustrial Sheffield." A local newspaper may have no qualms about describing the visiting Duchess of York as "astonishingly frumpish," yet still her befreckled visage adorns at least three magazine covers in a single week. And even as the tattoo-and-bare-skin crowd is crowding in to see Mick Jagger (who once acted as the country's favorite outlaw, Ned Kelly) perform at the National Tennis Center, hundreds of well-behaved families are lining up to visit Prince Andrew's boat, docked down the coast in Tasmania.

Today, in many ways, Australia seems to reflect the eccentric ways of a Western European society set down in the middle of a Lonely Place: hotels as imaginatively designed as pavilions in some world's fair; cities that offer Balkan, Burmese, Mauritian, Uruguayan, and Seychellian cuisine; casinos that are typically down-home affairs where neither solemnity nor discretion is held in high regard ("Not a Poker Face in Sight," promises the Adelaide casino). Nearly all the heads in Australian bars are frothy, and tattooed bikers down 3.3-pint "stubbies" of Foster's in dusty outposts like the Humpty Doo Bar, where a bulletin board advertises pigs and a sign warns customers tersely, "Don't Ask for Credit as Refusal Often Offends." Australian entertainment, in fact, is nothing if not straightforward: a slim tourist brochure in Melbourne includes 22 full ads for escort agencies.

For the historically minded traveler, the main lure of the place may well be Tasmania, the oldest convict settlement after Sydney, and one of those out-of-the-way places that many people want to visit because of their vague sense that no one has visited them before. With its blustery skies and lowering, snowcapped Mount Wellington, Tasmania is in some respects an inversion of the mainland, itself an inversion of England, and so ends up a little like the mother country. But its green and pleasant land is scarred with the remnants of its gloomy penal past: the gutted gray buildings at Port Arthur, the graves on the Isle of the Dead, and all the other grisly mementos of a place once known as "Hell on Earth."

By contrast, the social history of modern Australia—and of many places like it—is summarized most tidily in the main shopping street in Adelaide, the wondrously compact little town laid out in a square by a man named Light. The thoroughfare begins life as Hindley Street, a rough-and-tumble desolation row of sailors' haunts—video arcades, take-away joints, and tawdry souvenir shops. The names say it all: the Box Adult Book Shop, Joynt Venture smoking paraphernalia, For Roses Tattoo Studio, the Sweetheart cocktail lounge, the Pop-in Coffee Lounge, and Crazy Horse Striptease Revue. Then, downtown, it turns into Rundle Mall, a gleaming, pedestrian-only monument to civic order, the sort of middling Middle Australian area you expect to find in any suburban center: Florsheim Shoes, Thomas Cook Travel, Standard Books, and—on both sides of the central intersection—the Golden Arches.

Finally, on its eastern edge, Rundle Mall opens up into Rundle Street, a SoHoian anthology of today: the Appar-allel boutique, Known Space books, the Campari bistro, Al Fresco gelateria, the Australian School of Meditation, Bryan's Hairdressers, the Bangkok restaurant, Kelley's Grains and Seeds—one long neon-and-mannequin line of vintage clothes stores and veggie restaurants, culminating (as it must culminate) in the New Age Emporium. This street alone, it seems, tells the story of how the twenties became the fifties became the eighties, or how raffishness turned into Standard Shopping Center and then was reborn as Authentic Renovated and Redecorated Raffishdom.

As for the booming present tense, it is best inspected in the one area that contradicts the quiet and unpeopled air of the continent—and also, not coincidentally, the one area expressly designed for foreigners: the 21-mile Floridian motel-and-minigolf seaside strip known as the Gold Coast, an hour south of Brisbane. Centered on the town of Surfers Paradise, a place as self-effacing as its name, the Coast has become a furious riot of development, disco music pulsing through its glassy new arcades, Porsches cruising along its jungle of high-rises, a seemingly unending stretch of traffic-choked boulevards littered with ice cream parlors, Spanish-style motels, and Pizza Huts. There is a Ripley's Believe It or Not! here, and Kenny Koala's Dreamworld. And in truth, Surfers Paradise—or should it be called Surface Paradise?—has all the wound-up frenzy of an amusement park writ huge, a neo–Atlantic City tricked up in Miami Vice colors and high-tech accessories. Nothing is missing here, it seems, except surfers, perhaps, and paradise.

In the end, the greatest marvels of Australia reside simply in its land—the silence and the sky. For more than a day, you can travel through the Outback, a parched white land of ghosts, of blanched trees twisted at odd angles across a plain as vast and mysterious as Africa. Nothing breaks the vacancy but a dead cow, an upturned car, a stray eagle. Everywhere there is only emptiness and flatness. And then, rising up unanswerably against a diorama-bright landscape of shocked blue and thick red, Ayers Rock, old and mute and implacable, in powerful counterpoint to the young, pretty, somewhat uninflected society all around. The sacred rock is one of those rare places with a genuine sense of mystery: it casts a larger shadow than any postcard could suggest.

Or awaken one Edenic morning in Kakadu to see the sun gilding the swampy billabong, jabirus hovering above the water in the golden, gauzy early light. Two hours later, on the South Alligator River, listen to a guide reciting names as if riffling through the multicolored pages of some children's picture book: pelicans and egrets and snakebirds are here; pied herons, masked plovers, and migrant warders from Siberia; lotus birds are among the mango trees, and white-breasted sea eagles (with a wingspan of 6 feet), glossy ibises (with sickle-shaped beaks), and whistling ducks ("not capable of quacking"). There are blue-winged kookaburras in the sky, and sulphur-crested cockatoos; frill-necked lizards along the river-bank, and even lazy crocodiles sun-bathing just 10 feet from the boat. At dusk, the birds honk and squawk above a huge, pink-flowering lily pond, and flocks of black magpie geese and silver-winged corellas fly across the face of a huge full moon that sits in the middle of the darken-ing sky, catching the silver of their wings. In the daily enchantment of dusk, a visitor begins, at last, to catch the presence of an Australia within, a *terra incognita* deep inside, and a loneliness that will stay with him even when he leaves. In the twilight of Australia, the foreigner can catch an intimation of what Melville calls the "great America on the other side of the sphere," and so a sense of how everything brings him back to the natural state where he began: a lonely person in a Lonely, Lonely Place.

— Pico Iyer

Pico Iyer is a longtime essayist for Time *and a contributing editor to* Civilization *and* Tricycle: The Buddhist Review. *His books include* Cuba and the Night, Falling off the Map, *from which this excerpt was taken,* The Lady and the Monk, Video Night in Kathmandu, *and* Tropical Classical.

PILLARS OF FIRE ACROSS THE PLAINS

The western plains of New South Wales are grasslands. Their vast ex-panse flows for many hundreds of miles beyond the Lachlan and Mur-rumbidgee rivers until the desert takes over and sweeps inland to the dead heart of the continent. In a good sea-son, if the eyes are turned to the earth on those plains, they see a tapestry of delicate life—not the luxuriant de-sign of a book of hours by any means, but a tapestry nonetheless, designed by a spare modern artist. What grows there hugs the earth firmly with its ex-tended system of roots above which the plant life is delicate but deter-mined. After rain there is an explo-sion of growth. Nut-flavored green grass puts up the thinnest of green spears. Wild grains appear, grains which develop bleached gold ears as they ripen. Purple desert peas weave through the green and gold, and bright yellow bachelor's buttons cover acres at a time, like fields planted with mus-tard. Closest to the earth is trefoil clover, whose tiny, vivid green leaves and bright flowers creep along the ground in spring, to be replaced by a harvest of seed-filled burrs in au-tumn—burrs that store within them the energy of the sun as concentrated protein. At the edges of pans of clay, where the topsoil has eroded, live waxy succulents bearing bright pink and purple blooms, spreading like splashes of paint dropped in widen-ing circles on the earth.

Above the plants that creep across the ground are the bushes, which grow wherever an indentation in the earth, scarcely visible to the eye, allows for the concentration of more moisture from the dew and the reluctant rain. There is the ever-present round mound of prickly weed, which begins its life a strong acid green with hints of yel-low, and then is burnt by the sun or the frost to a pale whitish yellow. As it ages, its root system weakens so that on windy days the wind will pick it out of the earth and roll it slowly and majestically about like whirling suns in a van Gogh painting.

The creatures that inhabit this earth carry its colors in their feathers, fur, or scales. Among its largest denizens are emus, 6-foot-high flightless birds with dun-gray feathers and tiny wings, and kangaroos. Kangaroos, like emus, are silent creatures, 2 to 8 feet tall, and ranging in color from the gentlest dove-gray to a rich red-brown. Both species blend with their native earth so well that one can be almost upon them before recognizing the familiar shape. The fur of the wild dogs has the familiar yellow of the sun-baked clay, and the reptiles, snakes, and goannas look like the earth in shadow. All tread on the fragile habitat with padded paws and claws that leave the roots of grass intact.

On the plains, the earth meets the sky in a sharp black line so regular that it seems as though drawn by a creator interested more in geometry than the hills and valleys of the Old Testament. Human purposes are dwarfed by such a blank horizon. When we see it from an island in a vast ocean we know we are resting in shelter. On the plains, the horizon is always with us and there is no retreating from it. Its blankness travels with our every step and waits for us at every point of the compass. Because we have very few reference points on the spare earth, we seem to creep over it, one tiny point of consciousness between the empty earth and the overarching sky. Because of the flatness, contrasts are in a strange scale. A scarlet sunset will highlight gray-yellow tussocks of grass as though they were trees. Thunderclouds will mount thousands of feet above one stunted tree in the foreground. A horseback rider on the horizon will seem to rise up and emerge from the clouds. While the patterns of the earth are in small scale, akin to complex needlepoint on a vast tapestry, the sky is all drama. Cumulus clouds pile up over the center of vast continental spaces, and the wind moves them at dramatic pace along the horizon or over our heads. The ever-present red dust of a dry earth hangs in the air and turns all the colors from yellow through orange and red to purple on and off as the clouds bend and refract the light. Sunrise and sunset make up in drama for the fact that there are so few songbirds in that part of the bush. At sunrise, great shafts of gold precede the baroque sunburst. At sunset, the cumulus ranges through the shades of a Turner seascape before the sun dives below the earth leaving no afterglow, but at the horizon, tongues of fire.

The primal force of the sun shapes the environment. With the wind and the sand it bakes and cleanses all signs of decay. There is no cleansing by water. The rivers flow beneath the earth, and rain falls too rarely. In the recurring cycles of drought the sand and dust flow like water, and like the floods of other climates they engulf all that lies in their path. Painters find it hard to capture the shimmer of that warm red earth dancing in the brilliant light, and to record at the same time the subtle greens and grays of the plants and trees. Europeans were puzzled by the climate and vegetation, because the native eucalyptus trees were not deciduous. The physical blast of the sun in hot dry summers brought plants to dormancy. Slow growth followed in autumn, and a burst of vigorous growth after the brief winter rainy season. Summer was a time of endurance for all forms of life as moisture ebbed away and the earth was scorched. Winter days were like summer in a northern climate, and spring meant the onset of unbroken sunshine. On the plains, several winters might go by without a rainy season, and every 20 years or so the rain might vanish for a decade at a time. When that happened, the sun was needed to cleanse the bones of dead creatures, for the death toll was immense.

The oldest known humans on the continent left their bones on the western plains. Nomadic peoples hunted over the land as long as 40 thousand years ago. They and their progeny left behind the blackened stones of ovens, and the hollowed flat pieces of granite they carried from great distances to grind the native nardoo grain. Their way of life persisted until white settlers came by bullock wagon, 130 years ago, to take possession of the land. They came to graze their flocks of sharp-hooved sheep and cattle, hoping to make the land yield wealth. Other great inland grasslands in Argentina, South Africa, or North America were settled by pastoralists and ranchers who used forced labor: Indian peons, Bantus, or West African slaves. On Australia's great plains there were no settled native people to enslave. The settlers moved onto the plains long after the abandonment of transportation from Great Britain, the last form of forced labor available in the Antipodes. As a result, the way of life that grew up for white settlers was unique.

A man could buy the government leasehold for hundreds of thousands of acres of grassland at a modest price if he settled the land and undertook to develop it. Others, beyond the reach of government scrutiny, simply squatted with their flocks on likely looking land. The scale of each holding was beyond European dreams of avarice. Each settler could look out to the vacant horizon knowing that all he saw was his. To graze the unfenced land required a population of sheepherders, or, as they came to be called, boundary riders. A settler would need 12 to 15 hands for his several hundred thousand acres, but most would live out on the "run" (sheep run) at least a day's ride from the main settlement. The hands were solitary males, a freewheeling rural proletariat, antisocial, and unconcerned with comfort or the domestic pleasures. Their leisure went in drink and gambling, and their days in a routine of lonely and backbreaking work. The main house would be spare and simple also, its roof of iron and its walls of timber laboriously transported from the coast. The garden would be primitive and the boss's recreations would be little different from his hands'. If he shared his life with a wife and children, they lived marginally on the edge of his world of male activity. There was no rain for orchards, no water for vegetable gardens, and no society for entertaining. Women worked over wood stoves in 100° heat and heated water for laundry over an open fire. There was lit-

tle room for the culinary arts, because everyone's diet was mutton and unleavened bread, strong black tea, and spirits. The ratio of women to men was as distorted in this wave of settlement as anywhere in the settlement of the New World.

The pattern of the year followed the seasons. If the rains came, they fell in the winter. Lambing was planned for the spring, when the grass was at its best, and the last winter showers might have left some tender growth for young lambs to nibble before their teeth developed. If seasons cooperated, the lambs were well grown, able to walk great distances for their food and water by the time the summer set in. In February, before the summer reached its peak, the lambs were shorn, and the faces and withers of the grown sheep were trimmed so that flies could not infest the places where sweat and urine soiled their fleeces. In June, in midwinter, when it was less harmful to move the animals over distances and hold them penned in yards, the grown sheep were brought to a shearing shed and shorn. If there had been an uninterrupted supply of nourishment through the year, their fleece would be 7 inches thick, unstained by dust, and carrying an unbroken staple that meant it could be easily combed to spin the finest yarn. If the land they grazed did not carry enough herbage throughout the year, the staple of their fleeces would show a break to mark the point where the food supply had faltered. When the staple was broken it could not be so easily combed, and the yarn it produced, being of less high quality, sold for less. If there were too many breaks it might not repay the cost of producing it.

A pastoralist could follow several economic strategies. Fewer sheep could be grazed over a set area of land, moved to fresh pasture whenever their nourishment required, and thus produce smaller amounts of more valuable wool. More sheep could be grazed over land they would crop bare in a year, for a larger volume of less valuable wool. The land that was grazed out each year succumbed quickly to drought. The land that was grazed in careful rotation might not succumb for as long as four or five years, for the unbroken root systems of the plants would hold the ground. One thing was certain. If the drought was long enough, sheep and cattle would, in their hunger, drag up the roots of the herbage, their sharp hooves would loosen the topsoil, and it would begin to blow away in the wind. The grasslands the earliest settlers saw had never been cropped by ruminant animals. No sharp hooves had ever disturbed the soil. It looked rich and indestructible, but in reality it was one of the most delicately balanced environments on the planet.

The chance to acquire title to a western land lease was the chance of a lifetime. In the expansive environment of the 1900s, men who felt lucky to be alive looked at the plains and dreamed about finally achieving economic independence. Perhaps, if things went well, their children could live the life of Australia's pastoral elites. For the returned soldiers [from the 1914–1918 War], class consciousness was more or less set aside, but most knew they wanted private schools for their children, fashionable clothes for their wives to wear to the races, a fancy horse or two in the stables, and freedom from worry about money.

The voices that exclaimed over the follies of brass hats or swore poetically about the stubborn ways of sheep and cattle did so in a melange of accents. Some carried a Scots burr, some a trace of a Yorkshire flat a; some spoke grammatically and displayed the manners produced by attendance at one of Australia's private schools. Most spoke broad Australian: picturesque in image, laced with the rhyming slang of Cockney London and the poetic black humor of the Irish. Their manners and their clothes were deliberately working-class. At night when they sat with their wives beside their crackling static-blurred radios, they waited for Big Ben to chime and then heard the impeccable British accents of the BBC announcer reading the news. With that voice they absorbed a map of the world that placed their near neighbor, Japan, in the Far East, and located distant Turkey in the Near East. So far as Australia was concerned its map was also clear and idiosyncratic. There were Sydney, Melbourne, and Adelaide on the southeast coast, and the bush. Other places existed—small country towns, the new federal capital planned at Canberra, the Snowy Mountains with their huge areas of snow and ice, industrial seaports like Newcastle, near the coalfields. They did not register because there were really only two places in the westerner's consciousness: the bush, and the metropolis at the end of the railway line where the wool was sold.

The city was a place of unaccustomed leisure for people who labored hard seven days a week. For the men there were cheerful drinking occasions before the wool sales or the agricultural shows. For the women there were the shops, the doctors and dentists for the children, and the luxury of restaurants, fresh fruit and vegetables, seafood, flower stands. For the children there were the marvels of electric lights, neon signs, moving pictures, and unlimited candy stores. These were balanced but not outweighed by the ministrations of the dental and medical professions and the ominous crowds. For everyone there were the sore feet and aching legs that came from wearing one's best shoes on hard pavements, and the unaccustomed feel of city clothes.

Everyone much preferred the rare occasions of leisure and festivity at home. There were picnic races, a bush festivity that involved horse racing by day, cheerful and alcoholic gambling and dances by night. A district might band together to stage a gymkhana, where the jockeys were not professionals and the horses were local products. Every half-dozen stations would have somewhere a vestigial racetrack, barely a trace in the soil, with some rickety shelters from the sun and some kind of access to water. Bookmakers thrived as people cheerfully gambled away the year's profits in big bets, unconsciously recognizing that there were few other really satisfying diversions. Old lumber and battered corrugated iron would be pieced together to make a community hall in the middle of nowhere, and dances would be arranged by the Country Women's Association, or the Returned Soldiers' League. Musicians would materialize, and the men would appear in unaccustomed suits accompanied by wives in long dresses. People starved for company danced happily till dawn, reluctant to go home. Supper would be a feast at which every woman's prowess in the kitchen was assessed, and none of the hardworking revelers needed to worry about dieting.

Before they set out in the lightening sky, they stood to attention for "God Save the King," and if the evening had become an occasion for remembering 1914–1918, they sang "Land of Hope and Glory," evoking the memory, not so much of England, but of her mighty Empire, of which Australia was the proudest part. Anyone who mocked these loyalties learned quickly that he or she did not belong.

The cars would sweep home over the dusty roads, their lights visible like pillars of fire across the plains. If one arrived home first, one could stand on one's veranda and watch the other departures, visible for 20 miles or so. On regular nights there were only the stars, the cry of a fox, and the sound of the wind. Then if a car traveled very late at night it meant an emergency. Distant watchers would crane their heads to see where it went, and wonder what had gone wrong.

— Jill Ker Conway

Born in Hillston, New South Wales, Jill Ker Conway graduated from the University of Sydney in 1958 and received her Ph.D. from Harvard University in 1969. From 1964 to 1975 she taught at the University of Toronto and was vice president there before serving for 10 years as President of Smith College. Since 1985 she has been a visiting scholar and professor in MIT's Program in Science, Technology and Society. She now lives in Milton, Massachusetts.

WHAT TO READ AND WATCH BEFORE YOU GO

Books

Most of the following books are available in bookstores in the United States or Australia.

ABORIGINAL CULTURE

In the acclaimed *Australian Dreaming: 40,000 Years of Aboriginal History,* author Jennifer Isaacs has paired stunning color photographs with the story of the original Australians. Geoffrey Blainey's *Triumph of the Nomads* is a highly readable appraisal of the knowledge and technology that allowed the Aborigines to live in their harsh environment.

One of the most celebrated recent works by an Aboriginal writer is *My Place,* by Sally Morgan. Bruce Chatwin's *The Songlines* is a fictional rendering of the Aboriginal relationship with the earth.

FICTION

Peter Carey's inventive novels have won many awards, including the 1988 Booker Prize, the British Commonwealth's highest literary award. His work includes the novels *Jack Maggs, Illywhacker, Bliss,* and *Oscar and Lucinda.* Elizabeth Jolley is another leading contemporary author whose often humorous novels and stories, such as *The Sugar Mother* and *Woman in a Lampshade,* are set in her home state of Western Australia. Also recommended are *The Chant of Jimmie Blacksmith* and *The Playmaker,* Australian-subject books by Thomas Keneally, the author of *Schindler's Ark,* which became the film *Schindler's List.* Patrick White is Australia's most celebrated novelist, winner of the Nobel Prize in 1973. Among his works are *Voss* and *Flaws in the Glass.*

HISTORY AND SOCIETY

Published in 1994, Barry Hill's generously illustrated *The Rock: Travelling to Uluru,* weaves together oral and natural history in its account of The Handback, when white Australians gave ownership of Uluru back to the Aborigines.

Robert Hughes weaves Australia's convict origins into a fascinating narrative web in *The Fatal Shore.* The book traces the birth of the nation from the arrival of the First Fleet in 1788 through the end of convict transportation in 1868. Marcus Clarke's classic, *For the Term of His Natural Life,* was written in 1870 and brings to life the grim conditions endured by convicts.

If you're interested in the history of the Outback, *Frontier Country: Australia's Outback Heritage* is acclaimed as a definitive work. It encompasses the continent's 40,000 years of evolution. *We of the Never Never,* written in 1908 by Aeneus Gunn, describes her life as the wife of a pioneering homesteader in the Northern Territory. Henry Lawson also captured the spirit of Australian life at the turn of the century in books such as *While the Billy Boils* and *The Country I Come From.* Dame Mary Durack grew up in the Kimberley, daughter of a pioneering pastoralist family. Her many books include *Kings in Grass Castles* and *Sons in the Saddle.*

Ross Terrill's *The Australians* offers a penetrating look at the social fabric of today's Australia. *Sydney,* by Jan Morris, is a brilliant portrait of the contemporary mood, manners, and morals of the city.

Videos

From its early appearance on the world film scene with Charles Tait's 1906 *The Story of the Kelly Gang,* widely held to be the first feature-length moving picture, Australia didn't always hold its own against Hollywood. In the past several decades, however, it has come to reclaim its international stature, with popular and critical successes alike. Looking past the megahit comedy *Crocodile Dundee* (1986), there are a number of great Aussie films to choose from at your local video rental store. *Muriel's Wedding* (1995), *Strictly Ballroom* (1991), *The Man from Snowy River* (1981), and *My Brilliant Career* (1977) are spirited dramas that stand out for their big-heartedness, and Peter Weir's tragic *Gallipoli* (1980) and his eery *Picnic at Hanging Rock* (1975) are in a class of their own. *Oscar and Lucinda* (1997) is a lush adaptation of the Peter Carey novel by the same name, and *Shine* (1996) features an Oscar-winning performance by native son Geoffrey Rush. The computer-animated *Babe* (1995) and sequel *Babe: Pig in the City* (1998) delight and astonish adults and children alike.

ESSENTIAL INFORMATION

The major gateways to Australia include Sydney, Melbourne, Perth, Brisbane, and Cairns. Flights leave from Los Angeles, Honolulu, New York, Toronto, and Vancouver, as well as from London, Frankfurt, and Rome. Depending on your airline and route, you can elect to stop over in Honolulu, Fiji, Tahiti, or Auckland from the U.S.; Singapore or Bangkok from Europe. Nonstop service is available to Sydney from Los Angeles.

BOOKING YOUR FLIGHT

Price is just one factor to consider when booking a flight: frequency of service and even a carrier's safety record are often just as important. Major airlines offer the greatest number of departures. Smaller airlines—including regional and no-frills airlines—usually have a limited number of flights daily. On the other hand, so-called low-cost airlines usually are cheaper, and their fares impose fewer restrictions, such as advance-purchase requirements. Safety-wise, low-cost carriers as a group have a good history—about equal to that of major carriers.

When you book, **look for nonstop flights** and **remember that "direct" flights stop at least once.** Try to **avoid connecting flights,** which require a change of plane. Two airlines may jointly operate a connecting flight, so ask if your airline operates every segment. International flights on a country's flag carrier are almost always nonstop; U.S. airlines often fly direct.

CARRIERS

When flying internationally, you must usually choose between your domestic carrier, the national flag carrier of the country you are visiting, and a foreign carrier from a third country. You may, for example, choose to fly Air New Zealand to Australia. National flag carriers have the greatest number of nonstops. Domestic carriers may have better connections to your home town and serve a greater number of gateway cities. Third-party carriers may have a price advantage.

Now that it's no longer government owned, Australia's Qantas refers to itself as a national carrier, the other one being Ansett, which also operates an international service.

➤ TO AND FROM AUSTRALIA: **Air New Zealand** (☎ 800/262–1234 in the U.S., 800/663–5494 in Canada, 0181/741–2299 in the U.K., 13–2476 in Australia); **British Airways** (☎ 800/AIRWAYS in the U.S. and Canada, 0345/222–111 in the U.K., 09/366–3200 in New Zealand); **Canadian Air International** (☎ 800/426–7000 in the U.S., 800/665–1177 in Canada); **Cathay Pacific** (☎ 0171/747–8888 in the U.K.); **Delta** (☎ 800/221–1212 in the U.S. and Canada, 0800/414767 in the U.K.) to Sydney; **Japan Airlines** (☎ 0171/408–1000 in the U.K.); **Qantas** (☎ 800/227–4500 in the U.S., 0345/747–767 or 0800/747–767 in the U.K.) to Sydney, Melbourne, Brisbane, Cairns, and Perth; **Singapore Airlines** (☎ 0181/747–0007 in the U.K.); **United** (☎ 800/538–2929 in the U.S.) to Sydney and Melbourne.

➤ WITHIN AUSTRALIA: **Ansett** (☎ 800/366–1300 in the U.S. and Canada, 0171/434–4071 in the U.K.) and its regional subsidiaries such as **Kendell** (☎ 13–1300 in Australia) and **Hazelton** (☎ 13–1713), and **Qantas** (☎ 13–1313 in Australia) and its subsidiaries of **Eastern Australia, Southern Australia, Sunstate,** and **Airlink,** are the major domestic airlines. **Air Kangaroo Island** (☎ 13–1301) and **Airlines of South Australia** (☎ 08/8234–3000) cover South Australia.

CHECK-IN & BOARDING

Assuming that not everyone with a ticket will show up, airlines routinely overbook planes. When that happens, airlines ask for volunteers to give up their seats. In return these volunteers usually get a certificate for a free flight and are rebooked on the next flight out. If there are not enough volunteers, the airline must choose who will be denied boarding. The first to get bumped are passengers who checked in late and those flying on discounted tickets, so **get to the gate and check in as early as possible,** especially during peak periods.

Always **bring a government-issued photo ID to the airport.** You may be asked to show it before you are allowed to check in.

CUTTING COSTS

The least-expensive airfares to Australia must usually be purchased in advance and are nonrefundable. It's smart to **call a number of airlines, and when you are quoted a good price, book it on the spot**—the same fare may not be available the next day. Always **check different routings** and look into using different airports. Travel agents, especially low-fare specialists, are helpful.

Discount passes are also available from major airlines. Qantas has a Discover Australia fare, which gives a 30% discount off the normal full economy fare on its domestic routes. These fares can either be purchased before arrival or in Australia.

Qantas' Boomerang Pass is a discount air-travel pass valid for a minimum of two and a maximum of 10 sectors of economy-class air travel. Two price levels apply to Australian cities and those in other Qantas destinations, such as New Zealand and Fiji. Flights to the less-expensive one-zone cities cost $200 per sector. Flights to two-zone locations, such as Perth, Ayers Rock, some of the resort islands, and flights to New Zealand and Fiji, cost $250 per sector. The zone options can be combined to suit your flight plans. The pass must be purchased outside Australia.

Ansett's Visit Australia/New Zealand Pass must also be purchased overseas, and a minimum of two and maximum of 10 sectors also applies. The basic one-zone pass costs $200 and allows travel between any two points in *either* eastern *or* western Australia, as well as sectors *within* New Zealand with the exception of Auckland–Queenstown and Rotorua–Queenstown flights. Two-zone flights that cross zones—for example, flights from eastern to western zones in Australia and flights from Australia to New Zealand—cost $250 per flight. Ansett's See Australia fare cuts up to 30% off normal economy-class fares without restrictions; tickets must be purchased before you leave home or within 30 days of your arrival. The company's flights between Sydney and Auckland, New Zealand, are not included in Visit Australia discounts, only the sector-based passes mentioned above.

When you **fly as a courier** you trade your checked-luggage space for a ticket deeply subsidized by a courier service. There are restrictions on when you can book and how long you can stay.

CONSOLIDATORS

Consolidators are another good source. They buy tickets for scheduled international flights at reduced rates from the airlines, then sell them at prices that beat the best fare available directly from the airlines, usually without restrictions. Sometimes you can even get your money back if you need to return the ticket. Carefully read the fine print detailing penalties for changes and cancellations, and **confirm your consolidator reservation with the airline.**

➤ CONSOLIDATORS: **Cheap Tickets** (☎ 800/377–1000), **Discount Airline Ticket Service** (☎ 800/576–1600). **Unitravel** (☎ 800/325–2222), **Up & Away Travel** (☎ 212/889–2345), **World Travel Network** (☎ 800/409–6753).

ENJOYING THE FLIGHT

All flights to Australia from the U.S. are nonsmoking. Between Europe and Australia, only a few airlines permit smoking, including Alitalia and Olympic Airlines. Since flights from the U.S. to Australia cross the International Date Line, travelers lose a day on the outward leg of their travels and regain it on the journey home. However, crossing the International Date Line does not exacerbate jet lag. Experienced travelers try to minimize jet lag by changing their watches to the time at their destination as soon as they board the flight, and by planning their sleeping and eating around that time as far as flying allows.

For more legroom **request an emergency-aisle seat.** Don't sit in the row in front of the emergency aisle or in front of a bulkhead, where seats may not recline. If you have dietary concerns, **ask for special meals when booking.** These can be vegetarian, low-cholesterol, or kosher, for example. On long flights, try to maintain a normal routine, to help fight jetlag. At night **get some sleep.** By day **eat light meals, drink water** (not alcohol), and **move around the cabin** to stretch your legs.

FLYING TIMES

Flying times from New York to Sydney (via Los Angeles) are about 21 hours; from Chicago to Sydney (via Los Angeles) about 19 hours; from Los Angeles to Sydney (nonstop) about 15 hours; from Los Angeles to Melbourne (via Auckland) around 16 hours; and from London to Sydney or Melbourne about 20½ hours via Singapore or Bangkok.

HOW TO COMPLAIN

If your baggage goes astray or your flight goes awry, complain right away. Most carriers require that you **file a claim immediately.**

➤ AIRLINE COMPLAINTS: U.S. Department of Transportation **Aviation Consumer Protection Division** (✉ C-75, Room 4107, Washington, DC 20590, ☎ 202/366–2220), **Federal Aviation Administration Consumer Hotline** (☎ 800/322–7873).

RECONFIRMING

Airlines usually advise that it is not necessary to reconfirm international flights; however itís advisable to call regardless, usually 72 hours in advance. Particularly if you've changed your flight booking after the com-

mencement of your journey, you should reconfirm all following flights. Domestic flights in Australia require no reconfirmation.

AIRPORTS

The major airports are Brisbane Airport, Cairns International Airport, Sydney Kingsford-Smith Airport, and Melbourne Tullamarine Airport. There are no cost advantages to flying into one city as opposed to another, although there's certainly a greater choice of flights into Sydney, since this is the major international gateway. Car-rental rates from discount operators are similar in all cities, and rates are exactly the same from the the large agencies such as Avis, Budget, and Hertz. As for convenience, Sydney has more hotels in the vicinity of the airport, as well as a greater choice of accommodations, than any other city. Getting into town is easiest from Sydney and Brisbane airports. Melbourne's airport is farther away from the city, and the highways between are prone to rush-hour delays.

➤ AIRPORT INFORMATION: **Brisbane Airport** (☎ 61-3/3860–8600), **Cairns International Airport** (☎ 61-7/4052–3877), **Sydney Kingsford-Smith Airport** (☎ 61-2/9667–9111), **Melbourne Tullamarine Airport** (☎ 61-3/9297–1600).

DUTY-FREE SHOPPING

In Australia, visitors have no limits on what they can purchase; they are subject only to the limitations imposed by the country where they intend to travel with the goods.

BIKE TRAVEL

A network of rural trails for cyclists is being developed, and several books, such as *A Guide to Cycle Touring in the Southern Highlands and Adjacent Coastal Area of N.S.W.,* by Richard D. Kenderine, can help guide you.

BIKES IN FLIGHT

Most airlines accommodate bikes as luggage, provided they are dismantled and boxed. For bike boxes, often free at bike shops, you'll pay about $5 (at least $100 for bike bags) from airlines. International travelers can sometimes substitute a bike for a piece of checked luggage at no charge; otherwise, the cost is about $100. Domestic and Canadian airlines charge $25–$50.

➤ BIKE MAPS: A "Bicycle Touring Australia" map is available from **Breakaway Bicycle** (☎ 1877/829–8899).

➤ BIKE RENTALS: **Bicycle New South Wales** (✉ GPO Box 272, Sydney, NSW 2001, ☎ 02/9283–5200, FAX 02/9283–5246) can advise you on cycling in NSW and also provide contacts for other states.

BOAT & FERRY TRAVEL

Although there are no ferries operating within Queensland, many tour-boat operators make day trips out to the Great Barrier Reef from the mainland. The central points of departure are Townsville, Cairns, and Port Douglas. A ferry service runs between Melbourne and Devonport on Tasmania's north coast; however, this service is mainly used by Australians to transport their vehicles—for visitors, it's far more convenient to simply fly and pick up a rental car. You'll need to book or arrive early during the busy school holiday periods, in particular December–January for Tasmania and July for Queensland.

BUS TRAVEL

Most Australian towns are well served by bus. Route networks of large express companies cover the nation's major highways and link up with regional operators that serve smaller communities. Buses are usually air-conditioned, with toilets and, on some routes, hostesses. Drivers run videos from time to time on overhead monitors. One advantage of bus touring is that drivers also act as guides, sharing their considerable knowledge of the countryside and blending illuminating descriptions of the areas you traverse with anecdotes about local characters.

Following are some travel times and approximate one-way costs at press time: Sydney–Melbourne (15 hours, $60); Sydney–Adelaide (23 hours, $105); Sydney–Brisbane (17 hours, $85); Brisbane–Cairns (25 hours, $145); Melbourne–Adelaide (10 hours, $56); Adelaide–Perth, (35 hours, $229); Adelaide–Alice Springs (20 hours, $140); Alice Springs–Ayers Rock (6 hours, $59).

CLASSES

All bus lines in Australia offer a reasonable standard of comfort. Most have toilets and video systems, and all are required by law to provide seat belts, which passengers are advised to use. Where a choice of bus lines offer different fares on the same route, passengers can generally expect to get what they pay for.

CUTTING COSTS

Greyhound Pioneer Australia operates a national bus network and offers passes that result in considerable savings, especially when purchased overseas. Most can be bought on arrival in Australia, but at a 10%–15% higher price.

The Aussie Pass offers a variety of unlimited travel itineraries over the entire Greyhound Pioneer network for periods ranging from 7 to 21 non-consecutive days, within time limits of 30–60 days. Prices range from $499 to $982 for adults, with 10% discounts applying to children, YHA card holders, and VIP and ISIC Backpacker card holders. Holders of International Student Cards are eligible for a 20% reduction. McCafferty's offers comparable Travel Australia passes, along with a number of regional passes. Tasmanian Wilderness Transport offers the Tassie Wilderness Pass, which is valid for 5, 14, or 30 days. Costs range from $99 to $220. Many passes, some of which include discounts for accommodations and sightseeing, are available in the United States and Canada through ATS Tours and in Canada through Goway Travel.

➤ PASSES: **ATS Tours** (☎ 800/423–2880, FAX 310/643–0032), **Goway Travel** (☎ 800/387–8850).

RESERVATIONS

Travelers are advised to make advance reservations for bus travel, but there are no surcharges for this service. Provided they book in advance, passengers are never off-loaded due to overbooking.

SMOKING

Smoking is not permitted on buses in Australia. The penalty is a fine (and perhaps a sharp crack across the ear from the driver).

➤ BUS INFORMATION: **Greyhound Pioneer Australia** (☎ 13–2030 in Australia). **McCafferty's** (☎ 13–1499).

BUSINESS HOURS

As a rule, business hours in Australia are weekdays 9–5; this applies to post offices as well. In the Northern Territory, hours are most commonly 8:00–4:40 for government departments.

BANKS & OFFICES

Banks are open Monday–Thursday 9:30–4, Friday 9:30–5. In some states a few banks are open on Saturday mornings.

GAS STATIONS

Around urban areas and major highways, many gas stations are open 24 hours. In rural areas, however, gas stations are usually open between 8 AM and 6 PM

MUSEUMS & SIGHTS

In the cities, most museums and major sights are open 7 days, including public holidays. Outside metropolitan areas, opening hours for museums and sights may vary considerably; visitors are advised to check in advance.

SHOPS

Shops are normally open weekdays 8:30–5:30, with late closing at 9 PM on either Thursday or Friday. On Saturday shops are open from 8:30 to between noon and 4. Some stores, particularly those in the tourist areas of major cities, may be open a few hours on Sunday.

CAMERAS & PHOTOGRAPHY

Photographers will discover that the light in Australia is particularly harsh. In the middle of the day in particular, contrast is extreme, with washed-out highlights bleached of color and dense shadows that are beyond the contrast range of film. For these reasons, early morning and evening are generally preferable for taking photographs. For general outdoor photography, a film speed of around 200 ASA is practical.

As for protocol, Aborigines might resent a camera being pointed in their direction; however, they will seldom refuse a request for a photograph if you have already established friendly contact. If in doubt, ask first. There are no restrictions on photographing government buildings in Australia.

EQUIPMENT PRECAUTIONS

Always **keep your film and tape out of the sun.** Dust is also a problem in the Outback, but a camera bag that seals well will help protect equipment and lenses. Otherwise, wrap gear in a large plastic bag and seal or tie the top closed. Carry an extra supply of batteries, and **be prepared to turn on your camera or camcorder** to prove to security personnel that the device is real. Always **ask for hand inspection of film,** which becomes clouded after successive exposures to airport X-ray machines, and **keep videotapes away from metal detectors.**

FILM & DEVELOPING

Film is widely available throughout Australia. All pharmacies sell film, and Kodak and Fuji brands are widely available. A 36-exposure roll costs around $12. In tourist areas, one-hour processing for prints is usually available; otherwise, the standard processing and printing time varies from one to three days. Videotapes can be found at most places that sell film. The cost is around $15 for a two-hour tape.

VIDEOS

Beware of leaving video gear in a vehicle in the hot sun, where temperatures can reach extreme highs. At the beach, take care to protect video cameras from sand and salt spray.

➤ PHOTO HELP: **Kodak Information Center** (☎ 800/242–2424). *Kodak Guide to Shooting Great Travel Pictures,* available in bookstores or from Fodor's Travel Publications (☎ 800/533–6478; $16.50 plus $4 shipping).

CAR RENTAL

Rates in Sydney begin at $24 a day and $168 a week for an economy car with air conditioning, manual transmission, and 100 free kilometers. This does not include tax on car rentals, which is 1.5% in Sydney. Larger agencies such as Avis, Budget, Hertz, and Thrifty are the most likely to have rental desks located at airport terminals. Rates for car hire from larger operators are identical for all the major cities; however, you can expect to pay more if you hire a vehicle in a remote location. Discount operators offer vehicles at about the same rate in major cities. Travelers renting a car in Sydney must purchase mandatory collision insurance, which is included in the price.

Car rental procedures are similar to those of North America and Europe. A similar range of models is available, from luxury vehicles to family-size sedans and people-movers to two-door compacts. Most rental vehicles in Australia are Japanese-designed vehicles. Britz specializes in four-wheel-drive vehicles fitted out as campervans, which are an ideal solution for visitors who plan to travel off the beaten track.

Renters are generally prohibited from driving non-four-wheel-drive rental vehicles on unsealed roads. If you do and you have a collision, you may find that insurance will not cover the damage.

➤ MAJOR AGENCIES: **Alamo** (☎ 800/ 522–9696; 0181/759–6200 in the U.K.), **Avis** (☎ 800/331–1084; 800/ 879–2847 in Canada; 02/9353–9000 in Australia; 09/525–1982 in New Zealand), **Budget** (☎ 800/527–0700; 0144/227–6266 in the U.K.), **Dollar** (☎ 800/800–6000; 0181/897–0811 in the U.K., where it is known as Eurodollar, 02/9223–1444 in Australia), **Hertz** (☎ 800/654–3001; 800/ 263–0600 in Canada; 0181/897–2072 in the U.K.; 02/9669–2444 in Australia; 03/358–6777 in New Zealand), **National InterRent** (☎ 800/227–3876; 0345/222525 in the U.K., where it is known as Europcar InterRent).

CUTTING COSTS

In Australian cities, most airports and train and bus stations are well supplied with tourism literature and even tourist information offices that will help you track down discount car rentals. In other areas, check in the Yellow Pages under "Car Rental." The vehicles offered by these agencies are usually older than those from the major agencies, generally between two and three years old. Also, there are no provisions for one-way rentals; vehicles must be returned to the office where they were hired. To get the best deal, **book through a travel agent who will shop around.**

Do **look into wholesalers,** companies that do not own fleets but rent in bulk from those that do and often offer better rates than traditional car-rental operations. Payment must be made before you leave home.

➤ LOCAL AGENCY: **Britz** (☎ 1800–331–454).

➤ WHOLESALERS: **Auto Europe** (☎ 207/842–2000 or 800/223–5555, FAX 800–235–6321), **Kemwel Holiday Autos** (☎ 914/835–3000 or 800/678–0678, FAX 914/835–5126).

INSURANCE

When driving a rented car you are generally responsible for any damage to or loss of the vehicle as well as for any property damage or personal injury that you may cause. Before you rent see what coverage your personal auto-insurance policy and credit cards already provide.

Although insurance is included with standard rental vehicles in Australia, you are still responsible for an "excess" fee—a maximum amount that you will have to pay if damage occurs. Fines can be incurred for such accidents as a cracked windshield, which is common occurrence on Australian roads. The amount of this "excess" is generally between $500 and $1,000, but you can have this figure reduced by paying a daily fee.

REQUIREMENTS & RESTRICTIONS

In Australia your own driver's license is accepted at some rental companies. An International Driver's Permit is required at others; it's available from the American or Canadian automobile association, and, in the United Kingdom, from the Automobile Association or Royal Automobile

Club. These international permits are universally recognized, and having one in your wallet may save you a problem with the local authorities.

In Australia you must be 21 to rent a car, and rates may be higher if you're under 25. There is no upper age limit for rental.

SURCHARGES

Before you pick up a car in one city and leave it in another **ask about drop-off charges or one-way service fees,** which can be substantial. Note, too, that some rental agencies charge extra if you return the car before the time specified in your contract. To avoid a hefty refueling fee **fill the tank just before you turn in the car,** but be aware that gas stations near the rental outlet may overcharge.

CAR TRAVEL

Driving is easy in Australia, once you adjust to traveling on the left. The catch-phrase is: **Drive left, look right.** "Look right" is the pedestrian's caveat—and a serious one. For Americans, stepping into the street means looking left for oncoming traffic. Do that Down Under and you could be in trouble. Repeat: Drive left, look right.

Speed limits are 60 kilometers per hour (kph) in populated areas, and 100–110 kph on open roads—the equivalent of 37 and 62–68 mph, respectively. Surveillance of speeders and "drink-driving" (the legal limit is a tough .05% blood alcohol level) is thorough and penalties are high. Seat belts are mandatory nationwide for drivers and all passengers. Children must be restrained in a seat appropriate to their size. These can be hired from car-rental agencies.

When planning a driving itinerary, it's vital to **bear in mind the huge distances involved.** Queensland's Brisbane is 1,031 kilometers (640 miles) by road from Sydney, 1,718 kilometers (1,067 miles) from Melbourne, and almost the same distance from Cairns. The journey from Sydney to Alice Springs, the gateway to Ayers Rock, is 2½ hours by jet and a grueling 52 hours by bus. Between major cities, flying is usually advised.

AUTO CLUBS

➤ IN AUSTRALIA: **Australian Automobile Association** (☎ 02/6247–7311).

➤ IN CANADA: **Canadian Automobile Association** (CAA, ☎ 613/247–0117).

➤ IN NEW ZEALAND: **New Zealand Automobile Association** (☎ 09/377–4660).

➤ IN THE U.K.: **Automobile Association** (AA, ☎ 0990/500–600), **Royal Automobile Club** (RAC, ☎ 0990/722–722 for membership; 0345/121–345 for insurance).

➤ IN THE U.S.: **American Automobile Association** (☎ 800/564–6222).

EMERGENCIES

If you have an emergency requiring an ambulance, the fire department, or the police, dial 000. Many major highways now have telephones for breakdown assistance. Otherwise, flag down a passing motorist and ask them to call the nearest motoring service organization for you—most Australian drivers will be happy to assist, particularly in country areas.

➤ CONTACTS: Each state has its own motoring organization that provides assistance for vehicle breakdowns. When you hire a vehicle, you are entitled to assistance from the relevant motoring organization, free of charge. A toll-free, nationwide number (☎ 13–1111) is available for roadside assistance.

GASOLINE

Service stations are generally plentiful, although full service is common only in rural areas. The cost of gasoline ("petrol") varies around the country from about 70¢ per liter in Sydney to about 90¢ per liter in the Outback. American Express, MasterCard, and Visa are accepted at most service stations. Pumps are easy to operate and will be familiar to most drivers from North America and Europe.

ROAD CONDITIONS

Except for some expressways in and around the major cities, the majority of highways are two-lane roads with frequent passing lanes. Roads are usually paved and well maintained, though traffic lanes are narrower than in the United States. Always **take precautions when you drive through the Outback,** however. Road Trains (i.e. truck trains) can get up to 50 yards long, and passing them at that length becomes a matter of great caution, especially on roads in the bush. There are **no speed limits** on the open road in the Northern Territory.

Many Outback roads are unpaved, traffic is very light, and temperatures can be extreme. **Carry plenty of water and always tell someone your itinerary and schedule.** Flash floods from sudden rain showers can occur on low-lying roads. Don't try to outdrive them—**get to higher ground immediately when it rains.**

ROAD MAPS

Road maps are available at most gas stations, although the choice may be limited. For more detailed maps, look in bookstores in the major cities. For travelers who plan extensive road journeys, a comprehensive road atlas—such as the annual, widely available *Explore Australia* atlas published by Viking—is recommended.

RULES OF THE ROAD

Road regulations differ from state to state and even city to city. At designated intersections in Melbourne's Golden Mile (the central business district), you must get into the left lane to make a right-hand turn—watch for the sign RIGHT HAND TURN FROM LEFT LANE ONLY. Traffic circles are widely used at intersections throughout Australia; cars that have already entered the circle have the right-of-way. It's wise to **pick up a copy of the Highway Code** of any state or territory in which you plan to drive from the local automobile club. The Australian Automobile Association has a branch in each state, known as the National Roads and Motorists' Association (NRMA) in New South Wales and Canberra, the Automobile Association in the Northern Territory (AANT), and the Royal Automobile Club (RAC) in all other states. It is affiliated with AAA worldwide and offers reciprocal services to American, Canadian, and British members, including emergency road service and discounts on car rental, accommodations, and other services. Reservations must be made through an NRMA or RAC office.

CHILDREN IN AUSTRALIA

Australia is a wonderful place for children; however, parents should prepare them for several environmental and safety precautions. Be especially vigilant at the beach, where strong waves and currents can quickly overpower a child. Children are also likely to ignore the dangers of excessive exposure to sunlight, so protect their skin with a hat and a sunblock. As for activities, be on the lookout for special children's events at museums, theaters, cinemas, and national parks during school holidays.

FOOD

In Australia, eating out with children is no problem in family restaurants, which cater to children with high chairs and booster seats. This type of restaurant is usually found in suburbs rather than city centers. For more casual eating, coffee shops, delis, bistros, and fast-food eateries, both international chains and Aussie versions such as Hungry Jack's, welcome children.

LODGING

Most hotels in Australia allow children under a certain age to stay in their parents' room at no extra charge, but others charge them as extra adults; be sure to **ask about the cutoff age for children's discounts.** Roll-away beds are usually free, and children under 12 sharing a hotel room with adults either stay free or receive a discount rate. The Hyatt hotels in Sydney, Sanctuary Cove, Coolum Beach, Perth, Melbourne, Canberra, and Adelaide allow children under 18 to stay free when sharing a room with parents. The Hyatt Regency Sanctuary Cove and Hyatt Regency Coolum Beach both have a Camp Hyatt program for children. In general, however, few hotels have separate facilities for children. Exceptions include some of the Great Barrier Reef resorts.

Home hosting provides an ideal opportunity for visitors to stay with a local family, either in town or on a working farm. For information on home and farm stays, home exchange, and apartment rentals, *see* Lodging, *below*.

SIGHTS & ATTRACTIONS

Places that are especially good for children are indicated by a rubber duckie icon in the margin.

SUPPLIES & EQUIPMENT

Department stores and drugstores (called chemists locally) in Australia carry a wide range of baby products such as disposable diapers (ask for napkins or nappies), formula, and baby food.

TRANSPORTATION

If your children are two or older **ask about children's airfares.** As a general rule, infants under two not occupying a seat fly at greatly reduced fares or even for free. When booking **confirm carry-on allowances** if you're traveling with infants. In general, for babies charged 10% of the adult fare, you are allowed one carry-on bag and a collapsible stroller; if the flight is full the stroller may have to be checked or you may be limited to less.

Experts agree that it's a good idea to use safety seats aloft for children weighing less than 40 pounds. Airlines set their own policies: U.S. carriers usually require that the child be ticketed, even if he or she is young enough to ride free, since the seats must be strapped into regular seats. Do **check your airline's policy about using safety seats during takeoff and landing.** And since safety seats are not allowed just everywhere in the plane, get your seat assignments early.

When reserving, **request children's meals or a freestanding bassinet** if you need them. But note that bulkhead seats, where you must sit to use the bassinet, may lack an overhead bin or storage space on the floor.

If you are renting a car don't forget to **arrange for a car seat** when you reserve.

CONSUMER PROTECTION

Whenever shopping or buying travel services, **pay with a major credit card** so you can cancel payment or get reimbursed if there's a problem. If you're doing business with a particular company for the first time, **contact your local Better Business Bureau and the attorney general's offices** in your state and the company's home state, as well. Have any complaints been filed? Finally, if you're buying a package or tour, always **consider travel insurance** that includes default coverage (☞ Insurance, *below*).

➤ BBBs: **Council of Better Business Bureaus** (✉ 4200 Wilson Blvd., Suite 800, Arlington, VA 22203, ☎ 703/276–0100, FAX 703/525–8277).

CUSTOMS & DUTIES

When shopping, **keep receipts** for all purchases. Upon reentering your home country, **be ready to show customs officials what you've bought.** If you feel a duty is incorrect or object to the way your clearance was handled, note the inspector's badge number and ask to see a supervisor. If the problem isn't resolved, write to the appropriate authorities, beginning with the port director at your point of entry.

IN AUSTRALIA

Australia has strict laws prohibiting or restricting the import of weapons and firearms. Anti-drug laws are strictly enforced, and penalties are severe. All animals are subject to quarantine. Most canned or preserved food may be imported, but fresh fruit, vegetables, and all food served on board aircraft coming from other countries is forbidden. All food must be declared on your customs statement. Nonresidents over 18 years of age may bring in 250 cigarettes, or 250 grams of cigars or tobacco, and 1.125 liters of liquor, provided this is carried with them. Other taxable goods to the value of A$400 for adults and A$200 for children may be included in personal baggage duty-free.

Australian Customs Service (Regional Director, ✉ Box 8, Sydney, NSW 2001, ☎ 1300–363–263, FAX 02/9213–4000).

IN CANADA

Canadian residents who have been out of Canada for at least 7 days may bring home C$500 worth of goods duty-free. If you've been away less than 7 days but more than 48 hours, the duty-free allowance drops to C$200; if your trip lasts 24–48 hours, the allowance is C$50. You may not pool allowances with family members. Goods claimed under the C$500 exemption may follow you by mail; those claimed under the lesser exemptions must accompany you. Alcohol and tobacco products may be included in the 7-day and 48-hour exemptions but not in the 24-hour exemption. If you meet the age requirements of the province or territory through which you reenter Canada, you may bring in, duty-free, 1.14 liters (40 imperial ounces) of wine or liquor *or* 24 12-ounce cans or bottles of beer or ale. If you are 16 or older you may bring in, duty-free, 200 cigarettes and 50 cigars. Check ahead of time with Revenue Canada or the Department of Agriculture for policies regarding meat products, seeds, plants, and fruits.

You may send an unlimited number of gifts worth up to C$60 each duty-free to Canada. Label the package UNSOLICITED GIFT—VALUE UNDER $60. Alcohol and tobacco are excluded.

➤ INFORMATION: **Revenue Canada** (✉ 2265 St. Laurent Blvd. S, Ottawa, Ontario K1G 4K3, ☎ 613/993–0534; 800/461–9999 in Canada).

IN NEW ZEALAND

Homeward-bound residents 17 or older may bring back $700 worth of souvenirs and gifts. Your duty-free allowance also includes 4.5 liters of wine or beer; one 1,125-ml bottle of spirits; and either 200 cigarettes, 250 grams of tobacco, 50 cigars, or a combination of the three up to 250 grams. Prohibited items include meat products, seeds, plants, and fruits.

➤ INFORMATION: **New Zealand Customs** (Custom House, ✉ 50 Anzac Ave., Box 29, Auckland, New Zealand, ☎ 09/359–6655, FAX 09/359–6732).

IN THE U.K.

From countries outside the EU, including Australia, you may bring home, duty-free, 200 cigarettes or 50 cigars; 1 liter of spirits or 2 liters of fortified or sparkling wine or liqueurs; 2 liters of still table wine; 60 ml of perfume; 250 ml of toilet water; plus £136 worth of other goods, including gifts and souvenirs. If returning from outside the EU, prohibited items include meat products, seeds, plants, and fruits.

➤ INFORMATION: **HM Customs and Excise** (✉ Dorset House, Stamford St., Bromley Kent BR1 1XX, ☎ 0171/202–4227).

IN THE U.S.

U.S. residents who have been out of the country for at least 48 hours (and who have not used the $400 allowance or any part of it in the past 30 days) may bring home $400 worth of foreign goods duty-free. U.S. residents 21 and older may bring back 1 liter of alcohol duty-free. In addition, regardless of your age, you are allowed 200 cigarettes and 100 non-Cuban cigars. Antiques, which the U.S. Customs Service defines as objects more than 100 years old, enter duty-free, as do original works of art done entirely by hand, including paintings, drawings, and sculptures.

You may also send packages home duty-free: up to $200 worth of goods for personal use, with a limit of one parcel per addressee per day (and no alcohol or tobacco products or perfume worth more than $5); label the package PERSONAL USE and attach a list of its contents and their retail value. Do not label the package UNSOLICITED GIFT or your duty-free exemption will drop to $100. Mailed items do not affect your duty-free allowance on your return.

➤ INFORMATION: **U.S. Customs Service** (inquiries, ✉ 1300 Pennsylvania Ave. NW, Washington, DC 20229, ☎ 202/927–6724; complaints, ✉ Office of Regulations and Rulings, 1300 Pennsylvania Ave. NW, Washington, DC 20229; registration of equipment, ✉ Resource Management, 1300 Pennsylvania Ave. NW, Washington, DC 20229, ☎ 202/927–0540).

DINING

Some Australian restaurants offer a fixed-price dinner, but the majority are à la carte. It's wise to **make a reservation** and **inquire if the restaurant has a liquor license** or is "BYOB" or "BYO" (Bring Your Own Bottle). Some are both BYOB and licensed to sell beer, wine, and liquor.

Down Under, entrée means appetizer and main courses are American entrées—more logical than what we call them in the States, in fact. You'll also encounter the term "silver service," which indicates upscale dining. "Bistro" generally refers to a relatively inexpensive place. French fries are called chips; if you want ketchup, ask for tomato sauce.

All capital cities have a well established café culture, which means that you can always find somewhere to sit down and eat at lunchtime in metropolitan areas. Try to dine outside the peak hours between 12:30 and 2, when many office workers are doing the same. In rural areas most pubs serve lunch and dinner.

MEALTIMES

Breakfast is usually served between 7 and 10, lunch 11:30–2:30, and dinner service begins around 6:30. In the cities, a variety of dining options are available at all hours; however, the choices are far more restricted in the countryside.

RESERVATIONS & DRESS

Reservations are always a good idea: we mention them only when they're essential or are not accepted. Book as far ahead as you can, and reconfirm as soon as you arrive. We mention dress only when men are required to wear a jacket or a jacket and tie.

DISABILITIES & ACCESSIBILITY

The Australian Council for Rehabilitation of the Disabled is one source of information on facilities. However, since provisions vary from state to state, for additional information contact the ACROD offices in the states you plan to visit. The National Roads and Motorists Association (NRMA) publishes the $10 *Accom-modation Directory,* indicating which properties have independent wheelchair access and which provide wheelchair access with assistance. Another source of information is the "Disabled Travellers Guide to Australia, Accessible Motels and Hotels" available for about $30 including postage from the Council of Disabled Motorists.

➤ LOCAL RESOURCES: The **Australian Council for Rehabilitation of the Disabled** (⌧ ACROD, 33 Thesiger Ct., Deakin, ACT 2605, ☎ 02/6282–4333; ☎ 02/6282–4333 in Australian Capital Territory; ☎ 02/9743–2699 in New South Wales; ☎ 08/8945–2270 in the Northern Territory; ☎ 07/3366–4366 in Queensland; ☎ 08/8244–5529 in South Australia; ☎ 03/6223–6086 in Tasmania; ☎ 03/9362–0800 in Victoria; ☎ 08/9221–9066 in Western Australia). **Council of Disabled Motorists** (⌧ 2A Station St., Coburg, VIC 3058, ☎ 03/9386–0413). **National Roads and Motorists Association (NRMA)** (⌧ 151 Clarence St., Sydney, NSW 2000, ☎ 13–2132).

LODGING

The major hotel chains (such as Regent, Sheraton, InterContinental, Ramada, Hilton, Holiday Inn, and Hyatt) provide several rooms with disabled facilities in all of their properties. The National Roads and Motorists Association (NRMA) and the Council of Disabled Motorists (☞ *above*) are also good sources of lodging information.

When discussing accessibility with an operator or reservations agent **ask hard questions.** Are there any stairs, inside *or* out? Are there grab bars next to the toilet *and* in the shower/tub? How wide is the doorway to the room? To the bathroom? For the most extensive facilities meeting the latest legal specifications **opt for newer accommodations.**

TRANSPORTATION

Major airlines are generally accustomed to accommodating passengers with disabilities. In addition to making arrangements for wheelchair-using passengers, both Qantas and Ansett Airlines accommodate trained dogs accompanying sight- and hearing-impaired passengers. On Air New Zealand, wheelchairs for in-flight mobility are standard equipment; seat-belt extensions, quadriplegic harnesses, and padded leg rests are also available. Ask for the company's brochure "Air Travel for People with Disabilities."

As for road transportation, only Budget offers cars fitted with hand controls, but supplies are limited. Hertz will fit hand-held controls onto standard cars in some cities. Wheelchair-accessible taxis are also available in most state capitals.

Passengers on mainline passenger trains in Australia can request collapsible wheelchairs to negotiate narrow interior corridors. However, compact toilet areas and platform access problems make long-distance train travel difficult. Both Countrylink, the New South Wales state rail company, and V/Line (Victoria) issue brochures detailing assistance available on metropolitan, country, and interstate trains. Countrylink's (New South Wales) XPLORER and XPT trains have specially designed wheelchair-access toilets, and ramps for boarding and disembarking are provided.

➤ AIRLINES: **Air New Zealand** (☎ 202/514–0301; 800/514–0301; 202/ 514–0301 TTY; 800/514–0301 TTY), **Quantas** (☎ 202/366–4648).

➤ CAR RENTAL: **Budget** (☎ 800/527– 0700 in the U.S., 0800/181181 in the U.K.), **Hertz** (☎ 800/654–3001, 800/ 263–0600 in Canada, 0345/555888 in the U.K., 03/9222–2523 in Australia, 03/358–6777 in New Zealand).

➤ TAXIS: **Adelaide** (☎ 08/8211– 8888), **Brisbane** (☎ 07/3391–0191), **Darwin** (☎ 08/8981–8777), **Melbourne** (☎ 03/9345–3455 or 13– 2227), **Perth** (☎ 08/9333–3377), **Sydney** (☎ 02/9332–8888).

➤ TRAINS: **Countrylink** (13–1500 Sydney metropolitan and 13–2232 for NSW country and interstate). **V/Line** (03/9619–2189 in Melbourne).

➤ COMPLAINTS: **Aviation Consumer Protection Division** (☞ Air Travel, *above*) for airline-related problems, **Disability Rights Section** (✉ U.S. Department of Justice, Civil Rights Division, Box 66738, Washington, DC 20035–6738, ☎ 202/514–0301; 800/514–0301; 202/514–0301 TTY; 800/514–0301 TTY, FAX 202/307– 1198) for general complaints, **Civil Rights Office** (✉ U.S. Department of Transportation, Departmental Office of Civil Rights, S-30, 400 7th St. SW, Room 10215, Washington, DC 20590, ☎ 202/366–4648, FAX 202/ 366–9371) for problems with surface transportation.

TRAVEL AGENCIES

In the United States, although the Americans with Disabilities Act requires that travel firms serve the needs of all travelers, some agencies specialize in working with people with disabilities.

➤ TRAVELERS WITH MOBILITY PROBLEMS: **Access Adventures** (✉ 206 Chestnut Ridge Rd., Rochester, NY 14624, ☎ 716/889–9096), run by a former physical-rehabilitation counselor; **CareVacations** (✉ 5-5110 50th Ave., Leduc, Alberta T9E 6V4, ☎ 780/986–6404 or 780/986–8332) has group tours and is especially helpful with cruise vacations; **Flying Wheels Travel** (✉ 143 W. Bridge St., Box 382, Owatonna, MN 55060, ☎ 507/ 451–5005 or 800/535–6790, FAX 507/ 451–1685); **Hinsdale Travel Service** (✉ 201 E. Ogden Ave., Suite 100, Hinsdale, IL 60521, ☎ 630/325– 1335).

DISCOUNTS & DEALS

Be a smart shopper and **compare all your options** before making decisions. A plane ticket bought with a promotional coupon from travel clubs, coupon books, and direct-mail offers may not be cheaper than the least expensive fare from a discount ticket agency. And always keep in mind that what you get is just as important as what you save.

DISCOUNT RESERVATIONS

To save money **look into discount-reservations services** with toll-free numbers, which use their buying power to get a better price on hotels, airline tickets, even car rentals. When booking a room, always **call the hotel's local toll-free number** (if one is available) rather than the central reservations number—you'll often get a better price. Always ask about special packages or corporate rates.

When shopping for the best deal on hotels and car rentals **look for guaranteed exchange rates,** which protect you against a falling dollar. With your rate locked in, you won't pay more, even if the price goes up in the local currency.

➤ AIRLINE TICKETS: ☎ **800/FLY–4–LESS.**

➤ HOTEL ROOMS: **Steigenberger Reservation Service** (☎ 800/223–5652), **Travel Interlink** (☎ 800/888–5898), **VacationLand** (☎ 800/245–0050).

PACKAGE DEALS

Don't confuse packages and guided tours. When you buy a package, you travel on your own, just as though you had planned the trip yourself. Fly/drive packages, which combine airfare and car rental, are often a good deal.

ELECTRICITY

To use your U.S.-purchased electric-powered equipment, **bring a converter and adapter.** The electrical current in Australia is 240 volts, 50 cycles alternating current (AC); wall outlets take slanted three-prong plugs (but not the U.K. three-prong) and plugs with two flat prongs set in a V.

If your appliances are dual-voltage, you'll need only an adapter. Don't use 110-volt outlets, marked FOR SHAVERS ONLY, for high-wattage appliances such as blow-dryers. Most laptops operate equally well on 110 and 220 volts and so require only an adapter.

EMBASSIES AND CONSULATES

➤ CANADA: **Canadian Embassy** (✉ Level 5, Quay West 111, Harrington St., Sydney, ☎ 61/2364–3050).

➤ NEW ZEALAND: **New Zealand High Commission** (✉ Commonwealth Ave., Canberra, ☎ 61/6270–4211), **Consulate General** (✉ Watkins Place Building, 288 Edward St., Brisbane, ☎ 61/7221–9933), **Consulate General** (✉ 60 Albert Rd., South Melbourne, ☎ 61/39696–0501).

➤ UNITED KINGDOM: **British High Commission, Consular Section** (✉ SAP House, Akuna St., Canberra City 2601, ☎ 1902 941 555), **Consulate General** (✉ Level 26, Waterfront Place, 1 Eagle St., Brisbane, ☎ 07/3236–2575), **Consulate General** (✉ 17th Floor, 90 Collins St., Melbourne, ☎ 03/9650–3699), **Consulate General** (✉ Level 26, Allendale Sq., 77 St Georges Terrace, Perth, ☎ 08/9221–5400), **Consulate General** (✉ Level 16, The Gateway, 1 Macquarie Place, Sydney Cove, ☎ 02/9247–7521), **Consulate General** (✉ Level 22, Grenfell Centre, 25 Grenfell St., Adelaide, ☎ 08/8212–7280), **Honouary Consul** (✉ Trust Bank Tasmania, 39 Murray St., Hobart, 03/6230–3647).

➤ UNITED STATES: **U.S. Embassy** (✉ Moonah Place, Yaralumla, ☎ 02/6214–5600), **Consulate General** (✉ MLC Centre, Level 59, 19–29 Martin Place, Sydney, ☎ 02/9373–9200), **Consulate General** (✉ Level 6, 553 St. Kilda Rd., Melbourne, ☎ 03/9526–5900), **Consulate General** (✉ 16 St. George's Terrace, 13th Floor, Perth, ☎ 08/9231–9400).

EMERGENCIES

Dial ☎ 000 for fire, police, or ambulance services.

➤ CONTACTS: In Sydney, you can make nonemergency police inquiries through the **Sydney Police Centre** (☎ 02/9281–0000). On the Great Barrier Reef islands, emergencies are handled by the front desk of the resort on each island. Each resort can summon aerial ambulances or doctors.

GAY & LESBIAN TRAVEL

Politically and socially, Australia is one of the gay-friendliest countries in the world, ranking right up there with the Netherlands, Denmark, and Canada. Queer tourism associations are well established and have plenty to offer lesbian and gay tourists.

Australia is famous for its many festivals and parties, several of which are gay-oriented. In March, more than 500,000 onlookers attend the Sydney Gay and Lesbian Mardi Gras. Sydney is the country's leading lesbian and gay destination, with Melbourne not far behind. Midsumma is Melbourne's queer festival, with parties and events running from January through early February. Most other Australian cities and resort areas, especially on the east and southeast coasts, are fairly tolerant. In the west, Perth has a relatively small community, but there still is plenty going on. The one part of the country still rather closed-minded about queer life is Tasmania; however, the island still has a number of gay guest houses and B&Bs. Darwin and the Outback are also areas where same-sex traveling companions might want to exercise discretion.

There are several publications detailing gay and lesbian activities available. You'll find plenty of information on nightlife, travel, and queer life in *Campaign,* a monthly magazine on gay Australia. Gay Maps Australia provides maps of gay attractions and businesses in Sydney, Brisbane, and Melbourne. Some newspapers and magazines are also available at lesbian and gay bookstores in North America and the United Kingdom. Additionally, most major cities—including Sydney, Brisbane, Melbourne, Perth, and Adelaide—publish queer newspapers and/or have gay and lesbian business directories.

➤ GAY- AND LESBIAN-FRIENDLY TRAVEL AGENCIES: **Different Roads Travel** (✉ 8383 Wilshire Blvd., Suite 902, Beverly Hills, CA 90211, ☎ 323/651–5557 or 800/429–8747, FAX 323/651–3678); **Kennedy Travel** (✉ 314 Jericho Turnpike, Floral Park, NY 11001, ☎ 516/352–4888 or 800/237–7433, FAX 516/354–8849); **Now Voyager** (✉ 4406 18th St., San Francisco, CA 94114, ☎ 415/626–1169 or 800/255–6951, FAX 415/626–8626); **Skylink Travel and Tour** (✉ 1006 Mendocino Ave., Santa Rosa, CA 95401, ☎ 707/546–9888 or 800/225–5759, FAX 707/546–9891), which serves lesbian travelers; **Yellowbrick Road** (✉ 1500 W. Balmoral Ave., Chicago, IL 60640, ☎ 773/561–1800 or 800/642–2488, FAX 773/561–4497).

➤ LOCAL AGENCIES: **Australian Gay and Lesbian Tourism Association** (✉ Box 2174, Fitzroy BC, Victoria, 3065, ☎ 0411/22–0617).

➤ PUBLICATIONS: *Campaign* (☎ 02/9332–3620, FAX 02/9361–5962), **Gay Maps Australia** (✉ Box 1401, Bondi Junction, NSW 2022, ☎ 02/9369–2738).

HEALTH

In general, hygiene standards in Australia are high and well monitored, so **don't worry about drinking the water or eating fresh produce in the major cities.** The primary health hazard is sunburn or sunstroke: Australians suffer the world's highest incidences of skin cancer from overdoses of sun. Even people who are not normally bothered by strong sun should cover up with a long-sleeve shirt, a hat, and long pants or a beach wrap. Keep in mind that at higher altitudes you will burn more easily. **Apply sunscreen liberally** before you go out—even for a half hour—and wear a visored cap and sunglasses.

You are also advised to protect yourself from mosquito bites during the summer months (particularly in the north of the continent) by applying a reliable insect repellent. Although Australia is free of malaria, several cases of Ross River fever (dengue fever), a mosquito-transmitted virus, were reported recently in northern Queensland.

Dehydration is a serious danger that can be easily avoided, so be sure to carry water and drink often. Above all, **limit the amount of time you spend in the sun** for the first few days until you are acclimatized, and always avoid sunbathing in the middle of the day.

You may take a four weeks' supply of prescribed medication into Australia (more with a doctor's certificate).

DIVERS' ALERT

Do not fly within 24 hours of scuba diving.

FOOD & DRINK

In Australia the major health risk is traveler's diarrhea, caused by eating contaminated fruit or vegetables or drinking contaminated water. So **outside the major cities, watch what you eat and drink.** Stay away from ice, uncooked food, and unpasteurized milk and milk products, and **drink only bottled water** or water that has been boiled for at least 20 minutes, even when you're brushing your teeth. Mild cases may respond to Imodium (known generically as loperamide) or Pepto-Bismol (not as strong), both of which can be purchased over the counter; paregoric is another antidiarrheal agent. Drink plenty of purified water or tea—chamomile is a good folk remedy. In severe cases, rehydrate yourself with a salt-sugar solution (½ teaspoon salt and 4 tablespoons sugar per quart of water).

MEDICAL PLANS

No one plans to get sick while traveling, but it happens, so **consider signing up with a medical-assistance company.** Members get doctor referrals, emergency evacuation or repatriation, hot lines for medical consultation, cash for emergencies, and other assistance.

➤ MEDICAL-ASSISTANCE COMPANIES: **International SOS Assistance** (✉ 8 Neshaminy Interplex, Suite 207, Trevose, PA 19053, ☎ 215/245–4707 or 800/523–6586, 𝔽𝔸𝕏 215/244–9617; ✉ 12 Chemin Riantbosson, 1217 Meyrin 1, Geneva, Switzerland, ☎ 4122/785–6464, 𝔽𝔸𝕏 4122/785–6424; ✉ 331 N. Bridge Rd., 17-00, Odeon Towers, Singapore 188720, ☎ 65/338–7800, 𝔽𝔸𝕏 65/338–7611).

➤ HEALTH WARNINGS: **National Centers for Disease Control** (CDC, National Center for Infectious Diseases, Division of Quarantine, Traveler's Health Section, ✉ 1600 Clifton Rd. NE, M/S E-03, Atlanta, GA 30333, ☎ 888/232–3228, 𝔽𝔸𝕏 888/232–3299).

HOLIDAYS

New Year's Day, January 1; **Australia Day,** January 26; **Canberra Day,** March 20, 2000, March 19, 2001; **Good Friday,** April 21, 2000, April 13, 2001; **Easter,** April 23, 2000, April 15, 2001; **Easter Monday,** April 24, 2000, April 16, 2001; **ANZAC Day,** April 25; **Christmas,** December 25; **Boxing Day,** December 26.

INSURANCE

The most useful travel insurance plan is a comprehensive policy that includes coverage for trip cancellation and interruption, default, trip delay, and medical expenses (with a waiver for preexisting conditions).

Without insurance you will lose all or most of your money if you cancel your trip, regardless of the reason. Default insurance covers you if your tour operator, airline, or cruise line goes out of business. Trip-delay covers expenses that arise because of bad weather or mechanical delays. Study the fine print when comparing policies.

If you're traveling internationally, a key component of travel insurance is coverage for medical bills incurred if you get sick on the road. Such expenses are not generally covered by Medicare or private policies. U.K. residents can buy a travel-insurance policy valid for most vacations taken during the year in which it's purchased (but check pre-existing-condition coverage). British citizens need extra medical coverage when traveling abroad.

Always **buy travel policies directly from the insurance company**; if you buy it from a cruise line, airline, or tour operator that goes out of business you probably will not be covered for the agency or operator's default, a major risk. Before you make any purchase **review your existing health and home-owner's policies** to find what they cover away from home.

➤ TRAVEL INSURERS: In the U.S. **Access America** (✉ 6600 W. Broad St., Richmond, VA 23230, ☎ 804/285–3300 or 800/284–8300), **Travel Guard International** (✉ 1145 Clark St., Stevens Point, WI 54481, ☎ 715/345–0505 or 800/826–1300). In Canada **Voyager Insurance** (✉ 44 Peel Center Dr., Brampton, Ontario L6T 4M8, ☎ 905/791–8700; 800/668–4342 in Canada).

➤ INSURANCE INFORMATION: In the U.K. the **Association of British Insurers** (✉ 51–55 Gresham St., London EC2V 7HQ, ☎ 0171/600–3333, 𝔽𝔸𝕏 0171/696–8999). In Australia the **Insurance Council of Australia** (☎ 03/9614–1077, 𝔽𝔸𝕏 03/9614–7924).

LANGUAGE

To an outsider's ear, Australian English can be mystifying. Not only is the accent thick and slightly slurred, but Australians have developed a vibrant vernacular quite distinct from that of any other English-speaking country. You can soon learn the idiom and how to speak "strine"—as Aussies (who also call themselves "Ozzies") pronounce "Australian"—with a copy of Danielle Martin's *Australians Say G'Day,* which comes with a cassette tape recording to help you interpret the book's dialogues. Other useful guides to the intricacies of Australian terminology are *Australian Slang,* by Lenie Johansen, and *The Best of Aussie Slang,* by John Blackman. All of these books are available in Aussie bookstores.

LODGING

The lodgings we list are the cream of the crop in each price category. We always list the facilities that are available—but we don't specify whether they cost extra: when pricing accommodations, always ask what's included and what costs extra. Properties indicated by an ✕🖾 are lodging establishments whose restaurant warrants a special trip. Except for designated bed-and-breakfasts and farm stays, the majority of prices listed by hotels are for room only, although resorts in remote areas may offer American Plan (three meals included) or Modified American Plan (two meals). Surcharges sometimes apply on weekends, long weekends, and during holiday seasons.

Assume that hotels operate on the **European Plan** (EP, with no meals) unless we specify that they use the **Continental Plan** (CP, with a Continental breakfast daily), **Modified American Plan** (MAP, with breakfast and dinner daily), or are **all-inclusive** (including all meals and most activities).

APARTMENT & VILLA RENTALS

If you want a home base that's roomy enough for a family and comes with cooking facilities **consider a furnished rental.** These can save you money, especially if you're traveling with a group. Home-exchange directories sometimes list rentals as well as exchanges.

➤ INTERNATIONAL AGENTS: **Europa-Let/Tropical Inn-Let** (✉ 92 N. Main St., Ashland, OR 97520, ☎ 541/482–5806 or 800/462–4486, ⅏ 541/482–0660), **Rent-a-Home International** (✉ 7200 34th Ave. NW, Seattle, WA 98117, ☎ 206/789–9377, ⅏ 206/789–9379).

CAMPING

Think twice before camping outside of designated campgrounds, particularly in the Outback, where such unexpected, and potentially fatal, dangers as flash floods and bushfires can catch you by surprise. A four-wheel-drive vehicle may be necessary for a safari into the bush. Once there it is equally important to know what to look out for. Be sure to speak with the nearest park rangers before setting out.

The National Roads and Motorists Association (NRMA) puts out the booklet "Outback Motoring" (free to members, $4 for nonmembers). Another NRMA publication, "Caravan and Camping Directory," lists campgrounds and costs $10 for nonmembers.

➤ CONTACT: **NRMA** (✉ 151 Clarence St., Sydney, NSW 2000, ☎ 13–2132).

HOME EXCHANGES

If you would like to exchange your home for someone else's **join a home-exchange organization,** which will send you its updated listings of available exchanges for a year and will include your own listing in at least one of them. It's up to you to make specific arrangements.

➤ EXCHANGE CLUBS: **HomeLink International** (✉ Box 650, Key West, FL 33041, ☎ 305/294–7766 or 800/638–3841, ⅏ 305/294–1448; $88 per year), **Intervac U.S.** (✉ Box 590504, San Francisco, CA 94159, ☎ 800/756–4663, ⅏ 415/435–7440; $83 per year).

HOME & FARM STAYS

Home and farm stays, which are very popular with visitors to Australia, offer not only comfortable accommodations but a chance to get to know the lands and their people. Most operate on a bed-and-breakfast basis, though some also offer an evening meal. Farm accommodations vary from modest shearers' cabins to elegant homesteads. Guests can join in farm activities or explore the countryside. Some hosts offer day trips, as well as horseback riding, hiking, and fishing. For two people, the cost varies from $100–$250 per night, including all meals and some or all farm activities. Home stays, the urban equivalent of farm stays, are less expensive.

U.S. agencies that provide information and make reservations include Australian Home Accommodation, Australian Farm Host and Farm Holidays, Pacific Destination Center, Victoria Host Farms, and Bed & Breakfast Australia. Pacific Destination Center also represents Grand Country Estates and Houseguest, which offer B&B accommodations in private homes. A number of Queensland sheep and cattle stations offering farm and country vacations have banded together as the Queensland Host Farm Association. For information and reservations, contact the Royal Automobile Club of Queensland (RACQ) Travel Service.

➤ RESERVATION SERVICES: **Australian Home Accommodation,** represented by ATS/Sprint (☎ 800/423–2880), **Australian Farm Host and Farm Holidays,** represented by ATS/Sprint, SO/PAC (☎ 800/551–2012), **Pacific Destination Center** (☎ 800/227–5317), **Royal Automobile Club of Queensland** (RACQ) Travel Service (✉ Box 537, Fortitude Valley, QLD 4006, ☎ 07/3361–2390, FAX 07/3257–1504).

HOSTELS

No matter what your age you can **save on lodging costs by staying at hostels.** In some 5,000 locations in more than 70 countries, Hostelling International (HI), the umbrella group for a number of national youth-hostel associations, offers single-sex, dorm-style beds and, at many hostels, couples rooms and family accommodations. Membership in any HI national hostel association, open to travelers of all ages, allows you to stay in HI-affiliated hostels at member rates (one-year membership is about $25 for adults; hostels run about $10–$25 per night). Members

also have priority if the hostel is full; they're also eligible for discounts around the world, even on rail and bus travel in some countries.

➤ ORGANIZATIONS: **Australian Youth Hostel Association** (✉ 10 Mallett St., Camperdown, NSW 2050, ☎ 02/9565–1699, FAX 02/9565–1325), **Hostelling International—American Youth Hostels** (✉ 733 15th St. NW, Suite 840, Washington, DC 20005, ☎ 202/783–6161, FAX 202/783–6171), **Hostelling International—Canada** (✉ 400–205 Catherine St., Ottawa, Ontario K2P 1C3, ☎ 613/237–7884, FAX 613/237–7868), **Youth Hostel Association of England and Wales** (✉ Trevelyan House, 8 St. Stephen's Hill, St. Albans, Hertfordshire AL1 2DY, ☎ 01727/855215 or 01727/845047, FAX 01727/844126), **Youth Hostels Association of New Zealand** (✉ Box 436, Christchurch, New Zealand, ☎ 03/379–9970, FAX 03/365–4476). Membership in the U.S. $25, in Canada C$26.75, in the U.K. £9.30, in Australia $44, in New Zealand $24.

HOTELS & MOTELS

All hotels listed have private bath unless otherwise noted. Hotel and motel rooms generally have private bathrooms with a combined shower/tub—called "en suites"—although some bed-and-breakfast hotels and hostels require guests to share bathrooms. Tea- and coffeemakers are a fixture in almost every type of accommodation, refrigerators are found in virtually all motels, and stocked minibars are the norm in deluxe hotels. You can expect a swimming pool, health club, tennis courts, and spas in many resort hotels, some of which also have their own golf courses. Motel chains, such as Flag International, are usually reliable and much less expensive than hotels. You often can check into a motel without booking ahead, but reservations are required for weekends and holidays. Reservations for many Great Barrier Reef and beach resorts can be made in the United States through such groups as Utell International.

➤ TOLL-FREE NUMBERS: **Adam's Mark** (☎ 800/444/2326), **Baymont Inns** (☎ 800/428–3438), **Best Western** (☎ 800/

528–1234), **Choice** (☎ 800/221–2222), **Clarion** (☎ 800/252–7466), **Colony** (☎ 800/777–1700), **Comfort** (☎ 800/228–5150), **Conrad International Hotels and Hilton International** (☎ 800/445–8667), **Days Inn** (☎ 800/325–2525), **Doubletree** (☎ 800/222–8733), **Embassy Suites** (☎ 800/362–2779), **Fairfield Inn** (☎ 800/228–2800), **Federal Hotels & Resorts and P & O Resorts** (☎ 800/225–9849), **Flag International Hotels & Resorts** (☎ 800/624–3524), **Forte** (☎ 800/225–5843), **Four Seasons** (☎ 800/332–3442), **Hilton** (☎ 800/445–8667), **Holiday Inn** (☎ 800/465–4329), **Howard Johnson** (☎ 800/654–4656), **Hyatt Hotels & Resorts** (☎ 800/233–1234), **Inter-Continental** (☎ 800/327–0200), **La Quinta** (☎ 800/531–5900), **Marriott** (☎ 800/228–9290), **Le Meridien** (☎ 800/543–4300), **Nikko Hotels International** (☎ 800/645–5687), **Omni** (☎ 800/843–6664), **Pan Pacific Hotels Corporation** (☎ 800/937–1515), **Quality Inn** (☎ 800/228–5151), **Radisson** (☎ 800/333–3333), **Ramada** (☎ 800/228–2828), **Red Lion Hotels** (☎ 800/RED–LION), **Regent International** (☎ 800/545–4000), **Renaissance Hotels & Resorts** (☎ 800/468–3571), **Ritz-Carlton** (☎ 800/341–3333 in the U.S., 800/341–8565 in Canada), **Sheraton** (☎ 800/325–3535), **Sleep Inn** (☎ 800/221–2222), **Southern Pacific Hotel Corporation** (☎ 800/835–7742), **Utell International** (☎ 800/44–UTELL), **Westin Hotels & Resorts** (☎ 800/228–3000), **Wyndham Hotels & Resorts** (☎ 800/822-4200).

MAIL & SHIPPING

POSTAL RATES

Mail service in Australia is normally efficient. Postage rates are 45¢ for domestic letters, $1.05 per 20-gram (28.35 grams = 1 ounce) airmail letter, and 95¢ for airmail postcards to North America; the same airmail services cost $1.20 and $1 to the United Kingdom. Overseas fax service costs around $10 for the first page plus $4 for each additional page. You can send printed material by Economy Air, which travels via surface mail within Australia but by airmail across the Pacific, at a cost of $19 for up to a kilogram (a little more than 2 pounds).

RECEIVING MAIL

You can receive mail care of General Delivery (known as Post Restante in Australia) at the General Post Office or any branch post office; the service is free and mail is held one month. It is advisable to know the **correct Australian postcode (zip code)** of the area you are visiting; these are available from the Australian Consulate General. The zip code will allow you to receive mail care of Poste Restante (General Delivery) at the area's General Post Office. You will need identification to pick up mail. Alternatively, American Express offers free mail collection at its main city offices for its cardholders.

➤ RESOURCES: **Australian Consulate General** (☎ 713/629–9131 Houston; 213/469–4300 Los Angeles; 212/245–4000 New York; 415/362–6160 San Francisco; 202/797–3222 Washington; 613/236–0841 Ottawa; 416/323–1155 Toronto; 604/684–1177 Vancouver), **American Express** (☎ 800/528–4800; 212/477–5700 in the NY metropolitan area).

MONEY MATTERS

Prices for goods and services can be volatile. Still, those cited below may be used as an approximate guide, since variation should rarely exceed 10%.

Despite the growing perception in North America that Australia is an expensive destination, it has become more price-competitive. Although prices appear high at Sydney's five-star hotels, virtually all offer discounts of up to 30% on published "rack" rates. There are also plenty of cheaper dining and lodging alternatives. Medium-priced hotels and hotel-apartments abound in city centers and inner suburbs. For example, double-occupancy rates at the luxury Regent of Sydney start about $300 a night, whereas the tariff at Victoria Court, a bed-and-breakfast hotel classified as a landmark by the National Trust, is in the region of $135, including breakfast. Melbourne and Sydney tend to be more expensive than other cities.

Fares on international flights are usually lower between June and September, and many hotels offer lower tariffs in their off-peak season: April–September in the south, November–March in the Top End. Another way to save money is to buy passes, available for everything from hotels and interstate transportation to local bus and train services (☞ Bus Travel, *above*, and Train Travel, *below*).

The following are sample costs in Australia at press time:

Cup of coffee $2–$3; glass of beer in a bar $2.50–$6; take-out ham sandwich or meat pie $3.50–$6; hamburger in a café $4–$9; room-service sandwich in a hotel $12–$15; a 2-kilometer (1¼-mile) taxi ride $7.

Prices throughout this guide are given for adults. Substantially reduced fees are almost always available for children, students, and senior citizens. For information on taxes, *see* Taxes, *below*.

CREDIT CARDS

Should you use a credit card or a debit card when traveling? Both have benefits. A credit card allows you to delay payment and gives you certain rights as a consumer (☞ Consumer Protection, *above*). A debit card, also known as a check card, deducts funds directly from your checking account and helps you stay within your budget. When you want to rent a car, though, you may still need an old-fashioned credit card. Although you can always *pay* for your car with a debit card, some agencies will not allow you to *reserve* a car with a debit card.

Otherwise, the two types of plastic are virtually the same. Both will get you cash advances at ATMs worldwide if your card is properly programmed with your personal identification number (PIN). (For use in Australia, your PIN must be four digits long.) Both offer excellent, wholesale exchange rates. And both protect you against unauthorized use if the card is lost or stolen. Your liability is limited to $50, as long as you report the card missing.

Throughout this guide, the following abbreviations are used: **AE,** American Express; **DC,** Diner's Club; **MC,** Master Card; and **V,** Visa.

CURRENCY

All prices listed in this guide are quoted in Australian dollars. Australia's currency operates on a decimal system, with the dollar (A$) as the basic unit and 100 cents (¢) equaling $1. Bills come in $100, $50, $20, $10, and $5 denominations; which are differentiated by color and size. Coins are minted in $2, $1, 50¢, 20¢, 10¢, and 5¢ denominations.

CURRENCY EXCHANGE

For the most favorable rates, **change money through banks.** Although ATM transaction fees may be higher abroad than at home, ATM rates are excellent because they are based on wholesale rates offered only by major banks. You won't do as well at exchange booths in airports or rail and bus stations, in hotels, in restaurants, or in stores. To avoid lines at airport exchange booths **get a bit of local currency before you leave home.**

At press time, the exchange rate was about A$1.60 to the U.S. dollar, $1.04 to the Canadian dollar, $2.70 to the pound sterling, and 84¢ to the New Zealand dollar.

➤ EXCHANGE SERVICES: **International Currency Express** (☎ 888/842–0880 on East Coast; 888/278–6628 on West Coast), **Thomas Cook Currency Services** (☎ 800/287–7362 for telephone orders and retail locations).

TRAVELER'S CHECKS

Do you need traveler's checks? It depends on where you're headed. If you're going to rural areas and small towns, go with cash; traveler's checks are best used in cities. Lost or stolen checks can usually be replaced within 24 hours. To ensure a speedy refund, buy your own traveler's checks— don't let someone else pay for them: irregularities like this can cause delays. The person who bought the checks should make the call to request a refund.

OUTDOORS & SPORTS

BOATING & SAILING

➤ CONTACT: **Australian Yachting Federation** (✉ Locked Bag 806, Milsons Point, NSW 2061, ☎ 02/9922–4333, FAX 02/9923–2883).

DIVING

➤ CONTACT: **Australian Underwater Federation** (✉ 42 Toyer Ave., Sans Souci, NSW 2219, ☎ 02/9259–6496).

GOLF

Generally speaking, clubs can be rented, but you'll need your own shoes. In Australia, greens fees at public courses are generally under $20 for 18 holes.

➤ CONTACTS: **Classic Australian Golf Tours** (☎ 800/426–3610), **ITC Golf Tours** (☎ 800/257–4981), and **Swain Australian Tours** (☎ 800/227–9246).

HIKING

Despite the term, "national," parks are operated by the individual states in which they are located. For information, contact the National Parks and Wildlife Service in the capital of the state in which you are interested. In Western Australia, contact the Department of Conservation and Land Management. Organized hiking tours can be arranged through the bushwalking clubs listed in the telephone directory of each capital city. In this guide, national parks most often appear in a separate section at the end of each chapter.

To protect your skin against the sun, **wear a hat and sunglasses and put on sunblock**. At higher altitudes, where the air is thinner, you will burn more easily. Sunlight reflected off of snow, sand, or water can be especially strong. Apply sunscreen liberally before you go out—even if only for a half hour—and wear a visored cap and sunglasses.

Out in the hot Aussie sun, **beware of heatstroke.** Symptoms include headache, dizziness, and fatigue, which can turn into convulsions, unconsciousness, and can lead to death. If someone in your party develops any of these symptoms, have one person seek emergency help while others move the victim into the shade, wrap him or her in wet clothing (is a stream or lake nearby?) to cool him or her down.

Likewise, **avoid dehydration.** This underestimated danger can be very serious, especially considering that one of the major symptoms is the inability to swallow. It may be the easiest hazard to prevent, however: Simply **drink every 10–15 minutes,** up to a gallon of water per day in intense summer heat.

Temperatures can vary widely from day to night. Be sure to **bring enough warm clothing** for hiking and camping, along with **wet-weather gear.** Weather in a number of hiking hotspots in Australia can change quickly at almost any time of year. If you are not dressed warmly enough, hypothermia can be a problem. Exposure to the degree that body temperature dips below 95°F (35°C) produces the following symptoms: chills, tiredness, then uncontrollable shivering and irrational behavior, with the victim not always recognizing that he or she is cold. If someone in your party is suffering from any of this, wrap him or her in blankets and/or a warm sleeping bag immediately and try to keep him or her awake. The fastest way to raise body temperature is through skin-to-skin contact in a sleeping bag. Drinking warm liquids also helps.

Remember to **never drink from streams or lakes,** no matter how clear they may be. Giardia organisms can turn your stomach inside out. The easiest way to purify water is to dissolve a water purification tablet in it. Camping equipment stores also carry purification pumps. Boiling water for 15 minutes is always a reliable method, if time- and fuel-consuming. (For information on camping, *see* Lodging, *above*).

PACKING

The wisest approach to dressing Down Under is to **wear layered outfits.** Frequently, particularly at the change of seasons, weather can turn suddenly. You'll appreciate being able to remove or put on a jacket. A light raincoat and umbrella are worthwhile accessories, but remember that plastic raincoats and nonbreathing polyester are uncomfortable in the tropics. **Don't wear lotions or perfume in the tropics** either, since they attract mosquitoes and other bugs. It is also recommended that you carry insect repellent. Bring a hat with a brim to provide protection from the strong sunlight.

Dress is fairly casual in most cities, though top resorts and restaurants may require a jacket and tie. In Melbourne and Sydney, the younger set tends to be trendy; women might want to take along a cocktail dress for evening dining. In autumn, a light sweater or jacket will suffice for evenings in coastal cities, but winter demands a heavier coat—a raincoat with a zip-out wool lining is ideal. **Comfortable walking shoes are a must.** You should have a pair of running shoes or the equivalent if you're planning to trek, and rubber-sole sandals or canvas shoes are needed for walking on reef coral.

If you need to pack for both the tropical north and the cooler south, try to put the woolen clothes in one suitcase and lighter clothes in another, so you don't have to delve into both at each stop. Valuables, such as jewelry, should always be kept with you.

Also in your carry-on luggage **bring an extra pair of eyeglasses or contact lenses** and **enough of any medication you take** to last the entire trip. You may also want your doctor to write a spare prescription using the drug's generic name, since brand names may vary from country to country. In luggage to be checked, **never pack prescription drugs or valuables.** To avoid customs delays, carry medications in their original packaging. And don't forget to copy down and carry addresses of offices that handle refunds of lost traveler's checks.

CHECKING LUGGAGE

How many carry-on bags you can bring with you is up to the airline. Most allow two, but not always, so make sure that everything you carry aboard will fit under your seat, and get to the gate early. Note that if you have a seat at the back of the plane, you'll probably board first, while the overhead bins are still empty.

Keep in mind that **weight limits are stricter within Australia** than they are for entering the country.

If you are flying internationally, note that baggage allowances may be determined not by piece but by weight—generally 88 pounds (40

kilograms) in first class, 66 pounds (30 kilograms) in business class, and 44 pounds (20 kilograms) in economy.

Airline liability for baggage is limited to $1,250 per person on flights within the United States. On international flights it amounts to $9.07 per pound or $20 per kilogram for checked baggage (roughly $640 per 70-pound bag) and $400 per passenger for unchecked baggage. You can buy additional coverage at check-in for about $10 per $1,000 of coverage, but it excludes a rather extensive list of items, shown on your airline ticket.

Before departure **itemize your bags' contents** and their worth, and label the bags with your name, address, and phone number. (If you use your home address, cover it so that potential thieves can't see it readily.) Inside each bag **pack a copy of your itinerary.** At check-in **make sure that each bag is correctly tagged** with the destination airport's three-letter code. If your bags arrive damaged or fail to arrive at all, file a written report with the airline before leaving the airport.

PASSPORTS & VISAS

When traveling internationally **carry a passport even if you don't need one** (it's always the best form of ID), and **make two photocopies of the data page** (one for someone at home and another for you, carried separately from your passport). If you lose your passport, promptly call the nearest embassy or consulate and the local police.

ENTERING AUSTRALIA

All U.S. citizens, even infants, need a valid passport to enter Australia for stays of up to 90 days. A visa is also required.

Qantas passengers may obtain an Australian visa from that airline; otherwise, application forms are available from one of the offices listed below. Children traveling on a parent's passport do not need a separate application form, but should be included under Item 16 on the parent's form. The completed form and passport must be sent or brought in person to an issuing office, together with a recent passport-type photograph signed on the back (machine photographs are *not* acceptable).

Visitors planning to stay more than three months must pay a fee. Check with the Consulate-General to ascertain the cost, since it varies with the exchange rate. At press time, a visa costs $21. If you travel on an under-three-month visa and decide to extend it while in Australia, the fee rises; currently it's $200. If applying by mail, enclose a 12½" x 9½", stamped, self-addressed envelope and allow 21 days for processing.

PASSPORT OFFICES

The best time to apply for a passport or to renew is during the fall and winter. Before any trip, check your passport's expiration date, and, if necessary, renew it as soon as possible.

CANADIAN CITIZENS

Canadians need a valid passport to enter Australia for stays of up to 90 days. Australian visa requirements for Canadians are the same as for Americans. Visitors planning to stay more than three months must pay a $30 processing fee. (If you travel on an under-three-month visa and decide to extend it while there, the fee rises to about $150.) Contact the nearest Australian Consulate-General for visa application forms.

➤ PASSPORTS: **Passport Office** (☎ 819/994–3500 or 800/567–6868).

➤ VISAS: **Australian Consulate-General** (✉ Australian High Commission, 50 O'Connor St., Suite 710, Ottawa, Ontario K1P 6L2, ☎ 613/236–0841, FAX 613/236–4376); ✉ 175 Bloor St. E, Suite 314, Toronto, Ontario M4W 3R8, ☎ 416/323–1155, FAX 416/323–3910; ✉ World Trade Center Office Complex, 999 Canada Pl., Suite 602, Vancouver, British Columbia V6C 3E1, ☎ 604/684–1177, FAX 604/684–1856).

NEW ZEALAND CITIZENS

With a valid passport, New Zealand citizens may enter Australia without a visa and remain for an unlimited period of time.

➤ PASSPORTS: **New Zealand Passport Office** (☎ 04/494–0700 for information on how to apply; 04/474–8000

or 0800/225–050 in New Zealand for information on applications already submitted).

U.K. CITIZENS

Contact the London Passport Office for fees and documentation requirements and to request an emergency passport. Citizens of the United Kingdom need only a valid passport to enter Australia for stays of up to 90 days.

Australian visa application forms for longer stays are available from most travel agents and in the Australian Tourist Commission's brochure "Australia, A Traveller's Guide." You may also apply in person at the Australian High Commission or at the Australian consulates in Manchester and Edinburgh. Visitors planning to stay more than three months must pay a £15 processing fee. (If you travel on an under-three-month visa and decide to extend it while there, the fee rises to about £45.) Apply at least two weeks in advance if making your application by mail.

➤ PASSPORTS: **London Passport Office** (☎ 0990/210–410).

➤ VISAS: **Australian High Commission** (✉ Australia House, Strand, London WC2B 4LA, ☎ 0171/379–4334, FAX 0171/465–8217).

U.S. CITIZENS

U.S. citizens need a valid passport and visa to enter Australia for stays of up to 90 days.

➤ PASSPORTS: **National Passport Information Center** (☎ 900/225–5674; calls are 35¢ per minute for automated service, $1.05 per minute for operator service).

➤ VISAS: **Australian Consulate-General** (✉ 1000 Bishop St., Penthouse, Honolulu, HI 96813-9998, ☎ 808/524–5050, FAX 808/531–5142; ✉ 19th floor, Century Park Towers, Los Angeles, CA 90067, ☎ 213/229–4800, FAX 213/277–2258; ✉ International Bldg., 630 5th Ave., New York, NY 10111-0110, ☎ 212/408–8400, FAX 212/408–8401; ✉ 1 Bush St., San Francisco, CA 94104-4413, ☎ 415/362–6160, FAX 415/986–5440; ✉ **Australian Embassy**, 1601 Massachusetts Ave. NW, Washington, DC 20036-4673, ☎ 202/797–3222, FAX 202/797–3168).

SENIOR-CITIZEN TRAVEL

To qualify for age-related discounts **mention your senior-citizen status up front** when booking hotel reservations (not when checking out) and before you're seated in restaurants (not when paying the bill). When renting a car ask about promotional car-rental discounts, which can be cheaper than senior-citizen rates. Unfortunately, though, few—if any—of the discounts that Australian senior citizens enjoy are available to visitors, because an Australian "pensioner's card" is usually required as proof of age.

➤ EDUCATIONAL PROGRAMS: **Elderhostel** (⊠ 75 Federal St., 3rd fl., Boston, MA 02110, ☎ 877/426–8056, FAX 877/426–2166), **Folkways Institute** (⊠ 14600 Southeast Aldridge Rd., Portland, OR 97236-6518, ☎ 503/658–6600 or 800/225–4666, FAX 503/658–8672), **Interhostel** (⊠ University of New Hampshire, 6 Garrison Ave., Durham, NH 03824, ☎ 603/862–1147 or 800/733–9753, FAX 603/862–1113).

SHOPPING

Bargains are not hard to come by in Australia, although as a visitor you might not have the time it takes to look for them. Quality is good and prices are competitive, particularly in such clothing as hand-knitted wool sweaters, wool suits, and designer dresses and sportswear. Bargain hunters are best advised to **join one of the shopping tours in Melbourne and Sydney,** which visit one or two factory outlets. Check with your hotel concierge or the state tourist office for information about these tours.

Currently, there is no sales tax added to purchases in Australia, but an excise tax is levied on some luxury goods. Some specialty shops will deduct this tax—allowing you substantial savings of up to one-third the retail price—upon presentation of your passport and airline ticket. You can also **avoid paying excise tax** by shopping in one of the many duty-free stores scattered through the main cities. Prices on many items compare favorably with those in duty-free ports such as Singapore and Hong Kong. In some Australian cities you don't even have to go to the store if you buy from certain duty-free shops—you can order goods by phone, and your purchases will be delivered to the airport for your departure.

STUDENTS IN AUSTRALIA

Students and backpackers are entitled to reductions on the Greyhound Pioneer Australia unlimited travel Aussie Pass (☞ Bus Travel, *above*). These 10%–20% discounts are obtained by presenting an International Student Card, YHA cards, and VIP or ISIC Backpacker cards. Some accommodation discounts are also available in conjunction with the pass.

Victoria Street in Sydney's Kings Cross, near the rear entrance to the Kings Cross subway station, is a gathering spot for international backpackers. There you can sometimes find drivers looking for a rider to share car expenses while exploring the country, or someone heading home who is selling a car. However, several backpackers were murdered in New South Wales in the early 1990s, and backpackers are strongly advised against hitchhiking anywhere in the country. If you are sharing a car and expenses, it would be prudent to let someone know the vehicle's registration number, the people you will be traveling with, and your estimated time of arrival before you depart. Also, as best you can, be sure that your aims and personalities are compatible.

For a guide to backpacker hostels, contact V.I.P. Backpackers Resorts of Australia. This organization sells a V.I.P. Kit which includes the V.I.P. Backpackers Resorts guide plus a V.I.P. card which entitles you to discounts at all Australian backpacker hostels and on Greyhound Pioneer Australia and several other bus lines. The cost of the kit is $30, including postage.

The NSW Discovery Pass YHA, available for $199 to any member of the YHA or its overseas affiliates, allows unlimited economy travel on all Countrylink rail and coach services throughout New South Wales for one month. The pass is available from Countrylink Travel Centres. To save money, **look into deals available through student-oriented travel agencies.** To qualify you'll need a bona fide student I.D. card. Members of international student groups are also eligible.

➤ STUDENT IDs & SERVICES: **Contiki Holidays** (✉ 300 Plaza Alicante, Suite 900, Garden Grove, CA 92840, ☎ 714/740–0808 or 800/266–8454, FAX 714/740–2034), **Council on International Educational Exchange** (CIEE, ✉ 205 E. 42nd St., 14th fl., New York, NY 10017, ☎ 212/822–2600 or 888/268–6245, FAX 212/822–2699) for mail orders only, in the U.S., **Countrylink Travel Centres** (☎ 13–2232 for details) in New South Wales, **Travel Cuts** (✉ 187 College St., Toronto, Ontario M5T 1P7, ☎ 416/979–2406 or 800/667–2887) in Canada, **V.I.P. Backpackers Resorts of Australia** (✉ Box 600, Cannon Hill, QLD 4170, ☎ 07/3268–5733, FAX 07/3268–4066).

TAXES

Everyone leaving Australia pays a departure tax (now known as a Passenger Movement Charge) of $27; this amount is prepaid with your airline ticket. Hotels in the central area of Sydney charge a 10% room tax. In the Northern Territory, a 2.5% room tax applies.

Australia's excise tax is equivalent to the value-added tax (VAT) of other countries. The tax is usually included in the cost of the merchandise, but you may be able to deduct it with your passport and airline ticket.

TELEPHONES

COUNTRY & AREA CODES

The country code for Australia is 61. From the U.S., dial 011, then 61, then the local area code. From the U.K., dial 00, then 61. When dialing an Australian number from abroad, drop the initial 0 from the local area code.

Area codes for the major cities are: Sydney and Canberra, 02; Melbourne and Hobart, 03; Brisbane and Cairns, 07; Adelaide, Darwin, and Perth, 08.

DIRECTORY & OPERATOR INFORMATION

For international directory assistance call 1225; for information on international call costs, call 12552.

INTERNATIONAL CALLS

Calls from Australia to the United States, Canada, and the U.K. cost between 35¢ and $1 per minute (plus a 12¢ connection fee) in off-peak hours. These are Mon.–Fri. 6 PM–9 AM, and all day on weekends. Operator-assisted calls can be made from any phone with IDD (International Direct Dialing) access—check local telephone directories for international operator numbers. For a person-to-person call to the United States, the initial connection fee is $3.50, plus $2.29 per minute. In Australia, a collect call is known as a "reverse charge" call.

LOCAL CALLS

Australian numbers with a 13 prefix can be dialed country-wide for the cost of a local call: 40¢. For example, dialing a 13-number for a company in Melbourne when you are in Sydney will be billed as a local call. Toll-free numbers in Australia have an 1800 prefix. Unless otherwise noted, toll-free numbers in this book are accessible only within Australia.

LONG-DISTANCE CALLS

Long-distance calls can be dialed directly using the city code or area code. Rates are divided into three time periods: day (weekdays 8–6); night (weekdays 6–8); and economy (weekdays 8 PM–8 AM and all weekend, from Fri. 8 PM to Mon. 8 AM). A $3 service fee is charged for operator-connected calls when direct dialing is possible. Area codes are listed in the white pages of local telephone directories.

A note on phone numbers: since 1994, all telephone numbers in Australia have gradually been converted to eight-digit numbers. Exceptions are toll-free numbers (☞ *below*) and numbers with the prefix 13. The latter are country-wide and thus carry no area code at all. When you are calling long-distance numbers within Australia, remember to include the area code, even when you are calling from a number with the same area code. For example, if you are making a call from Sydney to Canberra, you need to include the area code even though both have the same 02 prefix.

LONG-DISTANCE SERVICES

AT&T, MCI, and Sprint access codes make calling long distance relatively convenient, but you may find the local access number blocked in many hotel rooms. First ask the hotel operator to connect you. If the hotel operator balks, ask for an international operator, or dial the international operator yourself. One way to improve your odds of getting connected to your long-distance carrier is to travel with more than one company's calling card (a hotel may block Sprint, for example, but not MCI). If all else fails, call from a pay phone.

➤ ACCESS CODES: **AT&T Direct** (☎ 800/435–0812), **MCI WorldPhone** (☎ 800/444–4141), **Sprint International Access** (☎ 800/877–4646).

PHONE CARDS

Australian phone cards can be used with silver public phones.

PUBLIC PHONES

Pay phones accept either coins (40¢ for a local call on a public phone) or locally purchased phone cards (for use with silver phones).

TIME

Figuring out what time it is Down Under can be dizzying, especially with cross-hemisphere daylight savings times and multi-time-zone countries. Without daylight savings times, Sydney is 15 hours ahead of New York; 16 hours ahead of Chicago and Dallas; 18 hours ahead (or count back six hours and add a day) from Los Angeles; and 10 hours ahead of London.

From Canada and the States, in order to avoid waking up some Aussie in the middle of the night, **call Australia after 7 PM.** If you're calling Western Australia, call after 9. From the U.K. or Europe, it isn't quite as complicated: call early in the morning or very late at night. When faxing, it's usually not a problem to ring discreet fax numbers at any time of day.

TIPPING

Hotels and restaurants do not add service charges, but it is a widely accepted practice to tip a waiter 10%–12% for good service, although many Australians consider it sufficient to leave only $3 or $4. It is not necessary to tip a hotel doorman for carrying suitcases into the lobby, but porters could be given $1 a bag. Room service and housemaids are not tipped except for special service. Taxi drivers do not expect a tip, but you may want to leave any small change. Guides, tour bus drivers, and chauffeurs don't expect tips either, though they are grateful if someone in the group takes up a collection for them. No tipping is necessary in beauty salons or for theater ushers.

TOURS & PACKAGES

On a prepackaged tour or independent vacation everything is prearranged so you'll spend less time planning—and often get it all at a good price.

BOOKING WITH AN AGENT

Travel agents are excellent resources. But it's a good idea to collect brochures from several agencies because some agents' suggestions may be influenced by relationships with tour and package firms that reward them for volume sales. If you have a special interest **find an agent with expertise in that area**; ASTA (☞ Travel Agencies, *below*) has a database of specialists worldwide.

Make sure your travel agent knows the accommodations and other services of the place they're recommending. Ask about the hotel's location, room size, and beds, and whether it has a pool, room service, or programs for children, if you care about these. Has your agent been there in person or sent others whom you can contact?

Do some homework on your own, too: local tourism boards can provide information about lesser-known and small-niche operators, some of which may sell only direct.

BUYER BEWARE

Each year consumers are stranded or lose their money when tour operators, even large ones with excellent reputations, go out of business—so **check out the operator.** Ask several travel agents about its reputation, and try to **book with a company that has a consumer-protection program.** (Look for information in the company's brochure.) In the United States, members of the National Tour Association and United States Tour Operators Association are required to set aside funds to cover your payments and travel arrangements in case the company defaults. It's also a good idea to choose a company that participates in the American Society of Travel Agent's Tour Operator Program (TOP); ASTA will act as mediator in any disputes between you and your tour operator.

Remember that the more your package or tour includes the better you can predict the ultimate cost of your vacation. Make sure you know exactly what is covered, and **beware of hidden costs.** Are taxes, tips, and transfers included? Entertainment and excursions? These can add up.

➤ TOUR-OPERATOR RECOMMENDATIONS: **American Society of Travel Agents** (☞ Travel Agencies, *below*), **National Tour Association** (NTA, ✉ 546 E. Main St., Lexington, KY 40508, ☎ 606/226–4444 or 800/682–8886), **United States Tour Operators Association** (USTOA, ✉ 342 Madison Ave., Suite 1522, New York, NY 10173, ☎ 212/599–6599 or 800/468–7862, FAX 212/599–6744).

GROUP TOURS

Among companies that sell tours to Australia, the following have a proven reputation and offer plenty of options. The classifications used below represent different price categories, and you'll probably encounter these terms when talking to a travel agent or tour operator. The key difference is usually in accommodations, which run from budget to better, and better-yet to best.

➤ SUPER-DELUXE: **Abercrombie & Kent** (✉ 1520 Kensington Rd., Oak Brook, IL 60521-2141, ☎ 630/954–2944 or 800/323–7308, FAX 630/954–3324), **Travcoa** (✉ Box 2630, 2350 S.E. Bristol St., Newport Beach, CA

92660, ☎ 714/476–2800 or 800/992–2003, FAX 714/476–2538).

➤ DELUXE: **Globus** (✉ 5301 S. Federal Circle, Littleton, CO 80123-2980, ☎ 303/797–2800 or 800/221–0090, FAX 303/347–2080), **Maupintour** (✉ 1515 St. Andrews Dr., Lawrence, KS 66047, ☎ 785/843–1211 or 800/255–4266, FAX 785/843–8351), **Tauck Tours** (✉ Box 5027, 276 Post Rd. W, Westport, CT 06881-5027, ☎ 203/226–6911 or 800/468–2825, FAX 203/221–6866).

➤ FIRST-CLASS: **AAT King's Australian Tours** (✉ 9430 Topanga Canyon Blvd., #207, Chatsworth, CA 91311, ☎ 800/353–4525, FAX 818/700–2647), **Brendan Tours** (✉ 15137 Califa St., Van Nuys, CA 91411, ☎ 818/785–9696 or 800/421–8446, FAX 818/902–9876), **Collette Tours** (✉ 162 Middle St., Pawtucket, RI 02860, ☎ 401/728–3805 or 800/340–5158, FAX 401/728–4745), **Down Under Answers** (✉ 12727 NE 20th St., Ste. 5, Bellevue, WA 98005, ☎ 425/895–0895 or 800/788–6685, FAX 425/895–8929), **Gadabout Tours** (✉ 700 E. Tahquitz Canyon Way, Palm Springs, CA 92262-6767, ☎ 619/325–5556 or 800/952–5068), **Newmans South Pacific Vacations** (✉ 6033 W. Century Blvd., Ste. 1270, Los Angeles, CA 90045, ☎ 310/348–8282 or 800/421–3326, FAX 310/215–9705), **South Pacific Your Way** (✉ 2819 1st Ave., #280, Seattle, WA 98121-1113, ☎ 206/441–8682 or 800/426–3610, FAX 206/441–8862), **Swain Australia Tours** (✉ 6 W. Lancaster Ave., Ardmore, PA 19003, ☎ 610/896–9595 or 800/227–9246, FAX 610/896–9592).

➤ BUDGET: **Cosmos** (☞ Globus, *above*).

GROUP TOURS

Like group tours, independent vacation packages are available from major tour operators and airlines. The companies listed below offer vacation packages in a broad price range.

➤ AIR/HOTEL: **Qantas Vacations** (✉ 300 N. Continental Blvd., #610, El Segundo, CA 90245, ☎ 800/641–8772, 800/268–7525 in Canada, FAX 310/535–1057), **United Vacations** (☎ 800/328–6877).

➤ FLY/DRIVE: **Budget WorldClass Drive** (☎ 800/527–0700, 0800/181181 in the U.K.) for self-drive itineraries, **Qantas Vacations** (☞ Air/Hotel, *above*), **United Vacations** (☞ Air/Hotel, *above*).

➤ HOTEL/SIGHTSEEING: **AAT King's Australian Tours** (☞ Group Tours, *above*), **Down Under Answers** (☞ Group Tours, *above*), **Newmans South Pacific Vacations** (☞ Group Tours, *above*), **South Pacific Your Way** (☞ Group Tours, *above*), **Swain Australia Tours** (☞ Group Tours, *above*).

➤ FROM THE U.K.: **British Airways Holidays** (☒ Astral Towers, Betts Way, London Rd., Crawley, West Sussex RH10 2XA, ☎ 01293/723–191), **Kuoni Travel** (☒ Kuoni House, Dorking, Surrey RH5 4AZ, ☎ 01306/740–500), **Qantas Holidays** (☒ Sovereign House, 361 King St., Hammersmith, London W6 9NA, ☎ 0990/673–464), **Virgin Holidays Ltd.** (The Galleria, Station Rd., Crawley, West Sussex RH10 1WW, ☎ 01293/617–181).

➤ ADVENTURE: **Alaska Wilderness Journeys** (☒ Box 220204, Anchorage, AK 99522, ☎ 907/349–2964 or 800/349–0064, FAX 907/344–6877.

➤ CUSTOMIZED PACKAGES: **Australia/New Zealand Down Under Travel** (☒ 4962 El Camino Real, Ste. 107, Los Altos, CA 94022, ☎ 650/969–2153 or 800/886–2153, FAX 650/969–3215), **Down Under Connections** (☒ 6640 Roswell Rd. NE, Atlanta, GA 30328, ☎ 404/255–1922 or 800/937–7878), **Pacific Experience** (☒ 63 Mill St., Newport, RI 02840, ☎ 401/849–6258 or 800/279–3639).

➤ FISHING: **Anglers Travel** (☒ 1280 Terminal Way, #30, Reno, NV 89502, ☎ 702/324–0580 or 800/624–8429, FAX 702/324–0583), **Fishing International** (☒ Box 2132, Santa Rosa, CA 95405, ☎ 707/539–3366 or 800/950–4242, FAX 707/539–1320), **Rod & Reel Adventures** (☒ 566 Thomson Ln., Copperopolis, CA 95228, ☎ 209/785–0444, FAX 209/785–0447).

➤ GOLF: **Australia/New Zealand Down Under Travel** (☞ Customized Packages, *above*), **ITC Golf Tours** (☒ 4134 Atlantic Ave., #205, Long Beach, CA 90807, ☎ 310/595–6905 or 800/257–4981).

➤ HORSEBACK RIDING: **Equitour FITS Equestrian** (☒ Box 807, Dubois, WY 82513, ☎ 307/455–3363 or 800/545–0019, FAX 307/455–2354).

➤ LEARNING: **Earthwatch** (☒ Box 9104, 680 Mount Auburn St., Watertown, MA 02272, ☎ 617/926–8200 or 800/776–0188, FAX 617/926–8532) for research expeditions, **Natural Habitat Adventures** (☒ 2945 Center Green Ct., Boulder, CO 80301, ☎ 303/449–3711 or 800/543–8917, FAX 303/449–3712), **Nature Expeditions International** (☒ 6400 El Dorado Circle, Suite 210, Tucson, AZ 85715, ☎ 520/721–6712 or 800/869–0639, FAX 520/721–6719), **Naturequest** (934 Acapulco St., Laguna Beach, CA 92651, ☎ 714/499–9561 or 800/369–3033, FAX 714/499–0812), **Questers** (☒ 381 Park Ave. S, New York, NY 10016, ☎ 212/251–0444 or 800/468–8668, FAX 212/251–0890), **Smithsonian Study Tours and Seminars** (☒ 1100 Jefferson Dr. SW, Room 3045, MRC 702, Washington, DC 20560, ☎ 202/357–4700, FAX 202/633–9250), **Victor Emanuel Nature Tours** (☒ Box 33008, Austin, TX 78764, ☎ 512/328–5221 or 800/328–8368, FAX 512/328–2919).

➤ MUSIC: **Dailey-Thorp Travel** (☒ 330 W. 58th St., #610, New York, NY 10019-1817, ☎ 212/307–1555 or 800/998–4677, FAX 212/974–1420).

➤ PHOTOGRAPHY: **Joseph Van Os Photo Safaris** (Box 655, Vashon, WA 98070, ☎ 206/463–5383, FAX 206/463–5484).

➤ SCUBA DIVING: **Down Under Answers** (☞ Group Tours, *above*), **Rothschild Dive Safaris** (☒ 900 West End Ave., #1B, New York, NY 10025-3525, ☎ 800/359–0747, FAX 212/749–6172), **Scuba Diving & Snorkeling Worldwide** (☒ Box 471899, San Francisco, CA 94147, ☎ 415/922–5807, FAX 415/922–5662), **Tropical Adventures** (☒ 111 2nd Ave. N, Seattle, WA 98109, ☎ 206/441–3483 or 800/247–3483, FAX 206/441–5431).

➤ SINGLES AND YOUNG ADULTS: **Contiki Holidays** (☒ 300 Plaza Alicante, #900, Garden Grove, CA 92840,

☎ 714/740–0808 or 800/266–8454, FAX 714/740–0818).

➤ SPAS: **Spa-Finders** (✉ 91 5th Ave., #301, New York, NY 10003-3039, ☎ 212/924–6800 or 800/255–7727).

➤ SPORTS: **Championship Tennis Tours** (✉ 8040 E. Morgan Trail #12, Scottsdale, AZ 85258, ☎ 602/443–9499 or 800/468–3664, FAX 602/443–8982), **Steve Furgal's International Tennis Tours** (✉ 11828 Rancho Bernardo Rd., #123-305, San Diego, CA 92128, ☎ 619/675–3555 or 800/258–3664).

➤ YACHT CHARTERS: **Alden Yacht Charters** (✉ 1909 Alden Landing, Portsmouth, RI 02871, ☎ 401/683–1782 or 800/662–2628, FAX 401/683–3668), **Huntley Yacht Vacations** (✉ 210 Preston Rd., Wernersville, PA 19565, ☎ 610/678–2628 or 800/322–9224, FAX 610/670–1767), **Lynn Jachney Charters** (✉ Box 302, Marblehead, MA 01945, ☎ 617/639–0787 or 800/223–2050, FAX 617/639–0216), **The Moorings** (✉ 19345 U.S. Hwy. 19 N, 4th fl., Clearwater, FL 34624-3193, ☎ 813/530–5424 or 800/535–7289, FAX 813/530–9474), **Ocean Voyages** (✉ 1709 Bridgeway, Sausalito, CA 94965, ☎ 415/332–4681 or 800/299–4444, FAX 415/332–7460).

TRAIN TRAVEL

Australia has a network of interstate, country, and urban trains offering first- and economy-class service. The major interstate trains are the *Indian-Pacific* from Sydney to Perth via Adelaide (26 hours Sydney–Adelaide, 38 hours Adelaide–Perth); the *Ghan* from Adelaide to Alice Springs (20½ hours; ☞ Chapter 10); the *Overland* (night service) and *Daylink* from Melbourne to Adelaide (12 hours); and the *XPT* (Express Passenger Train) from Sydney to Brisbane (15 hours). Service between Melbourne and Sydney is on the daytime or overnight *XPT* (10½ hours). Book early whenever possible, especially for the *Indian-Pacific* and the *Ghan* during peak times (August–October and Christmas holidays). For more information on Australia's network of rural and urban trains, or to make reservations or purchase discount passes, contact Rail Australia.

DISCOUNTS & PASSES

With the exception of the NSW Discovery Pass, the following rail passes are available only to overseas visitors. However, they can be purchased in Australia on presentation of your passport. Passes must be presented to the ticket office prior to the commencement of any journey. Rail passes do not include sleeping berths or meals.

The Austrail Pass allows unlimited economy travel on any passenger train in the country. Passes are available for 14, 21, or 30 days at prices ranging from US$407 to US$634.

The Austrail Flexipass allows unlimited travel on the national rail network. However, since its value is not ebbing away on days when you are not traveling, many will find this more cost-effective than the Austrail Pass. Four passes are available, from 8 to 29 days. The 8-day pass allows eight days of economy-class travel in a 6-month period and costs US$336. The 29-day pass allows 29 days of travel in the same period and costs US$878. The 8-day pass does not allow travel west of Crystal Brook in South Australia, which means that this pass is not valid for service to Perth or to Alice Springs.

The East Coast Discovery Pass allows economy-class travel between any two points from Melbourne to Cairns, with unlimited stops along the way. The pass is valid for six months, and for travel in one direction only. The cost of the pass is $215 from Sydney to Cairns, $295 from Melbourne to Cairns.

The NSW Discovery Pass allows unlimited economy class travel on all Countrylink rail and coach services throughout New South Wales for one month; the pass costs $249.

Advance purchase fares, which afford a 10%–40% discount between some major cities, are better bought before departure for Australia, as they tend to be booked up far in advance. It is advisable to make all rail reservations well in advance, particularly during peak tourist seasons. Contact your travel agent or the appropriate Rail Australia office.

TICKETS & SCHEDULES

➤ TRAIN INFORMATION: **Rail Australia** (☏ 800/423–2880, 818/841–1030 ATS Tours, and 800/633–3404 Austravel Inc. in the U.S.; 800/387–8850 Goway Travel in Canada; 0171/828–4111 in the U.K.)

TRAVEL AGENCIES

A good travel agent puts your needs first. Look for an agency that has been in business at least five years, emphasizes customer service, and has someone on staff who specializes in your destination. In addition **make sure the agency belongs to a professional trade organization,** such as ASTA in the United States. If your travel agency is also acting as your tour operator, *see* Buyer Beware *in* Tours & Packages, *above.*

➤ LOCAL AGENT REFERRALS: **American Society of Travel Agents** (ASTA, ☏ 800/965–2782 24-hr hot line, FAX 703/684–8319), **Association of British Travel Agents** (✉ 55–57 Newman St., London W1P 4AH, ☏ 0171/637–2444, FAX 0171/637–0713), **Association of Canadian Travel Agents** (✉ 1729 Bank St., Suite 201, Ottawa, Ontario K1V 7Z5, ☏ 613/521–0474, FAX 613/521–0805), **Australian Federation of Travel Agents** (✉ Level 3, 309 Pitt St., Sydney 2000, ☏ 02/9264–3299, FAX 02/9264–1085), **Travel Agents' Association of New Zealand** (✉ Box 1888, Wellington 10033, ☏ 04/499–0104, FAX 04/499–0786).

VISITOR INFORMATION

For general information contact the national and regional tourism bureaus below. For a free information-packed booklet "Destination Australia," call 800/333–0262. If you have specific questions about planning your trip, the Australian Tourism Commission runs the Aussie Help Line from 8 AM to 7 PM, Central Standard Time. Before you go, contact Friends Overseas—Australia to be put in touch with Australians who share your interests. Membership is $25.

➤ COUNTRYWIDE INFORMATION: **Aussie Help Line** (☏ 847/296–4900), **Australian Tourist Commission US:** (✉ 2049 Century Park E., Los Angeles, CA 90067, ☏ 310/229–4870,

FAX 310/552–1215). U.K.: ✉ Gemini House, 10–18 Putney Hill, Putney, London SW15 6AA, ☏ 0990/022–000 [information] or 0990/561–434 [brochure line], FAX 0181/940–5221). New Zealand: (✉ Level 13, 44–48 Emily Pl., Box 1666, Auckland 1, ☏ 09/379–9594), **Friends Overseas—Australia** (✉ 68–01 Dartmouth St., Forest Hills, NY 11375, ☏ 718/261–0534).

➤ REGIONAL INFORMATION: **Australia's Northern Territory** (✉ 3601 Aviation Blvd., Ste. 2100, Manhattan Beach, CA 90266, ☏ 310/643–2636, FAX 310/643–2637), **Australian Travel Headquarters** (✉ 1600 Dove St., Ste. 215, Newport Beach, CA 92660, ☏ 714/852–2270 or 800/546–2155, FAX 714/852–2277) for information on South Australia, **Queensland Tourist & Travel Corporation** (✉ 1800 Century Park E, Suite 330, Los Angeles, CA 90067, ☏ 310/788–0997).

➤ U.S. GOVERNMENT ADVISORIES: **U.S. Department of State** (✉ Overseas Citizens Services Office, Room 4811 N.S., 2201 C St. NW, Washington, DC 20520; ☏ 202/647–5225 for interactive hot line; 301/946–4400 for computer bulletin board; FAX 202/647–3000 for interactive hot line); enclose a self-addressed, stamped, business-size envelope.

WHEN TO GO

Australia is in the Southern Hemisphere, so **remember that the seasons are reversed**—it's winter Down Under during the American and European summer.

The ideal time to visit the north, particularly the Northern Territory's Kakadu National Park, is early in the dry season (around May). Bird life remains profuse on the drying flood plains, and waterfalls are still spectacular and accessible. The Dry (April–October) is also a good time to visit northern Queensland's beaches and rain forests. You can swim off the coast without fear of dangerous stinging box jellyfish, which infest ocean waters between November and March. In rain forests, heat and humidity are lower than later in the year, and crocodile viewing is at its prime, as the creatures tend to bask on riverbanks rather than submerge in the colder water.

During school holidays, Australians take to the roads in droves. Accommodations and attractions are crowded and hotel rooms and rental cars are unlikely to be discounted during these periods. The busiest period is mid-December to the end of January, which is the equivalent of the U.S. and British summer break. The dates of other school vacations vary from state to state, but generally fall around Easter, mid-June to July, and late September to mid-October.

CLIMATE

Australia's climate is temperate in southern states, such as Victoria and Tasmania, particularly in coastal areas, and tropical in Australia's far north. The Australian summer north of the Tropic of Capricorn is a steam bath—remember that by comparison no parts of North America or Europe are anywhere near as close to the equator. From the end of October to December (the Australian spring), or from February through April (late summer–autumn), southern regions are generally sunny and warm, with only occasional rain in Sydney, Melbourne, and Adelaide. Perth and the south of Western Australia are at their finest in springtime, when wildflowers blanket the land. Some people would say that spring and fall are the best times to travel to Australia, unless you're dying to get away from a northern winter.

The following are average daily maximum and minimum temperatures for some major Australian cities.

Climate in Australia

SYDNEY

Jan.	79F	26C	May	67F	19C	Sept.	67F	17C
	65	18		52	11		52	11
Feb.	79F	26C	June	61F	16C	Oct.	72F	22C
	65	18		49	9		56	13
Mar.	76F	24C	July	61F	16C	Nov.	74F	23C
	63	17		49	9		61	16
Apr.	72F	22C	Aug.	63F	17C	Dec.	77F	25C
	58	14		49	9		63	17

MELBOURNE

Jan.	79F	26C	May	63F	17C	Sept.	63F	17C
	58	14		47	8		47	8
Feb.	79F	26C	June	58F	14C	Oct.	67F	19C
	58	14		45	7		49	9
Mar.	76F	24C	July	56F	13C	Nov.	72F	22C
	56	13		43	6		52	11
Apr.	68F	20C	Aug.	59F	15C	Dec.	76F	24C
	52	11		43	6		54	12

HOBART

Jan.	72F	22C	May	58F	14C	Sept.	59F	15C
	54	12		45	7		43	6
Feb.	72F	22C	June	54F	12C	Oct.	63F	17C
	54	12		41	5		47	8
Mar.	68F	20C	July	52F	11C	Nov.	67F	19C
	52	11		40	4		49	9
Apr.	63F	17C	Aug.	56F	13C	Dec.	70F	21C
	49	9		41	5		52	11

CAIRNS

Jan.	90F	32C	May	81F	27C	Sept.	83F	28C
	74	23		67	19		65	18
Feb.	90F	32C	June	79F	26C	Oct.	86F	30C
	74	23		65	18		68	20
Mar.	88F	31C	July	79F	26C	Nov.	88F	31C
	74	23		61	16		70	21
Apr.	85F	29C	Aug.	81F	27C	Dec.	90F	32C
	70	21		63	17		74	23

ALICE SPRINGS

Jan.	97F	36C	May	74F	23C	Sept.	81F	27C
	70	21		47	8		49	9
Feb.	95F	35C	June	67F	19C	Oct.	88F	31C
	70	21		41	5		58	14
Mar.	90F	32C	July	67F	19C	Nov.	94F	34C
	63	17		40	4		65	18
Apr.	81F	27C	Aug.	74F	23C	Dec.	97F	36C
	54	12		43	6		68	20

DARWIN

Jan.	90F	32C	May	92F	33C	Sept.	92F	33C
	77	25		74	23		74	23
Feb.	90F	32C	June	88F	31C	Oct.	94F	34C
	77	25		70	21		77	25
Mar.	92F	33C	July	88F	31C	Nov.	94F	34C
	77	25		67	19		79	26
Apr.	92F	33C	Aug.	90F	32C	Dec.	92F	33C
	76	24		70	21		79	26

PERTH

Jan.	85F	29C	May	69F	20C	Sept.	70F	21C
	63	17		53	12		50	10
Feb.	85F	29C	June	64F	18C	Oct.	76F	24C
	63	17		50	10		53	12
Mar.	81F	27C	July	63F	17C	Nov.	81F	27C
	61	16		48	9		57	14
Apr.	76F	24C	Aug.	67F	19C	Dec.	83F	28C
	57	14		48	9		61	16

➤ FORECASTS: **Weather Channel Connection** (☎ 900/932–8437), 95¢ per minute from a Touch-Tone phone.

INDEX

NOTES

NOTES

NOTES

NOTES

Looking for a different kind of vacation?

Fodor's makes it easy with a full line of specialty guidebooks to suit a variety of interests—from adventure to romance to language help.

Fodor's. For the world of ways you travel.

L@@king
© FOR A
great place to go?

We know just the place. In fact, it attracts more than 125,000 visitors a day, making it one of the world's most popular travel destinations. It's previewtravel.com, the Web's comprehensive resource for travelers. It gives you access to over 500 airlines, 25,000 hotels, rental cars, cruises, vacation packages and support from travel experts 24 hours a day. Plus great information from Fodor's travel guides and travelers just like you. All of which makes previewtravel.com quite a find.

Preview Travel has everything you need to plan & book your next trip.

air, car & hotel reservations

vacation packages & cruises

destination planning & travel tips

24-hour customer service

previewtravel.com

preview travel℠

aol keyword: previewtravel
www.previewtravel.com

FODOR'S AUSTRALIA 2000

EDITORS: Jennifer L. Kasoff, Holly S. Smith

Editorial Contributors: Tony Baker, Jane Carstens, Terry Durack, Peter Forrestal, Michael Gebicki, Josie Gibson, Chips Mackinolty, Beverly Malzard, Anne Matthews, Helayne Schiff, Graham Simmons, Gary Walsh

Editorial Production: Linda K. Schmidt

Maps: David Lindroth Inc., Mapping Specialists, *cartographers*; Robert Blake and Steven Amsterdam, *map editors*

Design: Fabrizio La Rocca, *creative director*; Guido Caroti, *art director*; Jolie Novak, *photo editor*; Melanie Marin, *photo researcher*

Cover Design: Pentagram

Production/Manufacturing: Rebecca Zeiler

COPYRIGHT

"Five Thousand Miles from Anywhere" is excerpted from *Falling Off the Map*, by Pico Iyer. Copyright © 1993 by Pico Iyer. Reprinted by permission of Alfred A. Knopf, Inc.

"Pillars of Fire Across the Plains" is excerpted from *The Road from Coorain*, by Jill Ker Conway. Copyright © 1987 by Jill Ker Conway. Reprinted by permission of Alfred A. Knopf, Inc.

SPECIAL SALES

IMPORTANT TIP
Although all prices, opening times, and other details in this book are based on information supplied to us at press time, changes occur all the time in the travel world, and Fodor's cannot accept responsibility for facts that become outdated or for inadvertent errors or omissions. So **always confirm information when it matters**, especially if you're making a detour to visit a specific place.

PHOTOGRAPHY
Photographers/Aspen, Inc.: *Paul Chesley, cover (Great Barrier Reef).*

Auscape: Kathy Atkinson, 24B. Kevin Deacon, 25E. Jean-Paul Ferrero, 9C, 10A, 11B, 11D, 25D. Brett Gregory, 8A. Dennis Harding, 15D. Glenn Tempest, 12C. Rob Walls, 14A, 15 bottom left. Sorrel Wilby & Chris Ciantar, 14B.

Australian Tourist Commission: A. Bruzzone, 20B.

The Big Banana, 9D.

Brisbane Tourism, 16A, 29F.

Jan Butchofsky-Houser, 23A.

Corbis, 2 top left, 2 top right, 2 bottom left, 2 bottom right, 3 top left, 3 top right, 3 bottom left, 3 bottom right, 6B, 26A, 27D, 29 top, 30D, 30H.

Dave G. Houser, 1, 12A.

The Image Bank: John Banagan, 12D, 13E, 17D, 17 center, 18A, 21E. Walter Bibikow, 32. Andy Caulfield, 13F, 17E, 19C. Flip Chalfant, 13G, 21D. Giuliano Colliva, 7 bottom left. Michael Coyne, 24C. Peter Hendrie, 7D, 8B, 16C, 30F. Jeff Hunter, 16B. Lionel Isy-Schwart, 18–19 top. David Jeffrey, 23B. Anthony Johnson, 18B. Lupe Productions, 9E, 12B. Robbi Newman, 11C, 21 top. Andrea Pistolesi, 20C, 23C. Marc Romanelli, 19D. Guido Alberto Rossi, 30C. Thomas Schmitt, 15E. Alvis Upitis, 6C. Simon Wilkinson, 4–5, 24A.

Catherine Karnow, 22A.

James Lemass, 7E.

Lizard Island Lodge, 30I.

Melbourne Wine Room Restaurant, 30G.

Pier 9 Oyster Bar & Seafood Grill, 30B.

Rockpool, 30J.

Royal Botanic Gardens Sydney: Jaime Plaza, 6A.

Silky Oaks Lodge, 30A.

Skyrail Rain Forest Cableway, 30E.

South Australian Tourism Commission, 2 bottom center, 20A, 27C, 28 top, 28E.

Tourism Tasmania: George Apostolidis, 14C. Joe Shemesh, 26B.

ABOUT OUR WRITERS

Every Y2K trip is a significant trip. So if there was ever a time you needed excellent travel information, it's now. Acutely aware of that fact, we've pulled out all stops in preparing *Fodor's Australia 2000*. To help you zero in on what to see in Australia, we've gathered some great color photos of the key sights in every region. To show you how to put it all together, we've created great itineraries and neighborhood walks. And to direct you to the places that are truly worth your time and money in this important year, we've rallied the team of endearingly picky know-it-alls we're pleased to call our writers. Having seen all corners of the regions they cover for us, they're real experts. If you knew them, you'd poll them for tips yourself.

Tony Baker is a newspaper columnist, author, and publisher. He has been writing about the Australian good life for 30 years. He has written and published 10 restaurant guides and is a contributor to numerous newspapers and magazines.

After writing travel articles while being based in London, Singapore, and Jakarta, **Jane Carstens** returned to her native Queensland, where she covered that vast state top to bottom for Fodor's. A self-confessed foodie, she used to review restaurants in Southeast Asia, and has of course included ever-so-tempting Thai, Malaysian, and Indonesian restaurants in the Queensland chapter.

As the restaurant reviewer for the *Sydney Morning Herald*, food columnist for *Vogue Entertaining and Travel*, and co-editor of the *Sydney Morning Herald Good Food Guide*, **Terry Durack** is Australia's most influential food critic. He has written five cookbooks, including the widely acclaimed *Yum: A Voyage Around My Stomach*, and the just-released *Noodle*. He also writes a Sunday column for the *London Independent*.

British by birth, American by education, and Australian since 1979—after a stint as a Kiwi, as well—**Michael Gebicki** is a freelance travel writer and photographer now based in Sydney. Dashing articles about his global wanderings appear regularly in travel publications in North America, Europe, and Asia.

Josie Gibson got the travel bug young, as an exchange student in Japan, and she hasn't stopped traveling since. She has worked in London, the United States, and Australia as a radio and print journalist (including nine years at Radio Australia) and in government and public relations. Her favorite holiday spot is a sunny beach with a good book—and proximity to a good curry would make it perfect.

Beverly Malzard, an Australian travel writer based in Sydney, has spent many years as a journalist and editor. She was previously the managing editor of *Travel Vacations* and the editor of *Sydney WHERE* magazine. Her accolades include the prestigious Best International Travel Writer award from the Singapore Tourism Bureau in 1993 and the 1998 Travel Writer of the Year award from Air New Zealand and the Australian Society of Travel Writers.

Graham Simmons is a freelance travel photojournalist based in Melbourne. He is a full member of the Australian Society of Travel Writers whose work has been published regularly in several Australasian and international newspapers and magazines.

Don't Forget to Write

We love feedback—positive and negative—and follow up on all suggestions. So contact the Australia editor at editors@fodors.com or c/o Fodor's, 201 East 50th Street, New York, New York 10022. Have a wonderful trip!

Karen Cure

Karen Cure
Editorial Director